ISBN 978-0-265-92122-7
PIBN 10234751

FB &c Ltd, Dalton House, 60 Windsor Avenue, London, SW19 2RR.
Company number 08720141. Registered in England and Wales.

For support please visit www.forgottenbooks.com

ANNALS

OF THE

AMERICAN PULPIT;

COMMEMORATIVE NOTICES

OF

DISTINGUISHED AMERICAN CLERGYMEN

DENOMINATIONS,

WITH HISTORICAL INTRODUCTIONS.

BY WILLIAM B. SPRAGUE, D. D.

VOLUME III.

NEW YORK:
ROBERT CARTER & BROTHERS
530 BROADWAY.
1858.

ANNALS

OF THE

AMERICAN PULPIT;

OR

COMMEMORATIVE NOTICES

OF

DISTINGUISHED AMERICAN CLERGYMEN

OF

VARIOUS DENOMINATIONS,

FROM THE EARLY SETTLEMENT OF THE COUNTRY TO THE CLOSE OF THE YEAR EIGHTEEN HUNDRED AND FIFTY-FIVE.

WITH HISTORICAL INTRODUCTIONS.

BY WILLIAM B. SPRAGUE, D. D.

VOLUME III.

NEW YORK:
ROBERT CARTER & BROTHERS
530 BROADWAY.
1858.

PRESBYTERIAN.

VOL. III.

PREFACE.

The first two volumes of this work were issued somewhat less than a year ago. Considering the peculiar character of the work, I could not but await the public verdict upon it with some degree of anxiety, and now that it has been rendered in part, I am not disposed to dissemble the high gratification I have received from it. That my own partial friends should have looked kindly on the effort, perhaps I had a right to expect; but that the tone of the press should have been so uniformly indulgent,—ignoring even imperfections of which I was myself painfully sensible, after having done the best that I could,—was certainly more than I could reasonably look for. I hardly need say that I have already realized the good effect of this kindly reception, in the increased vigour and alacrity with which I have been able to carry forward the work.

I am indebted to several friends, especially to the Rev. J. L. Sibley, the present Librarian of Harvard College, for directing my attention to a few small errors, chiefly in respect to dates, nearly all of which have been already corrected in the stereotype plates.

I am willing to hope that the two volumes now published will not fall below the preceding ones in point of interest; but of this it is for the public, and not me, to judge. Of this at least I am certain,—that there has been no less of care and vigilance in the preparation of them; and they have required a much greater amount of labour, owing chiefly to the fact that, in the latter case, a large proportion of the biographical material has been necessarily gathered by correspondence with the surviving relatives and friends of the parties commemorated, whereas, in the former, much the greater part of it had already been embodied in printed documents, most of which were easily accessible.

There is one circumstance that has rendered the selecting of the subjects for these volumes a much more difficult task than for the previous ones,—namely, that the Presbyterian Church is so much less compact than the Congregational. It does not indeed reach back so far in point of time, but it covers a much wider space; and though I have corresponded extensively with prominent clergymen in the different States, with a view to make the best selection possible, I have little doubt that even *their* obliging efforts in my behalf have left the veil upon a goodly number of names that I should have delighted to honour. And then there are others of which I have been able, after the most diligent search, to find out only enough to make me regret that the ravages of time have put it out of my power to embalm them. I hope this statement will induce those who miss honoured or cherished names, which they may have expected to find, to regard the omission in any other light than as even a negative reflection on the memories of their friends.

It will, I doubt not, occur to some that there is a disproportionate relative importance given to some names in the measure of space which is devoted to them. I am quite aware that this, in one point of view, is an imperfection; and yet every one who reflects must perceive that it was inseparable from my general plan. I have not much fear that any of the numerous communications with which my friends have honoured the work will be found too long; but there are a few which I doubt not that others as well as myself will wish had been longer. In one or two instances, I have been obliged to dismiss a very eminent name, with a bare epitome of the character, because I have been utterly unable to find any one whose recollections would enable him to render a more extended testimony.

Notwithstanding the work is limited by its title to the close of the year 1855, I have allowed myself occasionally to introduce in *notes* names incidentally occurring, that have been added to the list of the dead since that period. They have, however, necessarily been treated so briefly, that they still remain legitimate subjects for biography.

The numbers under the name, at the commencement of each article, denote, so far as I have been able to ascertain, the commencement and the close of the individual's ministry. Where one has belonged successively to two denominations, he is placed in connection with the one in which he died. In that case, though the history of his whole ministerial life is given, the numbers indicate only the period of his latest ministerial connection; except in those cases in which the denominations are more immediately allied to each other,—as for instance the different branches of the Presbyterian family, and the Congregationalists; and then the numbers, as well as the sketches, range through the whole period of their ministry.

Notwithstanding I have mentioned, in the General Preface, the names of several persons to whom I am largely indebted for biographical material, independently of the commemorative letters, that number has since so much increased that I may be allowed to mention several more in connection with the Presbyterian department, as specially, though by no means exclusively, entitled to my grateful acknowledgements. To Dr. Krebs, Stated Clerk of the Presbytery of New York, to Dr. Rodgers, Stated Clerk of the Presbytery of New Brunswick, and to Dr. Howe, Professor in the Theological Seminary at Columbia, S. C., who has in his possession the Records of the Presbytery of South Carolina, and a great amount of other biographical material, I am indebted for much statistical information, which, otherwise, would either have been entirely wanting, or would have lacked its present character of perfect authenticity. Among others who have rendered me most important service which the work itself might not at first reveal, are the Rev. Daniel Dana, D. D., Newburyport, Mass.; Thomas W. Blatchford, M. D., Troy, N. Y.; Rev. John Forsyth, D. D., Newburgh, N. Y.; the late Rev. William Hill, D. D., Winchester, Va.; the Rev. William H. Foote, D. D., Romney, Va.; Mrs. Dr. John H. Rice, Prince Edward County, Va.; Rev. R. H. Morrison, D. D., Cottage Home, N. C.; Rev. Thomas Cleland, D. D., McAfee, Ky.; Rev. Joel K. Lyle, Paris, Ky.; Rev. Joseph H. Martin, Knoxville, Tenn.; J. G. M. Ramsey, M. D., Mecklenburg, Tenn.; and Rev. F. A. M'Corkle, D. D., Greenville, Tenn.

In the General Preface I have expressed my obligation to the Rev. Richard Webster, for the use of a large collection of valuable manuscripts in regard to the early history of the Presbyterian Church. Those manuscripts, together with much other valuable matter, have since been published in an octavo volume; and, as the printing of that work was contemporaneous with the revision of mine, the publisher kindly sent me the proof sheets in advance, that I might avail myself of the author's latest corrections. I have, however, retained my original reference,—"Webster's MSS.;" but it will be understood that they are identical with a portion of "Webster's History of the Presbyterian Church in America."

Of the other works to which I have been more or less, and in some instances largely, indebted for material for these two volumes, are Dr. Hodge's History of the Presbyterian Church; Dr. Foote's Historical Sketches of Virginia and North Carolina; Dr. Davidson's History of the Presbyterian Church in Kentucky; Dr. Smith's Old Redstone, or Historical Sketches of Western Presbyterianism; Dr. Alfred Nevin's Churches of the Valley; and Rev. James H. Hotchkin's History of Western New York. All these works possess great value, and evince extensive research. The three noble volumes of Dr. Foote especially, covering, as they do, a large tract of country in which Presbyterianism has been most at home, and made up, to a great extent, of material on which the pall of oblivion had long rested, and which nothing but his persevering industry could have exhumed, justly entitle him to a high and enduring place among the benefactors of his denomination. I must not omit to say that I have derived important aid from Dr. Allen's American Biographical Dictionary, the last edition of which is so much enlarged and improved as to be almost a new work; and from the new edition of Dr. Blake's Biography, in superintending which he performed his last earthly labours.

I have stated so explicitly, in the General Preface, the principles on which the work is constructed, that I deem it unnecessary either to repeat or to add any thing here on that subject. But I may be allowed to refer with satisfaction to that feature of it, which makes it the depository of the treasured reminiscences of so many eminent living persons, and which the public judgment has so unanimously approved,—as an occasion of renewing my hearty thanks to *all*, who have lent the influence of their names and their pens in aid of my enterprise. It is to this wide and generous coöperation especially, that I have been indebted, not less for the spirit to sustain so arduous and protracted a course of labour, than the means necessary to a successful result.

ALBANY, AUGUST 5, 1857.

P.S.—The publication of this and the next volume has been delayed several months, on account of the embarrassed financial condition of the Country.

February, 1858.

HISTORICAL INTRODUCTION.*

The Presbyterian Church of the United States must undoubtedly be considered as of Scottish origin. From about the period of the Revolution of 1688, which issued in the establishment of William and Mary on the British throne, Presbyterians began to emigrate from Scotland and the North of Ireland to these American Colonies; and they quickly manifested a desire to reproduce, in the land of their adoption, their own peculiar institutions. As the Quakers in Pennsylvania, and the Roman Catholics in Maryland, were the only denominations in America who, except the Baptists in Rhode Island, at that time, extended a cordial welcome to emigrants of other sects, it was in these two Colonies that the earliest and largest Presbyterian Churches were established. The Puritan element was early introduced into the Body, by way of New England, and contributions have, from time to time, been made to it from the Reformed Churches on the Continent of Europe; but though this may have served, in some degree, to modify, it has never essentially changed, its organization.

The early history of the Presbyterian Church in this country is involved in no little obscurity,—owing principally to the fact that those who originally composed it, instead of forming a compact community, were widely scattered throughout the different Colonies. It is evident, however, that several churches were established some time before the close of the seventeenth century. In Maryland there were the Churches of Rehoboth, Snow Hill, Upper Marlborough, Monokin and Wicomico,—the first mentioned of which is commonly considered the oldest, and was probably formed several years before 1690. The Church on Elizabeth River, in Virginia, is supposed by some to date back to nearly the same period, but the exact time of its origin cannot be ascertained. The Churches in Freehold, and Woodbridge, N. J. were constituted in 1692; and the First Church in Philadelphia, as nearly as can be ascertained, in 1698. In Newcastle, De., in Charleston, S. C., and in some other places, Presbyterian

* Hodge's History of the Presbyterian Church.—Krebs' Outline of the History of the Presbyterian Church.—Parker's do.—Article on the History of Presbyterianism in the United States, in the Encyclopedia of Religious Knowledge.—Greenleaf's Sketches of the Ecclesiastical History of Maine.—MSS. from Rev. Samuel Miller, D.D., Rev. Daniel Dana, D. D., Rev. Alexander Blaikie, Rev. J. H. Bates, and Rev. T. S. Childs.

Churches were planted at a very early period. In the latter part of 1705, or early in 1706, a Presbytery was formed under the title of the Presbytery of Philadelphia,—all whose members were from Scotland or Ireland, except the Rev. Jedediah Andrews, who was born and educated in New England.

In 1716, the Presbyterian Body had so far increased that some new organization was thought desirable. Accordingly, instead of one Presbytery, there were constituted four,—namely, the Presbytery of Philadelphia, the Presbytery of Newcastle, the Presbytery of Snow Hill, and the Presbytery of Long Island; and, at the same time, a Synod was formed, under the title of the Synod of Philadelphia. Shortly before this, several churches, with their ministers, in East and West Jersey, and on Long Island, originally Congregationalists, had connected themselves with the Presbyterian Church.

Notwithstanding the growth of the Church from this period was constant and rapid, it soon became manifest that the fact of its gathering its ministers and members from different countries, where, to some extent, different modes of thinking and acting on the same subjects prevailed, was likely to interfere with the general harmony of the Body. The points on which the difference of opinion chiefly developed itself, were the examination of candidates for the ministry on experimental religion, the strict adherence to Presbyterial order, and the amount of learning to be required of those who sought the ministerial office. These subjects were discussed with great, and often intemperate, zeal in the different Presbyteries. Two distinct parties were now formed—those who were more zealous for orthodoxy, for the rigid observance of Presbyterial rule, and for a thoroughly educated ministry, were called the "Old Side;" while those who were more tolerant of departures from ecclesiastical order, and less particular in respect to other qualifications for the ministry, provided they could have the evidence of vital piety, were called the "New Side" or "New Lights."

In 1729, after several years of diligent exertion on the part of the strict Presbyterians, and in consequence of an overture drawn up and prosecuted with great zeal the year before, by the Rev. John Thompson of Delaware, the Synod passed what was commonly called "The Adopting Act." This Act consisted of a public authoritative adoption of the Westminster Confession of Faith and Catechisms, and made it imperative that not only every candidate, but every actual minister of the Church, should, by subscription or otherwise, in the presence of the Presbytery, acknowledge these instruments respectively as their Confession of Faith. This Act had to encounter great opposition, especially from those ministers of the Synod, who had come from England, Wales, and the New England Colonies.

The strict Presbyterians having thus gained their main point, the other Side thought themselves entitled to be gratified in *their* favourite object. Accordingly, in 1734, they brought an overture to the Synod, directing "that all candidates for the ministry should be examined diligently as to the experience of a work of sanctifying grace on their hearts, and that none be admitted, who are not, in a judgment of charity, serious Christians." Though this overture was adopted unanimously, it afterwards proved the occasion of great disquietude.

These two Acts embraced the favourite objects of both parties—the main difficulty lay in carrying them into execution. The practice of the several Presbyteries was decided by the accidental circumstance of one party or the other being the majority, and this occasioned much debate and collision at the Synodical meetings,—each party charging the other, and commonly not without reason, with some violation, in the several Presbyteries, of the order of Synod.

In 1738, the strict Presbyterians, with a view to remedy what they regarded as a serious evil, prevailed on the Synod to pass an Act, directing "that young men be *first* examined respecting their literature by a Committee of Synod, and obtain a testimonial of their approbation before they can be taken on trial before any Presbytery." The Presbytery of New Brunswick, in the face of this Synodical decision, proceeded almost immediately to take Mr. John Rowland on trials, and a few weeks after licensed him to preach. The Presbytery of Philadelphia protested against the measure, and refused to admit Mr. R. to preach within their bounds; and the Synod, at their next meeting, formally annulled it, declaring that he could not be regarded as a regular candidate. Notwithstanding this, however, William Tennent, (the elder,) a member of the Presbytery of Philadelphia, publicly recognised the validity of Mr. R.'s licensure by admitting him to his pulpit; and when some of his congregation complained of it to his Presbytery, he earnestly justified his course, denied the authority of the Presbytery in the case, and "contemptuously withdrew"—whereupon the Presbytery censured his conduct as "irregular and disorderly." This took place in September, 1739. In October following, the Presbytery of New Brunswick, adhering to its first offence, proceeded to ordain Mr. Rowland to the work of the ministry; and he continued a member of that Presbytery until 1742, when he was dismissed to join the Presbytery of Newcastle. All this served to exasperate feelings already excited, and formed, in no small degree, the legitimate preparation for an open rupture.

It was at this juncture that Whitefield, in 1739, paid his second visit to America. The great revival that ensued, in connection with his labours, found its friends in the Presbyterian Church chiefly with the New Side; while the Old Side, or the strict Presbyterian party, perceiving some really censurable irregularities in the active friends and promoters of the revival, were not slow to pronounce the whole a delusion. This brought on the crisis. The controversy waxed more and more violent until 1741, when the highest judicatory of the Church was rent into two parts—the Old Side constituting the Synod of Philadelphia,—the New Side, the Synod of New York.

Soon after the separation, the Synod of New York began to perceive the necessity of providing for the education of their *future* ministers; and the result of their consultations on the subject was the establishment of the College of New Jersey. This institution commenced its operations in Elizabethtown, in 1746; was removed to Newark, in 1747; and thence to Princeton, in 1757. Meanwhile the Old Side patronized the Academies of New London and of Newark in Delaware, under the Rev. Francis Alison and the Rev. Alexander McDowall, and also the Academy and College of Philadelphia. The rivalship between these literary institutions served to render more intense the mutual hostility of the two parties.

But violent as the controversy was, it was not proof against the subduing, healing influence of time. Both parties gradually became sensible that they had acted rashly and uncharitably, and began at length to meditate a reunion. The first overtures in that direction were made by the Synod of New York in 1749; but it was nine years before the desired consummation was reached. In 1758, mutual concessions having been made, and the articles of union agreed upon, the two Synods were happily united under the title of the Synod of New York and Philadelphia. At the time of the disruption, the Old Side was the most numerous; but before the reunion, the New Side had become so.

From this time, the Presbyterian Church went on in as much prosperity as could consist with the disturbed state of the country, until after the Revolutionary War,—when it was judged proper to enter into some new arrangements. Accordingly, in 1785, the Synod of New York and Philadelphia began to take those steps for revising the public standards of the Church, which led to their adoption and establishment on the present plan. A large and respectable Committee, of which Dr. Witherspoon was Chairman, was appointed to "take into consideration the Constitution of the Church of Scotland and other Protestant Churches," and to form a complete system for the organization of the Presbyterian Church in the United States. The result was that on the 28th of May, 1788, the Synod completed the revision and arrangement of the public standards of the Church, and finally adopted them, and ordered them to be printed and distributed for the government of the several judicatories. This new arrangement consisted in dividing the Old Synod into four Synods—namely, New York and New Jersey, Philadelphia, Virginia, and the Carolinas,—and constituting over these, as a bond of union, a General Assembly, in all essential particulars after the model of the General Assembly of the Church of Scotland. The Westminster Confession of Faith was adopted with three small alterations. The Larger and Shorter Catechisms were adopted with one slight amendment. And a Form of Government and Discipline, and a Directory for public worship, drawn chiefly from the standards of the Church of Scotland, with such alterations as the form of our civil government and the state of the Church in this country were thought to demand, completed the system.

In 1801, a "Plan of Union between Presbyterians and Congregationalists in the New Settlements" was formed, with a view to prevent disagreement between the two denominations, and to facilitate their coöperation for the support of the ministry and other Christian institutions. This arrangement continued thirty-six years; and under it were formed hundreds of Churches in the States of New York and Ohio.

For some time previous to 1830, it had been apparent that there were really two parties in the Presbyterian Church, which, though not often brought into actual collision, had occasion, sometimes, in meeting a test question, to indicate their distinct existence. But the celebrated case of the Rev. Albert Barnes, which occurred about that time, developed more decidedly the opposing elements, and marked the formal commencement of a controversy which was destined, after a few years, to result in another division of the Church. Of this controversy I forbear entering into any details; partly because it would be irrelevant to my purpose, and partly because the controversy is too recent to form a legitimate subject for impartial history. Suffice it to say that, after a scene of intense and protracted conflict, continued till the year 1837, the "Plan of Union" was abrogated, and the four Synods of Genesee, Geneva, Utica, and the Western Reserve, were adjudged as no longer "constituent parts" of the Presbyterian Church; and the division thus commenced was consummated the next year. Since that period, the Presbyterian Church has consisted of two distinct Bodies, entirely independent of each other.

In 1837, previous to the exscinding of the four Western Synods, the Presbyterian Church contained 23 Synods, 135 Presbyteries, 2,140 ministers, 2,865 Churches, and 220,557 communicants. In 1857, the Old School Body contained 31 Synods, 155 Presbyteries, 2,411 ministers, 3,251 Churches, and 244,825 communicants. The New School Body, at the same date, contained 26 Synods, 114 Presbyteries, 1,595 ministers, 1,679 Churches, and 139,115 communicants. The aggregate of both Bodies is as follows:—57 Synods, 269 Presbyteries, 4,006 ministers, 4,930 Churches, and 383,940 communicants.

Notwithstanding Presbyterianism has never prevailed extensively in New England, it has had a distinct and independent existence there from a very early period. The French Church in Boston, which was formed of Huguenots, in or about the year 1687, was the first church organized on a Presbyterian basis; but it was continued no longer than while their public worship was conducted in the French language. The first Presbyterian organization in New England, of any permanence, dates to about the year 1718, when a large number of Presbyterians, with four ministers, migrated to this country from the North of Ireland. For some time, in cases of difficulty, the ministers and elders were wont to assemble informally, and hold what might be called *pro re nata* meetings; and occasionally, where they were unable to reach a satisfactory result, they asked advice of the Synod of Ireland.

This state of things continued without much modification till the year 1745, when the ministers resolved, as preparatory to the step they were about to take, to observe, in connection with their congregations, the third Wednesday of March, as a day of fasting, humiliation, and prayer. On the 16th of April following, the Rev. Messrs. John Moorhead of Boston, David McGregore of Londonderry, and Ralph Abercrombie of Pelham, with Messrs. James M'Keon, Alexander Conkey, and James Hughes, met in Londonderry, and being "satisfied as to the Divine warrant, with dependance upon God for counsel and assistance, they, by prayer, constituted themselves into a Presbytery, to act, so far as their present circumstances will permit them, according to the Word of God and the Constitutions of the Presbyterian Church of Scotland, agreeing to that perfect rule." This Body was called "the Boston Presbytery" and met according to adjournment, in that town, on the 13th of August, 1745.

There is a chasm in the Presbyterial Records, from the close of the year 1754 till the 24th of October, 1770. At this time, the Presbytery consisted of twelve congregations, and as many ministers. At a meeting held at Seabrook, N. H., on the 31st of May, 1775, the Presbytery resolved to divide itself into three distinct Bodies—namely "the Presbytery of Salem," "the Presbytery of Londonderry," and "the Presbytery of Palmer;" and the three Presbyteries, thus organized, were then formed into a Synod, called "the Synod of New England," which held its first meeting at Londonderry, on the 4th of September, 1776.

At Boothbay, Me., on the 27th of June, 1771, a new Presbytery was erected, called "the Presbytery of the Eastward,"—consisting of three ministers, and four ruling elders, representing four churches. It had no connection with the Boston Presbytery, and its origin is said to have been in some way connected with the removal of the Rev. John Murray to Boothbay. It never exhibited on its roll above eight ministers. Its last recorded adjournment (now known) was "to meet at New Boston, N. H., on the first Wednesday of October, 1792." The only relic of this Presbytery that I have been able to discover, is a curious old volume in the possession of the Rev. Dr. Jenks, of Boston, printed in 1783, with the following title:—"Bath-Kol. A Voice from the Wilderness. Being an humble attempt to support the sinking truths of God against some of the principal errors raging at this time. Or a joint testimony to some of the grand articles of the Christian Religion, judicially delivered to the Churches under their care. By the First Presbytery of the Eastward."

In September, 1782, the Synod of New England, finding their numbers considerably reduced in consequence of existing difficulties, agreed to dissolve, and form themselves into one Presbytery, by the name of "the Presbytery of Salem." For two succeeding years, this Presbytery met regularly in different parts of Massachusetts Proper; but after this, its meetings were held only in the District of Maine. Its last meeting was held at Gray, September 14, 1791, at the close of which it adjourned *sine die.*

The Third Associate Reformed Presbytery, afterwards called the Associate Reformed Presbytery of Londonderry, was formed in Philadelphia, October 31, 1782, and held its first meeting within its own bounds, at Londonderry, N. H., on the 11th of February, 1783. It ceased to belong to its original denomination in 1802, and was an independent Presbytery until 1809, when it was received into the Synod of Albany, and has since continued under the name of the Presbytery of Londonderry.

The Presbytery of Newburyport was formed by the concurrent action of the Presbytery of Londonderry and the Synod of Albany. It held its first session in Boston, on the 27th of October, 1826, and its last on the 20th of October, 1847,—when it became reunited to the Presbytery of Londonderry.

The Presbytery of Connecticut, consisting of several ministers and churches previously belonging to the Presbytery of New York, was constituted by the Synod of New York on the 15th of October, 1850, and held, its first meeting at Thompsonville on the 29th of the same month.

CHRONOLOGICAL INDEX.

[On the left hand of the page are the names of those who form the subjects of the work—the figures immediately preceding denote the period, as nearly as can be ascertained, when each began his ministry. On the right hand are the names of those who have rendered their testimony or their opinion in regard to the several characters. The names in Italics denote that the statements are drawn from works already in existence—those in Roman denote communications never before published, and, in nearly every instance, specially designed for this work.]

SUBJECTS.	WRITERS.	PAGE.
1683. Francis Makemie		1
1692. Josias Mackie	Rev. I. W. K. Handy	5
1698. Jedediah Andrews	*Dr. Franklin*	10
1705. George McNish		13
1708. Jonathan Dickinson	*Rev. David Austin.*	
	Rev. Thomas Foxcroft	14
1712. George Gillespie		19
1717. Robert Cross		21
1718. William Tennent	*Rev. George Whitefield*	23
1718, 1737, James and David McGregore	*Rev. E. L. Parker*	27
1719. Ebenezer Prime	S. I. Prime, D. D	30
1725. Gilbert Tennent	*Rev. Thomas Prince*	
	President Samuel Finley	35
1729. John Tennent	*Rev. Gilbert Tennent*	41
1730. John Moorhead	A. W. McClure, D. D	44
1730. Jonathan Parsons		47
1732. William Tennent (Second)	*Hon. Elias Boudinot*	
	General J. N. Cumming	
	John Woodhull, D. D	
	Hon. Thomas Henderson	
	S. J. Forman, Esq	52
1733. Samuel Blair	*President Davies*	
	President Samuel Finley	62
1735. David Cowell	*President Davies*	66
1736. Aaron Burr	*Rev. Caleb Smith*	68
1736. Francis Alison, D. D	*Rt. Rev. William White, D. D.*	
	President Stiles	
	John Ewing, D. D	73
1736. John Elder	W. R. Dewitt, D. D	77
1738. James Davenport		80
1740. William Robinson	*President Davies*	
	William Hill, D. D	
	Archibald Alexander, D. D	92
1740. Samuel Finley, D. D	*John Woodhull, D. D*	
	Hon. Ebenezer Hazard	96
1741. Samuel Buell, D. D	Henry Davis, D. D	
	Hon. Alfred Conkling	102
1742. David Brainerd	*Rev. Jonathan Edwards*	113
1742. John Blair	*Assembly's Magazine*	117
1742. Charles Beatty	*Dr. Franklin*	
	C. C. Beatty, D. D	119
1743. James Sproat, D. D	*Ashbel Green, D. D*	
	Thomas Bradford, Esq	125

	SUBJECTS.	WRITERS.	PAGE.
1744.	John Roan		129
1745.	David Bostwick	Hon. D. S. Boardman,	
		Hon. William Smith	
		Preface to his Treatise on Baptism	131
1745.	Jacob Green	*Ashbel Green, D. D*	135
1746.	Samuel Davies	*President Samuel Finley*	140
1747.	Caleb Smith		146
1747.	John Brainerd,	D. D. Field, D. D	149
1747.	John Rodgers, D. D	Samuel Miller, D. D	154
1748.	Elihu Spencer, D. D	Samuel Miller, D. D	165
1748.	John Miller		169
1749.	Robert Smith, D. D	*Assembly's Magazine*	172
1750.	Samuel Kennedy	S. K. Talmage, D. D	175
1754.	Matthew Wilson, D. D	Samuel Miller, D. D	178
1755.	Hugh Knox, D. D		180
1756.	George Duffield, D. D	George Duffield, D. D	186
1756.	Samson Occum	Rev. D. Waldo	192
1757.	Henry Patillo	Mrs. Dr. J. H. Rice	196
1758.	James Latta, D. D	Rev. R. P. Du Bois	199
1758.	Alexander McWhorter, D. D	Hon. Jacob Burnet	
		Rev. Aaron Condict	208
1759.	John Strain	Archibald Alexander, D. D	
		Samuel Martin, D. D	
		Charles Hodge, D. D	215
1759.	John Ewing, D. D	Samuel Miller, D. D	216
1760.	John Joachim Zubly, D. D	Hon. E. J. Harden	219
1760.	James Caldwell	Nicholas Murray, D. D	222
1760.	John Carmichael	*J. N. C. Grier, D. D*	228
1760.	Azel Roe, D. D	John McDowell, D. D	232
1761.	James Waddel, D. D	*Hon. William Wirt*	
		Rev. William Calhoon	
		Archibald Alexander, D. D	235
1762.	David Rice	Thomas Cleland, D. D	242
1763.	Alexander Hewat, D. D	Thomas Smyth, D. D	
		Hon. Mitchell King	246
1763.	John Rosbrugh	Mrs. Lettice Ralston	250
1763.	Patrick Allison, D. D	Robert Purviance, Esq	
		Matthew Brown, D. D	253
1763.	David Caldwell, D. D	Hon. J. M. Morehead	259
1764.	William Tennent (Third)	*Rev. Hugh Alison*	264
1764.	Samuel Blair, D. D	William Neill, D. D	268
1765.	Robert Cooper, D. D	John Moodey, D. D	270
1767.	Joseph Smith	Joseph Smith, D. D	274
1767.	John King, D. D	David Elliott, D. D	281
1767.	Charles Cummings	Hon. David Campbell	285
1768.	John Witherspoon, D. D	Ashbel Green, D. D	288
1768.	Thomas Read, D. D	Hon. Kensey Johns	
		Rev. James Latta	301
1768.	John Woodhull, D. D	John McDowell, D. D	304
1769.	Hezekiah Balch, D. D	Charles Coffin, D. D	308
1772.	Daniel McCalla, D. D	*William Hollingshead, D. D*	320
1772.	Robert Davidson, D. D	Robert Davidson, D. D	322
1772.	James Power, D. D	James Carnahan, D. D	326
1773.	Thomas Reese, D. D	*Dr. David Ramsey*	
		Chancellor James	
		Dr. J. R. Witherspoon	331
1773.	Nathaniel Irwin	J. P. Wilson, D. D	333
1773.	Samuel Stanhope Smith, D.D. LL.D	Philip Lindsley, D. D	335
1774.	Samuel Eusebius McCorkle, D. D	E. W. Caruthers, D. D	346
1774.	John McMillan, D. D	James Carnahan, D. D	350
1775.	Thaddeus Dod	*Rev. Cephas Dod*	356
1775.	John Rankin	Rev. I. W. K. Handy	360
1775.	William Graham	Archibald Alexander, D. D	365
1775.	John McKnight, D. D	George Duffield, D. D	371
1776.	John Linn	Robert Baird, D. D	375
1776.	Samuel Taggart	Rev. Theophilus Packard, Jr	
		Samuel Willard, D. D	377
1776.	James Hall, D. D	R. H. Morrison, D. D	381
1777.	Archibald Scott		387

	SUBJECTS.	WRITERS.	PAGE.
1777	James Francis Armstrong	Rev. I. V. Brown	389
1777.	Samuel Doak, D. D	J. G. M. Ramsey, M. D	392
1778.	John Blair Smith, D. D	William Hill, D. D.	
		Eliphalet Nott, D. D	397
1778.	Caleb Alexander	Hon. Oliver R. Strong	405
1779.	Stephen Bloomer Balch, D. D	Elias Harrison, D. D	408
1780.	Francis Cummins, D. D	S. K. Talmage, D. D	418
1781.	James Dunlap, D. D	Robert Baird, D D.	
		Andrew Wylie, D. D	422
1781.	Moses Hoge, D. D	W. S. Reid, D. D	426
1781.	James Mitchel	Mrs. Dr. J H. Rice	430
1782.	Samuel Carrick	R. B. McMullen, D. D	433
1782.	William Morrison, D. D	Daniel Dana, D. D	436
1782.	William McWhir, D. D	C. C. Jones, D. D	439
1783.	William Boyd	John McDowell, D. D	444
1783.	Joseph Clark, D. D	Rev. I. V. Brown	446
1785.	Charles Nisbet, D. D	Samuel Miller, D. D	450
1785.	John Durburrow Blair	Mrs. Dr. J. H. Rice	459
1786.	Nathan Grier	David McConaughy, D. D	462
1786.	Aaron Woolworth, D. D	Lyman Beecher, D. D	
		R. S. Storrs, D. D	
		Calvin Colton, D. D	468
1786.	Joseph Badger	T M. Cooley, D. D	
		G. E. Pierce, D. D	473
1786.	Ashbel Green, D. D	J. J. Janeway, D. D	
		Nicholas Murray, D. D	479
1786.	David Porter, D. D	G. N. Judd, D. D	
		Rev. G. A. Howard	496
1787.	Drury Lacy	Mrs. Dr. J. H. Rice	506
1787.	Ebenezer Fitch, D. D	Chester Dewey, D. D.	
		Hon. D. D. Barnard	511
1788.	James Muir, D. D	Elias Harrison, D. D	
		James Laurie, D D	516
1788.	Joseph Patterson	George Potts, D. D	
		William Neill, D. D	522
1788.	Robert Henderson, D. D	R. B. McMullen, D. D	
		Isaac Anderson, D. D	
		J. G. M. Ramsey, M D	528
1788.	Asa Hillyer, D. D	G. N. Judd, D. D	533
1788.	John Brown, D. D	Rev. R. C. Smith	
		S. K. Talmage, D. D	536
1789.	Samuel Porter	James Carnahan, D. D	539
1789.	James White Stephenson, D. D	Rev. William Mack	
		James Holmes, D. D	550
1790.	William Paxton, D. D	David McConaughy, D. D	554
1790.	Robert Cathcart, D. D	Rev. D. H. Emerson	559
1790.	William Hill, D. D	Rev. W. N. Scott	
		A. H. H. Boyd, D. D	563
1791.	Lewis Feuilleteau Wilson	R. H. Morrison, D. D	570
1791.	Jonas Coe, D. D	Hon. John Woodworth	
		Eliphalet Nott, D. D	
		T. W. Blatchford, M. D	
		Mark Tucker, D. D	576
1791.	James Turner	S L. Graham, D. D	
		W. S. Plumer, D. D	
		Rev. J. H. Turner	581
1791.	John Anderson, D. D	Samuel McFarren, D. D	588
1791.	James Blythe, D. D.	William Hill, D. D	
		E. D. McMaster, D. D	591
1791.	Samuel Miller, D. D	James Carnahan, D. D	
		Nicholas Murray, D. D	600
1791.	Archibald Alexander, D. D	John Hall, D. D	
		H. A. Boardman, D. D	
		Rev. W. E. Schenck	612
1792.	John Poage Campbell, M. D	Hon. C. S. Todd	626
1792.	Matthew Lyle	Drury Lacy, D. D	629

FRANCIS MAKEMIE.*

1683—1708.

Francis Makemie was born in the neighbourhood of Rathmelton, Donegal County, Ireland; but the date of his birth is not known. It is supposed that he prosecuted his academical, if not his theological, course, at one of the Scottish Universities. All that is known of his early religious exercises is that he became hopefully pious at the age of fourteen, chiefly through the instrumentality of an excellent school-master, under whose instruction he was placed. He was introduced by his pastor, the Rev. Thomas Drummond, to the Presbytery of Laggan, in January, 1681, and was licensed by the same Presbytery some time before the close of that year.

In 1678, application was made to that Presbytery, by a Captain Archibald Johnson, for assistance in procuring a minister for Barbadoes; and in December, 1680, Colonel Stevens, from Maryland, made a similar application in behalf of that Colony. Mr. Makemie was designated as a suitable person to undertake this mission; and, having consented to do so, he received ordination, *sine titulo*, with a view to coming to America. He preached for a while at Barbadoes; but how long does not appear. He was also, for some time, in Somerset County, Md., and is supposed to have been the founder of the church in Snow Hill. In this latter place his memory has always been gratefully cherished; and there are still many traditions there, illustrative of the good work which he performed, and the reverence with which he was regarded.

Mr. Makemie was married about the year 1690, to Naomi, the eldest daughter of William Anderson, a wealthy merchant of Accomac County, Va. By his marriage he became possessed of considerable property, so that he was afterwards quite independent in his circumstances. His residence from this time was in Virginia. In connection with his professional duties, he seems, for a time, to have carried on mercantile business; and there is a record of several suits which he instituted about the year 1690, to recover debts which were contracted in his commercial transactions.

In 1691, Mr. Makemie made a visit to England, and returned either the same year, or the beginning of the next. In July, 1692, he was visited by the celebrated George Keith, who had separated from the Society of Friends, and was travelling in the Southern Provinces, with a view to promulgate and give currency to his peculiar views. Having seen a Catechism written by Makemie, he professed to consider it as containing very grave errors; and the avowed object of his visit was to endeavour to expose and refute them. Makemie declined a public discussion with Keith, from an apprehension that his false reasonings and show of learning would mislead and injure many who might be present. Keith then wrote an examination of the Catechism, charging the author with "denying or wholly overlooking our need of the influences of the Holy Spirit, and of running to the Pope and Church of Rome." Not long after this, Makemie issued from the press

* Webster's MSS.—Smith's Hist. N. Y.—Miller's Life of Rodgers.—Spence's Letters.—Hodge's Hist. Presb. Church.

at Boston "An Answer to George Keith's Libel on a Catechism, published by Francis Makemie." It was recommended by Increase Mather, and several other leading clergymen in Boston, as "the work of a Reverend and judicious minister."

In October, 1699, Mr. Makemie obtained a formal license to preach, agreeably to the requirements of the Toleration Act,—having previously received a certificate of his qualifications at Barbadoes. There is a tradition that, through the influence of some of the clergy of the Established Church, he was arrested and carried to Williamsburg, to answer for the alleged irregularity of preaching without a license; and that he made so favourable an impression on the Governor, that he immediately became his friend, and not only licensed his dwelling-house as a place of worship, but also gave him a general license to preach any where within the limits of the Colony. In this same year, he published at Edinburgh a pamphlet entitled "Truths in a new light, in a Pastoral Letter to the Reformed Protestants in Barbadoes;" which contains an able and earnest vindication of the Non-conformists.

Mr. Makemie was, at this period, at once abundant and successful in his labours; and his heart was much set on procuring from the mother country a number of competent persons to engage in the work of the ministry in Maryland and Virginia. He made preparations for a voyage to England in the summer of 1703; but was prevented by some unexpected occurrence from carrying out his purpose. He went, however, the next year, and was absent nearly a twelve month. He visited London, and made arrangements for the supply of the congregations with evangelical clergymen; and at least two ministers from Ireland accompanied him on his return. During his stay in London, he published a work entitled "A plain and loving Persuasion to the inhabitants of Virginia and Maryland, for promoting towns and co-habitation." He notices it as an unaccountable humour, that, in these Provinces, no attempts were made to build up towns; and one of the objections to it he supposes to be, that, if there were towns, there would be ordinaries, and that would lead to drunkenness. His answer to this is, that "the giving away of liquor makes drunkards—if there were ordinaries, liquor could only be obtained by purchase—if there were towns, there would be stocks, and sots would be placed in them."

The two ministers who returned with Mr. Makemie were John Hampton* and George McNish. In the autumn of 1705, we find Mr. Makemie before the County Court of Somerset, endeavouring to procure the requisite certificates for the unmolested exercise of their ministry; for though, when he began his labours there, some twenty years before, there was the fullest religious liberty in Maryland, the Church of England had become the Established Church in 1692, and it was therefore necessary that these gentlemen should obtain a license in order to the safe and quiet exercise of their ministerial functions. The application in their behalf met with strong opposition, but was finally referred to the Governor, who decided in their favour.

Not long after Mr. Makemie's return from Europe, the Presbytery of Philadelphia was formed; but whether this took place in the year 1706, or

*It is not known whether JOHN HAMPTON was born in Scotland or Ireland. He was called to Snow Hill in March, 1707, and was "inaugurated" by his friend McNish. He was for a long time afflicted with ill health, and in 1717, made a visit to his native country, in the hope that it might contribute to his restoration; but it seems to have been to little purpose, as he asked and obtained leave of the Synod, in the autumn following, to demit his pastoral charge on account of his continued indisposition. He died sometime before February, 1721.

at the close of 1705, it is impossible now to determine, on account of a defect in the Presbyterial Records. The ministers who formed this Presbytery, or united with it previously to December, 1706 were Francis Makemie, George McNish, John Hampton, Samuel Davis,* John Wilson,† Nathaniel Taylor,‡ and Jedediah Andrews. Mr. Makemie was Moderator of the Presbytery in December, 1706.

In January, 1707, Mr. Makemie and his friend and fellow labourer, the Rev. John Hampton, stopped a few days in New York, on their way to New England. Lord Cornbury, the Deputy Governor, hearing of the arrival of these strangers, invited them to the castle to dine with him. No preparation had then been made for either of them to preach, nor was there any regular Presbyterian congregation in the city. After dining with the Governor, Mr. Makemie was invited by some of the citizens to preach on the ensuing Sabbath; and he consented to do so. Without his knowledge, application was made to the Governor for permission for him to preach in the Dutch church; but the answer was promptly in the negative. When the Sabbath came, he preached in the house of one William Jackson, on Pearl street, and baptized a child. Mr. Hampton preached on the same day at Newtown, L. I., to a regular congregation, which had already conformed to the requirements of the Act of Toleration. Mr. Makemie remained in New York on Monday, and went the next day to Newtown, intending to preach there on the day following. Immediately on his arrival, both these ministers were arrested on a warrant signed by Lord Cornbury, charging them with having "taken it upon them to preach in a private house, without having obtained any license for so doing; which is directly contrary to the known laws of England:"—and, as they were reported to have "gone into Long Island with intent there to spread their pernicious doctrine and principles, to the great disturbance of the Church by law established, and of the government of this Province," the Sheriff was directed to bring the bodies of both of them to Fort Anne. The next day, (Wednesday,) they were taken by a circuitous route through Jamaica to New York, where they were carried before the Governor, and, by his order, imprisoned; and, in consequence of the absence of the Chief Justice, they continued there nearly two months. At the end of that time, they were brought before that officer by a writ of *habeas corpus*, and admitted to bail; though no bill was found by the Grand Jury against Mr. Hampton, as he had not preached in the city,—and he was therefore discharged. In June following, Mr. Makemie returned from Virginia to New York to stand his trial; "in the course of which," says Dr. Miller, "it is difficult to say whether he was most conspicuous for his talents as a man, or for his

* SAMUEL DAVIS was residing in Delaware as early as 1692, for at that time, George Keith visited him; but the date of his arrival in this country has not been ascertained. The scene of his labours from 1705 or '06, onwards, was the churches planted by Mr. Makemie in Maryland, or those in their immediate vicinity. He finally succeeded Mr. Hampton as minister of Snow Hill, and died in the summer of 1725.

† JOHN WILSON is supposed to have been a native of Scotland. As early as 1702, he preached in the court-house at Newcastle, De., but remained there for only a short time. The next year, he returned, to the dissatisfaction of a portion of the people. But he seems not to have sustained the pastoral relation to that congregation. In 1708, the Presbytery directed him to preach alternately at Newcastle and White Clay. In 1710, he ceased preaching at Newcastle, and probably devoted his whole time to White Clay, till his death which occurred in 1712. He conducted—partly at least—the correspondence of the Presbytery with Scotland.

‡ NATHANIEL TAYLOR came to this country from Scotland with his congregation, and settled in Upper Marlborough, Md., about the year 1690. Both history and tradition are nearly silent concerning him.

dignity and piety as a minister of the Gospel." The result of the trial was an acquittal by the jury. But the court would not discharge him from his recognisance till they had obliged him to pay all the fees of his prosecution, which, together with his expenses, amounted to little less than three hundred dollars.

Soon after his liberation, Mr. Makemie preached again in the church in which the French were allowed to worship—his sermon was printed, and another great excitement was produced; insomuch that the Governor issued a new process, and employed his officers, during the whole of one Sabbath, to arrest and confine him again, with a view to another trial. He had, however, meanwhile, made his escape from the Province, so that the attempt was unsuccessful. He seems to have pursued his journey to New England; as he addressed a letter to Lord Cornbury from Boston, in July, 1707, expostulating with his Lordship for thus making him the object of a protracted persecution. This is the only letter of Makemie's that has been published; though there are two others, addressed to Dr. Increase Mather in 1684 and 1685, preserved in the archives of the Massachusetts Historical Society.* An account of this whole affair, supposed to have been written by Makemie, or at least under his superintendence, was published at the time, and was republished at New York, in 1755.

Mr. Makemie, after his release from confinement, on being admitted to bail, attended the sessions of Presbytery on his way to Virginia, and preached, agreeably to previous appointment. This was the last meeting of Presbytery which he ever attended; though it appears from the record of the next meeting that he had, in the mean time, obeyed an order of Presbytery to write to the Rev. Alexander Colden of Oxnam, Scotland, (father of Lieut. Governor Colden,) to endeavour to persuade him to come to this country, with special reference to taking the pastoral care of the people in and about Lewistown, De.

Mr. Makemie died at his residence in Virginia, in the summer of 1708, leaving a widow and two daughters. One daughter survived him less than a year, and her mother quickly followed her. The other daughter was married to a Mr. Holden of Accomac, and died without issue, in 1787, leaving a large property, part of which she bequeathed to the support of the Gospel and the relief of the poor. Makemie himself also made liberal bequests to charitable objects, and distributed his valuable library among his family, and two or three other friends. An original portrait of him was destroyed in the burning of the house of the Rev. Dr. Balch of Georgetown, D. C.

What gives Makemie his grand distinction is, that he was undoubtedly the first regular and thorough Presbyterian minister in this country; and he may justly be regarded as the father of the Presbyterian Church. His influence in the region in which he chiefly exercised his ministry, was extensive and powerful. Though no particular testimony remains concerning him from any contemporary writer, Dr. Miller, upon the authority of some venerable men of the generation immediately succeeding him, speaks of him as "a man of eminent piety, as well as strong intellectual powers, and an uncommonly fascinating address."

* Since this sketch was written, these letters have been printed in the History of the Presbyterian Church, by the Rev. Richard Webster.

JOSIAS MACKIE.

1692—1716.

FROM THE REV. I. W. K. HANDY.

PORTSMOUTH, Va., February 26, 1857.

Rev. and dear Brother: I regard myself as quite fortunate in being able, after some considerable search, to furnish you even with a few items, sufficiently authentic, to redeem from uncertainty a name which was beginning to be pronounced as a sort of myth. It has long been admitted by those familiar with the old Records of our Church, that a Presbyterian minister of the name of "*Macky*," was labouring at an early period, somewhere ou Elizabeth River in Virginia; but there has scarcely been a conjecture in relation to his attainments, labours, or even the length of time he was located on the River. Some, indeed, have suggested that he was probably a Scotchman; and as his name does not appear in the body of the Minutes, it has been thought that he could not have been in regular connection with the "Mother Presbytery." It is true that the particulars which have now come to light are very meagre; but they are not without interest; and will, no doubt, be received with great satisfaction, by all who would trace out the small beginnings of the Presbyterian Church in the United States.

The only item of history heretofore found concerning this ancient minister, appears in the Minutes of the Presbytery of Philadelphia, published by the Presbyterian Board. During the sessions of that judicatory, in September, 1712, "a complaint of the melancholy circumstances Mr. John Macky, on Elizabeth River, Virginia, labours under, being made by Mr. Henry,* the Presbytery was concerned. And Mr. John Hampton saying that he designed to write to him on an affair of his own, the Presbytery desired him to signify their regard to and concern for him." We learn nothing from this record, save the fact that Macky was living on the River; that he was in melancholy circumstances; and that he had the cordial sympathy of the members of Presbytery; with some of whom, at least, he was on terms of special intimacy and friendship.

It had often occurred to me that if access could be had to the Records of Norfolk County, something more might be learned of this early minister. It was in this way, I remembered, that much valuable information had been obtained concerning Makemie. Accordingly, as soon after my settlement in Portsmouth as circumstances would allow, I obtained permission of our obliging clerk, to search all the old files and registers. I had been examining but a short time, before, much to my gratification, I found

* JOHN HENRY was ordained by the Presbytery of Dublin, and came to Maryland in 1709, having been invited, on the death of Makemie, to be his successor. He was admitted a member of Presbytery in 1710; and the next year became pastor of the church at Rehoboth, Va. He died in 1717. He was married in 1690 to a daughter of Sir Robert King, the agent of Maryland, and the widow of Colonel Francis Jenkins. He had two sons,—*Robert Jenkins*, who resided in Somerset, and was Judge of the Provincial Court in 1754, and *John*, who was a Colonel, and a member of the House of Delegates for Worcester County. Mr. Henry had a high reputation as a citizen and a divine. He left a large manuscript volume, enforcing the leading doctrines of the Westminster Confession of Faith.

Mackie's name indexed. This led to the discovery of his recorded oaths; and, afterwards, of his will,—first as transcribed in the "Will Book;" and then the original document, among the files, signed by his own hand.

It appears from these various sources, that the Rev. JOSIAS MACKIE was among the earliest of the Presbyterian ministers who came to America. He was here as early as 1692;—the first notice I have found of him, bearing date, June 22, of that year. We have no recorded notice of Makemie, earlier than February 14, 1690; and we should yet have been in darkness as to the probable year of his migration to this country, but for the discovery in the Massachusetts Historical Library, of two letters written from Virginia in 1684 and 1685. As it is true that Makemie was labouring on the Eastern shore of Maryland, in South Carolina, and in Virginia, in all, some seven or eight years prior to the appearance of his name in the Records of Accomac County, so also there is nothing improbable in the supposition that Mackie may have been some time in America, before taking the oath of fidelity, &c., in Norfolk County. It was my original impression that Mackie might have crossed the Atlantic with Makemie, or very soon after him. But, upon reflection, I can find nothing to sustain this opinion; and I now think it more probable that he came to America soon after Makemie's visit to Elizabeth River, in May, 1684; where he found a "poor desolate people," mourning the loss of their "dissenting minister from Ireland," whom the "Lord had been pleased to remove by death," the summer before. It had been the great aim of this persevering and active servant of God to search out localities, to which he could invite ministers from his own country; and it is quite probable that, after supplying this field for a time, he gave place to his countryman, Mackie; whom he could now conscientiously advise to settle among such friends as "Colonel Anthony Lawson, and other inhabitants of Lower Norfolk County." According to this view—which I am well persuaded is correct—he was, indeed, the *successor* of Mackemie, on Elizabeth River; though not, as imagined by some, in 1712, *subsequently* to the death of that great man.

On the 22d of June, 1692, the Rev. Josias Mackie appeared before two magistrates,—Thomas Butt and James Wilson,—and by formal oath, renounced all connection with the Roman Catholic Church; and declared his approbation, according to law, of the "Articles of Religion," with certain exceptions, as allowed in the case of Dissenters. The oaths, as preserved upon the County Records, are in the following words, namely:—

"I, JOSIAS MACKIE, do solemnly and sincerely, in the presence of God, profess, testify, and declare that I do believe that, in the sacrament of the Lord's Supper, there is not any transubstantiation of the elements of bread and wine into the body and blood of Christ, at, or after, the consecration thereof, by any person whatsoever; and that the invocation or adoration of the Virgin Mary, or any other saint, and the Sacrifice of the Mass, as they are now used in the Church of Rome, are superstitious and idolatrous; and I do solemnly, in the presence of God, profess, testify, and declare that I do make this Declaration, and every part thereof, in the plain and ordinary sense of the words read unto me, as they are commonly understood by English Protestants, without any evasion, equivocation, or mental reservation whatsoever, and without any dispensation granted me, for this purpose, by the Pope, or any authority or person whatsoever, or without thinking that I am, or can be, acquitted before God or man, or absolved of this declaration, or any part thereof, although the Pope or any person, or persons, or power whatsoever, should dispense with or annul the same, or declare that it was null and void from the beginning.

"JOSIAS MACKIE.

"I do farther, as a minister of the Gospel, declare my approbation of, and do subscribe unto, the Articles of Religion mentioned in the statute made in the thirteenth year of the reign of the late Queen Elizabeth; except the thirty-fourth, about the traditions of the church; the thirty-fifth, concerning homilies; the thirty-sixth, of consecration of bishops and ministers; and the words of the twentieth article, viz: the church hath power to *decree* rights and ceremonies, and *impose*. I say, I do hereby declare my approbation of, and subscribe, the aforesaid Articles of Religion, excepting above, expressed by act of Parliament. JOSIAS MACKIE."

On the same day, Mackie took the oath of fidelity; and received permission to preach at certain designated places. This oath is as follows:—

"I do sincerely promise and swear that I will be faithful, bear true allegiance to their Majesties, King William and Queen Mary—so help me God.

"I do swear that I do from my heart, abhor, detest, and abjure, as impious and heretical, that damnable doctrine and position, that princes, excommunicated or deprived by, on any authority of the See of Rome, may be deposed, or murthered by their subjects, or any whatsoever; and I do declare that no foreign princes, person, prelate, state, or potentate, hath or ought to have any power, jurisdiction, superiority, pre-eminence, or authority, ecclesiastical or spiritual, within this realm—so help me God."

There is evidence that Mackie was no drone. As soon as he had obtained permission to preach, he selected three different places at which he might regularly conduct public worship. These were many miles apart, in different directions, on the river; and were, no doubt, visited at such intervals, as brought into frequent requisition the services of a choice "riding horse," and his "great riding coat;" both of which are carefully remembered in his will. These several appointments were held in "a house at Mr. Thomas Ivy's, in Eastern Branch; a house belonging to Mr. Richard Phillpot, in Tanner's Creek precincts; and a house belonging to Mr. John Roberts, in the Western Branch." On the 18th of November, 1696, he certifies that he had selected another "place of meeting, for preaching the Gospel;" which was at the house of Mr. John Dickson, in Southern Branch.

It is probable that Mackie, like his cotemporary Makemie, was, to a considerable extent, employed as a planter and merchant. It is certain, at least, that he owned "one hundred and fifty acres of land, lying and being in Princess Anne County, near the Back Bay;" and as it is stated in the will, that this was "the remainder of a tract of land, purchased of Capt. Francis Moore," it is to be presumed that he had once owned a farm of much larger dimensions, and which, perhaps, he had recently sold, that the proceeds might be sent to his relatives in Ireland. He appears, also, to have been possessed of a "valuable stock of horses, which he kept at the sea-side." From this stock, he bequeaths eight choice *mares* to various friends; and gives his "riding horse, bridle, and saddle, to Thomas Butt, son of Thomas Butt, deceased."

I suppose Mackie to have been a merchant, from the various debts due him, as mentioned in the will, and from the character of various items referred to. On the 19th of May, 1697, he was fortunate in a suit against the estate of George Newton, who was indebted to him in a bond for £40. For this, he was allowed, by an arbitration, 5223 lbs. of tobacco. Various sums were due him from merchants in London,—probably for tobacco which he had received in payment for goods: all of which money is devised to the children of his sisters in Ireland. To Elizabeth and John Wishard, and William and Mary Johnson, he bequeathed all his "new goods, both woolling, and linning," with certain exceptions, "to be equally divided between them; and the said Wishards to have their parts, immediately after his decease, and the said Johnsons, when they shall come of age, or married." To Richard Butt, he gives his "great riding coat, with twenty yards of brown linning that is in the chest of goods."

A library is not always the test of one's scholarship; but it is quite unlikely that a Presbyterian minister, in the seventeenth century, would have brought to the wilds of America a cumbrous load of books, simply for the sake of owning them. The several references which are made in the will to this property, indicate that Mackie's library must have been just such a one as would be valuable to a well educated divine. "I give," says he, "my more scholastic books, of learned languages, as Latin, Greek, Hebrew, to be equally divided between Mr. Henry, Mr. Hampton, and Mr. Mackness,* non-conforming ministers, at Pokamoke, or thereabouts." For the proper disposal of the rest of his books, he left a paper of "directions," and requests his executors "well and truly to observe" them. Mr. Richard Butt is requested to attend to the payment of certain debts; and as a remuneration for his services, his "will and desire" was, "that the said Richard Butt have a good portion of his English good books."

It is difficult to say whether Mackie was, or was not, a member of the Mother Presbytery. It is true that his name does not appear in the Records; nor is any mention made of his church in the body of the Minutes. In a letter, however, addressed "to the Rev. Presbytery of Dublin," and recorded in the Letter-Book—dated September, 1710, the "small congregation at Elizabeth River" is recognised as being within the bounds of Presbytery; and it is farther stated that this congregation, with various others, in Maryland, Pennsylvania, Jersey, and New York, "make up all the bounds, from which there were any members." Vacancies are spoken of; but Elizabeth River could not be one of them,—as it is known that Mackie was there until 1716. Another letter, of the same date, addressed to the Synod of Glasgow, speaks of ten members in the Provinces; but, in the specification, Virginia is not mentioned. Now, as the church on Elizabeth River is mentioned in the first letter among the churches having members; and as we know that Mackie was in connection with that church in 1710,—is it not probable that the Virginia church, being at so great a distance from each of the two places of meeting—Philadelphia and Newcastle—was overlooked, in the count? The probability is that Mackie and his church were regarded as being in connection with the Presbytery; but such would be the "great toil and labour, and great difficulty—by reason of [his] great distance from" the place of meeting, that he found it impossible to attend; and as his difficulties were well known to the brethren, he was not called to account, as was the Rev. Samuel Davis; who, though comparatively convenient, was frequently absent. If this were so, then his name would not appear in the Minutes, as no list of absentees was kept. It is at least cer-

* Generally spelt McNish.

tain from the notice taken of Mackie by the Presbytery, and the deep sympathy manifested towards him, under his "melancholy circumstances"—as well as from the disposition which he made of his "more scholastic books," that some special intimacy existed; and that he was known and recognised with more than a casual interest. What those "melancholy circumstances" were, we cannot determine; but, in the absence of a better supposition, and, with our present dim light,—it is not unreasonable to suppose that they may have been closely connected with, and afforded some painful reason for, his continued absence from the meetings of the Presbytery.

The question in relation to the place of Mackie's nativity has been agitated with no little interest;—some contending, from the name, that he was from Scotland; and others strenuously urging that he was a native of Ireland. The will throws all the light on this subject that we need. He was the son of "Mr. Patrick Mackie, sometime of St. Johnstone, in the County of Donegal, of the Kingdom of Ireland." At the time of his death, there were yet living his "three sisters, Mary, Margaret, and Rebecca." In his will, he directs that "all the remaining part of his money, which is in ready cash, in Virginia, should be equally divided" between these sisters; and he wishes that it may be transmitted "in bills of exchange, at his own cost and charge, direct to such person or persons as his executors should think best, in the city of London; and from thence, to Mr. John Harvey, of Londonderry, merchant, and from him transmitted to the children" of his three sisters.

Mackie was an unmarried man; and, as neither wife or children are mentioned in the will, it is more than probable that he was an old bachelor.

It is worthy of note that the name of this early Presbyterian divine was not "John Macky," as heretofore written, but *Josias Mackie.* As I have already stated, I have had the pleasure of examining the original will, as signed by his own hand. The first name,—*Josias*—is written in a large, bold hand. The *Mackie* is also large; but it bears evident marks of having been written *in extremis*, and without much control of the pen.

The Rev. Josias Mackie died sometime between the 7th and the 16th day of November, 1716. The will is dated on the 7th, and was proved on the 16th. From these dates and the date of his first oath—June 22d, 1692,—it is certain that he had been living on Elizabeth River, not far from a quarter of a century.

I am not able to communicate any thing concerning the *labours* of Mr. Mackie. Something valuable may yet come to light. It is certain, however, that he was a good man, a true Presbyterian,—bold, active, and laborious. With the care of a farm and a store, he found time to preach at four places of meeting; and in prospect of death, he leaves this solemn and interesting record:—"Being heartily sorry for my sins past, and most humbly desiring forgiveness of the same, I commit my soul to Almighty God, trusting to receive full pardon, and free justification, through the merits of Jesus Christ." I am, my dear Sir,

With great respect and friendship, truly yours,

ISAAC W. K. HANDY.

JEDEDIAH ANDREWS.*

1698—1747.

JEDEDIAH ANDREWS, son of Captain Thomas Andrews, was born at Hingham, Mass., July 7, 1674, and was baptized by the Rev. Peter Hobart, five days after. He was the youngest but one of ten children. He was graduated at Harvard College in 1695. In consequence of the schismatic influence of George Keith among the Society of Friends in Philadelphia, the way was opened for the commencement of religious services there, by Baptists, Presbyterians, and Episcopalians. There were nine Baptists and a few Independents in the town. After the "Barbadoes Company" gave up their store, the building was used by the two denominations in common, whenever the services of a minister could be procured.

The Rev. John Watts, a Baptist minister, began, by request, to officiate at regular intervals, and the Rev. Dr. Clayton, an Episcopal clergyman, entered into an amicable correspondence with him to effect a union with the National Establishment. In the summer of 1698, Mr. Andrews, having been licensed in New England, went to Philadelphia, and Mr. Watts and his friends, feeling uneasy at what they regarded as coldness on the part of their Episcopal brethren, proposed to Mr. Andrews, that he, with his infant congregation, should unite with them, and that the worship should be conducted by ministers, in good standing, of either body, as might be convenient, and both denominations should join in it. Some negotiation on the subject was attempted, but it ended in nothing satisfactory to any body concerned; but rather served to put the two denominations at a greater distance from each other.

Mr. Andrews was ordained in Philadelphia, probably in the autumn of 1701; for at that time commences his record of baptisms and marriages. A Mr. Talbot, Church missionary at Burlington, writing to the "Venerable Society for propagating the Gospel in foreign parts," says,—"The Presbyterians here come a great way to lay hands on one another, but, after all, I think they had as good stay at home, for all the good they do. . . In Philadelphia one pretends to be a Presbyterian, and has a congregation to which he preaches."

In 1704, Mr. Andrews and his congregation left the "Barbadoes Store" to worship in the new edifice they had erected in Buttonwood [now Market] Street. Five adults were baptized in 1705, and four in 1706.

The church is said to have been in some sense Congregational, but it was represented by elders in Presbytery from the first. Mr. Andrews was punctual in his attendance on every meeting, and never failed to be accompanied by an elder.

In 1707, the Presbytery directed each minister to read and comment upon a chapter in the Bible every Lord's day, "as discretion and circumstances of time and place would admit." All the ministers except Mr. Andrews complied, and, in 1708, it was "recommended to him to take into serious consideration the reading of a chapter, and making a comment on the same;" but there is no evidence that he ever fell into the practice. A

* Webster's MSS.—Hodge's Hist. Presb. Church.

strong prejudice prevailed against it in New England, where he had been educated, as it was considered an approximation at least to Episcopal usage; and Mr. Andrews' reluctance in the case was no doubt to be set down as a prejudice of education.

It is evident from the record of his baptisms that he must have performed, at different times, a considerable amount of missionary labour. Hopewell, Gloucester, Burlington, Amboy, and Staten Island, all seem to have been in turn favoured with his occasional ministrations.

He was also the Recording Clerk of the Presbytery and of the Synod, as long as he lived. He conducted most of their correspondence, especially with New England, and was considered as signally gifted in bringing to a successful termination angry disputes, both in congregations and among individuals.

There is a tradition that he gave up his Independency in 1729, and became thoroughly Presbyterian. This tradition, however, seems to be rendered somewhat doubtful by the fact, that it was just at that time that his congregation were asking aid from Boston to enlarge their place of worship. And, in addition to that, nothing of the kind is even hinted at in a letter which he addressed to Dr. Colman of Boston, the same year, asking advice as to his duty in relation to the "Adopting Act." "As to affairs here," he says, "we are engaged in the enlargement of our house, and, by the assistance we had from Boston, I hope we shall go on comfortably with that work."

In September, 1733, he preferred a request to the Synod that he should be allowed an assistant in the ministry. The request was unanimously granted, on condition that "sufficient provision should be made for his honourable maintenance, during his life among them." This was subsequently modified, the better to meet the views of the congregation, and they were allowed to call an assistant. But the Synod directed that those who desired an assistant should not diminish, but rather increase, their subscriptions for Mr. Andrews, because the existing subscription was scanty; that no part of what was already subscribed should be alienated from him, and that all the monthly collections should be appropriated to his benefit. In May of the next year, the Presbytery gave him leave to resign his charge, if he saw fit. In the autumn, the Rev. Samuel Hemphill came to this country from Ireland, was received as a member of the Synod, and took up his abode in Philadelphia, until he should obtain a settlement. Mr. Andrews invited him to occupy his pulpit a part of each Sabbath; but he soon regretted it; for he found that free-thinkers, deists, and in general the worst part of the community, flocked to hear him, while the better part of the congregation staid away. Mr. Andrews attended his service regularly during the winter; but felt himself bound to "article" against him, and a commission, appointed for the purpose of investigating the case, tried and suspended him. In writing to Dr. Colman, Mr. Andrews says that he had never suffered so much as during this period, and that his mind was made up to leave his charge, although the better part of them were desirous that he should remain. Mr. Hemphill finally sunk into obscurity and disgrace, in consequence of being detected in preaching other men's sermons.

The congregation could not agree in the choice of an assistant,—the preference of some being for Jonathan Dickinson, and of others for Robert Cross; but, while the matter was in debate, the friends of the latter asked of the Synod that they might be erected into a new congregation, and authorized to call a minister for themselves. Their request was granted by a large majority, with the understanding that they were not *obliged* to form a distinct Society, but *might* do so, if, upon mature reflection, they thought best.

The Commission met in June, 1736. The endeavours to effect a re-union of the congregation having been unsuccessful, they persuaded the friends of Robert Cross to make a further effort, and Mr. Andrews heartily approved of the design, but his friends would not consent to it. The new congregation had various supplies until 1737, when Robert Cross accepted their call. The two congregations were then united, and were allowed fifty pounds out of the funds of the Synod to buy a burying-ground. On the division of the Synod, in 1744, Mr. Andrews remained with the Old Side. He wrote to Dr. Colman—"Tennent is much more moderate, and lets me alone."

It is sad to be obliged to record that, near the close of a long and useful life, a cloud settled over this venerable man, that had scarcely passed off at the time of his death. He was arraigned by his Presbytery on a charge of gross immorality; and though he denied any criminal intent, he made a confession which, in the opinion of the Presbytery, so far involved his character, that they felt constrained to pass upon him the sentence of suspension;—a sentence which he himself recorded, thus closing his labours as Clerk of the Presbytery. He was, however, restored after a few months, and died in the year 1747.

The following estimate of Mr. Andrews as a preacher, from Dr. Franklin's Memoirs, is perhaps quite as illustrative of the character of the writer, as of the subject:—

"I regularly paid my subscription for the support of the only Presbyterian minister or meeting we had. He used to visit me sometimes as a friend, and admonish me to attend his ministrations. I was now and then prevailed on to do so—once for five Sundays successively. Had he been, in my opinion, a good preacher, perhaps I might have continued, notwithstanding the occasion I had for the Sunday's leisure in my course of study. But his discourses were chiefly either polemic arguments, or explanations of the peculiar doctrines of our sect, and were all to me very dry, uninteresting, and unedifying, since not a single moral principle was inculcated or enforced,—their aim seeming to be rather to make us Presbyterians than good citizens. At length, he took for his text Phil. iv. 8. "Finally, Brethren, whatsoever things are true, &c.;" and I imagined, in a sermon on such a text, we could not miss of having some morality. He confined himself to five points only, as meant by the Apostle: Keeping holy the Sabbath day; Being diligent in reading the Scriptures; Attending daily the public worship; Partaking of the Sacraments; and Paying due respect to God's ministers. These all might be good things; but as they were not the kind of good things I expected from that text, I despaired of ever meeting with them from any other, was disgusted, and attended his preaching no more. On Hemphill's defeat, (in 1735,) I quitted the congregation, never attending it further, though continuing my subscription many years for the support of its ministers."

GEORGE McNISH.*

1705—1723.

GEORGE MCNISH was born and educated, according to one authority,† in Ireland; and, according to another, in Scotland;‡ and he became a minister of the Gospel before leaving his native country. He came to America in 1705, with the Rev. Francis Makemie, of Virginia, who, after residing here a number of years, returned to Europe, expressly to induce ministers to come over, and meet the constantly increasing demand for the preaching of the Gospel. In June, 1706, by order of Governor Seymour of Maryland, he received the necessary license to preach, from the Somerset County Court. He was one of the original members of the Presbytery of Philadelphia.

His first labours, after his arrival in this country, were among the people of Monokin and Wicomico, in Maryland. They gave him a call to settle among them, probably some time before 1710; and, in the spring of that year, he received another call from Jamaica, L. I. He had evidently the two calls under consideration at the same time; for, at a meeting of the Presbytery in 1711, the call from Jamaica was put into his hands, and "'twas determined to leave his affairs respecting Jamaica and Patuxent to himself, with advice not to delay to fix himself somewhere." Sometime in 1711, he was actually installed pastor of the church in Jamaica, though he seems to have preached there frequently during the preceding year.

In 1717, the Presbytery of Long Island was formed, chiefly through Mr. McNish's instrumentality; and, as this was the first Presbytery formed in the Province of New York, he may fairly be considered as the father of Presbyterianism in that State. He was Moderator of the Presbytery of Philadelphia in 1710, and again in 1716; and consequently preached the Synodical Sermon at the first meeting of the Synod of Philadelphia in 1717. His text was John xxi. 17,—"Lovest thou me?" The same year, as he contemplated making a visit to Great Britain, the Synod deputed him to act in their behalf, during his absence, in promoting, as far as he could, the interests of religion in this country. He was prevented from making his contemplated visit; but the fact that he was appointed to such a service shows that he was one of the more influential ministers of his day, and enjoyed in a high degree the confidence of his brethren. Tradition ascribes to him much more than an ordinary degree of both talent and usefulness. In the Records of the Synod for 1723, there is the following entry:—"Upon reading the list of ministers, the Synod found to their great grief that Mr. McNish was dead." In the church register of Newtown it is stated that he died March 10, 1722–23.

During the whole of Mr. McNish's ministry, there was a violent controversy carried on in reference to the place of worship in Jamaica, which, though originally built for the Presbyterian Church, was appropriated, by Lord Cornbury, to the use of the Church of England. Though Mr.

* Hodge's Hist. Presb. Church.—Prime's Hist. L. I.—Macdonald's Hist. Presb. Church at Jamaica, L. I.—Webster's MSS.

† Dr. Reid.

‡ Mr. Poyer of Jamaica.

McNish was the minister of the congregation, some ten or eleven years, it is supposed that he never preached in the house of worship belonging to it, after his installation, as it was not restored till some time after his death. The particulars of this controversy form an interesting chapter in American Church History.

JONATHAN DICKINSON.*

1708—1747.

Jonathan Dickinson was descended from a highly respectable family. He was a grandson of Nathaniel Dickinson,—one of the first settlers of Wethersfield, Conn., who removed to Hadley, Mass., in 1659. He was a son of Hezekiah and Abigail Dickinson, and was born in Hatfield, Mass., April 22, 1688. At a very early age he lost his father,—after which, his mother was married to Thomas Ingersoll, and removed to Springfield—she is said to have educated her sons by assistance derived from the estate of her second husband. He was graduated at Yale College in 1706, after which he gave himself for a time to the study of Theology, and was licensed to preach the Gospel. He went to Elizabethtown, N. J., in 1708. He was ordained by the ministers of Fairfield County, Conn., September 29, 1709. His field of labour embraced not only what is now Elizabethtown, but Rahway, Westfield, Connecticut Farms, Springfield, and a part of Chatham. He met with the Philadelphia Presbytery, as a corresponding member, in 1715, and, at the ordination of Robert Orr†, actually joined the body, in 1717.

Here Mr. Dickinson continued to exercise his ministry during a period of nearly forty years. Dr. Green, in the notice which he has taken of him in his History of the College of New Jersey, expresses the opinion that he was accustomed, during a considerable portion of his ministry, to receive young men for instruction in the different branches preparatory to their entering on the study of some one of the liberal professions. He had also more to do with the public concerns of his denomination than almost any other man ; and especially in the great controversy by which the Synod of Philadelphia, then representing the whole Presbyterian Church, was so much agitated, and at length actually divided, he bore a most prominent part. For this he was eminently qualified, not merely by his great familiarity with the rules of ecclesiastical procedure, but by his uncommon sagacity, his calm judgment, and his unshrinking firmness,—tempered, however, by the spirit of Christian forbearance and moderation. And

* Pierson's Fun. Serm.—Miller's Retrospect, II.—Chandler's Life of Johnson.—Appendix to Green's Discourses.—Murray's Hist. Elizabethtown.—Webster's MSS.

† Robert Orr, came as a probationer to this country from Scotland or Ireland. Having preached for some time to the people of Maidenhead and Hopewell, he presented his credentials to the Presbytery, in 1715, and they were approved. He was ordained and installed at Maidenhead on the 20th of October, of that year. His field embraced the ground covered by Pennington, Lawrence, Trenton, (First Church), Trenton City, Titusville, and perhaps Amwell. He was dismissed from his charge in 1719, and received a general Synodical recommendation, being uncertain where Providence might cast his lot. On account of the loss of the Records of the Philadelphia Presbytery, his subsequent course cannot be traced.

besides the numerous and various duties devolving upon him, at home and abroad, in connection with his office as a minister, he was a practising physician, and acquired considerable reputation in the medical profession.

In the conflict of opinion that prevailed in relation to the revival in which Whitefield had so prominent an agency, Dickinson was found an unflinching assertor of the genuineness of the work; and few, if any, in the denomination to which he belonged, had more to do than he in sustaining and promoting its interests. Whitefield is known, on one occasion at least, to have visited him, and to have preached in his parish to a very large audience, collected upon the short notice of two hours. Brainerd, the field of whose most important labours was at no great distance from Elizabethtown, was Dickinson's intimate friend; and they were cordial coadjutors in promoting all the great interests of truth and godliness. But, notwithstanding Dickinson was the earnest friend and promoter of the revival, no one was more careful than he in discriminating between the precious and the vile in Christian experience, and no one set his face more resolutely against the spirit of fanaticism and extravagance by which the revival was, in many cases, so materially marred.

He published a tract bearing on this subject under the following extended title:—"A display of God's special grace, in a familiar Dialogue, between a minister and a gentleman of his congregation, about the work of God in the conviction and conversion of sinners, so remarkably of late begun and going on in these American parts: wherein the objections against some uncommon appearances among us are distinctly considered, mistakes rectified, and the work itself particularly proved to be from the Holy Spirit: with an addition in a second conference, relating to sundry Antinomian principles, beginning to obtain in some places." This pamphlet was widely circulated, and produced a great effect. It was published at first anonymously, but it soon became known who was the author, and it drew forth a strong recommendation from most of the clergymen in Boston, with Dr. Colman at their head, and subsequently a corresponding recommendation from some of the brightest lights of the Presbyterian Church,—such as the Tennents, Blairs, &c. It is written with great vigour and discrimination, and in a tone not unlike that which characterizes the works of Edwards, written about the same time, and on the same general subject.

The division of the Presbyterian Church, which resulted in the formation of the separate Synods of New York and Philadelphia, occurred in the year 1741. From this period, each of the Synods was intent upon making provision to train up young men for the ministry; and as nearly all the ministers of New Jersey attached themselves to the Synod of New York, and as the Presbyterian interest was stronger in New Jersey than in any other part of the Synod, it was proposed to establish a College, if possible, and to fix it within the limits of New Jersey. Dickinson had been the acknowledged leader in the old Synod of Philadelphia, when that constituted the entire Presbyterian body; and he was no less the leader of the Synod of New York, after the separation; and no doubt he had more to do in originating the College of New Jersey than any other man. The business of teaching had been familiar to him for years; and this, taken in connection with his confessed intellectual superiority and commanding influence, naturally directed the attention of the community to him, as the individual most suitable to preside in so important an undertaking. A charter for a College having been granted by John Hamilton, at that time acting Governor, the infant institution which, in due time, took the name of Nassau Hall, forthwith went into operation at Elizabethtown, with Dickinson at its head. Still he did not relinquish, in any degree, his pastoral charge, but connected with his accustomed duties as a minister the oversight and instruction of the new College: indeed it is probable that the office which he now formally assumed as President, occupied scarcely more of his time than he had previously devoted to the young men whose education he had undertaken to superintend. He, however, sustained this office but for a brief period; for the College did not commence its operations till the charter was given in October, 1746, and his death occurred on the 7th of October, 1747. But, though his Presidency lasted but a single year, there is no doubt that he left upon the institution the permanent impress of his own character.

He died of an attack of pleurisy, in the sixtieth year of his age, and at a time when his usefulness was probably greater than it had been at any period of his life. Mr. Johnes* of Morristown, who was with him in his last illness, asked him, just before his death, concerning his prospects, and his reply was—"Many days have passed between God and my soul, in which I have solemnly dedicated myself to Him, and I trust what I have committed unto Him, He is able to keep until that day." These were his last words. His Funeral Sermon was preached by the Rev. John Pierson† of Woodbridge, and was published. He was buried among his flock, where is still to be seen a venerable old monument, with a long poetical inscription, marking the place of his grave.

That President Dickinson's intellect was of a very high order, no one can doubt who reads half a dozen pages of any thing that he has written. There is a vigour and perspicuity of both thought and expression, an accuracy of discrimination, and an ability to grapple with the most difficult problems, that mark him at once as an extraordinary man. His style compares well with that of the best theological writers of his day. He possessed great energy and decision, as well as great conscientiousness; and, though he had no relish for controversy, for its own sake, he never hesitated to engage in it, when he supposed the interests of truth required it. Hence a considerable portion of his published works bear a controversial character, and are designed to defend what he regarded the cardinal doctrines of Christianity. It may be doubted whether, with the single exception of the elder Edwards, Calvinism has ever found an abler or more efficient champion in this country, than Jonathan Dickinson.

* TIMOTHY JOHNES was of Welsh extraction, and was born at Southampton, L. I., May 24, 1717. He was graduated at Yale College in 1737, and was ordained and installed at Morristown by the New York Presbytery, February 9, 1743. There were several extensive revivals in connection with his labours, and four hundred and twenty-four were added to the church, on a profession of their faith, during his ministry. While the American army was encamped in Morristown in the winter of 1777, Washington, on one occasion, communed with Mr. Johnes' church. He received the degree of Doctor of Divinity from Yale College in 1783. The late Rev. Dr. James Richards preached to the aged man (then near the close of life) in his own dwelling, that he might judge of his fitness to succeed him. He received a call just before the death of Dr. Johnes, who was removed by dysentery, September 19, 1794, aged seventy-eight.

†JOHN PIERSON was a son of the Rev. Abraham Pierson—first President of Yale College; was graduated at Yale in 1711; was ordained and installed pastor of the church at Woodbridge, N. J., in 1714; was dismissed at his own request, after a ministry of about forty years; and died at the house of his son-in-law, the Rev. Jacob Green of Hanover, in the month of August or September, 1770. It is stated on his tomb stone that he was a minister of the Gospel fifty-seven years. Besides the Funeral Sermon already mentioned, he published a Sermon preached at Newark before the New York Presbytery, entitled "Christ the Son of God, as God-man Mediator," 1751.

He was eminent for the warmth and strength of his devotional feelings, and for the uniform consistency and purity of his life. He was bland and courteous in his manners, and though sufficiently easy of access, was never tolerant towards undue liberties. He had great power in the pulpit, and enchained the attention of his audience by both his matter and his manner. His memory is still fragrant on the spot where he lived, and the children and children's children of those who knew and loved him, cherish an hereditary reverence for his name and his grave.

Forty-six years after his departure, the Rev. David Austin, one of his successors in the pastoral office, wrote thus concerning him:—

There are those now living who testify that he was a most solemn, mighty and moving preacher; a uniform advocate for the distinguishing doctrines of grace; industrious, indefatigable and successful in his ministerial labours. His person was manly and of full size, his aspect grave and solemn, so that the wicked seemed to tremble in his presence.

The Rev. Thomas Foxcroft, of Boston, in a Preface to his work on the "Five Points," says:—

I'm of opinion a book of this nature has long been wanting among us; and I give unfeigned thanks to God, which put this same earnest care for us into the heart of our brother, whose praise is in the Gospel throughout the churches, particularly by means of his elaborate writings, in vindication both of the faith and order of the Gospel, and other more practical publications. * * * * Now, as Paul said of Timothy, 'I have no man like-minded,' so I will presume to speak it, without any design of flattery or offence,—I know no man better accomplished (in my opinion) for a work of this kind than Mr. Dickinson; and without entering into recommendation of his performances, I doubt not the superior and established character of the Reverend author, with the improvement of the Divine subjects, is enough to invite a general reading, and solicit the attention of every serious and impartial reader.

Dr. Bellamy speaks of him as "the great Mr. Dickinson." Dr. John Erskine, of Edinburgh, said that the British Isles had produced no such writers on Divinity in the eighteenth century as Dickinson and Edwards. Dr. Rodgers, of New York, who knew Dickinson well, used to say that he was one of the most venerable and apostolical looking men he ever met with.

Mr. Dickinson was married at Elizabethtown, shortly after he went thither to reside, to Joanna Melyne, a descendant of Joseph Melyne, one of the associates in the purchase of the Elizabethtown tract under Governor Nicoll's grant. She died April 20, 1745, aged sixty-three. She was the mother of a large family, of whom only three daughters survived her. The third child, who was named after his father, was born September 19, 1713, and was graduated at Yale College in 1731. His youngest daughter, *Martha*, married the Rev. Caleb Smith, of Newark Mountains (now Orange). Another was the second wife of Jonathan Sergeant of Princeton, the grandfather of the Hon. John Sergeant of Philadelphia, and Mrs. Dr. Miller of Princeton. The third married Mr. John Cooper, probably of West Hampton, L. I.

David Brainerd was Dickinson's intimate friend,—the latter having interested himself deeply in his behalf, when he was refused a degree from Yale College. Brainerd spent part of the last year of his life under Dickinson's roof, and solemnized his second marriage at Newark, April 7, 1747. He rode back to Elizabethtown in the evening "in a pleasant frame, full of composure and sweetness."

The following is a list of President Dickinson's published works:—Remarks upon Mr. Gale's Reflections upon Mr. Wall's History of Infant Baptism, in a Letter to a friend, 1716. A Sermon preached before the

Synod on I. Timothy iii. 17, 1722. Defence of Presbyterian ordination in answer to a pamphlet entitled, "A modest proof of the order and government settled by Christ and his Apostles in the Church," 1724. Reasonableness of Christianity: Four Sermons, 1732. A Funeral Sermon on Mrs. Ruth Pierson, wife of the Rev. John Pierson, 1733. Remarks upon a pamphlet entitled, "A Letter to a friend in the country, containing the substance of a Sermon preached at Philadelphia in the congregation of the Rev. Mr. Hemphill"—(Defence of the commission of Synod by Mr. Dickinson), 1735. The vanity of human institutions in the worship of God: A Sermon preached at Newark, 1736. A Defence of the above Sermon, 1737. The Reasonableness of non-conformity to the Church of England, in point of worship: A second Defence of the same Sermon, 1738. The Witness of the Spirit: A Sermon preached at Newark, N. J., wherein is distinctly shown in what way and manner the Spirit Himself beareth witness to the adoption of the children of God, on occasion of a wonderful progress of converting grace in those parts, 1740. Observations on that terrible disease, vulgarly called the throat-distemper, 1740. The true Scripture Doctrine concerning some important points of Christian faith, particularly Eternal Election, Original Sin, Grace in Conversion, Justification by Faith, and the Saints' Perseverance. Represented and applied in five Discourses, 1741. A Display of God's special grace, in a familiar Dialogue, 1742. The Nature and Necessity of Regeneration considered in a Sermon from John iii. 3, preached at Newark, N. J., at a meeting of the Presbytery there. To which is added some Remarks on a Discourse of Dr. Waterland's, entitled "Regeneration stated and explained, according to Scripture antiquity," 1743. Familiar Letters to a gentleman upon a variety of seasonable and important subjects in religion, 1745. Reflections upon Mr. Wetmore's Letter in Defence of Dr. Waterland's Discourse of Regeneration. With a Vindication of the received doctrine of Regeneration, and plain scriptural evidence that the notion of Baptismal Regeneration is of a dangerous and destructive tendency, 1745. A Vindication of God's Sovereign free grace. In some remarks on Mr. J. Beach's Sermon, with some brief reflections upon H. Caner's Sermon, and on a pamphlet entitled a letter from Aristocles to Anthades, 1746. A second Vindication of God's Sovereign free grace, &c., 1748. An Account of the deliverance of Robert Barrow, &c., when shipwrecked among the cannibals of Florida.

GEORGE GILLESPIE.*

1712—1760.

GEORGE GILLESPIE was born in Glasgow, Scotland, in the year 1683, and was educated at the University in his native city. He was licensed to preach by the Presbytery of Glasgow early in 1712, and came to New England in the spring of the same year, bringing a letter of recommendation from Principal Sterling to Cotton Mather.

The congregation at Woodbridge, N. J., was at that time in a distracted state, and the ministers of Boston, having been made acquainted with it, judged Mr. Gillespie to be a suitable person to be introduced there, with a view to heal existing divisions. He accordingly *was* introduced by their recommendation; but, though his course was altogether prudent and conciliatory, and he was received at first in a way that seemed to promise the happiest results, circumstances still more adverse to the harmony of the congregation subsequently occurred, that left him with little hope of accomplishing the desired end.

In September following, the Presbytery approved of his credentials; and if Providence should open the way for his ordination by a call from any congregation, Messrs. Andrews, McNish, Anderson† and Morgan,‡ were

* Hodge's Hist. Presb. Church.—Webster's MSS.

† JAMES ANDERSON was born in Scotland, November 17, 1678; was educated in his native country; and was ordained by the Irvine Presbytery, November 17, 1708, with a view to his settlement in Virginia. He arrived in the Rappahannoc, April 22, 1709; but being disappointed in the state of things in Virginia, he came Northward and settled at Newcastle. In 1717, he was invited by the then recently organized Presbyterian congregation in New York to become their pastor. He accepted the call, and shared with the church its early adverse fortunes until 1726, when he resigned his charge with a view to become pastor of a church at Donegal, on the Susquehanna, in Pennsylvania,—though he was not actually installed there till the latter part of August, 1727. In 1738, he was commissioned by the Synod to go to Virginia to solicit the favour of the government in behalf of the Presbyterian Church there, and performed his mission satisfactorily. He married a daughter of Sylvester Garland of the Head of Apoquinimy, in February, 1712-13. She died December 24, 1736; and, in just about a year after, he was married to Rachel Wilson. He died July 16, 1740. A worthless fellow sought, after his death, to bring a reproach on his memory; but the Presbytery promptly came to his vindication.

‡ JOSEPH MORGAN was a grandson of James Morgan, who came to Pequot, New London, Conn., about 1647, with the first settlers—the younger John Winthrop being their head. He was the son of Joseph and Dorothy Morgan, and was born in New London (the part of it which is now Groton) November 6, 1672. In December, 1699, arrangements were made by the town of Bedford, Westchester County, N. Y. to secure him for their minister, and he acceded to their proposals. In the following year, he was ordained by the ministers of Fairfield County. Two years after, (1702,) he received the degree of Bachelor of Arts, as one of the first class of graduates at Yale; thus rendering it probable that, in one instance at least, a degree was given when the usual course of study had been accomplished before the College possessed corporate privileges. When he commenced preaching—contrary to the practice of the times, he used notes; but some of his brethren protested against it so strongly, that he quickly abandoned them. Having ministered at Bedford, and during part of the time at the neighbouring town of East Chester, for more than four years, he removed about the close of the year 1704, to Greenwich, Conn., and preached there till 1708. In 1709, he settled as pastor of the Presbyterian church in Freehold, N. J. In September, 1728, complaints were made to the Synod that he "practised astrology, countenanced promiscuous dancing, and transgressed in drink;" but the Synod dismissed them for want of proof. As, however, he had little prospect of further usefulness among his people, he tendered his resignation, and took charge of the churches of Maidenhead and Hopewell. In 1736, he was again charged with intemperance by the Presbytery of Philadelphia; and the evidence of his guilt was such that he was suspended from the ministry. But he was now far advanced in life, and seemed wholly insensible to the alleged delinquency. In 1738, the Presbytery, at the request of many excellent people who held him in high estimation, restored him, and the act was approved by the Synod. His name does not appear in any Presbyterial or Synodical Record after 1740. Mr. Morgan published a Sermon at the ordination of Jonathan Dickinson in Elizabethtown, 1712; a Treatise on Baptism, entitled "The Portsmouth Disputation examined," 1713; Remedy for mortal errors, showing the

designated to perform the ordination service. The Presbytery recommended him again to the congregation at Woodbridge:—They say, "We shall strengthen his hands, and encourage his heart, to try awhile longer, waiting for the effect of our renewed essays for peace and quietness among you."

Shortly after this, he received a communication from the Presbytery, informing him that the people of White Clay had petitioned for a minister; and, if he left Woodbridge, he was ordered first to supply that people.

He received a call from the congregation of White Clay Creek, and on the 28th of May, 1713, was ordained by a Committee of three; having preached the day before on Galatians iv. 4, 5; and delivered an Exegesis on—"An Christus pro omnibus et singulis sit mortuus?" These exercises, as well as his examination in the original languages, philosophy, and theology, were highly acceptable. His charge seems to have embraced, for several years, besides White Clay,—Red Clay, Lower Brandywine, and Elk River.

He was zealous for strict discipline, and three times entered his protest, when he thought offenders were too leniently dealt with. In one instance he informed his Presbytery that he would publish animadversions on the undue tenderness of the Synod, but they absolutely prohibited his doing it.

He was remarkably punctual in his attendance on meetings of the Presbytery and Synod, as well as in bringing a contribution to the fund.

On the great question of the Protest, he did not vote. Having, in all the previous trying sessions, laboured earnestly for the peace of the Church, he withdrew with the excluded brethren, and signified his willingness to be of their number, though he does not appear to have met with them afterwards. He remained neutral till 1744, when he returned to the Old Synod. In discussing the terms of union, he objected to being required to acknowledge what was generally styled—"the great revival," to be "a glorious work of grace." He had seen so many sad issues from hopeful beginnings, so much that he deemed reprehensible in the course of some of the leaders in the work, such wild confusion and wide spread division connected with it, that he could not conscientiously give it his unqualified sanction.

Mr. Gillespie died January 2, 1760, aged seventy-seven. Dr. Francis Alison, who knew him, speaks of him as "that pious saint of God."

necessity of the annointing of the Spirit to guard us from error; a Discourse on Original Sin; a Discourse on the death of his son, Joseph Morgan, 1723; Reply to an Anonymous railer against the doctrine of election, 1724; a Discourse entitled "Sin its own punishment," 1728; a Discourse entitled "Love to our neighbour recommended," 3d edition, 1749. His son *Joseph* graduated at Yale College in 1723, and died the same year.

ROBERT CROSS.*

1717—1766.

Robert Cross was born near Ballykelley, in Ireland, in the year 1689. He received both his academical and theological education in his native country, and came to America, when he was not far from twenty-eight years of age. On the 19th of September, 1717, at the first meeting of the Synod of Philadelphia, he presented his testimonials as a probationer, lately from Ireland, which having been approved, he was recommended to the Presbytery of Newcastle. On the 17th of March, 1719, he was ordained and installed at Newcastle, as successor to the Rev. James Anderson, who had then lately removed to New York. On the 18th of September, 1723, he received a call to settle over the Presbyterian congregation in Jamaica, L. I., as successor to the Rev. George McNish, and between that date and the 10th of October following, he left Newcastle, and took charge of the church in Jamaica. It was during his ministry that the people recovered their church property, including their place of worship, from which they had been ejected by Lord Cornbury, about a quarter of a century before.

In 1734, it appears that the First Church in Philadelphia had given Mr. Cross a call to become their pastor, as the matter of his removal was then a question before the Synod. The Commissioners from Jamaica and Philadelphia were heard at length; "and after the most critical examination of the affair, and the solemn imploring the Divine assistance, the matter was put to vote, and carried against Mr. Cross's transportation." The call from Philadelphia was by no means unanimous,—there being a large party in the congregation opposed to Mr. Cross; and, the next year, the part who were favourable to him, petitioned to be erected into a distinct congregation. The Synod having granted the petition, the new congregation presented him a call in 1736, and the Synod called upon him to express his views concerning it. Mr. Cross stated, in reply, that he thought the Synod could not properly come to any decision until his people had been duly informed on the subject; and that, as circumstances then were, he believed that he ought to remain at Jamaica. After a long discussion, the Synod finally resolved to defer the whole matter until their next meeting, that the people of Jamaica might be apprized of the movement, and might have an opportunity of presenting their objections against Mr. Cross's removal. Meanwhile, Mr. Cross was appointed to supply the new congregation at Philadelphia, for two months previous to the next meeting of Synod, provision being also made for the supply of the people of Jamaica during his absence. The next year, (May 27, 1737,) the subject of Mr. Cross's removal came again before the Synod, and reasons were urged by representatives of the two congregations respectively, why the proposed change in his ministerial relations should, and should not, take place. Mr. Cross having referred the case entirely to the judgment of the Synod,—they proceeded to deliberate upon it, and finally came to the unanimous conclusion

* Macdonald's Hist. of the Jamaica Church.—Prime's Hist. L. I.—Hodge's Hist. Presb. Church.—Webster's MSS.

that Mr. Cross should be "transported" to Philadelphia; after which, at Mr. C.'s request, they appointed a committee, consisting of Messrs. Thomson* and Anderson, to prepare a suitable letter to the congregation in Jamaica, "signifying what was done in the affair." He joined the Philadelphia Presbytery, May 29, 1737, and was installed on the 10th of November following. In the Minutes of Synod for 1738, there is the following entry:—"It is reported that Mr. Robert Cross was installed since our last, according to the Synod's appointment, and that the two congregations in Philadelphia were since united." The installation sermon was preached by the Rev. Mr. Andrews, with whom Mr. Cross was settled as a colleague.

Mr. Cross's ministry at Jamaica is said to have been highly successful, and attended by a considerable revival of religion. The Rev. James M. Macdonald, lately pastor of the same church, where he had the best opportunity of gathering up traditions respecting his ministry there, says that "it is evident that he was very highly esteemed," and "was one of the most prominent and influential ministers of the day in which he lived." Elizabeth Ashbridge, a celebrated Quakeress of that day, has rendered a somewhat equivocal testimony concerning him, in saying—"His people almost adored him, and impoverished themselves to equal the sum offered him in the city; but failing in this, they lost him."

The occasional labours of Whitefield in Philadelphia are said to have been not wholly in accordance with the views and feelings of either Mr. Cross or his colleague; and many who had been their friends, became alienated from them, on the alleged ground that they did not preach either alarmingly or fervently enough. Whitefield, when about to sail for England, wrote from Reedy Island, De., May 19, 1740,—"Mr. Cross has preached most of his people away from him. He lashed me most bravely, the Sunday before I came away. Mr. Andrews also preached against me." But subsequently, when the snow prevented the roofless "Great House" from being used, Cross offered his meeting house to Whitefield, and he preached in it.

After the death of Mr. Andrews, in 1747, the Rev. Francis Alison became Mr. Cross's assistant; and, in 1753, application was made to both Edinburgh and London for a colleague. Mr. Cross resigned his pastoral charge, June 22, 1758. He died in August, 1766. His wife, who was

* JOHN THOMSON came from Ireland to New York, as a probationer, in the summer of 1715. Being recommended by the Presbytery to the people of Lewes, De., he went thither to preach, received a call from them in the autumn of 1716, and was ordained and installed as their pastor in April, 1717. He resigned his charge in 1729, for want of support. The next year he accepted a call from Middle Octorora; but, in consequence of the distracted state of his congregation, he removed, in 1732, to Chestnut Level. In 1733, he was in such straitened circumstances that collections for his relief were made in the congregations in Donegal Presbytery. In the winter of 1738, he visited the Valley of Virginia, and passed through the Rockfish Gap to Concord, Buffalo, and Cub Creek. It was his wish to settle in Virginia, but his Presbytery would not release him from his charge until July, 1744; when he made his way back to the Valley, and was engaged, under Presbytery, in directing the missionary operations in Western Virginia. He visited North Carolina in 1744, and again in 1751; and in his latter visit he met with Henry Patillo, (afterwards a distinguished clergyman,) and advised him to study for the ministry. In 1749, while he was labouring in the County of Amelia, he published at Williamsburg an Explication of the Shorter Catechism. He also published a work on the Government of the Church, and a Sermon on Conviction and Assurance, which were highly commended by Gilbert Tennent. He spent his last years with his son-in-law at Buffalo, in Prince Edward, where, according to Dr. Foote, he died in 1753; though Dr. Alexander states that "he lies in the Buffalo grave yard without a stone." He participated largely in the difficulties that issued in the rupture of the Church, and in both his convictions and acts was very strongly on the Old Side.

born in the city of New York, in the year 1688, died the same year with her husband.

Mr. Cross maintained a correspondence with the ministers of the South Carolina Presbytery.

The following testimony to his character appears on his grave-stone:—

"He excelled in prudence, and gravity, and a general deportment, was esteemed for his learned acquaintance with the Holy Scriptures, and long accounted one of the most respectable ministers in the Province."

In 1735, Mr. Cross published a Sermon, preached before the Commission of Synod at Philadelphia, which he dedicated to his people at Jamaica, in terms expressive of strong regard and attachment.

WILLIAM TENNENT.*

1718—1746.

William Tennent was born in Ireland, in the year 1673. He received a liberal education in his native country, and was probably a graduate of Trinity College, Dublin. He entered the ministry originally in the Episcopal Church: he was ordained Deacon by the Bishop of Down, July 1, 1704, and Priest, September 22, 1706. After receiving orders, he acted as Chaplain, for some time, to an Irish nobleman; but it does not appear that he ever had charge of a parish, previous to his coming to this country; and the reason that has been assigned for it is, that he could not conscientiously conform to all the terms imposed on the clergy of the Established Church.

On the 15th of May, 1702, he was married to a daughter of the Rev. Gilbert Kennedy, who, having been ejected from his charge in Ayrshire, Scotland, went to Holland, where he exercised his ministry for some time, and thence went to Ireland, where he spent his latter years, and died February 6, 1687-88.

As Mr. Tennent's family was increasing, and his prospects of usefulness in his own country were somewhat dubious, he resolved, after a few years, to migrate to America, where he was encouraged to hope for more liberty of conscience, and greater facilities for doing good. He landed at Philadelphia on the 6th of September, 1718, with his family,—consisting of his wife, four sons, and one daughter; and was most hospitably received and entertained by James Logan, who was his cousin on the mother's side, and who, at different times, held several of the most important offices in the State.

Mr. Tennent seems to have come to this country with an intention immediately to change his ecclesiastical relations; and, accordingly, he soon applied to the Synod of Philadelphia, to be received as a minister into their connection. The Synod, after due deliberation, agreed to receive him;—not, however, till he had laid before them in writing the reasons which had induced him to withdraw from the Episcopal Church. The minute of the

* The General Assembly's Missionary Magazine or Evangelical Intelligencer, II.—Dr. Alexander's Hist. of Log College.—Tennent's Family Record, in his own hand-writing.—Webster's MSS.—MS. from the Rev. I. W. K. Handy.

Synod is as follows:—"Mr. William Tennent's affair, being transmitted by the committee [of overtures] to the Synod, was by them fully considered, being well satisfied with his credentials, and the testimony of some brethren here present; as also they were satisfied with the material reasons which he offered concerning his dissenting from the Established Church of Ireland; being put to a vote of the Synod, it was carried in the affirmative to admit him a member of the Synod. Ordered that his reasons be inserted on the Synod book *ad futuram rei memoriam*. The Synod also ordered that the Moderator should give him a serious exhortation to continue steadfast in his now holy profession—which was done." This transaction took place on the 17th of September, 1718,—within less than a fortnight after he arrived in the country.

Mr. Tennent, thus being introduced into the Presbyterian Church, went, in November following, to East Chester, N. Y., where he continued, probably as a stated supply, for about eighteen months. In May, 1720, he removed thence to Bedford, in the same neighbourhood, where he laboured for a short time; but soon after, probably in the year 1721, he left Bedford, and went to preach at Bensalem and Smithfield, in Bucks County, Pa. Here he continued until the year 1726, when he accepted a call from the church at Neshaminy, in the same county, where he remained till the close of his life. The Presbytery did not send a minister to install him; but the people, in answer to an inquiry made of them in the meeting-house, signified their acceptance of him as their pastor. He had two congregations, distinguished as the Upper and Lower.

Some time after his removal to Neshaminy, Mr. Tennent, being deeply impressed with the importance of a well educated as well as pious ministry, resolved on establishing a school at which young men might acquire the requisite qualifications for the sacred office. He was admirably fitted to conduct such a school, being a fine general scholar, as well as a thoroughly read theologian; and with the Latin language he was so familiar, that he could write and speak it, not only with perfect ease but with remarkable elegance. He is said to have delivered a Latin oration before the Synod, not long after he was admitted a member, which was greatly praised for its correct and splendid diction, and which showed the more finished education which, at that time, was obtained, in the mother country.

Mr. Tennent, with a view to carry his benevolent purpose into effect, erected a humble building, within a few steps of his own dwelling, for the accommodation of those who might offer themselves as students. His kinsman, James Logan, had presented him, in 1728, with fifty acres of land; and on this lot stood the building referred to. His expectations in this enterprise were more than realized; for here, before many years had passed, had been educated a considerable number of the most distinguished Presbyterian ministers of their time. Among them were Tennent's own sons, *Samuel* and *John Blair*, *Wm. Robinson*, &c. It may safely be said that the establishment of this institution, known as the "Log College," marked an epoch in the history of clerical education, at least in the Presbyterian Church, in this country.

In the year 1737 a portion of Mr. Tennent's congregation had become dissatisfied that he had so long acted as pastor of the church at Neshaminy, without having been formally installed. This part of the congregation made a complaint against Mr. Tennent before the Synod; but it was answered by another part of the congregation, who fully justified the course of their pastor. After both papers had been read, and both parties heard, the Synod adopted a minute expressive of their strong disapprobation of the conduct and probable motives of the complainants, and exhorting them to "lay aside their groundless dissatisfactions, and return to their duty."

Mr. Tennent seems to have been a man of great zeal, and a warm friend to revivals of religion. When Whitefield first visited Philadelphia, Mr. T., though living at a distance of thirty miles, hastened to the city, that he might enjoy the privilege of communion with one whom he considered so truly a kindred spirit. What impression he made upon Whitefield, may be inferred from the following entry in his journal:—

"At my return home [from visiting a family] was much comforted by the coming of one Mr. Tennent, an old gray-headed disciple and servant of Jesus Christ. He keeps an Academy about twenty miles from Philadelphia, and has been blessed with four gracious sons, three of which have been, and still continue to be, eminently useful in the Church of Christ. He brought three pious souls along with him, and rejoiced me by letting me know how they had been spoken evil of for their Master's sake. He is a great friend of Mr. Erskine of Scotland; and, as far as I can learn, both he and his sons are secretly despised by the generality of the Synod, as Mr. Erskine and his friends are hated by the judicatories of Edinburgh; and as the Methodist preachers (as they are called) are by their brethren in England."

Whitefield, on his return from New-York, visited Mr. Tennent at his own house, and spent some days with him. His account of this visit is as follows:—

"November 22. [1739.] Set out for Neshaminy, (twenty miles distant from Trent Town,) where old Mr. Tennent lives and keeps an Academy, and where I was to preach to-day, according to appointment. About twelve [o'clock] we came thither, and found about three thousand people gathered together in the meeting house yard. Mr. William Tennent (Jr.), an eminent servant of Jesus Christ, because we staid beyond the time appointed, was preaching to them. When I came up, he soon stopped; sung a hymn, and then I began to speak, as the Lord gave me utterance. At first, the people seemed unaffected; but, in the midst of my discourse, the power of the Lord Jesus came upon me, and I felt such a struggling within myself for the people as I scarce ever felt before. The hearers began to be melted down immediately, and to cry much; and we had good reason to hope the Lord intended good for many. After I had finished, Mr. Gilbert Tennent gave a word of exhortation to confirm what had been delivered. At the end of his discourse, we sung a psalm, and dismissed the people with a blessing—*O that the people may say amen to it!* After our exercises were over, we went to old Mr. Tennent's, who entertained us like one of the ancient patriarchs. His wife, to me, seemed like Elizabeth; and he like Zachary; both, so far as I can learn, walk in all the commandments and ordinances of the Lord blameless. Though God was pleased to humble my soul, so that I was obliged to retire for a while, yet we had sweet communion with each other, and spent the evening in concerting what measures had best be taken for promoting our dear Lord's Kingdom. It happened very providentially that Mr. Tennent and his brethren are appointed to be a Presbytery by the Synod, so that they intend bringing up gracious youths, and sending them out from time to time into the Lord's vineyard. The place wherein the young men study now, is, in contempt, called THE COLLEGE, &c. Friday, November 23d, parted with dear Mr. Tennent and his other worthy fellow labourers; but promised to remember each other publicly in our prayers."

Mr. Tennent, previous to the division of the Synod, had been a member of the Presbytery of Philadelphia; but, at that time, he joined the Presbytery of New Brunswick, to which also his sons, Gilbert and William, were attached.

His health, for some time before his death, was so infirm, that he was obliged to withdraw from his pastoral duties, and his pulpit was supplied by the Presbytery. His connection with his congregation is supposed to have been dissolved in 1742; but his name is enrolled among the members of the New Brunswick Presbytery in the following year, (1743,) and he is mentioned also as being present, the same year, at the ordination of his successor. He died at his own house, in Neshaminy, May 6, 1746, aged seventy-three; and was buried in the Presbyterian burying-ground, where his grave is still to be seen. Mrs. Catharine Tennent, his widow, died in Philadelphia, May 7, 1753, aged seventy.

Mr. Tennent had five children,—four sons and one daughter. Three of his sons, *Gilbert*, *William* and *John*, form the subjects of distinct sketches in this work.

CHARLES, the youngest son, was born at Colrain, in the County of Down, Ireland, on the 3d of May, 1711; and was, therefore, at the time of his father's emigration, seven years of age. He, like his elder brothers, received his education at the Log College. He was taken on trial by the Philadelphia Presbytery, in May, 1736, and was licensed to preach on the 20th of September following. After preaching for twenty-six years to the people of White Clay Creek in Delaware, by whom he was highly esteemed as a faithful minister, he resigned his charge, owing to their inability to fulfil their engagements in respect to his support; and, shortly after, in 1763, was installed pastor of the united congregations of Buckingham and Blackwater. Here he remained four years, during which time he had the supervision of a boarding school for boys, in which employment he seems to have been assisted by his son, Mr. William Mackay Tennent. Having lost his wife, Mr. Tennent, shortly after his settlement at Buckingham, was married a second time to a widow lady in Philadelphia,—a member of his brother Gilbert's church; and this marriage was fruitful of evils that seem to have continued till the day of his death. After being dismissed from Buckingham, he accepted an invitation to supply the congregations of Broad Creek and Little Creek, in Sussex County, De.; and here he continued his labours till November, 1769. It is due to historic truth to state that his manifold trials, in connection no doubt with the prevailing fashion of moderate and even immoderate drinking, led Mr. Tennent to excessive indulgence in this way, until the case attracted public attention, and finally brought him into painful relations with his Presbytery. The facts, as they are presented in a document before me, while they are highly monitory, are fitted to awaken the deepest sympathy. His health gradually declined during several of his last years, and he died on the 25th of February, 1771, aged fifty-nine years.

Charles Tennent had a son, WILLIAM MACKAY, who became a distinguished minister. He was graduated at the College of New Jersey in 1763, and began to preach when he was in his twenty-third year. He was ordained on the 17th of June, 1772, as pastor of the Congregational church in Greenfield, Conn. In December, 1781, he resigned his charge, and accepted an invitation from the Presbyterian church in Abington, near Philadelphia, where he continued till his death, which took place about the beginning of December, 1810. He was one of the Trustees of the College of New Jersey from 1785 till 1808, when he resigned his office. He received the degree of Doctor of Divinity from Yale College in 1794. He was Moderator of the General Assembly of the Presbyterian Church in 1797. His wife was a daughter of the Rev. Dr. Rodgers of New York. Dr. Alexander, who knew him personally, represents him as "a man of great sweetness of temper and politeness of manner," and as "distinguished for his hospitality." He states also that, during his last illness, which was protracted, though not attended with much pain, he was "blessed with an uninterrupted assurance of the favour of God." An Address was delivered at his funeral by the Rev. Dr. Green of Philadelphia, which was published.

THE McGREGORES.*

James, 1718—1729.
David, 1737—1777.

James McGregore received a thorough classical and theological education, and had the care of a Scot's Presbyterian Church in the North of Ireland. The sufferings to which Protestants were there subjected, in connection with his inextinguishable love of religious liberty, led him, with three other ministers, and a part of their respective congregations, to migrate to this country. As they were on the eve of embarking, he addressed a discourse to them, on the text—"If thy presence go not with me, carry us not up hence."

Mr. McGregore, with about one hundred families, arrived at Boston, on the 14th of October, 1718. The next winter he spent at Dracut; and, in the spring following, sixteen of the families who had accompanied him from Ireland, commenced a settlement on a tract of land near Haverhill, which was then called Nutfield, but which they named Londonderry. Mr. McGregore now joined the party from whom he had been temporarily separated, and on the 12th of April preached to them, under a large oak tree, the first sermon ever delivered in that place, from Isaiah xxxii. 2. The spot is known, and regarded with veneration, to this day.

As soon as the settlers had become organized as a religious Society, they proceeded according to the order of the Presbyterian Church, to invite Mr. McGregore to become their pastor. He accepted their call; but, as no Presbytery then existed in New England, the formality of an installation was dispensed with. On a day appointed for the purpose, the people met, and he solemnly assumed the pastoral charge of the church and congregation,—they in turn recognising him as their pastor and spiritual guide. He preached to them on the occasion from this very appropriate text—"Moreover, I will make a covenant of peace with them; and it shall be an everlasting covenant with them; and I will place them and multiply them, and will set my sanctuary in the midst of them forevermore."

There is a tradition that it was through the influence of Mr. McGregore with the Marquis de Vaudreil, then Governor of Canada, that the Colony, at an early period, was signally preserved from savage depredation. The two are said to have been intimate friends and correspondents; and the Governor, from respect to the wishes of his friend, directed the Catholic priests to charge the Indians not to molest or injure any of these people, as they were different from the English; and to assure them that not only would no bounty be paid for their scalps, but that the sin of murdering

* Parker's Hist. Londonderry.—Tracy's Great Awakening.—MS. from Rev. Dr. Whiton.

any of them would not be forgiven. Such is the tradition; and there are some circumstances that give to it, to say the least, an air of probability.

The church of which Mr. McGregore became pastor, was the first Presbyterian church in New England. It is not known how many composed it originally, but its increase was evidently rapid. At a Communion season in 1723, there were one hundred and sixty communicants; at another, a few months later, two hundred and thirty; and at the one immediately preceding his death, three hundred and seventy-five.

Mr. McGregore died, from a violent attack of fever, on the 5th of March, 1729, aged fifty-two. His Funeral Sermon was preached by the Rev. Samuel Phillips of Andover, from Zachariah i. 5.

Dr. Belknap, in his History of New Hampshire, represents him as "a wise, affectionate and faithful guide to his people, both in civil and religious matters."

The Rev. E. L. Parker, in his History of Londonderry, says,—

"His name and memory were most tenderly cherished by his bereaved flock, and succeeding generations; and the effects of his labours among them were long and widely felt. He possessed a robust constitution, and had enjoyed firm and uninterrupted health. He had never been visited with sickness, until seized with that which terminated his life. Though at the time but a youth, he was among the brave defenders of Londonderry in Ireland, and discharged from the tower of the Cathedral the large gun which announced the approach of the vessels that brought them relief. * * From traditional remarks, as well as from some few manuscripts of his which have been preserved, we are led to consider him a man of distinguished talents, both natural and acquired. He evidently possessed a vigorous and discriminating mind. He was strictly evangelical in his doctrinal views, and peculiarly spiritual and experimental in his preaching. During his short but severe sickness, he manifested a firm unshaken faith in the Saviour, and a lively hope of his interest in the promises of the Gospel. In the immediate prospect of death, he remarked to those around him that he trusted he had known Christ from the fourteenth year of his age, and would cheerfully confide to his hands his immortal interests. * * * His personal appearance was commanding; his stature tall and erect; his complexion rather dark; and his countenance expressive."

In October, 1706, Mr. McGregore was married to Marion Cargill, in Londonderry, Ireland. They had ten children, seven of whom, with their mother, survived him.

David McGregore was the third son of the Rev. James McGregore, and was born in Ireland, November 6, 1710. He received his literary and theological education, chiefly under the direction of the Rev. Matthew Clark,* his father's successor in the ministry. A new parish, called the West parish in Londonderry, having been formed, he was invited to take the pastoral charge of it. He was ordained in 1737; but the Society of which he became pastor was not actually incorporated till 1739. A controversy soon arose between the old and new parish, which lasted nearly forty years.

In the "great awakening" that took place in 1741, Mr. McGregore felt a deep interest, and took an active part. He visited Boston and some other

* Matthew Clark came to this country from Ireland, soon after the death of the elder McGregore, and immediately repaired to Londonderry, where he found many of his countrymen and former acquaintance. At the request of the church and congregation, he consented to supply the pulpit, and take the pastoral care of the people, though he was not formally installed. Being a fine scholar, he officiated also as an instructer in the higher branches of education. Though about seventy years of age, when he came to this country, he continued to labour in the ministry with great vigour for more than six years. He had served as an officer in the Protestant army, during the civil commotions in Ireland, and received a wound in the memorable seige of Londonderry; but, after those agitations had subsided, he quit the military service, and prepared himself to wield the sword of the Spirit. He was thoroughly Calvinistic in his religious views, genial in his temper, independent in his feelings, and retained a good deal of the martial spirit as long as he lived. He married, as his third wife, the widow of his predecessor. He died January 25, 1735, aged seventy-six.

places where the revival prevailed, and returned to his people with a full purpose to do what he could, by the Divine blessing, to bring about a similar state of things in his own charge. He accordingly delivered a series of very impressive discourses from Ephesians v. 14,—"Awake, thou that sleepest, and arise from the dead, and Christ will give thee light." With this effort commenced a remarkable awakening among his own people, which resulted in large additions to the church. Mr. McGregore showed himself a firm friend to the revival of that period, and, as an evidence of it, his name appears affixed to the Testimony of an Assembly of pastors at Boston, July 4, 1743, expressing their belief "that there had been a happy and remarkable revival of religion in many parts of the land, through an uncommon Divine influence." And, in a letter accompanying his Testimony, afterwards published in Prince's History, he says,—

"For my own part, I have seen little or no appearance of the growth of Antinomian errors, or any thing visionary or enthusiastic, either in my own congregation, or among the people in the neighbourhood where I live. Indeed, if asserting justification by faith alone, and denying it by the law, as a covenant of works, while the eternal obligation of the law, as a rule of life, is strongly maintained in practice as well as profession,—if this, I say, be Antinomian doctrine, then we have a great growth of Antinomianism. Again, if asserting the necessity of supernatural influence or Divine energy in conversion, or the reality of the immediate witnessing and sealing of the Spirit, be enthusiasm, then we have a remarkable spread of enthusiasm; and, in these senses, may Antinomianism and enthusiasm grow more and more, till they overspread the whole land."

In January, 1755, the Presbyterian congregation in the city of New York gave a call to Mr. McGregore to become their pastor. This call was regularly prosecuted before his Presbytery, which met at Pelham in April of that year, and afterwards at Boston in May following. Mr. McGregore, partly on account of his strong attachment to his own people, and partly from a conviction that the divided state of the church to which he was called, gave little promise of either ministerial comfort or usefulness, declined the call. In 1764, he received the degree of Master of Arts from the College of New Jersey.

Mr. McGregore did not survive his active usefulness. The last Sabbath that he spent on earth was a Communion season in his church. He preached on that occasion with his accustomed interest and animation, and then, exhausted by the effort, was carried out of the house. He was able, however, after a short time, to return and conclude the services; and this was the last meeting which he had with his people. He died in the utmost peace, on the Friday following, May 30, 1777, aged sixty-eight years. The Funeral Discourse was preached by the Rev. Dr. Whitaker, pastor of the Tabernacle Church in Salem, from II. Kings ii. 12.

The following is a list of Mr. McGregore's publications:—A Sermon entitled "Professors warned of their danger," 1741. The Spirits of the present day tried: A Sunday evening Lecture at Boston, 1741. A Sermon entitled "The believers all secured," 1747. The Christian Soldier: A Sermon at the ordination of Alexander Boyd,* 1754. A Sermon on the death of the Rev. John Morehead, 1773.

*Alexander Boyd studied Theology at the University of Glasgow, and came to this country, probably, early in 1748. In June of that year, at the suggestion of Mr. McGregore, he was taken under the care of the Boston Presbytery, and, having gone through the prescribed trials, was licensed to preach the Gospel. He was sent to preach first at Georgetown, Me., and in August, 1749, he received a call to settle in that place. But the Presbytery, having in the mean time heard some unfavourable reports from Scotland respecting him,—when the call came into their hands, returned it to the church, and cited their candidate to appear before them.

The Rev. E. L. Parker writes thus concerning Mr. David McGregore:—

'He was greatly respected, and his death sincerely lamented by the people of his charge. He stood deservedly high in public estimation, as a preacher and a divine. Few, if any, then upon the stage, were considered his superiors. His praise, as a bold, faithful, successful minister, was in all the surrounding churches, and his services eagerly sought. Though not favoured with a collegiate education, yet under the private instruction of Rev. Mr. Clark, and by his great assiduity and application in the acquisition of knowledge, he became a scribe well instructed unto the Kingdom of Heaven, and was able at all times and on all occasions to bring forth out of his treasure things new and old. He was an animated and interesting preacher. His pulpit talents were considered superior to those of his father. His voice was full and commanding, his delivery solemn and impressive, and his sentiments clear and evangelical. His house of worship was usually thronged. Many from the neighbouring towns attended regularly upon his ministry. He excelled not only as a preacher but as a pastor. In the discharge of parochial duties, especially in catechising his flock, he was eminently distinguished.... He possessed in an eminent degree, a spirit of firmness and independence, which deterred him from shrinking from duty on account of apparent danger or difficulty."

Mr. McGregore was married to Mary Boyd, a lady of fine personal appearance and accomplishments, who, having been early left an orphan, was brought up by his mother. She died September 28, 1793, aged seventy. They had nine children. One son, *Robert*, was aid-de-camp to General Stark, at the surrender of Burgoyne. Another son, *David*, was graduated at Dartmouth College in 1774, held the office of Captain in the Revolution, afterwards engaged in the business of teaching, and died in 1827. A third son, *James*, settled in Londonderry, was in the earlier part of his life much engaged in public business, sustaining not only the office of a magistrate, but various offices of the town, and was for some years a Representative in the General Court. He posessed a well endowed and well cultivated mind. He died much lamented on the 23d of June, 1818, aged seventy.

EBENEZER PRIME.

1719—1779.

FROM THE REV. SAMUEL I. PRIME, D. D.,

New York, April 26, 1852.

My dear Sir: I send you, agreeably to your request, the following notice, from such materials as I have been able to gather, of my venerable great-grandfather. As there is nobody now living who remembers him, I have to depend of course chiefly upon family records and traditions.

The Primes came from England,—three brothers of them, in the latter half of the seventeenth century. One settled in Rowley, Mass.; and from him descended the Primes who have been known in the mercantile circles

Upon his making what seemed penitent acknowledgments of the sin with which he was charged, the Presbytery continued his license, at the same time administering to him a sharp rebuke. After a while, he returned to Georgetown, and in June, 1750, the people renewed their call to him, and about the same time he was also invited to settle at Newcastle, Me. The Presbytery recommended both calls to his consideration; but he thought proper to decline them both. In 1751, the call from Georgetown was a second time renewed, and, in November of that year, he accepted it. Difficulties, however, arose, either on the part of the people or of the Presbytery, which prevented his becoming the pastor of that church. In 1754, he accepted a call from the church in Newcastle, and, as a matter of convenience, was ordained at Newburyport, on the 19th of September of that year. He remained at Newcastle, constantly involved in difficulties, and labouring to very little acceptance, until the latter part of the year 1758, when his dismission was finally effected. I find no trace of him afterwards.

of New York for the last fifty years. Another went to North Carclina, and the name is there perpetuated to this day. A third brother was one of the first settlers of the old town of Milford, Conn. Of this last mentioned brother, whose name was *James*, my great-grandfather was the second son, and was born July 21, O. S., 1700. The stormy period of the Revolutionary war destroyed the records of those early years, of which I should be glad to say more than is now possible; for I can learn nothing of his youthful training till he graduated at Yale College in 1718. He was probably licensed to preach by an Association in Connecticut, very shortly after his graduation; for, at the early age of nineteen, he was preaching at Huntington, L. I., as an assistant to the Rev. Eliphalet Jones,* pastor of the church of that town. After a service in this capacity of four years, he was ordained as colleague of Mr. Jones, by a council of ministers, half of them from Connecticut, and half from the Eastern part of Long Island. Happily settled over his first, and as it pleased God, his only, charge, he took to himself a wife—Margaret Sylvester, of Shelter Island, October 2, 1723. She died September 26, 1726; leaving two children. He was subsequently married to Experience, daughter of Benjamin Young of Southold. She died January 1, 1734,—the mother of three children. The eldest child, bearing his father's name, was a lovely youth, remarkable for his piety. While a member of Yale College, but at home during vacation, he fell sick and died, having completed his eighteenth year. After seventeen solitary years, Mr. Prime was married, a third time, to Mrs. Hannah Carle, a widow, who died February 9, 1776.

Only one of the children by either marriage, and he a child of the second wife, left motherless at the age of three weeks, survived the father. His name was *Benjamin Young Prime.* He was born December 20, 1733; entered the College of New Jersey, then in its cradle at Newark, in July, 1748, and graduated at Princeton in 1751. After pursuing the study and practice of medicine several years, he became a Tutor in the College at which he graduated in 1756, and continued in the office about a year. In 1762, he went to Europe for the purpose of enjoying higher advantages than our country then afforded, for the study of medical science. After a residence abroad of between two and three years, he took his degree in medicine at the University of Leyden, on which occasion he delivered a Latin Dissertation which was published there in a handsome quarto pamphlet. He became a highly accomplished scholar,—eminent for his mathematical, philosophical and classical attainments. He was in the habit of writing with great facility both prose and poetry, in the Hebrew, Greek, Latin, French, and Spanish languages; and in the opening of the Revolutionary struggle, his patriotic and popular songs spread like wildfire over the land, and helped to kindle the sparks of liberty into a flame. In the Curiosities of American Literature, appended by Dr. Griswold to D'Israeli's Collec-

* Eliphalet Jones is supposed to have been a son of the Rev. Mr. Jones, who was episcopally ordained in England, came to this country at an early period, and became the first minister of Fairfield, Conn.; but, in consequence of the burning of the first Records of Fairfield, neither the time of his installation, nor of his death, can now be ascertained. He, *Eliphalet*, was born at Concord, Mass., in the year 1640. He was invited to Huntington in January, 1676, having previously declined an invitation to the congregation of Jamaica. He was, at that time, residing at Greenwich, Conn. After some hesitation, he consented to spend a year with the people, and at the end of that time was settled with great unanimity. He continued in that relation more than half a century, and died June 5, 1731, in the ninety-first year of his age. He is said to have been "a man of great purity and simplicity of manners, and a faithful and successful preacher."

tion, among the Revolutionary odes and songs, some of Dr. Prime's are gathered,—more remarkable, however, for patriotic feeling than poetical merit.

After his return from Europe in 1764, he became a practitioner of medicine and surgery in the city of New York; but, after a few years, being the only surviving son of his father, who was then becoming infirm, he returned to Huntington, and resumed his residence with his father; where both employed the little leisure which their respective professions afforded, in the pursuits of elegant letters, for which their tastes and education admirably fitted them. Dr. Prime lived through the Revolutionary war, and died suddenly, October 31, 1791, leaving two sons and three daughters. The youngest son is the Rev. Nathaniel Scudder Prime, D. D., who still survives in a green old age.*

* This venerable man, since this letter from his son was written, has been gathered to his fathers. He was born in Huntington, L. I., on the 21st of April, 1785. He inherited from his father and grandfather a taste for letters, which he cultivated through life, and transmitted to his posterity. In 1800, he first embraced Christianity, as he believed, in its life and power. He graduated at the College of New Jersey in 1804; and on the 10th of October, 1805, was licensed, by the Presbytery of Long Island, to preach the Gospel. For a few years, he laboured on the East end of the Island, especially at Sag Harbour, where his ministry was attended by a powerful revival of religion. He subsequently preached, for some time, at Freshpond and Smithtown; and, in 1812, became the pastor of the Presbyterian Church in Cambridge, N. Y. Here he spent nearly twenty years of eminent usefulness, exerting a powerful influence through the whole region in the several departments of learning, benevolence, and religion. After a pastorate of seventeen years in Cambridge, he was induced to take charge of a literary institution in that place, where he became greatly distinguished as a teacher, while, at the same time, his services as a preacher were almost constantly put in requisition.

In 1830, he removed to Sing Sing, N. Y., to take charge of the Mount Pleasant Academy, and supplied the Presbyterian Church there for two years. He established at the same place a large and flourishing Female Seminary. In November, 1835, he removed this Seminary to Newburgh, where he resided chiefly for nearly eight years. In April, 1843, he removed to Williamsburg; in April, 1846, to Newark, N. J.; in May, 1847, to Ballston Spa, where he preached as a stated supply for about two years; in December, 1849, to Scotchtown; and in April, 1851, again to Williamsburg. From June, 1851, to October, 1852, he supplied the first Presbyterian Church in Brooklyn, and the rest of that year supplied at Yorkville. During a part of 1854, he supplied at Wyoming, Pa.; and in 1855, for several months, at Huntington, L. I. In April of this year, he removed to Mamaroneck, to the house of his son-in-law, Mr. A. P. Cummings, where he died in great peace on the 27th of March, 1856.

He was a Trustee of Middlebury College from 1822 to 1826; and of Williams College, from 1826 to 1831. The degree of Doctor of Divinity was conferred upon him by the College of New Jersey in 1848.

The following is a list of Dr. Prime's publications:—The pernicious effects of Intemperance in the use of ardent spirits: A Sermon delivered at the opening of the Presbytery of Long Island, at Aquebogue, 1811. An Address before the Cambridge Branch of the Moral Society of the County of Washington, 1815. Divine Truth the established means of Sanctification: A Sermon delivered at the Annual meeting of the Washington County Bible Society, 1817. A familiar illustration of Christian Baptism, in which the proper subjects of that ordinance and the mode of administration are ascertained from the Word of God and the History of the Church, and defended from the objections usually urged by the opponents of Infant Baptism and the advocates of Immersion, 1818. The year of Jubilee, but not to Africans: A Sermon delivered on the forty-ninth Anniversary of American Independence, 1825. Charge to the Rev. Samuel Irenæus Prime, delivered at his Installation as Pastor of the First Presbyterian Church in Mattewan, 1837. A History of Long Island from its first settlement by Europeans to the year 1845, with special reference to its ecclesiastical concerns, 1845.

On the 5th of July, 1808, he was married to Julia Ann, daughter of Major John Jermain of Sag Harbour, L. I. They had seven children,—five sons and two daughters. Two of his sons became clergymen, one of whom is the Rev. Dr. Prime, Editor of the New York Observer.

I knew the venerable Dr. Prime quite well during the latter years of his life, and always regarded him as a noble specimen of a man and a minister. He was compactly built, rather inclined to be stout, had a fine intelligent face, was quick and easy in his movements, and most agreeable in conversation. He had a mind of uncommon force and discrimination; a noble and generous spirit; simple and engaging manners; an invincible firmness in adhering to his own convictions; an earnest devotion to the best interests of his fellow men; an excellent talent for the pulpit; great tact at public business; and a remarkably graceful facility at mingling in a deliberative body. In private he had the gentleness of a lamb; but sometimes, in public debate, the lamb disappeared, and the lion came in its place.

To return to the main subject of my narrative. With the weight of increasing years and increasing labours, Mr. Prime began to feel the need of assistance. As he had been settled originally as a colleague with his predecessor, so now an associate was sought for him; and the Rev. John Close* was set apart to that work, October 30, 1766. He continued to labour with Mr. Prime nearly seven years; but in 1773 was dismissed. From this time onward, the aged pastor had no regular aid in the ministry. Though he was very infirm, the state of the congregation, distracted by the war of the Revolution, rendered it impracticable to provide him any relief.

The invasion of the enemy compelled the pastor and his son, with their families, to fly from their home: throwing their plate into a well, from which it was recovered when the war was over, and taking with them only what they could most readily carry in their hands. The son, with his young family, fled from the Island, and his aged father found an asylum in a retired part of the town.

"Though the whole Island, especially the Western parts, suffered greatly from the insolence and oppression of the soldiery, and still more from the depredations of the Tories, under their authority and protection, no town was subjected to equal outrages on their feelings and property with Huntington. The seats in the house of God were torn up, and the building converted into a military depot. The bell was taken away, and, though afterwards restored, it was so injured as to be useless. Subsequently, (1782,) when the contest was virtually ended, the church was entirely pulled down, and the timber used to construct barracks and block houses for the troops, one of the former being erected on Mr. Prime's home lot, directly overlooking his house. And to wound the feelings of the inhabitants most deeply, these structures were erected in the centre of the burying ground, the graves levelled, and the tomb-stones used for building their fire places and ovens. I have often heard old men testify, from the evidence of their own senses, that they had seen the loaves of bread drawn out of these ovens, with the reversed inscriptions of the tomb-stones of their friends on the lower crust.

"The redoubtable commander in these sacrilegious proceedings was Colonel Benjamin Thompson, a native of Massachusetts, and the same man who was afterwards created by the Duke of Bavaria, and known to the world as *Count Rumford.* But his acts in this place have given him an immortality, which all his military exploits, philosophical disquisitions, and scientific discoveries will never secure to him, among the descendants of this outraged community. It would seem that, during the whole war, no stone was left unturned to annoy the persons, and injure the property, of the inhabitants. Their orchards were cut down, (Mr. Prime's among the first,) their fences burned, and the scanty crops which they were able to raise under these embarrassments, were often seized by lawless force for the use of the soldiers, or ruthlessly destroyed to gratify their malice. The aged pastor of the Congregation, while he lived, was peculiarly obnoxious to the enemy, on account of his known patriotic views and feelings. When the troops first entered the town, at an early period after the battle of Long Island, the officers housed their horses in his stable, and littered them

* John Close was graduated at the College of New Jersey in 1763. After resigning his charge at Huntington, he removed to New Windsor, N. Y., and, without being installed, preached there, and in the neighbouring places, from 1773 to 1796. He afterwards resided at Waterford, where he died in 1813.

with sheaves of unthreshed wheat, which they did not need, tearing leaves out of his most valuable books, or casting one volume of a set into the fire, to render them valueless, without taking the trouble to destroy the whole. While recording these worse than Vandal transactions, I am sitting in the identical chair which my grandfather occupied before me, and which still bears the deep marks of British outrage. And I have books lying before me, with the impress of the same savage hands upon their mutilated covers and leaves."*

The aged patriarch, when sinking under the numerous afflictions of a long and laborious life,—now approximating to fourscore years, having deserted his own dwelling, was compelled to live in retirement, and die an exile in a solitary neighbourhood of his congregation. But even here he was neither inactive nor unhappy. In his diary under date of August 2, 1779, (only two months before his death,) we find the following record:—"Through the good hand of God upon me, I have lived to the close of my seventy-ninth year, and am entered upon my eightieth year, this being my birth day, according to the new style. What a monument am I of sparing mercy!" On the 25th of September, (or, according to another account, on the 3d of October,) he entered into his rest. He was buried in the old grave yard, the outrages upon which, a few years afterwards, I have already detailed; and tradition has handed down to us the following incident, which testifies to my ancestor's patriotism, and the distinction it earned for him in those days of trial. When Col. Thompson, (Count Rumford,) with a detachment of the enemy, took up their quarters in the Huntington grave yard, the Colonel pitched his *marque* at the head of my ancestor's grave, in order, as he said, that he might have the pleasure of treading under foot the *old rebel*, every time he went out or in.

Mr. Prime, according to the testimony of his contemporaries, was "a man of sterling character, of powerful intellect, and possessed the reputation of an able and faithful divine." He was a man of great system in all his habits, public and private. Having gathered around him a large and valuable library, he was constantly adding to the stores of his own learning, and enriching the minds of his people with the fruits of his patient, unremitting labour. It appears from a register which he kept till the close of his life, that he had written nearly four thousand sermons. He had some peculiar views on the subject of the Gospel commission. Believing, as he did, that the same qualifications and authority were required to preach the Gospel as to administer its ordinances, he would not consent to license men to preach, without, at the same time, ordaining them to the ministry. These views he defended in two sermons, and several members of the Presbytery of Suffolk adopted the same. His opinion on this subject was subsequently so far modified by the paucity of ministers, and the necessities of the times, that he did, before the close of his life, admit licentiates to preach in his pulpit; but he would never allow them to pronounce the benediction, which he considered an official act, in as high a sense as the administration of special ordinances.

Mr. Prime was eminently devotional in his spirit, and earnest and successful in his work. He sympathized deeply, and his people shared largely, in the great revivals which took place in his day, especially that in 1741.

* The above paragraphs are from the pen of my father, Rev. Dr. Prime.

In his diary he has detailed many interesting facts in connection with these periods, which show that a rich blessing attended his labours.

Mr. Prime published A Discourse on the nature of Ordination, delivered immediately previous to the ordination of Mr. Benjamin Tallmadge.*

It would be easy to extend this notice of my venerable ancestor, but as I suppose that I have written enough for your purpose, I will only add that

I am very sincerely yours,

S. I. PRIME.

GILBERT TENNENT.†

1725—1764.

GILBERT TENNENT, the eldest son of the Rev. William Tennent, Senior, was born in the County of Armagh, Ireland, February 5, 1703. He was about fourteen years old, when his father migrated to America. He received his education under the paternal roof, and afterwards assisted his father in conducting the education of others. The honorary degree of Master of Arts was conferred upon him by Yale College in 1725. His first permanent religious impressions were received in his fifteenth year, through the exertions of his father, on his passage across the Atlantic; but it was several years before he gained comfortable evidence of being spiritually renewed. In this interval, he pursued a course of theological reading, and subsequently devoted a year to the study of medicine, under an apprehension that his spiritual state would not justify his entering the ministry. But, about 1724 or 1725, his experience became more decided and satisfactory, so that he had no longer any doubt that he was called to preach the Gospel; and, in due time, he presented himself as a candidate to the Presbytery of Philadelphia, of which his father was a member. In his trials before the Presbytery, he appeared to uncommon advantage, and was licensed to preach in May, 1725. Shortly after his licensure, he preached for some time at Newcastle, De., and received a call to settle there; but he took his leave so abruptly as to excite no small displeasure among the people. The congregation and the Presbytery of Newcastle complained to the Synod on the subject, and a letter was produced declaring his acceptance of the call. The Synod decided that his conduct was too hasty, and the Moderator reproved him, and exhorted him to greater caution in future. He is said to have received the rebuke with great meekness. He was ordained at New Brunswick, by the Philadelphia Presbytery, in the autumn of 1726. He would have been called, shortly after, to Norwalk, Conn., had not the Fairfield Association interposed their judgment that he ought not to be taken from "so destitute a region as the Jersies." From the

* BENJAMIN TALLMADGE was born in New Haven, Conn., January 1, 1725; was graduated at Yale College in 1747; was ordained and installed pastor of the church in Brookhaven, L. I., October 23, 1754; was dismissed June 15, 1785; and died February 5, 1786, aged sixty-one years. He was a fine scholar and an able divine. He was the father of the late Colonel Benjamin Tallmadge, of Revolutionary fame.

† Dr. Finley's Sermon on his death.—Gillies' Hist. Coll.—Assemb. Miss. Mag. I.—Hist. Log Coll.—Webster's MSS.

commencement of his ministry, his preaching excited great attention; and his popular and commanding powers were acknowledged, even by those who disrelished the doctrines he preached, or thought him chargeable with undue severity.

When he settled at New Brunswick, he found there several very godly persons, who had been brought into the church under the ministry of the Rev. Theodore Jacobus Frelinghuysen,—one of the most eminent ministers of the Reformed Dutch Church; and that excellent man sent him a letter on "the necessity of rightly dividing the word," which made a powerful impression on his mind, and greatly quickened his zeal in his Master's cause. During the first year and a half after his settlement, though he was much admired as an able and impressive preacher, there seems to have been little visible fruit from his labours. A severe illness, which occurred about the close of that period, brought him into the attitude of deep humiliation in view of his want of success, and, from that time, he became far more earnest and pungent in his preaching, and had the pleasure soon to witness a corresponding change in the state of his congregation.

In 1738, he laid before the Synod "sundry large letters," which had passed between him and the Rev. David Cowell of Trenton, in regard to the true motive that should influence our obedience to God;—whether it should be wholly a desire for his glory, or whether there should also be a desire for our own happiness;—in other words, whether disinterested benevolence is the essence of holiness. The large committee, to whom the papers were referred, heard both parties, and delayed their decision for a year. The result to which they came, did not satisfy Tennent; and he again introduced the matter in 1740, but the Synod, by a large majority, refused to consider it. This he represented, in a paper which he read a few days after, on the deplorable state of the ministry, as sanctioning the doctrine that there is no difference between seeking the glory of God and our own happiness, and that self-love is the foundation of all obedience.

In the year 1740, he was prevailed on by Whitefield to accompany him on a "preaching tour" to Boston; and this tour undoubtedly constituted one of the great events of his life. With a fixedness of purpose which was proof against all obstacles, he set off, in the winter season, to visit a part of the country where he was an entire stranger, and where he knew his ministrations must prove to many exceedingly unwelcome. He reached Boston on the 13th of December, and continued there for nearly three months, preaching almost every day with great power, and producing of course a divided public opinion corresponding to that which already existed in respect to the labours of Whitefield. The effect of his preaching in Boston is thus described by the Rev. Mr. Prince, minister of the Old South Church, and the well known author of the Christian History:—

"It was both terrible and searching. It was for matter justly terrible, as he, according to the inspired oracles, exhibited the dreadful holiness, justice, law-threatenings, truth, power and majesty of God, and his anger with rebellious, impenitent and Christless sinners; the awful danger they were in every moment of being struck down to hell, and damned forever, with the amazing miseries of that place of torment. By his arousing and spiritual preaching, deep and pungent convictions were wrought in the minds of many hundreds of persons in that town; and the same effect was produced in several scores, in the neighbouring congregations. And now was such a time as we never knew. The Rev. Mr. Cooper was wont to say that more came to him in one week in deep concern, than in the whole twenty-four years of his preceding ministry. I can say also the same as to the numbers who repaired to me."

It appears from a letter which Mr. Tennent addressed to Whitefield, preserved in Gillies' Historical Collections, that a similar effect attended his preaching during his whole tour; and that, not only in the region of Boston, but at New Haven and Milford in Connecticut as well as on Long Island, there were multitudes addressing themselves with the utmost anxiety and earnestness to the work of their salvation.

Mr. Tennent had much to do in bringing about the division of the Presbyterian Church, in 1741: indeed it was owing, in a great measure, to his indiscreet and impetuous course, and especially to one sermon called the "Nottingham Sermon," which Dr. Alexander declares to be "one of the most severely abusive sermons that was ever penned," that that schism occurred. Being naturally a man of strong feelings, and fully convinced that a large portion of the ministers of the Presbyterian Church were opposed to the revival of which he was so zealous a promoter, he took it upon himself to denounce them in terms of most unsparing reprobation; and his conduct, viewed at this distance, though dictated no doubt by an honest regard to the cause of Christ, cannot be regarded otherwise than deeply reprehensible. It is to his honour, however, that, while he was a principal instrument in occasioning the division, he was no less active, seventeen years after, in healing it. He wrote and published a pamphlet, the design of which was to bring about a re-union of the two parties; and it was not without very considerable effect.

Whitefield's disciples and admirers in Philadelphia, having formed a new Presbyterian congregation, turned their eyes to Gilbert Tennent as a suitable person to become its pastor; and in May, 1743, just two years after the rupture of the Synod in the same city, they presented their call to him. He accepted it at once, from a conviction that his field of usefulness would thereby be greatly enlarged; and, accordingly, he was regularly released from the church in New Brunswick, which he had served for sixteen years. With the church to which he was now introduced, he continued during the residue of his ministry and of his life, which was about twenty years. He seems to have learned wisdom by his previous experience; for he never afterwards manifested any thing of a controversial spirit, but lived in much harmony with his brethren, and with all around him. His ministry at Philadelphia was marked by great diligence and fidelity, and was attended by many manifest tokens of the Divine blessing. It may be doubted, however, whether his preaching was, to the mass of hearers, so acceptable after his removal as before; for, instead of preaching from short notes, as he had been accustomed to do, he subsequently wrote his sermons out, and read his manuscript somewhat closely; the consequence of which was a considerable loss of force and animation. He displayed his great energy and perseverance, shortly after he went to Philadelphia, in procuring the erection of a spacious and very expensive church edifice for the use of his congregation. He called on Dr. Franklin, and asked him to give him the names of persons to whom he might apply for aid in his enterprise, and Franklin told him to call on every body. He did so, and soon accomplished his object.

In 1753, by request of the Trustees of New Jersey College, the Synod of New York appointed Mr. Tennent, in conjunction with the Rev. (afterwards President) Samuel Davies, to cross the Atlantic, to solicit funds for that institution. The mission was eminently successful; but the only account of it that remains is found in the diary of Mr. Davies. Nothing is known concerning the impression that Tennent produced in England; but there can be no doubt that, with his comparatively rough exterior, and unpolished manners, he must have suffered not a little from a comparison with his highly accomplished and attractive colleague.

About three years before his death, he became so infirm as to be unable to meet the demands which were made upon him by a large congregation; and, accordingly, in December, 1762, the Rev. George Duffield, then of Carlisle, was called to the co-pastorship with him. This call Mr. Duffield declined; and the congregation remained without another pastor as long as Mr. Tennent lived. He died on the 23d of July, 1764, in the sixty-second year of his age.

Of the circumstances of his death it is believed that the only record that remains is in Dr. Finley's Commemorative Discourse. He says,—

"He had an habitual, unshaken assurance of his interest in redeeming love, for the space of more than forty years; but, eight days before his death, he got a more clear and affecting sense of it still. And though he lamented that he had done so little for God, and that his life had been comparatively unprofitable, yet he triumphed in the grace of Jesus Christ, who had pardoned all his sins, and said his assurance of salvation was built on the Scriptures, and was more sure than the sun and moon."

President Finley's Sermon just referred to was preached on the 2d of September following his death. This, together with an Appendix, and a Funeral Eulogy by a young gentleman in Philadelphia, was soon after published. The inscription on the monumental stone, which his congregation placed over his remains, was written by his friend Dr. Finley, and is in classic Latin. Mr. Tennent was one of the original Trustees of the College of New Jersey, and held the office till his death.

Of Mr. Tennent's first marriage I find no record, but his wife died a short time before he made his tour to Boston; and he is said to have been "so much supported, that he was able to preach her Funeral Sermon, while she lay before him in the coffin." His second wife, whose maiden name was Cornelia De Peyster, and who, at the time he was married to her, was the widow of Matthew Clarkson of New York, died on the 19th of March, 1753, aged fifty-seven. He was afterwards married to Mrs. Sarah Spafford, widow of a Mr. Spafford of New Jersey. He had three children by the last marriage. He made his will, October 20, 1763, giving three hundred pounds and his library to his son *Gilbert*, and directing that he should be "put to learning," in the hope that he might be qualified for the ministry. He provides also for his daughters, *Elizabeth* and *Cornelia*. He constituted his wife, his brother William, and the Worshipful John Lyal of New Brunswick, the guardians of his children. His son was lost at sea. One daughter, *Elizabeth*, died early; the other,—*Cornelia*, was married to Dr. William Smith, a respectable physician of Philadelphia.

The following is a list of Gilbert Tennent's publications:—Solemn Warning to the secure world, from the God of terrible majesty; or, the presumptuous sinner detected, his pleas considered, and his doom displayed, (a volume,) 1735. The necessity of receiving the truth in love, considered in a Sermon preached at New Brunswick, with enlargements, 1735. The dark depths of Divine Providence opened and vindicated from the impertinent cavils of foolish men: In a Sermon on II. Thess. ii. 12, preached at New Brunswick, with enlargements, 1735. Memoir of his brother, John Tennent, and an Expostulatory Address to saints and sinners, 1735. Seven

Sermons in a volume of "Sermons on Sacramental occasions, by divers ministers," 1739. The Righteousness of the Scribes and Pharisees considered in a Sermon, 1740. The danger of an unconverted ministry, considered in a Sermon on Mark vi. 34, preached at Nottingham, Pa., 1740. A Sermon on Justification, preached at New Brunswick, 1740. The Espousals, or a Passionate Persuasive to a marriage with the Lamb of God:—In a Sermon preached at New Brunswick, 1741. Remarks on a Protestation presented to the Synod of Philadelphia, 1741. Two Sermons preached at New Brunswick, on the Priestly office of Christ, and the virtue of Charity, 1742. The necessity of holding fast the truth, represented in three Sermons in New York. With an Appendix relating to errors lately vented by some Moravians, &c., 1743. The Examiner Examined, or Gilbert Tennent harmonious. In answer to a pamphlet entitled "The Examiner, or Gilbert against Tennent," &c., 1743. A Sermon at the ordination of Charles Beatty, 1743. Twenty-three Sermons upon the chief end of man, the Divine authority of the Sacred Scriptures, the Being and Attributes of God, and the doctrine of the Trinity, preached in Philadelphia, (a volume, 4to,) 1744. The necessity of thankfulness for wonders of Divine mercies: A Sermon preached at Philadelphia on occasion of the important and glorious victory obtained by the British arms in the Mediterranean, under the conduct of Admiral Matthews, over the united States of France and Spain, and likewise the frustrating a detestable attempt to invade England by a Popish Pretender, 1744. The necessity of keeping the soul: A Sermon preached at Philadelphia, on Deuteronomy iv. 9, 1744. The danger of spiritual pride represented: A Sermon preached at Philadelphia on Romans xii. 3, 1744. The necessity of studying to be quiet and doing our own business: A Sermon preached at Philadelphia, 1744. An Account of a Revival of Religion, published in Prince's Christian History, 1744. A Discourse at the Opening of the new Presbyterian Church. The necessity of praising God for mercies received: A Sermon occasioned by the success of the late expedition, (under the direction and command of General Pepperell and Com. Warren,) in reducing the city and fortresses of Louisburgh on Cape Breton, to the obedience of his Majesty, King George the Second, preached at Philadelphia, 1745. Discourses on several subjects—on the nature of Justification, on the Law, and the necessity of Good Works vindicated, (a volume, 12mo.,) 1745. A Sermon on the lawfulness of defensive war, 1747. A Sermon preached at Philadelphia on the day appointed by the Honourable President and Council, to be observed throughout this Province as a day of Fasting and Prayer. With some enlargement, 1748. Brotherly love recommended by the argument of the love of Christ: A Sermon preached at Philadelphia before the Sacramental Solemnity. With some enlargement, 1748. The consistency of defensive war with true Christianity, 1748. The late Association for defence further encouraged; or defensive war defined, and its consistency with true Christianity represented. In a reply to some exceptions against war, in a late composure, entitled, "The Doctrine of Christianity as held by the people called Quakers, vindicated," 1748. (Printed by Franklin.) Irenicum Ecclesiasticum; or a humble impartial Essay upon the Peace of Jerusalem, 1749. A Sermon on the Salvation of God, 1749. The substance and scope of both Testaments, or the distinguishing glory of the Gospel: A Sermon on the displays of Divine justice in the propitiatory sacrifice of Christ, preached at Philadelphia, 1749. A Sermon preached at Burlington, N. J., on the day appointed by his Excellency, the Governor, with the advice of his Majesty's Council, for a Provincial Thanksgiving. Before the Governor and others upon texts chosen by his Excellency. With a Prefatory Address to Philip Doddridge, D. D., 1749. Two Sermons preached at Burlington, N. J., on a day of Public Fasting, on Matthew vi. 16, 17, 18, and Jonah iii. 8. Dedicated to Governor Belcher, 1749. The happiness of rewarding the enemies of our religion and liberty, represented in a Sermon preached at Philadelphia, to an independent company of Volunteers, at the request of their officers, 1756. A Sermon preached in Philadelphia, on the death of Captain William Grant, 1756. Sermons on important subjects adapted to the perilous state of the British nation, lately preached in Philadelphia, (a volume,) 1758. A Persuasive to the right use of the Passions in Religion; or the nature of Religious Zeal explained, its excellency and importance opened and urged, in a Sermon on Revelations iii. 19, preached at Philadelphia 1760.

The following testimony concerning Gilbert Tennent's character is extracted from Dr. Finley's Sermon above referred to:—

"As to his person, he was taller than the common size, and every way proportionable. His aspect was grave and venerable; and though, at first view, he seemed reserved, yet, upon nearer acquaintance, he was ever found to be eminently affable, condescending and communicative; and what greatly endeared his conversation, was an openness and undisguised honesty, at the greatest remove from artifice and dissimulation, which were the abhorrence of his soul while he lived. Besides, he was tender, loving and compassionate; kind and agreeable in every relation; an assured friend to such as he esteemed worthy of his regard, and a common patron to all who, he apprehended, were injured or distressed.

"He was of a truly public spirit, and seemed to feel the various cases of mankind in general; but very sensibly partook in all the good or ill that befell his country; and while he guarded against being unministerially pragmatical, yet, so far as he judged it consistent with his character, he warmly interested himself in whatever seemed to contribute to the safety and advantage of this Province in particular. He needed no other motive to exert himself, than only to be persuaded that the matter in question was an important public good; and, in such cases, he was much regarded, not only because of his known integrity, but his generous and catholic disposition. For, although he was a great lover of truth, and very zealous for its propagation, yet he was so far above a narrow party spirit, that he loved and honoured all who seemed to have the root of the matter in them, and made it their business to promote the essentials of religion, though they were, in various points, opposed to his own sentiments.

"He was, moreover, an example of great fortitude and unshaken resolution. Whatever appeared to him subservient to the advancement of the Redeemer's Kingdom, the salvation of souls, or the common good of mankind, he pursued with spirit; and what he did, he did with his might. If the end seemed to be attainable, great obstructions and difficulties in the way were so far from dispiriting, that they rather animated, him in his efforts; nor would he give up the point, while one glimpse of hope remained. Hence he accomplished many important matters, which one less determined and enterprising would presently have abandoned as desperate. He would go through honour and dishonour, through evil report and good report; and though he had sensibility with respect to his personal character, as well as other men, yet, if preserving it seemed, at any time, to require the omission of duty or sinful compliances, he readily determined to expose himself to all risks; and if adhering to the will of God should be accounted vile, he resolved he would yet be more vile.

"A great part of his life was a scene of unremitted labour. He studied hard, travelled much, and preached often, while his health and other circumstances permitted. He was instant in season and out of season,—always about his Master's business. They who have journeyed or been often with him in company, could not but observe his constant endeavours to do good by his conversation; to introduce some convincing or edifying topics; and his watching for proper occasions for speaking of God. And very faithful was he in warning sinners of their danger, and persuading them to seek salvation in earnest. Thus he plainly shewed how much religion was his element, and promoting it the delightful business of his life; how benevolent towards mankind he was, and how precious immortal souls were in his esteem. Every advantage accruing to them, or to the interests of religion in general, he reckoned as clear gain to himself; nor were they who divide the spoil ever more joyful than I have known him to be, on occasion of the hopeful conversion of sinners, whether by his own or the ministry of others; and often has his soul wept in secret places, for the pride and obstinacy of those who refused to be reclaimed.

"His great reading, with his various and long experience of the workings both of grace and corruption in the heart, made him a wise and skilful casuist, who could resolve perplexing exercises of mind with clearness, and comfort others with those consolations wherewith he himself, in like cases, had been comforted of God.

"He was a faithful attendant on the judicatures of the Church, as is natural for one so anxiously concerned for the interest of religion as he was; and, having accurately observed the effects of a lax and negligent government in some churches, he became a more strenuous assertor of due and strict discipline. But, above other things, the purity of the ministry was his care; and therefore, at the hazard of the displeasure of many, and in the face of reproach, he zealously urged every scriptural method, by which carnal and earthly-minded men might be kept from entering into it, and men of piety and zeal as well as learning introduced.

"As a preacher, few equalled him in his vigorous days. His reasoning powers were strong; his thoughts nervous and often sublime; his style flowery and diffusive; his manner of address warm and pathetic,—such as must convince his audience that he was in earnest; and his voice clear and commanding; and in a word, all things conspired to make him a judicious, zealous, popular and pungent preacher. With admirable dexterity, he detected the bold presumer, discovered the vanity of his confidence, and exposed the formal hypocrite to his own view."

JOHN TENNENT.*

1729—1732.

JOHN TENNENT, the third son of William Tennent, (Senior,) was born in the County of Antrim, in Ireland, November 12, 1706. He was but twelve years old, when his father came with his family to this country.

He had naturally strong feelings and a somewhat hasty temper, which often occasioned him sore trouble and bitter repentance. His mental exercises, previous to and at the time of his hopeful conversion to God, were most intense, and for a while he seems well nigh to have yielded to the conviction that his case was hopeless. His brother Gilbert, in describing his situation at that time, says,—"I have, through the riches of free grace, been favoured with the sight of many a convinced sinner, but never did I behold any other in such a rack of acute and continued anguish, under the dismal apprehensions of impending ruin and eternal misery, from the vengeance of a just and holy God." So bitter was his agony, that, at one time, he lay speechless for some minutes, and was supposed to be actually in the article of death; but, a few hours after, his countenance kindled with a glow of rapture, and he requested his brother to sing the thirty-fourth Psalm, in which he also joined with uncommon clearness and energy. His brother William was at that time exceedingly ill, and supposed to be past recovery; but such was the fervour of his spirit, that he walked a distance of thirty rods to see that sick brother, that he might communicate to him, on this side the grave, the surprising deliverance of which he had been the subject. Subsequently to this, he was subject to intervals of great doubt in respect to the genuineness of his religious experience; though his mind soon settled into an habitually trusting and happy state.

* Memoir by Gilbert Tennent.—Hist. Log. Coll.—Webster's MSS.

He was educated, both classically and theologically, at the Log College. He was taken on trial by the Newcastle Presbytery, November 21, 1728, and was licensed to preach on the 18th of September, 1729. Shortly after his licensure, he visited the congregation of Freehold, Monmouth County, N. J.,—a congregation originally formed of some Scotch people, who, in escaping from a shipwrecked vessel, were cast upon the Jersey shore. These people being Presbyterians, and wishing to enjoy the ordinances of public worship, after the manner to which they had been accustomed in their own country, set themselves to building a church with reference to this object; and, for some time, the Rev. Joseph Morgan was employed to preach to them; but he having left them in the year 1729, they invited John Tennent to preach as a candidate. Being a young man of great modesty and humility, it was with no small reluctance that he yielded to their request; and he even regretted his engagement, after it was made, believing, as he said, that they were a people whom God had given up for the abuse of the Gospel. He was, however, agreeably disappointed in his visit; for his very first labours were instrumental of bringing many of his hearers to serious consideration and inquiry. This greatly encouraged him, insomuch that he told his brother William that, though they were a poor, broken people, yet if they called him, he would go to them, even though he should be under the necessity of begging his bread. They gave him a unanimous call on the 15th of April, 1730, and he was solemnly set apart as their pastor on the 19th of November following.

He had but a brief ministry; for his death occurred on the 23d of April, 1732; and, for six months previous, owing to his enfeebled health, (he died of consumption,) his brother William had supplied his pulpit.

Gilbert Tennent has given the following account of the closing part of his life:—

"As he drew nearer to his end, his love for his people and concern for their welfare increased. He would often express himself to one of his brothers in such language as the following:—'I am grieved for my people; for I fear they will be left to wander as sheep without a shepherd; or get one that will pull down what I have poorly endeavored to build up.' His brother, who watched with him in his sickness, has frequently overheard him in the deep silence of the night, wrestling with God by prayer, with sobs and tears, for his people. Yea, when so reduced by consumption that he could scarce walk alone, he bore the pains of this lingering disease with unbroken patience, and silent submission to his Father's pleasure, until it pleased God to open a door of escape to his captive soul, through the ruins of his decayed frame.

"On Saturday evening,—the last evening of his life, he was seized with a violent pang of death, which was thought by his attendants to be the last; from which unexpectedly recovering, and observing a confusion among them, he addressed one whom he saw uncommonly affected, with a cheerful countenance, in the following words:—'I would not have you think the worse of the ways of holiness, because you see in me such agonies of distress; for I know there is a crown of glory in Heaven for me, which I shall shortly wear.' Afterwards, in the night, he often prayed,—'Come Lord Jesus! Oh Jesus, why dost thou linger?' Sometime before day, he repeated, with humble confidence, the last words of David,—'Although my house be not so with God, yet hath he made with me an everlasting covenant, ordered in all things and sure; for this is all my salvation and all my desire.' II. Sam. xxiii. 5.

"About the break of day, he called his brother William to prayer, and earnestly desired him to implore Heaven for his speedy removal; for, he said, he longed to be gone. About eight or nine o'clock of the next day, which was the Sabbath, his desire was granted, when it pleased his Master to translate him to that great assembly of the just, 'the Church of the first-born,' there to celebrate an eternal Sabbath in praises and songs of triumph.

"A few minutes before he expired, holding his brother William by the hand, he broke out into the following rapturous expressions:—'Farewell, my brethren; farewell, father and mother; farewell, world, with all thy vain delights. Welcome, God and Father, welcome, sweet Lord Jesus! Welcome death, welcome eternity. Amen!'

Then, with a low voice, he said, 'Lord Jesus, come, Lord Jesus!' And so he fell asleep in Christ, and obtained an abundant entrance into the everlasting Kingdom of his God and Saviour."

He was buried in the grave yard near the church in which he had preached, and a monument was erected to his memory, which still remains. It bears the following inscription,—more honourable to the character of the subject, than to the poetical talent of the writer,—by the Rev. Jonathan Dickinson of Elizabethtown.

"Who quiet grew old in learning, virtue, grace,
"Quick finished, well yielded to death's embrace:
"Whose mouldered dust this cabinet contains,
"Whose soul triumphant with bright seraphs reigns;
"Waiting the time till Heaven's bright concave flame,
"And the last trump repairs his ruined frame."

The session of his church made the following entry concerning him in their Church Record:—

"A mournful providence and cause of great humiliation to this poor congregation, to be bereaved in the flower of youth, of the most laborious, successful, well qualified and pious pastor this age afforded; though but a youth of twenty-four years, five months, and eleven days."

Gilbert Tennent published a short memoir of his brother John, in connection with one of his sermons, the subject of which is Regeneration. This discourse evinces a clear and discriminating mind; and there is much reason to believe that, had his life been spared, he would have been in no wise less distinguished than either of his brothers.

His brother Gilbert, in the memoir already referred to, thus describes him as a preacher:—

"In his public discourses, not to mention the justness of his method, the beauty of his style, and the fluency of his expression, by which he chained his not unwilling hearers to his lips, he was very awakening and terrible to unbelievers, in denouncing and describing, with the most vehement pathos and awful solemnity, the terrors of an offended Deity, the threats of a broken law, and the miseries of a sinful state. And this subject he insisted much upon, because he, with many others, found it the most effectual and successful means to alarm secure sinners. He used a close, distinguishing and detecting method, in the application of his sermons, which, with his pungent mode of expression, was very piercing and solemn. But, as Dr. Watts observes of Mr. Gouge, 'he knew the pity of Immanuel's heart, as well as the terrors of Jehovah's hand.' He was as tender and compassionate in his addresses to gracious souls, as faithful to brandish and apply the law's lancet to the secure; and he was as willing to do the one as the other. But, indeed, he was very cautious of misapplying the different portions of the word to his hearers; or of setting before them only a common mess, and leaving it to them to divide among themselves, as their fancy and humour directed them; for he well knew that was the bane of preaching.

"He was a successful preacher. * * * It may truly be said of him that he gained more poor sinners to Christ in that little compass of time which he had to improve in the ministerial work, which was about three and a half years, than many in the space of twenty, thirty, forty, or fifty years. But though he was thus honoured with the smiles of Heaven upon his labours, and though favoured with the kind regards of a loving and generous people, who, had it been possible, would have plucked out their own eyes and have given them to him,—so that no minister before was ever the object of a more respectful regard and sympathy; yet was he far from being exalted in his own mind, but, through grace, retained a just, grateful and humble sense of God's distinguishing goodness and his own unworthiness."

JOHN MOORHEAD.

1730—1773.

FROM THE REV. A. W. McCLURE, D. D.

JERSEY CITY, September 19, 1854.

My dear Sir: In compliance with your request, I send you the following sketch of my venerable ancestor, the Rev. John Moorhead, which I have compiled, partly from original documents, and partly from family traditions. I believe it embraces every thing concerning him that is at once sufficiently important and sufficiently authentic, to be used for the purpose which your request contemplates.

In the year 1729, a large number of families landed at Boston, having left the Counties of Londonderry, Donegal, Antrim, and Down, in Ireland. They were of the race generally called "Scotch Irish," which emigrated from Scotland to Ireland in the time of James the First. Their descendants came to New England for the double purpose of mending their worldly circumstances, and enjoying more fully the blessings of religious liberty. Most of them settled in Boston; but many of them founded the towns of Ellington, in Connecticut, Colerain in Massachusetts, Londonderry in New Hampshire, and other places in New England.

That portion of this people which found a home in Boston, made it their first care to provide for the worship of God, according to the doctrines and usages of the Scottish Kirk, so dear to them and their fathers. From one of their number, John Little, they purchased a lot of land, at the corner of what are now called Federal and Channing Streets. Either before they left Ireland, or very soon after their arrival in Boston, they invited Mr. Moorhead to become their minister; and he joined them in the year 1730.

JOHN MOORHEAD was born of pious and respectable parentage, in Newton, near Belfast, in the County of Down. His father, a farmer, afforded him the best opportunities in his power for a liberal education, which he completed at one of the Scotch Universities. He came to Boston about the twenty-third year of his age. There is no record of his ordination, and the presumption is that it took place previous to his leaving Ireland. This little "Church of Presbyterian strangers," as they styled themselves, worshipped at first in a *barn*, which stood on part of the ground they had purchased, and which was cheaply fitted up for their accommodation. They professed not to be ashamed to worship Him in so humble a sanctuary, who, for our salvation condescended to be born in a stable. As their numbers were enlarged by other emigrations from Scotland and Ireland, they practised "church extension" by adding two wings to their unpretending tabernacle. In 1744, they were able to erect, on the same spot, a very decent and commodious house of worship. This again gave place, early in this century, to a spacious and elegant Gothic edifice.

The first meeting held for the election of elders,—Mr. Moorhead being present,—was on the 14th of July, 1730. The elders then chosen were John Young, Robert Patton, Samuel McClure, Richard McClure, and Thomas McMullen, who were solemnly ordained to the office. This church session maintained watch and discipline over all baptised persons, as well as over members in full communion. The discipline was exercised with great strictness and solemnity. In 1744, there were twelve elders, and the congregation was divided into twelve districts; each of which was assigned to the care of an elder, whose duty it was to visit and pray with the sick within his bounds, to advise and reprove, as occasion might require, and to provide pecuniary aid for the suffering poor.

Once or twice in each year, Mr. Moorhead, taking with him one of the elders in rotation, visited every family of his flock,—whether in town, or scattered in the country. In these visits, he inquired into the spiritual state of the heads of the family, catechised the children and servants, and closed by kneeling in prayer, and earnestly pleading for the members of the household, according to the spiritual state of each. In addition to this, and the frequent visitation of the sick, he twice in the year convened all the families in each district, respectively, at the place of worship, where he questioned the older persons on the doctrines of the Confession of Faith, and again catechised the children and youth.

At the age of twenty-six, Mr. Moorhead was married to Sarah Parsons, an English lady of a bright and poetic turn, and highly educated. None of their children left issue except one daughter, who was married to Alexander Wilson of Boston. Mr. Moorhead's ministry lasted about forty-four years, till his death, December, 1773, at the age of seventy. He was a warm friend of liberty, but died at the opening of the Revolutionary war. He received from John Hancock substantial tokens of satisfaction at his course in reference to the rights of America. According to his portraits, one of which is finely engraved, he was tall in stature, of a commanding presence, with an agreeable and benignant aspect. His Funeral Sermon was preached by the Rev. David McGregore of Londonderry, N. H., from the text,—"Behold an Israelite indeed, in whom there is no guile." He published nothing except, in connection with Jonathan Parsons and David McGregore, "A fair Narrative of the proceedings of the Presbytery of Boston, against the Rev. Robert Abercrombie, 1756." His papers were destroyed or lost, when Boston was evacuated by General Gage.

The Rev. Dr. David McClure, who was, for many years, pastor of the church in East Windsor, Conn., and who, when a youth, was well acquainted with Mr. Moorhead, gives the following estimate of his character:—

"He was unwearied in his endeavours to promote the edification and salvation of his people. His thoughts and plans of benevolence extended also to their temporal concerns. He encouraged the industrious by such small pecuniary aids as were within his ability to bestow; or solicited assistance for them. Virtuous strangers from North Britain and Ireland were sure to find a friend in him. As a good Bishop, he was given to hospitality. As a sample of this benevolence, allow me to mention that it was his custom, when he heard of ministers from the country who were strangers in Boston, at public houses, to go or send for them to come to his hospitable roof.

"He was faithful and impartial in his duty, as a reprover of error and vice in all their forms. While he rebuked with sharpness, he showed an affectionate concern for the offender, and by meekness and condescension laboured to reclaim him. With equal cheerfulness he visited the hut or the garret of the poor, and the parlour of the rich, to do them good. Some were offended at the severity of his reproofs, and withdrew from his society to others where they could find more indulgence. He was universally respected by the good, and feared by those of the opposite character. He appeared less ambitious of fame than of faithfulness as a minister of Christ.

"Mr. Moorhead was a plain, evangelical and practical preacher. He paid very little attention to the ornaments of style in his pulpit performances. His discourses appeared to be extemporaneous. He expounded the Scriptures in course in the morning, and delivered a sermon in the afternoon. He preached the Law and the Gospel in their spirituality and purity. He insisted principally on the peculiar doctrines of the Gospel—the deep depravity of human nature; the Divinity of Jesus Christ, and the efficacy of the atonement; the special agency of the Divine Spirit in regeneration; the necessity of repentance, of faith in Christ, and of good works.

"He possessed strength of mind, sprightliness of imagination, and readiness of expression; but appeared indifferent to the choice of the most appropriate phraseology. His manner was solemn, affectionate and pathetic. His language and manner were the index of his mind. He spoke from the heart. His tears flowed in the earnest, alarming, or persuasive application of his sermons. He was an 'Israelite, in whom was no guile.' Such was the success of his faithful labours, and the accession of foreign Protestants, that, in six years after the founding of the church, the communicants were about two hundred and fifty. Four times in the year he celebrated the Lord's Supper. They were seasons of great solemnity. On these occasions, Mr. Moorhead commonly had the assistance of one or two of his brethren, particularly the Rev. Mr. McGregore, and afterwards the Rev. Mr. Clarke, of Londonderry, and once of the celebrated Mr. Whitefield, when every heart was moved by his solemn and enrapturing performances. On these occasions, each minister served a table in rotation.

"At those seasons of fervent zeal in religion, the house could not contain the multitudes eager to hear the words of eternal life. The doors and windows were crowded with spectators.

"The Society in general were respectable for good morals, industry, sobriety, attention to the duties of family religion, and the government and education of their children."

I think it proper to state that, if a uniform tradition can be relied on, my ancestor had a full share of that good humour and keen wit, which are generally understood to form a leading trait in the Irish character. There are many anecdotes illustrative of this characteristic, still current among his descendants, some of which I might venture to relate, if I did not fear that I should give too great a shock to the gravity of your readers. The propensity seems to have been as natural as his breath, but never to have been indulged at the expense of treating irreverently any thing of a serious nature.

With great respect and affection,

Yours most truly,

A. W. McCLURE.

JONATHAN PARSONS.*

1730—1776.

JONATHAN PARSONS was born at West Springfield, Mass., November 30, 1705. He was a son of Ebenezer Parsons, who was a deacon in the First Congregational church in that place; and a grandson of Benjamin Parsons, who emigrated from England to this country, and settled at Springfield about the year 1635. His mother's name was Margaret Marshfield.

In his early youth, he was put to a mechanical trade; but so decided were his intellectual tastes that, in connection with the labours of the workshop, and without any other assistance than he derived from books, he contrived to carry forward his preparation for College. At the age of twenty, he became a member of Yale College, and was graduated there in 1729.

It does not appear that, at the time of his entering College, he had any intention to devote himself to the ministry, or even that his mind had been formed to any decided habit of seriousness. Indeed, it would rather appear from his own recorded testimony, that he was averse to the contemplation of religious subjects, and that he imposed little restraint upon his vicious inclinations. After he joined College, though he was not lacking in application to study, he still gave no attention to the one thing needful; and he more than intimates that his decent appearance before the world was a mere cover to a course of habitual wickedness.

When he had reached about the middle of his college course, he was the subject of a dangerous illness, which led him to consider his ways, and at least to form a purpose of entering on a religious life. He now became serious and exemplary in his deportment, and shortly after, made a public profession of his faith in the Gospel. Though he fully believed, at the time, that a radical change had passed upon him, he was afterwards equally convinced that he had been the subject of a mere delusive experience.

Having resolved to give himself to the ministry, he commenced a course of theological study, shortly after he left College, under the direction of the Rev. Elisha Williams,—then Rector of the College, and subsequently completed it at Northampton, under Jonathan Edwards. Within less than a year after he was graduated, he was licensed to preach, and his early services in the pulpit marked him as among the more promising young preachers of the day. Not long after he was licensed, he was invited to the pastoral charge of the Congregational church in Lyme, Conn., and was ordained there in March, 1731.

After his settlement in the ministry, his mind underwent a great revolution in regard to both the doctrines of the Gospel, and the nature of Christian experience. The following account of the commencement of his labours, together with the severe conflicts which issued in the change above referred to,—a change which gave a new complexion to his character and ministry,—is from his own pen:—

* Searle's Fun. Serm.—Coffin's Hist. Newbury.—Amer. Quart. Reg., XIV.—Stearns' and Vermilye's Hist. Disc.

'Soon after my settlement, there was a great and general concern about religion, especially among the young people. I was very zealous in my work, and urged them to come to the Lord's table, and, in less than ten months, fifty-two persons joined the church.

"After I had been settled nigh two years, I was convinced that I had built my hopes of Heaven upon the sandy foundation of my own righteousness. The terrors of the law were very dreadful upon me for several months. Sometimes I thought I must be in hell in a few minutes. I thought every one who saw me must see my wretchedness, and often wondered how they could treat me with common respect,—much more with the respect due to a minister; and yet I believe my people were never so respectful to me, as at the time when I had those apprehensions of misery. If I had any quiet at this time, it was when I was upon my knees, begging for mercy or reading the Bible. These duties I attended much of my time. But when I read Mr. Stoddard's 'Safety of appearing in the righteousness of Christ,' especially his use of reproof to men trusting their own righteousness, and not submitting to God, I could plainly read my own character. Still I dare not let go my self righteous hold, till, one morning, as I came out of my study to attend family worship, I found myself naked, and saw the justice of God, though he cast me off forever. My struggles were all hushed in a moment, and I think I submitted to sovereign mercy. It was not ten minutes, I believe, before I saw the justice of God fully satisfied in Christ, and how he could save the chief of sinners. I saw the sufficiency of Christ as the Surety of the covenant of grace, to redeem the most helpless, wretched and hell-deserving. This put an argument in my heart to plead with God in prayer, and afforded some relief for a time. Still I was not satisfied of a change of heart till several months afterwards. Some time after this, I preached to the Indians at Nehantic, on the nature and necessity of regeneration,—Mr. C—— and Mr. A—— being present. After service, Mr. A. told me he was afraid I was not converted. My heart said there was reason to fear it. I had been several days in distress about it, and his discourse increased my distress. I went home eight miles very pensive. Slept but little that night and rose early. Mrs. Parsons, taking notice of something extraordinary, asked what was the matter. I told her I could not live so; and, after I had attended family worship, I retired into a secret place in the field, resolving never to see any body till I had my state cleared up, whether good or bad. I had not been alone with my Bible and upon my knees more than two hours, before light broke in with such assuring satisfaction, that I could not doubt of the safety of my state. This was a time (1741) of the outpouring of the Spirit in the land, and eminently so at Lyme, when many I believe were savingly converted."

From this period, Mr. Parsons' ministry gathered an unwonted degree of earnestness, and he became identified with the party who were technically known as the "New-Lights" of the day. Whitefield was then traversing the land, and preaching everywhere with an effect that was supposed by many to forebode the speedy ushering in of the millenial day. Gilbert Tennent also was, about that time, making his famous "preaching tour" through New England, and operating upon immense masses of people with scarcely less power than Whitefield himself. Both these illustrious itinerants (for such Tennent for a season became) repeatedly visited Lyme, and they were always Mr. Parsons' guests; and while they laboured abundantly in his parish, he joined them in their visits to several of the neighbouring congregations. In September, 1742, Mr. Parsons made a visit to Boston, and accepted an invitation from the Rev. Mr. Foxcroft to preach the Thursday Lecture. Entering fully, as he did, into the views and feelings of those who favoured Whitefield and the revival, and being deeply impressed with the conviction that a considerable portion of the ministers in that neighbourhood, as well as in New England generally, were opposed to what he believed were the genuine operations of the Holy Spirit, he availed himself of that occasion to bear a decisive testimony in respect to the state of both the ministry and the churches. The sermon was published shortly after, and occasioned considerable excitement, and some controversy. The author in a preface of no moderate length, recognises the fact of its bearing somewhat of a controversial aspect, and urges several considerations in justification of the uncompromising stand which he had felt himself called upon to take. It does not, by any means, justify the gross irregularities and excesses which the ultraists of the day (such as Davenport and his coadjutors) had introduced; but it denounces, in no measured terms, the substitution of a more lax system of doctrine for the faith of the Puritan fathers, and finds in this the reason of the prevailing opposition to the revival. It breathes a spirit of glowing zeal for the Redeemer's cause and honour, but, along with this, it must be acknowledged, somewhat less of the meekness and gentleness of the Gospel than could be desired.

The change in Mr. Parsons' character, and the corresponding change in his preaching, as might be expected, occasioned no small degree of speculation, and even agitation, among his people. Though many of them, as he had reason to believe, had been born into the kingdom under his ministry, and were bound to him by the strongest spiritual ties, yet there were not a few whom the earnestness and pungency of his rebukes, not less than his zealous co-operation with Whitefield and others of the same school, threw into an attitude of intense hostility. As he was himself naturally of an irritable spirit, he was but ill fitted to arrest an incipient contention; the consequence of which was, that, after having, for some time, struggled ineffectually against the current, he was dismissed from his charge by a council called at his own request, in October, 1745.

He was then invited, at the suggestion of Mr. Whitefield, to visit Newbury, (the part that is now Newburyport,) Mass., with reference to taking charge of a new congregation in that place. He accepted the invitation, and reached Newbury early in the month of November. But, when he became acquainted with a portion of the materials of which the new congregation was to be composed, he seems to have regarded it, as far at least as his own comfort was concerned, as no very promising enterprise. "I found" (says he in his journal) "a number of serious Christians in the congregation which I came to visit, who appeared to be understanding, solid, and in some measure established in the main points of Christian doctrine. But many others appeared of an Antinomian turn, full of vain confidence, self-conceit, false affections, &c., and some, that were the greatest Christians in their own esteem, appeared to be worldly and covetous." Still he was led to believe, in view of all the circumstances of the case, that it was his duty to remain there; and, accordingly, in March following, he formally took charge of the congregation. The persons originally composing his church, consisted of a secession from the Rev. Mr. Lowell's and the Rev. Mr. Tucker's; and, as it was considered, at that time, a decided infringement of ecclesiastical decorum to form a new church within the territorial limits of one of the same denomination, they determined to take, and actually did take, the Presbyterian form. But it was not merely in its form of government that the new church differed from those out of which it had chiefly grown, but in the more strongly marked character of its orthodoxy, and in a more cordial sympathy with the great religious movements of that period.

Mr. Parsons' ministry was blessed to the gathering of one of the largest churches and congregations in New England. Not less than two hundred were supposed to have been converted here through his instrumentality. He laboured in season and out of season: but he laboured in comparative quiet,—enjoying in a high degree the affection of his people, and the respect and confidence even of those whose religious views were not in accordance with his own.

Some years before Mr. Parsons' decease, the Rev. John Murray* was invited to become colleague pastor with him; but for several reasons, among which was the fact that his reputation was suffering from injurious reports, he declined the application. He, however, ultimately became Mr. Parsons' successor.

As Whitefield had been his intimate friend in the early part of his ministry, and had no doubt exerted more influence than any other person in deciding its character, so their intimacy continued, without interruption, till it was invaded by death. Whitefield had reached Newbury, on his return from a short journey to the East, and had stopped at Mr. Parsons' house with the expectation of supplying his pulpit on the succeeding Sabbath; but, scarcely had the Sabbath dawned, before that wonderful man was summoned to join in the service of the eternal temple; and Mr. Parsons preached, on that day, to an immense congregation from Phil. i. 21—"To die is gain."

Mr. Parsons survived Whitefield but a few years. His constitution gradually gave way; and, after a protracted and distressing illness, which he endured with the utmost resignation, he fell asleep in great peace, on the 19th of July, 1776, aged seventy-one years. His Funeral Sermon was preached by the Rev. Jonathan Searle† of Salisbury, N. H., and was published. His remains were deposited in the vault beneath his pulpit, which had previously received those of Whitefield; and there they continue to slumber together till this day.

Mr. Parsons was an excellent classical scholar, and was thoroughly versed in History. He was also, to some extent, a proficient in medicine, and occasionally practised it. He had a ready command of his pen; and no one was

* JOHN MURRAY was born in Ireland, May 22, 1742, and was educated at the University of Edinburgh. He came to this country when he was hardly twenty-one years of age, and shortly after was settled as pastor of the Second Presbyterian Church in Philadelphia. But having been guilty of a serious misdemeanor in regard to the signatures to his credentials, he was obliged, in consequence of the fact being discovered, to leave the city; and his next settlement was at Boothbay, Me., where a Presbytery was formed, called "the Presbytery of the Eastward," of which he became the most prominent member. Though the Presbytery of Boston refused fellowship with him, Mr. Parsons, after having thoroughly investigated the unfavourable reports, became satisfied that the faults committed, taken in connection with his own humble acknowledgments, ought not to be considered as disqualifying him for the exercise of the ministry. He was installed as Mr. Parsons' successor at Newburyport, on the 4th of June, 1781, and died on the 13th of March, 1793, aged fifty-one. He was regarded as one of the most eloquent preachers of his day. A full account of the unhappy affair that did so much to mar both his reputation and his usefulness may be found in the Rev. A. G. Vermilye s admirable Historical Discourse. Mr. Murray published An Appeal to the impartial public in behalf of the oppressed, 1768; The last solemn scene: A Sermon, preached at Boston, 1768; A Fast Sermon, at Newburyport, 1779; Bathkol: A voice from the wilderness, 1783; Jerubbaal or Tyranny's Grove destroyed, and the altar of liberty finished: A Thanksgiving Sermon, preached at Newburyport, 1783; The origin of evil traced in a Sermon, preached at Newburyport, 1784; Happy voyage completed, and the sure anchor cast: A Sermon preached at Newburyport on the death of Captain Jonathan Parsons, who died at sea, 1784; Grace and glory, or Heaven given only to saints: A Sermon preached at Newburyport, on the Death of Ralph Cross, 1788; Justification of believers by imputed righteousness: Three Sermons preached at Newburyport, 1788; The diligent Servant excited: A Sermon preached at Newburyport on the death of the Rev. Joseph Prince, [who was born at Boston, April 12, 1723; became totally blind and hopefully pious at the age of fourteen; commenced preaching at nineteen; preached three years at Durham, N. H.; five at Madbury, N. H., sixteen at Barrington, N. H.; thirteen at Pownalboro' Me.; seven at Candia, N. H.; and more or less in various other places, until the 15th of January, 1791, when he died at Newburyport, and was buried by the side of Whitefield and Parsons. He lived and died in total darkness, but was distinguished for fervent piety and impressive eloquence.]

† JONATHAN SEARLE was a native of Rowley, Mass.; was graduated at Harvard College in 1765; was ordained pastor of the church in Salisbury, November 17, 1773; was dismissed November 8, 1791; and died in 1819, aged seventy-four.

put in requisition for such service more frequently than he, by ecclesiastical bodies. He was a fluent and graceful extemporaneous speaker,—able to communicate his ideas on all occasions with great freedom and ease; and when his mind became excited, his unpremeditated efforts were often characterized by the most stirring eloquence.

He had many natural and acquired advantages for being a popular preacher. With a good person, a commanding and strongly marked face, great readiness of utterance, and freedom of gesture, and a command of the selectest language, he could scarcely fail to hold the attention of a congregation, independently of the truths which he delivered. At the commencement of his ministry, he bestowed great labour upon the composition of his sermons; and, though he afterwards became less careful for the graces of style, yet, having once acquired them, they remained with him, and formed a leading characteristic of the productions of his pen as long as he lived. When the change in his religious character occurred,—which he supposed was the great change from a sinful to a holy state, so thoroughly convinced was he that he had never preached the Gospel in all its richness and glory, that he actually burnt every sermon he had previously written. From that period, whatever his ministrations may have lost in refinement, they are said to have gained in unction and impressiveness. His devotional exercises, as might be expected from such a mind and heart, were distinguished for a graceful flow of appropriate language, animated by deep and strong feeling. In short, both the matter and manner of his prayers and sermons were such, as to secure the earnest attention, and awaken the devout feelings, of his audience.

Though Mr. Parsons' character was marked by no common cluster of excellencies, it was marred, to some extent, by a natural temper of more than ordinary severity. This occasionally abated somewhat from the pleasure of intercourse with him, and possibly it may have modified, in some measure, the complexion of some of his public acts. But to his praise it can be said that he was quite aware of this evil tendency, and was in perpetual conflict with it, so that, towards the close of his life, it existed in greatly diminished strength.

Mr. Parsons was married, on the 14th of December, 1731, to Phebe daughter of John Griswold of Lyme. By this marriage he had thirteen children, six of whom died in infancy; and of those who survived, one was *Samuel Holden*, who was born at Lyme, May 14, 1737; was graduated at Harvard College in 1756; settled as a lawyer in Middletown, Conn.; and was a Major-General in the war of the Revolution. He was subsequently appointed by Washington, Governor of the North Western Territory, and was drowned in Big Beaver Creek, in Ohio, November 12, 1789. Mrs. Parsons died December 26, 1770; and, in the following year, he was married to Mrs. Lydia Clarkson, widow of Andrew Clarkson, of Portsmouth, N. H., who survived him. The late Hon. Simon Greenleaf, an eminent jurist, and, for some time, Professor of Law in Harvard University, and the Rev. Jonathan Greenleaf of Brooklyn, N. Y., are among his descendants of the second generation.

The following is a list of Mr. Parsons' printed works:—Letters in the Christian History, 1741. Wisdom justified of her children: A Sermon preached at the Boston Lecture, 1742. Lectures on Justification, 1748. Good news from a far country: Seven Discourses, 1756. Rejoinder to R.

Abercrombie's Remarks on a fair Narrative of the proceedings of the Pres bytery of Boston against himself, 1758. A Sermon on true Godliness, &c., 1759. Manna gathered in the morning, 1761. Infant Baptism from Heaven: Two Sermons, 1765. A Sermon on the death of the Rev. George Whitefield, 1770. Letters on Baptism addressed to the Rev. Hezekiah Smith, 1770. Freedom from civil and ecclesiastical tyranny, the purchase of Christ: A Sermon, 1774. Sixty Sermons: 2 volumes, octavo, (posthumous,) 1784.

Mr. Parsons is now chiefly known as an author by his two volumes of posthumous Discourses,—most of those published in pamphlet form having been long out of print. They are characterized by very considerable mental vigour, by an imagination prolific of striking imagery, by great copiousness of diction and depth of feeling, and a most uncompromising adherence to that system of faith, to which, during the greater part of his ministry, he was so earnestly devoted.

WILLIAM TENNENT (SECOND).*

1732—1777.

WILLIAM TENNENT (Second) was born in the County of Antrim, Ireland, January 3, 1705. He came to this country at the age of thirteen, with his father, the Rev. William Tennent, who arrived with his family at Philadelphia, in the summer of 1718. He early evinced an uncommon thirst for knowledge, and made rapid progress in the languages, particularly the Latin. Being also, as it was hoped, the subject of an early conversion, he determined to devote himself to the Christian ministry. His elder brother, Gilbert, was already a popular preacher, settled in New Brunswick, N. J.; and William, after having gone through a preparatory course under the instruction of his father, went to New Brunswick to avail himself of the aid of his brother in the prosecution of his theological studies. When he left home, his father, with his parting blessing, gave him a small sum of money, telling him that, if he behaved well, it would be all he would need; and if he did not behave well, it was more than he deserved. When he had nearly completed his theological course, and was preparing for his examination by the Presbytery, he was the subject of the remarkable trance which has perhaps given him his greatest celebrity, and of which a particular and authentic account is given in two of the letters connected with this sketch.

After Mr. Tennent's gradual recovery from the effects of his trance, he still adhered to his purpose to preach the Gospel, and in due time received licensure from the Philadelphia Presbytery. His first efforts in the pulpit gave promise, if his life should be spared, of eminent fidelity and usefulness. His brother John, who had for some time been settled over the Presbyterian Church at Freehold, Monmouth County, N. J., having then recently deceased, application was made to the subject of this sketch, to supply the pulpit which his brother's death had vacated; and, after having served them

* Assemb. Miss. Mag. II.—Boudinot's Narrative.—Hist. Log Coll.—Webster's MSS.

a year in the character of a supply, he was, on the 25th of October, 1733, regularly constituted their pastor by the Philadelphia Presbytery.

Though the salary of Mr. Tennent, with proper management, was abundantly adequate to his support, yet, in consequence of his entrusting all his pecuniary concerns to a servant, he very soon became seriously embarrassed, and found that he had debts to a considerable amount, which it was quite impossible for him to cancel. Happening one day to mention this circumstance to a friend who was on a visit to him from the city of New York, his friend suggested, as the most suitable remedy for his difficulty, that he should get married; and when Mr. Tennent smiled at the suggestion, as if it were an utterly hopeless matter, the gentleman told him that there was a lady within his knowledge,—a Mrs. Noble,—his own sister-in-law, whom he thought eminently qualified for such a station; and intimated his willingness, if he would come to New York, to render him any aid in the matter that might be in his power. He accepted the proposal; accompanied his friend to NewYork the next day; was introduced to the lady; offered himself to her, and was accepted; and, within one week from the time of the introduction, she was the mistress of his house. His friend's recommendation was fully justified by her character; for, while she proved a most affectionate and devoted wife, she assumed, in a great degree, the management of his temporal concerns, and within a short time, under her skilful superintendence, he was not only free from debt, but was quite easy in his worldly circumstances. Besides several children who died in infancy, they had three who lived to mature age:—*John*, who was a physician, and died in the West Indies, at the age of about thirty-three; *William*, who forms the subject of a distinct notice in this work; and *Gilbert*, who was also a practising physician, and died at Freehold, before his father, at the age of twenty-eight. They were all men of fine appearance, and of excellent education and character.

Mr. Tennent, though he did not live till the close of the Revolutionary war, was yet deeply interested in the American cause, and by his prayers at least, strove earnestly for its promotion. He was on a visit to some friends near New York, when a British frigate attempted to pass the batteries, and proceed up the North River, while General Washington lay with the American army in the city. A heavy cannonading took place, which was mistaken, in the surrounding country. for a general attack on our army. Mr. Tennent was deeply affected, and, after pausing for a moment, turned to a friend or two present and said—"Come,—while our fellow citizens are fighting, let us retire for prayer." They accordingly went up into his room, where, for half an hour, he poured out his fervent supplications in behalf of his suffering country.

In the winter of 1776–77, the British overran a great part of the State of New Jersey, and particularly the County of Monmouth, where there were a large number of Tories. Encouraged by the adverse prospects of the American cause, a party of these people arose, and dragged numbers of their fellow citizens to the British Provost, by whom they were treated with the utmost rudeness and cruelty. Mr. Tennent now regarded his own situation as one of great peril; but, as he had no place to flee to, he remained at home, committing himself to the Divine protection. In December, 1776, a number of the inhabitants called upon him, and urged him to hasten to Princeton, and avail himself of General Howe's then recent proclamation, offering a pardon to those who should seek it within a limited time. He refused, till he became satisfied that he should stay at the peril of his life, and that if he did stay unmolested, it would be to little purpose, as he should have no opportunity of exercising his ministry. Under these circumstances, he at length very reluctantly consented to go to Princeton. On his way, he lodged at the house of a young clergyman, and, when he arose in the morning, manifested great depression of spirit. On being asked what troubled him, he answered with a sigh,—"I am going to do a thing for conscience sake, directly against my conscience." Soon after his return home, a change favourable to the American interest occurred, and the whigs of Monmouth County, who had been driven away, came back in force. Mr. Tennent continued to reflect severely upon himself for what he regarded as an act of timid and unworthy submission.

But the days of this good man were now almost numbered. About the latter end of February, or beginning of March, 1777, he was seized with a violent fever, which, after a few days, terminated fatally. He died on the 8th of March, 1777, and was buried in his own church at Freehold,—an immense concourse of people attending his funeral.

Mr. Tennent published a Sermon entitled "An exhortation to walk in Christ," preached at New Brunswick, August 8, 1737, upon the Monday after the Sacramental solemnity. It is included in a volume entitled "Sermons on Sacramental occasions by divers ministers," printed in 1739. Also, a Sermon upon Matthew v. 23, 24, 1769.

Judge Boudinot relates the following, among other anecdotes of Mr. Tennent, illustrative of his eminent piety:—

"He was attending the duties of the Lord's day in his own congregation as usual, where the custom was to have morning and evening service, with only a half hour's intermission to relieve the attention. He had preached in the morning, and in the intermission had passed into the woods for meditation,—the weather being warm. He was reflecting on the infinite wisdom of God, as manifested in all his works, and particularly in the wonderful method of salvation, through the death and sufferings of his beloved Son. This subject suddenly opened on his mind with such a flood of light, that his views of the glory and the infinite majesty of Jehovah were so inexpressibly great as entirely to overwhelm him, and he fell almost lifeless to the ground. When he had revived a little, all he could do was to raise a fervent prayer that God would withdraw Himself from him, or he must perish under a view of his ineffable glory. When able to reflect on his situation, he could not but abhor himself as a weak and despicable worm, and seemed to be overcome with astonishment that a creature so unworthy and insufficient had ever dared to attempt the instruction of his fellow men in the nature and attributes of so glorious a Being. Overstaying his usual time, some of his elders went in search of him, and found him prostrate on the ground, unable to rise, and incapable of informing them of the cause. They raised him up, and after some time brought him to the church, and supported him to the pulpit, which he ascended on his hands and knees, to the no small astonishment of the congregation. He remained silent a considerable time, earnestly supplicating Almighty God (as he told the writer) to hide Himself from him, that he might be able to address his people, who were by this time lost in wonder to know what had produced this uncommon event. His prayers were heard, and he became able to stand up by holding the desk. He now began the most impressive and pathetic address that the congregation had ever received from him. He gave a surprising account of the views he had of the infinite wisdom of God, and greatly deplored his own incapacity to speak to them concerning a Being so infinitely glorious beyond all his powers of description. He attempted to show something of what had been discovered to him of the astonishing wisdom of Jehovah, of which it was impossible for human nature to form adequate conceptions. He then broke out into so fervent and expressive a prayer, as greatly to surprise the congregation, and draw tears from every eye. A sermon followed that continued the solemn scene, and made very lasting impressions on all the hearers."

Judge Boudinot elswhere says of him—and he could testify from an intimate acquaintance:—

"He hated and despised sloth. He was almost always in action—never wearied in well-doing, nor in serving his friends. His integrity and independence of spirit were observable on the slightest acquaintance. He was so great a lover of truth that he could not bear the least aberration from it, even in a joke. He was remarkable for his candour and liberality of sentiment with regard to those who differed from him in opinion. His hospitality and domestic enjoyments were even proverbial. His public spirit was always conspicuous, and his attachment to what he thought the best interests of his country was ardent and inflexible. He took an early and decided part with his country in the commencement of the late Revolutionary war. He was convinced that she was oppressed, and that her petitions to the Sovereign of the mother country were constitutional, loyal, moderate and reasonable; that the treatment they received was irrational, tyrannical and intolerable. As he made it a rule, however, never to carry politics into the pulpit, he had no way to manifest his zeal for the public measures, but by his private prayers, and by his decided opinions delivered in private conversations. But in this way his sentiments became universally known, and he was considered as a warm friend to the American cause. * * * He was well read in Divinity, and professed himself a moderate Calvinist. The doctrines of man's depravity; the atonement of the Saviour; the absolute necessity of the all-powerful influence of the Spirit of God to renew the heart and subdue the will,—all in perfect consistence with the free agency of the sinner, were among the leading articles of his faith. * * * His people loved him as a father; revered him as the pastor and bishop of their souls; obeyed him as their instructer; and delighted in his company and private conversation as of a friend and brother."

The three following letters which came into my possession several years ago, contain notices of some of the most interesting events of the life of Tennent, not included in the preceding narrative. I have chosen to subjoin the letters, as being original documents, and of the highest authority. They were addressed to the venerable Judge Boudinot, and constituted part of the material out of which his memoir of Tennent's Life was formed. The first is from General J. N. Cumming, of Newark, N. J., of Revolutionary memory; the second is from the Rev. Dr. John Woodhull, Tennent's successor at Freehold, from whose lips I once heard a statement of the same facts; and the third is from Dr. Thomas Henderson, Tennent's family physician, a distinguished civilian of New Jersey, and a member of the Old Congress. A fourth letter is added, addressed to myself, by S. J. Forman, Esq., of Syracuse, N. Y., who is one of the very small number now living, who have any personal recollections of that remarkable man.

FROM GENERAL CUMMING.

NEWARK, January 3, 1804.

Dear Sir: The Rev. William Tennent once related to me that, after lying ill with the lung fever six weeks, in the midst of winter, about the year 1723, and when he was about nineteen years old, he apparently died. This happened on Sunday, whilst his brother Gilbert, with whom he lived in the city of New Brunswick, was gone to church. His body was laid out in the usual manner, in the back part of a room, in one of the old fashioned Dutch houses. On Monday morning, when they went to put him into the coffin, a man by the name of Duncan, who was assisting, called out to the others to lay him down, for he felt his heart beat, and was sure there was life in him. His brother Gilbert derided the assertion of Duncan, and indeed there was every thing to induce a belief that he was dead. The length of time that he had been sick, his emaciated body, his black lips, his sunken eye,—all appearances were against remaining life. But after this declaration of Duncan, it would not do to bury him, and the funeral was postponed till Tuesday, when the people assembled for the burial. In the mean time, all means had been used to restore life. They were again about to put the body into the coffin, when again Duncan called out,—"Lay him down, for I am sure there is life in him." No other person believed there was life, and yet so long as *he* retained this opinion, they would not allow the funeral service to proceed. The funeral was again postponed until Wednesday, and the means of restoring life meanwhile applied with the utmost diligence and vigour. At the time appointed, the people again assembled, and the Doctor was sitting on the bed-side with a looking glass in one hand, and a feather in the other, trying them alternately at his mouth and his nose. At the very last moment, to the unspeakable surprise of all, he opened his eyes, gazed on them, and swooned away for about two hours. Again he gazed, and again fainted. Shortly after, his whole body broke out in boils to such an extent that it seemed throughout a complete ulcer; insomuch that his nurses were obliged, for nearly a whole year, to sew up sheets, and stuff them with wool, in order to absorb the humours. It was more than a year before he could stand upon his feet, and his intellectual faculties seemed to be gone. He informed me that his eldest sister, named Catharine, was one day teaching him his letters, and he observed her to turn her head from him, and weep with great apparent agitation; and when he asked her what was the matter, she replied,—"I am distressed to think that your sickness has been so severe that, notwithstanding you have had a good education, you have forgotten all you ever knew." Upon this information, he said, there was a sudden return of the use of his faculties, but he was well convinced that his memory was never so good after as before his sickness. I did not ask him whether he saw any thing in his trance. My mother told me that he always said he should live to old age.

Thus, my dear Sir, you have all on this subject that I recollect to have heard. My memory was always strong; and the conversation I had with this good old man, in regard to his trance, was so impressive and extraordinary, that it is one of the last things that can ever fade from my recollection.

Yours affectionately,

J. N. CUMMING.

FROM THE REV. JOHN WOODHULL, D. D.

MONMOUTH, N. J., December 10, 1805.

Dear Sir: Agreeably to your request, I now send in writing the remarkable account which I some time since gave you verbally, respecting your good friend, my worthy predecessor, the late Rev. William Tennent of this place.

In a very free and feeling conversation on religion, and on the future rest and blessedness of the people of God, (while travelling together from Monmouth to Princeton,) I mentioned to Mr. Tennent that I should be highly gratified in hearing from his own mouth an account of the *trance*, which he was said to have been in, unless the relation would be disagreeable to himself. After a short pause, he proceeded, saying that he had been sick with a fever,—that the fever increased, and by degrees he sunk under it; and, after some time, as his friends informed him, he died, or appeared to die, in the same manner as persons usually do;—that, in laying him out, one happened to draw his hand under the left arm, and perceived a slight tremor in the flesh—that he was laid out—was cold and stiff—the time for his funeral was appointed and the people collected; that a young Doctor,—his particular friend, plead with great earnestness that he might not then be buried, as the tremor under the arm continued;—that his brother Gilbert became impatient with the young gentleman, and said to him—"What! a man not dead, who is cold and stiff as a stake!" The importunate friend, however, prevailed—another day was appointed for the burial, and the people separated. During this interval, many means were made use of to discover, if possible, some symptoms of life; but none appeared, excepting the tremor. The Doctor never left him for three nights and three days, when the people again met to bury him, but could not even then obtain the consent of his friend, who plead for one hour more; and when that was gone, he plead for half an hour; and then he plead for a quarter of an hour; when, just at the close of this, on which hung his last hope, Mr. Tennent opened his eyes. They then pried open his mouth which was stiff, so as to get a quill into it, through which some liquid was conveyed into the stomach, and he by degrees recovered.

This account, as intimated before, Mr. Tennent said he had received from his friends.

I said to him, "Sir, you seem to be one indeed raised from the dead, and may tell us what it is to die, and what you were sensible of while in that state." He replied as follows : "As to dying, I found my fever increase, and I became weaker and weaker, until all at once, I found myself in Heaven, as I thought. I saw no shape as to the Deity, but Glory all unutterable!" Here he paused, as though unable to find words to express his views, let his bridle fall, and, lifting up his hands, proceeded,—"I can say as Saint Paul did, I heard and I saw things all unutterable! I saw a great multitude before this glory, apparently in the height of bliss, singing most melodiously; and I was transported with my own situation, viewing all my dangers and all my troubles ended, and my rest and glory begun; and was about to join the great and happy multitude, when one came to me, looked me full in the face, laid his hand on my shoulder, and said,—'*You must go back.*' These words went through me,—nothing could have shocked me more—I cried out, 'Lord, must I go back?' With this shock, I opened my eyes in this world. When I saw I was in the world, I fainted; then revived and fainted several times; as one probably would naturally have done in so weak a situation."

Mr. Tennent further informed me that he had so entirely lost the recollection of his past life, and the benefit of his former studies, that he could neither understand what was spoken to him, nor write nor read his own name; that he had to begin all anew, and did not recollect that he had ever read before, until he had again learned his letters, and was able to pronounce the monosyllables, such as *thee* and *thou;* but that, as his strength returned, which was very slowly, his memory also returned. Yet, notwithstanding the extreme feebleness of his situation, his recollection of what he saw and heard while in Heaven, as he supposed, and the sense of Divine things which he there obtained, continued all the time in their full strength; so that he was continually in something like an ecstacy of mind. And said he, "for three years, this sense of Divine things continued so great, and every thing else appeared so completely vain, when compared to Heaven, that could I have had the world by stooping down to pick it up, I believe I should not have thought of doing it."

Having thus complied with your request, it may not be improper for me to add that, since Mr. Tennent's death, I conversed with his son, the Rev. William Tennent of South Carolina, on this subject, and he agreed in every particular, with one exception—namely, he understood that his father recovered his memory instantaneously.

I am, Dear Sir, affectionately yours,
In the dear Immanuel,
JOHN WOODHULL.

FROM DR. HENDERSON.

FREEHOLD, Monmouth, March 30, 1805.

Dear Sir: As I understand you have already been informed by Dr. Woodhull of the remarkable vision or trance of which Mr. Tennent was once the subject, I shall omit all allusion to that memorable event in the few notices of his character that I am about to furnish.

With regard to the manner in which he discharged the duties of the pastoral office, I can say something from actual knowledge, having lived chiefly under his ministry from my infancy to his death,—a period of between twenty and thirty years. I think I may say with confidence that he was regarded by all classes as a fervent, impressive, and successful preacher of the Gospel; and I doubt not that the Records of his church will prove that a greater number were received to communion, during his ministry, than in any other church in the then Province. His labours in spiritual concerns were far from being confined to the pulpit: he was indefatigable in his endeavours to do good in private. A considerable part of his time he appropriated to visiting his congregation, and would apply the truths of the Gospel personally to individuals of every age, rank, and character; and he was particularly attentive to the little children of his charge, taking care that they were early taught the Catechism, and explaining the various doctrines of the Gospel to their comprehension, as they were able to receive them. He was remarkable for his great attention to the particular situation of persons afflicted either in body or mind, and would visit them often, and with as much care as a physician would do, and proved frequently a very comforting spiritual physician to their souls. As a peace-maker, I am of opinion that none in our day have excelled,—few have equalled, him. If he heard of any difference arising in his congregation, he would scarcely give sleep to his eyes, before he would attempt to bring about a reconciliation between the parties; and he hardly ever remitted his efforts till his object was accomplished. Thus much concerning the general character of our mutual and dear friend I am able to state from my own knowledge.

With regard to any striking facts or anecdotes in the history of Mr. Tennent, I will mention two or three, though there is perhaps only one of them that you will deem worthy of much notice. Though I did not have it immediately from Mr. Tennent himself, yet I have heard the particulars so frequently stated by my parents, who were members of his church, and my father an elder, that I am confident I cannot be mistaken in respect to them. The circumstances were as follows: Mr. Tennent, while young in the ministry, had a contemporary of the name of John Rowland,* who had preached once or more in a church in the County of Hunterdon, N. J., but not often enough, or recently enough, to be readily known by the congregation. Mr. Tennent and Mr. Rowland had both gone on a preaching tour into Maryland or Virginia; and, in their absence, a certain young man by the name of Tom Bell, who knew Mr. Rowland, and who strikingly resembled him in his outward appearance, but who was a most artful and accomplished scoundrel, dressed himself as much like Mr. Rowland as he could, changed his name to that of John Rowland, and professing to be a minister of the Gospel, went into the congregation above alluded to, and passed himself off as the minister who had preached to them some time before. He accepted an invitation to pass the rest of the week with one of the members of the church, and to preach on the succeeding Sabbath. The impostor was treated with every

* JOHN ROWLAND was a native of Wales; came to this country in early life, and received his education for the ministry at the Log College. He was taken under the care of the New Brunswick Presbytery at its first meeting, August 8, 1738, in disregard of a standing rule of the Synod, which required that every candidate, before being taken on trials by any Presbytery, should undergo an examination on his classical and scientific attainments by a Committee of Synod. The Presbytery, believing this rule to be an undue infringement of the rights of Presbyteries, and considering it as designed to operate particularly against the Log College, determined to resist it; and hence arose the violent dissension between this Presbytery and the Synod, which issued in a division of the latter body into two parts,—the Old and the New Side. Mr. Rowland, having gone through the prescribed trials, was licensed to preach on the 7th of September; but the Synod refused to consider him a member of their body. On the very day of his licensure, an application was made for his services by the united Congregations of Maidenhead (Lawrence) and Hopewell (Pennington). He accepted the invitation, and a great revival of religion attended his labours. After some time, he removed from New Jersey into Pennsylvania, where he had charge of a congregation in what is called "the Great Valley," and also of New Providence, near Norristown, though much of his time seems to have been spent in itinerating. He died before the autumn of 1747. Dr. Henderson of Freehold says—"He possessed a commanding eloquence and many estimable qualities." Whitefield said—"There was much of the simplicity of Christ discernible in his behaviour."

mark of respect by the family who had thus proffered him their hospitality; and, in order the more effectually to blind them to his character and his purpose, he occupied a room by himself as a study, in which he was professedly making his preparation for the Sabbath. When the Sabbath morning came, and the family had got ready to go to church, it was proposed that the pretended minister should take a seat in the wagon in which the family were to be conveyed, while the gentleman of the house would ride on horseback. Thus they went to church· but when they arrived there, the clerical rogue suddenly made the discovery that he had left his notes behind, and begged his host to allow him to mount his horse, (a remarkably fine one,) and return to his house and get his notes, promising to be there to commence the service within a short time. The proposal being readily consented to, the imposter rode back to the gentleman's house, and, having rifled the desk of whatever he could find in it that was valuable, went off with all speed in a different direction, and thus made his escape. Several persons saw him on the horse, and addressed him as Mr. Rowland. When Mr. Rowland, after some time, returned to the Province, he was immediately prosecuted for horse-stealing; and when the case came to trial, Mr. Tennent appeared as a witness, proving that he and Mr. Rowland were, on that very Sabbath, at a particular place in Maryland or Virginia, and that one or both of them preached there. In consequence of this testimony, Mr. Rowland was honourably acquitted.

At that time, there were many leading families in that part of the Province, who evinced a deadly hostility to the Gospel, and who were upon the lookout for opportunities to bring its ministers into contempt. Perceiving the great and increasing influence of Mr. Tennent, and the remarkable success that attended his labours, they entered into a conspiracy against him, and succeeded in getting him indicted, by a grand jury of the County of Huntingdon, for perjury. Mr. Tennent was charged upon his indictment, and plead "not guilty." The trial was put off as usual to another term. His enemies, who were also the enemies of religion, had engaged distinguished counsel, whose anti-christian sympathies were entirely with their own. Mr. Tennent or his friends secured the best counsel they could get. At the time when the trial was to come on, Mr. Tennent attended at Trenton, and, in the morning, before the court was opened, was asked by his counsel, where his witnesses were; and his reply was, "I have no witnesses, Gentlemen, that I know of, but God and my own conscience." "You *have* no witnesses, Sir," replied the attorneys, with the utmost astonishment,—"then you had better have the trial put off:—you know what testimony will be brought against you, and what efforts will be made to ruin you; and you will inevitably be convicted, unless you are able to meet them with an opposing testimony." Mr. Tennent answered,—"I know it well; but I will never put it into the power of my enemies to charge me with a wish to delay the trial, or with being afraid to meet the law or justice. I know my innocence; and my God, whose I am, and whom I serve, and in whom I place all my confidence, knows it, and he will never suffer me to fall by the snares of the devil, or the wicked machinations of his agents—go to trial, Gentlemen." His attorneys informed him that his confidence in God as a Christian or a minister of the Gospel was no doubt well founded, and before a Heavenly Tribunal would be all-important to him; but that it would avail him nothing before a Court of Law, and again urged his consent to have the trial put off. He, however, persisted in his determination to let the trial take its course, assuring them that he had such entire confidence that God would bring about his deliverance in some way or other, that he did not wish for a moment's delay. They were so out of patience with him, that they did not hesitate to tell him that his conduct was more worthy of a wild enthusiast, or a downright madman, than of a prudent Christian. But he still charged them to go to court, and let the case come to trial without loss of time, and left them in a state of utter perplexity as to what course they should pursue; for the bell was then ringing for the Court to assemble. He had not walked far in the street, before he met a gentleman and lady, the former of whom inquired whether his name was William Tennent. He replied in the affirmative, and asked the gentleman if he had any business with him. The answer was, "You will best know, when I tell you whence I came, and what has brought me hither; but I should like to know whether you were in Maryland [or Virginia] at such a time, in company with Mr. John Rowland, minister of the Gospel." Upon being answered in the affirmative, he asked him if he recollected their lodging, a certain Saturday night, at the house of a person by the name of ——— and going to church on the ensuing Sabbath with the family, and one or both preaching, &c. Mr. Tennent said he did. The gentleman replied,—"I am that man in whose house you lodged that night, and this is my wife." Mr. Tennent took them by the hand, and expressed his great satisfaction at seeing them; for the Sabbath referred to proved to be the very one on which Mr. Tennent had sworn that Mr. Rowland was with him in Maryland or Virginia;—on which oath was based the accusation of perjury. The gentleman then explained the reason of his being there: he said that, several nights before, he and his wife awoke in the night at the same time,—each having had the same singular dream; which was, that he (Mr. Tennent) was at Trenton in the greatest possible distress, and that it was in their power alone to relieve him. They, however, suffered it to pass as an ordinary dream, and both went to sleep again; but they had the same dream a second, and even a third, time; and they were then so much impressed with the extraordinary circumstance, that they immediately arose from bed, prepared for their journey, and had travelled with all speed till they had reached Trenton. "And now," said the gentleman, "you can tell whether we have any business with you or not." Mr. Tennent begged them instantly to accompany him to the court house, the Court then being in the act of meeting. The case was forthwith called; the witnesses on both sides examined; the cause submitted to the jury; Mr. Tennent triumphantly acquitted; and his adversaries overwhelmed with confusion.

Another anecdote occurs to me, illustrative of Mr. Tennent's knowledge of human nature, and of his disposition always to be about his Master's business. On a certain occasion, he was travelling with a brother minister on a missionary tour at the South, when they stopped at an inn, and engaged lodgings for the night. At supper they met several gentlemen who were strangers to them; and when the cloth was removed, Mr. Tennent and the other minister withdrew from the table. A pack of cards was immediately brought forward; and one of the gentlemen, not knowing that there were any ministers present, asked Mr. Tennent and his clerical brother if they would take a cut with them; meaning thereby to determine by lot who should play. Mr. Tennent replied,—"With all my heart, Sir, if you can convince us that we are thereby serving our Master's cause, or doing anything in aid of the object of our mission." This drew some observations from the stranger, which were replied to by Mr. Tennent in substance as follows:—"This gentleman" (meaning his companion) "and myself are ministers of the Gospel: we both profess ourselves Christ's servants: we are sent out on his business, which is to persuade men to become reconciled to God." These remarks, made with great sincerity and kindliness of manner, produced such an effect upon the company, that the cards were immediately removed, and a willingness manifested to listen to Mr. Tennent and his friend on the most momentous of all concerns. They gladly availed themselves of the opportunity of doing their Master's work, and spent the evening in explaining to the company, into which they had been thus providentially thrown, the great truths and duties of religion.

I recollect another anecdote which I had from Governor Livingston, which shows how entirely Mr. Tennent's will was swallowed up in the will of his Heavenly Father. The Governor stated that, when, at a certain time, Mr. Whitefield was travelling in Jersey, Mr. Tennent accompanied him to Bound Brook, (if I remember right,) and after Divine service on a week day, a Mr. Van Horne invited Messrs. Whitefield, Tennent, Livingston, and some other gentlemen to dine with him. In the course of the conversation that occurred at the dinner, Mr. Whitefield introduced the subject of death,—expressing himself as weary of the trials and labours of life, and desiring to depart and be with Christ. Turning to Mr. Tennent, he said, "And what do you say, Brother Tennent—don't you want to get your dismissal too?" Mr. T. replied,—"I have no wish about it: I have nothing to do with death: my business is to live as long as I can, as well as I can, and to serve my Lord and Master as faithfully as I can, until it shall be his pleasure to call me to my rest." "But," says Mr. Whitefield, if it were left to your own choice, would you not wish to depart and be with Christ, rather than to encounter the fatigues and trials of this mortal state?" Mr. Tennent replied, "I wish to have no choice about it; I am God's servant, and am engaged to do his business as long as he pleases to continue me therein. But, Brother Whitefield, permit me to ask you one question:—What would you think of a person who had engaged to serve you with all fidelity to the end of his life, if he should, without any breach of covenant on your part, and before he had one-half performed the service allotted him, become weary of your service, and be constantly expressing a wish for some easier condition—would you not say that he was a lazy, unfaithful creature, and as such dismiss him entirely from your service?" Mr. Livingston told me that Mr. Whitefield appeared to feel the force of the reproof, and to receive it as a Christian; and that the company seemed much pleased at the ingenious and Christian-like manner in which it was administered.

I will close my communication (already too long) by detailing one more circumstance which fell within my immediate knowledge, illustrative alike of Mr. Tennent's love of country, and submission to the Divine will. He took the deepest interest in our Revolutionary struggle, believing, as he did, that the great cause of the world's civil freedom was bound up in it. When he was attacked with his last illness, I was sent for as his family physician; but it happened to be just at the moment that I was setting off for Haddenfield, to wait upon the Legislature of the State on important public business. I called on Mr. Tennent, after setting out on my journey, and, having learned the particulars of his case, I told him that I had but a few moments to stay, as it was then night, and I had more than twenty miles to ride before I slept; but that his case was an alarming one,—that it required the strictest attention, and that I advised him to avail himself at once of the best medical aid that could be procured. He replied that he was fully aware of the violence of the attack, and thought it more than probable that it would have a fatal result; "but, blessed be God," says he, "I have no wish to live, if it should be the good pleasure of my Heavenly Father to call me hence." After a moment's pause, he seemed to recollect himself, and varied the expression somewhat in this way—"I have no wish to live longer, unless it should be to see a happy issue of the conflict in which my country is now engaged; but the will of the Lord be done." On my return from Haddenfield, I hastened to see him, and was with him during the last twenty-four hours of his life. His death was worthy of his life,—full of Christian serenity and joyful hope. I believe it may be said of our departed friend, as truly as of any man who has lived during the present age, that he lived habitually under the influence of the powers of the world to come.

I am, dear Sir, with respect,

Your obedient, humble servant,

THOMAS HENDERSON

FROM S. J. FORMAN, Esq.

Syracuse, 25th October, 1847.

Rev. and dear Sir: I regret to say that my reminiscences of the celebrated William Tennent are too scanty and unimportant to be of any use to you. Nevertheless, since you ask for them, such as I have, give I unto you.

My parents were members of Mr. Tennent's church, and my very early years were spent under his ministry. I distinctly recollect to have seen him once at my father's house, in company with some of my relatives, with whom he was there visiting. In person he was tall—of a large frame, but spare, and of a long thin visage. He wore a large white wig. I remember that his manners were very pleasing to me. When he came into the house, I heard him say to some person behind him—"in spite of your teeth;" and at the same time, he shut his own teeth, and shook the curls of his long wig, twisting his hands together, and seemed to be in very high spirits. As my mother met him at the door of her room, he clasped both her hands with both of his, in the most cordial and affectionate manner. There was a facetiousness about his whole appearance that I never could forget. The party had come for a sleigh ride, about fourteen miles, in the month of April, and returned after candle light, for fear that the snow would leave them. I have always thought that Mr. Tennent resembled the likeness of Lord Chatham.

One of Mr. Tennent's sons was a physician. At one time, he inoculated a large number for the small pox, in a spacious farm house; and, while his patients (of whom I was one) were yet under treatment, he was himself taken sick and died suddenly. The patients had to scatter to their respective homes. One of his sons was a clergyman in Charleston, S. C., where he died. While I was yet a minor in a counting-house in New York, I was sent to Charleston as a supercargo, and, during my stay in the city, Mrs. Tennent heard of me, and sent for me to come to her house. Though I was an entire stranger to her, her intimacy with some of my connections in New Jersey led her to show me that civility.

With much esteem and respect,

I am, Rev. and dear Sir,

Your very obedient servant,

S. J. FORMAN.

SAMUEL BLAIR.*

1733—1751.

Samuel Blair was born in Ireland, June 14, 1712. In early youth he became hopefully a subject of renewing grace. He came to America while quite young, and received his education at the Log College, at Neshaminy, under the Rev. William Tennent. He must have been among the earliest pupils of that institution, as he was afterwards among the most distinguished men whom it sent forth. Having completed his preparatory course of both classical and theological study, he was licensed to preach, on the 9th of November, 1733, by the Presbytery of Philadelphia, and in May of the next year, was called to Middletown and Shrewsbury, and also, to Millstone

* Miller's Ret. II.—Mass. Miss. Mag. III.—Hist. Log Coll.—Webster's MSS.

and Cranberry, N. J. He accepted the former call in September following, and shortly after was ordained.

Here he continued about five years; but there are no records remaining to indicate the amount of success that attended his labours. He was one of the original members of the Presbytery of New Brunswick, which was formed in 1738. In 1739, he was earnestly solicited to settle in New Londonderry, otherwise called Fagg's Manor, in Pennsylvania. Not being willing to decide the question of duty which this call presented to him, he referred it to the Presbytery; and, after mature deliberation, they advised him to accept the call, on the ground that it would be the means of extending his usefulness. He acted in accordance with their advice; but his installation did not take place till April, 1740, though he removed to his new residence, and commenced his labours among the people in November, 1739.

Shortly after his settlement at New Londonderry, he established a classical school of the same general character with that of Mr. Tennent, in which he had himself been educated. At this school were trained several young men, who afterwards ranked among the most prominent clergymen of the Presbyterian Church; and one at least,—the Rev. Samuel Davies, among the greater lights of his generation.

In connection with Mr. Blair's ministry at New Londonderry, there occurred, in the year 1740, a very remarkable revival of religion, of which a minute account is preserved in a letter from Mr. Blair to the Rev. Thomas Prince of Boston, published in the "Christian History."

Mr. Blair was a prominent actor in those scenes which, in his day, agitated and finally divided the Presbyterian Church. He agreed with Gilbert Tennent in his opinions, and co-operated with him in his measures; and of course rendered himself obnoxious to the "Old Side" party in the Church.

In his doctrinal views he was a thorough Calvinist, as appears from his Treatise on Predestination and Reprobation. As a preacher he was distinguished for solemnity and impressiveness: his very appearance, before he opened his lips, is said to have struck his hearers with awe. The opinion which Mr. (afterwards President) Davies entertained of his preaching, may be inferred from the following anecdote which is given upon the authority of the late Dr. Rodgers of New York:—When Mr. Davies returned from Europe, his friends were curious to learn his opinion of the celebrated preachers whom he had heard in England and Scotland. After dealing out liberal commendations on such as he had most admired, he concluded by saying that he had heard no one, who, in his judgment, was superior to his former teacher, the Rev. Samuel Blair.

Mr. Blair's last illness was contracted from his going, upon an urgent call, and in an enfeebled state of body, to meet the Trustees of New Jersey College. As he approached his end, he expressed the strongest desire to depart and be with Christ; and but a minute or two before his departure, he exclaimed, "The Bridegroom is come, and we shall now have all things." He seemed to breathe the atmosphere of Heaven, before he had actually passed the Heavenly portals. His remains lie in the burying ground of Fagg's Manor, where his monument is yet to be seen. It bears the following inscription:—

"HERE LIETH THE BODY OF
THE REV. SAMUEL BLAIR,
WHO DEPARTED THIS LIFE
THE FIFTH DAY OF JULY, 1751,
AGED THIRTY-NINE YEARS AND TWENTY-ONE DAYS.

"In yonder sacred house I spent my breath,
"Now silent, mouldering, here I lie in death;
"These lips shall wake, and yet declare
"A dread Amen to truths they published there."

In the year 1754, the principal writings of Mr. Blair were collected by his brother John, and published in Philadelphia, together with an Elegy by the Rev. Samuel Davies, and Dr. Finley's Funeral Sermon. The volume contains Seven Sermons on important practical subjects, an elaborate Treatise on Predestination and Reprobation, and a "Vindication," written by the direction of the Presbytery of New Brunswick, in answer to "the government of the church," &c., by the Rev. John Thompson. As a writer, Mr. Blair seems to have been distinguished rather for profound thought, methodical arrangement, and perspicuous style, than for the graces and elegances of composition.

The following extracts from Mr. Davies' Elegy and from Dr. Finley's Funeral Sermon, show the estimate which they had of Mr. Blair's character:—

FROM MR. DAVIES' ELEGY.

"— Blair is no more—Then this poor world has lost
As rich a jewel as her stores could boast;
Heaven, in just vengeance, has recalled again
Its faithful envoy from the sons of men;
Advanced him from his pious toils below,
In raptures there in kindred plains to glow.

"O, had not the mournful news divulged,
My mind had still the pleasing dream indulged—
Still fancied Blair with health and vigour blessed,
With some grand purpose labouring in his breast.
In studious thought, pursuing Truth Divine,
Till the full demonstration round him shine;
Or from the sacred desk, proclaiming loud
His Master's message to the attentive crowd,
While Heavenly truth with bright conviction glares,
And coward error shrinks and disappears;
While quick remorse the hardy sinner feels,
And Calv'ry's balm the bleeding conscience heals.

"Oh! could the Muse's languid colours paint
The man, the scholar, student, preacher, saint,
I'd place his image full in public view,
His friends should know more than before they knew.
His foes astonished at his virtues, gaze,
Or shrink confounded from the oppressive blaze.
To trace his bright example, all should turn,
And with the bravest emulation burn.
His name should my poor lays immortalize,
Till he, to attest his character, arise,
And the Great Judge the encomium ratifies."

FROM DR. FINLEY'S FUNERAL SERMON.

"He was blessed with early piety. On his dying bed, he could recollect with delight, various evidences of gracious influences in his tender years. By this means, he was happily preserved from being ever engaged in vicious courses; and at once grew in stature and in grace. Religion, far from being a flashy thing with him, was rational and solid, manifesting itself in unreserved obedience to all God's commandments.

"To a holy disposition was added a great genius, capable of the highest improvement. He had a deep and penetrating judgment, a clear and regular way of conceiving things, and a retentive memory. He was an indefatigable student, a calm and impartial searcher after truth. He thought for himself, and was determined in his conclusions, only by evidence. He had a very considerable store of critical learning, and was especially conversant with the Scriptures in the original languages. How great his attainments in philosophy were, was known by few; for in his last years, his thirst for knowledge did sensibly increase, and he greatly improved himself therein. He studied several branches of the mathematics, and especially geometry and astronomy; nor will these seem tasteless studies to one who had such a savour of living piety, when it is considered that he saw the glory of God in all his works, and admired and adored Him in all. He delighted to see the 'invisible things of Him, even his eternal power and Godhead, manifested by the things that are made.' It was edifying to him to trace the footsteps of the Divine wisdom in particulars, and the infinite reach of projection in the frame and structure of the whole.

"But his critical and philosophical learning, and his large acquaintance with geography and history, were exceeded by his knowledge in Divinity. This was the business of his life, and herein he made such proficiency as few of his standing in the ministry have attained unto. Here he found what perfectly answered his refined spritual taste. The contemplation of redeeming love did much more elevate his soul, than that of the works of creation; for therein he saw the wisdom, the power, the justice, and the love of God, more clearly displayed. On every subject he had a set of most accurately studied thoughts. He had often weighed in an impartial balance every theological controversy; and was a solid disputant, and able to defend all necessary truth. He was a judicious casuist, and could very satisfyingly resolve dubious and perplexed cases of conscience. He was not only a proficient in systematic Divinity, which is comparatively a small attainment, but a great textuary. He studied the sacred oracles above all other things, and that it was not in vain, manifestly appeared from his great ability in dividing the word of truth. He could "bring out of his treasure things new and old." How clearly and fully would he explain his subject! with what irresistible arguments confirm the truth! with what admirable dexterity accommodate it to his audience! and with what solemn pungency did he impress it on the conscience! He spoke like one who knew the worth of souls, and felt in himself the surest constraints of love to God and man.

"As to his religious principles, he was of noble and generous sentiments. He had not so learned Christ as to be furious in his zeal for mere circumstantial or indifferent points. He understood the nature of religion better than to place it in things in which it does not consist; and was too much exercised about the great matters of the law, to be equally zealous for 'mint, anise and cummin.' Though sacrifice be good, yet he had learned that 'mercy is better.' He believed, and that in accordance with the Scriptures, that the communion of saints is of much greater importance, than many of those things in which Christians differ in judgment, and was, therefore, far from such narrowness, as to make every principle and practice which he thought to be good and true, a term of communion; and he was as far from the contrary extreme of indifference to the truth, and laxness of discipline. As he was diligent in the exercise of his ministerial office, to the utmost of his strength, not sparing himself, so did God very remarkably succeed his faithful ministrations to the conversion of many souls. He was the spiritual father of great numbers. I have had acquaintance with Christians in different places, where he only preached occasionally, who gave all hopeful evidences of a sacred conversion, and acknowledged him to be the instrument of it. He was strict in discipline, yet so as to be still candid; and severely just, yet so as to be still compassionate and tender. And with what wisdom and circumspection he judged in difficult cases, his brethren of the Presbytery well knew. We waited for his sage remarks, and heard attentively his prudent reasonings; and after his words, how seldom had any one occasion to speak again! 'His speech dropped upon us, and we waited for him as for the rain.' He has been eminently serviceable to the Church, by assisting several promising youths in their studies for the ministry; who, becoming learned by his instructions, and formed by his example, are now wise, useful and faithful ministers.

He was remarkably grave and solemn in his aspect and deportment; yet, of a cheerful, even, and pleasant temper. And in conversation with his intimate friends, facetious and witty, when the season and concurring circumstances would allow him to indulge in that way; in respect of which, his prudence could well direct him. He was of a generous and liberal disposition,—far from being niggardly or covetous; was foremost in acts of charity to the indigent, according to his ability, and in all his conduct discovered a noble indifference toward earthly things.

"If we consider him as a friend, he was as firm and steadfast, and might as much be depended upon, as any I ever knew. He was remote from precarious and fickle humours; his approbation was not easily obtained, nor easily lost. Nor was he a friend only in compliment, but would cheerfully undergo hardships, and suffer disadvantages, in order to do a friendly office. He was conscientiously punctual in attending ecclesiastical judicatures, Presbyteries or Synods. His presence might be depended upon if nothing extraordinary intervened, as certainly as the appointed day. He was not absent on every trifling inconvenience. In this respect his conduct was truly exemplary, and demonstrated his constant care for the public interests of religion. So great was his attention to matters of common concern, as to incline him rather to expose himself, than balk an opportunity of doing good.

"In social life also, he was worthy of imitation. As a husband, he was affectionate and kind; as a father, tender and indulgent. In him, condescension and authority were duly tempered. There was *that* in him that could engage love and command reverence at the same time. Who that was acquainted with him, would not be ready to say,—'happy was the family of which he was the head, and happy the congregation that enjoyed his ministry—happy the judicature of which he was a member, and happy the person who was favoured with his friendship!' He was a public blessing to the Church, an honour to his people, an ornament to his profession, who 'magnified his office.' He spoke as he believed; he practised as he preached; he lived holy, and died joyfully.

"For a long course of years, he had a habitual, increasing assurance of his interest in the favour of God, and that a blessed and glorious eternity would one day open upon him; which were his own emphatical words on his dying bed. This his assurance, was solid and scriptural, arising from the many and clear experiences he had of gracious communications to his soul. He was made sensible in his early years of his guilty state by nature as well as practice; felt his inability to deliver himself; saw plainly that he lay at mercy, and that it was entirely at God's pleasure to save or reject him. This view of the case created in him a restless concern, until the way of life through Jesus Christ was graciously discovered to him. Thus he saw that God could save him in consistency with all the honours of governing justice; for that the obedience and sufferings of Christ in the room of sinners have made a sufficient atonement for sin. He saw that Christ was a Saviour every way complete and suitable for him. His soul approved the Divine and glorious plan; and freely disclaiming all dependance on his own righteousness, wisdom and strength, most gladly accepted the offer of the Gospel, that Christ should be his 'wisdom, righteousness, sanctification, and redemption.' Strict holiness was his choice, and it was the delightful business of his life to do always those things which pleased his Heavenly Father. And on his dying bed, he had the full approbation and testimony of his conscience, as to the general bent and tenor of his life. These particulars are the heads of what he himself told me in his last sickness, and are delivered in the same order, as near as I can possibly recollect."

DAVID COWELL.*

1735—1761.

David Cowell was born in Wrentham, Mass., in the year 1704. He was graduated at Harvard College in 1732. Having studied Theology, and received license to preach, he went to Trenton, N. J., in the autumn of 1735, where he was employed to supply a vacant pulpit. On the 7th of April, 1736, he received a call to settle there, which he accepted; and the Presbytery of Philadelphia ordained and installed him on the 3d of November following. The sermon on the occasion was preached by the Rev. Jedediah Andrews of Philadelphia.

In the division of the Presbyterian Church in 1741, Mr. Cowell maintained a somewhat neutral position. He remained with the Old Side, and had no sympathy with what he regarded the extreme measures of the New Brunswick party; but he still remained in intimate relations with President Burr, and others belonging to the same side. The Commissions of the two Synods met at Trenton, in 1749, to consult in regard to a re-union, and Mr. Cowell was chosen Moderator; but nothing more decisive was done at the meeting, than to agree that each Synod should more fully prepare proposals of reconciliation, and that there should be, in the meantime, a mutual endeavour to cultivate a friendly and fraternal spirit.

* Hodge's Hist. Presb. Ch.—Webster's MSS.—Rev. Dr. Pierce's MSS.—MS. from Rev. Dr. John Hall.

Mr. Cowell was a devoted friend to New Jersey College, and was one of its Trustees from its foundation till his death. He was a great admirer of Davies, and had much to do in securing his election to the Presidency of the College. To induce his acceptance of the place, he wrote thus to him:—

"The College ought to be esteemed of as much importance to the interests of religion and liberty as any other institution of the kind in America. God, at first, in a most remarkable manner, owned and blessed it. It was the Lord's doing. He erected it; for our beginning was nothing. He carried it on till it was marvellous in our eyes. But it hath been under terrible frowns of Divine Providence; first in the loss of Mr. Burr,—the life and soul of it; and then of Mr. Edwards, from whom we had such raised expectations. May the Father of mercies look with pity and compassion on the work of his own hands! I am sensible that your leaving Virginia is attended with great difficulties; but I cannot think your affairs of equal importance with the College."

On the union of the two Synods, Mr. Cowell joined the New Brunswick Presbytery, and continued in relation with it till his death. He died, in his fifty-seventh year, on the 1st of December, 1760,—having never been married. President Davies preached his Funeral Sermon, from Hebrews iv. 11,—from which the following is an extract:—

"During the short time I have been a resident of this Province, he [Mr. Cowell] has been my very intimate friend; and I have conversed with him in his most unreserved hours, when conversation was the image of his soul. I had only a general acquaintance with him for ten years before.

"The characteristics of his youth were a serious, virtuous, religious turn of mind, free from the vices and vanities of that thoughtless age, and a remarkable thirst for knowledge; and I am witness how lively a taste for books and knowledge he cherished to the last. He appeared to me to have a mind steadily and habitually bent towards God and holiness. If his religion was not so warm and passionate as that of some, it was perhaps proportionally more even, uniform and rational. His religion was not a transient passion, but appeared to be a settled temper. Humility and modesty, those gentle virtues, seemed to shine in him with a very amiable lustre. He often imposed a voluntary silence upon himself, when he would have made an agreeable figure in conversation. He was fond of giving way to his brethren with whom he might justly have claimed an equality, or to encourage modest worth in his inferiors. He was not impudently liberal of unasked advice, though very judicious, impartial, and communicative, when consulted. He had an easy, graceful negligence in his carriage,—a noble indifference about setting himself off; he seemed not to know his own accomplishments, though they were so conspicuous that many a man has made a brilliant appearance with a small share of them. He had a remarkable command of his passions; he appeared calm and unruffled amid the storms of the world,—peaceful and serene amid the commotions and uproar of human passions. Remarkably cautious and deliberate, slow to determine, and especially to censure, he was well guarded against extremes. In matters of debate, and especially in religious controversy, he was rather a moderator and compromiser than a party. Though he could not be neuter, but judged for himself to direct his own conduct, he could exercise candour and forbearance without constraint or reluctance; when he happened to differ in opinion from any of his brethren, even themselves could not but acknowledge and admire his moderation.

"His accomplishments, as a man of sense and learning, were very considerable. His judgment was cool, deliberate and penetrating; his sentiments were well digested, and his taste excellent. He had read not a few of the best modern authors, and was no stranger to ancient literature. He could think as well as read; and the knowledge he collected from books was well digested, and became his own. He had carefully studied the Sacred Scriptures, and had a rational theory of the Christian system.

"He had an easy, natural vein of wit, which rendered his conversation extremely agreeable; he sometimes used it with great dexterity to expose the rake, the fop, the infidel, and other fools of the human species: it was sacred to the service of virtue, or innocently volatile and lively, to heighten the pleasures of conversation.

"He was a lover of mankind, and delighted in every office of benevolence. Benevolence appeared to be his predominant virtue, and gave a most amiable cast to his whole temper and conduct.

"That he might be able to support himself without oppressing a small congregation, he gave some part of his time to the study and practice of physic, in which he made no inconsiderable figure. A friend of the poor, he spared neither time nor expense to relieve them.

"I never had the happiness to hear him in the sacred desk. In prayer, I am sure he appeared humble, solemn, rational and importunate, as a creature,—a sinner in the presence of God.

"In the charter of the College of New Jersey, he was nominated one of the Trustees; and but few, invested with the same trust, discharged it with so much zeal, diligence, and alacrity. His heart was set upon its prosperity; he exerted himself in this service, nor did he forget it in his last moments.

"The Church has lost a judicious minister, and, as we hope, a sincere Christian; the world has lost an inoffensive, useful member of society; this town an agreeable, peaceable, benevolent inhabitant; the College of New Jersey a father; and I have lost a friend."

AARON BURR.*

1736—1757.

Aaron Burr was a descendant of the Rev. Jonathan Burr, who migrated to New England in 1639, and was, for some time, pastor of the church in Dorchester, Mass. He was the youngest son of Daniel Burr, of Upper Meadows, Fairfield, Conn., where he was born on the 4th of January, 1715-16. His early developments indicated a mind of uncommon power and versatility. He was graduated at Yale College in 1735, having been, during his whole course, distinguished for his proficiency, in both the languages and the sciences. He remained in College, a resident graduate on the Berkeley foundation, for one year; and, during this period, his mind underwent a revolution in respect to religion, of which the following account was found, after his decease, among his private papers:—

"This year (1736) God saw fit to open my eyes, and show me what a miserable creature I was. Till then I had spent my life in a dream; and as to the great design of my being, had lived in vain. Though before I had been under frequent convictions, and was drove to a form of religion, yet I knew nothing as I ought to know. But then I was brought to the footstool of sovereign grace; saw myself polluted by nature and practice; had affecting views of the Divine wrath I deserved; was made to despair of help in myself, and almost concluded that my day of grace was past. These convictions held for some months; greater at some seasons than at others; but I never revealed them to any, which I have much lamented since. It pleased God, at length, to reveal his Son to me in the Gospel, an all-sufficient and willing Saviour, and I hope inclined me to receive Him on the terms of the Gospel. I received some consolation, and found a great change in myself. Before this, I was strongly attached to the Arminian scheme, but then was made to see those things in a different light, and seemingly felt the truth of the Calvinian doctrines."

This change in his religious views and feelings was quickly succeeded by a determination to devote his life to the Christian ministry. And, having gone through the requisite preparation, he received license to preach in September, 1736. He preached his first sermon at Greenfield, Mass., and then went to New Jersey and laboured a short time at Hanover. His uncommon powers in the pulpit attracted no small attention, and the church at Newark, then in a somewhat depressed state, invited him to officiate as a stated supply for one year, commencing with January, 1736-37. At the expiration of that term,—January 25, 1737-38,—he was ordained and installed pastor of the church,—Mr. Pierson preaching the Sermon, and Jonathan Dickinson giving the Charge.

* Smith's Sermon occasioned by his death.—Livingston's Eulogy.—Miller's Ret., II.—App. to Green's Disc.—App. to Dwight's Life of Edwards.—Memoir of Aaron Burr.—Stearns' Hist. First Church in Newark.

In August, 1739, about a year and a half after his ministry commenced, a remarkable revival of religion began in his congregation, which increased gradually from month to month, until it pervaded all ages and all classes of society. In the winter of 1840–41, was another similar season, in respect to which, says an eye witness, "there is good reason to conclude that there were a greater number now brought home to Christ than in the former gracious visitation."

In June, 1742, the First Church in New Haven—in consequence, it is said, of some difficulties, which it was thought might best be terminated by the settlement of a colleague,—presented a call to Mr. Burr to become associated with their pastor, the Rev. Mr. Noyes; and, in pursuance of this call, a committee was appointed, with President Clap at its head, to go to Newark, and lay the call before Mr. Burr, and prosecute it before the Presbytery to which he belonged, with directions likewise "to treat with the good people of Newark, and obtain their consent to Mr. Burr's removal to New Haven." Of the result of this application nothing more is known than that it was unsuccessful.

Mr. Burr entered warmly into the great revival that took place in the early part of his ministry, and was in intimate relations with Whitefield, the Tennents, and many of the principal promoters of the work, though he was by no means insensible to the incidental evils by which it was marred. In a letter to Dr. Bellamy, dated June 28, 1742, he says,—

"I have so many things lying on my mind, that I know not how to communicate them with pen and ink. I long to have you alone a few hours, that I might unbosom myself freely; but 'tis good to have no will of our own. 'Tis glad tidings of great joy we hear from Southberry. But some things that I have heard from there I don't see through, which, in some measure, damps my joy. The bearer has given me more satisfaction. Glory be to God that he carries on his work in any way; I do rejoice and will rejoice. However, there are some things that persons are apt to run into at the present day, that we ought not to encourage:—1. Their being led by impressions and impulses made on their minds, with or without a text of Scripture, and taking their own passions and imaginations for the operations of God's Spirit. 2. Giving heed to visions, trances, and revelations. 3. Speaking of Divine things with an air of levity, vanity, laughter, &c. 4. Declaring their judgment about others openly and freely in their absence, whether they are converted or not. 5. Making their own feelings a rule to judge others by. 6. For laymen to take upon them to exhort in a public assembly. 7. Separating from their minister under a notion of his being unconverted."

The Rev. Jonathan Dickinson, first President of the College of New Jersey, having died at Elizabethtown in the autumn of 1747, the students whose education he had been conducting, were removed to Newark, and placed under the care of Mr. Burr, who had previously been in the habit of instructing in the classic languages, and had had under his direction a large Latin School. Whether he was formally appointed President under the first charter of the College, is a matter of doubt; but it seems he had charge of the youth who had been collected as the beginning of a College, for about a year before the charter was obtained, under which they were graduated. He was appointed President under the new charter on the 9th of November, 1748; and, on the same day, conferred the Bachelor's degree upon a class who were prepared to receive it. On that day also he delivered his Inaugural, which is spoken of in the record of the Corporation, as "a handsome and elegant Latin Oration." Either the original manuscript, or a copy in the handwriting of the author, is still in existence.

In 1754, Whitefield, who was then paying a visit to Governor Belcher, at Elizabethtown, attended the Commencement at Newark, on which occasion President Burr had the pleasure of conferring upon him the degree of Master of Arts. Immediately after the Commencement, Mr. Burr accompanied Whitefield to Boston, having a high esteem for his character, and a deep interest in the success of his labours.

Mr. Burr's devotion to the College was most constant and exemplary. He served it not only as the principal instructer and presiding officer, but in soliciting donations for the purchase of a library and philosophical apparatus, and for erecting a building for the accommodation of the students. In this agency, which he undertook by request of the Trustees, he was remarkably successful. He discharged the duties of both President of the College, and Pastor of the Church, until the autumn of 1755, when his pastoral relation was dissolved, and he gave his whole time to the service of the College.

The village of Princeton having been fixed upon as the most convenient situation for the College, the new edifice was erected there, under the superintendence of Mr. Burr. In the Autumn of 1756,—the building being so far completed as to be ready for the reception of the students, they removed thither, about seventy in number, and commenced the occupancy of it.

But Mr. Burr's life was now rapidly approaching its close. In the latter part of July, or the beginning of August, 1757, he made a hasty visit to Stockbridge, and, on his return to Princeton, went immediately to Elizabethtown, where he made an attempt before the Legislature to procure the legal exemption of the students from military duty. Thence he went to Newark, and preached an extemporaneous Funeral Sermon. He then returned to Princeton, and proceeded immediately to Philadelphia on the business of the College, and on his way contracted an intermittent fever. On his return, he received the news of the death of his friend Governor Belcher, at Elizabethtown, and was informed that he was designated to preach at his funeral. Having devoted the afternoon of September 2d to preparation for this service in the midst of a high fever, he rode the next day to Elizabethtown; and, on the day succeeding that, in a state of extreme exhaustion, preached the sermon. He returned to Princeton on the 5th, and his disease, from that time, made constant progress, until the 24th, when it terminated in death. His mind was entirely composed in the prospect of his departure, and he died rejoicing in the consolations of the Gospel. A Eulogy was pronounced upon him by Governor (William) Livingston, and a Funeral Sermon was preached by the Rev. Caleb Smith, of Newark Mountains, by appointment of the Trustees, and printed at their expense.

During the first fifteen years of his ministry, Mr. Burr remained unmarried. On the 29th of June, 1752, he was united in marriage with Esther, daughter of the Rev. Jonathan Edwards,—she being, at that time, only nineteen years of age. She was distinguished for an attractive exterior, for a richly endowed and highly cultivated mind, and for earnest and consistent piety. It was a somewhat novel circumstance that, after the preliminaries of the marriage had been settled, the bride was sent for with her mother to come to Newark, and the wedding took place there, amidst the congratulations of the people among whom she was to live. She survived her husband less than a year, and died on the 7th of April, 1758, in the twenty-seventh year of her age. They left two children—a daughter and a son—both born during their residence in Newark. The former was married to the Hon.

Tapping Reeve, Chief Justice of the Supreme Court of Connecticut; and the latter, bearing his father's name, and inheriting his talents, and rising to great political distinction, nevertheless had a history more sad and monitory than almost any other man of the age.

Mr. Burr published a Latin Grammar; a pamphlet entitled "The Supreme Deity of our Lord Jesus Christ maintained in a Letter to the dedicator of Mr. Emlyn's Inquiry into the Scripture account of Jesus Christ,"—reprinted in Boston, 1791; a Fast Sermon on account of the encroachments of the French, 1755; a Sermon preached before the Synod of New York, 1756; and a Sermon on the death of Governor Belcher, 1757.

The character of President Burr is thus sketched in the Funeral Sermon by the Rev. Mr. Smith:—

"It may not be improper here to take a more distinct view of his character as a divine, and his qualifications as a preacher. He was certainly an adept in Divinity, a scribe well instructed unto the Kingdom of Heaven, who out of his plentiful treasure could bring forth things new and old. In the Scriptures of truth he was thoroughly versed; read them by turns with the eye of a critic, to search out their sense, and in a devotional way, to obtain their salutary influence on his own heart. The Oracles of God were the standard of his Divinity, his ultimate Confession of Faith, the measure of his practice, and the man of his counsel, in all the parts of his ministry. He was greatly a master of systematical, casuistical and practical Divinity; understood polemical, but cared not much to wield the sword of religious controversy. His inclination led him to a field which wore a milder face, and where there is less danger of hurting that faith which is our own, and losing a good conscience ourselves, while we are attempting to rectify the faith and mend the consciences of others.

"In the pulpit, he verily shone like a star of the first magnitude, and appeared a wise master-builder in the house of God. He dwelt upon things of the highest moment, and cautiously built, not with wood, hay and stubble, but with gold, silver and precious stones. His public discourses were calculated to convey light to the mind, warmth to the affections, and health to the heart. His subjects, being well chosen, were handled with judgment and solidity; for he had, to an eminent degree, a masterly skill in dividing the word of truth, and gave with wisdom and faithfulness a portion to each in their season.

"When leisure would permit, his sermons were usually penned at large; yet if duty called, and he was not otherwise provided, he would cheerfully enter the pulpit without his notes. And indeed so very extraordinary was his talent for extemporary preaching, that the most competent judges approved his conduct, and heard him with pleasure and profit. A rich fund of Divine knowledge, command of his thoughts, surpassing quickness of invention, and remarkable readiness of expression, together with a heart commonly warm in the cause of God, and engaged by desires of doing good to the souls of men, rendered him truly a master-piece in performances of this kind.

"He never ascended the desk, but those who knew him had raised expectations, which were rarely, if ever, disappointed, and often exceeded. His gesture in the pulpit was easy and natural, and there was an air of mild gravity and genuine benignity in his aspect, that tended greatly to engage the favourable regard of his hearers. He was blessed with an easy door of utterance, and his deliverance was graceful and harmonious. * * * His diction was expressive, and his style neat and flowing; his language was well suited to the language of a Christian orator. When he thought proper, and occasion required, it was either plain or polished; for he could speak freely with such simplicity as a child might understand, or with elegance that would please the politest ear.

"In the gift of prayer he much excelled; for a spirit of prayer and supplication seemed always to rest upon him; and there appeared such marks of unfeigned sincerity, suitable affection and fervency, added to a rich variety and exact pertinency of expression, on all occasions, in his performance of this duty, that few, if any, were more fit to lead in public acts of devotion, or be the mouth of others to God. It may also be observed here that, in all the exercises of religion, both in public and in the family, he carefully avoided a tiresome prolixity, and was rather short and animated.

"If we now turn and survey the figure which this worthy man made in another great employment,—I mean as President of this School of the Prophets, we shall find no less cause to admire his character, revere his memory, and lament his death.

"When he entered upon this station, though he had then a large stock of learning of the scholastic kind, having been before, for a number of years, a constant instructer of youth in the learned languages and liberal arts; nevertheless he applied himself more closely to those branches of literature, which he judged a man ought to be accurately acquainted with, in order to discharge the trust faithfully, or appear with reputation and a requisite dignity as a head teacher in such a public school. He also viewed it, not as a part of ease, but of weighty business, and accordingly filled it with application and unwearied industry, much to the benefit of the students, satisfaction of the Trustees, credit of the College, and his own honour.

"The abundant store of useful knowledge with which he had been carefully enriching himself from his youth up, and to which he was continually making large additions, was here improved to the most valuable purpose. His mind was well replenished with ideas; and these he had an inimitable faculty of communicating with clearness and ease. His aptness to teach was almost without parallel. He laboured exceedingly that the youth committed to his tuition and care might be sent abroad with such a foundation of knowledge, as might be honorary to the place of their education, and fit them for future service in Church or State; aud it was a real grief to him, when these his painful endeavours failed of their desired success, which it can hardly be supposed but they too often did.

"As the piety of President Burr was as conspicuous as his erudition, he took indefatigable pains to cultivate the hearts of his pupils as well as their heads; and equally concerned himself to dismiss them as good Christians and good scholars. They who have had the happiness of being educated under his inspection, can bear witness with what zeal, solicitude, and parental affection he has often pressed upon them the care of their souls, and in the most moving manner, even with melting tenderness, urged the importance of their becoming true disciples of a holy Jesus. A gracious God was mercifully pleased, as we trust, to grant success, in some instances, to these pious attempts: for he had good hope concerning a number that they were really initiated into the school of Christ. The winter season of the last year of his life was his most joyful harvest, when a very remarkable Divine influence appeared among the students in this house; the good impressions that were then made, we have grounds to believe, are yet abiding with many.

"In matters of government in the College, he discovered great wisdom and sagacity. In judgment and natural temper he was inclined to soft and moderate measures; but, where these failed of their desired efficacy, he gave way to a requisite severity. * * As to his manner of presiding at the public Commencements, I imagine none who were fit judges, but will readily acknowledge that, in moderating the disputes and all the other exercises, which, on those days, belonged to his office, he acquitted himself with high honour and deserved applause. * * * * * * * *

"In ecclesiastical judicatures and councils, his assistance was often desired, and his judgment deservedly esteemed. He was cool and dispassionate in all debates, and had the felicity in general to have his sentiments embraced, or at least his measures come into; for there seldom an occasion presented, but he either overcame those who were of an opposite opinion by the force of his reasoning, or won them by such engaging persuasions as few were able to resist.

"He was a great friend to liberty, both civil and religious, and generously espoused this noble cause on every suitable occasion. As he abhorred tyranny in the State, so he detested persecution in the Church, and all those anti-christian methods which have been used by most prevailing parties, somehow or other, to enslave the consciences of their dissenting brethren. He was very far from indulging a party spirit, and hated bigotry in all its odious shapes. His arms were open to a good man of any denomination, however he might in principle differ or in practice disagree, as to what he himself, in the lesser matters of religion, judged to be preferable. He was no man for contention, and at a wide remove from a wrangling disputant; these bitter ingredients came not into the composition of his amiable character. His moderation was well known to all men that knew any thing of him. A sweetness of temper, obliging courtesy, and mildness of behaviour, added to an engaging candour of sentiment, spread a glory over his reputation, endeared his person to all his acquaintance, recommended his ministry and whole profession to mankind in general, and greatly contributed to his extensive usefulness."

FRANCIS ALISON, D. D.*

1736—1779.

Francis Alison was born in the parish of Lac, County of Donegal, Ireland, in the year 1705. He received an excellent classical education at an Academy in the North of that kingdom, under the particular inspection of the Bishop of Raphoe, and was afterwards, for some time, a student of the University of Glasgow. He came to America in 1735, and was, for a while, engaged as tutor in the family of the father of John Dickinson, Governor of Delaware, who placed his son under his care, and allowed him to receive a few other pupils. The exact date of his licensure cannot be ascertained; but he is spoken of as a licentiate, in the Records of the Synod of June 18, 1736. Between this date and the 25th of May, 1737, he was ordained by the Newcastle Presbytery, and installed pastor of the New London Congregation, in Chester County, Pa., where he continued fifteen years.

In the year 1743, he opened an Academy at New London, with a view to the general improvement of the community in which he lived, which was, at that time, exceedingly destitute of the means of intellectual culture; but it was rendered, by some concurring influences, a powerful auxiliary to the cause of theological education. About this time, the Synod of Philadelphia began to take measures for establishing a school on a permanent foundation, with special reference to training young men for the ministry. It appears from their Records that, as early as 1739, an overture for erecting a Seminary of learning was unanimously approved, and a committee appointed to visit Great Britain with a view to "prosecute this affair." The breaking out of a war between England and Spain occasioned the postponement of the matter for a time; but, in 1743, it was revived by the Presbyteries of Philadelphia, Newcastle, and Donegal, acting conjointly by a committee which met at the Great Valley in Chester County, by whom it was again referred to the Synod. The next year, (1744,) the school was established by the Synod, on the following plan: 1. That all persons who please, may send their children and have them instructed *gratis*, in the languages, philosophy, and divinity. 2. That the school be supported for the present by yearly contributions from the congregations under their care. 3. That if any funds remain, after paying the salaries of the Master and Tutor, they shall be expended in the purchase of books and other necessaries for the school. Mr. Alison was appointed Principal; and thus the new school was engrafted upon the grammar school, which he had established three years before. It became a justly celebrated institution; and served not only to aid in furnishing the Church with well qualified ministers, but the State with able civilians. Amongst those who were either wholly or partially educated here, were Charles Thompson, Secretary of the First Congress; Rev. Dr. John Ewing, Provost of the University of Pennsylvania, Dr. Ramsey, the Historian; Dr. Hugh Williamson, one of the framers of the Constitution of the United States, and Historian of North Carolina; Rev. Dr.

* Miller's Ret. II.—Holmes' Life of Stiles.—Stiles' MSS.—Webster's MSS.—Allen's Biog. Dict.

James Latta, eminent as a divine and a teacher; and Thomas McKean, George Read, and James Smith, signers of the Declaration of Independence.

In 1749, Mr. Alison was invited to become a teacher in the Philadelphia Academy. He was disposed to accept the invitation, and applied that year to the Synod for leave to join the Presbytery of Philadelphia. His request, however, was not granted; but, in place of it, some improvement was made in his situation as Principal of the Synod's school. We hear no more of this until May, 1752, when it seems that he had actually left his congregation, and removed to Philadelphia, without a dismission from the Presbytery. The matter being brought before the Synod by the Presbytery, the Synod, whilst declaring his conduct in the case anti-presbyterian, and "contrary to their known approved methods in such cases," yet regard it "in a great measure excusable," on account of the pressing circumstances in which he was placed, and its being almost impracticable for him to apply for the consent either of the Presbytery or the Synod in the usual way.

On his removal to Philadelphia, he took charge of the Academy; and when, in 1755, a College was added, he was appointed Vice Provost and Professor of Moral Philosophy. He was also assistant minister of the First Presbyterian Church. He discharged his duties, both as a preacher and a teacher, with acknowledged fidelity and success. The degree of Master of Arts was conferred upon him by Yale College in 1755, and by the College of New Jersey in 1756; and the degree of Doctor of Divinity, by the University of Glasgow in 1758. So highly was this latter honour then appreciated, that the Synod to which Mr. Alison belonged, made a formal acknowledgment of it to the University.

In the year 1755, Dr. Alison made a journey into New England, where he received great attention, and made many valuable acquaintances. He passed some time at Newport with the Rev. Dr. Stiles, in whom he found a kindred spirit, in respect to literary and scientific pursuits. In reference to these, Dr. Alison writes to him:—"I am highly pleased that you continue so unwearied in the pursuit of knowledge. I pray God that he may long spare you a blessing to his Church, and a useful instrument to promote knowledge and learning." He then proceeds to mention his own unsuccessful attempts to discover the comet expected about that time, and the injury which he hence derived to his health, which brought him to a resolution that effectually destroyed his star-gazing; and adds,—"As I hope, with more certainty and less trouble, to acquire this kind of knowledge in the next stage of my existence, if it be necessary, I have determined to give myself no further trouble, till I be allowed to converse with Newton, Halley, Whiston, and Flamstead, and some others of the same complexion, if these names be allowed to shine in one great constellation in Heaven. Yet I am far from blaming you for your careful and accurate researches; they may make you more useful here, and form your taste to examine the works of God with a higher satisfaction in the coming world."

Dr. Alison lived during a period of great agitation in the Presbyterian Church; and, possessing a naturally active mind, and ardent temperament, it was not to be expected that he would be a mere spectator of the passing scenes. His influence was deeply felt in both the Presbytery and the Synod; and whatever he undertook, became with him, for the time, all-engrossing. About the period of his settlement at New London, the controversy between the "Old Side" and the "New Side" was raging in all its violence. His views and sympathies were all with the "Old Side." He complained to the Donegal Presbytery of the Rev. Alexander Creaghead,* for intruding into his congregation, "to rend and divide it against his mind, the mind of the session, and the declared opinion of the congregation in general." The Presbytery having suspended Mr. Creaghead, and he refusing to submit, Dr. Alison carried the complaint up to the Synod, in 1741; and, when a hearing of the case was resisted there, on merely technical grounds, and thus "the last effort at accommodation failed," the famous "*Protestation*" was produced, signed by twelve ministers, one of whom was Dr. Alison,—and seven elders. This was immediately followed by what was called the "Great Schism"—the Church was rent into two parts, and remained thus divided for seventeen years.

In 1765, the people of New London, who had remained vacant from the time that he left them, sent him a call to come and resume his labours among them; but, after due consideration, he declined it.

Dr. Alison died on the 28th of November, 1779, in the seventy-fourth year of his age. A sermon was preached on the occasion of his death, by the Rev. Dr. Ewing, with whom he had been associated in the ministry, an extract from which was, many years after, published in the General Assembly's Magazine.

Dr. Alison was married to a lady whose maiden name was *Armitage.* They had six children,—four sons and two daughters. Two of his sons died in boyhood; a third died in his twenty-eighth year; and the rest survived their father. One of the sons was a physician. Though he left his family in indigent circumstances, he made provision in his will for giving his slaves their liberty.

Dr. Alison's only publication is a Sermon delivered before the Synods of New York and Philadelphia, May 24, 1758, entitled, "Peace and union recommended." It contains a note, suggesting that "as, in the perusal, it may to many seem long, they may conveniently divide it by pausing on the twenty-eighth page."

There are various testimonies remaining, to Dr. Alison's high character, as a man, a Christian, a scholar, and a preacher. Bishop White, who was

* ALEXANDER CREAGHEAD is supposed to have been born in this country. He was licensed to preach by the Donegal Presbytery on the 8th of October, 1734, and was ordained and installed minister of Middle Octorora, on the 18th of November, 1735. He entered warmly into the Whitefieldian revival, and being naturally ardent and impetuous, fell into some irregularities which, in 1740, became the subject of Presbyterial investigation. In 1741, the case was carried up to the Synod, where it was debated with great earnestness. It was, however, lost sight of by the action consequent upon the famous protest brought in by the Rev. Robert Cross, by means of which the conflicting parties in the Synod were separated. Mr. Creaghead withdrew with the New Brunswick Presbytery; and we do not find his name in connection with the Synod of either New York or Philadelphia until the year 1753, when he appears upon the roll of the Synod of New York as an absentee. He was, for a time,—between 1745 and 1753, associated with the Cameronians. About 1749, he removed to Virginia, and took up his residence in the County of Augusta, on the Cow Pasture River, within the bounds of the present Windy Cove Congregation. On the defeat of Braddock in 1755, his congregation was in a great measure dispersed; and, crossing the Blue Ridge, he found a more quiet resting place in what is now Mecklenburg County, N. C. In April, 1758, a call was presented to him from Rocky River, which he accepted, and his installation took place in September following. Here he passed the rest of his days in the arduous duties of a frontier minister of the Gospel, and died in March, 1766, then the only minister between the Yadkin and the Catawba. During his residence in Pennsylvania, he was charged with being the author of an anonymous political pamphlet, which was so offensive to the Government that, in 1743, one of the Justices for the County of Lancaster, in the name of the Governor, laid it before the Synod of Philadelphia. But the Synod disowned both the pamphlet and the supposed author, agreeing with the Justice that it was of a disloyal and rebellious tendency.

a student in the College of Philadelphia, while he was a Professor in it, says of him in his Memoirs,—

"Dr. Alison was a man of unquestionable ability in his department, of real and rational piety, of a liberal mind;—his failing was a proneness to anger; but it was forgotten,—for he was placable and affable."

President Stiles says of him—"He is the greatest classical scholar in America, especially in Greek—not great in Mathematics, Philosophy, and Astronomy, but in Ethics, History, and general reading, is a great literary character. I have had a long and intimate acquaintance with him."

The following is an extract from the Funeral Sermon by Dr. Ewing:—

"All who knew him acknowledge that he was frank, open and ingenuous in his natural temper; warm and zealous in his friendships; catholic and enlarged in his sentiments; a friend to civil and religious liberty; abhorring the intolerant spirit of persecution, bigotry, and superstition, together with all the arts of dishonesty and deceit. His humanity and compassion led him to spare no pains nor trouble in relieving and assisting the poor and distressed by his advice and influence, or by his own private liberality; and he has left behind him a lasting testimony of the extensive benevolence of his heart in planning, erecting and nursing, with constant attention and tenderness, the charitable scheme of the widow's fund, by which many helpless orphans and destitute widows have been seasonably relieved and supported; and will, we trust, continue to be relieved and supported, so long as the Synod of New York and Philadelphia shall exist.

"Blessed with a clear understanding and an extensive liberal education; thirsting for knowledge, and indefatigable in study, through the whole of his useful life, he acquired an unusual fund of learning and knowledge, which rendered his conversation remarkably instructive, and abundantly qualified him for the sacred work of the ministry, and the painful instruction of youth in the College. He was truly a scribe well instructed into the Kingdom of Heaven, a workman that needed not to be ashamed,—for he rightly divided the word of truth, and was peculiarly skilful in giving to every one his portion in due season. In his public exhibitions he was warm, animated, plain, practical, argumentative and pathetic; and he has left a testimony in the consciences of thousands who attended upon his ministry, that he was willing to spend and be spent to promote their salvation, and that he failed not to declare to them the whole counsel of God, while he endeavoured to save himself and those that heard him. And we have reason to hope that the bountiful Redeemer, whom he served in his spirit, has greatly honoured him by making him instrumental in the salvation of many, who shall be the crown of his rejoicing in the day of the Lord.

* * * * * * * * *

"He is now discharged from the labours of mortality, and is gone, we trust, to receive the approbation of that compassionate Redeemer whom he so faithfully served. For he often expressed his hopes in the mercy of God unto eternal life, and told me, but a few days ago, 'that he had no doubt but that, according to the tenor of the Gospel covenant, he would obtain the pardon of his sins through the great Redeemer of mankind, and enjoy an eternity of rest and glory in the presence of God.' It was this comfortable prospect that animated him to uncommon fidelity and industry in all the duties of life, and enabled him to bear the lingering dissolution of his body with patience and resignation, until he fell asleep in Jesus."

JOHN ELDER.*

1736—1792.

John Elder was born in the County of Antrim, Ireland, in the year 1706. His father, Robert Elder, migrated to America about the year 1730, and settled a few miles North of what is now Harrisburg, Pa. He brought all his family with him, except his son *John*, the eldest of his children, who was left with his uncle, the Rev. John Elder of Edinburgh, to complete his studies for the ministry. He (the son) was licensed to preach in the year 1732; and, some time after, (probably in 1736,) agreeably to previous arrangements, followed his father and family to America. In August, 1737, the churches in Pennsboro' and Paxton, Pa. applied to the Newcastle Presbytery for a candidate, and Mr. Elder was sent in answer to the request. On the 12th of April, 1738, the people of Paxton and Derry invited him to become their pastor; and, about the same time, he was called to one or two other places. He accepted the call from Paxton and Derry, and was ordained and installed on the 22d of November following.

About two years after his settlement, he was charged with teaching doctrines at variance with the standards of the Church; and, though the charge was groundless, it occasioned great agitation, and, in consequence of it, his congregation was divided. Mr. Elder seems to have continued with the part of his congregation who adhered to the "Old Side;" and, on the death of the Rev. John Roan, the congregation of Derry united with that of Paxton in receiving him as their minister.

As Mr. Elder resided on the frontier of the Province, the members of his congregation were generally trained as "Rangers" in defence against the Indians. Many a family mourned for its head, shot down by a concealed foe, or carried away captive. The men were accustomed to carry their rifles with them, not only to their work in the field, but to their worship in the sanctuary; and their worthy minister kept his beside him in the pulpit. It was no uncommon occurrence for death to overtake them, as they returned from the public services of the Sabbath to their scattered plantations. In 1756, the meeting house was surrounded with Indians, while Mr. Elder was preaching; but the spies having noticed the large number of rifles that the hearers had brought for their defence, the party silently withdrew from their ambush, without making an attack. In 1757, an attack was actually made, as the people were leaving the church, and two or three were killed. During the summer, they had some security by means of the visits of friendly Indians; but, at other seasons of the year, murders frequently occurred, and they found it impossible to discover the criminals. Mr. Elder himself superintended the military discipline of his people, and became Captain of the mounted men, widely known as the "Pextony boys." He afterwards held a Colonel's commission in the provincial service, and had the command of the block-houses and stockades from the Susquehanna to Easton. His apology for this extraordinary course lies in the extraordinary state of things which led to it. It is not easy to over-estimate the

* MS. from J. Wallace, Esq.—Webster's MSS.—Day's Hist. Coll. Pa.—Colonial Records of Pa. VI.

suspense and terror in which the inhabitants of that frontier region lived from 1754 to 1763. Elder besought the Governor to remove the Conestoga Indians, because they harboured murderers; and he engaged, if this were done, to secure the frontier without expense to the Province. This being refused, a party of his Rangers determined to destroy the tribe; and they called on Elder to take the lead in the enterprise. He was then in his fifty-seventh year. Mounting his horse, he commanded them to desist, and reminded them that the execution of their purpose would inevitably involve the destruction of the innocent with the guilty; but their prompt reply was—"Can they be innocent who harbour murderers?"—at the same time, pointing indignantly to instances in which their wives and mothers had been massacred, and the criminals traced to the homes of the Conestogas. He still earnestly opposed the measure, and at last placed himself in the road, that they might see that they could advance only by cutting him down. When he saw that they were preparing to kill his horse, and that all his entreaties were entirely unavailing, he withdrew and left them to take their own course. The persons engaged in this desperate enterprise, were chiefly Presbyterians, who resided in that neighbourhood, and not a few of them were men far advanced in life. They performed their work thoroughly and mercilessly, destroying in Lancaster and Conestoga every Indian they could find. On the 27th of January, 1764, Elder wrote to Governor Penn, as follows:—

"The storm which had been so long gathering, has, at length, exploded. Had Government removed the Indians, which had been frequently, but without effect, urged, this painful catastrophe might have been avoided. What could I do with men heated to madness? All that I could do was done. I expostulated; but life and reason were set at defiance. Yet the men in private life are virtuous and respectable; not cruel, but mild and merciful. The time will arrive when each palliating circumstance will be weighed. This deed, magnified into the blackest of crimes, shall be considered as one of those ebullitions of wrath, caused by momentary excitement, to which human infirmity is subjected."

The Indians were at length removed, by the Governor, from every exposed place, to Philadelphia; and many apprehended that the "Pextony boys," in the overflowing of their wrath, would pursue them thither. The Governor issued a proclamation, setting a reward on the head of one Stewart, supposed to be the ringleader, and some of his associates. Elder wrote to the Governor in their defence, stating the true characters of the men, and the palliating, if not justifying, circumstances under which they acted. Several pamphlets were published, commenting on the case with great severity, and some of them representing the Irish Presbyterians as ignorant bigots or lawless marauders. But, amidst all the violent attacks and retorts, Elder is never stigmatized as abetting or conniving at the massacre; nor is his authority pleaded by the actors in their defence.

The union of the Synods brought Mr. Elder and the other members of Donegal Presbytery into the same body with the leading members of the "New Side" Presbytery of Newcastle. For a while, they maintained, ostensibly, union of action; but, at length, the "Old Side" men withdrew from the Synod, on account of dissatisfaction in respect to certain cases of discipline, and formed themselves into a separate Presbytery. They, however, finally returned, and were scattered, with their own consent, in Donegal, Newcastle, and Second Philadelphia, Presbyteries.

Mr. Elder joined the Second Presbytery of Philadelphia, May 19, 1768. In the formation of the General Assembly, he became a member of the

Presbytery of Carlisle. He died in the year 1792, at the age of eighty-six; having been a minister of the Gospel sixty years, and the minister of the congregations in Paxton and Derry, fifty-six.

Mr. Elder was married, about the year 1740, to Mary, daughter of Joshua Baker, who was armourer under King George the Second; and, by this marriage, he had four children,—two sons and two daughters. After her death, he was married to Mary, daughter of Thomas Simpson, and sister of General Michael Simpson of Revolutionary memory, who was a Captain under General Montgomery at Quebec. By his second marriage he had eleven children. The last of the whole number (fifteen) died in April, 1853, at Harrisburg, in his eighty-seventh year.

FROM THE REV. W. R. DEWITT, D. D.

HARRISBURG, Pa., March 17, 1854.

Dear Sir: The Rev. John Elder, concerning whom you inquire, died twenty-six years before my settlement over my present charge. On my first coming to Harrisburg, there were several persons residing here, who recollected him well, having sat under his ministry and been members of his church. They all spoke of him with great respect, and to some his memory was dear.

From what I could learn of him, I should judge that he was a man of that decided and resolute character which still distinguishes the Scotch Irish of Pennsylvania and Ohio,—a man of robust constitution, of great courage and indomitable strength of purpose—something of an Andrew Jackson man, as to the prominent characteristics of his mind. The people with whom he was identified, belonged to the same race of sturdy, sterling men, whose native energies were nurtured by the dangers, toils and sufferings incident to the first settlement of our country. The history of his connection with scenes of Indian warfare would well illustrate the iron qualities for which he was distinguished, while, at the same time, it would show that he neither encouraged nor justified a vindictive spirit.

Mr. Elder's congregation embraced a large district of country of which the old Paxton Church was the centre. In good weather, and especially on Communion occasions, the house was too small to contain the people that assembled for worship. But extensive as was his pastoral charge, he was exceedingly jealous of any interference on the part of his ministerial brethren, and resisted to the last every attempt to establish other congregations within the field he regarded as his own. On one occasion I have heard it said that a Rev. Mr. Hogg*, (now Hoge,) who then lived on the outskirts of his congregation, preached for a time within the bounds of his parish. At the next meeting of Presbytery, Mr. Elder indignantly complained that "a *hog* had been rooting in his fields." It was some time after Harrisburg was incorporated, before Mr. Elder would allow any preaching here. The Presbytery sent several commissions to endeavour to settle the conflicts that arose out of the effort to establish a church in Harrisburg, between Mr. Elder and his people. Mr. E. never yielded, until he thought his authority was vindicated, and his pastoral rights admitted. In the controversy that divided the Presbyterian Church at that time, he was a strong Old Side man, distinguished more for orthodox theology, than for any strong demonstration of religious feeling. He looked with little indulgence on the New Lights,

* JOHN HOGG was a son of William Hogg, whose father emigrated from Scotland, and settled first in Amboy, N. J. He was graduated at Nassau Hall in 1749, and was licensed to preach by the New Side Presbytery of Newcastle, October 10, 1753. He was ordained in 1755, and first settled in Pennsylvania, near the Susquehanna, but afterwards removed to the neighbourhood of Winchester, Va., where he supplied Opeckon and Cedar Creek, in Frederick County. But he subsequently returned to Pennsylvania, and was one of the first members of the Huntington Presbytery. He died at a very advanced age.

and had little sympathy with any of their extraordinary movements for the promotion of the Gospel.

A gentleman of this place, a remote relative of Mr. Elder's, to whom I have applied for information concerning him, writes thus:—"As to Mr. E's personal appearance and habits, I would not venture any thing from my own knowledge; for though I may have seen him frequently, I was too young (only six years old) when he died, to retain any distinct recollection of him. But as my grandfather and he were full brothers, I have heard many of the relatives and friends speak of his personal appearance and manners, and they uniformly represented him as a large, fine looking man, above six feet high, well formed and proportioned, dignified in manner, a fine specimen of an educated gentleman, beloved and respected by the people of his congregation, and having great influence for good among them."

I am sorry that I cannot give you fuller and more detailed information of Mr. Elder, as he must have acted an important part, both as a citizen and a minister, in the first settlement of this portion of Pennsylvania. Should, however, the above answer your purpose, to any extent, I shall be gratified.

With much respect, yours sincerely,

WILLIAM R. DEWITT.

JAMES DAVENPORT.*

1738—1757.

JAMES DAVENPORT was a great grandson of the Rev. John Davenport, who was the first minister of New Haven, and was afterwards settled in Boston, where he died in 1670. He was a son of the Rev. John Davenport of Stamford, Conn., who was graduated at Harvard College in 1687, was ordained pastor of the church in Stamford in 1694; and died February 5, 1731, aged sixty-one. He (the father) was an eminently faithful and useful minister, and was so familiar with the original languages of the Scriptures, that he was accustomed to read them in the family in place of the English translation.

James Davenport was born in Stamford in the year 1710, and was graduated at Yale College in 1732. From letters addressed to his brother-in-law, the Rev. (afterwards Dr.) Stephen Williams of Longmeadow,—which are still extant, it appears that he was very seriously inclined, and probably a professor of religion, during his college life. He continued to reside at New Haven for two or three years after his graduation, and, during this time, it is supposed that he prosecuted his theological studies under the direction of Rector Williams. He was, at this period, the subject of some very troublesome, if not dangerous, disease: and, after having made trial of the skill of Dr. Hubbard of New Haven, without receiving any material benefit, he went to Killingworth, and spent some time in the family of Dr. Jared Eliot, distinguished alike as a physician and a clergyman,—that he might have the benefit of his medical attentions. Under Dr. Eliot's treatment, he very soon began to amend, and after two or three months, we find

* Miller's Life of President Edwards.—Prime's Hist., L. I.—Webster's MSS.—Various pamphlets connected with the Revival of 1740.—Tracy's Great Awakening.—Autograph letters of Mr. Davenport to Rev. Stephen Williams.

him again pursuing his studies at New Haven, and, for aught that appears, in his usual health. He seems to have taken a very serious view of the dispensation, and to have been deeply solicitous that it might turn to his spiritual benefit.

His letters at this period show that he was the subject of great spiritual conflicts, and was intent upon making high attainments in religion. Some of them show also, that he was far from having any sympathy with that extravagant spirit,—of which he afterwards gave so humiliating an example. In a letter dated Yale College, January 27, 1734, he writes thus—"I find need of continual supplies of grace and strength from above, that I may maintain a close walk with God; Divine wisdom and prudence to behave aright to and before others, so as to give no offence,—so as to do no hurt to religion, or to my own soul. Oh, Sir, a great thing I find it to be wise as a serpent, and harmless as a dove. I would repeatedly ask your prayers for me on this account. I am very sorry to hear what you write concerning Mr. R——, fearing it may be no small damage to religion. I should be sorry if, upon examination, you should find that there was real ground to fear, as you mention in your letter, with respect to Sir Pomeroy. Sir Wheelock, I hope, and am very well satisfied, thinks right in these matters, and has no wild notions, and I should be glad to hear that Sir Pomeroy has not."

It is not known where, or by what body, Mr. Davenport was licensed to preach; but, as he pursued his theological studies at Yale, and as his father was a prominent clergyman in Connecticut, there is little doubt that it was by an Association in his native State. In the spring of 1738, he was applied to, to preach at Maidenhead and Hopewell, (Lawrence and Pennington,) N. J., and the Philadelphia Presbytery wrote to him in behalf of those congregations; but he received a call from Southold, L. I., about the same time, to which he gave the preference. Southold was the oldest town on the Island, and had been left vacant, in 1736, by the removal of the Rev. Benjamin Woolsey.* His ordination took place on the 26th of October, 1738. Among the ministers composing the council was his brother-in-law, the Rev. Stephen Williams of Longmeadow.

Mr. Davenport's settlement was just at the time when the indications of what has been called the "Great Awakening," were beginning to appear in different parts of the Church. It was the custom of those who deplored the prevailing religious indifference, to draw the line with great distinctness between the converted and unconverted, and to express to individuals personally the judgment they had formed of their spiritual condition. Davenport, who seems to have been of an excitable temperament, and to have hailed the earliest signs of the new state of things with intense inter-

* Benjamin Woolsey was a grandson of George Woolsey, who emigrated from Yarmouth, England, to America, between 1630 and 1640; and was a son of Captain George Woolsey, who was born in New York, October 10, 1652, and died at Dosoris, L. I., January 19, 1740–41, in his ninetieth year. He was born at Jamaica, L. I., November 19, 1687; was graduated at Yale College in 1709; and was ordained as the third pastor of Southold, L. I., by an ecclesiastical council, in July, 1720. In 1736, he resigned his charge, and removed to Dosoris, in Queens County, where he had a large tract of land, which came to him through his wife. Here he spent the remainder of his life, preaching, as opportunity offered, in the surrounding country. He died on the 15th of August, 1759, in the seventy-second year of his age. He had two sons,—*Mèlancthon Taylor*, who was a Colonel in Abercrombie's expedition, and died during the expedition, in 1758; and *Benjamin*, who was graduated at Yale College in 1744, led a quiet country life, and died in 1771. The latter was the grandfather of the Rev. Dr. Woolsey, President of Yale College.

est, practised the severest scrutiny in regard to the religious character of the members of his church. He went so far as to pronounce upon them, almost with the confidence of Omniscience,—calling those, of whom he formed a favourable judgment, *brethren*, and the rest, *neighbours*,—at the same time, by a strange inconsistency, having as little intercourse with the latter class as possible. He subsequently went so far as to forbid the "neighbours" to come to the Lord's table,—a measure which of course was followed by excitement, distress, and exasperation.

There was no one who sympathised more fully in the state of mind into which Mr. Davenport was now brought, than the Rev. Jonathan Barber,* who was at that time officiating in the neighbouring parish of Oyster Ponds, (now Orient.) Mr. Barber visited Southold in March, 1740, on which occasion a meeting was held there for twenty-four hours, accompanied by demonstrations of—to say the least—a very doubtful character, and foreshadowing the yet more extravagant movements that were to follow. Davenport and Barber went together to East Hampton, and the effect of their labours there was a prodigious excitement—of which Dr. Davis, late President of Hamilton College, and a native of that town, says—"Many untoward and ever to be lamented circumstances occurred; yet lasting good was done amid a great shaking and commotion." Shortly after this, Davenport went to Philadelphia, where he was present at a meeting of Synod, and about the same time became acquainted with Whitefield, who speaks of him as "one of the ministers whom God has lately sent out,—a sweet, pious soul." Here he seems to have been not a little strengthened and encouraged in the course on which he had entered, by the bold and earnest preaching of Gilbert Tennent and Samuel Blair. The summer following he spent with his own people at Southold, during which time he supposed about twenty of them were converted; and in the autumn he preached for a while, amidst a powerful excitement, at Basking Ridge, N. J., and made another brief visit, in company with Whitefield, to Philadelphia. After spending the next winter, as is supposed, in his own parish, he went in July, 1741, into Connecticut, preaching in various places, as he had opportunity, and everywhere exciting great attention, and often the most violent opposition; while some excellent and eminent men seemed, on the whole, to countenance him,—being willing to tolerate the evil for what they considered the greater good. At Stonington, one hundred are said to have been awakened under his first sermon. From Stonington he seems to have gone to the neighbouring town of Westerly, R. I., and was accompanied by the people, in solemn procession, singing as they went. At Branford, he was invited to preach by the Rev. Philemon Robbins, and on their way to meet-

* JONATHAN BARBER, a son of Thomas Barber, was born at West Springfield, Mass., January 21, 1712, and was graduated at Yale College in 1730. He was licensed to preach by the Association of his native county in 1732, and commenced his ministerial labours in the neighbouring parish of Agawam. After leaving there, he seems to have exercised his ministry for some years on Long Island, though he was not regularly settled. In 1740, he accompanied his intimate friend, Mr. Whitefield, to the South, where he remained for seven years, Superintendent of the Orphan House in Georgia. About 1748, he returned to Long Island, and became pastor of the church to which he had previously ministered. Here he continued nearly ten years. In the autumn of 1758, he was installed pastor of the Congregational Church in Groton, Conn. Having discharged the duties of a pastor with fidelity and acceptance for eight years, he fell into a deep and settled melancholy, which prematurely closed his labours. After suffering under this distressing calamity for nearly eighteen years, he died suddenly, on the 8th of October, 1783, in the seventy-second year of his age. He had an extensive correspondence, both in this country and in Europe, and was held in high estimation as an exemplary Christian, and a faithful minister.

ing on Sabbath, he proposed that they should sing; and he did sing, despite of Mr. Robbins' objections and expostulations. At New Haven, he came in conflict with the pastor, the Rev. Mr. Noyes, who refused to submit to his examination; but he preached notwithstanding, and produced a powerful effect upon the mind of David Brainerd and many others; though an effect which was at best of a mixed character. At Saybrook, the Rev. William Hart, who had been his classmate in College, declined admitting him into his pulpit, chiefly on account of his severe and almost indiscriminate censures of the standing ministry.

In May, 1742, the Legislature of Connecticut passed a most extraordinary law, designed to regulate the conduct of ministers. If any minister preached without express invitation, in a parish not under his care, he was denied his salary for a year; and the ministers who licensed a candidate, or counselled a congregation, not under their particular Association, were also deprived of their support. No minister could draw his salary, till he had a certificate of the clerk of the parish, that he had not been complained of for either of these offences. Any minister of the Colony, preaching in any place beside his own parish, without the consent of the pastor and the majority of the people, was bound over in the penal sum of one hundred pounds not to offend again: those not inhabitants of the Colony, were to be carried out of it as vagrants. The law allowing "sober dissenters from the standing order" to form congregations, was repealed.

It can easily be imagined that such a man as Davenport was, at this period, could not be very safe within the range of the operation of this law. Accordingly, we find that in June, 1742, when Davenport and his friend, the Rev. Benjamin Pomeroy of Hebron, had met at Ripton, by request of the Rev. Mr. Mills, minister of the place, to consult in regard to carrying forward the revival, complaint was made to the General Assembly, of the disorders to be apprehended in consequence of their inflammatory proceedings, and they were immediately taken up and carried to Hartford, to answer for having committed various irregular acts in violation of the law. During their examination the greatest excitement prevailed, insomuch that the Sheriff found it difficult to conduct his prisoners from the meeting house, where the Assembly seems to have held its session, to the house where they were to be lodged; and it was found necessary to order out a militia force, of forty armed men, to protect the Assembly from the hostile demonstrations that were going forward. On the third day from the commencement of the examination, the Assembly decided "that the behaviour, conduct, and doctrines, advanced by the said James Davenport, do, and have a natural tendency to disturb and destroy the peace and order of this government. Yet it further appears to this Assembly that the said Davenport is under the influence of enthusiastical impressions and impulses, and thereby disturbed in the rational faculties of his mind, and therefore to be pitied and compassionated, and not to be treated as otherwise he might be." They, therefore, ordered him to be sent home to Southold. On hearing their decision, he said, "Though I must go, I hope Christ will not, but will tarry and carry on his work in this government, in spite of all the powers and malice of earth and hell." About four o'clock, P. M., the Sheriff, with two files of men armed with muskets, conducted him to the bank of the Connecticut, and put him on board a vessel, the owner of which agreed to carry him to his home. Pomeroy, who seemed "almost orderly and regular," in comparison, was discharged.

Shortly after this, Davenport went to Boston, but was very generally discountenanced by the ministers in that region. He attended public worship at Charlestown, on Sabbath morning after his arrival, and partook of the Lord's Supper, but in the afternoon remained at his lodgings, from an apprehension that the minister was unconverted. He appeared before the Boston Association, and gave them an account of his experience, which, on the whole, led them to believe that he was "truly pious," while yet they felt constrained to issue a public testimony disapproving his course. But he availed himself of the first opportunity publicly to denounce them, representing some of them as unconverted, and the rest as Jehosaphats in Ahab's army, and exhorted the people to separate from them without delay. In consequence of his erratic proceedings, he was seized by the Sheriff, and, on refusing to give bail, was committed for trial. The Sheriff offered him his liberty till the day of trial came, on condition that he would promise good behaviour; but he refused, and was accordingly kept in close quarters. When the trial came on, the ministers made intercession in his behalf with the Court, and the verdict was, that while he actually uttered nearly all the defamatory expressions that were charged upon him, he was at the time *non compos mentis*, and therefore *not guilty*.

During all this time, it is not to be supposed that his people had nothing to say in view of his long absences from them, or that they were satisfied with what he was doing abroad. So far from it, that, on the 7th of October following, a Council was convened at Southold, by request of his congregation, to take into consideration the peculiar state of things in respect to them and their pastor, and advise as to the proper course to be pursued. Though I have not met with any particular account of the doings of that Council in print, I have in my possession the following document in manuscript—the Result of the Council—in the handwriting of Jonathan Dickinson. From the fact that the manuscript is largely interlined and altered, it is presumed that this is the original draft, and that Dickinson of course was a member, and probably the Scribe, of the Council.

"At a Council of ministers convened at Southold, October, 1742, upon the desire and invitation of the congregation there, there being a variety of complaints exhibited by the committee of the First Parish in Southold against the Rev Mr. James Davenport, the pastor of the church there,—the Council, after distinctly hearing both the allegations of the said committee, and Mr. Davenport's answers to their several complaints, and after repeated and solemn addresses to God for his directing and assisting influences, came to the following conclusions:

"In the first place, we think it our duty to declare our firm and undoubted persuasion that the Glorious God has, as well in these as in several other parts of the country, made an uncommon display of the power of his infinite free grace in the conviction of sinners, and in the saving conversion of many to himself; and that he has improved our said Rev. brother, Mr. Davenport, as a successful instrument in carrying on this blessed and glorious work; and it is grievous to us to observe that some irregularities in Mr. Davenport's conduct have, as we apprehend, in a great measure hindered his usefulness, and been the unhappy occasion of prejudicing many against the work of God that has been carried on in the land.

"Upon the several articles of complaint that are laid before us, we propose our following opinions and advice. We can't but suppose that his barring sundry members of his church, of good reputation for religion, from Communion at the Lord's table, and his suspending one of his deacons, without any other reason against them than his own private apprehension of their internal state, was a proceeding too arbitrary and uncharitable; and that his refusing baptism to the children of some who have been communicants at the Lord's table, and to others of a blameless and regular conversation, only from a suspicion that they were unconverted, is a just cause of objection against him.

"We also think that his congregation have just cause to complain of his leaving them at several times, for so long a space as he has done, without their consent—whereby he has not only left them destitute of Gospel ordinances, but has been too unmindful of the obligations he lies under by his pastoral relation to them.

"If, by his declaring, both in praying and preaching, that he knows not beforehand what subject he shall preach upon until he comes into the pulpit, be intended that he makes no previous preparation for his public preaching, this is what we cannot justify. And we must likewise testify against the confusions and disorders sometimes brought into public worship, when there is praying, and singing, and exhorting, carried on at the same time in the same congregation, as being directly contrary to the Apostle's directions in I. Cor. xiv., and must therefore be displeasing to that God, who is a God of order, and not of confusion, in all the churches of the Saints.

"We likewise think that his method of censuring and condemning those ministers of the Gospel, whose conduct and conversation are unexceptionable, is that censorious judging, so frequently and in such plain and strong terms condemned in the word of God. And his encouraging separate meetings, in consequence of such censoriousness, is such a rending of the mystical body of Christ, and such a promoting of schism and uncharitableness, contention and confusion, as is utterly unwarrantable.

"We cannot approve of his singing along the streets, on the Sabbath, and other days,—there being too much appearance of ostentation herein, and we having no precept or example in the word of God to warrant such a practice.

"We, in like manner, highly disapprove of Mr. Davenport's making immediate impulses upon his mind the rule of his conduct in many cases, and declaring publicly that he is herein acted by the immediate influence of the Spirit of God; this being a pretence to such degrees and kind of inspiration as he brings no credentials to justify; and this having also a tendency to lead him and others off from a due attendance to the word of God, as the only safe and sure rule of our faith and practice.

"We also think that his refusing to let orderly ministers preach in the meeting house, in his absence, when desired by the congregation, is contrary to that charity and brotherly love, which he ought to live in the exercise of; and his improving and encouraging unqualified teachers to publicly preach and exhort, without any orderly introduction to the exercise of the sacred character, is a practice of a most mischievous and dangerous tendency, and directly contrary to the directions of the word of God.

"Upon the whole, as we cannot but be pleased to find such good affection in the whole congregation to Mr. Davenport, and such a desire that he should continue their minister, if he would leave off those irregularities, so we advise them to exercise some forbearance, praying and hoping that he may yet be convinced of these mistakes. But if, after their waiting upon him, he yet perseveres in those irregularities, we think they cannot continue under further special obligations to him as their minister; but we advise them to take the most peaceable methods they can in procuring another minister. In the mean time, we earnestly entreat them to conduct towards their minister, and any others that differ in their sentiments from them, with all possible kindness and respect, and to be very much in prayer to the Great Head of the Church, that he will heal their breaches, bring order out of their confusion, and carry on a work of grace with power among them."

How this Result was received by Mr. Davenport does not appear; though it is quite certain that it did not have the effect which either the council or his people desired. It is supposed that he spent the winter of 1842-43 at Southold; but he was not yet by any means cured of his delusions. In the beginning of March, 1743, he went to New London, by request of a company of his partisans, to organize them as a church. Immediately on his arrival, in obedience to messages which he said had been communicated to him from God, in various ways, he began to purify the company from evils which prevailed among them. To cure them of their idolatrous love of worldly things, he ordered wigs, cloaks and breeches, hoods, gowns, rings, jewels and necklaces, to be brought together into his room, and laid in a heap, that they might, by his solemn decree, be committed to the flames. To this heap he added the pair of plush breeches which he wore into the place, and which he seems to have put off, on being confined to his bed by the increased violence of a complicated disease. He next gave out a catalogue of religious books, which must be brought together and burned, as unsafe in the hands of the people. On the afternoon of the 6th of March,—the requisite preparations having all been made, his followers carried a quantity of books to the wharf and burned them, singing around the pile, "Hallelujah" and "Glory to God," and declaring that, as the smoke of those books ascended up in their presence, so the smoke of the torment of such of their authors as died in the same belief, was now ascending in Hell. Among the authors were Beveridge, Flavel, Doctors Increase Mather, Colman and Sewall, and even Jonathan Parsons of Lyme. The next day, more books were burned, but one of the party persuaded the others to save the clothes.

For some time after this, he was laid aside from his labours by a distressing illness; and this, in connection with two expostulatory letters which he received from Mr. Williams of Lebanon and Mr. Wheelock, seems to have been the means of bringing him to reflection and penitence. In 1744, he published in the Boston Gazette an ample retraction of his errors, which served, in a great measure, to restore to him the confidence of his brethren and of the Church at large. I take it from a manuscript copy which he sent to his brother-in-law, the Rev. Dr. Williams of Longmeadow, probably previous to its being published. It is as follows:—

"Messrs. Kneeland & Green: Please to give the following paper of my Retractation a place in the Gazette, and you will oblige

"Your humble servant,

"JAMES DAVENPORT.'

"Although I don't question at all but there is great reason to bless God for a glorious and wonderful work of his power and grace in the edification of his children, and the conviction and conversion of numbers in New England, in the neighbouring government, and several other parts, within a few years past, and believe that the Lord hath favoured me, though most unworthy, with several others of his servants, in granting special assistance and success, the glory of all which be given to Jehovah, to whom alone it belongs; yet, after frequent meditation and desire that I might be enabled to apprehend things justly, and I hope I may say mature consideration, I am now fully convinced and persuaded that several appendages to this glorious work are no essential parts thereof, but of a different and contrary nature and tendency; which appendages I have been, in the time of the work, very industrious in, and instrumental of promoting, by a misguided zeal; being further much influenced in the affair by the false spirit which, unobserved by me, did (as I have been brought to see since) prompt me to unjust apprehensions and misconduct in several articles, which have been great blemishes to the work of God, very grievous to some of God's children, no less ensnaring and corrupting to others of them, a sad means of many persons questioning the work of God, concluding and appearing against it; and of the hardening of multitudes in their sins, and an awful occasion of the enemies blaspheming the right ways of the Lord, and withal very offensive to that God, before whom I would lie in the dust, prostrate in deep humility and repentance on this account, imploring pardon for the Mediator's sake, and thankfully accepting the tokens thereof.

"The articles which I especially refer to, and would, in the most public manner, retract, and warn others against, are these which follow, viz:—

"The method I used, for a considerable time, with respect to some, yea many, ministers in several parts, in openly exposing such as I feared or thought unconverted, in public prayer or otherwise, herein making my private judgment (in which also I much suspect I was mistaken in several instances)—I say, making my private judgment the ground of public action or conduct, offending, as I apprehend, (although in the time of it ignorantly,) against the ninth commandment, and such other passages of Scripture as are similar, yea, I may say, offending against the laws both of justice and charity, which laws were further broken.

"2d. By my advising and urging to such separations from those ministers, whom I treated as above, as I believe may justly be called rash, unwarrantable, and of sad and awful tendency and consequence. And here I would ask the forgiveness of those ministers, whom I have injured in both these articles.

"3d. I confess I have been much led astray by following impulses or impressions, as a rule of conduct, whether they came with or without a text of Scripture, and my neglecting also duly to observe the analogy of Scripture. I am persuaded this was a great means of corrupting my experiences, and carrying me off from the word of God, and a great handle which the false spirit has made use of with respect to a number, and me especially.

"4th. I believe, further, that I have done much hurt to religion, by encouraging private persons to a ministerial and authoritative kind or method of exhorting, which is particularly observable in many such, being much puffed up, and falling into the snare of the devil, while many others are thus directly prejudiced against the work.

"5th. I have reason to be deeply humbled that I have not been duly careful to endeavour to remove or prevent prejudice, (where I now believe I might then have done it consistently with duty,) which appeared remarkable in the method I practised of singing with others in the streets, in societies frequently.

"I would also penitently confess and bewail my great stiffness in retaining these aforesaid errors a great while, and unwillingness to examine into them with any jealousy of their being errors, notwithstanding the friendly counsels and cautions of real friends, especially in the ministry.

"Here may properly be added a paragraph or two taken out of a letter from me to Mr. Barber at Georgia, a true copy of which I gave consent should be published lately at Philadelphia. I would add to what Brother T. hath written on the awful affair of books and clothes at New London, which afford ground of deep and lasting humiliation, I was, to my shame be it spoken—the ringleader in that horrid action. I was, my dear Brother, under the powerful influence of the false spirit, almost one whole day together, and part of several days; the Lord showed me afterwards that the spirit I was then acted by, was in its operations void of true inward peace, laying the greatest stress on externals, neglecting the heart, full of impatience, pride, and arrogance; although I thought, in the time of it, that 'twas the Spirit of God in an high degree. Awful indeed! My body, especially my leg, much disordered at the same time,* which Satan and my evil heart might make some handle of. And now may the Holy, Wise and Good God be pleased to guard and secure me against such errors for the future, and stop the progress of those, whether ministers or people, who have been corrupted by my word or example, in any of the above mentioned particulars; and if it be his holy will, bless this public recantation to this purpose. And oh! may He grant withal that such as, by reason of the aforesaid errors and misconduct, have entertained unhappy prejudices against Christianity in general, or the late glorious work of God in particular, may, by this account, learn to distinguish the appendage from the substance or essence,—that which is vile and odious from that which is precious, glorious and Divine, and thus be entirely and happily freed from all those prejudices referred to; and this in infinite mercy through Jesus Christ. And to these requests, may all God's children, whether ministers or others, say Amen.

"July 18, 1744. J. DAVENPORT."

It was not only through the press, but in a more private manner, that Davenport strove to repair the injuries he had done to his brethren and the churches. The church at Stonington had been rent by his disorderly proceedings; and, after his recantation, he took occasion to revisit it, with a view to undo, as far as he could, the mischief which he had done by his former visit. "He came," says the Rev. Mr. Fish, the minister of that parish, "with such a mild, meek, pleasant and humble spirit, broken and contrite, as I scarce ever saw excelled or equalled. He owned his fault in private, and in a most Christian manner asked forgiveness of some ministers he had treated amiss, and in a large assembly publicly retracted his errors and mistakes."

It would seem that he resigned his pastoral charge at Southold, shortly after he published his "Retractation;" for between that time (June, 1744) and April, 1745, he had (as appears from his letters to Dr. Williams)

* I had the long fever on me, and the cankry humour raging at once.

preached for some time at Plainfield, Conn.,—probably with reference to a settlement, and was, at the latter date, supplying his former charge at Southold, with the expectation of soon removing with his wife to the "Jersies." On the 22d of September, 1746, he became a member of the New Brunswick Presbytery, having, probably, for some time, been preaching within their bounds. In 1748, he transferred his relation to the New York Presbytery, with a view to settle at Connecticut Farms, near Elizabethtown; but I find no evidence that this purpose was ever fulfilled.

In 1750, he was residing at Hopewell, N. J. He made a preaching tour to Virginia in the course of that year, of which I find the following account in a letter which he addressed to Dr. Williams, on the 16th of October:—

"At the meeting of the Synod of New York, the appointment that I should go and preach sometime in Virginia was renewed, whereupon, on the week following, and on the 21st day of May, I set out. I delayed no longer, because I might, going then, enjoy the Rev. Mr. Davies' company into Virginia. On the 30th of May, we came to his house in Hanover, three hundred and seven miles distant from hence. I went above a hundred and twenty miles farther, even to Roanoke River, and came within thirty miles of North Carolina. It was four months complete before I returned home. After I began to preach in Virginia, I did not omit one Sabbath in the whole journey, and generally preached once every week, and sometimes twice or thrice: by this you may see that my bodily state was considerably rectified through Divine goodness. I rode, in the whole journey, fifteen hundred and ninety miles. The first two months of the journey, I was bravely in health; but the latter part of the time, more poorly, and often feverish, by reason of my being catched several times in the rain, as I was travelling. As to religion, I observed encouraging appearances in most places where I preached, and found reason to hope there were some abiding effects of the ministrations of the word. In and about Hanover County, where dear Mr. Davies preaches, the Lord's people seemed generally engaged in searching—quickened and stirred up, and some particularly comforted. I understood, further, that there were some souls there under conviction, but more in Cumberland and Amelia Counties in my way to Roanoke. The Lord be pleased to carry on his own work more and more, and take all the glory to Himself, to whom only it belongs."

In the autumn of 1752, he was preaching at a place in New Jersey, called Philippi. In a letter dated September 19th, he says,—"My continuance in these parts is at present doubtful, or rather likely to be but short, by reason of this place, (where I now am) Philippi's, not continuing to bear one third part of my support above one year; and this, so far as I can learn, not out of any disrespect to me, (for their respect seems rather to increase,) but an earnest desire to have a minister wholly to themselves. If I go from hence, I expect to go Southward; but where I shall fix is at present very uncertain. Oh that this and all Divine dispensations may be sanctified in order to lasting and spiritual benefit!"

On the 22d of October, 1754, he was installed pastor of the New Side Church of Hopewell and Maidenhead,—the Rev. William Tennent preaching the Sermon, from Acts xxv. 18. Referring to this occasion, he says,—"Through pure mercy, I found it a day of solemnity, sense of great unworthiness and insufficiency, sweet serenity and rest of soul in God through Christ, and dedication of myself to God, particularly in the affair of the day." At this time, it appears that one of his cousins, who had "thoughts of the ministry," was residing with him, and that he was expecting several more pupils in a short time. His health had now become quite confirmed—more vigorous, in his own judgment, than it had been for about twenty years.

He was Moderator of the Synod of New York in 1754, and preached the opening Sermon the next autumn, from II Cor. iv. 1. It was printed at Philadelphia, at "the newest printing office on the South side of the Jersey market," with the title, "The faithful minister encouraged."

In a letter to Dr. Williams, dated November 14, 1754, he writes thus:—"It is indeed matter of deep lamentation that it is at present a season of such awful security and neglect of God, of Christ, and of men's souls, in our land and nation in general, notwithstanding the loud calls and warnings the Lord gives us. Yet, blessed be God that there is some degree of a revival of religion in some places in your parts of late; that there are some also in our parts, both in respect of quickenings among God's people, and awakenings among others. Something of this nature I have had the comfort of observing lately in my place, and of hearing of in several other places. Dear Mr. Whitefield has had some encouragement our way; sundry by his means awakened, and some I heard of as hopefully converted,—especially one that was graduated this fall. We had the pleasure of Mr. Whitefield's company at the New Jersey Commencement, this fall, at Newark, and at the meeting of the New York Synod, the day following, in the same place. The Trustees of New Jersey College expressed something, though but a small part, of their love and esteem of Mr. Whitefield, by inviting and admitting him to the degree of Master of Arts. He preached to us, as he was much desired, on the Commencement day, and the following day; and the Lord was with him of a truth. I'm persuaded many of God's people, and especially of his ministers, found their hearts not a little warmed and enlivened by the preaching as well as conversation of his servant. I don't think there was one of the ministers of our Synod convened, but what rejoiced much in the opportunity of seeing and hearing Mr. Whitefield. (When the ministers of our Synod are all together, they are above sixty.) Oh that the pleasure of the Lord may prosper abundantly in his servant's hand, and that the name of our God may be praised for its prospering in such a measure already; as also for the success of the Messrs. Tennents and Davies, who have obtained, as we hear, £1500 sterling in England, beside books and mathematical instruments, and an order for a collection in the congregations throughout Scotland for the benefit of New Jersey College. Something valuable was obtained in Dublin, besides a collection throughout the bounds of the Synod of Ulster in Ireland. The Lord grant that this and other Colleges may be fountains of piety as well as learning; that there may yearly issue from them such streams as may make glad the city of our God."

I make an extract from one more of Mr. Davenport's letters, illustrative of his patriotism. It was addressed to his brother-in-law, Dr. Williams, who was, at that time, serving in the army as Chaplain, at Crown Point. It is dated July 11, 1755.

"I cannot help rejoicing that you are called out to bear fruit in old age, in the service of your God, your King, and your country. The Lord be, according to your desire, with your dear family and flock, which you have committed to his care. And oh may He give you, Dear and Reverend Sir, much of his presence and blessing! May He strengthen you in body and soul to go through all the services, fatigues and trials, you may be called to in this important enterprise; and make all easy and sweet to you comparatively, by firing your soul, from time to time, with love to God and Christ, to King and country.

"May the Lord God of Israel go before you, and the army you are with, and be your rereward. May He save you from all sin, cover your heads in the day of battle, cause your enemies to fall before you, give desired and happy success, and get all the glory to Himself! And oh may He lead us to repentance, gratitude, and fruitfulness by his goodness; cause our Popish and perfidious enemies, that are or shall be taken captive by us, to turn to Himself, and cause Anti-Christ's reign soon to come to its final period!

"Ungrateful indeed shall we be who tarry at home, if we don't pray hard for them who are gone to fight for us;—gone to fight, we trust courageously, for us and our families; for our lives, our properties, our liberties and privileges, our King and our Religion—in a word, our *every thing* that ought to be held dear and valuable by us—gone to play the man in fighting for us, and for the cities of our God.

"My soul is even now drawn out in longings in this momentous affair.

"Oh may the Lord God of gods, the Lord God of his Protestant and English Israel,—the God who has very lately and remarkably succeeded our forces to the Eastward, on the land and water;—the God who, just ten years before, delivered up Cape Breton into our hands;—the God who suppressed a rising formidable rebellion;—the God who defended and destroyed the French fleet, when big with hopes of our destruction;—the God who delivered and preserved our forefathers, when surrounded with a multitude of enemies;—the God who hears prayers, and will not suffer the Gates of Hell to prevail against his Church;—oh may this God be with you and succeed you, and all the British forces, by sea and land, abundantly, notwithstanding our many and aggravated offences, for his name and mercies' sake; defeat the designs of the French, and all that join with them against the Lord and against his Anointed; destroy the man of sin; cause Mahometan imposture to cease; bring in the Jews with the fulness of the Gentiles; and bring on the latter day glory, through Jesus Christ, to the eternal praise of the Infinitely glorious and blessed Three—One; Amen and Amen.

"So prays, Rev. and dear Brother,

"Yours in the dear Lord Jesus,

"JAMES DAVENPORT."

His ministry at Hopewell, especially after he became a settled pastor, seems not to have been a very happy one. There was evidently, from some cause or other, disquietude among his people; for we find that a portion of them asked leave of the Presbytery to join adjacent congregations, and, a few months before his death, a petition was presented for his removal. He died on the 10th of November, 1757, aged forty-seven years.

The following is the inscription upon his tomb stone:—

"In memory of the Rev. James Davenport, who departed this life, November 10, 1757, aged forty-seven years.

"Oh Davenport, a seraph once in clay,
"A brighter seraph now in Heavenly day.
"How glowed thy heart with sacred love and zeal,

"How like to that thy kindred angels feel.
"Cloth'd in humility thy virtues shone,
"In every eye illustrious but thine own.
"How like thy Master on whose friendly breast,
"Thou oft hast leaned and shalt forever rest."

His wife, Mrs. Parnell Davenport, died on the 21st of August, 1789, aged sixty years. They both lie buried in a small burying ground, about a mile West from Pennington, N. J.

They had two children. The eldest,—a daughter, by the name of *Elizabeth*, was married to a Mr. Kelley, who resided at Princeton, N. J. The son, *John*, was born at Philippi, N. J., August 11, 1752; was graduated at the College of New Jersey in 1769; studied Theology, partly under Dr. Bellamy, and partly under Dr. Buell of East Hampton, L. I.; was ordained June 4, 1775, and served the congregation of Southold as a stated supply for two years; preached for some time at Bedford, N. Y.; was installed at Deerfield, August 12, 1795, and was dismissed on account of ill health in 1805. In 1809, he returned to the State of New York, and died at Lysander, July 13, 1821. He was, in early life, an intimate friend of Aaron Burr. While Davenport was studying Theology under Dr. Buell, and Burr was residing with Dr. Bellamy, the former wrote to the latter a letter which is in my possession,—of which the following is an extract:—"I hope you are by this time fully resolved to engage in the sacred work of the ministry, and that you see your way clear to do it. You are placed under a very judicious as well as pious divine, whose instruction and conversation have, I hope, proved to your spiritual benefit. I rejoice to find you are pleased with your situation, and wish it may continue."

WILLIAM ROBINSON.*

1740—1746.

William Robinson was the son of a Quaker,—a man of wealth, and an eminent physician, and was born near Carlisle, England, a little after the beginning of the eighteenth century. He expected to inherit considerable property, not only from his father, but from an aunt in London; but, on going to London to visit that aunt, he greatly overstaid the time which had been allowed him, and plunged into the dissipations of the city, thereby contracting debts which his aunt refused to pay, and which he knew would excite the indignation of his father. Being unable to remain in London, and fearing to return home, he resolved to seek his fortune in America. To this proposal his aunt gave a reluctant consent, and furnished him with a small sum of money to assist in carrying out his purpose. On his arrival in this country, he found it necessary to engage in some active business for his support; and he betook himself to teaching a school in Hopewell, N. J., within the bounds of the Presbytery of New Brunswick. It seems probable that he taught a classical school in the State of Delaware also; for Samuel Davies, whose parents resided in Delaware, was, at one time, one of his pupils. We hear nothing of his erratic tendencies after he left England;

* Hist. Log Coll.—Foote's Sketches of Va., I.—Webster's MSS.

and his habits, from the time that he came hither, seem to havé been those of a correct and sober man.

He had been engaged in his school for some time, before his mind was practically directed to the subject of religion; and the manner in which this was finally brought about, was somewhat remarkable. As he was riding at a late hour one evening, when the moon and stars were shining with uncommon brightness, he was saying to himself,—"How transcendently glorious must be the author of all this beauty and grandeur!" And the thought struck him with irresistible force,—"But what do I know of this God? Have I ever sought his favour, or made Him my friend?" This impression never left him, until he found peace and joy in believing. He soon resolved to devote himself to the work of the ministry; and with reference to this, prosecuted his academical and theological studies at the Log College, while he went on with his school. He was received under the care of the New Brunswick Presbytery on the 1st of April, 1740; and, on the 27th of May following, was licensed to preach the Gospel. On the 4th of August, 1741, he was ordained at New Brunswick *sine titulo.*

In August, 1742, he received a call to settle at Neshaminy, as successor to the Rev. William Tennent, but declined it. The next winter, he was sent as an evangelist, by the Presbytery of Newcastle, in consequence of an earnest request from the people, to visit the Presbyterian settlements in the Valley of the Shenandoah, and on the South side of James River, in Virginia; and the numerous settlements of North Carolina, on the Haw. Soon after entering Virginia, he was seized, near Winchester, by the Sheriff of Orange County, and required to go to Williamsburg to answer to the Governor for preaching without a license. Before he had proceeded far, however, the Sheriff, finding that he was evidently a sensible and well disposed man, released him, and suffered him to pursue his mission unmolested. He passed the winter in Carolina, and, in consequence of imprudent exposures, contracted a disease from which he never recovered. On his return, he preached with great effect to the Presbyterian settlements in Charlotte, Prince Edward, Campbell, and Albermarle, Counties. Here he was waited upon by a deputation, that persuaded him, instead of pursuing his contemplated route to the head of the Shenandoah, to return to Hanover. The people in whose behalf his services were solicited, were far from being agreed in their religious views; some of them having reached the point of denying not only the efficacy but the expediency of good works, and of doubting whether it was right to pray, as prayer could not alter the Divine purposes. The delegates who waited upon him, having heard him preach, (as they were instructed to do, before extending to him an invitation to return with them,) were somewhat divided in opinion concerning his doctrines; but they finally gave him a cordial invitation in the name of the congregations. He at first declined; but their importunity at length prevailed, and he made his arrangements to visit Hanover.

On his arrival at Hanover, several prominent individuals had an interview with him, and examined his testimonials, and satisfied themselves in regard to his views of Christian doctrine and practice, and the measures which he proposed to adopt. He submitted to their examination with the utmost meekness and readiness, and led them to form high hopes in regard to the success of his labours. He preached to them, for the first time, on Sabbath, July 6, 1743; and it was the first sermon from a Presbyterian minister ever heard in Hanover County. He continued preaching for four successive days; during which the congregation regularly increased, and the impression became constantly deeper. An individual, who was present, giving an account of this series of exercises, seven years after, says—"There is reason to believe there was as much good done by these four sermons, as by all the sermons preached in these parts before or since." And he adds—"Before Mr. Robinson left us, he successfully endeavoured to correct some of our mistakes, and to bring us to carry on the worship of God more regularly at our meetings. After this, we met to read good sermons, and began and concluded with prayer and singing of Psalms, which, till then, we had omitted."

Mr. Robinson, having passed four days, labouring publicly and privately among these people, was constrained to take his departure, in order to meet other engagements; and besides, it began to be rumoured that measures were about to be taken to arrest him as an itinerant. The people, partly to compensate him for his arduous labours, and partly to testify their gratitude towards him, made him a handsome present in money; but he refused to receive it; and when they urged it upon him, he still persevered in his refusal, believing that the peculiar circumstances of the case would not justify him in any other course. The committee to whom the matter was entrusted, being still resolved to carry their point, put it into the hands of a gentleman with whom he was to lodge the night before leaving the county, with instructions that he should deposit it privately in his saddle-bags, not doubting that when he found it there after his departure, he would appropriate it to his own use. This was accordingly done; but, in the morning, when Mr. Robinson came to lift his saddle-bags, he found them much heavier than usual, and, on opening them, immediately discovered the cause. He smiled at the benevolent artifice, and said,—"I see you are resolved I shall have your money; I will take it; but, as I have told you before, I do not need it; I have enough, nor will I appropriate it to my own use; but there is a young man of my acquaintance, of promising talents and piety, who is now studying with a view to the ministry; but his circumstances are embarrassing; he has not funds to support and carry him on without much difficulty; this money will relieve him from his pecuniary difficulties: I will take charge of it, and appropriate it to his use; and, as soon as he is licensed, we will send him to visit you; it may be that you may now, by your liberality, be educating a minister for yourselves." The young man here referred to was Samuel Davies, afterwards the illustrious President Davies. Mr. Robinson applied the money as he had promised; and, in due time, Mr. Davies went to Hanover,—chiefly it is said, in consideration of his peculiar obligations to the people, and remained there ten years, making so broad and deep a mark in the character of the community, that time has done little to efface it.

Mr. Robinson's labours, during this tour, were arduous and unremitted, and withal eminently successful. His health, after this, visibly declined; but still he kept at his work, being employed part of the time in the State of New York, and part of the time in Maryland;—and a rich blessing seems everywhere to have attended his labours. Mr. (afterwards President) Davies renders the following testimony concerning him:—

"In Maryland also there has been a considerable revival, (shall I call it?) or first plantation of religion. * * * * In Kent County and in Queen Anne's, a number of careless sinners have been awakened and hopefully brought to Christ. The work was begun, and mostly carried on, by the instrumentality of that favoured man, Mr. Robinson, whose success, whenever I reflect upon it, astonishes me. Oh, he did much in a little time; and who would not choose such an expeditious pilgrimage through this world? There are in these places a considerable congregation, aad they have made repeated efforts to obtain a settled minister. But the most glorious display of Divine grace in Maryland has been in and about Somerset County. It began, I think, in 1745, by the ministry of Mr. Robinson, and was afterwards carried on by several ministers who preached transiently there."

On the 19th of March, 1746, Mr. Robinson was dismissed from the Presbytery of New Brunswick to the Presbytery of New Castle, with a view to his becoming the pastor of the congregation in St. George's, De.;—a congregation which had been gathered under his labours, in connection with those of Mr. Whitefield. But in April following, before he had yet been installed over his charge, his earthly course was finished. His Funeral Sermon was preached on the 3d of the succeeding August, by the Rev. Samuel Blair. He bequeathed his library to his friend and beneficiary, the Rev. Samuel Davies. There remains little documentary testimony concerning him; but there is a uniform tradition that he was an eminently devout and benevolent man, and one of the most vigorous and effective preachers of his day.

The following anecdote is related on the authority of the late Rev. Dr. Hill of Virginia:—

"On the night before Mr. Robinson was to preach in Hanover for the first time, he rode late to reach a tavern within some eight or ten miles from the place of preaching. The tavern keeper was a shrewd, boisterous, profane man. When uttering some horrid oaths, Mr. Robinson ventured to reprove him for his profanity; and although it was done in a mild way, the innkeeper gave him a sarcastic look, and said, 'Pray, Sir, who are you to take such authority upon yourself?' 'I am a minister of the Gospel' says Mr. Robinson. 'Then you belie your looks very much,' was the reply. [It is said that Mr. Robinson had the small pox very severely, which had given him a very rough visage, and deprived him of the sight of one of his eyes. It was with reference to his forbidding appearance that the innkeeper seemed to question his ministerial character.] 'But,' says Mr. Robinson, 'if you wish certainly to know whether I am a minister or not, if you will accompany me, you may be convinced by hearing me preach.' 'I will,' says the innkeeper, 'if you will preach from a text I will give you.' 'Let me hear it,' says Mr. Robinson, 'and if there is nothing unsuitable in it, I will.' The waggish innkeeper gave him the passage from the Psalms—'I am fearfully and wonderfully made.' Mr. Robinson agreed that it should be one of his texts. The man was at Mr. Robinson's meeting, and that text was the theme of one of his sermons. Before it was finished, the wicked man was made to feel that he was the monster, and that he was fearfully and wonderfully made. It is said that he became a very pious and useful member of the church."

Dr. Alexander says,—

"Probably Mr. Robinson, during the short period of his life, was the instrument in the conversion of as many souls, as any minister who ever lived in this country. The only circumstance relating to his person which has come down, is, that he was blind of one eye; so that by some he was called 'the one-eyed Robinson.'"

SAMUEL FINLEY, D. D.*

1740—1766.

SAMUEL FINLEY was born in the year 1715, in the County of Armagh, Ireland, and was one of seven sons, all of whom were esteemed pious. His parents were of Scottish descent, and were distinguished for an elevated Christian character. Finding that their son was fond of learning, and withal was gifted with an uncommon facility for acquiring it, they gave him the best advantages which their circumstances would allow; and, after having obtained the rudiments of an English education, they sent him to a school at some distance from home, in which he distinguished himself by his successful application.

When he was in his nineteenth year, he left his native country with a view to find a home on this side the Atlantic. He arrived in Philadelphia on the 28th of September, 1734. He seems to have been the subject of serious impressions from early childhood; and he used to say that, when he was only six years old, he heard a sermon which wrought powerfully upon his mind, and awakened in him an earnest desire to become a preacher of the Gospel; and this desire gradually became a purpose, and was never lost sight of in any of his subsequent arrangements. On his arrival in this country, he resumed his studies with reference to the ministry; and though there seems to be no certain evidence of the fact, yet it is supposed that he studied at Mr. Tennent's Log College;—partly because there was at that time no other institution in the Presbyterian Church in which young men were trained for the ministry, and partly because he put himself under the care of the New Brunswick Presbytery, most of the members of which had here received their education. After having gone through the prescribed trials, he was licensed to preach on the 5th of August, 1740. As this was a period in which the public mind was greatly awakened to religious things, he travelled extensively for some time after his licensure, and co-operated vigorously with the friends of the revival. He laboured, for a considerable time, and with great success, in West Jersey; in Deerfield, Greenwich, and Cape May. He preached likewise, with much acceptance, for six months, as a stated supply, to the congregation in Philadelphia, over which Gilbert Tennent was afterwards settled. He was ordained, probably as an evangelist, by the Presbytery of New Brunswick, on the 13th of October, 1742.

In August, 1743, several calls were presented to him,—one of which was from Milford, Conn.; and the Presbytery sent him to Milford "with allowance that he also preach for other places thereabouts, when Providence may open a door for him." Having preached at Milford, he went, by request of Mr. James Pierpont, to preach to the Second Society in New Haven; but, as that Society was not recognised by the civil authority, or the New Haven Association, it was an indictable offence to preach to it. Accordingly, on the 5th of September, as he was on his way to meeting, he was seized by a constable and confined. A few days after, he was presented by

* Assemb. Miss. Mag. I.—Panop. I.—Christ. Mag. I.—Mass. Miss. Mag. IV.—App. to Green's Discourses.—Hist. Log. Coll.—Smith's Old Red-Stone, or Historical Sketches of Western Presbyterianism.—Webster's MSS.

the grand jury, and judgment was given that he should be carried out of the Colony as a vagrant. The sentence was executed; and, though he petitioned the Assembly, in October following, to review the case, his prayer was denied.

In June, 1744, Mr. Finley accepted a call from the congregation in Nottingham, Md., on the borders of Pennsylvania, where he continued in the faithful discharge of the duties of his office nearly seventeen years. Here he instituted an Academy, with a view chiefly of preparing young men for the ministry, which acquired great reputation, and was resorted to by many from distant parts of the country. Among those whom it numbered as its pupils, at one time, were Governor Martin of North Carolina; Dr. Benjamin Rush of Philadelphia, and his brother, Jacob Rush,—an eminent judge; Ebenezer Hazard of Philadelphia; Rev. James Waddel, D. D. of Virginia; Rev. Dr. McWhorter of Newark, N. J.; Colonel John Bayard, Speaker of the House of Representatives; Governor Henry of Maryland, and the Rev. William M. Tennent of Abington, Pa. He was an accomplished teacher, and among his pupils were some of the very best scholars of the day. He boarded most of them in his own house. At table, he often indulged a vein of pleasantry with them, and used to say that nothing was more promotive of digestion than a hearty laugh.

Before Mr. Davies was chosen to the Presidency of the College of New Jersey, Mr. Finley was seriously thought of for the place; and when Mr. Davies at first declined, he recommended him as a person every way qualified for that important station. Upon the death of President Davies, in 1761, Mr. Finley was chosen his successor. So strong was the attachment between him and his congregation at Nottingham, that it was not without a severe struggle that he made up his mind to accept the appointment; and it was only the prospect of increased usefulness, that finally determined him. Having signified his acceptance of the Presidency, he removed to Princeton in July, 1761. This event was regarded as highly auspicious to the interests of the College; and his administration, which continued for five years, fully met the highest expectations that had been indulged in regard to it. His reputation, which before was very considerable, now became much increased and extended: he corresponded largely with eminent men, not only in this country, but in Europe. Among his foreign correspondents was the Rev. Dr. Samuel Chandler, a celebrated Dissenting minister in England, who estimated so highly his theological and general attainments, that in 1763, he procured for him the degree of Doctor of Divinity from the University of Glasgow;—the first instance, it is believed, in which this honour was ever conferred on any Presbyterian clergyman on this side the Atlantic.

Dr. Finley's unremitted application to the duties of his office began, after a while, to perceptibly impair his health, and an obstruction of the liver was induced, which proved beyond the reach of medical skill. When he found himself seriously ill, he went to Philadelphia to avail himself of the prescriptions of the best physicians there; but he seems to have had little apprehension that his disease was to have a fatal issue;—for he remarked to his friends,—"If my work is done, I am ready—I do not desire to live a day longer than I can work for God. But I cannot think this is the case yet. God has much for me to do before I depart hence."

About a month before he died, his physician expressed to him the opinion that his recovery was hopeless; upon which, he seemed entirely resigned to the Divine will; and, from that time till his death, he was employed in the immediate preparation for his departure. On being told by one of his physicians that, according to present appearances, he could live but a few days longer, he lifted up his eyes and exclaimed, "Then welcome, Lord Jesus!"

On the Sabbath preceding his death, he was informed by his brother-in-law, Dr. Clarkson, one of his physicians, that there was a decisive change in him, from which he apprehended that his end was near. "Then," said he, "may the Lord bring me near Himself. I have been waiting with a Canaan hunger for the promised land. I have often wondered that God suffered me to live. I have more wondered that ever He called me to be a minister of his word. He has often afforded me much strength, which, though I have often abused, He returned in mercy. O, faithful are the promises of God! O that I could see Him as I have seen Him heretofore in his sanctuary! Although I have earnestly desired death, as the hireling pants for the evening shade, yet will I wait all the days of my appointed time. I have often struggled with principalities and powers, and have been brought almost to despair—Lord, let it suffice!" Here he sat up, and closing his eyes, prayed fervently that God would show him his glory before he should depart hence,—that He would enable him to endure patiently to the end, and particularly that he might be kept from dishonouring the ministry. He then resumed his discourse, and spoke as follows:—"I can truly say I have loved the service of God. I know not in what language to speak of my own unworthiness. I have been undutiful; I have honestly endeavoured to act for God, but with much weakness and corruption." He then lay down, but continued to speak in broken sentences. "A Christian's death," said he, "is the best part of his experience. The Lord has made provision for the whole way; provision for the soul and for the body. O that I could recollect Sabbath blessings! The Lord hath given me many souls as crowns of my rejoicing. Blessed be God, eternal rest is at hand; Eternity is but long enough to enjoy my God. This has animated me in my secret studies; I was ashamed to take rest here. O that I could be filled with the fulness of God,—that fulness that fills Heaven." Being asked whether he would choose to live or die, he replied, "to die, though I cannot but say I feel the same strait that Paul did, that he knew not which to choose;—'for me to live is Christ, and to die is gain.' But should God, by a miracle, prolong my life, I would still continue to serve Him. His service has ever been sweet to me. I have loved it much. I have tried my Master's yoke, and will never shrink my neck from it. 'His yoke is easy and his burden light.'" One said to him—"You are more cheerful and vigorous, Sir." "Yes, I rise or fall, as eternal life seems nearer or farther off." It being remarked that he always used the expression 'Dear Lord,' in his prayers, he answered, "O, He is very dear, very precious indeed."—"How pretty is it for a minister to die on the Sabbath. I expect to spend the remainder of this Sabbath in Heaven." One of the company said,—"You will soon be joined to the blessed society of Heaven; you will forever hold intercourse with Abraham, Isaac, and Jacob, and with the spirits of the just made perfect—with old friends and many old-fashioned people." "Yes, Sir," he replied with a smile, "but they are a most polite people *now*." He expressed great gratitude to friends around him, and said, "May the

Lord repay you; may He bless you abundantly, not only with temporal but with spiritual blessings!" Turning to his wife, he said, "I expect, my dear, to see you shortly in glory." * * * * Seeing a member of the Second Presbyterian Church present, he said,—"I have often preached and prayed among you, my dear Sir, and the doctrines I preached to you are now my support, and blessed be God, they are without a flaw. May the Lord bless and prosper your church. He designs good for it yet, I trust." To a person from Princeton he said,—"Give my love to the people of Princeton, and tell them that I am going to die, and that I am not afraid to die." He would sometimes cry out, "The Lord Jesus will take care of his cause in the world!" Upon awaking the next morning, he exclaimed, "O what a disappointment I have met with—I expected this morning to have been in Heaven!" On account of extreme weakness, he was unable to speak much during the day, but what he did say was the language of triumph. The next morning, with a pleasant smile on his countenance, he cried out,—"O, I shall triumph over every foe. The Lord hath given me the victory, I exult—I triumph. O that I could see untainted purity. Now I know that it is impossible that faith should not triumph over earth and hell. I think I have nothing to do but to die. Yet perhaps I have—Lord, show me my task." He then said,—"Lord Jesus, into thy hands I commend my spirit—I do it with confidence—I do it with full assurance. I know that thou wilt keep that which I have committed to thee. I have been dreaming too fast of the time of my departure, for I find it does not come; but the Lord is faithful, and will not tarry beyond the appointed time."

In the afternoon of this day, the Rev. Elihu Spencer called to see him, and said,—"I have come, dear Sir, to see you confirm by facts the Gospel you have been preaching: pray, Sir, how do you feel?" To which he replied,—"full of triumph. I triumph through Christ. Nothing clips my wings, but the thoughts of my dissolution being prolonged. O that it were to-night! my very soul thirsts for eternal rest." Mr. Spencer asked him what he saw in eternity to excite such vehement desires. "I see," said he, "the eternal love and goodness of God; I see the fulness of the Mediator. I see the love of Jesus. O to be dissolved, and to be with Him. I long to be clothed with the complete righteousness of Christ." He then desired Mr. Spencer to pray with him before they parted, and said,—"I have gained the victory over the devil. Pray to God to preserve me from evil—to keep me from dishonouring his great name in this critical hour, and to support me with his presence in my passage through the valley of the shadow of death."

He spent the rest of the evening in taking leave of his friends, and in addressing affectionate counsels and exhortations to those of his children who were present. He would frequently cry out,—"Why move the tardy hours so slow?" The next day brought him the release for which he had panted so long. He was no longer able to speak; but a friend having desired him to indicate by a sign whether he still continued to triumph, he lifted his hand, and articulated,—"Yes." At nine o'clock in the morning, he fell into a profound sleep, in which he continued, without changing his position, till about one, when his spirit gently passed away to its eternal home. During his whole illness, he manifested the most entire submission to the Divine will, and a full assurance of entering into rest. His death occurred on the 17th of July, 1766, in the fifty-first year of his age.

It was the intention of Dr. Finley's friends to carry his remains to Princeton for burial; but the extreme heat of the weather forbade their doing it, and he was buried by the side of his friend, Gilbert Tennent, in the Second Presbyterian Church in Philadelphia. His Funeral Sermon was preached by the Rev. Richard Treat,* of Abington. When the church, at a subsequent period, was taken down, the remains of both these venerable men were transferred to the burying ground belonging to the Second Presbyterian Congregation, in which they still repose. Many of the students of the College went to Philadelphia to attend his funeral, and eight members of the Senior class, agreeably to a request which he made upon his death bed, carried him to the grave. The Trustees of the College testified their respect for his memory, by causing a cenotaph to be erected in the cemetery at Princeton, in a line with the tombs of the other Presidents whose remains repose there.

Dr. Finley was twice married;—first, to Sarah Hall, a lady of rare excellence, who died in the year 1760, previous to his leaving Nottingham; and afterwards, in 1761, to Anne, daughter of Matthew Clarkson, an eminent merchant of New York, who was a lineal descendant of the Rev. David Clarkson B. D., one of the two thousand ministers ejected for non-conformity in England, in 1662. He had eight children,—all by the first marriage. His second wife survived him forty-one years, and died in January, 1808. For several of her last years, she was totally blind; but she bore the affliction with the utmost cheerfulness. His son, *Ebenezer*, was graduated at Princeton College in 1772, and was afterwards a highly respectable physician in Charleston, S. C. One of his daughters was married to Samuel Breeze, Esq., of Shrewsbury, N. J., who was the mother of the wife of the Rev. Dr. Morse, the American Geographer.

The following is a list of Dr. Finley's publications:—A Sermon on Matthew xii. 28, entitled "Christ triumphing and Satan raging," preached at Nottingham, 1741. A Refutation of Mr. Thomson's Sermon on the doctrine of Convictions, 1743. Satan stripped of his angelic robe: the substance of several Sermons preached at Philadelphia, showing the strength, nature, and symptoms of delusion; with an application to the Moravians, 1743. A Charitable Plea for the speechless in answer to Abel Morgan's "Antipædobaptism, 1747. A Vindication of the preceding, 1748. A Sermon at the ordination of John Rodgers at St. George's, 1749. A Sermon entitled "The Curse of Meroz, or the danger of neutrality in the cause of God and our country," 1757. A Sermon on the death of President Davies, 1761.

The Rev. Dr. Woodhull, late of Monmouth, N, J., who was one of Dr. Finley's pupils, writes thus concerning him:—

"Dr. Finley was a man of small stature, and of a round and ruddy countenance. In the pulpit, he was always solemn and sensible, and sometimes glowing with fervour. His learning was very extensive: every branch of study taught in the College appeared to be familiar to him. Among other things he taught Latin, Greek, and Hebrew, in the Senior year. He was highly respected and greatly beloved by the students, and had very little difficulty in governing the College. He died in my Senior year, of a

* Richard Treat, a descendant or near relative of Governor Robert Treat, was born at Milford, Conn., September 25, 1708; was graduated at Yale College in 1725; was ordained and installed pastor of the church in Abington. Pa., by the Philadelphia Presbytery, December 30, 1731; was honoured with the degree of Doctor of Divinity from his *Alma Mater* in 1776; and died in 1778, aged seventy years.

complaint of the liver; and requested to be carried to the grave by some of the Senior class. This was accordingly done, and I was one of those who were the bearers of his corpse."

Ebenezer Hazard, Esq., of Philadelphia, formerly Postmaster General of the United States,—another of Dr. Finley's pupils, says of him,—

"He was remarkable for sweetness of temper, and politeness of behaviour. He was given to hospitality; charitable without ostentation; exemplary in the discharge of all relative duties; and in all things showing himself a pattern of good works. As a divine, he was a Calvinist in sentiment. His sermons were not hasty productions, but filled with good sense and well digested sentiment, expressed in language pleasing to men of science, yet perfectly intelligible by the illiterate. They were calculated to inform the ignorant, to alarm the careless and secure, and to edify and comfort the faithful."

Dr. Finley had a brother, *James*, who became a useful minister of the Gospel. He was born in the County of Armagh, Ireland, in February, 1725, and was nine years of age when he came with his parents to this country. His education was obtained chiefly under the direction of the Rev. Samuel Blair. After receiving license to preach, from the Newcastle Presbytery, (as is supposed), he was ordained and installed pastor of the church in East Nottingham, (now called the Rock,) by the same Presbytery, in 1752. About eight years after his settlement, his pastoral charge was enlarged, by the union of Elk with East Nottingham. In 1777, and again 1782, he asked his Presbytery to dismiss him, but, in consequence of the united and earnest opposition of his people to the measure, the Presbytery in each case refused his request. After the second refusal, he appealed to the Synod, and they dismissed him by their own act; but his dismission to the Presbytery of Redstone, of which he afterwards became a member, was not effected till the 26th of April, 1785. He removed with his family to Western Pennsylvania in 1783, and the next year accepted a call from Rehoboth and Roundhill,—two Societies in the Forks of Youghiogheny. It does not appear that he was ever formally installed over these churches, and yet he was recognised as virtually sustaining the pastoral relation. He continued to labour here diligently and successfully till his death, which occurred on the 6th of January, 1795. After he removed to the West, the Supreme Executive Council of Pennsylvania commissioned him as a Justice of the Peace, and a Judge of the Common Pleas. He had the reputation of being an eminently devout and godly man, but much inferior to his brother Samuel in point of talents and acquirements. He published a pamphlet entitled—"An attempt to set the Levitical Prohibition in relation to marriage in a true light." Three of his sons were elders in the church at Rehoboth, and one,—*John Evans*, was graduated at Princeton in 1776; was licensed to preach by the Newcastle Presbytery; and went to Kentucky about the year 1795, and became pastor of the church in Bracken, Mason County, where he exercised his ministry during the great revival.

SAMUEL BUELL, D. D.*

1741—1798.

SAMUEL BUELL was born at Coventry, Conn., September 1, 1716. His father, who was a respectable and wealthy farmer, designed him for agricultural pursuits; but, at the age of seventeen, a change occurred in the views and feelings of the son in connection with the subject of religion, which gave a new complexion to his pursuits and prospects for life.

It does not appear that his childhood and youth had been marked by any particular moral delinquencies, or unusual tendencies to evil; but, at the time above referred to, (about the year 1733,) he became deeply impressed with a sense of his sinfulness, and of his absolute dependance for salvation on the sovereign mercy of God through Christ. His views of his own character were so deeply abasing, and his sense of ill desert so pungent, that, for a season, he was upon the borders of despair. But these exercises, having continued several months, at length gave place to a calm and humble trust in the merits of the Redeemer. From this time, the ruling passion of his soul was to serve God in the best manner he could; and if he could gain reasonable evidence that such was the Divine will, to serve Him in the ministry of reconciliation.

He felt, however, that the office of a minister of the Gospel was too important to be approached lightly; and he did not determine to enter upon it without taking much time for deliberation and prayer. For more than two years, he held the question of duty constantly before him, availing himself of the advice of judicious friends, and whatever other helps were within his reach, to enable him to form a conclusion that he could justify to his conscience. The result was a determination to spend his days in preaching the Gospel; and, with a view to this, he at length set about his preparation for entering College.

After devoting a little more than a year to his preparatory course, he entered Yale College in 1737. Notwithstanding the multiplied temptations incident to college life, he seems to have lived continually in the fear of God, and, for the most part, in the comforts of the Holy Ghost. From some written memoranda of his experience at that time, which have been preserved, it would appear that, sometimes, for months together, he had an uninterrupted and most delightful sense of the presence and grace of God. Here he formed an intimate acquaintance with that devoted Christian, and afterwards eminent missionary, David Brainerd;—an acquaintance which was mutually and gratefully cherished, till Brainerd was taken to his reward. Mr. Buell's application to his studies, while in College, was most exemplary,—as was evinced by his highly respectable improvement in the various branches of study. He was graduated in September, 1741.

It had been his intention, from the commencement of his literary course, to pass several years, before entering the ministry, under the theological instruction of Jonathan Edwards, at Northampton; but, in consequence of the peculiar state of things which existed at the time of his leaving Col-

* His Anniversary, Eucharistical, and Half Century Sermon.—Daggett's Fun. Serm.—Conn. Evang. Mag., II.—Narrative of the remarkable Revival of religion.—Prime's Hist. L. I.—Thompson's do.

lege, involving a pressing demand for ministerial labour, he determined to apply immediately for license to preach. This peculiar state of things was nothing less than the extensive revival which prevailed at that time in various parts of the country, in which Whitefield had so prominent an agency. No doubt Mr. Buell had devoted himself much to theological reading, and especially to the study of the Scriptures, while he was in College; but, after all, he must have entered on his work with very imperfect qualifications, as he was licensed to preach, by the New Haven Association, within about a month from the time he was graduated.

Mr. Buell's ardent temperament, acting under the influence of an earnest piety, rendered him at once much at home in the scenes in which he was called to mingle. His first efforts in the pulpit showed that his whole heart was in his work; and they promised nothing which was not realized in his whole subsequent life. Whatever may have been the defects of his sermons, growing out of the want of mature preparation for the ministry, there was a deeply evangelical tone pervading them, and a fervour and impressiveness in the manner in which they were delivered, that rendered him at once one of the popular preachers of the day. Shortly after he was licensed, he journeyed to Northampton, preaching frequently and very effectively on the way. Here he spent several weeks,—with what acceptance, and with what effect, may be learned from the following extract of a letter from Mr. Edwards, to the Rev. Thomas Prince of Boston, dated Northampton, December, 1742:—

"About the beginning of February, 1741-42, Mr. Buell came to this town, I being then absent from home, and continued so till about a fortnight after. Mr. Buell preached from day to day, almost every day, in the meeting house, (I having left to him the free liberty of my pulpit, hearing of his designed visit before I went from home,) and spent almost the whole time in religious exercises with the people, either in public or private,—the people continually thronging him. There were very extraordinary effects of Mr. Buell's labours; the people were exceedingly moved, crying out in great numbers in the meeting house, and great part of the congregation commonly staying in the house of God for hours after the public service. Many also were exceedingly moved in private meetings where Mr. Buell was; and almost the whole town seemed to be in a great and continual commotion, day and night; and there was indeed a very great revival of religion. When I came home, I found the town in very extraordinary circumstances,—such, in some respects, as I never saw it in before. Mr. Buell continued here a fortnight or three weeks, after I returned, there being still great appearances attending his labours."

One may form some idea of the usual effect of his preaching from the following entry in his diary, made some time after this, in reference to one of his sermons:—

"The first time I ever preached to an assembly, where tears of affection under the word were not to be seen; and almost the first, when the Lord was not manifestly present with the people."

After having spent about a year in visiting different parts of New England, he was ordained in 1743, by an ecclesiastical council, as an evangelist, and in this capacity continued to prosecute his labours in various places, until he was obliged temporarily to suspend them on account of enfeebled health. It is due to his memory to say that, unlike some other evangelists, both of early and later times, he was always cheerfully subject to the will of the pastors in whose congregations he laboured; and while he was earnestly engaged in the promotion of what he fully believed to be a genuine revival of religion, he utterly disapproved of the rash and fanatical measures by which some of its friends attempted to sustain it.

The illness by which his labours were now interrupted, proved a somewhat serious one; and, for a considerable time, both he and his friends believed that his course was nearly finished. During this period of trial, his spiritual exercises were of the most satisfactory kind; and he was accustomed afterwards to recur to this stage of his Christian experience, as the ground of a subsequently increased confidence in the genuineness of his religious character. It pleased God graciously to interpose for his deliverance from expected death, and, after being taken off from his labours for the greater part of a year, he was permitted to return to them with renovated health, and to continue them with little interruption for more than half a century.

It was a somewhat noticeable providence that directed Mr. Buell to the field of labour which he was destined ultimately to occupy. The church at East Hampton, L. I., owing to the infirmities of their pastor, the Rev. Mr. Huntting,* had, for some time, been wishing to call to their service some young man, but had become divided by their ineffectual attempts to accomplish their purpose. A majority, however, at length agreed upon a candidate; and they went so far as to convoke an ecclesiastical council for the purpose of ordaining him. But, when the council convened, they found so formidable an opposition, that they did not feel justified in proceeding to the ordination. Many of the people complained of their decision, for this among other reasons,—that they could not afford to incur the additional expense of looking after another minister;—but to this objection it was answered by Mr. (afterwards President) Burr, and some other members of the council from New Jersey,—that they should be at no additional expense in the matter, as they would themselves undertake to furnish them a minister who should be acceptable. A short time after this, Mr. Buell, having set out on a preaching tour to the South, stopped at Newark, where he met Mr. Burr, who persuaded him to direct his course to East Hampton, and gave him an introduction to that vacant church. He had preached to them but a few Sabbaths, before they gave him a unanimous call, and on the 19th of September, 1746, they had the happiness of seeing him regularly installed as their pastor. The Sermon on the occasion was preached by Jonathan Edwards from Isaiah lxii. 4, 5, and was published.

Notwithstanding the great success which had attended Mr. Buell's early labours, he was himself quite aware that his intellectual preparation for his work had been too superficial; and was glad to avail himself of the opportunity furnished by a more settled mode of life, to engage more vigorously and systematically in the appropriate studies of a minister. Accordingly, he became at once a diligent student; and his profiting quickly appeared

* Nathaniel Huntting was a son of John and Elizabeth (Payne) Huntting, and a grandson of John Huntting who came from England in September, 1638, and settled at Dedham, Mass., where he died April 12, 1682. He (Nathaniel) was born at Dedham, November 15, 1675; was graduated at Harvard College in 1693; began to preach at East Hampton in September, 1696; was installed pastor of that church, September 13, 1699; was dismissed at his own request, on the settlement of his successor, September 19, 1746; and died September 21, 1753, in his seventy-eighth year. He was friendly to the great revival, but because he opposed the irregularities that attended it, he was unjustly charged with hostility to the revival itself. Dr. Beecher in his History of East Hampton, says,—"Mr. Huntting was a man of strong and distinguishing mind—firm and independent without rashness and obstinacy; an hard student, an accurate scholar, and of extensive theological reading." He was married to Mary Green, and had ten children,—six sons who reached maturity—two of whom, *Nathaniel* and *Jonathan* entered the ministry, but were obliged to desist from preaching on account of ill health. The former was graduated at Harvard College in 1722, and died in 1770; the latter was graduated at Yale College in 1735, and died in 1750.

unto all. As a proof of the uniformity of his application, it is noted in his diary, at the close of a number of the first years of his ministry,—"This year have written all my sermons, and have preached them without notes."

But, though he was careful to stir up the gift that was in him by a due degree of intellectual culture, his favourite maxim was "usefulness is life;" and his acquisitions were always turned to the best practical account. He could never content himself in his study, when he saw that there was a special demand for active labour in his congregation. Besides the stated services of the Sabbath, he preached once or twice in different parts of his parish during the week, and in seasons of special attention to religion, much more frequently. His sermons are represented as having often been of extraordinary length, insomuch that, not unfrequently, he found it difficult to detain his whole audience to the close of the service.

There are some amusing traditions in respect to the manner in which he sometimes contrived to prevent his hearers from leaving the church before the sermon was over. The two following I received from Dr. Miller. On one occasion, after preaching nearly two hours,—as long as he could feel secure of the presence of all his hearers,—he remarked that he had done preaching to sinners, and they were at liberty to go—the rest of his discourse would be addressed to good people. A gentleman, who once went to hear him, stated that, when the hour glass was nearly ready to be turned a second time from the commencement of his sermon, he said,—(much to the relief of the person who related it,) "*Once more*"—after going on some eight or ten minutes longer, he said—"*To conclude*"—and after another about equal interval, he said—"*Lastly:*" the gentleman added that he expected every moment to hear him say—"*Everlastingly.*"

The most striking characteristics of his preaching through life were solemnity and fervour; and one great secret of his power lay in the fact that he made his hearers feel that every word he uttered came from his inmost soul. His sermons were rich in scriptural instruction; but they were especially distinguished for the vigorous grasp with which they laid hold of the conscience. As a theologian he belonged to the same school with Edwards and Bellamy, and the former particularly he regarded as having spoken and written with almost superhuman wisdom.

As might be expected of a man so distinguished for his piety, he attached the highest importance to the efficacy of prayer; and, while his own prayers always showed that he was under the influence of a baptism of the Holy Ghost, he laboured earnestly to infuse the same spirit into the hearts of his people. It was part of the economy of his religious life to acknowledge God's hand in every thing. In a sermon preached upon the death of his first wife, (but not published,) after alluding to the sad changes which had occurred in his family, he says,—"I hope your candour will not deem it ostentation for me to add that my comforts were received with prayer, praise, and the joy of trembling, and have been parted with, (however nature might oppose,) with prayer, submission, and, at last, praise."

His success as a minister was fully answerable to his zeal and fidelity. He was privileged, at three different periods, to witness a remarkable attention to religion in his congregation. The first revival which occurred in 1764, was far the most extensive and powerful: ninety-nine were added to the church at one time, and many others subsequently, as the fruits of the same work. A similar state of things existed in 1785, and in 1791; and, at various other periods, his congregation was pervaded, in a greater or less degree, by an awakening and quickening influence. The remoter effect of these several revivals was to promote the credit of religion, and to increase the stability and extend the influence of the church.

At no period of his ministry was Mr. Buell's situation at once so trying and so responsible as during the Revolutionary war. The taking possession of the Island by the British occasioned the utmost consternation among the inhabitants, and not a small portion of them fled for safety. But this excellent man remained firm and constant at his post, resolved that nothing but death should remove him from his field of labour. By his uniform urbanity, discretion, and conscientiousness, he acquired no inconsiderable influence with some of the British officers, which he was enabled to turn to good account for the interests of the town and the neighbourhood. In some cases, his life was in imminent danger; but every one saw that he counted not his life dear to him, if, in the discharge of his duty as a minister of Christ, he were called to surrender it.

His usefulness was far from being confined within the limits of his own congregation. Of the Presbytery to which he belonged he was an active and highly influential member; and, even in his old age, he was uniformly punctual in his attendance upon its meetings. His sound judgment and incorruptible integrity gave great value to his opinions and counsels. He was extensively known, not only by his general influence but by his writings, and particularly by a Narrative of the great revival of religion which occurred among his people in 1764. He received the degree of Doctor of Divinity from Dartmouth College in 1791.

Dr. Buell was intent on promoting not only the spiritual but the intellectual interests of his people. A few years before his death, he was instrumental of establishing, at East Hampton, Clinton Academy,—an institution over which he exercised a parental supervision as long as he lived, and which has been, and still continues, a great public blessing. In this Academy he was accustomed to deliver a lecture, as long as his strength was adequate to the effort, once a week. It is still regarded in that neighbourhood with no small reverence, as a monument of his public spirit and philanthropy.

As he possessed great natural cheerfulness and vivacity, he was a most agreeable companion, and the young as well as the old were always glad to be in his society. He had an inexhaustible fund of anecdote, which, however, he dealt out with great discretion, and never at the expense of diminishing his own dignity, or forfeiting the respect of others. In his domestic relations, he was an example of whatever is tender, amiable and attractive. He was distinguished for his hospitality, and his visitors were sure to meet with a cordial and joyous welcome.

Dr. Buell was married three times. His first wife was Jerusha, daughter of the Rev. Joseph Meacham of Coventry, Conn., with whom he lived about twelve years. His second was Mary, daughter of Elisha Mulford of East Hampton, with whom he lived twenty-two years. And his third was Mary, daughter of Jeremiah Miller of East Hampton, whom he married but a short time before his death, and who survived him about forty years. He had ten children—only two of whom survived him.

Dr. Buell was distinguished for his patience and fortitude in suffering; and it was no common degree of suffering, especially in the way of domestic bereavement, that was allotted to him. During the time that he was the head of a family, no less than fourteen deaths occurred in his house; eight of which were of his children. But, in times of the deepest sorrow, he stayed himself upon God the Comforter; and no personal affliction was ever suffered to interfere with the discharge of his public duties. He was accustomed to avail himself, in the pulpit, of these sad events, as furnishing matter of instruction and admonition to his people; and two of his sermons, preached on these occasions,—one after the death of a son, the other after the death of a daughter,—were published, and still remain to testify to the strength of his parental sensibility and of his religious affections.

His faculties, both physical and intellectual, retained their vigour, in an uncommon degree, to the last of his days;—a blessing for which he was no doubt much indebted to his rigid observance of the rules of temperance. On the day that completed his eightieth year, he rode fourteen miles, preached, and returned home in the evening. His last illness was short, and but a single Sabbath passed, after he left his pulpit, before he was in Heaven. But he had no painful misgivings,—not a chill of apprehension, in the prospect of encountering the king of terrors. He knew in whom he had believed, and felt assured that his Redeemer would keep what he had committed to Him against the day of his appearing. He died on the 19th of July, 1798. The following extract from the Sermon preached at his Funeral by the Rev. Herman Daggett, and afterwards published, will show more particularly what were his exercises in the immediate prospect of his departure:—

"He said that his mind was in perfect peace, and seemed never to have enjoyed a more triumphant faith. He appeared to have impressions upon his mind concerning the glory of the Church, as hastening on, which he wished to communicate, but could not for want of strength. He desired also to speak much to those about him upon the subject of having an interest in Christ, the importance of which, as it then appeared to him, he said, was unutterable. He had no desire to recover, but to depart and be with Christ. He viewed himself, he said, as now passing Jordan's flood, and within a step, as it were, of the promised land, and the thought of returning again into the wilderness was painful to him. When asked, at one time, concerning the state of his mind, he requested his friends, in order to obtain it, to read the seventeenth chapter of John, repeating several times the twenty-fourth verse—'Father I will that they also whom thou hast given me be with me where I am; that they may behold the glory which thou hast given me.' Towards the last, he observed that he felt all earthly connections to be dissolved; and his soul appeared to be drawn with such strength and pleasure to the glorious world of light, that he could not bear to be interrupted by the assiduities of his friends, who were seeking to administer to his perishing dust, frequently putting them aside with one hand, whilst the other was raised to Heaven, where his eyes and his soul were fixed. And in this happy frame he continued, till the progress of his disorder wholly deprived him of the power of speech."

The following is a list of Dr. Buell's publications:—A Sermon preached at Brookhaven, at the ordination of Mr. Benjamin Tallmadge, 1754. A Sermon occasioned by the decease of Mrs. Esther Darbe, 1757. A Sermon preached at East Hampton at the ordination of Mr. Sampson Occum, a missionary among the Indians, 1759. A Sermon occasioned by the lamented death of the Rev. Mr. Charles Jeffrey Smith, 1770. A spiritual knowledge of God comprehensive of all good and blessedness: A Sermon preached at Enfield, 1771. A Sermon occasioned by the death of his daughter, Mrs. Jerusha Conkling, 1782. A Sermon occasioned by the death of his only son, 1787. A Sermon delivered at the ordination of the Rev. Aaron Woolworth, to the pastoral charge of the church in Bridgehampton, 1787. An Anniversary, Eucharistical, and Half-century Sermon, delivered at East Hampton, 1792. A Sermon delivered immediately after the funeral of Samuel Buell Woolworth, 1794. A Sermon preached at the ordination of Joseph Hazard* at Southold, 1797.

FROM THE REV. HENRY DAVIS, D. D.

PRESIDENT OF MIDDLEBURY AND HAMILTON COLLEGES.

CLINTON, N. Y., July 12, 1848.

Rev. and dear Sir: I cheerfully comply with your request to furnish you, as far as my very infirm health will admit, my reminiscences of the late Dr. Samuel Buell. He was pastor of the church in East Hampton, my native place, at the time of my birth. By him I was baptized; and though absent subsequently for a number of years, yet, when still a youth, I returned, and became one of his parishioners. My recollections of him, and of many scenes that I witnessed during his ministry, have scarcely begun to fade, even after the lapse of more than half a century.

Some of the most interesting events of Dr. Buell's ministry were anterior to my recollection, and in connection with the Revolutionary war. The struggle for independence had but recently commenced, when Long Island fell into the possession of the British, and so it remained till its termination. Many families fled for refuge to the Continent; and among them several from East Hampton, who were the Doctor's most cordial and able supporters. Such, at this time, was his reputation, that there was scarcely a vacant church in New England, of his denomination, but would gladly have opened its doors to him. He could not but foresee the dangers and sufferings which awaited him and his people who remained behind, but still he deemed it his bounden duty to stay at his post. During the entire period of the war, he continued to exercise his ministry among them,—not only preaching to them regularly on the Sabbath, but doing his utmost to alleviate their sufferings, and guard them against the multiplied temptations to which their circumstances necessarily exposed them. The situation of East Hampton was somewhat peculiar: it was not only the constant residence of a portion of the British land forces, but a large squadron of the navy was, during a considerable part of the time, stationed in Gardiner's Bay, which is but a short distance from the North shore of that town. This rendered the intercourse of the British with the inhabitants constant and unavoidable, and subjected the latter to very serious evils. But though the Doctor took no pains to conceal from the enemy his entire sympathy with the Colonies in their struggle, he was greatly respected by the officers for his gentlemanly deportment and general intelligence; and, while they actually sought his society, he was always ready to meet them with every suitable expression of good will. Some anecdotes are told that strikingly illustrate the high estimation in which he was held by them, as well as the fearlessness of his spirit and the quickness of his wit. The Commander-in-chief of the land forces remarked to him that he had commanded some of his farmers to appear on a certain day, (I believe on the Sabbath,) with their teams, at Southampton, twelve miles distant. "So I have understood," said the Doctor; "but I have countermanded your orders;" and, in consequence of this countermand, the project was relinquished. A young British officer, recently arrived, rode to his door and said, "I wish to see Mr. Buell." The Doctor soon appeared. "Are you Mr. Buell?"—was the question. "My name is Buell, Sir," "Then," said the officer, bowing with great respect,—"I have seen the god of East Hampton." On one occasion he was invited by the officers to accompany them on a deer-hunt. The invitation was accepted. But the Doctor, perceiving that one of the company was dissatisfied on account of some delay, at the commencement of the excursion, pleasantly asked him—"And what portion of his majesty's troops, Sir, have you the honour to command?"

* JOSEPH HAZARD was ordained and installed the seventh minister of Southold, June 7, 1797; was dismissed in April, 1806; and died at Brooklyn, L. I., in 1817.

"A legion of devils direct from hell," was the answer. The Doctor, assuming an attitude of profound respect, replied, "Then I presume, Sir, I have the honour of addressing Beelzebub, the prince of the devils." The officer, as if about to revenge what he considered an insult, drew his sword. But, at the smile and nod of his superior, he instantly sheathed it again. Before the excursion was ended, however, he became greatly interested in the Doctor, and it was evident that whatever unpleasant impression the occurrence had occasioned, was entirely removed. There can be no doubt that Dr. Buell possessed, in an extraordinary degree, the qualities, both natural and acquired, that were fitted to give him influence in the peculiar circumstances in which he was placed, during this stormy period; and it may reasonably be doubted whether his usefulness as a minister was, on the whole, ever greater, during a period of equal length.

In the year 1785, and not long after my return to East Hampton, it was my privilege to witness a powerful revival of religion under Dr. Buell's ministry. Within six or eight months, more than one hundred, who were hopeful subjects of the work, made a public profession of religion. Many more were thought by some to give evidence of having experienced a radical change, and were not entirely without hope for themselves. But, in the judgment of the pastor, the prosperity and efficiency of a church are not in exact proportion to its numbers; and he deemed it of vital importance that there should be much opportunity for reflection and self-communion, before so important a step should be taken as coming into the visible Church. On this subject, as indeed on every other in connection with his ministry, he uniformly observed the most exemplary caution. His whole course, not only during that revival, but throughout his subsequent ministry, impressed me deeply with the conviction that he was eminently a man of God, and devoted unreservedly to his service. His church had large experieuce of his wisdom and faithfulness. They walked together in the love and fellowship of the Gospel, and were seldom called to the painful duty of disciplining offenders.

In his stature the Doctor was of the medium height. His frame was somewhat slender, but possessed great strength and elasticity. He was unusually quick in all his movements. In his natural temper he was ardent, yet amiable, frank, and uncommonly cheerful. Few men were more discreet and circumspect: he perceived intuitively what was fitting on every occasion, and in his intercourse with men of all classes and conditions. I cannot call to mind that, in relation to pecuniary or other secular concerns, there was ever the least difficulty or misunderstanding between him and any one of his parishioners, or that he was ever complained of by any for neglecting them, or for bestowing too much attention upon others, or for being too much or too little occupied in his worldly concerns. He possessed great power of voice as well as physical vigour, and was favoured with uniformly excellent health. His sermons were never less than an hour, and not unfrequently from an hour and a half to two hours, in length. They were, for the most part, unwritten, and were delivered without notes, and with great force and animation. Yet he never complained of being fatigued by speaking, or, in any other way, as far as I know, gave the least indication of it. He was much in the habit of taking out his watch, and would often remark, "Brethren, time fails me," and excuse himself for not saying all on the subject that he had intended. He remarked to me, not long before his death, that, for a period of fifty years, he had not been prevented by ill health from preaching on a single Sabbath; and added that he had preached ten thousand times—a greater number he presumed than any other man in America.

In his intellectual habits he was remarkable for industry; and he was especially diligent in the discharge of all his professional duties. He studied the subjects of his discourses with great care, and I doubt not bestowed more time upon them than many clergymen do who write out every word. He had, for those times, an extensive and valuable library; and few men used their books more thoroughly or to better purpose. He was conversant, in no small degree, with the writings of the early fathers, and especially was a close student of Church History. From the former he was in the habit of quoting much in his public discourses. He once told me that he had devoted about twelve of the best years of his ministry to the study of the prophecies, and had prepared an extended treatise on the subject for the press; but he added, "as I was about putting my manuscript into the hands of the printer, Bishop Newton's work on the same subject appeared, and finding his plan and general views to coincide with my own, I was induced to abandon the idea of publishing what I had prepared."

Though social and hospitable in his feelings, and courteous and affable in his manners, he seldom visited his people, and had but little personal intercourse with them, except in seasons of revival. In his study, however, he always welcomed those who wished for religious instruction; and, in cases of sickness, he was ever at hand to administer needed counsel and consolation.

In spending the most of his time in his study, preparing for the services of the sanctuary, he thought he could do most to accomplish the great ends of his ministry. He was regarded as eminently a man of prayer. The intimate fellow-labourer with Edwards, Whitefield, and Brainerd, he imbibed a large measure of their spirit. He had little action in the pulpit, and yet he preached with great power and directness, and kept back nothing which he believed to be the counsel of God. His usual services in the church were two sermons on the Sabbath. He preached much, however, during the week, in the three neighbouring villages within the town, and spent no little time in regular catechetical instruction. But he seldom preached himself, or attended any religious meeting in the evening, except when there was an unusual attention to religion. His people, however, were in the habit of holding, regularly, meetings for prayer and religious conference, and they were favoured with much preaching in the church besides the sermons on the Sabbath. Few ministers of his day, I imagine, were visited by so many of his brethren from abroad, either from curiosity or other motives, as Dr. Buell. His visitors were principally from New England. To his clerical brethren he always gave a most cordial welcome; but one or more sermons to his people was the tax which each one had to pay for his hospitable reception. From this tax no minister, of regular standing, and of sufficient strength to preach, was exempt. But there was this amusing difference—Baptists and Methodists must address his people from the deacons' seat, while those of his own denomination only were admitted to the pulpit—the "sanctum sanctorum," as he was wont to call it. The ringing of the bell, at one or two o'clock in the afternoon, or a little before sunset, was the signal that a minister was in town, and that public worship would commence in about one hour; and in due season a respectable audience was always collected. He was once visited by two licentiates of the names of Cramm and More. Cramm preached in the afternoon. At the close of the exercises, the Doctor informed the congregation that there would be preaching in the evening. He then turned to the young men in the pulpit, and said, with his characteristic pleasantry, though certainly with questionable propriety,—"My people have been *Cramm'd* but they want *More*."

He was distinguished for self-control; seldom, if ever, thrown off his balance, on occasions which furnished strong ground for provocation, and seemed to invite to high excitement. Even in seasons of deep affliction, he was enabled to sustain himself with wonderful composure, not merely from natural self-command, but from the perfect confidence which he felt in the rectitude of the Divine administration. A striking illustration of this occurred in connection with the death of his only son,—a youth of uncommon promise, and greatly beloved, who died of the small-pox at the age of sixteen or seventeen. Though he was but a short distance from the town, the Doctor was not able to be with him during his sickness, or at his death. The Rev. Mr. Woolworth of Bridgehampton, (subsequently Dr. Woolworth, and son-in-law of Dr. Buell,) was present to preach at the funeral. After the remains were interred by the few who could attend to the painful duty without exposure, the people collected for worship.—The Doctor arose, and, with uplifted hands,—a gesture very common with him,—and eyes directed to Heaven, broke the profound silence of the great congregation in the language of Job—"I know that my Redeemer liveth, and that He shall stand in the latter day on the earth." With deep emotion, but perfect self-command, he addressed the audience for fifteen or twenty minutes. The effect cannot be described: his own were the only tearless eyes in the assembly.

Dr. Buell once remarked to me that there was not, to his knowledge, a single individual in the town, professing to be of any other denomination than the Presbyterian. It would have been strange indeed, considering the great age to which he lived, had he experienced no abatement of his influence before his death. At my last interview with him,—I believe when he was eighty-two or three,—he remarked, alluding to the change in the times,—"There was a time when, if a question arose touching the boundary between this town and Southampton, I could go and tell them where I thought it ought to be, and the matter was settled; but," he added, not without some degree of feeling, "it is not so now."

Without endorsing the opinion entertained of him by President Stiles, who remarked to a young gentleman, after reading a letter which he had handed him from Dr. Buell, "This man has done more good than any other man that has ever stood on this Continent,"—I think it cannot be doubted that his character and labours present many striking points of interest, and that he was, on the whole, among the most remarkable and useful men of his generation. If he may not be regarded as, in all respects, a proper and safe model for ministers of the present day, yet they may find much in his history that furnishes admonition and encouragement to unwearied diligence and fidelity in the performance of their duties. I remain, my dear Sir,

With unfeigned affection and respect,

Your friend and brother,

HENRY DAVIS.

FROM THE HON. ALFRED CONKLING,

JUDGE OF THE DISTRICT COURT OF THE UNITED STATES, AND AMBASSADOR TO MEXICO.

MELROSE, near Auburn, September 6, 1848.

Rev. and dear Sir: In acceding to your request, some months ago, that I would communicate to you my recollections of the Rev. Dr. Samuel Buell, who, for more than half a century, was the sole minister of the Gospel in my native town, I was not altogether unaware that I was acting with more complaisance than prudence. You will, I am sure, do me the justice to remember, however, that I took special care to warn you against indulging any other than very moderate expectations touching the fulfilment of my promise. But, along with my misgivings, I did, I confess, entertain the hope that when I came, as I have this morning for the first time done, to tax my memory on the subject, I should be somewhat more successful than my letter will show me to have been, in recalling something concerning this remarkable man, which it might interest you to know. The result, nevertheless, with regard to my own personal reminiscences, has been exactly what I ought to have foreseen it would be; for, at the time of his death, I was less than nine years old, and the residence of my parents was three miles from his, and from the church where he officiated. I do not remember, therefore, ever to have heard him preach more than two or three times. But I heard much of him, both before and after his decease, especially from my mother, who regarded him, while he was living, with the liveliest sentiments of esteem and veneration, and cherished his memory with affectionate and reverential regard. I have heard her speak also still more frequently and affectionately of his deceased daughter, *Jerusha*, whose rare intellectual and moral endowments and glowing piety justly entitle her name to be associated with that of her distinguished father. She was, at the time of her death, the wife of one of my paternal uncles, and I have in my possession an affectionate but apparently a very impartial tribute to her memory, entitled "Memoirs of the life and death of Mrs. Jerusha Conkling," written by her father. Judging from all I have heard and read of her, she seems indeed to have been one of the very noblest specimens of female character.

I remember Dr. Buell only as a venerable looking old man, wearing a large, remarkably neat white wig, rather small of stature and of slight frame, but of dignified mien and serene aspect. The portraits I have seen of him are expressive of great firmness and decision; and he was unquestionably a man of uncommon energy and boldness as well as of uncommon sagacity. I have often heard it related of him that while, during the Revolutionary war, Long Island was in possession of the British forces, he was unwearied and eminently successful in efforts to protect the inhabitants against those oppressive exactions and injuries of every sort, to which their situation exposed them. He was, at that time, upwards of sixty years old; and his ability to render these important services to the inhabitants of that part of the Island, (where a considerable body of troops were long stationed,) arose chiefly from the great respect and esteem in which, though an unflinching Whig, he was held by the better class of the British officers. His sprightliness, wit, and gentlemanly manners, are said to have made him a favourite with them, notwithstanding the independence of his spirit, and his firm adherence to his political as well as religious principles. I have heard my father speak with lively interest of a conversation of a religious cast at which he was present in a village church-yard, at a funeral, between Dr. Buell and an English officer, who, I am nearly certain, was the celebrated Major Andre, whose romantic character and unhappy fate awakened so painful a sympathy on both sides of the Atlantic. Dr. Buell seems indeed to have been hardly less attentive to the temporal than to the spiritual welfare of his people. He may, with unusual propriety, be said to have been a father to them; and the patriarchal character of his intercourse shows that he regarded himself in that light.

Soon after the conversation I had the pleasure of having with you respecting Dr. Buell, meeting my friend Sylvanus Miller, Esq., also a native of East Hampton, I made some inquiries of him concerning the Doctor. Among other things, he mentioned an incident which occurred at the time of the removal of his father from that town. Mr. Miller was then, as I think he told me, eleven years old. After all the arrangements for the removal had been completed, and the family were about to depart, Dr. Buell came to take a final leave of them; and, after bidding adieu to the senior members, he caused my informant and his little brother to kneel down before him, and laying his hands upon their heads, he "blessed" them. That blessing must have sunk deep into the young heart of my old friend, unless I misinterpreted the visible emotion with which, after the lapse of seventy years, he narrated the incident; and it may not have been with out its fruits, in enhancing the moral beauty of his blameless and highly useful life. He related also several other anecdotes of Dr. Buell, illustrative of the extraordinary versatility of his talents, of his enterprising spirit, and of the healthful and buoyant tone of his mind.

It was these qualities, added to his ardent piety, that inspired his people with the almost unbounded confidence they appear to have reposed in him, and made him what he undoubtedly was in his day and generation,—a distinguished public benefactor.

Believe me, dear Sir,

With high respect and regard,

Faithfully yours,

A. CONKLING.

DAVID BRAINERD.*

1742—1747.

DAVID BRAINERD was born at Haddam, Conn., April 20, 1718. His father was Hezekiah Brainerd, a man of considerable note in the Colony. His mother was a daughter of the Rev. Jeremiah Hobart, who, in the latter part of his life, was a settled minister in Brainerd's native place.

While he was quite a child, he was the subject of strong religious impressions, and was accustomed to meet with several others of about his own age, for purposes of devotion and Christian improvement. But, though he evidently imagined himself, at the time, the subject of a radical spiritual change, he was subsequently convinced that this was but a delusive experience. And this conviction was accompanied with the most humbling sense of his own sinfulness, and of the justice and holiness of God. After a protracted season of mental agony, which he describes as arising from inward resistance to the terms of the Gospel, he found peace and joy in believing. As he was walking in a retired place, on a summer evening, in 1739, for purposes of serious meditation, fully convinced of his absolute ruin and entire dependance on God's grace, a great and wonderful change came over his mind, which he considered as marking, at least, the first perceptible operation of the renovated nature. His views of the character of God, of the character and mediation of Christ, and of the office of the Holy Spirit, became clear, elevating and rapturous; he breathed a new atmosphere; he lived for new objects; in every action that he performed he desired to hide himself, that God might be all in all.

In September, 1739, shortly after this stage of his experience, he was admitted a member of Yale College. The extravagance which prevailed in connection with the great revival of that period, had the effect, as was to be expected, of driving a portion of the religious community to the opposite extreme; and Yale College, with President Clap at its head, seems to have been thrown into somewhat of an opposing attitude. Hence the religious atmosphere about the College was cold; and the government even went so far as to enact severe penalties against those students who should be heard of at a "New-Light" meeting. Brainerd, from the natural fervour of his spirit, as well as from his deep sense of the importance of eternal things, was inclined to sympathize with the more zealous party, and looked upon this procedure of the government as an unreasonable and tyrannical infringe-

* Brainerd's Journal.—Edwards' Fun. Serm.—Life by Edwards.—Do., by S. E. Dwight.—Do., by W. B. O. Peabody.—Assemb. Miss. Mag. II.—Bacon's Historical Discourses.

ment of his liberty; and he attended the "Separate" meeting, without any regard to the offensive enactment. About the same time, he was overheard to say, in conversation with several of his fellow-students, in respect to one of the Tutors, that he did not believe he had any more religion than the chair on which he sat. The individuals with whom he was conversing having been required by the Rector to state the conversation, Brainerd was ordered to make a public confession of his fault in the chapel. But, regarding the requirement as unreasonable and vindictive, he refused to submit to it; and, in consequence of this, was expelled from College. There is no doubt that the course which the government adopted in relation to him, was, in some measure, the result of sensitiveness to the prevailing religious excitement, and was designed as a strong expression of their opposition to Whitefield and his coadjutors; but, however much they may have been in fault, it must be acknowledged that Brainerd's course was justly liable to reprehension. Indeed, he was himself afterwards fully sensible of it; and, though he always considered himself as having been treated with undue severity, he never hesitated to acknowledge his fault, and it is evident that he profited not a little by his reflections upon it.

This untoward circumstance occurred while he was in his Junior year; and, as he never returned to College afterwards, he of course failed to receive a degree. In the spring of the same year in which he left College, he commenced the study of Divinity under the direction of the Rev. Jedediah Mills of Ripton, Conn., and, on the 20th of July following, (1742,) was licensed to preach by the Association of ministers holding its session at Danbury. From the commencement of his theological course, he had felt a deep interest in the deplorable condition of the heathen, especially the aborigines of our own country—his heart burned to follow in the footsteps of the apostle Eliot, in bringing the Gospel in contact with their darkened understandings; and, accordingly, in the autumn after he was licensed, he went to New York, by invitation from the Correspondents of the Society for promoting Christian Knowledge, and, after being duly examined, received a regular appointment from them as a missionary among the Indians.

The first scene of his missionary labours was at an Indian village called Kaunaumeek, about half way between Stockbridge and Albany. Here he lived in the woods nearly a year, lodging, during a part of the time, in a wigwam with the Indians, and subsisting altogether upon Indian fare. Though he was subject to the greatest deprivations, and often suffered not a little from bodily debility and disease, he persevered, without interruption, in his benevolent labours, until the Indians, among whom he resided, agreed to remove to Stockbridge, and place themselves under the care of the Rev. Mr. Sergeant. In consequence of this arrangement, he was obliged to look out for another field of labour, and forthwith directed his attention towards the Delaware tribe.

Having been ordained by the Presbytery of New York, at Newark, N. J., in June, 1744,—on which occasion the Rev. Mr. Pemberton of New York preached,—he immediately stationed himself near the Forks of the Delaware, in Pennsylvania, where he laboured, with comparatively little apparent effect, for about a year. At the end of this period, he visited the Indians at a village called Crosweeksung, in the neighbourhood of Freehold,—the residence of the celebrated William Tennent. Here was the scene of his greatest success. A wonderful Divine influence accompanied his labours, and, in less than a year, he baptized seventy-seven persons, thirty-eight of whom were adults, whose subsequent life furnished satisfactory evidence of a true conversion. There seems no reason to doubt that this was not only a very powerful, but very genuine, revival of religion. In a letter addressed to the Rev. Dr. Wheelock, he says—"The good work which you will find largely treated of in my journal, still continues among the Indians; though the astonishing Divine influence that has been among them is, in a considerable measure, abated. Yet there are several instances of persons newly awakened. When I consider the doings of the Lord among these Indians, and then take a view of my journal, I must say 'tis a faint representation I have given of them. Among those who witnessed to the remarkable character of this work were the Rev. William Tennent and the Rev. Charles McKnight,* both of whom lived in the immediate neighbourhood, and could testify from actual observation.

During his residence at the Forks of the Delaware, he twice visited the Indians on the Susquehanna; and he paid them a third visit in the summer of 1746. But, on his return to the village where he had been recently labouring, his physical energies were so far exhausted, that he found it exceedingly difficult to preach, and, in pursuance of medical advice, he determined to travel, and visit his friends in New England. He went as far as Boston, and in July returned to Northampton, and became domesticated in the family of Jonathan Edwards, to whose daughter he was engaged to be married. Here he continued, undergoing a gradual decline, accompanied, towards the close, with the most intense suffering, till October 9, 1747, when he closed his earthly course at the early age of twenty-nine.

His last illness is represented as a most calm and yet triumphant exhibition of Christian faith. His views of Divine truth were never so vivid and glorious, as when he had nearly reached the threshold of that world, where the objects of his faith were to become the objects of his vision. He saw nothing but worthlessness and emptiness in himself, nothing but worthiness and fulness in his Redeemer; and while he was yet lingering at the gate of death, he seemed to be entranced with the glories of Heaven. He forgot not, even amidst his dying agonies, and the anticipation of the crown that awaited him, the prosperity of Christ's Church on earth; and the poor Indians especially, among whom he had laboured, came in for a

* CHARLES MCKNIGHT was the son of a Presbyterian clergyman in Ireland, and is supposed to have come to this country about the year 1740. He was taken under the care of the New Brunswick Presbytery, June 28, 1741, and was probably licensed before the close of that year. Having received calls from both Staten Island and Basking Ridge, he was ordained, October 12, 1742. In May, 1744, he was called to the united congregations of Cranberry and Allentown, and was installed, at the latter place, as pastor of these two churches, on the 19th of July following. In 1748, his pastoral relation to Allentown was dissolved, and he became the pastor of Cranberry alone. Here he remained till October, 1756, when he requested to be liberated from the pastoral charge of Cranberry, which the Presbytery accordingly granted, as the state of his health was deemed insufficient for the full discharge of his duties. Where he laboured during the eight or ten following years, does not appear—possibly his health was too infirm to admit of his accepting a pastoral charge. About 1767, he became the pastor of the united neighbouring congregations of Shrewsbury, Middletown, and Shark River, and remained in this charge about nine years. On account of his warm sympathy with the cause of American Independence, and the active part which his sons took in the contest, he was imprisoned by the British, and subjected to the most barbarous treatment. He died, soon after his release, January 1, 1778. He left two sons—*Richard*, who held a commission as Captain in the American army, and became one of the "prison ship martyrs," at the age of twenty-five; and *Charles*, who was a Surgeon in the Revolution, and was afterwards distinguished as a surgical and medical practitioner in the city of New York. Mr. McKnight was a member of the Board of Trustees of the College of New Jersey from 1757 till his death.

share of his tender remembrances, as he was on his way through the dark valley. With his last breath he exclaimed—"My work is done—Oh to be in Heaven, to praise and glorify God with his holy angels!"

The funeral of Mr. Brainerd, at which Mr. Edwards preached, was an occasion of the deepest interest to the inhabitants, not only of Northampton, but of the whole surrounding country. His mortal remains repose in the burying place at Northampton, and the spot is hallowed to the hearts of thousands by the most grateful associations. The stranger who only passes through the town, is often heard inquiring the way to "Brainerd's grave;" and many a Christian, and many a minister, whose home is on the other side of the ocean, has stood over the spot with tender and sublime emotions, and with a moistened eye. It is within the last few years that, on some public occasion at Northampton, which called together a large number of ministers, a clerical procession walked early in the morning into the grave-yard, to visit this hallowed spot, and, as they stood over it, they offered up thanksgiving to his God and their God, for having made him what he was, and supplications that the remembrance of his example might cheer them onward in their labours, and assist them to win the immortal crown.

The following is an extract from the Sermon preached at Brainerd's funeral:—

"His convictions of sin, preceding his first consolations in Christ, (as appears by a written account he has left of his inward exercises and experiences,) were exceeding deep and thorough: his trouble and exercise of mind, through a sense of guilt and misery, very great and long continued, but yet sound and solid; consisting in no unsteady, violent and unaccountable hurries and frights, and strange perturbations of mind; but arising from the most serious consideration and proper illumination of the conscience to discern and consider the true state of things. And the light let into his mind at conversion, and the influences and exercises that his mind was subject to at that time, appear very agreeable to reason and the Gospel of Jesus Christ; the change very great and remarkable without any appearance of strong impressions on the imagination, sudden flights and pangs of the affections, and vehement emotions in animal nature; but attended with proper intellectual views of the supreme glory of the Divine Being, consisting in the infinite dignity and beauty of the perfections of his nature, and of the transcendent excellency of the way of salvation by Christ. This was about eight years ago, when he was about twenty-one years of age.

"Thus God sanctified and made meet for his use that vessel that he intended to make eminently a vessel of honour in his house, and which he had made of large capacity, having endowed him with very uncommon abilities and gifts of nature. He was a singular instance of a ready invention, natural eloquence, easy flowing expression, sprightly apprehension, quick discerning, and a very strong memory; and yet of a very penetrating genius, close and clear thought, and piercing judgment. He had an exact taste. His understanding was (if I may so express it) of a quick, strong and distinguishing scent.

"His learning was very considerable. He had a great taste for learning, and applied himself to his studies in so close a manner, when he was at College, that he much injured his health, and was obliged, on that account, for a while, to leave the College, throw by his studies, and return home. He was esteemed one that excelled in learning in that Society.

"He had an extraordinary knowledge of men, as well as things; had a great insight into human nature, and excelled most that ever I knew in a communicative faculty. He had a peculiar talent at accommodating himself to the capacities, tempers, and circumstances of those that he would instruct or counsel.

"He had extraordinary gifts for the pulpit. I never had opportunity to hear him preach, but have often heard him pray. And I think his manner of addressing himself to God, and expressing himself before Him, in that duty, almost inimitable; such (so far as I may judge) as I have very rarely known equalled. He expressed himself with that exact propriety and pertinency, in such significant, weighty, pungent expressions, with that decent appearance of sincerity, reverence, and solemnity, and great distance from all affectation, as forgetting the presence of men, and as being in the immediate presence of a great and holy God, that I have scarcely ever known paralleled. And his manner of preaching, by what I have often heard of it from good judges, was no less excellent; being clear and instructive, natural, nervous, forcible and moving, and very searching and convincing. He nauseated an affected noisiness and violent boisterousness in the pulpit; and yet much disrelished a flat, cold delivery, when the subject of discourse and matter delivered required affection and earnestness.

"Not only had he excellent talents for the study and the pulpit, but also for conversation. He was of a sociable disposition, and was remarkably free, entertaining and profitable in his ordinary discourse, and had much of a faculty of disputing, defending truth, and confuting error.

"As he excelled in his judgment, and knowledge of things in general, so especially in Divinity. He was truly, for one in his standing, an extraordinary divine. But, above all, in matters relating to experimental religion. In this, I know I have the concurring opinion of some that have had a name for persons of the best judgment. And, according to what ability I have to judge of things of this nature, and according to my opportunities which, of late, have been very great, I never knew his equal, of his age and standing, for clear, accurate notions of the nature and essence of true religion, and its distinctions from its various false appearances; which I suppose to be owing to these three things meeting together in him;—the strength of his natural genius, and the great opportunities he had of observations of others, in various parts, both white people and Indians, and his own great experience.

"His experiences of the holy influences of God's Spirit were not only great, at his first conversion, but they were so, in a continued course, from that time forward: as appears by a record or private journal he kept of his daily inward exercises, from the time of his conversion until he was disabled by the failing of his strength, a few days before his death. The change which he looked upon as his conversion, was not only a great change of the present views, affections, and frame of his mind, but was evidently the beginning of that work of God on his heart, which God carried on in a very wonderful manner, from that time to his dying day. He greatly abhorred the way of such as live on their first work, as though they had now got through their work, and are thenceforward, by degrees, settled in a cold, lifeless, negligent, worldly frame. He had an ill opinion of such persons' religion."

JOHN BLAIR.*

1742—1771.

JOHN BLAIR was born in Ireland in the year 1720. He was a younger brother of the Rev. Samuel Blair, and like him was an alumnus of the Log College, and a pupil of the elder William Tennent. He was licensed to preach by the New Side Presbytery of Newcastle, and was ordained, December 27, 1742, pastor of Middle Spring, Rocky Spring, and Big Spring, in Cumberland County, Pa. During his ministry here, he made two visits to Virginia,—the last in 1746,—preaching with great power in various places, organizing several new congregations, and leaving an enduring impression of his piety and eloquence. As he had his residence in a frontier settlement, exposed to the hostile incursions of the Indians, he found it necessary, after a while, to retreat into the more populous and civilized part of the Colony. Accordingly, he resigned his pastoral charge on the 28th of December, 1748; and he seems to have remained without a settlement till 1757, when he accepted a call from the church at Fagg's Manor, which had been rendered vacant by the death of his brother. Here he continued nearly ten years; and succeeded his brother not only as pastor of the church, but as head of the school which his brother had established. In this latter capacity, he assisted in the preparation of many young men for the ministry.

* Hist. Log Coll.—Webster's MSS.

As New Jersey College was originally founded for the specific purpose of training young men for the sacred office, the classical and theological schools, both at Neshaminy and Nottingham, were given up, after the College had gone into operation; though the latter school was continued until Dr. Finley was chosen President of the College. In 1767, shortly after Dr. Finley's death,—a sum of money having been left for the support of the Professor of Divinity in Nassau Hall, Mr. Blair was elected to that Professorship. He accepted the appointment and removed to Princeton. He was also appointed Vice President of the College, and was its acting President, until Dr. Witherspoon, who had been previously appointed to the Presidency, arrived to enter on the duties of his office.

As the funds of the College proved inadequate to the support of a Theological Professor, and as Dr. Witherspoon was both able and willing to discharge the duties of that office, in connection with those of the Presidency, it was deemed expedient that a distinct Professorship of Divinity should not be continued. Accordingly, Mr. Blair resigned his office as Professor, in 1769, and accepted a call from the Presbyterian congregation of Walkill, Orange County, N. Y., on the 19th of May of that year. Here he continued his labours as a pastor, until his death, which occurred on the 8th of December, 1771, when he was about fifty-one years of age.

During the excitement growing out of the question concerning the examination of candidates on their experience of saving grace, one of the Old Side published "Thoughts on the examination and trials of candidates." On this pamphlet Mr. Blair published "Animadversions," dated "Fagg's Manor, August 27, 1766. He published also a Sermon entitled "The new creature delineated," 1767; a Reply to Harker's* Appeal to the Christian world, entitled "The Synod of New York and Philadelphia vindicated;" a Treatise on Regeneration, which is thoroughly Calvinistic, and marked by no inconsiderable ability; and a Treatise on the Scriptural Terms of admission to the Lord's Supper,—in which he maintains that ministers and church officers have no more authority to debar those who desire to attend, from the Lord's table, than from any other duty of God's worship. This latter Treatise was republished in a small selection of Treatises on the Lord's Supper, by the late Rev. Dr. J. P. Wilson of Philadelphia.

The following testimony in respect to the character of Mr. Blair is from a writer in the Assembly's Magazine:—

* SAMUEL HARKER (or *Harcour* as the name is sometimes spelt in the New Brunswick Records,) is supposed to have been of Huguenot extraction. He was taken under the care of the New Brunswick Presbytery, December 6, 1749; was licensed to preach November 6, 1751; and was ordained at Roxbury, Morris County, N. J., October 31, 1752. In October, 1757, the Presbytery heard that he had imbibed and was propagating certain erroneous doctrines, and were about to proceed against him, when they learned that he had left his charge, and gone as a Captain in the army. In May following, they brought the matter before the Synod, who appointed a committee "to deal with him as shall appear to them most suitable for his conviction." The result was that the committee were satisfied that his sentiments were not essentially wrong, though they were incautiously expressed, verging somewhat towards Arminianism; but they could not convince him that even his mode of expression was not entirely correct. The Synod appointed another committee to confer with him, but no satisfaction was obtained by the conference. Having committed his views to writing, he asked the Synod, in 1761, to read the paper he had prepared, which they refused to do, at the same time expressing their disapprobation of some of his opinions. He published, shortly after this, what he had written, and, in 1763, the Synod condemned portions of it, and declared him "disqualified for preaching or exercising his ministry any where." Mr. Harker was married to Rachel Lovel, daughter of a French Protestant, residing at Oyster Bay, L. I. One of his daughters was married to Dr. Caldwell of Lamington, who, dying early, left her with an infant, who became the Rev. Dr. Joseph Caldwell, President of the University of North Carolina. Another daughter married Judge Symmes of Marietta, Ohio.

"He was a judicious and persuasive preacher, and through his exertions sinners were converted and the children of God edified. Fully convinced of the truth of the doctrines of grace, he addressed immortal souls with that warmth and power which left a witness in every bosom. Though he sometimes wrote his sermons in full, yet his common mode of preaching was by short notes, comprising the general outlines. His labours were too abundant to admit of more; and no more was necessary to a mind so richly stored with the great truths of religion. For his large family he amassed no fortune; but he left them what was infinitely better,—a religious education, a holy example, and prayers which have been remarkably answered. His disposition was uncommonly patient, placid, benevolent, disinterested and cheerful. He was too mild to indulge bitterness or severity; and he thought that the truth required little else but to be fairly stated and properly understood. Those who could not relish the savour of his piety, loved him as an amiable, and revered him as a great, man. Though no bigot, he firmly believed that the Presbyterian form of government is most scriptural, and the most favourable to religion and happiness.

"In his last sickness, he imparted his advice to the congregation, and represented to his family the necessity of an interest in Christ. A few nights before he died, he said,—'Directly I am going to glory—my Master calls me, I must be gone.'"

Dr. Alexander expresses the opinion that Mr. Blair, "as a theologian, was not inferior to any man in the Presbyterian Church in his day."

Mr. Blair was married to a daughter of John Durburrow of Philadelphia. He had one son, *John Durburrow*, who is elsewhere noticed in this work, and another, *William Lawrence*, who was graduated at Princeton, became a lawyer, and settled in Kentucky. His daughter, *Rebecca*, became the wife of the Rev. Dr. William Linn, of the Reformed Dutch Church in the city of New York.

CHARLES BEATTY.*

1742—1772.

CHARLES BEATTY was born in the County of Antrim, Ireland, about the year 1715. His father, John Beatty, was also a native of Ireland, of the Scotch-Irish stock, and was an officer in the British army. His mother, whose maiden name was Christiana Clinton, was of English descent,—the family having removed from England to the County of Longford, during the great rebellion, in consequence of being attached to the Royalists. She was a sister of Charles Clinton, the father of George Clinton, who was successively General in the army of the Revolution, Governor of the State of New York, and Vice President of the United States. Having lost his father at an early age, his mother, with her brother Charles and several other relatives and friends, resolved to find a home in America. They were Presbyterians, and it is said that they were influenced in their emigration by religious considerations. They embarked for Philadelphia in the latter end of May, 1729, but, owing to some adverse circumstances, did not arrive until the month of October, when they were landed at Cape Cod. For several days before they landed, they were reduced to half a biscuit, and half a pint of water, for twenty-four hours. Several of the passengers, and among them a sister of the subject of this sketch, perished from famine. It was supposed that the Captain had been bribed thus to subject them to privation and hardship, with a view to discourage emigration. Cape Cod was the first land they discovered on the American coast, and there they

* Miller's Life of Rodgers.—Presb. Mag., II.—Smith's Old Redstone.—Webster's MSS.—MS. from Rev. Charles Beatty, D. D.

prevailed on the Captain, by offering him a pretty large pecuniary consideration, to land them.

Young Beatty, before leaving his native country, had enjoyed the advantages of a good classical school, and had acquired a very competent knowledge of the languages. He had also had the benefit of an excellent religious training, under which he had become established in the ways of virtue and piety. And he was withal very respectably connected. But he was far from being rich in this world's goods. He was a merchant on a very humble scale, and used sometimes to carry his goods for sale about the country. On one of these excursions, he stopped at the Log College, then under the care of the elder William Tennent. In the course of the conversation, Mr. Tennent discovered, much to his surprise, that the young man was well acquainted with Latin, besides having otherwise a good education; and when, in addition to this, he found that he manifested a spirit of fervent piety, and a good degree of religious knowledge, he proposed to him to quit the employment in which he was engaged, and enter on a course of study preparatory to the ministry. The advice, thus given, was duly heeded; and young Beatty, having disposed of his articles of merchandise, returned to the Log College, and prosecuted his studies under the venerable man who had thus interested himself in his behalf, and whom he afterwards succeeded in the pastoral office.

At the time he commenced his studies, the Presbyterian Church was agitated by the differences respecting the examination of candidates on experimental religion, and some other matters, which resulted in the division of the body. The influence of the Log College was all on the strict side. Mr. Tennent's great object was to promote the purity of the Church, and to form a spiritual and earnest ministry; and Mr. Beatty sympathized fully with the spirit and aims of his revered instructer.

He was licensed to preach the Gospel on the 13th of October, 1742, by the Presbytery of New Brunswick, which took the lead on the New Side, and which had withdrawn from the Synod two years before. He was sent first to preach at Nottingham; but as Mr. Tennent's increasing infirmities led him, about this time, to seek a release from his pastoral charge, Mr. Beatty was called to succeed him, at the Forks of Neshaminy, on the 26th of May, 1743; and was ordained and installed there on the 14th of December following,—on which occasion Gilbert Tennent preached, and his father sat in Presbytery for the last time.

Mr. Beatty's labours at Neshaminy commenced under somewhat inauspicious circumstances. To a portion of the church Mr. Tennent's ministry, as well as the not infrequent services of his zealous friends, had become distasteful; while Mr. McHenry* of Philadelphia, who had been for several years employed as an occasional assistant to Mr. Tennent, and whose views on some of the great questions of the day seem to have differed materially from his, had become a favourite with them. From this portion of the church, as well as from the church at Deep Run, Mr. M. received a call, and was installed as pastor of the two churches, March 16, 1743. Though

* FRANCIS MCHENRY emigrated from Ireland to this country. He appeared before the Philadelphia Presbytery, November 10, 1737, with recommendations from the Monaghan Presbytery in Ireland, and was examined and licensed on the same day. In May, 1742, he was called to the church at Nottingham, but, though he supplied them for a season, he declined their call. In the spring of 1750, he spent eight weeks as a missionary in Virginia. He died in 1757.

this state of things could not have been otherwise than embarrassing and painful to Mr. Beatty, he seems to have met it with great prudence and dignity, and his labours, then as well as afterwards, were attended with a manifest blessing.

Mr. Beatty possessed a large measure of the missionary spirit, and sympathized most freely with David Brainerd in his efforts to evangelize the Indians. When Brainerd visited Philadelphia in 1745, to confer with the Governor on business connected with his mission, President Edwards says—"In his journey to and from thence, he lodged with Mr. Beatty, a young Presbyterian minister. He speaks of seasons of sweet spiritual refreshment, which he enjoyed at his lodgings." In June, 1745, there occurred a memorable Communion season at Mr. Beatty's church, in which Brainerd participated, and of which he has left in his journal a minute and highly interesting record. When Brainerd's health failed in 1746, and he was about to leave New Jersey, Mr. Beatty was one of the friends who came to bid him farewell.

Mr. Beatty was a punctual attendant on the judicatories of the church. He attended the first meeting of the Synod of New York, at Elizabethtown, in 1745, when Jonathan Dickinson was chosen Moderator, and the first meeting of the united Synods of Philadelphia and New York, at Phildelphia, in 1758, of which Gilbert Tennent was Moderator. His name is omitted on the Synodical Records, only in the years 1760–61 and 1768–69, when he was in England, or elsewhere engaged in public services.

On the 24th of June, 1746, he was married to Anne, daughter of John Reading, President of the Council of New Jersey, and afterwards Governor of the Province.

In 1754, he was appointed, with Mr. Bostwick and others, to make a missionary tour of three months in Virginia and North Carolina. He fulfilled this appointment, and reported accordingly to the Synod at their next meeting.

In 1755,—having been invited to become Chaplain, for a season, to the Pennsylvania troops that were about to be sent under the command of Dr. Franklin, to defend the North-western frontiers of the State, after the burning of the Moravian missionaries at Guandenhuetten, near Lehighton,—he asked the Synod's advice on the subject, and they decided in favour of his acceptance of the invitation, and at the same time appointed a supply for his pulpit during his absence. In respect to that campaign, Franklin makes the following rather amusing record:—

"We had for our Chaplain a zealous Presbyterian minister, Mr. Beatty, who complained to me that the men did not generally attend his prayers and exhortations. When they enlisted, they were promised, besides pay and provisions, a gill of rum a day, which was punctually served out to them, half in the morning and half in the evening; and I observed they were punctual in attending to receive it: upon which I said to Mr. Beatty—'It is perhaps below the dignity of your profession to act as steward of the rum; but if you were to distribute it out only just after prayers, you would have them all about you.' He liked the thought, undertook the task, and with the help of a few hands to measure out the liquor, executed it to satisfaction, and never were prayers more generally and more punctually attended. So that I think this method preferable to the punishment inflicted by some military laws for non-attendance on Divine service.

After the union of the two Synods, in 1758, measures were taken to establish "the fund for the relief of poor Presbyterian ministers, and ministers' widows and their children." Mr. Beatty was placed on the committee to digest a plan for its regulation and management,—the other members being Dr. Alison, Gilbert Tennent, Samuel Finley, and John Blair. In 1760, he was appointed by the Synod to go to England to solicit contributions in aid of this fund. He was very successful in executing the commission. He witnessed the coronation of George III., was presented at Court, and received a handsome donation from his Majesty for the fund. He visited Holland before his return.

In 1763, he was commissioned, with the Rev. John Brainerd, by the Synod, to take a missionary tour into the destitute frontier settlements. But the Indian war breaking out in Western Pennsylvania about that time prevented him from fulfilling the appointment.

In 1764, he was chosen Moderator of the Synod, and opened its next meeting with a Sermon from Titus iii. 8.

In 1766, the Synod again took up the subject of sending a mission to explore the frontier settlements, and to ascertain the condition of the Indian tribes. Messrs. Beatty and Duffield were appointed on the expedition. Mr. Beatty left Philadelphia on the 12th of August, 1766, and on the 4th day reached Carlisle, where Mr. Duffield was settled. It was then arranged that Mr. Beatty should go and preach to the destitute settlements on the Juniata, whilst Mr. Duffield should explore Path Valley, Fanet, and the Cove. They met on the 29th at Fort Littleton, and then proceeded to Pittsburg, where they arrived on the 5th of September. After remaining here a few days, and preaching with considerable effect, they passed on to the Indian town called Kighalampegha on the Muskingum, where the Chief of the Delaware tribe lived. They set out on their return on the 24th of September, and Mr. Beatty reached Neshaminy on the 15th of the next month. At the next meeting of the Synod, they report that

"They performed their mission to the frontiers and among the Indians;—that they found on the frontiers numbers of people earnestly desirous of forming themselves into congregations, and declaring their willingness to exert their utmost in order to have the Gospel among them, but in circumstances exceedingly distressing and necessitous, from the late calamities of the war in these parts; that they visited the Indians at the chief town of the Delaware nation, on the Muskingum, about one hundred and thirty miles beyond Fort Pitt, and were received much more cheerfully than they could have expected;—that a considerable number of them waited on the preaching of the Gospel with peculiar attention, many of them appearing solemnly concerned about the great matters of religion;—that they expressed an earnest desire of having further opportunities of hearing those things;—that they informed them that several other tribes of Indians around them were ready to join with them in receiving the Gospel, and earnestly desiring an opportunity—upon the whole, that there does appear a very agreeable prospect of a door opening for the Gospel being spread among those poor benighted savage tribes."

In the autumn of 1767, Mr. Beatty crossed the ocean, a second time, with a view to obtain the best medical aid in the case of his wife, who was afflicted with a cancer. She, however, died at Greenock, to which port the vessel was bound,—shortly after their arrival.

Mr. Beatty's last public service was in behalf of the College of New Jersey. He had been appointed one of its Trustees in 1763, and had ever evinced a deep interest in its welfare. The College being greatly in need of funds, he consented to visit the West Indies in its behalf; but soon after reaching the Island of Barbadoes, he took the yellow fever, which almost immediately terminated his life. He died at Bridgeton, on the 13th of August, 1772.

Mr. Beatty published a Sermon entitled "Double honour due to the laborious Gospel minister," preached at the ordination of the Rev. William

Ramsey,* 1756; the Journal of a two months tour among the frontier inhabitants of Pennsylvania, 1768; a Letter to the Rev. John Erskine, D. D., in which the theory that the Indians are the descendants of the Ten Tribes is maintained by a variety of arguments; and Further Remarks respecting Indian affairs, containing an historical account of what has been done for the Indians in America.

Mr. Beatty was the father of eleven children, eight of whom reached mature life. His four elder sons served their country in the army of the Revolution. *John* was graduated at Princeton in 1772, and studied medicine, but, early in the war, raised a company, was taken prisoner at Fort Lee, and, after his exchange, succeeded Dr. Boudinot as Commissary General of Prisoners. He resided principally at Trenton, N. J., where he was a ruling elder in the Presbyterian Church. He was a member of Congress from 1783 to 1785, and from 1793 to 1795. He died in May 1826. *Charles Clinton*, the second son, was graduated at Princeton in 1775, and, instead of entering the ministry, as he had intended, entered the army, and was accidentally shot by a brother officer in October, 1776. *Reading*, the third son, was studying medicine with his eldest brother, when the war commenced, and received an Ensign's commission in his brother's company. He was taken prisoner at Fort Lee, and, during two years' captivity, continued his studies, and afterwards was Surgeon till the close of the war. He was, for many years, an elder in the church at Newtown, Pa., and died in October, 1831. *Erkuries*, the fourth son, was preparing for College when the war broke out, and he immediately entered the army, in which he continued till 1793. He was in many engagements, and was severely wounded at Germantown. He afterwards resided at Princeton, N. J., where he died February 3, 1823. The Rev. Charles C. Beatty, D. D. of Steubenville, O., is his son, and only living descendant. Mr. Beatty's fifth son, *George*, entered the navy, and was lost at sea.

FROM THE REV. CHARLES C. BEATTY, D. D.

STEUBENVILLE, Ohio, February 21, 1857.

Dear Brother: As my grandfather has been dead nearly a hundred years, the knowledge that I have concerning him is chiefly traditional. Accounts agree in representing him as a minister of great activity, enterprise, and industry, both in his own congregation, and as a missionary through the churches; often visiting and preaching in distant vacant places, and bringing their cases before the judicatories of the Church. He seems to have been a very constant attendant on these judicatories, and to have been appointed on many and important committees. Almost always was he on the committee on the College of New Jersey;

* WILLIAM RAMSEY was the son of James Ramsey,—an excellent man, who emigrated from Ireland; and a brother of Dr. David Ramsey of South Carolina, the distinguished historian. He was born in Lancaster County, Pa.; was graduated at the College of New Jersey in 1754; and, while preparing for the ministry, was selected as a suitable person to unite the congregation in Fairfield, N. J., then in a divided state. From considerations of expediency, bearing on the peculiar state of the congregation, he went to Connecticut, and was licensed by the Association of the Eastern district of Fairfield County. He was received by the Abington Presbytery, May 11, 1756, and was ordained and installed at Fairfield, on the 1st of December following. He was married to Sarah Sealy of Cohanzy. He died November 5, 1771, aged thirty-nine; and a glowing Eulogy was pronounced upon him by his brother-in-law, Dr. Jonathan Elmer, which was published. The inscription upon his monument is—"Beneath this stone lie interred the remains of the Rev. William Ramsey, M. A., for sixteen years a faithful pastor of the Presbyterian Church in this place, whose superior genius and native eloquence shone so conspicuously in the pulpit, as to command the attention and gain the esteem of all his hearers. In every situation of life he discharged his duty faithfully. He lived greatly respected, and died universally lamented."

on the missions to the Indians; on the funds of the Church; and other various business,—as appears from the Records of Synod. The esteem in which he was held by his brethren for zeal, fidelity, and ability, appears from his being entrusted with the most important and delicate interests of the Church.

He was a warm friend of his country and its liberties, and being also of a martial spirit, which he inherited from his father, and communicated to his children, he was their appointed Chaplain to the Provincial forces raised for the defence of the frontiers. On one of these occasions, the following incident is said to have occurred:—A recruiting officer had been sent to his neighbourhood. After some time, Mr. Beatty met him, and asked after his success—when he was informed that he was greatly discouraged, as very few seemed willing to engage for the service. I am sorry to hear it, said Mr. Beatty—it ought not to be so,—but what is to be done? Then he asked the officer if he should be at church on the next day, which was the Sabbath, and was answered in the affirmative. The next day, at the close of the exercises, he said to his congregation,—" The savages have attacked the frontier settlements and are murdering our fellow citizens. The Governor has made a call for volunteers to march with a view to resist and drive them back, but I regret to learn that it is not very promptly met. It is certainly somebody's duty to go; and I have determined, if the Presbytery allows me, to offer my services as Chaplain, and thus do my part. Of course it will be very pleasant for me to have the company of any of the congregation, or my neighbours, who may feel it their duty to go." The result was that, during the next week, the recruiting officer was able to enrol about a hundred volunteers from that vicinity. A passport, which he received a few years after, from Governor Penn of Pennsylvania, commences thus:—" Whereas the Rev. Mr. Charles Beatty hath informed me that he proposes to go on a voyage to the West India Islands, in order to solicit benefactions for a public seminary of learning, in a neighbouring Province, and hath requested my passport and recommendation—these are to certify that the said Mr. Beatty hath resided many years in this Province, within a few miles of this city, and during the last war, from a spirit of loyalty and love to his country, he exposed himself to great dangers as a volunteer, and served in the capacity of Chaplain to the Provincial forces, and that he is a minister of undoubted reputation for integrity, candour, and moderation; Now, &c." This was dated April 14, 1772; and similar language is used by Governor Franklin of New Jersey, in a like document.

It is about thirty-five years ago that, after preaching in a small vacant church in the North part of Bucks County, Pa.,—having been invited to the house of an aged member, he made to me the following remarks:—" The first sermon I ever heard in America, was from the Rev. Charles Beatty of Neshaminy—the last I have heard, is from his grandson of the same name. I landed at Philadelphia, a youth of twenty years of age, and, having some relatives in Neshaminy, went immediately there. The day after my arrival was the Sabbath, and I went with my friends to hear Mr. Beatty preach. He was greatly esteemed by his congregation. When he came into the church, I observed that he stopped and spoke to several persons on his way to the pulpit, and learned afterwards that this was his custom,—to enquire where there was sickness, or any particular circumstances, so that he might offer prayer for the especial case. He was a very lively and animated speaker, used no notes, and his eye was passing constantly and searchingly over every part of the assembly. It was said that he could thus detect at once the absence of any of his congregation, or the presence of any stranger. Of the latter fact I had some knowledge: for, immediately after the close of the service, he came up to me, and said,—" Young man, I perceive you are a stranger in these parts." I told him that I had just arrived from Ireland. " You have done well," said he—" this is a better country for you; and if you are industrious, steady, and God-fearing, you cannot but succeed here." This was about fifty-five years ago, and I never saw him again,—having soon after left that neighbourhood; but I have not forgotten his manner and words, and the impression they made upon me. Being desirous of hearing his grandson, I have come out with difficulty, and may never hear another sermon. It so happened that he never was out again, and died not long after.

Mr. Beatty seems usually to have made his preparations for the pulpit without writing, as no manuscript sermons have been found among his papers; yet he was one of the most popular preachers of his day, though not probably a profound theologian. The daughter of Dr. Sproat of Philadelphia said that no minister, who assisted her father, was more universally acceptable than Mr. Beatty, both to that congregation and to others, and that her father was always pleased to have his services among them.

Mr. Beatty was particularly desirous that his children should have the best education which the times and the country afforded, and his training of them at home was of the most thorough kind, both intellectual and religious. All felt the impress of his character upon them in their future lives. At his death, he left to his children a considerable estate, which was almost entirely evaporated in the subsequent depreciation of continental money, so that none of them derived much benefit from their patrimony.

Very truly and affectionately yours,

CHARLES C. BEATTY.

JAMES SPROAT, D. D.*

1743—1793.

JAMES SPROAT was born at Scituate, Mass., April 11, 1722. He was graduated at Yale College in 1741, in the same class with Governor William Livingston of New Jersey, Dr. Samuel Hopkins of Newport, and Dr. Buell of Long Island. He entered College, careless of his immortal interests, and continued so during the greater part of his course; but, some little time before he graduated, Gilbert Tennent, on his memorable tour through New England, visited New Haven, and preached in a manner that, by the blessing of God, gave a new direction to his thoughts and feelings, and changed the entire complexion of his life. Tennent was afterwards settled in Philadelphia, and Mr. Sproat became his successor. It was a noticeable providence that Tennent, in preaching a sermon, in a part of the country remote from his residence, and to an audience who were all or nearly all strangers to him, should have been instrumental of the conversion of an individual, who was destined to enter into his labours, after he had himself entered into his rest.

Having gone through the requisite course of preparation for the ministry, he was licensed to preach, and soon received a call to settle in the Fourth Congregational Church in Guilford, Conn. He accepted the call, and was ordained August 23, 1743. Here he laboured with great zeal, popularity, and success, for about twenty-five years. After the death of Mr. Tennent, the church in Philadelphia, of which he had been pastor,—as has been

* Green's Fun. Serm.—Assemb. Miss. Mag. I.—Allen's Biog. Dict.—Mass. Hist. Coll. X.—Original Letters and Diary of Dr. Sproat.

already intimated,—directed their attention towards Mr Sproat, as a suitable person to be his successor; and, accordingly, in October, 1768, he resigned his charge at Guilford, and, shortly after, was installed over the church to which he had been called. He continued sole pastor till 1787, when he was relieved from a portion of his labours by the settlement of Mr. (afterwards Dr.) Ashbel Green.

In 1780, the degree of Doctor of Divinity was conferred upon him by the College of New Jersey.

The year 1793 was signalized by the prevalence of the yellow fever in Philadelphia, in its most malignant form, and to an appalling extent. The family of Dr. Sproat was almost annihilated by it. Himself, his wife, his eldest son and *his* wife, and his youngest daughter, became its victims. He remained in the city, ministering to the dying and the afflicted, as far as his waning strength would permit, until the disease attacked him in all its virulence. I find among my papers the following letter to his son *John*, who was then absent from home, dated "Friday, October 11th, one o'clock P. M."—just one week before his own death. From a postscript added by his daughter, it appears that the fever was upon him at that time.

"Dear John: Your poor old trembling father must be the sorrowful messenger of grief upon grief to you. Your brother William is no more—he departed this life about ten o'clock this morning, I trust for a better. I was there when he died. I shall attend his remains to his lonely house, the grave, at six o'clock. Your sister Olive has been with him all the time of his sickness, night and day. Poor creature,—God has hitherto supported her, and I pray He may still. Maria, very sick, knows not of her husband's death: there are some hopes of her. Your mother, exceedingly feeble, has not been able to see her son. I am so myself, but have seen him twice a day. His child is at our house with a nurse. We are all dying in the city daily. The Lord prepare us. Oh, my son, you have often heard the necessity of repentance towards God, and faith towards the Lord Jesus Christ. Now, now, it is abundantly necessary. Oh, pray for it; turn all your attention to it. What is the world and all the things in it, to an interest in Christ and his great salvation! The Lord have mercy on you all. Pray, pray for yourself, and pray for us. You'll stay where you are, and may God preserve you. JAMES SPROAT."

On the 23d of August preceding the date of this letter, he completed half a century as an ordained minister; and, from that period, he had seemed to be living in constant expectation of death, and a large portion of his waking hours were spent in private devotional exercises. His domestic afflictions, severe as they were, he endured without the least repining. At the funeral of his son, whose death is referred to in the above letter, he evinced the very sublimity of Christian mourning. Trembling with age, with disease already fastened upon him, he followed the corpse of his beloved son to the grave, and, after it was deposited, leaning on his staff, he pronounced only these words,—"The Lord gave, and the Lord hath taken away, blessed be the name of the Lord, Amen." His own death took place on the 18th of October, 1793, in the seventy-second year of his age. He continued in possession of his mental faculties to the last. After he had lost the power of speech, he was asked if he still experienced the sustaining influences of the Gospel, and he answered affirmatively, by lifting up his hand and his eyes to Heaven.

There were the most substantial demonstrations of grief in connection with his funeral. The more common mode of conveying a corpse to the grave, during the ravages of the pestilence, was on a cart,—sometimes on a hearse; and the attendants consisted only of the person who drove the carriage, the grave digger, and, in a few instances, two or three mourning friends. But, in the case of Dr. Sproat, the people who had met at the church for prayer, formed a procession of about fifty persons, and some pious negroes voluntarily offered to carry the bier.

Dr. Sproat's colleague, Dr. Green, was absent from the city at the time of his death; but, immediately on his return, he preached a Funeral Sermon, from Psalm cxvi. 15, which was published.

Dr. Green, in the sermon above referred to, thus describes the character of his venerable colleague:—

"In his natural temper, he used often to tell me that he was easily susceptible of passion. If it was so, it is certain that, like the sage of antiquity,* *he was remarkable for his victory over it*, and for those virtues which are its opposites. Patience, moderation, indulgence, and forbearance, were leading features in his general character. Meekness and affection distinguished him highly. Not only in the near relations of husband, father, and master, did they render him most dear and exemplary, but in all his intercourse with the world they shone out in the mildest and most amiable light. His candour, charity, and tenderness appeared on all occasions, and gained him, in a peculiar degree, the respect and affection of almost all descriptions of persons. He was free from all disguise. He was 'an Israelite indeed, in whom there was no guile.' You saw, at once, the man you would always see. Such a man was peculiarly formed for lasting friendship and unreserved confidence. They could scarcely be avoided by one who was often with him. Between him and myself, therefore, they subsisted in a manner which fills me with a mournful pleasure to recollect, and the loss of which I most sensibly realize and deplore. In a collegiate charge of nearly seven years, not one cold, or distant, or formal word ever passed between us; not the slightest alienation interrupted our harmony. On all occasions, he treated me like a father, and like a father, I can truly say, I loved and honoured him. His usual appellation in addressing me was, 'my son:'—and had I been his son by the ties of nature, as well as in the bonds of the Gospel, he could scarcely have treated me with more affection, or more sincerely regarded my interest as his own. * * * * * *

"In scholastic attainments he was a good proficient. Of those which are denominated the learned languages, he was a considerable master. He loved all the pursuits and interests of science; and I have heard him lament that his urgent calls to active service in early life left him so little time to become accurate in some of the departments of literature.

"In the study of Divinity he had made a progress that was truly great and enviable. It was his delight, and he pursued it incessantly. A man has seldom been seen, who had a more complete knowledge or a more familiar acquaintance with the Holy Scriptures. His great readiness in quoting and applying them in a pertinent manner, in his public addresses, you have all observed, and many of you, I trust, will remember as the means of your spiritual edification. He had made deep researches into systematic, casuistic and polemic Divinity. On these subjects he read much in some of the last years of his life. 'My own sentiments,' said he, 'in regard to the essentials of religion, I believe, are fixed. But I find much entertainment, and I think some advantage, in reading books of this description.'

"In his discourses from the pulpit, he loved to dwell on the fundamental and peculiar doctrines of the Gospel, which he regarded as a system of pure grace and mercy, abasing the sinner to the dust, and exalting God in the highest. When the train of his address led him to speak on the experimental part of religion, he was excellent and edifying in a singular degree. * * * * His public prayers were remarkable for a vein of piety and fervour seldom equalled. He had a certain copiousness of expression and engagedness of manner in this Divine service, which could arise from no other source than the familiar intercourse of his own soul with Heaven.

"In his personal religion he was truly eminent. His life and example exhibited a most amiable view of the influence and efficacy of the Gospel principles on the human heart and character. Unfeigned humility,—that ornament of every other grace, had become a habit of his soul, and appeared in all his deportment. Having studied long and made great proficiency in the School of Christ, he had learned the hard lesson of

* Socrates.

thinking in a very lowly manner of himself. His charity for others was uncommonly extensive. It led him to hope the best, where there was any probability on which hope could be founded. His faith was built on the sure foundations of the Gospel, and it supported him in the most trying hour. In some of his last moments he said, 'All my expectations for eternity rest on the infinite grace of God, abounding through the finished righteousness of the Lord Jesus Christ.'"

FROM THOMAS BRADFORD, Esq.

PHILADELPHIA, December 31, 1850.

Rev. and dear Sir: My reminiscences of the Rev. Dr. Sproat, concerning whom you inquire, have respect to a period when I was quite young, and of course are not very extended; but the little that I do remember concerning him, I am happy to communicate, in compliance with your request. My parents were both members of his congregation, and my mother a member of his church; and one of my early recollections of him is his coming to my father's house in the autumn of 1785, to officiate at the baptism of my youngest sister. At that day, it was common to administer the ordinance in private.

Dr. Sproat, as I remember him, was a venerable looking man. He always wore the wig and the cocked hat, according to the usage of aged ministers at that period. He possessed a benevolent countenance; his manners were gentle and courteous; his speech conciliating and kind, especially towards the youthful part of his flock, who were attracted to him by his paternal and affectionate treatment of them. He was accustomed to hear them say their Catechism; and if any one was not perfect in his lesson, instead of severely reproving him, he would gently lay his hand upon his head and say,—"Take care, my dear child, and get your lesson better next time." As the venerable man declined in strength and vigour, his preaching, of course, lost, in some degree, its interest, and the junior pastor, Mr. (afterwards Dr.) Ashbel Green, who was then in his early prime, became, especially to the younger part of the congregation, the chief object of attraction; and sometimes they even absented themselves from church in the afternoon, when it was known that Dr. Sproat was to occupy the pulpit. Some of the Doctor's friends indiscreetly alluded to this circumstance in conversation with him, by way of finding fault; but he mildly, and with the kindest spirit, replied,—"This is natural, and therefore not to be complained of: he must increase, but I must decrease."

I never knew of Dr. Sproat's publishing more than a single sermon, and that was one preached on the death of Whitefield, in October, 1770. It is highly evangelical in its character, and contains a lively and graphic delineation of Whitefield's prominent qualities. I will give you a brief extract from it:—

"Being a good man, full of the Holy Ghost and of faith, fired with a flaming zeal for his Lord and Master, filled with bowels of tenderness and compassion to immortal souls, and favoured with more than Ciceronian eloquence, he soon became the wonder of the world, as a preacher.

"As a speaker, he was furnished with such admirable talents, with such an easy method of address, and was such a perfect master of the art of persuasion, that he triumphed over the passions of the most crowded auditory with all the charms of sacred eloquence.

"Such were the impressions of the Eternal Majesty upon his mind, that he habitually lived as seeing Him who is invisible. He lived with a wise reference to futurity, and maintained a close walk with God. Prayer was his soul's delight. * * * Praise was an employment in which his soul was exceedingly delighted. In this exercise, he often appeared to anticipate the sacred pleasures of the upper world. His work was done, and we have good reason to believe it was well done. He lived long enough to perform an excellent part on this stage of action; to exemplify a life of virtue and piety; to sound the Gospel trumpet through almost the whole of the British empire; and to gather in a plentiful harvest of precious souls to the Redeemer, that shall be as so many sparkling diamonds in that untarnished crown of glory, which adorns his victorious brow. He lived God's time, which is the best time."

Regretting my inability to comply more fully with your request,

I remain your friend and brother in Christ,

THOMAS BRADFORD.

JOHN ROAN.*

1744—1775.

JOHN ROAN was born in Ireland, about the year 1716, and was brought up a weaver. He came to this country in his youth, and studied for some time at the Log College. He was licensed to preach by the "New Side" Presbytery of Newcastle. As early as 1741, he was engaged in teaching a grammar school on the Neshaminy; for Dr. Rodgers of New York (according to Dr. Miller) entered his school there that year, and continued in it several years afterwards.

In the winter of 1744, the Presbytery of Newcastle with which Mr. Roan was connected, sent him on a missionary tour to Virginia. He preached with great effect in Hanover, and the neighbouring counties; and many in different places were awakened and hopefully converted through his instrumentality. He was bold, energetic, earnest, but had less of caution and prudence than the peculiar circumstances in which he was placed, required. He inveighed against the clergy of the Established Church with great freedom, charging them not only with neglect of their official duties, but with gross moral delinquencies. His offensive statements and scathing satire quickly attracted the attention of the parish clergy and their friends; and they resolved that he should no longer be tolerated. Affidavits were laid before Governor Gooch, representing that this man was not only earnestly engaged in efforts at proselytism, but had actually been guilty of blasphemy. The matter came before the Grand Jury; and, after the Govcruor had delivered a vehement charge, they agreed to "present John Roan for reflecting upon and vilifying the Established Religion, in divers sermons, preached at the house of Joshua Morris in James City Parish, on the 7th, 8th, and 9th of January, before a numerous audience unlawfully assembled." Mr. Roan returned to Pennsylvania, before the meeting of the Court at which this charge was given. The charge was published, and an order forbidding any meetings of "Moravians, Muggletonians, and New Lights," was issued. The people of Hanover laid the case before the Synod of New York in May, 1745; and the Synod sent, by the hands of Messrs. Gilbert Tennent and Samuel Finley, an address to the Governor. These gentlemen were very graciously received by His Excellency, who readily granted them liberty to preach at Hanover. Before their arrival, the individual who had been chiefly instrumental in inflaming the government against Mr. Roan, and who was believed to have done it at the expense of perjuring himself, had fled never to return. The trial came on, on the

* Hodge's Hist. Presb. Ch.—Webster's MSS.

19th of October; but the six witnesses cited by the Attorney General, fully proved that he had uttered none of the expressions imputed to him, and the indictment was dropped.

In 1745, Mr. Roan was settled over the united congregations of Paxton, Derry, and Mountjoy. The union of the Synods placed him in Donegal Presbytery, and points of difference continually arose, which admitted of no concessions. The licensing of a young man by the name of William Edmeston was a trial of strength. He was a student of Sampson Smith,* and had been a prominent witness in his defence,—which was any thing else than a recommendation in the view of Roan; and, at the close of his examination for licensure, Roan expressed his dissatisfaction with what the majority had accepted as evidence of the young man's piety. Edmeston subsequently prosecuted Roan for various offences; the sum of which, however, was that he was a party and a principal mover in a conspiracy to destroy Smith by perjured or dishonest witnesses. The trial was protracted; trivial questions almost without number were asked; and the whole was apparently a matter of studied annoyance. In 1765, Edmeston appealed to the Synod, and the Presbytery also referred the case to them, and a large and respectable committee was appointed to determine the affair. The matter was finally dropped, and Edmeston went to England for holy orders.

Mr. Roan continued his labours with the congregations over which he was first placed, during the rest of his life. He informed the Presbytery, on one occasion, that his congregations were deeply indebted to him; and there is also a record of his having been sent as a missionary for eight weeks, to the South Branch of the Potomac. But the notices of him that remain are so few and scattered, that they only give us a clue to his character and his course.

He died on the 3d of October, 1775, aged fifty-nine years. He lies buried at Derry, beneath a stone that bears the following inscription:—"Beneath this stone are deposited the remains of an able and faithful, courageous and successful minister of Jesus Christ."

* SAMPSON SMITH came from Ireland, and was received by Donegal Presbytery, April 3, 1750. His ordination was reported to the Synod in 1752, and in the spring of that year, he spent eight Sabbaths in Virginia. He was settled at Chestnut Level, and was married to a daughter of the Rev. Adam Boyd of Octorora. He taught an Academy, for many years, with great success. The union of the Synods placed him in connection with the New Side ministers; and a charge of intemperance being preferred against him, he regarded them as the movers of it; while they viewed the Old Side men as determined to clear him, by excluding all the evidence on which the prosecution relied. The result was that he was acquitted; and the prosecution appealed to the Synod, who, by a committee, took up the whole matter *de novo*, and ultimately judged that he was worthy of at least a degree of censure. He withdrew from the Synod; joined the Newcastle Presbytery in 1768; and was suspended the next year, but was restored in 1771. The Synod then sent him to the South Branch of the Potomac for six months, and the next year for two months. His suspension was renewed in 1774, and was never removed. His death was in consequence of being struck by lightning.

[ADAM BOYD, mentioned above, was born at Bally-money, Ireland, in 1692. He came to New England as a probationer about 1723. He had formed a purpose to return to his native country, and with a view to this, had received from Cotton Mather a commendatory certificate, dated June 10, 1724. Having, however, formed an attachment to a young lady on this side the water, he subsequently changed his purpose, and determined to remain in this country. He was taken under the care of the Newcastle Presbytery in July, 1725, and in September following received a call from the congregations in Octorora and Pequea, Pa. This call he accepted, and in October following was ordained at Octorora. The Forks of Brandywine composed part of his field, till 1734. In the division of the Presbyterian Church, a large part of his congregation went to the New Side, and as his own sympathies were with the Old Side, he asked leave (August, 1741) to accept of an invitation given him by a fraction of the Brandywine Congregation, which adhered to the Old Side, and offered to pay for half his time. His relation to this part of his charge was dissolved (very irregularly according to his own statement) in 1758. He died on the 23d of November, 1768. On his tomb-stone is inscribed—"Forty-four years pastor of this church."]

DAVID BOSTWICK.*

1745—1763.

DAVID BOSTWICK was grandson to John Bostwick, who was of Scotch extraction, but came from Cheshire, England, to Stratford, Conn., about the year 1668, and subsequently removed, with a numerous family, to New Milford, of which he was one of the first settlers. The father of David Bostwick was Major John Bostwick, who was a deacon of the church, and was elected eighteen times (the elections being then semi-annual) as a Representative of the town to the General Assembly of the State. David was born at New Milford on the 8th of January, 1721. Dr. Miller, in his Life of Dr. Rodgers, states that, "at the age of fifteen, he entered Yale College, and graduated after the usual course of study." As, however, his name does not appear on the catalogue, it is presumed that this is partly a mistake: the Hon. David S. Boardman, who is a remote relative of Mr. Bostwick, after having explored every source of information on the subject, says,—"My belief is (and I have very little doubt of its correctness) that he was, for the greatest part of a college course, a member of Yale College; and that he finished his academical, and commenced and probably completed his theological, course, with a somewhat eminent Scotch scholar and divine in Southbury, (then part of Woodbury,) by the name of Graham. I am strengthened in this belief by the fact of Mr. Bostwick's having married a Miss Hinman of that place; with whom he probably became acquainted while a student." Previous to his engaging in the active duties of the ministry, he was, for some time, a teacher in an Academy at Newark, N. J., under the care of the Rev. (afterwards President) Aaron Burr. On the 9th of October, 1745, he was ordained to the work of the ministry, and installed pastor of the church in Jamaica, L. I. The Sermon on the occasion was preached by Mr. Burr, and was published. Here Mr. Bostwick remained more than ten years, in great repute, among not only his own people, but his brethren in the ministry, and the surrounding churches.

In July, 1755, the First Presbyterian Church in New York,—having become vacant by the removal of Mr. Cumming and Mr. Pemberton, who had been colleague pastors, gave a call to Mr. Bostwick, a member of their own Presbytery, to fill the vacancy. The people of Jamaica, who highly appreciated his character and services, strongly opposed his removal; and the church in New York being agitated with dissensions, especially on the subject of Church Psalmody, he was little predisposed to take a step that should put at hazard his own peace and comfort as a minister. The Presbytery, when the call was laid before them, referred the matter to the Synod, which was to meet in Newark in September following. The Synod appointed a committee to meet at Jamaica, a few weeks after, that they might deliberate on the subject under circumstances more favourable to their arriving at a correct conclusion. At the meeting of the committee, a memorial was presented from the elders, deacons, and trustees of the church in New York, earnestly praying that they would not only put the call into

* Smith's Hist. N. Y.—Miller's Life of Rodgers.—Preface to Bostwick's "Rational Vindication," &c.—MS. from Hon. D. S. Boardman.

Mr. Bostwick's hands, and encourage him to accept it, but that they would also take some measures for the settlement of the existing controversy in the congregation respecting the use of Watts' Psalms. The committee, however, were divided in regard to both the call and the question concerning Psalmody; and, instead of coming to any decision upon either, they determined to refer both questions to the regular Commission of Synod, which they requested the Moderator to convene without unnecessary loss of time. The Commission accordingly met at Princeton, on the 14th of April, 1756; when the call was put into Mr. Bostwick's hands; but, as he declared himself at a loss as to his duty in respect to it, the Commission, after having heard full representations on the subject from both New York and Jamaica, decided in favour of his removal to New York. Mr. Bostwick acquiesced in the decision; and his pastoral relation to the church of Jamaica was accordingly dissolved. He had previously, during his residence at Jamaica, rejected several calls from other churches; and he evidently went to New York, not without many misgivings and considerable reluctance.

Mr. Bostwick was installed shortly after, and about the same time removed his family to the city. But though he was unusually popular in the congregation, the controversy in respect to Psalmody was not quieted, and, after a few months, the brethren who were dissatisfied with the introduction of Watts, withdrew, and formed a distinct church, of which the Rev. (afterwards Dr.) John Mason became the pastor. This secession left the congregation in an harmonious state, and rendered Mr. Bostwick's labours far more easy and agreeable.

In 1760, Mr. Bostwick was laid aside for some time by ill health. Dr. Wheelock was then meditating the removal of his Indian School from Lebanon, and he wrote to Mr. Bostwick to enlist his aid in the enterprise. Mr. B. assured him of his good wishes on the subject, and promised him his aid, if he should ever have health enough to attempt any further labour; but he seemed to think that his health and even life were too uncertain to justify much reliance upon his efforts. After this, however, he so far regained his health, as to be able to attend to his ordinary pastoral duties.

In May, 1762, the Congregation purchased a parsonage, and gave the use of it to Mr. Bostwick, as an addition to his stated salary. As they had no charter, they were obliged to convey this property to certain individuals to be held in trust.

In the autumn of this year, (1762,) Mr. Bostwick being too feeble to discharge all the duties demanded of a pastor by so large a congregation, the Rev. Joseph Treat,* a member of the Presbytery of New Brunswick, was associated with him in his pastoral charge. But Mr. Bostwick's course was now nearly finished. He died after a severe illness of a few days, November 12, 1763, aged forty-three years.

He published a Sermon preached at Philadelphia before the Reverend Synod of New York, entitled "Self disclaimed and Christ exalted, 1758, which was reprinted in London, 1776; also "an Account of the life, charac-

* JOSEPH TREAT, was graduated at the College of New Jersey in 1757; was a Tutor in the College from 1758 to 1760; was licensed to preach by the Presbytery of New Brunswick in 1760; and retained his connection as pastor with the Presbyterian church in New York till 1784, when, in pursuance of an application to the Presbytery by the congregation, it was dissolved. In 1785, the Presbytery of New York report that they had, during the preceding year, dismissed Mr. Treat to the Presbytery of New Brunswick; but I find no further trace of him.

ter and death of President Davies," prefixed to Davies' Sermon on the death of George II, 1761. After his death, there was published from his manuscripts "A fair and rational Vindication of the Right of infants to the ordinance of Baptism; being the substance of several Discourses from Acts ii. 39." This Tract was reprinted in London, and a second American edition of it was printed in 1837.

The degree of Master of Arts was conferred on Mr. Bostwick by the College of New Jersey, in 1756; and he was one of the overseers of the same institution from 1761 till his death.

Mr. Bostwick had a numerous family of children,—four sons and six daughters, all of whom lived to adult years. One of his sons (*Andrew*) was a Colonel in the Revolutionary war. One of his daughters married General McDougall of the Continental army, and afterwards the Rev. Azel Roe; and another married General Roberdeau, a member of the old Congress from 1777 to 1779.

The Hon. David S. Boardman of New Milford, says of him—"His traditionary reputation as a preacher, as derived from the old people of this place, who occasionally heard him preach, when visiting his relations here, was very high."

The Hon. William Smith, in his History of New York, which was published in 1757, in speaking of Mr. Bostwick, says,—

"He is a gentleman of a mild, catholic disposition; and being a man of piety, prudence, and zeal, confines himself entirely to the proper business of his functions. In the art of preaching, he is one of the most distinguished clergymen in these parts. His discourses are methodical, sound and pathetic; in sentiment and in point of diction, singularly ornamented. He delivers himself without notes, and yet with great ease and fluency of expression; and performs every part of Divine worship with a striking solemnity."

The following notice of Mr. Bostwick's character is from the Preface to his Treatise on Baptism, which was published the year immediately succeeding his death. It is anonymous, but was evidently written by one who knew him well.—

"But though Mr. Bostwick's superior talents for the work of the ministry had spread his praises in the Gospel throughout these Western churches, yet he was personally known (comparatively) to but few; his fixed charge having always confined him within the verge of his incumbent duty, and his great humility and entire freedom from all ostentation ever concealed him as much from public view, as eminency of his station would permit. But as he is now no more, and some strictures of his person and character may be agreeable to many of the distant readers of this treatise, they may be pleased to take them briefly thus.

"As a man, he was something above middle stature, comely and well-set, his aspect grave and venerable; formed by nature with a clear understanding, quick apprehension, prompt elocution, and solid judgment; his imagination strong and lively, and his memory very tenacious. Of all these he gave the most convincing proofs, both in public and private life.

"He directed the course of his studies in a close and intimate subserviency to the great business of his profession. *En toutois isthi* [I Tim. iv. 15] might have been his motto. In Divinity his great strength lay. He had an admirable discerning of truth and error, in their causes, connections, and consequences; and believed and taught the pure doctrines of Christianity, as contained in the Holy Scriptures, and as declared in the public Confessions of the Reformed Churches, in their original and genuine meaning. He beheld his Bible with reverence, as the grand charter of life eternal. He knew it to be a revelation from God, and the most wonderful Book in the world. He saw its external and internal evidence, by Nature's light, aided by human learning, and by a special illumination from above. He beheld the majesty, glory, reality, and importance of the subject of it; discerning therein an admirable display of the infinite perfections of the Deity, with a perfect accommodation to the various states of man. He considered it not only as a system of Divine knowledge, but as revealing a practical and experimental discipline; and felt its vital energy, and had its truth sealed on his heart, with that kind of evidence, as would doubtless have stood the fire upon the severest trial.

"After this, I scarce need add that he was a divine of the old stamp, and could well defend his system against all gainsayers. In these things he was a scribe well instructed, and with great sagacity and penetration could discern the spirit of error in its most distant approaches. He knew its connections and tendencies, (ever aiming at God's dishonour or man's ruin,) and, therefore, as a faithful watchman, always gave the speediest warning of the danger.

"He had those gifts which rendered him a very popular preacher. With a strong, commanding voice, his pronunciation was clear, distinct and deliberate; his speech and gesture decent and natural, without any affectation; his language elegant and pure, but with studied plainness, never below the dignity of the pulpit, nor above the capacity of the meanest of his auditory. The strength of his memory and the flow of his elocution enabled him to preach without notes, but seldom or never extempore. He furnished the lamps of the sanctuary with beaten oil, and the matter and method of his sermons were well studied.

"In treating Divine subjects, he manifested an habitual reverence for the majesty of Heaven, a deep sense of the worth of souls, an intimate knowledge of the human heart and its various workings in its twofold state of nature and grace. He dealt faithfully with his hearers, declaring to them the whole counsel of God, shewing them their danger and remedy. And none will perish from under his ministry, but their blood must lie upon their own heads. He always spake from a deep sense of the truths he delivered, and declared those things which he had seen, and which he had heard, and his hands had handled of the word of life; and delivered nothing to his auditory but with a solemnity that discovered its importance.

"His mind had a poetic turn. His style was copious and florid. He sometimes soared, when his subject would admit of it, with an elevated wing, and his imagination enabled him to paint his scene, whatever it was, in very strong and lively colours. Few men could describe the hideous deformity of sin, the misery of men's apostacy from God, the wonders of redeeming love, the glory and riches of Divine grace, in stronger lines, and more affecting strains, than he.

"In the conduct of life, he was remarkably gentle towards all men, vastly prudent and cautious, and always behaved with the meekness of wisdom, and filled up every relation in life with its proper duty, and was a living example of the truth of that religion which he taught to others. He preached not himself, but Christ Jesus his Lord. In this view, his eye was single, and he regarded no other object. He knew in whose place he stood, and feared no man. He dared to flash the terrors of the law in the face of the stoutest transgressor, with the same freedom as he displayed the amiable beauties and glories of the Gospel for the comfort and refreshment of the penitent believer.

"As he highly honoured his Divine Master, he was highly favoured by Him, of which, take one instance.

"In a former illness, from which it was thought he could not recover, which happened some months before he died, he was greatly distressed by a deep concern for his widow and his great family on the event of his death. But God was pleased, in a time of great extremity, to grant him a glorious and astonishing view of his power, wisdom and goodness, and the riches of his grace, with a particular appropriation to himself and his, such as dispelled every fear, and at that time rendered him impatient to live; but, at length, on his recovery, which commenced immediately on the removal of this distress, his mind settled into a Divine calm. He perceived himself equally willing to live or die, as God pleased. In which temper he continued to his last moment, when placidly he resigned his soul and all his mortal interests, into the hands of his Saviour and his God. Such intercourse sometimes passes between the Father of Spirits and the human spirit, and such honour have they that fear God."

JACOB GREEN.*

1745—1790.

JACOB GREEN, a son of Jacob and Dorothy (Lynde) Green, was born at Malden, Mass., on the 22d of January, (O. S.) 1722. He lost his father when he was about a year and a half old, after which, his mother was married to John Barret, also a resident of Malden. When he had reached the age of about seven, his parents removed from Malden to Killingly, Conn., and he accompanied them. At fourteen, he chose a guardian, and was put out to a trade. Having lived about nine months with a Mr. Green of Killingly, and about a year with an uncle at Stoneham, and another year with another uncle at Malden, and having, from some peculiar circumstances, failed, in each case, of being bound out till he was twenty-one, it was proposed to him by a brother-in-law who had come from Connecticut, that he should endeavour to obtain a collegiate education. He caught eagerly at the idea; and an arrangement was soon made by which he could so far anticipate his patrimony, which lay in real estate, as to proceed at once to the accomplishment of his object. Just before he had completed his seventeenth year, he entered a grammar school, and pursued his studies till July, 1740, when he was admitted a member of Harvard College, at the age of eighteen and a half.

Under the influence of the excellent instructions and example of his mother, his mind was early directed to the subject of religion, and sometimes he had deeply serious feelings, and formed resolutions in favour of a religious life; but his evil propensities, aided by powerful temptations, prevailed over his better purposes; and his experience, for several years, was little better than a constant conflict between the power of conscience and the power of sin,—the latter, however, always gaining the victory. The clergyman, in whose family he resided, while he was fitting for College, having gathered from some incidental remark that fell from him, that he was not altogether indifferent to religion, came to him shortly after, and told him that he should propound him the next day for admission to the church; and though the young man was shocked at the suggestion,—not having at all contemplated such an act, he yielded to the proposal, and was actually received to Communion. He seems, for some time after, to have had little comfort in his religious exercises; and he ultimately had no doubt that, at that period, he was deceived in regard to his true character.

Not long after he entered College, Whitefield made his first visit to New England, and preached at Cambridge, among other places. Young Green heard him with wonder and delight, and he actually followed him, listening to his sermons, from place to place, as far as Leicester, where he left him, and went to visit his mother at Killingly. This was the last visit he paid to his mother, as she died in 1741. On his return to College, he found but little sympathy with his own religious feelings among the students, though about a dozen of them formed themselves into a religious society, and met once a week for devotional exercises. The state of things, however, soon underwent a great change; for, in January, 1741, Gilbert Tennent, whose

* Autobiography, &c., in the Christian Advocate, X.—Webster's MSS.

preaching tour through New England is one of the well known events of that period, came to Cambridge, and produced, by his ministrations, both in and out of the College, a most powerful religious excitement. Previous to this time, Mr. Green had allowed himself to hope that he had been the subject of a radical change; but, under the preaching of Tennent, he was led to account that experience as delusion. His exercises, for some time after this, were of the most awful and agonizing kind; but he was brought at length to repose in the mercy of God through Christ; and found great joy and peace in believing. His mind gradually settled into a calm and equable frame, though, from a portion of the record of his religious exercises which still remains, it seems to have been habitually in a high state of spirituality and devotion. And yet it is somewhat remarkable that, with all his glowing zeal, he had little disposition to take part in public religious exercises; and when he attempted it, he found, for the most part, neither freedom nor enjoyment.

He pursued his studies, during the whole of his college life, with most untiring diligence; and though he had an uncommonly vigorous constitution, it was considerably impaired by his excessive application and neglect of exercise. His studies, however, never interfered with his devotions—every thing else he regarded as subordinate to the cultivation of a spiritual mind. He was admitted to the degree of Bachelor of Arts in July, 1744. Among his classmates were Dr. Mayhew, Bishop Bass, and the Hon. Thomas Cushing, a distinguished statesman of the Revolution.

As his patrimony had been nearly or quite exhausted by his education, he found it necessary, on leaving College, to betake himself to some employment, as a means of support. Accordingly, he accepted an invitation to teach a school at Sutton, Mass., where he remained for nearly a year. Before the year had expired, he was earnestly solicited by some of his friends to commence preaching, and the committee of a vacant congregation actually applied for his services. He was not then licensed, nor at all predisposed to be; but that he might not mistake in respect to his duty, he determined to ask the advice of a minister in or near Boston, in whose judgment he had great confidence; and, on referring the matter to him, he was advised to defer entering the ministry till he had devoted a year or two to preparation for it. In this opinion he cordially acquiesced.

Having closed his school at Sutton, and being on a visit to his friends, waiting to know what might be the indications of Providence in respect to him, Whitefield, happening to pass through that part of the country, invited him to accompany him to Georgia, to take charge of his Orphan House. He accepted the invitation, and promised to meet Whitefield in New York, within about a month from that time, and proceed with him to his Southern destination. Accordingly, he followed him in due time, and overtook him at Elizabethtown, N. J., but was disappointed to learn from him that he had received letters from Georgia, informing him of the failure of certain subscriptions, in consequence of which he should not be able to manage the Orphan House as he had expected. He told him, however, that if he chose to go on with him, he would fulfil his agreement with him for half a year, or if he chose to stop, he would defray the expense of his journey thus far. Having consulted Mr. Dickinson, at whose house he found Whitefield, he determined, on the whole, to accept the latter side of the alternative; and then, by the advice of Mr. Dickinson, and Mr. Burr of Newark, he was induced to remain in that region, and receive license to preach. Accordingly, he was licensed in September, 1745, at Elizabethtown, and was immediately invited to preach at Hanover, Morris County. Here he preached a year on probation, received a call to settle, and was ordained and installed, in November, 1746. Some months previous to his ordination, he fell into deep spiritual darkness, and had, at one time, nearly determined to abandon the ministry, from a conscious unfitness to pursue it; but a conversation with Mr. Burr relieved him, in a good degree, of his apprehensions, and encouraged him to persevere in the work which he had undertaken.

In June, 1747, Mr. Green was married to Anna Strong of Brookhaven, L. I. She died of consumption in November, 1756. By this marriage he had four children. In October, 1757, he was married, a second time, to Elizabeth, daughter of the Rev. John Pierson of Woodbridge, N. J., and granddaughter of the Rev. Abraham Pierson, first President of Yale College. By this latter marriage he had six children,—one of whom was the Rev. Dr. Ashbel Green, President of the College of New Jersey. His second wife survived him many years, and died in August, 1810.

Mr. Green received but a slender support from his congregation, and, during the first twelve years of his ministry, kept himself, as far as possible, from being entangled with worldly cares. After that, feeling the necessity of making some provision for his family, he engaged, to some extent, in secular business,—chiefly in the practice of medicine, which he continued some thirty years. The physician and the minister he found little difficulty in uniting; but engagements of a more decidedly worldly character he considered as interfering with his ministerial comfort and usefulness.

In 1764, there was a powerful revival of religion in his congregation, which extended also to many other congregations in the region. A revival, still more powerful, occurred in 1774. While he was rejoicing in thus witnessing the fruit of his labours, he was attacked with a most serious illness, which threatened his speedy dissolution. He gathered his family around him in the evening, and gave them his parting counsels and blessings, in the full expectation that he should not see the light of another morning. It happened that, on the afternoon of the same day, several of the neighbouring ministers had met in his parish to hold a "public lecture," as it was called, with special reference to the interesting state of religion among his people; and, instead of having a sermon on the occasion, as usual, they spent the time in earnest prayer that the life of their apparently dying brother might still be preserved. The next morning, to his own surprise, and the great delight of his family, his disease had evidently formed a favourable crisis; and from that time he continued to mend, till he was able to resume his accustomed labours. In 1790, he witnessed yet another similar season of revival, in the midst of which he passed from his labours to his reward.

In 1780, Mr. Green was concerned in a movement which, at the time, excited considerable attention,—the formation of the Morris County Presbytery. He was not in principle strictly a Presbyterian, nor yet strictly a Congregationalist; but he sympathized with some of the peculiarities of each;—that is, he was in favour of Presbyterian Ordination, and of Independent Church Government. Accordingly, he united with several of his brethren in forming a Presbytery upon this basis; but it seems, in its practical results, never to have fulfilled his expectations.

Of his religious opinions, he gives the following account:—

"From my youth, I had heard much said upon the principles that are called Calvinistic and Arminian; and when I thought at all, I approved moderate Calvinism, before I had any religion; and when I got my religion in the *New Light* time, I became a more zealous Calvinist. I had a great aversion to the opposers of the New Light religion, and those opposers in New England, where I then lived, were generally supposed to be Arminian, or tinged with Arminian principles. When I settled in the ministry, I was led into Mr. Stoddard's notions of the Sacraments, by Messrs. Dickinson, Burr, and some others, that I had a high opinion of. They were in other respects strong Calvinists, and zealous promoters of the Reformation, or New Light religion, and opposite to those I had been troubled with as opposers in New England. Hence I was influenced to think they were right in their notions of the Sacraments. My prepossession in their favour, together with some plausible arguments they used, induced me to embrace Stoddard's sentiments, which before I had thought were not right, and for some time, I practised on his scheme in the admission of church members. But my church was not generally in that opinion, and I was not zealous to urge Mr. Stoddard's principles.

"After I had been settled a few years, I was inclined to some notions that were Arminian, or that bordered upon Arminianism, especially as to the power of the creature, the freedom of the will, the origin of action, &c. I seemed also to have some notion that there might be a degree of acceptableness to God in the religious duties of the unregenerate; which well agreed with the Stoddardian notion of unregenerate persons covenanting and coming to the Sacrament. But I continued not long in these notions; for, when I came to weigh and consider things well, I found I held several inconsistent sentiments. My sentiments in general were Calvinistic—I was founded and established in the principles; and yet I found that I had, in a measure, given in to several things that were Arminian, and quite inconsistent with my Calvinistic principles. I had been inclined to such notions of human freedom, the sufficiency of the creature, origin of power, duties of the unregenerate, their covenanting and using Sacraments, as were not consistent with other sentiments which I firmly believed, which I had the fullest evidence of, and could clearly demonstrate. When I came to look thoroughly into things, I found that all the Arminian notions or doctrines were so connected, that they must and would stand or fall together—the same connection I also found to be in Calvinistic sentiments. Dr. Watts' Terms of Christian Communion, Edwards' Inquiry concerning qualifications for Sacraments, and his book on the Will, were assistances to me in studying these points; and were a considerable means to help to bring me off from all the notions that bordered on Arminianism."

Mr. Green was a most vigorous and uncompromising opposer of African Slavery. He opposed it in public and in private, from the pulpit and the press, with the utmost zeal, though he stood almost alone in doing so. It was even made a term of Christian fellowship in the church of which he was pastor, that no Christian brother or sister should hold a human being in bondage.

He was an earnest advocate for American Independence. He even published a pamphlet to show its reasonableness and necessity, at a period when such an opinion was very extensively branded as a political heresy. He was elected, though contrary to his strongly expressed wishes, a member of the Provincial Congress of New Jersey, which set aside the Royal government of that Province, and formed the present constitution of the State; and he was Chairman of the committee which drafted the constitution. He published a series of able articles in a newspaper, designed to put his fellow citizens on their guard against the disastrous results of the paper currency, with which the country was then inundated. These essays were republished in many of the newspapers of the day; and the plan which they prescribed for the redemption of the "Continental currency," was very nearly the same which Congress ultimately adopted. When the British troops overran the State of New Jersey, in the autumn of 1776 and the beginning of 1777, it was thought that his prominence as a Whig peculiarly exposed him to hostile incursions and depredations; but he remained at his post nearly the whole time, and suffered no injury, and no material inconvenience.

Mr. Green published three Sermons, the subjects of which were,—"The nature of natural and moral inability;" "The sins of youth visited with punishment in subsequent life;" and "The nature of an acceptable Fast"—the latter was preached on a Fast day appointed by Congress. He published also the following miscellaneous pamphlets:—An Inquiry into the constitution and discipline of the Jewish Church, in order to cast some light on the controversy concerning qualifications for the Sacraments of the New Testament. With an Appendix, 1768. A Reply to the Rev. George Beckwith's Answer to Mr. Green's Sermon, entitled Christian Baptism, in a Letter to a friend, 1769; A small help offered to heads of families on the religious instructions of their households; A vision of Hell, consisting chiefly of a Dialogue between the devils on the temptations which they had found most successful in ruining immortal souls. This pamphlet was anonymous, and passed through several editions. A Reply to the Rev. George Beckwith's Answer to Mr. Green's Sermon entitled "Christian Baptism," in a Letter to a friend, 1769.

Mr. Green's last illness was short. In May, 1790, he had an attack of influenza, which, however, was not considered serious, until a short time before its fatal termination. Then he became suddenly comatose, and though he continued to answer questions intelligently, he manifested little disposition to converse. Being apprized that his end had nearly come, he was asked by his wife what were his views as to his future well-being, and he replied,—"I have a hope,"—and after a short interval, added,—"and some fear." Having uttered these words, his spirit gently passed away.

His son, the Rev. Dr. Green, wrote the following epitaph, containing an epitome of his character, which is inscribed on his tomb-stone:—

"Under this stone are deposited the remains of the Rev. Jacob Green, A. M. First Pastor of the Hanover Church, who died, 24th of May, 1790, aged sixty-eight years, of which forty-four were spent in the Gospel ministry. He was a man of temper, even, firm and resolute; of affections, temperate, steady and benevolent; of genius, solid, inquisitive and penetrating; of industry, active and unwearied; of learning, various and accurate; of manners, simple and reserved; of piety, humble, enlightened, fervent and eminent. As a preacher, he was instructive, plain, searching, practical; as a pastor, watchful, laborious; ever intent on some plan for the glory of God and the salvation of his flock; and, by the Divine blessing, happily and eminently successful."

Mr. Green left in manuscript, an autobiography reaching down as far as 1777. His son, the Rev. Dr. Green, published this in a series of numbers in the tenth volume of his "Christian Advocate;" and supplied the remaining part of the history from his own recollections.

SAMUEL DAVIES.*

1746—1761.

Samuel Davies was born near Summit Ridge, Newcastle County, De., November 3, 1723. He was, on both sides, of Welsh extraction. His father was a farmer, in humble circumstances, and of moderate intellectual powers and attainments, but of unexceptionable Christian character. His mother was distinguished for both talents and piety; and, from his birth, she sacredly devoted him to the service of the Lord in the Christian ministry. The father died in 1759, aged seventy-nine years. The mother survived her son several years, and passed the latter part of her life in the family of the Rev. Dr. Rodgers of New York.

The rudiments of his education he received from his mother, there being no school in the neighbourhood in which the family lived; but when he was about ten years old, he had an opportunity of attending a school some distance from home, where, for two years, he studied diligently, and improved rapidly. His mother had given the strictest attention to his religious education, and, by the blessing of God upon her unwearied efforts, in connection with her earnest prayers, he became, at the age of twelve, deeply and permanently impressed with the great truths of religion; though he did not make a public profession of his faith till after he had entered his fifteenth year.

His classical course was commenced under the tuition of a respectable Welsh Baptist minister,—the Rev. Abel Morgan; but he was transferred to Mr. Blair's famous school at Fagg's Manor, soon after its establishment. Here, under excellent advantages, he devoted himself to the study of the classics and the sciences, as well as Theology; and, in consequence of excessive application, his health, before the close of his course, was not a little impaired. He was licensed to preach by the Newcastle Presbytery, on the 30th of July, 1746. On the 23d of October following, he was married to Sarah Kirkpatrick, supposed to have been a daughter of John Kirkpatrick, of Nottingham.

On the 19th of February, 1747, he was ordained as an evangelist, with a view to a mission among some of the destitute congregations in Virginia, especially in Hanover County. This was, on several accounts, an unpromising and difficult field, especially in consideration of the fact that the Episcopal Church was then the Established Church of Virginia, and the Dissenters were, for the most part, extremely obnoxious to the civil authorities; but Mr. Davies is said to have undertaken the mission, partly from a feeling of gratitude towards certain persons in that region, who, through one of his friends, had contributed to meet the expenses of his education. On his arrival at Williamsburg, in April, he petitioned the General Court for a license to officiate at four different places of worship in and about Hanover. The petition was granted, chiefly through the influence of the Governor; though, at that time, there were pending several civil suits against Dissenting ministers, for holding religious worship in a manner not

* Finley's Fun. Serm.—Gibbon's do.—Assemb. Miss. Mag. I.—Panop. II.—Lit. and Evang. Mag.—Green's Hist. of N. J. Coll.—Foote's Sketches of Va. I.

recognised by the law of the Province. He immediately entered upon his labours, and was received with great enthusiasm, and listened to by multitudes with profound attention. The people were quickly resolved on securing his services permanently, and, after three or four months, they sent a call for him to the Presbytery. He returned from Virginia to Delaware about the close of summer; and, on the 15th of September, was suddenly bereaved of his wife, under circumstances peculiarly afflictive. His own health was now greatly reduced, and there was every thing to indicate that he was the subject of a confirmed consumption. He, however, continued his labours, preaching during the day, even when he was so ill at night as to need persons to sit up with him.

In the spring of 1748, there was some slight improvement in his condition, insomuch that his friends began to regard his recovery as at least possible. Many requests were now put in for his services; and that from Hanover was renewed with increased importunity. This he was, on every account, predisposed to accept; and, accordingly, he did accept it, though without any expectation that his health would allow him long to retain the charge. On this second visit to Virginia, he was accompanied by his intimate friend, Mr. John Rodgers, afterwards the Rev. Dr. Rodgers of New York, who, however, failed in his application for a license to preach in the Province.

On the 4th of October, 1748, he formed a second matrimonial connection with Jean, daughter of John Holt of Hanover, who became the mother of six children, and survived him many years.

About the same time, his license to preach was extended to three additional meeting-houses, so that his labours were now divided between seven places of worship, in five different counties, and some of them forty miles distant from each other; but his health was by this time restored, so that he was able to meet his manifold engagements. His residence was in Hanover, about twelve miles from Richmond. By his glowing zeal, combined with exemplary prudence, and an eloquence more impressive and effective than had then perhaps ever graced the American pulpit, he made his way among all classes of people, and was alike acceptable to all, from the most polished gentleman to the most ignorant African slave. A manifest blessing from on high attended his labours; and within about three years from the time of his settlement, no less than three hundred had been gathered to the communion of the church.

Though Mr. Davies succeeded, with little difficulty, in obtaining a license from the civil authorities to occupy so wide a field by his professional labours, he was subsequently engaged in controversy with Peyton Randolph, the King's Attorney General, on the question whether the Act of Toleration, which had been passed in England expressly for the relief of Protestant Dissenters, extended also to Virginia; he vigorously maintaining the affirmative, and the Attorney General *as* vigorously the negative. On one occasion, he appeared personally before the General Court, and replied to the Attorney General in a strain of eloquence, which is said to have won the admiration of the most earnest of his opponents. He maintained his position with the utmost firmness; and when, on his visit to England, he had an opportunity to bring the matter before the King in Council, he received a declaration, under authority, that the Act of Toleration did extend to the Colony of Virginia.

On the 4th of October, 1753, a request was presented to the Synod of New York, then in session in Philadelphia, by the Trustees of the College of New Jersey, that they would appoint two of their members, Messrs. Gilbert Tennent and Samuel Davies, to make a voyage to Europe to solicit benefactions in aid of the College. The appointment having been made and accepted, and every thing having been arranged for their departure, they embarked in a vessel for London on the 17th of November, where they arrived on the 25th of December. They visited Scotland together, but parted at Edinburgh, Mr. Tennent to visit Glasgow and Ireland, and Mr. Davies the principal towns in England. They subsequently met in London, in October, 1754; and the next month embarked for America,—Mr. Tennent immediately for Philadelphia, and Mr. Davies for York, Va. The latter had a rough and protracted passage, and did not reach Virginia till the 13th of February, 1755. He was received with great favour in both England and Scotland, and preached to not only universal acceptance, but universal admiration. The object of the united mission was also happily accomplished, in much larger collections being made for the College, than even the most sanguine friends of the enterprise had ventured to hope for.

Mr. Davies, on his return, immediately resumed his pastoral labours, though he found himself in the midst of a state of things that forbade him to confine his labours to his own congregation. The French and Indian war was at this time occasioning the greatest agitation throughout that part of the country; and even the idea of abandoning a part of the Colony of Virginia to the enemy had been suggested. On the 20th of July, 1755, occurred General Braddock's memorable defeat, and the remnant of his army was saved only by the skill and courage of Colonel Washington, then but twenty-three years of age. Ten days after this, Mr. Davies preached a Sermon "On the defeat of General Braddock going to Fort Du Quesne;" in which he called upon his hearers, in the most impassioned strain, to show "themselves Men, Britons and Christians, and to make a noble stand for the blessings they enjoyed." It was apprehended that the negroes might join the Indians and French; and Mr. Davies, who had perhaps more influence with them than any other person, exerted himself to the utmost to prevent such a movement. In August of the same year, he delivered a Sermon in Hanover to a company of Independent Volunteers, which was afterwards published, and in a note to which he alludes prophetically to Washington—"That heroic youth," says he, "Colonel Washington, whom I cannot but hope Providence has hitherto preserved in so signal a manner, for some important service to his country." On another occasion, he preached a Sermon to the Militia of Hanover County, with a view to raise a company for Captain Samuel Meredith; and such was the enthusiasm produced by the Discourse that, within a few minutes after it was concluded, the company was made up, and the preacher was well nigh overwhelmed with demonstrations of respect and admiration.

But, notwithstanding these patriotic efforts, which the circumstances of the times evidently demanded, Mr. Davies suffered nothing to diminish his exertions, or damp his zeal, in his appropriate work as a Christian minister. He preached the Gospel continually; in season and out of season; among the negroes as well as the white population; and his labours were attended with marked success. The Presbytery of Hanover,—the first Presbytery in Virginia, was founded shortly after his return from Europe, and chiefly through his instrumentality. The Act of the Synod of New York for this purpose bears date September 3, 1755; and Mr. Davies was appointed to open the Presbytery, which was directed to meet at Hanover on the 3d of December of that year.

Mr. Davies may be considered as having been the soul of the Dissenting interest in Virginia. The Presbytery of Hanover originally comprehended the whole of Virginia, and the greater part, if not the whole, of North Carolina; and throughout this extensive region were scattered settlements that were not in sympathy with the Established Church. Over this wide tract of country Mr. Davies' influence was diffused. So great was his popularity that his labours were called for abroad, much too often to satisfy his own people; and they even warmly remonstrated with the Presbytery for directing him to supply so many vacancies.

On the 16th of August, 1758, Mr. Davies was chosen to succeed Jonathan Edwards, as President of the College of New Jersey; but he declined the appointment. He was, however, on the 9th of May, 1759, elected a second time; and, though he still felt strong objections to leaving that extensive and important field, yet, as this was a second appointment, and the Synod had meanwhile given it as their judgment that he ought to accept it, and as he had long felt the deepest interest in the welfare of the College, he was constrained to think that the indications of Providence were in favour of a removal. He, therefore, signified his acceptance of the appointment, resigned his charge on the 13th of May, 1759, removed to Princeton shortly after, entered upon the duties of his office on the 26th of July, and was formally inducted into the Presidential chair on the 26th of September.

As Mr. Davies brought with him to the College the highest reputation for wisdom, piety, and eloquence, so he fully sustained it while his connection with the College continued. He had now the best opportunity for the exercise of his varied gifts; and he used them in such a way as to give new efficiency and lustre to the institution. But, while every thing seemed to promise a protracted career of usefulness, he was suddenly called away to exercise his powers on a nobler field. His habit being somewhat plethoric, he had been accustomed in Virginia to the exercise of riding, as a means of preserving his health. His duties at Princeton led him into a sedentary life, and his application to study was intense and unremitted. Towards the close of January, 1761, he was bled for a severe cold, and the next day transcribed for the press his Sermon on the death of George the Second. The day following, he preached twice in the College chapel. His arm became inflamed, and a violent fever ensued, to which he fell a victim in ten days. He died on the 4th of February, 1761, at the age of thirty-six, and after having held the office of President of the College a little more than eighteen months. His disease, in its progress, was accompanied by delirium; but, in his lucid intervals, and even amidst the wanderings of his mind, it was manifest that the tendencies of his spirit were towards immortality. A Sermon on the occasion of his death was preached in London on the 29th of March by the Rev. Dr. Thomas Gibbons, and another at Princeton on the 28th of May, by the Rev. Dr. Samuel Finley; both of which were published.

The following is a list of President Davies' publications:—A Sermon on man's primitive state, 1748. The state of religion among the Protestant

Dissenters in Virginia, in a Letter to the Rev. Joseph Bellamy, 1751. A Sermon preached before the Presbytery of Newcastle, 1752. A Sermon preached at the installation of the Rev. John Todd,* 1752. Religion and Patriotism, the constituents of a good soldier: A Sermon preached before a company of Volunteers, 1755. Virginia's Danger and Remedy: Two Discourses occasioned by the severe drought, and the defeat of General Braddock, 1756. Letters, showing the state of Religion in Virginia, particularly among the negroes, 1751–1757. A Sermon on the "vessels of mercy and the vessels of wrath," 1757. A Sermon on "Little children invited to Jesus Christ," 1757. The Curse of Cowardice: A Sermon before the Militia of Virginia, 1758. A Valedictory Discourse to the Senior class in the College of New Jersey, 1760. A Sermon on the death of George II., 1761. He was also the author of several important documents of a public nature, and various Hymns and other pieces of poetry, of no small degree of merit.

A collection of his Sermons, including most of those which had been printed during his life time, was published after his death, in three volumes, octavo. They have passed through several editions, both in Great Britain and in America, and are generally regarded as among the most able and eloquent sermons in the English language.

Though it is not to be supposed that there is any person now living, who has any recollections of President Davies, many of the last generation remembered him well, and the testimony which they rendered concerning him is a matter of authentic record. The Rev. Dr. John H. Rice, in the notices of his life and character which appeared in the Literary and Evangelical Magazine, has brought together various well authenticated traditions concerning him, which of themselves are enough to prove that he was one of the most gifted men of his time. The Rev. Dr. John H. Livingston, the Patriarch of the Reformed Dutch Church, informed me that he once heard him preach at Princeton, and that he was without exception the first pulpit orator to whom he had ever listened. His voice, his attitudes, his ges-

* JOHN TODD was graduated at the College of New Jersey in 1749, and was licensed by the Presbytery of New Brunswick in 1750. Shortly after his licensure, he went to Virginia, and preached to great satisfaction in some of the houses that had been licensed for the Rev. Samuel Davies. In 1751, he returned to the North, was ordained by the Presbytery of New Brunswick, and then went back to Virginia, where he was regularly licensed by the General Court "to officiate as an assistant to Samuel Davies, a Dissenting minister." He was installed on the 12th of November, 1752—the Sermon on the occasion was preached by the Rev. Mr. Davies, and was published, the next year, with a Dedication "to the Reverend Clergy of the Established Church of Virginia." After Mr. Davies' removal to Princeton, Mr. Todd was, for many years, the leading man in the Hanover Presbytery, East of the Blue Ridge. He was a staunch Whig during the Revolution, and was always zealous in defence of religious liberty. He took a deep interest in the early immigration to Kentucky, and exerted himself to the utmost to obtain from the Virginia Legislature a charter for a College in that new country; and, after the Transylvania Seminary was established, he was instrumental in furnishing it with a small but valuable library, and a scientific apparatus. He superintended a classical school which was in high repute for many years, but declined, and was finally given up, after he became far advanced in life. He grew prematurely old, in consequence of his excessive labours in the early period of his ministry; and, for several years previous to his death, he was not able to perform all the

unjust charges. Having accomplished his object, he set out for home on Saturday the 27th, and the same day was found dead in the road. Whether he died from apoplexy, or in consequence of being thrown from his horse, could only be conjectured. Mr. Todd preached in Virginia about forty-two years. A son, bearing his name, was licensed by the Hanover Presbytery, September 13, 1800, preaching his first Sermon where his father preached his last. For some time he occupied the churches left vacant by his father, but in 1809 removed to Kentucky.

ture, every thing pertaining to manner, he said, came up to the most perfect ideal that he was able to form.

The following is an extract from Dr. Finley's Sermon occasioned by his death:

"As to his natural genius, it was strong and masculine. His understanding was clear, his memory retentive, his invention quick, his imagination lively and florid, his thoughts sublime, and his language elegant, strong and expressive. And I cannot but presume that true and candid critics will readily discern a great degree of true poetic fire, style, and imagery, in his poetical compositions; and will grant that he was capable to have shone in that way, had his leisure permitted the due cultivation of his natural talent.

"His appearance in company was manly and graceful, his behaviour genteel, not ceremonious: grave yet pleasant; and solid but sprightly too. In a word, he was an open, conversable and entertaining companion, a polite gentleman, and devout Christian, at once.

"In the sacred desk, zeal for God and love to men animated his addresses, and made them tender, solemn, pungent and persuasive; while, at the same time, they were ingenious, accurate and oratorical. A certain dignity of sentiment and style, a venerable presence, a commanding voice, and emphatical delivery, concurred both to charm his audience, and overawe them into silence and attention.

"Nor was his usefulness confined to the pulpit. His comprehensive mind could take under view the grand interests of his country and of religion at once; and these interests, as well as those of his friends, he was ever ready zealously to serve. It is known what an active instrument he was in stirring up a patriot spirit,—a spirit of courage and resolution in Virginia, where he resided during the late barbarous French and Indian ravages.

"His natural temper was remarkably sweet and dispassionate; and his heart was one of the tenderest towards the distressed. His sympathetic soul could say 'Who is weak, and I am not weak?' Accordingly, his charitable disposition made him liberal to the poor, and that often beyond his ability. He was eminently obliging to all, and very sensible of favours conferred, which he could receive without servility, and manifest his grateful sense of them with proper dignity.

"To his friends he was voluntarily transparent, and fully acted up to the poet's advice:

"'Thy friend put in thy bosom: wear his eyes,
Still in thy heart that he may see what's there.'

"And perhaps none better understood the ingenuities and delicacies of friendship, or had a higher relish for it, or was truer or more constant in it, than he. He was not easily disgusted; his knowledge of human nature in its present state, his candid heart and enlarged soul, both disposing and enabling him to make allowances for indiscretions, which narrower and more selfish minds could not make. He readily and easily forgave offences against himself, whilst none could be more careful to avoid offending others; which, if he at any time inadvertently did, he was forward and desirous to make the most ample satisfaction.

"He was amongst the first and brightest examples of filial piety; a very indulgent parent and humane master. As a husband, he was kind, tender, cordial and respectful, with a fondness that was manly and genuine. In a word, think what might rationally be expected in the present imperfect state, in a mature man, a Christian in minority, a minister of Jesus, of like passions with others, in a gentleman, companion, and cordial friend, and you conceive of President Davies.

"It would hardly be expected that one so rigid, with respect to his own faith and practice, could be so generous and catholic in his sentiments of those who differed from him in both, as he was. He was strict, not bigoted; conscientious, not squeamishly scrupulous. His clear and extensive knowledge of religion enabled him to discern where the main stress should be laid, and to proportion his zeal to the importance of things,—too generous to be confined to the interests of a party as such. He considered the visible Kingdom of Christ as extended beyond the boundaries of *this* or *that* particular denomination; and never supposed that his declarative glory was wholly dependent on the religious community which he most approved. Hence he gloried more in being a Christian than in being a *Presbyterian*, though he was the latter from principle. His truly catholic address to the Established Clergy of Virginia is a demonstration of the sincere pleasure it would have given him to have heard that 'Christ was preached,' and substantial religion, common Christianity, promoted by those who 'walked not with him,' and whom he judged in other points to be mistaken. His benevolent heart could not be so soured, nor his enlarged soul so contracted, as to value men from circumstantial distinctions, but according to their personal worth.

"He sought truth for its own sake, and would profess his sentiments with the undisguised openness of an honest Christian, and the inoffensive boldness of a manly spirit;

yet, without the least apparent difficulty or hesitation, he would retract an opinion on full conviction of its being a mistake. I have never known one who appeared to lay himself more fully open to the reception of truth, from whatever quarter it came, than he; for he judged the knowledge of truth only to be real learning, and that endeavouring to defend an error was but labouring to be more ignorant. But, until fully convinced, he was becomingly tenacious of his opinion.

"The unavoidable consciousness of native power made him bold and enterprising. Yet the event proved that his boldness arose, not from a partial, groundless, self-conceit, but from true self-knowledge. Upon fair and candid trial, faithful and just to himself, he judged what he could do; and what he could, when called to it, he attempted; and what he attempted he accomplished.

CALEB SMITH.*

1747—1762.

Caleb Smith, a son of William and Hannah (Sears) Smith, was born at Brookhaven, L. I., December 29, O. S., 1723. The family was one of considerable wealth, and of high respectability.

As he discovered, from early childhood, more than common vigour of mind, and love of learning, his father resolved on giving him a collegiate education; and accordingly placed him at a grammar school, where he made such improvements that, in 1739, in his fifteenth year, he became a member of Yale College. His standing, during his whole college course, was highly respectable, and he graduated, an excellent scholar, in 1743. He remained at College, for some time, as a resident graduate.

During the second year that he was in College, there was a very general attention to religion among the students, in which he also had a share. From that time, his mind seems to have been permanently and habitually directed to his religious interests; though he looked with no little distrust upon his own exercises, on account of their having been less distinct and vivid than he supposed was necessary to give them the stamp of genuineness. To others, however, the evidence of his piety was very satisfactory; and several clergymen, to whom he communicated his religious views and feelings, had no hesitation in expressing the opinion that his conversion was radical, and that he ought to direct his attention to the Christian ministry.

In 1746, about the time he took his second degree, Mr. Burr of Newark, afterwards President of New Jersey College, applied to him to assist him in the instruction of a large Latin school, of which he had the charge; but Mr. Smith's engagements did not allow him to go to Newark till Mr. Burr was otherwise supplied. However, he went some time after to Elizabethtown, where he instructed several young men in the languages, while he pursued the study of Theology under the direction of the Rev. Jonathan Dickinson. At length, by the advice of Mr. Dickinson and some other ministers, he presented himself before the Presbytery of New York as a candidate for the ministry; and, having creditably gone through his several trials, was licensed to preach in April, 1747.

His preaching, from the beginning, was more than commonly acceptable; and, within about a year from his licensure, he received several unanimous

* A Brief Account of his Life.—Stearns' Hist. First Ch., Newark.

calls from different places to settle in the ministry. He requested the Presbytery to decide which call he should accept; but, as they chose to refer the matter to his own judgment, he decided in favour of Newark Mountains, (now Orange); and was accordingly ordained and installed there, November 30, 1748.

Though Mr. Smith evidently laboured with great diligence, and in a spirit of most intense devotion, his ministry was not signalized by any extraordinary immediate results. It was, however, during a period of uncommon religious apathy in the country at large, that he exercised his ministry; so that, even among men of his own views and spirit, he was not singular in not being permitted to witness an extensive revival of religion in connection with his labours. It seems to have been a source of constant uneasiness and grief to him, that his success was so limited; and yet there were a goodly number who connected their hopeful conversion with his instrumentality.

But Mr. Smith's usefulness was by no means confined to his own immediate congregation. In 1750, shortly after his settlement in the ministry, he was appointed a Trustee of the College of New Jersey, and exerted an important influence in aid of the interests of that infant Seminary. He was also early chosen Clerk of the Board of Trustees, and continued in that office till the removal of the College to Princeton. After the death of President Edwards, he was chosen President *pro tempore*, and for several months occupied that important station with much dignity and ability.

He was an active and useful member of the ecclesiastical bodies with which he was connected. He not only judged correctly but spoke well. He was, for many years, Stated Clerk of the Presbytery, and usually conducted its correspondence, especially in regard to all matters of peculiar delicacy or difficulty. He had a happy talent at reconciling differences—at preventing threatened disruptions, and restoring harmony where it had been temporarily interrupted.

Mr. Smith ranked among the more popular preachers of his day. In the early part of his ministry, he wrote his sermons out with great care; but, in the latter part of it, a large portion of his preaching was extemporaneous, so far as the language was concerned, though he never failed carefully to consider and digest his subject. His voice was clear and pleasant, though somewhat monotonous; and his manner in the pulpit was affectionate and fervent, without any of the show of oratory. He became, at one period, the subject of violent nervous and vertiginous affections, which occasioned him serious embarrassment in his public services, and sometimes even obliged him to support himself by holding to the pulpit. The only Sermon he ever published, was one on the death of President Burr, which is said to have been written at a peculiarly inauspicious moment, and to have been but a poor sample of his ordinary preaching. It is, however, a very respectable performance.

In the beginning of October, 1762, he was seized with a dysentery, which proved the means of terminating his life. In the early part of his illness, his mind, though not greatly clouded, was not entirely free from anxious thoughts; but, at a later period, he obtained a degree of confidence in the merits and the promises of his Redeemer, that cast out all fear, and put him in possession of a serene and triumphant joy. His people evinced their warm attachment to him, and their interest in the preservation of his life, by observing the Tuesday preceding his death as a day of fasting and prayer; on which occasion, they called in the assistance of several of the neighbouring ministers, to one of whom he expressed an undoubting assurance that he should soon be mingling in the praises and enjoyments of Heaven. On the Friday morning following, at a very early hour, perceiving that the closing scene had come, he gathered his family around him, and took his final leave of them, commending them in fervent prayer to the providence and grace of God. After this, he requested that his little son should be brought and laid in his arms; and, as he was too weak to be able to lift his arm, he desired some one to raise it and lay it over the child; which being done, he very affectionately invoked the Divine blessing upon him. He expired about six o'clock, the same morning, (October 20, 1762,) aged thirty-eight years and ten months.

His funeral was attended, on the Sabbath following, by a large concourse of people, among whom were a number of ministers. In the morning, one of the ministers preached from Philippians i, 21; in the afternoon, another preached from Ezekiel xxii, 30.

In September, 1748, Mr. Smith was married to Martha, youngest daughter of the Rev. Jonathan Dickinson of Elizabethtown,—a lady whose character is thus described by one of her contemporaries:—"She was superior to most of her sex in strength of genius; her intellectual powers were quick and penetrating; she had a thirst for knowledge, and was greatly delighted in reading. Kindness, care, and friendship, composed her natural temper: she was an agreeable companion, very obliging in her behaviour, and admired and loved by all who had the happiness of her acquaintance. As she was blessed with an early religious education, so the things of eternity began betimes to exercise her: she had serious impressions upon her mind even from her childhood, and began a course of secret prayer while young. And, although she was subject to melancholy at seasons, and consequently to fears and doubts about her spiritual state, yet, towards the latter part of her life, she had much greater satisfaction." With this excellent lady Mr. Smith lived nearly eight years, when, after a lingering disease of about a year, she was taken from him, in August, 1757, at the age of thirty-one,—leaving three children, all of them daughters. A little more than two years after this bereavement,—in October, 1759, he was married to Rebecca, daughter of the "Honourable Major" Foote of Branford, Conn. She is spoken of as having been "endowed with many agreeable virtues to render her an amiable companion;" but the fact that she was still living, when this reference to her character was made, was doubtless the reason why nothing more remains concerning her than this passing allusion. He had one son by his last marriage,—the child above referred to, as being lifted into his father's arms to receive his dying benediction. The descendants of Mr. Smith are among the most respectable people in New Jersey, one of whom is the Hon. Henry W. Green, the present (1849) Chief Justice of the State.

The only extended notice of Mr. Smith that remains, is a pamphlet of about sixty pages, printed at Woodbridge, N. J., in 1763, entitled "A Brief Account of the life of the late Rev. Caleb Smith, A. M., minister of the Gospel at Newark Mountains, who died October 22, 1762; chiefly extracted from his diary and other private papers. Heb. vi. 11, 12." The pamphlet contains comparatively few facts, being chiefly occupied with the record of his private religious exercises, evincing a remarkable degree of spirituality and devotion.

JOHN BRAINERD.*

1747—1781.

John Brainerd, a son of the Hon. Hezekiah and Dorothy (Mason) Brainerd, was born at Haddam, Conn., February 28, 1719–20. He was probably fitted for College by his brother, the Rev. Nehemiah Brainerd† of Eastbury, a parish in the town of Glastenbury. He was graduated at Yale College in 1746. During his collegiate course, his brother David, in his letters, warned him against that spurious religious experience that is too often found in connection with great religious excitements. But when he supposed himself to be converted, or when he made a public profession of religion, or with what church he originally connected himself, cannot now be ascertained. Probably his first membership was with the church in his native place; but, as the Records of that church at the period referred to are lost, nothing beyond conjecture is now attainable. It would seem, however, that he must have had the ministry in view during his college course; for within a few months after his graduation, he had commenced preaching, and was actually engaged as a missionary among the Indians.

The following letter, covering a considerable part of John Brainerd's missionary life, was addressed by him to Mrs. Elizabeth Smith, the wife of the Hon. William Smith, and previously the wife of Colonel Elisha Williams, once Rector of Yale College. It has never before been published, and doubtless contains the fullest, as well as most authentic, narrative of his self-denying labours, that is now extant.

Brotherton in New Jersey, August 24, 1761.

Madam: According to my promise, I here send a particular account of the Indian mission in this Province, which, for some years, has been the object of my care. I shall take a brief view of it from its first rise and foundation.

In 1743, my brother and predecessor, Mr. David Brainerd, being employed by the Corresponding members of the Honourable Society in Scotland for propagating Christian Knowledge, entered on the arduous business of Christianizing the Indians, and for that end, on the 1st of April, arrived at Kaunaumeek, an Indian settlement about twenty miles from Stockbridge Northwest. At this place he continued about the space of a year; and having so far gained upon these Indians as that he could persuade them to move to Stockbridge, and settle themselves under the ministry of the Rev. Mr. Sergeant, he, by the direction of the Correspondents, removed

* MS. from Rev. Dr. Field.—Allen's Biog. Dict.—Webster's MSS.

† Nehemiah Brainerd was a native of Haddam; was graduated at Yale College in 1732; was ordained pastor of the Second Congregational Church in Glastenbury, (Eastbury) Conn., in April, 1740; and died November 9, 1742.

to the Forks of Delaware in Pennsylvania. Among these Indians, he spent a little more than a year; had some encouraging appearances, but no very great success. He then took a journey of about thirty miles to a settlement of Indians at Crosweeksung in this Province; where it pleased the Lord greatly to smile upon his endeavours, and in the most remarkable manner to open the eyes of the poor savages, and turn them from the power of Satan to God, as appears at large by his printed Journal.

Partly with those Indians, partly at the Forks of Delaware, and partly on the banks of Susquehanna, (where he made no less than five journeys first and last,) he spent near two years, till he was so far gone in a consumption as rendered him utterly unable to officiate any longer.

But by this time a number of the Indians had removed from these Northern parts; the Indians also at Crosweeksung had left that place, and settled themselves on a tract of land near Cranberry, far better for cultivation, and more commodious for such a number as were now collected into one body.

In this situation I found the Indians when I arrived among them, at their new settlement called Bethel, which was about the middle of April, 1747. And this summer I officiated for my brother, who took a journey to the Eastward, thinking that possibly it might be a means of recovering his health. But his distemper had taken such hold of his vitals, as not to be diverted or removed by medicine or means. He was, on his return from Boston to New Jersey, detained at Northampton by the increase of his disorder, and there made his exit out of a world of sin and sorrow, and no doubt entered upon a glorious and blessed immortality, the October following.

The work of Divine grace still went on among the Indians, although those extraordinary influences that appeared for a time, had begun some months before to abate, and still seemed gradually going off, but the good effects of them were abiding in numbers of instances.

About this time, a mortal sickness prevailed among the Indians, and carried off a considerable number; and especially of those who had been religiously wrought upon; which made some infidels say, as in the days of Constantine, that it was because they had forsaken the old Indian ways and become Christians. This seemed to be a mysterious frown of Divine Providence.

Some time after my brother's decease, the Correspondents requested me to take the charge of the Indians, which I consented to; and in February, 1748, was ordained, and soon after had the Society's commission sent me from Scotland, and continued in their service for several years. And although we lost, at several times, by sickness, near or quite half that had been admitted to baptism when I came, yet, upon the whole, the church rather increased,—numbers being added from time to time. At one time, we had between forty and fifty members in full communion.

We likewise had a large English school, which sometimes consisted of above fifty children, who learned to read, write, repeat Catechisms, &c.; and some that gave hopes of being savingly converted while they were very young, but did not live to give us the best evidence of such a work of Divine grace.

We had likewise begun a spinning school for the girls, and were about forming a plan to bring up the boys to business, and several were already out to learn trades, when the proprietors laid claim to the land, and sued the Indians for trespass, which put an end to our schemes, and threw all into confusion.

We then turned our thoughts towards Susquehanna, and were attempting to provide a settlement for the Indians there, when, hostilities breaking out on the frontiers, the most barbarous murders were committed, which entirely defeated our design, and put a final stop to all further attempts of that nature.

And now things being in such a situation, the Correspondents thought proper to dismiss me from the Society's service, which they did in May, 1755.

I was then in New England, and upon my return had an invitation to Newark, which, with the advice of the Presbytery, I accepted; moved with my family, and continued there till June, 1756, when the Correspondents, thinking they had a prospect of procuring this land on which the Indians are now settled, requested me to resume the mission, with which I complied; and giving up the call I had, to settle at Newark, moved with my family to Brunswick, being the best place I could now fix upon to accommodate the Indians in their present situation, till the land for their settlement could be procured. In this situation I continued till September, 1757, when the Correspondents being disappointed, and seeing no way to procure the land, dismissed me a second time; and the congregation at Newark, having continued all this time unsettled, renewed their call to me the next week, which I soon after accepted, moved again with my family, and settled there. In this settled state, I remained but a little while; for in March, 1759, (in consequence of a treaty with the Indians, and this land purchased and secured to them by the Government,) I was requested by Mr. Bernard, the then Governor of this Province, and the Society's Correspondents, at a joint meeting at Perth Amboy, again to resume the mission. I took their proposals under consideration, and in the May following, laid the matter before the Synod at Philadelphia, and with the unanimous advice of that venerable body, gave up my charge at Newark, and embarked once more in the cause of the poor Indians.

About this time, I made the Indians a visit at their new settlement, and procured some supplies for them by order of Synod, during my absence in the army, and upon my return, the November following, fixed myself down among them, where I have steadily resided ever since.

I had repeated promises from Governor Bernard of a comfortable, decent house for the place of my residence, as also an house for the public worship of God. But promises were all I could ever get towards either: and when I came to think of moving here, was obliged to sell almost all my household furniture, because I had no place to put it in. And the loss I hereby sustained, together with the losses and expenses in my several removes was about £150 damage to my estate, besides all the fatigue and trouble that attended the same.

And as this movable state of affairs has been greatly to my disadvantage, it certainly has been no less to the congregation. The Indians have, every year, since the commencement of the war, enlisted into the king's service far beyond the proportion; and generally more or less, every campaign, have died in the army.

In 1757, we lost near twenty, taken captive at Fort William Henry, and but three or four have ever returned to this day, so that our number is greatly reduced.

On this spot, which is a fine, large tract of land, and very commodiously situated for their settlement, there are something upward of an hundred, old and young.

About twelve miles distant, there is a small settlement of them, perhaps near forty. About seventeen miles farther, there is a third, containing possibly near as many more. And there are some few scattering ones still about Crosweeksung. And if all were collected they might possibly make two hundred.

I spend something more than half my Sabbaths here at Brotherton; the rest are divided. At this place, I have but few white people. The reason is because this is near central between Delaware and the Sea, and the English settlements are chiefly on them. The other places are in the midst of the inhabitants, and whenever I preach there, I have a large number of white people, that meet to attend Divine service. But besides these, I have preached at eight different places on Lord's days, and near twenty on other days of the week, and never fail of a considerable congregation. So large and extensive is this vacancy.

Two large counties, and a considerable part of two more, almost wholly destitute of a preached Gospel, (except what the Quakers do, in their way,) and many of the people but one remove from a state of heathenism.

As to the success that has attended my labours, I can say but little. It is a time wherein the influences of the Divine Spirit are mournfully withheld. I think, however, I have ground to hope that some good has been done among both Indians and white people; and the prospects of further usefulness are very considerable, if proper means could be used. But such is the state of this country—there is such a mixture of Quakers and several other denominations, and so many that have no concern about religion in any shape, that very little can at present be expected towards the support of the Gospel. For my own part, I never have thought proper to take one single farthing yet, in all my excursions, fearing that it might prejudice the minds of some, and so, in a measure, frustrate the design.

At this place, where most of the Indians are settled, we greatly want a school for the children. When I built the meeting-house last year, I provided some materials also for a school-house, and in the fall addressed the Legislature of this Province for some assistance, not only for the support of a school, but for the erecting of a small grist-mill, a blacksmith's shop, and a small trading store, to furnish the Indians with necessaries in exchange for their produce, and so prevent their running twelve or fifteen miles to the inhabitants for every thing they want, whereby they not only consume much time, but often fall into the temptation of calling at dram-houses, (too frequent in the country,) where they intoxicate themselves with spirituous liquors, and, after some days perhaps, instead of hours, return home, wholly unfit for any thing relating either to this or a future world.

The Governor, the Council, the Speaker of the House of Assembly, and several of the other members, thought well of the motion, and recommended it; but the Quakers, and others in that interest, made opposition; and being the greater part of the House, it finally went against us. If the same could be done some other way, it would be the best step towards the end proposed, and be the most likely to invite not only the Indians at these other small settlements above mentioned, but those also who live in more distant parts of the country.

Thus I have touched upon the most material things relative to this mission, and I fear, tired your patience with my long epistle. And now, that all needed provision may be made for the promotion and perfecting of this good work among the Indians, and you among others be made an happy instrument of the same; that many faithful labourers may be thrust forth, and all vacant parts of the harvest be supplied; that this wilderness in particular may be turned into a fruitful field, and even the whole earth be filled with the knowledge of the Lord, is the fervent prayer of

Madam, your most obedient, humble servant,

JOHN BRAINERD.

P. S. Since my settlement here, I have been obliged to advance above £200 for the building of the meeting-house, for some necessary repairs of an old piece of an house that was on the spot, and for my support and other necessary expenses.

To Mrs. SMITH.

In January, 1758, Mr. Brainerd went, as the agent of New Jersey College, in company with the Rev. Caleb Smith of Newark Mountains, to solicit the Council convened at Stockbridge, to advise and sanction the removal of Jonathan Edwards to the Presidency of that institution. The Council, at the request of the English and Indian Congregations at Stockbridge, wrote to the Commissioners at Boston to appoint Brainerd to succeed Edwards; and also wrote to the Trustees of the College to exert their influence in the same direction; but the suggestion does not appear ever to have taken effect.

He resided for some time at Mount Holly, where he had a meeting-house, which was burnt by the British in the Revolutionary war. Several other places also shared his services, either regularly or occasionally. In 1767, the Synod granted him twenty pounds beside his salary for "his extraordinary services in forming societies, and labouring among the white people in that large and uncultivated country;" and the same grant was received the next year. From 1760 to 1770, he received from the congregations between Egg Harbour and Manahawken fifty-nine pounds and nineteen shillings,—having preached to them five hundred times. He continued to supply these numerous vacancies until 1777, when he removed to Deerfield, and preached there during the rest of his life. He died on the 18th of March, 1781, aged sixty-one years; and his remains repose beneath the floor of the Deerfield Church.

Mr. Brainerd was married in November, 1752, to Experience Lyon, who became the mother of three children, two of whom died very young. The surviving child,—a daughter, lived to become the mother of a family. Mrs. Brainerd died in 1757; after which, he was married to Mrs. Experience Price, who died August 28, 1793, leaving no issue.

The Rev. Dr. Field, who was for many years minister of the parish in which Brainerd's parents resided, and who has probably investigated the history of the family more carefully than any other person, says—"In person John Brainerd was rather tall. The tradition in Haddam is that he was as pious a man as his brother David, but not equal to him in ability.

He was distinguished for exactness and propriety in every thing; travelled much; conversed much on religion with Indians and whites, wherever he went, and did good to all men as he had opportunity. Of the death of his wife he writes as follows—'My dear wife, after a long and painful sickness, departed the 17th of September, 1757,—the greatest loss I ever sustained—the most sorrowful day my eyes ever saw. May God sanctify the heavy stroke to me and my little babes, support me under it, and make up the great loss to us in spiritual and Divine blessings. Dust thou art and unto dust thou shalt return. Having a desire to depart and be with Christ, which is far better. She has exchanged a vale of tears for a crown of glory. Blessed are the dead that die in the Lord; they rest from their labours, and their works do follow them.' "

JOHN RODGERS, D. D.*

1747—1811.

John Rodgers was born in Boston, on the 5th of August, 1727. He was a son of Thomas and Elizabeth Rodgers, who emigrated from Londonderry, Ireland, to Boston in 1721. In 1728, they transferred their residence to Philadelphia, when the subject of this sketch was a little more than a year old.

While he was yet a child, he evinced an uncommon love of knowledge, and a thoughtful habit of mind in respect to his eternal interests. It was under the preaching of Whitefield that he became first permanently impressed with the truths and obligations of religion. On one occasion, while Whitefield was preaching in the evening, on the outside of the steps of the Court House in Market Street, young Rodgers was standing near him, and holding a lantern for his accommodation; when he became so deeply impressed with the truth to which he was listening, that, for a moment, he forgot himself, and the lantern fell from his hand, and was dashed in pieces. Some time after he was settled in the ministry, Whitefield being on a visit to his house,—Mr. Rodgers alluded to this incident, and asked him if he recollected it. "Oh yes," replied Whitefield, "I remember it well; and have often thought I would give almost any thing in my power to know who that little boy was, and what had become of him." Mr. Rodgers replied with a smile,—"*I* am that little boy." Whitefield burst into tears, and remarked that he was the *fourteenth* person then in the ministry, whom he had discovered in the course of that visit to America, of whose hopeful conversion he had been the instrument.

From the period when he believed the principle of religion was formed in his soul, he set his heart upon the ministry as his ultimate profession; and to this his studies began immediately to be directed. Having remained a few months at a grammar school in Philadelphia, under the care of a Mr. Stevenson, a celebrated teacher then recently from Ireland, he was removed to another grammar school, established shortly before, on the Neshaminy, a few miles from Philadelphia, by the Rev. Mr. Roan, an eminent Presbyte-

* Memoirs by Dr. Miller.—Dr. Phillips' Two Discourses on the opening of the Presbyterian Church in Wall street.—Webster's MSS.

rian clergyman. Here he continued about two years, distinguished alike for his diligence in study, his exemplary deportment, and his fervent zeal in the cause of religion. In the summer of 1743, at the age of sixteen, he was transferred from Mr. Roan's school to an Academy of high reputation at Fagg's Manor, in Chester County, Pa., under the care of the Rev. Samuel Blair, one of the most respectable scholars and divines of his day. Here he completed his academical studies, and made some progress in Theology. While he was connected with this institution, he was brought into intimate relations with several individuals, who afterwards obtained very considerable celebrity in the ministry; among whom was the Rev. Samuel Davies, who died President of the College of New Jersey. Having pursued his theological studies for some time under Mr. Blair, he returned to his father's in Philadelphia, and completed his preparation for the ministry, under the direction of Gilbert Tennent. In June, 1747, he appeared before the Presbytery of Newcastle, and entered on the usual trials for licensure; and, having passed these trials, was licensed in October following.

During the winter after his licensure, he was occupied, by direction of the Presbytery, in supplying some of the vacancies under their care; but in the spring he accompanied his friend, Mr. Samuel Davies, to Virginia, with an intention to share with him, for a few months, the labours of the ministry in that destitute region. As the Episcopal Church was then established by law in Virginia, and no other denomination tolerated, except by explicit consent of the government, he made application, immediately on his arrival at Williamsburg, for permission to exercise the functions of the ministry; and though the Governor received him with great kindness, and did every thing in his power to further his wishes, yet the General Court utterly refused even to allow the reading of his testimonials,—a necessary pre-requisite to his receiving the desired license. Being thus disappointed in not obtaining permission to labour in Virginia, he passed over to Somerset County in Maryland, where he spent the summer of 1748, enjoying the hospitalities of many accomplished and excellent families, and preaching in various places, as he had opportunity. His labours during the season were generally highly acceptable, and in some instances were crowned with a signal blessing.

Early in the autumn of 1748, Mr. Rodgers returned to Pennsylvania, and when he attended the meeting of his Presbytery in October, he found no less than four calls waiting for his consideration. He chose the one from the Congregation of St. George's; which, though the least promising on the score of temporal support and comfort, still seemed to have the strongest claims upon him, on the ground that the prosperity, if not the continued existence, of the congregation was thought to depend upon his acceptance of it. Accordingly, he was ordained to the work of the ministry, and installed pastor of the church of St. George's, on the 16th of March, 1749. The sermon on the occasion was preached by the Rev. Dr. Finley.

His labours in his new charge were attended, from the beginning, with marked success. While he was most diligent in every department of pastoral duty, he had the pleasure to see the number of his hearers constantly increasing, and not a few, as he hoped, savingly profited by his ministry. The congregation soon became too numerous to be accommodated in their place of worship; and they enlarged it repeatedly in the course of a few years; while he was constantly growing in the affection and confidence of all around him. In one of the earliest catechetical exercises which he held for the benefit of the children of his congregation, he met a youth by the name of Alexander McWhorter, the promptness and correctness of whose answers attracted his particular notice, and laid the foundation of an affectionate intimacy between them that was terminated only by death. This lad afterwards became the Rev. Dr. McWhorter of Newark, N. J.

Besides the Congregation of St. George's, Mr. Rodgers had under his care a small congregation near the village of Middletown, De., then generally known as "the Forest Congregation." Here he laboured one-third of his time, and with manifest tokens of the Divine favour.

In the great controversy which, for many years, agitated the Presbyterian Church, and in 1741 rent it asunder, Mr. Rodgers was not a mere spectator. His sympathies were altogether with the "New Side," or the "New Lights," as they were called; and, considering that he had been trained in the school of Whitefield, it would have been strange if it had been otherwise. When a reunion took place in 1758, he had been about nine years in the ministry. It was an event in which he felt the deepest interest, as having in his view a most important bearing on the welfare of Christ's Kingdom.

In September, 1752,—between three and four years after his settlement at St. George's, Mr. Rodgers was married to Elizabeth, eldest daughter of Colonel Peter Bayard, of Cecil County, Md. She was every way fitted for her station, and became the mother of four children; one of whom was Dr. John R. B. Rodgers,—an eminent physician of New York, and another was the wife of the Rev. Dr. William M. Tennent of Abington, Pa.

In 1753, the Rev. Messrs. Samuel Davies of Virginia and Gilbert Tennent of Philadelphia were commissioned by the Synod of New York to visit Great Britain, with a view to solicit contributions in aid of the College of New Jersey. As the Synod undertook to supply their respective pulpits during their absence, Mr. Rodgers was sent, in the spring of 1754, to supply the pulpit of Mr. Davies. In consideration of the rude treatment to which he had been subjected on his previous visit to Virginia, he was apprehensive that he might still meet with some embarrassment from the same source. But herein he was agreeably disappointed: he was received with marked respect and kindness, and suffered to proceed in the discharge of his duty without molestation. He remained in Virginia several months.

Mr. Rodgers had now acquired such general popularity that, towards the close of the same year, (1754,) he was earnestly requested to visit New York, with reference to finding there a permanent settlement. The Presbyterian Church in that city had fallen into a state of unhappy disunion; and it was hoped that a person of his popular talents and conciliatory dispositions and manners might be instrumental in restoring peace. His attachment to his people, however, together with the doubt which he felt in respect to the issue of the proposed change, led him to decline the invitation.

In 1762, Mr. Rodgers was appointed by the Synod of New York and Philadelphia to visit Great Britain, to solicit benefactions in aid of the establishment of a "fund for the relief of poor and distressed Presbyterian ministers, their widows and children." This important and honourable mission, however, the state of his family obliged him to decline; and the Rev. Charles Beatty, another eminent minister, was appointed in his place.

On the 20th of January, 1763, Mr. Rodgers was called to mourn the death of his wife,—an affliction of which he often spoke, to the close of his life, with the utmost tenderness and sorrow. After somewhat more than a year and a half from the time of her death, he entered into a second matrimonial connection with Mrs. Mary Grant, the widow of William Grant, an eminent merchant of Philadelphia. By this marriage, he had one child, a daughter, who died several years before her parents. Mrs. Rodgers survived her husband, and died on the 16th of March, 1812, in the eighty-eighth year of her age. Of this lady Dr. Miller, who knew her well, says,—

"Her great firmness of mind, her remarkable prudence, her polished and dignified manners, her singular sweetness and evenness of temper, joined with fervent piety, endeared her to all that had the happiness of her acquaintance, and rendered her an excellent model for the wife of a clergyman."

In 1765, he was elected one of the Trustees of the College of New Jersey. This office he continued to hold, discharging its duties with most scrupulous fidelity, till 1807, when, with characteristic disinterestedness, he resigned it, that a younger and more active person might be appointed in his place.

In the early part of the year 1765, he received two calls,—one from the Congregation in New York then just vacated by the death of the Rev. David Bostwick,—and another from a large and important Congregational Church in Charleston, S. C. Mr. Whitefield, who happened to visit him about that time, gave it as his decided opinion that the indications of Providence were in favour of his removal, but was doubtful in which direction he ought to go. The question,—which call he should accept, was finally referred to the Synod; and after a patient investigation of the comparative claims of the two congregations, they decided almost unanimously in favour of the Congregation in New York. Accordingly, his pastoral relation to the Church of St. George's was dissolved in May, and his installation as pastor of the Church in New York took place in September following. The Installation Sermon was preached by the Rev. James Caldwell of Elizabeth-town.

Scarcely was Mr. Rodgers introduced to his new sphere of labour, before the influence of his ministrations became perceptible, not only in the rapid growth of the congregation, but in a greatly increased attention to religious things. It became necessary, at no distant period, to erect a new place of worship; and measures were accordingly taken for this purpose early in the spring of 1766. Within about fifteen months, the building was completed, —the same which still stands at the corner of Beekman and Nassau Streets, and is known as "Dr. Spring's Church." A large part of the funds requisite for this enterprise were collected by the personal applications of Mr. Rodgers. The Congregation, though now worshipping in two buildings, was still considered as one body. The ministers preached alternately in each building; and there was but one Board of Trustees, and one Eldership.

In 1768, Mr. Rodgers was honoured with the degree of Doctor of Divinity by the University of Edinburgh. Dr. Franklin, who was at that time in London, wrote, at the suggestion of Mr. Whitefield, to Principal Robertson, recommending Mr. Rodgers as a suitable person to receive such an honour; and, without any unnecessary delay, the request was complied with.

In the summer of 1768, Dr. Witherspoon arrived from Scotland, having a short time before been called to the Presidency of the College of New Jersey. Dr. Rodgers was among the first to do him honour; and he never ceased to regard him with the most affectionate respect. The year after his arrival, he accompanied him on a visit to Boston, and other parts of New England, from which both of them seem to have derived great enjoyment. Dr. Rodgers, who survived his venerable friend many years, preached a Sermon on the occasion of his death, by request of the Trustees of the College over which Dr. Witherspoon had presided. The Sermon was published, and is thought to have been the most creditable, in a literary point of view, of Dr. Rodgers' printed productions.

In 1774, Dr. Rodgers was appointed by the Synod to make a missionary tour of a few weeks during the summer, through the Northern and Northwestern parts of the Province of New York. He fulfilled the appointment in a laborious and faithful manner, and with considerable success. This mission occurred just at the time of the violent controversy between the settlers of the territory which is now Vermont, and the government of New York, in respect to the matter of jurisdiction. Some of the incensed Vermonters suspected, as he came from New York, that he had some political end to accomplish, adverse to their interests; and in one or two instances, there was a serious purpose formed to arrest him. But the individuals who had meditated it, were prevailed on to suspend its execution till he had fulfilled an appointment to preach; and, after hearing him, they were so much impressed with his Christian sincerity, that they were disposed to bid him God speed in his mission.

Dr. Rodgers was an early and devoted friend to his country's independence. Previous to the commencement of hostilities, he was associated with several other clergymen, among whom were Doctors Mason and Laidlie, in a weekly meeting for friendly intercourse and mutual improvement. As things were seen to be approaching a crisis, these excellent men determined to make this meeting an occasion for special prayer that the struggle in which the country was about to engage might be successful; and the meeting was continued, with reference to this object, until the ministers composing it, and the great mass of the people, were obliged to fly for safety from the city. Dr. Rodgers removed his family to a place in the neighbourhood, in February, 1776. They remained there for about two months; and he, in the mean time, visited the city, whenever his professional duties required. On the 14th of April of that year, General Washington took possession of New York for its defence. Shortly after his arrival, Dr. Rodgers, with several other gentlemen friendly to the American cause, called to pay him their respects. The General received him with marked attention, and, as he was about to retire, followed him to the door, and remarked that he had been mentioned to him in Philadelphia as a person who might be able to render him important service in reference to the cause of his country, and asked if he would allow him to apply to him for information whenever he might find it desirable. The Doctor assured him that he should do with the utmost alacrity whatever might be in his power. The General subsequently availed himself of the privilege of consulting the Doctor on more than one occasion, and it is hardly necessary to add that all his suggestions and requests received the most prompt attention.

In May, 1776, Dr. Rodgers removed his family from the neighbourhood of New York to Greenfield, Conn., as a place where they would be more out of the reach of the din and perils of war. Having been just before appointed a Chaplain to General Heath's Brigade, which, for several months, was stationed near Greenwich on York Island, he returned immediately from Greenfield, and entered on the duties of his Chaplaincy. These duties he performed with great zeal and fidelity, exhibiting at once a spirit of earnest piety and glowing patriotism.

In November of that year, having important private business to transact in Georgia, he resigned his Chaplaincy, and travelled by land through the whole Southern country to Savannah. He, however, took care to make his journey instrumental, as far as he could, of the furtherance of the Gospel; preaching not only on the Sabbath, but also on week-day evenings, whenever there was an opportunity. At Savannah he remained for some time with his friend, the Rev. Dr. Zubly, who had shortly before visited him in New York. Here also he met many of the friends of Whitefield; and the intimate relations in which he had stood to that eminent man, were a passport at once to their affectionate regards and devoted attentions.

In April, 1777, Dr. Rodgers returned from Georgia, and on his way home was informed of his election to the Chaplaincy of the Convention of the State of New York, then in session in Esopus. Having paid a short visit to his family at Greenfield, he immediately repaired to the Convention, and entered on the duties of his office. Subsequently, when the power of the State was lodged in a Council of Safety, which also held its meetings in Esopus, he served as Chaplain to that Body also. And at a still later period, when the first Legislature of the State, under the new constitution, convened, he was a third time elected to the same office. Meanwhile, he removed his family from Greenfield to Esopus, where they spent the whole of the summer, and part of the autumn, of 1777. They were, however, at length driven from Esopus by the burning of the village by the British; and the Doctor determined then to select for them a more retired and less exposed situation. Accordingly, towards the end of October, he removed them to Sharon, Conn., where he passed the following winter. During his sojourn here, he preached repeatedly for the Rev. Cotton Mather Smith, the minister of the parish in which he resided; and still more frequently to a congregation in the town of Amenia, in Duchess County, N. Y., in the neighbourhood of Sharon,—where he afterwards made a temporary settlement. This latter congregation had, for many years, been agitated by serious divisions; but, through the healing influence of Dr. Rodgers' ministrations, it was restored to its former harmony, besides being in other respects greatly benefitted and improved.

In April, 1780, the Doctor, to the great grief of the people among whom he had laboured in Amenia, accepted an invitation to remove to Danbury, and preach to the Society in that town. Here again he found a divided congregation; and by his prudence, zeal, and fidelity, he accomplished the same harmonizing work as in the congregation to which he had previously ministered. He declined being installed pastor of the church, on the ground that he wished to hold himself in readiness, on the return of Peace, to resume his pastoral charge in New York. He, however, joined the Congregational Association within whose bounds he resided, and cheerfully co-operated with his brethren around in all their plans for the general advancement of religion.

After remaining at Danbury somewhat more than two years, he was led, by some adverse circumstances, to determine on a change of residence; and, accordingly, in the spring of 1782, he accepted an invitation from the Church of Lamington, N. J., to minister to them, as long as Providence should continue the separation between him and his own people. In May of that year, he removed from Danbury to Lamington, where he continued, discharging all the duties of a pastor, till the autumn of 1783, when the close of the war permitted him to resume his connection with his Congregation in New York, from which he had so long been exiled.

On their return to the city after their dispersion, they found their numbers greatly diminished, their parsonage burnt, and both their houses of worship in a state of almost total ruin. They, however, rallied their energies with a view to recover themselves; and their first object was to obtain accommodations for public worship during the time that must elapse before their church edifices could be repaired. The Vestry of Trinity Church, with most honourable liberality, offered them the use of St. George's and St. Paul's Churches, as long as their necessities should require. This offer they gratefully accepted, and were thus accommodated by their Episcopal neighbours, from November, 1783, till the following June. One of Dr. Rodgers' earliest sermons, after resuming his ministry in New York, was delivered on a day of National Thanksgiving and Prayer, and was afterwards published, bearing the title "The Divine goodness displayed in the American Revolution."

The church in Beekman Street was first repaired, and as it was immediately ascertained that one building was quite inadequate to accommodate the applicants for pews, they set about repairing the church in Wall Street also; and in due time both were ready for occupancy. The expense of repairing the two buildings was very considerable; but Dr. Rodgers, with his accustomed magnanimity, volunteered, as he had done on a former occasion, to do a large part of the drudgery of collecting the requisite funds.

The Rev. Mr. Treat, with whom Dr. Rodgers had been associated as co-pastor, did not, owing to some personal considerations, return to the city after the close of the war; and the congregation having signified their willingness to dispense with the services of a second pastor, he was dismissed by the Presbytery in October, 1784. Subsequently, however, as their numbers increased, it was found that another pastor was needed; and the congregation, in April, 1785, called Mr. James Wilson, a licensed candidate for the ministry, who had then just arrived from Scotland. He was installed in August following, as colleague with Dr. Rodgers; but, after labouring very diligently and acceptably for about three years, his health became so much impaired that he was obliged to seek a Southern climate, and consequently resigned his pastoral charge.*

In the summer of 1789, the Rev. (afterwards Dr.) John McKnight, pastor of the Church in Marsh Creek, Pa., was invited to succeed Mr. Wilson; and, having accepted the invitation, was installed as a collegiate pastor of the Uni-

* Mr. Wilson, about the time of resigning his charge, received a call from the Presbyterian Church in Charleston, S. C., where there was reason to believe that both the climate and the service required of him would be more favourable to his health than those of New-York; and he accordingly signified his acceptance of the call on the 22d of January, 1788. After spending several years of ministerial comfort and usefulness in Charleston, he returned to Scotland where he remained a year or two, and then came again to America. He never took a pastoral charge after this; but, after struggling with ill health for several years, died in Virginia, in the year 1799, in the forty-eighth year of his age.

ted Churches with Dr. Rodgers, in December following. In the year 1792, Dr. McKnight's health became so much impaired that he was unable to preach, as he had been accustomed to do, three times on the Sabbath, in consequence of which, they called a third pastor, Mr. Samuel Miller, now (1849) the Rev. Dr. Miller, Professor in the Theological Seminary at Princeton. Dr. Miller remained pastor of the church for several years after the death of Dr. Rodgers, and still cherishes his memory with a truly filial veneration.

The Legislature of New York, shortly after the Revolution, passed an Act establishing a Board, styled, "The Regents of the University of New York,"—whose office it is, in general, to watch over the interests of literature throughout the State. Of this University, Dr. Rodgers was chosen Vice Chancellor, and he held the office as long as he lived.

In the revision of the public standards of the Presbyterian Church, and in all those measures which led to their adoption and establishment on the present plan, Dr. Rodgers had a highly important agency. And when the first General Assembly, under the new arrangement, met in Philadelphia, in May, 1789, he had the honour of being chosen Moderator of that Body.

In December 1803, Dr. Rodgers gave notice to the Session of his Church that, "on account of his age and growing infirmities, he was no longer able to preach more than once on the Lord's day," and requested that the requisite additional supply for the pulpit might be furnished. The request was of course acceded to with the utmost alacrity. Previous to this time, he had been accustomed to deliver his Sermons *memoriter;* but finding that his memory had begun to fail him, he commenced preaching with his sermon before him, and continued this practice as long as he continued to preach. In 1809, he had become so far enfeebled in both body and mind, that it was not without much difficulty that he could go through the service; and in September of that year he preached his last sermon. He subsequently attempted, on one occasion, to officiate at the administration of the Lord's Supper; but the great imperfection of his memory rendered the service alike difficult to himself, and painful to those who witnessed it. He continued gradually to decline, though he occasionally walked abroad, till about the close of the succeeding year, when he became too feeble to leave his house. For six weeks previous to his death, he was confined to his bed nearly the whole time; and after his memory had ceased to do its office in respect to all temporal objects and interests, and even his dearest friends, it was almost as vigorous as ever in regard to spiritual and eternal realities. He prayed with his family for the last time on the evening preceding his death, and sunk calmly to his rest on the 7th of May, 1811, in the eighty-fourth year of his age, and the sixty-third of his ministry. His funeral was attended two days afterwards, and an Address delivered on the occasion by the Rev. Dr. Milledoler. A Funeral Sermon was preached on the succeeding Sabbath by Dr. Miller, which was published some time after, in connection with the Memoirs of Dr. Rodgers, in an octavo volume.

Besides some miscellaneous articles in connection with the Episcopal controversy, and several Sermons in the "American Preacher," Dr. Rodgers published A Sermon before a Masonic Lodge, at Stockbridge, Mass., 1779; A National Thanksgiving Sermon, 1783; A Sermon on the death of Dr. Witherspoon, 1794; and A Sermon at the opening of the Cedar Street Church, 1808.

FROM THE REV. SAMUEL MILLER, D. D.,

PROFESSOR IN THE THEOLOGICAL SEMINARY AT PRINCETON.

PRINCETON, May 30, 1849.

Rev. dear Brother: When you request me to prepare for your forthcoming biographical work some brief memorials of the late venerable Dr. Rodgers of New York, I feel as if I were called not to the performance of a task, but to the enjoyment of a privilege. If there be a man living who is entitled to speak of that eminent servant of Christ, I am that man. Having been long and intimately acquainted with him; having served with him twenty years as a son in the Gospel ministry; and having enjoyed peculiar opportunities of contemplating every phase of his character, personal and official; so my ardent attachment and deep veneration for his memory make it delightful to record what I knew with so much distinctness, and remember with so much interest.

My acquaintance with Dr. Rodgers began in 1792, when he was more than sixty years of age, and when I was a youthful and inexperienced candidate for the ministry. He recognised in me the son of an old clerical friend, and from that hour till the day of his death treated me with a fidelity and kindness truly paternal. And when, next year, I became his colleague, he uniformly continued to exercise toward me that parental indulgence and guardianship which became his inherited friendship, as well as his Christian and ecclesiastical character.

Without attempting in this connection to enter into the details of his history, which I have already done at large in my "Memoir" of this beloved man, I shall content myself with recounting in a brief manner those features in his character which I regard as worthy of special commemoration, and which rendered him so conspicuous among the pastors of his day.

One of the great charms of Dr. Rodgers' character was *the fervour and uniformity of his piety*. It not only appeared conspicuous in the pulpit,—dictating his choice of subjects, his mode of treating them, and his affectionate earnestness of manner; but it attended him wherever he went, and manifested itself in whatever he did. In the house of mourning it shone with distinguished lustre. Nor was this all. He probably never was known to enter a human dwelling for the purpose of paying an ordinary visit, without saying something before he left it to recommend the Saviour and his service. Seldom did he sit down at the convivial table, without dropping at least a few sentences adapted to promote the spiritual benefit of those around him. In all the domestic relations of life, piety pervaded and regulated his conduct; controlling a temper naturally hasty and irascible, and prompting to the affectionate courtesies of Christian benevolence. I well remember a circumstance which, though small in itself, was considered by an impartial observer as not a little significant. A young clergyman, who had paid a short visit to the city, and who had enjoyed two or three pleasant interviews with Dr. Rodgers, a few years before his death,—at the close of the last interview, rose and offered his hand for the purpose of bidding him farewell. The Doctor took it, and squeezing it affectionately, with a very few simple words expressive of pious hope and tender benediction, dismissed him. The clergyman, on retiring, inquired whether what he had just witnessed was the Doctor's *common* manner of taking leave of his friends; adding that he had seldom seen any thing so much like the pious and primitive style of an Apostle before.

Another quality in Dr. Rodgers which, next to his piety, contributed to his high reputation, was *prudence*, or *practical wisdom*. Few men were more wary than he in foreseeing circumstances likely to produce embarrassment or difficulty, and in avoiding them. Few men were more cautious of "giving" unnecessary "offence that the ministry might not be blamed," or more watchful with respect to all those modes of exhibiting truth or of performing duty, which are calculated to conciliate the differently constituted minds of men. Hence he was able to do a thousand things without exciting the least resentment, which many others would not have accomplished without encountering the most determined opposition and animosity. And hence he rarely found himself in those perplexing and painful situations, to which the indiscreet and unwary are so frequently reduced, to the interruption of their own peace, and to the discredit of religion.

He was remarkable also for the *uniform, persevering and indefatigable character of his ministerial labours.* In preaching, in catechizing, in attending on the sick and dying, in all the arduous labours of discipline and government, and in visiting from house to house, he went on with unceasing constancy, year after year, from the beginning to the end of his ministry. He not only abounded in ministerial labours, but he laboured systematically, uniformly, and with unwearied patience. Difficulties did not usually appal him; delays did not discourage him. Those who found him busily engaged in pursuing a certain regular and judicious course at one period, would be sure to find him, after a series of years, pursuing with steady and undeviating steps the same course. In short, as his learned friend, Dr. Livingston, has remarked concerning him, he was literally "*forever the same.*"

The character of Dr. Rodgers' *preaching* was another of the leading elements of his popularity and usefulness. The two qualities most remarkable in his preaching were *piety* and *animation.* His sermons were always rich in evangelical truth; and they were generally delivered with a solemnity and earnestness which indicated a deep impression on his own heart of the importance of what he uttered. And hence, though he was never remarkable for that variety, either in the choice or the illustration of his subjects, which some would have preferred; and though he never gave himself the trouble to attain that polish and elegance of style to which many lend a large share of their attention, still, in the days of his vigour, he was one of the most popular as well as useful preachers in the American Church. No one ever found him affecting novelty in the representations which he gave of Divine truth, either with respect to their substance or their modes of expression, because he considered *the old as better;* and in the old track he was found forever walking.

Dr. Rodgers was *eminently a disinterested man.* Few men have ever been more free from private and selfish aims in acting their part in the affairs of the Church, than he. Of ecclesiastical policy, other than that which sought to promote the peace, the order, the purity, the extension, and the happiness, of the Church, by the most fair and honourable means, he evidently knew nothing. In petty schemes for diminishing the influence of his brethren that he might increase his own, or in the arts of intrigue, to play off contending parties or individuals, as engines for promoting his personal elevation, he was never suspected of engaging. He was always a peace-maker, never a divider. He rejoiced in the honour and success of his brethren. And when, towards the close of his life, some of the young men whom he had been instrumental in introducing into the ministry enjoyed a measure of popularity, which might be said in a degree to eclipse his own, his most intimate friends never saw him manifest on this account the smallest uneasiness. On the contrary, he appeared to take unfeigned pleasure in witnessing the acceptance of their labours, and in contributing to raise rather than depress their reputation.

Dr. Rodgers was further distinguished by a *punctual attendance on the judicatories of the Church.* He made it a point never to be absent from the meetings of his brethren, unless sickness or some other equally imperious dispensation of Providence rendered his attendance impossible. And when present in the several ecclesiastical courts, he gave his serious and undivided attention to the business which came before them, and was always ready to take his full share, and more than his share, of the labour connected with that business. The consequence was that he became personally known to almost all his brethren in the ministry of his own denomination in the United States; that he enjoyed their friendship and confidence; that he kept up a connected and thorough acquaintance with the affairs of the Church; that he contributed to strengthen the hands of those with whom he acted; and that thus the sphere both of his honour and his usefulness was greatly extended.

The great *liberality of sentiment* which Dr. Rodgers habitually discovered, endeared him to thousands, and contributed not a little to the extension of his influence. Though he was a firm Presbyterian, and a decided Calvinist, he was far from being a bigot. He seldom mentioned the opinions of others in the pulpit; but contented himself with declaring, illustrating, and endeavouring to recommend, what he believed to be the doctrines of Scripture. And on one occasion, when he was urged by some of the officers of his church to preach against what he regarded the errors of a particular sect, and to warn his people against them by name, he utterly refused, saying, "Brethren, you must excuse me. I cannot reconcile it with my sense either of policy or of duty to oppose these people from the pulpit, otherwise than by preaching the truth plainly and faithfully. I believe them to be in error; but let us out-preach them, out-pray them, and out-live them, and we need not fear."

Dr. Rodgers was remarkably prompt in obeying the calls of *humanity and benevolence.* Besides attending to his duty in several religious Societies, of all which he was President, he found time to be one of the most active and useful members of the "Society for the relief of distressed prisoners," and of the "Board of Trustees of the City Dispensary," in both of which, for a number of years, he presided. He was also a member of the "Manumission Society" of New York, and manifested a deep interest in the abolition of slavery, and in the success of plans for meliorating the condition of slaves. Nor did he, as is too often done, content himself with being a mere nominal member of those Associations. As long as he retained his vigour of body and mind, few persons in the community took a more active part than he in promoting and executing plans of enlightened and diffusive benevolence.

Both the reputation and usefulness of Dr. Rodgers were doubtless promoted by the *peculiar and uniform dignity of his manners.* This part of his character was not only remarkable but pre-eminent. If his manners had sometimes a degree of formality in them which excited the smile of the frivolous, they always manifested the polish of the well-bred gentleman, as well as the benevolence of the Christian, and never failed to command respect. He was habitually cheerful, and often facetious and sportive; but his sportiveness was always as remarkable for its taste and dignity as it was for the perfect inoffensiveness of its character. There was a uniformity, an urbanity, and a vigilance, in his dignity, which plainly showed that it was not the result of temporary effort, but the spontaneous product of a polished, benevolent and elevated mind.

I may say also in this connection that he was always *attentive to his dress.* Like his manners and his morals, it was invariably neat, elegant and spotless. He appeared to have an innate abhorrence of every thing like slovenliness or disorder about his person. And while there was nothing that indicated an excessive or finical attention to the material or adjustment of his clothing, it was ever such as manifested the taste of a gentleman. In this respect, he resembled his friend and spiritual father, Mr. Whitefield, whose sayings and example on the subject he not unfrequently quoted, and who often remarked that a minister of the Gospel, in his dress, as well as in every thing else, ought to be "*without spot.*"

The *personal appearance* of Dr. Rodgers, like every thing else about him, was remarkable. His *stature* was very little, if any, above the middle size. But his person was expanded and thick set, and whenever he appeared in the street, his neat and becoming professional costume, his large white wig, his venerable figure, and his dignified, slow, composed walk, all proclaimed the grave, apostolic man of God, who was going to and fro on errands of mercy.

I am, my dear Sir,

Sincerely and affectionately yours,

SAMUEL MILLER

ELIHU SPENCER, D. D.

1748—1784.

FROM THE REV. SAMUEL MILLER, D. D.

PRINCETON, April, 20, 1849.

Rev. and dear Sir: I am happy, in compliance with your request, to send you some notices of the Rev. Elihu Spencer, D. D., who was for many years the respected and beloved pastor of the Presbyterian Church in Trenton, N. J., and whose decease in that city, took place in the year 1784.

The ancestors of the family from which this eminent man descended, were five brothers, who emigrated from England to Massachusetts early in the seventeenth century. The eldest of these brothers, *John Spencer*, appears to have been a large landholder, a magistrate, a member of the General Court, and a high military officer in Newtown, now Cambridge, from 1634 to 1638, when he returned to England, and seems to have left no descendants on this side of the Atlantic. *William Spencer* the second brother, also settled in Cambridge, where he was a member of the General Court, and a landed proprietor. He afterwards removed to Connecticut, where he died in 1640, leaving a numerous family. He was the ancestor of the Honourable *Ambrose Spencer*, late Chief Justice of the State of New York. *Thomas Spencer*, the third brother, was also first settled in Cambridge, but removed to Connecticut in 1638; and died in Haddam, the residence of his family, in 1685, leaving a numerous posterity. The Rev. *Ichabod S. Spencer*, D. D., pastor of the First Presbyterian church in Brooklyn, N. Y.; the Honourable *Joshua Austin Spencer* of Utica, and several other eminent men bearing that name in the same State, are among his distinguished descendants. The fourth brother, *Jared Spencer*, originally settled with his brothers at Cambridge. He removed thence in a few years to Lynn, and not long afterwards to Connecticut, when he became one of the first settlers of the town of Haddam. He died in 1685, leaving a large family of children. The Rev. *Elihu Spencer*, the subject of this article, and General *Joseph Spencer*, a distinguished and active military officer during the Revolutionary war, were among his descendants. The fifth brother, *Michael Spencer*, was a joint proprietor with his brother *Jared*, and removed with him to Lynn, where he died in 1653. It is not known to me that any of his posterity remain.

ELIHU SPENCER, the subject of this sketch, was born at East Haddam, Conn., February 12, 1721. He was the son of Isaac and Mary Spencer, and early manifested an active and energetic mind. He commenced a course of literary study, with a view to the Gospel ministry, in the month of March, 1740; entered Yale College in September, 1742; and was graduated A. B. in September, 1746. After his graduation, he was recommended and urged to undertake a mission among the Indians of the Six Nations. His designation and recommendation to this office came from such men as David Brainerd, whose zeal and labours among another portion of the Indian population of our country are known and celebrated throughout the evangelical world; and Jonathan Edwards the elder, whose reputation and influence, as a great as well as a good man, are, if possible, still more widely diffused. On their recommendation, and under the sanction of the Society in Great Britain, which had fostered the other missions among the Indians, he undertook the arduous task. With this view, after leaving College, he spent a number of months with the Rev. John Brainerd, the surviving brother of David, who was also an eminent missionary among the Indian tribes. Under his direction he employed much time in studying the language of the Indian tribes, to which he contemplated devoting his labours; and with so much success that members of his own family have assured me that he spoke several of the Indian languages with great ease and fluency. And it is particularly recorded of him that he formed a large and accurate vocabulary of the language of the Oneida Tribe, which was deemed of great value. Nor was the study of the Indian languages the only object of his attention, appropriate to the missionary enterprise which he had undertaken. He spent some time in the family of President Edwards at Northampton, availing himself of his experience in Indian missions, and accompanied that eminent man to Albany, for the purpose of being present with him at the solemnities of an Indian treaty of much interest, which was held in that city. He appears also to have spent some months in actual missionary labour in the Western part of the Province of New York. And in pursuance of his favourite object, he was solemnly ordained to the work of the ministry, with a special view to an Indian mission, by an ordaining council in Boston, in September, 1748.

The leadings of Providence, however, appear to have been such as prevented his accomplishing what he and his friends had anticipated in this department of evangelical labour. After leaving Mr. Edwards, he came to Elizabethtown, in New Jersey, where he found the Presbyterian Church vacant in consequence of the death of President Dickinson. Here his preaching was so acceptable that the congregation gave him a call to become their pastor, which he was constrained to accept, and was installed in that office February 7, 1750, in the twenty-ninth year of his age.

In a little less than a year after settling in the pastoral office in Elizabethtown, Mr. Spencer was married to Miss Joanna Eaton, daughter of John Eaton, Esquire, and Joanna his wife, of Shrewsbury, in New Jersey. This took place on the 15th day of October, 1750, when he was in the thirtieth year of his age, and when the lady whom he married was in her twenty-first year. He remained the pastor of the Church in Elizabethtown about six years. While there, in 1753, he was invited by Governor Belcher to become the Chaplain of the New Jersey regiment, employed in the war then waging with the French and Indians; which he does not appear to have accepted. It was during his residence in Elizabethtown that his character for piety and public spirit prompted the Trustees of the College of New Jersey, then temporarily placed at Newark, to elect him one of the Corporate Guardians of that Institution. This occurred in 1752; and he held this honourable office as long as he lived. In 1756, he left Elizabethtown, and accepted a call to the pastoral charge of the Presbyterian Church at Jamaica,

L. I., where he remained, acceptably and usefully, two years or more. At the end of that time, he was appointed by Governor De Lancey of New York to the Chaplaincy of the New York troops, then about to march and take their place in the French war still raging. This appointment he appears to have accepted; and the Congregation of Jamaica reluctantly gave their consent to his leaving them for that purpose, because they expected their children, who had enlisted in the military service, to be under his spiritual care.

When his services as Chaplain in the army were closed, he transferred his relation from the Presbytery of Suffolk with which he had been connected, to that of New Brunswick, and laboured several years in the contiguous Congregations of Shrewsbury, Middletown Point, Shark River, and Amboy. It was about this time that he addressed a Letter to the Rev. Ezra Stiles, D. D., afterwards President of Yale College, then Pastor of a Church in Newport, R. I., which was published, and attracted no small share of public attention. The subject of it was "The state of the Dissenting Interest in the Middle Colonies of America." This Letter was originally dated at Jamaica, July 2, 1759, and there were some Amendments and Additions to it at Shrewsbury on the 3d of November following. So far as is known to me, this is the only formal important work that he ever committed to the press.

In the year 1764, the venerable Synod of New York and Philadelphia, having reason to believe that a number of their congregations in the Southern parts of our country, and especially in North Carolina, were in an unformed and irregular state, deemed it of great importance to send among them some divines of known wisdom, prudence, and popular talents, who might instruct, counsel and guide them aright, and prepare them for a more orderly and edifying organization. For this important, confidential and arduous service, the Synod selected the Rev. Messrs. Elihu Spencer, and Alexander McWhorter of Newark, N. J. They accepted the appointment; were employed a number of months on this mission; and were considered as having rendered, with much skill and efficiency, a very important service to the Southern Churches.

Soon after Mr. Spencer's return from the South, the Congregation of St. George's in Delaware having become vacant in consequence of Dr. Rodgers, their former pastor, having accepted an invitation to New York, he was called to succeed him in the pastoral charge. This call Mr. Spencer accepted, and spent about five years in St. George's, greatly to the acceptance and benefit of the congregation. Finding the climate, however, unhealthy to himself, and that his large and growing family was every year suffering more and more from epidemic disease, he felt constrained to remove, and in October, 1769, accepted a call to the city of Trenton, in New Jersey, in the pastoral charge of which church he continued, greatly popular, useful and beloved, until he was removed by death.

When the Revolutionary struggle came on, it found Mr. Spencer diligently engaged in his pastoral duties at Trenton. He not only took the course which almost all the Presbyterian ministers in the United States did, decisively in favour of the claims of the Colonies; but, with his constitutional zeal and energy, he became warmly and conspicuously engaged on the patriotic side. This led to another call which was made upon him in 1775, again to visit North Carolina. When he visited that Colony, ten years before, by order of the Synod, he and his companion, Dr. McWhorter, left such an impression of their talents and piety, and especially of their power in addressing and moving large masses of men, that there was a strong popular desire to engage their services again for a different purpose. The Provincial Congress of that Colony, having reason to believe that the population of several important settlements within their limits, were, partly from ignorance and partly from prejudice in favour of the British government, unfriendly to the cause of Independence, conceived the plan of employing the influence and the patriotic eloquence of the same gentlemen, who had before so ably served them on an evangelical mission. The request was made. It was accepted. Dr. McWhorter accompanied Mr. Spencer, and very valuable services to the cause of Independence were supposed to have been rendered in that part of the Southern country.

It is hardly necessary to say that these active and conspicuous services of Mr. Spencer to the cause of the Whigs greatly embittered towards him the feelings of the Tories. They hated him, threatened him, and on one occasion committed to the flames a large part of his books, and all his most important papers, which happened to fall into their power.

In 1782, the degree of Doctor of Divinity was conferred upon him by the University of Pennsylvania.

His last illness was an inflammatory fever, which terminated his life after a few days, during which he enjoyed abundant Christian support and consolation. His tomb stands in the cemetery connected with the church in Trenton, and bears the following inscription:—

"Beneath this stone lies the body of the Rev. Elihu Spencer, D. D., Pastor of the Presbyterian Church of Trenton, and one of the Trustees of the College of New Jersey, who departed this life on the 27th of December, 1784, in the the 64th year of his age. Possessed of fine genius, of great vivacity, of eminent active piety, his merits as a minister and a man stand above the reach of flattery. Having long edified the Church by his talents and example, and finished his course with joy, he fell asleep full of faith, and waiting for the hope of all Saints."

The accomplishments prominently dwelt upon in this epitaph were really those which shone conspicuously in Dr. Spencer. His piety was ardent; his manners polished, attractive, and full of engaging vivacity; his public spirit and activity in doing good indefatigable; and his character as a preacher singularly prompt, popular and impressive. Whenever, at the meeting of any judicatory, the ministers were at a loss about a preacher, when *he* appeared, the remark was,—"Here comes ready-money Spencer; now we shall have a sermon.' To all this may be added that in the various relations of life he was peculiarly amiable, exemplary and beloved. But on such a character there is no need of enlarging in further detail. It has been justly remarked by a respectable minister of the Gospel, who had well considered his history, "We cannot hesitate to place far above the ordinary grade, a man whom such men as David Brainerd and Jonathan Edwards, the elder, loved and strongly recommended; who was deemed worthy to succeed in their pastoral labours such ministers as Jonathan Dickinson and John Rodgers; whom two Governors, one not of his own denomination, successively appointed to Chaplaincies of a trying and arduous character; who was selected by a venerable Synod to perform a service, evidently calling for peculiar piety, wisdom, and address; and whom an enlightened Provincial Congress deemed the fittest instrument they could find, for accomplishing a most important and delicate patriotic service."

Dr. Spencer had a large and interesting family of children, a number of whom survived him. He had only one son who reached adult age,—*John Spencer*, Esquire, who was bred to the bar, and who died, a number of years since, leaving several children. His second daughter, *Sarah*, married Stephen Lowrey, Esquire, a merchant of Maryland, of which marriage only one daughter now survives. His third daughter, *Margaret*, married Jonathan Dickinson Sergeant, Esquire, a distinguished member of Congress, and Counsellor at the Philadelphia Bar. Of that marriage only three children survive, namely,—the Hon. *John Sergeant*, and the Hon. *Thomas Sergeant*, eminent Jurists, now residing in Philadelphia, and the eldest daughter, *Sarah*, now living in Princeton, the wife of him who gives this account. Dr. Spencer's fourth daughter, *Elizabeth*, married George Merchant, Esquire, an eminent classical teacher, long since deceased, leaving several children. His fifth daughter, *Valeria*, was allied in marriage to Richard Fullerton, Esquire, a broker of Philadelphia, of whom no issue survive. His sixth, *Lydia*, was married to William M. Biddle, Esquire, also a broker of Philadelphia. She is the only one of her father's children still living. She survives, an aged widow, and the mother of several amiable and promising children. Dr. Spencer's eldest and youngest daughters died unmarried.

I am, Rev. and dear Sir,
Very sincerely and respectfully yours,
SAMUEL MILLER.

JOHN MILLER.*

1748—1791.

John Miller was born in Boston, December 24, (O. S.) 1722. His father was John Miller, a native of Scotland, who migrated to America, and settled in Boston in the year 1710, and not long afterwards married Margaret Bass of Braintree, Mass. He was bred a Presbyterian in his own country, but connected himself in Boston with the Old South Church, then under the pastoral care of the Rev. Dr. Pemberton. Little more is now known of him, than that he was a remarkably grave, shrewd, discreet man, and that he carried on, for a number of years, and with great success, a sugar refinery and distillery in Boston.

John Miller, the elder, had two children; *John* was the eldest—*Joseph*, a younger brother, was never married. Soon after reaching mature age, he embarked on a voyage of commercial enterprise to Great Britain. But the ship in which he sailed is supposed to have foundered at sea. He was never heard of afterwards.

John, the subject of this sketch, was never graduated at any College. He received an excellent classical education at a public school of high

* MS. from his son, Rev. Dr. Samuel Miller.

repute in Boston, then under the care of Mr. John Lovell, who for a number of years maintained a very high character as a classical teacher, and was the honoured preceptor of a large number of the most eminent men of New England. Here young Miller studied with great diligence, and became a very accurate Latin and Greek scholar. Toward the latter part of his connection with Master Lovell's institution, he became decidedly pious, under the ministry of the Rev. Dr. Sewall, whose praise was in all the Churches, as a man of pre-eminent piety and devotedness in the sacred office, and who had now come into the pastoral care of the Old South. With this church he became united. Not long afterwards, he determined to devote himself to the Christian ministry; and soon commenced a course of study preparatory to entering on that office. He now engaged in the study of the Hebrew language, in which he became a proficient.

In May, 1748, Mr. Miller was licensed to preach the Gospel by the Association in the bounds of which he resided. Soon after receiving license, he travelled into the Colonies of Delaware and Maryland, and, having received a unanimous call from the Presbyterian Church at Dover in Delaware, he returned to Boston; was ordained to the work of the Gospel ministry, by a Council of which Dr. Sewall, Mr. Webb, Dr. Mather Byles, and several other eminent ministers of Boston, were members, and which convened in the Old South Church. This ordination was with a particular view to his taking charge of the Church in Dover, which had called him.

Immediately after his ordination, he repaired to Delaware, and commenced his evangelical labours in Dover, and soon afterwards received a call from the Presbyterian Church of Smyrna, twelve miles North of Dover. In the service of these two churches, he fixed his residence between them, four miles from Dover. Here, in the retired and exemplary discharge of his duties as pastor, he spent more than forty years.

Not long after Mr. Miller became fixed in his pastoral relation, he directed his views to a matrimonial connection; and, accordingly, on the 3d of November, 1751, he was married to Margaret, the eldest daughter of Allumby Millington,—a native of England, who had, a number of years before, settled as a planter in Talbot County, Md., seven or eight miles from the town of Easton. Of this lady, Dr. Rodgers of New York has often been heard to say that she was one of the most beautiful women he ever saw. However this might have been, nothing is more certain than that her moral beauty was eminently conspicuous, and acknowledged by all who knew her. She proved such a rich blessing to her husband, her children, and all with whom she associated, as the pen of biography has rarely an opportunity of recording. Her good sense, her pre-eminent prudence, her skill and fidelity in every domestic relation, her active benevolence, and, above all, her unaffected, fervent, consistent piety, rendered her the most conspicuous ornament of every circle and of every neighbourhood in which she moved.

Soon after Mr. Miller's settlement as a pastor, he purchased a small farm of a hundred acres, on which he resided during the remainder of his life. This he so managed as to make it contribute something toward the support of his family, and also to furnish amusement during the intervals of study.

Mr. Miller's life as a pastor was passed in retirement, and with few other occurrences than those which were connected with the unwearied discharge of the duties of the sacred office. When he first settled as a pastor, within the bounds of the Presbyterian Church, in 1749, he found it rent into two parties known as the *Old* and *New Side.* Being a great lover of peace, he did not at once seek a connection with either party; but, at the end of eight years,—namely, in 1757, he became a member of the Presbytery of Newcastle, and thus connected himself with the Old Side.

Mr. Miller was a punctual attendant on church judicatories as long as he lived. He was twice elected Moderator of the Old Synod, then the highest judicatory of the Church;—an honour which, it is believed, has been conferred in one other instance only, in the whole course of the history of the Presbyterian Church. He was always a diligent student. He gathered round him a much larger library than almost any of his brethren in the ministry possessed; and on all occasions appeared the friend of learning.

In 1763, the College of Philadelphia conferred upon him the degree of Master of Arts.

As the claims and conflicts of the Colonies with respect to the mother country drew on, Mr. Miller, like almost all his brethren in the ministry of the Presbyterian Church, with zeal and decision, took the side of the Colonies; and though naturally of a nervous and timid temperament, yet here he appeared to be animated with unwonted decision. He was so far from making any secret of his patriotic ardour, that a few days before the Declaration of Independence, he so far anticipated the spirit of that memorable movement, as to address the people of his pastoral charge from the decisive language of the revolting Tribes in the days of Rehoboam: (I. Kings xii, 16.) "We have no part in David, nor any inheritance in the Son of Jesse; to your tents, Oh! Israel!" He continued, to the end of life, a thorough, zealous, uncompromising Whig.

The temporal circumstances of this venerable man were never affluent, and sometimes were uncomfortably straitened. Yet he made out to give all his sons who reached mature age, a liberal education. He instructed them himself with great care in the Greek and Latin languages; and, when he saw that it was desirable, sent five of them to College, where they were all graduated.

Mr. Miller was a thorough and zealous Calvinist of the Old School. And though, having been bred a Congregationalist, he was not so warmly zealous with regard to Presbyterian Church order, yet he cordially fell in with that form of ecclesiastical government, and declined to co-operate with his intimate and beloved friend, the Rev. Dr. Matthew Wilson of Lewistown, in opposing it.

When the Old Synod was dissolved in 1788, and the first General Assembly met in 1789, Mr. Miller was becoming too infirm to take an active part in the public affairs of the Church with which he was connected: and he continued to decline in strength until the 22d of July, 1791, when he was removed by death in the sixty-ninth year of his age. He was never robust in health. Yet such was his uniform and strict temperance, and such the vigilance of his self-denial, that he was seldom sick, and enjoyed a large share of physical comfort to the close of life. And he expired at length in the arms of his children and friends, perfectly resigned to the disposal of Heaven, and looking with steadfast eyes and humble confidence to the hopes of a glorious immortality,—after having lived to complete, in an uncommon degree, all the essential and various duties of a good citizen, a father of a family, a fervently pious and exemplary Christian, and a faithful and devoted minister of religion.

He had, in all, nine children,—seven sons and two daughters. Of these, two died in infancy, and six survived him. His eldest son, who bore his own name, was bred a physician, and, under the impulse of a governing patriotism, he entered the American army, early in 1776, as a surgeon; and, on a hasty journey from the camp to visit his parents, he was taken ill and died on the road, February 28, 1777, in the twenty-fifth year of his age. His second son, *Edward*, was an eminent physician. He exercised his profession for a number of years in the city of New York, and was Professor of the Practice of Medicine in the University of that city, and died March 17, 1812, aged fifty-one years. The third son, *Joseph*, entered the profession of Law, held a high standing at the Bar in Delaware, his native State, and was more than once a member of the State Legislature: he died of yellow-fever, September 4, 1793. The fourth son, *Samuel*, was, for twenty years, pastor of the Wall Street Church in New York, and during the rest of his life was Professor of Ecclesiastical History and Church Government in the Theological Seminary at Princeton. The fifth son, *James*, was bred to the Law, and, soon after his admission to the Bar, with the highest promise of intellectual and moral excellence, fell a victim to pulmonary consumption, April 15, 1795, in the twenty-second year of his age. The daughters both married early and are long since deceased.

ROBERT SMITH, D. D.*

1749—1793.

ROBERT SMITH was born in Londonderry, Ireland, in the year 1723. His family, who had first emigrated from Scotland to Ireland, came to this country, when Robert was about seven years old. His ancestors, on both the father's and mother's side, had been, for several generations, substantial farmers, and distinguished for good sense and earnest piety. The family, on coming to America, settled at the head waters of the river Brandywine, about forty miles from Philadelphia. At the age of fifteen, his mind became deeply impressed with the subject of religion, under the preaching of Whitefield, during his first visit to this country. Having, as he believed, received the Gospel in its sanctifying power, he had a strong desire to devote himself to its ministry; and being encouraged by his parents to do so, he placed himself under the instruction of the Rev. Samuel Blair, who was at that time the head of an institution at Fagg's Manor, Chester County, Pa., designed especially for the education of young men for the ministry. Here he made very rapid improvement in both classical and theological knowledge. On the 27th of December, 1749, he was licensed to preach by the (New Side) Presbytery of Newcastle. On the 9th of October, 1750, he accepted a call from the churches in Pequea and Leacock, Pa., and on the

* Assemb. Miss. Mag. II.—Timlow's Hist. Serm.—Webster's MSS.—MS. from Mrs. A. M. Jones.

25th of March, 1751, was ordained to the work of the ministry, and installed pastor of those churches. The Rev. John Rodgers, then minister of St. George's,—afterwards the Rev. Dr. Rodgers of New York, was Moderator of the Presbytery on the occasion of his ordination.

Shortly after his settlement, he founded a school, designed chiefly for the instruction of youth in the Latin, Greek and Hebrew languages. In this school he employed the most respectable teachers; and it was soon resorted to by a large number of young men from different parts of Pennsylvania and Maryland, some of whom were afterwards greatly distinguished in the different professions. He exerted a strong religious influence on the minds of his pupils, and a large part of those entrusted to his care became exemplary professors of religion. Not a few whose early classical education he had conducted, returned to him, after they had completed their collegiate course, to pursue their theological studies under his direction.

In 1759, he was released from the care of the congregation of Leacock; and he subsequently asked leave to resign the charge of Pequea, on account of inadequate support; but the congregation finally prevailed on him to withdraw the application.

In 1760, he received the degree of Doctor of Divinity from the College of New Jersey. In 1772, he was appointed one of the Overseers of that College, and held the office during the rest of his life. He was the second Moderator of the General Assembly, and preached the opening Sermon the next year (1791) from Isaiah lxii. 8.

Dr. Smith was distinguished for his activity, being in labours most abundant. He not only attended with great punctuality on all the judicatories of the Church, but was often abroad visiting vacant and feeble churches, and endeavouring to strengthen the things that remained, that were ready to die. He was generally blessed with vigorous health, insomuch that never but in a single instance during his whole ministry, was he prevented from preaching on the Sabbath. And then, though confined to his chamber by a fever, he assembled the principal members of his church, and being placed in an easy chair, spoke to them of the hopes and joys of religion.

The last public act of his life was attending a meeting of the Board of Trustees of the College of New Jersey, distant more than a hundred miles, after his health had become greatly enfeebled. On his return, he suffered much from both debility and pain; and when he had nearly reached his own church, where he had expected to officiate, he stopped at the house of a friend to endeavour to recover strength for the exercise; but he began immediately to sink away, and in a few minutes life was extinct. He died on the 15th of April 1793, in the seventy-first year of his age.

He was married on the 22d of May, 1750, to Elizabeth, a sister of the Rev. Samuel Blair, his preceptor. They had seven children,—two of whom died young, two became physicians, and three ministers of the Gospel. *Samuel Stanhope* and *John Blair* are commemorated in separate articles in this work. *William R.*, the other son who entered the ministry, was born May 10, 1752; was graduated at Princeton in 1773; was licensed to preach by the Presbytery of Newcastle in 1776; was settled as pastor of the Second Church in Wilmington, De., about 1786; resigned his charge in 1796, and became pastor of the Reformed Dutch Churches of Harlingen and Shannock, N. J., in which relation he died about the year 1815. The

Rev. Dr. Thomas Dewitt writes me—"I remember him, while I was studying Theology at New Brunswick, 1810–1812. He was plain in his manners, a judicious and instructive preacher, without much power of elocution, a faithful pastor; and amiable and exemplary in his spirit and deportment."

Ebenezer Smith, M. D., another son of Dr. Robert Smith by his first marriage, settled in Wilmington, De., where was born *his* son, *William R.*, who also became a minister of the Gospel. He (the son) was hopefully converted during a revival in the year 1814; was interrupted in his collegiate course at Princeton, by ill health; was licensed to preach by the Presbytery of Northumberland in April, 1820; became Pastor of the united Congregations of Northumberland and Sunbury, in May, 1822; resigned his charge in October, 1831; and after passing two years in Ohio, returned to his former charge, and continued their Pastor till his death,—September 19, 1849.

Dr. Smith was married a second time to the widow of the Rev. William Ramsey of Fairfield, N. J. She was a native of Cohansey, and her maiden name was Sarah Sealy. By this marriage he had one daughter, born in the year 1780.

Dr. Smith published A Sermon preached on the union of the Old and New Side Presbyteries of Newcastle, entitled "A wheel in the middle of a wheel, or the Harmony and connection of the various acts of Divine Providence;" Two Sermons on Sin and Holiness, 1767; A Sermon entitled "The bruised reed bound up, and the smoking flax inflamed; or the weak oppressed believer victorious through the tender care and grace of Christ," 1774; Three Sermons in the American Preacher on Saving Faith, 1791.

The following testimony to the character of Dr. Smith, is from a notice of him published in the General Assembly's Missionary Magazine for January, 1806. It is supposed to have been written by one of the fathers of the Presbyterian Church, who could speak from actual knowledge.

"Few men in the holy ministry have been more useful or more esteemed than Dr. Smith. He entered it with the purest zeal for the glory of his Redeemer and the salvation of mankind; and his whole soul was devoted to the faithful discharge of the duties of his sacred office. * * * Though remarkably modest and even diffident in the deliberative assemblies of the Church, he has often been heard to say that in the pulpit he never knew the fear of man. He was so occupied with the solemnity and importance of his duties, that the opinions of men were forgotten: his mind was so filled with the Divine presence before which he stood, that wealth, station, talents, whatever is most respected by the world, was lost to him in the majesty of God. The character of his preaching, therefore, as was to be expected from a frame of mind so habitually devout, was remarkably solemn and fervent. The Holy Scriptures, in which God has been pleased to convey his will to mankind, he regarded as containing the happiest language in which to interpret Divine truth to the people. With the sacred volume he was perfectly familiar. And his sermons were usually filled with the aptest allusions and illustrations drawn from this precious source. The doctrines of the Gospel he delighted to express in the terms of Scripture; those doctrines especially which have been in any degree the subjects of disputation, and the cause of division in the Church. An enemy to controversy, he believed that Christians were more nearly united in sentiment than in the expression of their several creeds. In the copious use, therefore, which he made of Scripture language, he hoped to gain a double advantage: on controversial subjects he would create less offence and irritation; and in illustrating and enforcing Divine truth on the hearts of his hearers, he thought that the language of the inspired writers would come home with more authority to the conscience than the finest periods of human eloquence. In this perhaps he was not deceived, particularly in that field of labour which he had especially marked out for himself; for he was uncommonly successful in convincing secure sinners, in comforting and establishing believers in the faith of the Gospel, and in conciliating the affections and confidence of pious persons of all denominations. Preaching the Gospel and publishing the grace of the Redeemer was his most delightful employment; in which he exhibited an example of the greatest diligence and zeal, not only among the people with whom he was more immediately connected as their pastor, but throughout an extensive district of country, in every part of which he was often employed in these pious labours. He was indeed incessant and indefatigable in the service of his Divine Master, till at length he wore down to a slender thread a constitution originally vigorous, and his death at last which took place in the midst of the most active discharge of his duties, was not the effect of any particular disease, but of the gradual waste of nature occasioned by continual and extreme exertions."

SAMUEL KENNEDY.*

1750—1787.

Samuel Kennedy was born in Scotland, in the year 1720; and received his education in the University of Edinburgh. The circumstances which led him to migrate to this country are not known; but he seems to have come hither not long after the completion of his collegiate course, and to have engaged in studies immediately preparatory to the sacred office, by advice of the Presbytery of New Brunswick. He was received under the care of that Presbytery, on trials for the ministry, on the 6th of December, 1749; and was licensed by the same Body to preach the Gospel, on the 18th of May, 1750. He was ordained to the work of the ministry, and installed pastor of the Congregation of Basking Ridge, N. J., on the 25th of June, 1751.

Notwithstanding much the greater portion of the Scotch and Irish clergy in the Presbyterian Church in this country were found on the Old Side, in the memorable division of 1741, Mr. Kennedy's sympathies seem to have been decidedly with the other party; for while he did not undervalue human learning as one of the requisite qualifications for the ministry, he attached far more importance to experimental piety, and believed that the Church had a right to require the evidence of this in those who were to be commissioned to preach the Gospel. It was an evidence of his supreme regard to principle that he should have thus, in the choice of his ecclesiastical relation, disregarded what we may suppose to have been his national predilections.

Mr. Kennedy was one of the eighteen ministers who, in the year 1760, rendered themselves somewhat famous by an attempted interference in the concerns of the Episcopal Church. The Rev. William McClenachan, an Episcopal clergyman of Philadelphia, who had evinced somewhat more of religious zeal than most of his brethren, was, for that reason, more highly appreciated by one part, and less highly by another part, of his own denomination; and it was feared that the adverse influence would prevail to his exclusion from the Episcopal Church in that city. During a meeting of the Synod of New York and Philadelphia in May, 1760, Mr. McClenachan's embarrassed and somewhat doubtful position happened to become the subject of conversation among some of the members, and, with more zeal probably than prudence or delicacy, several of them agreed to address a letter to the Archbishop of Canterbury, requesting his official influence to enable Mr. M. to retain his place. The letter was accordingly written and

* Sketch of his life appended to Brown's Memoirs of Robert Finley, D. D.—MS. from Rev. Dr. Talmage.

despatched; but, as might be expected, the venerable dignitary to whom it was addressed, took no notice of it; and even the individuals who had subscribed it, were constrained, upon further reflection, to think that they had done an act of at least questionable propriety. The affair soon became public, and the letter found its way into the newspapers, accompanied by severe strictures; and, during the next meeting of Synod, it was hawked about the streets of Philadelphia in pamphlet form, with the ludicrous proclamation—"Eighteen Presbyterian ministers for a groat." It is certainly somewhat remarkable that the names of most of those concerned in the transaction, are among the most honoured in the history of the Presbyterian Church.

Mr. Kennedy was, for a considerable time, at the head of a classical school at Basking Ridge; and being a highly accomplished scholar, and possessing great wisdom and energy as a disciplinarian, his school was extensively patronized, and sent many of its pupils to the College of New Jersey. Some of them became distinguished men, and were often heard, in after life, to render a most grateful testimony to the ability and fidelity of their early instructer.

Mr. Kennedy was not only a clergyman and a teacher, but a physician also. For many years he practised medicine in his own congregation, and acquired no small reputation for his skill in detecting and treating diseases. He usually received the appellation of *Doctor*, but it designated the medical practitioner, and not the clergyman.

Mr. Kennedy was very diligent and faithful in the discharge of his pastoral duties, and his labours among his own people and elsewhere were eminently successful. Several extensive revivals of religion occurred under his ministry, in consequence of which his church greatly increased in both numbers and strength. And his influence was by no means confined to his own congregation—it extended to the whole surrounding region, and operated nowhere perhaps more powerfully than in the judicatories of the Church.

Mr. Kennedy's labours were terminated by death on the 31st of August, 1787, when he was in the sixty-eighth year of his age, and the thirty-seventh of his ministry at Basking Ridge.

FROM THE REV. SAMUEL KENNEDY TALMAGE, D. D.

PRESIDENT OF OGLETHORPE UNIVERSITY, GA.

OGLETHORPE UNIVERSITY, 27th February, 1855.

My dear Sir: You inquire after my knowledge of my "venerable ancestor, the Rev. Samuel Kennedy." My only relationship to him is the following,—and it is not slight. He was the spiritual father of my father and mother, who joined his church in youth, side by side, on the same day, and who were afterwards joined together by him in marriage. After he had gone to minister in a higher sphere, they gave me his name in token of their affectionate remembrance of him.

My father, though a plain unlettered man, was an elder in the church, and had more knowledge of his Bible than almost any private Christian I have ever known. He had an astonishing memory, and could repeat many of his old pastor's sermons almost verbatim; and in his old age he actually committed to writing some of them, after they had been treasured in his memory for a great many years. It is to him that I am indebted almost entirely for my impressions of Mr. Kennedy's character; for he never wearied in talking of him, and evidently regarded him as coming as near to his ideal of a Christian minister as any other man he had ever known.

Mr. Kennedy was, according to my father's representation, distinguished for the purity and elevation of his Christian character. He made it manifest to all by his daily conversation that he walked with God. He had naturally a strong mind, whose resources had been well developed by a thorough Scotch education. His knowledge of Theology was at once accurate and extensive; and he was not only a cordial believer but a vigorous defender of the Calvinistic system. He must have been distinguished for his activity and diligence; for besides being occupied part of the time as a teacher, he performed, to great acceptance, the duties of both a minister and a physician. And it is evident, from his increasing reputation as he advanced in life, that he must have spent no small part of his time in his study. As a confirmation of the fact that he was a ripe scholar and a profound theologian, I may mention that a brother of mine, many years ago, in travelling through Sussex County, N. J., came across some of Mr. Kennedy's books in the hands of an illiterate descendant, which were among the most learned works of the period immediately succeeding the Reformation, and which may fairly be considered as indicating the taste of their former owner. He purchased several of them, which are now in my possession, and which I highly prize, not more for their intrinsic value, than as precious memorials of my venerable namesake.

My father used to tell me that Mr. Kennedy was, in appearance and manner, one of the most simple and unostentatious of men, and that his great modesty kept him very much out of the range of public observation; but that, in the pulpit, the power of his thoughts and the fervour of his manner sometimes rendered him perfectly overwhelming. He has related to me instances of the astonishment created by his sermons at ecclesiastical meetings; how his audience, who had judged him, before he began the service, by his unassuming aspect, would, in the progress of it, become fixed and well nigh rapt by his noble conceptions, and bold and earnest appeals. One circumstance connected with his ministry evidently left upon the mind of my father,—if I could judge from the interest and frequency with which he used to relate it,—a very deep impression. There had been a season of unusual coldness in the Church at Basking Ridge, and the pastor had become not a little discouraged in view of the apparent fruitlessness of his labours. On a certain Sabbath, at the close of the public services, he resolved to spend the whole of the following week in earnest prayer and devout study, with a view to prepare a sermon that, by God's blessing, might rouse the congregation from their spiritual torpor, and bring them to feel the importance of eternal realities. He fulfilled his purpose,—immediately selecting his text for the next Sabbath, and devoting the whole intervening week to maturing and arranging his thoughts upon it. When the Sabbath came, he felt strong in the belief that he had produced something that would move his people, and he expected confidently to witness some special tokens of the Divine presence. After singing and prayer, he gave out his second hymn, and took his Bible to open to the text. But strange to tell, he could not call it to his mind—text, chapter, book, even subject, had deserted him. The congregation had finished singing, and in a half bewildered state he rose and gave out another hymn. He turned over the leaves of the Bible to find some passage on which to found an extemporaneous discourse; and his eye lighted repeatedly on one text upon which he thought he might say something—if my memory serves me, it was—"The wicked shall be turned into Hell, and all the nations that forget God." The singing being again concluded, he rose, overwhelmed with agitation and distress, and preached a sermon which melted down the whole congregation, and was the commencement of a wonderful revival of religion. He said he had never in his life before enjoyed so much freedom or exercised so much power in the pulpit. He went home alone weeping and rejoicing;—saying that God had answered his prayers in a manner fitted at once to humble the unworthy instrument, and to exalt the riches of his own grace.

I find it stated by another authority that "Mr. Kennedy was rather above the ordinary size of men, somewhat corpulent and plethoric. His manners were very plain, retaining much of their native Scotch simplicity, and sometimes approaching to bluntness. He was distinguished by an easy, copious and uniform flow of thought and expression on every subject. His remarks on all occasions were pithy, judicious and appropriate."

Very affectionately yours,

S. K. TALMAGE.

MATTHEW WILSON, D. D.

1754—1790.

FROM THE REV. SAMUEL MILLER, D. D.,

PRINCETON, November 20, 1848.

Rev. and dear Brother: It always gives me pleasure to call to mind the image and character of the Rev. Matthew Wilson, D. D., long since deceased. I can never recollect that excellent man without complicated emotions of reverence, gratitude, and love. He was the affectionate friend and correspondent of my venerated father; was often a guest at his house; and I may safely say, was never there without diffusing joy throughout the domestic circle.

MATTHEW WILSON was born in East Nottingham, Chester County, Pa., January 15, 1731. He was the son of James Wilson and Jean his wife, who intermarried in Ireland, and afterwards migrated to Pennsylvania, where they spent the remainder of their lives. He received his academical education under the direction of the Rev. Dr. Francis Alison, and the Rev. Alexander McDowall,* at an institution of high character at New London in his native State. I do not remember to have known under whom his theological studies were conducted. He was licensed to preach in April, 1754; was ordained to the office of the ministry in October, 1755; was installed pastor of the Congregations at Lewes and Cool Spring in Delaware, in April, 1756; and in August, 1767, by consent of his two congregations and of the Presbytery, took charge of another Congregation, devoting to them every third Sabbath, at Indian River. This latter arrangement was at first entered into only for a single year, but it was rendered permanent by a subsequent agreement. After a course of able and successful labours in that extensive charge, he died on the 30th of March, 1790, in the sixtieth year of his age, universally lamented.

The degree of Doctor of Divinity was most worthily bestowed on him by the University of Pennsylvania in 1786.

* ALEXANDER McDOWALL was born in Ireland, but his family, while he was yet young, migrated to this country, and settled in Virginia. He offered himself to the Donegal Presbytery, September 4, 1739, and was licensed to preach July 30, 1740. On the 29th of October, 1741, he was ordained *sine titulo*, with a view to his going to Virginia. He seems subsequently to have settled at Nottingham. He was appointed Principal of the school which was under the care of the Synod, first at Elk, and afterwards at Newark, De. He died January 12, 1782, having never married.

This great and good man was regularly bred to the medical profession, as well as that of a minister of the Gospel, and few physicians of his day manifested more learning, skill, or success, in the healing art. His medical practice occupied much of his time, and had he not exercised singular energy and diligence, would have drawn him away from the duties of the sacred office. But such were his perseverance and industry that he fulfilled the duties of both professions with great acceptance.

Dr. Wilson ever held a high place in public estimation. Ingenious, learned, pious, patriotic, and benevolent in an eminent degree, all that knew him respected him; and he had no enemies, but the enemies of truth and righteousness. Though every circumstance in his early life conspired to place him among those who were called Old Side men in the great controversy which divided the Church in his day, yet such were the fervour of his piety, and the amiableness of his temper, that both parties loved him; and he was taken by the hand by his New Side brethren, and heard by their Congregations, with as much pleasure as if he had been nominally with them. An ardent lover of peace, he lamented the divisions which agitated the Church, when he came into the ministry, and he was generally considered as one of the most influential instruments in bringing about the Plan of Union, which was consummated in 1758, and restored peace to the Presbyterian Church.

In the Revolutionary contest, which gave independence to the United States, Dr. Wilson took the side of his country with great decision and zeal. His patriotic efforts were unremitted, and, no doubt, exerted much influence wherever he was known. Some indeed thought that he carried his public activity in the great Whig cause rather further than became a minister of the Gospel; but his constitutional ardour prevented his taking counsel with the cold calculations of prudence, at a period which "tried men's souls."

Dr. Wilson was never fully reconciled to the plan of Presbyterian Church Government, exemplified in the Church of Scotland, and substantially adopted by our fathers of the Old Synod in 1788. He drew up and read before that body a plan of government, very considerably reduced in its tone, and more nearly resembling the Congregational system. Though his views were most respectfully listened to and deliberated on by the Synod, they were not adopted. The model of the Church of Scotland, though not servilely copied, was generally preferred; and a form of government and discipline, as nearly corresponding with that model as the different circumstances of the two countries rendered expedient, was finally established.

Dr. Wilson continued to be a diligent student to a late period of his life. Though he had the labours and cares of two important professions devolving upon him, he found time to be more of a reader than many whose occupations are less complicated and less pressing; and what is worthy of notice, he seems to have been in the habit of reading with pen in hand. I do not remember ever to have borrowed a book from his library, or indeed to have seen one of which he was the owner, without finding the margin filled, even to crowding, with manuscript notes,—some of them remarkably rich, graphic and interesting. By this practice, he rendered his books less sightly, and perhaps less valuable in the market; but more profitable to himself, more precious to his family and to all that loved him, and indeed more truly valuable to all the admirers of learning and of mind.

It was very common, about the middle of the last century, in printed volumes, to print emphatic words, especially in title pages and conspicuous positions, in red ink, to render them more attractive and conspicuous. Dr. Wilson was fond of introducing this practice into his letters. I have seen and now have in my possession a number of his letters, and in almost all cases, black and red ink are alternately employed, in order to give conspicuity and emphatic meaning to important words, names, or statements. I have no recollection of having observed this habit in any other man. He was said to have had two inkstands, one of black and the other of red ink, in every room in his house. Whether this were a fact, I know not; but for one thing I can vouch,—that I scarcely ever saw a letter from his hand, which did not, in some measure, corroborate the statement.

As a preacher, Dr. Wilson was not animated, or strikingly powerful. He was mild, instructive and persuasive. His voice was rather feeble and plaintive. His health was always delicate, and, toward the latter part of his life, he was habitually a valetudinarian. This his appearance in the pulpit generally indicated. Yet his ardent piety, his solemnity, and his manifest learning and intelligence, always made him an acceptable preacher to an enlightenod audience.

Dr. Wilson was married to Hester Gray in 1756. She died in 1762, having become the mother of two children, only one of whom survived her. In 1764, he was married to Elizabeth Creghead, a lady of uncommon energy of character, and eminent piety, who survived him many years, and died about 1813, in her eighty-fourth year. By this marriage he had five children, one of whom was the Rev. James P. Wilson, D. D., late pastor of the First Presbyterian Church in the city of Philadelphia, who, in piety, in learning, in talents, and in power as a preacher, had few equals.

It would give me pleasure to enlarge, without limit, on the reminiscences of a family so dear and so interesting to me and mine. But the infirmities of a man who has entered on his eightieth year, must be my apology for bringing this communication to a close.

Yours with great regard,

SAMUEL MILLER.

HUGH KNOX, D. D.*

1755—1790.

Hugh Knox was born in Ireland, but came to this country in 1751, when he was approaching manhood. It seems that he had some thoughts of entering the ministry, shortly after his arrival; for there is a record that the Synod of Philadelphia, having heard that he was desirous of being taken on trials, directed him to meet the Newcastle Presbytery; but as his views and feelings were at that time little congenial with the sacred office, so he quickly dismissed all ideas of seeking it, and resolved on a different course of life.

* Miller's Memoir of Rodgers.—Webster's MSS.—Original Letters of Knox.—Works of Alexander Hamilton, I.

Having letters to the Rev. Dr. Francis Alison, then Principal of the Academy at New London, Pa., he called upon him to see whether he could not employ him as an assistant teacher; but as Dr. Alison had no occasion for his services in that capacity, he gave him a note of introduction to the Rev. (afterwards Dr.) John Rodgers, who was then settled as pastor of the Churches of St. George's and Middletown, De., with a request that he would, if practicable, gather a school for Mr. Knox within the limits of one or the other of his congregations. Mr. Rodgers, being favourably impressed with the young man's appearance, immediately made an effort in his behalf, which resulted in the establishment of a school of which Mr. Knox became the head. Being a young man of fine personal appearance, and more than ordinary accomplishments, he became a very popular teacher, and was much esteemed throughout the neighbourhood.

After having been thus engaged for several months, a circumstance occurred which greatly changed Mr. Knox's condition and prospects;—a circumstance which, though involving criminality on his part, and bringing in its train immediate disaster, was nevertheless overruled to the most desirable and important results. When he went to reside at the Head of Bohemia, (for that was the place where he had his school,) he was exemplary in his morality, though he did not profess to know any thing of Christian experience. Unhappily, the strictness of his morals began to relax, and he became associated with a number of young men, who used to meet every Saturday afternoon for a frolic; and though these meetings were at first of a comparatively unexceptionable character, yet they gradually changed into a scene of boisterous and indecent revelry. On one of these occasions, some one of the company cried out to Knox—"Come, parson," (a title which they gave him on account of his being the gravest of their number, and withal a great admirer of the preaching of Mr. Rodgers,) "Come, parson, give us a sermon." At first, he declined; but, upon being urged, he actually met the demand in a very remarkable manner. Having an uncommon memory, great flexibility of voice, and withal a wonderful gift at mimicry, he began to preach the sermon which Mr. Rodgers had preached the Sabbath before, and went through it, so exactly imitating his tones and manner, that one of his elders who overheard it from another apartment in the house, declared that he could not distinguish between the original and the copy. But the most remarkable thing remains to be told. As he proceeded in the sermon, such was the interest which he contrived to counterfeit, that his auditors, who began to listen in merriment, gradually became serious, and, when he had finished, they left the spot disposed to any thing else than diversion or ridicule. And what was more, the mock preacher was overwhelmed with a sense of the criminality of what he had been doing, and deeply felt the power of those truths with which he had thus profanely trifled. Such was his mortification and his remorse in reflecting on his conduct, that he fled from the place the next morning, without stopping long enough to collect his dues, or arrange his affairs.

He went now to Newark, and applied to President Burr for admission to College; but, as he brought no testimonials, and stated that he had been living in the neighbourhood of Mr. Rodgers, the President told him that he might remain with him until the next Commencement, which Mr. R. would undoubtedly attend, and if his testimony concerning him were what could be desired, he should immediately be admitted. In due time Mr. Rodgers came; and much was he surprised at meeting the fugitive school-master, and much was the school-master embarrassed at meeting the minister, whose generous patronage he had so ungraciously and ungratefully requited. Mr. Knox watched his opportunity to get Mr. Rodgers to step aside with him, when he made a frank and penitent acknowledgment of his wicked conduct, and stated to him his circumstances in regard to becoming a member of College. He informed him, moreover, that reflection upon the ungrateful and wicked act which he had committed towards him, had led him, as he hoped, to deep reflection upon his character as a sinner, and to unfeigned repentance of all his sins; and that he wished to obtain a collegiate education with a view to devote himself to the Christian ministry. He begged Mr. R., provided he could consistently do so, to withhold from President Burr a statement of the sad affair which occasioned his leaving his school, lest, if it were communicated to him, it should prevent his being received as a member of College; and Mr. R. promised to comply with his request, unless the President should ask him questions that would render it impossible. Happily, no such questions were asked; and the President, having received such a testimony concerning his character as satisfied him, admitted him to College.

Mr. Knox graduated in the year 1754, and probably studied Divinity with President Burr. The Reformed Dutch Church in the Island of Saba having requested the New York Presbytery to send them a minister,—they selected Mr. Knox as a suitable person for the place, and he consented to their proposal. They accordingly proceeded to ordain him in the year 1755,—on which occasion he preached a Sermon on "the dignity and importance of the Gospel ministry," which was published by the unanimous request of the Presbytery. It is prefaced with a brief Address from the Presbytery to the Church of which he was to become the pastor, which commences as follows:—

"To the Dutch Protestant Reformed Church on the Island of Saba:—

"The Presbytery of New York send Greeting:

"When your request for an English Protestant minister was made known to us, we gladly embraced the opportunity of assisting so distant a part of the Lord's vineyard. And Divine Providence seasonably pointed out the ingenious author of the following Discourse, whom we can cheerfully recommend as a person we judge well qualified to supply your destitute church, and to promote the interest of the Redeemer's Kingdom among you."

It concludes thus:—

"We trust you will have reason with us to bless God, that has inclined his heart to accept your call; to forsake the society of his dear friends, and risk the danger of the sea, that he might carry the glad tidings of salvation to the distant Isles. That he may come to you in the fulness of the blessings of the Gospel of peace, and become the happy instrument in the hands of the great Head of the Church, of building you up in faith, peace and holiness, is and will be the prayer of

"Your brethren and servants in the Gospel of Christ.

"Signed by order, TIMOTHY ALLEN,* Presby. Cl."

* TIMOTHY ALLEN was graduated at Yale College in 1736; was ordained as pastor of the Congregational Church in West Haven, Conn., in 1738; and remained there till 1742, though in 1741 he was deposed by the New Haven Association for his alleged extravagances in connection with the revival, and especially for saying that "the Bible could not of itself, or by any man's efforts, do the unregenerate sinner any more good than the reading of an old Almanac." After the arrest of Davenport, by the Connecticut magistrates in 1742, many of the ultra revivalists were impressed with the importance of establishing a school for educating young men, after their own notions, for the ministry. Such a school was actually established at New London—called "The Shepherd's Tent;" and Mr. Allen was placed at the head of it; but, in consequence of an Act of the Legislature the same year, prohibiting the establishment of Seminaries "by private or unknown persons," it was removed to Rhode Island. The school quickly

After Mr. Knox's settlement in the Island of Saba, he not only retained his connection with the Presbytery of New York, but kept up a regular correspondence with them as a Body, besides frequently exchanging letters with several of the prominent members. From a letter in my possession, addressed to one of these brethren,* dated March 2, 1759, I make the following extract, as containing the only account I can find of Mr. Knox's situation after his removal to Saba:—

"As to my outward estate, it is such as I bless God I am well contented with, although it can never be considerable upon this Island. You can easily be convinced of this, when you consider that my stated salary and perquisites yearly do not amount to more than a hundred and forty pounds, your currency, and that fresh meat of almost every kind is seldom sold for less than from twelve to eighteen pence per pound; a good turkey for a heavy pistole or thirty shillings; a dunghill fowl, six or eight shillings, and every thing else in proportion; so that, all things considered, I reckon fifty pounds per annum upon the Continent equivalent to a hundred and fifty here.

"You have, I hope, before this time, heard, by my last to the Presbytery, of my being married to Governor Simmons' youngest daughter. I married her at the age of fourteen years and six months. She is a young woman of a good as well as an honourable family, of a comely outward form and good natural endowments, of a spotless character and a virtuous deportment. God only knows whether she is yet possessed of the one thing needful. I entreat your joint prayers with mine that what may be yet lacking in her, Christ would graciously supply out of the abundance of his grace; that, as we are one flesh by marriage, so we may be of one spirit in Christ. Since our union, we have lived under the Governor's roof, and have sat at his table,—so that our expenses in living are by this means greatly lessened. Dutch fortunes are never known nor given till the death of parents—however, I conjecture, by a general estimate of my father-in-law's circumstances and family, that that part which will come to me or my widow and family, may amount to about eight or nine hundred pounds, your currency, if not more."

In a letter addressed to the Rev. Caleb Smith of Newark Mountains, dated July 17, 1761, he writes thus:—

"In a letter enclosed with this, and which I beg you may forward to my pious and worthy friend, the Rev. Mr. Azariah Horton,† at South Hanover,

languished, and Mr. Allen removed to Long Island. He met with the Suffolk Presbytery, June 14, 1748, and laid before them the "absolution" by which the censure which he had incurred in New England was removed. He joined the New Brunswick Presbytery, October 12, 1748, and supplied the Churches of Hopewell and Maidenhead, three or four years. From 1753 to 1756, he laboured at Woodbridge, and was a member of the New York Presbytery till 1761, though he was installed at Ashford, Conn., October 12, 1757. He became the minister of Chesterfield, Mass., at the age of seventy, and preached, by request of the people, at his own installation, June 15, 1785. He died January 12, 1806, in his ninety-first year. He was a man of vigorous powers, a fervent preacher, and the author of several occasional Sermons.

* It does not appear to which of the members this letter is addressed.

† Azariah Horton was born at Southold, L. I., in the year 1715, and was graduated at Yale College in 1735. On being licensed to preach, probably by the New York Presbytery, he received a call to an eligible parish on Long Island, and was prepared to accept it. The Correspondents of the Scottish Society for propagating the Gospel urged upon his attention the case of the Indians on the Island, and finally prevailed on him to relinquish the call. He was ordained by the Presbytery of New York in 1741, and began his labours in the midst of the great revival. His charge extended along the whole Southern shore of the Island, for more than a hundred miles, upon which the remnants of once numerous tribes, at that time reduced to four hundred, of all ages, were scattered. Here he laboured with the utmost self-denial, and not without very considerable success, until 1750, when he accepted an invitation to supply

I have requested him to make a motion to the Presbytery that they should appoint a Committee of their members, or solicit the United Synod to appoint a Committee of their members, to draw up, print and publish a Plan of Church Government, and a Directory for Discipline, explaining the power of Church officers, the nature and reason of censures, suspension and excommunication, and giving plain and pertinent directions how to proceed with offending professors in a variety of cases. Such a public, authentic plan of procedure would, I am persuaded, be of great service to all our churches, more particularly to such of the members as are in my situation. If it should be objected that the Westminster Directory is adopted by the Synod, and is sufficient for this purpose,—I answer—the Westminster Directory, as it stands in our Confession of Faith, is too brief and general, and is no sufficient plan for procedure in particular cases. Besides, many of our people do not think themselves subject to the Church of Scotland, or belonging to it, and therefore are not willing to acknowledge its authority, or to be determined by its decisions. If you see any reason in this, Sir, I beg you would second the motion of the Rev. Mr. Horton. I am, for my part, fully persuaded that such a Directory, approved and published by the Synod, would add greatly to the authority of Church Councils, especially where there is not a concurrence of ministers to give force and weight to their decisions."

In a letter to the Rev. Jacob Green of Hanover, N. J., dated January 22, 1772, he writes as follows:—

"Although all matters of difference are reconciled long ago on this island, and the people of it, almost to a man, are solicitous for me to stay among them in the ministry, yet, from a variety of considerations too tedious for me to particularize here, I am induced to remove from them to the Danish Island of St. Croix, where there is a church provided for me, and a yearly salary of about twelve hundred *prs.* subscribed. I have acquainted my people here of this determination, and think of moving, (God permitting,) about the 1st of May next. I spent the months of September and October in that fine island, and found a number of Scotch, English, Irish, and North American, Presbyterians there, who gave me a cordial and unanimous invitation to come among them. Their first plan was a coalition with the Dutch Church, and a colleagueship with the Dutch minister; on which plan the most of the Dutch had become my subscribers. But the English party thought best to have a place of worship of their own, in order to avoid some inconveniences arising from the other plan."

In pursuance of the resolution intimated in the preceding extract, Mr. Knox, shortly after, resigned his charge at Saba, and settled at St. Croix, where he seems to have spent the rest of his days. The church in which he had preached at Saba was destroyed by a hurricane the same year that he left it; and the next year, (1773,) the Synod, by request of the New York Presbytery, appropriated fifty pounds out of "the collections for pious uses," to aid in rebuilding the edifice.

a church on Long Island, and became a member of the Suffolk Presbytery. After remaining here about a year, he accepted a call from South Hanover, or Bottle Hill, N. J., in 1751, where he contiued till November, 1776, when he was dismissed at his own request. On the 27th of March, 1777, he died of small pox, at the house of his son, in Chatham village,—aged sixty-two years. He was an earnest and faithful minister, an influential member, originally of the Synod of Philadelphia, and afterwards of that of New York, and had an important agency in establishing the College of New Jersey.

In the year 1767, the Rev. Jacob Green published a Sermon from Romans ix, 18, entitled "The Sinner's faultiness and spiritual inability,"—of which he sent Mr. Knox a copy. Mr. Knox dissented from some of Mr. Green's positions, which seem to have bordered on Hopkinsianism, and in 1769, he addressed a Letter to him through the press, in which he treats him with the utmost respect and kindness, states his objections to some of the views contained in his Sermon, and modestly advances what seems to him a more reasonable and scriptural theory. He maintains that God could not make a world of free agents without the possibility of their falling into sin. He also repudiates the Hopkinsian notion of benevolence, and of the necessity of sin to the highest display of God's glory. He writes as follows:—

"Make it appear clear, on your principles, [those of Edwards and Hopkins,] that God is exculpated from the charge of having any causality in producing sin, and I am satisfied. Consider me in the humble capacity of a learner. I have such a firm persuasion of your piety, and such a respect for your judgment and candour, as will keep me from uncharitableness in thought or language towards you. There breathes such a spirit of kindness and goodness through all your letters, as secures both my affection and my gratitude.

"The distinction between natural and moral inability I have ever thought an important and useful one, when well stated and explained. My worthy and excellent friend, President Burr, was the first who ever gave me an idea of this distinction. He did it in three sermons preached from Joshua xxiv, 19:—'Ye cannot serve the Lord, for He is an holy God.' He acknowledged they were the substance of Edwards' book relative to that subject, and expressed a pretty strong desire of having them printed, as some of the most useful and important he had ever preached. I would define *moral inability* thus:—a natural and contracted disinclination or aversion to the exercises of piety and moral virtue, which becomes faulty and criminal by our resisting the motives which would overcome it, and neglecting by prayer and other duties to apply to God through the Redeemer for those influences of the Holy Spirit by which it would have been wholly subdued, and our volitions and actions engaged on the side of piety and moral rectitude.

"The system of the ancient Calvinists is well jointed, and hangs together; but Calvinism, as held by President Edwards' admirers, seems to me as different from it as Arminianism—a middle thing patched up out of both, and ought to be called *Edwardism.*

"I greatly question what you say on p. 19:—'They have all the powers that can be conceived, in the nature of things, for a sinner to have; for they have light in the understanding, they see the reasonableness and fitness of things, and the obligations they are under.' I always thought the understanding was sadly darkened and blinded by the fall; that the natural man could not know nor discern the things of God, and that it required the power of renewing grace to cure this faculty of its blindness; but I find that Mr. Hopkins and you make out this faculty pretty sound and vigorous, as though it had suffered little, if any thing, by the original apostacy."

The celebrated Alexander Hamilton was placed in early boyhood under the instruction of Mr. Knox, and formed a strong attachment to him, while Mr. Knox, in return, watched and assisted, with the utmost fidelity, the development of the wonderful powers of his pupil. They kept up an active correspondence in after life; and two of Mr. K.'s letters are preserved in the first volume of Hamilton's works. Both were written during the Revolution, and breathe a spirit of earnest devotion to the American cause. From one of them, dated St. Croix, April 31, 1777, the following is an extract:—

"I have but a moment at command at present, and have not time to remark upon your letter. I can only inform you that it has given high satisfaction to all friends here. We rejoice in your *good character* and *advancement*, which is indeed only the just reward of merit. May you still live to deserve more and more from the friends of America, and to justify the choice, and merit the approbation of the GREAT AND GOOD GENERAL WASHINGTON—a name which will shine with distinguished lustre in the annals of history—a name dear to the friends of the liberties of mankind! *Mark this!* You must be the annalist and biographer, as well as the aid-de-camp, of

General Washington, and the historiographer of the AMERICAN WAR. I take the liberty to insist on this. I hope you take minutes and keep a journal. If you have not hitherto, I pray do it henceforth. I seriously, and with all my little influence, urge this upon you. This may be a new and strange thought to you; but if you survive the present troubles, *I aver*—few men will be so well qualified to write the history of the present glorious struggle. God only knows how it may terminate. But however that may be, it will be a most interesting story."

The degree of Master of Arts was conferred upon Mr. Knox by Yale College in 1768; and, at a subsequent period, he was honoured with the degree of Doctor of Divinity by the University of Glasgow.

Dr. Knox died in St. Croix in October, 1790. He had a son bearing his own name, who was graduated at Yale College in 1800.

Dr. Miller states that Dr. Knox "published five or six volumes, chiefly Sermons, which are highly esteemed." Two volumes of his Sermons, printed at Glasgow, in 1772, are in the Library of the College of New Jersey. In an autograph letter of his, written in 1761, I find him expressing his intention to publish a volume of Discourses, chiefly on Infidelity, but doubting whether the volume may be most advantageously brought out in this country or in Europe.

GEORGE DUFFIELD, D. D.

1756—1790.

FROM THE REV. GEORGE DUFFIELD, D. D.

DETROIT, February 29, 1848.

Rev. and dear Sir: In compliance with your request, I cheerfully give you what facts I have been able to collect, with regard to the history of my grandfather.

GEORGE DUFFIELD was the third son of George and Margaret Duffield, who had migrated to the Colony of Pennsylvania, somewhere from 1725 to 1730, from the North of Ireland. They were of English extraction immediately, but the family originally were French,—of the Huguenots, who were forced to fly from France, and take refuge in England and the North of Ireland, on account of their Protestant faith, and in consequence of the edict of Nantz, and the persecutions that ensued thereon. The name was originally *Du Fielde*, but was anglicised, after the settlement of the family in Great Britain. George Duffield (the father) first settled in Octorora township, Lancaster County, Pa., but shortly after sought a richer soil, and established himself in Pequea township, of the same county, where his son George was born; and on grounds which remain to this day in the possession of his descendants. He died at the advanced age of eighty-four years, and was noted for his stern integrity and devoted piety.

George Duffield, the subject of this sketch, was born October 7, 1732. He received his academical education at Newark, De., where he afterwards officiated as classical Tutor. He was graduated at Nassau Hall in 1752; and having, about that time, become hopefully pious, he joined the Church under the care of the Rev. Dr. Robert Smith, of Pequea, and soon after commenced the study of Theology under his supervision. From 1754 to 1756, he was Tutor at the College at which he was graduated. He was licensed to preach the Gospel by the Presbytery of Newcastle, March 11, 1756; having been married three days before to Elizabeth, daughter of the Rev. Samuel Blair of Fagg's Manor; who, on the 25th of September, 1757, died and was buried at Carlisle, along with the infant child to which she had given birth. He received a call from the united Churches of Carlisle, Big Spring, and Monahan, now called Dillstown, and was ordained at Carlisle, September 25, 1761, by the Presbytery of Donegal.

It is well known that the Presbyterian Churches had, for some time previously, been agitated by the revivals of religion that had prevailed, and were eventually divided,—the parties being vulgarly called "Old Lights" and "New Lights." In Pequea, Fagg's Manor, and Monahan, there had been gracious effusions of the Divine Spirit. Mr. Duffield was a zealous advocate and promoter of the revivals of that day, and was very popular as a preacher. His extemporaneous powers were remarkable, and his discourses rich in evangelical truth, and Christian experience. He sympathized with the friends and followers of Whitefield, and especially with Samuel Davies, and the Tennents, whose preaching was so effective. The church at Carlisle was one which had been recently formed in the village; the original settlers having built their church, and worshipped first in the house erected on their glebe, about two miles West of the borough of Carlisle, which became noted by the construction of extensive barracks as a frontier town. The formation of a new church in the borough, especially of one whose sympathies differed from those of the original church,—although it consisted chiefly of emigrants and settlers from other parts, who had participated in the revivals of religion of that day,—became the occasion of no inconsiderable difficulty; and there were obstacles thrown in the way of Mr. Duffield's settlement. Various reports of injurious tendency were put in circulation concerning him; and it was alleged especially that he had written a letter highly derogatory to the character and labours of the pastor of the original church. Much excitement prevailed, and he insisted that his letter should be produced, and the matter thoroughly investigated, previously to his reception and settlement. The result was a perfect acquittal from the offensive charges, after which his ordination took place.

During the pendency of his ordination and settlement in Carlisle, he was married, March 5, 1759, to Margaret Armstrong, sister of General John Armstrong, of Revolutionary memory, who was the father of the late General John Armstrong, Secretary of War during the administration of President Madison. By this marriage he had four children,—two of whom died in infancy. His youngest son, *George*, was, for many years, connected, as Register and Comptroller General, with the administration of the State of Pennsylvania, under the late Governor Thomas McKean.

At the time of his settlement in Carlisle and the united Congregations, each ten miles distant from the borough, the Indians were numerous in the vicinity, and often made hostile demonstrations, which required the body of the male members to arm themselves in self defence. In all these dangers he participated, cheerfully accompanying his flock to the camp, to administer to them there the consolations of religion. The Church at Monahan was in such an exposed situation, that, as a protection during the hours of worship, fortifications were thrown around it; behind which, while those stationed on the ramparts kept watch, the congregation might, without distraction or fear, engage in the worship of God. During this period of peril, the institutions of God's house were greatly prized, social prayer was much practised, and the members of the church were knit together by the strong ties of common faith in their guardian God, and brotherly affection for each other. The late Rev. Dr. John McDowell,* for some time Provost of the University of Pennsylvania, attributed, under God, his conversion, when but a youth of eight years of age, to a sermon preached by Mr. Duffield in the church at Monahan, from Zechariah ix. 12. "Turn ye," &c.; in which he took occasion to illustrate, from the surrounding fortifications, the only safe defence which sinners can find,—namely, the Lord Jesus Christ. His deep interest in and sympathy with a population thus perilled and suffering on the frontiers, rendered him, throughout the whole of that region, exceedingly popular. So strong was the attachment to him that, in all perilous adventures, especially during the Revolutionary struggle, the men who had to take up arms for their homes, their liberties, and their lives, always welcomed his visits in the camp with the most cordial good will.

Mr. Duffield was a bold and zealous assertor of the rights of conscience, an earnest and powerful advocate of civil and religious liberty. During the pendency of those measures which were maturing the Declaration of Independence,—while the prospects of the Colonies seemed most gloomy, his preaching contributed greatly to encourage and animate the friends of liberty. He was not in the habit of writing out his discourses in full; but, having made a skeleton, and arranged his thoughts, awaited the inspiration of the occasion for the filling up. Several of these unfinished discourses which remain, breathe a spirit of the most pure and lofty patriotism, and withal are strikingly prophetic of the glorious scenes which were to open out of all that darkness in which the country was then enveloped.

During his ministry at Carlisle, he was twice earnestly called by the Second Presbyterian Church of Philadelphia, then worshipping in the Northwest corner of Arch and Third Streets, to become their pastor; and the Commissioners, with great zeal, prosecuted their call before the Presbytery. Both the Presbytery and himself, however, judged that his presence at Carlisle was of more importance at that time than in Philadelphia.

In the year 1766, Mr. Duffield was deputed by the Synod, in connection with the Rev. Charles Beatty, to make a missionary tour, and visit the families that had pressed their way along the Great Valley that stretches through Pennsylvania, Maryland, Virginia, &c.,—commencing in the high lands in the vicinity of Newburgh, and running thence into Pennsylvania, and diagonally across that State. The object of this mission was to administer the offices of religion to those families. which had settled in what is now Franklin County, Pa., and through the range of country where Green-

* JOHN McDOWELL, a native of Pennsylvania, was graduated at the University of Pennsylvania in 1771; was for some time Principal of St. John's College, Annapolis, Md.; accepted the Professorship of Natural Philosophy in the University of Pennsylvania in 1806, and was elected Provost in the commencement of the following year, which office he also accepted; but the state of his health was found to be incompatible with the duties he had undertaken to perform, and in 1810 he was compelled to resign both offices, and retire into the country. He afterwards evinced his attachment to the institution by supplying a temporary vacancy occasioned by the resignation of his successor; and, at a still later period, by a very valuable bequest of books. He received the degree of Doctor of Laws from the University of Pennsylvania in 1807.

castle, Hagerstown, and other villages, now stand, as far as the Potomac, with a view to the organization of churches.

Some time after, Mr. Duffield was called to the Third Presbyterian Church in Philadelphia, where he officiated during the sessions of the Colonial Congress, anterior to and during the Revolutionary struggle. That church had been originally a branch of the First Presbyterian Church, under the care of the Rev. Dr. Ewing. A controversy arose between them and the parent church relative to their independence. Both the Presbytery and Mr. Duffield judged that it was his duty to accept the call, and remove to Philadelphia. The circumstances under which he was translated to that charge, in connection with the old feuds that had divided the entire Presbyterian Church,—not yet fully healed,—although the parts had again united, retaining their separate Presbyteries,—threw obstacles in the way of his labours at the commencement of his ministry. He was greatly admired as a preacher, and was well known as a bold, animated and decided Whig, resolutely contending against the encroachments on civil and religious liberty made by the government of Great Britain. On one occasion, shortly after his appearance in Philadelphia, the large church edifice, then standing on the corner of Third and Pine streets, which the First Church claimed to have under its control, was closed, and barred against his entrance, by their order, notwithstanding an appointment had been made for his preaching in it for the congregation accustomed to worship there, and by their direction. The house was opened by the officers of the Third Church, and Mr. Duffield was assisted through the throng that had assembled to hear him, and introduced through a window. News of the people assembling on Sabbath evening spread, and application was made to Mr. J. Bryant, the King's magistrate, to quell what was called a riot. The magistrate proceeded to the spot, and, shortly after the commencement of public worship, pressed his way into the aisle of the church, and before the pulpit,—ou the very spot where, afterwards, Mr. Duffield's remains were interred, and where they yet sleep, commenced, in the name of the King, to read the Riot Act, and require the people to disperse. The congregation was composed of zealous Whigs, who could not endure Tory influence or authority. The principal officer of the congregation, a Mr. Knox, rose and ordered the magistrate to desist. He refused, and went on with his reading. A second time, the zealous champion of liberty, in the hearing of all the congregation, with loud voice, demanded that the magistrate cease from disturbing the worship of God. He still refused; when, without further ado, he seized the magistrate, who was a small man, and lifting him up, carried him through the crowd out of the house, and ordered him to begone, and not come back there to disturb the worship of God. The magistrate bowed to the stern assertor of popular liberty, and Mr. Duffield went on with his preaching. But the next day he was arrested and brought before the Mayor's Court, and was required to plead to the charge of aiding and abetting a riot, and give bail for his appearance for trial. He politely and respectfully refused to put in any plea, or to give bail, averring that, as a minister of Christ, he was performing the duties of his office and was no way accessory to a riot, of the existence of which there was no proof. The Mayor,—the late excellent Mayor Willing, said that such a procedure would greatly embarrass the Court, who would be compelled to send him to prison, if he did not plead and offer bail. His brother, Samuel Duffield, M. D., or other of his friends whomsoever he might name, would be accepted by him as his bail. He still, with the utmost courtesy, declined. After some entreaty, the Mayor offered himself to be his bail, not wishing to remand him to prison. He cordially thanked his Honour for his unmerited kindness, but protested that he stood on the ground of principle, that he was called in the providence of God to assert the rights and liberty of a minister of Christ, and of a worshipping assembly, and denied the legitimate interference and cognizance of the King's government in such matters. The Mayor delayed, for several days, deciding in the case, and requesting him to take the subject into consideration, suffered him to withdraw to his own house, under the assurance that he must again appear before the Court, and give his definitive answer. The occasion and procedure were productive of great excitement. The news that the King's government were going to put Mr. Duffield into prison, spread through the city, and into the country, until it reached the region where he had formerly lived. Here the excitement became so great that the volunteer forces called the "Paxtony Boys," to whom he was well known and by whom he was much beloved, assembled, and resolved to hold themselves in readiness to march, though distant a hundred miles and more, to the city of Philadelphia, if he should be imprisoned, and set him at liberty, in opposition to the King's government. The occasion and opportunity for their valour were never afforded; for he was never again brought before the Mayor's Court. He was allowed to pursue his ministerial duties, uumolested, and the First Church settled their matters with the branch, and recognised their right to call the minister of their own choice, without dictation or control.

Attempts, however, were made to prevent his introduction into the Presbytery to which the First Church and their pastor belonged. He insisted on his right, according to the social compact, to be received by them, refusing to commence his ministry in Philadelphia, with allowed implications of his character and orthodoxy. Eventually, when he had been so received,—that his presence might not molest men who did not sympathize with him in ecclesiastical matters, he voluntarily applied for, and received, a dismission to the other Presbytery, with whose members he had more especial affinity.

During a part of the session of the Colonial Congress, he was employed, with the Rev. Mr. (afterwards Bishop) White, as Chaplain to that Body. John Adams attended regularly on his ministry, and communed with his church, during the sitting of Congress in Philadelphia.

Mr. Duffield was eminently a man of devotional feelings and habits, and was instrumental in establishing the first prayer-meeting in any Presbyterian Church in Philadelphia. It continued long after his death, and was held in the humble dwelling in which it was first instituted. So much did he value prayer, and so important did he feel it to be to excite and encourage the men that had left their homes and perilled their lives in the cause of freedom, to look to God and put their trust in Him, that he would occasionally, in the darkest hours of the Revolution, leave his charge, and repair to the camp, where the fathers and sons of many of his flock were gathered, and minister to them in the public preaching of the word, and personal converse. When the enemy were lying on Staten Island, and the American troops were on the opposite side of the Sound, on a Sabbath day, he preached to a portion of the soldiers gathered in an orchard, having ascended into the forks of a tree for his pulpit. The noise of their singing arrested the enemy's attention, who directed several cannon shot to be fired towards the place whence it proceeded. As the shot came rushing through the trees, he suggested that they should retire behind a hillock, not remote from the spot where they were,—which was done under the enemy's fire, without injury, and there they finished their religious exercises. He was with the army in their battles and retreat through Jersey, during that dark and nearly hopeless period of the Revolution, and was almost the very last man that crossed the bridge over the stream immediately South of Trenton, before it was cut down, by order of the American General. For this preservation he was indebted to a Quaker friend, whom he had essentially aided in his hour of trial,—though of politics opposed to his own,—and whose deliverance he had been the means of securing. The British officers had put a price upon his head, and were particularly anxious to destroy him, because of the influence he exerted among the soldiers of the American army. After the retreat from Princeton, he had retired to a private house in Trenton to seek repose, and was not aware that the American army had taken up their line of march, and had nearly all crossed the bridge, until his Quaker friend, having ascertained that he was in the town, sought him out, and gave him the alarm, just in time for him to escape, before the bridge was destroyed by the retreating army of Washington.

He continued the pastor of the Third Presbyterian Church until the day of his death, and was greatly respected and beloved by them. His death was occasioned by an attack of pleurisy, which ensued upon exposure at a funeral,—having officiated on one Sabbath in his pulpit in full health, and the next lying at the point of death. He died in Philadelphia among the people of his charge, February 2, 1790, aged fifty-seven years, and was interred in the middle aisle of the church which had been the scene of his labours. His Funeral Sermon was preached by the Rev. (afterwards Dr.) Ashbel Green, from Revelation xiv, 13.

There is, it is believed, a universally concurring testimony to the fact that he was an eminently devoted Christian, and an eminently faithful minister. In his natural temper he was buoyant and playful. He was the original of the "hot mush story," and one or two others of a similar character, when he was in College; and, at a still later period, he would sometimes have his joke, even at the expense of putting in jeopardy the feelings of a friend. He lived, however, habitually under the influence of invisible and eternal realities. He was perhaps not more remarkable for any thing than the strength of his faith. Frequently he was left without means to supply the immediate necessities of his family; but his faith failed not, and his gracious Lord never forsook him. On one occasion, his son had apprized him, on Saturday night, that the family were nearly destitute of provision, and that it would be necessary to repair to market early on Monday morning. He was absolutely without means, and knew not where to look for aid, as his people also were in a suffering condition; but he dismissed the subject from his mind for the Sabbath, remarking to his son,—"The Lord will provide." During that day, a sealed letter was put into his hands, which, according to his custom, remained unopened till Monday morning. On opening it, it was found to contain a sum of money sufficient to sustain his family, till they were otherwise relieved from embarrassment. But whence it came, or through whom it was sent, he never knew. The faith which, on

Saturday night, prompted him to say to his son,—"The Lord will provide,' he found, on Monday morning, had been most signally honoured.

He took an active part in the organization of the Presbyterian Church after the Revolution, and was the first Stated Clerk of the General Assembly. He published an Account of his tour with Mr. Beatty, along the frontiers of Pennsylvania, and also a Thanksgiving Sermon for the Restoration of Peace, December 11, 1783. He received the degree of Doctor of Divinity from Yale College in 1785.

I am truly yours,

GEORGE DUFFIELD.

SAMSON OCCOM.*

1756—1792.

Samson Occom was an Indian of the Mohegan tribe, and was born at Mohegan, an Indian settlement on the river Thames, between Norwich and New London, in the year 1723. His parents, like the rest of the Indians, led a wandering life, and supported themselves chiefly by hunting and fishing. None of the tribe could read, and none had any better dwellings than wigwams. When Occom was a boy, the Rev. Mr. Jewett,† minister of the parish that is now Montville, was accustomed to preach to these Indians once a fortnight; and, after a while, a person went among them to teach them to read. During the great religious excitement that prevailed about the year 1740, the Indians were brought somewhat under a religious influence by the visits of some of the ministers in that region, and a number of them were induced to repair to the neighbouring churches. Occom, among others, became deeply impressed by the truth which he heard, and, after some six months of anxiety and distress, believed himself to have gained "the good hope through grace." This change occurred in the year 1741, when he was in his eighteenth year.

From the time that his mind became enlightened, and his heart, as he hoped, renewed, he had a strong desire to become the teacher, especially the religious teacher, of his tribe. He applied himself diligently to learn to read, with such helps as he could command, and was soon able to read the Bible. In December, 1743, he obtained admission into the school kept by the Rev. Eleazar Wheelock of Lebanon; and he remained with him four years, evincing, during the whole time, the utmost docility and diligence. In 1748, he taught a school at New London; but soon left it, and was engaged in a school among the Indians, at Montauk, on Long Island, where he continued ten or eleven years. At first, he was there simply in the capacity of a teacher; and he devoted himself with great zeal and fidelity to the instruction of both children and adults; but having, after some time, received license to preach from the Windham (Conn.) Association, he joined to his office as teacher, that of preacher; and he preached not only to

* Buell's Ord. Serm.—Dwight's Trav., II.—Mass. Hist. Coll. IV, V, IX, X.—Allen' Biog. Dict.—Doc. Hist. New York, IV.

† David Jewett was graduated at Harvard College in 1736; was ordained pastor of the church in Montville, Conn., October 3, 1739; and died June 6, 1783, aged sixty-nine.

the Indians at Montauk in their own language, but also to the Skenecock and Yenecock Indians, distant some thirty miles. A considerable number of the Indians at Montauk were hopefully converted under his ministry. In speaking of the results of his labours here, after six years, he says,—"Many of them" (the Indians) "can read, write and cypher well, but they are not so zealous in religion now, as they were some years ago." His style of living, during his residence here, was well suited to the society with which he mingled. His house was covered with mats, and he changed his abode twice a year, that he might be near the planting ground in the summer, and the wood in the winter. As a means of obtaining his subsistence, he not only used his fish hook and gun freely, but bound old books for the people of East Hampton, stocked guns, made wooden spoons, cedar pails, and various other domestic utensils.

On the 30th of August, 1759, Mr. Occom was ordained by the Presbytery of Suffolk; and he retained his connection with the Presbyterian Church till the close of life.

In June, 1761, he went, under the direction of the Correspondents of the Society in Scotland for propagating Christian Knowledge, on a mission to the Onoyda (Oneida) Indians. The Correspondents, in a letter introducing him to Sir William Johnson,—after having set forth the importance of his mission, say—"We cannot doubt but that it will meet with your ready approbation, and therefore with the favour of your countenance and protection, and that you will be pleased to furnish Mr. Occom with such a pass, and such recommendations, as you shall judge proper to answer the great ends proposed." How long his mission continued does not appear; but it would seem to have been for only a short time.

In the beginning of the year 1766, Mr. Occom, by request of Dr. Wheelock, accompanied the Rev. Nathaniel Whitaker, then of Norwich, Conn., to England, to procure funds for Moor's Charity School. He was the first Indian preacher that ever appeared in Great Britain, and was of course an object of great curiosity and interest. The houses in which he preached were generally thronged with listening and gazing multitudes. He passed from England into Scotland; and from February 16, 1766, to July 22, 1767, he preached between three and four hundred sermons. He was eminently successful in regard to the object of his mission,—the amount of his collections in England and Scotland being upwards of ten thousand pounds sterling. The King himself subscribed two hundred pounds, and Lord Dartmouth fifty guineas. It seems, however, from the following extract of a letter which he wrote, after his return, that his object met with no great favour from the dignitaries of the Established Church; and the tone of the extract may help to illustrate his own character:—

"Now I am in my own country, I may freely inform you of what I honestly and soberly think of the Bishops, Lord Bishops, and Archbishops of England. In my view, they don't look like Gospel Bishops or ministers of Christ. I can't find them in the Bible. I think they a good deal resemble the Anti-christian Popes. I find the Gospel Bishops resemble, in some good measure, their good Master; and they follow Him in the example He has left them. They discover meekness and humility; are gentle and kind unto all men—ready to do good unto all—they are compassionate and merciful unto the miserable, and charitable to the poor. But I did not find the Bishops of England so. Upon my word, if I never spoke the truth before, I do now. I waited on a number of Bishops, and represented to them the miserable and wretched situation of the poor Indians, who are perishing for lack of spiritual knowledge, and begged their assistance in evangelizing these poor heathen. But if you can believe me, they never gave us one single brass farthing. It seems to me that they are very indifferent whether the poor Indians go to Heaven or Hell. I can't help my thoughts; and I am apt to think they don't want the Indians to go to Heaven with them."

After his return to this country, he resided at Mohegan, though he was often employed in missionary labours among distant Indians. In 1786, he removed with a number of the New England Indians, and a few from Long Island, to what was called the Brotherton Tract, in Oneida County N. Y., in the neighbourhood of the Stockbridge Indians, who were of Mohegan descent, and had been under the instruction of Mr. Sergeant and Mr. Edwards. His last years he spent with the Indians, chiefly at New Stockbridge, near Brotherton, though he was engaged for some time in teaching a school at Tuscarora. In 1790, he was set off from the Presbytery of Suffolk, with others, to constitute the Presbytery of Albany. He died suddenly, July 14, 1792, in the sixty-ninth year of his age. For some time previous, he had had a presentiment that his death was near. Having been accustomed, in early life, to the manufacture of pails and cooper-ware, he returned to this employment in his old age, as his leisure and strength would permit. He remarked to his wife, one day, that he must finish an article that he had commenced, soon, or he might not live to do it. He went to his work, finished the article, and set out to return. His wife saw him approaching the house; but, on looking a few moments after, noticed that he had fallen; and, on going to him, found that he was dead. His funeral was attended by more than three hundred Indians; and a Sermon was preached on the occasion by the missionary, Rev. Samuel Kirkland.

Mr. Occom, though generally exemplary in his deportment, occasionally yielded to excess in the use of intoxicating liquors. In one instance at least, this either drew upon him the discipline of the Church, or drew from him a voluntary confession; for, in a letter to the Presbytery of Suffolk, dated June 9, 1764, he says—"I have been shamefully overtaken with strong drink, by which I have greatly wounded the cause of God, blemished the pure religion of Jesus Christ, blackened my own character, and hurt my own soul." In his latter years, his life is said to have been entirely exemplary. His religious character was thought to have suffered for the time, at least in respect to humility, from the flattering attentions he received in England.

He published a Sermon at the execution of Moses Paul, an Indian, at New Haven, 1772. An account of the Montauk Indians, written by him, is preserved in the Collections of the Massachusetts Historical Society, vol. x. He occasionally tried his hand at poetry, and several of his Hymns are still extant.

The following testimony concerning him, is given by President Dwight, in his Travels—vol. II.:

"I heard Mr. Occom twice. His discourses, though not proofs of superior talents, were decent, and his utterance in some degree eloquent. His character at times laboured under some imputations. Yet there are good reasons to believe that most, if not all, of them were unfounded; and there is satisfactory evidence that he was a man of piety. During several years, (the last of his life,) he lived within the bounds of the Presbytery of Albany. By a respectable clergyman belonging to that Body, I have been informed that he was regularly received into their number; that he was esteemed by them a good man and a useful minister; that he was uncensurable in his life; and that he was lamented and honoured at his death."

About the time of his leaving Montauk, Dr. Buell, of East Hampton, wrote concerning him as follows:—

"As a preacher of the Gospel, he seems always to have in view the end of the ministry,—the glory of God and the salvation of men. His manner of expression, when he preaches to the Indians, is vastly more natural, free, clear and eloquent, quick and powerful, than when he preaches to others. He is the glory of the Indian nation."

FROM THE REV. DANIEL WALDO.

GEDDES, July 7, 1853.

Dear Sir: It is not much that I can tell you, from personal recollection, of the Rev. Samson Occom, though I distinctly remember to have heard him preach when I was about fourteen years of age. He preached, on one occasion, in an old meeting-house, in the part of Franklin, Conn., then known as Pettipaug; and, as it was only a few miles from my native place, I was attracted, in company with many others, by his reputation as an Indian preacher, to hear him. He made an impression on my youthful mind, which has remained in a good degree of vividness, through the long period of seventy-seven years,—an evidence that the impression must have originally been one of no inconsiderable strength.

Mr. Occom, at the time referred to, seemed to me to be a man between fifty and sixty years of age. He was of about the medium height, had rather a round face, and a bright intelligent expression, with a full share of the Indian look. There was nothing in his general manner, as far as I remember, to mark him as one of the sons of the forest; but his English education might naturally be expected to eradicate, in a great measure, his original Indian peculiarities. His voice was pleasant, but not very loud—sufficiently so, however, to accommodate any ordinary assemblage. His dress was entirely English. I do not remember his text, but I recollect that his subject led him to speak somewhat at length of what he called a traditionary religion; and he told an anecdote by way of illustration. An old Indian, he said, had a knife which he kept till he wore the blade out; and then his son took it and put a new blade to the handle, and kept it till he had worn the handle out; and this process went on till the knife had had half a dozen blades, and as many handles; but still it was all the time the same knife. I cannot be very particular as to the application he made of it, but the story I remember well, and it seemed to me at the time to be very pertinent to the object for which it was told.

His manner in the pulpit, as I remember it, was serious and manly; and he spoke without notes, and with a freedom which showed that he had a good command of his subject. He was undoubtedly a man of much more than ordinary talents, and though, for some time, a cloud rested over him, I believe those who had the best opportunity of judging, were disposed, on the whole, to think well of his Christian character.

Very truly yours,

DANIEL WALDO.

HENRY PATILLO.*

1757—1801.

Henry Patillo was born in Scotland, in the year 1726. He came to this country with an elder brother, when he was nine years old. He took up his residence, for a time, as a merchant's clerk, in the Province of Virginia; and notwithstanding he had received a religious education, yet, in the absence of the restraints to which he had been accustomed in his childhood, he now, for a time, yielded to the power of temptation. Leaving the counting-house, he engaged as a teacher of youth; and, while thus employed, became the subject of deep religious convictions. He continued his labours as a teacher, in two or three Presbyterian Congregations, successively; and, during the whole time, his mind seems to have been exercised in regard to his relations to God as a sinner; but it was not till after a year or two, that he obtained comforting and satisfactory views of evangelical truth. In a record which he has left of his own exercises subsequent to this, he states that, in the warmth of his feelings, he fell into the error of making his own experience too much a standard by which to judge of the experience of other professed Christians; but that further reflection and observation led him to correct the error.

After his hopeful conversion, he felt deeply anxious in respect to the spiritual condition of those around him, and in this state of feeling cherished the desire, and at length formed the purpose, of devoting himself to the Christian ministry. He now fell in with the Rev. John Thomson, of the Donegal Presbytery, Pa., who was on a visit to the Carolinas, and who invited him to go to Pennsylvania, and prosecute his studies preparatory to the ministry, under his care. He accepted the invitation, and actually set out on his journey, but, after a few hours, was arrested by a violent attack of pleurisy, which not only obliged him to return, but in its remoter effects, rendered him incapable of much exertion for several months. The result was that his project for going to Pennsylvania was given up; and the next year (1751,) the Rev. Samuel Davies, then residing in Hanover, Va., being on a preaching excursion to the Roanoke, met with Mr. Patillo, and, having learned his wish to enter the ministry, kindly offered to receive him under his care as a theological student. Mr. P. thankfully accepted the offer, and arrived at Mr. Davies' house in Hanover on the 1st of August.

He pursued his studies under the instruction of Mr. Davies, until 1753, when that eminent man went on a mission to Great Britain in behalf of Princeton College; and, on his return, about the beginning of 1755, Mr. Patillo resumed his studies under him, and continued to enjoy the benefit of his instruction until he was licensed to preach.

In the summer of 1755, he was married to a Miss Anderson. He had consulted Mr. Davies on the subject, and had received from him an opinion adverse to his forming the connection at that time; and though, at first, he was inclined to listen to Mr. Davies' advice, yet, on mature considera-

* Foote's Sketches of N. C.—MS. from Rev. Dr. Archibald Alexander.—Life of Dr. Alexander.—Webster's MSS.

tion, he felt constrained, in honour, to carry out his previous purpose. While he resided in Hanover, he was sustained partly by the kindness of friends, and partly by teaching a few children during several hours of each day; and, after his marriage, he seems to have depended somewhat on the pecuniary resources of his wife. They lived on a most economical scale; and in 1757, the small cabin which they occupied as a dwelling, was struck by lightning, and though it had in it eleven persons, they all escaped unhurt.

On the 28th of September, 1757, Mr. Patillo, having gone through all his Presbyterial examinations and trials, was licensed to preach by the Presbytery of Hanover. His ordination took place at Cumberland, on the 12th of July, 1758. On the 27th of September following, he accepted a call from the Churches of Willis Creek, Byrd, and Buck Island. Having remained with these Congregations about four years, he was dismissed from his charge, on the 7th of October, 1762, on the ground of an inadequate support. In May, 1763, he began to supply the Churches of Cumberland, Harris Creek, and Deep Creek, and continued with them two years. At a meeting of the Presbytery at Hico, on the 2d of October, 1765, a call was presented to him from Hawfields, Eno, and Little River. This call he accepted, and immediately removed to North Carolina, where he spent the remainder of his life. He, however, retained this charge only until the year 1774.

In 1775, he was elected one of the delegates for the County of Bute, (now Warren and Franklin,) to the first Provincial Congress of North Carolina. He accepted the appointment, and not only acted as one of the Chaplains of that body, but when, on a certain occasion of great interest, they resolved themselves into a Committee of the whole, he was unanimously appointed Chairman. It is hardly necessary to add that he was a zealous friend to those measures which hastened on the Revolution.

In 1780, he became pastor of the Congregations of Nutbush and Grassy Creek,—composed originally of emigrants from Virginia, who had been trained under the ministry of the Rev. Samuel Davies and his coadjutors. Here he continued his labours till they were terminated by death, in the year 1801; when he had nearly completed his seventy-fifth year. He died at a distance from home, in Dinwiddie County, Va., whither he had gone on a sort of missionary excursion. In his last moments, he evinced a triumphant faith. His Funeral Sermon was preached by the Rev. Drury Lacy.

Mr. Patillo, during several years of his ministry, was occupied partly in the instruction of youth. Though he never enjoyed the advantages of a collegiate education, as he had at one time hoped to do, he had the reputation of being a good classical scholar, and was a highly successful teacher. In 1787, the degree of Master of Arts was conferred upon him by Hampden Sidney College.

In 1787, Mr. Patillo published a small volume containing three Sermons—namely, on Divisions among Christians; on the Necessity of Regeneration; and on the Scripture doctrine of Election. A note appended to one of these Discourses broached the same doctrine concerning Christ's human nature, of which Edward Irving has since been so distinguished an exponent. At a later period, he published an Abridgment of Leland's Deistical writers, and a Sermon on the death of Washington. He also left in manuscript some Essays on Baptism, and on Universalism; a Catechism of doctrine for youth, and a Catechism or Compend in question and answer for the use of adults. He also prepared a Geography for youth, which is said to have possessed very considerable merit.

The following incident concerning Mr. Patillo is related by Dr. Alexander:—

"While I was minister in Charlotte, the old gentleman came once to pay his last visit to his friends in Virginia. I made a string of appointments for him, reaching from Cub Creek to Cumberland, and accompanied him the whole round. It was previously suggested to a few, as we passed from place to place, that it would be well to make a contribution to aid the aged servant of God. When we had finished our tour, I had in my saddle bags about thirty dollars, which the people had freely given. As I handed him the silver coin, (for we had then never seen a bank note,) the good old man appeared to be penetrated with gratitude."

FROM MRS. DR. JOHN H. RICE.

NEAR HAMPDEN SIDNEY COLLEGE, April 19, 1854.

My dear Sir: Though the Rev. Henry Patillo lived a considerable distance from my father's residence, he often travelled through our region, and came frequently to our house, where he was always a most welcome visitor. At a still earlier period, I have heard it said that he was familiar in my grandfather's house; so that he may be said to have been an acquaintance of the family during three generations. I was a girl of not more than fifteen, when I knew him, but there was so much in his appearance and manner that was striking and peculiar, that time has done little to efface the impressions I received respecting him. I have also many traditionary impressions of him, which I have received through some of his intimate friends; so that, on the whole, I may venture, with some degree of confidence, to say something, in compliance with your wishes, in respect to his character.

Mr. Patillo, if my memory serves me, had a large frame, and considerably more than the ordinary degree of flesh. I think his features were rather large and coarse, though his face easily lighted up with a smile of good-will. He seemed to be an eminently devout and godly man, and delighted to converse on subjects connected with experimental religion; and yet he was one of the most cheerful and good-humoured persons I ever knew. It seemed natural for him to say droll things; and he would sometimes keep a whole company convulsed, apparently without being conscious that he was doing it. He had great frankness of character, and would never even seem to dissemble in the smallest matters, though I have heard of cases in which he almost made himself ridiculous in avoiding the appearance of it. He was of a most contented and happy turn of mind, and though always poor, never seemed to regard his lot as a hard one. He was a great lover of books, and is said to have indulged his taste in that respect quite as much as his circumstances would warrant. His house, during his absence at a certain time, was burnt; and when he met his wife, on his return, his first exclamation was—"My dear, are my books safe?" and on receiving an affirmative answer, he thanked God, and seemed perfectly satisfied. I think he was uncommonly affectionate in his intercourse: he used always to address my mother as his daughter; and he was a great favourite with all the children.

I heard him preach, though I remember little more concerning it, than that, like his conversation, it was striking, and occasionally, I think, bordering on the ludicrous. He had a loud voice, spoke with great earnestness, and was listened to with much attention. I remember once seeing him at the house of my uncle, the Rev. Drury Lacy, for whom he had come to preach. Mr. Lacy had but one hand; and yet, by a dexterous use of it, he was able, with great facility, to make a pen. Mr. Patillo, as a matter of curiosity, handed him a quill, and asked him to make a pen for him. He immediately set about it, and in a short time gave him the pen. "Why," said Mr. P., "I could have done that as well as you." "And why did you not do it, then?" "Oh, because I wanted to see you work with your one hand."

That you may know in what estimation Mr. Patillo was held by Mr. Lacy, who was long his intimate friend, I subjoin the following extract of a Sermon which Mr. L. preached on the occasion of his death:—

"Possessed of an originality of genius, and endowed by nature with powers of mind superior to the common lot of men, he cheerfully determined to cousecrate them all to the service of the Saviour, in the Gospel ministry. That the Scriptures were his delight, and that he meditated on them day and night, so as to become well versed in their doctrines and precepts, all who had the pleasure of his acquaintance, all who ever heard him preach, and all who have read his printed works, can not be ignorant. That he devoted his time and talents to the service of God, his works of faith and labours of love among you, and as far as he had an opportunity of travelling to preach, abundantly testify. His zeal was so far from being diminished by age, that it evidently appeared to increase; as if the near prospect of obtaining the crown animated him to greater exertions to be found worthy of it. My hearers! Can you have forgotten the ardour and pertinacity of his prayers, the weight of his arguments, the fervour of his exhortations, and the persuasiveness of his counsels? Did he not visit your bedside when you were sick, and there communicate heavenly instruction, to revive your fainting spirits, and pour forth the fervent prayer to God that your affliction might be sanctified? And in the social intercourse of friendship, you must remember how readily he improved every occurrence to communicate useful and religious knowledge. That his life was a pattern of resignation and thankfulness has been remarked even by those who had but a slight acquaintance with him. Always cheerful, he seemed more disposed to bless the hand of Providence for the favours he enjoyed, than to think hardly of any afflictive dispensation he suffered. When was the tenor of his soul so lost and discomposed as to unfit him for the discharge of the sacred duties of his office?"

With best wishes for your success in every good word and work,

I remain truly yours,

ANNE S. RICE.

JAMES LATTA, D. D.

1758—1801.

FROM THE REV. ROBERT P. DU BOIS.

NEW LONDON, Pa., May 9, 1850.

Dear Sir: You have requested me to prepare a sketch of the life of the late Rev. James Latta, D. D., for insertion in your forthcoming work. In this request his only surviving son has joined. However incompetent for such a task, yet thus solicited, I feel encouraged to make the attempt. For the sake of your readers, who will naturally inquire how far they may confide in my statements, it seems necessary to observe concerning myself, that I am married to the eldest daughter of one of his sons,—the late Rev. John

E. Latta, and that my father, the late Rev. Uriah Du Bois,* was his successor for twenty-three years in his first charge. As Stated Clerk, I have access to the Records of the Newcastle Presbytery, of which he was a member for thirty years. I have also examined the printed Records of Synod. I have received communications from his son and daughter, his daughter-in-law, his successor in his second charge, and Mr. David Scott, a venerable elder in that church, who remembers him well. In addition to these, I have in my possession a copy of the "Christian's Magazine" for July 1810, which contains a memoir of him, in seven octavo pages, supposed, by his family, to have been written by an eminent divine, once his pupil, and afterwards his friend and co-presbyter, the late Rev. Dr. Samuel Martin, of Chanceford, Pa. Still, with all these sources of information before me, I have been surprised to find how few things connected with the life of this good man, so long prominent in the church and in society, relentless time has spared.

JAMES LATTA, was born in Ireland, in the winter of 1732. His family was Protestant, of the Scotch Irish Presbyterian stock. His mother's maiden name was Alison; and she was related to the Rev. Dr. Francis Alison. Nothing more is known of the family in Ireland. His parents migrated to this country, when he was about six or seven years of age, bringing him with them. The vessel in which they sailed from Ireland was wrecked upon the American coast, and the family records being then lost, the exact date of his birth is not known. They settled near Elkton, Md., and are believed to have been connected with the Elk River Congregation,—now called "the Rock." He, once, in riding by a graveyard belonging to that church, pointed it out to a daughter who was with him, as the place where his parents were buried.

The time of his spiritual birth is also uncertain. He appears to have been one of those few whose hearts are renewed in early childhood, if not from the beginning of their lives. When a mere child, he discovered a very serious and thoughtful turn of mind, and a pious gravity far beyond his years. Two illustrations of this are preserved in the family. One occurred at the time of the shipwreck referred to. During the three days and nights that he remained with others on board the foundering vessel, before they could be relieved,—so remarkable was his attachment to his Bible, that he kept it continually under his arm. He seemed to think *that* the most precious of his treasures, and if he should go down, that he must carry it with him. The other was about seven years later, when, from home at

*URIAH DU BOIS was a great-great-grandson of Louis Du Bois, who was driven from France on account of his religion, and settled in New Paltz, now in Ulster County, N. Y., about 1660. He (Uriah) was born in Pittsgrove township, Salem County, N. J., in 1768; was graduated at the University of Pennsylvania in 1790; was engaged chiefly in teaching from that time till 1796; completed his theological studies under the Rev. Ashbel Green, D. D. of Philadelphia; was licensed to preach by the Presbytery of Philadelphia, October 20, 1796; and was ordained and installed as pastor of the Churches of Deep Run and Tinicum, by the same Presbytery, December 16, 1798. In 1804, he resigned his charge at Tinicum, and removed from Deep Run to Doylestown, eight miles distant, where he became the head of a large and flourishing school, and, at the same time, established a Presbyterian congregation, to which, in connection with that of Deep Run, he continued to minister till the close of life. In June, 1798, he was married to Martha, second daughter of Robert Patterson, L. L. D. of Philadelphia, by whom he had five sons and three daughters. About two years before his death, he became the subject of a wasting disease, one effect of which was the almost total loss of sight. He still, however, continued his work,—some of his pupils reciting to him in a darkened chamber, and his sermons being preached in a sitting posture. He died September 10, 1821, in his fifty-fourth year. He was a man of great energy and industry, an excellent classical scholar, an accomplished instructer, and an earnest and attractive preacher.

school. So much was he esteemed for his piety by those who knew him, that families with whom he resided looked up to him to lead their worship, although but fourteen years of age; and he did it with an understanding that charmed and astonished all who heard him.

This pious turn of mind, together with his promising talents, his thirst for knowledge, and the advice of judicious friends, prompted his parents to give him a liberal education. He was, accordingly, placed under the care of the Rev. Dr. Francis Alison, at that time Pastor of the Church of New London, in Chester County, Pa., and also the Principal of a classical school at the same place. This was the school, which the Synod of Philadelphia, in 1744, adopted as their own, paying the salaries of the Master and Tutor by yearly contributions from their churches, and offering "*gratuitous* instruction in the languages, philosophy, and divinity, to all persons who may please to send their children." Here were trained up, under this deservedly famous teacher and scholar, many youth, who, in their turn, became eminent in the Church or the State. Amongst these the subject of this sketch made rapid improvement in useful knowledge, and in religious experience.

In the year 1752, Dr. Alison, having been chosen a Professor and Vice Provost of the College of Philadelphia, then being established, and now styled the University of Pennsylvania, removed thither. His young pupil soon followed him, and having there completed his collegiate education, he received his degree at the first Commencement that took place in this new seminary. As a proof of his high standing there, he had assigned to him on that occasion, the Salutatory Oration in Latin,—an exercise allotted to the member of the class reputed to be the best scholar. I have before me his diploma, as Master of Arts, bearing date May 1, 1760, and stating on its face that he had received his first degree of A. B. on the 17th of May, 1757.

The Trustees of the College, being favourably impressed with his character and attainments, offered him a situation as Tutor. This place he accepted and held for a few years, still pursuing his favourite study,—Divinity, under the same instructer, who had so long guided him in the pursuit of knowledge. Having put himself under the care of the Presbytery of Philadelphia, and passed his trials with much approbation, he was licensed by it to preach the Gospel on the 15th of February, 1758. He still remained, however, in the College as Tutor, pursuing his studies under Dr. Alison, and enjoying the advantage of submitting his sermons to the inspection of that venerable theologian. He acquired in this way, that accuracy in the style and structure of his sermons, for which he was ever after remarkable.

The Synod, at its meeting in May, 1759, directed him to "visit the Indians" in the summer of that year, and in November following, to go with several others on a mission to the then destitute settlements of Virginia and Carolina. The former of these appointments he did not fulfil, for reasons which were sustained by the Synod; but the latter he faithfully discharged, spending some time in those Southern parts.

Mr. Latta was ordained by the Presbytery of Philadelphia in October, 1759,—it would appear as an *evangelist*, and very probably in reference to the mission to the South, on which he was to go in the following month.

The Congregation of Deep Run, in Bucks County, Pa., having presented to him a call, it was accepted by him, and he was installed there in the year 1761. At that time, Deep Run was a Presbyterian settlement, and the church flourishing. In after times, the Germans took possession of that region, and the congregation became very small. During the pastorate of Mr. Latta, the lot of ground on which the church stands, and the parsonage house and farm, were deeded, by the Hon. William Allen of Philadelphia, to him and his successors in the ministry, for the use of the congregation.

On the 28th day of May, 1762, the Second Presbytery of Philadelphia was set off by the Synod from the Presbytery of Philadelphia. This consisted of five ministers, of whom Mr. Latta was one; and they were all strenuous advocates of what was called the Old Side. It appears from certain dissents and protests, in 1766, when an ineffectual attempt was made in Synod to reunite the two Presbyteries, that this Second Presbytery had been formed on the *elective affinity* principle, as its members professed to be conscientiously opposed to the practice of examining candidates for the ministry on their experimental acquaintance with religion, which the Synod had approved of; and had declared that sooner than remain in a Presbytery which pursued that practice, they would break off from all connection with the Synod.

In the year 1770, Mr. Latta resigned the charge of Deep Run. About that time, he was called to the pastoral care of the Congregation of Chesnut Level, in Lancaster County, Pa,—which belonged to the Presbytery of Newcastle. This call was accepted, and he was received as a member by that Presbytery on the 16th of May, 1771, and on the second Tuesday of November following, was installed in the pastoral office by Messrs. Alexander McDowell and William Foster.* The congregation, at that time, was widely scattered and very weak. The salary promised in the call was only one hundred pounds, Pennsylvania currency, which, "says Mr. Scott, (the elder above referred to,) "was never increased, and rarely all paid." Through the importunity of some friends, who wished to educate their sons, he was prevailed on (though not without great reluctance, lest it should interfere with his pastoral duties, to which he desired wholly to devote himself) to take a few pupils under his care. This led the way to numerous applications of the same kind, so that he was induced to employ an usher, that he might have more time to attend to his ministry. This school was continued under his direction for several years, and was acquiring celebrity; but the Revolutionary war, breaking out, arrested its progress. The usher and several of the older scholars joined the army, and he being unwilling to have the sole charge of it, it was closed. After the war, as soon as learning became again an object of pursuit, a Latin School was established at Chestnut Level by Mr. Sampson Smith; but Mr. Smith having been suddenly killed, by a stroke of lightning, his pupils were left without an instructer. Here, again, Mr. Latta was constrained to take up a charge which, in his own mind, he had resolved never to resume. The eyes of these young men were directed towards him, and their affecting solicitations to take them under his care, in their desolate situation, were irresistible. He continued to have charge of the school for several years, but

* William Foster (often spelled *Forster*) was graduated at the College of New Jersey in 1764; was licensed to preach by the Presbytery of Newcastle, April 23, 1767; accepted a call from Upper Octorora, where he was ordained and installed October 19, 1768; and died in September, 1780. He had a high standing as a minister, and occasionally received under his care theological students.

gave it up some time before his death. Several distinguished men were educated at this school. The income derived from it, added to his meagre salary, enabled him to purchase a farm, build a house upon it, and support his large family with decency and comfort.

Mr. Latta took a deep interest in the cause of American liberty, and firmly and zealously espoused that cause both by word and deed. He stimulated his people to defend their rights, and once, in the course of the war, when an unusual number of them were drafted to serve in the militia, with a view to encourage them, he took his blanket and knapsack, like a soldier, and actually accompanied them on their campaign. At another time, he served for a while in the army as a Chaplain.

About the year 1785, many congregations in this region were agitated upon the subject of procuring Acts of Incorporation from the State. Some of the people were in favour of this measure, whilst others vehemently opposed it, on the ground that if they were members of chartered bodies, their estates would be encumbered, as by a mortgage for arrears of salary. This controversy became very earnest at Chestnut Level. A petition was sent to the Legislature for a charter, in which, it would appear, the pastor concurred. This gave rise to a remonstrance against the petition, which was signed by a part of the congregation, and which had even the appearance of reflecting on the moral character of their minister. At least, it was so understood by him. The consequences were, great distress to his own mind, much strife and discord among the people of his charge, and the excluding from church privileges of some of the members. In this painful state of things, Mr. Latta called a special meeting of the Presbytery. It appears, from their Records, that they laboured in the matter, part of two days, patiently heard both parties, and, as the result, found (to use their own language) "that the evils complained of had taken their rise from mistaken apprehensions and injurious representations of the nature and design of the petition before mentioned; and that the persons complained of, whatever their paper might imply, disavowed all intention of impeaching Mr. Latta's character, or preventing his usefulness. The Presbytery, therefore, being desirous to adopt the most lenient and healing measures, agreed to take their solemn declaration to that purpose, as being a full justification of Mr. Latta's character and conduct. Accordingly, all the persons complained of, who were present, declared, one by one, in the most solemn manner, that they did not intend, by any means, to injure the character, interest, or usefulness, of Mr. Latta, as a minister of the Gospel." The Presbytery then, having restored them to their former standing, "exhorted all parties to unity, and to the cultivation of peace and brotherly love, and to the manifestation of a due respect to Mr. Latta." Thus was closed a breach that, at one time, threatened wide spread evil. This, so far as I can ascertain, was the only serious disagreement that Mr. Latta ever had with any of his people; and the result of it was certainly very creditable and honourable to him, and proved that, however some of them might, for a season, be led away by passion, he had in reality the confidence and heartfelt attachment of them all.

A few years afterward, some of the neighbouring churches began to introduce the Psalms and Hymns of Dr. Watts into their public worship. This was also an exciting subject in its day. Mr. Latta warmly advocated the new Psalmody, and laboured hard to have it brought into use among his people; but so earnest was the opposition, on the part of some of his leading members, that it never was accomplished in his day, and not until all these persons had been removed by death. At that time, the Rev. John Anderson, a minister of the Associate Church, wrote a Treatise on Psalmody, strongly reprobating the use of Watts, and challenging its friends to a vindication of it. This gave Mr. Latta an opportunity of publishing his views at large on the subject. He accepted the challenge, and sent forth a pamphlet of a hundred and eight octavo pages, the object of which was to show that the principal subjects of Psalmody should be taken from the Gospel. The pamphlet was never answered; and the high estimation in which it was held, at that time, is evident from the fact that it passed through four editions. This is the only work that he ever published.

The honorary degree of Doctor of Divinity was conferred upon him, about the close of the last century,—it is believed, by the University of Pennsylvania.*

Dr. Latta laboured on in the ministry, until very near the close of life. In December, a month before his decease, he attended a meeting of his Presbytery at New London, twenty miles from home. The circumstances of his death, as related by one of his daughters to my mother-in-law, were as follows:—Riding to church one Sabbath with his daughter Mary, he was thrown from the carriage, and falling on his head, he was somewhat stunned. He observed to her,—"I am killed; but do not tell your mother." He proceeded to church, preached with some difficulty, and returned home. He soon after fell into a sleepy, comatose state, until the daughter, the next day, alarmed, related to her mother what had happened. Help was immediately called in, but in vain. He continued a few days, almost insensible, and then died. Thus no opportunity was afforded to his family and friends to enjoy the advantages of his conversation in his last moments. He died on the 29th of January, 1801, near the close of his sixty-eighth year.

"His personal appearance," says Mr. Scott, "was not great,—slightly stooping, he appeared rather below the medium height—very spare of flesh, he always looked older than his years. There was in him a blending of cheerfulness and gravity rarely met with." An old lady, describing him as she had seen him alight from his horse, with his venerable countenance, and his long white hair hanging over his shoulders, said he seemed to her like the very impersonation of an old Apostle. Some aged people in my own congregation of New London, to which, when vacant, he, for many years, was accustomed, in company with Dr. Read of Wilmington, to administer the Communion, have spoken to me of the grave dignity of his appearance, and of his great solemnity in the pulpit. The writer of his Memoir says,—"though of a very delicate constitution, by a remarkable temperance and care, he attained to more than the ordinary age of man."

Dr. Latta was greatly blessed in his family. About the year 1765, he was married at Deep Run to Miss Mary McCalla of that congregation,—an aunt of the present Rev. William Latta McCalla of Philadelphia. She was a woman, eminent for her piety and amiability, and was truly a helpmeet for the man of God to whom she was united. She continued to reside

* In the Minutes of the Board of Trustees of that institution, there is a record of Mr. Latta's having been proposed for the degree, but not of its having been actually conferred, in 1799. The omission of the latter is supposed to have been accidental, as it was actually conferred by *some* College about that time, and his name is not found on the catalogue of any *other* College.

on the family farm at Chestnut Level until her death, which occurred February 22, 1810, in the sixty-sixth year of her age.

They were the parents of ten children, of whom eight survived them. Of these, four were sons, who all entered the ministry.

His eldest son, *Francis Alison*, was ordained on the 23d of November, 1796; was first settled at Wilmington, De., then at Lancaster, Pa., and afterwards at Chestnut Level,—his father's former charge. During a large part of his ministry, he also employed himself as a teacher, and in the latter part of his life, in that way alone. In this department, he was justly distinguished, and indeed there were few, if any, in his day, who excelled him as a classical scholar. He was a man of fine mind, and well cultivated, a poet, and an eloquent pulpit orator. In his disposition he was social and amiable. He was never married. He died April 21, 1834, in his sixty-seventh year, having served in the ministry nearly as long as his father.

His second son, *William*, was graduated at the University of Pennsylvania in 1794, was settled as a pastor over the united Congregations of Great Valley and Charlestown, in Chester County, Pa., and continued to have the charge of those Churches until his death, which occurred on the 19th of February, 1847, being then nearly eighty years of age, and in about the fiftieth year of his pastorate. He was also a fine scholar, was skilful in the use of his pen, and was occasionally occupied in teaching. He married Miss Mary Loyd of the Great Valley, who died about the same time with himself. By her he had four children,—one of whom is now the pastor of the Presbyterian Church at Waynesburg, in Chester County. The General Assembly, in 1847, paid a tribute to his memory, by speaking of him as "one of the venerable fathers of the Presbyterian Church." He was created a Doctor of Divinity by the La Fayette College, a few years before his death.

The third son of Dr. Latta was *John Ewing*. He received ordination on the 13th of August, 1800, and was the pastor, during the whole of his ministerial life, or over twenty-four years, of the united Churches of Newcastle and Christiana, in the State of Delaware. For a number of years, he had charge of an Academy at Newcastle, and several distinguished men were educated by him. An obituary, written by Dr. Gilbert, then a pastor at Wilmington, De., speaks of him as "intelligent, exemplary, and conscientious; attentive to the afflicted and the anxious, a man of enlarged views and liberal feelings, and a faithful, clear and instructive expounder of the word of God." He served the General Assembly, for several years, as their Permanent Clerk, and was honoured with other important offices in the Church. He was married to Catharine Van Voorhies of Philadelphia, and left behind him two sons and five daughters, who all, with their mother, still survive. He died on the 26th day of September, 1824, in his fifty-second year.

The following are his publications:—A Serious and affectionate Address to the Citizens of the United States, by a Society lately established for the suppression of vice and immorality. A Sermon preached on a day recommended by the General Assembly of the Presbyterian Church in the United States, to be set apart for Fasting, Humiliation, and Prayer, 1808. Christ's ministers, watchmen for souls: A Sermon delivered before the General Association of Connecticut, 1809. A Sermon delivered on a day recommended by the General Assembly of the Presbyterian Church in the United

States to be set apart for solemn Thanksgiving and Prayer, 1809. A Sermon preached on a day recommended by the President of the United States to be observed as a day of Humiliation and Prayer. 1812. A Sermon preached on a day recommended by the President of the United States to be observed as a day of Humiliation and Prayer, 1813. A Sermon preached at a meeting of a Committee of the Presbytery of Newcastle, and also at the opening of the Presbytery, 1814. A Sermon preached on a day recommended by the President of the United States to be observed as a day of Humiliation, Fasting, and Prayer, 1815. A Sermon preached at Newcastle, on a day recommended by the President of the United States to be observed as a day of Public Thanksgiving and Praise to God for the Restoration of Peace, 1815. An affectionate and earnest Address of a minister to the people under his care, on the important subject of Practical Religion: with short and easy Catechisms for children.

The youngest son of Dr. Latta, bearing his own name, *James*, was settled, at the time of his ordination, April 3, 1811, over the Congregation of Upper Octorora, in Chester County, Pa., where he continues to this day. He is now the oldest member of the Newcastle Presbytery. His congregation is large and flourishing, and has enjoyed several precious revivals of religion. He has had six children, of whom two sons and two daughters are now living. Any further notice, in this case, would be unseemly, as he of whom I write still lives.

The names of Dr. Latta's daughters were *Mary*, *Margaret*, *Elizabeth*, and *Sarah*. The first three were unmarried, and have all been removed by death within the last twelve years. They were intelligent, valuable women, sincerely attached to the Presbyterian Church, of which they were pious and useful members. The youngest, *Sarah*, is now living, and is the wife of Rev. Thomas Love, of Delaware State.

For a sketch of the *character* of Dr. Latta, in his different relations, I depend mainly upon the "Memoir" supposed to have been written by Dr. Martin, already referred to, and the reminiscences of Mr. Scott, the venerable elder of Chestnut Level, whose name I have before mentioned.

"As a *Teacher*," says the Memoir, "Dr. Latta was remarkably well qualified. Without severity, he had the faculty of governing well. He possessed the happy talent of making his pupils both fear and love him. They witnessed his fidelity, they saw his concern for their interests, and they reverenced him as a father. As a scholar, too, he had few equals: his erudition was general and profound. Such were his known abilities, and such his reputation as an instructer, that when any of his pupils were sent to the University over which the late Dr. Ewing presided, who has been so deservedly famed as a scholar, they were always received without examination. It was sufficient to know they had received their education with Dr. Latta."

"As a *man*," the writer of the Memoir observes, "Dr. Latta was truly amiable. 'An Israelite indeed' he was, 'in whom there was no guile.' Possessing a very affectionate heart, he was a steady, sincere and faithful friend. A fund of good sense and a natural cheerfulness which he possessed, rendered him both a profitable and an agreeable companion. His conversation was instructive and entertaining. It was indeed almost impossible to be long in his company without being both pleased and improved. Both old and young were fond of his society. When paying a visit to any of his people, it was pleasing to see the youth gather around him to enjoy his conversation. Though by his deportment he always inspired a reverence for his character, yet he was easy of access, and never failed to attract the attention, and add to the entertainment, of those with whom he conversed." Mr. Scott's testimony to this point is of the same character.

"As a *Christian* and *minister*," the memoir testifies, "he was exemplary to a remarkable degree. He was an ornament to religion, and his uniform deportment was such as to recommend it to all who knew him. When cheerful, there was nothing of levity about him; when grave, there was no austerity. His conduct was always manly and dignified, and calculated to inspire both reverence and love. The Scriptures were the rule of his life, and the glory of God the end for which he lived. He was conscientious in the discharge of every duty. And with such dignity did he support the sacred office which he bore, that there was scarce ever an instance of any person conducting himself profanely or rudely in his presence. The sight of him made folly blush, and vice cover its head." To this Mr. Scott adds, that "he was a man fully furnished, both by nature and education, for a Gospel minister of the first order; a most ardent lover of the Lord Jesus, and faithful in his Master's service to the last."

"As a *preacher*," too, we learn from the memoir, "he was highly eminent. He naturally possessed a strong and penetrating mind, and this was well furnished by reading and study. His style of writing was accurate, nervous, and often elegant. Though it was evident he sought not after refinement in his composition, yet the ornaments and graces of diction seemed occasionally to force themselves upon him. In the pulpit, he possessed an uncommon gravity. His countenance and mien bespoke him to be the man of God. His manner was plain and unaffected, but interesting and impressive. The vein of good sense which ran through all his preaching, and evidently flowed from a heart which deeply felt all that he said, powerfully arrested the attention of his hearers. He was faithful to declare the whole counsel of God. While he comforted and encouraged true Christians, he held up to sinners a glass in which they might see themselves; but, in addressing them, he always spoke as with the compassion of a father. The doctrines of Grace were the burden of his preaching. On them he delighted to dwell, and his manner of handling them was peculiarly interesting. His whole life and conversation showed how near he lived to his Master, how supremely he was devoted to his work, and how much he was concerned for the salvation of souls. He himself lived, and endeavoured to teach others to live, for eternity. Though on earth, his conversation was in Heaven. Few men indeed have discovered more indifference for amassing the wealth of this world, or more diligence in laying up treasures for another. Being set as a watchman on the walls of Zion, he devoted himself assiduously to his trust. He was willing to spend, and was spent, in his Master's service. He was instant in season and out of season. For upwards of forty years he laboured faithfully in the vineyard of the Lord."

I close this long letter, but for so eminent and worthy a man, comparatively brief sketch of his life, labours, and character, with a copy of his epitaph, written by the Rev. William Arthur* of Pequea.

* WILLIAM ARTHUR was born in Peebles, Scotland, in April, 1769, received a classical education at Edinburgh, and was ordained to the work of the ministry at Paisley. In 1793, he came to this country; and having preached, for some time, both at New York and Albany, he

"In memory of
THE REV. DR. JAMES LATTA,
Who died 29th January, 1801, in the 68th year of his age.
By his death, society has lost an invaluable member;
Religion one of its brightest ornaments, and most amiable examples.
His genius was masterly, and his literature extensive.
As a classical scholar, he was excelled by few.
His judgment was strong and penetrating;
His taste correct, his style nervous and elegant.
In the pulpit he was a model.
In the judicatures of the Church, distinguished by his accuracy and precision
After a life devoted to his Master's service,
He rested from his labours, lamented most by those who knew his worth.
Blessed are the dead which die in the Lord from henceforth;
Yea, saith the Spirit, that they may rest from their labours,
And their works do follow them."

With respect and affection,

Your brother in Jesus,

ROBERT P. DU BOIS.

ALEXANDER McWHORTER, D. D.*

1758—1807.

ALEXANDER McWHORTER was of Scotch extraction,—his ancestors, on both sides, having emigrated from Scotland to the North of Ireland. Both of his maternal grandparents lost their lives in the great Irish massacre of 1641, being hanged on a tree before their own door. None of the family survived this horrid scene, except his mother, who, being an infant at the time, was saved by being concealed by her nurse. His immediate parents, Hugh and Jane McWhorter, lived in the County of Armagh, where his father was, for many years, a linen merchant. Their eldest child, whose name was *Alexander*, was distinguished for his talents and piety, and spent two years at the University of Edinburgh, with an intention to devote himself to the Gospel ministry. At his solicitation the family removed to America, about the year 1730, and settled in the County of Newcastle, De., where his father was an extensive farmer, and an elder of the church of which the Rev. John Rodgers (afterwards Dr. Rodgers of New York), became pastor. Alexander died before he had completed his studies; and the subject of this sketch, being born about a month after, bore his brother's name.

The second *Alexander*, the youngest of eleven children, was born July 15, (O. S.) 1734. His parents being eminently pious persons, were especially solicitous for his moral and religious welfare, and lost no opportunity of impressing early upon his mind the great truths and duties of Christianity. In February, 1748, when he was in his fourteenth year, his father

went to Pennsylvania, and on the 5th of January, 1796, was installed pastor of the Church in Pequea, as successor to the Rev. Dr. Robert Smith. His relation with this congregation was dissolved, May 1, 1818. After this, he preached a few months in Lancaster, and occasionally supplied his former charge. In 1819, he removed to Cincinnati; and while there, was attacked with an affection of the eye, by which he partially lost his sight. In 1825, he removed from Cincinnati to Zanesville, where he died of hemorrhage of the lungs in February, 1827. He was distinguished for his common sense and firmness of purpose, and for the brevity, point, and effectiveness, of his sermons.

* Griffins Fun. Serm.—Stearns' Hist. First Ch., Newark.

died, leaving four children; and, as three of them were already settled in North Carolina, their mother, in the following autumn, removed into that Province, accompanied by Alexander, who left his paternal estate in Delaware, under the care of a guardian. Here he became most deeply impressed with a sense of his sinfulness, under a sermon preached by the Rev. John Brown, (I suppose of Timber Ridge, Va.,) and, for nearly three years, he was well nigh overwhelmed with anxiety and distress. After remaining in Carolina, probably between two and three years, he came to the North to receive his education under the direction of his guardian. Having studied for a short time at a school in the village of Newark, De., he became a member of Mr. Finley's famous school at West Nottingham, Pa.; and it was there that he first found relief from the spiritual burden that had so long oppressed him, and made a public profession of his faith by becoming a member of Mr. Finley's church.

He remained at this school for two years. In May, 1756, being in his twenty-second year, he joined the Junior class in the College of New Jersey, then at Newark, though removed the next year to Princeton. He graduated in the autumn of 1757,—a few days after the lamented death of President Burr.

Just as he was about returning to Carolina to visit his mother, and to seek her counsel in regard to his future course of life, he was met by the afflictive intelligence of her death; in consequence of which, he changed his purpose, and immediately commenced the study of Theology under the direction of the Rev. William Tennent of Freehold. He was licensed to preach by the Presbytery of New Brunswick in August, 1758. In October following, he was married to Mary, daughter of Robert Cumming of Freehold, High Sheriff of the County of Monmouth, and a relative of his instructer, Mr. Tennent. They had five children, two of whom entered the profession of Law.

The Congregation at Newark, N. J., had been in a distracted state from the time of Mr. Burr's dismission; and, though they had employed several candidates, they had found it impossible to unite upon any one of them. It was in this unhappy state of things that Mr. McWhorter went among them to preach in June, 1759; and they immediately and unitedly resolved to secure his permanent services. He had been previously designated by the Synod of New York and Philadelphia to a mission among his friends in North Carolina; and, with that view, he was ordained by his Presbytery at Cranberry, on the 4th of July. But, at that very meeting of Presbytery, Commissioners from Newark appeared, and by their solicitations, seconded by the influence of Mr. Tennent, obtained him for a supply. The result was that he, soon after, received a unanimous call to become their pastor, and was installed as such about the close of summer,—being then twenty-five years of age.

In 1764, the Synod renewed his appointment to the mission into North Carolina; but though this gave him an opportunity of visiting his friends, after a separation from them of twelve years, it came very near costing him his life. While in Carolina he was attacked with a bilious fever incident to the climate, which left him with an affection of the lungs which, for two years, seemed likely to have a fatal issue. But, in the midst of this scene of affliction, in the winter of 1764–65, he was permitted to hear of an extensive revival of religion in his own congregation. In the following summer, he received a call from the united Congregations of Center and Poplar Tent in North Carolina; which, though it afforded him an opportunity to settle among his father's children and descendants, he thought it his duty to decline. In 1766, he was induced to try the effect upon his health of a northern journey; and that journey, extended as far as Boston, proved unexpectedly the means of his entire restoration. And from that period, his health, with some very slight exceptions, continued vigorous until old age.

Shortly after his return from Boston, overtures were made to him from the congregation in that town, which had some time before become vacant by the death of his brother-in-law, the Rev. Alexander Cumming, to become their pastor; or rather, as they had scruples about calling a settled minister,—to resign his charge at Newark, with a view to accepting a call from them; but he declined the preliminary step, and the matter went no farther.

In 1772, a second revival of religion commenced, which proved even more extensive than the former, and continued about two years.

Mr. McWhorter partook largely of the sacrifices and hardships attendant on the American Revolution. In 1775, he was appointed by Congress to visit that district of North Carolina in which he had been before, with a view to do what he could to bring over the enemies of the Revolution to the American cause; but the enterprise seems to have been, on the whole, unsuccessful.

In 1776, he was honoured with the Degree of Doctor of Divinity by the Corporation of Yale College.

In the following winter, when the prospects of the American cause had become the darkest, and Washington had fled through New Jersey with a handful of troops, almost ready to perish from starvation, this patriotic minister hastened to the army encamped on the Pennsylvania shore, opposite Trenton, to concert, with the Commander-in-chief, measures for the protection of the State. And he was there on the memorable 26th of December, when the American troops crossed the Delaware, took the Hessians, and thus gave a new direction to the events of the war.

In the summer of 1778, at the solicitation of General Knox, he consented to become Chaplain of his brigade, which then lay with the main army at White Plains. During the few months that he was thus employed, Washington was often his hearer, and he was often Washington's guest. His resignation of the Chaplaincy was hastened by the fact that, in July of that year, Mrs. McWhorter was struck with lightning, and for the time was left without any symptom of life; and though she recovered her senses after a few hours, the shock to her constitution was such that her husband felt it necessary that he should return home earlier than he would otherwise have done, to attend to the concerns of his family.

In November of this year, he received a call from the Congregational Church in Charleston, S. C., to become their pastor. This call he was somewhat inclined to accept, and kept it under consideration till February following; but the state of his family, and the critical situation of Charleston, then threatened with invasion, finally determined him to decline it.

The next summer, (1779,) he received a call from the Congregation of Charlotte, Mecklenburg County, N. C., to become their pastor, and at the same time an invitation from the Trustees of Charlotte Academy, to become the President of that institution. The promising character of this infant seminary; the fact that it was situated among his relations; and in a part of the country supposed to be comparatively secure from hostile invasion; in connection with the fact that his salary, owing to the deranged state of his congregation, had become insufficient for the support of his family,—led him to think that it was his duty to accept the call; and his congregation did not feel at liberty, under existing circumstances, to oppose his removal. His pastoral relation to the church was accordingly dissolved, and in October following, he took his leave of Newark, amidst the warmest testimonies of affection and regret from his afflicted people.

This removal, however, proved any thing else than a fortunate affair. Scarcely was he settled in his new habitation, when the army of Cornwallis, scouring the country, entered Charlotte, and compelled him to fly with his family for safety. On his return, he found that his library, and furniture, and almost every thing that he possessed, had been sacrificed. Apprehending further attacks from the enemy, he determined again to set his face towards the North; and, accordingly, in the autumn of 1780, he came with his family to Abington, Pa., where he engaged to preach for the winter. The people of Newark, hearing of his misfortunes, invited him to make them a visit,—which he did in February, 1781. Soon after, they sent him a regular call, in consequence of which he returned in April with his family; and, though he was never reinstalled, he acted as pastor of the Congregation till his death.

In the summer of 1783, the Trustees of Washington Academy, in Somerset County, Md., offered him the Presidency of that institution, with a liberal salary. But, though the institution was specially designed for the education of young men for the ministry, and was in a part of the country where there was a wide field for ministerial labour, yet such was his attachment to his Congregation, especially in view of the then recent proofs of their affectionate regard, that he scarcely felt at liberty even to consider the application.

In 1784, another revival of religion occurred in connection with his labours, which continued also two years. Into this revival he entered with extraordinary interest,—preaching not only on the Sabbath, but several times in the week, and spending a part of almost every day in catechising, visiting from house to house, and holding private religious meetings.

Dr. McWhorter was one of those eminent men who, in 1788, had the principal agency in settling the Confession of Faith, and forming the Constitution of the Presbyterian Church of the United States; and in transferring the authority of the highest judicatory from the Synod to the General Assembly, which met first in May, 1789. When a Board of Trustees for the General Assembly was incorporated by the Legislature of Pennsylvania, ten years afterwards, he was named in the Charter as one of the Board; and he continued to hold this trust until 1803, when the infirmities of age induced him to resign it.

In 1796, another revival of religion occurred in his congregation, by means of which thirty or forty were added to the church. In 1802, there was yet another, and the last, revival under his ministry, which continued two years; during which a hundred and forty were admitted to communion beside those that were received from other churches.

After the burning of the Princeton College edifice in 1802, Dr. McWhorter was requested by the Trustees of that institution to visit New England, to solicit contributions in aid of erecting a new building. Such was the interest that he felt in the welfare of the College, that, notwithstanding the infirmities of age were upon him, he cheerfully undertook the mission, and was able, in due time, to make a report, creditable alike to his own sagacity and perseverance, and to the liberality of the people of New England.

The following beautiful incident in Dr. McWhorter's life was related, if I mistake not, by the Doctor himself, to the Rev. Dr. Miller of Princeton, who thus communicated it to the Rev. Dr. Murray of Elizabethtown:—

"After an absence of many years from his native place, he resolved, a little before his death, to visit once more the spot on which he was born. In his little carriage, driven by a coloured servant, he went, by slow stages, from his home in Newark to his early home in Delaware. Driving up to the door of the house in which he was born,—now old and dilapidated, he asked a woman who came to the door, *who* lived there. Being answered, he again asked, who lived there before *them*. Having received a reply, he again asked, 'who lived there before *them?*' The woman could not tell. He then asked if she had ever heard of a family who once lived there by the name of *McWhorter?* 'What name, did you say?'—said the woman. 'McWhorter,' replied the Doctor. 'I never heard of such a family,' said she. He then drove to a neighbouring house, where his uncle, a brother of his father, used to live. He asked the same questions, and received the same answers. Returning to the house of his birth, he left his carriage, and asked for a tumbler, saying,—'there is one place here that knows me, and that I know.' And, leaning on the arm of his servant, he hobbled to a spring at the bottom of the garden, from which he used to drink, when a boy. He stood over it for some time, and drank of its waters, until he could drink no more. He then hobbled back to his carriage, repeating these words, as he entered it,—the tears streaming from his eyes,—'The places that now know us, will know us no more forever.'"

On the evening of the 25th of December, 1806, he received an injury from a fall, from which he never recovered. In February following, when the dissolution of his aged wife was manifestly approaching, and he was himself rapidly sinking under manifold infirmities, one of his sons died so suddenly that his parents, though in the neighbourhood, were not apprized of his illness till they heard of his death. But he behaved with the most serene and dignified composure under the trial. On the 2d of April following, the beloved companion of his life finished her course with all the tokens of childlike piety; and this affliction he endured, like that which had preceded it, in the spirit of unqualified submission and humble trust. Nothing now remained but to make the immediate arrangements for his own departure. He sent an affectionate farewell to his brethren of the Presbytery; distributed his volumes of Sermons among his children, grandchildren, and other relatives, and gave directions in respect to his funeral. He lingered, in the utmost patience, and sometimes in the triumphs of a rapturous faith, till the 20th of July, 1807, when he gently passed away to the better world. His Funeral Sermon was preached by his colleague, the Rev. Edward D. Griffin, and was published.

Dr. McWhorter published a Sermon on the blessedness of the liberal, 1796; and two octavo volumes of Sermons, 1803.

FROM THE HON. JACOB BURNET,

JUDGE OF THE SUPREME COURT OF OHIO.

CINCINNATI, September 29, 1848

Rev. and dear Sir: You ask me for my recollections of the Rev. Dr. McWhorter. One of my very earliest recollections of any body or any thing, is the effect that was produced on my mind, by seeing that venerable man in the pulpit, in the clerical robes, and large full wig, worn by the clergy of that day. I knew him well, both in the pulpit and out of it, as I was growing up, and I am glad, even at this late period of my life, to testify my veneration for his character.

Dr. McWhorter was grave and dignified in his deportment—though far from being stern or repulsive, he seldom indulged in any very decided expressions of merriment. His temper was naturally quick, but was under such habitual control that the tendency to irritability was not often discovered, even by those who were most frequently in his company. His talents were much above mediocrity. He was a good classical scholar, and as a preacher, was among the most popular of his day.

The trait of character for which he was perhaps most distinguished was prudence. In the discharge of his duty to his congregation, individually as well as collectively, he showed himself at once very wise and very successful. Such was the confidence they reposed in him, that when they found themselves involved in any difficulty, they were almost sure to apply to him for advice, and the course he recommended, scarcely ever failed to secure the desired result.

During his unusually long ministry at Newark, controversies among the members of his church occasionally arose, which sometimes became widely extended, and were carried on with no inconsiderable warmth. On such occasions, each party resorted to the Doctor for counsel; and although, in some cases, it appeared impossible to interpose, without giving offence to one side or the other, yet his great practical wisdom always enabled him to get through the difficulty without losing the confidence of either party.

I will mention two occurrences which, though not important in themselves, may throw some light on the Doctor's general character.

A young respectable girl of his congregation fell violently in love with one of her associates, who, unfortunately, did not reciprocate her affection, and who therefore, very naturally, was not disposed to marry her. In the bitterness of her disappointment, she repaired to her minister for advice and assistance. After hearing her story, he made a visit to the young man, to ascertain the facts of the case, and was convinced that the young lady had no just claims on him, nor any grounds of complaint against him. This result he communicated to her; and at the same time advised her to banish the subject from her mind and forget him. This she declared was impossible. On a subsequent visit, she intimated to the Doctor a determination to put an end to her existence. He very promptly replied, "Why Rhoda, I admire your courage—it is the best thing you can do; and I advise you not to put it off a single hour, lest you should change your mind. Come, my chaise is at the door; I will take you to the river immediately, and see that the work is thoroughly done." She thanked the Doctor for his proffered kindness, but on the whole, thought she had better not just then avail herself of it.

The other circumstance to which I referred, took place very soon after Dr. Griffin became associated with him as colleague pastor. There was a very pious man belonging to the congregation, with whom I was personally acquainted, who had not formally joined the church, on account of some doubts which agitated his mind, but which I forbear to state, lest I might do it incorrectly. While this obstacle existed, his infant child was taken violently ill, during the temporary absence of Dr. McWhorter. The distressed father, who inclined to the opinion that baptism was essential to salvation, sent for Dr. Griffin, and requested him to baptize the child, which he declined to do, on the ground that neither of the parents was a member of the church; and he persisted in this refusal, regardless of the entreaties and tears of the father, till the infant expired, unbaptized. Dr. Griffin was himself deeply agitated and distressed,—fearing that he might have done wrong. In that state of mind, he called on his venerable colleague immediately after his return, and having stated the case, asked him what he would have done in the same circumstances. "Why," said Dr. McWhorter, "it is very likely that I should have baptized the child first, and then have examined the subject to satisfy my mind whether I had done right or not." I mention this as an illustration of the strength and tenderness of his sympathies.

Very respectfully your friend,

J. BURNET.

FROM THE REV. AARON CONDICT.

HANOVER, N. J., April 15, 1850.

Rev. and dear Sir: My acquaintance with Dr. McWhorter began, when I was about sixteen years of age. I was at that time placed in the Grammar School, as it was then called, which he had commenced with the view of aiding in the support of his family, during the hard times of the Revolutionary war, then in progress. My respect and affection were at once awakened towards him, and continued ever afterwards. There was a noble manliness in his countenance, person, and movements, which could not fail to impress me favourably.

As a teacher, I was, from the first, greatly delighted with him. He was remarkably a man of order and method. He was so communicative,—imparted instruction with so much ease, and was, in all respects, so paternal, that I considered it a high privilege to be under his instruction. He really impressed me with the idea that he knew almost every thing. To meet the difficulty of procuring books suitable for such a school, he wrote for his pupils, with his own hand, treatises on several of the sciences.

As a preacher, Dr. McWhorter was plain, instructive, practical. His discourses in the pulpit were generally written out. His language was correct, impressive, and often pathetic. His prayers in public were scarcely, if at all, less correct in language, than his sermons. There was much in his manner that was expressive of sincerity and fervour. His devotional exercises were uniformly very appropriate, and always characterized by becoming brevity. I never knew him fail to recognise very particularly Christ Jesus as the only ground and medium of acceptance with a holy God for sinful man. Though his style of delivery was dignified and agreeable, he did not abound in action. But I well remember one gesture,—a certain motion of his right arm, which, in connection with his expressive countenance, often gave great effect to what he uttered.

Dr. McWhorter was distinguished as a constant and punctual attendant on the judicatories of the Church. It was a rare thing for him to be absent from any meeting of Presbytery or Synod; and when he accepted an appointment as delegate to the General Assembly, I never knew him fail of fulfilling it. It seemed to me that whenever he entered a meeting of a church judicatory, it was his object, so far as he could do it without trespassing on the rights of others, to secure a seat where he could best *see* as well as *hear*, both the Moderator and the members who might have occasion to speak; and when seated, his attention seemed never, for a moment, to be withdrawn from the business in hand. He was always ready to express his own views of any subject that might arise, at the proper time; but could never be charged with occupying the time of the judicatory unnecessarily, by either too frequent or too long speeches. No man, it appeared to me, knew better than he, what to say, when to say it, and when to stop. He was eminently respected by the Presbyterian Church at large, and more than once had the most important public services entrusted to him.

I am, my dear Sir,

Very truly yours,

AARON CONDICT.

JOHN STRAIN.*

1759—1774.

It is somewhat remarkable that though few ministers in the Presbyterian Church enjoyed a higher reputation than JOHN STRAIN, during his lifetime, yet almost every memorial of him has perished; and, after having diligently explored every probable source of information concerning him, I have found it impossible to construct a continuous narrative of his life. Even the time and place of his birth are not known. The first that we hear of him is, his being graduated at the College of New Jersey in 1757. It has been supposed that he studied Theology under the Rev. Dr. Finley; but the fact, if it be one, is not, I believe, satisfactorily ascertained. He was licensed to preach by the Presbytery of Newcastle on the 29th of May, 1759; and was ordained *sine titulo*, by the same Presbytery, in 1761. He settled as pastor of the Churches of Chanceford and Slate Ridge, York County, Pa. Such was his popularity as a preacher, that, after the death of Gilbert Tennent, he was called to succeed him as pastor of the Second Presbyterian Church in Philadelphia; but so strong was the attachment existing between him and his congregations, that he was unwilling to leave them, and therefore declined the call. He died on the 21st of May, 1774.

The following estimate of Mr. Strain's character as a preacher was furnished me by the Rev. Archibald Alexander, D. D.:—

"The REV. JOHN STRAIN was a preacher of uncommon power and success. His manner, as I have heard from some who attended on his ministry, was awfully solemn. Many were awakened under his pungent and searching discourses; and his method of dealing with those who came to him under concern of mind, was thought to be very singular at that time. He would authoritatively exhort them to believe in the Lord Jesus Christ, and would then turn away from them. Sometimes, after preaching to the people, and offering Christ to them earnestly, when, after the benediction, they were going out of the house, he would rise up, and cry out in the most heart-piercing tone of inquiry— 'What! are you going away without receiving Christ into your hearts?'

"His plan of preaching was to represent to the sinner his ruined condition, and then urge him by every solemn and tender entreaty immediately to close in with the offers of mercy through the Lord Jesus Christ. I have often heard Hugh Weir, who was a subject of grace under the ministry of Mr. Strain, repeat whole sermons which he had heard him preach. His opinion was that he had never heard any preacher equal to him; and especially in the earnest and tender beseeching of sinners to be reconciled to God.

* MSS. from Rev. Archibald Alexander, D. D., and Rev. Richard Webster.

"Mr. Strain was near-sighted, and of a very grave and solemn aspect. An anecdote has been related of him and the Rev. George Duffield, D. D., for the truth of which I cannot vouch; but I will relate it as I have heard it, since it is characteristic of the men:—At the Synod (the old Synod) of Philadelphia, Mr. Strain acted as Clerk. One day, when he dined with Dr. Duffield, who was fond of a jest, the latter slipped into the coat pocket of the former, in which he had various papers of the Synod, a pack of cards, loosely rolled up in a paper. When they returned to the church, and the session was opened, Strain arose to read some paper or report, and thrusting his hand into his pocket, drew out the pack of cards, which, being loose, were scattered on the table and floor. Duffield of course enjoyed the fun. But Strain, no how embarrassed, but with awful solemnity, looking at Dr. D., said,—'When I see that man in the pulpit, I am so delighted and edified with his preaching, that I feel as if he ought never to come out; but when I see his levity out of the pulpit, I am disposed to think that he should never enter it again.'"

The late Dr. Samuel Martin, who ministered to the people, who, in youth, had heard Mr. Strain, writes thus of him:—

"He was of fervent piety, great zeal, and ardour: he could reach the passions by bursts of feeling and piety,—unexpectedly shooting aside of his subject, and taking his hearers unaware with a frightful or a rapturous exclamation. His subject could enchain him no longer than it could have effect: when it failed, he tried a new expedient. He was loved by many; but some, displeased with his fervour, left his ministry. All concurred in the belief that he was a man of great intimacy with his God and Saviour."

Dr. Hodge in his History of the Presbyterian Church says:—

"John Strain is still remembered as one of the most eloquent and impressive ministers our Church has ever produced."

JOHN EWING, D. D.

1759—1802.

FROM THE REV. SAMUEL MILLER, D. D.

PRINCETON, February 18, 1848.

Rev. and dear Brother: It gives me pleasure to contribute the least effort toward the erection of an humble monument to the memory of the Rev. Dr. JOHN EWING, late Provost of the University of Pennsylvania, whom I well knew, and whom I have much reason, on a variety of accounts, to remember with veneration and love.

He was a native of Maryland. He was born in the township of Nottingham, in Cecil County, in what is now that State, on the 22d day of June, 1732. Of his ancestors little is known. They emigrated from Ireland at an early period of the settlement of our country, and fixed themselves on the banks of the Susquehanna, near to the spot on which he was born. His father was in circumstances which enabled him to give his five sons as good an education as the state of the Colonies with respect to schools could then well furnish. After the first elementary school to which he was sent, he was placed at the Academy of the Rev. Dr. Francis Alison, an eminent Presbyterian clergyman, who had emigrated from Ireland, and who was greatly distinguished for his classical literature, and who became instrumental in forming a number of excellent scholars in the Middle Colonies. His literary institution at New London, in Pennsylvania, was long celebrated. There young Ewing passed the usual course of study; and, after completing it, remained three years longer in the Academy as a Tutor; directing special attention to the Latin and Greek languages, and mathematics, in all which he was eminent through life.

In 1754 he became a member of the College of New Jersey, then located at Newark, under the Presidency of the Rev. Mr. Burr; and, as he was so far advanced and matured in the principal studies of the College, he was graduated at the annual Commencement of the same year. At the same time he was the principal instructer in the grammar school, which was connected with the College, and spent a portion of almost every day in instructing others in the languages and mathematics. In 1756, he was chosen Tutor in the College in which he had been graduated, and continued in that station two full years, enlarging and maturing his knowledge. During this course of service as a Tutor, he removed with the College from Newark to Princeton, which removal took place in 1757. In pursuing the study of Theology, he returned to his former teacher and friend, the Rev. Dr. Alison, and was subsequently licensed to preach the Gospel by the Presbytery of Newcastle. At the age of twenty-six, before he undertook the pastoral charge, he was selected to instruct the philosophical classes in the College of Philadelphia, during the absence of the Provost, the Rev. Dr. Smith. While thus employed, he received, in the year 1759, a unanimous call from the First Presbyterian Church in the city of Philadelphia, to become their Pastor. This call he accepted, and was ordained to the work of the ministry, and installed as their Pastor, in the course of that year.

About this time, Mr. Ewing formed a matrimonial connection with Miss Hannah Sergeant, the eldest daughter of Jonathan Sergeant, Esq., of Princeton,—a lady of great beauty and domestic excellence, with whom he lived in happy union more than forty years, and who survived him a number of years.

In 1773, Mr. Ewing was commissioned, with the consent of his congregation, in company with Dr. Hugh Williamson, late a member of Congress from North Carolina, to solicit contributions in Great Britain for the support of the Academy of Newark, in Delaware. His high reputation in his own country, together with the ample supply of letters which he took with him, gave him access to a number of men eminent in Church and State, in Great Britain, and prepared the way for the formation of a number of acquaintances and friendships, which were highly interesting to him, and, in some cases, valuable, as long as he lived. He seems to have made a deep impression, especially in North Britain, in favour of American character. The cities of Glasgow, Montrose, Dundee, and Perth, presented to him their freedom; and from the University of Edinburgh, of which Dr. Robertson was then the Principal, he received the degree of Doctor of Divinity. Dr. Robertson, in presenting this diploma, declared that he had never before conferred a degree with greater pleasure. At this time the contest between the Colonies and the mother country was beginning to be serious. It was, of course, the theme of much conversation while he was in England. He had frequent interviews with the Prime Minister, Lord North, and with all the intelligence of one recently from the Colonies, and with all the firmness and zeal of an ardent Whig, he warned his Lordship against the prosecution of the contest, and confidently predicted its issue; but without effect.

But the narrative which Dr. Ewing, after his return to America, was wont to give with most graphic interest, was that of his first interview with the celebrated Dr. Johnson, at the table of Mr.. Dilly, the wealthy and hospitable Bookseller of London. Dr. Johnson, it is well known, was violent against the Colonies; had written a popular pamphlet against their claims; and heaped upon them and their advocates the coarsest abuse. Mr. Dilly, in inviting Dr. Ewing to dinner, apprized him that Dr. Johnson was to be of the party, and cautioned him against contradicting or opposing the great literary despot. During the dinner the contest with America became the subject of animated conversation. Dr. Ewing, the only American present, being appealed to, began, with his usual frankness, to defend the Colonies. Dr. Johnson, looking at him with sternness, said, "What do *you* know, Sir, on that subject?" Dr. Ewing calmly replied that, having resided in America all his life, he thought himself qualified to form and to express opinions on the situation and claims of the country. Dr. Johnson's feelings were roused. The epithets of *rebels* and *scoundrels* were pretty liberally applied to the population of the Colonies. At length Johnson rudely said, "Sir, what do *you* know in America? You never read. You have no books there." "Pardon me, Sir," replied Dr. Ewing, "we have read the *Rambler*." This civility instantly pacified him; and, after the rest of the company had retired, he sat with Dr. Ewing until midnight, in amiable, eloquent, and highly interesting conversation.

In the summer of 1775, Dr. Ewing returned from Europe. War was soon commenced between the United States and Great Britain. And he adhered to the cause of his country with all the firmness and zeal of an ardent Whig. In 1779, the Legislature of Pennsylvania revoked the charter of the old College and Academy of Philadelphia, and gave a new one, creating the University of Pennsylvania, on a large plan. At the head of this new institution Dr. Ewing was placed, under the title of *Provost*. In this station, united with that of pastor of a church, he continued to the end of life. Besides presiding over the whole University as its head, with dignity and commanding influence, he was Professor of Natural Philosophy in the institution, and every year delivered a course of learned and able Lectures on that branch of science. But this was not all. Perhaps our country has never bred a man so deeply as well as extensively versed in every branch of knowledge commonly taught in our Colleges as was Dr. Ewing. Such was his familiarity with the Hebrew language, that I have been assured by those most intimately acquainted with his habits, that his Hebrew Bible was constantly by his side in his study, and that it was *that* which he used of choice, for devotional purposes. In Mathematics and Astronomy, in the Latin, Greek, and Hebrew languages, in Logic, in Metaphysics and Moral Philosophy, he was probably more accomplished than any other man in the United States. When any other Professor in the University was absent, the Provost could take his place, at an hour's warning, and conduct the instruction appropriate to that Professorship with more skill, taste, and advantage than the incumbent of the chair himself. His skill in mathematical science was so pre-eminent and acknowledged, that he was more than once employed, with Dr. Rittenhouse, of Philadelphia, in running the boundary lines between several of the States, in which he acquitted himself in the most able and honourable manner. He was one of the Vice Presidents of the American Philosophical Society, and made a number of contributions to the volumes of their "Transactions," which do honour to his memory.

Dr. Ewing had a strong constitution, and for a long course of years enjoyed vigorous health; being very seldom kept either out of the pulpit, or from the Professor's chair by indisposition. In the early part of the year 1802, he was attacked with a chronic disease, which gradually undermined his health, and finally terminated his important and useful life on the 8th of September of that year, in the seventy-first year of his age.

Since the decease of Dr. Ewing, his "Lectures on Natural Philosophy" have been published in two volumes, octavo, and another octavo volume, containing twenty Sermons from his pen. He used to speak of Dr. Doddridge as a theological writer more to his taste than any other he could name in the English language. Every thing which the public has received from his pen, is considered as honourably sustaining his reputation, both as a Divine and a Philosopher.

Few preachers in his day were more popular than Dr. Ewing, especially with the more intelligent and cultivated classes of hearers. He sacrificed nothing to display in the pulpit. His merits were all of the solid, instructive, and dignified character. And as a Collegiate Instructer, I suspect he had no superior.

This venerable man had a large family of children, ten or eleven of whom survived him; but it is believed they are all now deceased. A number of respectable grandchildren still sustain the name and the honours of the family.

I am, Reverend and dear Brother, with the best wishes for the success of your biographical enterprise,

Very sincerely and respectfully yours,

SAMUEL MILLER.

JOHN JOACHIM ZUBLY, D. D.

1760—1781.

FROM THE HON. EDWARD J. HARDEN.

SAVANNAH, Ga., January 24, 1855.

My dear Sir: I have not been unmindful of your request for some account of the venerable Dr. Zubly, who was, for many years, pastor of a Church in this city; though I have been somewhat embarrassed by the difficulty of gathering the requisite material. For nearly all the facts connected with his history, I am indebted to our common friend, Mr. I. K. Tefft, who has been in correspondence with Dr. Zubly's descendants on the subject, and whose extraordinary perseverance and success in gathering materials for history and biography, entitles him to the good will and gratitude of the whole country.

JOHN JOACHIM ZUBLY (as appears from memoranda still in possession of his descendants) was born at St. Gall, in Switzerland, on the 27th of

August, 1724; was ordained to the Gospel ministry, on the 19th of August, 1744; and was married to Ann Tobler on the 12th of November, 1746.

The precise time of his arrival in the then Colony of Georgia is not known; but it is pretty well ascertained that in 1760 he took charge (as its first pastor) of what is now known as the Independent Presbyterian Church of Savannah. In this church he preached in English,—in which, the portions of his correspondence that still exist, show that he was a proficient. To one neighbouring congregation, it seems, he preached in German, and to another, in French. Of the many traditions that remain of "Parson Zubly," as he was called, there is none which does not accord to him great learning and ability; and there is no reason to doubt his entire devotion to the cause of his Divine Master.

The degree of Doctor of Divinity was conferred upon him by the College of New Jersey, in 1770.

At the commencement of the dispute between the mother country and her American Colonies, Dr. Zubly took a decided and active part with the latter. In the London Magazine for January, 1776, pp. 35, 36, 37, 38 and 39, may be found a fervid appeal, over his signature, in behalf of the Colonies, addressed to "the Right Honourable William, Earl of Dartmouth," who had, at the date of the letter, (3d September, 1775,) been appointed Secretary of State for the American department. This paper was published at the request of "an old correspondent," signing himself O, and who was no other, as is supposed, than the founder of Georgia,—General James Edward Oglethorpe. In the request for publication, the letter is styled an "Address to Lord Dartmouth;" and it is so creditable to the heart and head of Dr. Zubly that I will take the liberty to append some extracts from it. The address is worthy of being transcribed here entire, but its length forbids it. After alluding, in proper terms, to his Lordship's appointment, and the hope which had been entertained from his "religious character," and his "conscientious regard to justice and equity, as well as to the civil and religious liberties of this great Continent," the address proceeds:—

"Unhappily, during your administration, measures have been pursued very contrary to American hopes, and we easily conceive your Lordship may think it not less strange that many friends of religion in America should be so uneasy under laws which had your Lordship's concurrence and approbation. It is to the man and the Christian I wish to be permitted to address myself: your Lordship ranks among the highest subjects, and has a large share in all public measures; but anxiety for what may distress, and zeal for the welfare of the Empire, can be no crime, even in the meanest; and when a house is once in flames, every man is inexcusable, or must at least be so in his own breast, that does not contribute whatever he may think in his power, to their being extinguished. The effects of the present measures are visible, and it requires no sagacity to foresee what may be the consequence, should they be continued. Your Lordship may do much towards restoring and perpetuating the tranquillity of a great empire. Persons of my station have nothing to offer but hints and wishes; should these be beneath your notice, or stand in need of forgiveness, my sincere wish to contribute any thing towards a just, happy and perpetual connection between a parent state and an infant country, growing apace to the most astonishing importance, must be my only apology. *Pulchrum est bene facere republi-*

cæ, sed et bene dicere non est absurdum. 'To bind them in all cases whatsoever;' my Lord,—the Americans look upon this as the language of despotism in its almost perfection. What can, say they, an Emperor of Morocco pretend more of his slaves, than to bind them in all cases whatsoever? Were it meant to make the Americans hewers of wood, and drawers of water,—were it meant to deprive them of the enjoyment of their religion, and to establish a hierarchy over them similar to that of the Church of Rome in Canada, it would, say they, be no more than a natural consequence of binding them, (unseen, unheard, unrepresented,) in all cases whatsoever. My Lord, the Americans are no idiots, and they appear determined not to be slaves. Oppression will make wise men mad, but oppressors in the end frequently find that they were not wise men; there may be resources even in despair sufficient to render any set of men strong enough not to be bound in all cases whatsoever.

* * * * * * * * * * *

"Your Lordship believes a Supreme Ruler of the earth, and that the small and great must stand before Him at last—would your Lordship be willing, at the general meeting of all mankind, to take a place among those who destroyed or enslaved empires, or risk your future state on the merit of having, at the expense of British blood and treasure, taken away the property, the life and liberty of the largest part of the British empire? Can your Lordship think those who fear the Lord will not cry to Him against their oppressors? And will not the Father of mankind hear the cries of the oppressed? Or would you be willing that their cries and tears should rise against you as a forward instrument of their oppression?

* * * * * * * * * * *

"Proposals publicly made by ministerial writers relative to American domestics, laid the Southern Provinces under a necessity of arming themselves; a proposal to put it in the power of domestics to cut the throats of their masters, can only serve to cover the proposers and abettors with everlasting infamy.

"The Americans have been called 'a rope of sand,' but *blood* and *sand* will make a *firm cementation;* and enough American blood has been already shed to cement them together into a *thirteen fold cord*, not easily to be broken."

Such was the confidence of the people of Georgia in the intelligence and patriotism of Dr. Zubly, that he was appointed a delegate to the Continental Congress, of which he was a member in 1775–76; but, like many others of the Colonists who favoured the rights of the Colonies against the unjust exactions of the British Crown,—when the question of actual separation from, and independence of, the mother country came up for action, he was found opposed to extreme measures, and, suddenly quitting his post at Philadelphia, returned to Georgia. Here he took sides against the Colonies, and, in consequence, became very unpopular, and was finally compelled to leave Savannah. It appears, however, by his correspondence, that he was in Savannah during the siege of that place by the American and French armies in 1779, and that his losses of property, books, &c., during the war were considerable. Amidst all his sufferings, however, Dr. Zubly seems to have possessed a confiding and contented spirit. He died somewhere in South Carolina, on the 23d of July, 1781, and his remains were afterwards brought to Savannah and there interred. As he did not live to see the conclusion of the war which resulted in the independence of the Colonies, it cannot be known what course the dominant party in Georgia would have pursued towards him; but, when the occasions for that bitterness of feeling which characterized the conflict had passed away, there is every reason to believe that his memory was cherished, even by those against whom he took part, as that of one who had acted under strong convictions of the propriety of his course.

Dr. Zubly seems to have been of ardent temperament, devoted to his calling as a preacher of the Gospel, and zealous for the success of his labours. That he was a man of great learning and unaffected piety, is every where admitted; and that his conduct in opposing the cause of American independence was not uncharitably judged by those who knew him best, seems apparent from the fact that two of the streets of Savannah, *Joachim* and *Zubly*, still bear his name, and that one of the hamlets of the town (St. Gall) yet records the name of his native place in Switzerland.

Dr. Zubly left two daughters, whose descendants are amongst the most highly respected of the citizens of Georgia.

Dr. Zubly published a small volume entitled, "The real Christian's hope in death; or an account of the edifying behaviour of several persons of piety in their last moments; with a Preface recommendatory by the Rev. Mr. Clarke, Rector of St. Phillip's Church, Charlestown," 1756; a Sermon on the value of the faith without which it is impossible to please God, 1772; a Sermon on the death of the Rev. John Osgood of Midway, 1773; The law of Liberty: a Sermon on American affairs at the opening of the Provincial Congress of Georgia, with an Appendix, giving an account of the struggle of Switzerland to recover liberty, 1775.

Regretting that I am not able to recover more of the details of a life, which, in many respects, was one of great interest,

I am, my dear Sir, faithfully yours,

EDWARD J. HARDEN.

JAMES CALDWELL.

1760—1781.

FROM THE REV. NICHOLAS MURRAY, D. D.

ELIZABETHTOWN, N. J., November 18, 1847.

My dear Sir: I am happy to comply with your request in furnishing, as much in detail as I can, the facts connected with the eventful life of the Rev. James Caldwell. Though almost seventy years have passed since his death, his name is still fragrant, not only within the bounds of his congregation, but throughout this whole region; and there are not a few among us, who are alive to every effort to honour and perpetuate his memory.

The Caldwell family, if a uniform tradition can be relied on, are of French origin, and, at the time of the Reformation, became Huguenots. Driven from their country by the fierce persecutions which succeeded the revocation of the Edict of Nantz, they fled to Scotland, where they lived upon an estate called *Cold-well*, from a remarkably cold spring of water upon it.* Driven from Scotland by other persecutions, they fled to Ireland, where, as Presbyterians, they were permitted to worship God in peace. Early in the eighteenth century, John Caldwell came to this country from Ireland, bringing with him, besides his wife and children, four sisters,—all unmarried. Landing at Newcastle, De., he settled first in Lancaster County, Pa., but soon removed to a settlement called Cub Creek, in what is now Charlotte County, Va. There JAMES CALDWELL, the subject of this sketch, was born in 1734,—the youngest of seven children. And so numerous became the descendants of John Caldwell, that they gave their name to a place which I understand is called "*the Caldwell settlement*" to the present day.

He was sent to Princeton College, where he was graduated in the year 1759, —the first year of the Presidency of the eloquent Davies. In about a year afterwards he was licensed as a probationer for the ministry, and in 1761 was ordained by the Presbytery of New Brunswick, and, probably at the same time, installed pastor of the Presbyterian Church of Elizabethtown. He was married March 14, 1763, to Miss Hannah Ogden of Newark, whose piety and fortitude helped to cheer and sustain him through many a dark and trying scene.

Soon after his settlement in Elizabethtown, commenced the differences between Great Britain and her Colonies, which resulted in the war of the Revolution, and subsequently in our Independence. Descended from the Huguenots, and imbibing the spirit of the Scotch Covenanters, he may be said to have *inherited* a feeling of opposition to tyranny and tyrants. Possessing warm feelings, fine genius, great muscular energy, and sleepless perseverance, he entered with all his heart into the controversy. Connected with his congregation, at the time, were the Daytons, the Ogdens, Francis Barber, William Crane, Oliver Spencer, Elias Boudinot, William Livingston, Abram Clark, and others, who became eminent for their wisdom, piety, valour, patriotism, and whose names will long live in the annals of their country. Sustained by such men, and he in turn infusing into them his own spirit, he and his people were soon branded as rebels;—and richly did they deserve the name.

On the commencement of hostilities, and the formation of the Jersey Brigade, he was at once selected as its Chaplain.

In June, 1776, he joined the Jersey Regiment, then on the northern lines, under the command of his friend and parishioner, Colonel Dayton. His regiment was stationed at Johnstown, when the news of the Declaration of Independence reached it. Col. Ebenezer Elmer, then and there in the service, makes the following note of the ceremonies to which the news gave rise, on the 15th of July, 1776.

"At twelve o'clock, assembly was beat for, that the men might parade, in order to receive a treat, and drink the States' health. When, having made a barrel of grog, the Declaration was read, and the following toast was given by Parson Caldwell:—'Harmony, honour, and all prosperity to the Free and Independent United States of America: wise legislators, brave and victorious armies, both by sea and land, to the United States of America.' When three hearty cheers were given, and the grog flew round amain."

* This is said to be the origin of the name.

He did not remain with the army until the close of the campaign, but returned to New Jersey, where he was incessantly occupied by his public and parochial duties. His popularity with the army and the people was unbounded, and his practical wisdom and business talents were held in the highest estimation.

But his popularity with the friends of the Revolution was equalled, if not surpassed, by his unpopularity with its enemies. High rewards, it is said, were offered for his capture, and, to avoid the dangers to which he was constantly exposed from the Tories and the enemy, then in possession of Staten Island and New York, he removed his residence to Connecticut Farms,—a small place distant a few miles from Elizabethtown, where he continued until his death. Such were his own apprehensions and those of his friends, that he usually went armed; and, after the burning of his church, when preaching in what is yet spoken of as the Old Red Store, he was often seen to disencumber himself of a pair of pistols, and lay them by his side. To us, in these days, all this looks strange enough in a minister of the Gospel of peace; but there is an old proverb which well says that "Circumstances alter cases." He would not be a Tory—he could not be a neutral—his temperament forbade it; and the principles which led him to defend his country, taught him to defend himself also. He belonged to a class of ministers, who, almost to a man, considered it their duty to God, to aid their country in every way possible in the existing struggle; some of whom raised their own companies, and marched at their head to meet the enemy.

He was sustained in his political action by his congregation, with scarcely a solitary exception. The church in which he preached, was cheerfully yielded as a hospital for sick, disabled and wounded soldiers, as some of the aged people, still living, testify. It was its bell that sounded through the town the notes of alarm, on the approach of the foe; its floor was not unfrequently the bed of the weary soldier; and the seats of its pews, the table from which he ate his scanty meal. Its worshippers on the Sabbath were often compelled to stand through the service, because of the greasiness of their seats, and the fragments of bread and meat by which they were covered. In vengeance on the pastor and the people, this church was fired on the 25th of January, 1780, by a refugee named Cornelius Hetfield. On the 25th of June following, whilst General Knyphausen was on his way to Springfield, Mrs. Caldwell was shot by a refugee, through the window of a room to which she had retired with her children for safety and devotion,—two balls passing through her body. Her corpse having been drawn forth, and laid in the open street, the building was fired; and soon all the surrounding buildings were in ashes. Mr. Caldwell, on the night previous, had slept under his own roof. Hearing of the approach of the enemy, he mounted his horse, and proceeded to the quarters of Washington. After having gone a short distance, he returned to persuade his wife to accompany him; but she could not be induced to go. Whilst drinking a cup of coffee in his saddle, the enemy appeared in the distance; and he, bidding his wife farewell, galloped away. This, his last interview with her, took place in the morning before sunrise. On the evening of that day, he heard two soldiers talking in a whisper to each other, but the only words that distinctly fell upon his ear were "Mrs. Caldwell,"—and those were frequently repeated. Suspecting that all was not right, he besought them to tell him the worst: it was thus he first learned the tragic end of his wife.

On the subsequent attack upon Springfield he was present, and in every way he could, encouraged the troops. It is said that, during the conflict, the wadding of a company of soldiers failed: Caldwell flew to the Presbyterian Church, and filling his pockets and his arms with Watts' Psalms and Hymns, rode back to the company, and, as he scattered them about, throwing one here and another there, he cried out, "Now put Watts into them, boys."

When the army was reduced to a very low state, as to both pay and provisions, Caldwell was appointed Assistant Commissary General, and opened his office in Chatham. In this position his services were of immense value. Such was the confidence of the people in him, that provisions were soon supplied, and upon whatever guarantee he could give as to pay. And often, when the soldiers were under great excitement, because of the incapacity of Congress to pay them, the patriotic addresses of Caldwell allayed their feelings, and excited their enthusiasm to fight on to the last, under whatever trials and hardships.

Whilst New York and Staten Island remained in possession of the British, the war between the Royal and Republican armies was mainly at the South. New Jersey remained comparatively tranquil after the return of Knyphausen from Springfield, and the destruction of the bridge at Elizabethport. By flags of truce there were constant communications with New York, and the goods purchased there were sold in all our towns. And there were just soldiers enough left in New Jersey to act as sentinels at the main points, and to give due notice to the people in case of an attack. In this state of things, Mr. Caldwell was chiefly engaged in attending to the spiritual wants of his people.

There lived in the city of New York a family by the name of Murray, who greatly endeared themselves to many in New Jersey by their kindness to the Jersey prisoners in that city. Some of their relations resided in Elizabethtown. Arrangements were made for a visit from one of the ladies of the family; and, on the 24th of November, 1781, she came to Elizabethtown Point, under a flag of truce; and Mr. Caldwell went down in his carriage to meet her, and convey her to the town. As to the incidents which follow, there are conflicting statements; but that which I am about to give, is regarded, on the whole, as sustained by the most competent and numerous witnesses.

A sentry was kept up, at that time, at the Port. Tying his horse outside the sentinel, Mr. Caldwell proceeded to the wharf, and taking with him Miss Murray, placed her in his carriage, and then returned to the boat for a small bundle that belonged to her. Thus he passed three times the man who was keeping guard. With a small package in his hand he was returning a second time to his carriage, when the sentinel ordered him to stop, thinking probably that there was something contraband in the bundle. He replied that the bundle belonged to the young lady in his carriage. The sentinel said that it must be examined. Mr. Caldwell turned quickly about to carry it back to the boat, that it might be opened there, when the fatal ball struck him. The Captain of the guard hearing the report of a gun, looked round and saw Mr. Caldwell staggering before him. He ran and caught him in his arms, and laid him on the ground, and without speaking a word; he almost instantly expired,—the ball having passed through his heart.

The man who shot him was James Morgan, belonging to the Jersey Militia,—an Irishman by birth, and a man of the most debased and profligate character. He was always drunk when he could be; and liquor turned him into a savage. His family resided near a well in Elizabethtown, into which a child of his fell one day, and was drowned. When he returned, he found his child dead; and taking it by the arms, he beat its broken hearted mother with the dead body of her own child, until her cries brought some of the neighbours to her rescue.

Whether Morgan was on duty as a sentinel, when he shot Caldwell, is, to say the least, questionable. Many of the old people about Elizabethtown say that he was *not* on duty; and an aged person in Westfield, who witnessed the trial, declares that one of the main facts which led to the conviction of Morgan, was, that he was not on duty as a sentinel at the time: he was relieved but a few moments before the arrival of Mr. Caldwell.

The dead body of Mr. C. was laid on a bed of straw in a waggon, and thus was taken to the town, to the house of his devoted friend Mrs. Noel, whence it was buried on the following Tuesday,—November 28, 1781. The funeral was one of the most solemn scenes that this town has ever witnessed. The concourse assembled on the occasion was immense. The Rev. Dr. McWhorter of Newark preached the Funeral Sermon, from Ecclesiastes viii, 8; and, after the service was ended, the corpse was placed on a large stone, before the door of the house of Mrs. Noel, where all could take a last view of the remains of their murdered pastor. When this affecting ceremony was over, and before the coffin was closed, Dr. Boudinot came forward, leading nine orphan children, and, placing them around their father's bier, made an address of surpassing pathos to the multitude in their behalf. It was an hour of deep and powerful emotion; and the procession slowly moved to the grave, weeping as they went. And, as they lifted their streaming eyes to Heaven, they besought the blessing of God upon the orphan group, and upon their own efforts to resist and vanquish their oppressors.

Immediately after Mr. Caldwell was shot, Morgan was arrested, and sent to the quarters of Major Scudder, then the commanding officer of the station. Major S. delivered him to the civil authorities, and he was committed to answer to the charge of murder. Shortly after this, he was sent to Burlington for safe keeping, where he remained till January, 1782, when he was taken to Westfield for his trial. After a fair and full examination of the case, the Jury returned a verdict of murder against the prisoner; and he was sentenced by the Court "to be hung on the 29th of January, 1782, for the wilful murder of the Rev. James Caldwell." This sentence was duly executed in the presence of a vast crowd of spectators,—the poor wretch exhibiting the most shocking and profane levity up to the moment of his being launched into the eternal world.

As to the motives which induced Morgan to murder Caldwell, it is difficult, at this distance of time, and in the absence of all records of the trial, to decide. There are, besides, opposite statements on the subject. Some say he was drunk at the time. Others say that he was greatly irritated because he was not regularly paid his wages; and because Caldwell was the Commissary, he supposed that he was responsible for the neglect.

Others again say that he was bribed by the British or Tories. But whichever motive may have influenced him, nothing less can be made of the act than a wanton and wicked murder.

So vivid are the recollections of the old people of East Jersey concerning Caldwell, that, from their descriptions of him, an artist might almost paint him to the life. He was of middle size and of a strongly built frame. His countenance had a pensive, placid cast; but, when excited, was expressive of high resolution and energy. His voice was sweet and musical, and yet so strong that, when needful, he would make himself heard above the notes of the drum and fife. As a preacher, he was uncommonly eloquent and pathetic; rarely preaching without weeping himself, and at times he would melt his whole audience into tears. The venerable Dr. Ashbel Green states that the impressions made by one sermon that Caldwell preached in Chatham in 1779 or 1780, have never been effaced from his mind.

He was a man of unwearied activity, and of wonderful powers of both bodily and mental endurance. Feelings of the most glowing piety and the most fervent patriotism occupied his bosom at the same time, without at all interfering with each other. He was one day preaching to the battalion,—the next, providing the ways and means for their support,—the next, marching with them to battle;—if defeated, assisting to conduct their retreat,—if victorious, offering their united thanksgivings to God,—and the next, carrying the consolations of the Gospel to some afflicted or dying parishioner. Down to the present hour, the aged ones speak of him with tearful emotion. Never was a pastor more affectionately remembered by a people. And, as a token of grateful respect and veneration for his memory, one of the townships in the County of Essex has been called by his name.

Mr. Caldwell left behind him, as I have already stated, nine orphan children, with but a scanty patrimony for their support; and even that was unwisely managed. But God raised up friends for them, and they all lived to be respectable and useful, and some of them to occupy important places in Church and State. *John E.*, the third child, was taken by La Fayette to France, and was educated under the direction of the Marchioness. He subsequently returned to this country, and was, for many years, among the most distinguished philanthropists of the city of New York. *James B.*, the fourth child, was, for a long time, a Judge of the Courts of Gloucester County in this State. And *Elias B.*, the seventh child, was, for some years, Clerk of the Supreme Court of the United States; and because of his noble efforts in the cause of Colonization, one of the towns in Liberia is called *Caldwell*, in honour of him.

At a meeting of the Cincinnati of New Jersey, in Elizabethtown, July 4, 1844, it was intimated to them that a monument ought to be erected to the memory of this patriot minister, and that the suggestion, as to its erection, should come from *them*. The idea was kindly entertained, and a committee was appointed to consider the subject. A similar committee was appointed by the First Presbyterian Church of Elizabethtown, to co-operate with that of the Cincinnati. And, through the joint agency of these committees, a beautiful monument to the memory of Caldwell was erected over his remains, in the grave yard of the First Presbyterian Church, to transmit the memory of his patriotism, piety, and exalted worth to generations to come. That monument was dedicated, by appropriate ceremonies, on the 24th of November, 1845,—the sixty-fourth anniversary of Mr. Caldwell's death. An appropriate and impressive Address was delivered on the occasion by the Rev. Samuel Miller, D. D., which has since been published.

Hoping that these brief notices,—the best that I have been able to gather,—of one of the most honoured martyrs to American liberty, may avail to your purpose,

I am, dear Sir,

Truly and affectionately yours,

NICHOLAS MURRAY.

JOHN CARMICHAEL.*

1760—1785.

JOHN CARMICHAEL was born in the town of Tarbert in Argyleshire, Scotland, October 17, 1728. His parents, Donald and Elizabeth (Alexander) Carmichael, were both exemplary members of the Presbyterian Church. Circumstances of a personal nature induced them to migrate to this country in the year 1737. As they drew near the American coast, after a long voyage, a sudden gust well nigh overturned the vessel; and their son *John*, then a little boy eight years old, was precipitated overboard; but, happily, the waves bore him within reach of the Captain, and his life was saved. After remaining a short time at New York, they removed to Hackensack, a Dutch settlement in New Jersey, where they experienced much kindness from the people; but the irreligion, especially the profanation of the Lord's day, that prevailed there, led the pious father to seek, particularly on account of his children, a more congenial residence. Such a place he found in what was then called Ward Session, a few miles from Newark, N. J. Here the family attended the ministry of the Rev. Aaron Burr,—whose preaching made a deep impression on the mind of this son, and whose addresses at the Communion table he always remembered as having been characterized by great pathos and power.

In the year 1745, when he was between sixteen and seventeen years of age, death deprived him of his father; and his mother, being left with five or six children, of whom he seems to have been the eldest, (at least the eldest son,) she urged upon him, as the head of the family, the duty of maintaining domestic worship. It does not appear that he declined the service, though his mind had not yet been brought fully into harmony with the requisitions and spirit of the Gospel; but, shortly after this, in consequence of reading some excellent books which were put into his hands, his mind became fixed in evangelical views, his heart bowed in humble submission to the Divine requirements, and ultimately he not only cherished the desire, but formed the purpose, of devoting himself to the Christian ministry.

* MS. from his granddaughter, Mrs. Reigart.

He entered the College of New Jersey in the year 1755. In a letter dated February 23, 1758, he writes thus:—"Doubtless you have heard that Mr. Edwards has taken the Presidentship of our College. A dear gentleman, greatly loved of all the students,—one whose piety and learning is too well known to need my commendation. I will only say this much,—that my highest expectations have been more than answered in every thing. He delivers the clear and awful truths of our holy religion with a solemnity becoming their importance, and as one who is really entrusted with the souls of his fellow mortals. I hope he will be to this Society as the cherishing rays of the sun, which will expel the heavy gloom and nocturnal darkness which seemed impending over Nassau Hall, on the hiding from view that bright luminary, by the death of our President Burr." In November of the same year,—in reviewing some of the events of the year, he writes as follows:—"I have seen another very dear President" (Edwards himself) "breathing out his last expiring breath in the agonies of death. Oh, my soul, forget not the holy fortitude, the Christian magnanimity, with which he grappled with the tyrant, and his unshaken faith in the Great Mediator."

Mr. Carmichael finished his collegiate course, and was admitted to the degree of Bachelor of Arts, in August, 1759. In November following, he was summoned to the death bed of his mother, where he witnessed a scene of remarkable Christian triumph.

After studying Theology at Princeton, under the direction of the Rev. Samuel Davies, who had succeeded to the Presidency of the College the year he was graduated, he was licensed to preach by the Presbytery of New Brunswick, on the 8th of May, 1760. The next Sabbath, he preached both at Elizabethtown and at Newark, and during the week or two that he remained in that neighbourhood, his public services averaged about one each day. Towards the close of the month, he went to Philadelphia, to wait on the Synod for orders to supply vacancies, as they might judge proper. Speaking with reference to this journey, he says—"Dear, dear Mr. William Tennent gave me a refreshing, seasonable, but very humbling, lecture, by the way, in private, as we rode together, about my too frequent preaching."

From a letter of Mr. Carmichael's still extant, it appears that, even before his licensure, proposals were made to him to settle, at a suitable time, at a place called Salsborough; but, though he seems to have been not a little exercised in regard to it as a question of duty, he finally decided against the application. Sometime in the year 1760, he received a call from the church of the Forks of Brandywine, Chester County, Pa., to become their pastor. This call he accepted: and the Presbytery of Newcastle, then lately constituted from a part of the Donegal Presbytery, met at the Forks of Brandywine, April 21, 1761, and ordained him to the work of the ministry, and installed him pastor of that congregation. This connection continued until it was terminated by his death.

When the war of the Revolution came on, Mr. Carmichael showed himself an earnest and uncompromising friend to the liberties of his country. In the summer of 1775, the militia of the town of Lancaster requested him to preach a military sermon. In complying with their request, he gave them a discourse in which he endeavoured to establish the lawfulness of self defence; and so acceptable was it, that a copy was requested for the press, and it very soon passed to a second edition. In referring to it in his diary, he says,—"I desire to give God all the glory, if he enables me to throw even a mite into the offering to aid the great American cause against tyranny and wicked usurpation." So effectually did he succeed in instilling into the minds of his people his own patriotic spirit, that, whenever they were called into the service, it is said that not a man of them hesitated or faltered; and as it devolved on the females, in the absence of their husbands, and fathers, and brothers, to superintend the out-door concerns, he was accustomed to go around and render them needed advice and assistance; and, with such wise and efficient co-operation, they succeeded in securing at least the usual crops. A report was at one time current through the region in which he lived, that a premium had been offered to any one who would bring him to New York. This put his people upon the alert; and though there is no evidence that any attempts to carry out such a purpose were ever made, yet the rumour occasioned great anxiety to his family, and several times they were actually taken off in haste, under the influence of a false alarm. While the British still had possession of New York, he received a letter from there, stating that his uncle in Scotland had left him a legacy, which, if he would come on, he should receive, provided he would recant his treasonable oath of allegiance to a rebellious Congress; but, in case of his refusal, it should be confiscated. It is hardly necessary to say that he chose to sacrifice the legacy rather than his principles. He had also claims to a considerable amount of property in Albany; but, unfortunately, the attorney to whom he committed his papers, turned out to be a Tory, and passed over to the British, carrying the papers with him. His patriotic spirit comes out, perhaps in nothing more than in the following record of the birth of a son, which was made in his Family Bible:—"On the 18th of October, 1777, was born to me a son. Since it pleased the Great God of Providence to ordain he should be born the very day and hour that General Burgoyne and his whole army had to come forth, and ground their arms, and resign themselves prisoners of war to these United States of America; as General Gates was the instrument, in the hands of a kind and Divine Providence, to effect this deliverance; and as our great, judicious Commander-in-chief, General Washington, still continues to persevere amidst many difficulties, to head the American army, I thought it my duty, as a memorial of these events, to call my son *Washington Gates.*"

Mr. Carmichael was indefatigable in his labours as a Christian minister; not only discharging his various duties among his own flock with great punctuality and fidelity, but often assisting his brethren in extraordinary exercises, and sometimes performing short tours of missionary service. His health was feeble for many years previous to his death, but his active labours were scarcely ever intermitted. A few months only before he died, he preached a course of sermons on Haggai i. 10,—the design of which was to show that there are times when the servants of God should be more than ordinarily engaged for the promotion of religion. The disease of which he died (pneumonia) was induced by the fatigue which he underwent in assisting the Rev. Robert Smith of Pequea, at the Communion in his church, and by his exposure to the rain on his return home. Two Sabbaths before his death, he administered the ordinance to his own people, and, in serving the last table, expressed to them the belief that he should no more drink wine with them until he drank it new in his Father's Kingdom. He called upon all the communicants who were present, to join with him in devout thanksgiving for the great peace and consolation which he had enjoyed during his illness His death was a scene of uncommon triumph; and the last expression that fell from his lips was—" Oh that I had a thousand tongues that I might employ them all in inviting sinners to Christ." He died on the 15th of November, 1785, in his fifty-eighth year.

Mr. Carmichael was married on the 8th of May, 1761, to Phebe Cram of Newark, N. J. Her mother was the second wife of the Rev. Jonathan Dickinson, first President of the College of New Jersey. By this marriage he had three children, the eldest of which, a son, died in infancy. The second, *John Flavel*, studied medicine under Dr. Scott of New Brunswick, N. J.; practised for a time with acceptance in his native place, entered the army, as a surgeon, in 1788; and, after holding the office several years, settled in the State of Mississippi, where he died in 1807. A third child, by this marriage,—a daughter, still survives (1854) in her eighty-ninth year. Mrs. Carmichael died on the 21st of October, 1772, in her forty-second year.

On the 2d of June, 1773, he was married a second time, to Catharine Mustard. She died on the 5th of August, 1774, leaving an infant daughter, who afterwards became the wife of the Hon. Robert Jenkins, and still lives, a widow, on the paternal estate in Lancaster County, Pa.

On the 24th of April, 1775, he was married, a third time, to Sally, daughter of the Rev. Samuel Blair of Fagg's Manor. By this marriage he had three children,—a daughter who married the Rev. Samuel Donnel,* and migrated to Tennessee, but died shortly after she arrived there; a son,—*Washington Gates*, who entered the army with promising prospects, but soon died of yellow fever, at the mouth of the Mississippi, and another daughter who still survives as the widow of a Captain Allen. The mother died on the 11th of May, 1810.

The Rev. Dr. J. N. C. Grier, in a Discourse which he preached in 1849, containing the History of the Church of the Forks of Brandywine, pays the following tribute to Mr. Carmichael:—

"The Rev. John Carmichael was an eloquent man, in his day, and 'mighty in the Scriptures.' He was a man of ardent feelings, and what he did, he did with his might. He was the pastor of this congregation during the whole of the great American Revolution; and, like most of the Presbyterian clergymen of that day, he espoused the cause of his country, like one who would rather perish, battling for freedom, than live a slave. He was long spared to the affections and the prayers of his people, going in and out before them, as a burning and a shining light, breaking to them the bread of life; and being an example to the flock over which the Holy Ghost had made him an overseer, ever calling upon them 'to be followers of him, even as he also was of Christ.'

"The Congregation increased under his ministry, which lasted about twenty-four years. He died greatly respected, and deeply lamented, by his people,—and having in all the churches of his Presbytery the reputation of a man thoroughly furnished for his work—one who needed not to be ashamed, because he rightly divided the word of truth."

In addition to the above testimony, I may say that, through the kindness of Mr. Carmichael's granddaughter, Mrs. Reigart, of Windsor, Pa., I have been put in possession of large portions of his diary, which make it manifest, beyond all question, that he was an eminently devout and earnest Christian, as well as an uncommonly laborious and faithful minister. He seems to have been in the habit of acknowledging God in every thing, even in the most inconsiderable events of his life; and though his great constitutional ardour rendered him more than ordinarily sensitive to bereavement, or affliction of any kind, yet such was the depth and strength of his religious feel-

* Mr. Donnel joined the Cumberland Presbyterians.

ings, that his submission and confidence in God seem never to have failed him. I have had the opportunity of reading a few of his manuscripts, as well as the only Sermon of his which was ever printed, and they all bear the impress of a mind of much more than ordinary comprehensiveness and energy.

AZEL ROE, D. D.*

1760—1815.

Azel Roe, son of John Roe, was born at Setauket, on the East end of Long Island, on the 20th of February, 1738. His father was a man of considerable property, and of highly respectable standing in society. He was graduated at the College of New Jersey in 1756; and studied Theology under the direction of the Rev. Caleb Smith of Newark Mountains, (now Orange). He was licensed to preach the Gospel, by the New York Presbytery, in the latter part of the year 1759, or early in 1760; and, about two years after, was ordained to the work of the ministry, *sine titulo*, by the same Presbytery. After preaching, for some time, as a candidate, at Woodbridge, the congregation united in presenting him a call; and, having accepted it, he was installed in the autumn of 1763.

A few years after his settlement, a proposal was made to form a union between the congregation of which he was pastor and the upper congregation, (a branch or colony at Metuchin, called Second Woodbridge,) by which these churches were to be considered as one ecclesiastically,—that is, to have one Session, and to share equally in the services of the minister. A little before the year 1790, this united Church was visited by an extensive revival, which, in the course of two or three years, added to its numbers upwards of one hundred. The Congregation of the First Church became dissatisfied that the people of Metuchin should share equally with themselves the labours of their minister, and began to express the wish that the union to which they had consented, a few years before, might be dissolved; and this was finally effected, though not without strong opposition from the Congregation of Metuchin, nor until after repeated applications to the Presbytery. The dissolution of this union arose from an unbounded attachment to the pastor by both congregations. They both claimed him, and each desired to possess him wholly.

As his ministry included the period of the Revolutionary war, he showed himself, in various ways, an earnest friend to the liberties of his country. The part of New Jersey in which he resided, was much annoyed by marauding parties, sent out from the British troops encamped on Staten Island. On one occasion, a brave Continental Captain, who had done great execution in driving off or annoying these predatory bands, was very anxious to attack a party which had encamped near the Blazing Star Ferry, but could not induce his men to follow him. As many of them belonged to Mr.

* Records of the Church at Woodbridge.—MSS. from his grandson, Mr. A. S. Roe, and Rev W. M. Martin.

Roe's parish, he thought he would put in requisition *his* influence over them. Accordingly, he called and stated his difficulty, and found Mr. R. more than willing to second his efforts. The good minister accompanied the Captain to the place where the men were, and addressed a few words to them, exhorting them to their duty, and enforcing his exhortation by telling them that it was his purpose to go into the action himself. And into the action he went,—every man following readily. But when the bullets began to fly among them, they promised that if he would keep out of harm's way, they would do the business for the enemy. And seeing that their spirits were sufficiently excited, he did retire, and, as he afterwards acknowledged, very much to his own comfort.

But this was by no means the most serious point of his connection with the war. So active was he in stirring up all within his influence to enlist in his country's cause, that the Tories united with the British, and seized him one night while he was with his family, and carried him off as a prisoner to New York, where they shut him up in the "Sugar House." As they were on their way to New York, they were obliged to ford a small stream. The officer in command, who seemed to have taken a fancy to Mr. Roe, and treated him politely, insisted that the captured minister should allow him to carry him over upon his back. When they were in about the middle of the stream, Mr. Roe, who relished a joke, and was not wanting in ready wit, said to the officer,—"Well, Sir, if never before, you can say, after this, that you was once priest-ridden." The officer was so convulsed with laughter, that he had well nigh fallen under his burden into the water. The morning after he arrived at New York, when he was without food, and knew not how his necessities were to be supplied, an excellent breakfast was sent to him by the father of Washington Irving who had been informed of his imprisonment; and this same gentleman took care that he was rendered comfortable until he was exchanged. Shortly after this, in order to prevent a second surprise, he moved his family some miles back towards Piscataway, but, after the war, he returned to the old Stone Parsonage.

Mr. Roe was a Trustee of the College of New Jersey twenty-nine years—from 1778 to 1807. He was a member of the first General Assembly of the Presbyterian Church in 1789, and was Moderator of that body in 1802. He was honoured with the degree of Doctor of Divinity from Yale College in 1800.

At the close of the war of 1812, a celebration took place at Woodbridge, which was signalized by the roasting of an ox; and Dr. Roe consented to officiate as orator on the occasion. His highly patriotic address awakened the strongest enthusiasm in the community at large, not excepting some in the church from which he had been separated, whose attachment towards him had been somewhat cooled by his having been called to render testimony in a court of law, adverse to their interest.

He was first married in September, 1763, to Rebecca, daughter of Major Isaac Foote of North Branford, Conn., and widow of the Rev. Caleb Smith, under whom he prosecuted his theological studies. She died on the 1st of September, 1794. She was the mother of all his children,—two sons and six daughters. On the 24th of December, 1796, he formed a second matrimonial connection. The lady who now became his wife was Hannah, daughter of the Rev. David Bostwick, pastor of the First Presbyterian Church in New York. She had been twice married before. Her first husband was General McDougall of Revolutionary fame. Her second husband was Mr. Barret, Consul to France, and she was his widow when she was married to Dr. Roe. She was distinguished for a fine intellect, attractive manners, and consistent and elevated piety.

In November, 1815, Mrs. Roe was seized with lung fever, and died, after an illness of a few days, in perfect peace, in the sixty-seventh year of her age. When she saw that her husband seemed inconsolable in the prospect of her departure, she affectionately urged him to restrain his grief, and submit quietly to God's will. Up to the time of her death, which was on the 28th of November, his health had been uniformly good, and his ability to labour in no degree impaired. But the shock occasioned by her death was greater than he could bear. An affection of the throat, apparently caused by excessive grief, seized him; and, on the 2d of December,—four days after the death of his wife, he yielded up his spirit in a manner so peaceful that his children, who were aware that he had always been subject to a nervous dread of death, could hardly find it in their hearts to mourn his departure.

FROM THE REV. JOHN McDOWELL, D. D.,

PHILADELPHIA, January 29, 1857.

Rev. and dear Sir: I lose no time in replying to your request for my recollections of the Rev. Dr. Roe. He was one of my nearest ministerial neighbours for a number of years, and my relations to him were such as to give me a good opportunity of becoming acquainted with his character. I still hold him in grateful remembrance, and am in no wise reluctant to pay such a tribute to his memory as your request contemplates.

Dr. Roe was an old man when I first knew him; and his naturally fine appearance had been rendered venerable by age. He was of about the medium height—I should say, five feet and eight or nine inches, and well proportioned. His manners were more than ordinarily graceful and dignified, and indicated that he had been familiar with cultivated society. He was a person of excellent judgment and common sense, and though he is said to have possessed naturally strong feelings, he exercised, by means of either grace, or prudence, or both combined, remarkable self-control. He had a well disciplined and well cultivated mind, and had the reputation of being a good scholar. His preaching was distinguished for substantial excellence, rather than for those qualities which attract the multitude—his sermons were characterized by weighty, well digested and evangelical thought, so plainly expressed as always to be level to the humblest intelligence; but I cannot say that his manner of delivery was specially impressive. He was universally and highly esteemed as a pastor. He moved about among his people with great dignity, kindness, and faithfulness,—always evincing a watchful and earnest regard for their spiritual welfare. He was permitted, about a year before his death, to reap a rich harvest from his labours in an extensive and powerful revival of religion. He was a punctual attendant on the judicatories of the Church, and a useful and influential member; and continued his fidelity in his advanced age.

Dr. Roe was well known, and was held in high esteem, much beyond the neighbourhood in which he lived and laboured. That he must have had a high standing among the ministers of his own denomination, is sufficiently evinced by the fact that he was called to moderate its highest judicatory; and that he must have had a good reputation for talents and scholarship may be inferred from his having been honoured with the degree of Doctor of Divinity from Yale College.

You are doubtless aware of the remarkable proximity of Dr. Roe's death to that of his wife. I preached her Funeral Sermon on the 29th of November, 1815, and his on the 3d of December following,—there being an interval of only four days. My text at his funeral was—"The memory of the just is blessed;"—a sentiment which I am persuaded was heartily responded to, in its application to that honoured servant of God, by all who knew him.

With much esteem, yours,

JOHN McDOWELL.

JAMES WADDEL, D. D.*

1761—1805.

James Waddel, the son of Thomas Waddel, was born at Newry, in the North of Ireland, in July, 1739. His parents migrated to America in his infancy, and settled in the South-eastern part of Pennsylvania, on White Clay Creek. His mother was distinguished for her Christian knowledge and piety, and her attachment to Scottish Presbyterianism; and it was to her influence that he attributed his first religious impressions. In consequence of an injury which he received, at the age of twelve, upon his left hand, rendering it in a great degree useless, his father resolved to give him a liberal education. Accordingly he was sent to Nottingham, about fifteen miles distant, to the school of the Rev. Dr. Finley, where he enjoyed excellent advantages for both intellectual and moral culture. During the period of his connection with this school, he was the subject of very remarkable religious exercises, though they were not occasioned by any external means. He stated to Dr. Alexander that on two occasions in particular, he had such views of the glory and excellency of the Gospel as he never enjoyed afterwards. Dr. Finley rendered him important aid by his excellent counsel and instruction, and at length admitted him to the communion of the church.

Such was Mr. Waddel's proficiency, especially in the classics, that Dr. Finley took him, at an early age, to be his assistant. On leaving this school, he became an assistant teacher in another celebrated school of that day,—at Pequea, Lancaster County, Pa., under the care of the Rev. Robert Smith;—a school from which proceeded as many as fifty young men who were afterwards ministers of the Gospel. After having been engaged here a year or more, he set out to travel South, intending, as is supposed, to devote himself to teaching, and to settle in Charleston, S. C. On his way he stopped at Upper Marlborough, Md., where a Presbyterian church had already been founded; and though he was solicited to remain there, the inducements were not so strong as to detain him, and he pursued his journey till he reached Hanover County, Va. Here he had the pleasure of listening to the eloquence, and making the acquaintance, of that prince of pulpit orators, Samuel Davies; and it was this circumstance probably that gave the decisive direction to his life. Mr. Davies not only forbade him to go farther, but urged him to devote himself at once to the ministry.

* Notices of Dr. Waddel in the "Watchman of the South."—Foote's Sketches of Va., I.—Life of Rev. Dr. Alexander.—MS. from Rev. Dr. Hill.

Though he had been studying medicine before this, he was now persuaded to abandon it, and to act in accordance with Mr. Davies' advice. Shortly after this, he entered upon his theological studies, under the direction of the Rev. Mr. Todd of Louisa County, an eminent minister of his day, and meanwhile became engaged, for the third time, in the business of instruction. Here he remained until he was licensed as a probationer, at Tinkling Spring, on the 2d of April, 1761, by the (Old) Presbytery of Hanover. His acceptance as a preacher, from the beginning, may be estimated by the fact that, at the meeting of the Presbytery in October following his licensure, there were put into his hands five calls; but he did not think proper even to take any of them into consideration; as his mind was made up at that time to return to Pennsylvania, and he was not without some expectation of a settlement at York. He, therefore, left Virginia, and returned home to visit his parents; and when he revisited Virginia afterwards, it was with a view of obtaining a dismission from the Presbytery. When, however, the Presbytery met, there were present two gentlemen of great respectability as commissioners from the County of Lancaster, Va., who made such representations in regard to the spiritual destitution of the region in which they lived, that Mr. Waddel was constrained to admit the claim upon his services, and accordingly he suddenly changed his purpose. At a meeting of the Presbytery at Providence, on the 7th of October, 1762, he signified his acceptance of a call from the Churches of Lancaster and Northumberland; and, on the 16th of June, he was ordained at Prince Edward.

The people of Mr. Waddel's charge found in him every thing they could desire, and they showed him every mark of affectionate respect. He does not seem, at the time of his settlement, to have expected to remain long there; but various circumstances conspired to a different result. He found so much hospitality, intelligence, and piety in the region around, that the reluctance he had felt to making his permanent home there was quickly overcome. Besides, he was united in marriage, about the year 1768, with Mary, daughter of Colonel James Gordon, a gentleman of great respectability, and an elder in one of the churches to which he ministered. His father-in-law, shortly after his marriage, established him in a new and commodious house on Curratoman River; and here he would gladly have remained during his whole life, but for the ill effects of the climate upon his health. He passed no year without an attack of intermittent fever; and he often preached, when it was difficult for him to stand erect. This, in connection with the inroads of the Revolutionary war, led him, about the year 1776, to resign his charge, and remove to the Valley of the Shenandoah. Some two years previous to this, he had received a call from the Congregations of Opekon and Cedar Creek, which he declined.

On leaving Lower Virginia, his attention was directed to Tinkling Spring, in Augusta; and, on the 1st of May, 1776, a call from that congregation was presented to him, which he engaged to take into consideration for a year. In 1778, he removed his family to a place called Spring Hill, a few miles above Waynesborough, where he remained about seven years. For some time, his labours were confined to the Tinkling Spring Congregation, but they were afterwards shared by that and the congregation at Staunton. During his residence in Augusta, his health was entirely restored.

In 1785, Mr. Waddel removed to an estate which he had purchased at the eastern base of the Blue Ridge. This he named Hopewell. His house was in Louisa, but his property, amounting to nearly a thousand acres, lay chiefly in the Counties of Orange and Albermarle. He preached in several churches in the neighbourhood, and also became, for the fourth time, a classical teacher, and received pupils in his own house. The period of his residence in Louisa was about twenty years.

In 1792, the degree of Doctor of Divinity was conferred upon him by the Trustees of Dickinson College, Carlisle.

Some time after his removal to Louisa, he was overtaken with the calamity of blindness,—a cataract having seized first one eye, and then the other. He continued to preach, however, availing himself, in his preparations, of the assistance of different members of his family, in finding the text, consulting the commentaries, &c.; and the effect of his preaching was not a little heightened by the fact that he was seen to be speaking in total darkness. In 1798, his sight was partially restored, for a time, by means of the operation of couching; but the cataract speedily returned, and he saw the light of the sun no more.

Dr. Waddel's latter days were eminently serene and happy. The loss of his sight, though on many accounts a most severe deprivation, he submitted to with perfect resignation and cheerfulness. His mental faculties still remained as vigorous as ever; and he not only enjoyed intercourse with his friends, but entered with great interest into theological speculations. Before his death he gave orders that all his manuscripts should be committed to the flames; that his funeral should be conducted in the most simple manner; and that his body should be borne to the grave by his own servants. His death, which was a bright scene of Christian triumph, occurred on the 17th of September, 1805.

Dr. Waddel was the father of ten children, several of whom have occupied important positions in society. One of his daughters was married to the Rev. William Calhoon,* and one to the Rev. Dr. Alexander. His widow died at Staunton, in the year 1813.

Probably the best idea of Dr. Waddel's preaching, which it is possible now to obtain, is to be gathered from the following well known description by Mr. Wirt, which appeared early in this century, in the "British Spy:"—

"It was on Sunday, as I travelled through the County of Orange, that my eye was caught by a cluster of horses tied near a ruinous old wooden house in the forest, not far from the road side. Having frequently seen such objects before, in travelling through these States, I had no difficulty in understanding that this was a place of religious worship.

"Devotion alone should have stopped me to join in the duties of the congregation; but I must confess that curiosity to hear the preacher of such a wilderness was not the least of my motives. On entering, I was struck with his preternatural appearance. He was a tall and very spare old man; his head, which was covered with a white linen

* William Calhoon was born in 1772,—the son of an elder in the Briery Church, Prince Edward County, Va.; became a member of Hampden Sidney College, at the age of fourteen, and was hopefully converted while a member of that institution. He was licensed to preach by the Hanover Presbytery on the 12th of May, 1792, and in the succeeding autumn, went, under the commission of Synod, as a missionary to Kentucky. He resided in Kentucky for several years, and had a pastoral charge there; but returned to Virginia in 1799, and, after preaching at several different places, accepted a call from Staunton, and Brown's meeting house (afterwards Hebron). To these congregations he devoted his time and energies for a number of years, until, at length, the infirmities of advancing life admonished him to resign the charge, first of one congregation, and then of the other,—believing, as he did, that each of them required more service than he was able to render. He, however, continued to labour, to the full extent of his ability, while he lived. Dr. Foote represents him as a man of vigorous intellect, of great self command, of a ready mind, of fine conversational powers, and of an enlarged public spirit. He died on the 27th of August, 1851.

cap, his shrivelled hands, and his voice, were all shaking under the influence of a palsy; and a few moments ascertained to me that he was perfectly blind.

"The first emotions that touched my breast were those of mingled pity and veneration. But how soon were all my feelings changed! The lips of Plato were never more worthy of a prognostic swarm of bees, than were the lips of this holy man! It was a day of the administration of the Sacrament; and his subject was, of course, the passion of our Saviour. I had heard the subject handled a thousand times—I had thought it exhausted long ago. Little did I suppose that in the wild woods of America, I was to meet with a man, whose eloquence would give to this topic a new and more sublime pathos than I had ever before witnessed.

"As he descended from the pulpit to distribute the mystic symbols, there was a peculiar, a more than human, solemnity in his air and manner, which made my blood run cold, and my whole frame shiver.

"He then drew a picture of the sufferings of our Saviour; his trial before Pilate; his ascent up Calvary; his crucifixion and his death. I knew the whole history; but never until then had I heard the circumstances so selected, so arranged, so coloured! It was all new; and I seemed to have heard it for the first time in my life. His enunciation was so deliberate that his voice trembled on every syllable; and every heart in the assembly trembled in unison. His peculiar phrases had that force of description, that the original scene appeared to be at that moment acting before our eyes. We saw the very faces of the Jews; the staring, frightful distortions of malice and rage. We saw the buffet; my soul kindled with a flame of indignation; and my hands were involuntarily and convulsively clenched.

"But when he came to touch on the patience, the forgiving meekness, of our Saviour; when he drew to the life his blessed eyes, streaming in tears to Heaven, his voice breathing to God a soft and gentle prayer of pardon on his enemies, "Father, forgive them, for they know not what they do," the voice of the preacher which had all along faltered, grew fainter and fainter, until his utterance being entirely obstructed by the force of his feelings, he raised his handkerchief to his eyes, and burst into a loud and irrepressible flood of grief. The effect was inconceivable. The whole house resounded with the mingled groans, and sobs, and shrieks, of the congregation.

"It was some time before the tumult subsided, so far as to permit him to proceed. Indeed, judging by the usual, but fallacious, standard of my own weakness, I began to be very uneasy for the situation of the preacher: for I could not conceive how he would be able to let his audience down from the height to which he had wound them, without impairing the solemnity and dignity of his subject, or perhaps shocking them by the abruptness of the fall. But no! the descent was as beautiful and sublime, as the elevation had been rapid and enthusiastic.

"The first sentence with which he broke the awful silence, was a quotation from Rousseau: 'Socrates died like a philosopher; but Jesus Christ like a God!'

"I despair of giving you any idea of the effect produced by this short sentence, unless you could perfectly conceive the whole manner of the man, as well as the peculiar crisis in the discourse. Never before did I completely understand what Demosthenes meant by laying such stress on delivery. You are to bring before you the venerable figure of the preacher; his blindness constantly recalling to your recollection old Homer, Ossian, and Milton; and, associating with his performance the melancholy grandeur of their geniuses, you are to imagine that you hear his slow, solemn, well-accented enunciation, and his voice of affecting, trembling melody; you are to remember the pitch of passion and enthusiasm to which the congregation were raised, and then the few moments of portentous, death-like silence which reigned throughout the house: the preacher removing his white handkerchief from his aged face, (even yet wet from the recent torrent of his tears,) and slowly stretching forth the palsied hand which holds it, begins the sentence, "Socrates died like a philosopher"—then pausing, raising his other hand, pressing them both, clasped together with warmth and energy, to his breast, lifting his sightless balls to Heaven, and pouring his whole soul into his tremulous voice,—'but Jesus Christ—like a God!' If he had been indeed and in truth an angel of light, the effect could scarcely have been more Divine.

"Whatever I may have been able to conceive of the sublimity of Massillon, or the force of Bourdaloue, had fallen far short of the power which I felt from the delivery of this simple sentence. The blood which just before had rushed in a hurricane upon my brain, and, in the violence and agony of my feelings, had held my whole system in suspense, now ran back into my heart, with a sensation which I cannot describe—a kind of shuddering, delicious horror! The paroxysm of blended pity and indignation, to which I had been transported, subsided into the deepest self-abasement, humility, and adoration. I had just been lacerated and dissolved by sympathy for our Saviour, as a fellow-creature; but now, with fear and trembling, I adored him as a God.

"If this description gives you the impression that this incomparable minister had any thing of shallow, theatrical trick in his manner, it does him great injustice. I have never seen in any other orator such a union of simplicity and majesty. He has not a gesture, an attitude or an accent, to which he does not seem forced by the sentiment he is expressing. His mind is too serious, too earnest, too solicitous, and at the same time too dignified, to stoop to artifice. Although as far removed from ostentation as a man can be, yet it is clear from the train, the style and substance of his thoughts, that he is not only a very polite scholar, but a man of extensive and profound erudition. I was forcibly struck with a short yet beautiful character, which he drew of your learned and amiable countryman, Sir Robert Boyle: he spoke of him as if his noble mind had, even before death, divested herself of all influence from his frail tabernacle of flesh; and called him, in his peculiarly emphatic and impressive manner, 'a pure intelligence, the link between men and angels.'

"This man has been before my imagination almost ever since. A thousand times, as I rode along, I dropped the reins of my bridle, stretched forth my hand, and tried to imitate his quotation from Rousseau; a thousand times I abandoned the attempt in despair, and felt persuaded that his peculiar manner and power arose from an energy of soul, which nature could give, but which no human being could justly copy. In short, he seems to be altogether a being of a former age, or of a totally different nature from the rest of men. As I recall, at this moment, several of his awfully striking attitudes, the chilling tide with which my blood begins to pour along my arteries, reminds me of the emotions produced by the first sight of Gray's introductory picture of his bard:

'On a rock whose haughty brow,
'Frowns o'er old Conway's foaming flood,
'Robed in the sable garb of wo,
'With haggard eyes, the poet stood.
'(Loose his beard, and hoary hair
'Streamed, like a meteor, to the troubled air:)
'And with a poet's hand, and prophet's fire,
'Struck the deep sorrows of his lyre.'

"Guess my surprise when, on my arrival at Richmond, and mentioning the name of this man, I found not one person who had ever before heard of *James Waddel!*"

FROM THE REV. WILLIAM CALHOON.

AUGUSTA COUNTY, Va., November 23, 1848.

Rev. and dear Sir: I first became acquainted with the Rev. Dr. James Waddel about 1797, at which time he was an old man. He had then been restored to imperfect vision, by an operation on one eye, which operation had been performed by Dr. Tyler of Fredericktown, Md.

In person, he was tall, slender, erect,—in general deportment, dignified and commanding, but remarkable for politeness and gentlemanly manners—indeed I considered him a finished gentleman in the old Virginia acceptation of the term. In further description of his person, I may say, he had a long face, high forehead, Grecian nose, blue eyes, and small mouth and chin. He was partially affected with palsy; and the shaking of his head and hands, with a solemn countenance, produced in most minds a feeling of reverence and awe.

From the date just mentioned until 1805, I lived near his residence, and when not engaged in pastoral duties, usually spent an hour with him every day, attracted by his great knowledge and wonderful powers of conversation.

He exhibited a happy mixture of Christian cheerfulness with ministerial gravity. Owing to his partial vision, he seldom made excursions beyond his immediate neighbourhood,—still preaching, however, at the little meeting-house in the County of Orange, referred to by Mr. Wirt, and two miles from Hopewell,—his residence.

On one occasion, he preached at Milton, a village in Albermarle County, whither I had removed with my family; and this was the only sermon I remember to have heard from him,—owing to his habit of hearing others, instead of being heard by them. This sermon was preached in the presence of several infidels, and, after singing the last hymn, he arose and made an address on the importance of Christianity to a fallen world, as an evidence of its truth. I am satisfied that I never witnessed such a torrent of eloquence before or since.

He was a learned man, without ostentatious display, being more solicitous to present the Son of God to his audience, than to exhibit himself. His articulation was distinct, and his speech neither rapid nor slow. His gesture was not studied or uniform, but was such as was suggested by his feelings, and was always pertinent to the thought he was uttering. All in him seemed the result of a powerfully working mind, and of one constitutionally eloquent. His language was always neat, often elegant, evincing much cultivation. His delivery showed that he poured his soul into his words.

An old elder who once lived under Dr. Waddel's ministrations, informed me that he heard him preach, on a certain occasion, upon the glories of Heaven, and the introduction of saints there; when his descriptions were so vivid that he actually forgot himself, and involuntarily looked up to behold the amazing scenes, which the preacher, with such wonderful power, portrayed.

When I removed to this county, the parting of Mrs. Calhoon from her father was deeply affecting. He said, "My child, you weep, lest you may not see me again. Were I invited to a feast prepared for the honourable of this world, would you be distressed? Well, should you hear that your father is dead, comfort yourself with the thought that he has been called to the feast prepared by God for the redeemed." It was the last time she saw him. Shortly after our removal, (1805,) hearing of his illness, I visited him, and we had much conversation. He told me that he felt no personal interest in any thing earthly,—that he was convinced that he should soon leave the world. With a solemn countenance, without dejection, and in the perfect use of his mental faculties, he said,—"I feel no concern in view of death, of a painful kind, no more than when lying down to sleep." His mind was full of Heaven, because his confidence in Christ was firm and unshaken. He fell asleep in Jesus shortly after I left him.

With great respect,

WILLIAM CALHOON.

FROM THE REV. ARCHIBALD ALEXANDER, D. D.

PRINCETON, October 16, 1848.

Rev. and dear Sir: I do not know that I have much to add concerning Dr. Waddel to what has already been published. I may say, however, that he was as eloquent in private conversation as in the pulpit. He was very communicative, and, in the company of young persons, would go on for a quarter or sometimes half an hour, in the most animated and delightful discourse; and, on the subject of practical and experimental religion, these discourses were most edifying. I never heard him preach but once; and that was when he was perfectly blind. The subject was the "Parable of the Pharisee and the Publican." This passage of Scripture was repeated by him with perfect accuracy, and the discourse was masterly. The description of the Pharisee was striking, and in some respects new to me; as he exhibited him according to the character which he had among the people, who had no suspicion of his hypocrisy, but venerated him as a man of superior sanctity and elevated devotion. His manner was not harsh, but highly animated. This was the case in all his conversation. Whenever he discoursed on any subject, he entered into it with his whole soul. Even on metaphysical subjects he spoke with uncommon ardour.

He was a man of a most affectionate disposition, and in his treatment of strangers was remarkably courteous. In the expression of his own opinions he was as free and independent as any man I ever knew. Whatever sentiments he entertained he would express with perfect freedom, on all occasions, however they might differ from those of the persons with whom he conversed. In his person he was tall and very slender. At home he wore a white cap; in the pulpit, a large, full bottomed white wig,—which was the custom of the clergy in his day.

The most remarkable specimen of his eloquence which I ever heard, was in a speech delivered in the small church near his own house. The case was this—a clergyman, a member of the Presbytery of Hanover, had been maliciously prosecuted, as I believe, by two of his own elders. He was a man of great sensibility to any thing which touched the purity of his moral character; and this accusation produced in him a degree of anguish indescribable. Though unanimously acquitted, yet the idea of being charged with a base crime affected him much; and, as he feared that the decision of the Presbytery might not be known to all who had heard the accusation, he took pains to procure a copy of the proceedings, signed by the Moderator and Clerk. To this paper he attached certain severe remarks on the malignity of his accusers, mentioning them by name. This laid the foundation for a charge of forgery, as this had the appearance of being entirely an extract from the Records of Presbytery. It was on this second accusation that Dr. Waddel made the speech in defence of this clergyman. An intelligent elder present, who did not agree in opinion with Dr. W., and who had heard several of Patrick Henry's most celebrated speeches in criminal cases, declared that this was the most perfect specimen of eloquence which he ever heard. I had heard Mr. Henry on one occasion, and my opinion was that Mr. Henry's oratory was better adapted to produce its effect on the great body of the people, and Dr. Waddel's better suited to persons of refinement and education. You know that all attempts to describe oratory are vain—it must be heard to be understood.

James Madison, President of the United States, lived about seven or eight miles from the small church before mentioned, and frequently attended there with his mother, who was an eminently pious lady, and, as long as she was able to attend, a communicant in Dr. Waddel's little church. Mr. Madison often visited Dr. Waddel in his own house, and sometimes consulted him in matters relating to the welfare of the country. James Barbour, Governor of Virginia, was, in early life, the pupil of Dr. Waddel, and while he lived, cherished and expressed the highest admiration of his eloquence. Shortly before his death, he told an eminent physician in Philadelphia that Dr. W. had spoiled him, in regard to hearing other preachers. Philip Barbour, a Justice of the Supreme Federal Court, a brother of the former, entertained the same sentiments of admiration. Yet, while his preaching was so greatly admired by the intelligent and refined, it did not equally attract and move the illiterate and ignorant. Often such would prefer hearing an uneducated declaimer.

While Dr. Waddel was pastor of the Presbyterian Church in Lancaster County, in the Northern Neck, and on the Chesapeake Bay, he was visited by Mr. Whitefield, who spent a week in that region; preaching, as usual, very frequently, and with amazing power, and leaving behind him many seals to his ministry. Dr. W. was much pleased with the fervent zeal which glowed in Whitefield's bosom; but he thought he had great faults, among which self-exaltation was perhaps the most conspicuous and offensive. Soon after his departure, Mr. Whitefield wrote him an account of his wonderful success in preaching the Gospel, and annexed to almost every description several notes of admiration (! ! !). The gentlemen connected with Dr. Waddel's congregation greatly preferred the style of eloquence to which they had been accustomed, to the more fervid and impressive oratory of Whitefield. This sequestered congregation, almost insulated by the Rappahanock, Wicomico, and Chesapeake Bay, was several hundred miles from the nearest Presbyterian Church. While Dr. W. remained there, he had little intercourse with his brethren in the ministry; and his eloquence, when he was in full health, and in his prime, was seldom heard any where, except in this point of the Northern Neck. Before he moved up the country, his constitution was broken, and his voice much shattered.

It is perhaps proper to add that Dr. Waddel, while he held firmly the doctrines of the Bible as exhibited in the standards of the Presbyterian Church, was disposed to treat with great respect those who differed from him, even though he might consider them as holding serious errors. Neither did he make a man an offender for a word in matters pertaining to practical religion. Always exemplary in his life, he was as far as possible from pharisaic precision, and never frowned upon the buoyant spirits and innocent enjoyments of the young. There was great naturalness as well as great dignity pervading his whole character.

Yours truly,
A. ALEXANDER.

WILLIAM TENNENT (Third.)*

1762—1777.

William Tennent, a son of the Rev. William Tennent of Freehold, N. J., was born in Freehold, in the year 1740. He was graduated at the College of New Jersey, in 1758, and was admitted to the degree of Master of Arts, at Harvard College, in 1763. He was licensed to preach by the Presbytery of New Brunswick, sometime between the meetings of Synod in 1761 and 1762; and was ordained by the same Presbytery between the Synodical meetings of 1762 and 1763. Shortly after his ordination, he went, by appointment of Synod, to Virginia, and laboured within the bounds, and under the direction, of the Hanover Presbytery, for six months.

In 1764, the people of Norwalk, Conn., wishing to procure a colleague for their pastor,—the Rev. Moses Dickinson, then far advanced in life,—applied to Mr. Tennent to preach to them as a candidate for settlement; and, after he had preached several Sabbaths, they unanimously invited him, on the 13th of November, to become their junior pastor. He accepted their invitation, but expressed a wish to retain his connection with the Presbytery; to which the parish consented, on condition that he should conform practically to the rules of the Congregational Church. The Presbytery, however, not disposed to connive at any such arrangement, appointed a time and a committee of their own, for the installation. This the parish regarded as an undue assumption; and on the 12th of June, 1765, they held a meeting to consider the case, and, as the result of their deliberations, passed the following vote:—

"This Society, by a copy from the minutes of the Presbytery, are informed that Mr. Tennent declared his acceptance of the call of the Society, upon condition that he shall continue a member of the Synod of New York and Philadelphia, and of New Brunswick Presbytery; * * * but at the same time professed his desire and intention to hold communion and be in connection with the Reverend Association aforesaid, as far as is consistent with his continuing in his relation to the Synod: and that thereupon the said Presbytery had presumed that this Church and Society complied with the condition annexed by Mr. Tennent to his acceptance of their call, (which was made on very different terms); and accordingly have assumed to themselves a right to appoint, and did appoint, the time of instalment, and a committee of their own to officiate therein. On consideration of all which, this Society is of opinion that the annexing of the condition aforesaid to the acceptance of the call aforesaid, is a proposal subversive of the foundation on which the agreement and proceeding of the Society were predicated; and the proceedings of the Presbytery, in consequence

* Hall's Hist. Norwalk.—Ramsay's Hist. S. C., II.—Hist. Circ. Ch., Charleston.—Alison's Fun. Serm.—Hart's do.—MS. from Rev. W. S. Lee.

thereof, is an attempt to draw the Church and Society off from the constitution in which they are united, and to lead them to renounce the relations they stand in, and esteem too sacred to be violated; and do also view such appointment of the time and persons for instalment, as an imposition on the Society, and therefore is to be treated with neglect. Therefore, the Society do declare that they cannot comply with the above said conditions and appointment; but are obliged to look on Mr Tennent's annexing such embarrassment to his acceptance tantamount to a denial of the invitation made him, &c."

Mr. Tennent then declared that he never expected or intended that the Society should be under the power of the Presbytery; and signified his willingness to accept the call, if this explanation should prove satisfactory. Whereupon the Society voted their approval, and desired his settlement,—adding in their vote, June 19, 1765,—

"Nevertheless it is expected that, before his instalment, a certificate be produced from the Reverend Presbytery aforesaid, of Mr. Tennent's being released from them, agreeably to the tenor of the above proposals, in order to make way for a regular settlement here, and a full union with the Association here, on the constitution of this Colony."

The result was that Mr. Tennent was, in due time, installed; and, according to the agreement, he retained his connection with the New Brunswick Presbytery, and at the same time showed himself practically a good Congregationalist.

Mr. Tennent continued his ministrations at Norwalk with great acceptance for about six years and a half. At the end of that period, he received a call to become the pastor of an Independent Church in Charleston, S. C.; and, on the 8th of January, 1772, the Society met to decide whether they would concur with Mr. Tennent in calling a council to whom the question in respect to the call should be submitted. They peremptorily declined a concurrence, declaring that "there doth not appear any cause arising in the Society, or any matter subsisting between Mr. Tennent and the Society, that makes it necessary or expedient for the Society to desire a council." Just six days after this meeting, we find the Consociation of the Western District of Fairfield County in session, "to consider and determine a case of no less importance than the expediency of the Rev. Mr. Tennent's dismission from the pastoral relation to this Church and Society." The Society being called upon by the Consociation to state their views of the case, utterly refused their consent to Mr. Tennent's dismission, and declared their full conviction of the insufficiency of the reasons that were offered for it. They seem, however, subsequently, to have yielded to some considerations suggested by the Consociation, and on the 22d of January, they voted, evidently in a spirit of great dissatisfaction, that, if he desired a council for the dissolution of his pastoral relation, they had "nothing to object" to it. Shortly after this, his dismission was effected.

Mr. Tennent, as soon as he was released from his charge at Norwalk, went to Charleston, and was installed Pastor of the Church to which he had been called. Here he was received with great favour, and both in the pulpit and out of it, exerted a powerful influence. When the American Revolution commenced, he entered into it with great ardour, and his far-reaching mind seemed to comprehend, in an extraordinary degree, the wonderful results to which it was destined to lead. His glowing zeal and distinguished talents rendered him so great a favourite with the people, that, contrary to established usage, they, with much unanimity, elected him a member of the Provincial Congress. Such was the urgency of public affairs, that even good men, and ministers of the Gospel, sometimes considered themselves absolved from the obligation to the strict observance of the Sabbath; and Dr. Ramsay states that, "in the different hours of the same day, Mr. Tennent was occasionally heard both in his Church and the State House, addressing different audiences, with equal animation, on their spiritual and temporal interests." He rarely preached political sermons, but his prayers breathed a spirit of lofty patriotism, while they contributed not a little to awaken and cherish the same spirit in others. His vigorous pen was often put in requisition for his country's cause, though nothing was printed with his name, except two Sermons, and a Speech delivered in the Legislature of South Carolina, on the justice and policy of putting all religious denominations on an equal footing. In the year 1775, the adherents to the Royal government, in the back country, assumed an attitude of such decided hostility towards the friends of the Revolution, that serious consequences were apprehended. In this crisis, the Council of Safety despatched a deputation, consisting of William Tennent and William Henry Drayton, to endeavour to enlighten these people in regard to the nature of the dispute, and bring them to co-operate with the rest of the inhabitants. The committee not only had private interviews with them, but held public meetings in different places, and made several addresses, which were not without effect. The result of the mission was considered as decidedly favourable to the new order of things, and Mr. Tennent's shrewdness and eloquence had not a little to do with it.

Mr. Tennent was an earnest friend of religious liberty. Having been born and educated in a Province where there had never been any Church establishment, both conviction and habit rendered it difficult for him to accept toleration, as a legal boon, from those whose natural rights were not superior to his own. He drew up an argumentative petition in favour of equal religious liberty, secured the concurrence of different denominations in its favour, and when it was made the subject of legislative consideration, he delivered an able and eloquent speech in its support. It is understood that he exerted a powerful influence in aid of the reform which was ultimately effected.

In March, 1777, Mr. Tennent's venerable father died at Freehold, N. J. In the summer following, he made a journey to Freehold, with a view to conduct his aged and widowed mother to his own home, that the closing part of her life might be cheered by his filial attentions. He had reached the High Hills of Santee,—about ninety miles from Charleston, on his homeward way, when he was attacked with a violent nervous fever, which, after a short time, terminated fatally. He died on the 11th of August, 1777, in the thirty-seventh year of his age. The Rev. (afterwards Dr.) Richard Furman, in a letter to Mr. Tennent's widow, says,—

"I was with him in his last moments—his life went gently from him, almost without a struggle or a groan. He told me in almost the last words he spake that his mind was calm and easy, and he was willing to be gone."

He left a widow and five children,—two sons and three daughters.

Two Sermons were preached with reference to his death,—one by the Rev. Hugh Alison,* and the other by the Rev. Oliver Hart, Pastor of a Baptist Church in Charleston; both of which were published.

* Hugh Alison was a native of Pennsylvania; was graduated at the College of New Jersey in 1762, after which he was for some time engaged as a teacher, in Charleston, S. C. He was married to a daughter of Paul Smiser, a planter in South Carolina, and shortly after removed to James Island, taking with him a number of young men, with a view to superintend their

One of the two Sermons published by Mr. Tennent was entitled "God's Sovereignty no objection to the sinner's striving,"—preached in New York, 1765.

The following estimate of Mr. Tennent's character is from Mr. Alison's Discourse:—

"Do we view him in the pulpit? Few preachers had a more majestic and venerable presence, or a more winning and oratorial address. Animated with a sacred regard for the honour of his Divine Master, and the salvation of precious immortal souls, he spake the word with all boldness. I take you to record that he shunned not to declare unto you the whole counsel of God. A lively imagination, added to a careful study of the Scriptures, enabled him to bring forth out of his treasure things new and old; yet he never entertained his audience with scholastic niceties or subtle questions, which minister strife and endless disputation, rather than godly edifying which is in faith; but he entertained them with the plain uncontroverted truths of the everlasting Gospel. He preached Christ crucified our only wisdom, righteousness, sanctification, and redemption. He was careful and accurate in describing the nature of true religion, and in distinguishing the reality from the bare appearance. He spared not the secure and presumptuous sinner, but would thunder forth the terrors of the Divine law against him, that, if possible, he might awaken him from his dreadful slumbers; yet he was always ready, and well knew how and when, to administer the balm of the Gospel to the wounded spirit. Elegance of style, majesty of thought, and clearness of judgment, appeared in his discourses, and concurred to render them both pleasing and instructive. He laboured but a few years in this place, yet we trust he laboured not in vain.

"Or shall we view him as a patriot? His honest, disinterested, yet flaming, zeal for his country's good demands from us a tribute of respect. Impressed with a sense of the justice, greatness, and vast importance, of the American cause, he engaged in it with an ardour and resolution that would have done honour to an ancient Roman. For this, indeed, he was censured, and perhaps too liberally, even by his friends. * * *

"Early in the contest, Mr. Tennent magnanimously stepped forth as an advocate for this Continent. Here was a field suited to his great abilities, and here his abilities shone with increasing lustre. He first endeavoured to rouse his fellow citizens to a just sense of their inestimable rights, and a willingness to contend for them; and to his spirited exertions, among others, may, in a great measure, be attributed that noble, patriotic zeal, which so soon blazed forth to the immortal honour of this State In many of his speeches, which he delivered in the Provincial Congress and General Assembly, of which he was successively a member, he displayed great erudition, strength of argument, generosity of sentiment, and a most unbounded eloquence. He continued his fervent endeavours to the last, resolutely regardless of the attacks of envy and calumny which he met with; and particularly his strenuous efforts for abolishing religious as well as civil oppression in this country, deserve our sincerest acknowledgments.

"His natural genius was prodigiously strong and penetrating; and the unavoidable consciousness of his native power made him sanguine, bold, and enterprising. Yet the event proved that his boldness arose, not from a partial, groundless self-conceit, but from a true self-knowledge. Upon fair and candid trial, faithful and just to himself, he judged what he could do; and what he could do, when called to it, he attempted, and what he attempted he accomplished.

"But Mr. Tennent's principal ornament was his unaffected and substantial piety. His worst enemies could never charge him with a scandalous or immoral life. He honoured his Divine Master not only in word but in deed. The doctrines he taught and the duties he inculcated, were happily exemplified in his own life and conversation. Agreeable to the Apostle's charge to Timothy, he was an 'example of the believers in word, in conversation, in charity, in spirit, in faith, in purity.'

"He was remarkably humane and benevolent in his disposition, and possessed every personal grace and qualification that could attract the esteem and reverence of his fellow creatures. In domestic or social life, his character shines with peculiar lustre. He was a kind, affable and tender husband; a prudent, cautious and indulgent parent; a generous and compassionate master; and a faithful, affectionate and steady friend. His appearance in company was manly and graceful; his behaviour genteel, not ceremonious; grave, yet pleasant; and solid, but sprightly too. In a word, he was an open, conversable, and entertaining companion, a polite gentleman, and devout Christian at once."

education. He also became Pastor of the Presbyterian Church on that Island. Just before the Island was occupied by the British, during the Revolution, he returned with his family to Charleston, where he died of consumption in 1781 or 1782.

DAVID RICE.*

1762—1816.

David Rice was born in Hanover County, Va., December 20, 1733. His grandfather, Thomas Rice, who was an Englishman, but of Welsh extraction, migrated to Virginia at an early period. Having had a considerable estate left to him in England, he crossed the ocean with a view to receive it, but never returned; and it was supposed that he was assassinated on board the ship on which he took passage. He left in Virginia a widow with a large family of children, one of whom, *David*, was the father of the subject of this notice. He was a plain farmer, and both he and his wife were members of the Established Church. They would never hold slaves; he, because he considered it unprofitable; she, because she considered it morally wrong.

Their son, *David*, had religious impressions from a very early period, which never left him until he was hopefully the subject of a genuine conversion. He lived in a congregation which was under the pastoral care of the Rev. John Todd, and was occasionally, especially at Communion seasons, served by that eminent man, the Rev. Samuel Davies; and it was by the ministrations of the latter particularly, that he believed himself to have been savingly benefitted. He began his classical studies under Mr. Todd, and continued them under the Rev. James Waddel, D. D. "It seems probable, however," says the Rev. Dr. Archibald Alexander, who had the best means of forming a judgment on the subject, "that James Waddel was the teacher of the school kept at Mr. Todd's; and that the facts are that Mr. Rice began his studies before Mr. Waddel arrived, and completed his preparatory course under this teacher at the house of the Rev. John Todd; for it is believed that Mr. Waddel never taught a school any where else in Virginia, until long after Mr. Rice was graduated and licensed."

Mr. Davies having been appointed President of New Jersey College, Mr. Rice accompanied him thither in 1759, and became a member of the Junior class. Having taken the degree of Bachelor of Arts in 1761, he returned to Virginia, and studied Theology under the Rev. John Todd, and was licensed to preach by the Presbytery of Hanover, in November, 1762.

The first field of his evangelical labours was in the Southern part of Virginia and the Northern part of North Carolina. After labouring here, not without some evidence of success, for about six months, he visited Pennsylvania, where, agreeably to a previous engagement, he married Mary, daughter of the Rev. Samuel Blair. Thence he returned to Virginia, with the purpose of settling in North Carolina; but stopping at Hanover, then vacant by the removal of Mr. Davies, he received a call to settle there, and, having accepted it, was ordained and installed in December, 1763, at the age of thirty.

Here he laboured four or five years with considerable success, though his own impression was that his ministry accomplished more for the blacks than the whites. But an old dispute between two of the principal elders, which

* Memoir by Dr. Bishop.—Foote's Sketches, of Va. II.—Davidson's Hist. Presb. Ch. Ky.—MSS. from his relatives and Rev. Dr. Archibald Alexander.

originated in the time of Mr. Davies, having been revived,—in consequence of which the congregation were likely to be embarrassed in respect to his support, he obtained from the Presbytery a dissolution of his pastoral relation. He hated contention, was subject to depression of spirits, and was often fearful of the worst; and this probably had much to do with his determination to seek another field of labour. The separation from his charge was a painful event both to him and to them; for they were mutually and warmly attached.

After giving up his charge, Mr. Rice remained, for two or three years, unsettled, though he was, during this period, employed in his Master's work, as opportunity offered. At length he determined to fix himself in Bedford County, Va.,—a new and frontier settlement, in a mountainous region, with a population drawn from various parts of the world, and representing nearly all religious denominations. Here he took charge of three congregations; one of which was five, another eleven, and another twenty-five, miles from his dwelling. The last mentioned was called "the Peaks," as being near the Peaks of Otter. Here his labours were greatly blessed: without any extraordinary excitement, there was a lively and healthful state of religious feeling, and an earnest attention to the preaching of the word, which lasted, without any perceptible decline, for ten years. All classes and denominations were fond of attending his ministry. In due time, this congregation became sufficiently numerous to require all his labours, and, accordingly, he gave up the others and confined his attention to this. His ministry here was during the war of the Revolution, when many other congregations were scattered and separated from their pastors. It was much to the praise of the people that, during this disastrous period, they fulfilled their pecuniary engagements to him with punctuality.

When Kentucky was opened for settlement, Mr. Rice paid an early visit to that country, thinking it possible, as he had a rising family, that it might be his duty to remove thither, with reference to the more advantageous settlement of his children. His impression at first was adverse to a removal, and he returned to Virginia, resolved not to attempt it. In consequence, however, of some change of circumstances, particularly of his receiving a request, signed by some three hundred persons, to come and take charge of a religious Society in that region, he changed his purpose, and determined to cast in his lot with the new settlers of the West. He, accordingly, migrated thither in October, 1783.

The difficulties which he had to encounter, as a minister of the Gospel in this new country, were many and formidable. He took no special charge the first year; but, at the commencement of the second, a congregation was organized in what is now called Mercer County, with as much formality as circumstances would admit. They had three places of worship, which were known by the names of Danville, Cane-Run, and the Forks of Dick's River.

In this extensive field Mr. Rice laboured statedly and assiduously for fifteen years. He was now sixty-five years of age, and was troubled with an affection of the head, which incapacitated him for close and continuous thought, and subjected him to an almost habitual melancholy. He was also not a little tried by pecuniary embarrassments. He had purchased land, on the faith of his congregation guaranteeing the payment, which, however, was so long deferred, if not entirely forgotten, that the good man and his family would have been actually reduced to want, had it not been for the seasonable and kindly interposition of a benevolent individual in the neighbourhood.

Under these circumstances, in 1798, he removed to Green County, then a new settlement in the Southern part of Kentucky. He did not, however, take a pastoral charge, or attend much on Church courts, though he preached frequently, in the way of assisting his brethren, and of supplying vacant congregations. In 1805 and 1806, he performed an extensive missionary tour through Kentucky and Ohio, by appointment of the General Assembly, with a view to ascertain particularly the religious condition of the country. After his return, he addressed an Epistle to the Presbyterians of Kentucky, published the same year, and afterwards, in 1808, a Second Epistle, warning them with great fidelity and solemnity against what he believed to be the prevailing errors of the times.

During the last three years of his life, he was prevented from preaching and writing almost entirely. He had no complaints except what arose from the regular decay of nature, till the beginning of the year 1815, when he had a slight apoplectic stroke, from the effects of which he never recovered. On the day that completed his eightieth year, he preached, at his own house, his last sermon on Psalm xc. 12: "So teach us to number our days that we may apply our hearts unto wisdom." After this, he made no more appointments, except on the occasion of hearing of the death of his son, Dr. David Rice of Virginia, when he made a solemn address to his neighbours assembled at his dwelling. About the first of February preceding his death, he was seized with a difficulty of breathing, which he received as an admonition that his end was near. Early in the succeeding May, he was attacked with something like influenza, accompanied with fever and pain; and from this time till the close of his life, he had scarcely a momentary respite from bodily suffering. But he had the utmost tranquillity of mind, in the prospect of his departure, and his last expressions indicated an impatience to be absent from the body, that he might be present with the Lord. He died on the 18th of June, 1816, in the eighty-third year of his age. His excellent wife died a few years before him. They had eleven children,—six sons and five daughters. One of the daughters was married to the Rev. James Mitchel, and still (1857) survives, at the advanced age of more than ninety.

Mr. Rice was always the friend of liberal learning, and in more instances than one exerted himself in founding Seminaries. While in Virginia, he took an active part in the establishment of Hampden Sidney College, and had an important agency in obtaining the first two Presidents,—the Rev. Samuel Stanhope Smith, and the Rev. John Blair Smith. He was one of the first Trustees of the Transylvania University, and President of the Board from 1783 to 1787. The first Grammar School in Kentucky was opened in his house, in Lincoln County, in November, 1784.

The following is a list of Mr. Rice's publications:—

An Essay on Baptism, 1789. [This was probably the first pamphlet originating in Kentucky. It was printed in Baltimore.] A Lecture on Divine Decrees, 1791. Slavery inconsistent with justice and policy, 1792. A Sermon at the opening of the Synod of Kentucky, 1803. An Epistle to the Citizens of Kentucky, professing Christianity, especially those that are or have been denominated Presbyterians, 1805. A second Epistle, &c.,

1808. Letters on the Evidences, Nature, and Effects, of Christianity—composed for the use of his sons in 1812, in the seventy-ninth year of his age, and published in the Weekly Recorder for 1814.

FROM THE REV. THOMAS CLELAND, D. D.

SALVISA, Ky., March 20, 1852.

Dear Sir: I regret that my advanced age does not allow me to do all that I could wish in answer to your request; for, as David says,—"My strength faileth," both intellectual and physical; and yet I cannot refuse to give you, in the most general manner, my impressions concerning the venerable man in respect to whom you inquire. I had once a pretty good opportunity of knowing him, however little ability I now have of communicating the result of my observations.

Father Rice (for this is the appellation by which he is generally known) could hardly be considered as possessing talents of a very commanding order, though they were certainly highly respectable, and eminently adapted to usefulness. His distinguishing characteristic was sound judgment, and his disposition was conservative. He was remarkable for both the spirit and the habit of devotion. You could not be long in his company, without being deeply impressed with the idea that his affections had a strong tendency toward Heaven. In his general intercourse with society he was dignified and grave,—perhaps above most ministers of his day; insomuch that young people generally felt little freedom in his presence; but it was a characteristic of that period that ministers usually carried themselves with more reserve, and were less accessible to al. classes, and on all occasions, than they are now. He did, however, occasionally, unbend in familiar intercourse, and would, now and then, enliven conversation with an agreeable anecdote. He was a deeply earnest and effective preacher, delivering solemn and impressive thoughts in a solemn and impressive manner; and yet the effect of his manner was somewhat diminished by his occasionally taking on a sympathetic tone, which, to many of his hearers, seemed like a departure from the simplicity of nature. He had great executive powers, and he exerted them, in various ways, for the general improvement of the community in which he lived. He was not only eminently faithful in his stated ministrations, but acted the part of a father to the infant churches of Kentucky, besides devoting some share of his attention to literature and even politics.

Mr. Rice was tall and slender in person, quiet in his movements, and even at the age of seventy, he exhibited a remarkable degree of alertness. At that advanced period, I may safely say that no minister in Kentucky filled a wider space than he did. He was not like the eccentric comet, with its long fiery tail, which attracts the gaze and awakens the speculations of beholders for a few days and then disappears, but as the glorious sun, which, by its regular and constant influences, enriches our fields, illumines our horizon, and gladdens our hearts.

Affectionately yours,

THOMAS CLELAND.

ALEXANDER HEWAT, D. D.

1763—1776.

FROM THE REV. THOMAS SMYTH, D. D.

CHARLESTON, S. C., May 22, 1857.

My dear Sir: Your patient and patriotic labours, though most timely and even early, are nevertheless too late, as it regards many of the fathers, the founders of our Church. Many of these were men of note in their native land, thoroughly instructed in all the learning of the age, endued with heavenly gifts, and capable of occupying, as burning and shining lights, the most prominent positions. They left home, and country, and prospects, and not unfrequently positions of eminence, in the spirit of true missionary, self-sacrificing zeal. They were willing for a season to be obscure and unknown, having their record on high, and leaving their names written upon the fleshly tables of hearts regenerated and saved through their instrumentality, and in the book of God's remembrance. They sleep in our silent grave yards, around the sanctuaries erected for them in the wilderness, now often deserted for more convenient locations, and left to mouldering decay. In some cases, not even a stone marks the spot of burial—more frequently, where a rude stone, procured with difficulty, stands as a monument of the veneration of their bereaved flocks, no carved line tells the story of their lives. Living in tents or log cabins, and amid the daily vicissitudes of frontier life and Indian treachery, they had but little opportunity for study, and no inducements to write or publish.

As the winds that still breathe their soft requiem through the pine groves of the forest, collect the scattered leaves in some quiet eddy, there to slumber in decay, so will there be sometimes found garnered in the silent chambers of home, heart, public document, or private letter, fading memories of these forgotten worthies, waking up, like the echo of a far off trumpet heard amid the vallies of a range of hills, the tenderest emotions of the soul.

To these I love to listen, and these forest nooks I delight to visit. They are fruitful of suggestion, and pregnant with the most healthful and hopeful lessons. They link the past to the present, and the present to the future. They give reality to the unity of the Church in all ages. They enrol us among the glorious procession of the servants of God who have preceded us, and as they sowed the good seed, watered it with tears and prayers, and cultivated it with the most assiduous toil, and we have entered into their labours, so are we, while reaping their harvest, preparing the crop for a future in-gathering.

Surely, if every adventurous attempt to trace up the Nile to its source, and to fathom the depths of the African desert, is commendable, much more should every endeavour to glean the scattered leaves of traditionary history, and to interpret the soft, dying echoes of its distant events, be welcome to every Christian heart. You will, I hope, be encouraged in your artistic efforts to reproduce to the present and future generations the portraits of many of those prophets of the Lord, who, as the voice of one crying in the wilderness, have prepared the way for this glorious day of our country's progress in political and Christian civilization, and who, being dead shall thus continue to speak to us, and to look down encouragingly upon those who are bearing the burden and heat of the day.

Among the numerous names that dignify the early history of the Presbyterian Church in South Carolina, is that of its distinguished Historian, Alexander Hewat, who was born and educated in Scotland, and who, after occupying for many years the pastoral relation to the First—or as it is often called the Scotch—Presbyterian Church in the city of Charleston, returned to Great Britain,—for what causes is unknown, and most probably lived and laboured in London until his decease.

All that can be at present known concerning him from sources on this side the Atlantic, is contained in the following extract of a letter from my honourable friend, Mitchell King, a ruling elder in that church, and one of the oldest living residents in Charleston. His reminiscences and papers will constitute a very interesting and important chapter in the early history of our Church in this State. Judge King writes as follows:—

"The Rev. Dr. ALEXANDER HEWAT, the first Historian of South Carolina, was, it is believed, a native of Scotland. He received, as he tells us, (Sermons 1 vol. 386,) his grammatical education at Kelso. The first Presbyterian Church in Charleston, from the time of the Rev. Archibald Stobo,—a survivor of the ministers who accompanied the Scottish adventurers to the unfortunate Colony of New Caledonia, had usually been supplied with pastors from Scotland. Up to the time of the arrival of Stobo in Charleston, in 1700, the Presbyterians and Congregationalists had worshipped together. But within a few years after, they occupied different buildings, and adhered to the organization of their respective churches. The early Records of the First Presbyterian Church here—usually called, both before and since the Revolution, the Scotch Church—have not been carefully preserved, and only a few rather disconnected but authentic and precious relics of them remain. When the church required a minister, the congregation usually remitted funds to some friends in Scotland, to defray expenses, and solicited some distinguished gentlemen there to select and send an eligible pastor to them. This was, no doubt, done in the case of Dr. Hewat; as was afterwards done in the case of Buist. The Records of the Church in Dr. Hewat's own handwriting show that, on the 20th of March, 1763, he presided as Moderator at a meeting of the Session; and in the Record of the members of the St. Andrews' Society of Charleston, admitted in that year, his name is at the head of the list. From the day that he arrived in Charleston, until he finally left it, he continued devoted to his pastoral duties. The day on which he sailed, on his return to Europe, has not been ascertained. It appears from entries in the Records of the Church that he presided as Moderator at a meeting of the Session on the 22d of November, 1773, and again on the 23d of May, 1774. And on the 9th of May, 1775, it is recorded that the Rev. James Latta was married to Sarah Wilson—by virtue of a license from his Honour the Lieutenant Governor, (then the Honourable William Bull,) directed to the Rev. Alexander Hewat. So that no reasonable doubt can exist that on the 9th of May, 1775, he was still in Charleston. Indeed it is highly probable that he remained until some time in 1776; for, in his History, (2d vol. 299,) he states that the Capital of the South Carolina Society, in that year, "had arisen to a sum not less than £68,787 10s. 3d.;" and it is very unlikely that, after he left the country, he had the opportunity or the inclination to obtain such minute information. A tradition was prevalent fifty years ago among the senior members of his church—which is well recollected by some who are now seniors—that he was intimate in the family of Governor Bull, and was essentially aided by him in collecting the materials from which he wrote his History. It is believed that the near prospect of a war between the Colonies and the Mother country, induced him to leave South Carolina. His History appeared in London in 1779. His attachment to those who had been his flock in Carolina continued, and was cordially returned by them. The venerable Dr. Robert Wilson and Robert Rowand, who had been members of his Session from the time of his arrival, were spared to the Church for at least the first decade of the present century, and when the Congregation, in 1792, sent to Scotland for a pastor, Dr. Hewat was associated with the Rev. Doctors Robertson and Blair in the important commission. His absence from Edinburgh alone prevented him from joining in its execution. From this time until the 28th of September, 1820, we have little information of Dr. Hewat on which we can confidently rely, except what may be gleaned from his Sermons in two volumes, published in London in 1803–1805. He was married to a widow lady of Carolina, (Mrs. Burksdale,) who had visited Europe for the benefit of the health of two of her children.

"He certainly continued to correspond with some of his old friends. A copy of his Sermons sent to one of them, accompanied by a friendly letter, is now before the writer. But the friend to whom they were sent, has long since paid the debt of nature, and the letter is among the things that were. The Doctor is believed to have had a pastoral charge in or near London, and to have spent the latter part of his life principally in or near that city. On the 28th of September, 1820, from the Carolina Coffee House, Birchen Lane, Cornhill—a resort formerly well known to all gentlemen of Carolina who visited London, he addressed a letter to Mr. George Edwards, Charleston, S. C., and transmitted to him some memorials likely to interest him. That letter, by the kindness of a friend, has been presented to the Charleston Library Society, and is now preserved among their literary treasures. It is a touching proof of his affectionate memories, and closes in a manner worthy of a Christian minister—"Farewell, God bless you and all Friends in Carolina;" and that spirit animated him to the last. He is believed to have died in London in 1828, or early in 1829, and in his will he remembers the people of his Church in Charleston, and leaves them a legacy of £50 sterling, which, after the deduction of the English legacy duty, was, on the 4th of October, 1829, received by the Treasurer of the Church. An absence of more than fifty years had not chilled his affection for them, or effaced his relations to them from his memory. In his History of South Carolina, how unpretending soever it may be, he has erected a monument to himself that time will not destroy. May we not hope that the seeds of virtue and piety which in twelve years of faithful and acceptable ministry he planted among us, may, in obedience to the decrees of an overruling Providence, be yet producing good fruit, and lead to joyful recognitions between him and his Charleston friends in another and a better world.

The name of Dr. Alexander Hewat, or rather his surname *Hewat*, is an instance, to a very limited degree, of the differences that often occur in the spelling of proper names. No doubt can exist of the way in which he spelled his name. His entries by his own hand in the Record of the Presbyterian

Church of Charleston, his letter to Mr. Edwards, and the title pages of his published Sermons, leave no doubt that his uniform orthography was *Hewat.* It is so always given by the Historian, Dr. David Ramsay, who probably knew him well. Yet Mr. B. R. Carroll, in his valuable work—Historical Collections of South Carolina—always spells the name *Hewit;* and Watt, in that most laborious work,—Bibliotheca Britannica, gives us *Hewatt* as the author of the Sermons—*Hewit* as the author of the History. The mistake has probably arisen from the fact that the name of the author of the History was not given with it in 1779. There is not the least doubt that Dr. Alexander Hewat was the author of both the History and the Sermons.

The name of *Hewat* is not unknown in the early history of the Protestant Church of Scotland. In 1598, Mr. Peter Hewat, the precise orthography of our Hewat, was one of the ministers of the Presbyterian Church in Edinburgh. His name appears repeatedly in the 5th, 6th, and 7th volumes of Calderwood's History of the Kirk of Scotland, edited by the Wodrow Society, 1842, 1849. In July, 1617, he was tried at St. Andrews before James the First,—himself President of the Ecclesiastical Court, and condemned for opposing the Royal proclamation intended to impose Episcopacy upon Scotland. He was deprived,—(that is, deposed from his preferment,) and imprisoned in Dundee. Our Alexander Hewat may have been a descendant or kinsman of this Peter Hewat, as our Rev. Dr. John Forrest, now the Pastor of the Church once occupied by Dr. Alexander Hewat, is, I believe a descendant or kinsman of Thomas Forrest, Vicar of Dolor (Dollar,) who in February 1538–9 paid the penalty of martyrdom on the Castle Hill of Edinburgh for disobedience to what he believed to be the anti-christian commands of his ecclesiastical superiors. In 1617, James was urging Episcopacy on the good people of Scotland, and exercising that unhallowed authority which brought his son, the First Charles, to the scaffold, and in 1688 drove the second James and the legal heirs of the incorrigible and doomed race of Stuarts forever from the throne.

"It may be proper to remark that the surname of Peter Hewat in Calderwood, is occasionally spelled *Ewart*, but beyond doubt they belonged to the same man, and *Hewat* was the true common family name."

Judge King adds the following as a postscript to the letter of which the above is an extract:—

"Since writing the above, it has occurred to me to endeavour to verify the date of the arrival of Dr. Hewat in Carolina, by referring to some files of old newspapers which we have in the Charleston Library. I had so ascertained the time as to make an investigation for an indefinite period unnecessary. After spending nearly two weary hours in turning over the dusty numbers of the South Carolina Gazette for 1762–3–4, I discovered in a rather obscure place of the Gazette of the 5th and 12th of November, 1763, a notice of the arrival, in the course of the week, of the Rev. Mr. Hewitt for the Scots meeting. There can be no doubt that this is our Mr. Hewat. I know not how to reconcile this date with that of the 20th of March, 1763, in our old Church Records, which I still believe to be in his hand-writing. The entry of his name on the Roll of the St. Andrew's Society might very well have been made on the 30th of November, 1763. For he would in all probability join the Society at the next meeting after his arrival, on the day of the Patron Saint. The Pastor of the Scotch Church has generally, if not always, been the Chaplain of the Society."

I have little doubt that you have in the above extract, every thing concerning Dr. Hewat, that can now be recovered.

I remain very affectionately,

Yours in the Lord,

THOMAS SMYTH.

JOHN ROSBRUGH.*

1763—1777.

JOHN ROSBRUGH was born in Ireland in the year 1717; though his father's family had previously migrated thither from Scotland. He came to this country accompanied by a brother and sister in the year 1735. He was married early, and within less than a year lost his wife, who left an infant that survived her but a short time. This distressing bereavement was the means of awakening him to serious reflection, and of leading him to enter upon a religious life. He began now, though he was quite advanced in years, to turn his thoughts towards the Gospel ministry. He had already learned a trade; but had been so well educated in all the elementary branches, that he was capable of teaching a school; and it was by this means chiefly that he was enabled to prepare himself for College. He was graduated at the College of New Jersey in 1761, having, during his collegiate course, received aid from the fund for pious students collected by Tennent and Davies.

He studied Theology under the direction of the Rev. John Blair, then of Fagg's Manor. He was taken on trials by the New Brunswick Presbytery on the 22d of May, 1762, and was licensed to preach on the 18th of August, 1763. His first field of labour was in what is now Warren County, N. J.; and in October, 1764, he was called to Mansfield, Greenwich, and Oxford. He was ordained at Greenwich, December 11, 1764; was dismissed from the three congregations, April 18, 1769; and on the same day was called to the Forks of Delaware—Brainerd's "Irish settlement." [Forks West is now Allentown; Forks North is Mount Bethel.] The Synod transferred the Congregations in the Forks to the New Brunswick Presbytery, and he was installed as their pastor on the 28th of October, 1772. Here he remained during the rest of his life. He was married about 1766 to Jean, daughter of James Ralston, an elder in the Allentown Church. By this marriage he had five children.

Mr. Rosbrugh was a warm friend to his country's liberties, and finally fell a martyr to his patriotism. When Washington, with his dispirited and broken forces, retreated through New Jersey, before the superior army of the British, this excellent minister and devoted patriot joined with some of his neighbours of a like spirit, in forming a military company; and when they marched, he left his family and flock, and marched with them, in the capacity of a private soldier, and, like the rest, bearing his own musket. At Philadelphia he received the commission of a Chaplain to the regiment

* Notices in the Presbyterian by Rev. Archibald Alexander, D. D.—MSS. from Mr. Rosbrugh's his family, Rev. Smith Sturges, and Rev. Richard Webster.

to which these troops were attached. They joined the American army when retreating, and were in the rear of the army when several skirmishes took place with the advanced guards of the British. Mr. Rosbrugh proceeded with his company to Trenton; and, as he was going towards the river in search of his horse, he was met by a company of Hessians under British command. He immediately gave himself up as a prisoner, but begged, for the sake of his dear wife and children, that they would spare his life. He quickly found, however, that his request was to be denied, and that the bloody deed was to be performed without delay. He instantly knelt down, and, in imitation of his blessed Master, prayed for the forgiveness of his murderers. And scarcely had this prayer passed from his lips, before a deadly weapon pierced his body, and he lay struggling in death. They then took his watch, and part of his clothing, and left him weltering in his blood. The wretched creature who had committed the act, or had had a principal part in it, went, immediately after, with the fury of a madman, into one of the hotels in Trenton, and profanely boasted to the woman who kept it, that he had killed a rebel minister, and showed her his watch; but he added that it was too bad that he should have been praying for them while they were murdering him. "Oh," said she, "you have made bad work for his poor family." He answered with a frightful curse—"If you say another word, I will run you through." He then took up his sword and ran off, like a distracted person, and reported what he had done, to some of the British officers, who, it was said, justified and applauded the deed. Meanwhile a young man by the name of John Hayes, of Mr. Rosbrugh's congregation, took charge of the corpse, and buried it the next day in an obscure place in Trenton. The Rev. George Duffield of Philadelphia, having heard of the sad event, took measures to have the body removed to the church yard for its final interment. His widow, who had been informed of what had happened, by her brother, James Ralston,—then a member of the Provincial Congress, immediately came on, and saw the corpse of her husband; but the face was so mangled, and in every respect changed, that she found it difficult to recognise it. It was reported, at the time, that his murderers suspected, when they killed him, that it was Caldwell, whose glowing patriotism and commanding influence had rendered him specially obnoxious to the enemies of his country. His death took place in the early part of January, 1777. There is no monument to mark the place of his grave; nor is it possible in any way to identify it. The tradition is that Mr. Rosbrugh was "an able and eloquent preacher, though a defect in speech caused him sometimes to stammer."

FROM MRS. LETTICE RALSTON.

DANSVILLE, N. Y., December 28, 1850.

Rev. and dear Sir: It is but little that I can tell you of my revered father, from my own personal knowledge, as he died when I was only eight years old. But I have still some cherished recollections of him, which I am quite willing to communicate to you. The scene which imprinted itself more deeply upon my memory and my heart than any other in my earlier, and perhaps I may say my later, years, was his taking leave of his family, when he was going on that last fatal expedition. It almost broke my heart to witness his parting with my mother She threw her arms about his neck, and clung to him with such affectionate tenacity, that his own fortitude actually gave way, and he was obliged, by an almost violent effort, to disengage himself, and hurry out of the house. I saw him for the last time when he mounted his horse, and rode away to meet his company. It was only about two weeks before the astounding news of his death came back to us; and you can imagine what a dark day that was for his family. Our house was immediately filled with our neighbours and friends, who came to condole with us; and indeed the whole congregation seemed like a congregation of mourners. It is not easy to conceive of expressions of stronger attachment to a pastor, or of deeper sympathy with surviving relatives, than were witnessed on that occasion.

My mother told me that he had said that it had been impressed upon his mind for more than a year that he had but a short time to live: still he was the very picture of health, and she used to tell him that the way to get rid of such forebodings was to look in the glass. He was evidently, in the prospect of leaving home, not without serious apprehensions that he should never return. He wrote his will the night before he left us,—of which the following is an extract:—"Having received many and singular blessings from Almighty God in this land of my pilgrimage; more especially a loving and a faithful wife, and five promising children, I do leave and bequeath them all to the protection, mercy, and grace of God, from whom I received them. Being encouraged thereunto by God's gracious direction, and faithful promise—Jeremiah xlix. 11.—"Leave thy fatherless children, I will preserve them alive, and let thy widows trust in me."

After leaving home, my father wrote three letters to my mother, all of which breathe a spirit of glowing patriotism, as well as conjugal tenderness, and fervent piety. The last letter, which is dated December 27, 1776, is as follows:—

"My dear: I am still yours. I have but a minute to tell you that the company are all well. We are going over to attack the enemy. You would think it strange to see your husband, an old man, riding with a French fusee slung at his back. *This may be the last you shall ever receive from your husband.* I have committed myself, you, and the dear pledges of our mutual love, to God. As I am out of doors, I can write no more. I send my compliments to you, my dear, and to the children. Friends, pray for us. I am your loving husband."

In regard to my father's personal appearance, if I may trust either my own memory, or the testimony of many of his contemporaries, I may say that he was somewhat above the middle size, and altogether a portly, noble, fine looking man. His natural disposition was cheerful and lively, and he greatly enjoyed social life. As a preacher, I feel myself incompetent to speak of him any further than to say that he never read his sermons in the pulpit, and so far as I know, never wrote but one fully. He usually preached from short notes, many of which, together with the one finished discourse, are still in existence. I have always understood that he was greatly beloved by the people of his several congregations. A good old man,—an elder in the church in Allentown, has often told me how careful my father was to attend to all his pastoral duties. If any among his flock were sick, the physician was not more attentive than he; and if he saw any root of bitterness springing up among his people, he would not rest until the evil was effectually removed. From the statements received from him and others, I infer that there was perhaps nothing for which my father was more distinguished than his love of peace, and his ever vigilant and untiring efforts to promote it.

I cannot forbear to say a word of my dear sainted mother. From the time that she became a widow, she had but a feeble and broken constitution; but she was eminently faithful in the discharge of parental duty, carefully instructing and counselling her children, and endeavouring to imbue their minds with the knowledge and fear of God. She regularly maintained family worship, night and morning, by reading the Scriptures, singing, and prayer. I shall never forget the fervent prayer she offered the morning I left home to come to this State, that if we should never meet again on earth, we might meet where there will be no painful separations. To my great loss, but to her unspeakable gain, she died the following spring. She was one of the best of wives and mothers.

Affectionately and truly,

LETTICE RALSTON.

PATRICK ALLISON, D. D.

1763—1802.

FROM ROBERT PURVIANCE, ESQ.

BALTIMORE, 5th June, 1850

Dear Sir: Your letter, requesting some biographical notices, in connection with my personal recollections, of the Rev. Dr. Allison, formerly of this city, has been duly received; and I am the more willing to comply with your request from the fact that nearly all his contemporaries are gone, and if I were to decline, I should scarcely know to whom to refer you for the accomplishment of your wish. Indeed I acknowledge it is no unpleasant task to me to aid, in any degree, in perpetuating the memory of that venerable and eminent man. I was taught, from my childhood, to regard him with affection and reverence, and my earliest and best impressions were received under his ministrations.

PATRICK ALLISON was born in Lancaster County, Pa., in the year 1740. His father was a respectable farmer of that county, and was, I believe, a native of Ireland. He had several sons, and one or two daughters. As the sons grew up, his fortune not being sufficiently large to give to each a liberal education, and to leave an adequate portion besides, he proposed to them to commute what he intended to give them, for an education, which they were to consider as a discharge from any further claim on his estate. Patrick was the only one who accepted the commutation; and this became his only patrimony. He was, accordingly, by his own choice, sent to the University of Pennsylvania, at which, having very honourably sustained himself, he was graduated in 1760. He commenced his theological studies shortly after he left the University; but in 1761, was appointed Professor in the Academy at Newark, De., which office he accepted. He was licensed to preach, by the Second Presbytery of Philadelphia, in March, 1763. In August of that year, a few Presbyterians from Pennsylvania, who had, the year before, erected a log church in Baltimore, then containing between thirty and forty houses, and some three hundred inhabitants, sent a request to the Presbytery of Philadelphia that Mr. Allison, who had previously preached to them, might be appointed to supply their pulpit, on a salary of one hundred pounds *per annum*. He was, at this time, connected with the Newark Academy, at which several young gentlemen from Baltimore were pursuing their studies; and I rather think they were instrumental in directing the attention of the infant congregation towards him. Mr. Allison expressing his willingness to go, although he had a call to a larger church in Newcastle, De.,—the Presbytery complied with the request. He was ordained in Philadelphia, by the same Presbytery that licensed him, in 1765, but does not appear to have been ever installed in Baltimore, though he was always regarded as the pastor, during the long period that he continued to serve the congregation. He officiated at first, for some time, in a small edifice, to not more, it is supposed, than six families. In a few years, the number had so far increased as to require the erection of a new place of worship; to which, not long after, an addition was made to accommodate the influx of worshippers; and subsequently *that* was pulled down, and the present edifice erected,—one of the most expensive and elegant structures of that day.

Mr. Allison received the degree of Doctor of Divinity from the University of Pennsylvania in 1782.

Dr. Allison was married in March, 1787, to Wellary, daughter of William Buchanan, a gentleman who distinguished himself by his civil services during the war of the Revolution. She survived him about twenty years. He left an only child,—a daughter, who intermarried with Mr. George I. Brown, and died in 1849, leaving six children, the eldest of whom is quite eminent as a lawyer at our Bar.

The division which occurred in the Presbyterian Church into Old and New Side, had been healed a few years before he entered the ministry: his sympathies, however, on the controverted points, were strongly with the Old Side; and it is probable that this circumstance may have given, to some extent, the hue to his public character.

During the Revolutionary war, Dr. Allison felt that the great question at issue affected the interests of religion, as truly as any other interests which claimed the protection of society. He never concealed his own patriotic spirit, and lost no proper occasion to stimulate his countrymen to an unyielding resistance to the oppressions to which they were subjected. In the winter of 1776, Congress was removed to Baltimore; and this furnished him with many opportunities of exhibiting his warm devotion to his country. He became so popular with a large portion of the members, that he was often the object of their kind inquiries, after the removal of the body to another place. He was intimately acquainted with General Washington, and so great was the reverence with which he regarded his character, that the news of the General's death produced such an effect upon him, that his family felt a momentary apprehension in respect to the result.

Dr. Allison's connection with his church continued about thirty-five years. A year or two after he commenced his ministry, he received a call to become the Pastor of a Church in Philadelphia; but so earnest was the opposition made by his own flock to his acceptance of it, that he declined it almost immediately, and resolved to live and die with the people among whom Providence had already cast his lot. About two years previous to his death, his health began to decline, and, under the conviction that he should be inadequate to the discharge of his ministerial duties, he determined at once to relinquish his charge. Without previous consultation with any one, he announced this determination on a Sabbath, after preaching a sermon which gave no token of any thing like approaching intellectual decay. I was present when the announcement was made, and can never forget the almost electric shock which it sent through the assembly. The congregation utterly declined to accept his resignation, and, in compliance with their urgent wishes, he consented to retain the pastoral relation; though they proceeded, as soon as possible, to provide him with a colleague. Shortly after this, he made a journey to one of our western watering places, and returned with his health so much improved, that, on the succeeding Sunday, he preached, taking for his text the appropriate language of the Psalmist,—"Why art thou cast down, O my soul, and why art thou disquieted within me? Hope thou in God; for I shall yet praise Him who is the health of my countenance and my God."

Dr. Allison's disease was an affection of the nervous system, which had been gradually developing itself for some years, before it was perceived to have any material effect upon his mind. The first indication of this was in connection with the Sermon which he preached on the death of Washington. By request of his congregation, he yielded a copy of it for the press; and it came forth, very indifferently printed, and withal marred by some typographical errors. This circumstance, so trifling in itself, was observed to have a very great and disproportionate effect upon the Doctor's mind; and it was found impossible to account for it, without supposing some nervous derangement that had not before been perceptible, but which afterwards developed itself in the form of an incurable malady. Some few months before his death, it was thought desirable that he should be placed in a situation, where medical treatment could be more successfully applied than at home; and this was accordingly done. In three or four months, his mind seemed to have regained nearly its accustomed tone, but his frame was so shattered, as well by the medical treatment to which he had been subjected, as by the long continuance of his disease, that he sunk into the grave within two months after his return home. A short time before his death, he expressed a wish to close his eyes himself, at that solemn moment, and intimated, at the same time, to a lady who was kindly ministering around his death-bed, that when he felt himself about to make the transition, he would let her know it. Accordingly, just before the last moment came, he gave the promised intimation to his friend; he was assisted in raising his hands to close his eyes; and the place which had known him knew him no more. He died August 21, 1802, aged about sixty-two. Dr. Inglis paid a suitable tribute to his memory in a Funeral Sermon from I. Thess. iv. 13, which, some twenty years after, was published in a posthumous volume of Dr. I.'s Discourses.

Dr. Allison's personal appearance was highly commanding and impressive. He was of about the medium height, and in every way well proportioned. His manners combined grace with dignity in an uncommon degree,—so as to invite confidence on the one hand, and to repel all undue familiarity on the other. While there was nothing about him that savoured of ostentation, there was always that genuine self-respect, that considerate regard to circumstances, that cautious forbearance to give unnecessary pain, which never fail to secure to an individual a deferential respect from all with whom he associates. His moral character was entirely above reproach. Accustomed of course to move in the highest circles of society, he never forgot the sacredness of his calling, while yet he was a highly entertaining and agreeable companion. As he was himself remarkable for propriety of speech, he would never tolerate gross improprieties in others,—no matter what might be their standing in society; and if an expression bordering on profaneness, or even indecent levity, were uttered in his hearing, it was very sure to meet with a deserved rebuke. His intellectual character was universally acknowledged to be of a very high order. His early opportunities for the culture of his mind were among the best which the country then afforded;

and these, diligently improved, in connection with his fine natural powers, rendered him decidedly eminent even among the greater minds of his profession. He was always a diligent student; and his studies, instead of being strictly professional, took a wide range. He was an elegant belles lettres scholar, and was very familiar with both Ancient and Modern History. The versification of Pope, and the chaste beauties of Addison, had great attractions for him; and I rather think that the style of Robertson, the Historian, was the model on which he formed his own. His power of mental abstraction is said to have been so remarkable, that he experienced no interruption in the composition of a sermon, by the presence and conversation of company. In the delivery of his sermons he always had his manuscript before him; and though his manner could not be said to be attractive to a stranger, yet to those who were accustomed to it, it was very agreeable. His discourses were generally didactic, often profoundly argumentative. I once heard an Episcopal clergyman of some note expressing rather a low estimate of some of the ministers of the day, but of Dr. Allison he remarked with emphasis,—"*He* was a man of *matter*." He was especially eminent in the judicatories of the Church, and in all public bodies; being possessed of great penetration, the utmost self-control, and an admirable command of thought and language the most appropriate and elegant. I remember to have heard that Dr. Samuel Stanhope Smith, then President of Princeton College, remarked to a gentleman of our city,—"Dr. Allison is decidedly the ablest *statesman* we have in the General Assembly of the Presbyterian Church." And the late Dr. Miller of Princeton, as perhaps you are aware, has left behind him a similar testimony.

Dr. Allison, though he wrote but little for the press, yet sometimes wielded a pen of prodigious power. An occasion occurred, shortly after the Revolution, which led him to put forth his power as a controversial writer through the press, in defence of the great cause of equal rights among different denominations of Christians. During our Colonial dependance, the Episcopal Church in this State had been the favoured Church of the government; but the Revolution produced an important change in this respect, reducing the various religious denominations, in the eye of the government, to the same level. After the return of Peace, certain divines of the Episcopal Church invoked the aid of the Legislature, in reference to some matters of their own, in a way that seemed to recognise a distinction which the other denominations were not willing to concede to them; and the Legislature listened to their petition, and granted the desired aid. Dr. Allison regarding this legislative measure as characterized by an unworthy partiality, came out with a series of Essays over the signature, "Vindex," which contain a noble defence of religious liberty, and which procured an important modification and virtual defeat of the questionable bill. The following extract from one of these papers will show at once that he was a vigorous writer, and a champion for the cause of religious freedom:—

"An attempt of this sort will ever raise a powerful alarm, unless the people are enslaved or asleep. An attempt of this sort *has* raised a powerful alarm, and a prosecution of it shall, with the countenance of Heaven, be resolutely and successfully opposed."

In the conclusion of his introductory remarks, he says,—

"We have just accomplished a Revolution which is and will be the admiration of mankind, till all human glory passeth forever away. By our means, an uncommon illumination has spread over the whole civilized earth, penetrating even its dark and intolerant regions of gloomy superstition. The noblest prospects break around our enraptured views. We triumphantly anticipate degrees of national magnificence and grandeur, far superior to what the sun ever beheld. While the war continued, when weakening fear prevailed on almost every side, Maryland was distinguished by the wisdom and vigour of her councils, the unanimity of her citizens, the number and valour of her troops. Shall she tarnish her dear bought honours, and descend from her well earned fame? Shall she obscure the splendour of 'America's rising' by an admission of unjust distinctions and impolitic discriminations, which encroach upon the indefeasible privileges of her resolute, virtuous, obedient citizens? It must not, cannot, shall not, be. Their own liberal contributions and intrepid exertions in the late hostile scene, say, no; the blood of numerous heroes shed for equal, impartial liberty, says, no; an immortal leader says. no, who has been the chosen instrument of doing more for the salvation of his country, than ever before fell to the lot of a human being,—who has saved her to be an asylum for the poor and oppressed of all nations and religions, and who would have the residue of his days embittered by incurable anguish, if, looking across the river that enriches and adorns his peaceful retreat, he should behold ecclesiastical usurpation raising her hideous head, and spreading her hateful, malignant influence around; the God of Heaven says, no, who having heretofore signally interposed in their favour, and entrusted to their keeping the fair inheritance of impartial freedom, expects and commands them to stand fast in the liberty wherewith He has made them free."

About the year 1791 or 1792, an incident occurred, which brought Dr. Allison before the world in defence of American Protestantism. Dr. Carroll, who was a Roman Catholic divine, and who had also been so conspicuous as a patriot during the Revolutionary war, that he had been selected by Congress to act in the capacity of Secretary to the Mission to Canada, to induce that Province to join with the United States in their struggle against Great Britain,—had been appointed by the Pope, about the year 1789, the first Catholic Bishop in America. It became necessary for him to go to Europe to receive consecration, as that ceremony could not, at that time, be performed in this country. He went to London, and the Pope's Nuncio in that city was empowered to bestow it upon him. In the year 1790, he returned to his people in the new character of Bishop, to whom before he had been known only as a Priest. Dr. Carroll had been always highly esteemed by all denominations in Baltimore, as well for his decided patriotism, as for his exemplary Christian character; and Dr. Allison had long been on terms of great intimacy with him. It was very soon made known, after he had entered upon his new duties, that the title he assumed was *John, Bishop of Baltimore;* and to one who had shown himself so stern an advocate of religious liberty, and the equal rights of all denominations as Dr. Allison had done, it seemed too expressive of exclusiveness and supremacy, to be allowed to pass without animadversion. He accordingly arraigned it at the bar of public opinion, in a series of able Essays; though he aimed at nothing more than to show that, however much importance the Church which had adopted the title might ascribe to it, it was really worth no more than plain *Doctor* or *Mr.* in an unpretending Protestant Church.

I ought to add that Dr. Allison sustained all the domestic relations with the utmost dignity and affection: a more devoted husband and father than he was, it would be difficult to find. In the evening of his days, while his mind was undergoing the sad eclipse to which I have referred, he never intermitted family worship; and conducted it in such a manner as not to indicate the slightest mental aberration. His great aversion to appearing as an author induced him to leave, as one of his dying injunctions, that all his manuscript sermons should be committed to the flames: otherwise I doubt not there might have been a selection made from them for the press, which would have done honour to our American pulpit.

Dr. Allison's name is intimately associated, not only with the early history of the congregation of which he was pastor, but with many important measures of the Presbyterian Church, and with much that was done in his day for the general improvement of this city, and of society at large. From the origin of the Baltimore Presbytery, he was its leading member until he died. He was Chairman of the Committee of the Presbyterian Church on Psalmody, and a member of other leading committees at the organization of the General Assembly. He was one of the original founders of the Baltimore College and the Baltimore Library. He was also an active member of the Convention, that met first at Elizabethtown, in 1766, to oppose the establishment of Episcopacy in this country. Nearly half a century has elapsed since he passed away; but the memory of his talents and virtues is still fresh in some minds, and I rejoice that you are disposed to transmit some enduring notice of his life and character to future generations.

I am, with great respect,

Dear Sir, your obedient servant,

ROBERT PURVIANCE.

FROM THE REV. MATTHEW BROWN, D. D.,

PRESIDENT OF JEFFERSON COLLEGE.

CANNONSBURG, June 26, 1848.

Rev. and dear Sir: I regret that my personal knowledge of Dr. Allison of Baltimore is quite too limited to avail for the purpose which your request contemplates. I never saw him but once, though he certainly then made an impression upon me which the lapse of about half a century has left almost as distinct as ever.

The occasion on which I saw him, was a meeting of the Presbytery of Carlisle, at which he had been invited to sit as a corresponding member. It was about the time that I was licensed to preach; and knowing, as I did, the high standing of Dr. Allison in the Church, I was glad of an opportunity of even seeing him. Fortunately, something came up in the deliberations of the Presbytery, that drew from him some remarks; and, though he did not attempt any thing like a set speech, he said enough fully to justify the exalted opinion that I had previously formed of his great parliamentary skill and power. His personal appearance was remarkably dignified and commanding, and impressed me at once with the idea of intellectual superiority. His attitude, gesture, every thing pertaining to his manner, was in a high degree impressive, and seemed hardly to admit of improvement. And nothing could exceed the appropriateness and graceful elegance of his remarks. I have heard him spoken of by some of the fathers,—particularly the late Dr. John King; and they all agreed in ascribing to him talents and accomplishments of the highest order; though I am inclined to think that a deliberative body, rather than the pulpit, called them forth to the best advantage. On the floor of the General Assembly, I have often heard it said that he had no superior; and though he did not always carry conviction to all who heard him, it was not for want of the highest skill and address in managing his subject. Nearly all who have distinct recollections of him have passed away, but there must be a few still living who can tell you more about him than

Your friend and servant,

MATTHEW BROWN.

DAVID CALDWELL, D. D.*

1763—1824.

DAVID CALDWELL, the eldest son of Andrew and Martha Caldwell, was born in Lancaster County, Pa., March 22, 1725. His father was a farmer in comfortable circumstances, and was much esteemed in the neighbourhood in which he lived. The son, after receiving the rudiments of an English education, served an apprenticeship to a house carpenter; and he subsequently worked at the business four years, in the capacity of a journeyman. At the age of about twenty-five, he believed himself the subject of a true conversion, and made a public profession of his faith in Christ. Having resolved to devote himself to the ministry, he immediately commenced a course of study with a view to a collegiate education. Part of his preparatory course at least was under the instruction of the Rev. Robert Smith of Pequea, Pa. He was graduated at Princeton in 1761,—the year in which President Davies died; and he has been heard to say that he assisted in carrying him to his grave.

After leaving College, he was engaged, for a year, in teaching a school at Cape May; at the same time occupying his hours of leisure in the study of Theology. When the year had expired, he returned to Princeton, with a view to devote himself more exclusively to his preparation for the ministry; but, during a part of the time of his residence there, he acted as assistant teacher in College, in the department of languages. He was taken under the care of the New Brunswick Presbytery at its meeting in Princeton, September 28, 1762, and was licensed to preach the Gospel, by the same Presbytery, and at the same place, on the 8th of June, 1763.

Having supplied several vacancies within the bounds of the Presbytery that licensed him, he was commissioned by the Synod to spend at least one year as a missionary in North Carolina, and the Presbytery were ordered to ordain him with reference to this mission. He seems to have visited North Carolina first in the summer, or early in the autumn, of 1764; and then to have returned to the North for ordination. He was ordained at Trenton, N. J., on the 6th of July, 1765,— the sermon being preached by the Rev. William Kirkpatrick.† A call to him had been laid before the Presbytery at a previous meeting, from the Congregations in Buffalo and Alamance settlements in North Carolina; in consequence of which, he was dismissed to join the Presbytery of Hanover in Virginia. The Congregations to which he was called, included a considerable number of his friends, who

* Memoir by Rev. Dr. Caruthers.—Foote's Sketches of N. C.—MS. from Rev. Dr. Hall.

† WILLIAM KIRKPATRICK was graduated at the College of New Jersey in 1757; was licensed to preach by the Presbytery of New Brunswick at Princeton, August 15, 1758; and was ordained *sine titulo*, at Cranberry, July 4, 1759. In March, 1760, he was sent, in answer to a petition made to Presbytery, to preach at Trenton. In April, 1761, the people of Trenton gave him a call; and in April, 1762, by the advice of Presbytery, he accepted it; but, for some reason or other, his installation was postponed; and in December, 1764, the Presbytery refused to install him on the ground of inadequate support. He continued, however, to preach there, the greater part of the time, till June, 1766, when he accepted a call from Amwell, N. J., where he was installed in August following. In 1767, he was chosen a member of the Board of Trustees of Princeton College, and held the office until his death, which occurred on the 8th of September, 1769, in the forty-third year of his age. He was Moderator of the Synod in 1769. Tradition represents him as an eloquent man, and distinguished for his piety and usefulness.

had emigrated from Pennsylvania to North Carolina, and some of whom had been thoughtful enough to bespeak his services as a minister, while he was yet only in a course of training for the sacred office. One of his congregations belonged to the Old Side, and the other to the New Side, of that day; but, by his discreet and cautious management, he was enabled to keep them in friendly relations with each other.

He proceeded to Carolina immediately after his ordination; but, for some reason that is not now known, did not immediately join the Hanover Presbytery, or accept the call of the two Churches. It was not till the 11th of October, 1767, that he was received as a member of the Presbytery, and not till the 3d of March, 1768, that he was installed Pastor of the Churches. The installation sermon was preached by the Rev. Hugh McAden.*

As the salary which his congregations promised him, was only two hundred dollars, he found it necessary to make some other provision for his support; and, accordingly, he purchased a small farm, and, about the same time, commenced a classical school in his own house, which he continued, with little interruption, till the infirmities of age disqualified him for teaching. The number of scholars generally ranged from fifty to sixty; and among them were many who have since held some of the most important places in both Church and State.

Mr. Caldwell, at an early period in his ministry, directed his attention to both the science and the practice of medicine. He profited, in this way, by the residence in his family, for a year, of a practising physician, as well as by a constant correspondence with Dr. Rush, between whom and himself there grew up an intimacy while they were together in College.

Mr. Caldwell was identified with some of the most terrible events of the war of the Revolution. The territory that constituted the field of his labours, was repeatedly a scene of terror and bloodshed. His house was plundered, his library and furniture destroyed, and the most vigorous and insidious efforts were made to overtake and arrest him, when he had fled for his life. His people, like himself, were generally earnest patriots, and some of them lost their lives in battle, while all were subjected to the severest trials and privations.

After the return of Peace, Mr. Caldwell, besides attending faithfully to his duties as teacher and preacher, had much to do, in a more private way, with the political concerns of the country. He had been a member of the Convention that formed the Constitution of the State of North Carolina, in 1776, and had voted for a provision which forbade his being a member of the Legislature, while he was a minister of the Gospel; but still he was at liberty to express his opinion in regard to the measures which the public welfare demanded; and his opinion always carried with it great weight. As a testimony of grateful respect for the various public services he had ren-

* HUGH MCADEN was born in Pennsylvania, though his parents were from the North of Ireland. He was graduated at the College of New Jersey in 1753; studied Theology under the Rev. John Blair; was licensed to preach by the Newcastle Presbytery in 1755; was ordained by the same Presbytery in 1757; was dismissed to join the Hanover Presbytery in 1759, and the same year became the minister of the Congregations of Duplin and New Hanover in North Carolina; and, having remained there about ten years, removed to Caswell County, chiefly for the sake of a better climate, where he died January 20, 1781, leaving a wife and seven children. He suffered, not a little, during the Revolution,—his house being ransacked, and many of the most valuable things it contained, particularly his papers, being destroyed by the enemy; and, within two weeks after his death, they were encamped in one of the churches in which he had been accustomed to preach. He is represented as having been remarkably exact in his habits, and an eminently faithful and laborious pastor and missionary.

dered, when the present system of District Courts went into operation,—notwithstanding there were many applicants for the office of Clerk of Guilford County, Mr. Caldwell's son, in whose behalf no application had been made, received the appointment under circumstances the most gratifying to both the son and the father.

When the University of North Carolina was established, in 1791, Mr. Caldwell, it is understood, had the offer of the Presidency; but, owing to his advanced age, and to the peculiar state of his family, he saw fit to decline it. In 1810, the Trustees of that institution testified their respect for his character by conferring upon him the degree of Doctor of Divinity.

When the great religious excitement took place throughout the Southern country, about the commencement of the present century, Dr. Caldwell, though he believed that it was, on the whole, a genuine work of Divine grace, yet was convinced also that there was much about it which could not approve itself to an enlightened Christian judgment. He ventured cautiously, and yet firmly, to express this opinion; and, as might be expected, he was, for a time, set down by many as among the doubtful friends of the revival.

Dr. Caldwell continued to preach in his two churches, unless prevented by inclement weather, till the year 1820, though his infirmities had become so great that it was often with difficulty that he could reach his house, after a public service. For two or three years previous to his death, he never left the plantation on which he resided; but, during the whole progress of his decline, he uniformly evinced the utmost patience, equanimity, and gratitude for the Divine goodness. His death, which took place on the 25th of August, 1824, was attended with so little suffering, that his friends scarcely realized that he had entered the dark valley, when they saw that life was extinct. Had he lived seven months longer, he would have completed a century. A Sermon, with reference to his death, was preached, by appointment of the Orange Presbytery, in the Buffalo Church, by the Rev. E. Currie, one of his former pupils, from Eccl. vii. 1.

In the latter part of the year 1766, he was married to Rachel, the third daughter of the Rev. Alexander Craighead, minister at Sugar Creek, N. C. They had a large family of children: three of the sons entered the ministry, and one, the medical profession. Dr. C. suffered severe domestic afflictions,—three of his children, and one of them a clergyman of great promise, becoming irrecoverably insane. Mrs. Caldwell survived her husband less than a year, and died in the triumph of Christian faith. A marble slab near the Buffalo Church designates the spot where their mortal remains repose.

A somewhat extended biography of Dr. Caldwell, by the Rev. E. W. Caruthers, D. D.,—was published in 1842, at the close of which are two of Dr. Caldwell's Sermons,—one entitled "The character and doom of the Sluggard;" the other, "The doctrine of Universal Salvation unscriptural."

FROM THE HON. J. M. MOREHEAD,

GOVERNOR OF NORTH CAROLINA.

GREENSBORO', N. C., 4th August, 1852.

Dear Sir: The Rev. Dr. Caldwell, concerning whom you ask for my reminiscences, can hardly be said to have lived in my generation, but he seems rather to have belonged to a generation or two preceding

In November, 1811, my father took me, then in my sixteenth year, with a good common English education, from his residence in the County of Rockingham, to Dr. Caldwell's,—a distance of some thirty miles, for the purpose of putting me under his care and instruction. I had heard so much of him as an instructer and disciplinarian, that I had conceived of him as a man of great personal dignity, with a face the scowl of which would annihilate the unlucky urchin who had not gotten his lesson well. So I approached his residence with fear and trembling. We found, a few hundred yards from his house, and near a little mill on a small branch,—built rather to serve as a hobby for amusement than for any more practical purpose, an exceedingly old gentleman, bowed down by some eighty-six or seven winters, enveloped in a large cape made of bear skin, with a net worsted cap on his head, (for the evening was cool,) and supporting himself with a cane not much shorter than his own body—this was Dr. Caldwell. My fears of him and his authority were at once dissipated. The moment he was informed of our business, he remarked that he had long ago abandoned his school, and had taught but little since, and then only to oblige a neighbour or two; that he had no pupil at that time, and did not wish to engage in teaching again. My father reminded him of his promise made, many years before, and while he was not teaching, that he would educate his oldest son for him. The Doctor replied jocularly that he did not consider that that promise bound him to live always, that he might comply with it; and that my father ought to have presented his son long since. My father made some answer at which the Doctor laughed heartily, and said in a broad Scotch accent, which he often assumed, when he desired to be humorous, or to worry a laggard pupil with a bad lesson—"Weel mon, we must thry and see what we can do with the lad;" and turning to myself, said—"But mon, have ye an appetite for reading?" To which I replied, "I am not very hungry for it." The answer seemed to please him, and we then proceeded to his house.

I took boarding in the neighbourhood, and remained under his tuition until the fall of 1815, (losing a good deal of time, however, from the school,) when I went to the University of North Carolina, and was admitted a member of the Junior class. As I had nearly completed the prescribed course in the languages under Dr. Caldwell, I studied no Latin or Greek at the University, with the exception of Cicero, and that I studied privately.

I was not long in Dr. Caldwell's hands, before I became satisfied of his remarkable excellence as a teacher. He had but little to amuse him, except hearing my lessons. I applied myself to my studies with great zeal, with which he was much pleased; and often has he made me recite, from four to six hours a day, parsing every difficult word, and scanning nearly every line, when the recitation happened to be in any of the Latin poets. Indeed you could not get along with him, with any comfort, without knowing accurately and thoroughly every thing that you passed over.

The Rules of Prosody and Syntax in the Latin, and of Syntax in the Greek, with all the exceptions and notes, seemed to be as familiar to him as the alphabet. His memory had evidently failed to some extent; and I have sometimes found him, on my arrival in the morning, when I was studying the higher Latin and Greek classics, looking over my lesson for the day. He would apologize for doing so, by saying that his memory failed, and he was afraid I might *cork* him; meaning that I might ask him questions that he would not be able to answer. Hard words or difficult sentences in the various authors that he taught, seemed, for the most part, entirely familiar to him; and often, when he would ask me for a rule which I could not give, he would attempt to give it; and the phraseology having escaped his memory, he would bother at it, like a man with a tangled skein, searching for the end by which it can be unravelled, until some word or expression of his own would bring back to his memory some part of the rule, and then he would repeat the whole of it with great accuracy. Sometimes, when he could not repeat the rule in English, he would say—" Weel mon, let us thry the Latin;" and the Latin generally proved to be quite at his command.

Dr. Caldwell's course of studies in the languages,—Latin, Greek, and Hebrew, as well as in the sciences, was extensive for his day; and the facility and success with which he imparted his knowledge to others, in such extreme old age, was truly wonderful. Towards the latter part of the time that I was under his instruction, he had several more pupils, and among them was a student of medicine; and I noticed that he seemed just as familiar with that subject as any other.

During a part of the time that I was with him, he found great difficulty in reading, with the help of two pair of spectacles; but his sight returned subsequently, so that he could read the finest Greek print, without any glasses at all. I did not, however, observe much change in his intellect.

In stature, I suppose he must have measured about five feet, eight or ten inches; and in his younger days, he probably weighed from one hundred and seventy-five to two hundred pounds. He had a well formed head and strong features. He was an exceedingly studious man, as his great acquisitions in various departments of learning proved. The prominent characteristics of his mind were the power to acquire knowledge and retain it, and the power to apply it to useful and practical purposes. By some he was thought to be lacking in originality; but I think this questionable. He certainly possessed a strong mind; but the late day at which his education was commenced, the great extent and variety of his knowledge, and the active pursuits of his life, gave him but little time for that kind of reflection, without which originality of thought is not apt to be developed.

Dr. Caldwell was a man of admirable temper, fond of indulging in playful remarks, which he often pointed with a moral; kind to a fault to every human being, and I might say to every living creature, entitled to his kindness. He seemed to live to do good.

It would be difficult to duly appreciate his usefulness through his long life. His learning, his piety, and his patriotism, were infused into the generations of his day. An ardent Whig of the Revolution, he taught his people the duty they owed to their country as well as their God. Well do I remember, when, in 1814, the militia of Guilford were called together in this town to raise volunteers, or draft men to go to Norfolk, to have seen the old gentleman literally crawl up on the bench of the Court House to address the multitude, and in fervid and patriotic strains exhort them to be faithful to their country. The sermon had a powerful effect upon the soldiers. As an illustration, I may mention that a Quaker lad, who had been strictly educated in the faith of his denomination, after hearing the sermon, entered the ranks of the volunteers, served his tour, returned to the bosom of his own Church, which gladly received him, and lived and died an honoured and esteemed citizen.

From Dr. Caldwell's great age at the time I knew him, and the consequent failure of his voice, (never I think a very good one,) I could not form a very satisfactory opinion of his merits in the pulpit. All the sermons I ever heard him deliver were extemporaneous. But, if I were to hazard an opinion in respect to him as a preacher, in the vigour of his manhood, I should say he was a calm, strong, didactic reasoner, whose sermons were delivered with an earnestness that left no doubt with his hearers that he was uttering his own deep convictions, and with an unction that bore testimony to the Christian purity of his own heart.

Happy in the opportunity of thus bearing an humble testimony to the memory of my venerated friend I remain, your obedient servant,

J. M. MOREHEAD.

SAMUEL BLAIR, D. D.

1764—1818.

FROM THE REV. WILLIAM NEILL, D. D.

PHILADELPHIA, January 15, 1849.

My dear Brother: Agreeably to your request, I send you the following brief notice of the late Dr. Blair. I was not intimately acquainted with him; but having resided in Germantown, and preached some years in the house of worship which he very generously aided in erecting, I had an opportunity of learning his character and manner of life from reliable sources.

SAMUEL BLAIR was born in Fagg's Manor, Chester County, Pa., in the year 1741. His father, the Rev. Samuel Blair, then Pastor of the Church in that place, was a Presbyterian minister, of respectable talents and eminent usefulness; was a zealous friend to Whitefield, and ranked high among the New Lights in the memorable schism of the old New York and Philadelphia Synod. The son, as may be supposed from the character of the father, was early and carefully trained in the nurture and admonition of the Lord. When he was about ten years of age, his father was removed by death, and the care of his education devolved on his widowed mother and her advisers. The trust seems to have been faithfully discharged; for Samuel, in due time, entered the College of New Jersey, where he was graduated with honour, in 1760, at the age of nineteen. He afterwards served as Tutor there for about three years—from 1761 to 1764.

I can find no account of his first religious impressions; but the presumption is that he was hopefully pious before he entered College. The Christian ministry was his object; and, after passing the usual trials with credit, he was licensed to preach the Gospel, by the Presbytery of Newcastle, in 1764. He was popular as a preacher from his first appearance in the pulpit. His discourses were written out in full, with great care, and his elocution was at once chaste and impressive. Indeed, he seems to have been a young man of fine talents, and more than ordinary acquirements for his age. In proof of the justice of this remark, it may be stated here, that, in 1767, after Dr. Witherspoon had declined the first call of the Trustees of the College of New Jersey to the Presidency of that institution, young Blair, though not over twenty-six years of age, was elected to that office, with, as we have reason to believe, entire unanimity. But when the intelligence came from Scotland that, owing to a change of circumstances, Dr. Witherspoon would probably accept the call if it should be renewed, Mr. Blair immediately declined the invitation, and Dr. W. was re-elected. This was regarded, at the time, as a remarkable instance of self-sacrifice to the public good. He felt that the interests of the College demanded the services of a man of matured mind and eminent qualifications; and, therefore, gave way with a modesty and magnanimity worthy of record.

In November, 1766, Mr. Blair was installed pastor of the Old South Church in Boston, as a colleague of the Rev. Dr. Sewall. On his way thither, after his acceptance of the call, he was shipwrecked in the night, losing his wardrobe and manuscripts, and escaping narrowly with his life

His exposure, on this occasion, injured his health, and the loss of his sermons, which he had written with great care, depressed his spirits. In the spring of 1769, he took a journey to Philadelphia, and while there had a severe illness, which it was thought had given a shock to his constitution from which it could never recover. This, in connection with certain difficulties which had sprung up between him and his people, in relation to the Half-way Covenant,—as it was called, induced him, in September following, to proffer the resignation of his charge; and he was accordingly dismissed, October 10, 1769. About this time, he was married to Susan, daughter of the elder William Shippen, M. D.,—an eminent physician of Philadelphia. They had five children,—two sons and three daughters.

He received the degree of Doctor of Divinity from the University of Pennsylvania, in 1790.

After resigning his charge at Boston, he took up his residence at Germantown, near Philadelphia, where he passed the remainder of his life in retirement and devotion to his books; except that he served two years as Chaplain in Congress, and preached at other times, occasionally, as opportunity offered. He died in September, 1818, in the seventy-seventh year of his age. Mrs. Blair died in the spring of 1821.

Dr. Blair published two Sermons, one of which was occasioned by the death of the Rev. Dr. John Blair Smith, Philadelphia, 1799.

Dr. Blair was of about the medium size, of fair and ruddy complexion, and decidedly a fine looking man—not unlike, in his personal appearance, to the late Dr. Samuel Stanhope Smith. He was a man of polished manners and of amiable and generous dispositions. He was also a superior scholar, a well read theologian, and an eloquent pulpit orator. But, owing perhaps to excessive diffidence, and a tendency to melancholy, he was too much of a recluse. True, his health was feeble; but it would probably have been improved by more active service. He yielded too much to despondency, and did not rouse himself to labour in his profession with becoming energy and zeal. Hence the high expectations which his early promise had inspired, were, in a great measure, disappointed. But it should be mentioned to his honour that he was always liberal in his contributions to the support of religion, and of all evangelical enterprises. He was a principal agent, and one of the most generous contributors, in the erection of the Presbyterian church edifice in Germantown, where he laboured in word and doctrine, for some time, gratuitously, and with great acceptance. His services were also acceptable in Philadelphia, where he preached, by invitation, in several of the churches, when their pulpits happened to be vacant; but he rarely went abroad to preach, partly on account of infirm health, and partly because he deemed himself but poorly fitted for that sort of labour. Indeed, although he was a man of acknowledged talents, good education, and refined taste, he failed in energy and moral courage. He gave himself up to the luxury of private study, pondering the deep things of religion, waiting, it would seem, for a providential opening to some important station, when he might have been much more advantageously employed in the great practical duties of his office. I say this, because it is due to truth, and without the least disposition to dishonour his memory. While he was, in many respects, a noble specimen of a man, one cannot but wish, in contemplating his character, that his fine powers had been brought more fully into exercise, and that the history of his life had been a record of more extended and self-denying labours.

I am, my dear Sir,

Your brother and fellow servant in the Lord,

WILLIAM NEILL.

ROBERT COOPER, D. D.*

1765—1805.

ROBERT COOPER was born in the North of Ireland, in or about the year 1732. His father died in Ireland, while the son was yet a child. At the age of about nine, he, with two sisters, was brought by his mother to America. The family settled in Pennsylvania, probably in or near Lancaster or Carlisle. Their worldly circumstances were somewhat depressed, but his mother was active and frugal, and, in connection with what he was enabled to do for himself, managed to afford him tolerable facilities of education for that day. He was deeply sensible of the efforts which she made in his behalf, and manifested his gratitude in the most exemplary filial attentions till the close of her life. There is a tradition among his descendants that he learned the business of plough-making, in order to help himself in his education; but however this may have been, it is certain that he was obliged to labour at something to obtain the means, in part at least, of accomplishing this object; and that he occasionally left school, and engaged in manual labour, in order to meet his necessary expenses. It is supposed that he fitted for College chiefly under the instruction of the Rev. Mr. Roan, within whose congregation he resided during his earlier years, and for whom he always cherished a high regard. In due time, he became a member of the College of New Jersey, where he was graduated in September, 1763, under the Presidency of Dr. Finley.

Having determined to engage in the work of the ministry, he prosecuted a course of theological study, partly, it would seem, under the direction of his own minister, Mr. Roan, and partly under that of the Rev. (afterwards Dr.) George Duffield, then of Carlisle, afterwards of Philadelphia. He was received on trials for licensure by the (Old) Presbytery of Donegal, October 24, 1764, in little more than a year after his graduation. Having passed through his trials with great acceptance, he was licensed to preach by the Presbytery of Carlisle, February 22, 1765.

Immediately after his licensure, he was appointed by the Presbytery to supply, for a few Sabbaths, the vacant Congregation at Middle Spring; and, subsequently, a continuance of his labours was requested by that congregation: and some other congregations, particularly that at West Nottingham, then recently rendered vacant by the removal of Dr. Finley to the Presidency of New Jersey College, solicited his services. On the 18th of June, 1765, a call was presented to him by the Church at Middle Spring, accompanied with a request that, if he could not see his way clear to accept

* MSS. from Jonathan K. Cooper, Esq., Hon. Robert C. Grier, Rev. Isaac Grier, Rev. Dr. M'Conaughy, and Rev. Dr. Matthew Brown.

it at once, the Presbytery would appoint him, in the mean time, their stated supply; and though he was not prepared to give an *immediate* answer, he ultimately determined to accept the call. About the same time, the congregation at Martinsburgh, Va., to which Mr. Cooper had previously preached two or three Sabbaths, were actually moving to invite him to become their pastor, but were discouraged from proceeding, in consequence of being informed that any such application would be unavailing. He signified his acceptance of the call from Middle Spring on the 30th of October; and his ordination and installation took place on the 21st of the next month.

Here Mr. Cooper continued his labours, with great fidelity and usefulness, for thirty-one years. The church and congregation grew under his ministry, and the old wooden edifice, in which they had been accustomed to worship, gave place to a large and commodious building of stone, which was constantly and often densely filled. He watched with uncommon solicitude and assiduity over the interests of his flock, and was blest, in return, with their unwavering confidence and affection. He visited all the families in his congregation, frequently and systematically, and was especially attentive to the religious interests of the young. In these labours of love he found a most efficient coadjutor in his excellent wife, who was accustomed frequently to accompany him in his parochial visits, and often made herself very useful, especially in administering relief or consolation to the sick.

The degree of Doctor of Divinity was conferred upon him by Dickinson College, in the year 1792.

On the 5th of October, 1796, Dr. Cooper, in consequence of a decayed state of health, in which his mind had a sensible share, applied to the Presbytery for leave to resign his pastoral charge. The request was not at once decisively acted upon; but provision was made for rendering him the needed assistance in his labours, until the next meeting of the Presbytery. At that meeting, the Doctor renewed his request; and his church, having finally become satisfied that his infirmities were such as to cut off the hope of his being able to perform the duties of the ministry, signified to the Presbytery their assent to his proposal; whereupon, the pastoral relation was dissolved. This took place on the 12th of April, 1797.

The malady, which thus interrupted Dr. Cooper's public labours, was of the nature of dropsy; but it was attended with an inveterate depression of spirits, which, apart from physical infirmity, utterly unfitted him for the duties of his office. It was often with extreme difficulty that his family could persuade him to go into the pulpit; but sometimes the clouds would suddenly break away, and leave him to the full use of his faculties, so that he would preach with uncommon freedom and power. After he had resigned his pastoral charge, his bodily disease yielded to medical treatment, and, as a consequence, the general tranquillity of his mind was restored. He gladly availed himself of this favourable change to resume his ministerial labours; and, though he never afterwards had a stated charge, he often supplied vacant churches within the bounds of the Presbytery, and exerted himself not a little in gathering the means for sending the Gospel to the more destitute portions of the country, and even acted as a missionary himself. A short time before his death, there was a recurrence of at least the *mental* malady which had previously afflicted him; but it was only for a brief period, and he went down to his grave amidst the most cheering testimonies of God's gracious presence. He died April 5, 1805, in the seventy-third year of his age.

Dr. Cooper, as far as can now be ascertained, published nothing except a Tract, in 1804, entitled "Signs of the times;" in which he notices the progress of Infidel Philosophy in Europe, and the danger of its extending in this country; deprecates the spirit of fanaticism which was then becoming rife in many parts of the land; and carefully marks the distinction between a spurious excitement and a genuine revival of religion. A Sermon of his was also published, preached before a Regiment of troops, who were about to leave home to engage in the service of their country, during the Revolution; but this is believed to have been printed without any agency of his own, and perhaps without his knowledge.

Though Dr. Cooper had but limited means of support in his small salary and poor farm, he contrived, by rigid economy, to place himself in very comfortable worldly circumstances. He had also a very considerable library for that day; and by a memorandum in the hands of one of his descendants, it appears that a portion of his books were purchased for him by Dr. Witherspoon, in Scotland.

About the time that he entered the ministry, he was married to Elizabeth, eldest child of Jonathan and Jane Kearsley, then of Carlisle. They had four children,—two sons and two daughters. One son died in infancy. His eldest daughter, *Jane*, married a Mr. Samuel Nicholson, and has been dead many years. His second daughter, *Elizabeth*, was married to the Rev. Isaac Grier.* His youngest son, *John*, was liberally educated, and studied for the ministry; but was obliged, by a sudden decline of health, to give up study entirely, before he was licensed to preach. By relaxation and moderate exercise on a farm, however, he so far regained his health as to be able to teach a school, and was actually engaged in this employment upwards of thirty years. He removed to Peoria, Ill., the residence of one of his sons, in 1839, where he died, in 1848, in his seventy-third year.

FROM THE REV. JOHN MOODEY, D. D.

SHIPPENSBURG, PA., January 18, 1850

Rev. and dear Sir: My acquaintance with Dr. Cooper, my venerable predecessor in the ministry, concerning whom you inquire, was limited to the last years of his life. He lived but about two years after my acceptance of the call at Mid-

* ISAAC GRIER was born about the year 1763, in what is now Franklin County, Pa. His father, who was a farmer, was of the Scotch Irish emigrants, who settled in Pennsylvania at an early day. Having gone through his preparatory course under James Ross, a celebrated teacher, then at Chambersburgh, he entered Dickinson College, Carlisle, where he was graduated in 1790. He was licensed to preach about the year 1791, and, immediately after, spent a year in a missionary tour through the new settlements in Western New York. In 1794, he received a call from the Congregations of Lycoming, Pine Creek, and Great Island, in Lycoming County, Pa. In the spring of 1795, he purchased a small farm near the village of Jersey Shore, where he resided. Being but slenderly supported by his congregation, he, in 1802, opened a classical school, by means of which, together with his small farm, he managed to meet the expenses of his family. Having received a call to the Congregations of Northumberland and Sunbury, he removed to the town of Northumberland in April, 1806. Beside these congregations, he supplied a small church in Shamokin Valley, at least once a month. Here again, in order to make out a sufficient support for his family, he was compelled to assume the duties of teacher of an Academy. But his unceasing labours, both as pastor and teacher, in a few years, destroyed his constitution, and he died of dyspepsia, August 23, 1814. He was a man of high intelligence and great moral and Christian worth; and as a teacher of the Latin and Greek languages, he is said to have had no superior in Pennsylvania. He was the father of the Hon. R. C. Grier, one of the Justices of the Supreme Court of the United States, and the Rev. Isaac Grier of Mifflinburg, Pa.

dle Spring; and as he was absent from home during much of that time, supplying vacant congregations, and as most of my time was required in preparing for pastoral duties, and as our places of residence withal were seven miles apart, our intercourse was not very frequent. I was, however, occasionally a visitor at his house, especially during the period that intervened between my licensure and the acceptance of my call; and I uniformly found him a warm friend; given to hospitality; always ready to give advice where it was desired, and to explain any theological difficulty that was proposed to him.

In his religious views he was a thorough Calvinist, of the Old School, and adopted the Confession of Faith of the Presbyterian Church, in its legitimate import. He was well acquainted with Theology, and was a very competent theological teacher. Among those who resorted to him for instruction in this department, were Dr. McKnight of New York, Dr. Joshua Williams, for many years a distinguished minister in this region, Dr. Herron of Pittsburgh, and others of scarcely less celebrity. Of the estimation in which he was held by his brethren in the ministry, some opinion may be formed from the fact that, at the meeting of the Synod of New York and Philadelphia, the then supreme judicatory of the Presbyterian Church in the United States, in May, 1785, he was appointed, in connection with Dr. Witherspoon, Dr. Robert Smith, Dr. Samuel Stanhope Smith, and several other of the greater lights of the body, to frame a system of general rules for the government of the Church. Dr. Miller, in his Life of Dr. Rodgers, speaking of this Committee, has the following note under the name of Dr. Cooper:—"The Rev. Robert Cooper of Shippensburg, Pa., afterwards Doctor of Divinity. Dr. Cooper had a remarkably strong, sound mind; and although late in acquiring an education, and entering the ministry, he was a divine of great judiciousness, piety, and worth."

In the American Revolution, Dr. Cooper was a zealous Whig, and visited the army, for a short time, in the capacity of a minister, with a view no doubt to exhort them to activity and fidelity; and he was near being taken prisoner at Princeton. The political views which he held then, he retained through life; and sometimes, in his last years, when his mind, free from depression, rose into an opposite state of excitement, he dwelt upon these topics in the pulpit, more than was acceptable to a portion of his hearers.

As a preacher, Dr. Cooper seems to have been distinguished rather for the solidity and excellence of his matter, than for elegant diction, or an attractive delivery. He was, however, in the earlier part of his ministry particularly, a more than ordinarily popular preacher; and, with the more intelligent and reflecting portion of the community, he retained his popularity to the last. He was accustomed to write his sermons,—many of them at least, pretty fully; but had no manuscript before him in the delivery, unless it were a mere outline.

His personal appearance, whether in or out of the pulpit, was not very commanding. He was low in stature, and of a thin, spare habit. His face considerably resembled a print of melancholy, or hypocondriasis, which is given in Lavater's work on Physiognomy. This sadness of the countenance was undoubtedly an index to that peculiar habit of mind, if not original temperament, which subjected him to such serious inconvenience, and occasioned a premature separation from his people.

I am, dear Sir, yours with great respect,

JOHN MOODEY.

JOSEPH SMITH.

1767—1792.

FROM THE REV. JOSEPH SMITH, D. D.

ALLEGHANY CITY, November 1, 1850.

Rev. and dear Sir: In compliance with your request, I now send you the substance of all that I have been able to gather in respect to the history of my venerable grandfather, who was one of the early ministers of the Presbyterian Church in Western Pennsylvania.

JOSEPH SMITH was born in the year 1736, in Nottingham, Pa. His parents, who were natives of England, were not only professors of religion, but were regarded as eminently pious persons. Of his early education and religious exercises nothing is known; but there is reason to believe that he had passed his minority, when he first entertained the idea of devoting himself to the ministry. For he graduated at Princeton in 1764, when he was twenty-eight years of age. He was licensed to preach by the Presbytery of Newcastle, at Drawyers, August 5, 1767. Of his theological training I have been unable to gain any information. He seems, however, to have had considerable knowledge of the original languages of the Scriptures. The Hebrew Bible, the Greek Testament, Leigh's Critica Sacra, and Pool's Synopsis, were his constant companions, during his subsequent life.

On the 20th of October, 1768, he accepted a call from the Congregation of Lower Brandywine, and was ordained and installed their Pastor, April 19, 1769. A short time before he was licensed, he had married Miss Esther Cummins, daughter of William Cummins, merchant of Cecil County, Md.,—a lady of uncommon piety, intelligence, and refinement of manners,—who proved to be a help-meet indeed to the day of his death. Difficulties having sprung up in the congregation relative to the site of a church, his pastoral relation to them was dissolved, on the 26th of August, 1772. At the same meeting of the Presbytery, he received a call from the Congregations of Rocky Creek and Long Cane in South Carolina. This call he declined, and accepted an appointment as a supply to his former congregation, for one year. About this time, he began to preach in Wilmingtou, De., which was the occasion of great dissension among the people, as the Rev. William McKennan* was already preaching in that place. After a season of much excitement, during which various petitions and remonstrances were presented on the subject, the Presbytery, on the 12th of August, 1773, put into his hands a call from the Second Church of Wilmington. This he held till the autumn of the next year. In the mean time, the Congregation of Wilmington having united with that of Lower Brandywine, in seeking a portion of his labours, he accepted their united call, and became their Pastor, October 27, 1774. In these Churches he laboured till April 29, 1778, when, at his own request, the pastoral relation was dissolved, "by reason of the difficult state of public affairs." This expression alludes no doubt to the distracted state of the country, and especially

* WILLIAM MCKENNAN emigrated from the North of Ireland; was ordained as pastor of White Clay and Red Clay Creek Churches, in Delaware, in December, 1755, and served these Churches fifty-four years, during thirty-four of which he was also the Pastor of the First Church in Wilmington. He died on the 5th of May, 1809, at the age of ninety.

of that part of Delaware,—being then involved in some of the most harassing and bloody scenes of our Revolutionary war. Some time before he left Wilmington, a British army landed at the head of Elk, and soon after occurred the battle of Brandywine. The fearful cannonading on the field of slaughter shook many a window in Wilmington on that day. In June, 1776, soon after the battle, Mrs. Smith prematurely gave birth to their fourth child. The nervous excitement produced by the roar of the cannon threatened to prove fatal to both mother and child; but they were mercifully preserved,—the mother to sustain and increase the usefulness of her husband,—the feeble infant, to become, in future years, the wife of one minister, and the mother of another.

Soon after these events, he was urged by an imperative sense of duty, as a husband, parent, and minister, to retire with his family into the Barrens of York, where he resided for nearly two years, preaching with great success in the "region round about." At this time, one of his neighbours, who had recently been married, and had brought his wife home, was called upon by some of his acquaintances, on the Sabbath, and just as they were about setting out for public worship. The young man, who was pious, was not a little annoyed, but persuaded his friends to accompany them to their meeting-house in the neighbourhood, to hear Mr. Smith, of whom he gave them such an account as to awaken somewhat their curiosity. The result was the hopeful conversion of several of the party. During this period,—in the spring of the year 1779,—he paid a short visit to Western Pennsylvania. He preached several times within the limits of what were subsequently the Buffalo and Cross Creek Congregations, in Westmoreland, now Washington County. In June of that year, a call from these congregations was sent down to the Presbytery for him. He accepted it, and removed thither in December, 1780.

Here Mr. Smith spent the remainder of his life. Perhaps no pastor of a church was ever more blessed with devoted elders than he now was. A revival of religion quickly commenced under his labours, which never ceased till the day of his death—twelve years! And this too amidst the trials and perils of frontier life, where they were often in imminent danger from savage foes, and sometimes were compelled to retire to forts or block houses, to protect themselves from the merciless tomahawk. Besides Mr. Smith's abundant labours on the Sabbath, and his frequent preaching through the week, he instituted, at his own house, a Wednesday evening prayer meeting, to which persons would come from a distance of from three to fifteen miles.

Mr. Smith was not a man of robust health. In person he was tall, slender, of fair complexion, looking slightly askance with one eye. When he became animated, there was a piercing brilliancy about his eyes, that was peculiar and striking. His voice was adapted alike to the terrific and the pathetic. "I never heard a man," said the Rev. Samuel Porter, "who could so completely as Mr. Smith, unbar the gates of Hell, and make me look far down into the abyss, or who could so throw open the gates of Heaven, and let me glance at the insufferable brightness of the great white throne." His favourite subjects were the necessity of regeneration, and the immediate obligation of exercising faith in Jesus Christ. His ordinary style of speaking was quite removed from any thing like rhapsody—it was rather like free animated conversation. His sermons were generally written out with some degree of fulness. Many of the skeletons which he used on ordinary occasions, are so extended that they might, with little addition, be prepared for the press. But he would often, when speaking, rise to a pitch of uncommon sublimity, rendering himself quite irresistible to all classes of hearers. Yet, if it might be said that preaching was his forte, it is questionable whether his usefulness out of the pulpit was not even greater than in it. He was eminently a devout man, and often had special seasons of prayer. It was not uncommon for him to rise in the night, and spend hours in fervent intercession for his people, and especially for the youth of his congregation, and his own children. With reference to this, he kept a cloak at the foot of his bed during the cold weather, that he might have it in readiness to throw around him, when he wished to get upon his knees in the silent hours of night. His wife and himself often observed special fast days for the conversion of their children. Nearly all of them became hopefully the subjects of Divine grace, while they were quite young, and one was admitted to the fellowship of the church at the age of ten years. He was eminently faithful in catechising and conversing with his children. Sabbath evenings were generally spent in this way. Gathering them around the fireside, after the usual recitation of the Shorter Catechism, he would talk to them most earnestly and affectionately, and would sometimes close with solemn warnings, telling them that he would take the stones of the chimney to witness against them, &c. Yet there was nothing morose or forbidding in his character—on the contrary, he was cheerful, affectionate and uncommonly winning; and the children and youth of his church have some of them testified that, while he was among them, they were unconscious of the flight of time. Praise generally employed his lips, as soon as he opened his eyes in the morning. He was fond of singing, and he loved to sing a favourite verse or two before he rose from his bed.

He was a laborious and faithful pastor;—was particularly diligent in seeking out those who were neglecting the ordinances of religion. The tide of emigration, especially from Virginia, poured around him considerable numbers of the profane and openly irreligious. He was skilful in devising methods of access to persons, whom few would have thought it worth while to approach. On one occasion, he was at the house of one of his elders over night, and rising early in the morning, he observed a house half a mile distant. and inquired of his elder, *who* lived there. On being told that it was a person who had resided there but a few months, Mr. Smith asked if he came to church. The elder said he did not, but his wife and children came sometimes. Mr. Smith said that he would go and see him; and telling the elder not to delay breakfast for him, immediately set off. Arrived at the house, he found the man and his family at home. He introduced himself as the minister who preached at Buffalo, and as such had called to see them. The man said he knew him, though he had not been to church, but added that his wife and children sometimes went. Mr. Smith called the family together, and talked with them on the subject of religion; and, after some time, asked the man if he had had family worship that morning. He replied that he had not. "I suppose," said Mr. S., "that you pray in your family of course." He admitted that he did not. "Then," said Mr. S. "you ought to do it; and the sooner you begin, the better; you must begin immediately." He then asked for a Bible, and read a passage, accompanying it with suitable comments, and immediately asked the man to pray; and, without giving him time to express either his assent or dissent, he knelt down forthwith. A long silence followed. Mr. Smith then turned to the man and urged him to pray. He still remained silent. His importunate visitor again repeated his request. Under this process, his mind being deeply agitated, he cried out at length in agony,—"O Lord, teach me to pray, for I know not how to pray." "That will do," said Mr. Smith, as he rose from his knees; "you have made a good beginning, and I trust you will soon be able to extend your petitions." The result was such as Mr. Smith predicted. The tradition is that, from that time forth, he became a man of prayer, and he and his family were soon consistent and active members of the church.

One of his hearers,—a man of a worldly mind, and altogether careless on the subject of religion, yet very kind and respectful towards his minister, had often baffled his attempts to draw him into conversation on matters of a spiritual nature; but, on a Sabbath morning, as he was standing near the place of worship, conversing with others,—upon Mr. Smith's coming up, he observed to him that they had just been speaking of the vastness and grandeur of some rocks not far off. "Yes, Col. J.," said Mr. S., "the works of God are grand. And how hot will be those last fires that will melt down these rocks like wax—don't you think so?" "Very hot indeed, very hot indeed, Sir,"—said the Colonel, shrugging his shoulders, and edging away, manifestly with a barbed arrow in his conscience.

Mr. Smith was anxious, from the first, to assist in bringing forward young men to preach the Gospel. The Rev. Thaddeus Dod had, in the spring of 1782, moved into the village of Washington, and taught the town school or Academy in the old Court House for about a year, and then returned to Tenmile, where he had previously resided. During that time, two or three young men, having the ministry in view, received instruction from Mr. Dod, amongst whom were James Hughes* and John Hanna.† But the first school that was opened with a *special* view to the training of young men for the sacred office, is believed to have been begun by Mr. Smith, at Upper Buffalo, in 1785. The subject had pressed heavily on his mind for some time before. The great difficulty in his way was that he had no suitable house. But he had recently erected a building, adjoining his dwelling, to serve as a kitchen and out-house; and if his wife would consent to surrender that for a while, and fall back upon their former hampered domestic system, the object could be accomplished. Upon his stating the case to her, she cordially acquiesced in the plan, and warmly seconded his views. Almost

* James Hughes, the son of Rowland Hughes, an emigrant from England, was a native of York County, Pa.; was educated chiefly under the direction of the Rev. Joseph Smith; was licensed to preach the Gospel by the Presbytery of Redstone, April 15, 1788; and was ordained and installed pastor of Short Creek and Lower Buffalo Churches, in Ohio County, Va., on the 21st of April, 1790. Having laboured successfully here, upwards of twenty years, he resigned his pastoral charge on the 29th of June, 1814; and shortly after removed to Urbana, O., where, for three years, he acted as stated supply and missionary. In June, 1818, he was chosen Principal of what is now Miami University. This office he accepted, and held till his death, which occurred May 2, 1821, at Oxford, O. He was an earnest and faithful preacher, and a zealous promoter of the cause of missions.

† John Hanna presented himself for examination for licensure before the Presbytery of Redstone, on the 28th of December, 1790, and, in view of his very small capacities and attainments, "the Presbytery were unanimously of opinion that it was not their duty to encourage him to proceed any farther on trials, with a prospect of being licensed to preach the Gospel." Mr. Hanna, having been thus dismissed, went to New Jersey, and united himself with the Morris County Presbytery,—a small independent body, which has, for many years, been extinct. Here he was licensed and ordained, and is said to have been a useful minister.

immediately, the Latin School was opened, and Messrs. McGready,* Porter, Brice† and Patterson began their course. Soon after, James Hughes, who had already begun with Mr. Dod, joined them. About this time, the plan seems to have been adopted, of making this school, in some sense, itinerant; the brethren, Messrs. McMillan, Dod, and Smith, taking it in turn, and thus dividing the labour. It was found expedient, after a trial, to render it more fixed and permanent; and Chartiers, in the vicinity of Cannonsburg, was regarded, on many accounts, the most favourable location. This school afterwards became a public Academy, and grew at length into Jefferson College. But the original enterprise was undoubtedly set on foot by Mr. Smith.

Thus abounding in labours at home and abroad, and wearing himself out in his Master's service, the spring of 1792 found him still at his post. His health, though never vigorous, gave no token of his approaching end. He was in the pulpit on the first Sabbath of April, and was at Cross Creek, according to his alternate course, on that day. His text was, Galatians i, 8. "Though we, or an angel from Heaven, preach any other Gospel unto you, than that which we have preached unto you, let him be accursed." He took occasion, from this text, to give them a summary sketch of his twelve years' preaching. It seemed like the winding up of his ministry. It was remarked afterwards that he seemed to speak under the influence of a presentiment that it was to be his last sermon. The whole place was like a Bochim. How much

* James McGready was of Scotch Irish extraction, and was a native of Pennsylvania. The family, when he was quite young, migrated to the South, and settled in Guilford County, N. C. Here he passed several of his early years; and as he was a sedate and thoughtful youth, and in other respects promising, an uncle who was on a visit to his father's, conceiving that he ought to be educated for the ministry, prevailed on his parents to allow their son to accompany him to Pennsylvania, with a view to the accomplishment of this object. He went with him accordingly; and before he had time to begin his studies, he became convinced, under a sermon of the Rev. Mr. Smith, that his previous religious hopes had been delusive, and was brought, as he believed, to build on the only sure foundation. In the autumn of 1785, Mr. Smith opened a school to prepare young men for the ministry, in which Mr. McGready immediately became a pupil; and, after remaining there for some time, he became connected with another school, then recently opened by the Rev. Dr. McMillan, with whom he had resided for a short time immediately after his return with his uncle to Pennsylvania. Having completed his literary and theological course, he was licensed to preach by the Presbytery of Redstone, on the 13th of August, 1788, when he was about thirty years of age. In the autumn or winter following, he went to Carolina, and on his way stopped for some time at Hampden Sidney College, in Virginia, with Dr. John Blair Smith, who had had much to do with the great revival of religion in that neighbourhood; and his own mind seems to have been powerfully acted upon by what he saw and heard of the manifestations of Divine grace. On his arrival in North Carolina, he found the churches in a state of great spiritual apathy, and his preaching was the means of an increased attention to religion in many places. In 1796, he removed to Kentucky, and settled in Logan County, over the three Congregations of Muddy, Red, and Gasper, Rivers. Here his preaching produced the most powerful impressions, and he became a leader in that great excitement at the South-west, which, in some of its phases, has scarcely, to this day, ceased to be a subject of curious speculation. By his extreme measures, he brought himself into an embarrassed relation with his Presbytery, and was one of those who seceded to form the Cumberland Presbytery, though, after about two years, he withdrew from his new connection, and returned to the Presbytery of Transylvania. He shortly after removed to the town of Henderson, on the Ohio River, where he spent the remainder of his days, and died in 1817.

† John Brice was a native of Harford County, Md. He removed with his father's family, to Western Pennsylvania, and received his education chiefly under the direction of the Rev. Joseph Smith. He studied Theology, partly under Mr. Smith, and partly under the Rev. Thaddeus Dod. He was licensed to preach April 15, 1788, by the Presbytery of Redstone; and by the same Presbytery was ordained and installed pastor of the Congregations of Three Ridges and Forks of Wheeling, April 22, 1790. When the Presbytery of Ohio was formed in 1793, he was one of its members. Here he laboured till about the year 1807, when, on account of ill health, his pastoral relation was dissolved. He still continued, however, to preach the Gospel in Green County, Pa., and the adjacent parts of Virginia, as often as health would permit, until the 18th of April, 1810, when he was dismissed to connect himself with the Presbytery of Lancaster. He died August 26, 1811, aged fifty-one years. He was a man of nervous temperament, and subject to great despondency, but of an eminently devout spirit, and was greatly blessed in his labours.

more were his people affected, when it was found that he required assistance to get from the pulpit to his horse! He was obliged to remain for a day or two in the neighbourhood, and then was conveyed on a sled to his own house,—carriages of a more decent kind being then, at least in that region, almost unknown. His disease was inflammation of the brain. His sufferings, though short, were severe. In the earlier stages of his disease, his mind was enveloped, for a time, in thick darkness. His affectionate people poured in to see him. He asked them to pray for him. To a number of young people in whose conversion he had been instrumental, and who were permitted to approach his bedside, he said,—"My dear children, often have I prayed for you, when you were sleeping in your beds—now is your time to pay me back—pray for me that the Lord would shield me from the fiery darts of Satan. Deep calleth unto deep, and all his billows He maketh to pass over me." In such language, as I have been assured by one of the group who stood by his bedside, did he express the anguish of his spirit. But the conflict was at length over, and all was peace. His last day was spent in the land of Beulah. As long as he could speak, it was in accents of triumph and holy joy. He finished his course on the 19th of April. The tidings of his death spread gloom over a widely extended community. Such were the feelings of his people, as many of them have since testified, that it was a common remark among them that the sun did not seem to shine with his natural brightness for many days afterwards. The congregations in which he lived and died still experience the benefit of his influence, and are among the most flourishing in Western Pennsylvania.

Allow me, before I conclude, to mention one or two more anecdotes, illustrative of Mr. Smith's earnest devotedness to his work, and of the fearless and uncompromising spirit which he brought to it. Being on his way to the General Assembly, he stopped over the Sabbath in a congregation, where vital religion was at a very low ebb. The minister, having heard of Mr. Smith's terrific manner of preaching, intimated to him that one of his more moderate sermons would be most likely to prove acceptable to his people. Mr. Smith, after giving out an impressive hymn, and offering an unusually fervent prayer, arose to preach; and, as he arose, cried out with a strong voice, "Fire, Fire, Fire!" The congregation, alarmed and agitated, glanced towards every part of the building, above and around. "If the very mention of the word," continued the preacher, "so startles you,—if the mere apprehension of it excited by the voice of a stranger so disturbs you, what will it be to encounter the reality? 'Who can dwell with everlasting burnings?' This is my text." He delivered one of his most thoroughly awakening discourses;—a discourse which is said to have been the means of effecting an entire change in the spiritual views and ministerial labours of the pastor, as well as of producing an extensive revival of religion. The minister often mentioned the circumstance afterwards, with tears of gratitude to God for having thus sent his servant among them.

At one of the first Communion seasons in the Western wilderness, Mr. Smith was present. An immense concourse of people were drawn together from a widely dispersed settlement. The services were conducted in a grove adjoining the meeting-house; as this primitive sanctuary could scarcely have contained a tithe of the people. Such arrangements for conducting Sacramental meetings in the woods continued for many years afterwards. The Communion service, which was, at that time, generally more protracted than at present, was, in the case to which I refer, closed late in the afternoon of a long summer day. Mr. Smith rose to deliver the closing address. But the attention of the audience was not a little distracted. Considerable numbers, having many miles to go in order to reach their homes, were rising and dispersing,—some setting out on foot, some going to their horses, some disengaging their horses' bridles from the branches of the trees, and some already mounted and riding in different directions,—presenting altogether rather a picturesque and striking scene. Mr. Smith, struck with the whole aspect of things before him, raising his clear and piercing voice to a loud and thrilling pitch, commenced after this manner:—"One word to those who are now retiring, and who cannot remain longer with us—we are told that when this Supper was celebrated for the first time, none retired from the place until all was over, but Judas. If there be any Judases here, let them go; but let them remember that what they have seen and heard here this day will follow them to their homes, and to perdition, if they go there." The effect, it is said, was like an electric shock: they all, with scarcely an exception, returned to their seats, and hung upon his lips with fixed attention, until the benediction was pronounced.

If the foregoing account of this eminent servant of God be deemed worthy of a place in the work you have undertaken, and be thus rendered in any measure instrumental in promoting an increased degree of love to Christ and to the souls of men, among the living ministry, or those who are hereafter to enter the sacred office, it will be an abundant compensation for the time and trouble expended in its preparation by

Your brother in the Gospel,

JOSEPH SMITH.

Mr. Smith had a son, *David*, who was born in Wilmington, De., about the year 1772, and was seven or eight years of age, when his parents removed into Western Pennsylvania. About the age of sixteen,—there being no Academy in the West, he accompanied his father to one of the meetings of the Synod of Virginia, and was there transferred to the care of the Rev. Dr. John Blair Smith, then President of Hampden Sidney College. It was under the ministry of Dr. Smith that he became hopefully pious. Having graduated, probably in 1791, he returned to his father's, and after spending some time in the study of Theology, was licensed to preach the Gospel by the Presbytery of Redstone, November 14, 1792. He was ordained and installed by the same Presbytery, as pastor of the Congregations of George's Creek, and the Tent, in Fayette County, on the 20th of August, 1794. Having laboured here, with great success, for about four years, he removed to the Forks of Yough, in Westmoreland County, and took charge of the Congregations of Rehoboth and Roundhill, then vacant by the death of the Rev. James Finley. Here he remained until his death, which occurred on the 24th of August, 1803. He was a well read divine, and an earnest and faithful preacher. He was the father of the Rev. Joseph Smith, D. D., the writer of the preceding letter.

JOHN KING, D. D.*

1767—1811.

JOHN KING was born in Chestnut Level, Lancaster County, Pa., December 5, 1740. His father, Robert King, was a plain but respectable man, who emigrated from Ireland, and purchased the tract of land on which he resided till his death, which occurred a little after the year 1760. He was a ruling elder in the church to which he belonged.

At the age of thirteen, he commenced his classical studies at a grammar school, at which he continued till he had become in a good degree familiar, not only with the Latin and Greek Classics, but with Logic, Metaphysics, and Moral Philosophy. His father feeling himself unable immediately to bear the expense of giving him a collegiate education,—he engaged in teaching a school in West Conococheague, Cumberland County, Pa., and continued in this employment three years. Among his pupils, during this period, was John McDowell, afterwards the Rev. Dr. John McDowell, Provost of the University of Pennsylvania.

In 1763, the Indian war breaking out, his sister was killed by the savages; and as his school had considerably declined, he gave it up, and returned to his native place. Here he continued till the autumn of 1764, in no small perplexity as to the course of life he should pursue. He had not only had the benefit of a religious education, but had been the subject of early religious impressions, and had even joined the communion of the church, while he was engaged as a teacher at Conococheague; but still he seems to have been so distrustful of his religious experience, that he could not feel satisfied that it was his duty to direct his attention to the Christian ministry; and what added to his discouragement was that his voice was weak at best, and, for several preceding winters, he had suffered from extreme hoarseness. In these circumstances, after having earnestly sought the Divine guidance, and, as he thought, maturely revolved the subject in his own mind, he came to the conclusion that the Providence of God pointed him towards the medical profession. He went to Philadelphia, and had nearly perfected an arrangement for an apprenticeship with a physician there, when he was induced, by the advice of a friend, not to come to a definitive conclusion till he had taken the opinion of the Rev. Dr. Alison. Accordingly, he called on Dr. A., and stated his case to him; whereupon, the Doctor warmly advised him to give up all thoughts of the study of medicine, and to enter College with a view to the ministry. After due reflection on the way in which he had been led, and on what might reasonably be inferred in respect to the designs of Providence concerning him, he concluded to follow this advice; and, accordingly, entered College at Philadelphia in May, 1765. The College was then under the care of the Rev. Dr. William Smith as Provost, and the Rev. Dr. Francis Alison as Vice Provost; both of whom were acknowledged to be among the greater lights of their time. Mr. King, after a year's residence at College, commenced Bachelor of Arts in May, 1766.

*Autobiographical Notices.—MS. from Rev. Dr. Archibald Alexander.—Nevin's Churches of the Valley.

On leaving College, he returned home, and applied himself to the study of Theology till March, 1767, when he entered on his trials for the ministry, in the Second Presbytery of Philadelphia. He was licensed to preach in August following. The succeeding fall and winter he was engaged in preaching at New London, Pa., and within the bounds of the Newcastle Presbytery. On paying a visit to Conococheague, his former place of residence, he received an invitation to settle there; and having accepted it, was ordained to the work of the ministry, and installed Pastor of the Church in that place, by the Donegal Presbytery, in May, 1769. From this charge he never removed, till he resigned it shortly before his death.

For the last six years of his life, he was greatly afflicted and debilitated by a rheumatic affection, which baffled the skill of all his physicians, and finally brought him to the close of his earthly pilgrimage. During four years of this time, he continued his labours in the pulpit, and when unable to stand, delivered his discourses in a sitting posture. His death was accelerated by a fever which, in conjunction with his inveterate rheumatism, soon removed him from the earth. He died July 5, 1811, in the seventy-first year of his age.

In April, 1771, he was married to Elizabeth, daughter of John McDowell, one of the elders of the Church of which he was Pastor. She proved a tender and faithful help-meet to him during the residue of his life, and in the protracted illness which preceded his death, watched over him with most exemplary conjugal affection. He died without issue.

The Trustees of Dickinson College, in consideration of his high attainments as a general scholar and a theologian, conferred on him, in 1792, the degree of Doctor of Divinity,—a distinction well sustained by his public performances and by the public opinion.

FROM THE REV. DAVID ELLIOTT, D. D.,

PROFESSOR IN THE ALLEGHANY THEOLOGICAL SEMINARY.

Alleghany, February 22, 1850.

Dear Sir: Although I was the immediate successor of the Rev. John King, D. D., in the Congregation of Upper West Conococheague, at Mercersburg, Pa., my acquaintance with him did not commence until within a few years before his death. During that brief period, however, I had, from frequent intercourse with him, the most favourable opportunities for forming an estimate of his character and opinions. Being a man of very social habits, fond of conversing on theological and other subjects, and free and unreserved in the expression of his views, it did not require a long series of years to become familiarly acquainted with the prominent traits of his character, and to form a pretty accurate judgment of the variety and extent of his attainments. But even on this most favourable aspect of the case, I would feel some hesitancy in complying with your request in regard to a notice of this venerable man,—owing to the short period of my acquaintance with him,—were it not that I feel aided in the task by my recollection of the frequent recitals respecting him, which met me at every stage of my pastoral labours, among the intelligent people of his former charge, confirming and extending the opinions which I had formed from my own observation. The access also which I have had to some of the recorded memorials of his talents and learning, and to the testimony of many of his brethren in the ministry, has strengthened my convictions of the correctness of the views which I had taken of his character, and seems to render it proper that I should comply with your request, and furnish such statements as the truth will justify, and thus aid in perpetuating in the

Church the memory of an able and faithful minister of the Gospel of Jesus Christ.

Dr. King's mind was evidently not of the brilliant order. He was much more intellectual than imaginative. Nor were his intellectual efforts distinguished so much by great energy, as by their solidity and well sustained application to their appropriate objects. He was capable of close and logical processes of thought, and whenever he undertook to investigate a subject, however difficult and abstruse, he did it with marked ability. Evidence of the truth of this observation is found both in the published and unpublished productions of his pen.

As a preacher, Dr. King possessed but little popularity beyond the bounds of his own pastoral charge. This was owing chiefly to two causes. The one was a weakness of voice and hoarseness which totally disqualified him for producing any oratorical effect. The other was his style, which was too philosophical and involved for popular impression. That portion of his congregation, however, whose minds were disciplined to habits of thinking, and who had ceased to regard the defects of his manner, highly appreciated the rich evangelical instruction with which his discourses abounded, and the ability and earnestness with which he illustrated them, and enforced them upon the attention of his hearers.

As a theologian, his acquirements were fully recognised by his brethren and the churches. Hence he was frequently resorted to by candidates for the ministry, many of whom he assisted, by his instructions, in their preparation for the sacred office. Some of these, who afterwards attained considerable distinction in the Church—I have heard speak of him in terms of high commendation, as a man of strong mind, and an able and well read theologian.

But Dr. King was not a mere theologian—he had a taste for scientific pursuits, and his domestic cares being few,—having no children, he had favourable opportunities for improvement in the different branches of literature. With the Roman and Greek classics he was familiar, and had a considerable acquaintance with the Hebrew and French languages. He was well skilled in Mental and Moral Philosophy, and had paid more than usual attention to the Mathematics and Natural Philosophy, particularly to Astronomy and Chemistry. This last branch of science he seems to have cultivated with much care. Of this I find some evidence in a characteristic letter of his, under date of September, 1811, addressed to the celebrated Dr. Thomas Cooper, late President of South Carolina College, the countryman and friend of Dr. Priestly. Dr. Cooper was a man of various and extensive literary acquirements. Being a jurist as well as a physician and a chemist, he had been appointed to the Presidency of one of the District Courts of Pennsylvania, but was subsequently removed from that station by an Act of the Legislature. Not long after this occurrence, he was elected to the Professorship of Chemistry in Dickinson College, Carlisle, in opposition to the wishes of many of the Board of Trustees, particularly of the clerical members, who resisted his appointment on the ground of his reputed hostility to religion. It was known from his writings, published in England, that he was a Materialist, and that some of the positions which he assumed, bore strongly in the direction of Atheism. Dr. King, who was a member of the Board of Trustees, but too infirm to meet with them, finding that a very strong prejudice existed against Dr. Cooper, and that his appointment was not likely to be set aside, addressed to him the letter to which I have referred. In this letter, after noticing the importance of Chemistry as a branch of Natural Philosophy, and its practical utility, Dr. King enumerates the various absurd and impious theories which had been broached on the subject by different writers of the infidel school. He then refers to the favourable opportunity which Dr. Cooper would have, in his official position, "of counteracting these foolish and impious conclusions, and of inculcating the grand principle of all science," and concludes by suggesting the propriety of his preparing a course of Lectures, "shewing the uses and ends of the science, and pointing out its subserviency to religion, in common with all the other works of God." Although the letter, judging from the original draft which has fallen into my hands, is written without much attention to style, it shows a good measure of acquaintance with the subject, especially with the absurd reasonings and conclusions of those, who, through the promptings of infidelity, misapplied its principles. Dr. Cooper, as was reported at the time, received the letter kindly, spoke of it as the production of an able man, and expressed his intention to reply to it. No answer, however, was ever received.

As a writer, Dr. King was somewhat, though not extensively, known. The question respecting the lawfulness of a man marrying his deceased wife's sister was discussed by him in a Dissertation published in the Assembly's Magazine. He was also the author of a Catechism on the Evidences of the Christian Religion, for the benefit of young people; and of a Dissertation on the Prophecies, particularly in reference to the period in which he wrote. These various publications were all highly creditable to the author's learning and ability, although, in regard to the last, subsequent events proved that, like many others, he had mistaken the application of some of the predictions which he undertook to interpret.

During the progress of the great revival in Kentucky and Western Pennsylvania, Dr. King took a very lively interest in the work, and is known to have corresponded very fully on the subject with an intelligent and pious lady,—an intimate acquaintance and friend of his own, then residing in the West. I have made some efforts to recover this correspondence, but as yet without success. From scraps of it which I have seen among the Doctor's papers, I doubt not but it contains much that is valuable, and that his views were such as are in accordance with sound reason, and the decisions of the Word of God.

The Theology of Dr. King was strictly Calvinistic. And, although he cultivated a kind and fraternal spirit towards Christians of every name, he never sacrificed his principles at the shrine of a spurious charity. In the judicatories of the Church he was esteemed a wise and discreet counsellor. He was well acquainted with the government and discipline of the Church, and having been always punctual in his attendance on the meetings of her Courts, he had acquired much experience in the practical application of her laws. At an early period after the formation of the General Assembly, he was called to preside over that body,—his name appearing as *the fourth* on the list of her Moderators.

In his social intercourse, he was remarkable for the cheerfulness of his disposition, and the unaffected simplicity of his manners. In him religion appeared in her most agreeable and attractive forms. As exhibited in his example, her ways were indeed ways of pleasantness, and all her paths peace. His house was ever a place of desirable resort to the young people of his pastoral charge. And while, by the cheerfulness and vivacity of his conversation, he contributed to their enjoyment, he, at the same time, availed himself of the opportunity to impart to them some wholesome advice, and to lead their minds to a serious consideration of the interests of their immortal souls.

For a number of years before his death, Dr. King suffered severely from inflammatory rheumatism. But, although the bodily pain which he experienced from this source was often excruciating, his intellectual powers remained unimpaired to the last, with the exception of some transient disturbances, occasioned by the violence of the fever which accompanied his disease. It was my privilege to visit him, a few weeks before his death,—when he entered into an animated conversation in respect to his own religious views, feelings, and prospects. He said he could see nothing in his past life which afforded him any ground of dependance, and that he had no hope from any other quarter than the glorious scheme of redemption, as revealed in God's Word,—adding with emphasis—"No other way—nothing will do but this." During his illness, he spent much of his time in prayer for himself and others. His desire to depart was so strong that he greatly feared he did wrong in indulging it; but remarked that he strove and prayed against an improper solicitude, wishing to wait the Lord's time.

For some time after his disease had assumed a more threatening and dangerous character, his slumbers were almost constantly disturbed by frightful and distressing dreams. Being much perplexed on account of them, he prayed earnestly to God for deliverance, and it was not long until he found relief. And what led him to remark the special goodness of God in the case was, that he continued to enjoy tranquillity in sleep, although the fever, which might be supposed to have been the occasion of his dreams, remained in unabated force until a very short time before his death. "For so He giveth his beloved sleep."

About ten days before his death, I was present at his bedside, and upon his remarking that he suffered much, I observed that I hoped he received abundant support from above. "Oh, yes," said he, "I am greatly supported." He then went on to say that he had been strongly tempted to doubt with respect to the foundation of his hopes, and whether that system on which he had been accustomed to rely, was agreeable to the word of God; but, convinced that he had long before examined carefully into the grounds of his belief, he sought comfort in prayer to God, and it was but a short time until he found it. "I have now," said he, with a tear of joy sparkling in his eye,—"I have now no doubt of my love to God. He is the most glorious of all objects—no other can be compared to Him." For several days before his departure, he was able to converse but little; but, by detached expressions and significant gestures, he gave pleasing indications of the presence and sustaining power of religion in his soul. His latter end was peace; and in his death, as well as in his life, we have the most satisfactory evidence that though now "absent from the body," he is "present with the Lord."

I am, dear Sir, with great respect,
Yours in Christian bonds,
DAVID ELLIOTT.

CHARLES CUMMINGS.

1767—1812.

FROM THE HON. DAVID CAMPBELL,

GOVERNOR OF VIRGINIA.

MONTCALM, March 25, 1850.

My dear Sir: I have received your letter of the 11th inst., and will, with much pleasure, comply with the request contained in it, so far as I am able.

My father was among the first settlers on the waters of Holston, and I was born on the banks of that river, thirty miles East of Abingdon. In 1782, my father removed to Abingdon, and I have resided within the bounds of the Sinking Spring Congregation ever since. I was baptized by the Rev. Charles Cummings, the first Pastor of this Congregation, attended his preaching from early life, and was intimately acquainted with him for more than twenty years previous to his death, and with all his family. Since his death, I have had access to his papers and family records.

In early life, I was intimately acquainted with many of the old members of his congregation, who were living when he took charge of it in 1772. From them I learned some of the facts which you will find in the following sketch; but most of them were either within my own knowledge, or obtained from authentic records within my reach.

CHARLES CUMMINGS was an Irishman by birth, and came to America in early manhood. It is believed that he obtained his education chiefly in this country. On coming to Virginia, he took up his residence in one of the counties in the Northern Neck. Here, on the 13th of February, 1766, he married Miss Milley Carter, daughter of John Carter, Esq., of Lancaster County. He was now studying Divinity, and was licensed to preach by the Presbytery of Hanover, on the 18th of April, 1767. He was thoroughly educated,—well acquainted with Latin, Greek, and Hebrew, and possessed, for his day, a very large and valuable library. A call was presented for his services from the Congregation of North Mountain, in Augusta County, and he was ordained the 14th of May, 1767. Here he laboured in the ministry five years.

In 1772, he received a call from the people of Holston, forming the Sinking Spring and Ebbing Spring Congregations, and including all the Presbyterians of the Holston Valley, from the head of Holston to the Tennessee line, or as it then was,—the line of North Carolina. I have seen the original call. It was a most admirably drawn document of the kind, and was signed by about one hundred and thirty heads of families,—all members, I believe, of the church, and all men of highly respectable standing in society; many of whom afterwards became much distinguished. This call he immediately accepted, removed with his family, purchased land in the neighbourhood of where Abingdon now stands, and settled upon it. His first meeting-house at Sinking Spring was a very large cabin of unhewn logs, from eighty to one hundred feet long by about forty wide, and it stood near the middle of the present grave yard. It was there for some years after the second meeting-house was built, and had a very venerable appearance.

Mr. Cummings was of middle stature, about five feet, ten inches high, well set and formed, possessing great personal firmness and dignity of character. His voice was strong and had great compass; his articulation was deliberate and distinct. Without apparent effort, he could speak so as to be heard by ten thousand people. His mind was good, but not brilliant. He understood his own system well; spoke always with great gravity, and required it from all who sat under the sound of his voice. He would not tolerate any movement among the congregation after preaching commenced. He uniformly spoke like one having authority, and laid down the Law and the Gospel, as he understood them, with great distinctness.

When he came to Holston, he was about forty years of age. At this time the Indians were very troublesome, and continued to be so for several years; and, generally, during the summer months, the families were obliged, for safety, to collect together in forts. The one to which he always carried his family, was on the land of Captain Joseph Black, and stood on the first knoll on the Knob road South of Abingdon, and on the spot where my own gate now stands. In the month of July, 1776, when his family were in the fort, and he, with a servant, and waggon, and three neighbours, was going to his farm, the party were attacked by Indians a few hundred yards from the meeting-house. Creswell, who was driving the waggon, was killed at the first fire of the Indians, and, during the skirmish, the two other neighbours were wounded. Mr. Cummings and his servant man, both of whom were well armed, drove the Indians from their ambush, and, with the aid of some men from the fort, who, hearing the firing, came to their relief, brought in the dead and wounded. A statement has been published in a respectable historical work, that, on this occasion, Mr. Cummings lost his wig. I am able, from the testimony of one who was present when Mr. Cummings came into the fort, to say that the story has no foundation.

From the year Mr. Cummings commenced preaching at Sinking Spring, up to about the year 1776, the men never went to church, without being armed, and taking their families with them. On Sabbath morning, during most of this period, it was Mr. Cummings' custom—for he was always very neat in his personal appearance—to dress himself, then put on his shot pouch, shoulder his rifle, mount his dun horse, and ride off to church. There he met his gallant and intelligent congregation,—each man with his rifle in his hand. When seated in the meeting-house, they presented altogether a most solemn and singular spectacle.

Mr. Cummings' uniform habit, before entering the house, was to take a short walk alone, whilst the congregation were seating themselves. He would then return, hold a few words of conversation at the door with some one of the elders of the church, then would walk gravely through this crowd, mount the steps of the pulpit, deposit his rifle in a corner near him, lay off his shot pouch, and commence the solemn services of the day. He would preach two sermons,—having a short intermission between them, and then go home.

The congregation was very large, and preaching was always well attended. On sacramental occasions, which were generally twice a year, the table was spread in a grove near the church. Here he preached for many years, and until far advanced in life, to one of the largest, most respectable, and most intelligent, congregations ever assembled in Western Virginia. His Congregation at the Ebbing Spring was equally respectable and intelligent, but not so numerous. What portion of his time he devoted to this congregation is not known. It included the families at the Royal Oak, and for twenty miles in that direction. The meeting-house was built in the same manner as that at Sinking Spring, but not so large.

Mr. Cummings was a zealous Whig of '76, and contributed much to kindle the patriotic fire which blazed forth so brilliantly among the people of Holston in the war of the Revolution. He was the first named on the list of the Committee, appointed by the freeholders of Fincastle County, to prepare an Address to the Continental Congress, setting forth the wrongs and oppression of the British government. After the formation of Washington County, he was chairman of the Committee of Safety for that county, and took an active part in all its measures. He was also Chaplain of the first army that penetrated Tennessee against the Cherokee Indians.

Mr. Cummings was a leading minister of the Presbyterian Church in South-western Virginia, and that part of North Carolina which is now East Tennessee, and was, for many years, the Moderator of the Presbytery. The Rev. Samuel Doak and he might be called the fathers of that part of the Church in their day.

Mr. Cummings died in March, 1812, in about the eightieth year of his age, leaving many and most respectable descendants. He was a sincere and exemplary Christian, and a John Knox in his energy and zeal in support of his own particular Church. He never lost sight of his object, and always marched directly up to it, with a full front and determined will. He performed a great deal of missionary labour, through an extensive district of the country, beyond his immediate field, which was of itself large,—once, at least, going into Kentucky. The fruits of his labours still remain. He was a Presbyterian of the old stamp, rigid in his faith, strict in the observance of the Sabbath, and faithful in teaching his children and servants the Catechism.

With great respect,

I am your obedient servant.

DAVID CAMPBELL.

JOHN WITHERSPOON, D. D.*

1768—1794.

John Witherspoon was a son of the Rev. James Witherspoon, minister of the parish of Yester in Scotland, fourteen miles East of Edinburgh. He was probably the youngest child of his parents, and was born on the 5th of February, 1722. His parentage and family connections were highly respectable. His father was an uncommonly able and faithful minister, and was especially distinguished for the accuracy which marked his public discourses. On the mother's side, he traced an unbroken line of ministerial ancestry, through a period of more than two hundred years, to the great Reformer, John Knox. The father lived several years after the son was settled in the ministry,—probably till sometime after his removal to Paisley, and had the happiness of seeing him one of the ablest and most influential ministers of the Church with which he was connected.

There is reason to believe that the subject of this sketch experienced the power of religion upon his heart at a very early period; and that this was to be attributed mainly to the faithful instrumentality of a devoted Christian mother. At an early age, he was sent to the public school at Haddingtou, where he soon evinced remarkable powers; and so rapid was his progress in the various branches of study, that, at the age of fourteen, he was transferred to the University of Edinburgh, where he continued till he had reached his twenty-first year, when he was licensed to preach the Gospel. He was associated, at the University, with several persons, as fellow-students, who afterwards had a splendid career in life,—such as Blair, Robertson, John Erskine, &c., in the ministry, and many others distinguished in the other liberal professions. His collegiate course fully answered the expectations which had been awakened by his earlier developments; and, at the Divinity Hall particularly, he stood unrivalled for perspicuity of style, logical accuracy of thought, taste in sacred criticism, and

* Sketch of his Life by Rev. Dr. Samuel Stanhope Smith.—Dr. Rodgers' Sermon occasioned by his death.—MS. Memoir by Dr. Green.

all those intellectual qualities and accomplishments, which, in after life, conspired to render him one of the great men of the age and of the world.

Soon after he left the University, he was licensed to preach, and was invited to become assistant and successor to his venerable father in the parish of Yester; but having, in 1744, received a presentation from the Earl of Eglinton to the parish of Beith in the West of Scotland, he, with the unanimous consent of the people, was ordained in the early part of the following year as minister of that populous parish. Here he laboured with much acceptance, receiving many tokens of public and private regard, and many honourable testimonies to his distinguished usefulness. Not long after his settlement, he was married to Elizabeth, daughter of Robert Montgomery, of Craighouse, in Ayrshire. It is a somewhat singular fact that, previous to his marriage, he addressed an intelligent and excellent young lady of Edinburgh, who rejected his proposals; and yet not only a warm friendship, but a most interesting correspondence, was kept up between them, till the close of his life.

Soon after his settlement at Beith, the Pretender to the British throne landed in the North of Scotland, and was speedily joined by a devoted band of Highlanders, who espoused his cause; and a general alarm was spread throughout the country. The famous battle of Falkirk, which proved so disastrous to the Royal army, was fought, January 17, 1746; and among those whose curiosity carried them to witness the encounter with the rebels on that occasion, was Mr. Witherspoon, accompanied by a youth who went in the capacity of a servant. Unsuspicious of danger, he remained in a situation in which he was, with a number of others, made a prisoner. After continuing some time in custody elsewhere, the prisoners were confined in the castle of Donne, then in possession of the rebels. Having been kept in close confinement about a fortnight, and subjected to no small anxiety and some suffering, he at length succeeded in obtaining his release. It has been supposed by some that his nervous system, previously enfeebled by intense study, received a shock from the confinement occasioned by this curious and perhaps rash adventure, from which it did not soon, if ever, fully recover.

Mr. Witherspoon's first appearance as an author was in the year 1753, in an anonymous publication, entitled "Ecclesiastical Characteristics, or the Arcana of Church Policy." It was aimed at certain principles and practices, which then prevailed extensively in the Church of Scotland, and by its acknowledged ability, and particularly by the keenness of its satire, it produced a great sensation, and acquired immense popularity. Within less than ten years after it was first published, it had passed to a fifth edition. This was followed, soon after, by another able performance, entitled, a "Serious Apology" for the Characteristics, in which he avows himself the author of the work which he defends. In 1756, he published his "Essay on Justification," which has always been regarded as one of the ablest Calvinistic expositions of that doctrine in any language. The year after this, he published his "Serious inquiry into the nature and effects of the Stage,"—which also has had a wide and enduring popularity. This work had its origin in the fact that Mr. John Home, a clergyman of the Church of Scotland, had published his well known tragedy of Douglass, which was acted repeatedly in the Edinburgh Theatre, where a number of the author's clerical friends attended. An ecclesiastical procedure in respect to the case resulted in his relinquishment of the sacred office, and his devoting himself exclusively to literary pursuits.

In the year 1757, he was invited by the people of Paisley to become the Pastor of the Low Church in that town. But the Presbytery of Paisley, in consideration of his being the reputed author of the "Characteristics," (for he had not at that time avowed himself the author,) refused leave to grant even a call to be made to him, notwithstanding the unanimous and earnest application of all concerned. The matter, however, was referred, by way of complaint, to the Synod of Glasgow and Ayr; on which occasion he made a most masterly speech, (preserved in the American edition of his works,) in which, without either admitting or denying that he was the author of the work complained of, he managed with such address as not merely to obtain a formal acquittal, but to place his opposers in an exceedingly awkward and undesirable attitude. The Presbytery that had accused him, were obliged to sustain his call, to install him as Pastor of the Church to which he had been invited, and to receive him as a member in good standing, with their own Body; and he was chosen Moderator of the Synod of Glasgow and Ayr, the very next year after he had pleaded his cause before it. After having retained his pastoral charge in Beith for twelve years, he was installed at Paisley, January 16, 1757, as the successor of the Rev. Robert Finley, who was translated first to the North-west parish in Glasgow, and subsequently to the Theological chair in the University of that city.

During the period of his ministry in Paisley, besides discharging with great fidelity the ordinary duties of his office, he preached on various public occasions, and several of these Discourses were printed. In the early part of 1762, he published a Sermon, entitled "Seasonable advice to young persons,"—which subsequently involved him in no small difficulty. The following account of the affair is from a communication procured, in 1835, by Dr. Green, from a gentleman in Scotland, who in early life sat under Dr. Witherspoon's ministry, and who had access to the best sources of information on the subject on which he writes:—

"On Saturday evening, immediately preceding the dispensation of the Lord's Supper, in February, 1762, a few young men in the town connected with the higher ranks, were enjoying themselves in a convivial manner, when, amidst their madness and folly, they went through such religious forms of a profane celebration of that holy ordinance, as caused the inhabitants of the town to make the event that had taken place the subject of general conversation, and to denominate the profane action a mock Sacrament: and I well remember that when the affair was ever mentioned, it was always in strong terms of abhorrence of the blasphemous and wicked deed. In accordance with the general feeling of the respectable inhabitants of the town, Dr. W., a man of keen feelings, and actuated with laudable zeal for the interests of piety, in about a fortnight after the affair had happened, preached a Sermon on the subject of 'Sinners sitting in the seat of the Scornful,' in which he alluded in pointed terms to what had so lately taken place; and firmly believing the reports that had gone abroad, he published the Sermon with an introductory address to the public, with strong remonstrance, and giving the names of the persons accused. This gave great offence, and a prosecution was commenced against the Doctor for defamation of character, which went against him,—the proof having been considered by the judges defective; and he was subjected to a fine or expenses which brought him into pecuniary difficulties, which called his friends to come under engagements. From these engagements it has been generally understood his sureties were not relieved, when the Doctor left Scotland in 1768; and the impression on my own mind was, from the reports I heard in early life, that, had it not been for the friendly interference of those particularly interested in his welfare, he would have been prevented at the time from leaving the country."

The degree of Doctor of Divinity was conferred upon him, in 1764, by the University of Aberdeen; and the degree of Doctor of Laws, in 1785, by Yale College.

In 1764, he went to London and published his "Essays on important subjects," &c., in three volumes. These volumes were composed of pieces which had been previously published in Scotland, with the exception of his celebrated Treatise on Regeneration, which appeared now for the first time. By this means, he became more extensively known as a theological writer, and his fame reached far beyond his own country. Meanwhile, he was engaged in an extensive literary correspondence, both at home and abroad; and such was his reputation that he was invited to take charge of a congregation in Dublin, of another in Rotterdam in Holland, and of a third in Dundee in his own country; but he seems unhesitatingly to have declined them all. He made a brief visit to Holland, previous to his coming to America, but for what specific object does not appear.

Shortly after the death of President Finley, in 1766, the College of New Jersey chose Dr. Witherspoon to be his successor; and the letter informing him of his appointment was enclosed to Richard Stockton, Esq., a member of the Corporation of the College, then in England, with a request that he would visit him in Scotland, and deliver it in person. Dr. Witherspoon, however, owing, as has been said, chiefly to the reluctance of his wife to leave her native country, at first declined the appointment; but, as she became subsequently reconciled to such a step, and other circumstances also seemed favourable to it, he signified his willingness to accept the office, provided the invitation should be renewed. Accordingly, the Board of Trustees proceeded immediately to re-elect him, and, in notifying him of the appointment, expressed a wish that he would enter upon his office at the earliest period that might consist with his convenience.

It being now decided that he should cross the Atlantic, he was called to the painful office of taking leave of his pastoral charge. This he did on the 16th of April, 1768, in an excellent Farewell Discourse, which was published, first in pamphlet form, and afterwards as part of a volume. It was entitled "Ministerial fidelity in declaring the whole counsel of God." The volume referred to was published at Glasgow, on his leaving the country,—partly as an expression of regard for his congregation; and another was published at Edinburgh, about the same time, entitled, "Practical Discourses on the leading truths of the Gospel." The Discourses in the latter volume are so arranged as to form a concise system of Practical Divinity.

Dr. Witherspoon, having made all the arrangements requisite to his departure from the country, embarked from London, with his family, about the 20th of May. The precise date of his arrival in Philadelphia does not appear, though his voyage seems to have been a somewhat protracted one. From the friends of the College in Philadelphia he received a most cordial welcome, and, after having rested there for a short time, he was escorted to Princeton, where he was met with every demonstration of respect and kindness. On the evening of his arrival, the college edifice was brilliantly illuminated; and not only the whole village, but the adjacent country, and even the Province at large, shared in the joy of the occasion. To this most kind and gratifying reception the Doctor referred, with great modesty, and in a most appropriate manner, in the first sermon which he preached after his accession to the Presidency.

Dr. Witherspoon was inaugurated as President of the College, at a meeting of the Trustees, called specially for the purpose, on the 17th of August, 1768; and, either at that meeting or that which was held in connection with the Annual Commencement on the 28th of the following month, (it is impossible now to determine which,) he delivered an Inaugural Address in Latin, on the "Union of Piety and Science." It was soon ascertained that the highest anticipations which had been cherished in respect to his influence in promoting the interests of the College were likely to be realized. He introduced, at once, many important improvements in the system of education, and gave to the institution a more vigorous intellectual tone, and greatly increased its reputation abroad. Particularly, he introduced the method of teaching by lecture, which seems previously to have been unknown to our American Colleges; and he actually delivered Lectures on four different subjects;—namely, Eloquence and Composition, Taste and Criticism; Moral Philosophy; Chronology and History; and Divinity. Though it was impossible that he should go very much in detail into these several subjects, yet they were all handled in a luminous and able manner, and showed at once the versatility and the industry of the lecturer.

Dr. Witherspoon rendered most important service to the College by increasing its library and philosophical apparatus, and introducing the study of the Hebrew and French languages. When he came from Europe, he brought with him three hundred choice volumes as a donation to the College; and this number was afterwards considerably increased, by his influence with his friends in England and Scotland. He was also chiefly instrumental in obtaining the first Orrery constructed by the celebrated Rittenhouse, as well as a tolerable philosophical apparatus from Great Britain, the former of which was greatly injured, the latter nearly ruined, in the war of the Revolution. In 1772, a teacher of Hebrew was appointed in the College, but he seems never to have entered on the duties of his office, and instruction was given in this department by the Doctor himself. A teacher of French actually *was* employed, though it was left at the option of the students whether or not to avail themselves of his instruction. Dr. Witherspoon was himself an adept in French as well as Hebrew, and spoke and wrote the former with almost as much ease and elegance as his mother tongue.

When Dr. Witherspoon entered on his office, the funds of the College were so much reduced that the Trustees could not immediately fulfil their pecuniary engagements to him, and could only instruct their Treasurer to answer these engagements by the first money that should come into his hands. In this exigency, the Doctor made a journey through New England, preaching in several places, particularly in most of the churches in Boston, and soliciting private benefactions in aid of the College. Not less than a thousand pounds were contributed, as the result of his application. A subscription was opened also in South Carolina and Virginia, and some other of the Colonies, chiefly through the influence of Dr. W., which resulted in a yet further increase of the college funds. In consequence of this favourable change in the financial state of the institution, its debts were all paid, and a small surplus remained in the treasury. As the President had. in the mean time, accepted the Professorship of Divinity, in addition to his other duties, the Trustees added fifty pounds to his salary, making it then four hundred. As it was thought important to increase the number of active Professorships,—in order to which a still greater increase of the College funds was necessary, the Doctor was solicited to visit some of the West India Islands, to ask contributions; but, after he had consented to perform the mission, he was providentially prevented from undertaking it. His colleague, the Rev. Charles Beatty, actually went, and died immediately after reaching Barbadoes, and before he had had opportunity to make any collections. It was in connection with this enterprise, which was finally altogether abandoned, that Dr. Witherspoon wrote and published, in pamphlet form, "An Address to the inhabitants of Jamaica, and other West India Islands, in behalf of the College of New Jersey."

Dr. Witherspoon, in connection with his duties as President, discharged with great fidelity those of a Christian minister. In the third and fourth years of his administration, a remarkable revival of religion took place among his pupils, in which a considerable number, who subsequently occupied high places in both Church and State, were supposed to have a share. He sustained the office of Pastor to the Church and Congregation of Princeton, during the whole period of his Presidency,—preaching to them regularly twice on the Sabbath, and performing other duties incident to the pastoral relation. But, at the time when he seems to have been most zealous and abundant in his pastoral labours, a circumstance occurred which seriously threatened the termination of both his ministry and his life. In the midst of a discourse in the church at Princeton, he was seized with an affection of the brain, which obliged him to come to a sudden pause; and, supposing himself able to leave the church, he opened the pulpit door, and almost instantly fell helpless into the pew at the foot of the pulpit stairs, in which his family were sitting. He was but little injured by the fall, and the violence of the fit which occasioned it soon subsided,—followed, however. by a dizziness which, for some time, produced considerable embarrassment in public speaking. This is supposed to have been the first fit of the kind (Dr. Rush expressed the opinion that it was of the nature of apoplexy) that he experienced; though it would seem from a letter addressed by him to a friend in Scotland, that he was afterwards the subject of several similar attacks; which, however, were probably all included within quite a limited period.

The 17th of May, 1776, was appointed by Congress to be observed as a day of Fasting, with reference to the peculiar circumstances of the country. On this occasion, Dr. Witherspoon preached a Sermon, (afterwards published and dedicated to John Hancock, President of Congress,) entitled "The dominion of Providence over the passions of men." This Sermon went fully into the great political questions of the day, and was received on this side the water with the highest approbation; but it gave serious offence to his friends in Great Britain, and an edition of it was subsequently published in Glasgow, accompanied by notes, in which its author was represented as a traitor and a rebel.

The Provincial Congress of New Jersey met a few days after this sermon was preached, and Dr. Witherspoon was a member; though he retained his connection with it only eleven days. During this period, however, the important measure was adopted of arresting, and putting an end to the authority of, the Royal Governor of the Colony,—William Franklin. On the 22d of June, the day after the case of Governor Franklin had been disposed of, he was elected, in connection with five others, to represent the Colony of New Jersey in the Continental Congress;—with instructions, if it should be deemed expedient, to join with their associates in declaring the United Colonies independent. For this responsible place he was eminently qualified, not only by the clearness and vigour of his intellect, the calmness of his judgment, and his indomitable strength of purpose, but by an uncommon familiarity with the forms of public business, acquired from the position which he had held as a leader in the Church Courts in his native country.

Immediately after his new appointment, he left the Provincial Congress; and, having made the necessary preparation for leaving Princeton, repaired to Philadelphia, where he joined the General Congress, a few days before the Declaration of Independence. His mind had been previously made up as to the propriety and the necessity of that measure; and, after he became a member of the Body, he replied to a suggestion that there might be danger of precipitancy in coming to so important a result, that, in his judgment, the country was not only *ripe* for the measure, but in danger of becoming *rotten* for the want of it.

Dr. Witherspoon represented the State of New Jersey in the General Congress, for six years; that is, during the sessions of 1776, '77, '78, '79, '81, and '82. At the close of the year 1779, he resigned his place, from a conviction of his inability to sustain the burden of expense incident to holding it, as well as from a desire to give his particular attention to the revival of the College. He was, however, at the expiration of a year, prevailed on to return to the same field of duty; influenced no doubt chiefly by the critical state of the country, and the urgent solicitations of those who knew his wisdom in counsel, and his energy in action. It would be impossible, within the space allotted to this sketch, even to hint at the numerous important and diversified services which he rendered to his country, during this stormy period. He had great influence as a speaker, but he reserved it chiefly for great occasions. Notwithstanding he had the happiest talent at extemporaneous debate, all his more important speeches were maturely considered, and carefully written, and then delivered memoriter; and yet in a style of such perfect freedom, that no one would have suspected that he had written a word. Many of the most important State papers of the day, in relation to such intricate subjects of political economy as the emission of paper currency, the mode of supplying the army by commission, &c., were from his pen; and though he differed on some points from some of his illustrious associates, and was overruled by them, it has been remarked that he lived to see his own views, in almost every particular, justified by a mature and enlightened public sentiment. He was a leading member of various important committees, and many of the prominent measures adopted by Congress are understood to have had their origin with him. Neither his courage nor his confidence ever faltered in the darkest day; for it was sustained not only by a naturally heroic spirit, and unwavering Christian integrity, but by an undoubting conviction of the rectitude of his country's cause. During the whole period in which he was occupied in civil life, he never laid aside his ministerial character, but always appeared in every relation as became an ambassador of God. The calls for the observance of days of Fasting and Prayer were, commonly, if not always, written by him. He preached also, on the Sabbath, whenever opportunity offered, and always, when, for a short period, he visited his family. Nor would he consent, like some other clerical members of Congress, to change, in any particular, the dress which distinguished his order; wishing not only to remember, but to make others remember, that he was a "minister of God" in a sacred as well as in a civil sense.

During a considerable part of the Revolutionary war, the operations of the College had all been suspended; the principal edifice had been made a barrack, alternately for each of the contending armies; the library and philosophical apparatus had been destroyed; and the funds of the institution, which had always been scanty, had been reduced, by the depreciation of paper money, to a mere pittance. In these circumstances, the Trustees of the College resolved to send a commission across the water, to solicit donations, both in Great Britain and on the Continent;—a measure which, as the event proved, was premature and ill-judged, as the deep-rooted prejudice in Great Britain, occasioned by our national revolt, had not had time to subside. Dr. Witherspoon and the Hon. Joseph Reed, President of Pennsylvania, were appointed to this trust; and, in the month of December, 1783, they sailed for London with a view to execute it. But, on their arrival in England, they found every thing adverse to the object of their mission. Dr. Franklin, Mr. Jay, and Mr. Laurens, who had served with them in Congress, and who were then in Europe in a public capacity, strongly discouraged their application, on the ground that it was not merely unpromising but undignified. Many of Dr. Witherspoon's old friends were still living, but nearly all of them were more or less embarrassed by the change of relations which had occurred in consequence of the part he had taken in the American cause. It is not known that he preached, or was invited to preach, except in Paisley, his former place of residence. Having become fully satisfied that nothing of any moment was to be done for his main object, and probably also that a long visit was scarcely desirable even to his friends, he resolved on a speedy return to America; and, after a prosperous voyage, he reached this country, in the latter part of August, or the early part of September. Though he received a small amount from some few individuals, it was by no means sufficient to cover the expense of the mission.

In the autumn of 1789, Dr. Witherspoon was called to a severe domestic affliction in the loss of the wife of his youth. She was a person of distinguished piety, amiable temper, fine social and domestic habits, and endeared to all who had the privilege of her acquaintance. She had been the mother of ten children, all of whom were born in Scotland: only five of these, however,—three sons and two daughters, survived to accompany their parents to America. His son *James*, a young man of great promise, was Aid to General Nash in the Revolution, and was killed at the battle of Germantown. His son *John* was settled for several years as a practitioner of medicine at St. Stephens Parish, S. C., and is believed to have died at sea between New York and Charleston in the summer of 1795. His son *David*, who graduated with distinguished honour, at the early age of fourteen, married the widow of General Nash, and was successfully engaged for several years in the practice of Law at Newbern, N. C. The daughters of Dr. Witherspoon, by his first marriage, were *Anna* and *Frances*. The former was married to the Rev. Dr. Samuel Stanhope Smith, Dr. Witherspoon's successor in the Presidency of the College; the latter, to Dr. Ramsey, the Historian of South Carolina.

About a year and a half after the death of his first wife, he was married to a young widow, the relict of a Dr. Dill of Philadelphia, and the step-daughter of the Rev. William Marshall, of the Associate Church. The difference of age between him and his second wife was not less than five and forty years. By this marriage he had two daughters, one of whom died in infancy, and the other was married to the Rev. James S. Woods, a Presbyterian minister of Pennsylvania, and is deceased.

During the latter part of Dr. Witherspoon's life, he suffered much from pecuniary embarrassment, in consequence of having ventured some imprudent speculations in Vermont lands. The fact that he was unable to meet his pecuniary engagements subjected him, for a time, to no inconsiderable reproach; though there was never the slightest ground for questioning his integrity. Not long before his death, there was a rigid examination of all his accounts in connection with the College, of which, for many years, he had been almost the sole financial agent; and, though the result was not, in all respects, quite satisfactory, it left not the shadow of a suspicion upon his good name.

After his return from Europe, he was occupied till the close of life, in attending to the concerns of the College, in superintending the cultivation of his farm, on which he resided, two miles from Princeton, and in endeavouring to adjust his secular affairs in Vermont and other places. But, for some time previous to his death, he was utterly deprived of his vision. His blindness commenced first in one eye, from a contusion received in a storm at sea, on his voyage to Britain in 1784. It was occasioned in the other, some six or seven years afterwards, by a fall from a horse, when travelling through Vermont in search of lands which he had purchased in that State. His voyage to Europe, and his speculations in Vermont lands, may be regarded as, in several respects, the two most unfortunate enterprises of his life.

But even after he was thus providentially shut out from the light of day, the activity of his mind still continued, and his labours, in some departments, suffered little abatement. Particularly, he kept up an extensive correspondence, both in this country and in Scotland, in doing which he put in requisition an amanuensis, for at least one day in the week. He was accustomed also to preach every third Sabbath; and, on the preceding Saturday evening, he heard the sermon read which he had selected for the next day, and such was his power of memory that, though the sermon had been written many years before, he could, after a single reading, deliver it, without any embarrassment, and with little or no variation from the manuscript.

His descent to the grave was comparatively easy, and his views and feelings in reference to the approaching change were truly and sublimely Christian. The malady which terminated his life was the dropsy. He presided at the Annual Commencement on the 23d of September, 1794, with his usual propriety and dignity, and on the 15th of November,—less than eight weeks after, closed his earthly career. He was very little confined to his bed, and retained the full exercise of his mental faculties to the last. At the time of his death, he had advanced nine months and ten days in his seventy-third year. His Funeral Sermon was preached by one of the oldest Trustees of the College, and his particular friend, the Rev. Dr. Rodgers of New York: the character or memoir of Dr. Witherspoon, which appears in connection with the sermon, was, at Dr. Rodgers' request, supplied by the Rev. Dr. Samuel Stanhope Smith.

Dr. Witherspoon was undoubtedly one of the ablest, as well as one of the most voluminous, writers of his time. Beside the works already mentioned, he published a large number of Sermons, Lectures on Moral Philosophy, on Eloquence, on Divinity, on Education, Letters on Marriage, an Essay on Money, a work called the "Druid," in a succession of numbers, various Speeches in Congress, and other short articles having a bearing on the state of the country, &c., &c. Some of these, however, were not published till after his death. The only complete American edition of his works was published in three volumes, octavo, in Philadelphia, in the year 1803, under the supervision of the Rev. Dr. Green. An edition in nine volumes, duodecimo, was published in Edinburgh, in 1815.

The following sketch of Dr. Witherspoon's character is extracted from an unpublished Memoir of that eminent man, by the late Rev. Dr. Ashbel Green, who was, for many years, on terms of great intimacy with him, and had every advantage for estimating him correctly. I am indebted to the Hon. James S. Green of Princeton, for the privilege of making this use of his venerable father's manuscript.

"In person Dr. Witherspoon was of the middle size. He was fleshy, with some tendency to corpulence. His limbs were well proportioned, and his complexion was fair. His eyes were strongly indicative of intelligence. His eyebrows were large, hanging down the ends next his temples;—occasioned, probably, by a habit he had contracted of pulling them, when he was under excitement. Like many other clergymen in our country, he laid aside a full bottomed wig at the commencement of our national independence; and thenceforward wore his own natural hair, which covered the whole scalp, and at its lower extremity was confined in an artificial curl or buckle. His countenance united gravity with benignity, in its general expression; and this made the change in its aspect, when he frowned, more sensible and impressive. The features of his face possessed much of what painters denominate *character;* and of course he was a good subject for the pencil. His likeness by the elder Peale is striking. His public appearance was always graceful and venerable, and in promiscuous company he had more of the quality called *presence*, than any other individual with whom the writer has ever had intercourse, Washington excepted. His dress was becoming; avoiding equally the extremes of slovenliness and foppery. In the pulpit he always wore a band, and when he preached at Princeton, a gown likewise.

"It is believed that he was naturally of high temper, with ardent feelings and strong passions. These, however, had, in an eminent degree, been subdued by reason, religion, and habitual vigilance. In the numerous controversies and collisions of party in which he was engaged, especially in the earlier part of his public life, his antagonists never gained an advantage against him by provocation.

He withstood them with unembarrassed firmness, and replied to them with deliberation, sagacity, and consummate address. * * * Against a known enemy it appeared to be a maxim with him not to utter any thing unfavourable, unless it was plainly and imperiously demanded by duty. * * * His wit was never permitted to wound or embarrass the unoffending. He was not profuse in its use in the common intercourse of society; and when indulged among friends, its object was to enliven conversation, and promote innocent hilarity. Its severity was reserved to scourge vice, impertinence or arrogance, whether public or private. He conscientiously avoided every appearance of it in his sermons.

"Dr. Witherspoon was more a man of genius than of learning. He was indeed a scholar, and a ripe one; yet many have exceeded him in various and extensive erudition, whom he greatly excelled in native powers of mind, and in their vigorous, efficient and useful exercise. His reading was select rather than general and promiscuous. * * * What he had read he had well digested, and had formed a system of opinions for himself on various branches of knowledge. * * * That he was not deficient in imagination and wit, his satirical productions furnish unequivocal evidence; and that his memory was prompt and tenacious, was manifest from the facility with which he committed to it his precomposed sermons and speeches, and the confidence with which he could rely on its fidelity to enable him to deliver what he had committed, with accuracy and without embarrassment, before a public audience. His chief mental strength, however, lay in his reasoning faculty. He was a powerful thinker. When he took hold of a subject, he searched it to the bottom; and, in discussing it, he often treated it both analytically and synthetically. * * * His sagacity in discerning the character from indications which generally pass without notice, was truly wonderful. It was difficult for any individual, though previously a perfect stranger, to practise upon him any impositions. It was also surprising to observe with what readiness he could see through a complicated and perplexed subject, estimate its real merits and bearing, disentangle it, and present it in its true aspect. Prudence was a marked feature of his mind and character. He spoke and acted with great discretion, and readily perceived when speech or silence, action or forbearance, was demanded by circumstances. But when satisfied that an object was both proper and feasible, he pursued it with steady but cautious perseverance.

"In a notice of Dr. Witherspoon that appeared in the Edinburgh Christian Instructer of October, 1829, the following statement appears in respect to his Christian character:—'His personal religion is well known. Few men were ever more anxious to walk close with God, and by a solid, righteous and pious life, to adorn the doctrine of the Gospel. Beside the daily devotions of the closet and the family, he regularly set apart with his household the last day of every year for fasting, humiliation, and prayer. He was also in the practice of spending days in secret exercises of this kind, as occasions required.'

"Dr. Witherspoon's Theology was Calvinistic, according to the system of Calvin himself, subject only to the modification which it has received in the standards of the Presbyterian Church. Between him and Calvin, indeed, there was, in talents and improvements, no inconsiderable resemblance. Both were men of great intellectual powers, both eminent divines, both distinguished heads of literary institutions, both erudite civilians, and both keen satirists. Dr. Witherspoon certainly possessed a peculiar talent for presenting the Calvinistic doctrines in a popular form, and in a manner the least offensive to those who do not hold them; while he maintained them firmly in their substance. He was heard to say that the British critics who reviewed his works before he left Scotland, treated him with quite as much candour and respect as he had any right to look for from men whose religious sentiments so widely differed from his own.

"Dr. Witherspoon was among the very few *memoriter* preachers, whose manner is free from all indications that they are repeating what they have learned by heart. There was absolutely nothing of such an appearance in his delivery. This was doubtless in part owing to the simplicity of his language, and to the fact that he did frequently intermingle extemporary remarks, illustrative of what he had precomposed, or with a view to give it enforcement. He also made use of an expedient calculated to favour the appearance of unpremeditated address—it was this:—never to repeat from memory any considerable portion of Scripture, however perfectly recollected, but to open the Bible and read it from the sacred text. He earnestly recommended this to *memoriter* preachers, as calculated to increase the impression of the passages quoted, as well as to break the monotony of delivery. His own manner of doing it much resembled that of an eloquent lawyer, when quoting his authorities. * * * * His action in speaking never exceeded a graceful motion of his right hand, and the inclination of his body forward, when much in earnest. His greatest defect in public speaking was the lowness of his voice when he began. For, although his voice was remarkably articulate, the distant part of a large audience could not hear it distinctly, for a few sentences at first; afterwards, if profound silence was preserved, all that he said was easily audible by every attentive hearer. He affirmed that the nature of his voice required this gradual increase of its volume, to prevent its failing altogether. Yet, take his pulpit addresses as a whole, there was in them not only the recommendation of good sense and powerful reasoning, but a gracefulness, an earnestness, a warmth of affection and solemnity of manner, especially toward and at their close, such as were calculated to produce the very best effects of sacred oratory. Accordingly, his popularity as a preacher was great. The knowledge that he was to conduct a public service usually filled the largest churches in our cities and populous towns, and he never failed to command the profound attention of his audience. * * * * His public prayers were admirable; plain in language, correct, methodical, abounding in a choice selection of scriptural phrases, and uttered with the appearance of deep devotional feeling. When offered on special occasions, their appropriateness was singularly excellent. His manner of introducing and administering the Sacrament of the Lord's Supper surpassed any other performance of that sacred service which the writer has ever witnessed.

"As President of a College, it is believed that no one ever heard him utter a word in derogation of the merit of his predecessors. He lauded every thing in their arrangements, which he thought excellent. He made no violent or ostentatious changes; but introduced his improvements as silently and imperceptibly as was practicable. They mainly consisted in rendering the college course better adapted to qualify his pupils for active life, than it had been previously to his accession to the Presidency; and in this he was unquestionably and highly successful. He inculcated on the youth committed to his care, that transgressions directly contravening our duty to God, were always to be regarded as of the most aggravated kind; and, next to this, he placed deliberate offences against the authority of the College. These were in all cases to receive the severest discipline; while juvenile indiscretions, though not to be regarded as entirely innocent, were to be treated with great lenity. A sacred regard to truth, in an offender under discipline, was ever to be viewed as no inconsiderable mitigation of a delinquency. His official life was of considerably greater duration than that of his five predecessors, taken in the aggregate—their whole term of incumbency was less than eighteen years; his was more than six and twenty.

"Dr. Witherspoon, although habitually a student, and much given to profound thought, was nevertheless far from being a recluse. He greatly enjoyed social intercourse, and might justly be denominated a companionable man. That *presence* which has been mentioned, as attending him in formal company, or in intercourse with strangers, seemed, in a great measure to leave him, when among his friends and intimate acquaintance. With them he engaged in free conversation, permitting it to take its natural course, and promptly contributing his part to keep it up; yet never engrossing it, but allowing to others their proper share. He abounded in anecdote, and had a felicitous talent in giving it the full force of intended application. * * * * The young as well as the old loved his society; and when the company consisted exclusively, or chiefly, of the former class, it was his delight to impart such information or instruction as he thought might be useful to them; and this he did in a manner the most happily adapted to give impression to what he uttered, and to fix it in the memory. There was more of his Scotch dialect in his common conversation than in his public speaking—in both it was very perceptible, yet not extreme in either, nor to his friends unpleasant.

"Dr. Witherspoon professed to be fond of agricultural occupations. In the management of his Tusculum farm, however, it is believed, he did not excel. Of scientific farmers he once said, jocosely, that they could generally assign very good and plausible reasons why their experiments did *not* succeed. He not improbably belonged to this class himself. But in horticulture he was successful. He had practised it in Scotland; and few better kitchen gardens than his at Princeton were any where to be seen. Walking in this garden on a certain occasion with a lady of his acquaintance, she said to him,—"Why, Doctor, I see no flowers in your garden." "No, Madam," was the reply,—"no flowers in my garden, nor in my discourses either."

"He was fond of horseback exercise, and till he was blind, used it, in good weather, as a daily habit. Often, while a member of Congress, he preferred to make his journey to Philadelphia on horseback, rather than by stage. Indeed, the writer does not remember ever to have seen him, while his eyesight continued, in a vehicle of any kind. He accounted himself a good horseman, but, on a certain occasion, was reported to have remarked that, in Scotland, it would have been considered as a great indecorum to put a horse on a gallop; that he never did it there, nor in America, except on one occasion, and that was after Congress, on the approach of the British army to Philadelphia, had adjourned to Lancaster, and he, with other members, was fearful of being overtaken by the enemy's cavalry—a case of necessity surely, for which, even in Scotland, a dispensation might have been granted him.

"He was very punctual in the observance of all appointments, and very intolerant of those who were not. A man in his neighbourhood had made with him an engagement to meet him on some business at a certain place, on a day and hour that were specified. He, as usual, was punctual to his engagement—the other man did not attend at all. They shortly after met by accident, when it was found that the delinquent individual could assign no sufficient reason for his neglect, but said,—"I will positively meet you, Doctor, on such a day and hour," naming them. "No Sir, you will not,"—was the reply—"I must change my mind greatly, if I ever make with you another appointment, while I live."

THOMAS READ, D. D.*

1768—1823.

Thomas Read was born in March, 1746, in the then Province of Maryland, but within the present limits of Chester County, Pa. His parents, John and Eleanor Read, emigrated from Ireland to this country, several years before his birth. His father was a substantial yeoman in the old Country, and a landholder and prosperous farmer in this; and the children,—six in number, were trained up under a strongly religious influence, while they enjoyed some of the best opportunities which the country afforded for the culture of their minds. One of the brothers studied medicine, settled as a practitioner in Philadelphia, and was rising rapidly to eminence, when he was swept off, in 1793, by the yellow fever. Two others migrated, soon after the Revolution, to the Western part of Pennsylvania, where they have left large and highly respectable families.

The subject of this notice was educated at the old Academy of Philadelphia, since merged in the University of Pennsylvania,—then under the Presidency of Dr. Francis Alison. After graduating, in the year 1764, he commenced his career in life as a Tutor in the Classical Academy of Newark, but a few miles from the place of his birth. That institution,—the most distinguished in the State, continued an object of great interest with him till the close of life. He was early chosen its President, and held the office ever afterwards. The cause of Christian education was always near his heart, and he laboured for it almost as earnestly as if he had had no other vocation.

In 1768, having received license to preach, he commenced officiating as a supply for a small congregation, at a place called Drawyer's Creek, in Delaware. In 1772, he received from them a unanimous call, and was regularly installed by the Presbytery as their Pastor. He found them a small and feeble band; worshipping in a log-house in the midst of the wilderness; but within about six years after his installation, they had erected a capacious brick building, and ultimately became one of the most flourishing congregations in the State. During the many years that his connection with this congregation continued, he laboured zealously through the week as a missionary, taking a circuit of from thirty to forty miles; and these labours were attended often with manifest tokens of the Divine favour. He had several invitations, during this period, to settle over congregations that would have been considered in every respect more desirable; but his strong attachment to his people led him to decline them all, until, in the year 1798, he received a call from the Second Presbyterian Church in Wilmington, De., which he thought it his duty to accept. He accordingly did accept it, and removed thither the same year.

In the year 1796, he received the degree of Doctor of Divinity from the College of New Jersey.

As he entered his new field of labour, he quickly found that it was the scene of great disorder. Political disputes were conducted with extreme rancour, and embittered much of the intercourse of society. On one occa-

* MS. from his son, A. S. Read, Esq.

sion, not long after his settlement, a mob assembled around the church door, during the hour of service, and with the sound of drum and fife, and other tumultuous demonstrations, succeeded in interrupting the public worship. He paused in the midst of his sermon, left the pulpit, walked out of the house alone, and by the calm and solemn dignity of his appearance, joined to a kind and Christian expostulation, he succeeded in effectually dispersing the riotous assemblage. Some of the individuals concerned in this disgraceful affair, afterwards became his devoted friends.

In the war of the Revolution, he showed himself an earnest, active patriot. Early in 1776, he and forty or fifty others,—his neighbours and parishioners, fitted themselves out, shouldered their muskets, and marched to Philadelphia. Had they arrived a few days earlier, their services would have been gladly accepted; but the success which had attended the American arms at Trenton and Princeton, rendered it unnecessary that they should be enrolled.

On the 25th of August, 1777, the British army disembarked at Elk Ferry. General Washington was encamped near Stanton, about six miles below Wilmington, and nearly equidistant from the point of disembarkation of the British, and Chads Ford, where the battle was subsequently fought, on the 10th of September, about twenty miles from the camp. A smart skirmish at Couch's Bridge, between the outposts, and within four miles of Washington's encampment, gave the first intimation of the dangerous proximity of the enemy. To give battle in such a position, with our raw troops against disciplined veterans, would prove ruinous—to retreat by the high road, with a well appointed and regular army hanging on the rear, might prove more disastrous than a pitched battle. Every preparation was instantly made for departure; but how to retreat was the great question, and it demanded a speedy solution. The geographical knowledge of the immediate neighbours did not extend much beyond the limits of the contiguous farms, and the roads to the nearest markets; and no information that could be relied upon could be obtained. Between eleven and twelve o'clock at night, a council of war was called; and, while the greatest anxiety prevailed, Col. Duff, a gallant officer, then acting as one of Washington's staff, entered the room, and exclaimed instantly,—"I know the man that can extricate us." "Mount and bring him without a moment's delay," was the order; and immediately the Colonel was on his way to execute it. After travelling about five miles, he arrived at the house of Mr. Read, at twelve o'clock at night, roused him from his bed, and in ten minutes his horse was at the door, and he in the saddle, and both under whip and spur for the camp. In half an hour, they had gone over the whole distance, notwithstanding an exceedingly bad road,—and Mr. Read was introduced to Washington in his tent. He mapped out for the General, within a small space, the whole adjacent country, with all the cross and by-roads accurately marked; and by this means the General effected a safe retreat to the Brandywine. The above incident is related on the authority of Dr. Read himself.

Dr. Read resigned his pastoral charge in the year 1817,—the church having greatly increased in both numbers and moral influence under his ministry. After this, he preached, by request, as often as his health permitted, to the First Presbyterian Church in Wilmington, which had long been without a Pastor. In the year 1821, his right hip was partially dislocated by a fall, and he never afterwards fully recovered the use of it. He died in great peace, June 14, 1823.

Before he was yet of age, he married in Philadelphia a very accomplished lady,—the daughter of an English gentleman by the name of Stanley. She died in 1781, after having become the mother of six children,—three sons and three daughters. He was married a second time in 1788, to Mary, daughter of Alexander Stuart, of Bohemia Manor, in the State of Maryland. By this marriage he had five children,—two sons and three daughters. The second son by the first marriage was a physician, and died in the prime of life. The eldest by the second marriage commenced the practice of Law in Lancaster, Pa., but died unexpectedly a short time after. The other sons were farmers. Dr. Read left a widow who died as she had lived, a model of Christian character, on the 11th of December, 1845, in the eighty-fourth year of her age.

FROM THE HON. KENSEY JOHNS,

CHANCELLOR OF DELAWARE.

NEWCASTLE, February 26, 1852.

Dear Sir: I regret to say that my recollections of the Rev. Dr. Read, formerly Pastor of the Church at Wilmington, are not such as to enable me to express any opinion *of my own*, as to what he was in his various public relations. When he occasionally supplied the pulpit in the Presbyterian Church at Newcastle, he was generally the guest of my father, and was always highly esteemed and beloved by the whole family. I have always understood that he was a learned theologian, an instructive and useful preacher, and an affectionate, zealous and faithful pastor. His personal appearance I remember—it was such as was well calculated to leave an impression—like one of old, he stood above his fellows. His manners at once dignified and affectionate; his countenance expressive of intelligence and benevolence; his head covered with the wig of olden time, so becoming the aged,—altogether presented to your view the venerable minister.

Regretting that my recollections of him are so meagre, and so little to your purpose,

I am respectfully and sincerely yours,

KENSEY JOHNS.

FROM THE REV. JAMES LATTA.

PARKESBURG, Pa., April 22, 1851.

My dear Sir: It was not very long that I was in the ministry before the death of Dr. Read; but I had still some opportunities of knowing him, and my recollections and impressions, such as they are, I am very willing to communicate to you.

Dr. Read was a man of commanding appearance, of remarkably dignified manners, and altogether clerical in his deportment. He was a fine example of hospitality. His brethren were always most cordially welcomed to his house, and he never failed to make himself highly agreeable to them. Young ministers particularly received from him very special attention, and he seemed to delight in proffering them his counsel and aid in every way in his power. As a preacher, he was plain, instructive and impressive—his object evidently was not to gain popular applause, but to win souls to Christ;—not to please the fancy, but to enlighten the understanding, and improve the heart and life. And his every day deportment was a fine illustration of the truths which he preached—his example and his instructions both pointed in the same direction.

During the ministry of Dr. Read, there were several churches in the Newcastle Presbytery without a pastor. Over these he exercised a very watchful and tender care. He frequently visited them, administered to them the ordinance of the Supper, baptized their children, and encouraged and assisted their respective Sessions in the exercise of discipline. These churches reposed great confidence in him, and looked up to him with a sort of filial interest and affection. And his own church, though they regarded him with great esteem and reverence, and placed a very high estimate upon his labours, both in public and private, yet consented cheerfully that other less favoured churches in the region should share with them, to some extent, the benefit of his services. I will only add that Dr. Read was greatly respected throughout the region in which he lived, and the few who still remember him are ready to bear a grateful testimony to his substantial and enduring worth.

Yours very respectfully and affectionately,

JAMES LATTA.

JOHN WOODHULL, D. D.*

1768—1824.

John Woodhull was born in Suffolk County, L. I., January 26, 1744. His father was John Woodhull,—a man of great respectability and influence in the part of the country where he lived; and his mother was Elizabeth Smith, daughter of William Smith, of St. George's Manor, L. I. The Woodhull family emigrated from Great Britain to Long Island, at an early period, and are descended from illustrious ancestors through a long line which is traced back to the Norman conquest.

The subject of this notice was fitted for College in a grammar school, under the care of the Rev. Caleb Smith,—his maternal uncle, minister at Newark Mountains, (now Orange,) N. J. In the year 1762, he entered the Freshman class in the College of New Jersey. At the age of about sixteen, just as he was commencing his preparation for College, his mind was directed with some degree of earnestness to the subject of religion; but it was not till a powerful revival occurred in College, while he was an undergraduate, that he believed himself the subject of a spiritual renovation. His exercises then, and for some time afterwards, are represented as having been of a strongly marked, even extraordinary, character; and when he went to converse with President Finley with reference to making a public profession of his faith, the President is said to have regarded his case with uncommon interest, as furnishing a remarkable illustration of the power of the Gospel.

He graduated in 1766, and almost immediately after proceeded to Fagg's Manor, for the purpose of pursuing his theological studies under the direction of the Rev. John Blair. Here he continued till the summer of 1768, when he was licensed, (August 10th,) by the Presbytery of Newcastle, to preach the Gospel. He commenced his career as a preacher with much more than usual popularity; and on one occasion about sixty people became hopefully pious, in consequence of hearing him preach at a private house.

* MS. from his son, Rev. G. S. Woodhull.—Timlow's Hist. Serm.

He soon received several calls to settle in the ministry; but the one which he felt it his duty to accept was from the Leacock Congregation, Lancaster County, Pa. Here he was ordained and installed on the 1st of August, 1770.

In 1779, the large and respectable Congregation of Freehold, N. J. having become vacant by the death of the Rev. William Tennent,—Mr. Woodhull was called to be his successor. He accepted the call, and in due time was installed over his new charge. This connection was terminated only by his death.

In 1780, he was elected a Trustee of the College of New Jersey, and, during a few of the latter years of his life, was the oldest member of the Board.

In 1798, he was honoured with the degree of Doctor of Divinity from Yale College.

Dr. Woodhull, for many years, in connection with the duties of the ministry, conducted a grammar-school, near his residence, which produced many excellent scholars, some of whom have since risen to distinction. He was also, for a long time, in the habit of superintending the studies of young men in their immediate preparation for the ministry; but, after the establishment of the Theological Seminary at Princeton, in which he took a deep interest, he declined all service of this sort.

Dr. Woodhull enjoyed vigorous health, and continued his labours without interruption till near the close of life. He died suddenly at Freehold, November 22, 1824, in the eighty-first year of his age.

In 1772, he was married to Sarah Spafford of Philadelphia,—a step-daughter of the Rev. Gilbert Tennent. She was a lady of great excellence, and well fitted for the station she occupied. They lived together more than half a century. They had six children,—three of whom were in the liberal professions.

Dr. Woodhull published a Sermon in the New Jersey Preacher, in 1813.

In the winter of 1818–19, while I was yet a student at Princeton, though licensed to preach, I went, at the suggestion of Dr. Miller, to Freehold, to pass a Sabbath with Dr. Woodhull. It was my first acquaintance with him, and a letter from Dr. Miller was my introduction. I reached his hospitable but rather humble dwelling, on Saturday evening. He and his wife gave me a cordial welcome, and I soon found that I was to be amply rewarded for my journey. The house which he occupied, stood, I think, in an open field; and he quickly told me that it was on or near the spot on which was fought the famous battle of Monmouth. It was the house in which William Tennent had lived before him, and where Whitefield had often been a guest; and I remember his saying that when something of which he was speaking occurred, "Whitefield sat there, and Tennent sat there." His reminiscences of the olden time, and especially of the events of the Revolution, seemed inexhaustible; and what rendered them the more interesting was, that he scarcely spoke of any thing of which he was not himself a sharer or a witness.

I remember an interesting circumstance that he related to me in connection with his own personal history. He stated that, after he went to Fagg's Manor to study Theology with Mr. Blair, he was strongly urged by some pious young men from New England, who had been his classmates in College, to come and study with them under the direction of the celebrated Dr.

Bellamy. So urgent were they in their request, that he had concluded to make the change, provided it should meet the approbation of his father. He accordingly went home, obtained his father's consent, and made all his arrangements to set out on a particular day for Bethlem,—the residence of Dr. Bellamy. When the morning of the day came, he awoke, as he supposed, in his usual health, but, on attempting to dress himself, found that he was so ill that he could only fall back into his bed. It was the commencement of a severe and protracted illness, which prevented him from fulfilling his purpose to go to New England. When he recovered, he returned and finished his preparatory studies under Mr. Blair. He considered this circumstance as having given, in a great degree, the complexion to his subsequent life.

He told me that he had the story of Tennent's trance from his own lips. While he was an undergraduate at Princeton College, he said that a rebellion occurred among the students, and as it was thought desirable that there should be a meeting of the Trustees in reference to it, he was sent out to Monmouth to request Mr. Tennent's attendance. They started together just at evening to come to Princeton; and, shortly after they set out, Dr. Woodhull said that he ventured to say to Mr. Tennent, that he had heard that he had at some time been the subject of a remarkable trance, and, if he did not object, he should be much gratified, if he would give him some account of it. Mr. Tennent paused, and said that it was a subject on which he was always reluctant to speak; but still he was willing to state to him some of the particulars. He then went on and told the story at length; but it is not necessary that I should record it here, as it will be found in a letter from Dr. Woodhull, in connection with the notice of Mr. Tennent, in this work.

I attended church on the Sabbath with Dr. Woodhull, and stood over the spot where Tennent's remains rest. The old gentleman seemed as much awake to all the hallowed associations of the place, as I was, who had never been there before. My visit was altogether one of great interest, and on various accounts, never to be forgotten.

One of Dr. Woodhull's sons, *George Spafford*, entered the ministry. He was born at Leacock, Pa., on the 31st of March, 1773. Having received the elements of his classical education under the instruction of his father, he entered the Junior class of the College of New Jersey in the autumn of 1788, and graduated in 1790. After studying Law two years, and Medicine one year, he became hopefully pious, and immediately after resolved to enter the ministry. He commenced the study of Theology under the direction of his father, in the summer of 1794, and was licensed to preach the Gospel on the 14th of November, 1797. On the 6th of June, 1798, he was ordained to the work of the ministry, and installed Pastor of the Church at Cranberry, N. J. In the spring of 1820, he received a call to take the pastoral charge of the Church in Princeton, and having accepted it, was installed on the 5th of July of that year. Here he remained twelve years, and had an uncommonly successful ministry. In 1832, he resigned his charge, and shortly after accepted a call from Middletown Point, N. J., where he spent the last two years of his life. He died of scarlet fever on the 25th of December, in the sixty-second year of his age, and in the thirty-seventh of his ministry. He was eminently blameless and exemplary in his life—eminently peaceful and happy in his death.

FROM THE REV. JOHN McDOWELL, D. D.

PHILADELPHIA, June 10, 1852.

Dear Sir: My acquaintance with the Rev. Dr. John Woodhull commenced in the spring of 1802, when I began my course of theological studies under his direction. From that time I resided in his family for two years, and had an opportunity of knowing him intimately in his private as well as his public relations. After I entered the ministry, I had often the privilege of meeting him, and our intimacy continued unabated to the time of his death.

Dr. Woodhull had the advantage of most men in his personal appearance. He had a fine, tall, well proportioned frame, and his motions were easy and graceful. His countenance was expressive of vigour and intelligence, as well as honesty and strength of purpose. His manners were free and agreeable, but never lacking in dignity. He had fine powers of conversation, and could accommodate himself with great facility to any circle into which he might be thrown. You could not have been in his company, without feeling that you were in the presence of a well bred gentleman of the old school.

As a theologian, Dr. Woodhull was thoroughly Calvinistic. I do not think he was very extensively read in Theology—certainly his library was very limited; and yet he seemed to understand well the doctrines and the relations of his own system. As a teacher, he moved pretty much in the beaten track, and had a set of written questions from which he rarely departed in the examination of his students. Still, his remarks were always sensible and weighty, and were rather indicative of a naturally vigorous mind, than of a habit of close application. He generally had with him theological students, and among them were some who have since attained to eminence in their profession.

As a preacher, Dr. Woodhull was popular and useful, but it may reasonably be doubted whether he ever came up to the full measure of popularity or usefulness of which he was capable. He preached without very mature preparation, and there was less variety in his sermons than could have been desired; but there was always method, and appropriate scriptural illustration; while his style of elocution was free and attractive. The probability is that if he had been a more laborious student, his preaching would have commanded more attention, at least from the more intelligent part of the community; and yet his sermons were never otherwise than highly respectable.

Dr. Woodhull was distinguished for his skill and tact in ecclesiastical bodies. Here he exercised great influence, and his judgment was always highly respected. Indeed, his general influence in the Church, and in society at large, was exceeded by that of few of his contemporaries. He had a weight of personal character that made him felt wherever he was known.

He retained his vigour in an uncommon degree to old age. I remember hearing him deliver an Address, when he had reached fourscore, before the American Bible Society. I heard some person sitting near me remark, as the Doctor was about to speak, that he wondered they should have brought forward such an old man to speak on such an occasion; but I heard the same person say, at the close of the meeting, that the old man had proved to be the very best speaker of the day. He really put forth uncommon energy on the occasion, and acquitted himself with great credit.

Dr. Woodhull was not more remarkable for any thing than a habit of punctuality. He made it a matter of conscience to fulfil every engagement, even in respect to the least important concerns, and at the time appointed. It was this habit undoubtedly that formed a material element of his usefulness, and helped to give a complexion to his character.

With much respect, yours,

JOHN McDOWELL.

HEZEKIAH BALCH, D. D.*

1769—1810.

HEZEKIAH BALCH was born of pious parents in Harford County, Md., in the year 1741. While he was yet a child, his father removed his family to an elevated and salubrious tract of country in Mecklenburg County, N. C.; and it was here that the subject of this sketch passed most of his early years.

In 1758, he was admitted as a student of the College of New Jersey, at the recommendation of the Rev. John Rodgers, (afterwards Dr. Rodgers of New York,) and was graduated there in 1762. For a considerable time after his graduation, he was engaged in teaching a school in Fauquier County, Va. He was licensed to preach by the Presbytery of Newcastle between the meetings of Synod in 1768 and 1769. Soon afterwards we find him labouring as a missionary within the bounds of the Presbytery of Hanover, then reaching from the Potomac indefinitely towards the Pacific. For the increase of his usefulness, this Presbytery ordained him as an evangelist, on the 8th of March, 1770. The Synod of New York and Philadelphia, at their next sessions, constituted him and six other ordained ministers, the Presbytery of Orange.

It was during his ministrations in North Carolina that Mr. Balch first made his acquaintance with the young lady who became his wife. Her name was Hannah Lewis. She was a person of fine intellect and great personal attractions, but was, in after life, occasionally under some degree of mental derangement, which proved a great trial to her husband, and a serious embarrassment in the training of their younger children. They had six children,—four sons and two daughters. The eldest daughter became the wife of the Rev. (afterwards Dr.) Robert Henderson. After the death of Mrs. Balch,—about the year 1808,—he was married to Ann Lucky, a native of Pennsylvania, who removed to Tennessee in 1795 or 1796, and who was also a lady of excellent character, Her father was Robert Lucky, a native of New York. She died in Jonesborough, in 1835, aged seventy-two, having had no children.

Mr. Balch felt encouraged to bestow a portion of his labours on some of the destitute parts of Pennsylvania, and with a view to this, obtained a dismission from Orange Presbytery to join that of Donegal, between the meetings of Synod in 1774 and 1775. For about one year he supplied the Presbyterians in the village of York. After his return to the Presbytery of Hanover, which had ordained him, he received more frequent notices of the growing demands for ministerial services among the numerous Presbyterian settlers in the part of North Carolina, West of the Allegany mountains. Having made no small proof of his ministry, from 1769 to 1784, on the Atlantic slope near their Eastern side, and being urged by the zeal and enterprise of the Gospel pioneer to present himself where most needed, he formed his determination to cross the mountains, and cast in his lot with the people of God in the West.

*MS. from Rev. Dr. Coffin.—Foote's Sketches of N. C.

It was not much before the date of the charter of the Presbytery of Abingdon in 1785,—the first on the Western waters, within what is now Tennessee,—in which his name appears with those of two other petitioners and original members, the Rev. Messrs. Samuel Doak and Charles Cummings—that he removed with his family into the vast Western wilderness; where there roamed at large, in untamed ferocity, the Cherokee Indians,—furious with jealousy of the white population, that were then rapidly taking possession of their favourite hunting grounds. Here Mr. Balch, by reason of his age and experience, was called to take part in organizing churches. Among these was the First Presbyterian Church in Greenville, of which, ere long, he became the pastor; and it grew under his ministrations to be the largest in the Valley of the Holston and Tennessee. His most frequent exchanges of labour, as well as his most intimate consultations at this period, were with the Rev. Samuel Doak, who had settled somewhat earlier at Salem Church, Washington County; where he had opened a private classical school, which was the germ of one of the most important institutions that have been established in the South West.

It was mainly through the combined influence of these two brethren, that Dr. Watts' Version of the Psalms was introduced, instead of the former one by Rouse, into use in the churches in that region. The measure had to encounter violent opposition, and was not a little prejudiced by the indiscreet zeal of some of its advocates. Mr. Balch preached a Sermon on the subject, at the opening of the Presbytery of Abingdon, in October, 1786, which produced a great effect at the time, and which was published seven years afterwards, under the title—"Gospel Liberty in singing the praises of God, stated, illustrated, and urged." This sermon, with other concurrent means that were used, wrought a gradual change in public opinion, until the object which the Sermon contemplated was finally accomplished.

There was one procedure in which Mr. Balch and Mr. Doak were associated, after their removal to Tennessee, which was at once too remarkable and too characteristic to be omitted. By reason of very high waters keeping their brethren of the Presbytery away from them at the time and place of one of their fall sessions, they found themselves alone, except some few elders. The meeting was specially important, as the Presbytery had expected to license a candidate, whose trials had almost been gone through, and whose labours were impatiently called for by deplorable destitutions. After waiting in vain for absent brethren, they united with the elders present in prayer for Divine direction; and when they had held a free and satisfactory consultation, they opened and constituted as a Presbytery; finished the remaining trials of the candidate; licensed him to preach the Gospel, and appointed his labours for the next six months, or in other words, till the next stated sessions of Presbytery. They made a faithful record of their proceedings, and pledged themselves to each other, under consent and order of Presbytery, to attend together the next meeting of Synod; (for it was before the formation of the General Assembly;) submit their Records for review; meet any censure for irregularity; and state what they believed were the justifiable reasons of their procedure. A journey of six hundred miles on horseback brought them to Philadelphia, seasonably for the meeting of Synod. When the Committee, charged with the review of their Records, were called upon to report, the speaker and his fellow reviewer were thrown into such a convulsive and half suppressed titter, at what they regarded the wild vagrancy of their brethren in the backwoods, that they could scarcely compose themselves sufficiently to make an announcement of the irregularity. But though the Assembly were at first prepared to condemn the procedure, yet, upon hearing Mr. Balch's full and pathetic explanation, they were perfectly satisfied, and dismissed the matter with the most kindly spirit, and without a disapproving word.

Mr. Balch identified himself with the political troubles growing out of the formation of the State of Franklin. In consequence of this, he fell into a controversy with the Rev. William Graham of Virginia, who addressed a letter to him through the press, which was made the ground of an ecclesiastical process against the writer before the Old Synod; and when the General Assembly was formed, the cause fell under the jurisdiction of the Synod of Virginia.

About the year 1793, Mr. Balch had conceived, matured, and communicated to some of his friends, the plan of Greenville College. When the Territorial Legislature met in 1794, he applied for a Charter, and the granting of it—by which also he was constituted President and ex-officio a Trustee—was the first act of that Body; and he was allowed to have a plat of ground for the College near his own dwelling. When a copy of the Charter was delivered to Mr. B., an influential member of the Assembly said to him—"Now, Sir, you will have to travel and collect funds to put the College in operation, as George Whitefield did for his Orphan House." Mr. Balch replied that he had indulged no other expectation.

The next year, (1795,) he visited New England to collect funds for the new institution; and in that visit may be said to have originated a theological controversy which gave a somewhat polemical character to his whole future life. The full history of that controversy is to be gathered only from the Records of the different Ecclesiastical Bodies in which it was carried on; but some of the most prominent facts in connection with it will be found in the subjoined communication from the venerable Dr. Coffin, whose testimony will not be impaired, in the view of any body who knew him, by the fact that he is understood to have sympathized somewhat with Mr. Balch in his theological speculations. As his account, however, terminates with Mr. B.'s being acquitted with an admonition from the General Assembly in 1798, it may not be amiss to state that this was by no means the termination of the controversy. Previous to his trial before the Assembly, a civil suit had been instituted with a view to dispossess him and his adherents of the meeting house; and while this was pending, it was attempted to eject him from the pulpit by force. In the midst of a most tumultuous scene that occurred the Sabbath after his return from the Assembly, he retired with a large part of his congregation to a wide spreading tree, a short distance from the church, and there read the papers relating to his trial and acquittal by the Assembly. He subsequently performed Divine service there for several months; and such was his attachment to the spot that he intimated a wish to be buried there, provided it could be done without impropriety. Though his congregation was now divided into two, the greater part remained with him, and, as might have been expected, regarded both him and his theological system with increased favour. The decision of the law-suit restored the meeting house to him and his congregation, as the ascertained majority,—and in due time they resumed their worship in it.

In October following his trial before the Assembly, several charges were brought against him, before the Synod of the Carolinas, by a reference from the Union Presbytery,—the most grave of which was that he had acted with duplicity in making certain statements after his return from the General Assembly that were inconsistent with what he had said before that Body. Most of the charges were pronounced unsustained, but the one just mentioned was considered as proved, in consequence of which Mr. B. was suspended from his office as a minister, until the Presbytery of Union, to which he belonged, having become satisfied of his penitence, should see fit to restore him. At the same time the sentence of suspension from the office of elder and from the Communion of the Church was pronounced upon four of the elders who had appeared against Mr. Balch, "for the impropriety and irregularity of their course." Both parties expressed their submission to the judgment of Synod, and received a suitable admonition from the Moderator.

In 1800, Mr. Balch and several others, were constituted, by their own request, a New Presbytery, by the name of Greenville Presbytery. The same year he preferred a charge before the Synod against the Presbytery of Abingdon for having ordained his successor in the Mount Bethel Church, before they had settled their pecuniary accounts with himself, and for having ordained a man of questionable orthodoxy.

The degree of Doctor of Divinity was conferred upon him by Williams College in 1806.

When the Rev. (afterwards Dr.) Charles Coffin took up his permanent residence in Tennessee, about the beginning of the year 1805, he became associated with Dr. Balch in the labours of both the pulpit and the College. Dr. B. continued to labour in both relations as much and as long as he was able, though for the last two or three years of his life, his increasing infirmities rendered him incapable of severe or continuous exertion. He died after a brief but most distressing illness in Aprile, 1810.

It has already been stated that one of Dr. Balch's daughters was married to the Rev. Robert Henderson. She died, in her twenty-fifth year, on the 11th of March, 1795; and, according to the account of her last hours, written by her husband and published in the New-York Missionary Magazine of 1802, there has rarely been exhibited a more strongly marked scene of Christian triumph. Her father, who arrived just in time to see her die, asked her several questions designed to bring out the state of her mind in regard to his favourite doctrine of "unconditional submission;" and he expressed himself perfectly satisfied with her answers.

It is now (1857) several years since the last of Dr. Balch's children deceased. Several of his grandchildren entered the ministry, but not till some time after his death. His adopted son, the nephew and foster-child of his second wife,—*Seth J. W. Lucky*, was graduated at Greenville College; has been, for several years, on the Bench in Tennessee, first as a Circuit Judge, and now as a Chancellor, and is not only an exemplary and influential member, but an active and useful elder, of the Presbyterian Church in Jonesboro'. It was in his house that the second Mrs. Balch spent her last years.

FROM THE REV. CHARLES COFFIN, D. D.

PRESIDENT OF GREENVILLE COLLEGE.

GREENE COUNTY, Tenn., March 30, 1850.

Rev. and dear Brother: I have been casting about me for some time to see if I could not find some person more competent to do justice to the character of the Rev. Dr. Hezekiah Balch than myself; but time has made such desolating work with his contemporaries that I am almost ready to say that I am the only one left to testify concerning him. I have, therefore, determined to make an effort to comply with your request; though, in doing so, I feel bound to say that I am quite aware that I am undertaking a task of no small delicacy. Dr. Balch, more than almost any other man of his day, was involved in controversy; and was called to answer for alleged theological errors at each of the several Church Courts to which he was amenable. His most vigorous opposers were undoubtedly conscientious and excellent men, and I would not even seem to cast a shade upon their memories. But it is no reflection upon either him or them to admit that both were fallible, and *that* doubtless must appear in what I shall feel obliged to say in performing the service you have allotted to me. I cherish Dr. Balch's memory with affectionate veneration, and am glad that you propose to make him the subject of an enduring record. I knew him most intimately, having lived several years under his roof, and my family with me the latter and larger part of the time.

My first sight of this interesting man was in the summer of 1795, in the town of Newburyport, my native place, where I was then engaged in the study of Theology. The South Western Territory had recently been organized. At his suggestion, the charter of Greenville College had been granted by its first legislative Act, but without any provision of funds to enable him, as the President, to make it useful. After a successful visit to Charleston, S. C., to procure donations and endowments, he passed through the Middle and Eastern States, as far as Portland in Maine; and I afterwards found that both the President and Board of Trustees were well satisfied with the amount that was obtained. I heard him preach twice in different churches, and enjoyed his conversation at my father's house. His personal appearance was prepossessing,—with a dark coloured, lustrous, commanding eye, a full habit and erect frame of body; and his address was animating and full of benignity, both in the house of God and the private circle. His preaching was evangelical, hearty and impressive. The general bearing of his manner fastened itself on my memory as being well designated by the following words in his first sermon:—"I now come to the application, which I ever think to be the life of preaching." When he called the next day, my father, after making his donation, spread before him on the table Dr. Morse's first large map containing the South Western Territory; thinking to gain from him, as he did, some further knowledge of his country's Geography. I was myself very much interested while the President pointed out the ranges of the mountains, the beautiful valley of his residence, its water courses and fertile grounds; and described the climate as one of the most salubrious and delightful upon earth. The early concern for a College, amid the growing population soon to become a State, appeared to me a noble imitation of the patriotic care which made the founding of Northern Colleges so much a primary object. In about a year from that time, the new State of Tennessee was organized. In the spring of 1799, I was licensed to preach. A providential affliction in my eyes had been severely troublesome to me for two or three preceding years. I had suffered much from the wintry storms and piercing winds of the North, and from the overpowering reflection of the dazzling sunbeams from the snow and ice. A milder climate for the cold season was recommended by physicians. A conviction had likewise fastened upon my mind that some months might usefully be occupied in travelling, and gaining knowledge of the diversified population of our extensive Union, which might be followed with some important advantages through life. My recollections of President Balch were lively and pleasing. I passed the greater part of the subsequent winter preaching in the South, and wrote Mr. Balch a letter, intimating that I had some thoughts of visiting him in the spring. In his answer, he urged me to cross the mountains, and made the following somewhat startling communication:—"Since my return from New England, Sir, I have been cited to ecclesiastical trial for errors imputed to me by my prosecutors, sixteen times before Presbytery; four times before Synod; and once before the General Assembly. I had not far short of one hundred scholars in the College. But my interruptions and absences to attend my trials arrested the progress of the institution. The students were obliged to go home. Nevertheless, Sir, all that I have suffered has only served to confirm me more and more in the belief that what I have contended for is God's Bible truth, and will stand forever. My prosecutors have never yet taught me the doctrine of fear. Come over, Sir, and I hope God will so order it that you will fall in love with our country." My heart, I must confess, grew warm towards the man.

On the 11th of July, 1800, I rode up to his gate; and when he had ascertained my name, he said with tears filling his eyes—"I believe, Sir, there is a God in Heaven who hears prayer." In subsequent conversations he informed me that, long before his Northern journey, he had felt a confidence that clearer light than he had attained on the cardinal doctrines of grace, as to their agreement and harmony with each other, their fitness to honour God and feed and bless his people, was in all probability to be found somewhere; and that he had often thought he would account it but a small sacrifice to take his staff, and travel on foot to the ends of the earth, to find the man who could so unfold the mind of the Spirit, contained in the Sacred Scriptures, as to pour the desired light into his soul. He said it was impossible for him to travel under the rare advantages of improving conversation with the most enlightened ministers and other Christians, which he enjoyed, while soliciting for the College, without an earnest spirit of theological inquiry. "This," said he, "the great and good Dr. Green of Philadelphia did much to invigorate and direct by his kind, brotherly counsels to me on my way to the North, for which I have ever been thankful. He told me that I would find, as he did, in the Northern States, a class of ministers, some of whose religious sentiments were considered erroneous, while their main tenets were unquestionably Calvinistic. He advised me by all means to become acquainted with these men. 'I do not myself agree with them,' he said, 'in every thing; but in some things which are questioned, I know they are right. I found reason to esteem them as among the most laborious students, faithful pastors, successful preachers, and instructive writers in all New England.'" "Now," added Mr. Balch, and often did he take occasion to repeat it in my ears, —"these were the very ministers who most assisted me to obtain donations; and who afforded me, by conversations and books, my principal helps in the investigation of religious truth." He informed me that he preached, of course, boldly and explicitly, on his return, his most illustrative thoughts on Gospel doctrines, as had ever been his way; keeping nothing back of the whole counsel of God; fully persuaded that he had learned better to understand it by his opportunities of receiving additional light. "I took pains," said he, "to assure ministers and people, privately and publicly, that I believed more firmly, because more intelligently, than ever before, the cardinal doctrines of free and sovereign grace, which I had so long preached; but I blessed God He had led me into a clearer knowledge of them all in their inspired meaning and essential harmony; that I felt myself able to unfold them, and defend them, in a more consistent manner, and to preach the truth on one topic, without taking it back again, when discussing another."

As to the views which rendered Dr. Balch obnoxious to many of his brethren, it is impossible, in so brief a space as is allotted to me in this letter, to go into detail. It will perhaps be sufficient to say that he sympathized with that class of New England divines, who were and still are known as Hopkinsians. His most familiar and favourite sentiment was that all true holiness, both in God and his intelligent creatures, consists in impartial, disinterested good-will, love or benevolence to all beings capable of happiness; and a benevolent complacency in the moral excellence of all who possess this essential qualification for happiness, and for promoting its diffusion. The first impression which his preaching made upon his church and large congregation after his return from the North and East, as I received abundant evidence from many of them, was very generally favourable. But alarms were gradually excited among his people, and in due time, when he thought the case required it, he was heard by his Presbytery,—that of Abingdon; before whom he stated what were his views of Divine truth, which he fully believed were vindicated both by the Bible and the Confession of Faith. So satisfied were the majority of that body that he embraced nothing heretical, or dangerous to the souls of men, that they passed a vote to this effect; and agreed individually to do what they could to quiet any alarms existing among the people.

But so dissatisfied were the minority with this procedure, and so little did they expect any appeal could serve their cause, that they withdrew from the connection of the Synod and General Assembly, and constituted themselves an independent Presbytery. At their return to order, with due acknowledgment to Synod of the incautious step they had taken, the Presbytery of Union, composed of Mr. Balch and those ministers of Abingdon Presbytery, who had not taken ground against him, was constituted; and with what spirit, the very name by which they chose every where to be known, sufficiently and very truly indicates. Yet the alarms kept up by the remaining members of the Presbytery of Abingdon, extended to those who had removed from Washington and Greene Counties, to inviting lands below, within the bounds of Union. Yet the better spirit ultimately prevailed. Even the venerable fathers themselves, who saw most to disapprove in Mr. Balch's sentiments, and felt called upon to oppose them most sternly, were too good not to welcome the peaceful gales from Heaven, as they drew near to the promised land of light, love, and concord. They were able and faithful men, who held with intelligence and tenacity the views in which they had been educated; who rendered much important service to the Church in their day; and whom to know was surely to venerate and love. The opposing and the opposed, have, it is believed, already joined together in the never-ending song before the throne,—"Not unto us, but unto thy name be the glory," Oh God of our salvation!

In regard to Mr. Balch's most important trial at the bar of the General Assembly, representing the whole Presbyterian Church before its division, I have not one tenth part of the desirable space for rendering the honour most justly due to the ever present Head of his militant Church; to that faithful and enlightened judicatory which could do nothing against the truth, but for it; and its imperfect yet heroic witness, enjoying the privilege of answering for himself. After my first visit to Mr. Balch and his ministerial brethren in the Presbyteries of Abingdon and Union, I passed two or three times between Tennessee and my native State, and had opportunities of hearing frequently about the particulars of his trial. I was informed by ministers and others in the Middle States, that when the charges against him had been publicly read, and the testimony heard, and his time for defence was announced, he rose with humble boldness, and nobly exerted his powers to distinguish, explain, and prove from the Bible, what he had been contending for as the truth of God; that he was heard with profound attention by that venerable body, and a large crowd of spectators; and that he was much extolled by persons present for his frankness, intrepidity, perspicuity, and earnestness, combined with the submissive deference due to so respectable and numerous an assembly of ecclesiastical judges. In order to show something of the impression made at the time upon men of improved minds and deep thinking, it may suffice to state one anecdote, out of a number. The celebrated Dr. Rush, in the midst of extensive professional engagements, had received such information of the interesting trial of a Tennessee clergyman, that he chose to take time, and hear the defence. At the close of Mr. Balch's speech, the Assembly adjourned for dinner. The Doctor procured at the door an introduction to him; though he had seen him on his soliciting tour, and given him his patronage by his name and donation. He pressed him to go home and dine with him. Mr. Balch made his arrangements with reference to others, and went with the Doctor. "Sir," said the latter, "when a Gospel minister will come six hundred miles to face his prosecutors, and defend the assailed principles of his religious faith with the zeal and intrepidity which I have witnessed to-day, before the highest tribunal on earth to which he could be cited, my heart cannot but beat warmly in his favour, whether his sentiments and mine are identical or not." On my first return to the North, I had myself already read in Mr. Balch's papers the substantial history of the trial; but did not omit, while in Philadelphia, to call on the Rev. Dr. Milledoler who was at that time the Recording Clerk of the General Assembly, and, by his indulgence, to read in the folio book of Records the full account, in the corrected Minutes, of the whole trial and its result. Every thing was, as the certified extracts I had read before, attested. During my first visit, after spending a few months with Mr. Balch, and preaching and becoming acquainted in the general neighbourhood, I had got thoroughly to feel that he understood what he contended for; as he did not once, in all our conversations, give and take back any Gospel doctrine about which I found the controversy had been maintained. I began now to think seriously whether it might not be my duty to comply with his oft repeated request, and settle down by him as an instructer in the College, and a preacher in the town and vicinity. Having, from my early attachments, some reluctance on this point, and feeling some sense of obligation not to decide rashly, I became the more inquisitive to learn more distinctly, not merely from Mr. Balch, but from all accessible sources of information, what sentiments were supposed to be erroneous in his preaching; what he had been understood to maintain on the topics discussed, and especially, how the several judicatories that had tried him, had finally pronounced upon his religious views. I was now so happy as to find that it was not less his wish, than my determination, that I would hear every thing his opposers as well as friends might have to say. I was deeply impressed with the idea that my prospect of usefulness in the whole region, if I should settle in East Tennessee, would greatly depend upon my obtaining a correct knowledge of the minds of the people on the subjects so much debated. Hence I carefully sought and improved opportunities of free and friendly conversation with men of every class; with all the brethren in the ministry, old and young,—whether approving or disapproving Mr. Balch's views; also with his adherents and opponents among the people, and with serious observers in other denominations. After this extended and persevering investigation, I became satisfied that he was a vigorous and earnest defender of the leading doctrines of Hopkinsianism; that he had embraced the system intelligently as well as cordially, and that he had most unflinchingly and minutely defended before each judicatory what he had wittingly and confessedly held, and what he informed them he could not without new light renounce. Imprudences, in several instances, of speech and conduct were confessed; also some injudicious selections of words and phraseologies were reported by witnesses, and charged upon him. In these cases he seemed to have been ingenuous, docile and submissive; though he once or twice declared that he did not appear to have been understood. When the Assembly's Committee brought in their report upon his "creed," (See the Digest,) in which they pointed out three particulars as errors held by him, according to their understanding of words ascribed to him by witnesses, and after hearing his defence, he said he felt assured, when he heard them read, that he had never held or asserted them as truths. Hence the thought immediately struck him,—men appear now to be leaving you; if God should leave you, your condition would indeed be dreadful. "But," he added, "the very next thought that took possession of my soul, and nerved me afresh, was—I will at all events stick to God's truth." That very evening, a clergyman,—not of the Assembly, who had been a close observer of the whole course of the trial,—one who felt, as he perceived many others did, that the Committee had been led, by words reported as Mr. Balch's, to mistake his real sentiments, as he had unfolded them in his principal address to the Assembly, and in his more private communications to his friends, came to him in much excitement—we may hope with more love for the truth as it is in Jesus, than soundness of practical judgment, and thus addressed him—"Sir, I am afraid you will not get fair treatment. My advice to you is to go to-morrow morning, and tell the Assembly that you have been so misunderstood by their Committee that you do not see much prospect of getting justice from them as a judicatory; and that you therefore appeal from their fallible tribunal to the infallible tribunal of the Lord Jesus Christ." Mr. Balch had courage enough, and if left to himself, might, in his extremity, have had rashness enough, to have welcomed the suggestion. But from his large and righteous heart instantly burst forth the following Christian reply:—"A schism in the Church, Sir, is a dreadful thing. I should not like to be the guilty cause of any such curse. My shoulders are pretty broad—I trust they will spare my conscience. If they will only do that, Sir, I can bear for the truth's sake whatever burden they may think it their duty to put upon me." Others of better judgment came to advise him, and to pray with him for the favourable interposition of Heaven. At length, Mr. Irwin of Neshaminy, who had, with great vigour and boldness, sustained some of his controverted sentiments before the Assembly, called upon him, and put into his hand a small piece of paper, and asked him to consider its contents, and let him know whether he could, with a clear conscience, make the import of that writing his final answer to the Assembly, and rest the issue of his trial upon it. When he had read it, and felt assured that he correctly understood it, he replied that he readily could adopt it, without the smallest reserve; for it stated the truth of facts and nothing else; but that he had been so misapprehended by the Committee in their adopted report, that he was at a loss to know whether it would probably be accepted. His friend answered him—"I know so much of the minds of the members, that I have no doubt it would; and I entreat you to make use of it. Accordingly, when the Assembly called for his ultimate answer, he gave it nearly in the exact words of the paper handed him. I cannot tell who wrote it. Mr. Balch thought Mr. Irwin wished him to understand that he did not himself. From Dr. Green's personal friendship and conduct during the trial, he immediately said to him,—"It looks to me as coming from Dr. Green." "If so, it comes from a most estimable source," said Mr. I.; "and that is enough for me to say." The answer was accepted by such a majority as precluded any need of dividing the house to ascertain it. So soon as the Moderator, the Rev. Dr. John B. Smith, had declared, in the name of the Assembly, their vote of acceptance, and by obvious implication, of acquittal, in favour of Mr. Balch, and given him the admonition agreed upon, and a concluding prayer had been thankfully offered, Dr. Green arose with a majestic benignity in his commanding eye and face, and kindly said—"Moderator, Mr. Balch is now in as good and regular standing as any member of this Assembly; and I move you, Sir, that he and the minister and elder in Tennessee, now come forward in the presence of this judicatory and shake hands; in token that they will go home with the full purpose to live in Christian love and peace hereafter." Mr. Balch immediately stood on his feet, and, with his hand upon his generous and forgiving heart, said,—"Moderator, here is my heart; and here are both my hands,"—extending them earnestly. They did shake hands forthwith, to the general satisfaction of that truly Christian and enlightened Body. Thus amicably and providentially ordered was the most important ecclesiastical trial of Mr. Balch, leaving him, at its termination, in the unrestricted enjoyment of that faith which he had abundantly shown to the Church and the world was dearer to him than any thing else he could call his own. Should it not be considered an enduring honour to the widely extended Presbyterian Church, then an undivided whole, that under so persevering a course of prosecutions, carried through twenty-one trials or parts of trials, Presbyterial, Synodical, and of the highest Court, an upright conscience, even in an imprudent man, was thus safe beneath the outspread wings of its constitutional protection?

Yes, I must acknowledge that he was an imprudent man. His natural honesty and intrepidity were unsurpassed. All the movements of his soul seemed to be open and direct; but, under excitement, they sometimes savoured strongly of impulsiveness and indiscretion. His intrepidity was a bad counsellor in the moment of provocation and temptation. I could fill sheets with the details of his noble, self-denying and arduous exertions for the good of his fellow men. But I am sorry to add that even I, and certainly his opponents, if surviving, could fill pages in stating his rash steps, his unwise measures, and indiscreet words, where consummate prudence was demanded. His maxim, in all debates and controversies, was,—"I have no contention with any but about holiness." When he discovered his error in any thing, he was most ingenuous and thorough in repentance, confession, and making amends. As he did not always meet a similar return, he was sometimes thrown off his guard. From much knowledge of his life and conduct, I was obliged to conclude that when the fear of God was suspended in its rule over his lofty and intrepid soul, he feared nothing in the universe; and that of course Satan was at his elbow to take some advantage of him.

An impressive illustration of the influence of Mr. Balch's piety upon his principal prosecutor may here be stated. When they were about starting to a trial before the Synod of the Carolinas, he proposed to the elder, his neighbour, who was going there to prosecute him, that, for safety and convenience on their long journey, they should travel together. They did so. But rains had raised a particular stream so high that they saw it could not be forded without the swimming of their horses. Mr. Balch then said to his fellow traveller,—"Sir, you and I have families at home, to whom our deaths would be afflictive; we are in the hands of Divine Providence—don't you think we should do well to kneel down here on the bank of this deep and rapid stream, and pray God to help us over in safety?" "By all means, Sir," answered the elder—"please, Mr. Balch, offer a prayer." He did so. They passed over safely, and travelled on quietly together. This is the elder who shook hands with him before the Assembly; and once did so before the Synod. Soon after I came into the State, when Mr. Balch urged him, for his own satisfaction, to converse with me freely and fully on the disputed sentiments, which had cost him so much in their defence, he replied, and I doubt not candidly,—"Mr. Balch, it is not necessary; now I understand you better than I did. I have no serious objection to what you hold." And he was not the only opposing elder who gave Mr. B. substantially the same testimony.

I must say a word of the important service which Dr. Balch rendered to the cause of liberal education. By his exertions for Greenville College, interrupted, as we have seen, in a most unexampled manner, he provided a commodious two storied College-Hall, a considerable library, a well selected, though small, philosophical apparatus, daily instruction, the best text-books and improvements in teaching within his power to secure. He gave an important impulse to exertions in the same great cause throughout the whole South-western region, where there was before hardly a beginning. Greenville College had at one time students from nine different States and Territories; and a more than usual proportion of them rose to honourable eminence in the different walks of life.

To all persons who had any familiar and intimate acquaintance with Dr. Balch during his last years, the sunshine of his Heavenly Father's countenance seemed to irradiate his noble soul in a manner altogether uncommon. His numerous citations and trials were disastrous to his temporal interests. Pains of body and anxieties of mind, with irreparable injuries to his constitution, from his many journeys and exposures, were not their only consequences. The many imperious calls to attend trials, mostly at a distance from the whole circle of his home duties, as husband, father, master, pastor, and president, during the most exposed years of his younger children, the arrest given to instruction in the College, when most needed, the failing health of his wife and the increased expenses of his family, caused him to endure trials which touched the sympathies of his worthy opposers, and appeared to all exceedingly rare. Like his several brethren here in the ministry, he then had slaves in his family; who, from the kindness of his treatment, dearly loved him. He wished to do his duty to them. But the greater number were taken from him for family debts. The rest he liberated. One went to Liberia, and became useful there. Under all his afflictions, he so encouraged himself in his God, that, submissive and cheerful, he stood erect and unshaken, with an unbroken fortitude that struck all beholders. Once, late at night, when all were in bed, his large and well filled barn was struck with lightning. A large crop of hay and a valuable horse were consumed with the building. Some of his opposers observed him bathed in tears, and supposed that a troubled conscience was the cause—thinking that he interpreted the lightning's stroke, as they did, to be a token of God's anger against him for his errors and missteps. I was then absent in the counties below. Soon after my return, I heard of the above surmise. Some of the family had given me an account of the fire, and said they wished I could have witnessed the scene of their family worship the next morning, when Mr. Balch, having read a select portion of Scripture, and sung a few stanzas from Watts, with melting emotions, instead of kneeling, as was common, prostrated himself at his whole length on the floor; and offered what they considered the most admirable and affecting prayer to which they had ever listened. In our conversations before my absence, he had so condescendingly let me into his inmost soul, that I had a strong desire to hear what account he would himself give of his tears and emotions while his barn was burning. Taking opportunity one day when we were alone, I intimated my wish. "Sir," said he, with his emotions kindling afresh, "I was so filled with a sense of God's love, while, in his adorable sovereignty, he was burning down my barn and destroying my property, that I felt it, and still look back upon it, as one of the most favoured scenes of my life." It then seemed to me useless to ask why he prostrated himself in a family prayer the next morning. Considering the originality of his character, and the strength of his devotional feelings, I concluded, without the shadow of a doubt, that to exalt his God, and abase himself in the dust at his footstool, as unworthy of the love with which he had condescended to refresh him, was the joyful effort of his happy heart. Some years after that, I saw him in distress incomparably more extreme. The wife of his youth lay a corpse in his house. I found him silently and calmly pouring out a copious flood of tears. "Sir," said he, when he spoke,—"I have been in many a trying condition, where nothing but absolute submission to the will of God could reach my necessity; and I am now in one of the most trying in my whole life. But blessed be God, absolute, unconditional submission to his will is plaster sufficient for every sore."

Dr. Balch's retirement from his duties in the College was chiefly to the bed of languishment and death. But from that bed, on the lower floor of his log-house, shone forth all but the radiance of Heaven itself. When I first mentioned to him his approaching death, and his entrance into the world of retribution,—"Sir," said he, "with such a Redeemer as the Lord Jesus Christ for my dependance, I scorn to be afraid to die." Not many days afterwards, he resumed his soul-rejoicing theme:—"Sir," said he,—"if it were not for the infinite atonement of the Lord Jesus Christ, as the dependance of my soul before God, I would not go into eternity for ten thousand worlds. Without this, if I had strength, I would be running through the woods, and tearing the trees for very agony; but with this for my reliance, here I am, Sir, calmly waiting the Mighty Master's call." In another interview, he said to me, looking up with tears towards Heaven,—"Sir, I cordially submit to the righteous sentence of God's eternal law; the precepts of which I have no apology for breaking. At the same time, I trust I have a little—oh! how little, of that holy disinterested love which makes the life of a justifying faith in Christ; that love, Sir, that will bear the examination and meet the approving smile of the great Judge of quick and dead. Even in his last will and testament, he gave his soul to his God to be made for Christ's sake, in boundless grace, an eternal vessel of mercy in Heaven, or, in righteous judgment for his sins, a vessel of everlasting wrath in hell; just as seemed good in his sight. I said, Mr. Balch, will all who may read your will, understand your unshaken hope of salvation through Christ? "Sir," said he, "I cannot allow myself to make conditions with God; to Him I cordially submit, without any reserve, for time and for eternity. Let the words stand, Sir; they show the only way in which I mean to die. Those who have heard me insist on unreserved submission, as always involved in saving faith, may learn the importance of it in their own case, when they find how I choose to die." So, therefore, the words now stand in the Register's office in Greenville.

Such is, I believe, a faithful, though certainly a very inadequate, miniature of that truly venerable man of God, Hezekiah Balch, D. D. I shall be glad if it answers in any degree the purpose for which you have requested it.

That the Spirit of truth, grace, and holiness may preside over your important studies, and bless your diversified labours, is the fervent prayer, I doubt not of many, besides,

Dear Sir, your unworthy brother in Christ,

CHARLES COFFIN.

DANIEL McCALLA, D. D.*

1772—1809.

DANIEL McCALLA was born at Neshaminy, Pa., in the year 1748. His parents, who were worthy and pious people, paid great attention to his religious education, and, as the result of their faithful efforts, were privileged to see him admitted to the Communion table, at the early age of thirteen. He received the rudiments of his education at the grammar school in Fagg's Manor, in his native State, under the instruction of the Rev. John Blair. Here he acquired a very decided taste for classical learning; and, having gone through the requisite preparatory studies, he became a member of the College of New Jersey. During the whole of his collegiate course, which closed in 1766, he maintained a high reputation as a scholar; and when he graduated, in his nineteenth year, his attainments were regarded as very extraordinary.

On leaving College, he was induced, by the solicitation of several very respectable citizens of Philadelphia, to open an Academy in that city. In connection with his duties as a teacher, he prosecuted his studies with great vigour, making himself familiar with the science of medicine, mastering several of the modern languages, and pursuing a course of theological reading with reference to engaging ultimately in the ministry. He was licensed to preach, by the First Presbytery of Philadelphia, on the 20th of July, 1772.

His popular talents as a preacher very soon brought him invitations from several vacant congregations to settle among them; but he gave the preference to the united Congregations of New Providence and Charleston, in Pennsylvania; and, accordingly, was ordained and installed as their pastor in 1774. Here he preached with great acceptance till the commencement of the American Revolution, when his labours were put in requisition in a different and wider field. His heart was very much in the cause of independence, and he stood ready to obey any summons, whatever sacrifice it might involve, which he should receive from his country. Accordingly, at the commencement of hostilities, when the troops under General Thompson were ordered to Canada, he was appointed by Congress Chaplain of that corps,—the only Chaplain that Congress ever did appoint; for, by a subsequent arrangement, Chaplaincies were supplied by the commanding officers of each regiment. Soon after his arrival in Canada, he was made a prisoner, with General Thompson, and several other officers, at Three Rivers. Here he was confined, for several months, in a loathsome prison-ship, where he was subjected to the coarsest treatment, and suffered every thing but absolute starvation. At length, he was allowed to return, on parole, and was restored to his congregation in the latter part of 1776. In a short time, he was charged with having violated his parole in praying for his country. Finding himself in jeopardy, if he attempted to remain with his charge, he made his escape to Virginia; where, after some time, he was released from his parole by an exchange of prisoners. Meeting with much

* Memoir prefixed to his Sermons.—Hollingshead's Fun. Serm.—MSS. from Rev. Dr. Archibald Alexander, and Rev. W. S. Lee.

encouragement to institute an Academy in Hanover County, he was induced to engage in the enterprise; and, for a considerable time, he enjoyed a high degree of popularity in the capacity of a teacher. The congregation of which the Rev. Samuel Davies had been pastor being now vacant, Mr. McCalla succeeded to the charge; and as a preacher not less than a teacher he was highly acceptable. He became also, about this time, connected in marriage with Eliza, second daughter of the Rev. John Todd, of the County of Louisa,—an amiable and accomplished woman.

Mr. McCalla, being naturally of a social turn, had no aversion to scenes of conviviality, and was not always as discreet as might have been desired. This subjected him to severe remark, and finally brought him into some difficulties (of which I have not been able to ascertain exactly either the nature or the extent) which were the occasion of his leaving Virginia. About 1788, he went to South Carolina, and became the minister of a Congregational Church* in Christ's Church parish, near Charleston. Here he remained in retirement, a diligent student and faithful pastor, to the close of his life—a period of twenty-one years.

He was honoured with the degree of Doctor of Divinity from the College of South Carolina.

Dr. McCalla was afflicted with a protracted disease, which was supposed to have been hastened to its fatal consummation by the death of an only child, the wife of Dr. John R. Witherspoon, at the age of twenty-six. He died in great peace, and in the joyful confidence of a better life, in May 1809. Mrs. McCalla survived him. A Sermon on the occasion of his death was preached by the Rev. Dr. Hollingshead of Charleston, of which the following is an extract.

Speaking of him, after his removal to South Carolina, he says,—

"He was happy in the affections of his congregation; avoided rather than courted public notice, and never sought nor willingly consented that his friends should seek for him a more conspicuous situation than the one he occupied. * * * * *

"For many years before his death, Dr. McCalla's attention was principally directed towards the Sacred Scriptures. He read them diligently in the originals, and in several languages into which they had been translated; collected and compared various readings from many authorities, and had it in design, had his life been spared, to have digested his remarks and arranged them in an order, which would have rendered them useful to posterity.

"Dr. McCalla was in person a graceful figure; polite, easy and engaging in his manners; entertaining and improving in conversation; of a lively fancy and a generous heart; of unfettered liberality and undissembled candour. He was easy of access; a friend to mankind; but peculiarly attached to men of science and religion. On the subject of Church government he was liberal; but thought the popular plan of Congregational Churches the most consonant to apostolic and primitive practice, and best adapted to promote the interests of piety and religion."

Dr. McCalla published a Sermon at the ordination of James Adams† in 1799. In 1810, two volumes of his works were published with notices of his life by Dr. Hollingshead. These volumes contain nine Sermons on different subjects; twenty Numbers of Remarks on the "Age of Reason," over the signature of "Artemas;" Remarks on Griesbach's Greek Testa-

* It was not till the two preceding volumes were printed, that I discovered that Dr. McCalla died in connection with the Congregational Church. Rather, therefore, than omit so important a name, I have thought best to treat it as an exception from my general rule, and assign to him a place in the denomination with which he commenced, instead of that in which he closed, his ministerial career.

† JAMES ADAMS was born September 12, 1772; studied in his earlier days under the Rev. James Hall, D. D. of North Carolina, and studied Theology under the Rev. James McRee, D. D. of the same State; was licensed to preach by the Orange Presbytery in 1795; was employed by the Congregational Church of Dorchester, S. C., where he was ordained and

ment; An Essay on the excellency and advantages of the Gospel; Remarks on the Theatre and public amusements, in thirteen Numbers; Hints on Education, in fourteen Numbers; The Sovereignty of the People, in twelve Numbers; A Fair Statement and Appendix to the same in eighteen Numbers, containing an Address to President Adams; Servility of Prejudice displayed, in nine Numbers; Federal Sedition and Anti-democracy, in six Numbers; A Vindication of Mr. Jefferson, in two Numbers; and the Retreat, a Poem.

ROBERT DAVIDSON, D. D.

1772—1812.

FROM THE REV. ROBERT DAVIDSON, D. D.

NEW BRUNSWICK, N. J., September 7, 1848.

Dear Sir: In accordance with the promise given when I last saw you, I place in your hands the following biographical sketch.

ROBERT DAVIDSON was born at Elkton, Md., in 1750. He was graduated at the University of Pennsylvania in 1771. At the age of twenty-two he was licensed by the Presbytery of Newcastle; and the following year ordained by the Second Presbytery of Philadelphia. In the interim, he contracted a marriage, the circumstances of which may not be unworthy of notice.

While a student of Divinity, he was seized with a dangerous illness, at a farm house in the country, and owed his life to the assiduous care and kind nursing of a daughter of his host. She became so much attached to her patient, that, upon his recovery, he ascertained there was but one way in which he could repay her. Such was his gratitude, and such his nice sense of honour, that, finding her happiness seriously involved, he married her; although she was older than himself, had not the slightest pretension to beauty, and moved in an humble sphere of life. She made him, however, for upwards of thirty years, an excellent and devoted wife. She came to a tragical end, being killed by the overturning of a carriage.

When but twenty-three years of age, such was his reputation that he was appointed an instructer in the University of Pennsylvania, and soon after chosen Professor of History, and also assistant to Dr. Ewing, Pastor of the First Presbyterian Church of Philadelphia. In 1775, he composed a Dialogue in verse, with two odes set to music, which was performed as an exercise, at Commencement, in the presence of the Continental Congress. The Dialogue, which was published, was easy and flowing, and full of patriotic allusions. In July of the same year, he delivered a sermon on

installed, May 8, 1799; and was afterwards pastor of Bethel Presbyterian Church, York District, S. C., where he died on the 18th of August, 1843, aged seventy-one years.

JAMES MCREE, D. D., above mentioned, was born in the County of Iredell, N. C., May 10, 1752,—his parents having emigrated from the County of Down, Ireland, in 1730. He became a member of the Junior class in the College of New Jersey in 1773, and graduated in 1775. He studied Theology under the direction of the Rev. Joseph Alexander, D. D. of Bullock's Creek, S. C.; was licensed to preach by the Presbytery of Orange in April, 1778; became Pastor of the Congregation of Steele Creek in Mecklenburg County in September following, where he remained about twenty years; then, in 1798, took charge of the Congregation of Centre, thirty miles North from Steele Creek, where he spent the remainder of his life, and died in 1840. He was honoured with the degree of Doctor of Divinity from the University of North Carolina in 1810.

the War before several military companies, from I. Chron. v. 22.—"For there fell down many slain, because the war was of God." A month had not yet elapsed since the battle of Bunker Hill, and the sermon shared all the enthusiastic fervour of the times. It was repeated in a fortnight before the troops at Burlington. An extract will show how limited were the views of the Americans at that period:—

"*Independence we seek not*,—but our dependance must consist with liberty, and produce mutual good." "We mean to be on an equal footing with the Parliament of Great Britain, who are in truth but our brethren and equals. We mean to have, as the Constitution allows them to have, a voice, *in union with our King*, in all the laws which are to bind us, and to have the free disposal of that property we clearly earn, and which they pretend a right to extort from us, on what occasions and in what proportion they please."

One who spoke his mind so freely, could hardly be safe when the British forces took possession of Philadelphia two years after; and, accordingly, from that time till they evacuated the city, he was compelled to rusticate in Delaware.

In 1784, he published an Epitome of Geography in verse, for the use of schools, which was highly esteemed in its day. It was reviewed, as an Antiquarian curiosity, in Judge Hall's Western Monthly Magazine, (published in Cincinnati,) November, 1835. The Reviewer fell into a mistake, however, in confounding the author with Mr. James Davidson, who was altogether guiltless of the sin of poetry, but who was also a Professor in the same University, and sometimes called old Wiggie, from a habit he had of pulling off his wig, and beating delinquent pupils with it. Of the skill with which the poet mastered the difficulty of managing proper names, I may give the following specimen:—

"On the heights of the Alps much of Switzerland lies,
"The Alps, whence the Rhine and the Rhone take their rise,
"Schaffhausen, and Basel and Bern,
"Apenzel, and Zurich and Swisse,
"Uris, Zug, Underwald, and Lucerne,
"Solothurn, Fribourg, and Glaris."

Sometimes he met with names so intractable that he fairly gave them up.

'A Monomotapan, 'tis hard to describe,
"Or paint one of Mehenemugi's rude tribe,
"Of other rude nations strange things we might tell
"But time is too short, on such subjects to dwell.
"So rude e'en their names are, 'tis no easy thing,
"Of Matamau, Natal, and Souquas to sing;
"Or Sousiquas, Sofala, Sabia, press,
"With Consiquas, Odiquas, into my verse."

While the young Professor thus assiduously devoted himself to the interests of literature, his judgment was held in high estimation in the Church; and although not a ready debater, his name is found in the Minutes of the Old Synod on the most important Committees. But a new sphere of duty was now presented to him. Dickinson College was founded in Carlisle under the Presidency of the distinguished Dr. Nisbet, and he was invited to become one of his coadjutors. "His name will be of use to us,"—wrote Dr. Rush to Dr. Nisbet, "for he is a man of learning, and of an excellent private character." Upon taking leave of the University, the Trustees showed their sense of his merits and services, by conferring on him the degree of Doctor of Divinity.

Dr. Davidson was thirty-four years of age when he entered on his new and important duties. On the 1st of November, 1784, he was appointed Vice President of Dickinson College, and Professor of History and Belles Lettres; and, at the same time, became the Pastor of the Presbyterian Church of Carlisle. A serious division had recently occurred in that large congregation, but their new pastor, by his conciliatory manners, succeeded in harmonizing the discordant elements, and, for eight and twenty years, while he was connected with them, uninterrupted peace prevailed.

While he discharged his parochial duties with exemplary fidelity, he was indefatigable in meeting his engagements in the College. The year after his accession, he composed a Dialogue in blank verse, in honour of the patrons of the College, which was spoken in public and printed. Every moment was occupied. His maxim was "*a place for every thing, and every thing in its place.*" By means of his systematic habits, he was continually enlarging his acquisitions. He made himself acquainted with eight languages,—ancient, modern, and oriental; he was well versed in Theology; and was familiar with the whole circle of science. But Astronomy was his favourite study. He published some papers on this subject; and invented an ingenious apparatus, called a "*Cosmosphere, or Compound Globe,*" presenting the heaven and the earth to view on the same axis. By means of a movable horizontal plane, zodiac, solar index, &c., the relative positions of the sun and moon, the length of the day, the changes of the seasons, the time of eclipses, the precession of the equinoxes, and the rise and fall of the constellations, were rendered perfectly plain, and the solution of problems greatly facilitated.

He was also an amateur and composer of sacred music, and, in his earlier years, amused himself with executing pen drawings, some of which (Louis XIV., and Marie Antoinette particularly) are great curiosities. They have deceived connoisseurs, and have been taken for engravings, even by the distinguished painter, Mr. Nagle. But, from the early date of all these performances, it is evident that he had self-denial enough to sacrifice his elegant tastes at the shrine of those sterner duties which absorbed all his time and energy.

Called upon frequently to address the public on the great National Festivals, he always acquitted himself with credit, as his published Discourses evince. But, in 1794, he was placed in an unusually trying position. On the 28th of September of that year, he preached a sermon from Proverbs xiii, 34, on "the Duties of Citizens," before a large body of troops, on their way to suppress the Whiskey Insurrection; and again on the 5th of October, from II. Samuel vii, 23, on "the Freedom and Happiness of the United States," before President Washington, Governor Mifflin, and a large number of forces bound on the same expedition. The first of these, Dr. Miller describes as "a judicious but modest and mild discourse, which, though not very acceptable to the populace, gave but little offence." (Life of Nisbet, p. 223.) This modest and mild discourse, (which was very different from the caustic sermon that followed in the afternoon from Dr. Nisbet, his colleague, in the church, and which nearly provoked a mob,) nevertheless denounced the "*guilt of rebellion*" on the insurgents, and spoke freely of the wickedness of "countenancing mobs, riots, and seditions." If the populace was displeased, the authorities were highly gratified, and

Governor Mifflin tendered to the Pastor a Chaplain's Commission, which was however declined.

In 1796, Dr. Davidson attained one of the highest honours of the Church, in being chosen Moderator (the eighth in order) of the General Assembly,—an office which he filled with his accustomed mingled dignity and affability.

Upon the death of General Washington, in 1799, he pronounced a Funeral Eulogium, which is to be seen in a printed collection of Discourses, elicited by that melancholy occasion; and, upon the decease of Dr. Nisbet, in 1804, he paid a like tribute to his memory,—an extract from which may be found in Dr. Miller's Life of Nisbet, pp. 290–296.

After this event, the burden of the College devolved upon him, and for five years he discharged the duty of President. In 1809, he resigned, to devote himself exclusively to his pastoral charge, and received a vote of thanks from the Trustees for his long and faithful services. A few months previously, he had lost his second wife, after a brief union of two years—Margaret, daughter of the Hon. John Montgomery, of Carlisle. He gave vent to his grief in a touching Monody, which deserves mention as containing a prayer fulfilled long after its author was laid in the dust. The prayer was for his infant and only son, that, if spared to riper years, "*he might to holy office rise.*" What encouragement may pious parents derive from the recorded fulfilment of such prayers!

In 1810, April 17th, Dr. Davidson was married to Jane, daughter of the Hon. William Harris, Member of Assembly, and Commissioner to issue the old Continental money. This excellent lady, every way worthy of his choice, still survives.* In 1811, he published "The Christian's A. B. C.," or the 119th Psalm, in metre,—each octave commencing with the appropriate letter of the alphabet, with the exception of Q, X, and Z. This was followed, the next year, by a "New Metrical Version of the Psalms," with annotations. It does not pretend to compete with Watts, but is far superior to Sternhold and Hopkins, improved by Rouse. All the versification is not equally smooth. A stanza from the 148th Psalm, is as favourable as any, and will compare well, even with Dr. Watts:—

"Let bending age forget its cares,
"And count his mercies o'er;
"And lisping infancy attempt
"His goodness to adore."

But the time had now arrived, when this good man, pronounced by those who knew him best, "a blessing to the circle he occupied," was to take his leave of earth. He died of dropsy in the chest, after protracted agonies, which he bore as became a Christian, December 13, 1812, on the Sabbath day, in the sixty-second year of his age. A Funeral Sermon, afterwards printed, containing a sketch of his life and labours, was preached by his intimate friend, Dr. Cathcart, of York.

As a preacher, Dr. Davidson was instructive, clear and unaffected, but not fluent. He always had a better command of his pen than his tongue. He could not make the briefest address, without first committing it to paper, and then experienced great difficulty in remembering it. This embarrassment was owing to an unfeigned diffidence and extreme sensibility, which always prevented his making a figure as a debater or extempore speaker. His judgment, however, was so mature, and his opinions so well digested,

* She has deceased since this letter was written.

that he was in great request as a counsellor. Upon his tomb is engraved the inscription, more enviable than military trophies,—A BLESSED PEACE-MAKER.

As a man of letters, his standing was high. His clear intellect and extensive acquirements gave him great aptitude for communicating instruction. Of his diligent and studious habits, he left ample proof in twenty manuscript volumes of Sermons and Scientific Lectures, in addition to all that he had given to the public through the press.

I remain, dear Sir,

Yours truly,

R. DAVIDSON.

JAMES POWER, D. D.*

1772—1830.

JAMES POWER was born at Nottingham, Chester County, Pa., in the year 1746. His father was a substantial farmer, and had emigrated early in life from the North of Ireland, and settled amongst his countrymen, who composed the majority of the neighbourhood. He was fitted for College in his native place, at an Academy established and conducted by the Rev. Dr. Samuel Finley, afterwards President of Princeton College; and he was graduated at Princeton in 1766,—the last year of Dr. Finley's Presidency; so that his whole literary training seems to have been under that eminent man. He was one of the students of College, who visited Dr. Finley on his death-bed, in Philadelphia; and the affecting scene left a powerful and enduring impression on his mind. Among his classmates in College were Oliver Ellsworth, David Howell, Luther Martin, Nathaniel Niles, and several other eminent men.

He was licensed to preach by the Presbytery of Newcastle at Mill Creek, on the 24th of June, 1772,—having been somewhat delayed in the prosecution of his theological studies by ill health. On the 23d of December following, the Presbytery granted him leave to travel into Virginia; and this journey he evidently accomplished, as, in August of the next year, he received a call to settle over the united Congregations of Highbridge, Cambridge, and Oxford, in Bottetourt County, Va. This call, however, he did not accept, and whether he subsequently visited and supplied these congregations for a season is not known. But, in the summer of 1774, he crossed the Alleghany Mountains, and spent three months as a missionary, in what are now Westmoreland, Alleghany, Washington, and Fayette, Counties, in Pennsylvania.

At the expiration of this tour, he returned to the East, and preached as a stated supply for nearly two years,—it is believed at West Nottingham, and at another place within the bounds of Maryland. In the spring of 1776, however, he seems to have made up his mind to settle in the West; for on the 23d of May, of that year, the Presbytery determined to ordain him *sine titulo*, at their next meeting in August, "as he was about to

* Appendix to Elliott's Life of Macurdy.—Smith's Old Redstone.—MS. from Rev. Dr. Carnahan.

remove to the Western parts of this Province." In November following, having received ordination, he removed with his family to Western Pennsylvania, and fixed them at a place called Dunlap's Creek, near Brownsville. He became the Pastor of Mount Pleasant and Sewickly Congregations; but it seems to be a matter of question whether he took charge of them immediately after his arrival in 1776, or whether he divided his labours between them and other destitute churches in the region until the spring of 1779, when he assumed the pastoral relation; though the preponderance of evidence would seem to be in favour of the latter supposition. He retained the pastoral charge of these two congregations until April 22, 1787, when a dissolution of the connection between him and the Sewickly Congregation took place. But he remained in charge of Mount Pleasant, until April 15, 1817, when, on account of advanced age and infirmity, the pastoral relation between him and them was dissolved. He died August 5, 1830, in the eighty-fifth year of his age.

The degree of Doctor of Divinity was conferred upon him by Jefferson College in 1808.

Dr. Power was married to Mary Tanner, who was of German extraction, and a daughter of an elder in the church of the Rev. James Finley. They had eight daughters and no sons. The daughters were remarkably intelligent and active women. Three of them became the wives of Presbyterian ministers, and the others were married to respectable men in the neighbourhood.

FROM THE REV. JAMES CARNAHAN, D. D., L.L. D.,

PRESIDENT OF THE COLLEGE OF NEW JERSEY.

PRINCETON, October 25, 1848.

Rev. and dear Sir: After our conversation the other day in respect to the Rev. Dr. Power, it occurred to me that I probably knew him as well as any other person living, and perhaps have as many recollections that would help to illustrate his character. He frequently heard me say my catechism in my childhood, and sometimes lodged at my father's house. I will, in compliance with your request, as far as I am able, task my memory in respect to him.

In his person, Dr. Power was slender, erect, of a medium height, and at no period of life, corpulent. His manners were easy, graceful, free from affectation, and such as made him agreeable to all classes of society. In his dress, he was always plain, and at the same time remarkably neat; so that it was often marvelled at how he could ride on horseback, ten or twelve miles, in an uneven country, over muddy roads, alight from his horse, and appear in the pulpit, or on a preaching stand in the woods, with his clothes scarcely more soiled than if he had come from his toilet the moment before. He always rode a good horse, and it used to be said that he selected him with special reference to such a movement as would not throw mud and dust on the rider.

In his conversation and manners, he was dignified and somewhat precise; never indulging in levity, and seldom in wit; and yet he was sociable, and far from being morose or censorious.

His voice was not loud, but remarkably clear, and his enunciation so perfectly distinct that he could be heard at a great distance, especially when he spoke, as was not unusual, in the open air. In his manner and style of preaching, he had nothing of the vehemence and terror of his contemporary, the Rev. Dr. John McMillan, nor of the pungent and alarming address of the Rev. Joseph Smith—both of them pioneers in Western Pennsylvania. His sermons were clear and methodical, abounded in pertinent and evangelical thought, well expressed, and were delivered without notes, in a pleasing, rather than a remarkably forcible or striking, manner. To the sober and judicious part of his audience, who desired instruction in the doctrines and duties of Christianity, rather than strong appeals to the passions, Dr. Power's preaching was highly acceptable. His congregations and communicants gradually increased, although there was no remarkable revival under his ministry, except that of 1802, which extended to every part of Western Pennsylvania. In his doctrines, he was of the same school with the Tennents, Davies, Robert Smith, and Samuel Finley.

To the children and youth of his charge Dr. Power paid particular attention; and he was very successful in securing their affection and confidence, and in directing their attention to their immortal interests: especially, when he met a young person alone, it is believed he seldom failed to make a solemn and affectionate appeal to his heart and conscience. The remarkable talent which he possessed of remembering names and of recognising persons to whom he had been once introduced, gave him a peculiar advantage in his parochial duties. When he visited a family, or on any occasion entered a house, he was in the habit of asking the names of the children and domestics; and he would be able, afterwards, to call each one by name, and remember correctly their relative ages, even though the family was a large one. If any one was absent, he was sure to inquire for that one by name. The consequence was that he appeared to feel, and no doubt did feel, an interest in each individual, and no one thought himself overlooked or neglected. But it is a remarkable fact that, for three or four years before his death, while retaining in good degree his physical powers, this faculty of remembering and recognising persons so entirely failed, that he did not know his own children, who resided in the neighbourhood, and who visited him almost every week.

Dr. Power owned a large farm; but, leaving the management of the farm and other domestic concerns to his wife and daughters, he devoted his whole time to the duties of his sacred office. On account of the peculiar circumstances of the country, he received a very small pittance for his ministerial services; yet his farm was managed so judiciously, that, within a few years after their removal to the West, his family lived in a very comfortable and respectable manner.

To appreciate the labours and self-denial of Dr. Power, and other clergymen who settled in Western Pennsylvania, during the Revolutionary war, it is necessary to keep in view the difficulties and dangers to which, in common with other pioneers, they were exposed. The journey over the mountains—not less than a hundred and twenty miles—was not what it now is. There were no Macadamized roads, or canals, or railroads. A horse path over rocks, and precipices, and marshes, was the only way of access to what was significantly called "the Back Woods." Nor could the direct route through Chambersburg and Bedford be taken with safety. Parties of Indians hovered around, and murdered many families on their way to the West. On that road, there are places, whose names, (such as "the Burned Cabins," "Bloody Run," &c.,) to this day, indicate the barbarous acts of that period. To avoid the tomahawk and scalping-knife, a Southern route through Hagerstown, Hancock, and Cumberland, in Maryland, was usually taken, thence following Braddock's road over the mountains. And this road was not suitable to wheel carriages. Many, like Father McMillan, passed through the "Great Valley" to Staunton in Virginia, and thence over the mountains to Tiger's Valley. At present, a journey to Missouri or Iowa can be performed in less time, and with less than half the labour and danger, necessary, at that time, to reach "the Back Woods." When the mountains were passed, accommodations, not very attractive, were found. In the whole County of Westmoreland, then covering more than twice the space it now does, there was not, in 1781, a single stone, or brick, or frame, house. All the inhabitants lived in log cabins, more or less comfortable, according to the means of the occupants. The difficulty of obtaining articles necessary in carrying on farming operations was very great. Iron, with which that country now abounds, had to be carried on pack horses over the mountains; and salt, which now may be purchased for twenty cents, could not, at that time, be had for less than five dollars, per bushel. The want of mills to grind their bread was severely felt. In addition to these difficulties, and others which I omit, the inhabitants were not safe from the incursions of the Indians. In 1782, the year after Dr. Power arrived, Hanna's Town, the seat of County justice, twelve miles from Mount Pleasant, was burned, several persons killed, and the daughters of Hanna, the proprietor of the place, were carried off captive by the Indians. Between the years 1780 and 1785, the Indians made several incursions into the Sewickly settlements, murdered families, and retreated over the Alleghany River, before men could be collected to pursue them. The accommodations for public worship were also as rare and unsightly as the private dwellings of the people. They did not wait until they were able to erect a stone or brick building, costing from two to ten thousand dollars; nor did they send commissioners to ask aid from their wealthier brethren in the East. They took their axes, cut down trees, and, with their own hands, erected a log building, to protect them from the snow in winter, and from the rain in summer. Except in inclement weather, they worshipped in the open air, under the shade of the native forests.

Posterity will find it difficult to conceive of the rudeness of these primitive churches. They were constructed entirely with the axe. No saw, or plane, or even hammer to drive a nail, was used; for neither nails, or iron in any other shape, were employed. The roof was of clap-boards, kept in their places by logs laid upon them; and the doors were also clap-boards, fastened by wooden pins to cross-bars, projecting sufficiently far, at one side, to form a part of the hinge. The windows were small openings out, in two adjacent logs, and were glazed with oil paper or linen. The floors, when any they had, were cleft logs, smoothed by the axe. These churches were of different forms. The most simple and common were square or parallelogramic, having only four sides,—a single log extending from corner to corner. But when the congregation was large, and timber of sufficient length could not be had to make a four-sided structure of suitable dimensions, the cruciform was adopted; and there were twelve sides and twelve corners. In justice to these old fashioned Presbyterians, it must be understood that the twelve sides and the twelve corners were not intended to represent the twelve Apostles; nor was the cruciform adopted from a religious regard to the rules of ecclesiastical architecture, but to secure strength and convenience. And such buildings were both strong and convenient. The parts mutually supported each other, and one part of the transept was the preacher's stand, and the other part opposite accommodated a portion of the audience.

It need hardly be remarked that the style of both private and public buildings in that country has entirely changed. No people live more comfortably, or have more convenient houses of public worship, than the descendants of the pioneers of Western Pennsylvania.

The people to whom Dr. Power ministered, were chiefly the descendants of Scotch-Irish. Their forefathers had fled from Scotland to Ireland, and from Ireland to this country, to escape religious persecution. Educated under Presbyterian influence, and familiar with the doctrines of the Westminster Confession of Faith, they retained, in a good degree, the religious customs of their ancestors. The Shorter Catechism was learned at school, and was recited every Sabbath evening at home, by young and old. The pastor, accompanied by an elder, visited, as he was able, the families belonging to his charge, prayed with them, and gave them such advice as the case of each required. After he had gone from house to house, in a particular neighbourhood, he appointed a general meeting, which all the families in the district were expected to attend. And at these meetings he examined the heads of families, the young people, and the children, in separate divisions, as to their knowledge of the Catechism, and the doctrines and duties therein taught, and closed the whole with a discourse suited to the occasion.

Dr. Power punctually and faithfully continued this custom. The consequence was that both old and young were excited to diligence in the study of the Sacred Scriptures, and of the Catechisms of the Presbyterian Church; and among these hardy Back Woods people, you would find individuals much better instructed in the great truths of the Bible than many at the present day, placed in more favourable circumstances.

The part of the country in which Dr. Power exercised his ministry, was principally settled by young families. When he commenced his labours, few of the children in that region had been baptized; and, as the new settlers were a prolific race, he had much to do in administering the ordinance of baptism, so that he found it convenient to appoint set days for the purpose. On these occasions, he would sometimes have from thirty to forty children presented at once; and, on one day, he baptized as many as sixty. His services were also frequently put in requisition for performing the ceremony of marriage. In connection with this branch of his duty, the following anecdote is told of him:—As no bridges had then been erected, the streams were often quite impassable. Having to cross one of these swollen torrents to marry a couple, he found, when he reached it, that, it could not, by any possibility, be forded. In this dilemma, word was, by some means, conveyed to the young couple, when they immediately made their way to the river, and the minister standing on the one side, and they on the other, he solemnized the marriage. The law then required the publication of the bands, and on some Sabbaths, four or five announcements of this kind would be made.

Though a portion of this communication is not more applicable to Dr. Power than to some other of the early ministers of Western Pennsylvania, yet, as it relates to a state of things in which he largely shared, and which may be considered now of common interest, I thought I might as well introduce the facts, as illustrating the perils and trials amidst which, for a considerable period, he exercised his ministry.

Very sincerely and respectfully yours,

JAMES CARNAHAN.

THOMAS REESE, D. D.*

1773—1796.

THOMAS REESE was born in Pennsylvania, in the year 1742. When he was quite young, he removed, with his father's family to Mecklenburg County, N. C., where he prosecuted his studies preparatory to entering College, at an Academy, under the instruction of the Rev. Joseph Alexander† and a Mr. Benedict. In due time, he became a member of the College of New Jersey, where he received the degree of Bachelor of Arts, in 1768. After his graduation, he returned to South Carolina, and, having devoted some time to the study of Theology, was licensed to preach, and ordained to the work of the ministry, by the Orange Presbytery, in 1773. Soon after he commenced preaching, he accepted a call from Salem Church, Sumpter District, S. C., where he continued in the quiet and faithful discharge of his duties, till he was driven away by the storm of the Revolution.

It is well known that South Carolina was the scene of some of the most barbarous outrages that were perpetrated during the Revolutionary war. The whole order of things, social, civil, and religious, was interrupted. This was more especially the case during the years 1780 and 1781. From the time of the surrender of Charleston, public worship was almost universally suspended, and most of the churches, both in the town and in the country, were burnt, or occupied by the enemy as military depots, or in some other way shamefully desecrated. As there was no opportunity for ministers of the Gospel to exercise their vocation either in public or in private, and as an attempt to remain at their posts involved the utmost peril, the greater part of them went into exile; and among them was the subject of this sketch. It was in his congregation that the murders perpetrated by Harrison of Tory memory, and his followers, commenced; and some of the excellent members of his flock were among the victims. Knowing, as he did, that any attempt to administer consolation beyond his own family would be reckoned as sedition, and would be punished with death, he wisely fled before the storm, and took his family to Mecklenburg, N. C., where he continued to preach under many privations.

On the return of peace in 1782, Mr. Reese returned to his congregation in Salem, and resumed his pastoral duties with great ardour. He also devoted much time to study, and became distinguished for his acquirements, not only in Theology, but in Philosophy, and other kindred branches. About this time he commenced his admirable Essay on the influence of Religion on Civil Society, which was published in 1788,—a work which, it

* Ramsay's Hist. S. C., II.—South. Presb. Rev., VI.

† JOSEPH ALEXANDER was graduated at the College of New Jersey, in 1760; was licensed to preach the Gospel, by the Presbytery of Newcastle, in 1767; and in October of that year presented his credentials to the Hanover Presbytery, and accepted a call from Sugar Creek, N. C. His ordination took place at Buffalo on the 4th of March, 1768; and in May following, he was installed pastor of Sugar Creek. He subsequently removed to Bullock's Creek, S. C., where he exercised his ministry, and taught a school of a high order, as he had also done in North Carolina. He received the degree of Doctor of Divinity from the College of South Carolina in 1807. He died about the year 1808. A volume of his Sermons was published after his death. He was a man of small stature, but of fine talents and accomplishments, and an uncommonly animated and popular preacher. He was an ardent patriot in the Revolution. His wife was a daughter of President Davies.

has been said by high authority, would have been creditable to the pen of Warburton, or Paley; but, like most American productions of that day, it never passed to a second edition. It procured for the author the degree of Doctor of Divinity from the College of New Jersey, which is believed to have been the first instance of its being conferred on a Carolinian.

In the winter of 1792 or 1793, Dr. Reese accepted an invitation to a pastoral charge in Pendleton District, S. C., being among the first who removed from the low country to the upper. Here he had the care of two churches, one near Seneca River, and the other some ten or twelve miles distant. In these churches he laboured until the decline of his health, occasioned, as was supposed, by a change of climate, obliged him to desist. In the latter part of his life he was attacked with hydrothorax, which occasioned him great suffering, and prevented him from lying down for weeks previous to his death. He manifested the most exemplary patience during his illness, and died, sustained by the hope of a better life, in 1796, aged fifty-four years. His remains lie in the grave-yard, attached to the Old Stone Church, near the village of Pendleton.

Beside the Essay already referred to, Dr. Reese published two Sermons in the American Preacher, 1791, and a Farewell Sermon to his Congregation in Salem.

Dr. Reese, though very diligent in his profession, united with the minister of the Gospel, to some extent, both the teacher and the physician. For five or six years, and that after he had passed the meridian of life, beside preaching on the Sabbath, and lecturing to the coloured part of his congregation, he conducted, during the week, with very little assistance, a large classical school. He had also given considerable attention to medicine, and had made himself particularly acquainted with the more common diseases of the South; and this knowledge he was enabled to turn to good account, especially in a part of the country where it was difficult to command medical aid.

Dr. Ramsey, the Historian, who must have known Dr. Reese well, says of him,—

"He left behind him the character of a distinguished scholar, and an eminently pious man."

Chancellor James of South Carolina says of him,—

"In contemplating the meek and unobtrusive manners of this eminent servant of the Most High, we do not hesitate to say he was a pattern of Christian charity, as nearly resembling his Divine Master as has been exhibited by any of his contemporary fellow labourers in the Gospel."

Dr. J. R. Witherspoon, of Transylvania University, writes thus concerning him in the Presbyterian Review:—

"Dr. Reese was in person easy of access, a friend to human nature, but particularly attached to men of science and religion. With powers of mind equal to his benevolence and piety, he justly held a conspicuous station among eminent and good men. * * * * * * His appearance in the pulpit was graceful and dignified, his style flowing and elegant. He was in the habit generally of writing out his sermons with great care, and seldom, if ever, took the manuscript into the pulpit. His preaching was of the extempore kind, adding to the mature reflections of the study the powers of his native oratory. His flowing tears, and often suppressed voice, told the feelings of the heart, anxious only for the salvation of souls and the glory of God. Like Paul, he warned his hearers, day and night, with tears. His success in his ministerial labours evinced the power and presence of the Holy Spirit."

NATHANIEL IRWIN.

1773—1812.

FROM THE REV. JAMES P. WILSON, D. D.

NEWARK, N. J., June 15, 1857.

My dear Sir: I am glad that you are disposed to give to the Rev. Nathaniel Irwin, formerly the minister of Neshaminy, a place in your forth-coming work, and am more than willing to do any thing in my power to form a suitable memorial of him. You are aware that nearly all his contemporaries have passed away, and the few that remain have, for the most part, general impressions, rather than exact information, concerning him. My opportunities for becoming acquainted with his history and character were perhaps as good as they could be, considering that I was a little too late to have any personal knowledge of him. My first eight years of ministerial life were passed in connection with the Church of which he was the admired and beloved Pastor for thirty-eight years; and his memory there is fresh and fragrant to this day. My father, with whom he was in most intimate relations, used to talk much about him, and always expressed for him the highest respect and affection. He preached his Funeral Sermon, at the earnest request of the bereaved congregation.

NATHANIEL IRWIN was born at Fagg's Manor, Chester County, Pa., on the 17th of October, 1756. Of his parentage nothing can now be ascertained, though it is believed that he was of Scotch Irish descent. He was graduated at the College of New Jersey in 1770, being a contemporary and acquaintance there of James Madison, President of the United States, to whom he once paid a visit at the Capital, during his incumbency.

Soon after his graduation, he commenced the study of Theology, placing himself under the care of the Newcastle Presbytery, by which he was licensed to preach the Gospel between the meetings of Synod in 1772 and 1773. He took charge of the Neshaminy Church on the 1st of May, 1774, and was ordained and installed as its Pastor, by the First Presbytery of Philadelphia, on the 3d of November following. In this relation he continued till his death, which occurred on the 3d of March, 1812, in the fifty-sixth year of his age.

Mr. Irwin was not only in great favour with his own people, but was much esteemed and highly honoured by his brethren in the ministry. He was distinguished for his knowledge of human nature; for his great shrewdness in the management of difficult cases, and for a very uncommon facility at despatching public business. Scarcely any man exerted more influence than he in the General Assembly. His familiar acquaintance with all the forms of ecclesiastical procedure, his almost intuitive perception of the right and the wrong of every subject, in connection with the high respect that was felt for him, and the almost implicit confidence that was reposed in him, gave to his opinions and counsels a weight in that venerable Body, which rendered him at once one of its most prominent and useful members. One instance in particular is remembered in which, by his wise and timely interposition, he was instrumental of making clear an involved case, of cutting short a troublesome debate, and of securing the rights and vindicating the character of an individual, who, from misapprehension of his views on the part of the Assembly, seemed in danger for a time of suffering severe injustice. As an evidence of the estimation in which he was held for his talent at public business, I may mention that he was Clerk of the Old Synod of New York and Philadelphia from 1781 to 1785; was Moderator of the General Assembly in 1801; and was Permanent Clerk of the same Body from 1802 to 1807.

As a preacher, Mr. Irwin attained to a high rank among the excellent preachers of his time. He was clear, fluent, forcible, and often deeply pathetic. He was particularly distinguished for his felicitous services at funerals—not only for his tender and impressive style of address, but for his ability to meet the peculiar circumstances of each case in the most appropriate and impressive manner. He was accustomed to ride to church on his "mare Dobbin," and was in the habit of "letting her have her head," as he called it—that is, letting the rein lie loose upon her neck; and she went slowly along while he prepared his sermon. He commonly cut across the fields; and the neighbours on Sunday morning used to let the bars down that he might not find any difficulty in his way to church.

In private life, his manners were generally somewhat distant—certainly they were not lacking in clerical dignity—and yet it was not difficult for him to unbend amongst intimate friends, and he was by no means averse occasionally to a harmless joke. He was, too, notwithstanding his ordinary reserve, fond of the company of young people, especially of young ladies, and he sometimes had parties at his house for their amusement—indeed I think he saw no harm in some amusements which most of his brethren were inclined to reprobate. He was passionately fond of music, and often indulged himself in playing on the violin.

Mr. Irwin was probably the most thoroughly scientific man of his day in the county in which he lived; and he took pleasure in making his knowledge practical and useful. He was the first person who took John Fitch, (of steamboat memory,) who was a Bucks County man, by the hand, and encouraged him in his scientific investigations. And the autobiography of Fitch is now in the Philadelphia Library, in manuscript, addressed to the Rev. Nathaniel Irwin.

In the public and political concerns of the day, Mr. Irwin did not scruple to bear his part. A distinguished citizen of Bucks County, who knew him well, writes thus concerning him:—"He was a clear-headed, strong-minded and persevering politician; and amongst lawyers, a first-rate bush-lawyer—the last a favourite character—the foot on which he limped. He sent for me at the commencement of his last illness to write his will, and counselled me, among his last words, to have nothing to do with law-suits." At a time when the dispute ran high as to the location of the Court House of Bucks County, he entered with great zeal into the contest, and it was very much through his influence that it was ultimately fixed at Doylestown. There appeared at the time a printed caricature, representing Parson Irwin tugging, in his shirt sleeves and with his hat off, with all his might, to pull the building in the direction of Doylestown.

Mr. Irwin was twice married, and his second marriage was fruitful only of trouble. Indeed he was the subject of complicated domestic afflictions, which clouded his latter days, and finally broke his heart, and, as was generally supposed, occasioned his lamented death. He had not a large salary, but by careful management he placed himself in easy circumstances, and left behind him quite an estate.

Dr. Alexander, on his first attendance at the General Assembly in 1791, saw Mr. Irwin for the first time, and, as the Memoir of his Life informs us, made the following note concerning him:—"Nathaniel Irwin of Neshaminy was an influential member of this Assembly. He was very tall, and had a voice the sound of which produced alarm, on a first hearing. He always took his stand at a place the most remote from the chair, and seemed to utter every thing with the greatest sound he could command. It was easy to discern that as his head was literally long, so it was intellectually."

Yours very sincerely,

JAMES P. WILSON.

SAMUEL STANHOPE SMITH, D. D., L L. D.*

1773—1819.

Samuel Stanhope Smith was born March 16, 1750, at Pequea, Lancaster County, Pa. His father was the Rev. Robert Smith, a distinguished clergyman of the Presbyterian Church, who emigrated from Ireland, and established, and for many years superintended, an Academy, which supplied many able and excellent ministers to the denomination with which he was connected. His mother was Elizabeth, daughter of the Rev. Samuel Blair, and sister to Samuel and John Blair, all of whom were among the most prominent clergymen of their day. She was a lady of high intellectual endowments, as well as excellent moral qualities, and fitted to grace the most exalted station in society. The son, at a very early period, gave indications of possessing a mind of no common order; and the parents quickly determined to give him the best advantages within their reach for cultivating it. When he was only six or seven years old, he commenced the study of the languages in his father's school; and, as his father had employed some most accomplished teachers from abroad as his assistants, perhaps scarcely any school in the country, at that day, furnished better advantages for becoming thoroughly grounded, especially in the classics. The only language allowed to be spoken in the school was Latin; and whoever uttered a word in the mother tongue was marked as a delinquent. Young Smith made the best of his opportunities, and was distinguished for his improvement in every branch to which he directed his attention.

Of his earliest religious exercises it is believed that no record has survived him. He seems, from childhood, to have evinced a serious turn of mind, and to have taken little interest in the sports in which his schoolfellows indulged. He was accustomed to listen to sermons from the pulpit with great attention, and often, at the close of the service, could repeat a considerable portion of what he had heard. He also showed his predilection for the clerical profession, by sometimes gathering around him his brothers and sisters, and going through, as if he were a clergyman, with the various exercises of public worship. In the absence of his father, he some-

* Life by Dr. Beasley.—MS. from his daughter, Mrs. Breckenridge.

times took the lead in family prayer. He became a communicant in the Church under his father's care, while he yet remained under the paternal roof.

When he was in his sixteenth year, he was sent to College at Princeton: it was during the period that intervened between the death of President Finley and Dr. Witherspoon's accession to the Presidency, while the College was under the charge of several eminent Professors, and among them his maternal uncle,—the Rev. Dr. John Blair. Notwithstanding his youth, he entered the Junior class, and immediately took rank among the best scholars. Dr. Witherspoon arrived from Scotland, and entered on the duties of his office, while he was an undergraduate; and before he had completed his eighteenth year, he had received the Degree of Bachelor of Arts, under circumstances the most honourable to his talents and acquirements, and the most gratifying to his ambition.

During his collegiate course, Mr. Smith was in great danger of making shipwreck of his religious principles, in consequence of his intimacy with Mr. Periam, the Senior Tutor, who had embraced Bishop Berkeley's theory, denying the existence of the material universe. Mr. P. had so much influence over his pupil, that, for a time, he succeeded in making him not only a convert to his strange opinions, but an earnest advocate of them; insomuch that Mr. Smith's friends began to have the most serious apprehensions that he had become a permanent victim to one of the worst kinds of philosophical insanity. Happily, however, when Dr. Witherspoon arrived from Scotland, he brought with him the works of several distinguished Scottish philosophical writers, particularly Reid and Beattie, the influence of which was quickly perceptible, in bringing back this gifted young man into the regions of common sense. It was only for a short time that this aberration continued, and when his mind had once become steadfast in the right, it became so for life.

After taking his degree at Princeton, he returned to his father's house, and spent some time, partly in assisting him in conducting his school, and partly in vigorous efforts for the higher cultivation of his own mind. He read the finest models in polite literature, and the most accredited authors in intellectual and moral philosophy. He also occasionally tried his hand at writing poetry, but he was not much flattered by the result of his efforts, and he seems to have abandoned his devotion to the Muses on the ground that "*Poeta nascitur non fit.*"

He had not been long in this new sphere of labour, before he was invited to return to Princeton as a Tutor in the College, especially in the departments of the Classics and the Belles Lettres. Here he remained for upwards of two years,—from 1770 to 1773,—discharging his duties in connection with the institution with exemplary fidelity and to great acceptance, while, at the same time, he was pursuing a course of theological study in reference to the ministry. About the time of resigning his Tutorship, he was licensed to preach by the Presbytery of Newcastle.

As his health had suffered not a little from severe application, he determined, previous to assuming the responsibility of a stated charge, to spend some time as a missionary in the Western Counties of Virginia. When he reached that part of the country, he received a most cordial welcome from many Irish Presbyterians, who had settled there, and, at the same time, found a state of things that seemed to promise well to an earnest and faithful ministry. Religion was at an exceedingly low ebb in Virginia, and the professed ministers of the Gospel, with comparatively few exceptions, commanded but little respect. When, therefore, a preacher of strongly marked and elevated character appeared,—a man of not only cultivated mind and exemplary deportment, but evangelical spirit and captivating oratory, it was not strange that an intense and general interest should be awakened by his ministrations. Accordingly, he soon became an almost universal favourite. Persons, without distinction of sect or of rank, flocked to hear him; and those who had been entranced by the eloquence of Davies, seemed to feel as if *another* Davies had arisen. So powerful an impression did he make, that some of the most wealthy and influential persons soon set on foot a project for detaining him there, as the head of a literary institution; and in a short time the funds requisite for establishing such an institution were subscribed. The necessary buildings were forthwith erected, and the Seminary was subsequently chartered by the Legislature, under the name of Hampden Sidney College.

While these preparations were going forward, Mr. Smith was laboriously occupied in performing the missionary tour which had been the original object of his visit to Virginia. The new College being now nearly ready to commence its operations, he returned to the North, and formed a matrimonial alliance with the eldest daughter of Dr. Witherspoon. He then went back to Virginia, and took upon himself the double office of Principal of the Seminary, and Pastor of the Church; and the duties of each he discharged in such a manner as to fulfil the highest expectations that had been formed concerning him.

But, after three or four years, his constitution, which was never very vigorous, was found to be giving way, under the vast amount of care and responsibility to which his situation subjected him. A slight bleeding at the lungs commenced, which admonished him to take at least a temporary respite from labour; and, by the advice of his friends, he resorted to a watering place among the Western mountains, which was then acquiring considerable celebrity under the name of the "Sweet Springs." A residence there of a few weeks caused his unfavourable symptoms, in a great measure, to disappear, so that he returned to his family with his health in a good degree renovated.

At this period, (1779,) he was invited to the chair of Moral Philosophy in the College of New Jersey; and, notwithstanding his strong attachment to the infant Seminary in Virginia, of which he might be said to be the founder, the prospect of a more extended sphere of usefulness in connection with his *Alma Mater*, induced him to accept the appointment. Upon his arrival at Princeton, however, a most unpromising state of things presented itself. The College was then in ruins, in consequence of the uses and abuses to which it had been subjected by both the British and American soldiers, during the previous years of the Revolutionary war. The students were dispersed, and all its operations had ceased. Mainly by the energy, wisdom, and generous self devotion, of Mr. Smith, the College was speedily reorganized, and all its usual exercises resumed. For several years, Dr. Witherspoon, though retaining the office of President, was engaged as a member of Congress, in the higher affairs of the nation. After this, he spent some time in Great Britain, in endeavouring to collect money to replenish the exhausted funds of the institution. And, not long after his return, he was afflicted with total blindness, and many bodily infirmities, which, in a great measure, incapacitated him for the duties of his office as President. It is not too much to say, therefore, that, during this whole period, notwithstanding Dr. Witherspoon's name could not fail to shed glory over the institution, and he was always intent upon the promotion of its interests, whether present or absent, yet it was indebted for no small degree of its prosperity to the unceasing vigilance, the earnest efforts, the distinguished ability, of Mr. Smith.

Sometime after he had become established in his Professorship at Princeton, there was a recurrence of his former malady, in a greatly aggravated form, which, for a time, clouded the bright hopes which the commencement of his career had inspired. In November, 1782, he was suddenly overtaken with a violent hemorrhage from the breast, which was checked only by a copious bleeding in the arm and foot. The same thing occurred at a little later hour, the next day, and so, regularly, for several successive days; the blood being restrained, in each case, only by the use of the lancet. Mr. Smith, having remarked that the flux returned at stated intervals, proposed to anticipate its approach by opening a vein, a little before the time when he had reason to expect it. His physician objected to this, on the ground that his strength was so far gone that it would be preposterous to hazard the letting of blood beyond the absolute necessity of the case. He, however, remained steadfast in his own opinion, and at length obtained a lancet from his physician, with a view to his using it upon himself when he felt that the case demanded it. He used it the next day, and with the desired effect; and continued to use it, until he finally succeeded in subduing the disease. For a considerable time he was so far reduced as to be unable to help himself, or to speak above a whisper; but his strength gradually returned, so that he was able, at no distant period, to resume his duties in the College. For several years, however, he never ventured an effort in the pulpit, unless on some rare occasion, and then with the utmost caution and restraint. It is said that, during the whole of his subsequent life, whenever he felt any symptoms of a recurrence of his old complaint, he was accustomed to resort promptly to the lancet, and always with complete success.

In 1783, he was honoured with the degree of Doctor of Divinity from Yale College; and, in 1810, the degree of Doctor of Laws was conferred upon him by Harvard University.

In the year 1785, Dr. Smith was elected an honorary member of the American Philosophical Society in Philadelphia,—an institution distinguished not only for being the first of its kind, in the order of time, in the country, but for numbering among its members many of the most brilliant, profound, and erudite minds of which the country could boast. The same year he was appointed to deliver their Anniversary Address; and he met the occasion in a manner which, of itself, would have conferred lasting honour upon his name. The object of the Address was to explain the causes of the variety in the figure and complexion of the human species, and to establish the identity of the race. It was published in the "Transactions" of the Society, and was subsequently published in an enlarged and improved form, in a separate volume. With this work his reputation, as a philosopher, both at home and abroad, is, in no small degree, identified.

In 1786, he was associated with several of the most distinguished and venerable men in the Presbyterian Church, such as Witherspoon, McWhorter, Alison, Ewing, &c., in preparing the Form of Presbyterial Government, which continues to the present time. His comprehensive views and intimate acquaintance with all the forms of ecclesiastical procedure eminently qualified him for that important service.

Dr. Witherspoon died in 1794; and the same year Dr. Smith succeeded to the honours and responsibilities of the office which his death had vacated. Besides being highly popular as the head of the institution, he had now acquired a reputation as a pulpit orator which rendered it an object for many, even from remote parts of the country, to listen to his preaching. His Baccalaureate Discourses particularly, which were addressed to the Senior class, on the Sabbath immediately preceding their graduation, were always of the highest order; and it was not uncommon for persons to go even from New York and Philadelphia,—a distance of some forty miles, to listen to them. One of his most splendid performances was his Oration, delivered at Trenton, on the death of Washington: the occasion roused his faculties to the utmost, and the result was a production of great beauty and power. In 1779, he published a volume of Sermons, which were regarded as an important contribution to that department of our country's literature. They are characterized rather by general than particular views of evangelical truth, by a correct, elevated, and perhaps somewhat elaborate, style, by occasional bold and eloquent apostrophes, and by many stirring appeals to the heart and conscience.

In the spring of 1802, when the institution was at the full tide of its prosperity, the College edifice, through some instrumentality that was never fully ascertained, was burnt, together with the libraries, furniture, and fixtures of every description. Indeed all was gone, except the charter, the grounds, and the naked walls of brick and stone; together with the exalted character of the Seminary, and the commanding reputation of its President. After the first stunning effect of the calamity had passed away, but one sentiment pervaded all ranks of the people; and that was a determination to contribute the necessary funds to rebuild the house, and sustain the institution. The Trustees resolved to proceed immediately in the work of renovation; confidently relying on the support which the public feeling seemed so plainly to promise. They were not disappointed. Dr. Smith made a *begging* tour through the Southern States, and returned in the following spring, with about one hundred thousand dollars; which, with liberal collections made in other parts of the Union, enabled him to accomplish vastly more than he had ventured to anticipate. This was his crowning achievement. He had won new honours, and gained many new friends. The College was popular and prosperous, and numbered two hundred students. New buildings were soon erected, and several new Professors were added to the Faculty.

From this period, nothing occurred in Dr. Smith's life worthy of special remark until the year 1812, when, by reason of repeated strokes of palsy, he became too much enfeebled to discharge any longer the duties of his office. He, therefore, at the next Commencement, tendered his resignation as President, and retired to a place which the Board of Trustees provided for him, and there spent the remainder of his life. For several years, he occupied himself in revising and preparing for the press some of his works;

but, at length, disease had made such havoc with his constitution, that he was scarcely capable of any mental labour, though he was still visited by many of his friends, and, to the last, was the pride and joy of the domestic circle. After a long course of gradual and almost imperceptible decline, he died, in the utmost tranquillity, on the 21st of August, 1819, in the seventieth year of his age. A Sermon was preached on the occasion of his death, by the Rev. Dr. Woodhull of Freehold. His remains repose by the side of his illustrious predecessors. His wife died on the 1st of April, 1817. They had nine children, five of whom survived him.

When I entered the Theological Seminary at Princeton, Dr. Smith was still living, though too feeble to mingle in any of the concerns of active life. He was able, however, in pleasant weather, to attend public service on the Sabbath, and for some reason which I do not remember, if I ever knew it, he attended at the village church, and not at the College chapel, which was somewhat nearer to his residence. He used to walk up the aisle with great deliberation, partly, I suppose, on account of his advanced age and consequent feebleness, and partly, perhaps, from the solemn and reverent associations pertaining to the place. His face, though covered with the marks of decay, still revealed something of what it had been; and sometimes, under an exciting influence, there would seem to come forth, as if from a slumber, that beautiful and living radiance which had illuminated his features, and made him irresistibly attractive, in his better days. He wore a black cap, whenever he came to church, which rendered his appearance still more venerable. He always seemed to listen to the sermon with the utmost attention, but I never heard any thing to indicate that he was a captious hearer—though one of my friends told me that, as he was passing out of the church with him, after they had been hearing a sermon rendered somewhat misty by metaphysics, the Doctor turned round, and pointing to some coloured people who had been sitting in the gallery, said,—"I think that sermon must have been refreshing to those negroes." Though he had not then preached for several years, most of the people whom I met had been accustomed to hear him: and the uniform testimony was that he was surpassingly eloquent—some, I remember, who were capable of forming an intelligent judgment in such matters, and who never spoke at random, did not hesitate to say that, as far as their knowledge extended, his eloquence, in his best days, had no parallel.

Though I never had any intimacy with Dr. Smith, I was occasionally a visiter at his house, and always felt it a privilege to be in his company, even when he said the least; for there was an air of majesty about him, apart even from his being an interesting relic of the olden time, to which no one could be indifferent. I remember finding him once or twice busy in correcting his manuscript sermons, which he intended should be published, either before or after his death; and the appearance of the manuscript indicated that he had, at least, not outlived the ability to criticise his own writings. But the occasion that loosened his tongue, and quickened his intellect, more than any other upon which I ever happened to see him, was a visit that Dr. Kirkland, President of Harvard College, paid to him, I think in the winter of 1817–18. Dr. Kirkland was in one of his happiest moods, and Dr. Smith was delighted to see him; and it was really no small privilege to observe how the actual President, then in his full vigour, by his bright and pithy remarks, worked u the old Ex-President into something like what he must have been in the days of his greatest glory. All his other manifestations, that ever fell under my observation, were tame, in comparison with what I witnessed that morning. Once I recollect his speaking to me with some degree of warmth on what he considered the degradation of the pulpit by metaphysical preaching; and, in the same connection, he spoke of Buckminster's Sermons as being generally unexceptionable in point of religious doctrine, and as being, in a literary point of view, among the most splendid productions that he had met with. I might have told him that the admiration was reciprocal, for I well remember Buckminster's giving me Dr. Smith's Baccalaureate, on the Love of Praise, delivered in 1810, and speaking of it in no measured terms of approbation.

The following is a list of Dr. Smith's publications: —

VOLUMES.

An Essay on the causes of the variety of complexion and figure of the human species; to which are added Strictures on Lord Kaims' Discourse on the original diversity of mankind, 8vo., 1787. Sermons, 8vo., 1799. Lectures on the Evidences of the Christian Religion, 12mo., 1809. Lectures on Moral and Political Philosophy, 12mo., 1812. A Comprehensive View of the leading and most important principles of Natural and Revealed Religion, 8vo., 1816. Sermons, to which is prefixed a brief Memoir of his life and writings. Two volumes, 8vo. (posthumous), 1821.

PAMPHLETS.

A Funeral Sermon on the death of the Hon. Richard Stockton, 1781. A Sermon on Slander, preached in Brattle Street Church, Boston, 1790. A Discourse on the Nature and Danger of Small Faults, delivered in the Old South Church, Boston, 1790. Oratio Inauguralis, 1794. A Discourse on the nature and reasonableness of Fasting, and on the existing causes that call us to that duty, 1795. The Divine goodness to the United States of America: a Discourse delivered on a day of general Thanksgiving and Prayer, 1795. A Discourse delivered on the death of the Rev. Gilbert Tennent Snowden,* 1797. An Oration upon the death of General George Washington, 1800. A Discourse on the nature, the proper subjects, and the benefits of Baptism, with a brief Appendix on the mode of administering the ordinance, 1808. The Resurrection of the body: A Discourse delivered in the Presbyterian Church in Georgetown, 1809. On the Love of Praise: A Sermon delivered the Sunday preceding Commencement, 1810.

* GILBERT TENNENT SNOWDEN was the son of Isaac Snowden, who was an elder in the Second Presbyterian Church in Philadelphia, was a member of the first General Assembly in 1789, and was for thirty-six years a Trustee of Princeton College. He (the son) was born in Philadelphia, then the place of his father's residence; was graduated at Princeton in 1783; was settled as Pastor of the Church in Cranberry, N J., about the year 1790; and died in February, 1797. He had two brothers who were also ministers of the Gospel. *Samuel Finley Snowden* was born at Philadelphia, November 6, 1767; was graduated at Princeton in 1786; studied Theology under Doctors Witherspoon and Smith; was licensed to preach by the Presbytery of New Brunswick, April 24, 1794; was ordained to the work of the ministry, and installed Pastor of the Church in Princeton, on the 25th of November following; resigned his pastoral charge on account of ill health, April 29, 1801; was afterwards settled successively at Whitesborough, New Hartford, and Sackett's Harbour, in the State of New York; and died, without a moment's warning, at the last mentioned place, in May, 1845, at the age of seventy-eight. *Nathaniel Randolph Snowden*, the other brother, was born in Philadelphia; was graduated at Princeton in 1787; became Pastor of the Congregations of Harrisburgh, Paxton, and Derry, in Pennsylvania, in 1793; resigned his charge after about three years; afterwards supplied the Monaghan, and Petersburg, and various other, Congregations, and died at the residence of his son, Dr. C. G. Snowden, at Freeport, Armstrong County, Pa., November 3, 1850, in the eighty-first year of his age.

FROM THE REV. PHILIP LINDSLEY, D. D

PRESIDENT OF THE UNIVERSITY OF NASHVILLE.

NASHVILLE, February 2, 1848.

My dear Sir: You request me to communicate my impressions of the character of the late President Smith. I suppose you do not expect me to write an obituary notice or biographical sketch of this eminent person, nor yet a review of his several publications. What you ask for, if I mistake not, is my own individual estimate of the man, as spontaneously formed during the period of my personal intercourse with him. This, too, notwithstanding the elaborate "Memoir of his Life and Writings" prefixed to an edition of his posthumous Sermons, which appeared in 1821, and which has probably left little or nothing to be told. Rather, therefore, in compliance with the wishes of a friend, than with a hope of furnishing any additional matter of interest or moment, I am willing to make the attempt to revive and record some desultory reminiscences of my venerated instructer.

When I first became acquainted with Dr. Smith, he had already attained the summit of his well earned celebrity. Throughout the Middle and Southern States, he was regarded as the most eloquent and learned divine among his contemporaries. His reputation as a popular preacher had been long before established in Virginia, where *Samuel Davies* was still remembered by multitudes of his hearers, and while *Patrick Henry* was yet in the zenith of his brilliant career. There too he had founded a flourishing College; and to his sole agency and influence Hampden Sidney owed its origin and early prosperity. In the midst of his successful labours, as its Principal, and as the Pastor of a Church in its vicinity, he had been invited by his *Alma Mater* to return to the scene of his youthful studies, and his first essays as a Tutor. He had accepted the invitation, and for years, first as Professor, and afterwards as President, had contributed to elevate the College to a position of the highest usefulness and respectability.

It was in these auspicious circumstances,—just after the desolations occasioned by the fire in 1802 had been repaired,—that I began to attend his instructions, and to know him as the President. The opinion of college lads about men and institutions may be of little value in the great world; and yet it is oftentimes but the echo of the public voice, or a somewhat exaggerated expression of the popular judgment. They are apt to think and speak of their teachers as they hear others speak of them. From our childhood, we (the students) had never heard the Doctor's name pronounced but with praise. We came to the College, therefore, prepared to look up to him as the great man of the age. His superior talents and accomplishments, as a preacher, scholar, philosopher, and writer, were every where spoken of and acknowledged. And we never doubted that he possessed all the attributes and graces which could dignify and adorn the high station which he filled. Such were our prepossessions in his favour at the outset. And there was no subsequent reaction. He daily grew in our esteem. We thought not only that he was equal to every emergency, but that no other man could have succeeded so well. He seemed always to say and to do every thing in the happiest manner. In his various college performances, in the chapel, and in the recitation room, however brief and unpremeditated, or by whatever occasion suggested,—as well as in the more ornate and studied exercises of the pulpit,—he satisfied every expectation. It seemed natural for him "to put proper words in proper places," and to select the most expressive. There was no affectation, or mannerism, or artifice, or formality, about him. He was simple and unostentatious, and apparently regardless or forgetful of himself. We admired his personal appearance and deportment. And we always listened to his speech with pleasure, if not with profit. We never questioned his sincerity and uprightness. We revered him as a faithful Christian minister,—far above reproach or suspicion.

He was less obnoxious, probably than most other men in the like office, to the witticism, and ridicule, and swaggery, of the disorderly and mischievous portion of the students. That these should not have been always particularly gratified with his discipline, might be presumed. But I never witnessed any attempt to excite a laugh at his expense, or to play off a trick upon him in any fashion, or to exhibit him in a ludicrous attitude, or to caricature any of his remarks or actions. He never betrayed any foibles, or defects, or peculiarities, which could serve the purpose either of fun or abuse. He was the well-bred, courteous gentleman, every where, at all times, in all companies, on all occasions. The dignity of his bearing, though not repulsive or oppressive, was uniform and imposing. His very presence would rebuke, overawe, and silence the most turbulent assemblage of youth that ever met for sport or riot,—during my time at least.

Instead of reading his written Lectures on Moral Philosophy, and the Evidences of Christianity, they were previously placed in the hands of the students, and carefully studied in manuscript as text books. Each member of the Senior class possessed a copy,—transcribed by himself or some person whom he employed to do it, or purchased from a predecessor. Questions were asked upon the subject matter of the Lecture,—accompanied or followed by pertinent illustrations and explanations. I have already said enough to show how we appreciated these familiar instructions.

Of the government of the College, at this period of its greatest prosperity, under President Smith, I can hardly use language too favourable. It was maintained in rigid accordance with the spirit and letter of the printed code of laws, which every student, at his matriculation, promised to obey. I do not mean that there occurred no violations of law, or that every transgressor was duly punished. Such perfection has never been attained in any school or community, or under any system of government or administration. It is enough to say that we all fully believed that if we neglected our duties, or committed any offence, we should certainly be dealt with according to our deserts; and that all reasonable vigilance was exerted, both to prevent and detect every species of delinquency or disorder. We regarded the Doctor as a firm, resolute, fearless, decided man,—who would not wink at crime or folly,—but who, nevertheless, cherished towards us the most kindly and paternal feelings. My present deliberate opinion is, that he was one of the ablest and most successful disciplinarians of any age. I speak of him as he was in his best days; and these alone ought to testify as to his capacity and conduct.

Sometime after graduation, I returned to Princeton, when, as a Tutor in the College and student of Theology, (from 1807 to 1810,) I became more intimately acquainted with Dr. Smith: and again, from his resignation in 1812 to his decease in 1819, my intercourse with him continued without interruption.

Dr. Smith officiated as Professor of Theology, during the whole period of his Presidency, with the exception of two or three years, (from 1803 to 1806,) when that chair was occupied by the Rev. Henry Kollock, D. D. The "Divinity class" consisted, in my time, of some eight or ten young men, including the College Tutors,—to whose instruction he devoted two evenings of the week. He generally read a portion of his Lectures or notes as he called them; and then dilated upon the topics, in a free colloquial style, and always much to our edification. He directed our course of reading, heard our essays, and suggested subjects for investigation, dissertation, or oral disputation. The course included systematic Theology, ecclesiastical history and polity, pastoral duties, the Bible, and a large range in the fields of classic and general literature. He also attended and presided over an association, composed of the above and other resident graduates, who used to meet once a week for mutual improvement. This was a kind of philosophical as well as debating society. Here too, the learned President, in exhibiting the *pro* and *con* of controversy, in disentangling a knotty question, in distinguishing the real and practical from the cloudy and incomprehensible, in exposing error and sophistry, in sustaining truth and sound logic, or in "summing up,"—was the "great master,"—and the liberal umpire in all our wordy battles.

It will be seen from what has been said, that he must have been a working man. The stated preacher and pastor, the indefatigable teacher, (of sciences, too, usually distributed among several Professors,) the author of his own text books and of not a few others, the responsible Head and Governor of a College, which he had twice re-edified, the regular attendant and a most efficient member of the judicatories of the Church which he loved,—and more frequently invited or constrained to the performance of special and honourable services than any of his contemporaries,—verily he could seldom have laid aside his "harness," or known the comfort of repose.

Of his published works, though numerous and diversified, I shall take no further notice than to add the remark that few men, in any situation, have written so much and so well. These, however, do not fairly portray the man. Of their literary merit the critical reader will judge for himself. His philosophy and biblical exegesis, in some particulars, may be questioned or disallowed; but all will concede to him candour, honesty, habitual reverence for truth and righteousness, and great ability in the exposition and defence of his theories.

He was a diligent, persevering student through life. He knew how to employ usefully every leisure moment with pen or book. He was conversant with the literature, science, philosophy, and politics, of ancient and modern times. He was a classical scholar in the highest and best acceptation of the phrase. He was master, not merely of the mechanism and grammar of the Greek and Latin languages, but was deeply imbued with the spirit of the great authors. His delicate and cultivated taste enabled him to discriminate and to relish the finest and most exquisitely wrought passages, as well as the more obvious beauties and sublimities, of the poet and the orator. He wrote and conversed in Latin with great facility and was a first rate prosodist. In these accomplishments I have rarely met his equal.

He was not a recluse. His varied duties, public and professional, required him to be much abroad in the world, and to mingle with all sorts and classes of people. His house was frequented by the good, the great, the wise, the intelligent; and humble merit was always welcome at his board and fireside.

He was not ambitious, except in the apostolic sense. Instead of any leaning to covetousness, the tendency of his benevolent nature was rather to the opposite extreme.

He was free from envy, and jealousy, and resentment. Of these I could never detect in him the slightest indication. He had enemies, and he knew them. He was often misrepresented, and sometimes grossly slandered. But he uttered no words of complaint, or anger, or unkindness. I believe he forgave them and prayed for them. He was an Israelite indeed, in whom was no guile. He appeared incapable of deception, or intrigue, or crafty management, for any purpose.

He was no bigot or dogmatist. He cheerfully conceded to others the same liberty, with all the rights of conscience and judgment, which he claimed for himself. He could defend his own creed or opinions without arrogance or bitterness. He could demolish error or heresy, without abusing or denouncing men, or sects, or parties.

In the General Assembly, Synod, and Presbytery, of his Church, he was confessedly *primus inter pares*,—or at least second to none,—if report and tradition may be credited. But as my observation did not extend to these, I shall attempt no description.

There was a wide difference in the character of his eloquence, between his early and later years. I happened, while on a visit to Virginia in 1810, to meet with several elderly persons who had heard him preach, when a young man. They spoke of him as an impassioned orator,—like Whitefield or their own Davies and Henry. They spoke, too, of his patriotic speeches at the beginning of the Revolution, and of their marvellous effect upon the people. Now I never witnessed any thing of this sort. He had long before my day been disabled for such efforts. In the pulpit, when I heard him, he was comparatively calm and subdued in manner,—though the most dignified, graceful and impressive of preachers.

At the age of sixty-two, he was compelled, by ill health, to relinquish all public employments. During the remaining seven years he lived in retirement. This was perhaps the most beautiful and instructive period of his life. It often looms up before me like a bright, blessed, glorious vision,—such as we dréam of, but never realize. It seemed as though all the Christian graces and virtues, freed from every human imperfection, had now clustered around him, and blended together, like the colours of the rainbow, into a living form of chastened, hallowed, radiant loveliness.

His person, presence, and carriage were so remarkable, that he never entered the village church or college chapel, or walked the streets, or appeared in any company, without arresting attention, or creating a sensation, not of surprise or wonder, but of pleasing, grateful admiration,—a kind of involuntary emotion and homage of the heart,—a tribute as cordially yielded as it was richly deserved.

In a word, the venerable figure, the saintly aspect, the benignant smile, the ethereal spirit, the tranquil resignation, the humble faith, the cheerful temper, the habitual meekness, the generous sympathy, the comprehensive charity, the modest unpretending gentleness of his whole manner,—all proclaimed the mature and gifted Christian, ready to depart, and calmly expecting his final translation to a more congenial world.

To the last, this good man continued accessible and attractive to all; and he well knew how to engage in pleasant and profitable conversation persons of every variety of age, rank, and condition. Always the Christian gentleman, it was impossible for him to make an approach towards levity or coarseness, in word or act. I never heard from his lips an anecdote or allusion, a hint or expression, which might not have been whispered in seraphs' ears. This innate purity or acquired sense of propriety, I think, was peculiar and characteristic. It certainly is not always prominent even among divines.

He took great interest in the youthful candidates for the ministry. He delighted much in their society. His little parlour was often filled with them. And then, what words of wisdom, of kindness, of encouragement, of counsel,—and the prayer!—for he always concluded these meetings with prayer. The prayer of the dying patriarch,—of the ascending prophet!—for such to us he seemed. Thus blandly and peacefully passed away the latter years of the veteran invalid soldier of the cross,—doing what he could,—still, as ever, faithful to his vows, and zealous in his Master's service.

If he had faults, I saw them not; or if I did, I have long since forgotten them. Such are my recollections of Dr. Smith.

Very respectfully and truly yours,

PHILIP LINDSLEY.

SAMUEL EUSEBIUS McCORKLE, D. D.*

1774—1811.

SAMUEL EUSEBIUS MCCORKLE was born on the 23d of August, 1746, near Harris' Ferry, in Lancaster County, Pa. There he passed his earliest years; but when he was about nine, his parents, who were respectable and pious people, though in moderate worldly circumstances, removed with their family to North Carolina, and settled, some fifteen miles West of Salisbury, on lands which then belonged to the Earl of Granville. In this region he spent the rest of his life.

As his father had settled, with a pretty large family, in a part of the country where there was hardly a foot of land to cultivate, until the heavy growth of timber which covered it was removed, nor a shelter for man or beast, until it was erected, Samuel, with several brothers, most of whom were younger than himself, assisted his father in building the necessary tenements, and clearing and cultivating the farm. Samuel was also the instructer of the younger children of the family, and in a few years was employed as teacher of a public English school. At the age of about twenty, he commenced his classical studies. He was one of the first pupils in the school established by Dr. Caldwell, in Guilford County, in 1766 or 1767; and this was probably the beginning of his preparatory course.

He was graduated at the College of New Jersey, in the year 1772, in the same class with the Rev. Dr. McMillan of Western Pennsylvania, and Aaron Burr. He had made a profession of religion before entering College; but while there, he became satisfied, during a revival of religion, that his previous experience had been spurious, and then, as he believed, for the first time, really complied with the terms of the Gospel. He commenced the study of Theology, soon after he was graduated, under his maternal uncle, the Rev. Joseph Montgomery.† In the spring of 1774, he was licensed to preach the Gospel by the Presbytery of New York, and immediately after was appointed by the Synod to go Southward, and spend at least one year labouring in that region, under the direction of the Presbyteries of Hanover and Orange. After thus spending about two years in Virginia, during which time he seems to have become a member of the Hanover Presbytery, he accepted a call from the Congregation of Thyatira, in which his parents resided, and in which he had spent most of his early years. The Orange Presbytery, at a meeting in October, 1776, received him from the Presbytery of Hanover, and made arrangements for his ordination and installation in a fortnight from that time; though, owing to some unexpected occurrence, this arrangement did not take effect at the time specified, but was deferred until the 2d of August, 1777.

* MS. from Rev. Dr. Caruthers.—Foote's Sketches of N. C.

† JOSEPH MONTGOMERY was graduated at the College of New Jersey in 1755; was licensed to preach by the Presbytery of Philadelphia, between the meetings of Synod in 1759 and 1760; was ordained by the Presbytery of Lewes, between the meetings of Synod in 1761 and 1762; and became Pastor of the Congregations of Newcastle and Christiana Bridge, De. The Presbytery of Newcastle reported to the Synod, in 1785, "that, in consequence of Mr. Joseph Montgomery's having informed them that, through bodily indisposition, he was incapable of officiating in the ministry, and having also accepted an office under the civil authority, they have left his name out of their Records." His name appears on the list of members of Congress from Pennsylvania, from 1784 to 1788.

On the 2d of July, 1776, he was married to Margaret, daughter of William and Elizabeth Steele, of Salisbury, N. C.,—a lady of excellent character and highly respectable connections.

During the Revolutionary war, and especially from the summer of 1780, when the South became the theatre of conflict, the country was in a state of utter confusion, and vice of almost every kind prevailed to an alarming extent. The *civil* character of the war, too, gave it a peculiar ferocity, and produced a licentiousness of morals, of which there is scarcely a parallel at the present day. The municipal laws of the country could not be enforced, civil government was prostrated for a time, and society was virtually resolved into its original elements. Mr. McCorkle came out in reference to this state of things in his utmost strength. He preached, prayed, reasoned, and remonstrated—nor were his labours in vain. From the close of the Revolutionary war, and especially from the breaking out of the Revolution in France,—North Carolina, in common with other parts of the country, was overrun with French infidelity. Here again, he stood forth the indomitable champion of Christianity: he not only preached but published in defence of Divine Revelation; and infidelity quailed before him. It has been confidently asserted that more was done, in that part of the country, by his efforts, to arrest this tide of evil, which threatened at one time to sweep every thing before it, than by any or all other opposing influences.

About the year 1785, Mr. McCorkle commenced, in his own house, a classical school, to which he gave the name of *Zion-Parnassus;* but he discontinued it after ten or twelve years. He was a thorough scholar, and kept up his acquaintance, not only with the Latin and Greek Classics, but with Mathematics, Philosophy, and every important branch of learning. His salary being small, and not punctually paid, a school or some other source of income seemed necessary to the comfortable support of his family. But the drudgery of teaching, and the consumption of time and strength in the constant routine of mere preparatory studies, were foreign from the cast of his mind, and incompatible with not only his fondness for theological investigation, but his sense of obligation as a Christian minister.

In the year 1792, Mr. McCorkle was honoured with the degree of Doctor of Divinity from Dickinson College, Carlisle.

In the far famed revival, that existed at the South and West, about the beginning of the present century, in which bodily agitations were so strangely mingled with spiritual exercises, Dr. McCorkle, for a while, bore an active part. At its commencement, and for some time after, he had no doubt of its genuineness. and he laboured with much zeal for its promotion; but as extravagances began to develop themselves, he felt himself bound to oppose them, and to do what he could to save the churches throughout the region from a fanatical spirit. His efforts in this way were in a good degree successful.

Within a few years after the commencement of the revival, his health failed, and it was evident that he was approaching the end of his course. By several successive and severe attacks of fever, and other complaints, he was nearly disabled for public service; and though he lingered for some time, it was in a state of great infirmity and suffering. But he was fully sustained by those great Christian truths which it had been the business of his life to dispense to others. He wrote, with his own hand, very minute directions respecting his funeral, designating the minister whom he wished to preach his Funeral Sermon, the text which he desired him to use, (Job xix. 25,) the order of the funeral procession, and the hymns to be sung on the occasion; and he even wrote the epitaph for his own tomb-stone. He died on the 21st of January, 1811. His widow died not far from the year 1821. He had six children—five sons and one daughter, all of whom survived him.

The following is a list of his publications:—

A Sermon on Sacrifices, 1792. A Charity Sermon, delivered on several occasions, 1793. A National Thanksgiving Sermon, entitled "The comparative happiness and duty of the United States of America, contrasted with other nations, particularly the Israelites," 1795. A Sermon preached at the laying of the corner-stone of the University of North Carolina. Four Discourses on the great first principles of Deism and Revelation contrasted, 1797. Three Discourses on the terms of Christian Communion. A National Fast Sermon entitled "The work of God for the French Republic; and then her reformation or ruin; or the novel and useful experiment of national Deism, to us and all mankind." A Sermon entitled "The Angel's seal, set upon God's faithful servants, when hurtful winds are blowing in the Church militant."

FROM THE REV. E. W. CARUTHERS, D. D.

Greensboro', N. C., June 28, 1850.

My dear Sir: I was born within the limits of Dr. McCorkle's Congregation, was baptized by him in my infancy, and spent several of my early years under his pastoral care. And, although he died when I was young, I have neither forgotten his appearance, nor ceased to admire his character. His tall and manly form, his grave and solemn countenance, his impressive and thrilling tones, are still distinct in my recollection. I speak of him, not when he was in his full vigour, but during the last three or four years of his life, when he was often so afflicted that he could not preach regularly; but his afflictions, and the conviction which he had of his approaching dissolution, may have increased the solemnity of his manner and style of preaching. Though cheerful and pleasant in the social circle, or at the family fireside, he never indulged in levity, or seemed to forget for a moment that he was a minister of Jesus Christ. From looking over his manuscripts, I judge that he always wrote his sermons, but he never used his notes in the pulpit.

In addition to the ordinary duties of preaching, family visiting and catechising, he was in the habit of giving out every year a series of written questions, and allowing the people two or three months to prepare their answers. The elders were located in different parts of the congregation, and each one had his portion of the vineyard assigned him. He had the names of all the families and individuals within certain limits, and over these he was to have a special care, and at his house the examinations were to be held. The adults were examined on the written questions, and the children and youth were heard on the Catechisms, Shorter and Larger. Such occasions were a means of great improvement, and often of serious and lasting impressions on the minds of the people. I recollect being at one of these examinations, and also at one or two of his pastoral visits to my father's family. Though I was a mere child, I received impressions that have never been effaced; and I was made to feel, even then, the highest respect for the man. It has been remarked, and I believe justly, that the people of his charge were more thoroughly acquainted with the truths of Christianity, than those of almost any other congregation in that part of the country.

Dr. McCorkle was not made to be a missionary, even if he had lived at the present day, when the missionary spirit prevails so much more extensively than it did then. He was always ready to preach in destitute churches or regions, by direction of Presbytery, and often on his own appointment; but his delight was in his study, and thence emanated chiefly his usefulness. A minister's library is in general a good index to the cast of his mind and to his habits of study. If, on entering the study of a minister, with a small salary, and a large family to support, in this back country too, and in that period of its history when books were very expensive, and the difficulty of getting books from foreign countries was almost insurmountable,—you should find the shelves stocked with such authors in Theology, as Calvin, Turretin, Stackhouse, Stillingfleet, and Owen;—in Church History, as Hooker, Shuckford, Prideaux, and Mosheim (in Latin);—on Law and Civil government, as Puffendorff, Burlemaqui, Montesquieu, and Blackstone; besides the Universal History, Encyclopedia Brittanica, &c., it might be fairly inferred that he was a man who looked below the surface of things. Such was his library, and it was a good index to his mind and habits. He would not give a trifling book,—a mere novel or romance, a place on his shelves; but a work of real value that he wanted, he would spare no pains to procure. He rarely bought a work on experimental religion, if it were the production of a second or third rate man; but he delighted much in the practical works of such men as Owen, Edwards, and Doddridge.

As an evidence of the intensity with which he applied his mind to the investigation of truth, and especially to biblical research, it may be stated that not even the ordinary cares and interests of life were allowed to interfere with these favourite pursuits. If he had food and raiment, he seemed to be perfectly contented; and even the provision for that he left very much to others. His land was naturally fertile, and, with even tolerable culture, would have yielded an abundant supply for his family. He had also a number of servants,—the patrimony of his wife,—who, with moderate industry and good management, might have produced a surplus from his farm for market; but they were indolent and thievish, and he was indulgent to a fault. For several years, he employed overseers; but whether he was unfortunate in obtaining suitable persons for that business, or whether they could not make the negroes work, without such coercive measures as he would not sanction, does not now appear. The consequence, however, was, that almost every year there was a deficit; and he was obliged to buy at least a portion of his provisions. Under the pressure of necessity, he thought something must be done, and he concluded, in the spring, when the season for planting came, that, by taking a proper position on one side of the field, he could keep the servants at work, and attend to his studies, at the same time. The negroes, after ploughing across the field a few times until they found him so engaged that he did not notice them, stopped at the remote side of the field, and leaving their horses to graze, lay down and went to sleep. A neighbour, coming along, was surprised to find the negroes in such a predicament; but, at the other side of the field, on his way to the house, he found the Doctor in a corner of the fence, poring over a large volume, with several other folios, paper, inkstand, &c., by his side,—perfectly unmindful of his servants, and greatly surprised at being told that they were fast asleep at the other end of the row. That was the first and the last of his overseeing.

Dr. McCorkle had, on the whole, a very successful ministry. Many were hopefully converted through his instrumentality; and the general character of his congregation for intelligence and piety is a far better eulogium than any I could write, and a more enduring monument to his praise than the marble which covers his remains. With best wishes, I remain,

Your friend and servant,

E. W. CARUTHERS.

JOHN McMILLAN, D. D.

1774—1833.

FROM THE REV. JAMES CARNAHAN, D. D., LL. D.

PRINCETON, November 16, 1847.

Rev. and dear Sir: In reply to your letter requesting me to give you some account of the character and ministry of the late Rev. JOHN McMILLAN, D. D., I am happy to inform you that, a few years before the death of that remarkable man,—wishing to know something of his early life, and the progress of religion in Western Pennsylvania, as identified with his labours, I requested him to furnish me with a statement on these subjects. To my request he replied in the accompanying letter, which is at your service. You will see that this letter contains a fuller and more correct account of the introduction and establishment of Presbyterianism, and I may add of Christianity, in Western Pennsylvania, than can be found elsewhere. Presbyterians were the pioneers of that country. Within my recollection, there was hardly a congregation of any other denomination of Christians to be found West of the mountains. The letter I regard as a precious relic, not only on account of the facts which it contains, but as a remarkable specimen of penmanship. It was written when he was eighty years old, on three sides of half a sheet of small foolscap paper, and yet every word is legible, and nearly every letter complete.

DR. McMILLAN'S LETTER.

CHARTIERS, March 26, 1832.

REV. DR. CARNAHAN—Dear Sir: I received your friendly letter, and will endeavour to comply with your request.

I was born in Fagg's Manor, Chester County, Pa., November 11, 1752. I was first sent to a grammar school, kept by the Rev. John Blair, where I continued until he was removed to Princeton to superintend the College there. I was then sent to Pequea, to a grammar school kept by the Rev. Robert Smith. While there, the Lord poured out his Spirit upon the students, and I believe there were but few who were not brought under serious concern about their immortal souls; some of whom became blessings in their day, and were eminently useful in the Church of Christ; but they are all now gone to rest. It was here that I received my first religious impressions; though, as long as I can remember, I had at times some checks of conscience, and some alarms about the state of my soul: but these seasons were of short continuance;—like the early cloud and the morning dew, they quickly passed away. I never saw that I was a lost, undone sinner, exposed to the wrath of a justly offended God, and could do nothing for my own relief. My convictions were not attended with much horror: though I felt that I deserved hell, and that in all probability *that* must be my portion, yet I could not feel that distress which I ought to feel, and which I thought I must feel, before I could expect to obtain relief. I felt also much legality mingled with all the duties which I attempted to perform. In this situation I continued until I entered College at Princeton, in the spring of 1770. I had not been long there, until a revival of religion took place among the students, and I believe, at one time, there were not more than two or three but what were under serious impressions. On a day which had been set apart by a number of the students, to be observed as a day of fasting and prayer,—while the others were at dinner, I retired into my study, and while trying to pray, I got some discoveries of Divine things, which I had never had before. I saw that the Divine law was not only holy, just and spiritual, but that it was good also, and that conformity to it would make me happy. I felt no disposition to quarrel with the law, but with myself, because I was not conformed to it. I felt that it was now easy to submit to the Gospel plan of salvation, and felt a serenity of mind to which I had hitherto been a stranger. And it was followed by a delight in contemplating God's glorious perfections in all his works. I thought I could see God in every thing around me.

I continued at College until the fall of 1772, when I returned to Pequea, and began the study of Theology, under the direction of the Rev. Robert Smith, D. D. I had great difficulties in my own mind about undertaking the work of the Gospel ministry. I at last came to this determination,—to leave the matter wholly with God: if He opened the way, I would go on; if He shut it, I would be satisfied; and I think, if I ever knew what it was to have no will of my own about any matter, it was about this. I passed through my trials in the Presbytery of Newcastle, and was licensed by them to preach the Gospel, October 26, 1774, at East Nottingham.

The first winter after being licensed, I spent in itinerating in the vacant congregations of Newcastle and Donegal Presbyteries. In the summer of 1775, I took a tour through the settlements of Virginia, between the North and South mountains. In July, I crossed the mountains between Staunton and the head of Tyart's Valley, preached in the various settlements through which I passed, until I came to Chartiers, preached on the fourth Sabbath of August, and on the Tuesday following, at Pigeon Creek. I then turned my course eastward, and preached in the different settlements, as I passed along. In the winter, I again visited Augusta County, in Virginia, crossed the mountains in January, and preached at Pigeon Creek and Chartiers, until the latter end of March, 1776, when I returned home; and, at a meeting of Presbytery, on the 23d of April, accepted a call from the united Congregations of Chartiers and Pigeon Creek, and was dismissed to join the Presbytery of Donegal, and on the 19th of June, was ordained at Chambersburg. It being in the time of the Revolutionary war, and the Indians being very troublesome on the frontiers, I was prevented from removing my family to my congregations until November, 1778. I, however, visited them as often as I could, ordained elders, baptized their children, and took as much care of them as circumstances would permit.

When I came to this country, the cabin in which I was to live was raised, but there was no roof on it, nor chimney nor floor in it: the people, however, were very kind, assisted me in preparing my house, and on the 16th of December, I moved into it: but we had neither bedstead, nor table, nor chairs, nor stool, nor bucket. All these things we had to leave behind us: there being no waggon road at that time over the mountains, we could bring nothing with us but what was carried on pack horses. We placed two boxes on each other, which served us for a table, and two kegs served for seats; and having committed ourselves to God in family worship, we spread a bed on the floor, and slept soundly till morning. The next day, a neighbour coming to my assistance, we made a table and a stool, and in a little time had every thing comfortable about us. Sometimes, indeed, we had no bread for weeks together; but we had plenty of pumpkins, and potatoes, and all the necessaries of life; and as for luxuries, we were not much concerned about them. We enjoyed health, the Gospel and its ordinances, and pious friends: we were in the place where we believed God would have us to be, and we did not doubt but that He would provide for us every thing necessary. My wife and I lived comfortably together more than forty-three years; and on the 24th of November, 1819, she departed triumphantly to take possession of her house not made with hands, eternal in the Heavens.

When I had determined to come to this country, Dr. Smith enjoined it upon me to look out for some pious young men, and educate them for the ministry; "for," said he, "though some men of piety and talents may go to a new country, at first, yet if they are not careful to raise up others, the country will not be well supplied." Accordingly, I collected a few who gave evidence of piety, and taught them the Latin and Greek languages, some of whom became useful, and others eminent, ministers of the Gospel. I had still a few with me, when the Academy was opened in Cannonsburg, and finding that I could not teach, and do justice to my congregation, I immediately gave it up, and sent them there.

The first remarkable season of the outpouring of the Spirit, which we enjoyed in this congregation, began about the middle of December, 1781. It made its first appearance among a few who met together for social worship, on the evening of a Thanksgiving day, which had been appointed by Congress. This encouraged us to appoint other meetings for the same purpose on Sabbath evenings; and the appearances still increasing, Sabbath night societies were continued with but little interruption for nearly two years. It was then usual to spend the whole night in religious exercises; nor did the time seem tedious, for the Lord was there, and his work went pleasantly on. Many were pricked to the heart with deep convictions, and a goodly number, we hope, became the subjects of renewing grace. At the first sacramental occasion after the work began, forty-five were added to the church, many of whom continued bringing forth the fruits of righteousness, and filling important offices in the church, until they were removed to the world of spirits. This time of refreshing continued, in a greater or less degree, until the year 1794. Upon every sacramental occasion, during this period, numbers were added to the church, who gave comfortable evidence of having obtained a saving change of heart; but, as I neglected to keep a register of their names, I cannot now ascertain their number.

The next remarkable season of the outpouring of God's Spirit was in the year 1795. This, however, was not very extensive, nor of long continuance; yet, during this season, about fifty were added to the church, most of whom continued to manifest, by their walk and conversation, that they had experienced a real change of heart, and some of them became successful preachers of the Gospel, though there were some lamentable instances of apostacy.

In the spring of the year 1799, the Lord again graciously revived his work in this congregation. Many were at once awakened to a serious concern about their immortal souls, and made to inquire the way to Zion with their faces thitherward, weeping as they went. Of those that were then awakened, about sixty joined the church, and made a public profession of religion. This revival, as well as that of '95, was carried on without much external appearance, except a solemn attention and silent weeping under the preaching of the word.

From this time until the fall of 1802, religion was evidently on the decline; for though some were every year added to the church, yet they were generally such as had been brought under serious impressions in 1799, and there were few or none newly awakened. Sinners became more bold in sin, and floods of vanity and carnality appeared likely to carry all before them. Even the pious themselves became very weak and feeble in the cause of Christ, and much buried in the world, insomuch that when God returned to build up Zion, it might in truth be said, "We were as men that dream." Many stood astonished, not knowing what to make of it, and but few were prepared to meet the Lord, and bid Him welcome. This work differed from former revivals only in this,—that the body was more generally affected. It was no unusual thing to see persons so entirely deprived of bodily strength, that they would fall from their seats and off their feet, and be as unable to help themselves as a new born child. I have seen some lie in this condition for hours, who yet said that they could hear every thing that was spoken, and felt their minds more composed, and more capable of attending to Divine things, than when their bodies were not thus affected. As far as I could observe, the bodily exercise never preceded but always followed upon the mind's being deeply impressed with a sense of some Divine truth. Between fifty and sixty joined the church, as the fruits of this revival. After the close of the revival, which began in 1809,—though, upon every sacramental occasion, some joined the church,—yet nothing very remarkable took place until 1823, when God again visited this dry and parched congregation with a shower of Divine influences. About sixty joined the church, as the fruits of this revival; a number of whom were students in the College, and are now preaching the Gospel of Christ to their dying fellow men. Since that time, religion has rather been on the decline, though still we are not left without some tokens of the Divine presence. At every sacramental occasion, some have come out from the world, and professed to take the Lord for their portion. * * * * * * *

The First Presbytery that met on this side of the mountains, was held at Mount Pleasant, on the third week of October, 1783. The first Synod met at Pittsburg, on the last Wednesday of September, 1802. * * * I am now in my eightieth year, and have outlived all the first set of ministers who settled on this side of the mountains, all the second set who were raised in this country, and several of the third. I yet enjoy pretty good health, though sometimes troubled with rheumatic pains. I am yet able to preach, though my memory is much failed, so that I am obliged to make more use of notes than formerly; yet my lungs are still good, and I can bawl almost as loud as ever. * * * As I have given up my congregation, because I could no longer perform the duties of a pastor, if my life and health be continued, I design this spring and summer to visit some of the old congregations which I helped to collect, and see how they do, and once more blow the Gospel trumpet among them. JOHN McMILLAN.

The preceding letter nearly exhausts the subject of your inquiry, as it was written when the venerable old man had almost reached the end of his course. He received the degree of Doctor of Divinity from Jefferson College, in 1807. During the summer and autumn immediately preceding his death, he was occupied much in visiting the churches, and preaching in various places, and it was observed that he preached with almost the energy of middle life. In October, 1833, he attended the meeting of the Synod at Pittsburg, and preached twice during its sessions; and afterwards accompanied several of his brethren down the river to Wheeling. There he remained nearly a fortnight, preaching almost every day and evening. On Tuesday, the 5th of November, he went to Cannonsburg, and stopped at the house of a friend, in his usual health. In the course of the night following, he was taken seriously ill, and when the Doctor was called the next morning, Dr. M. made a remark to him, that was understood to imply a conviction on his part that his disease would have a fatal termination. And thus it actually resulted. He died, sustained to the last by the consolations of the Gospel, on Saturday morning, the 16th of November. His disease was paralysis of the prostrate gland, occasioned, as was supposed, by overtasking his strength in preaching. The day after his death, which was the Sabbath, his body was conveyed to the Chartiers Church, attended by a large concourse, where, after appropriate funeral services, it was laid in its last resting place.

In his personal appearance and manners, Dr. McMillan was as far from being attractive as you can well imagine. He was nearly or quite six feet high, when standing erect,—which, however, rarely happened, as he usually walked with his neck and head inclined forward. He was of a stout and clumsy form, his features coarse, his nose very prominent, and his general aspect somewhat forbidding.

He had, I think, no great talent at extemporaneous preaching,—at least in early life. He, therefore, wrote his sermons out in full, and committed them to memory. As he could put *multum in parvo* on paper, he had his sermon of such a size that he could put it into a small pocket Bible, and hold it under his thumb, so that very few of his hearers knew, or even suspected, that he had so much as short notes. His voice was strong and coarse, and he poured his words out in such a torrent, that it often offended delicate ears. He had but little gesture, seldom moving his hands in the pulpit. The body of his discourse was generally doctrinal, divided into two or three heads,—the whole an hour long,—not five minutes more or less,—embracing, at different times, the whole system of doctrine taught in our Confession of Faith. In the application of his sermons, which he never omitted, he made appeals to the hearts and consciences of his hearers, which were sometimes appalling. In describing the wretchedness of the lost, especially of those who had enjoyed the privileges of the Gospel, he was tremendous. And God blessed his preaching in a remarkable manner. He could not be called a man of genius, or of splendid talents. He wrote and spoke plain English, which the most illiterate could understand, and seldom introduced metaphysical discussion, either in the pulpit or out of it. I have often seen him, when preaching to fifteen hundred or two thousand people, in the open air, under the shade of the native trees, take off his coat and neckcloth or stock, in the midst of his discourse, and proceed without exciting a smile in one of the audience.

He was an excellent Latin and Greek scholar, and, at a very early period, opened a school in a small log cabin which he built near his house. Whenever he found a young man of piety, who appeared to have gifts promising extensive usefulness in the Church, he took him into his family, taught him without charge, and trained him up for the ministry. In this way Patterson, Porter, Marques, Hughes, and several other eminently useful ministers, were trained. After an Academy, through his influence, was established in Cannonsburg, three miles from his residence, he confined his teaching to Theology; and this he continued until Theological Seminaries were established.

He lived almost entirely on the products of his farm, and in a style of the utmost simplicity and plainness; and though he extended a hospitable welcome to his friends, they generally partook of the accustomed fare, and never heard an apology from his lips. No man ever valued money less, for his own use or that of his family, beyond what was necessary to render them comfortable. I have reason to believe that, in the latter part of his life, he gave, for benevolent purposes, more than he received from his congregation; and he did it so silently, that there were very few to whom it was known. He was in the habit of furnishing indigent young men with the means of prosecuting their studies for the Gospel ministry,—always as a loan,—telling them to return it when they were able, so that he might assist others. He also enlisted the co-operation of others with himself in this object, long before Education Societies were thought of. From a person who lived in his family, at the time of the occurrence, I learned the following interesting fact illustrative of his benevolence. Sometime between 1780 and 1790, there was a scarcity of bread, and great suffering in consequence, in the Western part of Pennsylvania. The scarcity of breadstuffs was not thought of until April or May; but, about that time, people began to go in every direction to purchase grain. When a stranger came to Mr. McMillan, wishing to buy, he would ask the applicant in a rough way if he had money to pay for it. On receiving an answer in the affirmative, he would say,—"I have no wheat or corn for *you*; you can buy elsewhere." He disposed of his wheat and corn, of which he had several hundred bushels, to such as he knew had no means to buy, on condition that they would return to him an equal quantity after harvest. To the vicious and idle his rebukes were often severe, sometimes scathing. To those in distress either of body or mind, he was kind and tender, beyond what a stranger would think possible in a man of his appearance.

Dr. McMillan's influence in preaching the Gospel himself, and in training others for the same work, it is not easy to estimate. With all his imperfections, he was just such a man as was suited to the field of labour assigned him. He lived to a good old age, and has left behind him a bright name on earth, and has gone, I doubt not, to a glorious reward in Heaven.

Very respectfully and truly yours,

JAMES CARNAHAN.

THADDEUS DOD.*

1775—1793.

THADDEUS DOD, the son of Stephen Dod, was born near Newark, N. J. on the 7th of March, (O. S.) 1740. His father, who was a native of Guilford, Conn., removed from Newark to Mendham in the same State, while this son was in his infancy; and there the son spent his youthful days. From early childhood he had strong religious impressions, and the private record of his exercises through a series of years shows that he was the subject of almost constant internal conflicts, until the year 1764, when he believed that he experienced a decisive change of character. The next year he was admitted to the Communion of the Church in Mendham.

At a very early period he began to develop an extraordinary taste and talent for Mathematics, and he was earnestly desirous of obtaining a collegiate education; but the straitened circumstances of his father forbade the expectation of it, except as it should be accomplished through his own efforts. By teaching school at different times, and studying as he could find opportunity, he at length succeeded in becoming fitted to enter College, and in acquiring the means of meeting his expenses there. He joined the Sophomore class of the College of New Jersey in the spring of 1771, and was graduated in the autumn of 1773, under the Presidency of Dr. Witherspoon. Soon after leaving College, he went to Newark, N. J., where he was married to Phoebe Baldwin, and about the same time entered on the study of Theology under the direction of the Rev. Dr. McWhorter. After remaining there about a year, he removed to Morristown, where he continued his studies under the Rev. Timothy Johnes, who had been his first teacher in Latin. He was licensed to preach by the New York Presbytery, in 1775.

In the winter of 1776–77, he was confined by a severe attack of inflammatory rheumatism; but in the month of March, though still unable to dress himself without assistance, he resolved on making a tour to the West. After preaching in parts of Virginia and Maryland, he crossed the mountains, and visited the settlements of George's Creek, Muddy Creek, and Dunlap's Creek, and proceeded thence to Tenmile. As there were, at the latter place a number of families, who had removed from Morris County, it is not improbable that they had invited him to visit them, and that his journey was undertaken with special reference to that purpose. This emigration had taken place about the year 1773, when there had been for several years peace with the Indian tribes; but, by a fresh outbreak in the spring of 1774, these people were driven back, and took refuge in a fort near Monongahela River. The next year, they returned and built a fort, to which they could resort in time of danger. In the summer season, for several years, they were compelled frequently to remain together in the forts,—the men going out in armed parties to work on their farms; and in the winter, when the Indians retired to their wigwams and hunting grounds, they returned to their habitations. Such was the state of things when Mr. Dod went among them; and as they were his old friends, and some of them had been associated with him in the scenes of an interesting revival in New

* Presb. Mag. IV.—Smith's Old Red Stone.

Jersey, in 1764, the meeting must have been, to both parties, one of no common interest. The frequent incursions of the Indians had put a stop to immigration, and prevented the increase of their numbers, and consequently delayed, what they most ardently desired,—the establishment of a church, and the administration of its ordinances among them. After preaching, for some time, in that comparatively desolate region, he returned to New Jersey in August, 1777.

The people at Tenmile, during his sojourn there, expressed a strong desire that he should take up his residence among them as their minister; and though there were not more than ten men within their bounds, who were professors of religion, and not one man of wealth among them all, they unanimously agreed to support him and his family, if he would cast in his lot with them, and share their simple and humble mode of living. Though he foresaw that his acceptance of their invitation would subject him to much self-denial and sacrifice, yet the interest which he felt in ministering to his early friends, and in seeing the Gospel planted in that new country, disposed and ultimately determined him to yield to their wishes; and accordingly he was ordained by the Presbytery of New York, *sine titulo*, in October, 1777, with a view to finding his home in that then distant part of the country.

Shortly after this, he left New Jersey, with his family, consisting of a wife and two children,—and also two of his brothers, with their families, to carry out his purpose in regard to an ultimate settlement. By the 10th of November, they had arrived at Patterson's Creek, in Hampshire County, Va., where Mr. Dod had made some acquaintance in his former tour. But hearing, while there, of a then recent formidable attack by the Indians on the Fort at Wheeling, and of the consequent confusion and terror prevailing throughout the West, they deemed it imprudent to proceed farther at that time. Mr. Dod, however, after remaining a few days with his family, left them, and crossing the mountains alone, proceeded to Tenmile, where he preached in the forts, and baptized the children, and after a week returned.

He remained at Patterson's Creek for nearly two years, during which time he was employed in preaching there, and in the adjacent counties in Virginia and Maryland, where, it would seem, no churches had yet been organized. His labours in this field were attended with a manifest blessing, and when he was about to leave, a vigorous effort was made to retain him, and a much better support offered him than he could expect at Tenmile; but he could not be diverted from his purpose. Accordingly, in September, 1779, he, with his wife and child, (for he had buried one child during his sojourn at Patterson's Creek,) and his two brothers, proceeded on their way, and crossed the mountains on pack horses, some of which had been sent from Tenmile. One of his brothers, however, accompanied him only a part of the way, and then returned to New Jersey.

On reaching the place of his destination, he found a dark and forbidding state of things; but he entered upon his labours with great zeal and self-denial. On the 15th of August, 1781, he organized a church consisting of twenty-five members; but it was some time before the Lord's Supper could be administered, on account of their being exposed to the incursions of the savages. Mr. Dod was the second minister who settled West of the Monongahela River, (Dr. McMillan only having preceded him,) and took a position farther on the frontier than any other. Tenmile, on the South, bordered on an unbroken wilderness. A line of forts from Pittsburg to Wheeling protected the places farther North; but from Wheeling to Point Pleasant all was open to the savage foe. But though there were frequent hostile demonstrations on the part of the Indians, and though many families in the neighbourhood fell under the tomahawk and scalping knife, not one of the little company that emigrated from New Jersey was killed. And what was still more remarkable, the ministrations of Mr. Dod, in the midst of these perilous circumstances, and while the people, during part of the time, were shut up in the fort, were attended by a revival of religion, as the fruits of which upwards of forty were admitted to the church. The first administration of the Lord's Supper was in a barn, in May, 1783; and it was an occasion of great solemnity, and accompanied by unusual tokens of the Divine presence. The first house of worship was erected in the summer of 1785; and though public worship was held alternately in two sections of the congregation, no other was erected till the summer of 1792. There was but one organization of church or congregation while Mr. Dod lived.

As he had an exquisite taste for music, and withal was well acquainted with it as a science, he caused special attention to be given to the performance of that part of public worship. He used no other than Watts' Psalms and Hymns from the first. He delivered sermons and addresses designed to illustrate the importance of sacred music, and the manner in which it should be performed. And in 1792, he introduced singing without reading the line; and though it was to some rather an offensive innovation, it seems to have occasioned no serious disturbance.

Mr. Dod was specially attentive to the interests of education,—frequently visiting schools, and counselling and encouraging the teachers. He had a building erected within a few steps of his own dwelling, in which he opened a classical and mathematical school, in the spring of 1782. This school, which was the first of its kind in the West, was in operation for about three years and a half. It was discontinued in the autumn of 1785; but for what reasons, cannot now be definitely ascertained. Messrs. Smith and McMillan, who were associated with Mr. Dod as pioneers in the ministry, also sympathized with him most fully in the educational enterprise; and as the result of their consultation and co-operation, an Academy was instituted at Washington, Pa., for which a charter was granted, September 24, 1787, with a donation of five thousand acres of land. Mr. Dod was urgently solicited to become the head of this institution, and he finally—though not without great reluctance—consented to serve in that capacity for a single year. The institution went into operation on the 1st of April, 1789, with between twenty and thirty students. In connection with his duties as Principal, he continued his labours as a minister—preaching one-third of the time at Washington, and dividing the other two-thirds between the two places at Tenmile.

Mr. Dod's labours, throughout his whole ministry, seem to have been attended with much more than an ordinary blessing. Besides a regular increase of his church from year to year, there were several seasons of special religious interest, which brought in larger numbers. It was during such a season that he was called to rest from his labours. In the summer of 1792, a revival commenced among his people, which continued through the succeeding autumn and winter. Encouraged by this state of things, Mr. Dod was abundant in his labours, notwithstanding he was then rapidly wasting under the influence of pulmonary consumption. At the fall meeting of Presbytery, he had been appointed to preach on the first Sabbath of April at Cross Creek, which had been rendered vacant by the death of the Rev. Joseph Smith. This appointment he insisted, contrary to the better judgment of his friends, on fulfilling; but it proved to be the last public service that he ever performed. In returning home, he was exposed to a violent storm, which, together with the fatigue occasioned by the exercise, effectually prostrated him. His disease now took on a more decided form, and he became convinced that the time of his departure was at hand. For a brief period, he was subject to distressing doubts in regard to his spiritual state; but before his death the joys of salvation were fully restored to him. He died on the 20th of May, 1793. A Discourse was preached at his funeral by the Rev. Dr. McMillan, from Rev. xiv. 13.

The following is an extract from an article written by his son, the Rev. Cephas Dod, of Amity, Pa., and published in the Presbyterian Magazine for August and September, 1854:—

"Mr. Dod in his early childhood evinced a love of learning, and it deserves particular notice that his attention was first turned to a careful reading of the Holy Scriptures, and seeking a knowledge of the doctrines of religion. At the age of about fifteen or sixteen years, he took to mathematical studies, which he pursued with great ardour, though without an instructer, and his attainments were probably not the less profound, because made with little assistance. Rev. Dr. Carnahan, in a letter dated July, 1841, wrote—'The following anecdote will show the estimation in which your father's mathematical talents and attainments were held by his contemporaries in the College. Before the death of Chief Justice Kirkpatrick, who was a Trustee of the College, Albert B. Dod, our present Professor of Mathematics, was nominated in the Board of Trustees for the Mathematical Chair, and the Judge remarked that he was not acquainted with the candidate, and did not know his reputation as a mathematician; nevertheless he would vote for him most cheerfully; he liked the name; that he never knew a Dod (and he was acquainted with many of them) that was not born a mathematician; that there was one Thaddeus Dod in College when he was a student, who seemed to understand mathematics by instinct; that all the students applied to him for aid when any thing difficult occurred in their mathematical studies. He presumed the candidate was of the same stock,* and he would vote for him.

"It does not appear that he was less eminent as a classical than a mathematical scholar. The Greek and Hebrew texts prefixed to some of his discourses,—each neatly written in its appropriate character,—show his familiarity with those languages. He had much versatility of talent, and could pursue with pleasure any branch of science; but the word of God, the doctrine of the Cross, was his favourite study.

"Rev. Dr. Eliot, in his Address at the Inauguration of Dr. Clark, as President of Washington College, uses the following language in reference to Washington Academy and Mr. Dod—namely:—'As an Academy, it soon acquired distinction, by having for its first President the Rev. Thaddeus Dod, one of the early literary pioneers of Western Pennsylvania, the associate of McMillan, Power, and Smith, in the formation of the first Presbytery West of the Alleghany Mountains,—probably, if we may trust tradition, the most accomplished scholar of their number.'

"In preaching he used notes, seldom entering the pulpit without them; but they were, for the most part, very short; few of his discourses, though studied with great care, were written out in full. Being a subject of pulmonary disease, his voice was not strong, and did not admit of loud and passionate declamation. His enunciation was exceedingly distinct, and his emphasis correct, so that he was easily heard even by a large audience. In his manner, he always showed that he felt the truths he delivered, and was anxious that those whom he addressed should feel them too. His preaching was spoken of by ministers and people as being of a remarkably close discriminating character. He took great delight in religious conversation, entering deeply into its spirit, and this practice he urged upon his people in all their communications together, as a means of growth in grace, and of stirring each other up to love and good works. With the young people of his charge he used great familiarity, and especially by affectionately urging upon them the claims of the Gospel."

* The Professor was a grand-nephew of Thaddeus Dod.

JOHN RANKIN.

1775—1798.

FROM THE REV. ISAAC W. K. HANDY.

PORTSMOUTH, Va., June 7, 1857.

Rev. and dear Brother: The name of John Rankin is well worthy of a record in your "Annals." He was a bright light in "the Peninsula;" and though it is now nearly sixty years since his candlestick was removed, the rays of that light are still reflected in the "lower counties," and children's children experience their continued influence. As I have had considerable opportunities of investigating his history, I am happy to furnish you the result in the following brief sketch.

JOHN RANKIN was a native of the same little "Diamond State," that gave to the Church such men as Davies, Miller the younger, McWhorter, James P. Wilson, and a host of others—earnest friends of the cause of Presbyterianism, as well as of our common Christianity. He was born at Newark, De., on the 22d of March, 1750, of—it is believed—poor but respectable parentage. He was a student in the "Old Academy" of his native village; where he acquired a knowledge of the languages, and made commendable progress in such other branches as were taught in the Presbyterian schools of that day. His theological studies were pursued under the direction of the Rev. Thomas Read, D. D., of Wilmington, for whom he seemed always to entertain the highest respect, and into whose hands we are informed by tradition were committed some of his manuscript sermons, intended for the press; but which, for some unknown reason, were not published. For these sermons I have made diligent search, but without success. I have, however, been fortunate enough to find, in possession of a son of the excellent Read, an autograph essay on the subject of Temperance, which is interesting, not only as a beautiful specimen of chirography, but as illustrative of the sound principles held by some good men, long before the day of Temperance pledges and associations.

In 1773, the Presbytery of Lewes, which had generally numbered about eight members, was found to be reduced just one half. The only ministers remaining to supply the destitute places of that portion of the Peninsula, lying South of the three upper counties, were Messrs. John Miller, Jacob Ker,* Alexander Huston,† and Matthew Wilson. These fathers had each of them two or three congregations to which they statedly ministered; and all of them rejoiced to perform as much missionary labour over the exten-

* JACOB KER,—a son of Walter Ker, an emigrant from Scotland,—was born in Freehold, N. J.; was graduated at the College of New Jersey, in 1758; was Tutor in the College from 1760 to 1762; was licensed to preach by the New Brunswick Presbytery between the meetings of Synod in 1762 and 1763, and was ordained by the same Presbytery between the meetings of Synod in 1763 and 1764; was received by the Presbytery of Lewes on the 29th of August, 1764; was called to the Churches of Monokin and Wicomico, Md., August 29, 1764; became Pastor of those Churches shortly after, and died in charge of them on the 29th of July, 1795. The following testimony to his worth is from the Records of the Presbytery of Lewes:—"The loss of this great and good man was sensibly felt by the Church in general, and by this Presbytery in particular. He was a bright luminary in the Church, who lived exemplarily, preached warmly, and prayed fervently—a pattern truly worthy the imitation of his brethren."

† ALEXANDER HUSTON was licensed to preach by the Presbytery of Lewes, April 12, 1763; was ordained and installed Pastor of Murtherkiln and Three Runs, De., October 9, 1764; and died January 3, 1785, greatly lamented.

sive surrounding wastes, as opportunity and health would allow. They were unable, however, to comply with half the calls that were made upon them to preach and to administer the ordinances. At this crisis, it was resolved to supplicate the Presbytery of Newcastle for aid. An urgent appeal was drawn up, (October 19,) setting forth the fact that "here are numbers of starving souls, crying to us for the bread of life, and we unable to assist them. We, therefore, apply to you, our dear Christian fellow-labourers, who are not only concerned for your particular churches, but for the whole Church of Christ, and earnestly request you, as you regard the common interest of our Lord Jesus, that you send us what supplies you possibly can."

Two noble-hearted young men caught the echo of this "Macedonian cry," and responded at once to the pressing appeal. These were Samuel McMaster* and John Rankin. McMaster came with a diploma from the Academy of Newark, De., and a certificate of recommendation from the Presbytery under whose care he had been previously received as a candidate for the Gospel ministry. Young Rankin was unable to reach the ground until the following spring. He came, too, under an embarrassment which his fellow-pupil had escaped — without a presbyterial recommendation. Early in the winter of 1775, he had applied to the Presbytery of Newcastle to be taken on trials for licensure; but some members, objecting to the reception of an individual who had not been honoured with a College diploma, it was determined to make the application an occasion for an overture to Synod upon the question—"May Presbyteries license persons to preach the Gospel who have not obtained a degree from some College?" The answer to this overture,—which may be found in the Synodical Record, was just such as might have been expected from a body of judicious and learned men; and, no doubt, such as Rankin himself was satisfied would be returned. "As Presbyteries," said they, "are the proper judges to determine concerning the literary and other requisite qualifications for the ministerial office, it is not intended to preclude from admission to trial those who have not had the opportunity of obtaining public testimonials, or degrees from public seminaries."

Rankin's circumstances were such, that he found it altogether inexpedient to wait a whole year for this announcement; and with the consciousness of a preparation which could be suitably attested by a Presbyterial examination, he resolved to make application without delay to the Presbytery of Lewes to be taken on trials for licensure. The application was favourably received; and at the meeting of Presbytery, held at Murtherkiln, November 29, 1775, he was regularly licensed as a probationer for the Gospel ministry.

Immediately after the licensure of Mr. Rankin, he was appointed to supply the Churches of Buckingham in Maryland, and Blackwater in Delaware, at intervals, until the next meeting of Presbytery. He appears to have interested these associated congregations at once; and in March, he was again appointed to supply them for the next three months,—with the exception of a few Sabbaths which were to be devoted to the Churches at Fishing Creek and Vienna, in Maryland.

* SAMUEL MCMASTER was licensed to preach by the Presbytery of Lewes, March 26, 1776; was ordained April 20, 1779; shortly after became Pastor of Snow Hill and Pitt's Creek Churches, in which connection he remained more than thirty years. He wrote a History of the Rehoboth Church.

The Churches of Buckingham and Blackwater were now anxious to have the entire services of Mr. Rankin; but expecting to be absent for a time from the bounds of the Presbytery, he could only promise to supply them on his return as heretofore. This he continued to do in compliance with their solicitations, and by regular appointment, until the summer of 1778. About a year before this, however, he had intimated to his brethren a desire to be dismissed from the Presbytery. To this proposal they could not accede; and at length, in submission to their authority, the idea was abandoned altogether. Up to this time, he had continued to exercise his gift, simply as a licentiate. This subjected the churches to much inconvenience. The difficulty, however, was unavoidable, as the Presbytery had not been able to assemble for about fifteen months, in consequence of the agitation occasioned by the Tories. This having at length subsided, an urgent appeal was made by the Churches of Buckingham and Blackwater for his ordination, "who also begged leave to present a unanimous call for his settlement with them." Mr. Rankin, having signified his disposition to accept the call, the ordination was effected according to their wishes on the 3d day of June, 1778, in the church at Murtherkiln. The minister preached his own ordination Sermon from II. Cor. ii. 16; and all the other services were performed by the Rev. John Miller. Arrangements were made for the installation, at Buckingham, April 20, 1779, but there is reason to believe that that service did not take place until the meeting of the Presbytery in October of the same year.

The comfortable relations existing between Mr. Rankin and his people are sufficiently apparent in the protracted service which he rendered them,—continuing through a period of more than twenty years. Coming amongst them at a time of great political distraction, and when, in consequence of the peculiar crisis, even the hearts of Christians had contracted an unwonted spiritual insensibility, it seemed as if he had little to hope. It was a time of prevailing iniquity—wicked men walked abroad in the unrestrained indulgence of every lust; infidelity was rife; strange sectarists were diffusing their erratic and even poisonous sentiments over the length and breadth of the Peninsula; and, at no time, perhaps, had so great a want of interest been manifested among all classes, on religious subjects. But Rankin was not discouraged. With strong confidence in the God of battles, he went forth to the contest. Whilst, as a Presbyterian, he was not backward to defend the distinctive principles of his Church, he was yet more earnest in his advocacy of what he regarded the fundamental truths of our common Christianity.

Rankin did not labour in vain. An intelligent and able theologian,—a zealous preacher, with a fervid and easy delivery, he was heard with attention wherever he went. Few men have enjoyed a greater popularity; or enjoying it, have turned it to better account. Instant in season and out of season, visiting the waste places and preaching to the destitute wherever he could find them,—he sowed broadcast the seed of the word; and God gave it increase. The savour of his good name was in all the churches; and whilst the memorials of his holy influence appear in various public and private records, there are those yet living who testify to the charm of his conversations, exhortations, and sermons. There are no means, however, of arriving with statistical accuracy at the results of his labours, even amongst the people of his own charge. About this time, the Sessions of Buckingham and Blackwater, were not particular in the preservation of their Records; and there are no data, by which we can reach even a probable estimate of the numbers brought into the Kingdom of the Redeemer during his long pastorate. We know, however, that the old frame building in which he entered upon his work, soon became too strait for the growing congregation; and that, long before his death, it became necessary to erect that very stately and commodious brick edifice, which, after resisting the storms of more than threescore and ten winters, was at length unroofed and dilapidated by the fearful tempest that brought distress to so many hearts on the night of the 18th of January last.

About the year 1791, the health of Mr. Rankin began seriously to fail, so that it became necessary for him to relinquish his Delaware charge, which, at a distance of some twenty miles, he had continued for years to serve with great diligence and constancy.

In May, 1792, he represented the Presbytery of Lewes in the General Assembly; and he was there again the next year, as a special commissioner, associated with the Rev. Jacob Ker, Major William Jones, and William Morris. The appointment of this extra delegation grew out of a report which had been made to the Presbytery by Mr. Rankin, in relation to a judgment of the Assembly, virtually censuring that judicatory for an action which had been taken in the case of the Rev. Francis Hindman.* Through the influence of these gentlemen, the Assembly was induced to review so much of their proceedings as related to this matter; and, "after considerable discussion, it was resolved, as the sense of this house, that no man or body of men, agreeably to the constitution of this Church, ought to be condemned or censured, without having notice of the accusation against him or them, and notice given for trial; and therefore that if the General Assembly of the last year so meant, by the minute in question, it was informal."

In 1796, we find Mr. Rankin again a member of the Assembly. During this year also, he was obliged to ask permission of the Presbytery to be absent part of the summer on an excursion for his health. Indeed, from this time onward, he appears to have gradually failed; until, at length, after two more years of toil and suffering, he bade farewell to the scenes of earth.

Nearly threescore years have passed since this excellent man went to his grave. But he is still gratefully remembered by some aged persons; and there are few in the vicinity of those ancient churches, in the "lower counties," who are ignorant of, or without reverence for, the name of Rankin. With that name is associated a character, presenting an interesting combination of cheerfulness, energy, piety, and great usefulness. There is not even a traditionary reminiscence of unfaithfulness as a pastor, nor of imprudence or indiscretion in any of the relations which he sustained,—ecclesiastical, civil or social. This is the more remarkable, as he is known to have been very deeply interested in the events of the Revolutionary struggle. At a meeting of Presbytery, held shortly after his death, the following memorial was entered upon the Minutes:—"The Rev. John Rankin was removed by death, on the 2d instant; by which event the Church has

* FRANCIS HINDMAN was ordained and installed Pastor of the united Congregations of Lewes, Coal Spring, and Indian River, De., by the Presbytery of Lewes, April 27, 1791, and was dismissed on the 21st of April, 1795.

lost a zealous advocate, the Presbytery a worthy member, and his country a warm patriot."

There are various traditions of Mr. Rankin's uncommon power as a preacher. The late General George Handy, of Somerset County, Md., has frequently remarked that he could distinctly remember a Communion season which occurred at Princess Anne, when the Pastor of that Church,—Rev. Jacob Ker,—was assisted by the minister from Buckingham; and such was the pathos and eloquence of the preacher, and the general solemnity of the scene, as to leave an impression upon his mind which remained vivid after the lapse of many years.

As an illustration of Mr. Rankin's powers of extemporaneous speaking, I may mention the following incident which is said to have occurred at Bishop's Mill, near the Southern line of Delaware,—a locality where, from time immemorial, on election and other public days, crowds of persons have resorted to engage in such sports as might be suggested by the excitement of the hour. On one of these occasions,—tradition does not say what,—a large concourse of people had assembled; and among the multitude of topics discussed, the wonderful *impromptu* talent of Parson Rankin—as he was familiarly called—was not forgotten. Some alleged that he could speak fluently and appropriately, on any subject, and at any moment, without the least premeditation—others doubted—and to settle the matter, certain parties ventured a wager. The Parson, though at a distance of a dozen miles, was immediately sent for, with the express understanding that he should not be informed of the object until his arrival. Finding him at home, the messenger returned, in haste, with his charge. As soon as Mr. Rankin reached the spot, he was informed that the crowd wished to hear him preach; and that, without any delay. The friends of the preacher had not mistaken his powers. Mounting a stump, or some other convenient elevation, he, at once, opened his Bible, and announced his text,—Acts x, 29,—"Therefore came I unto you without gainsaying, as soon as I was sent for: I ask therefore, for what intent ye have sent for me?" With so appropriate a text, caught up in a moment, it can easily be imagined that the sermon was correspondingly interesting and impressive.

Mr. Rankin is said to have been a man of fine musical taste. The flute and the violin were his favourite instruments; and with all the existing prejudice against "fiddling," he habitually performed on the condemned instrument, without bringing reproach upon either the church or the ministry.

He was also an ardent lover of nature; and his mind delighted in poetry. It was his habit to rise with the lark; and in the bright early morning to prepare his sermons,—oft-times, indeed, whilst walking in the fields or woods. There are several beautiful hymns extant which were composed by him; and these hymns are still sung to tunes which were also his own composition. One of his hymns, called "The Rising Sun," was composed—both words and music—during a walk in the morning at sunrise.

In 1780, Mr. Rankin married Mary Atkinson of Worcester County, Md., by whom he had several children,—two only of whom now survive,—namely, Mr. James Rankin, of Ohio, and Mrs. Sally Franklin,—widow of the late Major Henry Franklin of Berlin, Md. The Hon. John Rankin Franklin, of Snow Hill, Md., and George Franklin, M. D., of Donaldsonville, La. are grandsons of this worthy minister.

The remains of Mr. Rankin lie interred in the grave-yard of the church, which, for so many years, had been the scene of his labours. Over his grave is a marble slab, with the following inscription:—

"In memory of
THE REV. JOHN RANKIN,
Who departed this life, March 2d, 1798,
Aged 48 years;
A burning and shining light in this part of Christ's
Vineyard, 20 years.
In mental improvement, excelled by few;
As a divine, well instructed
In the mysteries of Christ's Kingdom;
Taught by his Master to give each their meat
In due season;
In private and public life beloved by all
Who knew him;
A faithful, diligent pastor;
A tender husband; an indulgent parent;
Lovely and pleasant in his life.
Servant of Jesus, here repose in peace;
Thy course is finished; won the heavenly prize;
Henceforth, a glorious crown of righteousness
And endless bliss await thee in the skies."

I am, with much respect,
Your friend and brother,
ISAAC W. K. HANDY.

WILLIAM GRAHAM.

1775—1799.

FROM THE REV. ARCHIBALD ALEXANDER, D. D.

PRINCETON, November 23, 1849.

Rev. and dear Sir: In complying with your request for some notices of the life and character of my former instructer and friend the Rev. William Graham, I shall avail myself chiefly of an Address which I delivered, some years ago, before the Alumni of Washington College, and which, upon examination, I find to be entirely in accordance with my present impressions.

WILLIAM GRAHAM was born on the 19th of December, 1745, in the township of Paxton, near Harrisburg, in Lancaster County, (now Dauphine,) in Pennsylvania. His father was a plain farmer, in moderate circumstances, and emigrated from the North of Ireland, as did also his mother, whose name before marriage was Susannah Miller. Mr. Roan was the Pastor of the Presbyterian Church in Paxton, which was much larger a hundred years ago than at present, owing to the fact that the Germans have bought out most of the original settlers, who were Scotch and Irish. Until the age of manhood, Mr. Graham was brought up in the business of agriculture, which he understood well, and of which he was always fond. But, at this period of his life, having undergone a great change in his religious views and feelings, he resolved to prepare for the work of the holy ministry. The obstacles in his way were indeed great: but being encouraged by the counsels, and aided by the efforts and prayers, of a most excellent mother, to whom he attributed, in a great measure, his success in this important enterprise, he ventured, under all discouragements, to go forward in endeavouring to obtain a liberal education, depending on the guidance and aid of Divine Providence. Having prepared himself for admission to the College of New Jersey, he entered that institution, in company with a number of young men, who became eminent in the Church or State. Among whom, as a scholar, he stood pre-eminent; for, during the college course, he gained a whole year; that is, he anticipated the studies of the Senior year before the class entered on them, and was permitted to retire from College till the time of the examination of his class, when he attended with them, and was graduated in the year 1773. As his father was unable conveniently to bear the expenses of his son, while at College, he contributed to his own support, by teaching in the grammar school, then under the special direction of Dr. Witherspoon, the President of the College. Having completed his college course, he pursued his theological studies under the tuition of the Rev. Mr. Roan, a divine of considerable distinction. But, during the whole period of his education, he was constantly engaged in the study of Theology. Among all his teachers, however, he gave the preference to his excellent mother; and has been heard to say that he learned more of practical religion from her, than from all persons and books beside. He was licensed to preach by the Presbytery of Hanover, on the 26th of October, 1775.

When the Hanover Presbytery determined to establish a school for the rearing of young men for the ministry, they applied to the Rev. Samuel Stanhope Smith, then itinerating in the State of Virginia, to recommend a suitable person to take charge of their school,—upon which, he at once recommended Mr. Graham, and at their request wrote to him to come on to the Valley of Virginia. Before this time, a classical school had been taught at a place called Mount Pleasant, near to the little town of Fairfield. Here Mr. Graham commenced his labours as a teacher; and here we find the germ whence sprung Washington College.

It was not long, however, before it was judged expedient to remove the infant school to Timber Ridge Meeting-House, where a convenient house for the Rector was built, and also an Academy, and other small buildings for the accommodation of the students. A considerable sum was now raised by subscription for the purchase of books and a philosophical apparatus, and Mr. Graham was entrusted with the business of selecting and purchasing such articles as he should judge most useful and necessary; and, accordingly, he took a journey to Philadelphia, and executed judiciously the trust reposed in him. He also travelled into New England, to solicit benefactions for the rising Academy, and not without some success, though not very considerable. At this time, the prospects of the infant institution were very encouraging, and if no untoward events had occurred, there is reason to believe that it would speedily have risen to great eminence and usefulness. But the Revolutionary war having burst on the country, threatening ruin and desolation, the attention of all *true* men was turned to the defence of the country; and from no part of the United States, it is believed, did more young men enter the public service, than from the region to which I am now referring. And it may truly be said that the patriotic fire burned in no bosom with a warmer flame, than in that of Mr. Graham himself. On a certain occasion, when, by invitation of the Executive authority of the State, it was resolved to raise a volunteer company of riflemen, to go into active service, there appeared much backwardness in the men to come forward,—he stepped out, and had his own name enrolled, which produced such an effect that the company was immediately filled, of which he was unanimously chosen Captain; and all necessary preparations were made for marching to the seat of war,. when General Washington signified to the Governors of the States, that he did not wish any more volunteer companies to join the army.

The abandonment of the houses erected at Timber Ridge, appears to have taken place,—though without authority,—as a matter of necessity. The income from the Academy was small, and his salary for preaching to the two Congregations of Timber Ridge and Hall's Meeting-House, (now Monmouth,) being paid in depreciated currency, it was impossible for him to support his family. He, therefore, resolved to return to farming, and, accordingly, he purchased a small farm on the North River, within a mile or two of the present site of Washington College.

The school at Timber Ridge was, however, continued for some time after Mr. Graham retired to his farm, and he endeavoured to perform the duties of a Rector, by visiting it, and giving instruction, several times in each week. But this being found very inconvenient to himself, and disadvantageous to the school, after due deliberation, he resolved to relinquish the establishment at Timber Ridge, and to open a school in his own house. It was here that, at an early age, I commenced my course of classical learning. Even at this time, there was a respectable number of students in the school, most of them having reached the age and stature of men. After some time, a frame edifice was erected on ground given for the purpose, and the school was continued until, in the year 1782, application was made to the Legislature for an Act of Incorporation, and, accordingly, a number of Trustees were formed into a body corporate, to have full charge of the Academy, which received the name of LIBERTY HALL,—which name it retained until it was endowed by General Washington, when his name was substituted for that which it had before borne. Before this donation was received, Mr. Graham had resigned his office as Rector or President, though it is understood that he used all his influence to secure this important endowment; and that he was the author of the letter addressed to General Washington, by the Trustees, in favour of this institution.

Though Mr. Graham had some formidable opposers, who had taken up strong prejudices against him, and although, after the close of the war, the character of the students who attended at the Academy was greatly deteriorated, and the difficulties which environed him were many and perplexing; yet it must be conceded that, in resigning his important post at this time, he was not guided by his usual wisdom. It is not expedient, perhaps, to bring distinctly into view, in this connection, the disappointment which attended his favourite scheme of planting in the West a little colony of select families of like mind, who might live in peace, far from the contentions, bustle, and turmoil of the world. All such schemes must fail in the present state of human nature.

Mr. Graham possessed a mind formed for accurate and profound investigation. He had studied the Latin and Greek classics with great care, and relished the beauties of these exquisite compositions. With those authors taught in the schools, he was familiar by a long practice in teaching, and always insisted on the importance of classical literature, as the proper foundation of a liberal education.

He had a strong inclination to the study of Natural Philosophy, and took pleasure in making experiments, with such apparatus as he possessed; and he had procured for his Academy as good a one as was then possessed by most of the Colleges. In these experiments much time was employed, on which inquisitive persons, not connected with the Academy, were freely permitted to attend.

As he was an ardent patriot and a thorough republican, the times in which he lived led him to bestow much attention on the science of government; and one of the few pieces which he wrote for the press was on this subject. By some he was censured for meddling with politics; but it should be remembered that, at that time, this country, having cast off its allegiance to Great Britain, and declared itself independent, had to lay the foundation of governments both for the States and for the Nation; and that the welfare of posterity, as well as of the existing inhabitants of the country, was involved in the wisdom with which this work was done. The talents of every man, capable of thinking and judging on such subjects, seemed to be fairly put into requisition. It is a sound maxim that men living at one time must not be judged by the maxims of an age in which all circumstances are greatly changed. At the adoption of the Federal Constitution, which, according to its original draft, he did not approve, he relinquished all attention to politics during the remainder of his life.

The science, however, which engaged his attention more than all others, except Theology, was the Philosophy of the Mind. In this he took great delight, and to it he devoted much time and attention. Though acquainted with the best treatises which had then been published, his investigations were not carried on so much by books, as by a patient and repeated analysis of the various processes of thought, as they arose in his own mind, and by reducing the phenomena thus observed to a regular system. I am of opinion that the system of mental philosophy which he thus formed, was, in clearness and fulness, superior to any thing which has been given to the public, in the numerous works which have recently been published on this subject. And it is greatly to be regretted that his Lectures were never fully committed to writing, and published for the benefit of the world. It was, however, a fault in this man of profound thought, that he made little use of his pen. And it was also a defect that, in the latter years of his life, he addicted himself little to reading the productions of other men, and perhaps entertained too low an opinion of the value of books.

But you will wish to know something more particularly of Mr. Graham as a theologian and a preacher. From the time of his ordination by the Presbytery of Hanover in 1775, he became a teacher of Theology. Most of those who entered the holy ministry in the Valley of Virginia, pursued their preparatory studies under his direction. And, after the great revival which commenced in the year 1789, he had a theological class of seven or eight members, under his tuition, which was kept up for several years. It was his custom to devote one day in the week to hearing the written discourses of these candidates, and to a free discussion of theological points. In these exercises he appeared to take great delight; and the students were always gratified, and commonly convinced, by his lucid statements and cogent reasonings. As most of those who enjoyed the benefit of his instructions in this incipient Theological Seminary are not now in the world, it may not be improper to say that some of them rose to eminence in the Church, and as Professors or Presidents of literary institutions. The influence which he gained over the minds of his pupils, while under his care, was unbounded. Yet he encouraged the utmost freedom of discussion, and seemed to aim, not so much to bring his pupils to think as he did, as to teach them to think on all subjects for themselves. A slavish subjection to any human authority he repudiated; and, therefore, never attempted to add weight to his opinions, by referring to a long list of authors, of great name; but uniformly insisted that all opinions should be subjected to the test of Scripture and reason. Some of his students have been heard to say that the chief benefit which they derived from his instructions, was that, by this means, they were led to the free and independent exercise of their own faculties in the investigation of truth.

Mr. Graham, in his theological creed, was strictly orthodox, according to the standards of his own Church, which he greatly venerated; but, in his method of explaining some of the knotty points in Theology, he departed considerably from the common track; and was of opinion that many things which have been involved in perplexity and obscurity, by the manner in which they have been treated, are capable of being easily and satisfactorily explained by the application of sound principles of philosophy. As a preacher, he was always instructive and evangelical; though in common his delivery was rather feeble and embarrassed than forcible; but when his feelings were excited, his voice became penetrating, and his whole manner awakening and impressive. And his profound study of the human heart enabled him to describe the various exercises of the Christian with a clearness and truth which often greatly surprised his pious hearers; for it seemed to them as if he could read the very inmost sentiments of their minds; which he described more perfectly than they could do themselves. When it was his object to elucidate some more difficult point, it was his custom to open his trenches, so to speak, at a great distance; removing out of the way every obstacle, until he was prepared to make his assault on the main fortress: thus, insensibly, he led his hearers along, step by step, gaining their assent, first to one proposition, and then to another, until, at last, they could not easily avoid acquiescence in the conclusion to which he wished to bring them. As a clear and cogent reasoner, he had no superior among his contemporaries; and his pre-eminence in the exercise of this faculty was acknowledged by all unprejudiced persons.

It has been hinted that Mr. Graham had enemies, who often had influence to impede or thwart his favourite schemes; and candour requires that it should be acknowledged that he sometimes imprudently made enemies of those who might have been efficient friends, by too free an indulgence of satirical and sarcastical remarks; which weapon he could wield with great power. And it must also be conceded that towards his opponents he never manifested much of a conciliatory temper, but seemed rather disposed to stand aloof from them, and to set them at defiance.

In the government of youth, Mr. Graham was, from the first, a rigid and unyielding disciplinarian. He laid it down as a principle that, at every risk, authority must be maintained; and when this was by any one resisted, however formidable the student might be in physical strength, or however many might combine to frustrate the regular exercise of discipline, he fearlessly went forward in the discharge of his duty, and generally triumphed over all opposition; and often inflicted severe castigation on the thoughtless persons, who dared to rebel against lawful authority. Whether his rigour might not, in some instances, have been extreme, is a question on which judicious men would differ in opinion.

As has been already hinted, the great error of his life was the relinquishment of the important station in which Providence had placed him, and for which he was so eminently qualified; and *that* at a time of life when he possessed the ability of being more useful than at any former period. Having removed to the banks of Ohio River, he fell into great embarrassments, in the midst of which he died, in consequence of a violent fever contracted by exposure to frequent drenching rains, while on a journey to Richmond. In that city he breathed his last, on the 8th of June, 1799, in the house of his friend, the late Colonel Robert Gamble; and his remains were deposited near the Episcopal Church on the hill, over which a plain marble slab, with a short inscription, is placed.

Mr. Graham was married to a young woman in Carlisle, by the name of Mary Kerr. They had two sons and three daughters who lived to mature age. His eldest son entered the ministry, and, after licensure, was stationed in Prince George County, below Petersburg, where he contracted a bilious fever that proved fatal. His only other son who grew to manhood, was his youngest child, and was taken by James Priestley, LL. D., and educated out of gratitude for Mr. Graham's kindness in giving him a liberal education. He studied medicine, lived in Georgia, and was hopefully converted among the Methodists, of which society he became a member, and died a few years since.

The extent of the influence exerted by this one man over the literature and religion of Virginia, cannot be calculated. As the stream which fertilizes a large district is small in its origin, but goes on continually increasing until it becomes a mighty river, so the influence of the Rev. William Graham did not cease when he died, but has gone on increasing by means of his disciples, who have been scattered far and wide over the West and South.

Yours truly,

A. ALEXANDER.

JOHN McKNIGHT, D. D.*

1775—1823.

JOHN McKNIGHT was born near Carlisle, Pa., October 1, 1754. His father, who served as Major in the French and Indian wars of that period, died during the early childhood of this son, and his mother subsequently contracted a second marriage. Little is known of his early life, except that he exhibited great loveliness and buoyancy of temper, which made him a general favourite with his associates. In due time he became a member of the College of New Jersey, where he graduated under the Presidency of Dr. Witherspoon, in 1773.

Shortly after leaving College, he went to Shippensburg, Pa., where he prosecuted his theological studies, under the direction of the Rev. Dr. Robert Cooper. He was licensed to preach by the Presbytery of Donegal between the meetings of Synod in 1774 and 1775, and was ordained by the same Presbytery in the latter part of 1776, or early in 1777.

In 1775, shortly after his licensure, he went to Virginia, and organized a Congregation on Elk Branch, embracing the country between Shepherdstown and Charlestown. Here he remained till 1783, when he resigned his charge, and accepted a call to the Lower Marsh Creek Presbyterian Church, in Adams County, Pa. This connection was eminently favourable to both his comfort and usefulness, and the years which he spent here he ever afterwards regarded as among the happiest of his life. He owned a farm of about one hundred and fifty acres; and such was the generous consideration of his large and respectable congregation towards him, that they actually left him little to do in cultivating it, while the voluntary offerings which they otherwise made him were more than double his stipulated salary.

A somewhat amusing incident occurred during his connection with this church, that was strikingly illustrative of one feature of his character. He had just ordained three ruling elders; and one of them was appointed to attend the meeting of Presbytery to be held the next week. He came to the Pastor on the evening of the day of his ordination, under a good deal of agitation, to inquire what were the duties that would be expected of him. Perceiving the state of his mind, Mr. McKnight assumed a serious air, and replied,—"You are to see that my horse is fed and saddled in time to start; to go before and have breakfast or dinner prepared for us; to pay the bills, and in Presbytery to vote as I do." This playfulness relieved the anxious elder, whose countenance changed from its solemn gravity to a smile,—when opportunity was given to inform him what his real duties would be as a member of the Body.

After labouring with the Marsh Creek Church for about three years, he was called in July, 1789, to be a colleague Pastor with the Rev. Dr. Rodgers of the united Presbyterian Congregation of the city of New York; and after mature deliberation, and by the advice of the Presbytery of which he was a member, he accepted the call, and was installed on the 2d of December of that year. The church, which had previously been in a somewhat divided state, in consequence of having had several candidates among them, now became harmonious, and Mr. McKnight entered upon his

* MS. from his son.—Miller's Life of Rodgers.

labours with great zeal and alacrity. He was accustomed to preach regularly three times on the Sabbath, and to lecture on the Shorter Catechism on a week-day evening, besides performing a large amount of more private pastoral labour.

In 1791, he was honoured with the degree of Doctor of Divinity from Yale College; and in 1795, was Moderator of the General Assembly of the Presbyterian Church.

Early in 1792, Dr. McKnight's health had become so much impaired by his arduous and incessant labours, that it became evident that he could no longer preach three times on the Sabbath; and, as the congregation were very desirous of keeping up the third service, they resolved on calling a third minister. They accordingly gave a call to Mr. (afterwards the Rev. Dr.) Samuel Miller, which he accepted; and his ordination and installation took place in June of the next year. In 1797 and 1798, a new Presbyterian Church was built in Rutgers street, in connection with the collegiate charge; and a large debt, contracted by the enterprise, was, to a great extent, discharged by the personal efforts of Dr. McKnight, in collecting funds for the purpose.

In 1806, Dr. McKnight was commissioned by the New York Missionary Society to visit the Tuscarora Indians, among whom that Society had previously had a missionary,—to decide upon the expediency of organizing a Christian church among them. He executed the commission, much to the satisfaction of the Society, as appears from their next annual Report. He found some serious difficulties in the way of the organization, partly growing out of the ignorance and dubious Christian character of some at least, who offered themselves as candidates for church membership, and partly from a difference of opinion, on some points, with the missionary who was on the ground; but, notwithstanding these embarrassments, he proceeded to organize the congregation, and the whole was performed in an orderly, peaceable and solemn manner.

Dr. McKnight remained in New York, in the earnest and faithful discharge of his ministerial duties, twenty years. In April, 1809, the collegiate connection was dissolved. Though Dr. McKnight had always been opposed to collegiate charges, from principle, yet he deemed the dissolution of that existing relationship, at that time, inexpedient, as he considered some of the measures employed to effect it, unjustifiable. Anticipating protracted collisions and jealousies as the result, and being considerably advanced in life, as well as reduced in health, he determined to resign, and, with the consent of the Presbytery, did resign, his pastoral charge.

On leaving New York, he removed to a small but beautiful farm, with modern improvements, in the neighbourhood of Chambersburg, Pa., which he had purchased for a residence. Shortly after this, the Presbyterian Church of Rocky Spring, one of the oldest congregations in that region,—then recently rendered vacant, and whose house of worship was about three miles from his dwelling, unanimously invited him to become their pastor. He dissuaded them from presenting him a regular call; but consented to serve them as a stated supply, as his health would permit; and as such he performed towards them all the duties of a pastor, with as much fidelity and punctuality as if the pastoral relation had actually been constituted. About this time, he received several pressing invitations from different churches in the State of New York, to take the pastoral charge of them;

but in each case he returned a negative answer. His removal from New York he always regarded as a happy event in his life. It not only loosened him from the cares and responsibilities of a heavy city charge, which had become exhausting by reason of advancing age, but brought him into a peaceful retirement, among a large circle of relatives and friends, and gave him leisure for those special devotional exercises so congenial with his feelings, and so fitting to his circumstances and prospects.

In 1815, he was invited to the Presidency of Dickinson College. Contrary to his own inclination, he yielded to the importunities of his friends, and accepted the invitation. But he soon found that the fiscal concerns of the institution were so much embarrassed, as to render the hope of its success, and even permanency, in his estimation, at best doubtful; and he accordingly resigned the office, after having held it for little more than a year. He now returned to his farm, and resumed his ministerial labours, and continued in the discharge of them, as opportunity offered or occasion required, until the commencement of the year 1822, when he had an attack of a bilious epidemic disease, which entirely prostrated his physical energies, already greatly reduced by age, and a long course of active ministerial labour. From the effects of this attack he never recovered; and on the 21st of October, 1823, in the seventieth year of his age, in the full exercise of his mental powers, and in the lively assurance of a future glorious life, he departed calmly and triumphantly to mingle in other scenes.

Dr. McKnight published six Sermons on Faith,* [recommended by Doctors Rodgers and Witherspoon,] 1790; a Thanksgiving Sermon, 1795; a Sermon before the New York Missionary Society, 1799; a Sermon on the present state of the political and religious world, 1802; a Sermon on the death of the Rev. Dr. John King, 1811.

On the 17th of October, 1776, he was married to Susan, daughter of George Brown, of Franklin County, Pa., who survived her husband about nine years. They had ten children. Two of them entered the ministry, one of whom is deceased, the other is still (1857) living. Another entered the medical profession, became a Surgeon in the navy of the United States, and died on the 14th of May, 1857, in the sixty-fifth year of his age.

Washington McKnight, the eldest son of the Rev. Dr. McKnight, was born near Millerstown, Adams County, Pa., January 29, 1779. He was graduated at Columbia College, New York, in 1798. Having prosecuted his theological studies under the direction of his father, he was licensed to preach by the Presbytery of New York, October 3, 1800. After his licensure, he spent considerable time in travelling through the State of New York, and some of the adjacent States, visiting vacant churches, forming an acquaintance with many Presbyterian ministers, and exercising his talents in preaching. Having declined invitations to settle in several places, he was at length invited to become the Pastor of the Presbyterian Church in Augusta, Ga., and President of the Academy in that place. This invitation he thought it his duty to accept; and, accordingly, he was ordained

* Dr. Archibald Alexander states that, in one of his preaching excursions in the early part of his ministry, he met with a Mr. Robert Campbell, who had formerly been a member of Dr. McKnight's congregation in Virginia, and whose memory was so prodigious that he could repeat many of his Sermons verbatim; that after the Doctor's removal to New York, when he resolved to publish his Sermons on Faith, he found the manuscript of one of them was missing, and on applying to Mr. Campbell, recovered the discourse, not only in substance, but nearly or quite to the very letter.

by the Presbytery of New York, April 26, 1804, and proceeded immediately to undertake the duties of the double charge devolved upon him. These duties he discharged in a manner that gave promise of extensive usefulness. But his career of activity was destined to be short. Within less than a year after his arrival at Augusta, he was attacked with a disease, known as "the strangers' fever," which, after a few days, terminated fatally. He died on the 5th of September, 1808, in the twenty-ninth year of his age. He retained the full use of his intellectual faculties to the last, and passed away under the sustaining influence of a hope full of immortality. He was uncommonly amiable in his dispositions, and bland in his manners; was a fine classical scholar, and an animated, earnest and popular preacher.

FROM THE REV. GEORGE DUFFIELD, D. D.

DETROIT, March 11, 1850.

Rev. and dear Sir: You ask me to communicate to you whatever recollections I may have of the Rev. Dr. John McKnight, which may serve to illustrate his character. It is but little that I knew personally in relation to him. He was far my superior in years and attainments. Although a resident of the same place with him for the greater part of a year, and associated in the same Presbytery for several years, in the latter period of his life, my opportunities for intercourse with him were perhaps scarcely sufficient to justify me in undertaking what you request. I will, however, do the best to meet your wishes that I can.

Dr. McKnight was a man of slender person, and rather above the medium height. His countenance indicated a considerate turn of mind, and at least a capacity for deep thought. His manners were graceful and dignified, without any attempt at the polish and courtier-like demeanor, sometimes assumed by popular and fashionable clergymen. He was at home in all society, and could adapt himself, in his native simplicity of character, to every variety of age, temper, and education. A shade had been cast upon his natural naivete and cheerfulness by advancing years, and possibly deepened somewhat by unexpected changes in his ministerial relations. In the circle of his friends and acquaintances, and among the people to whom he ministered, his manner was free and affable, and his conversation pleasant and instructive. As a preacher, he was calm and dispassionate. Although there was little variety in either his tones or gesture, yet his delivery was far from being dull or monotonous: it was well adapted to his matter, which was generally a lucid, logical exhibition of some important scriptural truth. He was a zealous assertor and advocate of the Calvinistic faith, which, however, he chose to present in connection with a "thus saith the Lord," rather than the subtleties of metaphysics. The bearing of Christian doctrine on Christian experience and practice, he carefully set forth; and a small volume which he published, on the subject of "saving faith," unfolds both his own influential belief, and his opposition to Antinomian peculiarities. He maintained the views which had been held and defended by Dr. Robert Smith of Pequea, Pa., in his controversy with Dr. Annan. This work was well received and extensively circulated, and was acknowledged, even by those who dissented from the views which it maintains, to evince a very thorough acquaintance with didactic theology, and no inconsiderable skill in conducting an argument.

The first time I recollect to have seen Dr. McKnight, was during the sessions of the General Assembly in Philadelphia, in May, 1812, if I mistake not, when the subject of the location of the Theological Seminary was under consideration. Princeton and Chambersburg were the places between which the competition was greatest. Dr. McKnight earnestly advocated the latter, deprecating various influences which he stated, and predicting (for he spoke thus confidently) that, in process of time, should it be placed in Princeton, it would become the great ruling head and motive power in the General Assembly. On this subject he displayed great zeal; but he was overruled by the judgment of his brethren. I think he seldom appeared afterwards in the General Assembly, but diligently confined his attentions and labours within the immediate region in which he lived.

Dr. McKnight finished his earthly career, surrounded by his family and friends, and among a people who still greatly reverence his memory. Having commenced his ministerial labours in the region where he died, at a very early period after its first settlement, his name was associated with the earliest and most important events connected with the Church and cause of Christ, within the bounds of the Presbytery of Carlisle. There are still living a considerable number, who cherish a grateful appreciation of his services, as an able and faithful minister of Christ.

Very respectfully yours,

GEORGE DUFFIELD.

JOHN LINN.

1776—1820.

FROM THE REV. ROBERT BAIRD, D. D.

New York, January 15, 1850.

My dear Sir: My personal recollections of the Rev. John Linn are not very extensive or minute; and yet, in my earlier days, I had some opportunities of knowing him, and I can truly say that he left an impression upon my mind which time has done little to impair. I regarded him as an uncommonly fine specimen of a man; and so, I am confident, he was generally regarded by those who were privileged to know him. The materials for the following brief notice of him, are derived from the most authentic source; though his life was of so even a tenor, that it could hardly form the subject of a protracted narrative.

John Linn was born in Adams County, Pa., in the year 1749. His parents were Presbyterians, and were connected with the Congregation of Lower Marsh Creek, in the Presbytery of Carlisle. He made a profession of religion while he was yet quite a youth. He was fitted for College by the Rev. Dr. Robert Smith of Pequea, Lancaster County, Pa., and was graduated at Nassau Hall, during the Presidency of Dr. Witherspoon, in the year 1773. He was a classmate of Henry Lee, Morgan Lewis, Aaron Ogden, John Blair Smith, William Graham, John McKnight, and several others, distinguished in their respective professions. After leaving College, he returned to Pennsylvania, and studied Theology under the direction of the Rev. Dr. Robert Cooper, minister of the Congregation of Middle Spring, within the limits of what was then Donegal (now Carlisle) Presbytery. He was licensed to preach by the Presbytery of Donegal in December, 1776. Not far from a year after his licensure, the Congregations of Sherman's Valley, in Cumberland (now Perry) County, invited him to become their pastor. He accepted the invitation, and was accordingly ordained and installed shortly after. Here he remained labouring faithfully and efficiently to the close of his ministry, and his life. He died in the year 1820, in the seventy-first year of his age. His death occurred in consequence of his being overtaken by a severe shower, on his way home from church. Being warm, from the exercise of preaching, he took a violent cold, which run into a typhus fever, and terminated in death, within a few days. His son, the Rev. James Linn, who resided at a distance, arrived at the paternal residence in time to attend his father's funeral; and, on the Sabbath succeeding, occupied the vacant pulpit.

Soon after his settlement in the ministry, he was married to Mary Gettys, a native of the neighbourhood in which he resided. She survived him a few years. They had seven children,—five sons and two daughters. One of them, the Rev. James Linn, D. D., born in 1783, is the Pastor of a Presbyterian Church in Bellefont, Pa.

Mr. Linn was about five feet ten inches in height, portly and symmetrical in his form, and muscular and active in his bodily movements. He had great strength of constitution, and uncommon powers of endurance. His disposition was social and cheerful; he could easily accommodate himself to persons of different characters and conditions in life, and was cordially welcomed by every circle into which he was thrown. He was distinguished for sobriety of mind rather than versatility; was reflective rather than imaginative. As his salary was inadequate to the support of his family, he was under the necessity of conducting a farm, and, at certain seasons of the year, of labouring upon it himself: this rendered him a less vigorous and diligent student than he would otherwise have been, particularly in the latter part of his life; but his mind was so trained to reflection, that his studies could hardly be said to be intermitted, even while he was engaged in manual labour. He was accustomed to write his sermons out at full length, and deliver them from memory; except that, in the summer, his morning discourse, which was a lecture on some portion of the New Testament, was usually delivered without written preparation. He had a remarkably clear voice, and uttered himself with great solemnity and impressiveness. One of his manuscript sermons,—a sermon occasioned by the death of the Rev. Samuel Waugh*—I have had the opportunity of perusing; and it shows that he was a correct writer, and an instructive, methodical and earnest preacher. He was uncommonly devoted to the interests of his flock, giving no inconsiderable portion of his time to pastoral visitation. In his family, and indeed in all his relations, he was a fine example of Christian dignity, tenderness, and fidelity.

Accept the assurance of my kind regard.

R. BAIRD.

* Samuel Waugh was a native of Carroll's Tract in Adams County, Pa.; was graduated at the College of New Jersey in 1773; was settled as pastor of the united Congregations of East Pennsborough and Monaghan, in 1782; and continued in this relation until his death, which took place in January, 1807. One of his parishioners (Judge Clendenin) says of him—"He was a sound divine, a very acceptable preacher, and highly esteemed by his people."

SAMUEL TAGGART.*

1776—1825.

SAMUEL TAGGART was born at Londonderry, N. H., March 24, 1754. His father was James Taggart, and his mother was a daughter of James Anderson, both of whom were born in Ireland, but migrated with their parents to this country,—the former, when he was eleven years old, the latter, when she was about eight. His father was for many years a ruling elder in the Second Presbyterian Church in Londonderry, but afterwards removed to Halifax, Vt., where he died at a very advanced age.

Samuel was the youngest of eleven children, the principal part of whom died in infancy. He had the advantage of a religious education, and at an early period became a vigorous defender of the doctrines of Calvinism, while yet religious truth had gained no permanent lodgement in his heart. Indeed, notwithstanding he had intervals of thoughtfulness in regard to his higher interests, he was in the main regardless of religion as a practical concern, and even yielded to some of the forms of open vice.

He commenced a course of study preparatory to College, a little before he had completed his fourteenth year, under the direction of a clergyman, supposed to be the Rev. Mr. McGregore, in his native place. In October, 1772, when he was in his nineteenth year, he became a member of the Junior class in Dartmouth College. His mind, at this period, seems to have acquired something like a settled aversion even to religious contemplation. But almost immediately after he entered College, through the earnest and faithful ministrations of the first President Wheelock, he was brought into a state of great anxiety in respect to his immortal interests. After this, however, there were, for several months, alternations of comparative indifference and deep concern, until, in April, 1773, he experienced a great change in his feelings, which he believed marked the period of his conversion. His health was not vigorous when he joined College; but so overpowering had been his religious feelings, and so much had he neglected bodily exercise, that his physical system became so reduced as to render it necessary for him, for a time at least, to give up his studies. This he did in June, 1773, with little prospect of ever resuming them. He availed himself of the first opportunity, after his return home, to connect himself with the church in his native place. As his health began gradually to mend, he determined to return to College, and to prosecute his studies with ultimate reference to the ministry. Accordingly, he did return in December following, and resumed his place in his class; but his health was still far from being perfect, and in the succeeding April, (1774,) it had declined so far as to render it necessary that he should again suspend his studies and return home. After this, his constitution seemed to recover its former vigour; and in July he again went back to College, and remained until his class graduated, which was but a little more than a month. Thus it appears that his college course was not only brief, but repeatedly interrupted.

* MS. Autobiography.—MS. from his son.—Packard's History of the Churches and Ministers in Franklin County.

Immediately after taking his Bachelor's degree, he returned to Londonderry, and commenced the study of Theology under the minister of the parish, the Rev. David McGregore. He was licensed to preach by the Presbytery of Boston, June 1, 1776. Not long after his licensure, he received a call to settle at Coleraine, Hampshire County, Mass., the population of which was made up, in a great measure, of emigrants from Ireland. On the 5th of September, 1776, the Presbytery advised him to accept the call from Coleraine; and he accordingly did accept it, and was ordained and installed Pastor of that Church, February 19, 1777.

Mr. Taggart, it would seem, was, in the early part of his ministry, brought into a somewhat serious difficulty with his Presbytery. It was his wish, at one time, to unite with the Associate Reformed Presbytery of New York; and he was actually holding some informal negotiations with them on the subject, without consulting the Boston Presbytery, of which he was a member; whereupon, the latter body, regarding his conduct as irregular, summoned him before them as an offender. A protracted discussion and correspondence ensued, which resulted in his being dismissed on the 2d of June, 1785, with a general recommendation. He afterwards joined the Presbytery of Londonderry.

In the summer and autumn of 1802, he performed a missionary tour of about three months and a half, under the Hampshire Missionary Society, in the Western Counties of the State of New York. His manuscript journal, which is still preserved, shows that he was not only attentive to his appropriate duties as a missionary, but was observant of every thing in respect to the general state of the country, that fell under his eye.

In the year 1803, Mr. Taggart was chosen to represent in Congress the district in which he lived; and he continued, by repeated re-elections, to represent it, till the year 1817—a period of fourteen years.

Mr. Taggart's frequent and protracted absences from his people, in the discharge of his duties as member of Congress, served to loosen, in some degree, the cord by which he was bound to them, and in October, 1818, he asked leave of the Presbytery to resign his pastoral charge. The result of the application is indicated by the following record of the Presbytery:—"The prospect of the Rev. Mr. Taggart's support and usefulness among the Church and people of Coleraine being, in our opinion, terminated, it is expedient that his pastoral relation to them be dissolved, and it is dissolved accordingly. We rejoice to find that, amid all the unhappy debates among the people of Coleraine, they have still been united in maintaining their esteem and respect for their pastor, against whose private and ministerial deportment no complaint has arisen from any quarter. * * * * We most cordially recommend him to the Christian public, as an eminently able and faithful minister of the Gospel of Christ."

After his dismission, he preached occasionally for the neighbouring ministers, and sometimes in the parish where he had resigned his charge. He preached and administered the Lord's Supper there, but a few weeks previous to his death.

He died after an illness of a few days, April 25, 1825, in the seventy-second year of his age. His Funeral Sermon was preached by the Rev. Dr. Packard of Shelburne.

On the 5th of October, 1778, he was married to Elizabeth, daughter of George Duncan, of Peterborough, N. H. She died March 14, 1815. He was married to Mary Ayers, at Washington City, March 25, 1816. By the former marriage he had fourteen children, eleven of whom lived to maturity. By the second marriage he had three children.

The following is a list of Mr. Taggart's publications:—A Treatise on the Evidences of Christianity. An Oration on the death of Washington, 1800. Scriptural Vindication of the doctrine of the Final Perseverance of all true believers, 1801. An Oration delivered at Conway on the anniversary of American Independence, 1804. A Sermon before the Hampshire Missionary Society, 1807. An Address to the independent electors of the Hampshire North District, 1811. Two Sermons delivered on the Public Fast, 1812. An Address to the author's Constituents on the subject of Impressments, 1813. A Sermon delivered at Brattleborough at the ordination of the Rev. Jonathan M'Gee, 1819. A Farewell Sermon at Coleraine, 1819.

FROM THE REV. THEOPHILUS PACKARD, Jr.

Shelburne, Mass., June 1, 1852.

Dear Sir: Though I was accustomed often to see and hear Mr. Taggart in my early years, yet, in complying with your request, I shall depend less upon my own recollections than upon the testimony of my father, who was his near neighbour, and intimately associated with him during a large part of his ministry. My father is now far advanced in life, but his recollections of his former friend are perfectly distinct and intelligent.

There is no doubt that Mr. Taggart possessed a mind of great strength and vigour. The few productions of his pen that remain, show that he was a bold, earnest thinker, and that he possessed the reasoning faculty in an uncommon degree. But I am inclined to think that the faculty for which he was most remarkable was memory. In relation to names, dates, the ages of people, and other things of that class, his memory was truly wonderful. Though he visited his people but little, and was not very familiar with them, yet he could tell their names and ages with surprising facility and accuracy. In large families, he would sometimes tell the exact dates of the births of the children, better than the parents themselves. He told my father that, during one winter, while he was in Congress, he wrote a series of Lectures on Sacred History, and that the first two might be thought to be copies of Jamieson's on the same subject; but that he had not read Jamieson for many years. He once said that he could not only remember the names of all who were members of Congress, during his own membership of fourteen years, but could give a description of every one of them.

He was a singularly absent minded man. He once rode on horseback from Coleraine to Shelburne, and dismounted at the house of the minister, Rev. Robert Hubbard, who met him, and seeing a large open pocket knife in his hand, said,—"Mr. Taggart, do you come armed for war?" Mr. Taggart was himself surprised at the presence of the knife, and explained by saying that, when he started from Coleraine, he cut a riding stick on the road, and was not aware that he had not returned the knife to his pocket, till reminded of it by Mr. Hubbard. The distance that he had travelled was six miles.

The quality to which I have now referred made him remarkably inattentive to little things, and sometimes also to matters of some importance. For instance, no Records of the church, during his ministry, have ever been found; and the supposition that he never kept any, comports with his general habits. His church being invited on one occasion to attend by their pastor and delegate a council at Greenfield, he neglected to present the letter to the church, and invited a neighbour, Major Chandler, who belonged to my father's church, to take him in his carriage to the council, and act as his delegate. This was done. My father, being on the same council, observed that, when Mr. Taggart was inquired of whether his church had received a letter missive and complied with its request, he said he had received such a letter, and *there* was Major Chandler who came with him. Nothing more was then said, and Major Chandler was enrolled as a member of the council. When the council had a recess, my father said to Mr. Taggart privately and humorously, "How came you to have one of my church members as your delegate?" Mr. Taggart then told him the whole story, and the matter passed off pleasantly.

He possessed remarkable shrewdness, and would sometimes confound an adversary, or silence an evil speaker, by a single word. When he was on his missionary tour in 1802, he lodged one night at a public house, not far from Albany. In the evening, a man from Albany came in, and gave an account of some rather striking event which had just occurred, accompanying his statement with many profane expressions. Mr. Taggart, after hearing him for some time, turned to him and said,—"Sir, you are a stranger to me; but you appear to be a person of intelligence and integrity, and I should be willing to take your word without an oath, and I presume the rest of the company would likewise." The man immediately apologized to Mr. T., and said that his mother had taught him better, and that he was ashamed of himself for using such language, and thanked the stranger for having reproved him.

Mr. Taggart's sermons were marked by vigorous thought, were extremely methodical, and abounded in Scripture quotations. They were also rather remarkable for their length. When about to preach to my father's people, on a very cold day, and requested by him not to make his exercises very long, he replied,—"I have no short sermons." In his delivery, he lacked animation, and was somewhat monotonous. He preached generally from short notes, but he seemed to make little use of them.

Mr. Taggart is understood to have acquitted himself honourably as a member of Congress, though his usefulness as a minister was no doubt essentially impaired by his going into political life. A number of his speeches in Congress were published, and excited very considerable attention. John Randolph, who was with him in Congress, having been told that he was pastor of a church, said to him with his characteristic keenness—"With whom hast thou left those few sheep in the wilderness?" (I Samuel xvii. 28.)

It is inscribed on his tombstone that "he had an amiable disposition, a discerning and well improved understanding, was an able divine, and preached the Gospel with delight, until a few days before he departed, as we trust, to be with Christ."

Yours with respect and esteem,

T. PACKARD, Jr.

FROM THE REV. SAMUEL WILLARD, D. D.

Deerfield, September 17, 1851.

Dear Sir: I cannot say that my acquaintance with the Rev. Mr. Taggart was very intimate, and yet, whatever recollections of him I have, I take pleasure in communicating to you. My first knowledge of him was at a meeting of the Trustees of the Deerfield Academy, after which, I met him on several different occasions, and had an opportunity of observing him, both in public and in private.

In person, he was above the middle size, thickly set, and in the latter part of his life, considerably inclined to corpulency; and his countenance, though expressive of intelligence, was marked rather by calm dignity and solidity than vivacity. In conversation he was free and agreeable; though I do not remember that he ever discovered very strông emotion. You got the impression that he was a thoughtful, sensible man, who considered well what he said, and usually spoke to good purpose. I heard him preach, so far as I recollect, but once, and that was at Greenfield, on some special occasion. I remember to have been much impressed by one peculiarity,—namely, that he preached with his eyes shut, and prayed with them open. His subject led him to the statement of various statistical facts and dates; and the accuracy and fluency which he exhibited, without any paper before him, showed either a very exact and ready memory, or great care in preparing for the exercise. His voice was good for public speaking, and his general manner was not otherwise than agreeable, though I think he had little or no gesture. He could not be considered a dull speaker, nor yet a very animated one. His Theology was the prevailing orthodoxy of New England.

Mr. Taggart, with strong powers of mind and good qualities of heart, was nevertheless distinguished for some eccentricities. Judge Smith, of Exeter, who was his early and intimate friend, related to me this anecdote concerning him:—Immediately after his admission to Dartmouth College, the acting Professor of Divinity delivered a lecture specially designed for the class which had then recently entered. During the delivery of the lecture, the Professor was not a little annoyed by observing that young Taggart was busying himself in catching flies; and, as soon as the exercise was over, he spoke to him with a good deal of earnestness, and asked him what he had been doing. "Hearing your lecture, Sir,"—was the answer. Said the Professor,—"I think you have heard very little of the lecture—let us hear what you can tell of it." To the Professor's great astonishment, Taggart arose, and repeated no inconsiderable part of it.

It is related of him, as an instance of what is called absence of mind, that, wishing to consult a book which he knew to be in his neighbour's library, he repaired to the house, and walked through a room in which a number of persons were sitting, without observing them, and went into another room, and took the book and carried it away with him. He was afterwards enquired of concerning it, by the owner, and he was not aware of having taken it at all.

There are many striking anecdotes extant concerning him, but the above are all that I now remember.

Yours faithfully,

SAMUEL WILLARD.

JAMES HALL, D. D.*

1776—1826.

JAMES HALL was born of Scotch Irish parentage, at Carlisle, Pa., August 22, 1744. When he was eight years old, the family removed to North Carolina, and settled in the upper part of Rowan (now Iredell) County, within the bounds of the congregation of which he afterwards became the pastor. The country was then new, and for its religious privileges depended chiefly on the labours of missionaries, who were sent thither by the Synods of New York and Philadelphia. But young Hall, being blessed with pious parents, early became familiar with the Bible and the

* Foote's Sketches of N. C.—Missionary Journals.

Assembly's Catechism, and was brought under a decided religious influence. His mind seems to have been religiously impressed from early childhood, but it was not till he had reached the age of about twenty, that he made a public profession of religion. From the time that he believed himself the subject of a spiritual renovation, he felt strongly inclined to the ministry as a profession; but the state of his father's family seemed to him, at the time, to oppose an insurmountable obstacle to it, and he postponed the idea, not, however, without hope that Providence might yet open a way for the accomplishment of his object. At the end of four years, he communicated his wishes to his parents, and, contrary to his expectations, found them entirely favourable to the project. About the same time, he entered into a solemn covenant with God that he would devote his life to the preaching of the Gospel, if he might be qualified for it by a suitable education.

It was nearly a year after this before he was able to enter on his preparatory course of education,—the delay being occasioned chiefly by a dangerous illness. During this period, an incident occurred, which was the occasion of no small vexation to him, and which doubtless had an important influence upon his subsequent life. He happened to meet at a wedding a young lady of uncommon attractions, by whom he became greatly fascinated; and, without reflecting seriously on the probable bearings of such a step on his future course, he rather hastily made to her proposals of marriage, which were accepted. It occurred to him, on further reflection, that the fulfilment of the engagement into which he had thus incautiously entered with the young lady, would at least greatly embarrass him in fulfilling the covenant into which he had entered with his God, to devote himself to the ministry; and the result of his reflections on the subject was, that he was thrown into a state, not only of deep solicitude, but of intense mental agony. He had an interview with his female friend, shortly after, in which he made to her a frank and full statement of his difficulties, in consequence of which they mutually agreed that the engagement should not take effect. This was the sum and substance of all that he ever had to do practically with the subject of matrimony.

He was in his twenty-sixth year when he commenced the study of the classics; though he had previously formed a habit of close mental application, by pursuing different branches of study in connection with his labours on the farm. At the age of seventeen, a Treatise of Geometry fell in his way, and he applied himself to it with great assiduity, until he had pretty thoroughly mastered it. By help derived from the plates, he constructed a quadrant with which he was accustomed to amuse himself, by measuring the height of trees and the distances of objects. He had always a passion for mathematics, a good knowledge of which he considered as an indispensable part of a thorough education.

Having prepared himself for College, he entered at Princeton, and graduated under President Witherspoon, in 1774, when he was in his thirty-first year. He had a high reputation in College, especially in the exact sciences; insomuch that, soon after he graduated, Dr. Witherspoon expressed a desire that he should be retained in the College as a teacher of Mathematics. This proposal, however, he declined, on the ground that he had sacredly devoted himself to the ministry of the Gospel, and could not feel at liberty to make any engagement that would even retard his entering on this chosen vocation.

He pursued his theological studies under the direction of Dr. Witherspoon, and was licensed to preach by the Presbytery of Orange, sometime between the meeting of the Synod in 1775 and 1776; the precise time being now unknown. There was, at this time, a great demand for Presbyterian ministers in both North and South Carolina; and it was this circumstance particularly that determined Mr. Hall to take a shorter theological course than would otherwise have been desirable to him. Various congregations immediately pressed him with invitations to become their pastor; but he finally determined to settle in the neighbourhood in which most of his early years had been passed. On the 8th of April, 1778, he was installed Pastor of the united Congregations of Fourth Creek, Concord, and Bethany; and as there is no record of his ordination, it is supposed to have taken place at the same time with his installation. He held the pastorship of these three congregations till the year 1790, when he was released from his connection with Fourth Creek and Concord Congregations, that he might have more time to devote to the cause of domestic missions. His connection with the Bethany Congregation continued during the remainder of his life.

He was honoured with the degree of Doctor of Divinity from the College of which he was a graduate, and subsequently, in 1810, from the University of North Carolina.

Dr. Hall was far from being an indifferent or idle spectator of the scenes of the Revolution. His heart went fully into the American cause, and he declined no service, whether secular or sacred, by which he might hope to promote it. He was accustomed to meet the people of his neighbourhood, when they had assembled to discuss the political topics of the day, and set forth to them their obligations as patriots, and make earnest and eloquent and highly effective appeals to them in favour of the cause of freedom. When South Carolina was overrun by the British forces under Cornwallis, he assembled his flock, addressed them with great fervour and pathos, and called upon them to take up arms in defence of their friends and neighbours, who were suffering such terrible wrongs at the hands of an invading foe. A select company of cavalry was immediately organized, and, by general consent, he was demanded for their leader, and actually accepted the command. In 1779, he led them on an expedition into South Carolina, performing the double office of Commander and Chaplain, and was absent for several months. When it was necessary, at a subsequent period, for the American forces to march into the Cherokee country,—Georgia, to encounter the Indians, Dr. Hall accompanied the army in the capacity of Chaplain. During the expedition, which lasted about two months, he had but one opportunity of preaching; and, in honour of that first sermon in the Indian territories, the adjacent country was named after the Chaplain,—Hall County. After the skirmish at Cowansford on the Catawba, between the forces of Cornwallis and the North Carolina militia, he was selected by General Greene as a suitable person to succeed General Davidson, who had fallen in that skirmish,—in the office of Brigadier General; and a commission was actually offered to him. He declined it, however, on the ground that others could fill that post, at least with as much advantage as himself, while he had solemnly pledged his life to the defence of the Gospel.

At the close of the Revolutionary war, he found religion on every side in an exceedingly decayed state, and the churches to a great extent a scene of lesolation. He now set himself, with all his energies, to repair the waste places of Zion, to restore the stated ordinances of the Gospel where they had been discontinued, and to elevate the standard of Christian feeling and character. His efforts were instrumental in bringing about an extensive revival of religion in his own congregations, as the fruit of which eighty persons were received to the Communion at one time, and sixty at another. Such was the severity of his labours that his health began seriously to decline, and he developed some pulmonary tendencies that were thought to be alarming. In consequence of this, and of the advice of physicians, he resolved on trying the effect of a sea voyage; and, accordingly, embarked at Charleston, S. C., for Philadelphia. The effect was decidedly favourable, and the more so, it was supposed, from his having a long and boisterous passage. After attending the meeting of the Synod of New York and Philadelphia, he returned home with invigorated health and spirits.

In the year 1793, he commenced his missionary excursions under the direction of a Commission of Synod. These were numerous, involved great sacrifices and hardships. and led to most important results. In the autumn of 1800, under a commission of the General Assembly, he commenced a mission to Natchez, together with two other brethren whom the Synod had appointed to accompany him. This was the first in the series of Protestant missionary efforts in the lower part of the Valley of the Mississippi. The report of this mission was made to the Synod of 1801, and a separate account of it was published by Dr. Hall in the newspapers of the day, which excited a very general interest throughout the Southern country.

He was a Commissioner to the General Assembly at Philadelphia from the Presbytery of Orange, sixteen times, and was Moderator of that body in 1803. He attended all the meetings of the Synod of the Carolinas from 1788 to 1812, with a single exception, and was the last Moderator. The Synod of North Carolina was then constituted, and his attendance upon its sessions was unintermitted, until the infirmities of age rendered it inconvenient to him to travel. His attendance on meetings of Presbytery was equally punctual.

Dr. Hall performed very important services for the whole Southern country, by his efforts in the cause of education. Very soon after he entered the ministry, he was connected with a literary institution on Snow Creek, in a neighbourhood that formed part of the Bethany Congregation. He subsequently opened an "Academy of the Sciences" at his own house, of which he was himself the sole Professor. This institution was continued for many years, and was considered as the best scientific school in the State, at that time. He formed a class of young people in his congregation, to meet him, once a week, to receive instruction in grammar; and, as they were unable to command the needful books, he wrote out a system of grammar, and allowed his class to take manuscript copies of it. It was afterwards published and gained an extensive circulation. He also conducted the theological education of a large number of young men who entered the ministry, some of whom have since occupied stations of commanding influence in the Church. Several distinguished statesmen of the South also were indebted to him chiefly for their literary and scientific training.

In July, 1819, Dr. Hall returned from the Anniversary of the American Bible Society,—an institution in which he felt the deepest interest, and from the sessions of the General Assembly, for the last time. The last seven years of his life were years of great weakness and depression; and not unfrequently his mind was enshrouded in spiritual gloom. He died on the 25th of July, 1826, in the eighty-second year of his age, and his body lies entombed in Bethany church-yard.

Dr. Hall published a Sermon on Proverbs xiv, 34, preached at the opening of a Court in South Carolina, and a Sermon preached at the ordination of Mr. Samuel C. Caldwell, as Pastor of Sugar Creek Church, 1792: also a Narrative of a most extraordinary work of Religion in North Carolina, 1802; and a Report of a missionary tour through Mississippi and the South Western Country.

FROM THE REV. R. H. MORRISON, D. D.

Cottage Home, N. C., May 19, 1848.

Rev. and dear Brother: The request contained in your letter places me in a delicate position. I must either refuse to give my estimate of Dr. Hall's character, and thus do violence to my feelings of veneration for an eminent servant of Christ, or I must attempt what I feel incompetent to perform in a suitable manner. I came into the ministry, when Dr. Hall's career of usefulness was drawing to a close. Though my recollections of him are associated with many solemn scenes of my youth, I was then unable to form a correct judgment of his character. I am indebted chiefly to several of his venerable contemporaries in the ministry, who survived him many years, and to the recollections of aged Christians generally in the region where he resided, for my impressions in regard to his qualities as a man, and his labours as a minister.

The most prominent trait of Dr. Hall's character was his devoted piety. This appeared not only from his constant exemplification of all the moral virtues, but from an entire and cheerful consecration of himself to the service of God. It was evidently the great purpose of his life to do good to his fellow men. The ministry of the Gospel was the work in which he most delighted,—a work, in which no sacrifices were counted too painful, no labours too arduous. For about forty years, his ministry was one glowing scene of untiring activity, and earnest zeal to win souls to Christ. This part of the Church has witnessed no such example of self-denied effort to diffuse the light and power of the Gospel as that presented by the life of this venerable man.

When he remained at home, his labours were most abundant in behalf of his people. His charge was composed of three churches, each of which has now its own pastor. When he travelled, it was to proclaim the Gospel to the destitute. He bore the messages of mercy from house to house. Christians were instructed and stimulated to their duty, and the careless were admonished and exhorted in the most affectionate and impressive manner. When he taught, it was to train up ministers for the Church; and some of our most useful and distinguished clergymen enjoyed the privilege of his instruction. When he led his neighbours and friends to the field of battle, it was in a conscientious defence of the liberties of his country; and when his services could be dispensed with, he promptly refused the most flattering offers of promotion in the army, and returned to his chosen work.

In nearly all our churches, precious memorials are to be found of Dr. Hall, as a warm and active friend of revivals of religion. During the dark period which succeeded the American Revolution, the churches belonging to his charge were cheered with copious effusions of the Holy Spirit, and large numbers gathered into the fold of Christ. In January, 1802, we find him travelling to Randolph County with about forty of his people, to hail the approach of that memorable work of God in the Southern States. From that day, for the next seven years, his voice was always heard, as that of a beloved and fearless leader in the wonderful scenes of that deeply interesting work. However useful other men may have been, all concede to him the honour of having been the most efficient champion of the truth, in a revival rendered dear to the Church by the conversion of thousands of souls. As he had no family, his circumstances permitted him to travel more extensively than others, and he was perhaps better qualified than any of his brethren for this particular kind of ministerial labour.

His preaching was distinguished for a clear, earnest and pungent exhibition of the truths of God's word, accompanied, I doubt not, by a very confident and humble reliance on the influences of the Holy Spirit to give it effect. His deep experience in the Divine life qualified him, in an eminent degree, to be a safe guide to the inquiring and heavy laden sinner, as well as to resolve the doubts and remove the perplexities of those who had indulged a hope in the Divine mercy.

I was too young to be a witness to the most wonderful scenes of the revival to which I have referred; but, as the camp-meetings connected with it continued till about 1812, I recollect very distinctly my own impressions under Dr. Hall's preaching. The recollection gives me sorrow, as certainly a recurrence to the follies and stupidity of my youth ought to do. When other ministers preached, I succeeded in preserving a good degree of indifference; but when Dr. Hall rose to speak, his looks, and voice, and solemn manner, filled me with an indescribable awe, and the most painful apprehensions. I dreaded the man, under a painful impression that he was a powerful instrument in the hand of God, and that I might be converted under his preaching. Another cause of my dismay was the fact that his solemn and fervid manner generally awakened the bodily exercises incident to that day. It was no uncommon thing for persons to cry out in distress, and plead aloud for mercy, or give thanks to God for their feelings of joy, and offer audible supplications for their families and friends. I looked upon such exercises at the time with no small degree of terror, and was reluctant to place myself in circumstances which would peculiarly expose me to become a subject of them.

Dr. Hall was eminently a man of missions. His heart was in the work of spreading the Gospel, and his life was devoted to it. In addition to many short excursions, he performed fourteen long and toilsome missionary tours, under the direction of the General Assembly, or the Synod with which he was connected. His journals show that these tours were of the most laborious, faithful and successful kind. He was not the man to be satisfied with passing over the country, and making appointments at those places only which seemed specially to invite attention. He went in search of the destitute, and he found them. He visited families and neighbourhoods, catechised the youth, organized churches, and circulated the Scriptures. He was often a member of the General Assembly, and the journeys which he made on these occasions were signalized by a great amount of faithful missionary labour, and by the hopeful conversion of many individuals and even families. In short, wherever he was, he was always about his Master's work; and, as his Master owned his labours in an eminent degree on earth, there is no doubt that He has conferred upon him a glorious reward in Heaven.

If these few recollections and impressions, in respect to a great and good man, shall avail, in any degree, to the object you have in view, it will be an occasion of real gratification to me.

Yours truly,

R. H. MORRISON.

ARCHIBALD SCOTT.*

1777—1799.

ARCHIBALD SCOTT was a native of Scotland, who migrated in his boyhood, and alone, to the Colony of Pennsylvania, about the year 1760. Being poor and friendless, he was cast entirely upon his own resources. He laboured for his livelihood in the field; and it is said that whilst, during the day, he followed the plough as a labourer for the wealthy farmers, he perseveringly devoted a part of every night, and all his leisure hours, to the acquisition of useful knowledge. So great was his love of learning that he was accustomed to take his Latin Grammar—written in Latin—with him into the field, and while his plough-team was resting or feeding, he would open it, and busy himself in endeavouring to understand its contents; and even when he was following his plough, his mind was still occupied with his grammar.

Dr. Cooper, a worthy physician in Pennsylvania, having been struck with the remarkable aptitude for learning evinced by this young man, was instrumental of his being introduced into the family and school of a Mr. Finley, who had a high reputation as a teacher at that day. Here he enjoyed the advantages of a thorough academical training, whilst he compensated for it, in some measure, by working on the farm—an occupation of which he was very fond, and which he pursued, as occasion offered, even after he entered the ministry. During the period of his connection with Mr. Finley's school, he joined the Presbyterian Church; and it is believed that he now, for the first time, made a public profession of religion. He began, about this time, to have some thoughts of entering the ministry; but several years must elapse before this cherished idea could be realized.

Some time after quitting Mr. Finley's school, he migrated to the Valley of Virginia, in company with two of his friends, one of whom,—Mr. Ramsey, afterwards became his father-in-law. He was, for several years, a student of Theology under the supervision of Principal Graham, of Liberty Hall Academy, and, during this period, supported himself by teaching a school. He was licensed to preach by the Hanover Presbytery, in Prince Edward County, October 31, 1777; and was ordained and installed Pastor of the united Churches of Hebron and Bethel, in Augusta County, in December, 1778,—the Rev. William Graham and the Rev. James Waddel officiating on the occasion.

Mr. Scott's charge was a very scattered one, comprehending a district some twenty miles square, and of course his pastoral labours were very arduous. Like most of his brethren also, during the Revolution, he had a very inadequate salary,—in consequence of which, he was obliged to cultivate a small farm to make out a support for his family. But he never suffered any thing to divert him from his appropriate duties as a minister. His great energy and unyielding perseverance, his glowing patriotism and earnest piety, fitted him pre-eminently for the period in which he lived. He entered warmly into the American cause, and exhorted his people to fight for freedom; but he felt that the more important work that devolved

* MS. from Rev. John A. Scott.—Foote's Sketches of Va. 2d Series.

upon him, was to assist in laying deep the foundations of our Republic on religious truth, and doing what he could, by instruction and example, to prepare the rising generation to enjoy and preserve constitutional liberty.

Mr. Scott attached much importance, and devoted much time, to the catechetical instruction of the young. Besides the "Shorter Catechism" which he used, he introduced what was known as "The Mother's Catechism,"—a work extending to thirty-two pages, octavo, (the Appendix of which he wrote himself,) which he caused to be printed under his own supervision. It was his practice to assemble all the children and youth of his charge, in different neighbourhoods, on week-days, to attend to this duty. It was in this employment that he was engaged on that memorable Saturday of June, when the alarm of the approach of Colonel Tarleton and his British dragoons spread consternation from Staunton throughout the surrounding Valley of Virginia. It is said that Mr. Scott, like his two neighbouring brethren, Graham and Brown,* exhorted the stripling youths of his congregation (their elder brethren were already with Washington) to arm themselves, and go with their neighbours, who were rising up simultaneously throughout the County of Augusta, to stand with their arms at Rock Fish Gap, on the Blue Ridge Mountains, to dispute the pass with the invader and his legion. The next day, after prayers in the three congregations for the success of the American arms, the old men and the striplings from the congregations of Graham, Brown, and Scott, united with others, and met at Rock Fish Gap, to resist the inroads of the marauding horsemen. William Graham was the master spirit; but he was heartily supported by Brown and Scott, his co-presbyters, in the movement. It was the recollection of this scene, so recently enacted under the patriotic spirit of these three pastors and their people, that gave occasion to those memorable words of General Washington—"If I should be beaten by the British forces, I will retreat with my broken army to the Blue Ridge, and call the boys of West Augusta around me, and there I will plant the flag of my country."

Mr. Scott continued the pastor of Bethel and Hebron for more than twenty years,—the relation being dissolved by death. He died at his residence, a few miles South-west of Staunton, after a short illness, on the 4th of March, 1799, leaving a widow and a large family of children. His widow died soon after, and the children were left orphans. But the eldest of his daughters (afterwards Mrs. McPheeters) assumed the headship of the family, and, by extraordinary energy and economy, succeeded in educating her younger brothers and sisters, all of whom became members of the Church,

* JOHN BROWN was graduated at the College of New Jersey in 1749; was licensed to preach by the Presbytery of Newcastle; and in 1753 became Pastor of the Churches of Timber Ridge and New Providence. In the division of the Church, which existed at that day, he was of the New Side. He taught, for some time, a celebrated school, which afterwards came under the care of the Rev. William Graham, and was the germ of Washington College. In 1767, for some reason that is not definitely understood, he resigned the charge of the Timber Ridge Congregation, and confined his labours to that of New Providence. In 1796, being weighed down by the infirmities of age, he relinquished New Providence also, and removed to Kentucky, to spend his remaining days with his children. He died at Frankfort in the year 1803, in his seventy-fifth year. He was married to Margaret, daughter of John Preston,—born in Ireland, in 1730, a lady distinguished for intellectual vigour and accomplishments,—who died in 1802. They had seven children who lived to maturity. One of the sons, *John*, was a student at Princeton College, when that institution was broken up by the British, became distinguished in civil life, and was a member of the old Congress in 1787 and 1788. Another son, *William M.*, was graduated at Princeton in 1786, became a physician, and died early, in South Carolina. Another, *James*, was an eminent lawyer; was a member of the United States Senate from Louisiana, from 1812 to 1817, and from 1819 to 1824; and was for several years American Minister to France.

as well as useful and excellent members of society. Mr. Scott was buried in the grave yard of the Hebron Church, and his memory is gratefully and reverently cherished by the children of those whose characters were moulded by his influence. Many of his descendants are members, and several of them are ministers, of the Presbyterian Church. His son, the Rev. William N. Scott, still survives, (1856,) as the patriarch of the Winchester Presbytery; and three of *his* sons have also entered the ministry, though one of them,—the Rev. William C. Scott, after a brief but brilliant course, has been called to his reward.

In person Mr. Scott was tall and manly—his features were prominent; his eyes large and blue; his nose aquiline; his hair rather light; and his skin slightly pitted by small-pox. He possessed a logical and discriminating mind, and was a strong, vigorous thinker—"a workman that needeth not to be ashamed." He was characteristically meek and humble, and had a low estimate of his own performances; but his preaching is said to have been in a high degree instructive, and often eloquent and powerful. He exerted great influence in the community at large, while, by his own people, he was regarded with an almost boundless esteem and veneration.

JAMES FRANCIS ARMSTRONG.*

1777—1816.

JAMES FRANCIS ARMSTRONG was of Irish extraction. He was a son of Francis Armstrong, and was born at West Nottingham, Md., April 3, 1750. His father was a ruling elder in the Presbyterian Church in that place. He received the elements of his education at Pequea, but was subsequently transferred to the celebrated school founded by the Rev. Samuel Blair, at Fagg's Manor. The school, during his connection with it, was under the care of the Rev. John Blair, a younger brother of its founder, who was afterwards chosen Vice President and Professor of Theology in Princeton College.

In the autumn of 1771, Mr. Armstrong entered the Junior class at Princeton, and had the privilege of living in the family of the President, Dr. Witherspoon. He graduated in the autumn of 1773; and, immediately after, commenced a course of theological study under Dr. Witherspoon's direction. On the 6th of June, 1776, he was received under the care of the Presbytery of New Brunswick, as a candidate for the ministry. Having passed his several examinations, and sustained the trials assigned him, he was to have been licensed at a meeting of the Presbytery appointed to be held at Shrewsbury; but this meeting was prevented by the invasion of the State by British troops; and, in the uncertainty of the future, Dr. Witherspoon certified the facts to the Presbytery of Newcastle, within whose bounds were Mr. Armstrong's paternal church and home, and they adopted him as their own candidate, and licensed him to preach, in January, 1777.

* Hall's Fun. Serm. for Mrs. Armstrong.—Murray's Hist. of Elizabethtown.—MS. from Rev. I. V. Brown.

This was an exciting period of the Revolution. The battle of Princeton took place in that month, and the seat of war had advanced to Philadelphia and Delaware. Even before his licensure, his patriotism prompted him to join a volunteer company; but now he was desirous of serving his country more consistently as a Chaplain to the army. With this view, he was ordained by the Presbytery of Newcastle, in January, 1778, and, on the 17th of July following, was appointed by Congress "Chaplain of the Second Brigade of the Maryland Forces." Before that date, he had proceeded with the army to the Southern campaign, and is supposed to have remained in the service till the decisive victory at Yorktown. In the exposures of this campaign, he contracted a rheumatic disease, which continued to the close of his life, and was attended, in his latter years, with intense suffering.

In June, 1782, Mr. Armstrong commenced preaching to the Church in Elizabethtown, N. J. On the 22d of August following, he was married by Dr. Witherspoon, to Susannah, daughter of Robert James Livingston. Her mother was a daughter of William Smith, an eminent lawyer, and Chief Justice of the Supreme Court of New York, and sister of William Smith, also Chief Justice of New York, and afterwards of Canada, and author of the History of New York. Mrs. Livingston, after the death of her husband, removed with her family from the city of New York to Princeton, for the sake of more conveniently educating her sons. Hence it was at Princeton that Mr. Armstrong was married to her daughter. He continued to supply the pulpit at Elizabethtown for nearly a year, when he was compelled to discontinue his labours on account of an enfeebled state of health, occasioned by an attack of the measles.

The Rev. Dr. Elihu Spencer having died at Trenton at the close of the year 1784, Mr. Armstrong preached his Funeral Sermon, and afterwards frequently supplied the vacant pulpit. On the 17th of October, 1785, a call was agreed upon by the Congregation, but, owing to some financial arrangements necessary to be made, it was not formally accepted until April, 1787. Meanwhile, however, Mr. Armstrong had taken up his residence in Trenton, and been received by the Presbytery of New Brunswick. The charge included, beside the church in town, one a few miles distant in the country, known in latter years as "Trenton First Church." He gave one third of his time to the country church, and the remainder to the one in town, till April, 1787, when the former found a separate supply, and the next year the inconvenient partnership of the two congregations was legally dissolved. He then served the town church alone, (unless he may have given part of his time in the interval to Lawrenceville,) until September, 1790, when the Lawrenceville Congregation called for half his time; and from that date until 1806, he was the joint pastor, preaching at Trenton and Lawrenceville on alternate Sabbaths. But through much of this period, he was so disabled for public effort by his rheumatic disease, that both pulpits were supplied by the Presbytery.

In 1806, a new church was built by the Trenton Congregation; and, during its erection, Mr. Armstrong preached on every alternate Sabbath in the Episcopal Church, the Rector then in office having a second charge at Bristol, Pa., as Mr. Armstrong had at Lawrenceville. This courtesy grew out of the habit of a large number of the two congregations worshipping with each other, in their respective churches, when their own pastor was at the other place. In 1815, Mr. Armstrong had an assistant provided for him;

for though he was still able to go out, and occasionally to enter the pulpit, he was never free from bodily suffering. It was in the summer of that year that he performed his last public service. There was no reason to suppose, at that time, that he might not be spared for years, and be able occasionally to bear a part in the services of the sanctuary. On the Sabbath referred to, his text was "Wo is me, if I preach not the Gospel;" and it was noticed that the only Psalm used in the singing was the third part of the seventy-first; the first half being sung at the beginning, and the remainder at the close, of the devotional exercises. Nothing could have been more appropriate to his circumstances, or more expressive of what seems to have been the habitual temper of his mind. A few months after this brought his sufferings to a close—he died on the 19th of January, 1816, in the sixty-sixth year of his age, the thirty-eighth of his ministry, and (counting from the date of his call) the thirty-first of his pastorship. The Sermon at his Funeral was preached by the Rev. Dr. Miller, Professor in the Theological Seminary at Princeton.

Mr. Armstrong was the father of six children, five of whom survived him, and three of whom still (1857,) survive. One of his daughters became the wife of Chief Justice Ewing. One son, *Robert Livingston*, was graduated at Princeton in 1802, settled as a lawyer at Woodbury, N. J., and died September 22, 1838. Mrs. Armstrong died on the 13th of February, 1851, in her ninety-third year. Dr. Hall, in a sermon preached on the occasion of her death, says,—"This venerable lady was characterized, to the last day of her life, by the dignity, yet gentleness, of her manners; her considerate and efficient benevolence; the quiet, yet faithful, discharge of her social and Christian duties."

FROM THE REV. ISAAC V. BROWN

TRENTON, 24th February, 1855.

My dear Sir: You ask for my recollections of my former neighbour and friend, the Rev. James F. Armstrong, of Trenton. I knew him intimately, and we were in the habit of frequently exchanging visits. He was an exceedingly interesting companion, full of intelligence and anecdote, frequently referring to past events and thrilling scenes, in many of which he had been personally interested. My recollections of him are very grateful, and I am happy to do any thing that may help to honour and perpetuate his memory.

He was by nature,—the evidences of it being very decisive, even in infirmity and old age,—a person of much ardour, activity, and decision. The interests of letters and of religion were, more than any thing else, impressive and absorbing with him. He was a highly acceptable preacher, and, had his health remained firm, I have no doubt that he would have been eloquent and attractive in the pulpit, far beyond most of his contemporaries. No man was more constant and untiring in his attendance on the judicatories of the Church, from the General Assembly down to his own Session; and he was always a vigilant, active and efficient member. He was equally exemplary in his attendance on other public bodies, especially the Board of Trustees of Princeton College,—in the welfare of which institution he always took the warmest interest.

Mr. Armstrong, in his personal appearance, was noble and striking, even in ruins. He had a princely, generous spirit, which always answered quickly to the claims of human wretchedness. Hospitality reigned in his heart and in his house. His noble partner in the cares of life manifested a cordial interest in the cause to which he was devoted, corresponding with his own. The same spirit has descended to his excellent surviving daughters, and is visible even in the generation following them, through the line of a deceased sister, who has left four children distinguished for usefulness in the different walks of life.

Mr. Armstrong had, in various ways, a decisive influence in advancing the prosperity of this place of his residence; and many of our citizens who still survive, retain grateful and vivid recollections of him. By his marriage, he became connected with one of the most distinguished families in the State of New York; and, in addition to this, he was the intimate friend and associate of a noble company of patriots, scholars, and Christians, in this State; such as General John Beatty of the Revolution, Colonel John Bayard, Dr. Boudinot, Judge Patterson, Dr. Samuel Stanhope Smith, Dr. McWhorter, Dr. Woodhull, and others, in whose society he moved as an ornamental and animating element. It was interesting to observe how the celebrations of the Cincinnati and other kindred Societies,—while they furnished an opportunity of reviving his old associations, and renewing his intercourse with many of his old friends, served also to quicken his patriotic zeal, and work up his spirit to the tone of other days. When, by reason of his infirmity, he was not able to sustain himself in a long march through the streets, I have given him my arm to prevent his falling by the way. And having a little of the old '76 spirit myself, it afforded me great pleasure to mingle with such groups, to hear their exciting speeches and music, and to partake of their hospitality.

I am, dear Sir, most respectfully yours,

ISAAC V. BROWN.

SAMUEL DOAK, D. D.*

1777—1830.

Samuel Doak was a son of Samuel and Jane (Mitchel) Doak, who emigrated, when they were very young, from the North of Ireland, and settled in Chester County, Pa.; but, soon after their marriage, removed to Virginia, and took up their residence in Augusta County, within the bounds of the New Providence Congregation. They were both members of the Presbyterian Church at the time of their marriage, and belonged to that division of it that was known as the Old Side. It was in August, 1749, after their settlement in Virginia, that their son Samuel was born. He remained at home, labouring upon his father's farm, till he was sixteen years old. He then made a profession of religion, and shortly after commenced a course of classical study in a grammar school, in the neighbourhood of his father's house, kept by a Mr. Alexander. This school, after a while, passed into other hands, and was removed to another place; and, subsequently, it underwent other changes still, until it finally grew into the institution which is now known as Washington College, in Lexington, Va. Such was his desire for an education that he proposed to relinquish his share of the patrimonial inheritance to his brothers, in order to obtain it. His father, for a time, dissuaded him from the attempt; but, observing that it threw him into a discontented and melancholy mood, he determined to gratify his wishes. His funds were low, and he *clubbed* with another similarly situated, erected a hut near the school house, lodged and boarded

* MSS. from Dr. J. G. M. Ramsey and Rev. S. W. Doak, D. D.

himself, and became at length assistant teacher, and thus acquired the means of defraying the expenses of his college course.

In October, 1773, young Doak entered the College of New Jersey, two years in advance, and in 1775 was admitted to the degree of Bachelor of Arts. He was subsequently, for a short time, an assistant teacher in the school of the Rev. Robert Smith of Pequea, Pa., and commenced the study of Theology under his direction. On his return to Virginia, he was married to Esther H. Montgomery, sister of the Rev. John Montgomery,* whose family belonged to New Providence. Shortly after this, he accepted the office of Tutor in the then new College of Hampden Sidney, which had been established by the Rev. Samuel Stanhope Smith. Here he remained about two years, pursuing the study of Theology under the Rev. John Blair Smith, President of the College; and afterwards continued his studies for some time, under the Rev. William Graham, at Timber Ridge. He was licensed to preach the Gospel by the Presbytery of Hanover, on the 31st of October, 1777; and having preached for some time in Washington County, Va., he removed to the Holston settlement, in what was then a part of North Carolina, but now a part of East Tennessee. Here he found the means of subsistence, especially meal, extremely scarce; and he was obliged to go thirty miles back in the direction of Abingdon, for supplies. On one occasion during his absence, the Cherokees, then in a state of hostility towards the whites, came near his cabin; and Mrs. Doak, apprized by the barking of the dogs, of their approach, retired stealthily to the woods with her infant asleep in her arms. From her hiding place she saw several of them enter the door, carry out a portion of the furniture, and then set fire to the building, and retreat with their plunder. She considered it a remarkable providence that her child did not awake; for if it had, the novelty of the passing scene would have produced fright and crying, and would thus have betrayed their place of concealment, and both the mother and child would have become victims to Indian barbarity. After the departure of the Indians, she went, by a blind path, ten miles to the nearest station, where she met, the next day, with her husband. Preaching one Sabbath on the frontier, a panic was produced by a messenger riding hastily up, and exclaiming "Indians, Indians,—Rogdale's family are murdered." Mr. Doak stopped abruptly in his discourse, referred to the case of the Israelites in similar danger, offered a short prayer that the God of Israel would go with them against these Canaanitish heathen,—called for the men to follow him, and taking his rifle, led his male hearers to the pursuit. At another time, after he had commenced teaching at Salem, and while his class was reciting, a similar alarm was given; and he immediately dismissed his school, and repaired with his students to the camp of General Sevier.

Mr. Doak was a member of the Convention of 1784, that formed the constitution of the ancient Commonwealth of Franklin; and tradition ascribes to him the paternity of a clause in the rejected constitution, making

* JOHN MONTGOMERY was graduated at the College of New Jersey in 1775; was licensed to preach by the Presbytery of Hanover, October 28, 1778; was ordained April 27, 1780; accepted a call in October 1781 from Winchester, Cedar Creek, and Opecquon, and after spending a few years here, resigned his charge in 1789, and took up his residence in "the Pastures," Augusta, where he had inherited property. Here he remained during the rest of his life. Previous to his ordination, he was associated with Mr. Graham in the instruction of Liberty Hall. He was an amiable man, a popular preacher, and a good scholar. During the latter part of his life, his ministry was interrupted by bodily infirmities.

provision for a University,—requiring the Legislature to erect it before the year 1787, and to endow it liberally.

After residing at the Holston settlement a year or two, he removed in the hope of finding a more promising field of usefulness, to the settlement on Little Limestone, in Washington County, and there purchased a farm, on which he built a log house for purposes of education, and a small church edifice, and founded a congregation known as the "Salem Congregation." The literary institution which he here established, was the first that was *ever* established in the great Valley of the Mississippi: in 1785 it was incorporated by the Legislature of North Carolina, under the name of "Martin Academy;" and in 1795, it became "Washington College." From its incorporation as an Academy till the year 1818, Mr. Doak continued to preside over it; and the elders of his congregation formed a part of the Board of Trustees. While he was attending a meeting of the General Assembly at Philadelphia, he received a donation of classical books for his infant institution, which he carried in a sack upon a pack horse, five hundred miles; and this constituted the nucleus of the library of the present Washington College.

Having organized a number of churches in the county in which he lived, also at Bethel and Timber Ridge, in Green County, he resigned the Presidency of the College in the year 1818, and was succeeded in the office by his son, the Rev. John M. Doak, M. D. He now removed to Bethel, where he opened a private school, which he called Tusculum Academy, and which, under his son, the Rev. Samuel W. Doak, D. D., has since grown into a flourishing College. He was honoured with the degree of Doctor of Divinity from both Washington and Greenville Colleges, in 1818. At Bethel he passed the residue of his life, in honour and usefulness, and died in his eighty-second year, on the 12th of December, 1830. The most respectful notice of his death was taken by his former pupils in Washington College, in a series of Resolutions, testifying their gratitude for his services, and their veneration for his memory.

Dr. Doak's ministry was attended with no small success. Several powerful revivals of religion occurred in connection with it, from the fruits of which proceeded a number of zealous and efficient preachers of the Gospel.

Dr. Doak's first wife died on the 3d of July, 1807. He was afterwards married to Margaretta H. McEwen, who died September 22, 1831. He had five children,—all by the first marriage. The eldest son, *John Whitefield*, was born, October 18, 1788; was educated by his father; was licensed to preach by the Abingdon Presbytery, when he was in his nineteenth year, and shortly after was ordained and installed pastor of New Dublin and Wythville Churches, in Virginia. He was subsequently Pastor of Mount Bethel and Providence Churches, in Tennessee. In the year 1809, he was installed Pastor of the Church in Frankfort, Pa. In consequence of the failure of his health, which rendered it doubtful whether he would be able to continue in the ministry, he studied medicine, returned to Tennessee, and became a very successful medical practitioner, and at the same time officiated as a stated supply of Salem and Leesburg Churches. He died on the 6th of October, 1820. He was distinguished for his talents and usefulness. Dr. Doak's other son, the Rev. *Samuel W. Doak*, D. D., is now (1857) the President of Tusculum College, Tenn.

FROM J. G. M. RAMSEY, M. D.

AUTHOR OF THE "ANNALS OF TENNESSEE."

MECKLENBURG, near Knoxville, Tenn., November 21, 1849.

My dear Sir: It costs me no effort to comply with your request for my reminiscences of the venerable Dr. Samuel Doak, my early friend and teacher. His name is associated with some of my most cherished and grateful recollections, as well as with the progress of knowledge and religion in East Tennessee, from its first settlement to the period of his death.

Dr. Doak, if my memory serves me, was somewhat above the middle stature, had a large muscular frame, well formed, and in later life a little inclined to corpulency,—full chest, wide shoulders, and short neck, indicating a strong tendency to apoplexy,—of which indeed he died. His appearance was grave and commanding; his voice stentorian to the extreme, and any thing but melodious; his eye deep blue, not entirely lustreless, but yet indicating little of passion or genius. The whole countenance expressed strong intellect, manly good sense, calm dignity, and indomitable firmness.

His habits were those of the student, teacher, and divine. The amount of his reading in the latter part of his life was small; that of his thinking immensely great. Though naturally very social and friendly, he spent little of his time in conversation, and none of it in conviviality. The very fragments of time he sacredly appropriated to preparation for the pulpit, and to his Presidential duties. The entertainment of his guests (except such as were clerical and professional) devolved upon other members of his family. When out of College, his whole time was spent in his study. There, reclining at his ease in an armchair, his head bending backwards, his eyes generally closed,—almost entirely abstracted from the world without, he cultivated the powers within, and prepared that rich intellectual and moral aliment, which it was at once his duty and his pleasure to impart to his class and his congregation. In the recitation room, his posture was nearly the same. Two or more classes, in the languages especially, would sometimes be reciting to him at once; and his practised ear seldom failed to detect an error. His fidelity as a teacher is beyond all praise. The students of Washington College, under his Presidency, were not, as is common in most similar institutions, subdivided into Freshman, Sophomore, Junior, and Senior classes; but each pupil studied, and learned, and disciplined his mind, for himself. One brilliant genius, one diligent student, could not, under this system, act as a ferry-man for the whole class, and carry over the incompetent or the indolent. Each one was permitted, without artificial restraint, to make as rapid progress in his studies as his industry or his abilities enabled him to do. The acquisition of knowledge,—mere literary attainment, was not the sole or even primary object of Dr. Doak's instruction—it was mental discipline—it was to train the intellect,—to teach the young man how to think,—to think accurately and profoundly,—to think for himself, and to beget a spirit of manly reliance upon his own powers of independent investigation and vigorous thought. "Nullius addictus jurare in verba," he inculcated as a favourite maxim; and his stern rebuke was never withheld from the exhibition of a blind subserviency to popular sentiment or antiquated usage.

As one instance of his indefatigable application to scientific and literary pursuits, I may mention that, though a tall son of Princeton, in some of its palmiest days, he had learned little of Chemistry, and nothing of the Hebrew language, at that ancient seat of learning. But, at the age of sixty-five, he commenced his chemical studies, and, though entirely self taught, he was soon well qualified to teach the science to others. About the same time, he commenced the study of Hebrew, and very soon was able to teach it; and the class which he graduated in 1815, were examined upon that language publicly before an admiring audience, —the first case of the kind that ever occurred in Tennessee. He read the ancient works on Theology in the languages in which they were originally written: Calvin's Institutes in Latin he always placed in the hands of his theological students; and the Presbytery usually confided to him the Latin exigeses of probationers for the ministry. He had a passion,—not a taste, but a passion,—for philology. He taught the languages to the last; and when the apoplectic tendency was upon him, his discourse to those around his dying bed, though incoherent, was in good Latin.

Commencement was the only gala-day in the year with Dr. Doak. On that occasion, he wore his antique wig, his shorts, and his old fashioned shoes: the muscles of his stern brow were relaxed, and he gave himself up to an unusual urbanity and kindliness of manner. He was still grave,—still dignified and venerable; but there was an air of self-complacency,—of benignity blended with conscious self-consequence, which he exhibited on no other occasion. His posture was erect; his movements less ungraceful; his manner calm and most respectful. His Board of Trustees, who were indeed his Faculty, were seated upon plain benches near and around his chair. The candidates for the Academic honours approached him deferentially, slowly, modestly, and with filial regard and consideration bowed to him. Returning the salutation, the old President arose, and holding the diploma in one hand, said in a solemn and impressive tone of voice, and with a paternal pride and solicitude in his eye,—"Præses et Curatores Washingtoniensis Collegii," &c. The scene was deeply interesting and impressive, and was never forgotten by a graduate.

The *amor habendi* that so much characterizes our countrymen and our age, and the belittling influences of which are unhappily sometimes seen in ecclesiastics, and other learned men, degrading the noble powers of the intellect down to the grovelling pursuits of mammon, was not even an emotion,—far less a passion, with Dr. Doak. He rose above it, and even in old age, when avarice sometimes gets in the ascendant, he considered the acquisition of wealth for its own sake as ignoble and disparaging. His tuition fee was five dollars a session of five months; and in this was included the use of the college library, and other facilities of instruction. His habits were frugal; his hospitality, though not elegant, was better—it was unpretending and cordial. The primitive simplicity of early times in the West, and of frontier life, was exhibited upon his farm, in his house, in his dress, and in his intercourse with the world. When a young man, the condition of things around him created a necessity of participating actively in the settlement and defence of the country, and in its civil and political affairs. He always voted; and the consideration in which he was held by the people, generally allowed him to open the polls,—in other words, to vote first.

As a minister of the Gospel, I hardly need say that his praise was in all our churches. He may well be considered the first apostle of Presbyterianism in Tennessee. No one has been more successful in training up young men for the ministry. The pupils of his charity are lifting up their voices in the abodes of refinement and civilization, and in the recesses of the wilderness. His style of preaching was original, bold, pungent, and sometimes pathetic. His delivery was natural and impressive, and well fitted to give effect to the truths which he uttered. It is a remarkable fact that he was a subject of that far-famed physiological phenomenon,—the "*Exercise*," or "*Jerks*," that prevailed so extensively in the Western country, about the beginning of this century. He had cautioned his people against it, privately and from the pulpit. He took it while preaching. He alluded to it afterwards, when lecturing to his classes; said he could not explain it satisfactorily, and called it "*the strange work of God.*"

On the whole, I think it may safely be affirmed that Dr. Doak was among the most useful men of the period in which he lived. His influence in the propaga tion of Christianity, and especially in the extension of the Presbyterian Church, in the West, it is not easy to estimate; while his students, in the early days of Tennessee, filled all the learned professions, and were almost the only teachers, for several years, in the infant settlements of the West and South-west.

The portrait of Dr. Doak is preserved in the library of Washington College. The contour of his face bears a strong resemblance to that of John Knox; and the strong points of character in the two men were strikingly similar.

I am, dear Sir,

Very respectfully yours,

J. G. M. RAMSEY.

JOHN BLAIR SMITH, D. D.*

1778—1799.

JOHN BLAIR SMITH was the fourth son of the Rev. Robert Smith, D. D., and was born at Pequea, Lancaster County, Pa., June 12, 1756. He received his name from a maternal uncle,—his mother being a sister of the Rev. Messrs. Samuel and John Blair. In very early life, he evinced a great thirst for knowledge, and an uncommon facility at acquiring it. At the age of fourteen, he became, under the most watchful and faithful parental training, hopefully a subject of renewing grace; and at sixteen was admitted to the Junior class in the College of New Jersey. During his whole college course, though he was naturally of a cheerful and social turn, his conduct as a Christian was always worthy of his profession, and his improvement in the various branches of study worthy of his acknowledged talents, and answerable to the high hopes which his earlier developments had awakened. He was graduated under Dr. Witherspoon in 1773, and was one of a class of twenty-nine, fourteen of whom became ministers of the Gospel, and three Governors of States.

An elder brother, Samuel Stanhope Smith, having become the head of the rising institution in Prince Edward County, Va., under the care of the Presbytery of Hanover, and also in 1775 been installed pastor of the Churches of Cumberland and Briery in Prince Edward,—the subject of this notice went, at his suggestion, in the early part of 1776, to join his brother as an assistant teacher, and at the same time to prosecute his theological studies under his direction. Having previously joined the Newcastle Presbytery, he transferred his relation from that to the Presbytery of Hanover on the 18th of June, 1777; and having gone through his several trials, was licensed to preach by the latter Body, at Tinkling Spring, on the 29th of April, 1778. He was ordained by the same Presbytery at Prince Edward Court House, on the 26th of October, 1779. At the same meeting of Presbytery, (October 28,) his brother, having received an invitation to the chair of Moral Philosophy in the College of New Jersey, asked leave to resign the Presidency of Hampden Sidney College, and also his pastoral charge; both which requests were granted. John Blair Smith was

*Assemb. Miss. Mag., 1805.—Foote's Sketches of Va., 1st Series.—Life of Rev. Dr. Ashbel Green.—MSS. from Archibald Alexander, D. D., and William Hill, D. D.

immediately appointed to succeed him as President of the College; and in the spring of the next year, (1780,) he became his successor also in the pastoral office.

About this time Mr. Smith was united in marriage with Elizabeth, daughter of Colonel John Nash, of Templeton, Prince Edward County,—a lady distinguished alike for her accomplishments and her piety. They had six children,—five sons and one daughter. One of the sons, (Robert,) entered the ministry, and for some time served the Church in Snow Hill, Md., where he died in 1824.

Though Mr. Smith, from the time he appeared in the pulpit, attracted much attention as a preacher, yet he was by no means at first so popular as his brother who had preceded him: before he left the State, however, he is said to have been at once more attractive and powerful than any other clergyman in Virginia from the time of Samuel Davies. But the earlier years of his ministry were much less distinguished for zeal and activity than those that followed. The times were most adverse to the progress of religion, and the success of ministerial labour. The State, and that very part of it, had been invaded by the British; and the minds of the people were occupied chiefly about their own safety, and their country's independence. Mr. Smith was an earnest patriot, and withal was a man of great activity and courage. The College suffered much in consequence of the war. Its resources were exhausted; and the youth who should have been pursuing their classical studies were hurried off to the army.

After the Peace, it was some time before religion and literature began to revive. The Methodists, about this time, began to pass through Virginia, and by their great zeal attracted no inconsiderable attention. In some places the members of the Presbyterian Church were induced in considerable numbers to join their Society. About the year 1786 or 1787, they came within the bounds of Mr. Smith's congregations, and were probably the means (so says Dr. Alexander) of giving a fresh impulse to both his religious feelings and his public ministrations. Instead of condemning what in them he disapproved, he endeavoured to imitate what he considered praiseworthy; and from this time he exhibited a degree of ardour, which had never been witnessed in him before. He preached with a power and frequency which, by the Divine blessing, soon began to produce visible effects. An extensive revival of religion ensued, which spread through the College, and the whole adjacent country. Mr. Smith entered into the work with such glowing zeal, and his preaching was so eloquent and powerful, that he was continually urged to extend his labours, and to places more and more remote from his residence. By this means, he was so often called away from the College, that some of his friends thought that he was less attentive to his duties there than could be desired; and this was felt the more, as the institution, being without funds, depended for its support on the fees of the students. He himself also was of the opinion that his first duty was to preach the Gospel; and as there seemed to be on every side a great demand for preaching, he determined to resign his office as President of the College, and give himself wholly to the appropriate work of a minister. This resolution he carried into effect in the year 1789; and, at the same time, bought a small farm in the neighbourhood of the College, and went to live upon it.

But Mr. Smith's own congregations began at length to feel that his numerous engagements abroad were hardly compatible with a proper attention to his pastoral duties at home. Meanwhile, owing to a great lack of domestic economy, he had become not a little embarrassed in his financial concerns; and the salary which he received from his congregations was not sufficient to meet the current expenses of his family. These circumstances prepared the way for his removal to another field of labour.

In April, 1791, he was appointed by his Presbytery one of the Commissioners to attend the General Assembly at Philadelphia. During the meeting of the Assembly, he was invited to preach in the Third, or Pine Street, Presbyterian Church, which was then vacant, and looking out for a pastor. So acceptable was his preaching that the congregation were called together, and made out a unanimous call for him, before he left the city, which he conditionally agreed to accept. When the circumstance became known to his own people, who regarded him with an affection amounting almost to idolatry,—they were greatly distressed, and threw every obstacle they could in the way of his removal; but they found it impossible to divert him from his purpose. He accordingly resigned his pastoral charge, removed to Philadelphia in the autumn following, and was installed over his new charge in December.

Shortly after Mr. Smith's settlement in Philadelphia, he became a member of an Association consisting of several of the most prominent clergymen of the city, designed to prevent the spread of infidel principles through the medium of certain newspapers. One article of his at least, over the signature of A. B., was published in a newspaper, which was followed by a pamphlet from Dr. Ashbel Green, full of scathing satire, that terminated the controversy, and, for the time being, arrested the evil.

In 1795, the degree of Doctor of Divinity was conferred upon him by the College of New Jersey. In the same year, Union College, at Schenectady, N. Y., was founded; and Dr. Smith was chosen its President. He accepted the appointment, and for three years presided over the infant institution with great credit and success. He then returned to his former charge in Philadelphia, and was formally reinstated among them in May, 1799.

The following extract of a letter from Dr. Smith to Major Morton, of Prince Edward County, Va., which is in my possession, discloses the reason of this last change:—

"I suppose that my return to my former charge in Philadelphia will excite some surprise amongst my friends. However, it can be explained upon a very natural principle, without ascribing it to fickleness of mind. It is simply because I prefer being Pastor of a Congregation before being President of a College, and think myself better qualified for the former than the latter; and because I have regained that health and strength, the want of which only prevented me from staying in Philadelphia when I was there. It is true that I shall run a great risk in the present circumstances and prospects of the city; but it is equally true that my post would have been there, and I should have had my chance with the other citizens, if the want of health had not compelled me to remove.

"The Trustees of the College have accepted my resignation in a manner very respectful to me, and have directed that my portrait be taken and preserved in their Hall. They insist upon my staying till after the Commencement, next May, though I wish to go about the beginning of April."

On his return to Philadelphia, he was cordially greeted, not only by his own congregation, who had parted with him most reluctantly, but by a large portion of the intelligent and excellent people of the city. But their joy was destined soon to be turned into mourning. About the middle of August, he was attacked by the yellow fever, and died on the 22d of the month,—one of the first victims of that terrible pestilence. He died in perfect tranquillity,—in a manner worthy of his Christian life and his Christian hopes. A Sermon was preached on the occasion of his death by his relative, the Rev. Dr. Samuel Blair.

Dr. Smith's only acknowledged publication was a Sermon entitled "The enlargement of Christ's Kingdom, the object of a Christian's prayers and exertions,"—delivered in the Dutch Church in Albany before the Northern Missionary Society in the State of New York, 1797.

FROM THE REV. WILLIAM HILL, D. D.

WINCHESTER, Va., June 15, 1848.

Rev. and dear Sir: My opportunities of acquaintance with Dr. John Blair Smith were confined to the period of his residence in Virginia—the period, however, in which he performed his greatest work, and earned his brightest laurels. I was a student at Hampden Sidney College, while he was its President; and, owing to some peculiar circumstances, was brought into nearer relations with him than were almost any of my college cotemporaries. I had an opportunity of marking his whole course from that time until he left the State.

My most interesting recollections of him have respect to the great Revival of religion that commenced in Hampden Sidney College in 1787, which was instrumentally sustained and carried forward chiefly by his efforts. Though he had always been an earnest and eloquent preacher, the commencement of that revival evidently gave a fresh impulse to his spirit, and a greatly increased fervour and power to his ministrations. He showed, from the very beginning, that his heart was in it, and that nothing that it was in his power to do for its promotion would be omitted. The most violent opposition was raised against it by a large part of the college students, and those who were known to be in an anxious state of mind were derided as miserable fanatics; but Dr. Smith immediately frowned the opposition into silence, and threw around the serious students the protection of his influence and authority. His preaching was marked by a clearness, directness, pungency, and tenderness withal, that the most hardened found it difficult to resist. Immense congregations would hang upon his lips in breathless silence, except as the silence would be interrupted by an occasional deep sigh. If he observed in his audience the least sign of undue excitement,—any thing not perfectly consistent with the decorum due to the services of God's House, he would instantly pause and say,—"You must compose your feelings, Brethren—God is not the author of confusion, but of peace in all his churches." And sometimes, on such occasions, he would give out a verse or two of some hymn for the people to sing, till perfect silence was restored, and then would go on with his discourse. When this came to be understood, all tendencies to noisy demonstration were suppressed; though it not unfrequently happened that when the congregation was dismissed, several would be seen remaining in their seats, because, from the overpowering effects of distress or joy, they were unable to rise until their friends came to their assistance.

Dr. Smith was unusually careful in avoiding hasty admissions to the church. He urged upon the consideration of those who were hopeful converts the importance of the most close and diligent self-scrutiny, and the great danger of becoming fixed on a false foundation. He required of them generally a probation of several months, and sometimes of a year or more, before being received as communicants. No anxious seats or inquiring meetings were used or thought of in those days; though no opportunity was suffered to pass unimproved for earnest and faithful conversation in private.

Dr. Smith had but a slender frame, and a feeble constitution; and his exertions, especially during the revival, were much greater than his strength would warrant. Not unfrequently he would go into the pulpit, and preach with wonderful animation and power, when his friends thought that he ought to be in his bed. On one occasion, he ruptured a blood-vessel, and fell in his pulpit, and had to be taken out and carried home. At another time, as he was preaching in a private house, and standing by a large open window, the same thing occurred again, and putting his head out of the window, he discharged such a quantity of blood that all who were present supposed that they had heard him preach for the last time. After this, he was urged by his physicians and friends to quit preaching altogether; but in a few weeks he had resumed his accustomed labours as if nothing had happened. The buoyancy of his spirit, and the all-absorbing interest which he felt in his work, gave to his feeble frame a sort of recuperative power, that made the passage a very short one back from a near approach to the grave to the fresh and vigorous discharge of his ministerial duties.

Notwithstanding Dr. Smith was earnestly devoted to his work as a minister of the Gospel, his influence was deeply felt also as a patriot and a citizen. When the war of the Revolution spread terror and agitation through the region in which he lived, and interrupted the regular exercises of the College, instead of finding an apology in his profession for remaining inactive at home, he raised a company of volunteers from among his students and the youth of his congregations, and with sword in hand marched at their head as Captain, joined the army, and performed a tour of military duty, in pursuit of the British legions who were carrying desolation through the sea-ports and lower counties of Virginia. He subsequently set out with a view to join a company of volunteers to assist General Morgan in a probable encounter with Cornwallis; but when he overtook the company, his feet were blistered by travelling, and he was, not without great difficulty, persuaded by Colonel Martin, one of his elders, to abandon the expedition and return home.

But Dr. Smith exerted an important influence in the civil concerns of the State also, especially as connected with the interests of religion. When the Legislature, in 1776, abolished the establishment of the Church of England in the State, they, at the same time, passed an Act, incorporating the Episcopal Clergy, and giving them a right to the glebes and churches which had been procured by a tax upon the inhabitants in general, including Dissenters of every description as well as Episcopalians,—notwithstanding the Bill of Rights had said—"The rights of conscience and the free exercise of religion shall be secured to all the citizens of the State, and no preference shall be given to one sect over any other." Another bill was introduced, but not yet passed, to extend the privileges of the Act of Toleration, as passed by William and Mary, to the State of Virginia. Dr. Smith framed a remonstrance against those Acts, which he induced the Presbytery of Hanover to adopt and send to the Legislature. It was a very able State paper, and had the effect of preventing any further proceedings in regard to the Act of Toleration, though the other Act remained in force a few years longer, until public sentiment loudly demanded and finally secured its repeal.

Another great excitement was raised in Virginia by a bill which was introduced in the Legislature, in the year 1784, for a general assessment of all the inhabitants of the State, to raise money for the support of religion in the State, leaving it to the different parishes to decide what denomination of Christians it should go to support. This bill was to be submitted to the voters. The inhabitants of the Eastern Counties, where the predilection was generally for the old establishment, were much in favour of this plan of assessment, and its operation in respect to them would have been nearly the same thing as the re-establishment of the Episcopal Church; whereas, in the upper counties, where the Dissenters were more numerous, and much divided into sects, it would only generate contention, and open a door for electioneering and intrigue. Then, too, each sect that was excluded from the assessment, would have to support its own minister, and pay the assessment besides. This, it was urged, would displease more persons than the former establishment, would encourage a spirit of intolerance, and would array the different denominations in a spirit of bitter hostility against each other.

Patrick Henry, who was at this time a member of the Legislature, was a strenuous advocate of the assessment, and it was confidently expected, as well from the wonderful power of his eloquence as from the general character of the Body, that the Bill would pass into a Law.

The subject now became one of intense interest, especially among Presbyterians, who were nearly unanimous in their opposition to the plan;—though Mr. Graham, a man of much distinction among them, favoured it. Dr. Smith, having succeeded in procuring what he deemed a suitable memorial to the Legislature, was appointed, with two others, to present it, and defend the side which it espoused; though it was generally regarded as a most unpromising, not to say hopeless, movement. It turned out that the conflict was almost entirely between Smith and Henry; and the result was that the assessment bill was defeated by a majority of three votes.

It is well known that our great Virginia Orator was originally opposed to the adoption of the Federal Constitution. When that noble instrument was submitted to the consideration of the people, Patrick Henry offered himself as a candidate for Representative of Prince Edward County in the State Convention; and he appointed a day to meet the people of the County at the Court House, to show the defects of the Constitution, and the grounds on which he opposed it. The Court House is not a half hour's walk from the College. Dr. Smith, who was an earnest friend of the Constitution, had made his arrangements to be present at the meeting, and defend it against his attacks; but, being called away at that hour to visit a sick person, he employed a young man who lived in his family, remarkable alike for memory, for shrewdness, and for the use of his pen, to take down Mr. Henry's speech in shorthand for his (Dr. Smith's) benefit. Within a week or two from that time, there was to be a public exhibition in the College Hall—an occasion which was always sure to draw together a large assembly. When the day arrived, Patrick Henry, who lived in the neighbourhood, came with the rest, little dreaming of the rod that was prepared for him. One of the best speakers among the students came forward upon the stage, and delivered Henry's philipic against the Constitution, almost exactly as he had himself delivered it, at the Court House. Another immediately followed with a speech prepared by Dr. Smith, in which he had put forth all his energies, in *defence* of the Constitution. There was no intimation given that the two speeches were not written by the individuals who had pronounced them. Henry was not a little annoyed by the procedure, and at the close of the exercises gave Dr. Smith to understand, in no equivocal terms, that he felt that an unfair advantage had been taken of him. Dr. Smith contended that he had no cause for complaint, unless his speech had been unfairly represented; and in that case, he declared himself ready to make any amends in his power. Henry said *that* was not the ground of his complaint; for the young man had certainly taken his speech down with great accuracy; but he thought it was indelicate and improper that he should be placed in such circumstances before that audience, without any intimation having previously been given him of what was intended. Dr. Smith replied that Colonel Henry knew it was his intention to have replied to him, when he spoke at the Court House, but was providentially prevented; that he had then spoken for public effect, and his speech became public property; that all that he could reasonably require was that it should be fairly reported; and if that had been done, he could not see that he had any just reason for complaint. Henry, however, was not at all satisfied, broke off all intercourse with him from that time, and would never hear him preach afterwards, though he had previously been one of his constant hearers.*

Leaving it to others to speak in regard to Dr. Smith after he left Virginia, I will only add that

I am very respectfully and truly yours,

WILLIAM HILL.

FROM THE REV. ELIPHALET NOTT, D. D.

UNION COLLEGE, April 10, 1857.

Dear Sir: My acquaintance with Dr. John Blair Smith was short; my reminiscences of him are therefore few, but precious—for they are reminiscences of a wise and good man;—of a man who, during our too short acquaintance, ever treated me as a son;—whose counsels gave a new direction to my opinions on Church organization; and whose efforts determined the ultimate field of my labours.

I came from the State of Connecticut in the summer of 1795, on a mission to the "new settlements" in Western New York, which could hardly be said to extend beyond Rome. Almost all beyond Rome—much this side of it—was wilderness.

My training had been in the Orthodox Congregational Church—my sympathies were with it; and so were my opinions in regard to Church government. And it was my purpose, and I deemed it to be my duty, to extend its influence, and to form churches to be in the same ecclesiastical connection, and under the same form of government.

In passing through Schenectady, I stopped over night at a public house opposite the Academy building, then occupied by the College, and learned that there was to be a prayer meeting or lecture there that evening. I felt it my duty to attend it, and was solicited to preach by Dr. Smith, then President of Union College, who, after sermon, invited me to his house to spend the night. He inquired concerning my views, and objects, and theatre of action. Having told him, he said to me,—"The Orthodox Churches of New England hold substantially the same faith as the Presbyterian, of which the Shorter Catechism is the common symbol. Now this being the case, is it wise, is it Christian, to divide the sparse population holding the same faith, already scattered, and to be hereafter scattered, over this vast new territory, into two distinct ecclesiastical organizations, and thus prevent each from enjoying those means of grace which both might much sooner enjoy but for such division? Would it not be better for the entire Church that these two divisions should make mutual concessions, and thus effect a common organization on an accommodation plan, with a view to meet the condition of communities so situated?"

The arguments employed by Dr. Smith were deemed conclusive by me, gave a new direction to my efforts, and led, through the influence of other Congregationalists whom I induced to co-operate, to the formation of those numerous Presbyterian Churches on this "accommodation plan," of which, though the plan has been abandoned, the fruits remain to the present day.

* Dr. Archibald Alexander expressed to me the opinion that Dr. Smith's treatment of Patrick Henry on this occasion was not such as his character and standing entitled him to.

My fixed purpose was, when I came into the State of New York, to settle in the country. From this purpose Dr. Smith availed himself of every opportunity that presented to dissuade me. He urged on me the consideration of the fact that the Apostles always sought the great cities as centres of influence. He urged my settlement in the First, then the only, Presbyterian Church in Albany; and it was owing to his untiring exertions that I was finally settled in that city.

Coming as I did from Connecticut, where the discourses of the clergy were, for the most part, argumentative, written discourses, and read calmly and deliberately from the pulpit, the impassioned and extemporaneous efforts of Dr. Smith filled me alike with admiration and amazement. His addresses to the hopes of Christians were most cheering,—his appeals to the conscience of sinners, terrific. He was the dispenser of the consolations of the Gospel to the righteous, the Boanerges of the Law to the wicked. He was ever ready, ever willing, to preach, and always commanded the rapt attention of the audience he addressed. His preparations for the pulpit were meditation and prayer. He seldom wrote his sermons—at most he wrote only a few brief hints on a slip of paper, which, as he rose in the pulpit, he placed under the thumb of his left hand, in which he held a small pocket Bible, which he raised instinctively to meet his eye, when he came to a new topic of discourse. Whether he read the hints written, when he so raised the Bible, or whether it was merely a habit necessary to the free workings of his mind, it would seem, was uncertain; for, on one occasion, when delivering an impassioned passage, the little brief slipped from beneath the thumb which held it, sailed away, and finally lodged on the floor of the middle aisle. Not the least embarrassed by this incident, the Doctor tore a small piece from a newspaper in his pocket, placed it under his thumb in the little pocket Bible in his left hand, and went on with his discourse, raising the Bible to his eye as frequently as before, and gathering from it apparently the same inspiration.

In private life, Dr. Smith was remarkable for his hospitality and conversational powers. His opinions on Slavery were substantially those of Washington, Jefferson, and other distinguished contemporary statesmen at the South. But though he spoke of it freely in conversation, and seemed to anticipate the divisions which it has since occasioned in the Church, I do not recollect to have ever heard him allude to it in the pulpit, where he seemed to know nothing but Christ and Him crucified.

He informed me that, during the prevalence of that terrible epidemic,—the yellow fever, in Philadelphia, in 1793, he remained in the city, kept his church open, and preached every Sabbath, and to audiences such as he had never addressed before.

He left his charge in Philadelphia chiefly on account of ill health, and under the promise, if he ever recovered his health, to return to them again. He did recover his health, and fulfilled his promise by returning to his former charge; but he returned there to die. There rest his ashes, and thence his sainted spirit ascended to his God. Though he left no published works of consequence, as memorials of his worth, behind him, his memory yet lives on earth, and will live honoured, and revered, and loved, by all who knew him, among whom are none who remember him with greater affection and veneration than the writer of this brief memorial.

Very truly yours,

ELIPHALET NOTT.

CALEB ALEXANDER.*

1778—1828.

Caleb Alexander was born in Northfield, Mass., on the 22d of July, 1755. He was a great-grandson of John Alexander, who, with several brothers, emigrated from Scotland, in the early settlement of New England, and planted themselves on Connecticut River. His grandfather, John Alexander, with twelve others, first purchased from the Indians the land that constituted the old town of Northfield. His father was Simeon Alexander, a respectable farmer, who, during the Revolution, rendered good service, in different ways, to his country. His mother's maiden name was Sarah Howe—she was a sister of Caleb Howe, who was killed by the Indians at Hinsdale, N. H., in July, 1775, and whose family were carried captives to Lower Canada. Both his parents were exemplary members of the church.

Young Alexander seems to have early conceived the idea of obtaining a liberal education, though he spent the period of his youth chiefly in labouring on his father's farm. He entered Dartmouth College, and remained there till his Senior year, (1776,) when he was recommended by President Wheelock to be admitted to the same standing in Yale College. The following is an extract from the President's letter:—"He is another of that number of which I have sent you several already, who was, in the judgment of Christian charity, the subject of God's saving mercy, in that special season of the outpouring of his Spirit here, the winter before last. The change appearing in the youth was very great, as, before it, he was considerably of the wild order; but ever since, as far as I have seen or heard, he has adorned his Christian profession by a truly religious and exemplary conversation. He has been a diligent student and a good scholar." He was graduated at Yale in 1777; and took his second degree at Brown University in 1789.

Mr. Alexander entered on the study of Theology soon after he left College, under the direction of the Rev. Ephraim Judson of Taunton; and on the 14th of October, 1778, was licensed to preach the Gospel, at Groton, Conn., by the Eastern Association of New London County.

On the 28th of February, 1781, he was ordained Pastor of the Church in New Marlborough; but this relation continued for only a short time. He seems to have given offence to a portion of his congregation by the great directness and pungency of his preaching,—which was strongly Calvinistic; though the council that dismissed him, in recognising this fact, bear an honourable testimony to his fidelity. His dismission took place on the 28th of June, 1782. On the 26th of December, 1785, he received a call to settle over the Church in Mendon, Mass.; and was installed as its Pastor, on the 12th of April, 1786,—the Rev. Dr. Emmons of Franklin preaching the installation sermon.

In 1801, he was appointed by the Massachusetts Missionary Society to visit the Churches and Indians in the Western part of New York. On his return, he sought and obtained a dismission from his congregation, partly on account of the inadequacy of his support, and partly from a conviction

* Hist. Mendon Association.—MS. from his son, W. H. Alexander, Esq.

that there was a field of usefulness open at the West, which it was desirable that he should occupy. The date of his dismission was the 7th of December, 1802. On his return to the State of New York, he divided his ministerial labours among the three Churches of Salisbury, Norway, and Fairfield, giving one third of the Sabbaths in the year to each Church. He was also instrumental in founding the Academy at Fairfield, and became its first Principal; and it enjoyed, under his direction, a large share of public favour. In 1807, he relinquished his charge of the Church in Norway, from their inability to fulfil their pecuniary engagements. He subsequently discontinued his labours at Salisbury; and in the summer of 1811, resigned his charge at Fairfield also, on account of the insufficiency of his salary. The officers of the Fairfield Church gave him, on his leaving them, the strongest testimony of their confidence and regard.

It was not merely as Pastor of the Church, but as Principal of the Academy, at Fairfield, that Mr. Alexander received but a stinted compensation for his services; and, accordingly, in January, 1812, he tendered his resignation as Principal, expressing, at the same time, his conviction that it was impossible to build up an institution at Fairfield of so liberal a type as he had projected and wished for. He now became interested in establishing a College, where the prospects seemed more encouraging; and, accordingly, he united with several other gentlemen to advance Hamilton Academy at Clinton to the dignity of a College. The effort proved successful; and, on the 22d of July, 1812, he was unanimously elected President of the new institution. He, however, did not accept the place; and, in the autumn of the same year, he removed his family to Onondaga Hollow, where he had been earnestly solicited to come and co-operate with several others in the establishment of an Academy. The Academy went into operation, and, for the first four years, he was its Principal. He then resigned the place, and retired to a farm in the neighbourhood; but he now became interested in the founding of the Theological Seminary at Auburn, and engaged in this enterprise also with great zeal and energy. In September, 1820, he was appointed General Agent to solicit donations for the endowment of Professorships in the institution; and he discharged the arduous trust with a good degree of success.

In 1822, the Connecticut Missionary Society appointed him missionary to the destitute churches within the bounds of the Onondaga Presbytery; and in this way he was occupied about nine months. During the last five years of his life, much of his time was devoted to writing for religious newspapers, and to efforts in other ways for the advancement of the cause of education and Christianity. He continued to preach, as his services were called for, till almost the close of his life.

His last illness was very short, or rather he may be said to have declined without any perceptible illness. He died at Onondaga, on the 12th of April, 1828, in the seventy-third year of his age. His Funeral Sermon was preached by the Rev. Washington Thacher.*

*Washington Thacher, a son of Deacon Moses Thacher, was born at Attleborough, Mass., February 23, 1794, but removed early with his father's family to Nine Partners (now Harford) Pa.; received his classical education under the Rev. Lyman Richardson; studied Theology under the Rev. John Truair; was licensed to preach by the Otsego Presbytery in 1821; was ordained in 1822; officiated as stated supply at Morrisville, N.Y., from 1822 to 1826; was Pastor of the Church in Jordan, N. Y., from 1826 to 1842; resigned his charge on account of ill health; was afterwards a stated supply at Eaton, N. Y., three years; was appointed Secretary and Agent of the Central Agency of the American Home Missionary Society in July, 1847; and died June 29, 1850. He was an eminently devout man, and an earnest and effective preacher.

Mr. Alexander was married in 1780, to Lucina, daughter of the Rev. Thomas Strong,* his predecessor at New Marlborough. She died in Onondaga, November 24, 1847, aged ninety-one. They had nine children. One of the daughters was married to the Rev. Dr. Lansing,† then of Auburn. One son, *William H.*, (the only one who arrived at maturity,) still (1857) survives, and resides at Syracuse.

The following are Mr. Alexander's publications:—An Essay on the real Deity of Jesus Christ, 1791. A Dissertation on the Psalms, showing them to be a pre-history of Jesus Christ, 1796. A Sermon preached at Mendon on the death of George Washington, 1800. English Grammar abridged, 1793. Grammatical System of the Latin language, 1795. A New Introduction to the Latin language, 1795. A Grammatical system of the Grecian language, 1796. A Spelling Book on an improved plan, 1799. The Columbian Dictionary, 1800. A new and complete System of Arithmetic, 1802. A Grammatical System of the English language, 1814. Virgil's works translated into literal prose. The Young lady's and Gentleman's Instructer.

FROM THE HON. OLIVER R. STRONG.

SYRACUSE, July 21, 1855.

Dear Sir: The early part of my life was passed at Pittsfield, Mass., a few miles from New Marlborough, where the Rev. Caleb Alexander, for some years, exercised his ministry; and this, in connection with the fact that Mrs. Alexander was remotely connected with my father, rendered his name and reputation familiar to me from my youth. It was not, however, until about the year 1810, when I came to reside in this State, (New York,) that I became personally acquainted with him. Our acquaintance commenced at the time when he first came to Onondaga,

* THOMAS STRONG was a native of Northampton, Mass., was graduated at Yale College in 1740; was ordained first Pastor of the Church in New Marlborough, October 31, 1744; and died August 23, 1777.

† DIRCK CORNELIUS LANSING was born at Lansingburg, N. Y., March 3, 1785, and was graduated at Yale College in 1804. He became hopefully pious during a revival in College and joined the College Church. He studied Theology under the Rev. Dr. Blatchford of Lansingburg, and was licensed to preach by the Presbytery of Columbia, on the 6th of January, 1806. In the autumn of the same year, he gathered a church, where now stands the flourishing town of Onondaga, and had the pastoral charge of it for eight years. He then, on account of the failure of his health, retired awhile upon a farm, but continued to preach, as he had opportunity, on the Sabbath, and soon became the acting Pastor of the Church in Stillwater, N. Y., where he remained two years and a half. In the summer of 1816, he supplied, for some time, the Park Street Church in Boston; and soon after accepted a call from the First Presbyterian Church in Auburn, N. Y. Here he acquired great popularity, and was instrumental of bringing upwards of one thousand persons into the church in twelve years. During a part of the time also he filled the chair of Sacred Rhetoric in the Theological Seminary. In July, 1829, he took charge of the Second Presbyterian Church in Utica, where he continued to labour with great zeal, and was, as he had previously been, an earnest friend to what were commonly called "protracted meetings" and other kindred instrumentalities for promoting revivals. On the 10th of February, 1833, he was installed Pastor of a Free Church in New York, then worshipping in Masonic Hall, and retained this charge until the spring of 1835, when ill health again obliged him to suspend his public labours. For the next ten years, he was not confined to any one place, but laboured in many pulpits in Central and Western New York, as an evangelist or stated supply, and spent one year in Illinois, where he was instrumental in organizing a church, and building a place of worship. In 1846, he returned to the city of New York, and took charge of a feeble Missionary Church in Chrystie Street. In the spring of 1848, he engaged in the enterprise of building up the Clinton Avenue Church, which had been organized in November of the preceding year. He was its first Pastor; but on account of his enfeebled health, the relation was dissolved on the 19th of December, 1855, and in the spring of 1856, he removed to Walnut Hills, near Cincinnati, O., where he died on the 19th of March, 1857, aged seventy-two. He published a volume of Sermons (octavo) in 1825; and received the degree of Doctor of Divinity from Williams College in 1826. An eloquent Sermon was delivered on the occasion of his death by the Rev. Dr. Thompson of the Broadway Tabernacle, which represents his character as combining many noble qualities, and his life as one of great activity and usefulness.

to take measures for establishing an Academy, over which he subsequently presided for some years; and being myself one of the Trustees of the institution, we were frequently brought together in relations of both business and friendship. I often heard him preach, and saw him in private under a great variety of circumstances; and, in his last illness, he appointed me one of the executors of his will.

In form, Mr. Alexander was thick set, and about five feet, nine or ten inches in height. He was slightly lame, and walked in a manner that would indicate that one leg was shorter than the other. His face was full, broad, of rather a florid complexion, and expressive of reflection and intelligence. His manners evinced a benevolent spirit, and yet he was distinguished for strength of purpose. I well remember that his tenacity and perseverance used to be indicated by his being called, "the old Scotchman,"—with reference to his Scotch descent. Though I cannot say that he was reserved in conversation, yet neither was he particularly communicative, except on some special occasions; and then he would make himself highly interesting. He was exceedingly amiable and exemplary in his private relations, and was pre-eminently a loved and loving husband and father.

I think Mr. Alexander never ranked among the more popular preachers of his day. His discourses were, I believe, always sensible and edifying; his voice was sufficiently full and clear, but not remarkable for smoothness; he had little or no gesture, and not much animation. Whenever I heard him preach, I think he read his discourses, though I believe it was very common for him to preach from short notes. The excellence of his preaching doubtless lay rather in the matter than in the manner.

I will only add that Mr. Alexander sustained a very high character as a teacher, and I believe pretty uniformly secured the confidence and affection of his pupils, as well as the approbation of their parents.

I regret that it is not in my power to give you a more extended description of the subject of your inquiry; but if what I have written shall be at all available to your purpose, I shall be highly gratified.

I am, my dear Sir, with great respect,

Your friend and servant,

OLIVER R. STRONG.

STEPHEN BLOOMER BALCH, D. D.*

1779—1833.

STEPHEN BLOOMER BALCH was a descendant of John Balch, who emigrated to New England, at an early period, from Bridgewater in Somerset, England, and became possessed of large property and extensive influence. A great grandson of his removed to Deer Creek in Harford County, Md.; and there the subject of this sketch was born on the 5th of April, 1747. He was the second son of James† and Anne (Goodwyn) Balch; both of whom were exemplary members of the Presbyterian Church. His father was a man of a highly gifted and cultivated mind, had a fine poetical talent, and was the author of some anonymous pieces that had no small celebrity in their

* Religious Telegraph, (Richmond, Va.,) 1833.—MS. from his son, Rev. T. B. Balch.

† According to another authority, James Balch emigrated directly from England to Maryland.

day. The youthful days of the son were spent, for the most part, under the ministry of the Rev. Mr. Strain, who was distinguished for his eloquence, and, who, but for his warm attachment to his people, would have been removed to a more conspicuous sphere of labour.

While he was yet a youth, his father removed with his family from Maryland, and settled in Mecklenburg County, N. C. Here he was employed for several years in assisting his father to cultivate his farm, but his heart was set upon going to College, and ultimately becoming a minister of the Gospel. For the accomplishment of this object, he alternately taught a school and pursued his own studies; and indeed he was a student at the same time that he was a teacher. When he was about twenty-five years of age, he was fitted for an advanced standing in College, and had, by his industry and economy, acquired the necessary means for defraying the expenses of his collegiate course.

In the autumn of 1772, he became a member of the Junior class in the College of New Jersey. Here he contracted an intimate friendship with his classmate, James Hall, afterwards the Rev. Dr. Hall, of North Carolina, who was for many years a prominent clergyman in the Presbyterian Church. He was admitted to the degree of Bachelor of Arts in 1774. The Hopkinsian controversy was, at that early period, not unknown, even at Princeton; but Mr. Balch seems to have had little sympathy with his brethren of that school. During one of his college vacations, he boarded at some farm-house in the neighbourhood with a Hopkinsian brother, who did his utmost to induce him to adopt Dr. Hopkins' peculiar view of disinterested benevolence. Finding him less docile than he could have wished, he made his case a subject of special prayer at the family worship, and continued the prayer in his behalf to a very unusual length. When they rose from their knees, Mr. Balch, not being greatly pleased with this kind of effort to convert him, turned to his fellow-student and said,—"If you wish to pray me into disinterested benevolence, go to your closet." This anecdote is related upon the authority of the late Rev. Dr. Samuel Stanhope Smith, who was a resident of Princeton at the time.

A short time before Mr. Balch graduated, President Witherspoon was applied to by the Trustees of the Lower Marlborough Academy, in Calvert County, Md., to recommend a suitable person for Principal of that institution. Dr. Witherspoon immediately offered the place to Mr. Balch, and advised him to accept it; giving him at the same time many important hints in respect to his conduct in subsequent life. Mr. Balch, having the utmost confidence in the judgment of his venerable friend and President, determined at once to accept the place. Accordingly, after making some little preparation, he set off upon his journey; but, on reaching Philadelphia, he found himself short of funds, and knew no person in the city to whom he could apply for aid. He resolved, however, to call for what he needed at the hotel, and, as a last resort, to exhibit his testimonials as evidence that he was worthy to be trusted. The next morning, he walked to the market house,—not in the best spirits, and, as he was passing through the crowd, he noticed a person apparently scrutinizing his countenance very closely, though he said nothing. At length, when he had set out to return to his lodgings, and had proceeded some distance, he heard a voice calling to him with some earnestness; and, on looking around, he saw that it was the same person who had just before been so intently gazing at him. He represented himself as an itinerant merchant, and stated that he knew him by his resemblance to his friends in North Carolina, from whom he had lately received great kindness during a severe illness ; and he then added,—"Perhaps I can now pay back the kindness of your friends." This unexpected overture led Mr. Balch to disclose to him his actual need, and the stranger lent him all the money that was necessary for his relief. Mr. Balch often related this circumstance with great satisfaction.

After reaching Calvert County, he entered at once upon his duties as teacher, and succeeded in gaining, in an uncommon degree, the confidence and affection of his pupils. The events of the Revolution were beginning now to excite great interest throughout the country; and the Preceptors of Academies were required to keep their pupils in a kind of military training, ready to exchange their books for muskets at a moment's warning. This state of things rendered Mr. Balch's office as a teacher far more difficult and responsible than it would otherwise have been ; and, on one or two occasions, the older members of his school were actually put in requisition for military service.

During his residence in Calvert County, he made the acquaintance of Bishop Claggett, from whom he received many kind attentions, and with whom he was ever after in very friendly relations, till the close of the Bishop's life.

He continued teaching for about four years, and received the greater part of his salary in Continental money—"rather a bright remuneration"—to use the language of his son, "for fighting with mosquitoes, and for being conquered quite frequently by the Tertian ague."

He then went to Pennsylvania, and was licensed to preach the Gospel, by the Presbytery of Donegal, on the 17th of June, 1779. Hearing, about this time, of the death of his father, he returned to the South, and spent some months in travelling as a sort of missionary in the Carolinas. On his way thither, he spent a Sabbath in Georgetown, and preached in the hamlet which had been founded in September, 1751, by George Beall, whose granddaughter he subsequently married. The people invited him to remain, promising to build him a church, but he declined at that time, though he gave some encouragement of returning to them after performing his projected tour at the South.

While Mr. Balch was itinerating in North Carolina, he was subjected to many privations and hardships. On one occasion, night overtook him when he was in a strange neighbourhood ; but he discovered a dwelling not far from the road, which he supposed, from its appearance, must be the residence of some wealthy man. He made his way to it, and was very hospitably received by the lady of the house, though her husband was not at home. Being greatly fatigued, he retired early, and soon fell asleep ; but it was not long before the gentleman of the house, who was no less a personage than General Williams of North Carolina, returned unexpectedly, entered his chamber, and intimated to him, in no equivocal terms, that he should allow no one who was not a Whig to sleep under his roof. "Let me rest in peace then," said his guest, "for I was educated under Dr. Witherspoon,—one of the Signers of the Declaration of Independence." The next day, the General entertained Mr. Balch with a poem which he had composed on the Stamp Act; and, on the following Sabbath, as the enemies of the Revolution laid great stress on the apostolic injunction to be subject to the higher powers, he earnestly requested his clerical guest to discourse upon that passage. He did so, much to the annoyance of the Royalists who were present, while the General, with several pistols in his belt, acted as Clerk.

Mr. Balch was invited to settle over a congregation in North Carolina; but he had made up his mind to return to Georgetown, with a view to establish there a Presbyterian Church. Accordingly, he went thither in March, 1780, and found as unpromising a field of labour as can easily be imagined. He preached for some time in a room rented for the purpose; and, in 1782, a few individuals interested in sustaining Divine institutions, joined in building a very plain house for public worship. There were seven persons, including the Pastor, who joined in the first celebration of the Lord's Supper. Shortly after this, he was instrumental of establishing a Presbyterian Congregation in Fredericktown, Md.

The return of Peace, at the close of the Revolution, contributed not a little to the growth of the village in which Mr. Balch was settled. His church gradually increased, and many Episcopalians who resided in the neighbourhood joined in their worship. Still he found his salary quite inadequate to the support of his family; and, in order to meet his current expenses, he was obliged to resort to some other business; and he chose that of instructing youth. Accordingly, he was in the habit, for many years, of conducting the education of young men; and among his pupils were not a few who have since attained to great usefulness and prominence.

After the removal of the seat of government to Washington City, the Episcopalians, who had been accustomed to worship in the Presbyterian Church, established a church of their own; and thus the number who contributed to Mr. Balch's support was temporarily somewhat diminished. The loss was, however, quickly much more than made up by fresh accessions from various quarters; insomuch that it became desirable that the place of worship should be enlarged. Into this project Mr. Balch entered with great resolution and vigour; and it was chiefly, if not entirely, by contributions obtained through his persevering efforts, that the enlargement was effected. Mr. Jefferson, who was then President of the United States, contributed in aid of his object seventy-five dollars. He applied to Albert Gallatin, Secretary of the Treasury, but he declined giving, on the ground of the excessive frequency of similar applications. Mr. Balch immediately dropped the matter, and began to converse on general subjects; and among other questions which he asked was one in regard to the success of Napoleon, in subverting the Genevese Republic. Mr. Gallatin said emphatically that his country was gone. "I am sorry to hear it," rejoined Mr. Balch, "for the city of Geneva has produced more illustrious men in Church and State than any other spot on the globe." He then rose and bade the Secretary good morning; but, before he had proceeded far, was called back to receive from Mr. Gallatin a handsome donation.

From this time Mr. Balch's congregation gradually increased until 1821, when the old church edifice was taken down, and a more commodious and more elegant house erected in its place. The night before the dismantling of the old building, Mr. Balch preached a sermon to an immense assemblage, in which he discoursed somewhat at large upon the history of the congregation. It was an occasion of deep interest to him; and while he rejoiced in it as marking a favourable epoch in the history of his congregation, it could not but awaken in his mind many sad and tender recollections.

In the year 1818, Mr. Balch was honoured with the degree of Doctor of Divinity from the College at which he was educated.

In the year 1831, Dr. Balch experienced a great calamity in the burning of his house. Some time before day, the watchman, in going his accustomed round, observed a light in one of the front rooms, but did not at first suppose that it was any thing out of the common course. When he came near the house again, he observed that it was wrapped in flames. The fire gained on the building so rapidly that, in a few moments, every way of escape was cut off, except by a slippery shelving roof which was under the window of his chamber. Several fruitless attempts were made to pass the stairway; but, as he opened the door that led to it, he saw nothing but a cloud of smoke mingled with sparks of fire. In this extremity, Dr. Balch, with great self-possession, resolved to lead the way on the roof. When the aged couple were discovered in these awfully perilous circumstances, a feeling of horror ran through the assembled multitude; but when it was perceived that their escape was effected, it gave way to a shout of generous exultation. He escaped with only the garments in which he slept; his apparel, furniture, library, manuscripts,—every thing which his house contained, was burnt to ashes. The loss was one which he ill knew how to sustain; but a circumstance occurred shortly after, by means of which he was saved from the embarrassment to which he might otherwise have been subjected. One of his early pupils suggested to him the idea that he was entitled to a pension, under the then recent law of Congress, providing for Revolutionary claims. An application was accordingly made, his claim was granted, and before his decease he drew the sum of twelve hundred dollars.

Dr. Balch, after he had passed the age of fourscore, retained so much vigour as to be able to preach occasionally without inconvenience. A few Sabbaths before his death, he had preached three times in Alexandria, besides attending a funeral. On the Sabbath immediately preceding his death, on returning from public worship, he showed manifest signs of indisposition, and found himself unable to walk home. He revived, however, and, during the week, evinced his accustomed cheerfulness. The next Sabbath morning, (September 7, 1833,) after having rested well during the night, he awoke and took some refreshment; but was immediately seized with a spasm of the heart, which caused almost instantaneous death. The tidings of his departure produced a great sensation in the whole community. The Aldermen and Common Council of the town passed a unanimous resolution to attend his funeral. The town Gazette was clothed in mourning; while funeral badges were displayed not only in the church, but upon the market house, and upon all the stores in the streets through which the immense procession passed. A Funeral Discourse was delivered on the following Sabbath, by the surviving Pastor of the Church; and there was subsequently another before the Presbytery of which he was a member, by the Rev. Elias Harrison of Alexandria. His ministry in Georgetown extended through a period of fifty-three years.

In 1782, Dr. Balch was married to Elizabeth, daughter of Colonel George Beall, of Georgetown,—a young lady of great beauty and rare accomplishments. She died in her sixty-second year. He was subsequently married to a Mrs. King, who lived but about twenty days after she became his wife. He was married a third time to a Mrs. Parrot. He had nine children,—four sons and five daughters,—all by the first marriage. One of his sons was a judge in Florida, two were lawyers, and one, the Rev. Thomas B. Balch, is a Presbyterian clergyman, well known as the author of "Christianity and Literature," "Ringwood Discourses," and various other works. His eldest daughter is the widow of the late General Macomb of the United States Army.

FROM THE REV. ELIAS HARRISON, D. D.

ALEXANDRIA, May 7, 1857.

Rev. and dear Sir: It gives me pleasure to comply with your request for my reminiscences of the Rev. Dr. Balch, late of Georgetown, partly because the very intimate relations in which we were placed towards each other, during the last seventeen years of his life, gave me the best opportunities of knowing him, and therefore enable me to speak of him with great confidence, and partly because my estimate of his character is such that I am glad to co-operate in any effort to embalm his memory.

The first time I ever saw him was in 1813, when I was a student at Princeton College, in company with his son Thomas. He came there on a visit,—the first he had ever paid to the institution, since he was graduated; and, as was to be expected, it was an occasion to him of much pleasurable excitement. He remained there for several days,—being frequently present both in the common dining hall, and in the recitation room; and moving about freely, as he did, among the students,—with some of whom he was acquainted, he became exceedingly popular. Their attention was particularly drawn to him by the *sly humour* which came out both in his language and in his countenance; while the anecdotes in which he abounded, concerning the scenes and incidents of bygone days, called forth peals of laughter, which were heard from one end of the College grounds to the other. In these explosions he himself always joined most heartily; and it was said that Dr. Green, who was then President of the College, and who was more than commonly tenacious in regard to ministerial propriety and dignity, took him to task in respect to the freedom of his demeanor, intimating that such loud "horse laughs," as he termed them, would lessen his influence and injure his reputation. To this Dr. Balch replied,—for he afterwards told me the story,—that for his own part, he always did love a good "horse laugh;" and that if he (Dr. Green) had indulged himself in that way a little more frequently, he never would have supposed that his own nose was the nozzle of a tea-pot, or that his head was made of glass—alluding to certain imaginings predicated of Dr. G., (whether true or false I know not) at a time when he was suffering under the influence of great nervous depression. In the end, however, our venerable President became so much interested in the Doctor and his irrepressible humour, that he not only relaxed somewhat from his accustomed dignity, but actually, in some degree, caught the contagion, and heartily shared in the laugh which at first he seemed to deprecate. Before Dr. Balch took his departure for home, he expressed to the occupants of a certain room an earnest wish to be permitted to sleep there one night, as it was the room which he had occupied during his whole college life, and it was not likely that he should ever be there again. His request was very cheerfully complied with; and this, with other pleasant circumstances, served to leave a most agreeable impression on the minds of the students, and to render his visit among them a delightful episode in the tedious monotony of college life.

After this I never saw him until I came to this city in the close of the year 1816. It was, I think, the last week in December of that year, when, in accordance with a long established rule for mutual convenience and prôfit, it was his turn to aid my venerable colleague, Dr. Muir, in the solemnities of the Lord's Supper. I then heard him preach for the first time; and though the discourse could not be called an eloquent one, there was still a *something*, both in matter and manner, that rivetted my attention so closely, as to leave an impression which the lapse of more than forty years has done little to efface. In person, he stood before us, large, tall, and rather commanding. His countenance, though solemn, seemed after all to have in it a tinge of dry humour. His language, though chaste and well adapted to his subject, was the suggestion of the moment,—for he never wrote his discourses. His method was lucid and natural, and yet peculiarly his own. And his manner was characterized by fervour, unction, and I would say, originality withal. The impression which he left upon me, was somewhat strange indeed, but it was on the whole highly favourable both to his intellect and his heart—an impression, I may add, which none of his subsequent exhibitions ever served to remove or impair. He was a great friend to loud as well as animated speaking in the pulpit; and in this, my first, interview with him, he counselled me most earnestly never to lose sight of that important requisite in a preacher;—adding, in his usual quizzical manner, that young ministers were little aware of its importance, for it was often accepted by the people as a substitute for good sense and sound argument.

Dr. Balch was also greatly in favour of preaching without a manuscript, and especially without writing at all; and he seemed, at that first interview, to take quite a fancy to me, because I had avowed my determination never to take even short notes into the pulpit, and so far as practicable, to avoid the common practice of always writing fully for the Sabbath. He told me, if I remember right, that he scarcely ever wrote a whole sermon, and had never written the half of one during his whole pastorate; and he certainly gave a somewhat remarkable reason for it. It was this:—When on his way from the Carolinas to the place of his final settlement,—Georgetown, he was invited to preach at a certain church in Virginia, at which there were several ministers of the Baptist denomination, and a very large gathering of people. The services had been opened by a discourse which, though delivered with great vehemence and boldness of manner, seemed to him very crude, disjointed and illogical. [The Baptist clergy were not then what they have become since—they were doubtless pious and devoted men, but few of them had anything beyond a common education.] Inasmuch as he had taken his diploma at College, and withal had several well prepared discourses with him, which he had carefully committed to memory, he indulged the rather self-complacent reflection that, as he was to follow the illiterate preacher, he should, to say the least, not suffer in a comparison with him. He acknowledged that the evil principle within him so far gained a momentary control, that he was expecting to hear his sermon spoken of in no measured terms of approbation; but, instead of that, as he was walking behind a large number of people, after the sermon had been delivered, he heard them speak of it as absolutely so poor a thing as not to be worth the time they had spent in listening to it; while his illiterate predecessor was extolled to the skies. "From that time," said the Doctor, "I firmly resolved never again to attempt either to preach a great sermon, or to write out another sermon for the pulpit"—a resolve to which I believe he adhered, without a single exception, till his dying day.

It would be a mistake, however, to suppose that he did not *study* his sermons. He did not study them in the ordinary way; and yet the orderly method and compact arrangement by which they were marked, showed that they were the product of no inconsiderable thought. He generally formed a brief outline of his discourse in the early part of the week, and then occupied himself leisurely in filling it up before the Sabbath. These skeletons were written in very small paper books, made for the purpose, each of which would perhaps hold a hundred or more; but they were never taken with him into the pulpit. I have seen many of them, and have remarked their apparent neatness and freedom from both erasures and blots; but was never able to decipher a solitary line, except by a vigorous effort of the imagination; for his handwriting was scarcely more legible to me than Arabic. His preaching was most frequently doctrinal, and was characterized by great fearlessness and energy. He evidently cared little for the praise of man, and I have sometimes thought, still less for his censure. I am inclined to think that the general character of his pulpit performances was such as to justify the remark said to have been made by a respectable and excellent old lady, that "it was always very good living."

In his dispositions he was kind, amiable and eminently social. I never saw him out of temper but once, and then but for a short time; while, during a long course of years in which I was familiar with him, and met him in almost every variety of circumstances, he was pre-eminently good natured, cheerful and buoyant. His exuberance of good humour continued with him till the close of life; and some of his friends of nervous temperament found it an excellent antidote to depression of spirits. He was, in relating humorous anecdotes, absolutely irresistible—neither the dignity of Dr. Green, nor the sobriety and quietness of my revered colleague, Dr. Muir, was proof against it. I must confess there was no man whom I welcomed more heartily than Dr. Balch, when I found the *blues* were gathering upon me; for though I was constrained to think, with the venerable President of Nassau-Hall, that his laughing explosions were perhaps too frequent and sometimes too violent, yet he actually did more for me in certain moods than any physician could do; and then there was such an air of naturalness about it, that you seemed to feel that, with such a constitution as he had, it could hardly be otherwise.

He was very urgent with young ministers to get married, if possible, as soon as they were settled. And as he was often appointed to charge the newly installed pastor, he not unfrequently hinted at what he regarded a duty on this subject, in that solemn exercise. He did so at my installation; and though, on the whole, the charge was very judicious, and unusually solemn, he could not resist the impulse to say,—and with an archness of tone and manner that was marked by the whole congregation, and created a universal smile,—that it would be well for me to remember that "a Bishop" must not only be "blameless," but "the husband of one wife." He saw me married not many months afterwards, and offered me his congratulations on the occasion, with a heartiness that could not have been greater, if he had supposed that I had got married merely out of respect to the advice he had given me at my installation.

Dr. Balch's pastoral relation seems to have been a happy one. His charge gradually increased from a mere handful of people to one of the largest congregations of our denomination in this whole region. His people respected and loved him; and those of them who still survive, never speak of him but with a feeling of profound veneration. He was always welcome in their families; and his open and cheerful manner, and freedom from all stateliness and reserve, made him a great favourite, especially with the young. I believe it is uncommon that a minister, during so long a period, retains in so high a degree the affection of his people.

A few years before his death, he was affected with a sudden paralytic stroke, while in the midst of his discourse on the Lord's day. It came without a moment's premonition, rendering him both stiff and speechless, but neither depriving him of consciousness, nor changing his bodily position. Taken home, he was soon restored to speech, and in a few weeks, by proper medical treatment, to about his accustomed health. While he was confined to his bed, I called to see him; and finding him at the moment alone, he seemed unusually gratified, and hardly able to express his feelings of joy that an opportunity was once more given him of speaking without restraint. "For," said he, "neither my family nor my physician, though transcendently kind, and earnestly seeking my recovery, have rightly understood my case; they have interdicted all company, and laid an embargo on my tongue ever since it has been restored to use: and I know very well that these two things, if persisted in, instead of curing me, will hasten me out of the world. I must see my friends, and I must talk, or I must die." And he did talk rapidly, though he saw my alarm at the announcement of the prohibition, and though Mrs. Balch, rushing in at the sound of his voice, urged every consideration she could to prevent it. Strange to say, he recovered rapidly from that hour; and often did he remind me afterwards of that accidental, or rather providential, circumstance of my finding him alone; "for I verily believe," said he, "it was the means, under God, of continuing my life a little longer."

This attack is supposed to have resulted immediately from his discontinuing the use of tobacco; to which he had been immoderately given for more than sixty-five years. In all other kinds of personal indulgence he was very sparing; and had never tasted ardent spirits, to the amount of a spoonful, from the age of twelve years. His physician had warned him of the probable issue of a sudden breaking up of this habit, and advised him, by all means, if he were to attempt it at all, to let it be a gradual process; but, being rather obstinately set in his resolves, when once made, he persisted, until he had well nigh experienced the worst. He then resumed the practice for three or four years, and during the whole period enjoyed uninterrupted health; when, relinquishing it again, he was again visited in the pulpit of a neighbouring brother with an attack similar to the other, though not so severe or protracted. He then returned to it once more, and continued it in moderation till his death.

One of the last Sabbaths of his life Dr. Balch spent with me, and assisted me in the administration of the Lord's Supper; and he was apparently in as good health, both of body and of mind, as at any time when I had seen him for a number of years. He preached for me that day twice, and preached also at the Protestant Methodist Church in the evening, in addition to the services rendered at the Lord's table. It was generally remarked that his sermons were not only longer, but far more solemn and impressive than usual; but he suffered no inconvenience from the labours of the day. He left me apparently in fine health and in excellent spirits, and I heard no more from him until the astounding news came that he was dead; and that was quickly followed by an urgent request that I should come and take part in the funeral solemnities. I did go and meet the sad demand that was made upon me,—sharing the service (so far as the addresses were concerned) with the Rev. Mr. Brooks of the Episcopal Church, with whom Dr. Balch had been in the most cordial relations. I was subsequently called upon by the Presbytery to preach his Funeral Sermon, which I did at its sessions in the First Church in Washington City, and in the presence of an immense audience, which had been attracted to the service from a desire to do honour to the memory of that venerable man.

I have already intimated that Dr. Balch was tall and well proportioned in his physical structure. His countenance was a fair index to his character. His eyes were rather small, though keen; his face perhaps a little too long for beauty, and his neck too short for the head that was above it. His gait was always slow and cautious, and his movements indicated either that he was very absent in mind, or that his faculties were intensely concentrated on some particular subject. His dress was never of the most fashionable kind; nor was he always so particular in respect to it as to escape the imputation of being a little slovenly; yet, on the whole, his personal appearance was very respectable, and in society he was not lacking in due attention to the rules of politeness. He was an early riser, and would often take a long stroll, before any of his family or neighbours were up; and in all ordinary circumstances, ten o'clock at night would find him either in bed, or in his room preparing for it. It was doubtless to the regularity of his habits, the cheerfulness of his spirits, and the utter absence of every thing like agitating or corroding passion, quite as much as to his native vigour of constitution, that was to be attributed not only his exemption from the ordinary maladies which prevail among men, but a state of scarcely interrupted usefulness or enjoyment to the close of an unusually long life.

Notwithstanding Dr. Balch's passion for the humorous and the ludicrous, he thought much and felt much on the subject of personal religion, and to his particular friends, he spoke of it with both freedom and feeling. I never heard him express a doubt of his personal interest in the merits of his Redeemer; and towards the close of life he seemed to dwell upon the prospects of the opening future with a greatly increased interest and solemnity. But the nature and permanency of his religious principles were most effectually tested by the purity of his life, the stern fidelity with which he rebuked the various forms of evil, and his readiness to make personal sacrifices for the cause of Christ. In view of all that I knew of him, I cannot doubt that when he was dismissed from his labours on earth, he went to receive the plaudit, "Well done, good and faithful servant."

Yours very truly,

ELIAS HARRISON.

Dr. Balch had an elder brother, HEZEKIAH JAMES BALCH, who had a somewhat brilliant, though brief, career. He was born at Deer Creek, then the residence of his father, in 1746; was graduated at the College of New Jersey in 1766; was licensed to preach the Gospel by the Donegal Presbytery in 1767; and was ordained by the same Presbytery previous to the meeting of the Synod in 1770. In 1769, he went on a mission to the Southern States, and shortly after became Pastor of the two Congregations,—Rocky River and Poplar Tent, which he continued to serve till the close of life. In the famous Mecklenburg Convention, (May 19, 1775,) he was present, and had an important agency in framing the well known "Declaration" which that patriotic body put forth. He died, unmarried, in the summer of the same year. He is said to have been a man of fine personal appearance, and an accomplished scholar, and to have disappointed, by his early death, many hopes of extensive usefulness in the Church.

There was yet another brother, JAMES BALCH, who became a clergyman, and lived and died in Kentucky, where he seems to have taken an active part against the movements of the Cumberland Presbyterians.

FRANCIS CUMMINS. D. D.*

1780—1832.

Francis Cummins was the son of Charles and Rebecca (McNickle) Cummins, and was born near Shippensburg, Pa., in the spring of 1752. His father and mother were both from Ireland—the former from the County of Tyrone, the latter from the County of Antrim: they were strangers to each other in Ireland; but, migrating to this country while they were young, they met and were married after their arrival here. They were members of the Presbyterian Church, and belonged to what was then called the "New Side;" being great admirers of Whitefield, the Tennents, and others of that school. His father was originally a cooper; but, by persevering industry, he became, at no distant period, an independent landholder and farmer.

The son spent his early years upon his father's farm; though he had the advantages of education common at that day, and in that part of the country. When he was in his nineteenth year, his father removed to Mecklenburg County, N. C., where the neighbouring College, then called "Queen's Museum," afforded him opportunity for a higher education. He was a pupil in that institution, both before and during the Revolutionary war, and a part of the time enjoyed the instruction of the Rev. Dr. McWhorter, who had then recently removed thither from New Jersey. Here he was graduated about the year 1776.

After leaving College, he was, for several years, engaged chiefly in the business of teaching. He was first employed as Preceptor of Clio Academy, then a respectable German Seminary, in Rowan County, now Iredell. He afterwards taught, successively at Bethel Church, York District, S. C.; at Smyrna Church, Wilkes County; at Lexington, Oglethorpe County; at Bethany Church, Greene County; and at Madison, Morgan County,—Ga. Many of the most distinguished men of South Carolina and Georgia were his pupils; and among them the late William Smith, an eminent Judge and United States Senator from South Carolina, and the late Andrew Jackson, President of the United States.

He was an active and zealous patriot in the war that gave us our independence. He was at different times in the army, and was engaged in several battles. He was present at all the Mecklenburg Whig meetings of 1775, and mingled in the exciting scene of the reading of the celebrated Declaration at Mecklenburg Court House. The interest which he thus early took in the welfare of his country, continued unabated to the close of life. When the controversy on the subject of "nullification" arose in South Carolina, though he had then numbered his fourscore years, the fire of his youth seemed to be re-kindled in favour of the Union; and to a brother clergyman who, in a moment of excitement, declared his readiness to draw his sword against the General Government, he replied, "If you dare do so, I will draw my sword again, and cut you down."

While Mr. Cummins was engaged in teaching, he was prosecuting his theological studies, under the direction of the Rev. (afterwards Dr.) James

* MS. from his grandson, Colonel William McKinley.—Foote's Sketches of N. C.

Hall. He was licensed to preach by the Presbytery of Orange, at Rocky River Church, in Mecklenburg County, December 15, 1780. During the year 1781, he preached at Hopewell, and various other places; and in the spring of 1782, accepted a call from Bethel Church in the adjacent district of York, S. C., where he was ordained towards the close of that year. In the spring of 1788, while residing at Bethel, both as the pastor of a church and the teacher of youth, he was elected by the people of York as a member of the South Carolina Convention, called to decide upon the Constitution of the United States; and though all his colleagues were for rejecting it, he voted in its favour.

He was never long stationary in any one field of labour, or rather his labours were never confined to a single congregation. There were about twenty congregations, which considered him as, in some sense, their pastor, during the whole period of his ministry. He laboured about one year in North Carolina, twenty-four years in South Carolina, and twenty-five years in Georgia. His time was almost always laboriously divided between teaching and preaching; and the churches in that region were, at that time, so generally missionary stations, that the ministers were obliged to resort to teaching in order to sustain themselves and their families. This necessity, however, was mercifully overruled, in the providence of God, to the education of many a man under religious influences, who, otherwise might have remained uneducated, or who might have been trained by an enemy of religion.

The degree of Doctor of Divinity was conferred upon him by the University of Georgia, at Athens, in the year 1820.

Dr. Cummins had great vigour of constitution, and, with the exception of occasional fevers, to which the country was subject, he scarcely ever suffered from ill health. In 1830, he stated to his grandson that the sun had never caught him in bed, when he was not confined by illness, for fifty years. In January, 1832, he was attacked by the influenza, which, on the 22d of February,—just about a month from the commencement of the disease,—terminated his life. His last sermon was preached on the 15th of January,—three days before he became seriously ill, on Romans viii. 16, 17, "If children, then heirs, &c." This passage ministered greatly to his comfort, as he was getting ready to put off his earthly house of this tabernacle. He expressed the utmost gratitude that he had been permitted to preach the Gospel, and the most joyful confidence that he was about to enter into rest. A Sermon with reference to his death was preached in April following, before the Hopewell Presbytery, by the Rev. Dr. John Brown. He lies buried beneath the oaks around the Male Academy in Greensboro', Greene County, Ga.

On the 26th of March, 1778, he was married to Sarah, daughter of David and Elizabeth Davis, who had emigrated from Wales, and were at that time members of the Presbyterian Church of Steele Creek. She was born in a place called *the Coves*, in Cumberland County, Pa. At that place, the Indians, on a certain Sabbath, attacked her father's fort. Her grandfather, Mr. James, a Baptist preacher, of the seventh day order, was shot dead, while trying to view the Indians from the head of the stairs. During the contest, her mother, Mrs. Davis, was all the time running bullets, though her father was lying a corpse. Some blasts of a conch-shell at last dispersed the savages.

His wife died December 10, 1790, the mother of eight children,—two sons and six daughters. All these had the best means of education, which that part of the country then afforded. His two sons were graduated, the one at Hampden Sidney College, the other at the College of New Jersey. He records it as an interesting fact in respect to his children, that the first married a native of Delaware; the second a native of Maryland; the third a native of South Carolina; the fourth a native of North Carolina; the fifth a native of Pennsylvania; the sixth a native of Massachusetts, the seventh a native of Virginia, and the eighth a native of Connecticut.

In October, 1791,—the circumstances of his family rendering it imperatively necessary that he should form a second matrimonial connection, he was married in Mecklenburg County, N. C., to Sarah Thompson, a native of Lancaster, Pa., with whom he lived forty years. She died the year after him, and sleeps by his side.

Dr. Cummins published, shortly after he went to Georgia, a pamphlet addressed to the Methodist and Baptist denominations, on the Doctrines and Polity of the Presbyterian Church; and, at a later period, two Sermons on Baptism, and a Sermon preached on the Fourth of July.

FROM THE REV. S. K. TALMAGE, D. D.

MILLEDGEVILLE, Ga., April 28, 1852.

Rev. and dear Sir: You ask for my recollections of the late Rev. Dr. Francis Cummins. My personal knowledge of him extends over only a few of his latter years; but such as it is, I cheerfully communicate it to you.

One of my earliest interviews with him was at the examination of an Academy. It was conducted principally by himself. As he was an aged man, I expected to find him rusty as a scholar. But, to my surprise, I found him exceedingly accurate and minute in his scientific knowledge, highly appreciating, and dwelling with enthusiasm upon, nice points of classical literature. On further acquaintance, I discovered that he was an admirable critical scholar. His biblical knowledge, and particularly his acquaintance with the Greek of the New Testament, was uncommon. Indeed, I incline to the opinion that the divines of the last century, though lacking in that varied and refined literature, which the educated clergy of the present age compass, yet far surpassed them in critical skill, and intimate knowledge of the sacred text. And just here, in my apprehension, lay their superior strength.

Dr. Cummins was an able and well read theologian. He held the Calvinistic system with great tenacity. He was always suspicious of any loose forms of expression, which seemed to him to rob God of his supremacy, and unduly to exalt man. It became young preachers to be on their guard in his company; for their careless quotations from Scripture, and incorrect forms of expression, were sure to draw forth his comments. I never heard him preach; but his addresses at ecclesiastical meetings, as well as his private conversations, gave abundant proof of profound thought, great originality, and nice discrimination. He was uncommonly gifted in prayer. His lofty conceptions of the Divine attributes, and his deep sense of the comparative nothingness of the creature, could not fail to strike every worshipper; and often, to this day, they form the subject of remark among those who used to listen to his devotional services. He had that clearness and vividness of conception, and that power of condensation in the use of language, which gave him great control of the minds of his hearers.

His physical man was in keeping with his intellectual. He was considerably above the common size, with broad shoulders, expanded frame, and large limbs

He had a high, capacious and intellectual forehead; and every thing in his appearance indicated that he was no ordinary man. His voice was guttural; but there was about it the remnant of a deep-toned power, indicating that, in the vigour of manhood, it must have been a very appropriate vehicle for his commanding thoughts.

Dr. Cummins was charged by some with a tendency to authoritativeness and pedantry. These appearances were, doubtless to a great extent, the result of his long experience as a teacher, and of the habits almost necessarily contracted thereby, in connection with the fact that his acknowledged superiority commanded the deference of nearly all his associates.

As a matter of principle, he was very severe against exhibitions of ignorance in the pulpit; and he had a strong antipathy to every thing that had the appearance of fanaticism.

He was greatly opposed to all Secret Societies, and had no patience with any of his clerical brethren who united with them. Among his little weaknesses,—and let him that is without sin cast the first stone,—he loved to advert to the fact that General Jackson had received part of his education under his sceptre.

He had one peculiarity which I must not omit to mention,—namely, his remarkable use of epithets, and especially his frequent employment of terms in a sense drawn rather from their etymology, than their common use. I remember his once characterizing a sermon in favour of immersion, which he thought very weak, as being "pregnant with windy, watery arguments." He wrote an apology for his absence from a meeting of Synod in Savannah; and, in relation to the remoteness of the place of meeting from the centre of our territory, spoke of its "eccentricity." His other reason was the lameness of his old horse. He congratulated a young clerical brother, who had lately taken a wife, on his "duplicity." He once said,—speaking of the composition and delivery of sermons,—"Some men thunder and some men lighten; but for my part, I think it is more natural for thunder and lightning to go together." I once saw a pamphlet that he wrote, about the time he came to Georgia, vindicating the Presbyterian denomination from various charges which had been made in relation to their creed. He commented on the origin of the name from *Presbyter*—elder. He dwelt upon their reverence for every thing scriptural, sacred, venerable, aged,—and rounded a paragraph with this unexpected sentence—"Now Methuselah was a *consummate* Presbyterian."

Though Dr. Cummins, when I first made his acquaintance, was an old man, and a subject of much physical infirmity, yet his death was deeply felt; for his kindness and sociability towards his junior brethren were a source both of enjoyment and of profit to them. He always said something in conversation that was strong, original, and suggestive of important thought. His great wisdom and experience made him very valuable in counsel.

Dr. Cummins published very little, and his influence will be transmitted to posterity chiefly through the living men whose characters he moulded. He has left a large and respectable circle of descendants, who reflect honour on their paternity by their own fine intellectual characteristics.

Yours very truly,

SAMUEL K. TALMAGE.

JAMES DUNLAP, D. D.

1781—1818.

FROM THE REV. ROBERT BAIRD, D. D.

NEW YORK, February 15, 1850.

My dear Dr. Sprague: You have requested me to furnish you some notices of the life and character of the Rev. James Dunlap, D. D. Herewith you will receive all that it is in my power to communicate, for a portion of which I am indebted to the only surviving member of his family.

Dr. Dunlap was my instructer in Latin and Greek, from the autumn of 1813 to midsummer, 1816, when he removed from Uniontown to Washington, as you will learn from the following narrative. He was Pastor, at a very early period, of the church of which my father was one of the ruling elders. And although this was long before my birth, yet this fact was the occasion of my hearing much in my early years, from my parents and other people, respecting him. In addition to this, he was Pastor of a neighbouring church for several years after my birth. I have therefore had considerable opportunities for forming a correct estimate of his character.

JAMES DUNLAP was born in Chester County, Pa., in the year 1744. He was the son of godly parents, and early manifested a more than ordinary desire for knowledge. From the best information that I can gain, I have reason to believe that he was fitted for College in the celebrated school at Fagg's Manor, which was for some time under the care of Dr. Samuel Finley, afterwards President of the College of New Jersey. Of that College he, in due time, became a member, and was graduated in the year 1773, under the Presidency of Dr. Witherspoon. From 1775 to 1777, he was a Tutor in the College at which he graduated; and, during this period, is supposed to have pursued his theological studies under the direction of its venerable President. He studied also for some time under the Rev. James Finley of East Nottingham. He was licensed to preach by the Presbytery of Donegal sometime between 1776 and 1781; and was ordained, *sine titulo*, by the Presbytery of Newcastle, August 21, 1781, at Fagg's Manor.

Not long after his ordination, he migrated to Western Pennsylvania, to which part of the great West many excellent people removed from Chester, Montgomery, Lancaster, and other Counties in the Eastern end of the State. In the autumn of 1782, he became a member of the Red Stone Presbytery, and Pastor of two congregations in Fayette County, called Dunlap's Creek and Little Red Stone. In 1789, his connection with these congregations was dissolved, and he accepted the charge of Laurel Hill Congregation in the same county, which he held till 1803, when he was called to succeed the amiable and accomplished Watson as President and Professor of Languages and Moral Philosophy in Jefferson College, Cannonsburg. In connection with his duties in College, he also preached to the Congregation of Miller's Run, as long as his health would permit.

In 1806, he was honoured with the degree of Doctor of Divinity from the College over which he presided.

In 1812, he resigned the office of President and of Professor, on account of his increasing infirmities, and removed to New Geneva,* in Fayette County, on the Monongahela River, about thirty miles distant from Cannonsburg. Here he engaged in teaching a small number of scholars in the classics. The next year, however, (1813,) he removed to Uniontown, where he had charge of the Academy (now Madison College) of that place. In this situation he remained till the summer of 1816, when he removed, with his wife and two unmarried daughters, to Abington, near Philadelphia, where his youngest son, the Rev. William Dunlap, was Pastor of a Presbyterian Church. He thus recrossed the Alleghany Mountains in his old age, to spend his last days almost amid the scenes of his youth.

But the veteran servant of Christ was now near the end of his course. On the 22d of November, 1818, he died in the joyful hope of a glorious immortality, in the seventy-fifth year of his age. Notwithstanding, in his last hours, he found much in the review of his life to lament, still his faith in the promises of God failed not. Just as the hand of death was falling upon him, he said with great humility,—"I know that I love God, and that I love his people for the likeness they bear to Him." One of his daughters, leaning over him, asked him if he knew her. He replied,—"Take my watch, and keep it as a memento of my love for you." His Funeral Sermon, agreeably to his own request, was preached by the Rev. Dr. Neill of Philadelphia.

Dr. Dunlap was certainly no common man. He possessed naturally a very amiable temper; and though, on account of his enfeebled health, somewhat prone, in his later years, to irritability, yet he was as far as possible from having an implacable spirit: a moment's reflection, a single word of explanation, was generally sufficient to allay all excitement. He was remarkably free from ambition, and was a beautiful example of Christian humility. I never heard a lisp from any human being, that even seemed to reflect upon his Christian character; and the most thoughtless and wicked, who were brought within the sphere of his influence, were constrained to acknowledge that he was a good man.

Notwithstanding Dr. Dunlap was highly respected as a faithful and even eloquent preacher, it was as a scholar and a teacher of youth that he was perhaps chiefly distinguished. His knowledge of the classics was exceedingly minute and accurate; and even in his old age, it was his delight to devote a part of each day, unless other more important engagements claimed his attention, to his favourite Latin and Greek authors. The copies of Homer, Horace, Virgil, Cicero, and above all, the Greek Testament, which he was accustomed to use, were witnesses to his great love of classical literature,—being almost literally worn out in his service. His influence in Jefferson College was very great, especially in this department of learning. He wrote but little, except sermons, and I am not aware that he published any thing; and yet the cause of sound learning as well as of religion found in him one of its most able and efficient friends. Many of his pupils have become distinguished in both Church and State, and some have become known as authors.

* This village of New Geneva was founded by the late Albert Gallatin, and derived its name from the birth place of its founder,—Geneva in Switzerland. It is remarkable that the manufacture of glass in the United States should have commenced in this little obscure town, at the foot of the Alleghany Mountains.

Mrs. Dunlap survived her husband nearly eight years, and died in Philadelphia, in 1826, full of faith and of peace.

Of their four daughters, the third only remains. The eldest was married to the late Rev. Stephen Boyer.* The eldest son of his second daughter, the Rev. Samuel Fulton, is Pastor of the Fourth Presbyterian Church in Pittsburgh. He is much respected as a man and a minister.

Of three sons, the eldest and second,—*Joseph* and *James*, studied law and practised for several years at Natchez, Miss. They were both men of superior talents and fine scholarship. *Joseph* died in 1821, and *James* the year following. *James* was, for several years, a Judge in the District Court. The third son, *William*, was graduated at Jefferson College in 1807, and was a Tutor in the College of New Jersey in 1809. He had a well balanced and well cultivated mind, and more than usual gravity of manners. He was for several years Pastor of the Presbyterian Congregation in Abington, Pa. He suffered much during the last year and a half of his life, and survived his father less than a month. He met death in the exercise of a joyful and triumphant faith.

Your sincere friend and brother,

ROBERT BAIRD.

FROM THE REV. ANDREW WYLIE, D. D.

PRESIDENT OF INDIANA UNIVERSITY.

BLOOMINGTON, Ind., April 1, 1849.

Rev. and dear Sir: I cheerfully comply with your request for my recollections of my venerated friend and instructer, the late Dr. Dunlap. When I first knew him, which was about the year 1808, I was but a lad. In the course of some following years, I had, it is true, a better opportunity of observing his ways than students generally have in respect to their teachers; and his character made a very distinct impression on my mind,—which, however, was not so intelligible to me then as it is now. The following imperfect sketch may give some idea of it.

Dr. Dunlap (the students, in speaking of him among themselves, generally called him *Neptune*, because his presence quelled the waves of noisy merriment, which occasionally rose among them,) was in his personal appearance somewhat remarkable, as he was also in some traits of his character. The one was a symbol of the other. About five feet, eight or ten inches, he appeared, as he walked along with slow and measured step, to notice nothing—his figure, straight as an arrow—his gait, regular and uniform—his form, perfect in its proportions—his dress, plain and neat. To a casual observer the most remarkable thing about him was his abstraction. He seemed generally lost in thought, and to take no interest at all in the outward world. Of course he talked seldom, and when he did, his words were elicited and few. He was a fine classical scholar, and when a happy translation was made by a student, you might see a gleam of intense delight in his looks, but he would say nothing. Two lads, one myself, and the other Charles Lucas, (alas he fell in a duel,) asked him to hear

* STEPHEN BOYER was born in New Brunswick, N. J., March 18, 1783; spent several of his early years as a merchant's clerk in Philadelphia; was graduated at Jefferson College in 1808; was licensed to preach in June, 1810; was settled as Pastor of the Church at Easton, Pa., in 1812; resigned his charge in 1814, and accepted a call from the Borough of Columbia, Pa., the same year. He subsequently removed to York, Pa., and divided his services between the three Churches of York, Columbia, and Wrightsville. He was, for a number of years, Principal of the York County Academy, and was an accomplished scholar and excellent teacher. He published several occasional Sermons. He died on the 10th of November, 1847.

them in an extra course of Greek, which he did in a manner which showed that he did not think it a trouble but a pleasure.

His temper was mild and patient; but when the ill conduct of any of his pupils, being persisted in for a long time, exhausted his patience, he became, as has been said of Washington, "terrible in his wrath." I saw him chase an ill-contrived, saucy, red-headed boy across a room, out of the one in which he was reciting, to the platform on which the stairs landed, kicking him or rather kicking at him, all the way. Some kicks probably touched him lightly, for the boy ran with all his might, and the way he got down stairs, and cut across the *campus*, would, with the other part of the scene, have set us "in a roar," but we suppressed it, till we were dismissed and out of sight. One other occasion I remember which cannot be briefly told so as to give the full impression. Yet I will try. A great, tall chap, whom we called *Doctus*, (he affected the reputation of a sage among us,) had an awkward fashion of lifting his feet alternately, in a swinging manner, as he stood up to recite. Another member of the class, a sly rogue, would contrive to introduce under the feet of *Doctus* a dry burnt coal from the hearth, the crunching of which he knew would affect the President's nerves unpleasantly. This trick he played several times so as to escape notice. At length, the President could bear it no longer, and shutting the book, he administered to poor *Doctus* such a cutting and terrible rebuke as fairly made him tremble. He was cured of his shuffling.

Dr. Dunlap preached regularly to a small congregation in the country,—never that I remember in the College; so that I seldom had the opportunity to hear him, and when I did hear him, it was on occasions for which he had likely made more than ordinary preparation. Judging from these occasional efforts, I should think him a good deal above the standard of ordinary excellence. His sermon was clear, plain, rich in thought, and, in some respects, impressive. But his voice always broke into the "falsetto," when he became highly animated; and these occasions, when they occurred, which was not often, were sure to be marked by something in his whole manner which was very peculiar and striking. I have never seen any thing like it in any other speaker. His arms would be thrown out suddenly towards the opposite poles; his face would beam with light,—not *glow;* and his whole person would exhibit for a moment the appearance of tension, as if for flight;—then perhaps he would stop short, as if he had forgot something, and then proceed in his usual calm, subdued tone. One occasion I remember well—it was on Monday after the Sacrament of the Lord's Supper had been administered, "on the hill"—the congregation was large; the day was fine; the air mild and calm. The preparatory parts of the service were finished. He stood up in the *tent*. His fine figure is now before me as it then was. There he stands, gazing into vacancy, over the heads of his people, as if he were looking into the Western horizon. He puts his hand into his vest pocket, as if feeling for his spectacles; and thus he stands till I begin to fear he has forgot himself altogether. Suddenly he brings down his eye to the holy page, announces his text, and proceeds to discuss and apply it in one of the best discourses that I ever heard.

I have understood that he once, for some time, quit preaching entirely. This took place when he was the Pastor of a congregation called "Laurel Hill." It was attributed to a fit of melancholy. I know not how it was. But I know that the spirit of Dr. Dunlap was, in its sensibilities, too delicate for the things,—and when I say things, I mean not material things,—with which he was in contact. He had no rugged strength. He was not a Luther but a Melancthon. He could hardly be said to be a resident of earth. He dwelt in a region of thought by himself, or in the company of those whom the eye of flesh sees not. Most assuredly he was a good man.

Very respectfully yours,

A. WYLIE.

MOSES HOGE, D.D.*

1781—1820.

The grandparents of MOSES HOGE came originally from Scotland, during the persecution of Charles the Second, and settled first at Amboy in New Jersey. Thence they removed to Delaware; thence to Pennsylvania, and thence to what is now Frederick County, Va., and settled on Cedar Creek, about the year 1735. Here also lived and died James and Mary (Griffith) Hoge, the parents of the subject of this sketch. And here too he himself was born on the 15th of February, 1752.

Young Hoge evinced an uncommon precocity of mind, and such was his thirst for knowledge that every leisure moment was devoted to his books. His father was a farmer in only moderate circumstances; but he was an intelligent as well as eminently pious man, and was disposed to gratify and cultivate the intellectual tastes of his son to the extent of his ability.

From his earliest childhood, under the influence of a Christian education, his mind had a serious direction, and he has been heard to say that he could not remember the time when the subject of religion was not grateful to his feelings. He did not, however, make a public profession of his faith till he was about twenty years of age. His father, though he had been a ruling elder in the Presbyterian Church near his own residence, for some reason transferred his relation to an Associate Church in Pennsylvania, distant more than a hundred miles; and though he and his family attended the usual Sabbath services in the church where they had been accustomed to worship, *he* went regularly once a year into Pennsylvania to attend the Communion. On one of these occasions, his son Moses accompanied him, and became a member of the same church with which his father was connected.

With his first desire to obtain a liberal education, and perhaps with his first distinct religious impressions, was connected the purpose, if Providence should open the way, to become a minister of the Gospel. He served, for a short time, as a soldier in the army of the Revolution; but under what circumstances cannot now be ascertained. Up to that time, nothing seems to have occurred that gave promise of his being able to carry out his favourite purpose of acquiring an education; but, shortly after, as is supposed, two clergymen called and passed a night at his father's, and were so much struck with the evidence of his intellectual superiority, that they encouraged him to commence at once a course of study, and persuaded his father to render him whatever pecuniary aid might be in his power. Accordingly, without much delay, he made his way across the Blue Ridge into Culpepper County, to a classical school, taught by a minister of the Associate Church. This school, however, owing to the troubles of the Revolution, was soon broken up; and, for a short time after this, he seems again to have been engaged upon the farm. In 1778, he repaired to Liberty Hall Academy, which Hanover Presbytery had then lately established at Timber Ridge, and of which William Graham was at that time the head. He completed his studies here in 1780; and meanwhile his mind

*MSS. from Rev. Dr. Hill and Rev. Dr. Alexander.—Foote's Sketches of Va., 1st Series.

had undergone a change in regard to his church connection. On the 25th of October of that year, he was received as a candidate by the Hanover Presbytery.

During the pendency of his trials for licensure before the Presbytery, he went to reside with the celebrated Dr. James Waddel, and prosecuted his theological studies still further under his direction. He was licensed to preach in the latter part of November, 1781; about one year after he left Liberty Hall Academy. It had been his purpose to settle in Kentucky; but this was deferred for a while, that he might visit the people on the South branch of the Potomac, within the present bounds of Hardy County; and finally, from his attachment to that people, his purpose was relinquished altogether. The Congregation in Hardy, which took the name of *Concrete*, called him to be their Pastor; and he was ordained at Brown's meeting house, Augusta, December 13, 1782,—the Sermon on the occasion being preached by the Rev. Archibald Scott. During his residence at this place, he devoted himself with great assiduity to study, especially the study of Hebrew; and at the same time taught a school, which not only helped to furnish him the adequate means of support, but secured to the youth in the neighbourhood important advantages which they could not otherwise have enjoyed.

On the 23d of August, 1783, he was married to Elizabeth, daughter of John Poage, of Augusta County,—a lady of the finest intellectual and moral qualities.

After having spent about five years on the South branch of the Potomac, he found the climate so injurious to his health, that it became necessary for him to seek another residence; and, notwithstanding the devoted attachment of his people, and their earnest wish that his labours among them might be continued, they could not conscientiously interpose any obstacle to his leaving them. Accordingly, in the autumn of 1787, he removed to Shepherdstown; and, though there was much in the religious state of things there that seemed unpromising, he very soon gathered a large congregation, and acquired great popularity throughout the whole region.

In 1793, he appeared for the first time as an author. A very popular Baptist minister, by the name of Jeremiah Walker, had suddenly passed, under somewhat peculiar circumstances, from ultra Calvinism to the entire rejection of the Calvinistic doctrines, and had written a pamphlet in defence of his new views. To this pamphlet Mr. Hoge wrote an able and somewhat extended Reply, in vindication of the doctrines of the Presbyterian Church.

In the year 1799, Mr. Hoge published another work which attracted very considerable attention, entitled, "The Christian Panoply." It was designed as an antidote to Paine's Age of Reason. It consisted of two parts—the first containing the substance of Bishop Watson's masterly Reply to the first part of Paine's work, and the second Mr. Hoge's Answer to the second part of it. It had a wide circulation, and exerted a very important influence.

In the autumn of 1801, Mrs. Hoge's health had become so delicate that her physicians advised that she should pass the winter in a more Southern climate. He accordingly set out to travel with her; and, after spending some time in North Carolina, they proceeded farther South, but without any perceptible improvement of her health. On their way home, they determined to visit the Sweet Springs in Bottetourt County; but, before they arrived there, she became so feeble as to be unable to proceed on her journey, and on the 18th of June, 1802, the fifth day from the time that they stopped, she died. She was full of peace and hope in her last hours; and her husband, though he was obliged to bury her in a desolate place, and in the midst of strangers, stood at the head of her grave, and preached Christ and Him crucified as the Resurrection and the Life. They had lived together in the conjugal relation upwards of nineteen years.

In October, 1803, Mr. Hoge attended the meeting of the Synod of Virginia, at Hampden Sidney College. During the sessions of the Synod, he renewed his acquaintance with an accomplished and pious lady, whom he had formerly known as the wife of William Pitt Hunt in Maryland, but who had been for several years a widow. He soon made proposals of marriage to her, which she accepted, and within less than a month she had become his wife. The union proved a source of much happiness to both parties, as well as to Mr. Hoge's family.

In 1805, he opened a classical school, partly as a necessary means of support, and partly with a view to the education of his own sons. In 1807, he was invited to take charge of the Academy in Charlestown, about ten miles from Shepherdstown; and to divide his ministerial labours between the two places; but, after due deliberation, he declined the offer. Shortly after this, he was appointed President of Hampden Sidney College, in place of Dr. Alexander, who had removed to Philadelphia; and at the same time was invited to be assistant preacher in Cumberland and Briery Congregations, each of them about ten miles distant from the College. After considerable hesitation, he consented to remove. He was inaugurated as President of the College during the sessions of Synod in the month of October, and was welcomed to his new field of labour with every expression of good-will and confidence.

In 1810, the degree of Doctor of Divinity was conferred upon him by the College of New Jersey.

The subject of education for the ministry having been discussed by the General Assembly in 1809, it was resolved to send down to the Presbyteries the inquiry whether there should be one or more Seminaries established. A divided answer was returned to the Assembly; but the Presbyteries in Virginia determined in favour of *Synodical* Seminaries; and the Assembly having consented to this, wherever it should be preferred, while yet they determined on establishing a central one,—the Synod of Virginia, in 1812, resolved to establish a Seminary within their bounds, and unanimously appointed Dr. Hoge their Professor.

From this time till his death, he held the two offices of President of the College, and Professor of Divinity under the appointment of the Synod. He had the pleasure of seeing about thirty of his pupils at Hampden Sidney, licensed and ordained ministers.

In 1819, Dr. Hoge's constitution, under his multiplied and onerous labours, was found to be giving way. For several months, he was confined to his chamber, and part of the time to his bed; but he still, even in his feeblest state, continued to hear the daily recitations of his class. In the course of the summer, his health was so far recruited that he paid a visit to his friends in the Valley about Shepherdstown and Winchester,—which proved to be his last. In the spring of 1820, he attended the meeting of his Presbytery in Mecklenburg County, and was appointed a delegate to the General Assembly to meet in Philadelphia. He extended his journey as far as New York, with a special view to attend the anniversary of the American Bible Society. This desire being gratified, he spent a little time at Princeton, and then proceeded to Philadelphia. He was able to attend the sessions of the Assembly for about a week, when he became so ill as to be confined to his lodgings. As soon as his case became alarming, his family were sent for, and his wife arrived, only, however, in season to witness his serene and triumphant departure. He died on the 5th of July, 1820, in the sixty-ninth year of his age. A Sermon on the occasion of his death was preached by the Rev. Ezra Stiles Ely, D. D. His remains repose in the burying ground attached to the Third Presbyterian Church in Philadelphia, by the side of those of his intimate friend, Dr. John Blair Smith, who had formerly been President of Hampden Sidney College.

Dr. Hoge had four children,—all by the first marriage, besides several that died in infancy. Three of his sons entered the ministry.

The year after his death, a volume of Sermons was published, from his original manuscripts; though, not having been prepared for the press by himself, they are thought, however excellent, scarcely to do justice to his character as a preacher. This at least was the opinion of Dr. John H. Rice.

FROM THE REV. W. S. REID, D. D.

LYNCHBURG, Va., April 14, 1853.

Rev. and dear Sir: Notwithstanding my health is feeble, and I find writing consequently somewhat laborious, I cannot decline your request for my recollections of my venerable friend, the Rev. Dr. Hoge.

My acquaintance with him did not commence until after I had graduated at Princeton in 1802. While struggling on my way to the ministry, by my personal exertions, aided by the beneficence of friends, I was providentially introduced to this excellent man. He was then a resident of Shepherdstown, in this State, and Pastor of the Church there. He kindly invited me to visit him. He opened to me, as he had done to many others in similar circumstances, the heart of affection and the hand of benevolence. He soon extended to me an invitation to come and make my home in his family; allowing me to prosecute my studies under his direction. I did so, and remained with him between one and two years; and of course had an opportunity of becoming thoroughly acquainted with his character. He was a member of the Winchester Presbytery, under the care of which I passed to my profession.

In person Dr. Hoge was of middle size, somewhat tending to a forward bodily inclination. His manners, though without much artificial polish, were familiar and agreeable: they expressed very strongly the kindness and benignity of his spirit. He possessed a mind of uncommon vigour, capable at once of accurate discrimination and profound research; and withal richly stored with the treasures of scientific knowledge. As a preacher, his manner was ungraceful, even uncouth; but there was so much depth and originality of thought, such richness and force of illustration, and such clear and cogent reasoning, that the awkwardness of his manner was very soon quite overlooked or forgotten. In his theological views, he was thoroughly Calvinistic, regarding the doctrine of salvation by free and sovereign grace, as the very substance of Christianity. He was profoundly read in Theology, and had accustomed himself to view the system which he held, in its various relations and bearings. As a teacher, he had not only great patience but great skill. He had an admirable facility at clearing up difficulties, and illustrating the harmony of the Christian system. At the same time, he was an eminent example to his pupils of the Christian spirit. He was concerned, not more to impart to them a knowledge of the truths of the Gospel, than to lead them to cultivate an ardent piety, and duly to appreciate the responsibilities of the work to which they were devoted. He was honoured as the instrument of bringing into the ministry many faithful labourers, some of whom, having served their generation, have already fallen asleep. He was eminently conscientious and useful in all his relations, and was much honoured and beloved wherever he was known. He was greatly blessed in his family, having three sons in the ministry, on whom his mantle may be said to have rested.

That God may eminently bless your labours is the earnest desire of

Your friend,

WILLIAM S. REID.

JAMES MITCHEL.*

1781—1841.

JAMES MITCHEL was born at Pequea, Pa., January 29, 1747. His father, Robert Mitchel, was born in the North of Ireland, but came to America when he was quite young. He was a man of vigorous intellect and earnest piety, was well acquainted with his Bible, and strong in his attachment to the Presbyterian Church. His wife, whose maiden name was Mary Enos, was of Welsh extraction, and was also distinguished as a warm hearted Christian. They removed from Pennsylvania to Bedford County, Va., where they resided many years. They both reached an advanced age, and of their thirteen children, not one lived to see less than threescore years and ten. The attention of the father is said to have been first awakened to the subject of religion, by overhearing his great-grandmother —who was then more than a hundred years old, and who lived to be a hundred and twelve,—praying in secret for his conversion.

Their son James made a public profession of religion when he was in his seventeenth year; though he dated the commencement of his religious life to a somewhat earlier period. Of the circumstances of either his classical or theological education little is known, though he was, for a time, previous to his entering the ministry, a Tutor in Hampden Sidney College. He was licensed to preach the Gospel, by the Hanover Presbytery at Concord, Va., in October, 1781.

Shortly after his licensure, he seems, by advice of his Presbytery, to have taken a missionary tour into the Western Territories. It does not appear how long he was absent, but it was probably somewhat less than a year, as there was an application made for his services from the united Congregations of Concord and Little Fallings, at the meeting of Presbytery in October, 1782.

Some time during this year, he was married to Frances, daughter of the Rev. David Rice, and granddaughter of that eminent scholar and divine, the Rev. Samuel Blair of Fagg's Manor. Soon after his marriage he removed to Kentucky, where he exercised his ministry as he had opportunity, and

* Foote's Sketches of Va., 2d Series.—MS. from Mrs. Dr. Rice.

supported his family chiefly by teaching a school. He remained in Kentucky, however, but a short time; for in October, 1783, the Presbytery agreed to send him to the Churches of Hat Creek and Cub Creek, and appointed a day for his ordination. Owing to peculiar circumstances, however, the ordination did not take place at the time first appointed, but was deferred till the 4th of August, 1784, when the service was performed at Buffalo.

Mr. Mitchel continued to preach to these congregations about three years. In March, 1786, the Congregation of the Peaks, in Bedford, made out a call for him, and the Presbytery gave him leave to supply them during the summer, and keep the call under consideration. He was ultimately installed over that congregation, though there is no record of installation services, and the exact date cannot now be ascertained. Here, with a congregation covering an indefinite extent of territory around the Peaks, he passed his long ministerial life.

In the spring of 1787, the degree of Bachelor of Arts was conferred upon him by Hampden Sidney College—why it was not conferred at an earlier period is not known.

Not long after Mr. Mitchel removed to Bedford, a revival of religion commenced among the Baptists in the County of Charlotte, and gradually spread over a large portion of the Hanover Presbytery, extending even into North Carolina. Into this work he entered with great alacrity; and he had the pleasure to see a rich blessing attending his labours. As the Presbyterians and Baptists were, to a great extent, fellow labourers in this revival, the different views of Baptism held by the two denominations, ultimately became very generally a subject of discussion; and Mr. Mitchel, after mature reflection, committed his thoughts upon it to writing, in the form of a brief treatise which he designed for publication. For some reason, however, it never saw the light, and it is understood that the manuscript has been lost.

After he had passed his fiftieth year, he suffered greatly from nervous derangement, and consequent spiritual depression. Doubting the genuineness of his piety, he questioned also his right to preach the Gospel. He set out, not without great reluctance, with some young friends, to attend a meeting of Synod at Winchester. Stopping for the night at a place called New Market, in Shenandoah County, he yielded to an importunate request from some of the people there to preach in the evening. He took for his text the words addressed to our first father by his Creator—"Adam, where art thou?" The following were the heads of his discourse—1. "All men have a place, like Adam, in which they ought to be. 2. All men, like Adam, are found out of their places, and where they ought not to be. 3. All men, unless they take warning, will soon find themselves in a place where they will not want to be." As he proceeded, he became greatly excited by his subject, and delivered himself with uncommon power; and this marked the breaking away of the cloud which had gathered around him. Many years after, at an ecclesiastical meeting, a repectable elder of a church, and a member of the judicatory, came to him, and asked if he remembered preaching at New Market, at such a time, on the text, "Adam, where art thou?"—Upon receiving an affirmative answer, the elder went on to say,—"Well, Sir, that sermon found me a poor ungodly sinner, and by the blessing of God effectually aroused me—I had no peace till I found it in Christ the

Lord." It is further stated that an old man whose Christian name was *Adam*, and who was an unbeliever, happened to be present at the meeting, and as often as the preacher cried out, "Adam, where art thou?"—the voice penetrated to his inmost soul, and he became convinced that he was in a place in which he could ill afford to remain; and the result was that he found no rest until he bowed to the requirements of the Gospel.

Mr. Mitchel often made missionary excursions, travelling for weeks and even months at a time, in the South-western Counties in Virginia. Wherever he happened to be, he was always ready to preach, and his preaching was always acceptable and often highly effective. He was jealous of all innovations, not only in the doctrines but the usages of the Church. When the members of the Hanover Presbytery began to dispense with the use of tokens at the Communion, he looked upon it with deep concern, as boding evil to the purity of the Church; and when he saw that the omission was likely to become general, he appeared before the Synod, and addressed his brethren on the subject in a tone of earnest expostulation, and even rebuke. Though his views were not practically heeded, his advanced age and truly apostolic character prevented any demonstration on the part of the Synod, that was not entirely respectful.

Mr. Mitchel's last sermon was preached at the house of his sister-in-law, Mrs. Margaret Mitchel, on the last Sabbath of December, 1840. Shortly after this, he became seriously ill,—the first time in his life that he had ever suffered severe indisposition. During the whole period of his illness, his mind was perfectly tranquil, and was evidently reaching forward in the exercise of a strong faith to the glory that was to follow. One of the last sentences he uttered was—"I want to live just as long as will be for the glory of God, and no longer." On waking from a gentle slumber, his countenance seemed lighted up with joy; while an increased difficulty of respiration told that the time of his departure was at hand. In a few moments, he calmly folded his arms, closed his eyes, and yielded up his spirit. He died on the 27th of February, 1841, aged ninety-four years and one month.

Mr. Mitchel was the father of thirteen children,—two sons and eleven daughters. His wife, who was twenty years younger than himself, still survives (1857) in great infirmity, having passed her ninetieth year.

FROM MRS. DR. JOHN H. RICE.

PRINCE EDWARD COUNTY, Va.,
near Hampden Sidney College, May 6, 1854.

My Dear Sir: I remember the Rev. Mr. Mitchel, concerning whom you inquire, only as an old man. I used to see him at my father's in my childhood, when he came to attend meetings of Presbytery and Synod; and when I was more advanced in life, I had other and better opportunities of observing his appearance, and judging of his character. I can give you in a few words my principal recollections of him.

He was an uncommonly small man, being low in stature, and having very little flesh; but he had great natural activity, and age had done little or nothing to lessen it. His face, though pretty well wrinkled, wore an intelligent expression, and easily brightened up into an agreeable smile. He was full of good humour, and never allowed his part of the conversation to flag. He seemed also to have much general intelligence, and he was looked up to by every body as a man of another age.

In the pulpit, perhaps, his most striking characteristic was animation. In his extreme old age, he would sometimes exhibit all the fire of youth; and would dash about, as if impatient of confinement to one spot. Though he had not a tooth in his head, his enunciation was remarkably distinct, and his voice, which was well adapted to public speaking, seemed to retain the clearness and force of middle life. His preaching was bold, earnest, and if I may judge from the specimens I have heard, was of a more than ordinarily alarming character. He quoted frequently the passage—"Upon the wicked He shall rain snares, fire and brimstone, and an horrible tempest," and many others of the same import.

Mr. Mitchel was a teacher of youth, as well as a preacher; and in the former capacity, as well as the latter, had a high reputation. I have heard it said, however, that his discipline was very severe; and I remember to have heard of one of his pupils whom he had whipped with a handful of flax, resolving that when he was grown up, he would give it back to him; but as I never heard of any encounter between him and the old gentleman in after life, I take for granted that his resolution did not very long survive his flogging.

Mr. Mitchel was undoubtedly always reckoned among the more respectable of the Virginia clergymen. In the later periods of his life, he became an object of interest from his extreme old age, in connection with his remarkable activity; and, though he has now been dead many years, he comes up before me, as if I had seen him but yesterday, in the exercise of his naturally joyous spirit, and yet as a sort of animated bounding skeleton.

Yours respectfully,

ANNE S. RICE.

SAMUEL CARRICK.

1782—1809.

FROM THE REV. R. B. McMULLEN, D. D.

KNOXVILLE, Tenn., June 22, 1855.

My dear Sir: As nearly half a century has passed since the Rev. Samuel Carrick closed his earthly career, many facts and incidents that might have legitimately formed part of the narrative of his life, have undoubtedly passed into oblivion; though enough remain to show that he was more than an ordinary man, and had much to do in giving direction, at an early period, to the ecclesiastical affairs of this State. What my opportunities have been for gaining information in respect to his history, as well as forming a correct judgment of his character, may be inferred from the fact that I am not only familiar with many persons who, in early life, were his contemporaries and associates, but am Pastor of the same Church with which he was connected during much the greater part of his ministerial life.

SAMUEL CARRICK was a native of York County, (now Adams,) Pa., and was born on the 17th of July, 1760. At an early age, he came to the Valley of Virginia, and there prosecuted his studies under that distinguished scholar and theological teacher, the Rev. William Graham. He was taken under the care of the Hanover Presbytery, the last Wednesday of November, 1781, as a candidate for the ministry, and having passed through his several trials, was licensed at New Providence as a preacher of the Gospel on the 25th of October of the next year. He was ordained and installed Pastor of Rocky Spring and Wahab meeting-house, at the house of James Hodges, on the fourth Wednesday of November, 1783.

In 1784, a memorial was sent to the Legislature of Virginia, that awakened no small interest, and occasioned considerable agitation. It was to this effect—"Should all the people of the State be taxed to support religion in their respective denominations?" The Presbytery of Hanover were unanimously against the measure; but say,—"Should it be thought necessary, at present, we would wish it to be done on the most liberal plan." In May following, the Augusta Church requested the Presbytery to explain parts of the memorial, and especially what they meant by the word "liberal." Mr. Carrick and Mr. Hoge were appointed a Committee to answer their inquiries.

On the division of the Presbytery in 1786, Mr. Carrick became a member of the Lexington Presbytery. On the 12th of April of that year, he applied for, and received, a certificate of good standing, with a view to travel, and the same year he was a member of the Synod of New York and Philadelphia, then the highest judicatory of the Church. He is supposed to have visited Tennessee, shortly after his return from Philadelphia.

For several years, Mr. Carrick seems to have divided his labours between Virginia and Tennessee; but he did not settle permanently in Tennessee, till about the year 1791, when he was regularly dismissed to join the Abingdon Presbytery. Sometime during 1789–90, he became greatly distressed in regard to his spiritual state, and doubted so much the genuineness of his own religious experience, that he actually withdrew temporarily from the duties of the ministry. But after protracted and painful struggles, the cloud passed off, and he returned to his accustomed labours with his former alacrity. This was but a short time previous to his final removal to Tennessee.

Before he was actually settled in this State, he preached upon a remarkable mound at the junction of the Holston and French Broad Rivers. It would seem also that in the year 1789, he was sojourning upon the Holston River, about four miles from Knoxville.

Before leaving Virginia, he was married to a Miss Moore, daughter of Robert Moore, of the Timber Ridge Church, by whom he had three children,—two sons and a daughter. The daughter (Elizabeth) became the wife of the Hon. Hugh Lawson White,—a member of the Senate of the United States, and at one time a candidate for the Presidency. Mrs. Carrick died on the 24th of September, 1793,—a day memorable in the annals of Tennessee. A body of one thousand Indians (one authority says fifteen hundred) were known to be within a few miles of Knoxville that night, on their march to destroy all the inhabitants of that place. Thirty-eight of about fifty men who were there, went two miles from the little fort, where the women and children were gathered, to meet this company of armed savages,—not doubting that they were in the path of duty, and willing to trust Providence for the result. Mr. Carrick felt obliged, notwithstanding his wife was a corpse, to go with the defenders; and the solemn duty of laying her remains in their last resting place, was actually performed by female hands. The Indians, after coming within three or four miles, halted to take counsel. They were divided in their opinions on the question whether or not they should make clean work of it by a general massacre, or whether they should spare the women and children; and, after con tinuing their debates till daylight, without coming to any agreement, they withdrew, and, going to a neighbouring station, murdered the inmates of the house in a most barbarous manner. The details of this shocking affair may be found in Dr. Ramsey's Annals of Tennessee.

Shortly after the death of his first wife, Mr. Carrick formed a second matrimonial connection, with Miss Hannah McClelland, by whom he had four children,—all of whom are deceased. She died on the 17th of August, 1809, in her fiftieth year.

In February, 1794, Mr. Carrick was in Knoxville, and at the opening of the Territorial Legislature, he preached before that Body, by their invitation, on the second day of the session. The same year, he was chosen, by the Legislature, President of Blount College, which office he held till his death. During this whole period, he had the pastoral charge of the Knoxville Church, and, until 1803, of the Lebanon Church also.

In January, 1796, when the delegates had met for the purpose of forming a State Constitution, we find this among their earliest records:—"On motion of Mr. White, seconded by Mr. Roddy, ordered that the session commence tomorrow with prayer, and a sermon to be delivered by the Rev. Mr. Carrick."

Mr. Carrick always took great interest in the general cause of education. Having a good education himself, and finding great need of it among the people, he was ready to do every thing in his power, both as a citizen and a presbyter, to bring the means of intellectual culture within the reach of all classes. In 1800, he was Chairman of a Committee appointed by the General Assembly to prepare a Pastoral Letter to the Churches, Dr. Blackburn being the other member associated with him. In the autumn of the same year, he was Chairman of a Committee, with Dr. Henderson, "to draft rules to regulate the conduct of the Presbytery in the exercise of discipline, and explanatory of our sense of the Constitution." In 1806, he was a Commissioner to the General Assembly, and was appointed on a Committee of which Doctors Green, Miller and Nott, were also members,—to report on the duty of the Church in reference to the subject of education. I mention these facts chiefly as illustrative of his acknowledged activity and public spirit, and of the important influence which he exerted in his more general relations to the Church.

In person Mr. Carrick was very erect, and altogether of a fine commanding appearance. He was extremely urbane,—even courtly, in his manners. In the pulpit his manner was grave, dignified and solemn. His views of Divine truth were clear and definite, and they lost nothing by his mode of exhibiting them. As a preacher, he undoubtedly commanded great respect throughout this whole community.

The circumstances of his death were impressive and startling. It was the season for the sacramental meeting in his church. He had spent much of the preceding night in preparatory thought and study. Very early in the morning, he was seized with apoplexy, and in a few moments his spirit had taken its upward flight. The Rev. Samuel G. Ramsey, his friend and co-presbyter, was sent for immediately, and he came and administered the Communion to his Church,—as it were, by the very side of the dead body of their beloved Pastor.

Yours very sincerely,

R. B. McMULLEN.

WILLIAM MORRISON, D. D.*

1782—1818.

WILLIAM MORRISON, a son of Daniel and Janette (McFarland) Morrison, was born in Perthshire, Scotland, in the year 1748. He early cherished a strong desire for the Christian ministry; but the circumstances of his father were so straitened as to forbid the idea of giving him a liberal education. In consequence of this, the son determined to migrate to this country, hoping that he should here find the requisite means for accomplishing his favourite object; and he accordingly came hither at the age of seventeen. As he brought with him letters of recommendation from ministers in Scotland, addressed to several ministers in New York and Philadelphia, he was received with kindness, and encouraged to pursue the design which had brought him hither. Resuming the humble employment in which he had been originally engaged, he soon acquired a sum sufficient to defray the expenses of a collegiate education. But his faith was destined to encounter other difficulties still. The College of New Jersey, to which his eyes had been fondly turned, had its operations suspended by the war of the Revolution. Being repelled by similar embarrassments from other scenes of collegiate education, he was constrained to have recourse to academic and private instructers. Having thus attained a competent share of classical and general knowledge, he placed himself under the care of the Associate Presbytery of New York. By their advice, he pursued and completed a course of theological study under the Rev. Robert Annan, then living in the vicinity of Philadelphia. He was soon licensed as a candidate for the Christian ministry, and entered with great delight and characteristic ardour on the duty of preaching.

Shortly after he was licensed, Providence directed his way to Londonderry, N. H. It was a congenial spot; for he found in the place a great number of his own countrymen and their descendants. The congregation to which he preached had enjoyed, for a long period, the labours of the excellent Mr. McGregore, under whom they had become well instructed in the truths of Christianity. Mr. Morrison's services were highly appreciated; and he soon received a unanimous call from the Church and Society to become their Pastor. He accepted the call, and was ordained and installed February 12, 1783.

The scene of Mr. Morrison's labours was extensive, and his duties were arduous. The energy and activity of his mind found ample scope among his numerous flock. But his ministerial services reached much farther. In various towns, both near and distant, which were settled in considerable measure by emigrants from Londonderry, his services were eagerly sought, and they were freely and frequently rendered, especially on Sacramental occasions. As these occasions were attended with a variety of public exercises, he often returned home, exhilarated indeed in mind, but labouring under great bodily exhaustion.

The degree of Doctor of Divinity was conferred upon him by Dartmouth *University*, about the year 1816.

He continued to occupy till the close of his life the same field of labour to which he was first introduced. But eight days before his death he preached

* Dr. Dana's Fun. Serm.—MS. from Rev. J. W. C. Bartley.

a Funeral Sermon for one of his congregation, from Psalm xxxix. 4, "Lord, make me to know mine end," &c. On Wednesday, the 4th of March, 1818, while visiting a school in one of the districts of his parish, he became suddenly indisposed; and this proved to be the commencement of his last illness. Within two or three days, it became apparent that his life was in serious danger. On Sabbath morning, he said to his wife—"You know that the Sabbath has always been my best day, and my employment then my best employment. But this is the last Sabbath I shall spend on earth. In a short time, I shall be spending an everlasting Sabbath." He added with a smile,—"Will not that be a blessed exchange?" In the evening of that day, he seemed quite exhausted; but in his bed, with his family around him, he uttered a most solemn and affectionate prayer, in the course of which he intimated that it would be the last prayer he should ever offer. After this, he took each of his family affectionately by the hand, and when he had so far recovered himself as to be able to speak, said,—"Now Lord, what wait I for?" Such was a sample of his death-bed exercises. He expired just as the words—"Come, come, Lord Jesus," had passed from his lips,—on the 9th of March, 1818, at the age of seventy. His Funeral Sermon was preached by the Rev. Dr. Dana of Newburyport, and was published.

Dr. Morrison published a Sermon preached before the Honourable General Court of New Hampshire at the Annual Election, 1792; a Sermon at the installation of the Rev. John Giles,* Newburyport, 1803; and a Sermon occasioned by the death of John Pinkerton, Esq., 1816.

He was married on the 28th of June, 1784, to Jane Fullerton, of Pequea, Pa. They had eleven children: two of the sons were graduated at Dartmouth College, and entered the profession of Law, and both of them died of consumption in Savannah, in the year 1831.

FROM THE REV. DANIEL DANA, D. D.

NEWBURYPORT, April 16, 1851.

My dear Sir: I was intimately acquainted with Dr. Morrison for many years, and feel perfectly free to render my testimony concerning his character for the purpose for which you ask it. Many years have passed since his departure, but they have done little to diminish the vividness of my impressions concerning him.

Dr. Morrison ranked well with the excellent preachers of his day. It was in the pulpit that his perceptions, his acquisitions, and the energies of his mind had full scope, and the affections of his heart poured themselves forth in a tide of devout and benevolent feeling. His sermons were full of Gospel truth; were luminous and instructive; faithful and searching; awfully alarming to the wicked, yet encouraging to the sincere, and tenderly consoling to the mourner in Zion. His prayers were no less impressive than his sermons. Replete with reverence and affectionate devotion; the breathings of a soul apparently in near communion with its God; full yet concise; adapted to occasions and circum-

* JOHN GILES was born in England; was ordained Pastor of a Dissenting Church in Wellington, (Somerset,) where he remained nine years; then had the charge, for a few years, of a church in Exeter; came to this country from his love of Republican institutions in 1798; preached for a short time in Elizabethtown, N. J., and Trumbull, Conn.; and on the 20th of July, 1803, was installed Pastor of the Second Presbyterian Church in Newburyport, where he continued till his death, which occurred in November, 1824. He published an Oration delivered at Newburyport on the Fourth of July, 1809; and Two Discourses delivered at Newburyport on occasion of the National Fast, 1812.

stances; they could scarcely fail to impress and edify the hearers. His manner in the pulpit was peculiar. It had something of patriarchal simplicity; something of apostolic gravity and authority. Yet it was mild, affectionate and persuasive. It indicated a mind absorbed in Heavenly things, deeply conscious of its awful charge, and anxiously intent to fasten eternal truths on the hearts and consciences of men.

As a Pastor, Dr. Morrison was faithful, assiduous and tender; instant in season and out of season; watching for souls as one that must give account; and finding his delight in the discharge of the most laborious and exhausting duties of his office. Little did he spare himself, even in those closing years of life, in which his emaciated form proclaimed the ravages of disease; and infirmity, combined with age, seemed to demand repose. Without exaggeration, it may be said that he was truly the father of his beloved people. He rejoiced in their joys, sympathized in their sorrows, counselled in their perplexities, adapted himself to their infirmities, and, without sacrificing dignity, or independence, or faithfulness, "became all things to all men," that he might promote their spiritual good.

But his cares and labours were by no means confined to his flock. The general interests of Zion, the peace and welfare of churches, near and remote, engaged his feelings, and frequently employed his exertions. In addition to his abundant solicitudes and efforts as a member of the Presbytery, he was frequently resorted to, in cases of difficulty, in Congregational Churches. Nor had he any reluctance, when requested, to unite in council with his ministerial brethren of those churches. And few have been so successful in promoting the interests of peace and order. His deep knowledge of human nature, the quickness and accuracy of his perceptions, his sound judgment, his consummate prudence, his unaffected kindness united with energy and independence, were eminently fitted to render him successful in mediating between contending parties, and becalming the agitated spirits of men.

He took an interested and energetic part in the variety of plans and institutions, which were commenced in his day, for disseminating the Scriptures and religious tracts, for extending the knowledge of the Gospel, for educating poor and pious youth, for promoting the power of godliness, and effecting a reformation of manners. Every design connected with the glory of God and the best interests of man, engaged his cordial concurrence, his active patronage, his fervent prayers. He was much animated and delighted with the signs of the times. He considered the multiplied revivals of religion in our country, and the unexampled exertions of Christians on both sides of the Atlantic, to evangelize the heathen, as intelligible and delightful indications of the approach of the promised Millenium.

Dr. Morrison had much of the spirit of genuine and exalted patriotism. Looking abroad on the country which he had made his own, he cherished the delightful hope that its institutions were destined, not only to conduct to exalted happiness its own inhabitants, but to elevate and bless the world. In an Election Sermon delivered by him before the Legislature and principal officers of the State, he manifested how pure and enlarged were his views of the nature of civil government and of its ultimate design. He watched with untiring and anxious assiduity the course of things in the Federal and State Departments, and gave his most cordial approbation to the measures of wise and disinterested rulers. The character and course of Washington early secured his entire confidence; nor was it ever withdrawn from the public men who followed in his path.

In the private walks of life, Dr. Morrison exhibited a character consistent and uniform, estimable and lovely. His piety was strict without austerity, and fervent without enthusiasm. If there was a trait in his character conspicuous above the rest, it was benevolence—a benevolence which prompted him to unwearied and self denying exertions in promoting the real happiness of his fellow creatures; which inspired candour for their failings, and compassion for their distresses; which could forgive the injurious, and overcome evil with good. It is scarcely needful to add that in the social and domestic relations he was signally exemplary and amiable; that he was a most affectionate husband, a most tender father, and a most faithful friend.

Such are my impressions of the venerable father of whom you have asked me to give you some account.

Very sincerely and affectionately yours,
DANIEL DANA.

WILLIAM McWHIR, D. D.*

1782—1851.

William McWhir was the son of James and Jean (Gibson) McWhir, and was born in the parish of Moneyrea, and County of Down, Ireland, on the 9th of September, 1759. His father was a farmer in comfortable circumstances, and both his parents were exemplary professors of religion. In his early childhood, he lost the sight of one eye, and came very near losing his life, by means of the small-pox. His father and grandfather had both been elders in the Presbyterian Church; and his parents were desirous that one of their children should be a minister; and contrary, as it would seem, to his own better judgment, they conferred the honour upon *him*. After having, for some time, attended a school in the neighbourhood of his father's residence, he was transferred to another school, of a higher order, in Belfast, to be prepared for College. Here he was brought into intimate relations, for some time, with an unprincipled and profligate young man, whose influence upon him, temporarily at least, was very disadvantageous. He remained at this school until 1778, when he was sent to the University of Glasgow, being then about nineteen years of age. Here he passed three sessions, which was the period prescribed to their candidates, by the Synod of Ulster. It does not appear that, even at this time, his mind was at all awake to a sense of Christian obligation, notwithstanding he had made a profession of religion, and his studies were directed with particular reference to the ministry.

Immediately after leaving the University, he put himself under the care of the Presbytery of Killileagh, in the County of Down, and having gone through with his trials and examinations, was licensed to preach the Gospel on the 24th of December, 1782. He was ordained by the same Presbytery on the 25th of September, 1783.

Having, from the age of about twelve years, been deeply interested in America, by reading Carver's Travels, he early formed a purpose, with the consent of his father, (his mother was now dead,) to find a home on this side the water. Accordingly, immediately after his ordination, he sailed from Belfast for Philadelphia, where, on his arrival, he received from various distinguished individuals a cordial welcome to the country. After a

* MS. Autobiography.—MS. from Edward J. Harden, Esq.

few weeks, he went, in compliance with a request that had been sent to him previous to his leaving Ireland, to engage as a teacher at Alexandria; and he now became the head of a large and flourishing Academy, which was liberally patronized by General Washington, and to which the General sent two of his nephews. This brought him into quite intimate relations with that illustrious man, as well as with many other men of note in that neighbourhood. The following is his account of his first visit to Mount Vernon:—

"A few days after General Washington's return to Mount Vernon, I visited him in company with a countryman of mine, Col. Fitzgerald, one of Washington's Aids. At the dinner table, Mrs. Washington sat at the head, and Major Washington at the foot—the General sat next Mrs. Washington on her left. He called upon me to ask a blessing before meat. When the cloth was about to be removed, he returned thanks himself. Mrs. Washington, with a smile, said,—'My dear, you forgot that you had a clergyman dining with you to-day.' With equal pleasantness he replied, 'My dear, I wish clergymen and all men to know that I am not a *graceless* man.'" He goes on to say—"I was frequently at Mount Vernon and saw him frequently at Alexandria; nor did I ever see any person, whatever might be his character or standing, who was not sensibly awed in his presence, and by the impression of his greatness. The vivacity and grace of Mrs. Washington relieved visitors of some of that feeling of awe and restraint which possessed them. He was uniformly grave, and smiled but seldom, but always agreeable. His favourite subject of conversation was agriculture; and he scrupulously avoided, in general society, topics connected with politics, or the war, or his own personal actions."

In the year 1792, Mr. McWhir was applied to by an influential friend in Georgia, to visit Augusta, with a view to taking charge of both an Academy and a Presbyterian Church in that town; and, as he found that his expenses of living in Alexandria were too great to justify the expectation of being able to lay up any part of his income, he was inclined to listen to the application. He, accordingly, after making arrangements for a temporary supply of his place in the Academy, proceeded to Augusta on horseback; but, on his arrival, found that the affairs of both the Church and the Academy, were so identified with the movements of political parties, that there was little encouragement to him to remain. He, therefore, returned almost immediately to Alexandria,—only, however, to resign his place in the Academy, and to get ready to seek a more Southern residence. As soon as he could make the necessary arrangements, he left Alexandria, and went to Savannah, and thence to Bryan County, to visit some of his friends. During his sojourn there, he accepted an invitation from the people of Sunbury, in Liberty County, to take charge of their Church and Academy, both of which were at that time vacant. Here his labours as teacher and minister, overtasked his strength, though his preaching was remarkably well attended, and his school grew constantly in numbers and popularity.

About this time, he was married to a Mrs. Baker, a lady of an excellent character, and of about his own age; and, shortly after, he purchased a plantation a few miles from Sunbury, to which he gave the name of *Springfield*. After continuing in his school about five years, he removed with his family to his plantation, in consequence of finding that his health suffered from the excessive labour which the two offices of minister and teacher devolved upon him. He, however, in compliance with the urgent solicitation of his friends, soon opened a select school at Springfield. For a while he continued to preach at Sunbury, but, as the school became large, he held religious services on the Sabbath at Springfield. This school he kept up for several years, until the labour and responsibility became so great that he resolved once more to abandon teaching.

Still, however, he was not willing to lead an inactive life; and the great destitution of the means of grace in the surrounding region impressed him with the obligation still to preach, as he had opportunity. About the year 1809, he commenced preaching at the Court House in McIntosh County, about twelve miles from Darien; where, in the midst of great darkness and the most violent opposition to religion, he succeeded in organizing a church. His labours here were almost entirely gratuitous. From this station he went to Darien, where he laboured for some time; and after the building of a new place of worship, the McIntosh Church was transferred to the latter place.

An event now occurred in the life of Mr. McWhir, which, to those who have followed his history to this point, will be a matter of no little surprise. Notwithstanding he had always been a minister, in regular standing, of the Presbyterian Church, he had been, even from the time that he commenced his education, *privately* a Unitarian. Having occasion to re-examine the Scriptures, about the year 1812, with a view to prove their Divine authority, he was led to take a new view of the doctrines which they contain, and, at no distant period, became thoroughly satisfied that the creed which he had before only *professed* to receive, really embodied the true sense of the Word of God. This change of religious opinion led of course to a corresponding change in his preaching, which did not escape the observation of those to whom he ministered.

In September, 1804, there was a tremendous hurricane, which desolated the coast of Georgia, sweeping directly over his plantation, and occasioning him a loss of about fourteen thousand dollars. Being now urged to take charge again of the Academy at Sunbury, he did so,—partly with a view to repair his fortunes. After a few years, he relinquished it again, on account of his health; but again returned to it, and continued his connection with it a while longer. On leaving it the third time, he gave up teaching as a profession, though he occasionally received a few pupils to instruct in a private way.

In 1819, he suffered a severe affliction in the death of his wife. After this, his health being much enfeebled, he determined on a visit to his native country. Accordingly, in the spring of 1820, having attended the sessions of the General Assembly at Philadelphia, he sailed for Liverpool, and, after remaining there a short time, passed on to London, where he was knocked down in the street by robbers, and so severely injured as to be confined to his room for a month. Thence he went to Ireland, and visited the few of his relatives and acquaintances that remained after the lapse of forty years; and, in the spring of 1821, proceeded to Scotland where he had the pleasure of making the acquaintance of Dr. Chalmers, and being present at the sessions of the General Assembly of the Church of Scotland. He returned to the United States in the autumn of that year, with renovated health.

In 1824, in consequence of a representation which had been made to him of the deplorable destitution of the means of grace in East Florida, was induced to visit St. Augustine, with a view to make an effort for the promotion of the Redeemer's Kingdom. He accordingly constituted a Presbyterian Church, and ordained elders there; and, for several years after this, was engaged in collecting the requisite funds for building a church edifice; and, in due time, he had the pleasure to see the object accomplished.

From 1827 to 1835, he was engaged in supplying vacant churches in Bryan, Liberty, and McIntosh Counties, and in various efforts for the promotion of the cause of education. In 1838, he disposed of his homestead, and went to Savannah, where he remained more than a year. He then accepted an invitation from his friend Major William J. McIntosh, of Bryan County, to reside in his family; and he actually lived there till 1847, when he returned to Savannah, and fixed his home in the family of his grandson, (by marriage,) Edward J. Harden, Esq. At the age of nearly ninety, he became a volunteer colporteur of the American Tract Society, and continued in this service till he was too feeble to labour. For several years previous to his death, he was unable to preach; but he never lost his interest in religious meetings, and was a regular attendant at church, even down to the Sabbath immediately preceding his death. He died at the house of a friend in Liberty County, in perfect peace, on the 31st of January, 1851, in the ninety-second year of his age. His funeral was attended at Midway Church, whence, in accordance with his own expressed wish, his remains were carried to Sunbury, and buried beside those of his wife. In the disposal of his property, which was not large, he made several bequests to charitable institutions. He left no descendant, and no relative in this country.

The degree of Doctor of Divinity was conferred upon him by Franklin College, in Georgia, in 1832.

FROM THE REV. C. C. JONES, D. D.

Riceboro', Liberty County, Ga., March 24, 1855.

My dear Sir: I knew Dr. McWhir in my childhood, as a friend and frequent visitor in our family, and was afterwards a pupil in his school. He was one of my examiners when received into the Presbytery of Georgia, and also when ordained by that Body. The friendship which he had entertained for my parents, he transferred to their son, and we were, for some twenty years, on terms of intimacy and confidential friendship.

He was a man of medium stature, of good proportions, muscular and quick in his movements, and with uncommon powers of endurance. He had a pure Irish face, and having been disfigured in childhood by the small-pox, was homely, and, becoming prematurely bald and gray, he carried the appearance in his countenance of a man advanced in years, when he was not as yet past middle life. His personal habits were the neatest imaginable. I do not remember ever having seen him dressed otherwise than as a gentleman and a clergyman. He possessed great self-respect, and a high appreciation of his office. He desired always to be recognised and treated as a clergyman. He never himself forgot, nor suffered others to forget, that he was one. His manners in the family, and in his association with all classes, were uncommonly polished and dignified, and aside from the politeness which appeared natural to him, he was formed upon the model of a gentleman seen in the Old Dominion at the period of the Revolution.

Dr. McWhir exacted in society much attention, but it was fully returned, and seemed a spontaneous movement, on his part, to preserve that elevation of manners, and that mutual respect, which add so great a charm to the intercourse of life. He was the most perfectly social man I have ever known. Warm and sincere in his attachments, it was a real heartfelt pleasure to him to be in the society of his friends, and to mingle with men of distinction; and his effort was, by cheerfulness of spirit and ready and easy powers of conversation, to convert the hour, or the day, as the case might be, into one of high social and friendly enjoyment. Fond of children, they never escaped his notice.

In intellectual power, he was perhaps not superior to the general mass of his brethren; yet an excellent scholar, well grounded in Latin and Greek, and in the usual branches of English education; and had no superior in his day as a teacher and a disciplinarian. His reputation as such was unbounded, and he is remembered more as a teacher and a friend of education and patron of learning, than as a minister; although he ranked among our first Presbyterian ministers, and bore his part reputably in the early efforts to establish our Church in the State. Of real courage and of mercurial temperament, of a high sense of honour and justice, and of strict integrity, energetic and prompt in decision and action, his schools were always models of morality and of order. He was a terror to evildoers. No fear of personal consequences to himself, nor family connections, nor wealth, nor friendly relations, nor poverty on the part of his pupils, served to screen the guilty. He used the rod sparingly, but when necessary, most effectively. He was long a teacher, and educated fathers and their sons. Scholars were sent to him from all parts of the State; and, when engaged in teaching, he travelled in our own country, and in England, and Scotland, and Ireland, to perfect himself, and to become master of improvements in that great art. His energy and perseverance were such as secured him success in whatever he undertook. Never having studied Theology systematically, and coming, as he believed, to a saving knowledge of the Lord Jesus Christ, some years after his migration to the United States, and when the period of study with him was waning, and much of his time occupied by teaching, and constant engagements adverse to close application, he could not be ranked among accomplished theologians,—although he was firmly settled upon the doctrines of our Confession of Faith. He adhered conscientiously to the Old School branch of our Church, through every trial and difficulty. His preaching, after I knew him, partook more of the practical and hortatory, than the doctrinal. He had a habit of yielding to his feelings in preaching, and most commonly was affected to tears. He contributed liberally to all our benevolent Societies and objects, while he had a special interest in the circulation of the Scriptures, and in our missionary operations, both at home and abroad. He was one of the earliest advocates of the Temperance Reformation, and adhered to its principles to the day of his death. Towards the close of life, his heart was more than ordinarily interested in the progress of the Gospel on the earth, and in its success he greatly rejoiced. His reading was chiefly religious and devotional, and he seemed to be rapidly maturing for Heaven. The lamp of life literally burnt to the socket, and mind and body wasted away in extreme age unto death. My last conversation with him, which occurred not many weeks before his death, found him fixed upon the "Rock of Ages." Said he, "My dear Friend, I cannot say that I have the faith of assurance, but I think I can say I have an assured hope."

Wishing you success and usefulness in your work,

I am very truly yours in our Lord,

C C. JONES.

WILLIAM BOYD.*

1783—1807.

William Boyd was the grandson of Robert Boyd, who was a native of Scotland, and, during a period of persecution in that country, fled to Ireland. He was a son of John Boyd, who was born in Ireland, but, after he had reached his maturity, removed with his family to America, and settled in Franklin County, Pa. Here William Boyd was born in the year 1758. When he was about fifteen years of age, his father was taken from him by death; and about the same time he became deeply impressed with religious things, and experienced, as he believed, the renewing influences of Divine grace. His mind was now directed towards the ministry of the Gospel; and, though his patrimony was small, he succeeded, by some means, in obtaining a liberal education. Whether he took the whole four years' course at Princeton, or entered an advanced class, does not appear; but he was graduated in 1778, in a class which numbered but four beside himself—its smallness being no doubt attributable to the fact that that was the period of the Revolution, when fighting was more in vogue than studying, and a College was a less attractive place than a battle field.

After leaving College, he was engaged for two or three years in teaching,—first an Academy in the city or vicinity of Annapolis, and then a family school in the neighbourhood of Baltimore. In connection with teaching, he pursued a course of theological study, and was licensed to preach the Gospel in 1783, by the Presbytery of Donegal, under the direction of which he continued till he entered that of New Brunswick. He remained for some time unsettled, preaching as Providence directed, in Pennsylvania, New Jersey, and New York; and his early ministrations were received with great favour, and attended with a manifest blessing. He was applied to by several important churches to settle over them; but he seems to have been afraid of the temptations involved in having a city charge; and besides, his taste led him to seek a more retired field of labour. The people of Lamington, N. J., having occasionally heard him preach, at length extended a call to him to become their Pastor; and, having accepted their call, he was ordained and installed on the 20th of October, 1784. Here he exercised his ministry till the close of his life.

In the year 1800, he was elected a Trustee of the College of New Jersey, and continued to hold the office while he lived.

Mr. Boyd, during the last twenty years of his life, never enjoyed vigorous health, and several times had some alarming symptoms of consumption; though he was able to go through the ordinary routine of ministerial duty without much interruption. Early in March, 1807, he had been appointed, by the Presbytery of New Brunswick, to preach to a vacant congregation in the neighbourhood. In fulfilling this appointment, he suffered from the severity of the weather, and, on his return home, was seized with an obstinate fever, which was the means of developing more fully the affection of the lungs which had troubled him so long. He continued gradually to decline for about two months—till the 17th of May

* App. to Life of Rev. Robert Finley, D. D.

when his earthly pilgrimage closed. During his last weeks and days, he exhibited an edifying example not only of Christian resignation, but of Christian triumph. Soon after the commencement of his more serious illness, he remarked to some friend—"I have for many years felt this weakness growing upon me; I have a long time apprehended that I should fall a victim to it; and now the time is coming." Being asked whether, if such were the appointment of God, he was ready to depart, he replied—"I have been examining myself, and searching out the evidence of my being in a state of grace, and upon the whole, I feel pretty well satisfied that I have really undergone a gracious change; and I am therefore willing to submit to God, knowing that his own time and way are best." With nearly his last breath, he exclaimed—"I am not afraid to die."

A Sermon was preached at his Funeral by the Rev. (afterwards Dr.) Robert Finley, and was published.

Mr. Boyd was married, shortly after his settlement, in 1784, to a Miss Taylor, daughter of Colonel Taylor, who lived in the vicinity of his residence. She died several years before her husband. They had six children, four of whom survived their father.

FROM THE REV. JOHN McDOWELL, D. D.

PHILADELPHIA, 11th June, 1852.

Dear Sir: The Rev. William Boyd of whom you wish me to furnish my recollections, was the minister of my father's family, and the first minister of whom I have any remembrance. I used to say my Catechism to him in my childhood, and I always sat under his preaching until I left home for College. My recollections of him extend down to the period of his death, which occurred after I had been in the ministry two or three years.

What would first strike you on seeing Mr. Boyd, especially in connection with the pulpit, was his remarkable gravity and dignity; and yet he was capable of unbending in free and pleasant intercourse. His appearance on the Sabbath impressed my youthful mind almost as if he had been an angel. He walked in and out of the church, looking directly before him, and never turning to the right hand or the left, unless there was some special occasion for it. There was an air of solemnity about him, that made you feel that he was a man of God; and this impression was so strong, that, before he opened his lips in the pulpit, you felt yourself pledged to listen reverently to whatever he might say. He was considerably above the medium height, and had a fine intellectual expression of countenance. His mind was cast in a superior mould. His memory was unusually retentive, his perceptions quick and clear, his judgment accurate, and his literary and general acquirements far more than respectable. He had a vein of keen wit, which he brought into exercise on suitable occasions, but never in a way to disparage in the least his ministerial character. His rich and varied attainments, and his happy power of adaptation, rendered him at once agreeable and instructive in any company.

Mr. Boyd was distinguished for an uncommon knowledge of the Scriptures. In his theological views, he was a thorough and earnest Calvinist, and was little tolerant of innovations, while yet he had no relish for controversy, and never engaged in it, unless impelled by a strong sense of duty. I remember that, in a conversation which he had with me on this subject, shortly after I began to preach, he remarked that he would give me one piece of advice;—and that was, never to raise a ghost, unless I was sure that I was able to lay him.

Mr. Boyd undoubtedly took rank among the best preachers of New Jersey. He never used notes in the pulpit—at least nothing more than a brief; and I do not think that he was accustomed fully to write out his sermons. Still, he always preached to the intelligence of his hearers, and his thoughts were well matured and luminously presented. His manner, as a public speaker, was animated and earnest, and well fitted to secure attention. I think he had no great taste or tact for public business, and my impression is that he had little to do with ecclesiastical bodies.

Yours truly,

JOHN McDOWELL.

JOSEPH CLARK, D. D.*

1783—1813.

JOSEPH CLARK was born near Elizabethtown, N. J., October 21, 1751. His parents were both persons of great worth, and his mother especially was distinguished for her piety. It was chiefly through the influence of his mother's instructions and example, that his mind early took a decidedly religious direction. While he was yet a youth, he was admitted a member of the Presbyterian Church in Elizabethtown, under the ministry of the Rev. James Caldwell.

Mr. Clark was trained to the carpenter's trade, but, after he had passed his twentieth year, he resolved to become a minister of the Gospel. He had many difficulties to contend with, but, by great patience and perseverance, he overcame them all. His progress was not a little retarded by the confusion occasioned by the American Revolution. When the British entered New Jersey, he was a member of Princeton College; but he nevertheless joined the American army, and continued, for a considerable time, in the service of his country. He then returned and completed his collegiate course, and was admitted to the degree of Bachelor of Arts in 1781, just at the close of his twenty-ninth year. He immediately entered upon his course of theological study, under the direction of the Rev. Dr. Woodhull of Monmouth, at the same time assisting the Doctor in conducting a highly respectable grammar school, which had been established through his instrumentality.

Having gone through the usual course of study prescribed to candidates for the sacred office, he was licensed to preach the Gospel on the 23d of April, 1783, by the Presbytery of New Brunswick. On the 21st of October following, he was appointed as a stated supply, for six months, to the vacant Congregation of Allentown, N. J. On the 15th of June, 1784, he was ordained, *sine titulo*, to the work of the ministry, by the Presbytery of New Brunswick. Shortly after this, the people of Allentown extended a call to him to become their pastor; but, though he laboured statedly among them from that time, he did not regularly accept their call until June, 1788, when his installation took place.

Here Mr. Clark continued, growing in the affections of his people, and the good-will and confidence of his brethren in the ministry, till January, 1796, when he was regularly translated from the pastoral charge of the Congregation in Allentown, to that of the Congregation in New Brunswick, where he continued till the close of life.

* App. to Life of Rev. Robert Finley, D. D.—MS. from Rev. I. V. Brown

In the years 1798 and 1799, the state of our Western frontier, and the destitute condition of many congregations in different parts of the country, became an object of attention and interest with the General Assembly, and with many prominent individuals in the Presbyterian Church. In the year 1800, the General Assembly fully matured their views on the subject, and appointed several agents, of whom Mr. Clark was one, to solicit donations, in various parts of the country, with a view to carry their benevolent purposes into effect. Mr. Clark addressed himself to the duties of his agency with great vigour, and collected upwards of seven thousand dollars,—a sum exceeding, by nearly two thirds, the greatest amount collected by either of his associates in the agency. He was, at the same time, performing very important service in reference to the same object, in connection with his own Presbytery.

In the year 1799, Mr. Clark was appointed by the General Assembly, in connection with several other gentlemen, to meet the General Synod of the Associate Reformed Church, in reference to their receiving and ratifying the system of correspondence and intercourse between the Associate Reformed, Reformed Dutch, and Presbyterian, Churches in the United States, which had been prepared and reported by a joint committee from these several sections of the Church, and unanimously agreed to by the preceding General Assembly. The effort, however, proved unsuccessful.

In March, 1802, the edifice, library, and philosophical apparatus, of the College of New Jersey were destroyed by fire. Here again, Mr. Clark's labours were put in requisition for collecting funds to repair the very extensive loss. He travelled into the interior of Virginia, and made liberal collections for his object, but his labours were prematurely interrupted by a serious illness, which obliged him to suspend all active exertion for a considerable time.

In 1802, he was elected a member of the Corporation of the College of New Jersey, and continued to discharge the duties of the office with great zeal and fidelity to the close of life. He was also, for many successive years, a member of the Committee of Missions, which acted by the appointment, and under the direction, of the General Assembly.

In 1809, he was honoured with the degree of Doctor of Divinity from Jefferson College.

Dr. Clark had at best a feeble constitution and imperfect health; but he was nevertheless among the most active ministers of his day. For a short time previous to his death, he had suffered from some increase of indisposition; but the evening before, he seemed much better, and had retired to rest with the expectation of setting off early the next morning to meet the Synod of New York and New Jersey. His wife, having her attention drawn to him by something unusual, hastened to his bedside, and found him in the agonies of death. Medical aid was instantly called, but it was unavailing—it was found that violent spasms had stopped the motion of his vital powers. He died on the 19th of October, 1813.

Dr. Clark's only publications were a Sermon occasioned by the death of the Hon. William Patterson, 1806, and two Discourses in the New Jersey Preacher, 1813.

He was married, not long after his first settlement in the ministry, to a Miss Imley, of Allentown, sister of the Hon. James H. Imley, who was for some time a Representative in Congress from New Jersey. They had four children,—one daughter and three sons. The eldest son was a clergyman, the second a lawyer, and the third a physician. The eldest, *John Flavel*, was graduated at the College of New Jersey in 1807, holding rank among the first scholars in his class. After his graduation, he was engaged for some time in teaching in the State of Georgia. He commenced the study of Divinity in the Theological Seminary at Andover; but, before his course was completed, was chosen Tutor in his Alma Mater at Princeton, and held the office three years, still pursuing his theological course under Dr. Green, President of the College. He was licensed to preach the Gospel by the Presbytery of New Brunswick, and by the same Presbytery was subsequently ordained and installed Pastor of the united Congregations of Flemington and Amwell. This connection continued more than twenty years. He was afterwards settled at Patterson, N. J., and was called thence to take charge of the Presbyterian Congregation of Cold Spring, Putnam County, N. Y. Leaving Cold Spring, he was for about one year at Oyster Bay, L. I., and then accepted a call from the Presbyterian Congregation of Fishkill, Dutchess County, N. Y.—he was installed May 18, 1847, and continued there till his death, which took place in 1853. He had the reputation of being a benevolent and excellent man, and an able and faithful minister.

FROM THE REV. ISAAC V. BROWN.

TRENTON, December 9, 1854.

Dear Sir: The Rev. Dr. Joseph Clark of New Brunswick, concerning whom you ask for my recollections, was one of the three or four most intelligent, active and influential ministers of the Gospel in this State, and so continued till his death. I had the best opportunities for knowing him in public and in private. I sat under his ministry more than a year. Being the teacher of his three sons, in connection with Bishop Croes, I was often in his family; and while he was absent, collecting funds for Princeton College, then recently burnt to the ground, I uniformly at night occupied a room in his house. Mrs. Clark was very amiable, kind and excellent, but very timid; and having four children in early years, and only female help, she needed some protection.

Dr. Clark possessed a mind originally of a superior order, and enlarged and accomplished by much reading and study. Such was the peculiar character of his mind, that he was eminently qualified to be a successful agent in business implicating the characters, involving the interests, and touching the sensibilities and passions, of men. He was independent and firm in his exercise of thought, and accustomed to rely very much on his own judgment; and, without appearing to be ambitious, presuming, or self-confident, he was always ready and forward to aid, and if need be, to direct, in any great and good work. He had much to do in accomplishing several important public objects in his day.

In the pulpit he was always solemn, dignified and instructive. His discourses were solid and judicious, and well fitted to leave a lasting impression on the mind of the attentive hearer. His representations of Scripture doctrine were thoroughly Calvinistic; but they were also in a high degree practical. His elocution was deliberate, and, on ordinary occasions, on account of the weakness of his lungs, he spoke with no great animation; but there were times when he seemed to rise above his bodily debility, and to display not a little of the spirit and energy of the Christian orator.

In debate, he had a remarkable talent both to scrutinize and to defeat the arguments and aims of his adversary. He had promptness without arrogance in advancing, and firmness without obstinacy or ostentation in maintaining, his opinions. If he had inadvertently deviated from order, or committed an error in his statements, it seemed to give him pleasure, when reminded of it, even by the most inconsiderable of his brethren, to make acknowledgment and reparation. The opinions and arguments of opponents in discussion he treated with the utmost respect. On the introduction of a new subject, he did not employ the artifice sometimes resorted to by those who aim only at triumph in debate, of waiting in silence to discover the popular impulse, that he might the more certainly espouse the successful side of the question—on the contrary, he was often, on such occasions, one of the first speakers; and, instead of betraying himself into the power of his antagonists for the want of previous thought, he generally showed himself prepared to speak at once appropriately and effectively.

In the details of business, few men probably have surpassed him. In giving thought an eligible form on paper for any specific purpose; in drawing an article of agreement between hostile parties; in sketching a resolution or report, or performing any kindred service, on a sudden emergency, he seemed to have an intuitive perception of what the occasion required. He was patient, indefatigable and accurate, far beyond what is usual even with men of his high character and standing.

Dr. Clark possessed extraordinary colloquial powers, and a strong relish for cultivated society; and his extensive and various information, his easy address and facility at communication, rendered him an uncommonly instructive and agreeable companion. In his person, he was of full the medium stature, but slender; his complexion was fair; his eyes sharp and blue; his hair light and not very abundant. In his manners, he exhibited a due proportion of dignity and familiarity, candour and affection. In all his walk through life, with the politeness and affability of the man of literature and the gentleman, he mingled that purity of conversation and that savour of devotion, which ought ever to characterize a minister of Jesus Christ. Hospitality always presided at his board. He welcomed the society of the excellent, the intelligent and honourable of every denomination, of all ranks, and from every quarter. He could accommodate himself with great ease to every kind of company, whether cultivated or uncultivated, and knew how to make persons of every description easy and happy in his presence and in his family. His memory well deserves to be honoured and embalmed.

I am, my dear Sir, truly yours,

ISAAC V. BROWN.

CHARLES NISBET, D. D.*

1785—1804.

CHARLES NISBET, the third son of William and Alison Nisbet, was born at Haddington, in Scotland, January 21, 1736. His elder brother, Andrew, was a minister of the Established Church, and was settled in the parish of Garvald, in the Presbytery of Haddington. Of the occupation and circumstances of his father little more is known than that they were not such as to enable him to defray the expenses of his son's education beyond a bare preparation for the University. But, notwithstanding the son was thus early cast upon his own resources, so intense was his thirst for knowledge, that he was enabled to accomplish his favourite object with comparatively little difficulty. He entered the University of Edinburgh in 1752, and at the same time made an engagement as a private tutor, by means of which he was enabled to meet the expenses of his whole college course. He is supposed to have graduated in the year 1754, in the eighteenth year of his age.

From the University he passed immediately to the Divinity Hall in Edinburgh, where he continued a diligent and successful student six years; during which time he supported himself chiefly by his contributions to one of the popular periodicals of the day. There still remain among his private papers some records of his religious exercises at that time, which show that, if he was enthusiastically devoted to Theology as a *science*, he was nevertheless an earnest and devout Christian. He was licensed to preach the Gospel, by the Presbytery of Edinburgh, on the 24th of September, 1760.

His first engagement, as a stated preacher, was with the Church in the Gorbals of Glasgow. The congregation stipulated, in addition to the salary promised in their call, to furnish him with a house; but, as he had no family to occupy a house, they failed to fulfil this part of their engagement. After having remained with them about two years, he received a call from the Church in Montrose, which he thought proper to accept. On taking leave of his congregation, he, with his wonted aptness, preached to them from Acts xxviii. 30—"And Paul dwelt two whole years in his own hired house, and received all that came in unto him."

The Church of Montrose was a large and intelligent one, and the right of patronage of the parish was vested in George the Third. Mr. Nisbet was ordained on the 17th of May, 1764, by the Presbytery of Brechin, within the bounds of which he had his pastoral charge. Notwithstanding he was settled as co-pastor with the Rev. John Cooper, yet the advanced age and consequent infirmities of his colleague devolved upon *him* nearly the whole amount of pastoral duty. He addressed himself to his work, however, with great energy and success, and quickly won not only the respect, but the admiration, of his extensive and influential charge.

About two years after his settlement in Montrose, he was married to Anne, daughter of Thomas Tweedie, of Quarter, about thirty miles South of Edinburgh. An attachment had existed between them for twelve years; but their marriage had been postponed from prudential considerations. Another distinguished personage was married at Montrose about the same

* Memoir by Dr. Miller.—Communication from Rev. Dr. Robert Proudfit.

time; and as they were both intimate friends of the celebrated Dr. Beattie, Professor at Aberdeen, he composed on the occasion a beautiful poem which he styled *Epithalamium Montrosianum*.

Not long after Mr. Nisbet's settlement at Montrose, Dr. Witherspoon, then Pastor of the Church at Paisley, was chosen to succeed Dr. Finley as President of Princeton College. His first impression was that he could not accept; and his first answer was in the negative. But Mr. Nisbet, though at that time only thirty-one years of age, was the person whom Dr. Witherspoon recommended as more suitable to fill that important station than any other within his knowledge. The Doctor, however, on more mature reflection, concluded to accept the place; and though his answer in the negative had already been communicated to the Trustees of the College, yet, on receiving an intimation of a change in his views, they immediately renewed the appointment, and he forthwith signified his acceptance of it. Witherspoon had had something to do in conducting Nisbet's early studies; and they always remained firm friends until death separated them.

It is well known that, at the time when Mr. Nisbet entered the ministry, the Church of Scotland was divided into two parties,—the *orthodox* and the *moderate*,—a division, which, it is believed, is recognised, to some extent at least, to this day. Mr. Nisbet was uniformly and decisively associated with the orthodox party; and though that party was then considerably in the minority, yet, in several instances, with the vigorous co-operation of Dr. Witherspoon, he made himself deeply felt in the General Assembly, and even succeeded in carrying certain measures which were regarded as adverse to the interests of the opposite party. One or two of his speeches in the Assembly have been preserved, which may be considered as models of eloquence in an ecclesiastical deliberative assembly; unless perhaps some might think them more highly spiced with wit than consists with the decorum due to such an occasion.

In the year 1771, Mr. Nisbet wrote a review of Wesley's System of doctrine, which was, at that time, attracting considerable attention from the theologians of Scotland. The article,—which, however, was not published till several years afterwards,—discovers a remarkably comprehensive and discriminating mind, though it deals with both the system and its author with no inconsiderable severity. Had it been written at a later period, it has been thought by a competent judge, who knew the writer well, that it would have borne a somewhat different character.

Mr. Nisbet, in common with many other distinguished men of his country, justified the claims of the American Colonies, which brought on the war of the Revolution. And, in the progress of the struggle, he hesitated not boldly to proclaim his views, both in public and in private; and sometimes with such scathing irony, that the partisans of government, while they could hardly repress a smile, were yet burning with indignation. He showed himself also the earnest friend of reform in the Established Church. The Patronage Act especially he opposed with great zeal, and in 1782 he drew up a series of resolutions which were adopted at a large meeting in Montrose,—designed to procure the repeal of that Act, and restore to the Churches the right to choose their own ministers. But, notwithstanding he was so often found, in reference to matters of Church, and of State, and of both united, on the unpopular side, his varied talents and acquirements, in connection with his acknowledged sterling integrity and worth, secured to him a very general and substantial popularity.

In 1783, the degree of Doctor of Divinity was conferred upon him by the Trustees of Princeton College;—an honour which, it is said, would probably have been conferred by the same institution at an earlier period, but for the temporary interruption of friendly intercourse between this country and Great Britain, occasioned by the war of the Revolution.

In 1783, a new College was founded at Carlisle, Pa., called Dickinson College, in honour of the celebrated statesman, John Dickinson, who, at least nominally, took the lead in its establishment. In April, 1784, Dr. Nisbet was chosen President of this institution; and his acceptance of the office was urged by Mr. Dickinson, Dr. Rush, and others, with great importunity. He was quite aware that the enterprise must involve serious difficulties; though there were some of which he was not, and could not be, aware till he should learn them by experience. After having had the invitation some time before him, and looked at it in various and somewhat conflicting lights, he, at length, in opposition to the judgment of many of his best friends, signified his acceptance of it; and shortly after set about preparing for his voyage to America.

He sailed from Greenock with his family, on the 23d of April, 1785, and landed at Philadelphia on the 9th of June following. He brought with him his wife, two sons, and two daughters; having buried four children previous to his leaving Scotland. After remaining a few weeks in the family of Dr. Rush, at Philadelphia, and in the mean time making a short visit to his old friend Dr. Witherspoon, at Princeton, he set out for Carlisle, and reached it amidst the usual patriotic demonstrations of the Fourth of July. He was received by the assembled multitude with the most marked testimonies of respect; and, on the next day, was formally inducted to his new office. His Inaugural Discourse,—the only Discourse he ever allowed to be printed,—was designed to illustrate the importance of the union between learning and piety. It was considered as well worthy of its able and accomplished author.

Scarcely had Dr. Nisbet entered on the duties of his office, before he and several of his family were attacked with a violent fever, from which their recovery was very difficult and gradual. The Doctor himself suffered more severely than the rest; and, after a confinement of several months, during which he was utterly inadequate to any mental or bodily exertion, he had so far yielded to discouragement as to resolve on returning to his native country. He, therefore, ou the 18th of October succeeding his arrival, tendered to the Board of Trustees of the College the resignation of his office; which, however deeply regretted by them, they, on the whole, felt constrained to accept. As the season was unfavourable to a voyage across the ocean, he determined to postpone his return until spring; and, in the mean time, he had so far regained his health and spirits, that he consented to be re-appointed to his office; and, accordingly, on the 10th of May, 1786, he was unanimously elected, a second time, President of the College. Though it was some time before his health was fully restored, yet it was never afterwards seriously interrupted, till the approach of the malady that, many years after, closed his life.

As soon as his health would warrant his return to vigorous labour, he not only resumed his official duties, but pursued them to an extent which would have seemed an over-match for any constitution. He immediately commenced the preparation and delivery of four different courses of Lectures;—one on Logic; another on the Philosophy of the Mind; a third on Moral Philosophy; and a fourth on Belles Lettres, including interesting views of the principal Latin and Greek classics. Each of these lectures was written, so far as it was written at all, on the evening immediately preceding the delivery; but his mind was such a storehouse of well digested and admirably arranged material, pertaining to every subject, that a few hints only, committed to paper, were all the preparation that he needed for a meeting with his class.

In addition to the amount of labour already referred to, he yielded to a request of several of the graduates of the College, who had in view the Christian ministry, to give them a course of lectures on Systematic Theology. He was accustomed to deliver one of these lectures every day in the week, except Saturday and Sunday, while the College was in session; and the whole course consisted of four hundred and eighteen lectures, and extended through a period of somewhat more than two years. They were all written out, and read with great deliberation, so that each student might take them down from the lips of the lecturer. He did not claim for them the merit of entire originality, but frankly told his students that he availed himself freely of the writings of the most approved theological authors. After this course was completed, he delivered another, consisting of twenty-two lectures, on the Pastoral Office; and these also were taken down by the students in the same manner as the others.

Besides his onerous labours in connection with the College, he regularly preached in the Presbyterian Church in Carlisle, alternately with the Rev. Dr. Davidson, who was at that time its Pastor. His services here, as well as in the College, were very generally and highly appreciated.

At the first Commencement in the College, which occurred on the 26th of September, 1787, there were nine young gentlemen admitted to the degree of Bachelor of Arts; and the institution, in its constantly increasing prosperity, showed the influence of its distinguished head. It must be admitted, however, that Dr. Nisbet's expectations in coming to this country were, by no means, fully answered. Notwithstanding the great object of the Revolution had been gained in our national independence, yet the intellectual, moral, and in some respects the civil, interests of the country had suffered greatly in the struggle; and he found such a state of things here as it was hardly possible for him to anticipate. He came when the elements were in a chaotic state, and were highly susceptible of the influence of any vigorous and plastic hand. His letters to his friends in Scotland breathe a feeling of disappointment; but he was not unwilling to submit to some inconvenience and self-denial for the sake of doing something to mould the character of an infant nation.

In the spring of 1792, Dr. Nisbet paid a visit to Governor Dickinson, in honour of whom the College was named, and who then resided at Wilmington, De. The Governor, who felt himself in some degree responsible for unredeemed pledges made to Dr. Nisbet, previous to his leaving Scotland, received him with every mark of hospitality and respectful attention; and the visit seems to have been mutually and highly gratifying. On the first evening after the Doctor's arrival, the conversation turned on the probable effect of an earnest prosecution of the study of the physical sciences on the religious character; and such was the impression made on the mind of the Governor by the remarks of his distinguished guest, that, at the close of the conversation, he said to him,—"Doctor, what you have said would form an invaluable octavo volume. I would give a large sum to have it in that form." The Governor urged him to pay him an annual visit; and Dr. Nisbet, shortly after his return home, received notice that Mr. Dickinson had deposited five hundred dollars in one of the banks of Philadelphia, subject to his order, to meet the expense of the visits which he had solicited. The President was not slow to avail himself of this proffered generosity; and, accordingly, for several years afterwards, paid an annual and most welcome visit to his distinguished friend. His journeys were always made on horseback.

In the year 1793, Dr. Nisbet was subjected to some peculiar trials, in consequence of what was called the "Whiskey Rebellion;"—a rebellion in Pennsylvania, occasioned by the tax laid by the government of the United States on ardent spirits. Feeling that it was one of those occasions on which the pulpit had a right to be heard, Dr. Nisbet, while the tumultuous scene was in progress, preached a sermon that was designed to discountenance the rebellious procedure, and that contained some sarcastic allusions that gave great offence to the insurgent party. A few days after, when a company of the rebels came into Carlisle from the adjacent country, to erect a Whiskey or Liberty Pole, serious apprehensions were entertained that Dr. Nisbet's house would be assailed by the mob; and several respectable individuals offered to remain in it, for the purpose of aiding in its defence, if there should be occasion; but the Doctor declined their offer, on the ground that their presence might serve to invite attack. The result, however, justified the apprehension of his danger; for the mob were actually on their way to accomplish a work of destruction upon his dwelling, when they were met by some one who informed them that the President's younger daughter was seriously ill, and were persuaded, in consequence of this information, to forego their contemplated outrage.

Early in January, 1804, Dr. Nisbet took a severe cold, which grew into a fever and inflammation of the lungs, and finally terminated his life. He died on the 18th of the month, after an illness of less than three weeks. During the greater part of the time, his bodily sufferings were intense, but his patience and fortitude were most exemplary. Even after he lost the power of conversing with those around him, his mind was evidently absorbed in communion with his God. He died with "Holy, Holy, Holy," upon his lips, wanting only three days of having completed the sixty-eighth year of his age. His funeral was attended by a large concourse, who evinced the most affectionate respect for his memory, and an appropriate Sermon was delivered on the occasion by the Rev. Dr. Davidson.

Dr. Nisbet left a widow who survived him more than three years, and died in the hope of a better life, May 12, 1807. He left four children. The eldest son, *Thomas*, who had been graduated at the University of Edinburgh, died shortly after his father. His second son, *Alexander*, after graduating at Dickinson College, studied law, and settled in Baltimore, where, for many years, he has held the office of Judge of the City Court. The eldest daughter, *Mary*, was married, in 1790, to William Turnbull, Esq., a native of Scotland, but at that time a resident of Pittsburg, and survived her father about twenty years. The youngest daughter, *Alison*, who was married to Dr. Samuel McCoskry, an eminent physician of Carlisle, in 1795, was left a widow in 1818, and is still (1849) living. Her only surviving son is the Rt. Rev. Samuel McCoskry, Bishop of the Protestant Episcopal Church in the Diocese of Michigan.

Dr. Nisbet's valuable library, consisting of many of the rarest works, fell into the hands of his two grandsons, Bishop McCoskry and Mr. Henry C. Turnbull, who, with most commendable liberality, presented it to the Theological Seminary at Princeton.

Dr. Nisbet, while in Scotland, was in intimate relations with many distinguished individuals in that country, and he maintained a constant correspondence with several of them after he came to America. Among his most devoted friends were the Countess of Leven,—a lady distinguished for her intelligence and piety, the Earl of Buchan,—well known in this country as Washington's correspondent, and the Rev. Dr. John Erskine of Edinburgh,—for a long time a leader of the orthodox part of the Established Church. The latter left as a legacy to Dr. Nisbet a considerable part of his library; but before the fact was known in this country, the venerable legatee had departed.

FROM THE REV. SAMUEL MILLER, D. D.

PRINCETON, April 30, 1849.

Rev. and dear Sir: Your proposal to include some account of the Rev. Dr. Charles Nisbet, late President of Dickinson College, in your projected biographical work, gives me much pleasure. And when you call upon me for some reminiscences of that great and good man, I feel myself honoured and gratified. You have called me not to the performance of a task, but to the enjoyment of a privilege; for I can never think of his revered name, without a throb of veneration, gratitude, and love, which it is not easy fully to express in language.

My acquaintance with this excellent and venerable man commenced in the autumn of 1791. He had arrived in America from Scotland six years before; had established a high reputation as President of a College; had delivered a course of Lectures on Systematic Theology, which were deemed by the best judges to be eminently able and instructive; and was extensively regarded as the most learned divine of the United States. These considerations induced me, after having studied Theology two years with a beloved father, on his decease, to spend a large part of the third under the counsel and guidance of Dr. Nisbet. Accordingly, I went to Carlisle, spent a few months in the immediate vicinity of his residence, and enjoyed opportunities of listening to his instruction and studying his character, which I shall always remember with grateful pleasure. I regard very few of the months of my life, as having been either so pleasantly or profitably spent.

My Memoir of this eminent man, published a few years ago, contains the results of my observation upon his character; and I know not how I can serve your purpose better than by availing myself of some portions of that in my present communication.

Dr. Nisbet's intellectual powers were universally acknowledged to be of a very high order. That his memory was all but prodigious, and his wit seldom equalled, all who knew him, with one voice, conceded. His memory extended to words as well as things, and seemed to serve him without effort on all occasions. This being the case, some may be ready to doubt whether one so remarkable for the power of recalling past impressions, and of tracing unusual and striking associations of ideas, would be likely to be a sound or strong reasoner,

But his power in the judicatories of the Church, and many of his sermons, as well as several things which have appeared from his pen, especially his Review of the system of Mr. John Wesley, clearly evinced that his reasoning powers, as well as those of retention and imagination, were remarkably clear and vigorous. The rapidity, as well as the vigour, of his mental operations, was noticed as striking by all who conversed with him. If controversy had more strongly called his reasoning talents into exercise, there can be no doubt that there would have been a display of them of the most honourable kind.

In love of knowledge and in solid learning, this eminent man undoubtedly exceeded even most of those denominated the learned men of his age. He had been a devoted student from his boyhood. He read books, (as I have often had occasion to observe,) in half, if not one third, of the time, which it cost any other person I ever saw. And he seemed to forget nothing that he read. Studies of this kind could not fail of leading to an accumulation of knowledge of the rarest extent and value. He seemed to have read every book, and to have studied every subject, which the best informed person in his company could ever mention. He perhaps more fully deserved the title that was given him before he left Scotland,—*a walking library*,—than any other man in the United States.

His familiarity with the Greek and Latin classics was especially remarkable. Of this many striking proofs and examples were continually occurring. A single one will suffice. Once, not long after his settlement in Carlisle, when he was dining with a select literary circle, a lawyer of considerable eminence, who greatly prided himself on his acquaintance with the Latin and Greek languages, was of the company. In the course of conversation, this gentleman quoted several lines in the original Greek from Homer's Iliad. When he had finished his quotation, Dr. Nisbet said to him,—"Well, mon, go on; what you've left is just as good as what you've taken." The gentleman confessed that his memory did not serve him for repeating more. The Doctor then began where he had ended, and with the greatest ease repeated a considerable additional portion.

But his knowledge of languages was not confined to the Latin and Greek. He was an excellent critic in Hebrew literature. He also read French, German, Italian, Spanish and Portuguese—the two first named, with perfect ease and familiarity, and all in such a manner as to understand the scope, and to relish the beauties, of the principal writers in those respective tongues. Here were nine languages possessed and used by one man. To some of them he did not apply his mind until late in life; and in making his acquisitions in this field, he proceeded almost entirely by his own unassisted efforts, without enjoying any of those facilities which much travel, large libraries, and the constant society and aid of great linguists, so richly afford.

As a Preacher, Dr. Nisbet's excellence was great and peculiar. In early life, he was in the habit of preparing for the pulpit by writing a portion, and sometimes a considerable portion, of what he intended to deliver. But it was only on special occasions that he wrote the whole. What he wrote he commonly committed to memory, which, with him, was a very short and easy process. Two or at most three readings of that which had been recently written, would enable him to repeat it verbatim. He was probably never known to carry a paper, or any kind of help to his memory, into the pulpit. Such a mind needed no such aid. After he came to America, he wrote but two sermons, one at his Inauguration as President of the College, which was printed, and the other on the death of Washington, which, though solicited by many to be published, was never committed to the press.

In the later periods of his life, when I enjoyed the privilege, not only of hearing him, but also of being much with him in private, his preparation for the pulpit seemed to cost him very little labour. Indeed there appeared to be no particular portion of time set apart for it. Even the members of his own family never knew when it was done. The truth is, his mind was so richly furnished with knowledge, his memory so extraordinary, his imagination so much under his command, and all his powers so prompt and obedient to his will, that it seemed almost as easy for him to preach as to breathe. Nor was his preaching, by any means, of that common-place, declamatory character, which too generally belongs to the extemporary speakers, in which words are more abundant than thoughts. On the contrary, his sermons abounded in thought, always weighty and instructive; often new, striking and deeply interesting.

His delivery in the pulpit was not remarkably graceful, or conformed to the rules of art. His voice was small, scarcely sufficient to fill a large house, without extraordinary effort. He made very little gesture. He seldom rose to much vehemence, but poured out a flood of precious truth, good sense, and unaffected piety, with a uniformity and solidity which never failed to fix and reward the attention of those, who were more intent on richness of thought and sound theological instruction, than on the ornaments of rhetoric, or the graces of a fascinating delivery. His style of speaking was remarkably clear, manly, unaffected, direct, and adapted to please all classes of intelligent and serious hearers. His powers of argument and of illustration seemed to be inexhaustible; and when the hour (to which his sermons were usually confined) was out, he closed, not from the least failure of matter, but rather from the unexpected and regretted failure of time. On one occasion, when visiting a friend in the ministry, that friend having left the discussion of an important subject unfinished in his morning's discourse, Dr. Nisbet, in the afternoon, took it up at the point where it had been left, and brought it to a close in a manner equally instructive and interesting;—and all this, without retiring a moment for study, or appearing to devote any time to preparation.

As a Divine, Dr. Nisbet was a thorough old school Calvinist. He was a devoted friend of the Westminster Confession of Faith; considering it as a lucid and most happy exhibition of the system of doctrine taught in the Holy Scriptures. The arrangement of his course of Theological Lectures was in conformity with the chapters of this Confession.

As the President of a College, Dr. Nisbet had many peculiar difficulties to contend with; but amidst them all, he maintained an honourable standing in the estimation of all sober and competent judges. With respect to one branch of discipline, that is, inflicting the penalties prescribed by the laws on individual students, the tendency of Dr. Nisbet's mind was to err on the side of undue lenity, rather than that of over strictness. His peculiar benevolence often led him—as some thought, too often—to overlook irregularities and disorders, or to arrest the stroke of justice, when the interests of the College demanded that it should fall on the head of the offender. But in regard to the discipline of his wit and sarcasm, he was the terror of disorderly students. Frequently, when the lash of the law either could not be inflicted, or failed of making the proper impression, he could, by a single sentence of caustic wit, cover the delinquent with mortification and shame. Indeed, there is reason to believe that, in more than one instance, young men were so deeply and painfully stung by an unexpected stroke of satire or sarcasm, that they had no other refuge from the ridicule which it brought upon them, than to leave the College.

Dr. Nisbet, after he came to America, for various reasons, which need not here be stated, seldom attended the General Assembly of the Church to which he belonged; and when he did attend, seldom took an active part in its proceedings. He sometimes, indeed, came to Philadelphia during the sessions of the Assembly, but it was more frequently for the purpose of relaxing himself during a collegiate vacation, or of meeting clerical friends, than for taking a seat in the Body as a member. This was once humorously recognised by himself in a conversation with the late Dr. Mason of New York, with whom he happened to meet on one of these visits. Dr. Mason said to him in that free and jocular manner for which he was remarkable,—" Well, Doctor, I find you sometimes come to Philadelphia during the sessions of the General Assembly." " Yes," said he, " I am not a member, but I like to meet my friends, and see a little of what is going on." *Mason*—" But do you not sometimes go into the Assembly, and listen to its proceedings?" *Nisbet*—" Yes, I sometimes go in for the *benefit of hearing*, and then I come out for the *benefit of not hearing*." *Mason*—" Well, Doctor, which is the greater benefit?" *Nisbet*—" Indeed, mon, it's hard to strike the balance."

As the wit of Dr. Nisbet was exuberant and inexhaustible, and as, on some occasions adapted to call it forth, he could wield with power the weapons of ridicule and sarcasm, it might be supposed by such as did not know him, that he was wanting in tenderness and sympathy. This, however, was far from being the case. On the contrary, few men were ever more remarkable than he, for their feeling and benevolent hearts. Of this I have myself witnessed many striking examples, but will advert to only one. In the winter of 1791, the melancholy defeat of General St. Clair, by the Miami Indians, occurred, to the distress of the nation. A large part of the American army, which was engaged in that expedition, had, on its way Westward, encamped for a number of weeks in the neighbourhood of Carlisle, and became considerably acquainted with the inhabitants of the borough. I was in Carlisle when the disastrous event occurred, and had for weeks before heard the Doctor indulging his wit at the expense of the government of the United States, and of that army, and its prospects in particular. When the news of its sanguinary defeat arrived, instead of receiving it, as those who did not know him well, might have expected, with more than his usual sarcasm, he was affected, melted, nay almost overwhelmed, by the sad intelligence. If he had lost any of his nearest and most beloved relatives on that field of national disaster, he could not have manifested more deep or heartfelt grief than he expressed, not merely in a single short paroxysm of feeling, but for a number of days together. Indeed, his whole history exhibited him as kind hearted and sympathetic to a degree greatly beyond what is common in those who are popularly called benevolent men.

The domestic character of Dr. Nisbet was eminently amiable and exemplary. In the relations of husband, parent, and master, he exhibited a bright example of the most vigilant fidelity, affection, and benevolence. No one could enter the door of his dwelling without perceiving that his family was the abode, not merely of order and harmony, but of the most endearing attention and love.

Dr. Nisbet, however, with all his accomplishments, was not so well qualified as many inferior men, to meet the exigencies, and encounter the difficulties, which attended his transfer of residence to America. The Countess of Leven was undoubtedly correct, when she intimated to him in one of her letters that he was not fitted to engage in scenes of hardy endurance and conflict. He laboured under a nervous timidity, which rendered it difficult for him to meet physical danger with composure. He had no taste nor fitness for resisting injuries, or contending with the unfeeling or unjust. His wit, too, not being always under the government of cautious reserve, sometimes led him to attack popular prejudices or iniquitous actions, in a style which many who did not know his sterling honesty and benevolence, were not always ready to excuse. To which may be added, that the first fifty years of his life having been spent amid European scenes and habits, he never acquired a facility in making such allowance for American scenes and habits as the situation of our country really required.

Dr. Nisbet's person was, in height, rather below the middle stature, and in early life slender, and full of agility. He often said that, in his youth, in walking, it was easy for him to keep pace with an ordinary horseman; and that he frequently, on a winter's morning, walked twenty or thirty miles before break fast, without any painful effort. Before his arrival at middle age, however, he became corpulent, and continued so to the end of life. It came upon him suddenly, like a disease, and no degree of abstinence which he could adopt, appeared to arrest or diminish it. Yet his corpulence did not interfere much with activity, even in advanced age. His motions were habitually rapid, and such as might have been expected in one who had been once so remarkably agile. He was characteristically quick in every movement, physical and intellectual. Neither did his corpulence interfere with his health. This was seldom interrupted. He was, indeed, occasionally troubled with some disorder of the stomach, somewhat similar to the modern fashionable disease called *dyspepsia*. He, however, very seldom took medicine; but generally found himself entirely relieved by a fast of twenty-four hours, to which he uniformly resorted.

Many other virtues besides those which have been mentioned, might be celebrated as shining in the character of this remarkable man. His perfect integrity; his freedom from all hidden policy or concealment; the disclosure of his sentiments on all subjects with the simplicity of a child; and his habitual disinterestedness, formed a charm of the most attractive kind in all his Christian and social intercourse.

To have had the opportunity of contributing any thing, however small, towards embalming the memory of this extraordinary man, I regard as one of the precious privileges of my life.

I am, Rev. and dear Sir,

Very sincerely yours,

SAMUEL MILLER.

JOHN DURBURROW BLAIR.*

1785—1823.

JOHN DURBURROW BLAIR was born at Fagg's Manor, Pa., October 15, 1759. He was a son of the Rev. John Blair, who was for a while settled in the neighbourhood of Carlisle, and afterwards succeeded his brother as both pastor of the church and teacher of the school, at Fagg's Manor. The subject of this sketch was graduated at the College of New Jersey in the year 1775, under the Presidency of Dr. Witherspoon. The Doctor, having been requested to name a suitable person to take charge of Washington Henry Academy in Virginia, which had been under the care of the Rev. Daniel McCalla, thought proper to recommend young Mr. Blair, who immediately repaired to Hanover, and entered on the duties of his office.

Mr. Blair had, early in life, made a profession of religion, and had formed a purpose to pursue the study of Theology. This purpose he continued to prosecute, without an instructer, after his removal to the South; and having passed through the prescribed trials in the Presbytery of Hanover, was licensed to preach the Gospel about the year 1785. Soon after this, he received a call from the Church in Pole Green, in Hanover, of which Samuel Davies had been pastor, while in Virginia; and, having accepted the call, was ordained to the pastoral office. He retained his connection with this church till within a few years of his death, when, by reason of the infirmities

* MS. from Rev. Dr. Archibald Alexander.

of age, he was no longer able to attend to his pastoral duties in connection with it. He was married to a Miss Winston, the daughter of a respectable gentleman in Hanover. The Academy not flourishing according to his wishes and expectations, he determined to remove his residence to the city of Richmond. Here he taught the classics to a number of boys in his own house, and preached on every alternate Sabbath in the Capitol, still giving the one half of his labours to the Church in Hanover, which was not more than nine or ten miles distant. His preaching in Richmond was in friendly association with the Rev. Dr. Buchanan, of the Episcopal Church. Between these two clergymen there subsisted a long and intimate friendship, which was terminated only by the decease of the latter. After the memorable calamity of the loss of so many valuable lives by the burning of the Richmond Theatre, in the year 1812, it was resolved by the inhabitants of Capitol Hill to build a Monumental Church on the site of the late Theatre. In this enterprise all the families, Presbyterian as well as Episcopalian, who had been accustomed to worship in the Capitol, enlisted, without, it would seem, any very definite understanding as to the ultimate destination of the edifice; though, after it was completed, it was thought best that it should be occupied exclusively by some one denomination, and the majority decided in favour of the Episcopalians. The friends of Mr. Blair, now animated by a more liberal and energetic spirit than ever before, proceeded to erect a handsome church edifice for themselves on Shockoe Hill, where he officiated during the remainder of his life. Before this time, the people had never been formed into a regular church: there were neither elders nor deacons, and the Lord's Supper had never been administered by Mr. Blair in Richmond; but such as were communicants were accustomed to go to the church in Hanover to join in the participation of that ordinance. As soon as their house was completed, a regular church was constituted, which still remains, and has been under the charge of several successive pastors since the death of Mr. Blair.

After he took up his residence in Richmond, he became intimate with the most enlightened men of the place, among whom were Judge Marshall and Judge Washington, who were remarkably fond of his company, and spent much of their leisure in a club of which he was an esteemed member.

His death came not suddenly, but gradually; and when he found his end approaching, he had his children called around his bed, and addressed them in the following manner:—"I have little to say to you,—much less than I expected, in consequence of weakness. In the contemplation of death, you are present to my mind. To part with you will be a painful scene. My manner of life, my doctrine, and the exhortations I have given you, you know. I have nothing new to add to these now. Your reliance for the pardon of your sins must be on the Lord Jesus Christ. To Him alone you must look. You must be sanctified. You were born in sin, as I was. This must be overcome; for nothing unholy can ever enter the Kingdom of Heaven. The grace of God alone is sufficient to sanctify you, to rectify the disorders which sin has introduced, and to implant in your hearts new principles, destroying the power and the love of sin. This grace is ever to be sought with humble, penitent, fervent hearts. In addition to this, and in consequence of this, you will find your highest delight in God, and your highest pleasure in his service. As for myself, I have reason to believe that I was early made a subject of Divine grace. I have not been without my faults. My aberrations are chiefly in practical religion. When I was young, I was very enthusiastic; had the folly to think that if they would let me preach, I could convert the world. But God was pleased to show me my insufficiency. When I began to preach, I converted nobody. I could not do it. Yet I hope God has made me an instrument of good to many souls. When I came to maturer years, my religion became rather a calm and settled conviction and habit, than a matter of feeling and an ebullition of love. And now, after I am gone, if it is asked whether I made any remarkable speech, you may answer, No; but that I am not without hope and confidence. I depend on Him in whom I have believed. I think I have a right to plead his promises of mercy. He has never left me nor forsaken me. He has supported me all along, and I believe, will do so still. I know that I must pass through the dark valley and shadow of death; but I think I am prepared for God's will, and that I shall be ready when He shall call me home. 'Lord Jesus, into thy hands I commend my spirit!' I should like once more to speak to this congregation; but I shall not be able to do that." His death occurred in January, 1823; and his Funeral Sermon was preached by the Rev. John Blair Hoge, in the church on Shockoe Hill, already mentioned.

Mr. Blair published a few occasional Sermons during his life, and after his death, a volume of his Sermons was published under the direction of his successor, the Rev. J. B. Hoge.

FROM MRS. DR. JOHN H. RICE.

NEAR HAMPDEN SIDNEY COLLEGE, May 3, 1854.

My dear Sir: I knew the Rev. J. D. Blair slightly before I removed to Richmond to reside in 1812; but from that time my acquaintance with him was intimate as long as he lived, and my relations to him such as to give me a good opportunity of judging of his character. Many years have passed since his death; but my recollections of him are still fresh, and I cheerfully comply with your request in communicating them to you.

Mr. Blair was one of the most gentlemanly and polished men that you would meet in any circle. He was not above the medium height, and was of rather a slender figure; but had great delicacy of person, and an uncommonly mild and benignant, and at the same time an intellectual, expression of countenance. He was much more than clergymen generally are, a man of the world; was fond of polished and fashionable society, and mingled in it perhaps more freely than was consistent with his highest Christian enjoyment or ministerial usefulness. He was always particularly welcome to such circles, as his bland, engaging manners, and fine social qualities, were well fitted to render him a favourite. He never seemed more in his element than at a wedding. And this brings to my mind one peculiarity of his which I never knew how to account for: he was never willing to marry any one who had not been baptized, and sometimes, when he discovered at the moment when the ceremony was about to be performed, that the bride had not received baptism, he would abruptly pause, and proceed to administer it. He was very fond also of making the wedding of an elder daughter the occasion for baptizing the younger children of the family. He was accustomed to administer the ordinance generally, if not uniformly, in private, and the occasion (called *a Christening*) usually brought together many of the friends of the family, and was often attended with no inconsiderable degree of hilarity. It was both his principle and practice to baptize all children, whether their parents were professors of religion or not.

Mr. Blair may be regarded as having been a more than commonly popular preacher. The staple of his sermons was good sense and sound orthodoxy, according to the standards of the Presbyterian Church. His style was graceful and polished, and his manner of delivery was in perfect harmony with his style. His voice was soft and pleasant, and fell like sweet music on the ear of his audience. My impression is that his ministrations were not remarkable for variety—certainly he had some favourite expressions which he repeated so often that I remember them to this day. For instance, when administering the Communion at Hanover, as he was accustomed to do, I have heard him say, I know not how often,—in addressing the coloured communicants, "Methinks your black faces will hereafter make a fine contrast with the white robes of Christ's righteousness, which you will wear in Heaven." Of course I do not hold myself responsible for the correctness of the sentiment, or the elegance of the expression—I only refer to it as a sentence which he often repeated.

Mr. Blair was always a benevolent man, but, in his latter days, he evidently grew in spirituality. I was not present at his dying scene, but was informed that it was characterized by great humility, peace, and confidence in the Saviour. His death produced no small sensation in the surrounding community; and all felt that a man of rare accomplishments and virtues had passed away.

Most respectfully,

ANNE S. RICE.

NATHAN GRIER.

1786—1814.

FROM THE REV. DAVID McCONAUGHY, D. D.,

PRESIDENT OF WASHINGTON COLLEGE.

WASHINGTON, Pa., June 25, 1849.

Rev. and dear Brother: The man whose memory you ask me to assist in embalming, is one to whose pious example, wise counsels and instructions, and earnest prayers, I was much indebted in my special preparation for the ministry. It will, therefore, be only a labour of love for me to comply with your request; and I am happy to say that my impressions of the venerable man are so distinct that I can state them without any doubt or misgiving as to their correctness. I have also in my possession the material facts necessary to a narrative of his life.

NATHAN GRIER was born in Bucks County, Pa., in September, 1760. His parents were John and Agnes (Caldwell) Grier, who, after their marriage, came to this country from Ireland. Without the wealth and distinction of this world, they were rich in faith and good works, and had that honour which cometh from God. By education, and by intelligent conviction, they embraced cordially and held firmly the faith and forms of the Presbyterian Church. They had three daughters and eight sons, who were highly esteemed for their intelligence, piety, and eminent worth. Their posterity, still numerous, honourably exemplify the virtues of their worthy ancestors.

The subject of this sketch "feared the Lord from his youth," and was remarkable for his piety while yet a boy. Parental example, prayers, and instruction, which were savingly blest to the rest of the family, were evidently the means of early kindling up in *him* a heavenly light, which shone more and more unto the perfect day. Devoted to God in his youth by humble faith, he chose the ministry of the Gospel as the best means of promoting the glory of God, and the benefit of his fellow-men. His classical education was conducted by his elder brother, the Rev. James Grier, of Deep Run. He entered the University of Pennsylvania about 1781, and was graduated in 1783. His standing in College was good, but not particularly distinguished. After leaving College, he taught a grammar school, for a short time, in Pitts Grove. He prosecuted his theological studies under the direction of his brother, who had previously aided him in his classical course. He was licensed to preach by the Presbytery of Philadelphia in 1786. In the same year, he received and accepted a call from the Congregation of the Forks of Brandywine, and was installed as their Pastor in 1787. It was in the purpose of God, and in fact, a union for life. To the spiritual good of this congregation his labours as a Pastor were all appropriated. To them the Head of the Church assigned him, as an important gift;—his time, his prayers, his cares, and his faithful efforts. Having become the Pastor of a congregation, he also became a husband, by taking as his wife, Susannah Smith, a member of his own Church, and daughter of Robert and Margaret Smith,—the grandparents of the distinguished General P. F. Smith, lately in the Mexican war, and now of California. This family was highly respectable, and in comfortable worldly circumstances; and Mr. Grier's choice of a partner there was by a kind direction of Providence. She was eminently a "help meet" in the duties and cares of that interesting relation. With great prudence and discretion, and exemplary domestic economy, she maintained a pious walk, and a life of intimate communion with God. By her prayers and example, she strengthened the hands and encouraged the heart of her husband in his official duties, his necessary worldly engagements, and the wise and pious government and instruction of their common offspring. Her society, counsel, and aid, he was not permitted to enjoy to the end of his natural life. She died in the faith and hope of the Gospel, January 2, 1812, about two years before he was summoned from his earthly labours.

For the large and important charge to which he was called, the Head of the Church had thoroughly trained and qualified him. The Rev. John Carmichael, a minister of very considerable eminence, had been his immediate predecessor; and the Congregation being highly intelligent and well instructed in Divine truth, were abundantly qualified to enjoy and appreciate an able and faithful ministry,—such as they found in the Pastor which God had now given them. His judgment was sound and discriminating, and his talents as a preacher eminently popular. With a voice clear, pleasant and commanding, he exhibited a solemnity of manner and a deep and tender earnestness, which never failed to secure attention, and often made a powerful impression. He spake as one who believed and felt the force of Divine truth, and the weight of ministerial responsibility. His sermons were usually short, and combined the Law and the Gospel in due proportions. He never failed to preach "Christ crucified," but he also faithfully exhibited to sinners their guilt and danger, that thus they might be prepared to welcome the gracious provision which the Gospel offers. His preparation for the pulpit was elaborated with devout and conscientious care. The arrangement of his discourses was natural and lucid, and the matter of them at once eminently evangelical and practical. While his style was correct, chaste and graceful, there was no attempt at the ornaments of a refined rhetoric; nor did he deal in perplexing and difficult questions, involving the subtleties of metaphysics. His governing aim was to declare "the whole counsel of God" so plainly that all could understand it, and so discriminately that each one might appropriate it. He sought not to exalt himself but Christ; not to be honoured or rewarded with the praise of men, but with the approbation of God, and the conversion and salvation of those in relation to whom he knew that "he must render an account." As might be expected, he held a high place in the confidence and affection of the people of his charge, and his labours were greatly blessed. To other churches also, in which he was occasionally called to minister, his services were eminently acceptable. In Theology, his views were clear, profound, well arranged, and evangelical. In all the duties of religion, he gave evidence that he understood their importance and solemnity. His individual attachments were strong, sincere and discriminating, though they were not cherished to the exclusion of those respectful attentions and benevolent feelings which he owed to his fellow men in general. His disposition was eminently social. In familiar intercourse with his friends he found much enjoyment, nor did he fail to impart as much as he received. Hilarity, always chastened by Christian decorum, shed a grateful influence over every circle in which he mingled.

One important characteristic which Mr. Grier possessed in an eminent degree, was firmness of purpose. His opinions were formed upon careful consideration, were maintained with unwavering confidence, and, if occasion required, defended with manly vigour and independence. And the same was true in relation to what he regarded as ascertained duty. It must be done, let the consequence be what it might. Of many facts illustrative of this feature of his character, I venture to refer to one. On meetings of the Presbytery, and other judicatories of the Church, he was a punctual attendant; and, in conducting business, was among the most efficient members. During my connection with the Newcastle Presbytery, by which I was licensed, troubles in Ireland caused the removal to this country of many Presbyterian ministers, who had been prominent in their opposition to the civil government at home. Their cherished habits of thought, and the leading part which they had previously acted, seemed to have been favourable to the growth of their self-esteem, and evidently led some of them to expect more deference than they could reasonably claim. They seemed also, in virtue of their being foreigners, to regard themselves as more skilled in matters civil and ecclesiastical, than the ministers who had had their training in this country. At such arrogant assumption none felt more indignant than Mr. Grier; and not seldom he manifested his independent American spirit, by resisting undue interference, and dispensing merited rebuke. In reference to such cases, he would jocosely remark, "a gentle picking to let off the wind seems expedient and may be useful." In all his relations as a pastor, a citizen, an ecclesiastic, and a man, he was earnest in his endeavours to know what was right, and inflexibly firm in his adherence to it.

Mr. Grier was not only eminently honoured of God as a Pastor in his Congregation, and as a faithful and very acceptable preacher of the Gospel in the churches generally, but had an important instrumentality in directing and aiding young men in their studies preparatory to the Gospel ministry. The Presbyterian Church in America had not then provided Theological Seminaries, and students in Theology availed themselves of the libraries and instructions of the pastors of churches, as they had opportunity. The estimation in which Mr. Grier was held as a pious, able and successful minister of the Gospel, induced many to avail themselves of his direction and aid. The quiet and order of his house; his example as a devoted Christian, a pastor, and a preacher; his pleasant manners; his kind and ready efforts to promote the piety, comfort, and knowledge of his students,—make the memory of those times and circumstances pleasant and imperishable. Those who studied under his direction, were accustomed to divide their time between the study of the Scriptures, Ecclesiastical History, and a series of questions—about one hundred in number—in the usual order of the System of Theology. On these questions they were required to write pretty fully, and submit the result to his examination and criticism. In like manner, they composed sermons, on which they had his opinion as to matter and manner. All this required much of his time and attention; which, however, he always gave with the utmost alacrity.

As a husband, a father, and guardian of his family, his whole demeanour was characterized by Christian dignity, condescension, affection, and faithfulness. And the God of his family crowned with his efficient benediction his efforts to train them up in the nurture and admonition of the Lord. He left five children,—three daughters and two sons. Two of his daughters became the very estimable wives of respectable Presbyterian ministers,—the former theological students of their father; and the third is the worthy and Christian widow of Dr. Robert Thomson, late of Fagg's Manor, Pa. His sons, in early life, entered on the responsibilities and duties of the Gospel ministry, in which they have proved themselves able and faithful. The elder, the Rev. Robert S. Grier, has long been the esteemed pastor of the Congregations of Tom's Creek and of Piney Creek within the Carlisle Presbytery. The younger son, the Rev. John N. C. Grier, D. D., was, soon after his father's demise, chosen unanimously as successor in the pastorate of the Congregation of the Forks of Brandywine. His settlement there was on the 24th of November, 1814. In that charge, of which he is now pastor, he has laboured continuously, faithfully and acceptably. I may add that there are very few stated pastors, whose labours have been more eminently blessed by repeated seasons of gracious visitation, and large accessions to the Communion of the Church. It is indeed a garden of the Lord, over which his special care has been exercised, and on which He has shed largely the refreshing influences of his grace.

The subject of this sketch lived and died in the bosom of the Congregation of the Forks of Brandywine. Twenty-seven years he served them with fidelity and success, until, having finished the work which was assigned him, he was summoned from his labours on earth to a glorious reward in Heaven. He died of a typhoid fever, of only eight days continuance, March 31, 1814, in the fifty-fourth year of his age. His Funeral Sermon was preached by the Rev. William Arthur, and was published.

The many years which have elapsed since my intimate association with this excellent man, and the remoteness of my residence from him during the latter part of his life, prevent me from recording many incidents in his history, which might have given additional interest to my narrative, and rendered this tribute to his memory more worthy of its venerated subject.

I am most respectfully and affectionately,

Your brother in the Gospel of Christ,

DAVID McCONAUGHY.

The Rev. Nathan Grier, as has been intimated in the preceding sketch, had an elder brother, JAMES GRIER, who was also a minister of the Gospel. He was a native of Deep Run; was hopefully converted under the preaching of Whitefield; was graduated at the College of New Jersey in 1772; was a Tutor there in 1773 and 1774; studied Theology under Dr. Witherspoon; was licensed to preach by the First Presbytery of Philadelphia in 1775; and was ordained by the same Presbytery, and installed Pastor of the Church in Deep Run, in 1776. This was his only pastoral charge, though he supplied for some years the neighbouring Church of Tinicum. He died on the 19th of November, 1791, aged forty-one years, from the rupture of a blood vessel in the lungs,—having, for some time previous to his death, on account of great bodily weakness, delivered his sermons in a sitting posture. He closed his pulpit labours on the Sabbath, and closed his earthly existence the next day. His Funeral Sermon was preached by the Rev. Nathaniel Irwin of Neshaminy, and was published.

The Rev. Dr. Andrews of Doylestown, Pa., who has had access to the best means of information concerning him, has kindly furnished me the following paragraphs as the result of his inquiries:—

"In person the Rev. James Grier was of medium height; exceedingly thin; erect and graceful in his movements, and neat in his dress; with a countenance remarkably sedate,—yet not sombre but winning, so that the children of his congregation loved his society, and were easy in his presence. His hair was jet black and abundant,—was parted in front and lay combed back over his temples. He was amiable and conciliatory in his disposition and manner; as one expresses it,—'making peace between God and man, and between man and his neighbour."

"His voice was deep and sonorous, and, in the latter years of his ministry, from failure of health, it acquired a peculiar solemnity in its tones. He spoke with due deliberation, and usually just loud enough to be distinctly heard. He ordinarily used but little gesture, and that of the milder kind; but his manner was always earnest, and at times it became deeply impassioned. Not in the terrors of the Lord so much as in the persuasive power of the Gospel did his strength lie. One of his congregation who lived to be aged, used to say of him that 'it was not possible to hear him preach and refrain from tears;' though, as is said of Dr. Archibald Alexander, I have never met with one who recollected ever seeing the preacher himself weep in the delivery of a sermon.

"He is represented as a very discriminating, instructive preacher, with a power over an audience to which few attain. An incident may illustrate this—He was at Tinicum on a Communion Sabbath, and followed up the Sacramental service with a Sermon on the text,—"And the door was shut." After reading the passage, he closed his Bible with an action somewhat energetic, and lifting up his hands, apparently in the deepest agony, exclaimed,—'My God, and *is* the door shut?' The impression upon the whole congregation was perfectly overwhelming; and I have been told that Mr. Grier himself regarded the sermon as having been more signally blest in the awakening of the careless than perhaps any other during his whole ministry. I once saw it in manuscript, and it was in no way remarkable for its thought or its structure.

"He never *read* his sermons in the pulpit. It is said that his custom usually was to write out on Monday the discourse of the preceding Sabbath. But an aged man,—not a member of his congregation,—told me, a few years ago, that in his youth he remembered hearing him preach at Deep Run, when—as a very unusual thing—he faltered in the use of a word, then tried a second time, and not being successful, drew a manuscript from his pocket, and turning over a few leaves, and finding the expression he wanted, replaced the paper and proceeded as before. Whether he sometimes preached memoriter, or always trusted to the inspiration of the moment for his language, I have never been able to ascertain.

"I cannot learn that his pastoral life was marked by what in these days would be denominated a Revival of religion; but he built up and strengthened the people of God; instructed the children of the Church; exemplified what a Christian minister ought to be; and elevated the standard of religious character in the view of the whole community. Fathers Stewart and Dunlap, brought into the church in his day,—afterwards ruling elders, and distinguished for their close walk with God, used to determine all difference of opinion between them and myself,—doctrinal and experimental, with simply this appeal—'Mr. Grier thought so.' No living man so controlled their minds as did James Grier, who had been in his grave for half a century."

Mr. Grier was first married to a Miss Tenbroeck of New Jersey, by whom he had one daughter. His second wife was Mary Ferguson of Deep Run, who had four children,—three daughters and one son.

The son was JOHN FERGUSON GRIER, who also entered the ministry. He was born at Deep Run in the year 1784; was fitted for College in the Brandywine Academy; entered Dickinson College in 1799, and graduated with the first honour of his class, in 1803; was a teacher successively of a classical school in Pequea, Pa., and in the Academy at Brandywine; prosecuted his theological studies under his uncle, the Rev. Nathan Grier; was licensed to preach by the Presbytery of Newcastle, June 26, 1810; was ordained and installed Pastor of the Church in Reading, Pa., November 23, 1814; received the degree of Doctor of Divinity from Meadville College; and died January 26, 1829. The circumstances of his death were peculiar. There had been, for a short time previous, indications of an increased attention to religion in his Congregation. On the evening on which he died, he had attended a meeting for prayer and conversation with those who were in an anxious state of mind. At this meeting there was great solemnity manifest, and he remarked to a friend, on his way home, that he was satisfied that a revival of religion had commenced. He retired about eleven o'clock, apparently in perfect health. Soon after he fell asleep, his wife, hearing a faint groan, spoke to him; but she received no answer. The reason was that he was dead. The religious interest increased greatly after his death, and nearly seventy persons were added to the church within a few weeks. A Eulogy was pronounced upon Dr. Grier, by C. B. Penrose, Esq., at the request of the Belles Lettres Society of Dickinson College, on the 27th of March succeeding his death, and was published.

AARON WOOLWORTH, D. D*

1786—1821.

Aaron Woolworth, a son of Richard and Lois Woolworth, was born at Longmeadow, Mass., October 25, 1763. His father cultivated a small farm, and, in connection with that, carried on the business of a tanner, currier, and shoemaker. He entered Yale College in 1780; had a highly respectable standing as a scholar during his whole course; and received the degree of Bachelor of Arts in 1784. It was while he was an undergraduate that his mind became deeply impressed with eternal realities, and he entered with fixed purpose on the religious life. About the time, and probably on the very day, of his joining the church, he committed to paper the following solemn engagements :—

"Yale College, August 4, 1783.

"I do this day lay myself under renewed obligations to surrender the remaining part of my life to the service of my Creator ; and, by Divine assistance, to walk according to the most holy religion of Jesus Christ, my most glorious Redeemer—in a full belief of the Sacred Scriptures of the Old and New Testament, to practise all duties therein required, according to my best knowledge ; to commence and carry on a warfare with every sin ; to use my utmost endeavours to promote the interests of religion and virtue among my fellow-men ; to take Christ's yoke upon me ; to take up his cross and follow Him through evil report and good report ; to hate father and mother, brethren and sisters, and even my own life, in comparison with my love to my Saviour ; to surrender up myself to be saved entirely by his merits and vicarious righteousness ; to deny myself of all good things which interfere with God's glory ; to resign myself entirely to his service, having no will of my own, contrary to his most holy will."

After leaving College, he taught school, for a short time, in Enfield, Conn.; after which, he devoted some time to the study of Theology, under the direction of the Rev. Dr. Hart of Preston. He was licensed to preach the Gospel by the Eastern Association of New London County. After preaching for some little time at East Hampton, Mass., he went to Long Island, in the beginning of the year 1787, and commenced preaching as a candidate to the Church in Bridgehampton. That church had been long destitute of a pastor, and was then in a distracted state ; and it was in consequence of a personal application from a committee of the church, that he was induced to visit them. His first sermon was from the text,—"I ask, therefore, for what intent ye have sent for me ?" He was received at once with great favour, and measures were soon taken which resulted in his permanent settlement. He was ordained and installed on the 30th of April, 1787,—the Sermon on the occasion being preached by the Rev. Dr. Buell of East Hampton, L. I. The Church was at that time Congregational, though it subsequently became Presbyterian.

Several powerful revivals of religion occurred under his ministry, particularly one in the year 1800, an account of which was published in

* Phillips' Fun. Serm.—Prime's Hist. L. I.—MS. from his son, S. B. Woolworth, LL. D.

connection with Dr. Buell's Narrative of an extensive Revival in East Hampton.

In 1809, he received the degree of Doctor of Divinity from the College of New Jersey.

Though his constitution was not very vigorous, his health was generally good, and he was seldom prevented from preaching by illness. He often said that he desired to go from his labours to his rest; and his prayer was signally answered. His last labours were on the Sabbath, March 25, 1821, when he preached and administered the Lord's Supper with unusual fervency and tenderness. He was then labouring under a severe cold, which terminated in a typhoid affection of the lungs, of which he died on the 2d of April following. His mind, during his illness, was in a state of great serenity, and one of his last expressions was—"Death has no terrors to me." A Sermon with reference to his death was preached to his bereaved flock, a short time after, by the Rev. Ebenezer Phillips,* of East Hampton, and was published.

On the 27th of August, 1788, he was married to a daughter of the Rev. Dr. Buell, who died at the residence of her eldest son, at Homer, in Cortland County, N. Y., September 10, 1846. He left five children, one of whom, *Samuel Buell*, graduated at Hamilton College in 1822, and is now (1854) Principal of the State Normal School at Albany.

FROM THE REV. LYMAN BEECHER, D. D

Boston, November 24, 1852.

My dear Brother: The name of Dr. Woolworth revives in my mind a flood of tender reminiscences. I was a youth of twenty-three, ardent and inexperienced, when our acquaintance commenced; he, a father whose love, guidance, and support were returned by filial affection, confidence, and gratitude. Our love, like that of Saul and Jonathan, was precious and mutual; and to me, in the novitiate of my public labours, his affection, example, and counsels, were inestimable.

His stature was a little below the medium. His countenance was the index of intellect, but mild and prepossessing. His manners were those of a Christian gentleman,—unaffected and winning. His intellect and scholarship were much above mediocrity. His judgment was remarkably sound; his piety deep and efficacious—all which rendered him among the most beloved and influential ministers on the Island.

As a preacher, he was intellectual, discriminating and argumentative. In his delivery he was earnest, and in his applications powerful and pungent.

He was extensively known beyond the limits of the Island, as a great and good and useful man in his day and generation. And the praises on earth cannot add to the honours and joys in which he has long been participating in Heaven.

The wife of Dr. Woolworth, who was the daughter of Dr. Buell, of revival memory, was indeed a help-meet for her husband, a mother in Israel, and to me also; and by me greatly beloved, as her children still are. She fulfilled her mission well, and lived long to be useful in the Church of God.

I am affectionately yours,

LYMAN BEECHER.

* Ebenezer Phillips was ordained and installed the fifth Pastor of the Church in East Hampton, L. I., May 15, 1811. Failure of health compelled him to resign his charge, and he was dismissed on the 16th of March, 1830. He removed to Carmel, Putnam County, N. Y., where he died not far from the year 1840.

FROM THE REV. R. S. STORRS, D. D.

Braintree, Mass., June 18, 1857.

My dear Sir : Pleasant as it is to throw back the mind on scenes that transpired fifty years ago, it is not a little humiliating to mark the imperfections of a memory, retaining vivid impressions of general facts, but failing in power to invest them with the freshness of passing realities. Yet, if ineffaceable impressions of moral worth made on an individual mind by early acquaintance, can be transferred in any measure to others, they will not be useless, even if not clothed in the drapery of instructive and amusing incident.

Dr. Woolworth, known, from early childhood, through my parents who loved him as a brother, and through the large circle of his relatives and friends, composing no small part of my honoured father's congregation,—known also personally in later youthful years, as a man of large heart, clear mind, and warm social affections,—was selected as my theological teacher on my leaving College. For a year, my home was in his family; and not even a father's house could inspire more of confidence, freedom, and affection, than filled the heart of his theological novitiate.

A more genial spirit has rarely, if ever, pervaded a human bosom: in all the relations of life, the law of kindness was ever on his tongue, while from large treasures of knowledge and love, he poured light and joyousness over every circle in which he moved.

In his insulated location, and through his excessive modesty, he was not often called to direct the course of students in Divinity; but whenever he yielded to solicitations of this kind, he showed himself a workman that need not be ashamed, and secured the highest respect of his pupils: his discriminating mind, familiar manner, spiritual unction, and evident anxiety to train up preachers like Paul and John, commanded the affectionate reverence of all who sat at his feet, and shared the ripe fruits of his diligent studies and varied experience. His preaching was eminently scriptural in form as well as spirit; his sermons were thoroughly prepared, and usually written out in full—logical, direct and persuasive in their construction, they were always heard with interest and profit, and formed a valuable model for the study of those under his instruction.

As a pastor, he was unwearied in his attentions to his flock,—not only discharging duty faithfully to the sick, the bereaved, the dying, and the otherwise afflicted, but, entering often every family of his congregation with the freedom and affection of a father, he invited the free communication of thought and feeling on all subjects of interest; and enjoying the confidence of all, and ascertaining their spiritual condition, he ministered instruction to godly edifying, with cheerfulness of spirit and aptness of speech strikingly impressive. No pastor, I venture to say, was ever more entirely trusted and tenderly beloved by all classes of the community—the result of a perfect transparency of character, and an overflowing sympathy with them in joy and in sorrow. And when the divisions and alienations that, under another ministry, had preceded his settlement, and the deep rooted prejudices of the "New Lights" on the one hand, and the inflexibility of the "Conservatives" on the other, are taken into consideration, it cannot be questioned that the skill with which he met the difficulties of his position, and the unlimited confidence he inspired, developed a peculiar fitness for his office. Always active and devoted, he was yet "wise as a serpent and harmless as a dove." In all good things he was zealously affected; but when the special presence of the Holy Spirit appeared, his zeal burst forth as a glowing flame; and in the lecture room, the praying circle, and the house of God, alike, his heart and lips were manifestly touched by a coal from the altar in Heaven. It having been my privilege to be with him during one of the first and most precious revivals I have ever witnessed, his course of procedure, whether with the Christian or the unbeliever, the awakened sinner or vain caviller, left on my mind impressions of his excellence as a spiritual guide, which are still fresh as in the spring-tide of youth, and scarcely less important in their practical bearings than the elaborated lectures, and convincing demonstrations, of the Theological Tutor.

Receiving licensure from the Long Island Presbytery, and labouring for many months within its bounds, I had opportunity to learn the high estimation in which he was held throughout the churches. Not a few of these were either partially or wholly destitute of regular ministrations—nearly all of them had been rent by divisions like those which had once distracted his own parish—on all sides they were assailed by the spirit of sectarianism, and needed counsel and encouragement from the few settled ministers of their own connection. Nor were these ministers the men to turn a deaf ear to the calls of the enfeebled churches; and their missionary tours through the Island were frequent, laborious, and refreshing "like a clear heat upon herbs, and like a cloud of dew in the heat of harvest." None sympathized more deeply in the afflictions of Zion, nor laboured more abundantly and successfully to relieve them, than Dr. Woolworth. His praise was in all the churches; they looked up to him as a father, spoke of him as an ever sympathizing friend, confided in him as a sagacious counsellor, and loved him as an elder brother. In his bodily presence, social converse, pulpit teachings, and fervent prayers, they delighted; but in the absence of these, his "letters" were always "weighty and powerful," even if they conveyed but a single item of information or advice, closing with the benediction—"Grace, mercy and peace from our Lord Jesus Christ, be with you all." His name is still as "ointment poured forth among those churches;" and though the lapse of years, and the passing away of generations, must bury its sweet odour in the same grave that treasures up his precious dust, it will be restored at the sounding of the Archangel's trump, and be had in "everlasting remembrance," as associated with the glory of having turned many to righteousness, and shining "as the stars forever and ever."

If I felt at liberty to take a more comprehensive view of Dr. Woolworth's character, and exhibit him as he appeared in the relations of a husband and father, a friend and companion, a Christian patriot and philanthropist, or if there were room for the detail of incidents illustrative of his theological erudition and acumen, and his pastoral fidelity and tenderness, other pages might well be filled. For in conjugal devotion to the incomparably meek and energetic companion of his life, and in prayerful solicitude for the children of his love, he was unsurpassed. Discriminating in his friendships, they were firm and enduring. Choice in his companionships, they were cheerful and humorous though grave. Ardent in his patriotism, he flinched in no struggle for his country's honour, though his convictions of the course to secure it differed ever so widely from those of his best friends. And boundless in his philanthropy, he spared no labour nor sacrifice to relieve suffering, and "give quietness and assurance forever," at home and abroad. To youthful preachers he never failed to give advice when asked, encouragement when needed, and monitory counsels when duty prompted—wounding the sensibilities of none, increasing the efficiency of all, and inspiring admiration of his delicacy and faithfulness. Among his people, whether he met errorists of one kind or another, at the fireside or in the social circle, he quickly made their misapprehensions visible to themselves, in a way that gave no offence, while it compelled their admission of the clearness of his mind, the pureness of his heart, and the beauty of the apples of gold he set before them in vases of silver. But I already trespass too far in indulging the sweet reminiscences of one whose upward flight has oft compelled the exclamation, "My father, my father! the chariots of Israel and the horsemen thereof."

Most respectfully and affectionately yours,
R. S. STORRS.

FROM THE REV. CALVIN COLTON, D. D.

NEW YORK, September 3, 1855.

Dear Sir: In compliance with your request, I herewith transmit to you a reminiscence of the character of my uncle, the Rev. Aaron Woolworth, D. D.

As you are doubtless already in possession of the most important historical points of his biography, I will confine myself to a brief record of my abiding impression of his *benevolence,* which, though natural to him, was doubtless, and in no small degree, improved and stimulated by the elevated tone of his Christian character. When I was at Yale College, I sometimes spent a vacation with my uncle at Bridgehampton, and being the son of a sister whom he loved, he took a lively interest in me, and showed me great kindness.

"Cousin," he used to say, "'*Suaviter in modo, et fortiter in re,*' is an infallible maxim for making ourselves agreeable and successful in life." The *suaviter in modo* he himself exhibited in a remarkable degree, and it arose from the never failing kindness of his heart. However I may have failed to profit by the maxim, I could never forget it; and through life, as often as I have read or heard it, or had occasion to use it, it has invariably brought my uncle to mind, with his own manner of uttering it; and his manner was always an exemplification of the first part of it. His feelings towards all persons were always kind, and actively so, as occasion invited or permitted. His domestic relations, as fashioned and cultivated by himself, presented a calm, reflected image of the impressions of his hand. A family thus trained was a beautiful model of that sphere of life, whence emanate the hallowing influences of society.

My uncle's pastoral relations were of a similar character; and he stood before his people on the Lord's day, not only to command their attention as hearers of the Word, but to impress upon them,—not studiously as a purpose cherished by himself, but unavoidably from his well-known character,—a sense of his own bright example of the doctrine he preached. The people of his parish, somewhat remote from the great bustle of the world, were primitive in their habits, and it needed no great stretch of imagination to conceive that they enjoyed the ministrations of a primitive pastor. Above all, his natural benevolence, prompted by the lofty motives of his sacred calling, was always conspicuous, because it was always active; and it stood out foremost, as well in his ministerial functions, as in his social relations. It is rare that we find so much of the man of God, in this lofty sense of the term,—whose great aim and constant endeavour are to reconcile men to God. We may well suppose *that* to have been the daily prayer of the closet, which was the constant and unrelaxed effort of the life. And in what field could the benevolence of such a heart be more advantageously exemplified?

With great respect, I am yours,

C. COLTON.

JOSEPH BADGER.*

1786—1846.

Joseph Badger was a descendant, in the fourth generation, of Giles Badger, who came from England about the year 1635, and settled in Newbury, Mass. He was the son of Henry and Mary (Langdon) Badger, who, after having resided at Norwich, Conn., and afterwards, for a while, in New Jersey, removed to that part of Springfield, Mass., which is now called Wilbraham. Here Joseph was born on the 28th of February, 1757. His parents were both professors of religion, and were careful in the religious training of their children. In 1766, the family removed to Partridgefield, (now Peru,) in Berkshire County, which was then a new and uncultivated place, and without any school or other means of intellectual improvement. The counsels and prayers of his parents at this period made a powerful impression upon his mind; though he was subsequently led by youthful vanities to the verge of ruin.

In February, 1775, when he had just completed his eighteenth year, he entered the army, about three weeks after the battle of Lexington, being enrolled in a company of Colonel John Patterson's regiment. He waited on the Chaplain of the regiment, the Rev. David Avery, for about two years. He was present at the battle of Bunker Hill, and was afterwards for some time with General Arnold in Canada, serving in the different capacities of soldier, baker, and nurse; suffering at one time from the small-pox, and at another from fever and ague; and often subjected to the most imminent perils. Having, in 1777, received his discharge from the service, he went to visit some friends in New Preston, Conn., and arrived there two days before the British destroyed Danbury. He immediately joined a party who went forth in pursuit of the enemy, under the command of a recruiting officer, and, after participating in one sharp contest with them in Wilton, and another in Fairfield, he returned to his friends in New Preston.

Shortly after this, he enlisted again as an Orderly Sergeant, until January, 1778, and was stationed first at Milford, Conn., and afterwards at White Plains, N. Y. At the expiration of this term, he visited his friends in Massachusetts, but returned to New Preston before the close of February, and hired himself out in the business of weaving, until the next October; in which time he wove more than sixteen hundred yards of cloth. Having earned a little more than enough to pay for his clothing, he resolved to spend the remainder in acquiring some more knowledge than he had of the elementary branches of spelling, writing, and arithmetic,—intending, after a short time, to return to the army. As there was no school in New Preston, which he could attend, with the prospect of much improvement, he placed himself under the instruction of the Rev. Jeremiah Day, in whose family he became a boarder. Here he spent the winter of 1779–80, engaged in study; but in the spring he found his funds so reduced, that he was under the necessity of again resorting to the loom.

About this time his mind became deeply impressed with the truths of the Bible. Without experiencing any great excitement, he gradually gained

* Autobiog.—Amer. Quart. Reg. XIII.—Kennedy's "Plan of Union."

the evidence, as he believed, of a thorough change of character, and, after a few weeks, became a member of Mr. Day's church. He now relinquished his intention of returning to the army, and resolved to enter on a course of study with a view to the ministry. He immediately commenced the classics under the instruction of Mr. Day, and, though he was repeatedly interrupted for a considerable time in his studies, both by sickness and by teaching a school to provide himself with necessary funds, he was enabled to enter the Freshman class in Yale College at the Commencement in 1781. During his college course he was dependant on his own exertions for support; but, through the indulgence of President Stiles in granting him all the favours in his power, and by teaching a school, and performing certain humble services in the College for which he received remuneration, he was enabled to advance respectably with his class to the close of his college course. In his senior year, he constructed a *Planetarium*, which cost him about three months' labour, and for which the Corporation paid him one hundred dollars. He was graduated in September, 1785.

The next year after his graduation, he taught a school in Waterbury, Conn., and studied Theology under the direction of the then aged Rev. Mark Leavenworth; after which, he was licensed to preach by the New Haven Association. During the next winter, he supplied the pulpit at Northbury, (now Plymouth,) Conn. On the 24th of October, 1787, he was ordained Pastor of the Church in Blandford, Mass.,—the Sermon on the occasion being preached by his friend, the Rev. Mr. Day.

While residing in Mr. Day's family as a student, Mr. Badger formed an intimate friendship with Lois, a daughter of Stephen Noble, of New Milford, and a sister of Mrs. Day. He was married to her in October, 1784,—a little less than a year before his graduation, and three years before his settlement in the ministry. By this marriage he had seven children—three sons and four daughters.

He continued Pastor of the Church in Blandford thirteen years. On the 24th of October, 1800, he was dismissed from his pastoral charge, having been appointed by the Connecticut Missionary Society to labour as a missionary in the Connecticut Western Reserve. Accordingly, on the 15th of November following, he set out for that new and distant field of labour; and, after a tedious and somewhat perilous journey, he reached Youngstown a little before the close of the year. He immediately commenced visiting the small settlements, and preaching to the few families that composed them. The winter and spring he spent in the Southern part of the Reserve; but, in June, as soon as the waters were fordable, he visited the interior settlements,—passing on from Hudson to Cleveland, and thence still farther to the North. He also made a tour to the Indians on the Maumee, to ascertain their condition with reference to the establishment of a mission among them. Returning to Hudson in October, and thence striking across to Austinburg, he organized a church in the latter place, on the 24th of that month, consisting of ten males and six females. This was the first church organized by a New England man, on the Reserve, and the second and only church after that at Youngstown, organized in this field before the year 1802. The church at Youngstown took the Presbyterian form; that at Austinburg, the Congregational.

Mr. Badger now set out to return to New England, by way of Buffalo. His health was feeble when he started on his journey; but the fatigue and exposure to which he was subjected, brought on a fever by which he was confined for some time at Buffalo, with only a doubtful prospect of recovery. He was enabled, however, at length, to proceed on his journey, and, after some further detentions by repeated attacks of illness, he reached his family and friends,—having been absent from them a year and forty-seven days. After spending a week or two with them, he repaired to Hartford, and made a report concerning his mission to the Missionary Board, which was accepted.

Having satisfied himself from actual observation that the soil of the Western Reserve was good, and would admit of a dense population, and that a door was open for extensive ministerial labours in that region, he resolved to remove his family thither; and, accordingly, having made the necessary arrangements, they set out, on the 23d of February, 1802, with all their movable goods, in a wagon drawn by four horses, to find a home in the wilderness. They reached Austinburg about the last of April, and shortly after got into a rude cabin of their own, with flooring enough to spread out their beds, but without chair or table, and without a door being hung, or the chinks stopped. In this plight he left his family to make their garden, and went on a missionary tour, from which he returned about the middle of June. After spending several weeks in providing for the comfort of his family, he sallied forth, in the early part of August, on another missionary tour of about two months, during which he visited nearly all the settlements in the South part of the Reserve. In December, he commenced his winter's tour, and, after a succession of arduous labours and perilous adventures, was with his family again in April, 1803. On reaching home, he found letters from the Missionary Board, renewing his appointment, but reducing his salary to six dollars per week. He regarded this reduction as unreasonable, and, after some correspondence on the subject, which did not result agreeably to his wishes, he came to the resolution in January, 1806, to resign his appointment from the Connecticut Board, and accept one from the Western Missionary Society at Pittsburgh. Under their patronage he laboured among the Wyandotte Indians, in the Sandusky region, for several years.

In the autumn of 1807, Mr. Badger moved his family to Sandusky; but, on account of the unhealthiness of the climate, he moved them back the next year. In November, 1809, he set out with his wife on a journey to New England, and while she stopped with her friends at New Preston, he proceeded to Boston, where he collected nearly eleven hundred dollars in aid of his mission.

On his return, he went to his missionary station at Sandusky, and, after making some necessary arrangements, repaired to Pittsburgh, and made a report to the Missionary Board, and then returned to his family. Before he reached home, he was met with the melancholy tidings of the death of one of his daughters. After spending a few days with his afflicted family, he went back to his missionary field, and pursued his labours with the Indians until about the middle of November, when he received a letter from his wife, informing him that their house had been burnt, with nearly all their provisions and furniture. He immediately hastened to his distressed family, and by aid kindly furnished by their neighbours and friends, he quickly succeeded in building another cabin, and placing his family again in comfortable circumstances.

In the spring of 1810, he removed with his family to Ashtabula. Here, and in the neighbouring settlements, he laboured in the ministry, receiving his support, partly from the people, and partly from the Massachusetts Missionary Society.

In September, 1812, General Perkins' brigade was ordered to the Westward to guard the frontier. A request came to Mr. Badger to visit the camp, and, shortly after, General Harrison, without consulting him on the subject, appointed him Brigade Chaplain,—which was almost immediately followed by a commission from the Governor. He was also, about the same time, appointed Postmaster for the army. He returned to his family about the middle of March, 1813; and had scarcely reached home when one of his sons was taken with an epidemic fever, and died the third day.

On the 4th of August, 1818, his wife, after a brief but severe illness, died in her sixty-fourth year. She was a person of uncommon excellence, and had proved an efficient coadjutor with her husband in the self-denying labours of missionary life. In April, 1819, he formed a second matrimonial connection with Abigail Ely,—a lady from Wilbraham, Mass., who was then on a visit to her sisters living in Salem, O.

Mr. Badger continued to preach as usual, without any stated support, until 1826, when he reported himself to the War department as a soldier of the Revolution, and was placed on the pension roll at ninety-six dollars a year. In the spring of this year, in compliance with an invitation from the people of Gustavus, in Trumbull County, he removed to that place; constituted a church of about thirty members, and was installed as Pastor by the Grand River Presbytery, in October following. Here he preached for eight years, and was privileged to see no inconsiderable fruit from his labours. About the close of that period, his voice began to fail, and his general health was somewhat impaired, so that he proposed to his people to allow him to give place to another minister. They, however, declined to do so, and he continued to preach, as he was able, until June, 1835, when he was, at his urgent request, dismissed by the Presbytery of Trumbull County. In October following, he removed to Wood County, to reside with his only surviving daughter. He died at Perrysburg, in perfect peace, in the year 1846, in the ninetieth year of his age.

Mr. Badger always retained his preference for Congregationalism, but united with the Presbytery of Ohio, on the Plan of Union, shortly after he went to the Reserve, and continued in connection with the Presbyterian Church till the close of life.

FROM THE REV. TIMOTHY MATHER COOLEY, D. D.

GRANVILLE, Mass., May 4, 1857.

My dear friend and Brother: You will not expect from a man who has passed eighty-five, a very extended communication on any subject; but I cannot decline your request for my recollections of Mr. Badger, especially as I am almost the only person left whose memory embraces the portion of his life that was spent in this neighbourhood. He was a member of the council that ordained me, and took part in the services of the occasion. And from that time till he migrated to the West, he was one of my nearest ministerial neighbours. I knew him intimately, and have always regarded him as an extraordinary man.

One of the most remarkable features of his character was his wonderful versatility. It seemed as if there was nothing to which he could not turn his head or his hand with perfect ease. I remember noticing in the museum of Yale College a beautiful *Planetarium* which he constructed while an undergraduate; and which was regarded as one of the most curious objects in the whole collection. He was a bookbinder, a weaver, a carpenter,—any thing that the present exigency might demand. An infidel in his parish sent him Tom Paine's Age of Reason to bind; but I do not remember to have heard how he treated either the book, or its unprincipled and impudent owner. When, at one time, he wanted the means of support, he betook himself to the loom, and earned them. When, at another time, he found himself in need of a barn, he took his broad axe, square and compass, and formed the frame work with his own hand. His universal genius seemed to render him independent of artificers of every kind.

You might suppose that this quality to which I have now adverted would be very likely to interfere with his spirituality, and to discover itself in ways hardly consistent with the highest degree of ministerial usefulness. But thus it was not. The duties of the ministry were evidently, in his estimation, paramount to every thing else; and the various kinds of handicraft to which he resorted, were all rendered subservient to the ulterior object of the "furtherance of the Gospel." In religious conversation he was pleasant, instructive, discriminating and experimental. In prayer he was eminently gifted, and apparently highly devout. In his sermons he made up in vigorous and well digested thought, for any defects which, owing to his imperfect early education, might be apparent in his style. He never hesitated to rebuke sin either in private or in public; and I doubt not that he could say with another distinguished minister now gone to his rest,—"I am not aware that, in preparing my sermons, I ever inquired what would please or displease my hearers." I well remember that in a sermon I heard him preach before the Hampden Association, he brought out some of the higher points of Calvinism, with a directness and pungency almost startling. One of the ministers present, whose orthodoxy was, to say the least, not of the most rigid type,—when it came to him to criticise the sermon, remarked as follows:—"Brother Badger's sermon reminds me of old Mr. Moorhead's third proposition—'I shall speak from the text,' said he, 'in three propositions—1. I shall tell you something that I know about, and you know nothing about. 2. I shall allude to something which you know about, but I know nothing about. 3. I shall speak of what we don't any of us know anything about.'"

Mr. Badger possessed a spirit of courage and perseverance, unsurpassed. His personal trials and sufferings, during much the greater part of his long life, exceeded those of any other minister in this country within my knowledge. Few, if any, clergymen could have been found in New England who would have thus cheerfully—I may say heroically—relinquished the charge of an intelligent people, to encounter the deprivations and perils of a missionary, in the then trackless wilds of Ohio. His record is in Heaven.

With the warmest affection,

your brother in Christ,

TIMOTHY MATHER COOLEY.

FROM THE REV. GEORGE E. PIERCE, D. D.,

PRESIDENT OF THE WESTERN RESERVE COLLEGE.

HUDSON, O., March 24, 1857.

Dear Sir: My opportunities for personal acquaintance with the Rev. Joseph Badger have not been great. I came to the Reserve in 1834, and he closed his labours, as Pastor of the Church in Gustavus, the following year,—after which, he preached but occasionally for the remaining ten years of his life. Having, however, resided upon his former field of labour, my own impressions in regard to him have been confirmed by intercourse with those who knew him more intimately.

In person, he was above the medium size, of a strong and muscular frame, and yet not peculiarly corpulent. The features of his countenance were strongly marked, bold, expressive and manly. In his manners he was frank, open, benevolent and sympathetic. A stranger soon felt at home with him, and prepared to receive with confidence information on all points of interest within the field of his labours.

His talents in the pulpit were above mediocrity. Though not eloquent according to the refined notions of rhetoric, yet, with a strong and vigorous intellect, and sincere devotion to the great end of preaching, he was clear, forcible and discriminating in the presentation of Gospel truth and Christian duty. His public labours were held in general estimation, as always instructive, and calculated to make a happy impression on the minds of his hearers. His Theology was in accordance with the best standards in Litchfield and Berkshire Counties, in the days of Griffin, Porter, Mills, Shepherd, and Hyde.

Though a Congregationalist in New England, he entered into cordial co-operation, upon the Plan of Union, with the Presbyterian ministers in this vicinity. In the spirit of peace and Christian fellowship, he assisted them in the administration of ordinances, according to their forms, and received their assistance in the Congregational Churches which he organized. At the beginning of his missionary labours, the Presbyterian Churches were in the enjoyment of powerful revivals of religion, attended with certain well known peculiarities. These peculiarities he ascribed to the power of God, and they were no hindrance in the way of co-operation. The great peace and prosperity of the Churches on the Reserve, for the first quarter of a century, were in a good degree the result of the wise and unsectarian arrangements of their first missionary.

As a man, Mr. Badger had some prominent traits of character, of much avail to him as a missionary in a new country. His powers of endurance, determination, and perseverance, were put in requisition, when, leaving his family scantily provided for, he traversed dense forests alone, with only an Indian trail or pocket compass to direct his way, and sought every remote settlement, to encourage and cheer the lonely inhabitants, and instruct and edify them with Gospel truth. His knowledge of human nature and power of adaptation made him, to the people, profitable and interesting. Though not a physician, he was often in families where other medical advice could not be had, and, in such circumstances, did not hesitate to administer medicine, and perform the minor class of surgical operations. By his mechanical skill, he could assist the farmer in repairing the broken implements of husbandry. If his horse lost a shoe in the woods, he could replace it, having the article, with nails and hammer, in his saddlebags. When a loaded wagon had broken an axletree, ten miles from any habitation, with an axe, an augur, and a pocket knife, he spliced it, fitted it to the wheel, and went on his way.

His medical and mechanical skill availed him in the camp, as well as on the missionary field.. He entered the Revolutionary army at the age of eighteen. In the hospital at Fort George, there were many sick and in very distressing circumstances. Not a dish of any kind could be found from which to administer drink or medicine. Resort was had to dishes made of bark and chips scooped out with a knife. The commanding officer sought for a man who could turn wooden dishes. Mr. Badger, who was acting the part of a nurse, volunteered for the service, tools were ordered, and soon a good supply of dishes were furnished.

When he served as Chaplain in the War of 1812, he was attached to a regiment stationed at Lower Sandusky, now Fremont, in this State. The settlement was small, and the army, encamped in the woods, was short of provisions, and suffered especially in that they had no means for grinding their corn. Mr. Badger, by boring and burning, scooped out a large oak stump in the form of a mortar. In this he placed an upright shaft, fitted at the end for a pestle, and gave it motion by means of a horizontal spring pole, fastened to the neighbouring trees, and thus the corn was pounded. When he had got his machinery in operation, he called on Colonel Darrow, the commanding officer of the station, now living in this township, and from whom I have the statement, and asked him if he ever heard of priestcraft? He replied, "Yes." "Would you like to see a specimen?" "Yes." So he took him to the woods and showed him his contrivance.

Many incidents might be related, showing Mr. Badger's labours and perils as a missionary. The story of his encounter with a bear is familiar in many families, and bids fair to be handed down, as one of the tales of the nursery. On the eve of a dark rainy night, the streams being much raised, he came to a ford on Grand River, and crossed, intending to encamp on the bank. He was prevented by the snapping and growling of some animal near. It soon became so dark that he could not see his hand holding the bridle, and he knew by the noise, that a bear was continually approaching. Having a horse shoe in his hand, and guided by the noise, he threw it, but without effect. He reined his horse right and left, that he might find a tree, and climb from danger. Succeeding in this, he fastened the bridle to the smaller limbs, rose upon his saddle, and ascended the tree. The bear came to the root, and, as he supposed, began to climb. Gaining a firm footing, he drew a sharp knife, and prepared for battle. But, as the bear did not approach, he ascended about forty feet into the top of the tree, found a convenient place to sit upon a limb, and tied himself to the tree with a large bandana, that he might be more safe, if he should fall into a drowse. The night was most dreary, with storm, and wind, and heavy peals of thunder. Providentially the horse was not frightened, but remained a quiet sentinel at the foot of the tree. Being drenched with rain, he shook his saddle, and so frightened the bear, that he retreated a few rods, where he remained growling and snapping his teeth till near daylight, when he left the premises, and the missionary went to his home in safety.

Yours respectfully,

GEORGE E. PIERCE.

ASHBEL GREEN, D. D.*

1786—1848.

Ashbel Green was born at Hanover, Morris County, N. J., July 6, 1762. His father was the Rev. Jacob Green, who was, for many years, minister of the Presbyterian Congregation in Hanover, and his mother was a daughter of the Rev. John Pierson, long Pastor of the Presbyterian Church in Woodbridge, N. J., and granddaughter of the Rev. Abraham Pierson, first President of Yale College.

He was prepared to enter College, chiefly by his father. It was his father's original intention that he should be a farmer; and he accordingly engaged a pious and respectable farmer of his congregation to take charge of him and his elder brother, with a view to their becoming acquainted with the different branches of husbandry. It being apparent that this son had a

* Autobiography edited by Rev. Dr. J. H. Jones.—MS. from Hon. James S. Green.

strong thirst for knowledge, and was bent upon obtaining a collegiate education, his father did not think proper to oppose it; but allowed him to pursue his preparatory studies under his own direction. He, afterwards, in accordance with his father's advice, engaged in teaching first an English, and then a Grammar, school, devoting his leisure hours to his own improvement. His father, who was a physician as well as a clergyman, sometimes put in requisition *his* services in the performance of his medical duties, and in this way the son acquired some knowledge of medicine, which proved an important advantage to him in after life.

The father being a zealous Whig in the Revolution, the son early imbibed the same spirit, and when a mere stripling, was enrolled in the lists of those who were fighting for their country's liberties. The highest office which he attained, was that of Orderly Sergeant in the militia; but he seems always to have been on the alert, at the call for military aid, and in one instance at least,—at the attack on Elizabethtown Point,—was exposed to imminent danger. His reminiscences, in old age, of Revolutionary times, were minute and interesting; not a few of which are happily preserved in his autobiography.

As young Green was remarkably intelligent for a person of his years, he became familiar, during the Revolution, with many of the officers of the American army; and, as infidelity prevailed extensively among them, he caught, in some degree, the sceptical spirit. Being, however, dissatisfied with the state of mind into which he had been brought, he resolved to make the Divine authority of the Scriptures the subject of candid investigation; and, accordingly, read some of the most able and popular works in defence of Christianity. Though he was now satisfied that the defenders of Revelation had the best of the argument, yet his mind was still in an unsettled state; and it occurred to him that the fairest way of settling the question was by an examination of the Bible itself. Accordingly, he took up the New Testament as if he had never read it before; and he had not gone through the Evangelists, before he was entirely cured of his scepticism. And this was but a preparation for his receiving the truth in the love of it. He gave much time now to private meditation and devotion; and at no distant period, as he believed, gave himself to God in an everlasting covenant.

During the period in which this mental and spiritual change was passing upon him, he was occupied in teaching a school; but in the month of November, 1781, he left his school, and returned to his father's, where he spent the ensuing winter in study, with a view to enter College at an advanced standing in the spring. So intense was his application during that winter, that his eyesight was very much impaired, and in the following spring he was compelled, for some weeks, to cease from study altogether. His predilection seems to have been for Yale College; and had it not been for the accidental delay of a letter in answer to one which he had written to a friend, making inquiries concerning the expenses, course of study, &c., at Yale, he would undoubtedly have gone thither for his education. The delay of that letter he was accustomed to consider as having given the decisive complexion to his life. He was admitted to the Junior class in the College of New Jersey, after it had gone through half its usual course, in the spring of 1782.

Notwithstanding Mr. Green had spent but about a year and a half in College as an undergraduate, so thorough had been his preparation, and so vigorous and mature was his mind, that, at the Commencement at which he graduated, he received the highest honour, in being appointed to deliver the Valedictory Oration. It was a circumstance of no small interest that Washington was present on the occasion; and the orator concluded by a direct address to that illustrious man. Washington met him the next day, and passed a high compliment upon his performance.

Immediately after his graduation, he was appointed a Tutor in the College, accepted the appointment, and continued to hold the office two years. He was then appointed to the chair of Professor of Mathematics and Natural Philosophy, and held that a year and a half. In November, 1785, he was married to the eldest daughter of Robert Stockton, of Princeton. Having pursued a course of study under Dr. Witherspoon, in connection with his duties as an officer of College, he was licensed to preach by the Presbytery of New Brunswick in February, 1786. He, at one time, had serious doubts whether to devote himself to the ministry, or to the profession of Law; and he seems to have been decided in favour of the former, by a casual remark addressed particularly to his conscience, by Dr. Samuel Stanhope Smith, then Vice President, and afterwards President, of the College.

His first sermon he preached in the church at Princeton, in the hearing of his venerable friend and instructer, Dr. Witherspoon, who, at the close of the service, expressed his approbation by tapping him on the shoulder, and saying,—"Well, well, continue to do as well as that, and we'll be satisfied"—"the only praise," said Dr. Green, "that he ever gave me to my face."

His first invitation to a settlement in the ministry was from the Independent Congregation of Charleston, S. C. Shortly after, he received a similar invitation from the Second Presbyterian Church in Philadelphia. In the former case, he was to be the colleague of Dr. Hollingshead, then a young man; in the latter, of the venerable Dr. Sproat, who was far advanced in life. It was in view of the difference of age between the two men, with whom it was proposed that he should be associated, that Dr. Witherspoon, whose opinion on all subjects he seems to have regarded as well nigh oracular, advised him to accept the call from Philadelphia. He did accept it, and was ordained and installed, in May, 1787. The Sermon on the occasion was preached by Dr. Ewing, and was afterwards published.

In 1787, he was elected a member of the American Philosophical Society. His certificate of membership bears the signature of Benjamin Franklin as President, and John Ewing, William White, and David Rittenhouse, as Vice Presidents.

In the year 1789, during the session of the First General Assembly, Mr. Green exchanged pulpits with Dr. Rodgers of New York, who was Moderator of the Assembly, and who was the more desirous of having his own pulpit well supplied, as Congress was then in session in New York, and a large part of the members were accustomed to attend his church. Dr. Rodgers' congregation, who were then looking out for a colleague to their pastor, were so favourably impressed with Mr. Green's public services, that they were about resolving to make an effort to secure them permanently, when,—the circumstance being communicated to him,—he interposed a peremptory prohibition of any such movement.

In 1790, Mr. Green was a member of the General Assembly, and made a motion that the intercourse between the Presbyterian and Congregational ministers, which had existed through a convention, previous to the Revolutionary war, should, with the approbation of the latter, be renewed. This motion was carried, and has taken effect in the correspondence which has subsisted between the Presbyterian and Congregational Bodies to the present time.

It was just at the close of this first General Assembly of which he was a member, that he received intelligence of the extreme illness, and apparently approaching death, of his father. He hastened to Hanover, but did not arrive till after his father's death and burial. His visit, however, was important, not merely as a visit of condolence to the surviving members of the family, but as it gave him an opportunity of counselling and instructing, in public and in private, many of his old friends and neighbours, who were anxiously concerned in regard to their salvation. His temporary labours among them were supposed to have been productive of the happiest consequences.

In the month of June, 1791,—his health being somewhat reduced,—he took a journey into New England, as far as Portsmouth, N. H., visiting most of the intervening places of any importance. He was absent from home nearly two months, during which time he mingled in many interesting scenes, and made the acquaintance of many distinguished men. His observations on the state of society, and especially on many prominent characters of the day, as they appear in his autobiography, are highly interesting. He returned to Philadelphia about the last of July, with his health and spirits much recruited, and with a large addition to the treasury of his grateful recollections concerning the land of his fathers.

In 1792, he was honoured with the degree of Doctor of Divinity from the University of Pennsylvania. The same year, he was elected Chaplain to Congress, and was re-elected by every successive Congress, till the removal to Washington in 1800; so that he held the Chaplaincy, in connection with Bishop White, for eight years.

In 1793, the yellow fever prevailed in Philadelphia with terrible mortality. Dr. Green and his wife were both seriously ill for some time, and finally left the city, and went to Princeton, not so much, however, to avoid the pestilence, as on account of having received intelligence that their child at Princeton was dangerously ill. This intelligence indeed proved erroneous; but, after they had once reached Princeton, the Doctor was urged by his friends in Philadelphia, and among them by his good old colleague, Dr. Sproat, by no means to venture a speedy return to the city. But scarcely had this advice been given before Dr. Sproat himself fell a victim to the disease. He died on the 18th of October; but Dr. Green delayed his return to Philadelphia till the 9th of the succeeding month. On Sunday, the 16th, he preached a Sermon with reference to the death of his colleague, which produced a powerful impression on the audience, and was afterwards published.

Dr. Green being now deprived of his first colleague, the burden of his duties was greatly increased; and, in the course of the succeeding winter, the Second and Third Presbyterian Churches of Philadelphia entered into an arrangement to obtain the services of the Rev. (afterwards Doctor) John N. Abeel, with an understanding that he should serve the Second Church two thirds of his time, and the Third Church the remaining third. He was accordingly installed as Colleague Pastor with Dr. Green; but the plan of union between the two churches did not work well, and it was but a short time before he accepted a call from the Reformed Dutch Church in New York. The relation between him and Dr. Green was mutually pleasant, not only while they held a common charge, but as long as Dr. Abeel lived. Dr. Green has left this strong testimony in his favour,—that "he was a most amiable man, and one of the best preachers in our country." His removal to New York was in the year 1795.

The yellow fever reappeared in Philadelphia in 1797. Dr. Green, having fixed his family at Princeton, remained in the city during nearly the whole time, ministering on the Sabbath to not more than one third of the number that usually composed his congregation. And, notwithstanding the peculiar impressiveness of his discourses in connection with the awful visitation of Providence, he had no evidence that, during the whole period, a solitary individual was brought to repentance. When the same disease commenced its ravages again in the succeeding year, (1798,) he had no hesitation in retiring from the city, and advising as many of his congregation as could, to do the same. He adopted the same course under similar circumstances in 1799 and 1802.

In the year 1799, Dr. Green was relieved from a portion of his clerical duties, by being allowed to receive as a colleague the Rev. (now Dr.) Jacob J. Janeway. With him, as with both his preceding colleagues, he lived on terms of the most affectionate intimacy; and no one of Dr. Green's contemporaries is more ready now than Dr. Janeway to pay a tribute to his extraordinary worth. The younger colleague continued his relation to the church, after the elder had resigned his charge, to occupy another field.

Dr. Green, as early as 1789, was attacked with a violent influenza, which ended in chronic rheumatism. This, with some other painful bodily affections, had produced an occasional melancholy, which interfered greatly, not only with his religious enjoyment, but with the free and comfortable discharge of his public duties. In the hope of obtaining relief from these complaints, he made a journey, in the summer of 1800, in company with a friend, to the Warm and Sweet Springs of Virginia. In this journey he made the acquaintance of Bishop Madison, the Rev. Dr. Baxter, and other excellent and distinguished persons, and made many interesting observations on the natural curiosities of the country through which he travelled. He reached home about the middle of October, after an absence of somewhat more than three months, with his bodily health materially benefitted, but without having experienced a proportional relief from mental depression. This continued, in a greater or less degree, for nearly two years, and gradually disappeared in consequence of a monthly blood-letting which he adopted without consulting a physician.

In March, 1802, the edifice of the College of New Jersey, with the exception of the walls, was reduced to ashes. The Board of Trustees,—of which Dr. Green had been one from the year 1790,—immediately assembled, and he was appointed to write an Address to the public, and to deliver another Address to the students; both of which duties he satisfactorily discharged, and both Addresses were published. Dr. Smith, the President of the College, was requested to visit South Carolina, to solicit benefactions. He consented to this proposal, only on condition that Dr. Green should have some oversight of the College during his absence. Accordingly, Dr. Green actually assumed this responsibility, and made several visits to Princeton, while the President was performing his tour; preaching on the Sabbath, attending examinations, and counselling the Faculty on various matters, and co-operating with them in the administration of discipline.

In January, 1807, he lost the wife of his youth, after having lived with her in the marriage state more than twenty-one years. Her death was preceded by a lingering and protracted illness, which kept his services in almost constant requisition. His own testimony in respect to her is, that "she was a patient and humble Christian." During her illness, and especially after her death, he suffered greatly from ill health, and from a return of the deep depression of spirits to which he had before been subject; but he continued his labours without interruption, and considered them, on the whole, as having been quite as useful as in any other period of his ministry.

In 1809, the first Bible Society in the United States was formed by several philanthropic individuals in Philadelphia, and Dr. Green wrote an Address to the public, stating the nature of the Association, and inviting other places to follow their example. This Address had a very extensive circulation, and did much to awaken the public mind to the obligation of giving the Bible to the destitute. Bishop White was the first President of the Society, and Dr. Green succeeded him, and retained the office as long as he lived.

In October of this year, Dr. Green was married to Christiana Anderson, the eldest child of Colonel Alexander Anderson. In speaking of this connection he says,—"The mending of a broken family is commonly a delicate affair, especially for a minister of the Gospel. But, on this occasion, I had the happiness to find that my three sons approved of the choice I had made; and that not an individual of my congregation, so far as known to me, was dissatisfied with it."

The proposal to establish a Theological Seminary in the Presbyterian Church was first introduced into the General Assembly in May, 1809; and the next year a resolution to this effect was adopted with great unanimity, and a committee appointed to draft a Constitution or Plan for the proposed Seminary. Of this committee Dr. Green was Chairman, and the important document that was produced was from his pen. In May, 1812, the General Assembly appointed a Board of Directors for the new institution, and *they* elected Dr. Green as their President, which office he continued to fill till his death. He evinced, in various ways, his devoted attachment to the Seminary, and never failed to be present at the meetings of the Board of Directors, until the infirmities of age rendered his attendance absolutely impracticable.

In August, 1812, he was elected President of the College of New Jersey. This appointment took him by surprise; but, after considerable hesitation, he concluded to accept it. On the resignation of his pastoral charge, instead of delivering a Farewell Sermon, as is common on such occasions, he circulated among the congregation a printed Address, containing appropriate counsels and exhortations. His pastoral relation was dissolved by the Presbytery of Philadelphia on the 20th of October, and on the 29th, he went to Princeton to enter upon his new field of labour. He received, this year, the degree of Doctor of Laws from the University of North Carolina.

At the close of the year 1813, he experienced a most severe affliction in the death of his eldest son. He was a young lawyer of great promise, settled in Philadelphia, and greatly respected and beloved by all his acquaintance. Being exhausted by heat and labour, he left the city with a view to recover his health. Having spent a little time at Ballston Springs, he passed over to Boston, in company with a friend, but on the way was attacked with more serious indisposition; and, after having been at Boston about ten days, during which no serious apprehensions were entertained respecting him, he suddenly died. His father's reflections on the occasion evinced the keenest sense of bereavement, mingled with the most profound submission to the Divine will.

But scarcely had the poignancy of this affliction ceased to be felt, before he experienced yet another in the death of his second wife. She died suddenly in March, 1814, in consequence of a premature confinement. She was a lady of uncommonly vigorous mind, great discretion, and earnest piety. Their connection was for a little less than four years and a half.

In the winter and spring of 1815, a very unusual attention to religion prevailed in the College of New Jersey, which resulted in the hopeful conversion of a large number of the students. One of the chief instrumentalities which Dr. Green recognised in connection with this work, was the study of the Sacred Scriptures, which he introduced soon after he came to the Presidential chair, and which constituted a regular Sabbath afternoon exercise. After the excitement attending the revival had passed away, the President made a long and able Report concerning it to the Trustees of the College, which was afterwards published, with an Appendix containing Questions and Counsel designed to aid those who believed themselves to have been subjects of the work. The pamphlet was widely circulated, and found its way into the hands of the Editors of the London Christian Observer, who, while they seemed to rejoice in the facts which it contained, doubted the expediency of the publication.

In October, 1815, he was married (for the third time) to a daughter of Major John McCulloch, of Philadelphia. In November, 1817, after a somewhat gradual decline, she also was taken from him by death. I was present at her funeral, and was struck with the fact that Dr. Green joined in singing the hymn, while the coffin of his wife lay by the side of him.

Dr. Green continued to occupy the Presidential chair till September, 1822, when, on account of the infirmities of advancing age, and other considerations which he deemed it not necessary to specify, he tendered the resignation of his office. The Trustees, in accepting his resignation, expressed their high appreciation of his services, and their regret that he had felt constrained to take such a step. The Congregation of Princeton, through their Trustees, signified their grateful sense of the many favours which he had shown them. And finally, the students of the College, by a committee, addressed him a letter, testifying, in the warmest terms, their respect for his character, their disappointment in being deprived of his instructions, and their wishes that the evening of his life might prove the serene harbinger of an eternal rest.

Notwithstanding one principal motive which induced Dr. Green to retire from the Presidency, was that he might be relieved from the great amount of care and responsibility which his official duties imposed upon him, he continued to labour for several years in a different field with unremitted activity.

He immediately took up his residence in Philadelphia and remained there, with occasional absences of a few weeks, till the close of life. He became the Editor of the Christian Advocate, a monthly religious periodical, which he continued for twelve years. A large portion of the articles were written by himself, and were marked by his characteristic perspicuity and vigour. Previous to his removal to Princeton, he had delivered a course of Lectures on the Assembly's Catechism; and, by the urgent request of his friends, he consented, after his return, to repeat them. They were now most of them either rewritten, or written for the first time: they were published originally in the Christian Advocate, but afterwards in two volumes, duodecimo, under the direction of the General Assembly's Board of Publication. In addition to these important services he preached to an African Congregation for two years and a half, besides frequently supplying the pulpits of his brethren, and meeting almost innumerable demands which were made upon his time by the general interests of the Church, and the various enterprises of Christian benevolence.

Dr. Green's decline, for several of the last years of his life, was exceedingly gradual; and, after he retired from public labour, and chiefly from public observation, he spent most of his waking hours in exercises of devotion. His last public appearance was in the General Assembly of 1846, where, without making his intention previously known, he, unexpectedly to the Assembly, showed himself. As he entered the door, supported by two individuals, the whole Assembly instinctively rose, and remained standing till he was conducted to his seat. The Moderator briefly addressed him, and he uttered a few appropriate words in reply, and shortly after retired. For several of his last months, his articulation was very indistinct, so that even those who were most accustomed to converse with him, found it difficult to understand him: and though his intellectual powers had greatly declined, yet his habit of devout meditation and prayer never forsook him. It was remarkable, however, that, a few days before his death, when his mind seemed burdened with its meditations, to which it was unable to give expression,—ou hearing read a portion of the first chapter of the Gospel by John, he was suddenly relieved from the difficulty of utterance, and burst out in a most fervent and eloquent strain of thanksgiving to God for all his mercies, and especially for his unspeakable gift. The power of distinct articulation then left him to return no more. His death occurred on the 19th of May, 1848, when he had almost completed his eighty-sixth year. The General Assembly of the Presbyterian Church was then in session in Baltimore; and when the news of his death reached them, they noticed it in a way which indicated at once their veneration for his character, and their gratitude for his services. His remains were removed to Princeton, to repose among the graves of his illustrious predecessors in the Presidency of the College of New Jersey. An appropriate Sermon was preached at his Funeral by his intimate friend and former colleague, the Rev. Dr. Janeway.

Dr. Green was the father of four children,—three by the first marriage, and one by the second. One of his sons, *Jacob*, was a Professor of Chemistry in Jefferson College, and died in February, 1841. Another, *James Sproat*, became an eminent lawyer, and resides at Princeton, N. J.

Dr. Green was identified with the history of the Presbyterian Church, far more than any man who survived to the period of his death. He was a Presbyterian from the strongest conviction; and whatsoever he found to do in promoting the interests of Presbyterianism, he did with his might. He was Moderator of the General Assembly in 1824. In the great controversy which issued in the division of the Church in 1837, he was firmly, sternly with the Old School; and is understood to have heartily concurred in the ultimate measures which were adopted. He watched the progress of the contest with the closest scrutiny and deepest concern, until he considered all the principles for which he had contended as settled; and then seemed gracefully to lay aside his armour, like a warrior retiring from the battle field. He was always an earnest friend of missions; and, though he was connected with different missionary associations, not under the care of the General Assembly, he was greatly in favour of a distinct Presbyterian organization, and exerted an important influence in effecting it.

Dr. Green's literary labours were considerable. In addition to those already mentioned, he superintended an edition of Dr. Witherspoon's works in 1802, and left in manuscript a somewhat extended biography of that eminent man, designed to be prefixed to a new and more complete edition of his works. For several years, beginning with 1804, he had the chief editorial responsibility of the General Assembly's Magazine,—a periodical which attracted considerable notice in its day. In 1822, he published an elaborate History of the College of New Jersey, in connection with a series of his Baccalaureate Discourses. These Discourses are marked by great ability, and are perhaps the noblest monument of the author's intellect, which he has left behind him. He published also a History of Presbyterian Missions.

Besides the larger works, and the contributions to periodicals above referred to, Dr. Green published the following:—A Sermon at the Funeral of the Rev. Dr. Duffield, 1790. The Address and Petition of a number of the Clergy of Philadelphia to the Senate and House of Representatives of the State of Pennsylvania, relative to Theatrical exhibitions, 1793. A Sermon occasioned by the death of the Rev. Dr. Sproat, 1793. Obedience to the laws of God: A Fast Sermon, 1798. An Address of the Trustees of the College of New Jersey, 1802. An Address to the Students and Faculty of the College of New Jersey, 1802. A Discourse at the Opening for public worship of the Presbyterian Church in the Northern Liberties of Philadelphia, 1805. An Address of the Bible Society of Philadelphia, 1809. Report of a Committee of the General Assembly, exhibiting the Plan of a Theological Seminary, 1810. Life and death of the righteous: An Address at the Funeral of the Rev. William M. Tennent, D. D., 1810. Advice and Exhortation addressed to the people of the Second Presbyterian Church in Philadelphia, on resigning the pastoral charge of that Congregation, 1812. A Report to the Trustees of the College of New Jersey, relative to a Revival of Religion among the students of said College in the winter and spring of 1815. Doing good in imitation of Christ: A Discourse delivered in the College of New Jersey, the Sabbath preceding the Annual Commencement, 1822. Christ crucified, the characteristic of apostolic preaching: A Sermon delivered at the opening of the General Assembly of the Presbyterian Church, 1825. The Christian duty of Christian women: A Discourse delivered at Princeton before a Female Society for the support of a female school in India, 1825. A Sermon (National Preacher, No. 39) delivered at the opening of the Synod of Philadelphia, 1826. An Address at the interment of Robert Ralston, 1836. A Sermon at the Whitefield Chapel, 1836.

My personal recollections of Dr. Green commence with the period of my becoming a member of the Theological Seminary at Princeton, in the autumn of 1816. He was then in the midst of his Presidential career, in his full vigour, and perhaps at the height of his usefulness. During the period of my course in the Seminary, I knew him chiefly as a preacher; and I can truly say that I have heard few preachers statedly, whose public services were equally edifying and impressive. His sermons were always fine specimens of logic, were richly imbued with the evangelical spirit, and abounded in mature and vigorous thought. His manner was deeply serious, but not for the most part highly impassioned, though there were passages in almost every sermon, that he uttered with great force and effect. There was nothing about his appearance in the pulpit, that seemed painfully artificial, and yet it was evident that his tones, his attitudes, his gesture, indeed every thing pertaining to his manner, were the result of careful study. I have understood that, in early life, his manner was much more free and more attractive to the mass of hearers than in his latter years; and this was probably owing, in a degree at least, to an affection of the head, which, in some instances, obliged him to sit down in the midst of his service, at other times to suspend his labours altogether, and once or twice was the occasion of his falling in the street. His sermons on the Sabbath were always written, and the manuscript lay before him; but he read with so much freedom that his reading did not at all impair the effect of his delivery. Some of his most edifying discourses were delivered at a Thursday evening lecture in the College, which most of the students of the Seminary were accustomed to attend. On these occasions he always sat, and never used notes; and though his expositions of Scripture were then more simple, and less formal and studied, than on the Sabbath, and indeed rose little above the tone of familiar conversation, yet they seemed to bring out the mind of the Spirit, and to come to the hearts of his hearers, quite as effectually as his more elaborate productions. His prayers were always varied to suit any occasion that might occur, and his last prayer always referred felicitously to the subject of his discourse; but the prayer that ordinarily preceded the sermon, was so nearly a form, that it soon became so familiar to me that I could repeat large portions of it. I have reason to believe that his public prayers were generally premeditated, and some of them, I know, were written.

I have said that I knew Dr. Green, while I was in the Seminary, chiefly as a preacher; but shortly before I finished my theological course, I was brought into pleasant social relations with him, which continued without interruption as long as he lived. I occasionally visited him at Philadelphia, and always found him dignified and stately indeed, but perfectly kind. I had occasion two or three times to ask important favours of him; and no man could have granted them more readily. On one occasion, when the Old and New School controversy in the Presbyterian Church was at its height, I got into a stage coach with him at Princeton to go to Philadelphia; and, as I knew how deeply his feelings were interested in the great questions at issue, I thought of nothing but that we should hear those questions discussed throughout the whole journey. But, to my great surprise, the good old man never opened his lips to make an allusion to the subject. He went back to the scenes of his earlier days, and related numerous anecdotes connected with the Revolution and subsequent periods, which not myself only, but all his fellow passengers, heard with the deepest interest. My last visit to him was not many months before his death. Having heard that his faculties had so far decayed that his friends could no longer have any enjoyment from intercourse with him, I had made up my mind that I would not even attempt to see him; but being told by his housekeeper that I was in the city, he very kindly sent for me. I found him sitting in his study, with his Greek Testament before him, which, even then, he occupied a part of every day in reading. A portion of his autobiography also lay by his side, which, I believe, was then in the process of being transcribed. He received me in his usual friendly manner, and though his articulation had become indistinct, and his words were few, he conversed intelligently upon every subject that was introduced. When we parted, I expected to see him no more; and did not. My eye lingered upon him, as upon a magnificent ruin. It was not long before I heard that the grave had taken him into its keeping.

FROM THE REV. JACOB J. JANEWAY, D. D.

New Brunswick, February 15, 1850.

My dear Sir: I am every way disposed to comply with your request for my recollections of my venerable friend and former colleague in the ministry,—the Rev. Dr. Green; but I do not know that I can meet your wishes better than by availing myself, with some slight alterations, of certain portions of a letter of considerable length, which I wrote at the request of the Rev. Dr. Jones, and which appears in connection with Dr. Green's autobiography.

My acquaintance with Dr. Green commenced in 1798. From the beginning of the year 1799, we laboured together as colleagues in the pastoral charge of the Second Presbyterian Church in Philadelphia, more than thirteen years,—till his pastoral relation to that church was dissolved, in consequence of his appointment to the Presidency of the College of New Jersey; and from that time till the day of his death, a friendship and intimacy that had never been interrupted, continued to exist. What I shall write, although intended as a tribute of friendship and affection to his memory, yet shall be, as far as I can make it, strictly true and free from exaggeration.

In stature, Dr. Green was of the middle size, but portly; having features well formed, a florid complexion, enlivened with dark, brilliant eyes; he was, in his youth, handsome. In subsequent life, he lost his florid complexion, and became somewhat corpulent. He still retained a commanding appearance.

The intellectual powers of Dr. Green were of a high order. The character of his mind is impressed on his writings. His Lectures on the Shorter Catechism, the Sermon on the Union of Science and Religion, which he preached and published, while President of the College of New Jersey, and the Christian Advocate,—a religious periodical which he, for a number of years, conducted with so much ability and usefulness, will long remain as proofs that he was endowed with a strong, vigorous and comprehensive mind.

With such commanding powers, it is natural to suppose his influence in the different ecclesiastical bodies with which he was connected, was great. It was; and, as an evidence of it, let me recite this anecdote. While an important measure was under debate in the General Assembly, the Doctor, who had been only an observer, obtained a seat in the house by the resignation of the principal in the commission. He soon arose, and made a motion that gave to the discussion a new and important turn. Dr. Speece of Virginia, who was sitting beside me, said to me, "See the influence of that man—he rises and makes a motion, and without offering a single argument, takes his seat, and his motion is carried."

He was characterized by much firmness and decision. On one occasion, while Philadelphia was the seat of government, and Dr. Green, Chaplain,—the Senate, being called to order for prayer, he saw a Senator still sitting and engaged in writing. Determined to exact at least an external reverence for that Almighty Being they were about to worship, he stood still, till the Senator, startled by the prolonged silence, arose upon his feet, and assumed a becoming attitude. He then proceeded to offer prayer.

When the news of the death of General Hamilton, who unhappily fell in a duel with Aaron Burr, reached Philadelphia, it produced a great sensation among the citizens. A public meeting was called to do honour to his memory. Resolutions were accordingly adopted, and published in the newspapers; and among them one calling on the clergy to notice the sad occurrence in their sermons on the coming Sabbath, with a view to eulogize that great man. Dr. Green immediately saw the impropriety of the resolution, and, with a view to extricate the clergy from the snare laid for them, and to save them from doing any thing unbecoming that holy religion of which they were the appointed teachers, he took measures for assembling them in a public meeting for consultation on what was proper to be done in the emergency. Resolutions were adopted and published, to counteract the injurious effect that was likely to result from the resolutions adopted by the meeting of the citizens, and to set every minister free from the ensnaring influence he might have felt, in conducting the services of the coming Sabbath. Every minister was left to act as his conscience might dictate to be right; to notice the death of that great man or not; and if he should choose to notice it, to do just as he deemed duty demanded. I recollect that I availed myself of the opportunity the sad occurrence afforded, for reprobating, in the course of my sermon on the Sabbath, the vile and barbarous practice of duelling. But I have no recollection that my colleague took any notice whatever of the event in his discourse.

In the year 1800, Dr. Green travelled for his health to the Sweet Springs in Virginia, where he remained for some time. While there, he determined to sustain his character as a Christian minister. He felt it proper that infirm mortals, seeking health from fountains God had been pleased to open and render medicinal, should acknowledge his bounty and their dependance on Him for the blessing they sought. He, therefore, resolved that it was becoming him, as a minister, to propose, with consent of the company, to offer prayer to God at their public meals. His wishes were gratified. It is remarkable that he received considerable aid in the accomplishment of his pious purpose from Major ———, a gambler. That man would call the company to order; and knocking loudly on the table, he would say, "Dr. Green will ask a blessing." So accustomed had they become to the religious ceremony, that no one would take his seat at the table till the arrival of this man of God, or, if he were prevented by indisposition, till it was announced he would not be present.

The intellectual powers of Dr. Green, being sanctified by the grace of God, were consecrated to the service of the Great Giver, and employed in the way for which they were bestowed. He was not only pious, but *eminently* pious and devout.

In imitation of his teacher, Dr. Witherspoon, for whom he always entertained a high veneration, he observed the first Monday of every month as a day of fasting, humiliation, and prayer. At what time he commenced this practice I do not know. The fact first came to my knowledge in 1802; when, during the prevalence of the yellow fever in Philadelphia, we were both staying at Mr. Ralston's country seat, Mount Peace, from which we went on the Sabbath and preached to that portion of our people, who were willing to assemble in the church. He had, it is probable, commenced the habit years before; and I think he continued it till the close of life.

Three times in the day, he retired to converse with his Heavenly Father, by prayer and supplication, thanksgiving and praise. His love for social prayer was manifested by his inviting his ministerial brethren to meet at his house every Monday morning for the purpose of reading the Scriptures, offering united prayer to God, and singing his praises.

His piety prompted him to acts of charity. He was ready, according to his ability, to relieve the needy, and aid in the accomplishment of all benevolent purposes. In the distribution of his charity, he acted not from impulse but from principle. He settled in his mind what proportion of his income he ought to consecrate to benevolent purposes. One tenth he deemed the proper proportion for himself. On occasions he went beyond this rule. Warmly attached to the Theological Seminary at Princeton, and ardently desiring its enlargement and prosperity, he purchased and gave to the Trustees two acres of ground additional to what they held, for that valuable institution.

Dr. Green was eminently qualified by his intellectual endowments, his devoted piety, and his talent for public speaking, for preaching the Gospel of Christ. And he preferred this above all other pursuits. His discourses on the Sabbath were uniformly written. Having judiciously selected his text, he confined himself to the thoughts it suggested. He never allowed himself to run away from his text, and deliver an essay or essays that had no connection, or a very slight one, with it. His intelligent hearers saw the thoughts he presented to be suggested by the portion of the Divine Word on which he was discoursing. There was such a close connection between the parts of his sermon, and such a unity given to the whole, that his hearers could easily recollect what they had heard, and treasure it up in their memories. He carefully wrote out what he intended to deliver; regarding it as wrong to enter the pulpit without due preparation, unless unexpectedly called by Divine Providence to speak;—when he thought a minister was authorized to make the attempt, and rely on assistance from on high. The discourses of Dr. Green, carefully prepared, were at once devotional, practical and experimental. They were always adapted to the occasion, and suited to the wants of the people.

His delivery was excellent and commanding. Favoured with a good voice, he modulated it so as to impart force to the thoughts he uttered, and being accompanied with graceful and appropriate gesticulation, his discourses were rendered at times very impressive.

On the whole, I have no hesitation in saying that, when he was in good health and good spirits, his sermons were so well prepared, and delivered with such eloquence, that I regarded him (my place of residence afforded opportunities for hearing the best preachers) as the first preacher of his day in the Presbyterian Church.

In fine, Dr. Green was a great and good man,—eminently pious and useful. His immediate successor in the Presidency of the College, the Rev. Dr. Carnahan, justly said, when his body had been laid in the grave, in the place of interment which holds the mortal remains of his illustrious predecessors, Dickinson, Burr, Edwards, Davies, Finley, Witherspoon, and Smith,—"He was by his talents fitted to fill any civil station; and by his eloquence to adorn the halls of our National Legislature."

Very respectfully, your brother,

J. J. JANEWAY

FROM THE REV. NICHOLAS MURRAY, D. D.

ELIZABETHTOWN, May 20, 1849.

Rev. and dear Sir: You ask me for my reminiscences of the Rev. Dr. Green, and my views as to his general character, as a minister and a literary man. And whilst feeling that there are many who are more competent to the task, because of their long and familiar acquaintance with him, I hesitate not to comply with your request. I shall arrange my views of his character under a few heads, and bring in my recollections of him by way of illustrating them.

1. He was a man pre-eminently of two characters, public and private; and to form a right estimate of him he must be known in both. To those who only knew him as a public man, he was stern, unyielding, dictatorial, and repulsive; to those who knew him both in public and in private, he was mild, pliable, and peculiarly attractive. Hence, by one class he was respected, but disliked; whilst by another he was greatly beloved, and regarded as an oracle.

Although I had heard much of him from my boyhood, and read some of his writings, I never saw him until 1826. And the sight of him, at that time, would induce any young man to resolve to keep at a respectful distance. His form was full and commanding; his appearance was stern; his eye, gleaming through shaggy eyebrows, was penetrating; his step was firm; and from his cane to his wig there was something which, to say the least, was more repulsive than attractive to a youth. And with this conclusion agreed many of the anecdotes which I had heard of him, whilst he was President of Nassau Hall. My acquaintance with him commenced in 1827, and in this wise—visiting Philadelphia as the agent of one of our National Societies, I felt his approbation of my plans necessary to my success. I called to see him, and was introduced into his study. I soon found myself in converse with a courteous, kind, but dignified Christian minister. He not only approved my plans, but tendered his own subscription to the object. Finding, on inquiry, as I was about to retire, that I was a candidate for the ministry, he invited me to a seat by his side, and the impressions made upon my mind and heart by his kind inquiries, by his paternal advice, are vivid to this hour. He dismissed me with his blessings upon myself and upon my object. Never was a revolution more entire wrought in the feelings of a man. And from that day forward he was my counsellor in cases of difficulty. And so pleasant and simple was he in private, that, on leaving my family, after an occasional visit of a few days, my little children would cling to his feet and to his garments, crying out—"You must not go, Dr. Green." I feel quite sure that those who only knew him in Presbyteries and Synods, and especially in the ardent conflicts of the General Assembly, of which he was almost a standing member, have the most erroneous views of his true character.

2. His was a truthful character. Truth was to him truth; and what he believed, he felt and acted out. It was not his policy to believe one way and act another. Such policy he scorned, and withheld his confidence from those who practised it. A man cast in such a mould is likely to be unpopular with that large class of persons who regard truth with less reverence; who stretch it or contract it to suit circumstances; who, in the bad sense of the phrase, are ready to become "all things to all men." They are prejudiced, obstinate, bigoted, sectarian. But there is a better and truer explanation of all this. There is a deep and heartfelt reverence for the truth as such, which, on all occasions and every where, forbids its compromise on the ground of mere worldly expediency. There is an inner reverence for it, in kind and degree, like unto that which is felt for God himself. This was conspicuous through the whole long life of Dr. Green. And often have I heard him censuring with far greater severity what he considered the crooked policy of some of his friends, who always acted with

him, than that of his opponents, who always pursued a different policy from his. His firmness was at an equal remove from fickleness and obstinacy, which are alike alien to a truly noble character. The one is barren of good as the yielding wave; the other, as the unyielding rock. Although holding his opinions strongly, he was ever willing to yield them for good reasons. A fool never changes his opinions, but a wise man always will, for sufficient cause.

3. He was a most fervent and instructive preacher. Although I never heard him preach until he had passed the meridian of life,—until, fearful of attacks of vertigo, to which he was subject, he generally declined the pulpit;—yet the few sermons I have heard him deliver, very deeply impressed his hearers, and very obviously indicated that, in the prime of his years, he was a man of no ordinary power. His utterance was distinct; his manner was calm and dignified—if he never rose to the higher style of action, he always attained its end,—attention and impression. He made you feel that he entirely believed every word he uttered, and that it was of infinite moment that you should believe it also. The minister that uniformly makes this impression, must be one of great power.

Nor was the impression which he made simply that of manner—his matter was always weighty, well arranged and instructive. If his topics were commonplace, they were always important. If his discussions were sometimes dry, they were clear as a sunbeam. If you could not always adopt his opinions, there was no mistake as to what he meant. In all my intercourse with him, I had never cause to ask, "What do you mean, Sir?" Nor do I remember a sentence in all his writings which is not entirely transparent.

His most valuable Lectures on the Shorter Catechism, and his published Sermons, give a fair specimen of his ordinary style of preaching. If they have not the amplitude of Chalmers, nor the polished eloquence of Hall, nor the warmth of Davies, they have the purity of Blair, in union with a natural simplicity which strongly fixes their truly evangelical sentiments in the mind and heart. Hence the devoted attachment both to him and his sentiments, of those who enjoyed his ministrations.

He greatly excelled as an expounder of the Word of God. Of his talent in this way I had abundant opportunity for forming a judgment. The Sabbath School teachers of Philadelphia adopted a rule to have the same Bible lesson taught on the same Sabbath in all schools of the city, and to have the lesson expounded to them by some clergyman. The Lecture room in Cherry Street was the place, and Dr. Green was the man, selected. On each evening, the large room was crowded by one of the most interesting and interested audiences I ever beheld; and, although the Doctor was then approaching his threescore years and ten, never did I hear more clear, and full, and fresh, and pleasing expositions of Divine truth. At the close of the lecture, opportunity was given for the asking of any questions upon any points that were left unexplained; which were always answered with a promptness that showed the remarkable fulness of his mind upon all topics connected with the exposition or the elucidation of the Scriptures. I know not that I ever attended a more instructive religious service. I have learned that it was greatly blessed of God to the conversion and edification of Sabbath School teachers. He served his generation in more dignified stations, but probably in none more usefully, than when expounding the Word of Life to nearly a thousand young men and women, who, on each successive Sabbath, sought to impress those views received from him on the minds of ten thousand children. Might not this plan be successfully revived in all our cities?

4. He was a truly devotional man. His public devotional services were always peculiarly impressive. They were solemn, pathetic, reverential, strikingly appropriate, and never unduly protracted. In the family, he always commenced morning and evening prayer by imploring a blessing upon the service, and whilst

engaged in it, all felt that he was conversing with God, as a man converses with a friend. I have more than once heard him express his regrets at the little preparation ministers often make for conducting the devotional services of a congregation; and I have heard him state that, in the early part of his ministry, he was in the habit of writing prayers with equal regularity as sermons. And whilst he never read them, nor committed them closely to memory, the writing of them furnished him with topics for prayer, and gave to those topics arrangement, and to the expression of them variety and appropriateness. For this thought he might have been indebted to his venerated teacher, Dr. Witherspoon, who always recommended devotional composition to his theological students, of whom Dr. Green was one.

My first sermon was preached in the Third Presbyterian Church, Philadelphia,—then under the pastoral care of the Rev. Dr. Ely, and from the text, "Compel them to come in." Dr. Ely was absent, and to my confusion, Dr. Green entered the church, just at the opening of the service. Feeling it better to have him behind me than before me, I sent a request to him to sit in the pulpit. In my ardour to stimulate ministers and Christians to do their duty, I omitted almost any allusion to the necessary agency of the Spirit to secure their success. He made the concluding prayer, in which, with his accustomed felicity, he converted the topics discussed into supplications, and then brought out, most prominently and emphatically, the essential truth which I had omitted. I felt that the whole congregation realized the defect of my sermon. His kindness was marked at the close of the service. I went to my study, rewrote my sermon, put into it the prayer of Dr. Green, and it is unnecessary to say that it was greatly improved by the addition.

My very last interview with him impressed me with the depth of that spirit of devotion which characterized his life. He was feeble, and forgetful, and in a mood to talk very little to any body. Hearing that I was in the city, he sent for me that I might attend to a matter of business for him, connected with the New Jersey Historical Society. I entered his study on a May morning, about nine o'clock. His Greek Testament was open before him—he requested me to be seated. The business ended, he waved his hand, saying—"My devotional reading is not yet concluded—I will be happy to see you at another time." And as I closed the door of his study, the prayer—"God bless you"—fell upon my ear,—the last words I ever heard him utter. All testify that the closing years of his life were marked by a spirit remarkably devotional.

5. He possessed a truly catholic spirit. This assertion perhaps will startle some who only knew his public character, and who have only heard of him as an impersonation of Old School Presbyterianism. Yet it is true to the letter. His own views he held strongly, but in perfect charity to those who differed from him. Although his contributions and exertions were mainly confined to the organizations of his own Church, it was out of consistency with himself, and not out of illiberality to others. More than once have I heard him detail an account of a visit made him by the venerable Dr. Woods, for so many years the ornament of the Andover Theological Seminary. They compared views on theological and other subjects; and whilst they differed a little in the explanations of some positions, they radically agreed. "Would to God," I have heard him say, "that all our ministers and churches held the sentiments of my Brother Woods." And after the disruption of our Church, he never permitted a day to pass without the most fervent prayers to God on behalf of the brethren to whom he was regarded as being so violently opposed. He had none of the narrow sectarianism that would confine the Church visible to those only who walked with him; and often have I heard him rejoice in the good that was done by Episcopalians, Baptists, and Methodists; while, on all suitable occasions, he could strongly maintain the positions on which he differed from them. There is not probably a

National Society for the spread of the Gospel in this land, to which he was not a contributor, and of which he was not a member or a manager; whilst he may be considered the father of nearly all the Boards and Societies of his own deeply venerated Church. "Nobody will question the Presbyterianism of Dr. Green," said an eloquent divine, during a debate in the General Assembly, "as he was dyed in the wool." "The brother mistakes," said Dr. Green, with that promptness of repartee which he possessed—"the Lord by his grace made me a Presbyterian." And although the principles of his Church were interwoven with his spiritual life, and formed a part of it, yet he had the most cordial love for the children of God, by whatever name called. Never have I heard him speak with more affection of any man, than of his friend, the amiable and venerated Bishop White.

6. He was remarkably gifted as a son of consolation to desponding souls. This perhaps was mainly owing to his own simple views of Divine truth, and his rich experience of its power. He had the ability to simplify every subject on which he spoke or wrote, and to do it in a few words. This is very apparent in his Lectures on the Shorter Catechism, prepared for the youth of his own congregation. When anxious or desponding souls applied to him for direction, he first sought out the cause of trouble, and then, like a well instructed scribe, he so simply presented and applied the remedial truth, as to give, if not immediate, yet speedy, relief. He acted upon the principle that "if the truth makes us free, we are free indeed." Hence, aged desponding Christians, and individuals asking what they should do to be saved, and from different congregations in the city, were often found in his study, seeking his counsels. On such occasions, there was a kindness and blandness in his manner, which formed the greatest contrast with his stern and unflinching position, when contending for principles on the floor of the General Assembly.

A case in illustration of this I will state. Twenty-five years ago, the name of Miss Linnard, whose memoir has since been published, was familiar to the pious female circles of Philadelphia. She shone conspicuously among them for her fine sense, great activity, and deep piety. A minister, still living, preached a preparatory lecture in the church in Spruce Street, of which she was a member, on the text "Lovest thou me?"—which cast her into the deepest gloom. Such were the strong and vivid representations which he made as to the necessary preparations for the right partaking of the Lord's Supper, that, conscious of not possessing them, she resolved not to commune. Her sense of duty and her deep depression of feeling came into conflict, and occasioned her the most intense anxiety. In this state, she had recourse to Dr. Green, who had heard the lecture." "My dear child," said he, "our excellent brother seemed to forget that the Lord's table is spread, not for angels, but for sinners. He has come not to call the righteous, but sinners to repentance. It is the weary and heavy laden He invites to Himself, and to the privileges of his house." It was enough. She left his study rejoicing in the Lord; and a more joyful Communion season she had never spent on earth. I heard the lecture; and the incident here narrated I have heard from both parties. And this, I feel persuaded, is a fair illustration of his skill and success as a comforter of the Lord's people, and as a director of the inquiring to the Cross of Jesus Christ.

It was during his Presidency that the revival occurred which, under God, brought into the church and into the ministry such men as Dr. John Breckenridge, Dr. Hodge, Bishops McIlvaine of Ohio, and Johns of Virginia.

It remains for me only to speak of him as a literary man. As his life and writings will do his memory full justice upon this subject, I need say but little in respect to it. When he graduated at Princeton, he was the Valedictorian of his class. He was soon made Tutor, and then Professor in his *Alma Mater* His academic habits he carried with him into his pastoral life, and always took rank in the very first class of the educated men of his own age,—with such men as Dwight, and Smith, and Mason, and Wilson. If he was excelled in brilliancy by these, and others with whom he ranked, he was fully their equal in all solid attainments. It was no ordinary tribute to his literary character, that he should be selected to succeed Dr. Smith as the President of Princeton College, in which position he discharged his duties as instructer with distinguished ability, and in a religious point of view especially, with distinguished usefulness. On retiring from the Presidency, he commenced the Christian Advocate, which he edited for many years; and whose twelve volumes give the most ample testimony to his rich scholarship, his keen discrimination, his metaphysical acumen, his sharpness as a critic, and the extent and variety of his reading. Some of the ablest productions of his pen were written after he had passed his fourscore years; and to the very close of his life his Greek Testament was his daily study, and he could repeat passages from the Greek and Roman classics with great interest and vigour. His habits of study he never surrendered to the last. And I have in my possession a note which he addressed to me on business, in his eighty-fifth year, written with as clear, bold and steady a hand, as if written in his fortieth year. In this respect he is an example worthy of imitation by all literary men in advanced years, to study, write, and work to the last. Still waters soon stagnate; running waters, never. The mind unemployed, like the blade of Hudibras,

> " Which eat into itself for lack
> Of somebody to hew and hack,"

preys upon itself, and soon passes away.

Such is my estimate of the character of Dr. Green. By others who knew him much longer, and more intimately, it might be sketched more strongly and truly; but such are the impressions which are left upon my mind and heart from an acquaintance with him of twenty years. On the whole, I esteem him as among the ripest scholars, the most able divines, the most useful men, which our country has produced. His name will be more closely connected with the history and progress of the Presbyterian Church, one hundred years hence, than that of any of his predecessors. He well deserves a name and a place among the Lights of the American Pulpit.

Yours affectionately,

N. MURRAY.

DAVID PORTER, D. D.*

1786—1851.

DAVID PORTER, the son of Increase and Mary (Niles) Porter, was born in Hebron, Conn., May 27, 1761. His mother died when he was four years old. With the exception of ten months, during which he served in the army of the Revolution, he lived in his father's family till he was about eighteen years of age.

Having resolved on a liberal education, and gone through his preparatory course, he entered Dartmouth College in 1780, and was graduated in 1784. He devoted himself to his studies with great assiduity, and ranked high as a scholar in every part of his collegiate course. Notwithstanding he had been the subject of serious impressions occasionally from his childhood, it

* MS. Autobiography.—MS. from his family.

was not till his second year in College that he supposed himself to experience a radical change. A powerful revival of religion commenced in the neighbourhood; and at first he was determined that he would not allow it to divert his attention in any degree from his studies; but he found himself unable to keep his resolution, and was soon borne down with a sense of his own sinfulness. After a few weeks, he was enabled, as he believed, calmly and gratefully to repose in the merciful provisions of the Gospel, and at no distant period made a public profession of his faith in Christ, by joining the church in Hanover connected with the College.

Shortly after his graduation, he went to Portsmouth, N. H., where he spent two years and a half in teaching a school, and at the same time was prosecuting his theological studies under the Rev. (afterwards Dr.) Joseph Buckminster of Portsmouth, and the venerable Dr. Stevens of Kittery. After being licensed to preach, he laboured several months in Sanford, Me., and was invited to settle there, but declined.

In February, 1787, he accepted a call from the Congregational Church of Spencertown, N. Y., and was ordained as its Pastor on the 24th of September following. Here he continued in the laborious discharge of his duties fourteen years. On account of the inadequacy of his salary to the support of his family, he was obliged to devote a portion of his time to teaching,—a service for which he was admirably qualified, and in which he was eminently useful. His ministry here was attended with an unusual blessing, and his church was greatly enlarged, as the result of several revivals of religion. He was also peculiarly happy in his ministerial relations, having for his neighbours such men as Doctors West, Catlin, Hyde, and Shepard, who were all regarded as lights in their day, and whose religious views were nearly or entirely in accordance with his own.

In June, 1803, Mr. Porter resigned his charge at Spencertown, and in October following, was installed Pastor of the First Presbyterian Church in Catskill, N. Y. Both the church and the village were at that time in their infancy, and for several years they were obliged to use the Court House as a place of public worship; but, in due time, and in no small degree through his instrumentality, a convenient church edifice was erected.

In the year 1811, he was honoured with the degree of Doctor of Divinity from Williams College.

His connection with the Church at Catskill continued till June, 1831, when, having entered his seventy-first year, he requested to be released from his pastoral charge. The request was acceded to by his church, and the relation dissolved. His ministry here was, on the whole, a highly successful one, and the very close of it especially was signalized by a revival of uncommon power, as the fruit of which, not less than one hundred were added to the church.

Dr. Porter, in resigning his pastoral charge, had no idea of retiring from the labours of the ministry. His heart was strongly set on many of the great benevolent objects of the day, and he wished to be able to render to some of them a more efficient aid than he could by continuing in his pastoral relation. In 1824, he was chosen a corporate member of the American Board of Commissioners for Foreign Missions; and with most of the other national institutions for the spread of the Gospel, he was connected, from their organization. Immediately after he resigned his charge, he engaged in the service of some of these institutions,—taking as his field of labour the county in which he lived, and several counties adjacent to it, and continued his agency till he had completed his eightieth year. He was an uncommonly successful as well as popular agent.

For several years previous to his death, Dr. Porter was gradually sinking under the infirmities of age, and the weakness of his limbs particularly rendered it difficult for him to go much beyond the limits of his own dwelling. On the 24th of September, 1843, the fifty-sixth anniversary of his ordination, he preached his last sermon on the text,—"Brethren, the time is short." It was not written, but was rendered highly impressive by its appropriate and weighty sentiments, and the solemnity and pathos with which it was delivered. His last visit to the house of God was on the 28th of July, 1847, on occasion of the Funeral of his eldest son. Then, as on similar preceding occasions, he evinced the most unqualified submission to the Divine will.

For nearly three years immediately preceding his death, Dr. Porter was confined to his house by reason of the infirmities of age. During this period, he maintained great equanimity of spirit, and never lost his interest in his friends or in passing events. He died on the 7th of January, 1851, of paralysis, after being confined to his bed twelve days. His reason was continued to the last, and he died in the utmost peace.

On the 11th of October, 1791, he was married to Sarah, daughter of the Rev. Daniel Collins* of Lanesborough, Mass. They had six children, all of whom are now (1857) deceased. The venerable widow is still living. One of his sons (William Augustus) was graduated at Williams College, and was Professor of Rhetoric and Moral Philosophy in the same institution from 1827 till his death in 1830.

The following is a list of Dr. Porter's publications:—An Anniversary Discourse occasioned by the death of four children of Daniel Sayre, who were consumed by fire on the night of the 28th of January, 1808, preached at Cairo, 1809. A Dissertation on Christian Baptism, and the subjects therewith immediately connected, comprised in a series of sections, 1809. A Sermon delivered at Cairo, at the ordination of the Rev. Richard Williams,† 1812. A Sermon preached at Lanesborough at the Ordination of the Rev. John Dewitt to the charge of that church as Colleague Pastor with Rev. Daniel Collins, 1812. A Sermon delivered at Ellsworth, (Sharon) Conn., at the Ordination of the Rev. Orange Lyman to the pastoral care of the Church and Society in that place, 1813. A Sermon at the dedication of the Presbyterian meeting-house in Hunter, N. Y., 1828.

I had the pleasure of an acquaintance with Dr. Porter during the latter part of his life. On my first introduction to him, I was much impressed by his large corporeal dimensions, the intelligent and yet benevolent expression of his countenance, and a certain indescribable peculiarity of manner, which not only predisposed me to good humour, but often excited a smile. My first meeting with him was at the Synod at Catskill, shortly after he had demitted his pastoral charge. I saw at once that he was one of the most influential members of the body: he was not often upon his feet, but when

* DANIEL COLLINS, was a native of Guilford, Conn.; was graduated at Yale College in 1760; studied Theology under the Rev. Dr. Bellamy; was ordained Pastor of the Church in Lanesborough, April 17, 1764; and died August 26, 1822, aged eighty-three.

† RICHARD WILLIAMS, the son of Nathaniel Williams, was born at Lebanon, Conn., April 27, 1780; was graduated at Yale College in 1802; was ordained and installed Pastor of the Church at Cairo, January 9, 1812; and died in 1844.

he did speak, his words were always apt and weighty, and were listened to with the utmost deference. It was not merely his venerable age and large experience that gave him his influence, but his exemplary moderation and sound judgment, and enlightened, discriminating and practical views of whatever subject presented itself. I afterwards heard him preach, though it was apparently without much preparation, and in my Lecture room. The discourse was sensible, characterized by great seriousness and unction, and delivered in a manner which secured an undivided attention. Owing, I suppose, to his bodily infirmities, he had his cane in one hand during the delivery of the sermon, and, at short intervals, we heard it come down upon the floor with no small force, and, though it seemed odd, it was really a very effective gesture. He passed several nights in my house at different times, and I was always delighted by his cheerfulness and good nature, not less than edified by his sensible and spiritual conversation. I remember his detailing to me certain parts of his history in connection with the Revolution, particularly some hair breadth escapes in Rhode Island, in which he seemed to live over the past with the most intense interest. The impression that he always left upon me was, that he had a comprehensive, discriminating and well furnished mind, a tender and generous heart, and above all a spirit of earnest and devoted piety.

FROM THE REV. GIDEON N. JUDD, D. D.

MONTGOMERY, N. Y., May 3, 1851.

My dear Brother: My acquaintance with the late Dr. Porter of Catskill, commenced in 1803. I then resided in my father's family in the adjacent town of Cairo. The Presbyterian Church there was then feeble and destitute of the stated administration of Divine ordinances. Over it the Doctor watched with paternal and benevolent solicitude. During the summer months, after performing the usual services of the Sabbath for his own people, he frequently delivered a third sermon in Cairo, at a late hour in the afternoon. When his own pulpit was supplied by a brother in the ministry, he not unfrequently spent the Sabbath in our place, and often preached there at other times, when his services were specially needed. As my mind had previously been brought under religious influences, I was deeply interested in both his preaching and conversation. After my attention was turned to the ministry, in every stage of my course of preparation for it, he was a most valued counsellor.

After I was graduated, and before I entered the Theological Seminary at Princeton, I spent six months in his family. That was a season of more than ordinary religious interest among his people, and I had a favourable opportunity to know his manner of addressing the understandings, the consciences, and hearts of men, in those solemn and interesting circumstances. His conversation and preaching evinced an intense interest in the spiritual welfare of those whom he addressed, and a deep sense of his own responsibility. He watched for souls as one that felt that he must give an account of his ministry. The claims of the law of God he exhibited with great clearness, and urged them with great power upon the consciences of the impenitent. He laboured to convince them that their moral depravity was entire, and that the only hope of their salvation was in the sovereign mercy and grace of God.

His treatment of the awakened and anxious was characterized by great tenderness and fidelity. And he was equally faithful in his treatment of those who indulged hope of acceptance with God. He presented the tests of genuine conversion with great clearness, and urged upon them the importance of diligent self-scrutiny and earnest prayer to God for unerring teaching and guidance.

After entering the ministry, I enjoyed only occasional intercourse with him, till I was called in 1840 to take the pastoral charge of his former flock. During a residence of nearly ten years in Catskill, my intercourse with him was frequent and intimate, and to me deeply interesting. His modesty and humility were remarkable. Notwithstanding he had sustained to the people of my charge the relation of Pastor for nearly thirty years, and had been my counsellor and intimate friend, he assumed no authority. When I consulted him, as I often did, he gave his opinion with modesty and frankness, and did every thing he could to encourage and assist me in my work. On theological subjects and Christian experience and practice, the general state of religion and the conversion of the world, he conversed with great freedom and interest. Upon these themes he delighted to dwell. At his advanced period of life, men often look upon the present with great dissatisfaction, and the future with dark forebodings. It was not so with him. He did not think the former days were better. In view of what God had done, during his ministry, for the spread of the Gospel at home and abroad, and what He has engaged to do for the extension of his Kingdom among men, he indulged joyous anticipations for the future.

In his domestic and social relations, Dr. Porter was eminently qualified to receive and communicate pleasure. Ardently attached to his family and friends, and deeply imbued with the spirit of benevolence, he took great delight in imparting happiness. His conversation, though frequently characterized by abruptness of manner and expression, was both pleasing and instructive, and occasionally enlivened by exhibitions of humour and wit, so controlled, however, by discretion and Christian principle, that they detracted nothing from the dignity either of the Christian or the minister.

His keen sensibility and great benevolence led him promptly to enter into the joys and sorrows of others. To the afflicted, especially of his flock, he was eminently a son of consolation. With great fidelity and tenderness he pointed them to the only source of true consolation, and urged the duty of acquiescence in the will of God, and joy in his government. His manner of doing this was peculiarly his own. Sometimes a single sententious remark or inquiry, uttered in his significant manner, contained volumes of instruction. Two examples, as specimens of his method of addressing persons in affliction, now occur to me. On one occasion, when visiting a deeply afflicted family,—after making a few appropriate remarks, he said to them with great solemnity and tenderness,—"You had better look up." At another time, to a young lady of his flock, whose heart was almost crushed with anxiety for a suffering sister, he put the significant and twice repeated inquiry—"Can you speak well of God? Can you speak well of God?"

Dr. Porter had an uncommonly vigorous intellect. His discernment was quick and keen, his discrimination accurate, his judgment sound, and his reasoning faculty of a very high order. It was for these solid and useful attributes of mind that he was distinguished, rather than for a splendid imagination, or an exquisite taste.

His style and manner of speaking were characteristic of his strong original mind, and adapted to make a deep impression. He never sought to adorn his style with flowers of rhetoric, or fascinating imagery. He aimed to make it clear, concise and forcible; and he succeeded. No one could hear or read his public discourses, without being convinced of his honesty of purpose, and his strong desire to communicate to other minds the thoughts and feelings which glowed in his own. In the arrangement of the topics of his discourses, his method of discussing them, and the perspicuity and energy of his language, he furnished a model of uncommon excellence.

In his preaching, he dwelt much upon the leading doctrines of the Gospel; but in connection with them he exhibited, with great clearness and pungency of application, the various branches of experimental and practical godliness. In the selection of his themes for the pulpit, he seems habitually to have kept in view the great end of preaching,—the glory of God in the conversion of men, and their subsequent growth in knowledge and holiness.

The soundness of his judgment and the ample stores of his theological learning led intelligent laymen and his brethren in the ministry to consult him in cases of difficulty, and on abstruse points of doctrine to pay great deference to his opinions. Both before and after the establishment of Theological Seminaries, many candidates for the ministry placed themselves under his instruction, whose Christian and ministerial character he was eminently instrumental in forming for usefulness.

Dr. Porter was sincerely attached to the doctrines and polity of the Presbyterian Church, but was remarkably free from a sectarian spirit. The division of the Church in 1838, and the causes which led to it, he deeply deplored. But strongly as he was convinced that the Exscinding Acts of 1837, which produced the division, were wrong, he never exhibited an unkind spirit towards their authors or their advocates. He was persuaded that both Bodies were agreed in a belief of all the essential doctrines of the Gospel, and that a practical demonstration of the fact would greatly subserve the interests of true religion.

Dr. Porter was indeed a man of great worth. His memory on earth is blessed, and I am persuaded his recompense is great in Heaven.

Very respectfully and sincerely yours in the bonds of friendship, and the Gospel of our adorable Lord Jesus,

G. N. JUDD.

FROM THE REV. G. A. HOWARD.

Catskill, March 15, 1855.

Rev. and dear Sir: I am but imperfectly qualified to give you the sketch of Dr. Porter's personal appearance and peculiarities you have requested. I did not see this remarkable man until his mind and body were broken down by disease and the infirmities of age. I well remember him, however, as he appeared when I first entered his room,—a man of great bulk, seated in an arm-chair, which was furnished with large wheels, his fine compact head sunk upon his breast in thought or slumber, and the soft breeze of June blowing in through the open window, near which he sat,—lifting and slightly disarranging his thin white hair.

When roused and made acquainted with my presence, he raised his head, looked at me inquiringly for a moment, and then a light of welcome and pleasure came into his eyes, and he extended his hand heavily with a cordial "How d'do?" His voice was deep and full. They placed a chair for me near him And, though he said but little, and occasionally dropped his head, and sunk into an apparent reverie, I discovered more than once, while conversing with others, that he was listening, watching my countenance, and examining me from head to foot. He praised his people—they were *his* until he died;—and said a few abrupt, kind words to me as associated with them; but entered into no connected conversation.

When I rose to take leave, he requested me to pray; and, uniting in the prayer with evident emotion, responded at the close with an audible *Amen*.

He lived until the following January, and I had frequent interviews with him. His words were always few; and at this time he conveyed his thoughts and wishes in short ejaculations. Once or twice he spoke more at length, and with great animation, and on one occasion with much enjoyment of his own humour.

His sensibilities were readily excited. He had three noble sons, and all of them were in the grave. Any allusion to them deeply affected him, and at times, attempting to speak of them himself, he would weep and sob in a manner which showed that time had done but little to mitigate his grief.

His people were strongly attached to him, and to his aged, afflicted and amiable wife, who was a model of the Christian gentlewoman. They loved to visit him; nor they only—persons of several denominations frequently met in his room. He spoke but little, yet received great pleasure from their respectful and affectionate attentions. He was fond of children; and when, every Sabbath afternoon, his grandchildren, as they were returning from church, came in to see him, it was pleasant to witness his enjoyment of their presence and affection.

Most of the time he sat by the window I have mentioned. He was unable to stand for a moment. His ankles were too weak to support his immense weight. He was wheeled into another room to his meals; and, occasionally, in pleasant weather, was drawn out upon the stoop of the front door, which commanded a fine view of the mountains. When he became more acquainted with me, he often spoke of his great sinfulness,—saying—"I'm a miracle of grace, Sir;—a miracle of grace." When I rose to leave him, he would usually fix his eyes upon me with a peculiar expression, for a moment, and then exclaim, with a decisive inclination of the head,—"Pray."

He declined very gradually; and died at last so peacefully that his wife who was holding his hand, only discovered his departure, by the cessation of his breath, which, in her blindness, her quick ear instantly detected.

Dr. Murdock of the Reformed Dutch Church was engaged in prayer at the time by his side; and at the same moment I was kneeling by one who had been his pupil, and friend, and elder, and who entered Heaven the same hour.

On the day of their Funeral, the stores of the village were closed. The church in which Dr. Porter formerly preached was crowded to excess; and many who came from a distance were unable to obtain an entrance. The esteem in which he had been held was so great, that the years of his incapacity and retirement had left him more than is possessed by most men, in the fulness of their strength.

You will see by what I have thus far written, how imperfectly I knew this revered and peculiar man.

In conversing with others,—I have frequently asked, "how did he look, and act, and speak, and what was the secret of his power?" But I cannot fully answer these questions. Those who knew him well, invariably smile, sometimes quietly laugh, when his name is mentioned, and say,—"I cannot describe him. He was the most peculiar man I ever knew. Nobody was like him in the least. You cannot put him into words. He was the oddest man you ever saw. A thousand infinitesimal peculiarities marked the expressions of his countenance, the inflexions of his voice, his gestures, and every thing about him." Then they will speak of his overflowing kindness, his generosity, his originality, his pure, ardent piety. And again, a smile will come upon their faces, and then there will follow some anecdote of his peculiarities, or his shrewdness.

He unquestionably exerted a very powerful formative influence upon the inhabitants of Catskill, and of the surrounding country. To this day his opinions are quoted as authority. His instructions are held as unquestionable truths.

His Theology was Hopkinsian. His mind was logical and clear; his opinions decided; his will indomitable. He well understood the springs of human action, and possessed a remarkable quickness and tact in touching and controlling them.

But with these traits he combined the simplicity and sincerity of a child. His heart was unusually gentle, and kind, and affectionate. And if you add to these characteristics, quiet assured reliance upon his own judgment, and the ability to exercise *the power of silence*, (which he frequently employed with no little effect,) you will have as correct an idea of his mental peculiarities as I can gather from conversations with those who knew him.

When he walked abroad, his personal appearance must have arrested the eye of every stranger. His head was like Napoleon's; his neck was short; his body large and fleshy; his legs were unusually small,—tightly encased in short clothes, and beneath these, in black silk hose. He carried a large cane; and his motions were quick, nervous and awkward.

When he stood in the pulpit and became interested in his sermon, his short, dense sentences, jerked out with a nod; his strange and violent gestures, and his stamping foot, called a smile upon the faces of all who were not accustomed to them. Even clergymen, sitting with him in the pulpit, were sometimes unable to control their countenances. But he was wholly unconscious of these effects,—he was absorbed in his subject, and soon gained entire control of his hearers.

In the lecture room, his manner was still more remarkable. He frequently spoke with his cane in hand, and brought it down with his emphatic foot, bending his whole body to give force to the gesture. He would walk to and fro, and becoming more excited as he spoke, he would sometimes descend to the floor of the room; step over a bench to arrive at an open space; walk up and down there for a while; step over another bench opposite to the former, and return to the desk on the farther side; continuing and closing his address, without exhibiting the slightest consciousness of what he was doing with his peripatetic body.

When he called upon any one to pray, he would sometimes add in a tone more of command than request,—"Be Short!" His own exercises were very brief; but they were very comprehensive and instructive. He wasted no words. His thoughts were new, fresh, and expressed in striking language. When speaking, he used periods, if I may speak so, between the clauses of his sentences, or as though he employed hyphens for commas;—and thus, though otherwise his utterance was rapid, every word that he delivered told upon the listener.

Notwithstanding his eccentricities, he was regarded with unbounded reverence No one dictated to him—no one remonstrated with him. He took counsel with himself, and, with some deference to forms, carried through that on which he had determined, without opposition. The children all regarded him as a superior being. One remembers,—and tells it with a smile at her former self,—how she thought his person and dress the standard of ministerial appearance, looking with low esteem and some suspicion upon small and thin men, who wore loose pantaloons. Another always associated him with the highest mountain in the Catskill range. Another had very confused and interchangeable ideas of Dr. Porter and the Saviour. Another, for a year or two, thought he was God. When he met them and stopped, as was his custom, and took their hands between his thumb and the tips of his fingers, and said in his kind absent-minded way, "How d'do child," it awed them, and was an event to be remembered. This reverence continued as they grew older, and began to understand his sermons, and a good degree of it remained as long as he lived. At one time, he catechised the children occasionally on Saturday afternoon. But he never got much beyond the first page, they say; and he had a pleasant habit of answering the questions himself, when there was the slightest hesitation, and saying "Very well, child, very well."

A few anecdotes chosen from the many which are told of him, may serve further to illustrate his eccentricities.

He never could be induced to converse, or to express an opinion upon any subject, when he thought silence the better course. With a dull, uninterested look he would seem unconscious of the speaker's words, and though his eye rested upon him, almost of his presence. When the questioner ceased, there would follow a dead pause. "Don't you think so, Doctor?" No answer—no consciousness. Then, waking suddenly from his apparent abstraction, he would speak of something wholly remote from the subject of the inquiry, or conveying a subtle reproof for meddling with it.

In these times of apparent reverie, he heard and weighed every word that was uttered; and not unfrequently quoted a remark against his baffled questioner, who thought at the time he uttered it, the Doctor, in his fit of abstraction, had not heard a single word.

In later years, he was singularly absent-minded. He was accustomed to pray with his eyes wide open. One evening, at a "neighbourhood meeting," his prayer was drawing to a conclusion, when he saw before him a young lady to whom he was greatly attached, and who had returned that day from a long absence. Suddenly, to the astonishment of all present, he crossed the room, and extended his hand, exclaiming with a voice of hearty pleasure—"*O! how d'do?*" He was totally unconscious of the irregularity, and no thought of it subsequently embarrassed him.

On another occasion, somewhat later in life, he was praying in the presence of several clergymen, and a large audience, at a union prayer meeting for Colleges. Always interested in the religious welfare of students, he had been excited by the statements which had just been made. He was pleading fervently for the spirit of prayer in our churches, and enforcing his petition with "arguments," when, suddenly changing from prayer to exhortation, he exclaimed to the standing assembly, bringing down hand and foot to enforce his words,—"Yes, brethren, we must *pray* more! That's what we want. More prayer! more prayer!"—and after adding a few more sentences, he turned to the clergyman who had been speaking, and said, "Go on Sir! go on."

To illustrate his "management;"—he had much of the harmless wisdom so useful to one who has to deal with men.

He never gave a direct reproof; but at times he suggested one that was not easily forgotten. A young man who had recently become a professor of religion, was standing one Sabbath with his companions near the church. The conversation became trifling, and he was laughing heartily at something which had been said, when the Doctor, who stood at a little distance with a clergyman who was to preach for him, called to the young man and beckoned him to approach. When he came near, he introduced him to the stranger, mentioning his name in full, and saying in a marked and serious manner—"*a member of the Church, Sir, a member of the Church!*" The youth, in later years, became an elder, and he told me that the influence of that rebuke had not left him for an hour since it was given.

When the Doctor was threescore years and ten, he determined to resign his charge. Its duties oppressed him. He spoke of it; but no one moved in the matter. They did not want to part with him. "It would hardly seem Sunday" to go to church and hear another man preach. At last, one Sabbath, he requested the congregation to remain after the benediction. The service being closed, he descended from the pulpit, and standing behind the Communion table with his hands upon a chair, looked round until all was expectation. His head sunk upon his chest for a moment. Then he raised his eyes, and exclaimed in a firm, earnest voice, "THREE THINGS!—I must have a colleague—I must resign—or I must die!"—and sat down.

The discussion which followed the Doctor's laconic address led to no action at that time. Subsequently it was agreed that he should put the question of his resignation to vote. He wished it, for the sake of his successor, to be decided without apparent reluctance, and without a dissenting voice. This he secured in the following manner. He contrived that the call to the Rev. T. M. Smith, and, after its acceptance, the arrangements for his installation, should be made without any reference to the fact that he was still Pastor of the Church. At the installation he was appointed to deliver the Charge to the People.

His Address, ardent and full of affection, and gratitude, and rejoicing, was calculated to draw out the hearts of his people toward himself; and near the close, after an animated reference to the revival then in progress, he suddenly paused. The house in the hush of expectation was perfectly still. Then, in an abrupt but subdued manner, he broke the silence by saying—"But,—brethren! before closing my remarks, I have one *request* to make. You may think I might have made it before. But for reasons in my own mind, I preferred to reserve it for this place. It is the last request I shall make as your Pastor. It is a request of mutual good will, for your sake not less than my own. It is not that I love you the less, but the more, that I make this request. It is but fitting that I do it. I am confident you will meet my views, which the Presbytery will ratify. The vote I ask you to pass is, *that I be dismissed, strictly so, from my pastoral charge of this Church and Congregation.* In this vote I hope there will be but one voice—I am persuaded there will not. The assembly are all seated; and I now put the question. Those of the Church and Congregation in favour of granting the request, will signify it *by keeping their seats*—they of the contrary mind will manifest it by rising." Before they had time to recover from their surprise, he added—"The Clerk will be so good as to record the vote as *unanimous!*"

After resigning the pastorate, he became the agent of several Benevolent Societies, and collected great sums for them in this village, and in the adjacent country. He approached each man in a different way. He would sometimes name a specific sum; saying, "Mr. X. it is a good cause, Sir; a good cause, but you must'nt give too much;—fifty dollars is enough, Sir." Mr. X. would probably have decided upon ten.

He was told of one man, a wealthy farmer, who had said he was "determined to give him nothing that year any way." Shortly before harvest, the Doctor made it convenient to stop at his house. He soon interested him in the operations of the Society for which he was then collecting; but nothing was said about a subscription. He remained to dinner. Before the repast was over, the man's mind was filled with the noblest missionary views. To spread the glad tidings of salvation was made to appear the great work and joy of the Christian's life. After dinner, they walked out upon the piazza. "Whose farm is *that* Sir?"—said the Doctor, extending his hand with a wide gesture towards a large tract, crowded with ripening grain. "That is mine." "Yours?—a large farm—beautiful farm!" After a pause, during which the Doctor was looking round with sincere admiration upon the scene of tilth and beauty, he exclaimed, "whose farm is that, way over by those woods, Sir?" "That is mine too." "Fine meadows—very large farm—very *valuable* farm." "Who owns the woods?" "They belong to me, Sir." "Umph!" Changing his position so as to command another view, he said, after a while, "your neighbour has a heavy crop there; very rich land; whose is that, Sir?" "Well," the man answered, growing a little restless, "my farm goes about as far as you can see, Doctor,—that's all mine." "All yours!" Then, turning upon him with a serious, almost reproachful, look, he said,—"God has done a great deal for you; what are you going to do for Him? A pause ensued which seemed to repeat the question, and demand an answer. I do not know the reply; but as a result of the interview, the Doctor carried away the farmer's subscription for a larger amount than ever. He was irresistible. Those who knew his way, when he began to draw out of them the proofs of their prosperity, often cut short his approaches by saying with a smile of surrender,—"How much shall I give, Doctor?"

The following anecdote, which I received from the lips of the person to whom it refers, is very characteristic. He had sold some valuable books to a young clergyman of another denomination, in the village. Some months had slipped by, and payment had been delayed. The Doctor was sitting on his 'stoop' one bright morning, when his debtor passed, politely saluting him. "Young man!"—cried the Doctor. He turned and came back to the gate, as the Doctor rose from his chair. "Those *books*." Then with a gesture of serious courtesy, he added,—"Pay for them when you please, Sir; pay for them when you please!" And, without waiting for an answer, turned, and went into the house. They were paid for the next day.

When speaking of personal piety, he always, to the end of his life, dwelt upon his great sinfulness. "It is an ocean without a shore," he would say. "My transgressions are like mountains piled upon mountains." "I *hope* to be saved, Sir," he once said to Dr. Dickinson,—"but I'm an awful sinner, Sir,—an awful sinner. If I am seen in Heaven, Sir, it will astonish the universe!" And this he said with such sincerity and earnestness, that, for a moment, his visitor was confused and unable to reply.

A few months before his death, an elder of his church called to see him, and, in the course of the conversation, remarked,—"Ah well, Doctor, when we go to Heaven we shall leave all these sorrows behind us." The old man sat up, and looked at him with apparent wonder—he scanned him once or twice from head to foot, and then exclaimed with an emphasis on every word,—"Do you expect to get to Heaven?" Then shaking his head, and withdrawing his gaze, he added, "It's a great thing to say, Sir;—a great thing to say."

He was greatly loved. "The *dear* old man!"—said one who had been speaking of his kindness and generosity. "He was one of the best men in the world," say many. I am often caused to regret that I did not share with my predecessors the pleasure of knowing him in his vigour and activity. I could then have replied to your request with a fuller and more accurate account of this singular, influential and venerated man.

With affectionate esteem,

G. A. HOWARD.

DRURY LACY.*

1787—1815.

Drury Lacy, the son of William and Elizabeth (Rice) Lacy, was born in Chesterfield County, Va., October 5, 1758. His father was a planter in comfortable circumstances, but was distinguished more for his hospitality than his carefulness in either the management of his estate or the education of his children. The son was about ten years old when the father died; and for a year or two previous to this event, he had attended the school of the Rev. Mr. McCrea, an Episcopal clergyman in the County of Powhatan. From the age of ten to sixteen, he lived with his mother, who was left, at the death of her husband, in very straitened circumstances, and found it extremely difficult to provide for her small family. When he was about fourteen or fifteen years old, (one authority says *ten*,) he met with a sad casualty, which, however, had a very propitious bearing upon his subsequent life. At a County muster of the militia, a man in the ranks had loaded a gun so deeply that he feared it would burst, if it were discharged; and in a most cowardly spirit, asked some one of the boys standing by to discharge it, without intimating that there was any danger. Young Lacy stepped forward, took the gun and fired it—the barrel burst, and his left

* MSS. from Rev. B. T. Lacy, and Rev. Dr. Archibald Alexander. Foote's Sketches of Va., 1st Series.

hand was frightfully mangled, and torn off. In after life, his wrist was protected by a silver cup which was fitted over it, and into the end of which a fork and other instruments prepared for the purpose were screwed; and thus the loss of the hand was, in some degree, supplied. From this circumstance, when, in after life, he became an instructer of youth, in connection with Hampden Sidney College, he received the nick-name of "Old Silver Fist;" and it also gave him the designation among his ministerial brethren, of "Lacy with the silver hand and the silver voice."

His mother, who was an eminently pious woman, died when he was about sixteen years old; and, being now cast upon his own resources, he engaged, with that slender stock of information which might have been expected from his hitherto very limited advantages, in teaching a school. It was, however, a school of the humblest class, and the compensation was barely sufficient to procure for him the plainest clothing. At the age of about eighteen, when he would have served in the war of the Revolution but for the loss of his hand, he procured another and more eligible situation as a teacher, in Cumberland County, in the family of Daniel Allen, an elder in the Presbyterian Church, which was at that time supplied by the Rev. John Blair Smith, President of Hampden Sidney College. Here he became acquainted with Mr. Smith, attended his ministry, and ere long joined the church of which he had the charge. While engaged in this school, he acquired, by his own efforts, a very good knowledge of Geography, English Grammar, Algebra, Geometry, and Surveying. He subsequently taught in the family of Colonel John Nash, of Prince Edward County, where he enjoyed the instruction of President Smith, one or two hours each week. With this slight assistance, he acquired such a knowledge of the Latin and Greek languages, that, at the age of about twenty-three, the office of Tutor in Hampden Sidney College was offered him. He accepted it, but still pursued his own studies privately. From the time that he commenced his religious life, he had cherished the purpose of devoting himself to the ministry; and, in due time, in connection with his other duties, he began his theological studies under President Smith, and prosecuted them until he was ready to receive license to preach. He was received under the care of the Hanover Presbytery with a view to being licensed, in April, 1787, and was actually licensed in September following, when he was not far from twenty-nine years of age. He was ordained by the same Presbytery that licensed him, in October, 1788.

In July, 1788, Mr. Smith informed the Trustees of the College that he found the united duties of President and Pastor quite too laborious, and asked to be excused from the former. The Board acceded to his request, but desired him still to continue his relation to the College, and appointed Mr. Lacy Vice President, devolving upon him a large part of the labour and responsibility which had previously fallen to the lot of Mr. Smith. The next year, Mr. Smith resigned the Presidency altogether, and then the whole supervision of the institution came upon Mr. Lacy. There was a concurrence of circumstances to render his situation one of great difficulty, as well as of great responsibility. He, however, continued his connection with the College till the year 1796, when he tendered his resignation, and retired to a farm which he had purchased in the immediate neighbourhood, and to which he gave the name of Mount Ararat.

On the 25th of December, 1789, Mr. Lacy was married to Anne, daughter of William Smith, of Montrose, Powhatan County,—a lady eminently fitted, by her fine intellectual and moral qualities, to minister to both his happiness and usefulness. They had six children,—three sons and three daughters. Two of the sons are Presbyterian clergymen, the third a physician.

After Mr. Smith left Virginia, Mr. Lacy succeeded him, not only as acting President of the College, but as one of the ministers of the churches with which he had been connected; though he seems never to have been regularly installed in the pastoral office. After he removed to his farm, he opened a small classical school, which he continued during the rest of his life. Among his pupils were many who have since become eminent men.

Mr. Lacy was often a delegate from the Hanover Presbytery to the General Assembly of the Presbyterian Church, and in the year 1809, was Moderator of that Body. He also served as Clerk of the Presbytery, during a large part of his ministerial life. His handwriting was not only beautiful but exquisitely so; insomuch that the volume of Presbyterial Minutes which he has left, is valued not merely as a Record but as a curiosity.

In the year 1815, Mr. Lacy was afflicted with a serious complaint, (the calculus,) which led him to make a journey to Philadelphia, to avail himself of the skill of some of the distinguished surgeons of that city. He accepted an invitation to stop at the house of his intimate friend, Robert Ralston; and there he finished his earthly course. The surgical operation was performed with entire success; but, after a few days, his strength began perceptibly to fail, and he quickly sunk into the arms of death. His wife, whom he left at home in her usual health, was seized with a violent fever, and died within a few days after his departure; but, though the tidings of her death had reached Philadelphia previous to his own death, it was thought unsafe that they should be communicated to him, and he was left to learn the fact first by meeting her beyond the vail. He addressed a letter to her in the immediate prospect of the operation he was to undergo, expressing a doubt whether they should ever meet again on earth, but the letter did not reach its destination, until the eye for which it was designed was closed in death. Mr. Lacy died in the exercise of the most serene trust in the mercy of God through Jesus Christ, on the 6th of December, 1815. His remains repose in the burying ground belonging to the Second Presbyterian Church in Philadelphia.

Mr. Lacy published a Sermon on the death of the Rev. Henry Patillo of North Carolina, 1801; and also a pamphlet of considerable size, containing an account of the great revival in Kentucky, and the strange appearances connected with it.

The following notice of Mr. Lacy's character as a preacher, has been kindly furnished me by his eldest son, the Rev. William S. Lacy, of Arkansas:—

"He left but few manuscript sermons, and those not entirely finished, and far inferior to his ordinary pulpit performances, having been written in the earlier years of his ministry. During the last fifteen years of his life, the period of his greatest ministerial success, he rarely, if ever, wrote his sermons, and but seldom prepared even short notes for the pulpit. His preparation was almost exclusively mental and spiritual. He thought intensely upon his subject, and arranged the matter carefully in his mind, and then trusted to the occasion to suggest the appropriate language. I have often, when a youth, been greatly impressed with the deep abstraction and awful solemnity depicted in his countenance, while engaged in meditation, as he was walking in his chamber or in the yard. And when, from these scenes of meditation and prayer, he went into the pulpit, there was frequently in his preaching a solemnity and pathos, a freshness and vigour, a penetrating, burning, melting eloquence, which I have never known surpassed. At the same time, candour compels me to say that not unfrequently there was a dryness, hardness, and confusion, in his preaching, with an utterance, hurried and painfully loud, which brought him, for the time, as far below the average of respectable preachers, as he usually rose above it. He was at times subject to deep mental depression; and then he was frequently unable to make any preparation for the pulpit; and the consequence was that his preaching was attended with pain and grief almost insupportable to himself, and with disappointment to his hearers. But, for the most part, he enjoyed the light of his Father's countenance in a remarkable degree. His style was formed very much upon the model of the sacred writers, and his discourses were enriched with large and pertinent quotations from the Word of God. In reading a chapter from the Bible in the presence of his congregation, his eye seldom glanced at the page, but was fixed on the congregation, as if he were speaking extemporaneously. The same was true of him, while reading or rather reciting the psalm or hymn. His utterance was rendered doubly effective by the expression of his beaming and flexible countenance, and the power of his flashing and melting eye."

FROM MRS. DR. JOHN H. RICE.

NEAR HAMPDEN SIDNEY COLLEGE,
PRINCE EDWARD COUNTY, June 7, 1849.

Dear Sir: I knew Mr. Lacy well from my very early years. He was a near neighbour of my father, and he often walked to our house for exercise, and to enjoy a conversation with my good mother, and I may say, a play with the children. By taking part in our little sports, he made us all love him, and by the good instruction which he took care to communicate, he made us respect and revere him. He contrived so to secure our confidence that we did not hesitate to impart to him any secret; and he would advise us in so gentle a way, that we were scarcely sensible that he was advising us at all. His grand aim evidently was to bring us to the Saviour. Often would he tell me how he longed to see my face glowing with an expression of love to God, and how dangerous it is to enter a world like this without being a true Christian. And after I became thoughtful on the subject of religion, nothing could exceed the interest which he manifested that my serious impressions might not pass away.

His person was very large and imposing, and his countenance, when lighted up, was most expressive and delightful. I can in no way bring him more plainly before me, than by thinking of him as he was listening with delight to Dr. Alexander's eloquence, and casting his deep blue eye over the congregation, with the tears streaming down his cheeks, to notice the effect which it produced. His own preaching was simple and natural, and sometimes very eloquent. His prayers, especially in his latter years, were peculiarly fervent; and he seemed, like Abraham, the friend of God, most reverently and devoutly speaking, as if face to face, to his Heavenly Father. He was uncommonly successful as a preacher to the coloured people; and his addresses to them at the Lord's table were most simple and impressive, and often highly pathetic. In his private intercourse he was cheerful and sociable, but never lost sight of what was due from him, and due to him, as a Christian minister. A good old lady remarked that he exceeded any one she ever saw at a Sacrament, and at a Wedding. When inquired of if he thought it was sinful to dance, he would say,—"Be warmly engaged in religion, and then you may dance as much as you please." My recollections of him, both in the pulpit and out of it, are most grateful and affectionate.

To supply in some measure the deficiency of my own account of Mr. Lacy, I take the liberty to add the following graphic account of him from the pen of his intimate friend, Dr. Alexander:—

"About the time that Mr. Lacy entered the ministry, commenced that remarkable revival of religion, which extended more or less through every part of Virginia, where Presbyterian Congregations existed. And although Dr. J. B. Smith was the principal instrument of that work, yet the labours of Mr. Lacy were, in no small degree, successful. His preaching was calculated to produce deep and solemn impressions. His voice was one of extraordinary power. Its sound has been heard at more than a mile's distance. His voice was not only loud, but clear and distinct: in the largest assemblies convened in the woods, he could always be heard with ease at the extremity of the congregation. On this account, Mr. Lacy was always one of the prominent preachers at *great meetings*. His preaching also was with animation. His address to his hearers, whether saints or sinners, was warm and affectionate. Indeed, according to his method of preaching, lively feeling in the speaker was an essential thing to render it either agreeable or impressive. Mr. Lacy was therefore a much more eloquent and impressive preacher on special occasions, when every circumstance combined to wind up the mind to a high tone of excitement, than in his common and every day discourses,—in which he was always evangelical, but sometimes flat and uninteresting. Upon the whole, it may serve to characterize his preaching, to say that it was better suited to the multitude, than to the select few who possess great refinement of taste; better adapted to satisfy and feed the plain and sincere Christian, than to furnish a feast for men of highly cultivated intellect. He enjoyed the unspeakable pleasure of knowing a considerable number of humble, exemplary Christians, who ascribed their first impressions to his preaching or conversation; for he excelled in the art of conversing on the subject of experimental religion. To inquirers and young converts he addressed himself in private in a very happy manner; which was to them often the means of important spiritual benefits. And on general subjects he conversed in an agreeable and instructive manner."

With great regard, sincerely yours,

ANNE S. RICE.

EBENEZER FITCH, D. D.*

1787—1833.

Ebenezer Fitch was a descendant, in the fourth generation, from the Rev. James Fitch, who came to this country in his youth, and was minister, successively, at Saybrook and Norwich, Conn. He was the second child of Jabez and Lydia (Huntington) Fitch, and was born in Norwich, September 26, 1756. His early years were passed in Canterbury, where he was fitted for College by the Rev. James Cogswell, who had married his father's sister. He entered Yale College in 1773, and was graduated in 1777. In the spring of his Senior year, College was temporarily broken up, in consequence of the turmoil and peril growing out of the Revolutionary war: the several classes were accompanied by their respective Tutors to different towns in Connecticut, that they might still continue to prosecute their studies; and that to which young Fitch belonged, passed the summer in Wethersfield under the instruction of Mr. (afterwards President) Dwight. This class, at the usual time for Commencement, returned to New Haven, met the government of College, and, without much formality, received their diplomas. During the whole of his college life, he was distinguished for good deportment, and for diligence and success in the various branches of study.

After receiving the honours of College, he spent about two years at New Haven, as a resident graduate. While on a visit to Canterbury, during this period, he was enrolled and drafted as a soldier to join the army. He resisted the requisition, on the ground that, as a resident graduate, he was still a member of College, and therefore exempt from military duty; and, though it was claimed that he could not *then* be considered a member of College, President Stiles, to whom the question was referred, returned an answer in his favour. On leaving New Haven, he spent nearly a year in teaching a select school in Hanover, N. J. In a letter dated January 4, 1780, he writes thus: "I am about five miles East of Morristown, and eight from the enemy. Week before last, I visited the camp, and had the pleasure of seeing many *old* and some *dear* friends. I found the Log House City on the declivity of a high hill, three miles south of Morristown. There the Connecticut line dwells in tabernacles, like Israel of old. And there the troops of the other States lie, some at a greater and some at a less distance, among the hills, in similar habitations."

In the autumn of 1780, Mr. Fitch was appointed a Tutor in Yale College. He accepted the office, and continued in it till 1783, when he formed a mercantile connection with Henry Daggett of New Haven. In consequence of this arrangement, he went to England the following winter, and made an extensive purchase of goods; but it proved a disastrous speculation, and subjected him to pecuniary embarrassment, from which he did not recover for many years. In 1786, he was again elected to the Tutorship, and continued to hold the office, in connection with that of Librarian, till 1791.

It would seem, from a journal kept by him in his earlier years, that he was the subject of serious impressions from his childhood, and that he him-

* Memoir by Rev. Calvin Durfee.—Pres. Stiles' and Rev. Dr. James Cogswell's MS. diaries.

self believed that he became the subject of a renewing influence, previous to his admission to College. He, however, delayed making a public profession of religion until May, 1787, during the second period of his Tutorship, when, as appears from the unpublished diary of President Stiles, he joined the College Church. He must, however, have previously been engaged in preparation for the ministry, for, before the close of the same month, he was licensed to preach the Gospel by the Association of New Haven West, at Oxford.

In October, 1790, Mr. Fitch was elected Preceptor of the Academy in Williamstown, Mass.,—a new institution which, it was understood, was destined ultimately to become a College. After considerable hesitation, he accepted the office, and entered upon its duties in October, 1791. The school consisted of two parts,—a grammar school, and an English free school; and, under the direction of Mr. Fitch, it soon became extensively and deservedly popular. In June, 1793, it was incorporated by the General Court of Massachusetts, as a College. In August of the same year, Mr. Fitch was elected President; and in October following, Williams College was regularly organized by the admission of three small classes.

In May, 1792, he was married to Mrs. Mary Cogswell, the widow of his cousin and classmate, Samuel Cogswell, who had been accidentally shot dead, while on a gunning party, in Lansingburg, N. Y. She was a highly intelligent and excellent lady, and well adorned the station to which this marriage introduced her. They had eleven children, ten of whom were sons. The oldest, a youth of great promise, died just after he had been admitted a member of College, and on the night preceding the Commencement of 1807. "The President," says the Rev. Dr. Robbins who was present on the occasion, "though deeply afflicted, appeared remarkably well. He performed the official duties of Commencement with great correctness and propriety. The Funeral of his son was attended the next day; and most of the students remained to sympathize with their deeply afflicted President and his family. When the corpse was deposited in the grave, the bereaved father, in a calm and collected tone, remarked,—'I do not deposit in this grave silver or gold, but my first-born, the beginning of my strength.'"

The first Commencement of Williams College was held on the first Wednesday of September, 1795. On the 17th of June previous, President Fitch was ordained to the work of the ministry, with special reference to his connection with the College, by the Berkshire Association,—the Sermon on the occasion being preached by the Rev. Ephraim Judson, of Sheffield.

In 1800, President Fitch received the honorary degree of Doctor of Divinity from Harvard College.

Dr. Fitch devoted himself to the welfare of the College with great fidelity, and no inconsiderable success,—as an evidence of which, at one period of his Presidency, there were enrolled upon the annual catalogue about one hundred and forty students; and the average of the twenty-one classes, which were graduated under him, was about twenty-two. During this period, an unusually healthful moral influence, for the most part, pervaded the College, and, in several instances, religion became, with a large portion of the students, a matter of paramount concern. It was here especially, that Mills, and Hall, and the Richardses, and others, received that plentiful baptism of the missionary spirit, which marked an epoch in the history of the American Church. But the time at length came, when Dr. Fitch thought that the interests of the College, as well as his own personal comfort, would be promoted by his resigning his office; and, accordingly, he did resign it in May, 1815. In consideration of the acknowledged inadequate compensation, which, for several years, they had been able to render for his services, the Trustees, on his vacating the office, voted him the sum of twenty-two hundred dollars; an act alike honourable to their sense of justice, and grateful to his own feelings.

In the succeeding autumn, Dr. Fitch was installed Pastor of the Presbyterian Church in West Bloomfield, N. Y.; and, though he had now nearly reached the age of sixty, and was beginning to feel the infirmities incident to advanced life, he addressed himself to the duties of a Pastor with great interest, punctuality, and zeal. And his labours were crowned with many tokens of the Divine favour. In his Farewell Sermon, preached November 25, 1827, he stated that there had been two seasons especially, when the Spirit had descended upon the congregation like rain, and that, during the whole period of his ministry there, there had been added to the church a hundred and ninety persons,—a hundred and forty-five of whom had been received on a profession of their faith.

After he resigned his charge, he continued to preach occasionally till almost the close of his life. In the summer of 1828, when he was in his seventy-second year, he, in company with his wife, made his last visit to New England,—to the scene of his childhood and youth, as well as manhood; and this visit was ever afterwards a subject of some of his most grateful recollections. Until within a few months of his death, his health, considering his advanced age, was quite comfortable; and he continued to move about with some degree of freedom, and to enjoy the society of his friends. He was subject, however, to occasional attacks of asthma, from which he experienced no inconsiderable suffering. His mind seemed uniformly in a peaceful state, and was evidently occupied chiefly on those invisible realities in which he expected soon to mingle. He died March 21, 1833, in the seventy-seventh year of his age. His Funeral Sermon was preached by the Rev. Julius Steele.* His widow died at Cleveland, O., in the family of one of her daughters, November 21, 1834.

Dr. Fitch published a Baccalaureate Discourse in 1799.

FROM THE REV. CHESTER DEWEY, D. D.

ROCHESTER, April 18, 1852.

Dear Sir: I became acquainted with Dr. Fitch on my admission to the Freshman Class in Williams College, in 1802. The acquaintance was of course very slight, (as it was my purpose, by good conduct, to escape any *particular* attentions from the Faculty, and especially from the President,) till I commenced the Senior year. Dr. Fitch was the sole instructer of the Senior class. When, afterwards, in the Tutorship, I lived in his family, and as Professor in the College I was associated with him, and in the habit of daily intercourse, till he resigned his office and left the College, in 1815.

Dr. Fitch was a man of fine personal appearance, of rather courtly manners and dignified carriage, of the most cordial and benevolent feelings, of the purest

* JULIUS STEELE was graduated at Yale College in 1811; was ordained and installed Pastor of the Church in East Bloomfield, N. Y., March 13, 1816; was dismissed on the 21st of January, 1829, and died in 1849.

morals and the most exemplary religious character. He was a Christian gentleman of the Puritanic form of New England.

His powers of mind were not the strongest or the most brilliant, but they were solid, investigating, and highly respectable. Graduated at Yale College, and for many years a prominent Tutor there, he was well versed in the languages, in philosophy, and in the general literature of that period. And his acquaintance with distinguished persons, on both sides of the Atlantic, added much to his influence, and gave interest to his intercourse with young men. He came to the Presidency of the College under decidedly favourable auspices.

As an instructer, he had, at that time, a high reputation. Well acquainted with the branches which he taught, and possessing a fund of racy anecdote, he was able to give much point and interest to the recitations.

Though he possessed an excellent temper, and was singularly devoted to the improvement of his pupils, he was not altogether equable in his management of young men, and perhaps was not always directed by the most discriminating knowledge of human nature, especially as it exists in collegians. There sometimes occurred a sudden exhibition of the terror of authority, which finally disappeared in the language used, or was modified by after consideration. In the management of the College, this was undoubtedly a serious evil.

There were a variety of reasons, external and internal, which I need not attempt to state—which led Dr. Fitch ultimately to resign his office as President. The Trustees, in accepting his resignation, rendered a cordial testimony to the purity of his intentions, and to the fidelity and zeal with which he had laboured to sustain the College, and advance its prosperity.

Dr. Fitch was eminently a good man. I never came into collision with him, though I may not always have approved his course or his reasonings. I cherished a hearty and affectionate regard for him while he lived, and his memory abides deep and dear in my heart.

With high regard,
Your obedient servant,
C. DEWEY.

FROM THE HON. DANIEL D. BARNARD,

MINISTER FROM THE UNITED STATES TO PRUSSIA.

ALBANY, April 9, 1850.

My dear Sir: I am afraid my recollections of Dr. Fitch are hardly of a character to be of much use to you, though, since you request it, I will give them to you with sincere pleasure.

When I entered Williams College, Dr. Fitch was no longer President of that institution. He was still, however, a resident of Williamstown, and I was a frequent visitor at his house. In subsequent years, and in another part of the country, he was a familiar visitor in my father's family, where I occasionally met him. I knew him well enough to have received a strong impression of his manners and character—an impression which I still vividly retain.

Dr. Fitch was a well-bred gentleman of the old school—not of the most formal class, yet with formality enough to give a certain air of dignity to his manners and conversation. In person, as I now recollect him, he was perhaps rather below than above the middle stature, but he was very erect, and his carriage quite commanding. His step was firm, and he moved like a man who had a fixed purpose in life, and had the resolution to pursue it. His motions were not quick, but composed and steady—they were prompt and ready, but there was nothing disturbed or hurried about them. He had something of the air of a man of business, but of one whose business was of a settled and stable character, perfectly comprehended and fully appreciated in regard to its high importance, and the length and breadth of its great duties. It was the air of one who had studied his position and his powers, and who was reasonably conscious of a certain degree of strength and capability. But whatever there was of apparent confidence in himself, was far enough removed from every thing like arrogance and presumption. I suppose there have been few men who have cherished a more habitual or abiding sense of dependance on a Higher Power. If there was any one thing which marked his demeanour more strongly than another, it was humility. He was eminently a meek man. But he was not of an abject spirit—he did not, because conscious of infirmities, think it necessary to set about degrading himself in his own estimation. Being single minded, and fully purposed to use his powers, his position and his calling, as became a scholar, a gentleman, a Christian, and a minister of the Gospel, he very justly respected himself, and as justly felt himself entitled to the respect and confidence of others. Something of all this was easily read in his deportment and manner.

Dr. Fitch bore commonly a grave countenance, as if the business of life, and life itself, were serious matters; yet his aspect was habitually hopeful and cheerful; not unfrequently it was glad and joyous. His face wore a peculiarly benevolent and kind expression, and though this was deepened into sadness on particular occasions, yet it was never clouded with gloom. Neither his temper nor his religion was one of gloom.

His conversation was usually sedate and earnest, but it was often seasoned with anecdote and pleasantry. He had an agreeable voice, the tones of which, in serious discourse, were solemn and impressive. He spoke with fluency, though not with rapid utterance; and his language was remarkable for its correctness, simplicity, and elegance. I should say he was a correct and good scholar, without being a profound one. His range of study and acquirement had been quite large. His learning was for every day use, and he threw enough of it into his conversation to make him both an agreeable and instructive companion.

He was, I believe, commonly regarded as a sensible and correct thinker, of considerable intellectual vigour, but he was not looked upon as a man of genius or of much originality. He had a well balanced mind, and his faculties had been so cultivated as to *preserve* the balance of his powers, and thus fit him for eminent service in the practical duties of the elevated sphere of life to which Providence had assigned him. I am sure that the quality which he cultivated more assiduously than any other, was goodness. His aim was to be pure in heart, and to lead a life void of offence towards God and towards men. His religious faith was probably held with as little doubt or wavering, as that of any enlightened Christian that ever lived. A thorough theologian, and master of all points of difficulty and difference among sects, as well as between Christianity and Infidelity,—still his own faith was held with all the simplicity of a little child. It was a hearty, trusting faith, which seemed incapable of being disturbed, and over which no shade of doubt seemed ever to pass. He believed, and he seemed to have no unbelief. And his faith was of that sort that it appeared to be a natural and necessary thing that he should be constantly growing in goodness, and in the daily beauty of a godly life. It is seldom, I think, especially in a person of such mark, that the genuine simplicity and humility of the Christian character is so well illustrated as in his case.

I do not know that I can add any thing to these very imperfect recollections and impressions; and it is more than I dare hope, that what I have thus briefly sketched, will be found of any considerable value or interest.

I am, my dear Sir, with great respect and regard,

Very sincerely yours,

D. D. BARNARD.

JAMES MUIR, D. D.*

1788—1820.

James Muir was a son of the Rev. Dr. George and Tibbie (Wardlaw) Muir, and was born on the 12th of April, 1757, in Cumnock, Scotland,—the place in which his father exercised his ministry. Both his father and his grandfather were highly respectable ministers of the Church of Scotland. Concerning his early years little can now be gathered; but from the manner in which the children of the Scottish clergy in those days were generally educated, it is fair to presume that there was no lack of parental care and vigilance in regard to his early intellectual or moral training.

Early in life, (the precise period is not known,) and under the preaching of his excellent father, his mind became deeply impressed with the importance of eternal things; and to use his own language a few days before his death, he "found no peace till he had fled for refuge to the ark of the everlasting covenant." His thoughts, which had previously been directed to the profession of the Law, were now fixed upon the Christian ministry.

After the usual course of classical and philosophical studies in the University of Glasgow, at which he graduated in March, 1776, he prosecuted the study of Theology at Edinburgh, but subsequently went to London, and is supposed to have completed his theological studies under the direction of his cousin, the Rev. Dr. Henry Hunter,† author of the "Sacred Biography." Here he was licensed to preach the Gospel on the 12th of May, 1779, by six clergymen, of whom Dr. Hunter was one, who style themselves "Dissenting Ministers in the City of London and neighbourhood, and conforming to the doctrine and practice of the Church of Scotland."

After his licensure, he was for some time engaged in teaching a school in London, and preaching as an assistant to Dr. Hunter. On the 10th of August, 1781, the same Presbytery that had licensed him, ordained him as an evangelist at the Scots Church in London, with reference to his acceptance of a call from a company chiefly of Scotch Presbyterians, in the Island of Bermuda, whither he was going for the benefit of his health.

He resided at Bermuda, as the Principal of an Academy, and as the acting Pastor of a Church, for nearly eight years. During this period, he was married (February 29, 1783) to Elizabeth Wellman, who was a native of the Island, and connected with one of its most respectable families. While on a transient visit to his friend and his father's friend, the Rev. Dr. Witherspoon, then President of Princeton College, he connected himself with the Presbytery of New Brunswick, sometime between the meetings of Synod in 1785 and 1786.

He had made his arrangements to return from Bermuda to his native country, and had actually embarked for the purpose; but the vessel in which he had taken passage was driven back in distress, and he was induced to change his direction for the United States. After his arrival in New York in 1788, he preached, for several months, about the same time with the

* MSS. from his daughters and Rev. Dr. Harrison.

† There is a tradition in the family that he preached for some time in Lady Glenorchie's chapel; but whether this was the chapel which she established in Edinburgh, or another chapel in London, has not been ascertained.

Rev. Jedediah Morse, (afterwards Dr. Morse of Charlestown, Mass.,) as a candidate in the Collegiate Church of which the late Dr. Rodgers was then Pastor. But as division was likely to ensue in consequence of the peculiar attachment of a portion of the congregation to each of the candidates, they both, from a regard to the harmony of the church, withdrew; and Mr. Muir, in the spring of 1789, accepted a call to the Presbyterian Church in Alexandria, where he continued during the residue of his ministry and of his life.

In 1791, the degree of Doctor of Divinity was conferred upon him, at the suggestion of Dr. Witherspoon, by the Corporation of Yale College.

About three years before his death, his health being considerably impaired, he made a visit of a few days to the Island of Bermuda, and, being there on the Sabbath, accepted an invitation to preach in the church where he had formerly ministered. He preached from the text,—"Our fathers, where are they?"—a discourse which excited an unusual interest, and was commented upon in a very laudatory manner by the public papers of the Island. On his return, he remarked to a friend that it was wonderful how he could ever have been contented to remain on such a little patch of earth for seven years, when it seemed to him that there was scarcely room sufficient for ordinary exercise, without coming in contact with the ocean.

In March, 1818, the Rev. (now Dr.) Elias Harrison, after having served as an assistant to Dr. Muir for more than a year, was installed as co-pastor. The Doctor's health, after his return from Bermuda, was generally good until the spring of the year 1820. The last sermon he preached was on the last Sabbath of May in that year, while his colleague was at the General Assembly in Philadelphia. About that time, the disease of which he died, which proved to be an ossification of the muscles of the stomach, began to develop itself. His physician, Dr. Dangerfield, supposing that the country air might be of service to him, had him removed to his own dwelling on the Maryland side of the Potomac, and, for more than six weeks, ministered to him with unceasing care, and all the appliances which medical skill could suggest, but without any favourable effect. As it was manifest that his life was wasting away, he was conveyed back, in a state of great feebleness, to the spacious dwelling of Jonathan Swift, one of his congregation, situated in the suburbs of the town, and there, after lingering some two or three weeks, with many of his beloved flock daily about him, he died in perfect peace on the 8th of August, 1820. Two days after, he was buried in the church, just beneath the pulpit he had occupied for more than thirty-one years. By his own request, he was dressed in his gown and bands, and his grave was thirteen feet deep.

Mrs. Muir survived her husband about ten years. They had had seven children; but, at the time of his death, only four were living,—one son and three daughters. The son, *Samuel*, was, for some years, a post surgeon in the United States army, stationed on the South-western frontier. He had, however, resigned his commission, and, having married a daughter of one of the Chiefs of the Sacs or Fox tribe of Indians, was, for several years, regarded as one of the greatest men of the nation. About three years before his death, he had settled in an extensive medical practice at Galena, Ill.; and, during, the Black Hawk war, when the cholera broke out in our army under General Scott, with such terrible violence, he boldly went out, a volunteer, to endeavour to stay its ravages. But, after saving the lives of many in the army, he was attacked by the disease himself, and in twenty-four hours was numbered among its victims. He was educated at Edinburgh, was a highly accomplished man, and a skilful physician.

Dr. Muir is the author of several books, all of which are highly creditable to his talents and piety. In 1795, he published a small volume entitled "An Examination of the principles contained in the Age of Reason: In Ten Discourses." In 1812, he published another volume, containing Ten Sermons, several of which were preached on special occasions, and each one having an Appendix, illustrative at once of the subject of the sermon, and of the character of the author. He published yet another, containing seven Sermons, which he preached while he was Pastor at Bermuda—also a Sermon at the ordination of the Rev. T. B. Balch, and it is believed some other Occasional Sermons, not even the titles of which can now be recovered.

In the autumn of 1815, immediately after my graduation at Yale College, I went to reside as a private tutor in the neighbourhood of Alexandria, and had the privilege of an early introduction to Dr. Muir and his family, and of frequent intercourse with them, during a period of about eight months—indeed I first made a public profession of religion in his church, and commenced the study of Theology under his direction. He was a short, thick-set man, rather heavy in his movements, of a grave but most kindly expression of countenance, and as gentle and guileless as any human being I ever met. There was an air of loveliness and simplicity about him that led me at first,—young and inexperienced as I was,—to underrate somewhat his talents and acquirements; but, as I became acquainted with him, I found myself in contact with an exceedingly well balanced, well disciplined, and well furnished mind. His appearance in the pulpit was certainly far from being graceful. He always wore the gown; but that served rather to make the disproportion between his breadth and his height the more noticeable,—though, to my eye at least, it gave additional solemnity and impressiveness to his manner. I can see him at this moment standing in that venerable old pulpit, holding up his little black Bible before him with both hands, and reading sometimes nearly half a chapter at a time by way of illustrating his subject, and in an accent so intensely Scotch that it seemed to my unpractised ear not only strange but ludicrous. But his sermons were always full of vigorous and condensed thought, and in point of style were very much of the Addisonian school. Though he had high ideas of Christian consistency and clerical propriety, he was always cheerful, and never averse to telling or hearing a humorous anecdote. His kindness towards me was scarcely less than paternal; and when I parted with him in June, 1816, to return to the North, he gave me letters to several of his friends in the cities through which I was to pass, that procured for me some of the most valued acquaintances of my life. I corresponded with him till near the time of his death, and I cannot imagine a more perfect representation of his mind and heart than his letters furnished.

FROM THE REV. ELIAS HARRISON, D. D.

ALEXANDRIA, January 10, 1849.

Rev. and dear Sir: You ask for my impressions of the character of our venerable friend, and my former colleague in the ministry, the Rev. Dr. Muir. I can truly say that my recollections of him are such as it gives me sincere pleasure to record; and I am glad to co-operate with you in an effort to honour and perpetuate his name and memory.

There was a peculiarity in Dr. Muir's preaching, in respect to both matter and manner, which it is not easy, by any single phrase or term, to characterize. A member of the United States Senate, after having listened to one of his sermons, remarked that he was "a short man, of short sermons, of short sentences." This was strictly true. His discourses rarely exceeded thirty-five minutes in length, and the sentences of which they were composed were unusually short, as may be seen in the published sermons which he has left behind him. He always spoke with a small Bible open and lying on the large one before him on the desk; and when he had occasion to refer to any part of it, (and his quotations were very frequent and long,) it was his uniform practice to take it up and read, even when his people generally believed, and some of them knew, that there was not the least occasion for it;—for few men probably ever committed more of the Bible to memory than he did. He carried it with him, both in the original and the translation, wherever he went, and rarely, if ever, failed to analyze, with critical accuracy, at least two chapters, each day. Indeed such was his familiarity with the Scriptures in the original languages, that he could quote the Hebrew and the Greek, almost as readily as he could the English. He always preached without notes. Until the last three years of his life, he wrote his discourses with great care, and with equal care committed them to memory. But he never could preach, as he has himself assured me, unless he had his manuscript in his pocket; and, on one occasion, having found, after he had commenced the service, that he had neglected to bring it with him, he was under the necessity of going back to his study to get it. Yet he could speak with as much ease and correctness without as with writing; and few, if any, could ever tell by his manner of delivery whether he was speaking memoriter or extempore. Owing to a pretty strong Scotch accent, and a slight defect in his utterance, he could not be called a popular preacher; and yet his sermons were rich in Divine truth, and were characterized by condensed thought, logical arrangement, and great simplicity and perspicuity of style.

Dr. Muir was a severe student. He could not tolerate the idea of addressing immortal souls on the most momentous of all concerns, without having prepared himself for it by careful study as well as earnest prayer; and few things would put down a ministering brother in his estimation more than to be told that his discourses were either almost or altogether unpremeditated. I rarely ever saw him more out of temper than he was with a young licentiate, who, burning with what he regarded as holy zeal, remarked that it seemed to him a waste of time to study and write sermons. The Doctor could not be called an active man, though he was always regular in visiting his people, and ministering to the sick and afflicted; and when he made an engagement either to preach or perform any other duty, it was never his own fault if it was not fulfilled.

But for nothing was he more distinguished than an exemplary Christian life. I lived in his family, and was in close intimacy with him, for more than three years; and, during the whole of that time, was never able to detect a word, an action, or even a feeling, which I would dare to pronounce decidedly wrong. And yet, during that period, his church was rent with factions, many of his congregation inflamed with bitterness and wrath, and in the issue, about half of the number separated and constituted a new church. Against all these untoward influences, he struggled hard and prayed much; and the result was that he sustained himself throughout with the utmost Christian forbearance and good will. He was often called, in reference to his large share of gentleness and meekness, in connection with his smallness of stature,—"the little Moses."

Dr. Muir enjoyed, in a high degree, the good opinion and affectionate regards of his brethren in the ministry, and great weight was given to his counsels in the judicatories of the Church. The whole community in which he lived, reverenced him for the purity of his life, and the memory of his exalted virtues is still dear to many, though he has long since passed away.

I will close this communication by referring to his death scene, which, for sublimity and impressiveness, has rarely, if ever, had a parallel, within my observation. A few hours before his departure, he called his whole family around him,—his wife and three daughters, (his son was absent,) and laying his hand on the head of each, and in order, according to age, beginning with his wife, he gave to each a most solemn and affecting word of exhortation, corresponding, it seemed to me, to each one's particular disposition; and then, like the Patriarch of old, commending them to his own covenant-keeping God, gave them his parting blessing, amid the tears and sobs of many of his beloved flock. After a few moments' rest, he called me also, and laying his hand upon my head, and invoking the blessing of the great Head of the Church upon my person and ministry, gave me one of the kindest, most affecting, and most impressive charges, to which I ever listened. He had always manifested towards me a strong affection, and the last energies of his life were given to this closing effort. It will never be forgotten; for though I cannot recall the precise language,—the spirit, the look, the impression, are scarcely less vivid at this hour, than they were the hour after the solemn spectacle had passed before me.

Ever fraternally yours,

ELIAS HARRISON.

FROM THE REV. JAMES LAURIE, D. D.

WASHINGTON, May 1, 1850.

My dear Sir: Your request for my recollections of our excellent and lamented friend, Dr. Muir, I have been prevented from complying with till now, partly by domestic affliction, partly by ill health, and partly by other causes which it is not necessary to mention. But I assure you that no part of the reason has been that I have been indifferent to the subject of your request,—for I can truly say that I have been associated with few men in the course of my life, whose memory I cherish with more reverence and affection than that of Dr. Muir. I became acquainted with him first, forty-seven years ago, on my arrival in this country from Scotland,—a number of years after his settlement in Alexandria; and, as I became almost immediately after a permanent resident of this city, distant from Alexandria but a few miles, my opportunities of intercourse with him were frequent during the remainder of his life. Our intimacy was probably greater from the fact that we were natives of the same country, and had, on that account, many common interests and associations.

Dr. Muir was one of those men in respect to whose characters there is likely to be very little difference of opinion. He was constituted with such perfect simplicity and ingenuousness of temper, that it would have been impossible for him, by any effort, to practise the least dissimulation. Every one who was brought in contact with him, felt that he was exactly what he appeared to be; his statements were all taken without any abatement on the score of designed exaggeration; though his unsuspecting disposition might sometimes perhaps have rendered him liable to the charge of credulity. It is not unlikely that Mrs. Hunter, the wife of the celebrated Dr. Henry Hunter of London, a relative of his, had this trait of his character in view, when she told him, as he was coming to this country, not to believe a word that he heard, and not more than half of what he saw. I do not mean to impute to him any extraordinary weakness in this particular, and yet it must be acknowledged that, in what commonly passes for worldly shrewdness and sagacity, he was not much distinguished. He was so conscious of the purity of his own motives, was so entirely "an Israelite indeed in whom there was no guile," that he would never impute evil motives when charity could possibly find out those of a different character. So uniformly gentle and benignant was his spirit, that I remember but a single instance in which he was betrayed into what would be considered as savouring in any degree of severity, and that was a remark addressed immediately to an individual, who, he had reason to believe, had, under the guise of friendship, acted a disingenuous and treacherous part towards him.

Dr. Muir retained too much of the Scottish accent to have any great popularity in this country as a preacher; and yet his sermons were always rich in evangelical truth, and written in a chaste, easy, perspicuous style. There was one peculiarity in his mode of preparing his discourses, which deserves to be mentioned. He used, at the commencement, to scatter all along over his paper key words, or words which were to begin paragraphs; and so thoroughly had he studied his subject, that he had never any difficulty in filling up his paper, making these several words subserve his original design.

In his theological and ecclesiastical predilections he was thoroughly a Presbyterian, both from education and conviction, and yet he was as far as possible from an intolerant spirit, and mingled freely and cordially with Christians of different communions. So amiable and generous a spirit as he possessed, sanctified withal by deep and consistent piety, could not but render him an object of attraction in every circle. In his family, he was a model of all the domestic virtues; among the people of his charge, he was the warm hearted and devoted Pastor; and in society at large, he was not only a well wisher to, but a diligent promoter of, all the great interests of human life. When I say that he had no enemies, I have stated only half the truth; no one could be brought in contact with him, especially in the sense of enjoying familiar intercourse, without regarding him with respect and veneration; and the deep and general lamentation which was witnessed at his death, was a sufficient testimony that the whole community in which he lived regarded him as among the excellent of the earth.

He had long been familiar with death before he was called to encounter it. It was a subject on which his thoughts were greatly prone to dwell, and though, in his latter years, the grave yard was a mile or more from his dwelling, he was accustomed frequently to resort thither, and yield himself to devout "meditations among the tombs." When his own turn to die came, his spirit was so disciplined to meet the event, that he could rejoice in the prospect of his departure, knowing in whom he had believed; but the physical agony attending the approach of death was well nigh overwhelming. A day or two previous to his departure, he sent for me to come and see him; but so extreme was his weakness, and so severe his bodily sufferings, that I found him incapable of holding much conversation. I remember he exclaimed—"Is this death?"—and then added, with reference to the torturing pains which he was enduring—"it is terrible;" but there was nothing to indicate that his spirit was not reposing with perfect confidence in the merits and promises of his Redeemer. Those who stood by his bedside, when the pulsations of life finally ceased, could not feel a doubt that Heaven was, at that moment, opening to receive a glorified spirit.

In calling up these reminiscences of my friend long since departed, I am glad if I have contributed to your object, as I am sure it has led me into a field in which it has been most grateful to me to linger. If my recollections are less extensive than you had expected, you will perhaps find a satisfactory reason for it in the fact that they are the recollections of a man whom age has brought near to the borders of the grave.

Yours truly and affectionately,

JAMES LAURIE.

JOSEPH PATTERSON.*

1788—1832.

JOSEPH PATTERSON, a son of Robert and Jane Patterson, was born in the North of Ireland, March 20, 1752. His father, though a lad at the time, was at the famous seige of Derry; and the sufferings to which the family were subjected in consequence of it have not often had a parallel. This branch of the Patterson family emigrated from Scotland to Ireland, in consequence of the terrible persecutions that were carried on by Claverhouse under Charles II.; and the father of Joseph Patterson was the son of John, in whom the family commenced in Ireland.

The parents of the subject of this sketch originally belonged to the Scottish Church, but joined the Secession under the Erskines, sometime before the middle of the eighteenth century. They were eminently pious persons, but were exceedingly strict in their religious views, and had little sympathy even with any other branch of the Presbyterian Church than their own. They came to this country with several of their younger children in 1774, and settled near Milestown, about seven miles North of Philadelphia, where Mr. Patterson died, aged a little more than seventy, about 1778. His wife survived him not far from three years.

Of Joseph Patterson's earliest years little is known beyond the fact that, when he was a mere child, he became deeply concerned in respect to his salvation, and joined with some other children in a private prayer meeting which was held under a thorn hedge. On the 27th of February, 1772, he was married to Jane Moak, he being less than twenty years of age, and she, less than eighteen. His elder brother had already migrated to this country; and not long after his marriage he formed the purpose of following him; in the expectation also that, at no distant period, he should be joined by other members of the family. Accordingly, he and his wife arrived at Philadelphia early in 1773; and, after stopping for a short time in Pennsylvania, they settled in Saratoga County, N. Y. In consequence, however, of the arrival of his parents the next year, he was induced to return to Pennsylvania, and was occupied for a year or two in teaching a school near Germantown. When the Revolutionary war commenced, he showed himself a vigorous patriot; he listened with enthusiasm to the first public reading of the Declaration of Independence, and immediately gave up his school and enlisted as a common soldier. But, though he entered the army, he did not leave his religion behind,—as is evident from the following incident. As he was engaged in his devotions one day in a rough shed, where the troops were quartered, the rifle of a neighbouring soldier was accidentally discharged, and shivered a board just in the line of his person. As he was remarkable for noticing providences, this must have left a strong impression upon his mind.

He retired from the army in 1777, and removed Westward to the County of York; and, having remained there two years, proceeded still farther West,—to the County of Washington. The region in which he now settled was a wilderness; and though he, in connection with a few other pious per-

* Record of the Patterson Family.

sons who accompanied him, built a rude church in the woods, yet they were in constant jeopardy from the surrounding Indians, even while they were engaged in worshipping in it.

In the autumn of 1785, the Presbytery of Redstone advised Mr. Patterson to direct his attention to the ministry, and to qualify himself for it without unnecessary delay. Agreeably to this advice, he engaged, with several others, in a course of preparatory study under the direction of the Rev. Joseph Smith; but, as Mr. Smith did not live in his immediate neighbourhood, he was obliged, in order to avail himself of his instruction, to become temporarily an exile from his own family.

Mr. Patterson continued his preparatory studies about three years. He was licensed to preach the Gospel in August, 1788; and in April following accepted a call to the charge of the united churches of Raccoon and Montour's Run, in Washington County,—the former being eighteen miles from Pittsburg. He served both these churches for ten or twelve years, when, each having become able to sustain a minister, he resigned the care of the latter.

Like other ministers of that day, he made frequent missionary tours, during which his labours were most abundant. In the year 1802, he spent several months among the Shawnee Indians, and kept a journal during the time, that is replete with interesting and surprising incidents, and strikingly illustrates the deep spirituality and glowing zeal of the missionary.

Mr. Patterson, on the 4th of February, 1808, was called to a great domestic affliction in the death of his wife. She seems to have been an eminently devout and godly person; and the death that she died was worthy to close the life that she had lived. In giving an account of her death in a letter to a friend, four years after it occurred, he writes as follows:—"On the Sabbath following, I preached on Job xiv. 14. Views of the glory she was advanced to, and hopes of being soon in it, dulled the edge of sorrow, so that I scarcely felt its sharp cutting. I think it was near two years before my affliction on account of my bereavement came to its height."

On the 9th of May, 1812, Mr. Patterson was married to Rebecca Leech of Abington, Pa., who was a person every way suited to render him happy. She survived him.

In the autumn of 1816, Mr. Patterson being in his sixty-fifth year, and withal considerably oppressed with bodily infirmities, resigned the charge which he had held for more than twenty-seven years. He now removed his residence to the city of Pittsburg, where he continued during the remainder of his life. But, though he had no stated charge, his zeal and activity in promoting the cause of Christ were unabated. He occupied himself as a sort of city missionary, distributing Bibles and tracts, ministering to the wants of the afflicted and destitute, and especially rendering counsel and aid to the poor emigrants, who were found thronging to the Western country from every part of the world.

In May, 1829, just after his recovery from a somewhat protracted illness, a false step on the pavement gave a wrench to one of his ancles, which occasioned him another season of confinement to his chamber of at least two months. On the 30th of January, 1832, at the close of a series of religious meetings in the church where he was accustomed to worship, he gave a solemn exhortation, which proved to be his last public act. Four days later, he took the final sitting for his portrait; and after the work was done, he turned to the artist, who was of infidel sentiments, and urged him with great solemnity to "apply to the Holy Spirit to draw the Divine image upon his heart." On the evening of the same day, he requested his wife to read the 103d Psalm; and when she had done so, he remarked,—"I have been trying all my life to come up to the tone and spirit of that Psalm; and at length I believe I can." He then knelt down and offered a fervent prayer; but was so weak, at the close, that he could not resume his seat without assistance. On the 4th of February, about one o'clock in the morning, he awoke unwell, and he very soon became sensible that the time of his departure had nearly come. Having requested that the physician should be called, and also his son, who occupied a dwelling adjoining his own, he said,—"The time is come; Lord, help," and closing his eyes, expired without a struggle.

Mr. Patterson had eight children,—all by his first marriage, and all born in America. *Robert*, his eldest son, born April 1, 1773, is an ordained minister of the Presbyterian Church, and was formerly Pastor of a Church about seven miles from Pittsburg.

FROM THE REV. GEORGE POTTS, D. D.

NEW YORK, May 29, 1852.

My dear Brother: I am sorry that, in attempting to comply with your request, I cannot give you the results of an intimate personal acquaintance with my venerated relative, Mr. Joseph Patterson. As I passed through the city of Pittsburg, on my way to and from the South, I saw and conversed with him in the latter years of his life, and this intercourse, brief and transient as it was, confirmed the previous high impressions of his excellencies, derived from those who knew him best. I will try to indicate to you, in a few words, the traits by which he was best known.

I think all his friends would agree, in selecting *childlike simplicity* as the most characteristic of his traits. It marked his natural and spiritual endowments. He was a transparent man, and a transparent Christian. Any one, thrown into his society, even for a short time, would quickly have discovered this. He was affable and social in a high degree, and had a quiet, simple, but forcible, way of uttering himself, which made you feel that you were in company with an Israelite in whom was no guile. This simplicity and directness of character gave to his manners an unartificial appearance, which might not altogether please those who count stiffness and reserve essential to dignity. But a just observer would see that this peculiar tone of character did not degenerate into weakness. He had the sagacious insight as well as the simplicity we often see in children, and which, when joined, as it was in his case, with the experience of age, entitles its possessor to the name of a *wise* man. He made no pretension to great learning and eloquence, in the ordinary meaning of the words, but he had what was better,—a thorough knowledge of the human heart, and a thorough knowledge of, and confidence in, the Christian methods of influencing it. He was a very *practical* man. Exact and punctual in his engagements of every kind, taking a common sense but well-considered view of all that he undertook, he said and did in a direct way what the occasion required. He knew well how to become all things to all men, without compromitting truth or duty: equally acceptable to the wise and experienced, and to little children with whom he was a great favourite. But his eminent usefulness to the various characters with whom he sought intercourse, was, in a large degree, owing to the fact that his childlike simplicity at once enlisted their confidence. He had striking things to say, and he said them often in a striking way, but you saw that there was no artifice about them,—no studied impromptus were they, but the spontaneous impulses of an active, pious, benevolent soul.

His *benevolence* was also a marked trait. Naturally, like many other men of strong sympathies, he was, as he often informed his friends, irritable and hasty. But those who knew him late in life, would never have suspected it. His social disposition, his great accessibility, his large fund of anecdote, his capacity to enjoy in moderation the humorous as well as the grave side of things, all betokened the strength of the sympathies which drew him to his fellow-creatures. No man was fonder of a quiet, genial laugh. With a truly Irish affinity for the ludicrous, he sometimes assumed a solemn jocoseness and gentle sarcasm of manner, which was highly entertaining. He used to condemn this disposition of his, unjustly, under the name of *levity*. But it ought not to be so arraigned, unless it become predominant, which was not the case in this instance. It has often been a marked trait in the character of men of eminent piety and benevolence. That you may know what I mean, I will give a specimen of his humorous sarcasm, mentioned to me by a friend. After hearing a young preacher, who evidently thought more of himself than his subject, and whose discourse was wanting in evangelical unction, my friend asked Mr. Patterson what he thought of the sermon. "Well," said he, with his quiet smile, "there were a good many good things which were not in that sermon." Even in these moods, the habitual spirituality of his mind was always apparent. He was no trifler: he said and did nothing "to court a grin;" but, living as he did under a profound, practical sense of Divine realities, and in an extraordinary degree upon the very borders of Heaven, he did not forget that he was in the flesh and among men. He was, on every account, strongly drawn to them: a true Christian socialist, he lived not for himself, but cheerfully and hopefully wrought in any of the departments of social benevolence. He was bent on doing good, not so much in the way of large and magnificent schemes, as in the laborious, minute, and often obscure, details of every day work. Thus, as a Pastor, he was one of the most indefatigable; and, after leaving his charge to reside among his children in Pittsburg, his last years were employed among the crowds of that large city in detailed labours,—the effects of which, like the effects of the silent dew, cannot be estimated by any arithmetic of ours. Pittsburg was and is a great thoroughfare for emigrants, and among them he did a vast deal of work, in ministering to their temporal and spiritual necessities, in a day when the name—*Colporteur* was as yet unknown. For this, as well as other works of mercy, his praise is in all the Churches of Pittsburg.

While prosecuting his work in this department, he showed himself eminently a fearless man. His firm trust in God and a good conscience prompted him to do many things from which other good men sometimes shrink. I will mention only one example. In one of his collecting rounds, an acquaintance met him, saying, "Well, Father Patterson, what errand are you on to-day?" "I am just going to the man who keeps store over there, to get a dollar for my Bible distribution." "Why, certainly you will not go to such a man as that—an open infidel and scoffer; you will not get a cent from him." "Yes I will, I'll get a dollar—come along and see." They walked into the store. The old gentleman made his request, in his usual bland way, and was met with scorn. "I won't give a cent for such a purpose." "Do you say you won't?" "I say I won't." "Well, I will go home with my subscription book, and lay it before the Lord, and I will tell Him that Mr. —— absolutely refused to give any thing towards the distribution of the Bible." There was a solemn reality in the good old gentleman's manner, which seemed to scare the man,—infidel as he was. Opening the money-drawer, he said, "Here, take your dollar."

Mr. Patterson was, in his religious views, a thorough-going, old-fashioned Calvinist. His piety was deep and earnest, blending the experimental and practical in due proportion. In all his abundant activity and success, he was a thoroughly humble man. His conversation and manner were of a piece with this single record which he made, when relinquishing his pastorate, after many years of the most exemplary fidelity—"I resigned my charge on account of bodily infirmity, after being Pastor of Raccoon twenty-seven years and six months, *for every day of which I need pardon through the blood of Christ.*" He was also a thoroughly trustful man. His natural simplicity of character showed itself in his habits of prayer and communion with our Lord. He conversed with Him as a man with his friend, carrying every thing that interested him, in the shape of joy or sorrow, to the Throne of Grace. He was a strong believer in such texts as the following—"Casting all your care upon Him, for He careth for you"—"Whatsoever ye shall ask the Father in my name, believing, ye shall receive."

Mr. Patterson entertained the opinion that the strong language in which Holy Scripture speaks of believing prayer, justifies us in expecting special answers to special prayers. And his own experience abounds with examples of such answers,—some very extraordinary indeed. I must content myself with giving you one or two in the language of another.

"Some time after his removal to the West, he and some others made a purchase of land, and paid the money. It was soon discovered that the seller was not the owner. How much Mr. Patterson's share in the investment was, is not known; but it was a greater loss than he could well bear. The other purchasers had recourse to law, and advised him to 'employ counsel.' 'No,' he replied quaintly—'I have read in the Bible of a Wonderful Counsellor, and I will apply to Him.' The man who had defrauded him, had absconded, but, not long after, as Mr. Patterson was passing his house, a child, running up to him, begged him to come in. When he did so, the wife, handing to him the identical bag with the identical dollars, said, 'My husband, when he went away, charged me to give you back this money, for, said he, I'm afraid the man will pray me to death.'"

Another instance is equally remarkable and suggestive. Mr. Patterson taught a school. The neighbourhood was poor and the people few and scattered. One morning he was about to proceed to the school-room, which was at some distance from his lodgings, when he discovered that his pen-knife was gone. He supposed he must have dropped it the evening before, as he was returning from school. He could not replace it, as the nearest store was many miles off, and perhaps even there, a pen-knife was not to be had. To make the matter worse, snow had fallen during the night, and covered the path. What could he do? Writing and arithmetic were the chief branches then taught. He was naturally troubled at his loss, and as he walked along made his trouble a subject of believing prayer. At length his mind was relieved, and he felt satisfied that in some way the "Lord would provide." As he proceeded, he saw a man riding towards him, and leading a horse by the bridle. When they got near him, the led horse suddenly started off the road on to the foot-path. When Mr. Patterson came up to the place where the horse had kicked off the snow from the foot-path, there lay the lost pen-knife. Mr. P. said to the narrator of this incident, that he never had had a more delightful sense of God's goodness and faithfulness, as a prayer-hearing God, than on this occasion.

But I must not extend this imperfect description of my venerable relative. He was, in fine, "a good man, and full of the Holy Ghost and of faith, and much people were added to the Lord." He entered and dwelt in the Kingdom of God, as a little child,—always full of the main thing,—always acting as seeing Him who is invisible. I think I see his fine benevolent face, with its bland smile, as he talked of heavenly things, and assured me of his prayers that I and my new companion might be prospered in the spiritual life. It was thus, in his most casual intercourse—he had always something heavenly to say. "I am afraid," said he, one day, with his benevolent smile, to one of his busy merchant friends, hurrying past him in the street,—"I am afraid you could hardly find time to-day—to die," and passed ou—a fine example of what is meant by being instant out of season.

I will only add that he took a deep interest in education, and especially in the rising ministry. The Theological Institution at Alleghany enlisted his prayers and efforts in a high degree. It was only a short time before his death, he said to a friend, "I have found a new prayer for the students. God, before whom my fathers,—Abraham and Isaac, did walk; the God which fed me all my life long unto this day; the Angel which redeemed me from all evil; *bless the lads.*" Gen. xlviii. 15, 16.

I need not say that Mr. Patterson was a *gentleman* in manners—with the characteristics I have mentioned, he could not have been otherwise. In stature, he was of the middle height, with an athletic frame. His voice was low and plaintive, his eye mild but clear, his nose aquiline, and his hair dark. His profile was marked.

You will not wonder that I esteem it a great honour to be related to such a man

Ever, my dear friend, yours truly,

GEORGE POTTS.

FROM THE REV. WILLIAM NEILL, D. D.

PHILADELPHIA, September 16, 1856.

My dear Sir: I spent my early years in the part of the country in which Joseph Patterson exercised his ministry. He had commenced preaching some time before I entered the Academy at Cannonsburg, and my principal knowledge of him was from the visits which he occasionally made there and in the neighbouring places, at Sacramental and other seasons, and from my being once or twice a guest in his family. The occasion which I have more particularly in mind was one of great interest to me. In those days the celebration of the Lord's Supper was reckoned much more than it is now as a grand religious festival. It usually brought together a large representation from several congregations in the neighbourhood; and it was looked forward to, and waited for, by pious people, as a season of refreshing from the presence of the Lord. The preaching was often marked by unusual power, and attended with a copious blessing; and it was a common thing for those who made a profession of religion, to date the origin of their serious impressions to one of these interesting seasons. It was on such an occasion that I, in company with several of my fellow-students, went to Mr. Patterson's, in a place called Raccoon, distant about twelve miles from the Academy. On reaching his house, we found that a large number of persons from different places had preceded us, and we began to apprehend that his accommodations in the way of lodging were already exhausted: I therefore ventured to propose to him that we should seek lodgings elsewhere; but, instead of assenting to my suggestion, he immediately stepped upon the piazza, and with a loud voice said,—"Not a soul will go away from this house to-night;" and, accordingly, there were probably between twenty and thirty who found lodging that night under his roof. The circumstance was illustrative alike of his hospitality and his decision.

Mr. Patterson was a man of a more than commonly grave and solemn aspect, and showed by all his conversation and deportment that he lived habitually under the influence of the powers of the world to come. He was naturally of a social turn, but his conversation was almost always, if not directly religious, at least tending towards a serious character; and he had a large fund of anecdote illustrative of Christian duty and experience, which he was accustomed often to draw upon to great advantage. I never knew a man whose heart seemed more intently fixed upon doing good. Wherever or in whatever circumstances he was placed, it was evident that he was always about his Master's business. It was difficult for him to meet a person, even in the most casual way, and to hold conversation with him on any subject, without dropping at least a word in relation to his higher interests. Nobody, I imagine, that knew him, ever doubted the strength of his faith, or the purity and consistency of his entire character.

Mr. Patterson commanded great attention as an earnest and powerful preacher. In the warm season, he more commonly preached in a tent,—the church edifice being much too small for the accommodation of the multitude who attended on his ministry. He regarded so little his personal appearance, that he used often to preach without his coat; but this was much less at variance with the tastes and habits that prevailed at that day in that part of the country, than those which exist at the present time. His preaching was always simple and plain, but it was always sensible and edifying, and rich in evangelical truth. His voice was loud and commanding, and he sometimes spake, especially in rebuking the popular vices of the times, as one having authority. He was, however, a son of consolation to Christians, and, indeed, he knew how to give to every one his portion in due season. The results of his preaching were manifestly great, and I doubt not that he is rejoicing in them in a better world.

Yours, forever, in the bonds of the Gospel,

WILLIAM NEILL.

ROBERT HENDERSON, D. D.

1788—1834.

FROM THE REV. R. B. McMULLEN, D. D.

KNOXVILLE, Tenn., March 31, 1857.

Rev. and dear Sir: The history of Dr. Henderson's life, considering the prominent place he held among the ministers of his day, as well as his comparatively recent death, is veiled in no inconsiderable degree of obscurity. After diligent and somewhat extended inquiry in respect to him, the following is the best account that I am able to give you of the leading events of his life, and the more striking traits of his character.

ROBERT HENDERSON was born in Washington County, near Abingdon, Va., on the 31st of May, 1764. Being left an orphan at an early age, and also in destitute circumstances, he received very little education until after the time of his conversion. The following is his own statement:—

"When a boy quite down in my teens, my attention was arrested and fixed to Divine things, in a very unusual and extraordinary way. After having been the subject of an almost indescribable distress for upwards of a year, I at length found peace through the great goodness and mercy of God, and became the subject of a delightful hope. Being filled with an ardent desire to preach the precious Gospel of Jesus, I was much distressed because the way seemed hedged up before me, as I deemed it impossible to obtain such a classical education as I believed to be essential to such an office. In this state of affairs, I tried to banish the thought from my mind for about six months; but finding all efforts of that kind unavailing, I at length gained the permission of my mother,—a poor widow, to make the trial. I undertook the expense of obtaining a classical education without a dollar in hand or in prospect."

He commenced his classical studies under the tuition of the Rev. Samuel Doak, D. D., who, a little while before, had opened an Academy in Washington County, East Tennessee, then known as Martin Academy, and now as Washington College. Here he pursued and completed his course of study preparatory to entering the ministry; and, in recording the fact, he adds,—"it was not upon charity either." He was licensed and ordained by the Abingdon Presbytery in or about the year 1788, and took charge of the two Churches of Westminster and Hopewell,—the latter of which was at Dandridge,—the present County seat of Jefferson County, Tenn. He was associated, in the First Presbytery formed in this part of the country, with Blackburn, Carrick, and Ramsey. He continued to minister to the churches just named for more than twenty years; and was then released from them to accept a call from the Churches of Pisgah and Murfrees Spring, in Rutherford County, West of the Cumberland Mountains. Ten years previous to this translation, he had requested a dissolution of the pastoral relation, on the ground that he was left sometimes in actual want from the neglect of his people to supply him with the necessaries of life. The facts in the case having been laid before the Presbytery, that Body charged him with "excessive modesty and unnecessary delicacy in not letting his wants be known;" and charged the churches with "shameful want of public spirit in *neglecting* to inquire into his necessities." The churches promised to do better, and the Presbytery unanimously advised him to withdraw his petition. He did so, and remained with them more than ten years longer. When he finally left them, their own statement concerning him was as follows;—"We part with our beloved pastor with regret, whose labours we have enjoyed for more than twenty years, and with whom we have lived in bonds of strictest love and union during that period, without the smallest interruption."

After remaining a short time with the Churches of Pisgah and Murfrees Spring, he left them, and preached a while at Nashville and Franklin, in adjoining Counties, and then returned and spent eight years more with them. He then left them again, and took up his abode at Franklin, where he taught a school, preaching there and in the surrounding country. Through his whole life, he seems to have suffered much from pecuniary embarrassment, and more especially toward its close.

During several of his last years, Dr. Henderson was gradually declining in health,—being alternately of a full habit, and then greatly emaciated. His death, which took place in July, 1834, was noticed by the Presbytery to which he belonged at their next meeting, in a manner that indicated a very high estimate of his talents and character.

Dr. Henderson was twice married—first, to a daughter of the Rev. Hezekiah Balch; and afterwards to a daughter of Major John Hackett, an elder in the Grassy Valley Church. Each of these wives he considered a paragon of excellence; and it is said that he sometimes even made an allusion to one or the other of them in his sermons, when he wished to present the highest idea of female loveliness. He had a large family of children.

He published two volumes of Practical Sermons in 1823, which contain many impressive and stirring thoughts, and bear the impress of a mind of superior mould.

Dr. Henderson was a man of great powers of address. Sometimes he was overwhelmingly solemn; at other times, witty and humorous; and then again, most severe and scathing. His appeals were bold and passionate, and at times awfully grand. He possessed a well nigh matchless power of mimicry, and could accomplish more by voice, countenance, attitude, and gesture, than almost any other man. He was accustomed to lash the vices of the times, as with a whip of scorpions; and yet he often spoiled his most solemn and pungent appeals by some flash of wit, that would bring a smile, if not a broad laugh, over his congregation. He was himself fully aware of this unfortunate propensity, and mourned over it; but it stuck to him as a part of his nature. In the prime of life, he had great reputation, not only as a pungent but a profound preacher; but his eccentricities, particularly that to which I have just referred, no doubt interfered not a little with his usefulness as a Christian minister. His passion for detailing humorous anecdotes seemed to gain strength with advancing years; and perhaps it is due to truth to say that, with the more pious portion of his hearers at least, his later labours were not his most acceptable. For many months before his death, however,—owing to his bodily infirmities, he preached but seldom.

Dr. Henderson was a most earnest and vigorous supporter of Gospel order,—especially as connected with the worship of God. He was, for instance, an uncompromising opponent of Camp-meetings. In a letter written to his very particular friend, Colonel F. A. Ramsey, in 1804, he says,—"I was with Mr. Blackburn at Little River last Saturday, Sabbath, and Monday. If the quantum of religion is to be estimated by noise, and the number of those people who pray very loud in the same circle at the same time, the people there have certainly more religion than all the other people of this country put together. They go incalculably beyond what I think right in these respects."

No man was more fearless than Dr. Henderson in the discharge of what he believed to be his duty. What Conscience dictated to him must be done,—no matter what obstacles might be in the way. He was invited to deliver a sermon in Nashville on Profane Swearing. This he appointed to do in the Court House,—no house of worship having been erected there at that time. Upon rising in the Judges' place, he saw sitting directly before him two men who were among the most notorious swearers in Tennessee; both of whom had rendered him substantial pecuniary aid in time of need. He afterwards said that worldly policy immediately suggested that he should postpone that subject till another time, lest he should offend those who had so kindly ministered to his necessities; but that Conscience sprang up and said,—"Robert Henderson, do your duty." He obeyed Conscience; and it is said that his delineations, and lashings, and denunciations, of profane swearers, were absolutely terrific. The subject was exactly suited to his descriptive and pantomimic powers, and he did it the most ample and fearful justice. He sat down feeling that he had satisfied his conscience, but not doubting that he had permanently alienated his friends. The next day they sent for him, and he went with the full expectation of receiving a torrent of abuse; but to his great surprise they met him with the utmost kindness, thanked him for his faithful reproofs, and presented him with a fine suit of clothes as an expression of their respect and gratitude. He received the degree of Doctor of Divinity from Greenville College in 1818.

Regretting that I have not more ample means of complying with your request, I remain your friend and brother,

R. B. McMULLEN.

FROM THE REV. ISAAC ANDERSON, D. D.

MARYVILLE, East Tennessee, January 8, 1849.

Dear Sir: I knew the Rev. Robert Henderson, D. D., concerning whom you inquire, but am apprehensive that my reminiscences of him are not sufficiently extensive to answer the purpose for which you ask them.

Dr. Henderson was gifted with pulpit talents of a high order. He explained the doctrines of the Gospel with great clearness, and enforced its duties with great power. He was an earnest and animated speaker, and his appeals to the hearts and consciences of his hearers were often of the most pungent character. His sermons were frequently two hours, and sometimes three hours, in length; but notwithstanding this, his congregation heard with attention and without weariness. He often introduced into his most solemn discourses such strange comparisons and illustrations, that those accustomed to hear him would involuntarily smile, and sometimes well nigh burst into a laugh. I have seen thousands hanging on his lips, with their eyes fixed intensely upon him, and the tears flowing profusely down their cheeks, and yet a smile playing on almost every face. He administered to vice the most scathing rebukes, which sometimes produced solemn awe, and sometimes bitter resentment. On one occasion, when his audience consisted, as was supposed, of more than two thousand persons assembled in a grove, he saw several rude men laughing and talking at some distance from him, and without a pause the following lines burst from his lips like a clap of thunder—

"Laugh ye profane, and swell and burst,
"With bold impiety,
"Yet shall you live forever cursed,
"And seek in vain to die;"

and then went on as if nothing had taken place. His oddities as a speaker seemed to have the same effect in keeping his hearers from weariness, that a recess commonly has under other speakers. As he often found it necessary to go into the grove, from the house being too small to contain the people who had assembled, he would state to them explicitly what sort of behaviour he considered as becoming a worshipping assembly, and would speak particularly of the great impropriety of wearing their hats; and then would conclude with some such remark as the following—"If, after what I have said, you will not take off your hats, you may nail them on for what I care." But notwithstanding he abounded in such oddities, he was still eminently useful, and is remembered by the aged Christians of East Tennessee with the most affectionate respect.

Yours truly,

ISAAC ANDERSON.

FROM J. G. M. RAMSEY, M. D.

MECKLENBURG, near Knoxville, Tenn., March 26, 1857.

My dear Sir: The "Annals of the American Pulpit" would certainly be incomplete without some notice of the Rev. Dr. Robert Henderson. He was one of the pioneer heralds of the cross,—an apostle of religion and learning, on the frontiers of both East and West Tennessee; in the early settlement of both which he acted a prominent and very useful part. I have a most distinct recollection of him. He was the bosom friend of my father,—the late Colonel F. A. Ramsey, and a very frequent guest at his house. He was the favourite preacher of both my parents, and it was the dying request of my sainted mother that her Funeral Sermon should be preached by him, and from a text of her own selection—(Hebrews vi. 18, 19, 20.) This was done, accordingly, at Lebanon Church in 1805, and with another Sermon preached in her bed-room a short time before her death, was published in pamphlet form, and extensively circulated in the Tennessee Churches. Up to 1811,—during all my boyhood, I had frequent opportunities of seeing him and hearing him preach.

Dr. Henderson was not a very learned, nor should I say in the highest sense, a very eloquent, preacher; and yet he was exceedingly methodical, instructive, and I may add, impressive. He adopted the old mode of sermonizing, and divided and subdivided his subject almost *ad infinitum*. He preached extempore, and without even short notes. He was very fluent, self-possessed, and always prepared. The architecture of his pulpit performances was very complete,—even classical—the *lucidus ordo* was perhaps the most prominent trait; but, in the application and improvement of his subject, he was often exhortatory and pathetic, sometimes caustic and denunciatory. In respect to these latter qualities he has had few equals. I have seen at the immense gatherings of earlier times, thousands of his hearers subdued and overwhelmed by his melting pathos. On such occasions, his indescribable earnestness, his emphatic tones, his bold and significant and striking gesticulation, were perfectly irresistible. His preaching was always sure to attract a crowd, and his longest sermons were listened to, not only without the slightest sign of impatience, but generally with the most fixed attention. His prayers were singularly impressive. His utterances were in a subdued, sometimes scarcely an audible, tone; and his whole manner took on an air of reverential solemnity and awe that I have rarely witnessed in any other man. He must have been a strangely constituted person indeed, whatever his character may have been, who could have listened to one of Dr. Henderson's prayers, especially in certain states of feeling, without being moved by it.

In his intercourse with the world, he had a good deal of the old-fashioned ministerial dignity and reserve; but in his own family he was most affectionate; and in the social circle was kind and communicative, and sometimes highly entertaining. On the frontier he had to contend against vice in high places; and there he displayed a spirit that was truly heroic. Against duelling and horse-racing, two of the popular evils of the day, he lifted up his voice like a trumpet; and that too, even when General Jackson was among his hearers. On one occasion, that distinguished citizen, an admirer not more of courage than of Christian consistency, sent him a valuable present, as a token of his grateful respect, for having sternly rebuked these vices in his presence.

Though many years have passed since Dr. Henderson's death, and many more since my opportunities of observing him terminated, he was a man to leave strong impressions, and hence I have great confidence in presenting him to you as he is retained in my memory.

Very respectfully, your obedient servant,

J. G. M. RAMSEY.

ASA HILLYER, D. D*

1788—1840.

Asa Hillyer was born in Sheffield, Mass., April 6, 1763. His father, who was a physician, was a native of Granby, Conn., but had removed to Sheffield to enter upon the practice of medicine, where he was married to a daughter of Deacon Ebenezer Smith. He returned with his family to his native place, when this son was about ten years of age, and there, with the exception of a residence of perhaps two years on Long Island, he remained till his death. In the Revolutionary war, he served in the American army as a Surgeon, and, during part of the time, was attended by his son, who was then probably about sixteen or eighteen years of age.

The subject of this sketch entered Yale College in 1782 and graduated in 1786, at the age of twenty-three. It was at this time that his father resided at Bridgehampton, L. I.; and as the son was returning home from College, the vessel in which he sailed was driven ashore on a stormy night, near the East end of the Island. There happened to be a mother with several small children on board, to whose preservation he devoted himself; and, as the morning dawned, he placed them in a boat, and, plunging into the water, pushed the boat ashore. This event had an important influence on his future character and course of life. Until that time he had been a stranger to the hopes of the Gospel; but he then consecrated himself, upon that solitary beach where his life had been jeoparded and mercifully preserved, to the service of his God and Redeemer. The resolutions which he then formed he was subsequently enabled to carry out; and, in due time, he commenced his theological studies under the direction of the venerable Dr. Buell of East Hampton, and completed them under Dr. Livingston of the Reformed Dutch Church in the city of New York.

Having been licensed to preach by the Old Presbytery of Suffolk, L. I., in 1788, he was appointed to supply the Churches at Connecticut Farms and Bottle Hill, (now Madison,) two Sabbaths each. The Congregation in the latter place, on hearing him preach, invited him with great unanimity to become their Pastor; and he was accordingly ordained and installed over them September 29, 1789.

In the summer of 1791, he was married to Jane, the only child of Captain Riker of Newtown, L. I.,—with whom he lived most happily for thirty-seven years. She died in 1828. They had seven children,—four sons and three daughters.

In the year 1798, while minister at Bottle Hill, he was appointed by the General Assembly a missionary to visit the Northern part of Pennsylvania, and the Western part of New York. On this tour he was engaged for nine weeks, and travelled upwards of nine hundred miles,—preaching almost every day, and sometimes twice a day, during the whole time. He preached the first Sermon *ever* preached in what is now the city of Auburn.

In the summer of 1801, he was invited to take the pastoral charge of the Church in Orange; and, having accepted the invitation, he was installed on

* Fun. Serm. in MS. by Rev. J. Gallagher.—MS. from Rev. Joseph M. Ogden.—Do. from Dr. Pierson.—Tuttle's Hist. Presb. Ch., Madison, N. J.

the 16th of December following. In this congregation,—one of the largest and most influential in the State, he laboured with great acceptance and success for upwards of thirty years. On several occasions after his removal to Orange, he visited, in company with a brother minister, the destitute settlements in the interior of the State, where his labours were always highly appreciated. He resigned his pastoral charge in 1833 ; and, from that time till his death, devoted himself to visiting, attending religious meetings in the week, and preaching on the Sabbath, as occasion or opportunity occurred, to the three Presbyterian Congregations of the town.

While sustaining the responsibilities, and performing the duties, of an extensive pastoral charge, he did not shrink from responsibilities and duties of a more public nature. He assisted in the formation of the United Foreign Missionary Society, (since merged in the American Board,) of which he was a Director. He assisted also in the formation of most of the great National Societies for extending the knowledge and influence of the Gospel, which came into existence during the period of his ministry. He took a lively interest in their operations, contributed freely of his time and money to their support, and always, unless providentially prevented, attended their anniversaries.

In 1811, he was chosen a Trustee of the College of New Jersey, and held the office till the close of life. In 1812, he was appointed one of the first Directors of the Theological Seminary at Princeton, and was re-elected regularly until after the division of the General Assembly.

In 1818, he received the degree of Doctor of Divinity from Alleghany College.

In the disruption of the Presbyterian Church in 1837, Dr. Hillyer fell on the side of the New School. But, though he regarded the division as an unwise measure, it never disturbed his pleasant relations with those of his brethren whose views and action in reference to it differed from his own. The Princeton Seminary, too, he regarded to the last with undiminished interest, and its honoured Professors, with whom he had so long been familiar, he never ceased to reckon among his best friends.

In the winter of 1839–40, he was attacked by a disease, under which his bodily energies soon began sensibly to decline ; and though his friends hoped that the return of warm weather might affect him favourably, they were doomed to disappointment. During the period of his decline, a revival of religion took place among the people to whom he had so long ministered, and it was a sore trial to him that he could not more directly participate in it; but he evinced at once the most thankful and submissive spirit. His last public address was delivered at the Communion less than four weeks before his death; and his last ministerial act in public was pronouncing the benediction on the Sabbath following. He witnessed the approach of death without the least sign of apprehension,—knowing in whom he had believed. He suffered considerably during the last day of his life, and it was the only day in which he was wholly confined to his bed. He died on the evening of the 28th of August, 1840, retaining his consciousness, as was supposed, till the moment the vital spark was extinguished.

Dr. Hillyer's only publications were a Sermon preached before the Presbyterian Education Society, 1820 ; and a Sermon on a day of Public Thanksgiving and Prayer, 1822.

I knew Dr. Hillyer slightly, while I was a student in the Seminary at Princeton; more, after I was settled in the ministry, and quite intimately, in some of his last years. He always seemed to me a rare specimen of Christian and ministerial dignity, consistency, and loveliness. He had a fine person, a face with regular features and benign and attractive expression, and in his manner and whole bearing he was exceedingly bland and genial. I used to love to converse with him, not because I expected to hear from him any thing specially striking or original, but because he always spoke out of a full, warm heart, and made me feel as if I was in the company of "the disciple whom Jesus loved." I do not remember to have ever heard him utter a word of questionable prudence or propriety. I have heard him talk freely concerning his brethren whose views on exciting and absorbing questions of church policy differed greatly from his own, but not a sentence fell from him, which might not have been communicated to them without jeoparding in the least their kindly feelings towards him. Dr. Miller and he for instance took opposite sides in the great Church controversy; but there was no man towards whom he continued to the last to manifest a more affectionate regard, and I had reason to know that that regard was fully reciprocated. While it was evident that he had no ambitious aspirations, and cared nothing for popular favour, except as it might be rendered subservient to his usefulness, it was impossible that a character formed under the influence of such high principles, and so uniformly consistent and benevolent as his, should not have left its mark on the community in which he lived, and should not be gratefully cherished in the remembrances of many others.

FROM THE REV. GIDEON N. JUDD, D. D.

MONTGOMERY, N. Y., March 2, 1857.

My dear Brother: In compliance with your request, I will state my general impressions concerning our venerated friend, Dr. Hillyer. During twenty years we were co-presbyters, fourteen of which we resided near each other, and had charge of intermingled parishes, and were often associated in labours designed to promote the spiritual welfare of our flocks, and the interests of the Kingdom of our adorable Redeemer.

His physical frame was above the ordinary stature, symmetrical and commanding, and his countenance an index of the benevolence of his heart. He was cheerful, without levity; dignified in his deportment, but not magisterial or forbidding; a pleasant companion and faithful friend. In his family, he was, as he justly deserved to be, an object of affection and veneration. As a preacher, he was highly respectable; and as a pastor, he had but few superiors or even equals. His sensibilities were keen. With his people, both in their joys and sorrows, he deeply sympathized. In the house of affliction, by the bedside of the dying, and among the bereaved, he was eminently a son of consolation. In visiting the families of his flock, he was assiduous, kind and faithful. To the thoughtful and anxious inquirers after the way of salvation, and to the people of God, in their conflicts, fears, sorrows and joys, he was a deeply interested, tender and faithful counsellor and guide. He was a fine specimen of a Christian gentleman, and in all his relations reflected honour upon his office, as an ambassador of the Lord Jesus Christ.

Very sincerely and fraternally yours,

G. N. JUDD

JOHN BROWN, D. D.

1788—1842.

FROM THE REV. ROBERT C. SMITH,

PROFESSOR IN OGLETHORPE UNIVERSITY.

MILLEDGEVILLE, March, 20, 1847.

Rev. and dear Sir: In complying with your request for some account of the life and character of the Rev. Dr. John Brown, late of Fort Gaines, in this State, it is due to truth to say that, though I preached his Funeral Sermon, I never knew him until his sun had verged far towards the West. From the testimony of those who had seen it in its meridian splendour, in connection with the beautiful tints which, even in setting, it threw upon the landscape, I shall be obliged to make out my biographical portrait.

JOHN BROWN was born in Ireland, Antrim County, on the 15th of June, 1763. His father was among the poor of this world, and therefore voluntarily became a subject of what was called the "Kings bounty;"—an arrangement by which the distressed of Ireland might obtain a gratuitous passage to America, and at the same time secure a title to a hundred and sixty acres of land in one of the Carolinas. He chose his location in Chester District, S. C.; and there lived to see his son John a distinguished minister of the Gospel. The mother of John, like Hannah, "lent her son to the Lord," and early taught him to read the Scriptures. In his sixteenth year, he enjoyed the advantages of a country school for nine months; and in his nineteenth year, he was sent for an equal period to a grammar school in the Waxhaw settlement. These eighteen months make the sum total of his educational advantages—the rest of his early years being spent in assisting an indigent and afflicted father to conduct a farm for the support of his family. During the latter nine months, which he devoted to study, he was associated with the destined hero of New Orleans; and, like that hero, he did not wait to be forced into the military service of his country. At the age of sixteen, he was seen voluntarily exchanging the Groves of the Academy for the noise and bustle of the Camp, and, under General Sumter, intrepidly fighting his country's battles.

But no sooner was Peace restored than young Brown was found again diligently engaged for the improvement of his mind. He also soon perceived that his country was invaded by another enemy, far more to be dreaded than British forces. The tocsin of alarm had been sounded; and the call, made by the great "Captain of our salvation," for volunteers, fell upon his ears in tones loud and long. For this service he felt wholly unprepared. His weapons in the previous warfare had been carnal. But such, he was assured, would not now answer. The sword of the Spirit must be wielded—the whole armour of God put on. But he was "not disobedient to the Heavenly call." "Immediately he conferred not with flesh and blood," but consented to enter the service, and, by prayer and supplication, sought those weapons which are "mighty through God to the pulling down of strong holds."

Having studied Theology under the instruction of the Rev. Dr. McCorkle, near Salisbury, N. C., he was licensed to preach in the year 1788, by the

Presbytery with which his venerable teacher was connected. In the course of the same year, he was married to a Miss McCulloch, in whose affections he lived for fifty years,—when she was taken from him by death.

Having laboured, both in teaching and preaching, for a few years after his licensure, he was invited to the Pastorship of the Waxhaw Church, S. C. He accepted the invitation, and remained there for ten years. A difference of sentiment among the members of his church led him to resign his charge; and again, for a few years, he resorted to teaching, which seems to have been a favourite employment with him. Notwithstanding his limited advantages already referred to, and the pressing duties of a popular preacher, he rose to very considerable literary distinction. In 1809, he was elected Professor of Logic and Moral Philosophy in the University of South Carolina; and in 1811, he was chosen President of the University of Georgia. The duties of these offices he discharged with much ability, and with a fidelity which many of the citizens of those and the adjoining States must long remember with gratitude.

The degree of Doctor of Divinity was conferred upon him by the College of New Jersey in 1811.

After leaving the Presidency of the College, he removed to Jasper County, Ga., and was soon after chosen Pastor of Mount Zion Church, in Hancock County, in the same State. This station he held for twelve years; and then removed to Fort Gaines, where he spent his remaining days. His wife died shortly after this last removal. His labours here were those of an evangelist.

About the 20th of November, 1842, he perceived symptoms of approaching dissolution. But such symptoms had no terrors for him. He loved dearly his children and friends; but he felt that "to depart and be with Christ was far better." He lingered till the 11th of December, when, in the eightieth year of his age, he departed to his eternal rest.

Dr. Brown's life was eminently devoted to the service of God, and regulated by the precepts of the Gospel. His religious feelings had both strength and ardour, but were ever subject to the control of reason. If, in matters of religion, the right lies between two extremes, Dr. Brown certainly occupied the proper point; for I know not whether he was more distant from extravagance and enthusiasm on the one hand, or from lifelessness and cold monotony on the other. His piety consisted in the steady and active operation of a holy principle rather than in the excitements of times and occasions. He had a strong aversion to every thing like ostentation; and hence he rarely spoke of his own spiritual exercises—indeed he seldom spoke of himself in reference to any thing. He did, however, occasionally disclose his religious feelings to his more intimate friends; and from what he said to them, as well as from the tenor of his daily deportment, it was quite manifest that "he walked with God." His belief of the doctrines contained in the Westminster Confession of Faith was firm and uniform. But he was far from a bigoted pertinacity. On the contrary, his mind was ever open to the force of reason, and ready to adopt any sentiment which seemed to him supported by sound argument. But he was as far from fickleness as from bigotry. He had no peculiar relish for what was new, and no disposition to become weary of a sentiment, because it had been long entertained.

Dr. Brown was no partisan in religion. He belonged to no sect, unless, by the abuse of that term, it is made to apply to the whole mass of devout Protestants. He laboured, and prayed, and felt at home, among all who love our Lord Jesus Christ in sincerity, by whatever name they might be called.

As a minister of the Gospel, he certainly possessed rare excellencies. He had that combination of intellectual and moral qualities, which gives stability and duration to a minister's usefulness. His perceptions were clear, his power of discrimination great, his imagination sufficiently fertile, and his heart susceptible of profound emotion. He was always serious and affectionate in his manner, insomuch that none who heard him could doubt that his object was the glory of God in the salvation of souls. His style was simple, clear and dignified; suited to convey to his hearers the plain and logical conceptions of his own self-cultivated intellect. His sermons were at once doctrinal and practical—while they exhibited the truth, they brought it to bear directly upon the heart and conscience. He lived to witness many revivals, and always had an important agency in carrying them forward.

He had high qualifications also as an instructer of youth. He possessed great kindness of disposition, sterling intelligence, and genuine decision. He exhibited politeness without affectation, dignity without haughtiness, and strict adherence to rules of order without a needless and belittling precision. In the prime of life, he was distinguished for his skill and despatch in business. In all his conduct, whether public or private, he was so free from self-importance and dogmatism, so benign, and circumspect, and conciliatory, that I am not aware that he ever needlessly wounded the feelings of any body.

Dr. Brown had ten children, only five of whom lived to maturity, and only three survived himself. At the time of his death, he had two sons and one daughter. His son *John*, who was a physician, has since died, more extensively lamented perhaps than almost any individual who has ever died in the vicinity of Fort Gaines.

Yours affectionately,

R. C. SMITH.

FROM THE REV. SAMUEL K. TALMAGE, D. D.,

Oglethorpe University, May 12, 1849.

Rev. and dear Sir: I knew Dr. Brown concerning whom you inquire, and certainly regarded him as a remarkable man. But I know not whether I can tell you any thing concerning him, which you have not already received from other sources.

He was a wonderfully fluent speaker—I am not sure that I have ever known the individual who was more so. He abounded in rich evangelical and experimental instruction. His humility was remarkable. He was ever ready to defer to the humblest of his young brethren. His modesty prevented him from acquiring that celebrity to which his talents, research, and intrinsic worth, entitled him. His indifference to the world and his unbounded generosity kept him always poor. His excessive confidence in men made him the dupe of many a deceiver. He was perfectly guileless and unsuspicious. He loved every body, and the law of kindness dwelt upon his tongue. I never heard him say an unkind word of any human being. Whilst truly liberal in his judgment of other denominations, and careful to offend no one, he was one of the firmest friends of the Presbyterian Church I ever knew. He believed its doctrines, polity, and order were purely scriptural; and his diligent examination of Scripture, pursued by a searching and discriminating mind, made him a powerful advocate of the system which he embraced.

He was well entitled to the appellation we used, when speaking of him,—"Our apostle John." A venerable lady, now deceased, wife of Joseph Bryan, leading elder of the Mount Zion Church, Ga., used to relate many anecdotes of him. Mr. Bryan was in the habit of collecting his salary, and providing his family supplies. He would not trust his beloved and venerable pastor with the keeping of his own money, or the making of his own bargains. When Dr. Brown needed a new hat, or a supply of clothing, he consulted his elder. When he needed a little money to go to Presbytery or Synod, Mr. Bryan furnished it. Mrs. Bryan said, if her husband gave him a twenty dollar bill, he would give it all away, if he saw an object that appealed to his sympathy, without reflecting how he was to pay his expenses on the journey. After dwelling, on a certain occasion, at considerable length, on his character, she closed her description by adding,—"In fact, Father Brown is good for nothing in the world, but just to go right home to Heaven, and take the highest seat there."

Yours truly,

SAMUEL K. TALMAGE.

SAMUEL PORTER.*

1789—1825.

Samuel Porter was born in Ireland, on the 11th of June, 1760. His parents were worthy members of the Reformed Presbyterian Church, commonly called Covenanters, and attached great importance to their distinctive peculiarities. His mother devoted him to the Lord, for the work of the ministry, from his birth; in reference to which she called him *Samuel*. Not, however, having the means of obtaining a liberal education, he learned the business of a weaver, without, at the time, having any other prospect than earning his livelihood by this humble occupation. Having, in due time, taken to himself a wife, he determined to seek a home on this side the ocean; and, accordingly, in the year 1783, when he was about twenty-three years of age, he succeeded in carrying out his purpose. On his arrival in this country, he went into the interior of Pennsylvania, and spent the first winter in the vicinity of Mercersburg, Franklin County, where a near relative of his then resided. The expense of his voyage and journey after his arrival had entirely exhausted his small funds; though he quickly found himself among kind friends, who generously contributed towards the support of his family.

As he had been very strictly trained in the peculiarities of his own Church, and had had little sympathy or intercourse with any other, he was not much predisposed to attend on any other ministrations. Being, however, in the neighbourhood of Upper West Conococheague, where the Rev. (afterwards Dr.) John King exercised his ministry, he was induced, on one occasion, to go to hear him preach; though his expectations of being edified

* Memoir prefixed to his Sermons and Dialogues.—Appendix to Life of Macurdy.—Old Redstone.

or profited seem to have been very low. He was, however, agreeably disappointed in the service, and heard nothing which was not fully in accordance with his own views of Christian doctrine and duty. This led him to go again and again; and the more he heard Mr. King, the more fully he was convinced that there was no difference between his own Church and the Presbyterian Church of this country, that need be an obstacle in the way of his passing from the one to the other. The next year, he went to live in Western Pennsylvania, and having settled in Washington County, he had frequent opportunities of hearing the Rev. Joseph Smith, and the Rev. (afterwards Dr.) John McMillan; and the result was that, at no distant period, he transferred his relation to the Presbyterian Church, from a conviction that his spiritual enjoyment would not thereby be diminished, while his Christian usefulness would be increased.

By the advice of Dr. McMillan, and some other ministers, who felt deeply the need of an increase of the means of evangelical instruction in that new country, and who withal had formed a very favourable opinion of the vigour of Mr. Porter's intellect, as well as the depth and strength of his religious feelings, he was induced to undertake a course of preparation for the Christian ministry. His studies were prosecuted, partly under Mr. Smith, and partly under Dr. McMillan; though he studied Theology exclusively under the latter. Dr. McMillan, in consideration of his indigent circumstances, made no charge for either his board or tuition; and one of Mr. Porter's own countrymen,—a man of great benevolence, who lived in the neighbourhood, kindly took charge of his family, and saw that they were comfortably provided for, while he was going through his preparatory studies.

Mr. Porter had inherited the strong feeling of disapprobation common to the denomination with which he was originally connected, of the use of any other than the "old version" of the Psalms in religious worship. In this state of mind, he resolved, during his residence with Dr. McMillan, to investigate the subject of Psalmody with great care, and to write an elaborate defence of the views which he had always held in respect to it. As he proceeded in his examination, his convictions grew weaker instead of stronger, and he finally felt constrained to abandon his previous views altogether, and actually betook himself, both in private and in public, to the use of Watts' Psalms, and continued to use them without scruple, ever afterwards.

As Mr. Porter had made Theology his study, in no small degree, from very early life, and had acquired considerable general knowledge, before he entered on a formal course of preparation for the ministry, the Presbytery allowed the usual course of study, in his case, to be somewhat curtailed. He was licensed to preach by the Presbytery of Redstone, on the 12th of November, 1789. At a meeting of the Presbytery, April 20, 1790, he had a call put into his hands from the united Congregations of Poke Run and Congruity, one from the Congregations of Dunlap's Creek and George's Creek, and one from Long Run and Sewickly. The first of these calls he accepted, and accordingly, on the 22d of September, 1790, was ordained and installed Pastor of the Congregations of Poke Run and Congruity. In these congregations he laboured with untiring diligence until the 11th of April, 1798, when, on account of ill health, he was released from Poke Run, though against the earnest wishes and remonstrances of that portion of his charge. The Congregation at Congruity now became responsible for his entire salary; and he continued their Pastor till the close of his life.

In the beginning of the year 1813, he was called to a deep affliction in the death of a son, of great promise, who bore his own name. He had been educated at Jefferson College, and was settled as a minister at Cumberland, Md., in the autumn of 1811. He was a young man of highly respectable talents, amiable disposition, and decided piety. But he was cut down when he had but just entered on his course: while his father, already in the decline of life, was spared, amidst constantly increasing infirmities, to labour yet many years in his Master's vineyard.

Towards the close of his life, Mr. Porter became so feeble that he was able to deliver his sermons only in a sitting posture; and at length the marks of decay began to appear in his mind, particularly in his memory. The last time he attempted to preach, he announced his text as usual, and the plan of his discourse, but was unable to recall the first head, and was obliged to relinquish the exposition of his subject. The circumstance deeply affected him as well as his audience, and he then announced to them, after a brief but pathetic address, that his public ministrations had come to a close. From this time he was confined chiefly to his house, and his strength gradually declined, till he passed from the scene of his labours to his reward. He died on the 23d of September, 1825, in the sixty-sixth year of his age, having been a Pastor thirty-five years.

The following is a list of Mr. Porter's publications:—A Discourse on the Decrees of God, the Perseverance of the Saints, and Sinless Perfection, being the substance of two Sermons, delivered at Congruity, 1793. A Revival of true Religion delineated on Scriptural and rational principles, in a Sermon delivered at the opening of the Synod of Pittsburg, 1805. A Discourse relative to the Atonement of Christ, delivered at the opening of the Synod of Pittsburg, 1811. Two Dialogues—one between Death and the Believer—the other between Death and the Hypocrite. [These were published many years after his death, and are said to have been written before he entered the ministry.] In 1853, these several Discourses and Dialogues were republished in a small volume, in connection with a Biographical Sketch of the author, by the Rev. David Elliott, D. D.

Mr. Porter occasionally contributed articles to the weekly journals,—among which, was one of a strongly satirical character, entitled "An Apology for the Drunkard," and another containing a Defence of the Synod of Pittsburg against some animadversions in the public papers on account of its action in regard to Freemasonry.

FROM THE REV. JAMES CARNAHAN, D. D., LL. D.

PRINCETON, N. J., May 13, 1857.

Rev. and dear Sir: In complying with your request to give you my reminiscences of the Rev. Samuel Porter of Western Pennsylvania, I have to say that my personal knowledge of him was very limited. As he was located thirty or forty miles from the place of my residence, I had the opportunity of seeing him but a few times, and of hearing him preach only once, and that, on an occasion so peculiar that the discourse could not be considered as a fair specimen of his ordinary ministrations. I have indeed heard much respecting his early history, his character as a man, and as a Christian, and of his ability and success as a minister of the Gospel. But I shall, agreeably to your suggestion, limit myself chiefly or entirely to my own rather scanty personal recollections.

My impression in respect to the personal appearance of Mr. Porter is, that he was a little above the medium height, stout and heavy built, indicating strength rather than activity. His hair was of a light brown, the muscles of his face full, and when at rest not indicating any uncommon degree of intellect; but when he was roused, every feature seemed illuminated with thought and feeling.

Notwithstanding the defects of his early education, and the late period at which he entered the ministry, few men were better qualified to interest and instruct a Christian audience. His ordinary sermons were said to be not declamatory and exhortative, but highly instructive and practical, bringing the great truths of the Bible to bear on the hearts and consciences of his hearers. His voice was loud but not harsh, and capable of being modified so as to express the various emotions and passions. He had a rich vein of humour, and abounded in pleasant and appropriate anecdotes. In the pulpit, this natural tendency was kept under restraint; yet it would sometimes break out and excite a smile in his audience; but these occasional episodes did not prevent him or his hearers from falling back at once into the most serious and solemn train of reflection.

The only occasion on which I ever heard Mr. Porter speak in the pulpit was one which required great constitutional and moral courage, as well as great talent in overcoming the prejudices of his hearers. It was during the insurrection in Western Pennsylvania, usually called the *Whiskey insurrection*, in 1794.

In order to appreciate the courage and talent necessary to resist the torrent of public opinion, we must have a knowledge of the agitated state of the four counties in Pennsylvania, West of the mountains, and of the causes which produced the commotion. The mountains, which were scarcely passable by wheel carriages, cut the people off from market for their produce at the East—the mouth of the Mississippi was in the hands of the Spanish; and the Indians, prowling on the banks of the Ohio, attacked boats, loaded with flour, as they floated down the river; so that the price which their produce would command in the market, was but a poor compensation for the expense and risk they incurred in conveying it thither. No way remained of getting any profit for their labour, except by distilling their grain, and reducing it into a more portable form. At that time, distilling and trading in whiskey was considered as honest and honourable an employment as any other. Distilleries became numerous, and a large amount of capital was invested in them. A heavy excise was laid on them and their products, by the general government, recently gone into operation. The excise bore very unequally and oppressively on the people West of the mountains, and was very unpopular. Deputy excise men were seized at night by men in disguise, carried into the woods, stripped and covered with a coat of tar and feathers. Guns were discharged at or towards the United States Marshal, returning in company with the Inspector of the excise, after serving a writ on a distiller who had not registered his distillery as the law required. The next morning, the house of the Inspector was surrounded by armed men, and his commission and papers demanded, which being refused, an assault was made, and repelled by the Inspector and his servants. Shortly after, a larger number of armed men made a second attack on the Inspector's house, then guarded by a few United States soldiers. The discharge of guns was brisk and fatal on both sides. A soldier in the house was shot, and the commander of the assailants killed. The house and barn of the Inspector were set on fire, and the guard was compelled to surrender. The United States mail from Pittsburg to Philadelphia was seized, and letters opened in order to ascertain who were opposed to these lawless transactions. In obedience to a call made by the leaders, five or six thousand men, armed and unarmed, assembled on Braddock's fields, about nine miles from Pittsburg. It was proposed to take possession of the United States Arsenal, near Pittsburg, and to burn the town, unless the obnoxious persons were surrendered. By the dexterous management of a committee from Pittsburg, a compromise was made,—namely, that the individuals named should be banished from Pittsburg, and from the district, in a fixed number of days. The insurgents marched into Pittsburg to show their strength, and dispersed without doing much mischief. Inflammatory hand bills were placarded over the country, calling on the people to resist, and threatening tar and feathers and destruction of property, to those who opposed the wishes of the mob. The distilleries which had been registered by their owners, as the law required, with an intention of paying the excise, were forcibly entered, and the distilling apparatus destroyed. There were many good citizens who disapproved of these lawless doings, and at first did not interfere; and when the frenzy reached its height, one was afraid to make known to another his opinion. The ministers of the Gospel, from an unwillingness to introduce into the pulpit a subject which had a political aspect, were generally silent. Not so with Mr. Porter. From the beginning, he spoke, publicly and privately, against the unlawful proceedings, and prevented his own people and others in the neighbourhood from participating in them.

When General Washington, then President of the United States, was advised that the officers of the General Government had been driven from the country, and that the Courts of the State did not and could not protect the persons of peaceable citizens from violence, and their property from destruction, he called out an army of fifteen thousand men, chiefly from New Jersey, the Eastern part of Pennsylvania, Maryland and Virginia. And while the army was on the march, he sent a proclamation West of the Mountains, offering an amnesty for what was past to all who, on a day named, would sign a solemn promise to abstain from further violence, and to obey the laws of the United States. The Governor of the State also offered a similar amnesty for the violation of the laws of the State previously committed.

When these proclamations arrived, meetings were called in different places to consider and decide what was to be done. In company with other students of the Academy at Cannonsburg, I attended one of these meetings in the bounds of Father McMillan's Congregation. Some hundred and fifty people were collected. A stage or platform was erected in front of a public house, and the audience stood in the road, or sat on logs before the platform. Two or three speeches in favour of non-submission and continued resistance were made and applauded. A very respectable man,—an elder in the Presbyterian Church, and an Associate Judge of the County of Washington, rose and advised calmness and moderation, and as soon as it was perceived that he was in favour of signing the conditions of amnesty, he was hissed and pelted with clods of earth and mud, and driven from the stage. This, no doubt, was a fair specimen of what occurred at other similar meetings. Many were determined not to sign the amnesty, and to prevent by force others who were willing to sign it. Father McMillan became alarmed; and as several of his congregation, and a few members of his church, were implicated in the disorders, he postponed the administration of the Lord's Supper, which ought to have taken place. Having learned that Mr. Porter had successfully opposed the lawless proceedings, he invited him to come and address his people on the subject. Mr. Porter accepted the invitation, and appointed a day when he would be present. As he had to cross the Monongahela, and to pass through the region where the insurrection commenced, and where the leading insurgents resided, many persons thought he would be mobbed on the way; or if he came and advised submission, the sacred desk would not protect him from insult and violence. Fully aware of these dangers, he came alone, on horseback, and was at the place of worship at the time appointed. It was on a week day, and a large congregation was collected, some from a distance, and many not in the habit of worshipping in that place. After preliminary devotional services, Mr. Porter rose, and with calmness and perfect self-possession, remarked in substance that he had come at the invitation of their venerable pastor to address them on a subject in which they and the whole community at that time were deeply interested; and that, as a minister of the Gospel, he had determined to say nothing but what the teachings of our Lord and his Apostles authorized—he would therefore read as a guide for his remarks the first seven verses of the thirteenth chapter of the Epistle to the Romans—"Let every soul be subject unto the higher powers," &c. He first referred to the occasion which led the Apostle to speak of the authority of civil rulers, and of the duties which private citizens owe to the existing government—he stated that the independence of the Jews as a nation was lost, and they were reduced into subjection to the Romans;—that their national pride was wounded;—that they thought no government, except that given immediately by God to their fathers, was lawful;—that, feeling oppressed by a foreign yoke, they were ready on every occasion to throw it off, and to follow any leader who promised to restore their national independence. They also looked for a victorious prince in the Messias promised to their fathers. Vast multitudes followed Theudas and others who pretended to be the Messias, and were destroyed by the Roman armies, as is recorded in the Acts of the Apostles. Jews who embraced Christianity were not wholly free from national prejudices, and were liable to be overwhelmed in the same terrible calamity which came upon that guilty and devoted nation. The doctrine taught by the Apostle was, that civil government was a Divine institution, established for the benefit of mankind; and to resist its authority was rebellion against God—that "the powers that be"—that is, the existing government, in whatever manner established, whether by conquest or usurpation, or by the suffrages of the people, or whatever form it might assume, ought, for conscience sake, to be obeyed in things not forbidden by God; and even if the laws were, in many respects, oppressive, private citizens ought nevertheless to submit. He maintained that to the general doctrine of obedience there are exceptions, and that passive obedience, in all cases whatsoever, cannot legitimately be inferred from the general precept. When human laws interfere with the rights of conscience, and require men to do what God has forbidden, or not to do what God has commanded, each individual is bound to obey God rather than men; and if such a penalty await them, to suffer imprisonment and death. On this principle the Apostles acted, when forbidden by the Jewish Sanhedrim to teach in the name of Jesus. On this principle Paul acted, and therefore could not intend to teach passive obedience. Nor did he intend to teach that the people, if they have the power, may not change their rulers and their laws, and adopt a new form of government, as was done in the late American Revolution. But among these exceptions is not found the right to withhold from the existing government the usual revenue. The main object in the passage under consideration, was to inculcate on Christians the duty of paying tribute, even under the reign of Nero,—as great a tyrant as ever existed. The paying of tribute affects the purse and not the conscience. The tribute may be oppressive and impoverish the body, but it does not ruin the soul. And to refuse to pay, when the individual or individuals have no power to resist, is folly, and madness, and rebellion against God. If they suffer for withholding the tribute imposed by "the powers that be," they will not receive the martyr's crown.

As Mr. Porter, in his exposition, kept close to the words of the Apostle, the audience listened with decorum and attention. But when he came to apply the principles which he had found in the inspired record to the state of the Western Counties,—to contrast the tribute imposed by Nero with the excise on distilleries and whiskey, and the absolute despotism of the Roman government with the elective franchise of the United States, there was a visible stir and commotion in the assembly. Some laid their hands on their hats, as if preparing to leave the house. Others frowned and seemed ready to rise and drag the speaker from the pulpit. Mr. Porter, who spoke without note or paper before him, saw the effect of what he was saying, and to illustrate his argument, he introduced a humorous anecdote, and in a short time changed the aspect of his audience, and then returned to the serious view of his subject. Again the same indignant feeling was manifested, and he calmed the commotion by another sally of keen wit. These changes from the serious to the ludicrous, and from the ludicrous to the serious, occurred several times. At length the attention of the audience became so absorbed in the subject, that the speaker was permitted to go on without interruption. He showed that the present course was both foolish and wicked, and that inevitable ruin awaited the people of Western Pennsylvania, if opposition to the Federal Government, and violation of the State laws were continued;—that for a small district,—not more than sixty miles from East to West and from North to South,—to attempt to resist the power of the United States, was folly and madness greater than that which actuated the Jews when they resisted the armies of the Roman Empire, and brought such a calamity upon their nation and their sacred city as the world had never witnessed;—that General Washington, who had successfully led our feeble army through a seven years' war with a powerful nation, was not the man to be turned aside from performing what he thought to be his duty by threats and blustering, and tar and feathers;—that an army of fifteen thousand men were on their march, and the people of Western Pennsylvania must submit, or they must fight. He knew and appreciated the valour and skill with the rifle, of the men West of the Mountains; but they could not perform impossibilities;—they could not hope for a miraculous interposition when they were in rebellion against the ordinance of God and man. What could an unorganized body of men, however brave, without the munitions of war, without money and without allies, do against an army regularly organized, and furnished with all the means of destruction? Many of their bravest and most prominent men would fall, and others would be taken captive and carried off to a distant part of the State, imprisoned and condemned as traitors, and hung. He described in thrilling tones the anguish of mothers, and wives, and sisters, when they saw those dearer to them than life torn from them as criminals. The hearts of the women, many of whom were present, were touched, and the sympathies of the sterner sex were not unmoved. He closed his discourse in an affectionate and soothing manner, stating that an opportunity was presented of averting these impending calamities ;—that by signing, in good faith, the conditions of amnesty offered by the General and State Governments, peace and order and happiness would be restored, and that he was confident the oppressive tax would, in a short time, be removed, and a more genial sun than had heretofore been seen, would dawn West of the Mountains. He added that their great sin, in this as well as in other matters, was against God, and called for repentance;—that the door of mercy was not yet closed, and the most vile and guilty might enter, assured that none who asked forgiveness in the name of their Advocate on high would be rejected.

The triumph of the speaker was perfect. When he came down from the pulpit, he was cordially taken by the hand by several who had entered the house, determined not to be convinced, and thanked for his able and timely discourse. Others whose obstinacy would yield to no arguments, seeing a large majority of the congregation were against them, departed in silence. These are a few of the fragments of the discourse in connection with the transactions of that day, which the storms of threescore and three winters have not swept from my memory.

In conclusion, let me remark that the power of Mr. Porter as a speaker is not to be measured by any thing that he has written. Like the great Virginia Orator, Patrick Henry, he could speak much better than he could write. And you, my dear Sir, as well as many others, have not forgotten that the ably written discourses of the late revered and beloved Dr. A. Alexander, were not equal in power and effect to the addresses which flowed spontaneously from his lips without note or paper before him. And if the words of Mr. Porter had been accurately written down as they were uttered, and read or spoken by another person, without his tones, and accents, and emphasis, and expression of countenance, they would have lost more than half their force and meaning.

Considering that my own personal recollections of this remarkable man are not more extended, I will add a few paragraphs in respect to him, written by the Rev. David Elliott, D. D., who has evidently formed a very just conception of his character.

"Those who were most familiarly acquainted with Mr. Porter agree that he was endowed with talents of a high order. He had great aptness both in acquiring and imparting knowledge. His memory was one of peculiar tenacity, enabling him to retain, for practical purposes, whatever was deemed valuable by him and worthy of preservation. This qualified him for acting with much efficiency in the public judicatories of the Church. It was there that he appeared to the greatest advantage; and it rarely occurred that he embarked in the advocacy of any measure, which he did not carry successfully through. He had a peculiar tact in argument, and his controversial powers were successfully tested on several occasions. He appears to have been qualified by nature for a dialectician, and with comparatively little educational training in the rules of logic, he evinced more than common skill in the syllogistic art. And had he enjoyed the usual advantages of liberal study and mental discipline in early life, he would doubtless have appeared to much greater advantage, and been entitled to a much higher rank as a writer and controversialist.

"By his contemporaries, Mr. Porter is represented to have been a very attractive and forcible public speaker. Of his power in this respect, the following graphic description from the pen of the Rev. Robert Johnston, furnished the writer several years ago, will give the reader some accurate conception:—'His qualifications as a public speaker were evidently of the first order. His voice was clear and strong; not harsh, but musical and commanding, possessing sufficient volume to be heard distinctly by thousands assembled in the open air. He spoke fast, but his articulation was so distinct, and his thoughts so clearly expressed, as to be easily understood. His was the eloquence of nature, and it was irresistible. Prompted by the energy of his thoughts,—the intonations of his voice, and the action of his body, gave emphasis to his theme, and held the attention of his audience entranced. I can never forget the first time I heard him preach. It was in the spring of 1793. He assisted Dr. McMillan at a Communion. It was also a time of refreshing from the presence of the Lord, and a very large assembly of people was present on the occasion. He preached on the afternoon of the Sabbath, from Isaiah xl. 1, 2,—'Comfort ye, comfort ye my people, saith your God. Speak ye comfortably to Jerusalem, and cry unto her that her warfare is accomplished.' The assembly were seated in a beautiful grove of young beech, gently ascending in front of the tent where he stood. He commenced, and for two hours held that large assembly in breathless attention, while a torrent of sweet, celestial eloquence, poured from his lips, with a rapidity and pathos that dissolved a large portion of the assembly in tears. The mildness and majesty of his countenance, softened by the feelings of his own heart, and glowing with the sublimity and grandeur of his theme, heightened by the flickering rays of the setting sun, breaking through the boughs of the beech trees on his face, as he spoke, combined with the energy of his voice and the thrilling power of his thoughts, left on my mind, and doubtless on that of others, an impression of intellectual and moral greatness, which I had never before attached to any human being. Such was the originality of his thoughts, and the commanding power of his eloquence, that, although he often spoke two hours with a rapidity of utterance rarely equalled by public speakers, the attention of his audience never appeared to relax.'

"Mr. Porter was distinguished for his ready wit, which he sometimes carried into the pulpit. In the use of rhetorical figures, he would occasionally startle his hearers by the boldness of his positions, from which it seemed impossible that he should be able to retreat, without injury to the cause of religion. One of his ministerial brethren, speaking of this trait in his manner of preaching, remarked to the writer, that he reminded him of a man angling for fish, who would sport with the fish at the bait, giving it line until it seemed almost beyond his power to draw it up; but at the proper juncture would arrest it and bring it safely to land. So he acted with his hearers. After indulging in bold sallies of wit, and leading them into scenes of levity, calculated to induce a state of mind adverse to religion, he never failed to bring them back to a proper tone of feeling. If, for a moment, he provoked a smile, by a sudden change of subject and manner, he soon restored them to seriousness, and often had them bathed in tears. The following well authenticated anecdote may serve to illustrate this feature of his character and style of preaching:—

"During the sessions of the General Assembly at Winchester, Va., in the year 1799, Mr. Porter, being present, was invited to preach. He accepted the invitation, and took for his text, Ecclesiastes xi. 9,—'Rejoice, O young man, in thy youth; and let thy heart cheer thee in the days of thy youth, and walk in the ways of thine heart, and in the sight of thine eyes: but know thou, that for all these things, God will bring thee into judgment.' In reading the text, he stopped suddenly when he reached the last clause, without announcing it, and commenced his discourse. He spoke of youth as the season of enjoyment; the period in which the animal spirits are buoyant and lively, and the whole man fitted to participate largely in the pleasures of sense. In the midst of this period was the person spoken of in the text. He was *young*, in the heyday of youth; and *a man*, not a child in leading-strings, under parental authority and control; but a man in stature and age, capable of judging and acting for himself,—a high-minded, independent, daring young man. He was a type of the whole race of such young men;—a model, an example. And according to the counsel given to such in the text, so the speaker urged every other young man to go and do likewise. Hence, he opened up to him the path of sensual pleasure; he sketched, in rich and attractive colours, its gay delights; he invited him to enter, and having entered, he urged him forward in his joyful career of folly and sin, by all the arguments which his powerful intellect could suggest, and by all the allurements which his vivid imagination could depict. At every step in his wild career, he presented him with new pleasures, and caused his soul to swell with new and indescribable joys. With such sober earnestness and overwhelming force did he describe the pleasures of sin, and urge young men onward in the indulgence of their depraved appetites and passions, that many of his ministerial brethren were startled and alarmed at the boldness of his positions, and the alluring richness of the drapery, which he threw around them; and the hearts of the young and profligate portion of his hearers swelled with delight. Such an advocate they had never had before. Their triumph they felt to be complete, and they were ready to go forth and proclaim that the ways of sin were ways of pleasantness, and all its paths were paths of peace; and that to indulge every sinful desire of their hearts was the true way to be permanently and truly happy.

"Having thus depicted the pleasures of sin, and carried the reckless youth into the midst of his sensual indulgences, where he was sporting and revelling in all the gaieties and extravagances of unbridled lust, the speaker suddenly paused, and dropping his eye upon the text, recommenced reading with slow and solemn emphasis,—'*But*,'—'ah,' said he, 'this BUT, is a strange and troublesome little word, and often obtrudes itself at a very unwelcome moment'—'But, know thou, that for all these things God will bring thee into judgment.' 'This,' exclaimed the preacher, 'is the other side of the picture. You have seen the one side, and it shall now be my business to let you see the other.' He then proceeded, with graphical skill, to present in all its terrible solemnity, the judicial consequences of such a course of sinful indulgence. He spoke of the throne of judgment; of the arrest of the criminal; of his appearance at the bar of justice; of the searching scrutiny of the Judge, whose 'eyes are as a flame of fire;' of the public exposure of the sinner's deeds of darkness; of the infliction of God's wrath; of the horrors of a guilty conscience; of the final sentence and the 'everlasting destruction' of the condemned culprit, 'from the presence of the Lord and from the glory of his power.' The scene was one of painful interest and overwhelming solemnity. Every mind was filled with awe; and while, with deep and mournful feeling, he followed the gay and misguided youth into the dark regions of despair, and spoke of the agonies of his never dying soul, and of the piercing cries which issued from the midst of 'the flame' in which he was 'tormented,' the whole assembly were moved and melted into tenderness, and gave vent to their feelings in a gush of tears.

"Mr. Porter was a bold and fearless reprover of vice in all its various forms. To him it made no difference whether it appeared in the tattered garments of poverty, or the fashionable and gaudy attire, with which wealth invests its subject; he everywhere met it with rebuke, and sought to expose its deformity, that men might be preserved from its destructive power. It was not his way to mince reproof, or to present it in so indistinct a form as not to be seen or felt by those for whom it was intended.

* * * * * * * * * * * *

"It is true that he had a peculiar method of doing things, and would sometimes resort to measures which it would have been hazardous in almost any other man to have attempted. An illustration of this is furnished in the following letter, written by William Redick, an Elder in the Presbyterian Church at Uniontown, Pa., and addressed to the editor of the Presbyterian Advocate, at Pittsburgh, bearing date August, 1852:—

"'The Dialogue which appeared in your paper of the 14th ult., from the late Rev. Samuel Porter, together with a brief sketch of the life of the author, naturally led back my thoughts to bygone days, and awakened the memory of incidents connected with the Reverend author of the Dialogue, and the Congregation of Congruity, from which fondly cherished neighbourhood I now have been many years absent.

"'It occurs to my mind that it may be of interest to your readers to learn something of the energy of character, and peculiar tact, of the author of the Dialogue for accomplishing what but few others could do. For this purpose, permit me to relate an anecdote of him as nearly as I can, just as it occurred under my own observation, some thirty-one or thirty-two years ago.

"'A new stone tavern house had been built on the turnpike, scarcely a mile from the church, and was just opened out by the owner, a very clever man. The young folks of the neighbourhood, many of them the children of church members, and even baptized members themselves, had agreed to have what was generally known as a *house-warming*, by holding a ball there. The arrangements were all made, the tickets distributed, and the guests invited.

"'On the Sabbath previous to the intended ball, this aged minister, after preaching an eloquent sermon, sitting in his old split bottom arm-chair, (for he was too feeble to preach standing, and for many a long day sat and preached in that old arm-chair, elevated in the pulpit for his accommodation,) and before dismissing the congregation, gave out the usual notices for the ensuing week and Sabbath. After stating that Presbytery would meet the next Tuesday in

Greensburgh, and making his usual appointments, he then gave notice that on the next Thursday evening, at early candle lighting, a ball was to be held about three-fourths of a mile from that place. He said it was to be hoped that all the polite young ladies and gentlemen would attend, as it was said to be a place where politeness and manners could be learned and cultivated, and that many other things could be said in favour of attending such places, which it was not necessary for him to mention at that time. However, it was to be hoped that as many as could, would attend at the time named—'next Thursday evening at early candle lighting!' He remarked that, for his part, if he did not attend, the young folks would excuse him, as it was likely he might be detained at Presbytery; yet, should Presbytery adjourn in time, and nothing else prevent, he expected to attend; and should he be present, he would open the exercises of the night, by reading a text of Scripture, singing a psalm, and offering up a prayer. But, as the strong probability was that he could not be in attendance, and lest he might not, he said he would then and there read the text, the congregation would sing a psalm, offer up a prayer and be dismissed. Then, with a full and solemn voice, and in the most solemn, impressive manner, he read the ninth verse of the eleventh chapter of Ecclesiastes,—'Rejoice, O young man, in thy youth, and let thine heart cheer thee in the days of thy youth, and walk in the ways of thine heart, and in the sight of thine eyes; but, know thou, that for all these things God will bring thee into judgment.' Then, with the same solemn, impressive voice and manner, he announced and read the seventy-third Psalm, 'Lord, what a thoughtless wretch was I,' &c. After this was sung by the congregation, he then offered up a fervent and affecting prayer; praying earnestly for the thoughtless and gay, and for the power of God's Spirit to guard them all from those vices and amusements which might lead the youthful mind to fritter away precious time, and neglect the one thing needful; and then, with his solemn benediction, the congregation was dismissed.

"'The result was, that it produced a seriousness throughout the congregation, that went into the community; and, notwithstanding the arrangements had all been made, and many were anxiously and impatiently awaiting the appointed evening, yet none had the hardihood to think of braving the impressive reproof, or dared to outrage the awakened moral sense of the community, and go on with the ball. The set evening arrived and passed away, but the ball never was held.'

* * * * * * * * * * * * *

"But although Mr. Porter was thus rigorous and uncompromising in his opposition to vice, even in its most fashionable and attractive forms, in his ordinary intercourse with society he was highly cheerful and familiar. He abounded in anecdote, by which he imparted animation to the social circles in which he moved, and which rendered him a very attractive companion. In his family, he was kind and indulgent, and for the accommodation or relief of a friend, he never considered any sacrifice too great.

"His personal piety, although consistent, was not as highly devotional in its type, as that of some others. This has been attributed to his severely intellectual habits and associations, and to his constitutional vivacity. But, that he possessed real piety, those best acquainted with him, never doubted. He himself did, sometimes, call in question the reality of his hope in Christ. His perplexity seems to have arisen from the fact that he was not conscious of any particular time in which he had experienced that change of heart, of which he knew every one who would enter into the Kingdom of God, must be the subject. This occasionally gave him uneasiness. But he was not without some substantial grounds of encouragement. For, although he could not mark the period of such a change,—neither could he recollect any period of his life, in which he did not love to contemplate the character, laws, and government, of God, nor in which he did not find comfort in the holy duties of religion. From his earliest years, also, he hated and shunned the society of the wicked. Being conscious of this habitual opposition of heart to the ungodly practices of wicked men, he was encouraged to hope that he would not be condemned to dwell forever with them in the world of woe. Accordingly, he was very frequently heard offering up the prayer of the man after God's own heart,—'Gather not my soul with sinners, nor my life with bloody men.' And as, on the other hand, he loved to think of God, and to hold fellowship with his people in the holy duties of religion, he was led to indulge the hope that, through riches of grace in Christ Jesus, he would be admitted at last to dwell with them in Heaven. Thus did he escape from the perplexities arising from his inability to designate the exact time in which he had experienced the regenerating grace of God upon his heart; and he was led to the conclusion that, if his hope was not utterly groundless, he must have been born into the Kingdom ot God, in early youth, probably when, on his knees at the side of his pious mother, she poured out her soul to God for his conversion and salvation. This, doubtless, was the true solution of his case. He had the true marks of a child of God in his hatred of sin, and his love of holiness. These furnished evidence of his regeneration; and his not being able to recollect the time when this occurred, could not disprove the fact."

Very respectfully and truly yours,

JAMES CARNAHAN.

JAMES WHITE STEPHENSON, D. D.*

1789—1832.

The parents of James White Stephenson were of Scotch-Irish extraction, and composed a part of that large body of Presbyterians that migrated to Virginia and the Carolinas during the latter half of the eighteenth century. They halted and sojourned for two or three years in Augusta County, Va., where the subject of this sketch was born, in the year 1756. Shortly after his birth, they removed to Lancaster District, S. C., and settled near the old Waxhaw Church, where they remained during the rest of their lives. Though little is now known of his youthful days, there is reason to believe, from several circumstances, that, through the sanctified influence of a pious education, he entered upon the Christian life at a very early period.

Where and under what instructer he had his early classical training, cannot now be ascertained; though there is little doubt of his having been graduated at Mount Zion College, Winnsboro', S. C., then under the Presidency of the Rev. Thomas H. M'Caule.† This institution, however, though having a perpetual charter, and being fully empowered to confer degrees, was merely an Academy of a high order.

* South. Presb. Rev. VI.

† Thomas Harris M'Caule was graduated at the College of New Jersey in 1774, and two years after was ordained and installed Pastor of Centre Congregation, N. C. He was uncommonly popular both as a man and as a preacher. He entered warmly into his country s cause during the Revolution, and in the time of the invasion went with his flock to the camp, and was beside General William Davidson when he fell. Such was his reputation in the walks of

After having completed his academical or collegiate course, he became the Principal of a classical school near the old Waxhaw Church, and continued his connection with it two or three years. One of his pupils was Andrew Jackson, who was destined in after life to the highest military and civil honours.

When the war of the Revolution invaded South Carolina, Mr. Stephenson recognised his country's claim to his services, by promptly enlisting for its defence: he immediately gave up his school, and knew no other life than that of a soldier till the return of Peace. With one of his brothers he joined the army under the command of General Sumter, and participated in several battles, particularly those at Blackstock's, and Hanging Rock. On one of these occasions, while the fight raged fiercely, a ball from the enemy struck the britch of his gun and broke it, and then glancing, killed the man that stood next to him. At another time, it became his duty in turn to stand as sentinel at a certain place, but being indisposed that night, a fellow soldier volunteered to serve in his stead, and was shot dead at his post. Thus, in two instances, was he the subject of a signal providential preservation from death.

Sometime after the close of the war, he commenced his immediate preparation for the ministry; and, having gone through a course of theological study, was licensed in 1789 by the Presbytery of South Carolina, which then embraced the entire territory of the State. Shortly after his licensure, he accepted a call to the pastoral charge of the Bethel and Indiantown Churches, in Williamsburg District.

A few years previous to this time, the Williamsburg Church had been greatly distracted by the alleged doctrinal errors and unministerial conduct of the Rev. Samuel Kennedy, a native of Ireland. The church was formed as early as 1736, and for many years enjoyed great spiritual prosperity; but for some time previous to the Revolution, its prosperity had declined, chiefly in consequence of its receiving large accessions from the North of Ireland, in which, to say the least, spirituality was not the predominant element. Then the church was vacant during nearly the whole period of the war; and the agitation and peril to which it was subjected, were most unfavourable to a healthful tone of Christian feeling and action. Such was the state of things when Mr. Kennedy was invited to take charge of it; and his ministry served only to aggravate the pre-existing evils. Though he was invited for the limited term of three years, yet the majority voted to continue him after that term had expired. A considerable minority, however, consisting of the descendants of the original founders of the church, earnestly remonstrated against his being retained, and when they found that their remonstrances were unavailing, they determined to devote to destruction that which they were unable to save from what they deemed desecration. And, according to a previous understanding, the dissatisfied party met one morning in the month of August, 1786, with about one hundred negro men, and in a few hours the entire building was razed to the ground, and the materials removed from the spot. The pulpit was carried a distance of three miles, and concealed in a barn.

These violent proceedings, as might be expected, drew after them a train of deplorable consequences. The minority, who had been the actors in this

civil life, that he was once run for the office of Governor, and failed in the election by a very small vote. He had fine classical attainments, and these, in connection with his great energy of character and popular address, marked him out as a suitable person to preside over Winnsboro' College. He had the training of a considerable number of eminent men.

work of destruction, withdrew, leaving the majority in possession of the name and property of the Williamsburg Church, and were, in due time, regularly organized under the name of the Bethel Church. To the pastoral charge of this church, in connection with that of Indiantown, Mr. Stephenson, then a licentiate, was called. He was ordained and installed sometime between the meetings of Synod in 1790 and 1791. Mr. Kennedy, a short time after the schism, removed into North Carolina, where he ended his days.

It was a high testimony to Mr. Stephenson's discretion, that he was enabled so to demean himself in the difficult and delicate position which he now held, as to avoid the censure, and gain the respect and confidence, not only of his own church, but of that from which his was a secession. This was the more remarkable, as the places of worship occupied by the two bodies were but about fifty paces from each other.

On the 4th of August, 1791, Mr. Stephenson was married to Elizabeth, daughter of Major John James, who was distinguished for some daring feats in the Revolution. She was every way qualified for the station to which she was thus called; but it pleased an Allwise Providence that the union should be of short duration. She died on the 29th of July, 1793, aged twenty-four years.

Mr. Stephenson was largely blessed in his ministry. He was diligent in every department of ministerial labour, and his churches grew proportionally in both numbers and spirituality. At length his attention, with that of a number of his people, began to be directed to the favourable openings in the West, and forthwith they determined on carrying the Gospel into that almost unbroken wilderness. Accordingly, about twenty families, with their minister, migrated to Maury County, Tenn., and jointly purchased a large tract of land belonging to the heirs of General Greene, of Revolutionary fame.

Mr. Stephenson preached his Farewell Discourse in Indiantown Church, on the 28th of February, 1808, and, on the 3d of March following, set out on his journey to the West. On the 20th of May of the same year, he was married to Mrs. Mary Flemming, a member of his own church, and one of the emigration from Williamsburg.

In 1815, the degree of Doctor of Divinity was conferred upon him by the Board of Trustees of the South Carolina College.

In his new field of labour, he exercised his ministry with undiminished zeal and fidelity, and his popular talents soon attracted the attention, and secured for him the friendship, of some of the most prominent men in the State. He possessed in a high degree the missionary spirit, and was especially intent on evangelizing the poor Indians. He possessed a naturally vigorous physical constitution, and was rarely, if ever, prevented by ill health from performing the services of the sanctuary, until he was far advanced in life. For about a year before his death, he was assisted by the Rev. James M. Arnell, who was unanimously chosen his successor. He died on the 6th of January, 1832, aged seventy-six, having been the pastor of a portion of his congregation for more than forty-two years. His death was an edifying scene of Christian hope and triumph. Only one child,—a son, survived him.

He left behind him several hundred manuscript sermons, but only two or three of his sermons were ever published.

FROM THE REV. WILLIAM MACK.

COLUMBIA, Tenn., May 18, 1857.

Rev. and dear Sir: The Rev. James White Stephenson, D. D. died several years previous to my removal to this place. The location of his church is a few miles West of this town, and I am well acquainted with several persons, who, for many years, enjoyed his ministry. From these I have gathered the statements which I am now about to communicate.

He was of medium height, and heavily built. The features were large, the eye grey, the expression grave. He was quite unique in his appearance. When once seen, he was apt to be remembered. Several have said that so distinct was the impression of him in their minds, if they were artists, they could furnish me with a picture, clearly showing the outward man.

His manners were grave and dignified. He was easily approached, yet something in him told you that it must be done respectfully. The kindness of the heart shone forth in the countenance. He was highly respected and much beloved.

As a preacher, Dr. Stephenson was solid and instructive. Flights of imagination were rarely, if ever, attempted. Under his preaching the people became well instructed in the leading truths of Revelation. His sermons abounded in scriptural expressions. While his pulpit efforts were always adapted to be useful, occasionally, when he became aroused by certain circumstances, he would deliver a discourse of a highly impressive character. There was this peculiarity in his preaching—that, whatever was the theme of his discourse, he almost uniformly closed with some invitation or urgent exhortation—such as, "Turn ye, turn ye, why will ye die?" "Ho every one that thirsteth, come ye to the waters," &c.

Dr. Stephenson was a consistent Christian. He evidently aimed to practise what he preached. His life spoke for God as well as his lips. He was doubtless well prepared for death. His last illness was brief, and unexpectedly to himself, if not to others, his spirit left its earthly tenement.

Very respectfully,

WILLIAM MACK.

FROM THE REV. JAMES HOLMES, D. D.,

PROFESSOR IN THE WEST TENNESSEE COLLEGE.

JACKSON, Tenn., June 25, 1857.

Dear Sir: Nearly the third of a century having passed since I saw Dr. Stephenson, and never having enjoyed an intimate acquaintance with him, I feel quite inadequate to write any thing that shall even seem to do justice to his character. At intervals I spent several nights with him on my missionary agency, and on one occasion had the privilege of accompanying him to his church and of hearing him preach. His white locks and very patriarchal appearance are distinctly before my eye. His solemn and intelligent countenance, dignified bearing, and conciliatory manners, could not fail to leave a favourable impression. Having read of the substantial character of the colonists who chose him as their spiritual guide in their new home, I was prepared to meet a man of mark, and such decidedly I found him to be. Time has shown the kind and degree of influence exerted by him in the formation of the "Frierson settlement"—a name by which that community has ever been designated. Few churches in the State have so uniformly maintained an enviable notoriety, particularly for the faithful private and public instruction of the blacks. An enduring record ought to be made of God's favour to that Christian colony, as well as of the exalted worth of the man who was chiefly concerned in giving it its early religious direction.

Very respectfully,

JAMES HOLMES.

WILLIAM PAXTON, D. D.

1790—1845.

FROM THE REV. DAVID McCONAUGHY, D. D.

WASHINGTON, Pa., March 29, 1850.

Rev. and dear Brother: I knew the venerable man concerning whom you inquire, very intimately, and esteemed and loved him very much; and it is no selfdenial to me to comply with your request, in furnishing you with a brief sketch of his life and character.

WILLIAM PAXTON was born April 1, 1760, in Lancaster County, Pa. His father was a respectable farmer, distinguished not so much by wealth, as by integrity of character, soundness of thought, and practical good sense. These mental attributes were the common characteristic of his family. William, the subject of this sketch, devoted his early life to agricultural employments. It was, however, somewhat identified with the struggles of our country for her independence. He served in two companies, at different times, during the Revolutionary war, in one of which he was present and participated in the battle of Trenton. Subsequently, his love of knowledge induced him to seek the advantages of a liberal education; and his love of God and man constrained him to consecrate all to the work of the Gospel ministry. He commenced his preparatory course when about twenty-four years of age; and prosecuted his classical, scientific and theological studies, chiefly at the Strasburg Academy, near Lancaster City, Pa., under the direction of the Rev. Nathaniel W. Sample,* then Pastor of the Congregations of Lancaster and Middle Octorora. He had not the advantages of a collegiate education; but, with a mature mind and diligent study, he made the needful acquisitions, and laid a foundation upon which he accumulated a more than ordinary amount of knowledge, literary, scientific and theological, as also of that various and more general acquirement which gives completeness to the highly cultivated mind. He was taken under the care of the Newcastle Presbytery, April 29, 1789; and, having passed, with great credit, through the several trials assigned him, he was licensed by that Presbytery, on the 8th of April, 1790, as a candidate for the Gospel ministry. On the 6th of October following, he was appointed

* NATHANIEL WELSHARD SAMPLE was born at Peach Bottom, York County, Pa., in 1752. His grandparents came from Ireland, and settled in the place where he was born. He pursued his academical studies under the direction of the Rev. Robert Smith of Pequea, and graduated at Princeton in 1776. He studied Theology under the Rev. Mr. Foster, of Upper Octorora, and was licensed to preach by the Newcastle Presbytery in 1779. Having supplied the Church at St. George's, De., for six months, and declined an invitation to become its Pastor, he accepted a call from the Church in Leacock, in connection with that of Lancaster and Middle Octorora. His pastoral relation to these Churches continued forty years, and was dissolved by Presbytery, September 26, 1821. He died at Strasburg, Pa., August 26, 1834, aged eighty-three years.

stated supply to the Churches of West Nottingham and Little Britain. In this service he continued more than six months, and received a call from those Congregations to become their Pastor. This, after mature consideration, he declined. In his probationary visitation and preaching to the Churches, he accepted an invitation to preach to the Congregations of Lower Marsh Creek and Toms Creek, in the Carlisle Presbytery. They had recently become vacant by the transfer of the Rev. John McKnight, their late Pastor, to the Collegiate Presbyterian Churches in the city of New York. Mr. Paxton's services were so acceptable to those vacant congregations, that they promptly and unanimously gave him a call to become their Pastor. It is no slender proof of his promising character and talents, that he was chosen by that respectable and intelligent people, as the successor of one who was so deservedly popular in the churches generally, and who stood so high in the esteem and affections of the Congregation which had most reluctantly parted with him. Mr. Paxton accepted their call on the 4th of April, 1792, and was accordingly dismissed from the Presbytery of Newcastle, to put himself under the care of the Presbytery of Carlisle. This took effect on the 7th of June, 1792; and on the 3d of October following, he was, by that Presbytery, ordained to the work of the Gospel ministry, and installed as Pastor of the Churches of Lower Marsh Creek and Toms Creek.

On the 20th of January, 1794, he was united in marriage with Miss Jane Dunlop, daughter of Col. James Dunlop, then residing near Shippensburg, Cumberland County, Pa. This family was among the most respectable in that community; and she who became his wife was to him a most valuable acquisition. She was, by her piety, intelligence, and other important accomplishments, eminently adapted to be a pastor's wife, and to conciliate the favour and respect of those with whom she was thus associated. In the knowledge of domestic and all like matters, having been well trained, she proved to be a very efficient auxiliary in making the most of a small salary for the support and comfort of her family, and for the numerous demands made upon the hospitality of her home by many visitors. She still survives, greatly honoured and beloved.

To the united congregations composing his charge, he ministered with great acceptance and usefulness for several years, until Lower Marsh Creek Congregation became desirous to have his entire pastoral labours. To this Toms Creek submitted with deep regret; and from that time until the resignation of his charge, a few years before his death, his labours were devoted to Marsh Creek alone. I may well say—*devoted*; for I think I have known no pastor whose labours among his people were so continuous and uninterrupted as his. Very rarely was he absent from the public duties of the Sabbath, unless to assist a brother in the administration of the Lord's Supper, and in one or two instances, when, by sickness, he was, for a short time, unable to render his ordinary services. Although afflicted often by a chronic bilious diarrhœa, yet he possessed such a degree of general health as made him competent to fulfil with great punctuality his various labours, through an unusually long term of ministerial service, amounting to fifty-three years. Of Marsh Creek Congregation he was Pastor forty-nine years; and he continued to supply them occasionally, until they obtained their present pastor, so that it may be said that that Church was favoured with his ministerial services for more than half a century. His ministrations were always characterized by decided ability and great faithfulness. By his congregation they were highly appreciated, and their attachment to, and estimation of, him suffered no abatement. To relinquish him as their Pastor was very unwelcome, even when his bodily infirmities rendered it not only expedient but absolutely necessary.

In 1826, the degree of Doctor of Divinity was conferred upon him by Dickinson College.

In person, Dr. Paxton was large,—six feet in height, and the whole frame in due proportion,—full, but not corpulent. His features, without much of what is usually denominated beauty, were open, regular, well developed, and expressive of benignity and intelligence. His mind was strong, vigorous and well balanced. Each faculty seemed to have its appropriate development. Warmth of affection, a delicate sensibility, and chaste imagination, were associated with uncommon power of discrimination, and a talent for profound research. None were less disposed than he to rest contented with an undefined and superficial knowledge of things. On metaphysical subjects he was thoroughly at home, though he rarely introduced any thing of this kind into the pulpit. He was, however, fond of holding philosophical discussions, and he often had the opportunity of doing so, with the Rev. John Black,* Pastor of an adjoining congregation, in whom he found a kindred spirit, and who was a man of much more than ordinary intellect.

Dr. Paxton possessed a high degree of critical talent, which he employed in the composition of his sermons, not for literary display, but to ascertain and present to his hearers the precise import of the passage that formed the theme of his discourse.

As a preacher, he was highly interesting and acceptable. His visits to neighbouring churches were always specially welcome. His sermons were distinguished for appropriate and well digested thought, natural and lucid arrangement, and thorough discussion. Far from being dry and merely intellectual, they were lively and impressive; and a well regulated imagination often added force and beauty to his scriptural illustrations. His habits, which were intensely studious, enabled him to bring forth from his treasures, in due season, " things new and old." In preparation for his public services he was conscientiously careful and punctual. His own good sense and piety, a practical conviction of what he owed to his people, the awful importance of the cause to which he was consecrated, with the

* John Black was a native of South Carolina, and was graduated at the College of New Jersey in September, 1771, having entered the Junior class half advanced, in May of the preceding year. He was licensed to preach by the Presbytery of Donegal, October 14, 1773, and on the 22d of June, 1774, a call was presented to the Presbytery for his ministerial labours from the Congregation of Upper Marsh Creek in York County. Having accepted this call, he was ordained and installed the Pastor of that Church, August 15, 1775. In 1786, he, with others, was set off to form the Presbytery of Carlisle. In consequence of some difficulties in his congregation, he applied to the Presbytery on the 10th of April, 1792, to have the pastoral relation dissolved. Some arrangement, however, subsequently took place, which led him to withdraw his application. But on the 5th of December, 1793, he renewed the request, and was accordingly released from his charge on the 10th of April, 1794. From this time till 1800, he exercised his ministry chiefly in a Reformed Dutch Congregation, near Hunterstown, in Adams County. On the 9th of October, 1800, he obtained a dismission from Carlisle Presbytery, to connect himself with the Presbytery of Redstone; and he afterwards became a stated supply to the Congregations of Unity and Greensburg, in which relation he continued until April 22, 1802, when he declined serving them any longer, and obtained leave to travel within the bounds of the Presbytery. He died August 16, 1802, in the exercise of a triumphant faith. He possessed a high order of talent, and was especially fond of philosophical disquisitions. He published a Discourse on Psalmody, in reply to the Rev. Dr. John Anderson of the Associate Church.

corresponding responsibilities, did not allow him to serve God and his Church with that which cost him little or nothing. His duty had his heart, his time, and his best efforts; and it was not strange that he was held by his people in almost unrivalled estimation. His manner of preaching was what is usually denominated *extempore;* but the matter was the result of mature thought and exact preparation. His method was, after having selected and thoroughly examined his subject, to reduce it to a pretty full outline, occupying usually a folded sheet of letter paper. This, by careful meditation, he thoroughly possessed himself of, and thus was able to present it to his hearers with accuracy and fulness. I am not aware that he ever used, in the delivery of his sermons from the pulpit, even this summary outline. In manner, he was solemn, dignified, commanding, graceful, without any theatric effort, and with only those gestures to which his feelings naturally prompted him.

As a pastor, he was affectionate and faithful. In the exercise of church discipline, he was strict and conscientious, yet considerate and wise. A bodily affliction already referred to, rendered his family visitations less frequent than his own wishes and those of his charge would have made them; but still they were performed in good season and measure.

His habits were more than ordinarily domestic. This resulted partly from love of retirement and study, partly from peculiar affection for his family, and partly also from the physical malady before mentioned, which required indispensably a strict regard to diet, and great regularity in all his habits. This was a reason why he felt obliged to deny himself, for the most part, an attendance upon the higher judicatories of the Church. Very few whose presence, counsels, and influence were so desirable, were present so seldom at the meetings of Synod; and with the General Assembly I believe he never met more than once or twice. But he was eminently social in his disposition, and was fond of the society of his brethren; and no one could enjoy the hospitalities of his house for ever so brief a period, without having the visit associated with many agreeable recollections.

As a husband and a father he was peculiarly affectionate. Some thought that he carried this to excess, especially as respected his children in their earlier years; but if so, still, under the favour of God, there was a controlling propitious influence, which gave the parents the elevated gratification of seeing their children, in mature life, sober-minded, prudent, honourable, and respected members of the Christian Church. Of those who lived to maturity there were four,—two sons and two daughters. The daughters early formed honourable matrimonial alliances, and had children, of whom I have no special knowledge. It pleased a sovereign God to remove both those daughters by death, before they had seen the midday of life. Of the sons, the elder only, Col. James D. Paxton, now survives, and he alone survived their common father. He is a highly honourable and respected gentleman, living in Adams County, Pa. The younger son early commenced a literary course, and, after due preparation, became an eminent physician, distinguished for his piety, as well as his professional skill. Many years since, his labours on earth terminated. He left a widow,—a lady highly respectable, and one son,—an educated youth of very fair promise, now a student of law.

Dr. Paxton was an eminently modest man, and little disposed to seek that distinction to which he might have attained, and which they who were most competent to judge, thought he deserved. As an illustration of this, I may mention his unwillingness to publish any of his sermons, or other literary productions. That such publications would have been honourable to himself, and a benefit to the world, no one doubts who knew him: yet I know not that he ever yielded to the wishes of his friends in this respect in a single instance. But his memory is deeply and affectionately embalmed in many pious hearts, and not least in those of his fellow-labourers, who were favoured to enjoy his society and friendship, and to hear him converse and preach in his own peculiarly interesting and striking manner. After an unusually long and faithful ministry, being enfeebled by age, and especially by a severe injury occasioned by a fall, he resigned his pastoral charge, between whom and himself there had always existed a strong affection. This took place on the 19th of October, 1841. His few remaining years were attended by considerable affliction, but cheered by the consolations of the Gospel, and an unabated desire to do good. He suffered much from a severe rheumatic affection; his eyesight became dim, which deprived him of one of his greatest pleasures: he enjoyed very much hearing others read his favourite authors, but the Holy Scriptures were his chief delight. He took great pleasure in explaining and commenting on the sacred text. His conversations and lectures on religious subjects were as beautiful, and lucid and methodical, as in his best days; and, to the last, his greatest delight was to instruct those around him, and recommend the religion of Jesus, and persuade them to embrace that Saviour, whom he had found so precious in his long pilgrimage. Although for some time unable to leave his arm-chair, he attended regularly to family worship, morning and evening, to the last day of his life. He retired at night feeling weaker than usual; he slept, but about the middle of the night, a person who was sleeping in the room to take care of him, was awakened by a slight noise or movement: he went immediately to his bedside, but found him unable to speak. The family were summoned; he remained speechless without pain for two days; and then passed away so quietly that some persons in the same room knew not that death had entered there, and that a "freed spirit had winged its flight to Heaven." This was on the 16th of April, 1845, and in the eighty-sixth year of his age. A few months before his death, I saw and conversed with him for a short time. His manly form was sadly changed, and his mind, especially his memory, had lost much of its former vigour; but still he was majestic even in ruin. The sky, though clouded, yet by occasional openings, still revealed the attributes of a superior mind, and the workings of a vigorous and elevated faith.

With great and affectionate regard, yours,

DAVID McCONAUGHY.

ROBERT CATHCART, D. D.

1790—1849.

FROM THE REV. DANIEL H. EMERSON.

York, January 18, 1850.

Rev. and dear Sir: I knew Dr. Cathcart as intimately as any son can know a father. I visited him every week during nearly five years, unless prevented by sickness; and, with the best opportunities for becoming acquainted with his character, my deliberate judgment is that he was among the purest and best of our American clergymen. His portrait hangs before me in the parsonage which I occupy,—a parsonage which his personal influence, foresight, and energy, erected; and as I gaze upon the calm majesty of that face and form, I recognise in it those noble qualities which, through Divine grace, rendered him so useful here, and which, I doubt not, are matured into qualities still more exalted in a better world.

Robert Cathcart, a son of Alexander and Mary Cathcart, was born in November, 1759, in the County of Londonderry, near the town of Coleraine, Ireland, where he studied with diligence, and laid the foundation of that accurate classical and general knowledge, for which he was, through life, distinguished. He afterwards attended the College of Glasgow for three sessions, in different years, and was there engaged in studying the sciences and Divinity. He was licensed to preach the Gospel by the Presbytery of Route, and laboured for several years within their bounds; during which he preached for every minister of that Body, all of whom he knew intimately, and all of whom died before him. He came to the United States in 1790, and was cordially received by the Presbytery of Philadelphia. It was but the year before, (1789,) that the first meeting of the General Assembly was held; and the fathers of that Assembly were the prominent men of the Presbytery of Philadelphia. They immediately took this stranger by the hand, welcomed him to their field of labour, introduced him to their churches, and appointed him to preach in their vacant congregations; and never did he forget this kindness, or lose his feelings of regard for these his early friends. While a member of the Presbytery of Philadelphia, he received a call to settle at Cape May, which, however, he declined, on account of the supposed unhealthiness of the situation. He subsequently accepted a call from the united Churches of York and Hopewell, and in October, 1793, was ordained and installed Pastor of the two Congregations, by the Presbytery of Carlisle.

Dr. Cathcart retained his connection with the Hopewell Congregation, until 1835,—a period of forty-two years, when, on account of his increasing infirmities, he resigned that part of his charge. The Hopewell Congregation was fifteen miles distant from York,—the Doctor's residence; and he preached in York and Hopewell on alternate Sabbaths; and it is quite remarkable that he was able to fulfil his appointments every Sabbath save one, for forty-two years. He retained his connection with the Church in York till 1839.

In Hopewell he was in the habit of visiting every family in his congregation one year, and catechising old and young the next; and this he continued to do for many years. He was also accustomed to lecture to both his congregations; and in the course of his ministry, he went through the whole of the book of Psalms, one or more of the Gospels, the whole of the Epistle to the Romans, the Epistle to the Hebrews, and parts of several of the other Epistles. This he considered as the most profitable mode of instructing the people in all the doctrines of the Scriptures; and he was surprised that, although so reasonable in itself, and so often recommended by the General Assembly, it was so little practised by the ministers of this land. His plan of catechetical instruction was introduced among his people in York also, and in both places was followed with equally favourable results.

Dr. Cathcart pursued his labours with unwearied diligence till the waning of his physical faculties obliged him to desist. For the last year or two of his life, he was confined to his house, and for a few of the last weeks, to his bed. For a year or more he suffered greatly from a singular sensation in his head, as if the most terrible storm were spending its violence there; and yet he was never heard to complain. The day before his death, it was remarked by one of his family that he was unusually well; and but a few moments before that event, he was conversing with his usual cheerfulness and vivacity, when suddenly he spoke to his daughter; and, on hastening to him, she found he was not, for God had taken him. Thus he died without a struggle, on the evening of the 19th of October, 1849, at the advanced age ot ninety years.

Dr. Cathcart was married in 1796 to Susannah Latimer of the State of Delaware. They had seven children, five of whom (two daughters and three sons) survived him. One of his sons practised medicine, the other two engaged in mercantile pursuits. Mrs. Cathcart died in the year 1810.

Dr. Cathcart was remarkable for his strict attention to business—his regularity and punctuality in the discharge of his duties. In describing his punctuality, one of his friends has remarked,—"He was as regular as the sun in the heavens: when the clock struck the hour of an appointment, we were certain the Doctor was there." And often has he been heard to say, when others failed of their appointments,—"Punctuality, if not a Christian grace, is certainly a great moral virtue." His punctuality was manifested in nothing more strikingly than in his attendance on all the judicatories of the Church. For more than forty years, he was but once absent from the meeting of the Synod of Philadelphia, and that was occasioned by sickness. He attended the meetings of the General Assembly, as a Commissioner from his Presbytery, for nearly thirty years in succession, and was one of its Clerks for nearly twenty; and so uniformly was he present in the Assembly, that his early friend, Dr. Green, pleasantly remarked to him,—"Brother Cathcart, you are always here; your Presbytery must have elected you as their *standing representative.*"

While a member of the General Assembly, he was sent as a delegate to the General Association of Connecticut, with which Body he was greatly delighted. He admired the simplicity of its forms, the spirituality of its exercises, the brotherly love prevailing among its members; and thought that some of the usages of the ecclesiastical bodies in New England might be beneficially adopted by the lovers of Presbyterianism. During this visit, he formed a friendly acquaintance with Dr. Dwight, and others, of which he ever afterwards spoke with great interest.

The degree of Doctor of Divinity was conferred upon him, in 1816, by Queens College, New Brunswick, N. J. He was a Trustee of Dickinson College, Carlisle, for thirty years, and attended all their Commencements during that period. About the year 1808, he obtained from Dickinson College the degree of Doctor of Divinity for the Rev. Thomas Scott, the author of the Commentary on the Scriptures, and for two or three other clergymen of acknowledged merit in Great Britain. The great modesty of Mr. Scott would not permit him to use this title, in connection with any of his works, and, accordingly, it is not recognised in the early English editions of his Commentary. On the second day after he received Dr. Cathcart's letter, informing him of the honour conferred on him by his friends in America, he wrote him a most interesting reply of seven or eight pages; in which he begs Dr. Cathcart to present his Christian respects to all those who had concurred with him in procuring the diploma; but adds that he is not certain whether he can with propriety make use of it, as this might appear presumption in one who was never educated at any College, except that of *St. David*, who, in following his flocks, sought after wisdom. In the diploma, he was designated as "Chaplain of the Lock Hospital;"—concerning which he observes,—"My brethren in America mistake my present situation. It is true I was Chaplain of the Lock Hospital for nearly eighteen years; but my plain, uncommonly plain, manner of preaching prevented me from being useful there, and I now preach in one of the smallest churches in England; but when the weather is good, the church is full and overflowing; and I have here a better opportunity of *attempting* to do good, than when in the city of London."

Dr. Cathcart was a great admirer of Scott, and agreed with him substantially in his theological views. He was in the habit of daily reading at least two chapters in the Bible in connection with Scott's Commentary; and not unfrequently he read many chapters in a day, with all the notes and observations. "Thus," he said,—"I lay a good foundation each morning, in the word of God, and I can then go on and build upon this foundation all the general reading I please." His reading, particularly for the last twelve years of his life, during which he had not the labour of a pastoral charge, was immense. Having a strong constitution, unimpaired eyesight, an insatiable thirst for knowledge, and a wonderfully retentive memory, he would read every thing valuable within his reach, and would delight his friends with the stores of information which he would pour forth, during a social interview. This habit of reading and of constantly exercising his mental powers continued to the last moment of life, and afforded him amusement during a confinement which, to many, would have seemed intolerable.

As a preacher, Dr. Cathcart was commonly didactic, and to a great extent doctrinal. He generally preached to his Hopewell Congregation without a manuscript; and in the same manner frequently preached, when occupying the pulpits of his brethren in Philadelphia and elsewhere. During the meeting of the Assembly at Philadelphia, he always preached once for the Rev. Dr. Wilson; and his form is vividly remembered by those who were children there thirty or forty years ago. At this season, he enjoyed fraternal counsel with such men as Nisbet, Wilson, Green, Rodgers, Milledoler, and McKnight; and from these delightful interviews he always returned with a gladdened spirit, to cheer his flock with the intelligence he had collected respecting the progress of the Kingdom of the Redeemer.

One subject that gave him no little annoyance was the exceeding ease with which the pastoral relation was broken up in this country. "Why,— in Ireland," he would often say, "the pastoral relation is considered as sacred and binding as the marriage relation." And on this subject he sometimes quoted a remark of the celebrated and witty Dr. Nisbet. Dr. Cathcart had expressed the hope that the situation of some young minister would now be a permanent one. "Permanent, Sir," exclaimed Dr. Nisbet, "let me tell you, Sir, there is nothing permanent in this country but *revolution!*" To the credit of Dr. Cathcart, however, it may be said that the idea of permanency in the pastoral relation was fully realized in his own case; for he retained the pastoral charge of the Hopewell Church forty-two years, and that of the Church in York, forty-four. He resigned his latter charge in 1837. But after that, he occasionally preached, and frequently took part in the services of the sanctuary, especially on sacramental occasions.

Dr. Cathcart published a Sermon on the death of the Rev. Dr. Davidson, 1812.

Dr. Cathcart was remarkable for a truly philanthropic spirit. To the various benevolent Societies of the day, he contributed with alacrity and liberality. In the Temperance reformation, as soon as convinced of its utility, he took an active part, and was among the first of the older citizens of the community in which he lived, to take a high stand on this subject, and to maintain it in all situations. He was distinguished also for his public spirit, for his zeal in the cause of education, and his active co-operation in all measures which had a tendency to benefit his fellow-citizens. His interest in the young continued to the last; and when it might have been supposed that almost a hundred winters would have chilled the current of genial feeling, it was delightful still to find the greenness of youth beneath the snows of age, and the freshness of boyhood mingling with his maturity of experience and wisdom.

I remain yours in the Gospel,

DANIEL H. EMERSON.

WILLIAM HILL, D. D.*

1790—1852.

William Hill, the son of Joseph and Joanna (Read) Hill, was born in Cumberland County, Va., on the 3d of March, 1769. His ancestors were from England. He lost his father when he was five years old; and, after the lapse of a few years, his mother gave him a stepfather in Mr. Daniel Allen, father of the Rev. Carey Allen,† and an elder in the Presbyterian Church in Cumberland County, at that time under the pastoral care of the Rev. (afterwards Dr.) Samuel Stanhope Smith. At the age of eleven, he lost his mother, who seems to have been a devout and exemplary Christian, and to have made impressions upon the mind of her son in favour of a religious life, that had a powerful influence in ultimately determining his character. One year previous to this, he was placed under the tuition of Mr. (afterwards Rev.) Drury Lacy, who, for three years, was employed by Mr. Allen as a teacher in his family. After his mother's death, he was placed under the guardianship of one who cared little for religion, and under whose influence he soon lost his serious impressions, and became absorbed, to a great extent, in the pleasures of fashionable life.

This habit of carelessness, however, was not destined to be of long continuance. In 1785, he entered Hampden Sidney College, then under the Presidency of the Rev. John Blair Smith. So low was the state of religion in the College at that time, that there was not a student who evinced any regard for it, nor one who was known to possess a Bible. During the early part of his collegiate course, he endeavoured to banish all thoughts of religion, and indulged freely in the vices common to his ungodly associates; but even then he had his moments of reflection, when he was haunted by the remembrance of his mother's counsels and prayers. Nearly two years elapsed, after he entered College, before his character seemed to undergo a

* MS. from Dr. Hill.—Presb. Quart. Rev., 1853.—Foote's Sketches of Va., 2d. Series.

† Carey Allen was born in Cumberland County, Va., in April, 1767. In early life, and through life, he was remarkable for a kindly disposition, and a great propensity to drollery, without seeming to be aware of it. At the age of about seventeen, immediately after his recovery from a violent attack of typhus fever, which was supposed to have so far crippled his constitution as to render him unfit for active labour, he commenced a course of study at Hampden Sidney, with a view to enter one of the professions. While at home during a vacation in the autumn of 1787, the Rev. Hope Hull, a distinguished Methodist clergyman, preached in the neighbourhood with great power, and young Allen became so deeply affected by the discourse that he actually fell prostrate on the floor. Before he rose upon his feet, he believed that he yielded up the rebellion of his heart, and became a new creature in Christ Jesus. In January, 1789, he was received by the Hanover Presbytery as a candidate for the Gospel ministry, and after going through one unsuccessful examination before the Presbytery, was examined a second time, and licensed to preach on the 8th of May, 1790. He passed the succeeding summer as a missionary in the counties along the Carolina line. In 1791, he engaged in another mission, under the direction of the Commission of Synod, in that part of Virginia which is now embraced in the State of Kentucky,—an exceedingly difficult and hazardous, but not unsuccessful, enterprise. On the 21st of April, 1792, a call was made out for him by a small congregation consisting of families who had settled on Silver Creek and Paint Creek,—from Virginia. Immediately after this, he returned to Virginia, but soon went back to Kentucky, and resumed his work as a missionary. In the autumn of 1793, we find him in Virginia again, attending a meeting of Presbytery; but in the spring of 1794, he made a final remove to Kentucky. On the 11th of October following, he was ordained and installed Pastor of the Churches of Silver Creek and Paint Creek, after he had kept the call in his hands two years. Shortly after his settlement, he took a severe cold, in consequence of preaching in a crowded room, which brought on a consumption of which he died on the 5th of August, 1795, at the early age of twenty-eight. With great natural eccentricity he combined a large measure of Christian benevolence, and a glowing zeal in his Master s cause.

radical change. After his mind had, for some time, been turned inward upon itself in silent and anxious thought, he retired to a secluded spot, where he gave vent to the agony of his spirit in earnest cries for the Divine mercy, and was enabled, as he believed, to devote himself without reserve to the service of God. Shortly after, two or three other young men connected with the College experienced a similar change of views and feelings, and associated themselves with him in a private devotional service, which, as it became known, excited the most bitter opposition from their fellow students, and even drew forth threats of vengeance, unless it were discontinued. This brought the matter to the ears of the President, who assured them not only that they should be protected in their rights, but that they should have the privilege of holding their meeting in his parlour, and that he would himself be present and assist in conducting it. A revival of religion now commenced, which soon included among its subjects half of the students in College. One of the most remarkable cases of hopeful conversion was that of Nash Legrand,* then a resident graduate, who passed from a state of absolute profligacy to a joyful confidence in the Saviour, and ultimately to a highly respectable standing in the ministry of the Gospel. The revival extended into neighbouring churches, and then into those which were more remote, and was more extensive and powerful than had been experienced in Virginia since the days of President Davies.

It was during the summer of 1787 that young Hill made a public profession of religion. He graduated at Hampden Sidney College in 1788; and shortly after commenced the study of Theology under the direction of President Smith. He was licensed to preach the Gospel by the Presbytery of Hanover, July 10, 1790. For the two years immediately succeeding his licensure, he acted as a missionary, under the commission of Synod, in the lower counties of Virginia, as far down as the Chesapeake Bay, and through the upper counties to the Blue Ridge, from Tennessee to Maryland, and especially in the counties in the lower part of the Valley.

In October, 1792, Mr. Hill was married to Nancy, daughter of Colonel William Morton, of Charlotte County, Va. They lived together sixty-one years,—Mrs. Hill having died on the 26th of May, 1851. They had two children,—both of them daughters.

Immediately after his licensure, Mr. Hill was invited to take charge of the congregations which had been under the care of President Smith; but he declined their call, and, after acting for two years as a missionary, settled

* NASH LEGRAND was a descendant of Huguenots who settled upon James River, at Manakin town, a few miles above Richmond, the latter part of the seventeenth century. His father, Peter Legrand, removed to Prince Edward County, and settled within two miles of Hampden Sidney College. His mother was sister to Colonel John Nash of Prince Edward County, and was distinguished alike for her accomplishments and piety. When the revival commenced in Hampden Sidney College, young Legrand was prosecuting his studies preparatory to the practice of medicine; but the change which then took place in his character gave a new direction also to the purposes of his life. Laying aside his medical books, he commenced the study of Theology under the direction of Dr. Smith, and on the 25th of April, 1789, he was licensed by the Hanover Presbytery to preach the Gospel. In April, 1790, he was appointed a missionary by the Commission of Synod, and laboured in that capacity very successfully from June till October, in seven or eight different counties in Virginia. In the autumn of that year, he commenced his labours in the Congregations of Cedar Creek and Opekon, where he continued an eminently devoted pastor for more than eighteen years. He finally resigned his charge on account of bodily infirmities; and returned to his native county (Prince Edward); but subsequently supplied vacant congregations till the autumn of 1814, when, being on a visit to Frederick County, he was attacked with an illness which quickly prostrated him, and he died in the month of October, at the age of forty-six. He was a zealous, popular, and uncommonly successful, preacher.

in Berkeley, now Jefferson County, Va. His stated field of labour was indeed missionary ground; and though his labours here were prosecuted amidst many discouragements, they were marked by great vigour and boldness, and were followed by highly important results. He had now acquired a high reputation as a commanding and effective pulpit orator; as an evidence of which may be mentioned the fact that he was appointed to deliver a Funeral Oration at Harper's Ferry, in commemoration of Washington,—a service which he performed to the great satisfaction and admiration of an immense auditory.

In January, 1800, Mr. Hill left his residence in Jefferson County, and took charge of the Presbyterian Church in Winchester. Though the call was unanimous, there were some subjects of interest upon which the people were by no means agreed among themselves; and though this rendered the position of the pastor a difficult one, he was enabled to adhere to his own convictions, without forfeiting the good-will of any party. Here his influence was widely and powerfully felt. His great strength of purpose, vigour of thought, and energy of utterance, gave him an advantage, both at home and abroad, over most of the preachers of his day. Among those who made a profession of religion under his ministry was Major General Morgan of Revolutionary memory, who not only regarded Mr. Hill as the instrument of his conversion, but was greatly comforted by his counsels and prayers in his last hours.

In 1816, the honorary degree of Doctor of Divinity was conferred upon him by Dartmouth *University*. Some of his brethren used jocosely to tell him that his title to D. D. was not valid, because the Institution that gave it had no legal existence, and subsequently died by a decree of Court.

In February, 1834, Dr. Hill accepted a call to the Briery Presbyterian Church, in Prince Edward County. Here he remained two years, and then resigned his charge, and became Pastor of the Second Presbyterian Church in Alexandria, as successor to the Rev. William C. Walton.* After two years more, he found himself becoming disqualified for active labour, by the infirmities of age, and therefore resigned his pastorship, and returned to Winchester to pass the residue of his life among those who had for many years enjoyed the full vigour of his ministry.

During his residence in Alexandria, and for two years after his return to Winchester, Dr. Hill was engaged in writing a History of the Presbyterian Church in the United States, designed to have been published in two octavo volumes. Owing, however, to circumstances connected with the disruption

* William C. Walton was born in Hanover County, Va., on the 4th of November, 1793. His father died an early victim to intemperance; and the youthful days of the son were passed under circumstances most unfavourable to the formation of religious character. In his eighteenth year, he went to reside in the family of a Presbyterian elder in Winchester, and shortly after had his mind earnestly directed to the subject of religion by a sermon which he heard from a Methodist preacher. After a short season of bitter remorse and fearful conflict, he believed that he made a sincere dedication of himself to God through Christ, and soon after became a member of the Presbyterian Church. He felt almost immediately a strong impulse towards the Gospel ministry, and his Pastor, the Rev. Dr. Hill, proposed to him that he should be educated with reference to it, by the Presbytery of Winchester. Accordingly, in the autumn of 1811 he repaired, under the direction of Presbytery, to Hampden Sidney College. On the 22d of October, 1814, he was licensed to preach the Gospel, though he was still a student at Hampden Sidney, and remained there a considerable time afterwards. After preaching for some time to the Congregations of Smithfield and Berryville, on the 25th of April, 1818, he was ordained by the Presbytery to the work of the Gospel ministry, and on the 6th of May was installed Pastor of the Presbyterian Church in Hopewell. Early in 1823, he accepted a call to the Third Presbyterian Church in Baltimore, where he remained about eighteen months, and then returned to Virginia. After labouring in various places, and suffering almost constantly

of the Church, he was diverted from his purpose, and determined to publish his work in Numbers; but a single Number only was ever issued, and *that* took its complexion very much from the then existing controversy. In the great contest that issued in the division of the Church, Dr. Hill's judgment, sympathies, and acts, were fully with the New School; and a message that he sent to the Synod a few days before his death, showed that his mind underwent no change on the subject to the last.

For eight years immediately preceding his death, Dr. Hill was chiefly engaged in reading his favourite authors, and in writing sketches of the lives of some of his early associates. He was much in the habit of conversing on personal religion, and seemed to live to a great extent amidst invisible realities. A few months before his death, he suffered a severe attack of illness, which he regarded as the probable harbinger of his release. Though he recovered partially from it, it was still evident that he was the subject of a gradual process of decay. Two weeks before his death, he was laid prostrate upon his bed. His mind immediately became unstrung, and never again recovered the power of connected thought; though there was that even in his delirium that showed the upward tendency of his spirit. He died on the 16th of November, 1852, in the eighty-fourth year of his age. His Funeral Sermon was preached by the Rev. A. H. H. Boyd, D. D.

Dr. Hill's publications are a Sermon on Confirmation; a Sermon on Ministerial Parity preached before the Synod of Virginia, 1819; a Missionary Journal from 1790 to 1792; and a work on American Presbyterianism; besides various contributions to periodicals.

FROM THE REV. WILLIAM N. SCOTT.

Luny's Creek, Hardy County, Va., January 30, 1855.

Rev. and dear Sir: I regret my inability to do justice to the subject upon which you have asked me to write. Although acquainted with Dr. Hill many years ago, and connected with him by marriage, still, for many years past, my intercourse with him and knowledge of him have been comparatively limited. Some thirty years since, I removed to a locality quite distant from him; and, as we took different sides in the division of the Church in 1837–38, our occasional intercourse was, in this way, interrupted—he meeting with one Presbytery and Synod, and I with other Bodies of the same order, we rarely got together. I will, however, cheerfully give you such information in respect to his person and character as my recollections supply.

Dr. Hill was a man of fine appearance and noble bearing. In size, he was considerably above mediocrity, and was inclined to corpulency. It was not

from bodily indisposition, he accepted a call in the spring of 1827 to the Second Presbyterian Church in Alexandria, and was installed as its Pastor on the 3d of July following. In August, 1832, he received an invitation to become the Pastor of the Free Church, in Hartford, Conn., and, having accepted it, removed thither in October, and entered at once his new field of labour, in which he continued until he went to his final rest. He was taken ill on the 20th of December, 1833, and, after a scene of Christian triumph, such as is rarely witnessed, died, on the 18th of February, 1834, aged forty-one years. The most prominent characteristic of his ministry seems to have been his unceasing direct efforts to promote revivals of religion, and the remarkable success by which they were attended; though it is understood that he adopted and pressed somewhat earnestly what were then called the "new measures." A very interesting Memoir of his life was published in 1837, by the Rev. Joshua Danforth, D. D., now the Pastor of the same Church in Alexandria of which Mr. Walton had the charge. He represents him as having been one of the most zealous and devoted of ministers. In a letter, he says of him, "He was gentle in temper, never denunciatory, remarkable for amenity of manners, opinions, life. He loved souls and the glory of God."

unusual to hear it observed that he would have made a noble general for an army, or admiral for a fleet. Indeed there was in the stern expression of his countenance, and the seeming austerity of his brow, when excited by his subject, something well calculated to awaken emotions of awe. In illustration of this, allow me to repeat an incident that occurred in my own house. Dr. Hill and his lady were in Martinsburg,—the place of my residence at that time. The Doctor had preached that day, but was called away afterwards, while his wife remained and dined at my house. It happened that a Mr. C., a worthy farmer from the neighbourhood, dined with us that day, and not knowing that the lady sitting with us at the table was Mrs. Hill, he began to give his opinion of the sermon to which we had been listening. He remarked that it was a very solemn and impressive discourse; "and yet, I confess," said he, "that the very looks of the man,—his fiery, piercing eye, and severe expression of countenance, destroy in a great measure the effect of his good sermons on my mind." Seeing that Mrs. Hill was as much amused as any of us, I turned to my friend, the farmer, and said,—"My dear Sir, you are a little too severe in your criticism, considering that the wife of Dr. Hill is sitting here with us at the table." The man seemed quite astounded, and his lips were sealed; but Mrs. Hill kindly relieved him by remarking that Mr. C. was not to blame for his impressions, and that more than once, similar remarks had been made by others in her presence, who knew the relation she sustained to the Doctor. My friend told me, many years after, that the incident was of great use to him, having taught him to be more cautious in his remarks upon the absent.

But, though such was the outward appearance of the man, especially when under the influence of mental excitement, still there were few more highly gifted with the social graces, and real pleasantry and suavity of manners. He had a general cheerfulness about him, which rendered him a highly agreeable companion.

His performances in the pulpit were of very various degrees of merit. Often, under favourable impulses, he would exhibit great pathos and power, and seem to rise quite above himself; and then he could enchain or melt his audience at pleasure; while, at other times, he would fall as far below himself, and seem to lose altogether the life and spirit of his theme. This latter sometimes happened in repeating the same sermon on a different occasion,—owing no doubt, partly at least, to the fluctuation of his animal feelings.

Dr. Hill never flinched from controversy, when he thought the occasion required him to engage in it. When he took his position, he generally held it with great firmness and tenacity. This trait he had often an opportunity of exhibiting in Presbyterial and Synodical discussions, and also in at least two paper controversies, which I now recollect,—in one of which his antagonist was of another denomination,—in the other, of a different profession.

I saw Dr. Hill once during his last illness. He was then, and had been for some time, confined to his room. Though much enfeebled, he was still cheerful in spirit, and lucid in intellect, and talked calmly and freely about the death of his wife and his own expected departure. It was but a few weeks after this that his earthly career was closed.

Respectfully and fraternally yours,

W. N. SCOTT.

FROM THE REV. A. H. H. BOYD, D. D.

WINCHESTER, Va., February 6, 1857.

Rev. and dear Sir: In complying with your request for my impressions of the character of Dr. Hill, it is proper I should say that I was most intimately associated with him for ten years previous to his death. Having served the

Church in various positions for a half century, he came to Winchester, the scene of his early labours in the ministry, to live and die among those whom he loved, and who would gladly minister to him during the closing period of his life. I shall confine myself to a brief expression of my views of his character, as based upon my daily intercourse with him.

Dr. Hill possessed an intellect of great clearness and vigour. No one need misunderstand him. His conceptions were strong and vivid, and his style of expression was terse and sententious. His active life, in the early part of his ministry, prevented that kind of mental discipline which results from severe study. His intellect was more remarkable for strength than for logical development. He grasped a subject with great energy. He sought to obtain large and comprehensive views of truth, rather than to indulge in vain speculations. His perceptions were quick, and his conclusions, which would prove to be correct, were often formed with great rapidity. He loved the truth, and hence, in his investigations, he brought his vigorous mind to contemplate it in its various relations, but not so to analyze it by metaphysical distinctions, as to lose sight of it in its moral bearings upon the human heart. His memory was remarkably retentive. His mind was capable of comprehending any subject to which it was directed; and, though his impatient nature would prompt him to forego the thorough investigation of subjects, step by step, in a logical form, he would nevertheless give such a degree of attention as was necessary to arrive at a right conclusion. His mind was well stored with first principles; and, therefore, making them the basis of his inquiries, he did not deem it indispensable, in order to ascertain the truth, to pursue with logical, metaphysical accuracy a subject in all its aspects.

Dr. Hill was a man of great firmness of purpose. When his judgment was convinced, he never wavered, unless new and powerful reasons were presented to him. He was not to be shaken from his purpose to pursue what he believed to be the right path, either by the flattery of friends or the threats of opponents. His mental constitution fitted him to be a leader rather than to be led. His indomitable will would never yield to the will of another through fear or favour. He must be fully persuaded of the propriety of the course recommended, before he would consent to change any plan of action upon which he had determined. It was his firmness and decision of character that occasionally impressed others with the idea that he was harsh and forbidding, when in truth his feelings may not have been excited in the slightest degree. He was often placed in a situation which called for a high degree of Christian decision. Had he lived in times of persecution, like Paul before Felix, or Luther before the Diet of Worms, he would have been unmoved by lordly power, or the threats of exalted wickedness.

His physical temperament was of a mercurial cast. He was ardent, fearless, and enthusiastic. This peculiarity of his constitution was known to himself as well as to others. It developed itself amid the conflicts of sentiment in Church and State, in different periods of his life, and, combined as it was with an inflexible will, it was sometimes the occasion of leading him to express his own convictions in a manner that would seem to evince unkindness of feeling. Such an inference, however, is by no means legitimate. Whilst, like other men, he was liable to excitement of temper, he was by nature magnanimous and kind. He lived a long life, passed through many scenes of excitement, came in contact with men of every class and character, and it would have been strange indeed, if, in the circumstances in which he was placed, his naturally excitable temperament had never been developed. He was ever ready to *defend* what he believed to be the truth. But I am not aware that he ever manifested a disposition unnecessarily to assail the views and persons of others. The grace of God had done much in softening the asperities of his natural constitution, so that, in the midst of high party excitement, he was enabled, in a great measure, to control a nature that otherwise might have been the source of deep mental disquietude. He had his faults—for he was a man. But they were the faults of that class who unite an ardent, excitable temperament with some of the most commanding virtues of humanity;—who, if, amid the vicissitudes and conflicts of life, they permit the waves of passion to obscure their vision, have imbedded in their moral nature the principles of right, and which, having a predominating control, will show themselves, sooner or later, in acts indicative of their heavenly origin.

As a friend, Dr. Hill was genial and pleasant. Those who had his confidence, found him one of the most agreeable companions. His conversation was instructive, and sometimes humorous. Undue familiarity he would not permit; but he delighted in a free and easy manner, and none who understood the proprieties of life need be restrained in his presence. Having been accustomed to mingle in all classes of society,—with the high and low, the rich and poor, he had a fund of anecdote which gave interest to his conversation. To his ministerial brethren particularly, his vivid narration of events and incidents connected with the history of distinguished men, both in Church and State, during the first part of this century, was always interesting and instructive. He loved the society of his brethren; and, after the infirmities of age interfered with his meeting them in the judicatories of the Church, and in protracted religious services, he was always gratified in receiving their visits. His social qualities were well adapted to enlist the affections of those in whom he reposed confidence.

As a preacher, Dr. Hill was clear, energetic and impressive. His power, as an extemporaneous preacher, was very remarkable. He had not the learning and the close, logical reasoning of Rice, nor the chaste and flowing style of Speece, nor the splendid imagination of Kirkpatrick. But there was a combination of excellencies in his preaching which made him a great favourite. His commanding person, his clear and powerful voice, the vividness of his conceptions, the directness and pungency of his appeals, and the deep earnestness visible in his countenance and manner of delivery, impressed his audience with the conviction that what he said was truth, and such truth as involved their most vital interests. He never aimed to please the fancy, or to gratify a fastidious taste. He sought to arouse the sleeping conscience, to melt the obdurate heart, and to save the undying soul. His illustrations were drawn chiefly from practical life, and they were, for the most part, so apt and striking, as to make a powerful impression upon his audience. He seldom wrote his sermons. Like most of his brethren in Virginia, he preached from brief notes. This habit was acquired in early life, partly from necessity, and partly because the state of society and public sentiment rendered it inexpedient to use a manuscript. His sentences were short and pithy; and when his soul was fired by his subject, he would throw out thoughts, that would fall upon the minds of his hearers with an almost irresistible power. Some of the most eloquent and impressive thoughts I have heard from the pulpit, were uttered by him when his mind was enkindled by his theme, and without any preparation. He loved to preach; and Christ and Him crucified constituted the great theme upon which he delighted to dwell.

As a member of the judicatories of the Church, Dr. Hill was conspicuous. He was regular in his attendance upon these convocations. His long experience had made him familiar with the rules of deliberative bodies. His powers as a debater were universally acknowledged. His advice was received with all the respect due to his talents, experience, and standing in the Church.

The piety of this venerated father was based upon fixed principles. It was neither the exuberance of animal passion, nor the heartlessness of a cold and formal sentimentalism. I have often heard him remark that he had not those ecstatic emotions, that intense and glowing rapture, which some experience. His religion was the religion of principle. He aimed to live according to the rule prescribed by his Divine Master. He loved the Scriptures of truth. During the last two years of his life, he read through the Bible with the Commentary of Dr. Scott. He had not the mildness of John, the beloved disciple, but he had, to a very great degree, the Christian fortitude of Paul and of recovered Peter. His sixty-six years of service in the cause of the Saviour were years of full devotion of both his intellect and heart to Him who redeemed him with His own blood.

It was my privilege to witness the closing scene of his life. For some years he had been anticipating death, and the grace of God was evidently preparing him for this event. On various occasions he expressed his entire confidence in the Saviour, and said, if it was God's will, he would prefer "to depart and be with Christ, which is far better." He was in a state of delirium for several days previous to his death, apparently unconscious of suffering. All power of connected thought was gone. And yet there was something in the character of that delirium which indicated his deep interest in spiritual things. Sometimes he spoke as if he was preaching that Gospel which he had proclaimed for sixty years. Then, again, he seemed to be transported to the portals of Heaven. Among other things, he said, "I hear music"—it seemed as if God was giving him a foretaste of the rich melody that would soon fall upon his ransomed spirit. He continued in this delirium until his soul was released from its clay tenement. His vigorous constitution resisted, with great tenacity, the assault of the ruthless destroyer. But it finally yielded the contest, and the oft-repeated wish of this venerable father was gratified—*his soul was at home with his Saviour.*

Yours fraternally,

A. H. H. BOYD.

LEWIS FEUILLETEAU WILSON.*

1791—1804.

LEWIS FEUILLETEAU WILSON was born at St. Christopher's, one of the West India Islands, in June, 1753. His father, a wealthy planter, wishing to give his sons a better education than the Island afforded, sent this son, then about four years old, and another who was two years older, to enjoy the better advantages that might be secured by a residence with their friends in London. The elder brother died on the voyage; but Lewis arrived safely, and was immediately put to school. Some time after, his father removed to London; and the son was continued at a grammar school until he completed his seventeenth year. At that time, an uncle of his migrated to America, and settled in New Jersey: young Wilson accompanied him, and soon after his arrival became a member of Princeton College.

He proved himself an excellent scholar during his college course, and was graduated with honour in 1773. His mind was first brought into sympathy with religious things, during a revival that took place in the College in 1772. At the commencement of the revival, he was disposed to keep himself aloof from every thing connected with it, and he even insulted one of the Tutors, who ventured to call his attention to his higher interests; but

* Dr. J. M. Wilson's Sermon occasioned by his death.—Foote's Sketches of N. C.

it was not long before he became a subject of the deepest anxiety. It was while listening to a sermon by the Rev. Dr. Spencer of Trenton, that he first awoke to a sense of his guilt and danger; and from that time he found no rest, till he found it in what he believed was a full and hearty submission to the terms of the Gospel. The opposition which he manifested to the revival, in its earlier stage, never ceased to be an occasion of lamentation and humiliation with him, as long as he lived.

A circumstance occurred in connection with his graduation, that was illustrative equally of his fine scholarship and his noble spirit. When the honours were distributed in his class by the Trustees of College, five were appointed to deliver orations, and the second oration fell to him. When the announcement was made by the President, he rose and made a most respectful and grateful acknowledgment of the honour that had been conferred upon him, but begged to decline it, and expressed a wish that it might be given to another. He was accordingly excused, and a person to whom he knew the appointment would be more acceptable, was substituted in his place.

After receiving his Bachelor's degree in September, 1773, he visited London, intending to take orders in the Established Church of England,—the Church in which he had been educated,—if he could see a reasonable prospect of comfort and usefulness. But not finding the National Church in such a state as he desired, he resolved to enter the ministry in connection with some other denomination, though his father, who was a man of large property, earnestly opposed it, and refused him all pecuniary aid. Having obtained possession of a bequest of three hundred guineas, left to him by an aunt, whose death had occurred a short time before, he furnished himself with a wardrobe and small library, and returned to America, after a residence in England of about five months.

Landing at Philadelphia, he went immediately to Princeton, and commenced the study of Divinity, under the direction of Dr. Witherspoon, in the spring of 1774. Soon after this, he was chosen Tutor in the College and held the office about one year. Being interrupted in his theological studies by the breaking up of the College, in consequence of the war of the Revolution, he was prevailed upon by a fellow-tutor to accompany him to Philadelphia, and to become associated with him in the study of medicine; and this resolution to change his professional studies is said to have been induced partly by some perplexity of mind—the nature of which is not known—into which he was thrown by the study of Church History.

After pursuing his medical studies about two years, he embarked in the cause of American Independence, and entered, as a Surgeon, the Continental army. In this capacity he continued several years,—being employed part of the time in the land service, and part of the time on board of vessels of war. In 1781, he was informed of the death of his father, and of his having left him a legacy of five hundred pounds sterling. In consequence of this, he made another visit to England; and, on his return to America, he settled as a practising physician in Princeton, N. J.

Mr. Wilson, amidst all the adverse circumstances attendant on his connection with the army, maintained an exemplary Christian deportment, not only discharging his various relative duties with great fidelity, but evidently living under an habitual impression of eternal realities. And now, having retired from the agitating scenes of military life, he gave himself, first of all, to a most careful and diligent study of the entire Scriptures. After being employed for a few years as a medical practitioner, and devoting much of his time to the direct culture of his Christian affections, he was induced, in the year 1786,—chiefly through the influence of the Rev. Mr. (afterwards Dr.) James Hall, who had formed a strong attachment to him in College,—to take up his residence in Iredell County, N. C., the scene of Mr. Hall's labours. Shortly after his removal thither, he became connected in marriage with Margaret, daughter of Hugh Hall, and a near relative of the friend by whose influence his removal to North Carolina had been effected.

Though Mr. Wilson rendered himself highly acceptable and useful in his new sphere, as a medical practitioner, he was not, nor had he been in preceding years, fully satisfied with himself for having abandoned the purpose of entering the ministry. Meanwhile, many of the good people around him, observing his excellent qualifications for the ministry, became urgent that he should change his profession, and direct his attention primarily to the maladies of the soul rather than those of the body; and some of the leading ministers in Orange County, among whom was his excellent and influential friend, Mr. Hall, very decidedly seconded this suggestion. After due deliberation on the subject, he determined to act in accordance with the judgment of his brethren, and he accordingly offered himself to the Orange Presbytery as a candidate for the Gospel ministry. Having passed his various trials with great credit, he was licensed to preach in the year 1791.

His efforts in the pulpit, from the first, were received with marked approbation; and, in a short time, several respectable congregations endeavoured to secure him as their pastor. He ultimately accepted a call from the Fourth Creek and Concord Churches; and in June, 1793, he was ordained to the work of the ministry and installed Pastor of those Churches. It was a peculiarly pleasant circumstance attending his settlement, that it brought him into the immediate vicinity of his friend, Mr. Hall, with whom he had long been in intimate and endeared relations. His connection with these two Churches continued about ten years with uninterrupted harmony.

Of Mr. Wilson's connection with the great Western and Southern Revival, which occurred about the commencement of this century, and of his views of the phenomena by which it was marked, some idea may be formed from the following extract of a letter to his intimate friend, the Rev. Dr. Ashbel Green, of Philadelphia, dated Iredell County, N. C., May 12, 1803:—

"In your letter you desire me to give you some account of the revival of religion. Several months have elapsed since your request, and I have no doubt but you have been particularly informed upon the subject. You must, notwithstanding this, allow me to narrate upon this subject, requesting that you will allow yourself to give me your candid thoughts upon what I shall relate.

"Fifteen or sixteen months ago, a number of us undertook a journey of eighty miles, in the most dreary part of the winter, to see religion in a new form. At that time, we had something among us that we called religion: the profession was general in our country, and I can, without hesitation, say that a number of us had the root of the matter in us; while, at the same time, we are now obliged to acknowledge that the wise and foolish virgins were shamefully slumbering and sleeping together. I can say, as to myself, that, although I was frequently rejoicing because I had been brought into the ministry of the Gospel, and flattered myself that I was making advances in holiness, there was much in me that needed reformation. Whilst I lamented the general decay of religion, I made no suitable effort to produce an alteration for the better. I continued to preach, but was under the influence of the same lukewarm spirit, which too generally pervaded our Southern Churches. In this state of mind, I received frequent accounts from the Transylvania country of a religion accompanied with all the unusual circumstances which you have often heard of. I reasoned upon them—I was able, in my apprehension, to account for them—I had no doubt but that the Spirit of God was among them; but, at the same time, was satisfied that there were enthusiastic extravagances, exceeding any thing I had ever heard of. In this state of mind, with these impressions, I went to Randolph, where I first got a view of it. The scene opened with an outcry from some hundreds at the same instant. The noise and confusion can neither be conceived nor described—you never can understand it till you see it. All my former reasonings were at once overturned. I found myself totally ignorant of that which, a few minutes before, I thought I could have explained to any reasonable mind. Astonishment seized me, and I sunk, in spirit, lower, if possible, than Bunyan's pilgrim, when in the middle of the slough of despond. In this state of mind, I spent the remainder of the day, the following night, and the succeeding day, when I was at last compelled, almost against my will, to receive it as a Divine work. The whole of this time,—two days and the intermediate night, I spent in going through the people, and examining their exercises. The circumstances which presented themselves were agitations of body, tremors, convulsions, suffocations, &c., which have no religion in them. Some were prostrate on the earth, crying for mercy—others shouting and exhibiting every demonstration of the most ecstatic religious joy; some exhorting sinners—others praying over those on the ground. My first object was to determine their sincerity,—to satisfy myself that there was no affectation in the business. I think there was none: if there was, I could not detect it. There was the greatest harmony between the language and the countenance. A circumstance pretty general with those who came through, as it is called, was a gloss, a splendour, a glory of countenance, a beauty in the human face, which I never before beheld. It is a something which, I suppose, will serve to give an idea of the shining of Stephen's face, when in the council. This splendour remains a longer or a shorter time, and is not, cannot be, dependant on the will of the creature. After satisfying myself with respect to the sincerity of those who were the subjects of the work, I reasoned with myself in the following way:—It is certainly possible for the Spirit of God to operate so powerfully upon the hearts of three thousand persons, as to compel them to speak aloud; in which case, all that is uttered will be according to the present state of mind of each individual. If we suppose this actually to take place in such a multitude at the same instant, those circumstances must take place which we have been attempting to detail. One prays under a sense of sin—another shouts with the apprehension of mercy. One, impressed with a view of the miserable case of sinners, exhorts all around him, and a fourth, under the same impression, makes his application to God in prayer. And that which appears at first view to be the most horrid confusion, will immediately become exact and necessary order. The objections against it are numerous. The most formidable comes from professors. The subjects of this extraordinary work, say they, are many of them incapable of giving any scriptural evidence of a saving change. In answer to this, I say, he that endures to the end shall be saved. It is to be feared that, among the stony ground hearers, we may be obliged hereafter to number some who, in our estimation, have given a satisfactory account of a work of grace upon their hearts. I believe there is a turning about time to every soul that is truly converted. Those who have had an opportunity of religious instruction, and have improved it, are sometimes able to tell a pretty consistent story; but as for those who were both ignorant and profane, what are we to expect from them at such a time, more than a general sense of sin, and general apprehension of mercy through the Redeemer? As to myself, I can say that if I was ever born to Jesus Christ, it was at College. When I first turned from sin to God, my mind was a perfect blank as to religious knowledge, and had I been obliged to undergo a critical examination, I could not have given a scriptural evidence of a saving change. I was ignorance itself. I could have told you what I had felt, and that I was determined to follow the Redeemer in the regeneration.

"The effect of the revival in our churches is truly astonishing. Although it appears to be remarkably owned by God, our churches are tending to dissolution—hardly a congregation where it has taken place, but there is opposition. Whatever may be the event to some, we have reason to rejoice in the day of visitation. It is a truth that many have turned from sin to holiness, and are now, in the most exalted strains, celebrating the praises of redeeming love. The children of God are animated to a great degree, and we are generally praying for and expecting more glorious days than we have as yet seen. I have now given you, as well as I could, an account of every thing that has led me to view this extraordinary work as Divine. I wish you, with your ancient candour and freedom, to remark not only upon what I have said, but upon what you have heard. I have cordially embraced religion in its present form. I am endeavouring to promote what many call confusion. If I am wrong, I wish to be convinced; if right, to be confirmed."

In connection with the revival, there sprung up a controversy between a portion of the Fourth Creek Congregation and Mr. Wilson on the qualifications for admission to the "sealing ordinances." This controversy does not seem to be very exactly defined; bnt it is said to have been substantially the same with that which existed between Jonathan Edwards and the people of Northampton. At any rate, it issued in Mr. Wilson's separation from the Fourth Creek Congregation, in 1803. It does not appear, however, that it was attended with any embittered state of feeling towards him, and his resignation is understood to have been a voluntary matter on his part, and to have resulted from his unwillingness to preside over a divided Session. During the short period of his life that remained, his labours were confined to the Congregation of Concord.

His last illness was a violent inflammatory fever. From its commencement, he seems to have had a full conviction that he should never recover; and the grounds of this conviction, as he stated to a friend, were that he had some symptoms which were entirely new to him, and that, during the preceding two months, he had realized a degree of deadness to the world, which had had no parallel in his previous experience. As he gradually sunk from day to day under the power of his malady, his mind was quickened to a state of unwonted spiritual fervour, and while every thing that he said and did seemed simple and natural, there was in it all a most impressive testimony to the all-sustaining power of the Gospel. He died in perfect peace, on the 11th of December, 1804, in the fifty-second year of his age. He left a widow and seven children, all of whom became members of the Church, and two of the sons ministers of the Gospel.

FROM THE REV. R. H. MORRISON, D. D.

COTTAGE HOME, N. C., February 19, 1857.

Rev. and dear Sir: As the Rev. L. F. Wilson, concerning whom you inquire, died in my childhood, of course I have no personal recollections of him that could avail to your purpose. Judging, however, from the estimate formed of him by ministers and Christians who knew him well, I have no doubt that he was a man of useful talents and sound learning; that he devoted himself to the work of Christ with great energy and wisdom; that his zeal and courage in the cause of truth were blended with remarkable humility and prudence. Public sentiment has awarded him a high claim to veneration as a faithful, devoted and successful minister of the Gospel. Perhaps the best testimony that can be given of his worth, is found in an Appendix to a Sermon preached on the occasion of his death by the Rev. John M. Wilson, D. D., who knew him personally, and whose judgment is entitled to the utmost confidence. He speaks of him in the following terms:—

"Mr. Wilson was a most entertaining and agreeable companion. His natural temper lively and cheerful, his education finished, his judgment penetrating, his acquaintance with the world large, qualified him at once to entertain and edify those that were conversant with him. Free from an useless round of ceremony, and unshackled by modes and forms, it was impossible not to be easy in his company.

"Our deceased friend, as a divine, certainly stood in a point of view highly respectable. He was not a wandering star, running off into eternal eccentricities. With respect to his system of faith, it was that which you might have expected from his profession. It was not like Nebuchadnezzar's image, composed of heterogeneous materials, which can never coalesce—he was firmly Calvinistic. In this respect, he believed, and many will believe with him, 'that he went his way by the footsteps of the flock, and fed his kids beside the shepherds' tents.'

"In the arrangement of his public discourses, he was clear and judicious; his gesture natural, indicating deep engagement of heart; his style elevated and nervous; his eloquence flowing and persuasive.

"The language of Mr. Wilson's precepts and practice was one. By a life and conversation conformed to the Gospel, he silently exhorted those to whom he ministered, as the great Apostle of the Gentiles did the Churches,—'My little children, be ye followers of me, even as I am a follower of Christ."

I have no doubt that the above extracts convey a faithful idea of that excellent man.

Very truly and affectionately yours,

R. H. MORRISON.

JONAS COE, D. D.*

1791—1822.

JONAS COE was a grandson of Samuel Coe, who migrated to this country from England, and settled at Newtown, L. I., about the year 1712; removed with his family to New Hampstead, Orange County, N. Y., in 1734; and died in 1742, aged about seventy years. He was a son of John and Hannah (Halstead) Coe, and was born at New Hampstead, the residence of his parents and grandparents, on the 20th of March, 1759. His father was an earnest patriot in the Revolution, and on one occasion took with him into battle five of his sons,—one of whom was the subject of this sketch, then only sixteen years of age. In due time, he became a member of Queen's (now Rutgers) College, New Brunswick, N. J., where he graduated in 1789. He spent his vacations in labouring on his father's farm, and occasionally at other times also, he returned home to render him temporary aid. He received the degree of Master of Arts from the College of New Jersey in 1792, and from Union College in 1797. He pursued his theological studies under the direction of the Rev. Dr. Rodgers of New York; was taken under the care of the Presbytery of New York, October 11, 1790; and was licensed to preach on the 7th of October, 1791.

On the 3d of May, 1792, a call from the Church in Stamford, Conn., was put into his hands, which, however, he declined.

The town of Troy originally comprehended two villages,—Troy and Lansingburg, distant from each other about three miles. While these villages were yet in their infancy, there were a number of individuals in each of them who were desirous of having the benefit of a preached Gospel, but the number was not sufficient in either place to enable them to support a minister. The inhabitants of the two villages, forming two separate congregations, therefore combined their strength, and invited Mr. Coe, then a highly respectable licentiate, to become their pastor,—preaching in the two places on alternate Sabbaths. He accepted the call, and on the 11th of October, 1792, was dismissed to the Presbytery of Albany, was received by that body on the 20th of February, 1793, (after an examination of two days!) and was ordained and installed on the 25th of June following. During the earlier years of his ministry, he resided in Lansingburg, but as early at least as 1802, he removed his family to Troy, and there spent the rest of his days.

In 1803, after he had held this united charge about eleven years his Congregation at Troy had so much increased in both numbers and pecuniary ability, that they felt themselves strong enough to support the ministry without sharing the expense with the sister village; and, accordingly, the union between the two congregations was dissolved, and Mr. Coe's sole charge thenceforth was in Troy.

At the time of his settlement over these congregations, almost the whole Northern part of the State of New York was a wilderness. As settlements commenced at various points, he visited them in the capacity of a mission-

* MS. from his daughter, Mrs. Brown.—Hon. John Woodworth's Reminiscences of Troy. Alden's Epitaphs, IV.

ary, endeavouring to aid them, as far as he could, to the establishment of Christian institutions. In one of these benevolent excursions, he went as far North as Plattsburg.

The degree of Doctor of Divinity was conferred upon him by Middlebury College in 1815.

Dr. Coe's ministry was not marked by any very striking events, except that it was attended by several remarkable revivals of religion. Its general character in this respect may be sufficiently indicated by the fact that between 1815 and 1818, no less than two hundred and sixty were received as members of his church.

It was Dr. Coe's daily prayer in his family, as well as his often expressed wish in conversation, that he might not survive his usefulness—nothing seemed to distress him more than the idea of becoming a superannuated clergyman, and a burden to his people. God mercifully granted him this desire of his heart. He was laid aside from his work but six weeks, and confined to his bed but a few days, prior to his death. His disease was a peculiar form of dyspepsia. In his decline as well as in his vigour, in his death as well as in his life, he bore an honourable testimony to the power and excellence of the Gospel. He died on the 21st of July, 1822, in the sixty-fourth year of his age. His Funeral Sermon was preached by his neighbour and intimate friend, the Rev. Dr. Blatchford. Twenty-five clergymen were in attendance at his Funeral.

Dr. Coe was first married on the 27th of September, 1794, to Eliza Huntting, daughter of Dr. Matthias B. and Phoebe Miller, and sister of the Hon. Morris S. Miller, who was for some time a member of Congress. She was a lady of great personal attractions, as well as uncommon loveliness and excellence of character. She was born in Dutchess County, N. Y. April 10, 1778, and died on the 19th of April, 1805. On the 14th of May, 1810, he was married to Abigail Wallace, also a native of Dutchess County, —who then resided in Lansingburg, and who still (1857) survives in her eighty-sixth year. He had three children,—two sons and one daughter,—all by the first marriage. The eldest son, *Edward M.*, was graduated at Union College in 1815; studied Law, and engaged in the practice of it at Troy, where he died February 12, 1828, aged thirty-one years. *John R.* was born in January, 1800; was graduated at Union College in 1816; became a student at the Princeton Theological Seminary in the autumn of 1817; was licensed to preach by the Presbytery of Troy in October, 1820; after labouring for some time as a missionary, was ordained and installed Pastor of the Church in Whitehall, N. Y., in July, 1822; and died in September, 1823. He inherited many of his father's excellent qualities, and many fond hopes were blasted by his early death.

FROM THE HON. JOHN WOODWORTH.

ALBANY, April 23, 1857.

My dear Sir: It gives me pleasure to bear my testimony to the great worth and usefulness of my former venerable friend and pastor, the Rev. Dr. Coe; and I do it with the more alacrity, as it is doubtful whether there is another person now living whose opportunities for knowing him at once reach back so far, and were so frequent and favourable as my own. I commenced the practice of Law in Troy in the year 1791; and Dr. Coe commenced his labours there, if I mistake not, in the spring of the next year; so that I knew him from the very beginning of his ministry. Troy was, at that time, little more than a hamlet, consisting perhaps of thirty or forty houses; but there were some excellent people there, who felt too deeply the value of the Gospel to be willing to live without it. The principal of these was Mr. Jacob D. Vanderheyden, a wealthy and influential man, and the owner of the ground on which Troy stands. He had been the subject of a very remarkable conversion—from being utterly indifferent to religion, and intensely devoted to the world, he had become one of the most earnest and exemplary Christians, and had acquired an amount of religious knowledge and true spiritual wisdom, that enabled him to preside at social meetings in a highly appropriate and edifying manner. It was through his influence, I think, more than that of any other person, that the labours of the young minister were secured for the two infant settlements. I was myself one of Dr. Coe's hearers from the beginning, and I first made a public profession of religion by joining his church, after a revival of religion in 1803.

Few men whom I have ever known have accomplished so much good as Dr Coe by that insensible influence which pertains to character. You could not say he was a great *preacher*, and yet he was always respectable—you could not say he was a great *man* in the popular acceptation of the word,—for with the exception of judgment and common sense, I do not know that he possessed any intellectual faculty in more than ordinary strength; but you could say, after all, that he possessed a great *character*;—by which I mean a character so formed as always to be accomplishing, silently indeed but most effectively, the true mission of a Christian minister. There was such a blending of the lovely qualities of nature with the higher qualities that are superinduced by grace, there was such an entire freedom from every thing that could give reasonable offence on the one hand, and such fidelity to his own convictions of truth and right on the other,—in short, there was such a graceful symmetry and elevation in his whole bearing, that he seemed to be doing positive good, even when he was absolutely doing nothing. You can hardly imagine any thing to exceed the tenderness of his sympathy in scenes of sorrow; and next to the Gracious Comforter above, his people looked to him in the hour of their trouble. Wherever he might be, or in whatever circumstances placed, it was evident that his heart was set upon doing good. He never needed a voucher for the purity or the benevolence of his intentions. In every circle in which he was known, his name was a synonyme for whatever is true, and pure, and lovely, and of good report. I am glad you have revived my recollections of him by your request; for though he has long since passed away, his memory will always be dear to my heart.

I am, with great regard,

Sincerely yours,

JOHN WOODWORTH.

FROM THE REV. ELIPHALET NOTT, D. D.

UNION COLLEGE, May 12, 1857.

Rev. and dear Sir: Though I am not able to furnish you with the facts concerning Dr. Coe for which you ask, permit me to say that I consider him as having been one of the most estimable and useful men with whom I have ever become acquainted. He exerted a powerful influence for good in this community, during the latter part of the last, and the first part of the present, century.

Dr. Coe was a man of great wisdom and goodness. His deep and uniform piety, and at the same time his kindly and affectionate manners, rendered him a welcome guest in every family, and thus he became emphatically a preacher of the Gospel from house to house.

During the early part of his ministry, he wrote his sermons fully, and with great care, and he delivered them memoriter as they were written. This habit he continued till an extensive revival, (I do not remember exactly at what period it occurred,) with which his labours in the cause of his Master were crowned. From that time till the close of life, he read from the pulpit the manuscript he had prepared,—giving as a reason for the change that time had become too precious to be employed in memorizing the discourses he had carefully written.

Dr. Coe was not distinguished for either flashes of wit, or bursts of eloquence, but he was distinguished for uniformity of conduct and completeness of character. He was never known to do a rash act, or utter a foolish expression. What he said was always suited to the occasion, and whatever he executed passed finished from his hand.

Wise in counsel and punctual in attendance, he had a controlling influence in the business that came before the judicatories of the Church to which he belonged.

For many years he was a member of the Board of Trustees of Union College, and took an active part in its organization, and in all its early transactions. He was also, for a long time, a member of its Examining Committee, and met the classes regularly three times a year, encouraging them by his presence, and guiding them by his counsel.

He was my own personal friend, and I owe much of my success to his constancy and fidelity. Peace to his sainted spirit! Few men have been more useful, lived more beloved, or left behind a more blameless character or cherished memory.

Yours very sincerely,

ELIPHALET NOTT.

FROM THOMAS W. BLATCHFORD, M. D.

TROY, March 17, 1857.

Dear Sir: I knew Dr. Coe well, and loved him dearly. My earliest religious impressions are associated with him. It is fifty-two years since I first heard him preach. He was in the habit of frequently visiting at our house, and of exchanging pulpits with my father. I often rode with him between the two places, Troy and Lansingburg, and it was a treat that I always coveted. His conversation was usually more or less of a serious character, and sometimes turned directly on personal religion. He was exceedingly mild and pleasant, warmhearted and affectionate, and seemed always to take a special interest in the young. He loved children, and children consequently loved him. One incident illustrative of this is particularly fresh in my recollection. On one occasion, my father sent me on an errand to him, very early in the morning; and after breakfast, (for I took my breakfast at his house,) as I was about to return home, he laid his soft warm hand upon my head, (I think I feel it now,) led me into an adjoining room, and there offered a most fervent and affectionate prayer in my behalf, supplicating for me the gracious presence and guidance of God's Holy Spirit.

In the pulpit he was always solemn, earnest and affectionate—often affected to tears, and sometimes quite overcome by his emotions. He had a mild tenor voice,—his delivery was somewhat rapid, though his articulation was very distinct. His prayers were fervent and impressive in manner, and rich and felicitous in evangelical thought and expression. His power in the pulpit consisted more in persuasion than in argument—his sermons, though by no means deficient in well digested thought, evinced more of practical and experimental religion than of extensive learning or profound investigation. But his great success as a minister was undoubtedly to be referred more to his labours out of the pulpit than in it—as a pastor I do not hesitate to say that, to this day, I have never known his equal.

His labours were rewarded by several seasons of refreshing from the presence of the Lord. One of these, which commenced in January, 1816, was followed by an addition to the church, after a few months, of more than a hundred persons. I was present on the occasion, having just returned from London, where I had been pursuing my medical studies; and the scene was perhaps the more impressive to me, from some peculiar circumstances under which I witnessed it. The church, though a large building, was crowded to its utmost capacity; and multitudes were standing on the outside, trying to catch occasionally a sentence, or through the open windows to get an imperfect view of the interesting scene that was passing within.

Though it is now thirty-five years since the death of Dr. Coe, his memory is still gratefully cherished, not only by the few surviving members of his charge, but by their children and children's children.

I remain, Rev. dear Sir,

Yours very sincerely,

THOMAS W. BLATCHFORD.

FROM THE REV. MARK TUCKER, D. D.

Ellington, Conn., March 9, 1857.

My dear Brother: Dr. Coe, concerning whom you ask for my reminiscences, was like a father to me, and I cherish his memory with something like a filial affection. My acquaintance with him commenced in 1815, during an extensive revival of religion with which the city of Troy was then blessed. I was at that time a student of Theology under Doctors Nott and Yates. I accompanied Dr. Yates to Troy, and we remained there for some time. I had an opportunity of observing Dr. Coe's movements in connection with the revival, and was most favourably impressed by his activity and zeal on the one hand, and his discretion and caution on the other.

Dr. Coe may be said to have been a finished gentleman. Without the semblance of any thing like artificial airs, his manners were bland, courteous, and altogether exceedingly attractive. I have somehow got the impression that there was a striking resemblance in respect to manners and general bearing between him and Dr. Rodgers of New York. As a preacher he did not aspire to any high literary excellence, but always presented Divine truth with great simplicity and clearness, so that a child would never hesitate in regard to his meaning, while yet his sermons were so instructive that the more intelligent might profit by them. As a pastor, few equalled, none probably exceeded, him. He seemed to look upon his people as a father upon his family, and was always upon the alert to do them good by every means in his power. At the bedside of the sick and dying, and at funerals—indeed wherever Christian sympathy and tenderness were demanded, no man's ministrations were more appropriate or effective than his. And his general influence through society was of the happiest kind—every body revered him—every body confided in him; for it was evident that the spirit of beneficence pervaded and controlled even his most common actions. The secret of his great influence lay not in any extraordinary intellectual powers, but in a perfectly symmetrical and well balanced character, by means of which each of his faculties was rendered in the highest degree available. What has been said of Washington may be applied to him—his moral virtues were all great talents. His actual power may be estimated by the fact that he built up a noble church and congregation, embracing a large amount of talent, learning, and wealth, and never in any degree lost his hold of them till the close of life. I was present at his funeral; and seldom is there witnessed more of respect, and love, and genuine sorrow, than was manifested on that occasion. His imperfections (and he had as few as any minister I ever knew) were like spots on the sun, covered with a rich robe of light.

Yours truly,

MARK TUCKER.

JAMES TURNER.*

1791—1828.

JAMES TURNER, the son of Richard and Nancy (Johns) Turner, was born in Bedford County, Va., May 7, 1759. His father was a farmer, and lived and died in the same county. His mother was a member of the Presbyterian Church, and, in her latter years particularly, was eminently devoted to religion.

While he was yet quite a youth, he studied the Latin and Greek languages, in both of which his progress was very remarkable. He seems, however. to have been arrested prematurely in his education, as his knowledge of many branches, particularly of Mathematics and Philosophy, was quite limited. At the age of seventeen, he was bearing arms as a soldier in the army of the Revolution.

He early formed the purpose of devoting himself to the study of the Law; but in this he was signally defeated. On his way to the place where he was to prosecute his studies, he was robbed of his money and clothes, and thus was induced to relinquish altogether the idea of the legal profession;—a circumstance to which he was accustomed, afterwards, to advert with the warmest gratitude.

At this period of his life, he was gay, profane, even profligate: he scrupled not to trifle with the most sacred things, if he could thereby minister to the merriment of those around him; though he was never addicted to those more degrading forms of vice, which almost necessarily render one an outlaw from decent society. At a gaming party, or a horse race, or almost any other scene of frivolity, he was always at home; and, on one occasion when engaged in a horse race, he was thrown from his horse, and for some time it was supposed that his neck was dislocated, and that he was actually dead; though he afterwards revived, and ultimately recovered.

In August, 1778, he was married to Sally, daughter of Colonel William Leftwich of Bedford. This proved a most happy connection, and it continued for fifty years, lacking a few months.

Soon after his marriage, he settled on a farm in what was then regarded the frontier part of the State, (Bedford County,) though it is now nearer the middle. It does not appear that he intended to take any part in public life; much less had he, at that time, any aspirations for either of the liberal professions: but such were his social habits, and so acceptable did he make himself to the community in which he lived, that, though still very young, he was elected to represent his county in the General Assembly of the State. He did not, however, in this capacity, as far as is known, particularly distinguish himself.

The hopeful conversion of Mr. Turner took place in the year 1789. Even when he professed to attend church, he rarely, if ever, entered the house. On one occasion, when the Rev. Drury Lacy was preaching at Bedford,—as the preacher had an uncommonly fine, commanding voice, Mr. Turner, who stood outside, was reached not only by the voice of the preacher, but by an arrow of conviction. He went home in the

* MS. from his son, Rev. J. H. Turner.—Foote's Sketches of Va., 2d Series.

deepest mental agony; and such was the anguish of his spirit, that, at midnight, the different members of the household were called together to join in prayer that he might be delivered from the burden that so oppressed and overwhelmed him. He availed himself of an early opportunity to acquaint his pious mother with the distress which had overtaken him; but, instead of expressing sympathy, as he expected, she burst forth in a tribute of devout thanksgiving to God, saying that that was the very thing for which she had been praying for years. At length the cloud passed away, and his mind became serene and happy. He was at first somewhat perplexed in regard to some of the doctrines of Christianity, but was ultimately led to repose with great strength of conviction in the Calvinistic system.

Soon after this change of character, he began a course of public exhortation. Nor, in this exercise, did he confine himself to his own neighbourhood, but, in company with his Pastor, the Rev. James Mitchel, performed extensive circuits of missionary labour in the destitute parts of the neighbouring counties. In this way, it soon became known that he had a remarkable talent for public speaking, as well as uncommon zeal for the promotion of Christ's Kingdom; and the Presbytery of Hanover, within whose bounds he was exercising his gifts, soon encouraged him to give himself formally to the work of the ministry. Accordingly, on the 29th of October, 1791, at the age of thirty-two, he was licensed by that Presbytery to preach the Gospel. The full literary course required by the Presbyterian Book of Discipline, was not exacted in his case, as it was judged to be one of those extraordinary cases which would justify a departure from the rule.

On the 28th of July, 1792, he was ordained to the work of the ministry, and installed as Colleague Pastor with the Rev. Mr. Mitchel, in what was then called the Peaks Congregation, but which was really three Congregations with one Session. He also took charge of the New London Congregation. Here he spent the whole of his ministerial life. He was several times urged to change his field of labour, but he seemed to regard his first charge as having peculiar claims upon him, and no considerations that could be presented, were powerful enough to induce him to leave them.

It was much to the credit of Mr. Turner that he always evinced the utmost respect and deference towards his aged and excellent colleague, the Rev. Mr. Mitchel. They were exceedingly unlike, in both their natural temperament and their style of preaching; but there existed between them the most perfect harmony, and there was nothing in Mr. Turner's deportment to indicate that he was even aware of his having any popularity as a preacher above that of his venerable associate.

Mr. Turner died on the 8th of January, 1828, within three months of being sixty-nine years old. His health had been undergoing a gradual decline, and the infirmities of age accumulating upon him, for several years. But, on the day of his death, he seemed unusually well and cheerful. He was suddenly seized with violent suffocation, supposed to be the effect of a disease of the heart; and he had only time to say that he was dying, and to commit his soul to God, before his spirit was dislodged from its earthly tabernacle.

Mr. Turner was the father of fourteen children, seven of whom survived him. One of them, *William Leftwich*, was for some time Pastor of the Church, and Principal of the Academy, at Raleigh, N. C.; and in 1809 removed to Fayetteville, where he was still engaged in both preaching and teaching. He received the degree of Master of Arts from the University of North Carolina in 1810. He died greatly lamented, on the 2d of October, 1813. He was a young man of strongly marked talents and character, and of great promise; and his brief ministry at Fayetteville was eminently blessed. The grief of his father, occasioned by his death, was well nigh overwhelming; but he submissively remarked that he knew not how he could do a better thing than raise up children for the Kingdom of Heaven. Another son, *Jesse H.*, entered the ministry, and is now (1850) a resident of Richmond, Va. One other son became a practitioner of medicine, and now resides in the Western country.

FROM THE REV. S. L. GRAHAM, D. D.,

PROFESSOR IN THE UNION THEOLOGICAL SEMINARY, VA.

UNION THEOLOGICAL SEMINARY,
PRINCE EDWARD COUNTY, Va., July 28, 1848.

Rev. and dear Sir: James Turner of Bedford County, concerning whom you inquire, was one of the most remarkable men of his day. His conversion, which took place after his marriage, was a signal triumph of Divine grace over a most unpromising subject.

He was a man of real genius. He was, to a great extent, self-made; and yet few men have, under the same circumstances, wielded a greater influence, or been regarded with a warmer affection. His illustrations were, for the most part, entirely original, and well adapted to his subject. And though, if uttered by others, many of them would have seemed tame, or perhaps excited a smile, yet they neither degraded the speaker by vulgarity or ludicrousness, nor detracted from the dignity of scriptural truth. Very few men of his age equalled him in originality. He was exceedingly attractive as a public speaker. Large congregations attended his preaching, and every body felt and acknowledged his wonderful power.

One of the most prominent characteristics of his preaching was its simplicity. He made you feel by his manner that his whole heart was open before you. The most pathetic parts of his sermons were those in which some story was told, or some appeal made, with all the artlessness of a child. I remember a striking example that once occurred at the College Church, in Prince Edward. He simply remarked that he did not personally know the audience before him, but he knew their fathers and mothers, and the children by their resemblance to them. The whole house was melted into tears. There was a magic power in the manner in which this simple sentence was uttered, which made it perfectly irresistible. Its force, it is true, depended, in a degree, on what had preceded; but the artless simplicity and impressive earnestness with which the whole was uttered cannot easily be imagined.

Mr. Turner, in his power over the passions of men, was acknowledged to be without a rival among the clergy of Virginia. Others probably excelled him in vigour and elegance of diction, but in his ability to move the heart he had no equal. The amount of emotion of which he was capable was amazing. The physical frame of almost any other man would have sunk under it; and life would have been destroyed. When his efforts in the pulpit were made under favourable circumstances, his appeals were absolutely overwhelming, and his command over his audience complete. His voice had sufficient compass to be heard in his conversational tones: it was soft and melodious, and yet sometimes so awful as to make one quake. He could so utter emphatic phrases as to create an impression which would never be lost. For example, on one occasion, he so pronounced the simple sentence,—"Lifted up above the world," in reference to the Christian's triumph, as to leave an indelible impression on my mind; and though a boy when I heard it, it rings in my ears to this day Still the tones of his voice were always those of kindness and love. There was nothing in his manner menacing, or harsh, or repulsive. He spoke as a father to his children. He was never deluded into the belief that insolence was Christian boldness, or uncharitable denunciation, ministerial faithfulness. I can only say that to have an adequate idea of his eloquence, it would be necessary to see and hear him.

But the crowning excellence of Mr. Turner was that he possessed an earnest piety. This appeared on every occasion. He did nothing for effect. He did not speak to shine, but to do good. Though he was one of nature's noblemen, and such was the fame of his eloquence that persons travelled far to hear him, yet he was never tempted to any thing like ostentatious display. To use one of his own sayings, his heart yearned over his people. He never forgot his commission as a minister of Christ, and was always serious in a serious cause. His habits were not what, in a strict sense, would be called studious, and he had no great amount of book-learning; yet the most cultivated listened to him with a respect felt for few others. It was his deep and fervent piety, in connection with his wonderful gifts, which made him so eloquent, and opened for him a passage to all hearts. Men of iron nerves were borne away by the gushing tide of his pious emotions. He seldom travelled beyond his own native county, and was therefore known only by fame in much the larger portion of the State.

Very truly yours,

S. L. GRAHAM.

FROM THE REV. W. S. PLUMER, D.D.

BALTIMORE, Md., November 27, 1849.

Rev. and dear Sir: You ask for some of my recollections of the late Rev. James Turner. I never was intimate with him, and never was at his house but once, and that for not more than half an hour. Some of the company inquired concerning his health. He repled,—"It is not pleasant to fill the ears of our friends with the tale of our infirmities, but I cannot tell a lie—I am not well;" and immediately began to inquire respecting the prospects of religion in a distant part of the country.

I never heard him preach but twice. He was then aged and quite infirm. The first time I heard him was at a meeting of Hanover Presbytery in Lynchburg, in the fall of 1826. My expectation was high. But he far transcended it. The last time I heard him was at a meeting of the Synod of Virginia, in the same place, not long before his death. Between him and the late Dr. Baxter had long existed a very strong and tender friendship. Though very different in their mental habits, yet their hearts were alike warm, tender and generous. Dr. Baxter offered the prayer before the sermon, and when he asked God to bless his aged servant, and enable him once more to bear a good testimony for Christ, his emotions were irrepressible. I believe every devout man in that house said *Amen* to that prayer. And it was answered. For although Mr. Turner's discourse had less logical connection than the one I had heard before, its spiritual power and its impressiveness were even greater. The audience was very large. There were present learned Doctors of Divinity, and many less distinguished clergymen, lawyers, physicians, merchants, farmers, wagoners, boatmen, negroes, persons of both sexes and of all ages. They all seemed to be deeply affected, and in the same way. He invariably put his hearers off their guard by making the most plain and simple remarks. A little child could not have seemed more artless. Indeed you were often smiling at the familiarity of his illustrations. Yet all of a sudden,—you knew not how,—but by remarks no less simple, yet inimitably pathetic, you would be bathed in tears, and even convulsed with weeping. But in the midst of a tumult of feeling, which I never saw surpassed, he would, by a sentence, relieve the whole audience. Indeed, some persons felt, at such sudden changes, a great desire to laugh. They were not their own masters. I felt greatly ashamed to be seen laughing, and covered my head. At last I saw the late Dr. John H. Rice affected just as I was. This relieved me for the time. Yet there was no levity there. The preacher was as solemn as any man I ever saw. Had he at any moment said,—" let us pray," I suppose every man in the house would have felt that it was proper. Indeed, in less than five minutes from the time I found myself laughing, I was weeping convulsively at his description of the love of Christ, and the joys of Heaven. I do not know that I have ever seen a more solemn impression made on a large congregation, than by that sermon.

Mr. Turner had great advantages as a preacher. He was a large man with noble features, and a very pleasant yet commanding voice. His emotions, however strong, never impaired the strength, sweetness, or clearness, of his tones. He was naturally what Quintilian calls a *good man*. His impulses were noble and generous. Even in the days of his irreligion, he had despised meanness, and maintained a high reputation for candour. Every one who saw him believed that he was a sincere and kind man. I think I have never seen any man, in whom there was such an exuberance of what the French call " bonhomie" as in Mr. Turner. Then he always regarded and spoke of himself as a miracle of grace. His gratitude to Christ seemed to be like the waters of a mighty river. He never appeared so joyous as when speaking of the love of Christ to his chosen people.

I never saw but one James Turner in the pulpit, and I do not expect ever to see another. I would readily travel a hundred miles to hear such a sermon as either of those I heard from him. I have never seen any man sway an audience as he did. Old and young, learned and unlearned, saint and sinner, the white man and the black man, felt and owned his power.

Mr. Turner had not read very much. Yet he was far, far removed from ignorance. He was well acquainted with the best practical writers, and he had studied his whole Bible with much prayer to God, and with a great love for the truth. He well understood the peculiar doctrines of the Gospel, and preached them constantly. He was a lover of good men, and a lover of peace. He practised on the principle that " one hour of brotherly love is worth a whole eternity of contention;" yet he firmly defended truth and righteousness, when they were assailed.

He saw great afflictions in his day, but they were sanctified to him. When I last saw him, he had buried seven of his children, but they had died in faith. His allusion to his shortly meeting them in Heaven produced in the audience a degree of emotion which it would have been dangerous to prolong. It will surprise no one to hear that he was quite unequal in his preaching. Though always humble, he seemed peculiarly mortified when he did not succeed. This I have heard from others.

He was a great friend of Theological Seminaries, and of all good institutions. Thousands remember his masterly, though brief, commendations of the Bible Society. In the last sermon which I heard from him, he greatly commended it. He was, in few words, a great, humble, eloquent, candid, affectionate, fearless man of God. He left few, if any, enemies behind him. Thousands on earth still remember his preaching as the most exciting exercise to which they ever listened.

Very respectfully and affectionately yours,

WM. S. PLUMER.

FROM THE REV. JESSE H. TURNER

RICHMOND, Va., December 23, 1847.

Rev. and dear Sir: Notwithstanding the delicacy that may seem to attach to the testimony of a son in respect to a venerated and beloved parent, I cannot bring myself to refuse your request for some reminiscences of my lamented father.

My father's early advantages for education, as you may have learned from other sources, were not very extensive. Nevertheless, from his constant perusal, or I should rather say careful study, of the best writers on Divinity, in connection with a naturally correct taste, his use of language in his public discourses did not offend even the most fastidious ear. I never saw any one who had a greater passion for reading than he. On several occasions, while I was with him on a visit, he asked me if I could not procure for him some new work, and remarked that he had read all the books in his own small library over and over again. Baxter, Bunyan, Owen, were among his favourite authors; but I distinctly recollect hearing him say that Robert Hall, in respect to both sentiment and style, came nearer to his *beau ideal* than any other man.

I would like to say something, and indeed I ought to say something, in regard to his manner in the pulpit; but it is so difficult to do him justice in this respect that I almost shrink from the attempt. However, I will do the best I can. In his exordium he was solemn, but perfectly natural and simple. You would have supposed that any child might say the same things in the same way. He seemed to seize at once upon whatever was prominent or striking in his text, and to present it in the most forcible and impressive manner. At the beginning, the tone of his voice was always low, strongly resembling a familiar conversation with his hearers. But gradually and imperceptibly warming with his subject, and at the same time elevating his voice, he frequently,—I may say generally, gained the entire control of his audience;—moving, melting, and swaying them just as he pleased; and all this without the slightest apparent effort on his part. I have, on more than one occasion, gone to hear him preach, resolved that I would not allow myself to be excited by him. But, notwithstanding my resolution, his simple and unpretending manner would throw me entirely off my guard, and, before I was aware of it, I found that he was leading me whithersoever he listed.

The subjects on which he preached were, I think, as varied as usual. But if there was one in which he delighted more than in any other, and which seemed to stir his soul to its lowest depths, it was the grace of God as displayed in the salvation of the sinner. His main object seemed to be to convince the sinner that God did not destroy him, but that he destroyed himself, and was therefore wholly responsible for his own ruin.

He was accustomed to prepare his sermons with very considerable care. It is true that he never wrote them out at full length, but usually wrote, on a very small piece of paper, and in as few words as possible, the leading ideas on which he was to dwell, including the divisions and subdivisions of his discourse. This paper, thus prepared, he placed between the leaves of a small pocket Bible, where it remained till it was needed for use. In the morning, before preaching, making use of these short notes, he carefully studied his subject—I mean the sentiment, not the words,—for I have heard him say that he trusted to the occasion for the form of expression. In preaching, he always held his little Bible in his hand, referring frequently to his notes. I think it probable that, without his notes for a security, he would often have found himself unable readily to recall the train of thought which he had projected.

My father was blessed with an eminently successful ministry. I distinctly recollect three extensive revivals among his people, as the result of which a very considerable number were gathered into the Church. In addition to this, a constant blessing seemed to attend his ministrations, in the frequent conversion of souls in a more quiet and silent way.

He was a pioneer in the cause of Temperance. In the year 1818, before there was any excitement on this subject, he preached earnestly in favour of the principle of total abstinence; and not without effect,—for several of the families in his congregation from that time adopted the principle. By the way, I believe this sermon on Temperance was one of the only two sermons which he ever wrote out. It was heard by an old and much valued friend of his, who had formerly been an elder in his church, but had removed to the "far West;" and he was so much interested in it, that, by his earnest request, my father wrote it out after it was delivered, and gave him a copy of it.

In his intercourse with his brethren in the ministry, he was always in a high degree cordial, confiding and affectionate. A little incident which I beg leave to relate, will illustrate this trait of his character. On a certain occasion, there was a considerable revival in one of his congregations. Dr. Baxter, who then lived in the Valley of Virginia, some forty miles distant,—well knowing how acceptable his services would be at such a time, came to pay my father a visit,—bringing with him a considerable number of his young people, that they might mingle in the revival, and become imbued with its spirit. At the first opportunity, the Doctor was requested to preach. The sermon was a good one,—a very good one, as all Dr. Baxter's were, but still, as my father thought, was marked by too little zeal and unction. As soon, therefore, as he took his seat, my father remarked to him,—"This wont do, Doctor, you must try again." The next day the Doctor preached again, and was then told that he had done better, but still it would not do yet. Before the third effort, his heart had become thoroughly warmed, and, under the influence of his lively feelings, he delivered a sermon which produced a powerful effect. When he sat down, my father laid his hand upon his shoulder, and said,—"This *will* do; now go home and preach in this manner to your own people, and I doubt not that you will soon be blessed with a revival." He was intimately associated with most of the more prominent Presbyterian ministers in Virginia of his day; but with no one did he maintain a more delightful fraternal intercourse than with Dr. Baxter. For a considerable time, they had their residence in the same neighbourhood; and when, afterwards, they were separated by a greater distance, in consequence of Dr. B.'s removal, they still cherished for each other the warmest affection, and welcomed their less frequent meetings as occasions of great and mutual interest.

With sentiments of sincere esteem,

I am, dear Sir, yours affectionately,

J. H. TURNER.

JOHN ANDERSON, D. D.*

1791—1835.

JOHN ANDERSON was the son of William and Ann (Denny) Anderson, and was born in Guilford County, N. C., on the 10th of April, 1767. His paternal grandfather emigrated from the North of Ireland to this country; and *his* father was a native of Scotland; so that his extraction is that which is commonly known as Scotch Irish. His ancestry, as far as it can be traced, was uniformly Presbyterian.

His father's occupation was that of a farmer; and he himself worked on a farm until he was sixteen years of age. When he was about seventeen, he entered the Academy of the Rev. David Caldwell, one of the most eminent teachers of his day, where he received his entire classical and theological education. His mind became first permanently impressed with Divine truth, during an awakening in the Academy, which occurred under the labours of the Rev. James McGready, who had himself been hopefully converted through the instrumentality of the Rev. Joseph Smith of Pennsylvania, and had wandered, on a preaching tour, as far South as North Carolina.

Mr. Anderson was licensed to preach by the Presbytery of Orange, N. C., in the year 1791, and shortly afterwards was ordained as an evangelist. He commenced his labours in the Southern part of North Carolina, and the Northern part of South Carolina; and in this field passed the first two years of his ministerial life. From 1793 to 1798 or 1799, he itinerated through the States of Tennessee and Kentucky, sometimes crossing the Ohio, and preaching to the settlements in what is now Ohio and Indiana. During these years, he travelled without aid from any missionary association, and was not only subjected to great privations and dangers, but actually suffered for want of the means of an adequate support.

In 1801, he began his labours in Upper Buffalo Church, Washington County, Pa., and was installed as its Pastor the next year. Here he continued to hold the pastoral relation, with great acceptance and usefulness, until it was dissolved, by his own request, on account of declining health, on the 15th of January, 1833.

He received the degree of Doctor of Divinity from Washington College, Pa., in the year 1821.

Dr. Anderson never had a vigorous physical constitution, and yet he so husbanded his strength as to perform a vast amount of labour. He continued to preach regularly until within eighteen months of his death, and occasionally until within four months of it. His last illness was a chronic affection of the throat and lungs—in fact the winding up of a disease under which he had laboured a quarter of a century. He died at his own residence, surrounded by all his children except one, on the 5th of January, 1835, in the sixty-eighth year of his age. His last hours were eminently peaceful, and his only hope and only glorying were in the cross of Christ.

He was married, March 10, 1800, to Rebecca, daughter of James and Elizabeth (Morrison) Byers, of Westmoreland County, Pa. They had ten

* MS. from his son, Rev. W. C. Anderson, D. D.—App. to Life of Macurdy.

children, eight of whom reached maturity. Two of them have been graduated at Washington College, Pa. *William C.* (now the Rev. Dr.) Anderson, who was graduated in 1824, is well known as a prominent clergyman in the Presbyterian Church; and *John*, a younger son, who was graduated at the same College in 1834, is engaged in commercial and other kindred pursuits. Mrs. Anderson died on the 15th of December, 1854.

Dr. Anderson conducted the theological education of a large number of young men, some of whom have since risen to eminence in the Church. He was also, during the whole of his pastoral life, extensively engaged in missionary operations. He was one, if not of the originators, at least of the most active members, of the Old Board of Trustees of the Western Missionary Society; and under its direction he made several tours to the Wyandotte Indians on the Sandusky River. He was also largely instrumental in founding the mission on the Maumee, and visited it once in company with the Rev. E. Macurdy, with a view to settle some existing difficulties. After the transfer of that station to the United Foreign Missionary Society, he became one of the most efficient supporters of that Society, and subsequently of the American Board of Commissioners for Foreign Missions, into which it was merged. In forming the present General Assembly's Board of Foreign Missions at Pittsburg, in 1831, he took a most lively interest, and extended to it his cordial and active support till the close of life.

It is not known that Dr. Anderson published any thing, except a series of articles on the Popish controversy, and another series on the Temperance question—both in the Pittsburg Recorder.

FROM THE REV. SAMUEL McFARREN, D. D.

CONGRUITY, Pa., October 16, 1855.

Dear Sir: My opportunities for becoming acquainted with the character of the late Dr. John Anderson, were abundant. My *personal* acquaintance with him, it is true, commenced when he was in the decline of life, and I quite a youth. But I enjoyed the acquaintance of many ministers and other persons, who knew him well, and were associated with him in the earlier part of his ministry, and of their estimate of his character I have no doubt. Though brought up at a distance of some twenty miles from his pastoral charge, I frequently heard him preach during my boyhood. When I was a student at College, he was President of the Board of Trustees. I afterwards prosecuted my theological studies under his direction, and, during one year, boarded in his family, and attended constantly on his ministry.

In person, Dr. Anderson was rather above the ordinary height; and, at least towards the close of his life, was inclined to stoop. His form was slender, his visage thin, and his complexion cadaverous. He had a small, dark eye, which was occasionally lighted up in conversation, and more especially in the pulpit, so as to be very animated and piercing.

As a man, he was characterized by great plainness and simplicity of manner, and by candour, sincerity, and straightforwardness, in all his intercourse with society. He had little taste for display or ceremony, and would never stoop to any thing approaching to finesse. Unassuming and unostentatious himself, the efforts of others to display themselves never deceived him. He had a keen discrimination of character, and easily penetrated any disguise that might be assumed. He was emphatically a lover of peace—kind and courteous towards all. While he rarely, if ever, gave offence, he was entirely free from that morbid sensitiveness which often takes offence where none is intended. But, with all his peaceable tendencies, he possessed great moral courage, and never hesitated to rebuke vice fearlessly, whenever there was occasion. A striking instance of this was his opposition to the use of intoxicating drinks, at a time when the practice of drinking was almost universal. Years before there was any general movement on the subject, he had succeeded in inducing a large part of his congregation to adopt the principle of total abstinence, and banish the bottle from their harvest fields.

As a pastor, he had the entire confidence of his people. That he possessed great power as a preacher was felt by all who heard him; and yet few of them perhaps could tell wherein his strength lay. In his appearance in the pulpit, in the tones of his voice, or the manner of his delivery, there was nothing peculiarly attractive or commanding. Nor had he a remarkably brilliant imagination; nor did he often make a direct attempt to arouse the passions of his audience; but yet there was something in his preaching which never failed to secure an earnest attention, and not unfrequently his hearers would be so absorbed as entirely to forget the preacher in the subject.

One characteristic which contributed much to the effect of his discourses, was their remarkable perspicuity. Having himself a perfectly clear perception of the ideas he wished to convey, he expressed them clearly, without repetition or circumlocution. He was never tedious,—never dwelt on an idea, turning it over and over until his audience became wearied.

And then there was a deep solemnity and earnestness in his manner. His eye and his countenance indicated that he felt himself to be standing between the living and the dead, and treating with man, as God's ambassador, on the most momentous of all subjects. Even the hardened profligate was not unfrequently moved by his solemn and earnest expostulations.

But that which more than any thing else gave power to his preaching, was his skill in dealing with the conscience—laying open to his hearers the secret workings of their own hearts. He was eminently what is sometimes denominated a searching preacher; and it was on this account perhaps as much as any other, that his preaching found so much favour, especially with serious Christians and anxious inquirers.

In his preparation for the pulpit, at least in the later years of his ministry, he made but little use of the pen; and never, it is believed, preached with even short notes before him. But no intelligent hearer could doubt that his subject had been thoroughly digested, and the matter of his discourse carefully and logically arranged, in his own mind. Hence the leading points of his subject were easily remembered and recalled by the attentive hearer. His manner of sermonizing was somewhat peculiar, and such as could not be safely copied by others. An anecdote illustrative of this latter remark now occurs to me:—One of Dr. Anderson's co-presbyters, who greatly admired him, and had undertaken, it appears, to make him his model in the pulpit, complained to a ministerial brother that, for several weeks, he had not enjoyed his ordinary freedom in preaching, and had, in his own estimation, fallen far below his common standard. "But at length," said he, "I have discovered the reason—I have been trying to work with John Anderson's tools." But notwithstanding the type of his sermons was peculiar, there was great variety, not only in the matter of which they were composed, but in their texture and form. And hence his people never grew weary of him,—never desired a change; but reluctantly consented to his dismission, when the infirmities of age compelled him to ask a release from pastoral duties.

As a teacher of Theology, he took a deep interest in developing the native talent of his pupils. Whilst he shunned that mawkish dislike for all controversy, which would allow the truth to suffer rather than incur opposition in its defence, his aim was to train his pupils for preaching the truth rather than figuring in polemics. "Preach the Gospel; put as much Gospel as possible into every discourse,"—was the substance of his oft-repeated advice.

In estimating the talents and attainments of Dr. Anderson, the disadvantages under which he laboured ought not to be overlooked. Several of the earlier years of his ministry were spent in itinerant labours. This seemed to be required by the feeble state of his health. He has been heard to say that the Presbytery, when they licensed him, expected him to preach a few sermons, and then die. That the work of an itinerant missionary is very unfavourable to habits of study, it is easy to see. After his settlement, the extent of his charge was such as to require much of his time for pastoral engagements. And even if other duties had not prevented, the state of his health was never such as to admit of intense and long continued application to his studies. Add to all this, that his library, owing to the scantiness of his support, was always small. That he should have attained, notwithstanding all these disadvantages, such eminence in the Church, and among his brethren, certainly proves that his natural endowments were of a high order. But his highest praise is that these endowments were consecrated to the service of that Blessed Master in whom he trusted for redemption, and whose glory he sought as the great end of his life and labours.

Very truly yours,

S. McFARREN.

JAMES BLYTHE, D. D.*

1791—1842.

JAMES BLYTHE, the son of James and Elizabeth Blythe, was born in Mecklenburg County, N. C., October 28, 1765. Both his parents were of Scottish extraction. His father seems to have designed him from his youth for one of the liberal professions, and hence he was early placed at a grammar school in his native county, to learn Latin and Greek. The study of Latin, however, proved so distasteful to him, that he begged to be permitted to lay it aside; and his father gravely assented, but, at the same time, directed him to be in readiness to drive one of his wagons to Charleston. The boy, knowing that there was no alternative, submitted to the requisition; but, on his return, assured his father that the journey had cured him of his aversion to Latin, and that he was more than willing to return to his studies. He, accordingly, did resume them, and, in due time, joined Hampden Sidney College, where he completed his scientific and classical course under the Presidency of Dr. John Blair Smith. He was a professor of religion before he went to College; but so adverse to the culture of the spiritual mind were all the influences by which he was there surrounded, that he cut loose from the restraints of a Christian profession, and passed among his gay associates for a thorough devotee to worldly vanities. It was a singular circumstance by which he was brought to reflection, and recovered from his wanderings. A student in College with whom he was intimate, and whom he had known only as a companion in levity and sin, had become deeply impressed with the importance of religion, and had shut himself up in his room for the purpose of reading his Bible, and supplicating the

* MSS. from his family.—Davidson's Hist. Presb. Ch., Ky.

renewing influence of the Holy Spirit. While he was thus engaged in these secret exercises, young Blythe came to the door and knocked, and as he received no answer, he continued knocking, and with so much violence that his comrade within feared that the door would be forced open; and, therefore, he unlocked it, and let him in. As he entered the room, he took up a book which lay upon the bed, and found that it was a Bible. "Do you read such a book as this?"—was Blythe's inquiry. His friend was strongly tempted for the moment to conceal his convictions, and turn the whole into ridicule; but he summoned resolution to acknowledge the truth, which was that his conscience was heavily burdened with a sense of his sinfulness. Blythe burst into tears, and told him that there was much more hope for him than for himself; for that he had been, for some time, a professor of religion, and had been living in open violation of his Christian obligations. From that time, however, Blythe broke away from the influences which had ensnared him, and engaged heartily and efficiently in the discharge of his various Christian duties; and this event marked the commencement of an extensive revival of religion.

Having graduated at Hampden Sidney, in 1789, and devoted some time to the study of Theology, under the direction of the Rev. Dr. Hall of North Carolina, Mr. Blythe was licensed by the Orange Presbytery; and in the fall of 1791, he visited Kentucky, and preached at Paint Lick, and other places. On the 25th of July, 1793, he was ordained and installed Pastor of Pisgah and Clear Creek Churches. At this time, there was great danger from the incursions of the Indians; and he has been heard to say that it was the custom of every man to attend preaching *armed*, and that even the minister carried his rifle and rode with his holsters. He resigned his charge, after having held it but a short time, and for a series of years was annually appointed a stated supply by the Presbytery. In this way he ministered to the Pisgah Church, upwards of forty years.

On the 1st of August, 1793, he was married to Margaret, daughter of James and Margaret (Irving) McElroy, who had removed to Kentucky from Rockbridge County, Va.

When the Presbytery of Transylvania were engaged in establishing the Kentucky Academy, Mr. Blythe and the Rev. David Rice were associated, in 1795, in an agency through the Eastern States, in aid of that object. Their effort was very successful, as they obtained upwards of ten thousand dollars. Of this sum President Washington and Vice President Adams contributed each a hundred dollars, and Aaron Burr, fifty. When, in 1798, the Academy was merged in the University of Transylvania, Dr. Blythe was appointed Professor of Mathematics, Natural Philosophy, Astronomy, and Geography; and subsequently he was the acting President of the Institution for twelve or fifteen years. When Dr. Holley was elected President, in 1818, Dr. Blythe was transferred to the chair of Chemistry in the Medical department. This place he resigned in 1831.

The degree of Doctor of Divinity was conferred upon him by the College of New Jersey, in 1805.

In connection with his Professorship he held a pastoral charge, being associated, for some years, with the Rev. James Welsh,* as Colleague Pas-

* JAMES WELSH was licensed to preach on the 27th of July, 1793, and recommended to the Synod of Virginia as a missionary. After labouring for a year in the bounds of the Redstone Presbytery, and declining a call in Mason County, Ky., he was ordained Pastor of the Lexing-

tor of the Church in Lexington. The co-pastorship is said to have been less harmonious than could have been desired.

He was strongly opposed to the war of 1812; and, in consequence of his political opinions, became involved in a controversy with Mr. William L. McCalla, then a candidate for licensure, and holding an opposite political creed. Mr. McCalla arraigned him at the bar of his Presbytery, on a variety of charges, and the case was finally referred to Synod. In respect to several points Dr. Blythe made due acknowledgments, and on the whole, was honourably acquitted.

In 1812, he commenced publishing a monthly periodical, called "The Evangelical Record and Western Review;" which, however, reached only to the second volume.

About the time that he resigned the Presidency of the College, he established a Seminary for young ladies, in which were introduced many of the higher branches of education, especially the Mathematics and Natural Science. He was exceedingly thorough in his instructions, and his influence in this department was widely and deeply felt.

In 1816, he was Moderator of the General Assembly of the Presbyterian Church.

In 1831, he attended the Convention of delegates from the Presbyteries, which met at Cincinnati, at the suggestion of the General Assembly, on the subject of Domestic Missions, and was chosen Moderator. In 1834, he signed the memorable "Act and Testimony;" and in 1835, was one of the standing committee of the Convention at Pittsburg, called by those who had signed that instrument. In 1837, he was one of the Convention of ministers and elders, which met in Philadelphia on the 11th of May, to deliberate on "some plan of reform" in the Church; and of this Body he was elected temporary chairman. In the great controversy that divided the Church, his sympathies and acts were with the Old School party.

In 1832, Dr. Blythe was chosen President of South Hanover College, Ind. He accepted the appointment; and, for several years, fulfilled the duties of the office to great acceptance, at the same time giving more or less gratuitous instruction in the Theological Seminary in the same place. In 1836, he resigned the Presidency of the College, and, wishing still to labour to the extent of his ability, he accepted an invitation in October, 1837, from the New Lexington Church, ten miles from Hanover, where he continued to preach until a few months before his death, when declining health obliged him to desist from labour.

In the autumn of 1841, Dr. Blythe's health began very perceptibly to fail, though he still preached occasionally, and was able to read and enjoy the society of his friends. After a few months, his disease, which was dropsy, took on a more decided form, and from that time he had only brief intervals of relief from suffering until his death. He viewed the approach of death with the utmost serenity of mind, and bore the fullest testimony to the all-sustaining power of Christian faith. He died on the 20th of May, 1842, aged seventy-seven; and was buried in a small enclosure on his own ground at Hanover.

ton and Georgetown Churches, February 17, 1796, in which charge he continued till 1804. On account of his inadequate salary, he was obliged to practise medicine for the support of his family. In 1799, he was appointed Professor of ancient languages in Transylvania University.

Dr. Blythe published the Sermon which he delivered on taking leave of his Church at Lexington, 1832, and one or two other occasional discourses.

Dr. Blythe had twelve children,—five sons and seven daughters. Three only of his sons lived to reach manhood. The eldest was killed in the battle of the River Raisin, at the age of eighteen. His second son died a few months previous to the completion of his college course. His third son (*Samuel Davies*) was born March 27, 1804; was graduated at Transylvania University in 1824; entered the Theological Seminary at Princeton immediately after his graduation, where he remained three years; was licensed to preach by the Presbytery of New Brunswick in 1827; acted as Agent of the American Bible Society during the winter of 1827–28; was settled in the autumn of 1828 as Pastor of the Church in Hillsboro', O., and resigned his charge after a few years for want of adequate support; became stated supply at South Hanover, Ind., for four years; was afterwards settled in the Tabernacle Church in Philadelphia, but remained there for only a short time; was settled at Woodbury, N. J., in 1837, where, in connection with his pastoral labours, he conducted a classical school; ruptured a blood vessel while preaching in Philadelphia, in 1841, in consequence of which he ceased preaching for a year, without giving up his school; resumed preaching at the end of a year,—shortly after which, decided symptoms of pulmonary consumption appeared, of which he died in June, 1843. His fourth son, *Joseph W.*, has been for many years Pastor of the Church in Cranberry, N. J. His fifth son, *James E.*, is a lawyer in Indiana. Mrs. Blythe, who was a lady of fine intellect, and most exemplary Christian character, died in January, 1835. She fell dead in the street, as she was returning home from a visit of mercy to a poor woman.

FROM THE REV. WILLIAM HILL, D. D.

WINCHESTER, Va., September 7, 1848.

Rev. and dear Sir: My knowledge of Dr. Blythe commenced when we were students together at Hampden Sidney College. Though he was three or four years older than myself, our acquaintance, after we both became specially interested in the subject of religion, grew into a most intimate friendship. But when we left College, he returned to North Carolina, his native State, and soon after removed to Kentucky, where he spent much the greater part of his life. As our fields of labour were so distant from each other, we seldom met after we parted at College; though we occasionally exchanged letters, and always retained a deep interest in each others' welfare. A few years before his death, we were thrown more together, and twice we served together as Commissioners to the General Assembly, where we had an opportunity of mutually reviving early recollections.

Dr. Blythe was unquestionably a man of superior talents, and of very considerable erudition. He was a fluent and ready speaker, and in the pulpit especially had a good degree of fervour and animation. I doubt not that his duties as Professor in the College considerably interfered with his success as a preacher and a pastor: and yet I believe he always considered the duties of the ministry as paramount to those of the Professorship. His lectures, especially on Chemistry, were highly popular and useful. He probably showed his strength as a lecturer, a disciplinarian, and a debater in ecclesiastical bodies, even more than in the pulpit. I have never heard the consistency or the purity of his Christian or ministerial character called in question by any one.

In person, Dr. Blythe was tall and straight; his face was broad and of ruddy complexion; and his gait and general appearance dignified almost to sternness. There was something in his manner, which at first would be very likely to leave an impression that he lacked affability; but it quickly disappeared on an acquaintance with him, and you felt that he was not wanting in a kindly and genial disposition. He had great tenacity of purpose, and was always candid, and sometimes a little abrupt, in the expression of his opinions. He was

> "A man resolved and steady to his trust;
> "Inflexible to all and obstinately just."

He commanded great respect wherever he was known, and filled an important place in society with marked dignity and usefulness.

Yours very respectfully,

WILLIAM HILL.

FROM THE REV. E. D. McMASTER, D. D.

PRESIDENT OF MIAMI UNIVERSITY.

Miami University, November 30, 1848.

Rev. and dear Sir: My personal acquaintance with the late Rev. Dr. Blythe was confined to the last three years and a half of his life,—I having previously seen him on only one occasion a few years before, as a member of the General Assembly of the Presbyterian Church. I, therefore,—though during this period my intercourse with him was frequent, intimate and cordial,—feel myself less competent to give a truthful and adequate delineation of his character, than if I had known him during his earlier years, and in the meridian of his life. The impression I received of him, I, under this disadvantage, send to you, in compliance with your request, to make such use of it as you may see fit,—only regretting that the representation is not more worthy of the subject.

One introduced to the acquaintance of Dr. Blythe, during the period I knew him, would have seen a gentleman advanced to a good old age, of portly person and commanding presence; of stature a little above the medium height; a frame stoutly built; a habit full but not corpulent, and of sanguineous complexion and temperament; a countenance, of features strongly enough marked, but regular and pleasing; and a large and well-formed head with a full covering of whitened locks,—the hoary head, in him a crown of glory, because found in the way of righteousness; though well stricken in years, erect and firm in posture; of stately gait and dignified mien, and of manners at first sight a little formal and stiff, but which soon relaxed into a demeanour bland, courteous and cordial.

If any one, admitted to his friendship and confidence, had the heart in cold blood to apply the dissecting knife to the character of this fine old gentleman, so venerable for years and his services to religion and learning, now gone to his reward with God, no doubt he might be able to indicate in that character some defects and infirmities; for some imperfections are implied in the possession of our common nature. I have no disposition to such an occupation; and I have no hesitation in saying that in our venerable friend, over any imperfections, whatever they were, which a critical eye might have discerned, those qualities worthy of approval and respect greatly predominated, and that his character was one of much and various excellence.

The *manners* of Dr. Blythe, in public bodies and in private life, exhibited a certain air which, to a casual observer, or to an unfriendly eye, might seem to savour of ostentatiousness and assumption of superiority. This appearance, however, scarcely existed beyond the threshold of intercourse. This passed, his whole deportment was in an unusual degree open, free, communicative and kind. Toward those for whom he had no respect, his bearing was apt to be such as to indicate in what light he viewed them; and where he thought there was impertinent obtrusiveness, he often put on an expression of contempt and scornfulness, which it were better to avoid even toward those who may provoke it. Yet one conciliatory word was at any time enough to dispel all this apparent severity, and to melt him into kindness, not less toward the humblest individual, than toward those who stood highest in his esteem. There was, in the expression of his sentiments, both on public occasions and in private intercourse, a positiveness, which, to those not fully acquainted with him, may have given the impression of dogmatism. But I have never known a man, by his years and standing so well entitled to have his own opinions respected, more ready to listen with candid attention, and yield all due respect, to the views of other men. Whatever partial exceptions may have at times appeared in this respect, his manners were habitually in an eminent degree urbane, social and cordial. Especially toward every *good* man,—by him apprehended to be such, his heart went out in expressions of warm and kindly affection.

In his *domestic relations*, he appeared to unusual advantage. For the memory of the wife of his youth and riper age, (deceased some years before I knew him,) who seems to have been a lady well worthy the regards he bestowed upon her, he, till the close of his life, cherished a deep, tender and most affectionate respect. Among his children who remained with him, and all of whom were grown up, he dwelt, as it becomes a father to dwell in the midst of his children,—his house affording a fine exemplification of what he himself was wont often to urge the priceless value of,—a well ordered and happy home,—and above all, a home sanctified and blessed by religion,—a Bethel wherein God is pleased to dwell.

If among men standing in the first rank of scholars, he would not have been eminently distinguished for the extent, the variety, or the depth, of his learning, such learning as he had, he possessed the happy faculty of turning to the best account in the service of sound education and true religion. Of his character as an instructer of youth in the academical situations which, for many years, he held in different institutions, I had no opportunity, from personal observation, to judge,—as he had retired from these employments before I knew him. The impression of himself which he left upon his pupils, so far as I have ever learned, was such as to induce, on their part, towards him, feelings of affectionate and respectful attachment, which continued throughout life. I recollect an incident illustrative both of this feeling, and of Dr. B.'s capacity for repartee. A late Governor of Kentucky had in his youth been a pupil of the Doctor, while at the head of Transylvania University, and was, during some part of his undergraduate course, more remarkable for his waggish propensities than for the studiousness of his habits. The Doctor had, on some occasion, called the student to his study, and at the close of some admonition, addressing him by his name, said with some emphasis,—"You will never do any good, Sir!" A few years ago, the Doctor being at Frankfort, was, with some other company, invited to dine with his quondam pupil, now the Chief Magistrate of his native Commonwealth. The Governor, in a style to draw the attention of the table, and in a tone of pleasant raillery, recited the occurrence, and added, "Now Doctor, I have proved that you are no prophet; for *I* am *Governor of the State of Kentucky*, and am entertaining *you* at my table." "Ha! Sir," said the Doctor, "the excellence of the *lecturer* has spoiled the credit of the *prophet; my lecture has made* you Governor of the State of Kentucky."

As a *preacher*, I presume that, during the few years that I occasionally heard him, he was scarcely equal to what he had been in an earlier period of his life. He preached sometimes from short notes, which lay before him, or were held in his hand; sometimes, I believe, without any written preparation at all. He was generally somewhat diffuse, and remarkable rather for the evangelical tone of his sentiment, the epigrammatic point of his style, the authoritativeness of his delivery, and the warmth and affectionateness of his manner, than for the fulness of his matter, the precision of his statements, the logical method of his arrangement, or the thoroughness of his discussion. I have been told by a venerable contemporary, and for many years a co-presbyter of his, that, in his earlier ministry, he was designated as "the tearful preacher." In the last years of his life, he was always earnest, often tender, sometimes truly impressive as well as instructive. From what I saw of him during this period, I can easily conceive that, in earlier life, he was what he is represented to have been for many years, one of the most zealous, active and efficient ministers in establishing institutions of learning, and in planting and rearing churches in the Commonwealth in which he spent the vigour of his days.

As *a member of the judicatories of the Church*, he took in their business a lively interest, and generally bore an active part. That he possessed consideration in these bodies appears, among other proofs, from the fact that he was at one time chosen the presiding officer of the highest judicatory in the Presbyterian Church. He was a member of the memorable Assembly of 1835, which another venerable member of that body predicted would be known in the History of the Church, as the "first Reforming General Assembly;" and of the still more memorable Assembly of 1837; and in the proceedings of both had an active participation.

Though called to act in troublous times, and repeatedly engaged in controversy, to *theological and ecclesiastical polemics*, Dr. Blythe was, I think, habitually averse. At an early period in his ministry, he became an actor in the scenes of that most extraordinary religious excitement, which prevailed in Kentucky and some adjacent States, in the beginning of the present century. To the extravagant and gross disorders which so largely entered into that excitement, he set himself in a very decided and uncompromising opposition, on account of which he was, by his people, excluded, for a whole year or more, from his own pulpit, and in other ways suffered reproach and obloquy. These disorders he undoubtedly continued, to the end of his days, to condemn as decidedly as ever. An analysis, however, of the complete phenomena of that marvellous movement, and a reduction of the different elements respectively to their proper principles, he had not, I think, been able to make to his own satisfaction; and his mind probably remained in doubt on the question, to what extent, in the midst of the phrenzy, and folly, and wickedness, of that strange tumult of the people, the Spirit of God, who out of darkness and chaos can bring forth light, and order, and life, may have been carrying on a work of saving grace in the conversion of men. It was a subject which appeared to be to him one of painful reminiscence, and of which he generally spoke with reserve. My impression is that there was left in his mind, as the result of his experience in that case, and in some occurrences of a later date, a feeling of reluctation toward all religious controversy. In the great controversy which, for many years agitated the Presbyterian Church, and which issued in the disowning by the Assembly of 1837 of four Synods, which had been in connection with it, and in the great schism of the following year, he was the advocate of moderate counsels. He, however, always contended for an adherence to the doctrine and order of the standards, and for the right and obligation of the Church, in her own proper capacity, to conduct the great work of Christian Missions committed to her by her Redeemer and King. When the controversy came to an issue and the division was effected, he, as a matter of conscientious preference, continued in the Body distinguished as the Old School Presbyterian Church. He nevertheless continued to be, as he had always been, a lover of every good man, in whatever department of the Church he might be found; and even when he could not approve of the means employed by men, to rejoice in whatever appeared to him adapted to advance the cause of true religion, and the Kingdom of God in the world.

Of the sincerity, truthfulness, and depth, of his *personal religion*, I believe it was those who knew him best who entertained the most confident persuasion. He ever evinced, in public and in private, in all those ways in which they who are born of God are usually wont to do so, a warm and lively interest in the things of religion; and on all suitable occasions was ready enough to enter into those freer communications which the best Christians reserve for the intercourse of intimate and confidential friendship. Christian principle evidently exerted a controlling and directing influence over his character and life. His personal religion bore, too, this mark of genuineness,—that it was progressive. His path was that of the just, which is as the shining light, that shineth more and more unto the perfect day. Planted in the house of the Lord, and spreading out his roots by the river of God, his leaf faded not,—he brought forth fruit in old age. This manifested itself in various ways, but was especially conspicuous in the increase of his zeal and labours to promote the great work of Christian missions, which appeared toward the close of his life. In the General Assembly of 1841, of which he was a member, and just about twelve months before his death, he earnestly exerted himself to effect the adoption of some measures for the better supply of the destitute in our own country with the Gospel. The result of his exertions appears in the action taken by the Assembly, and it is to him and another aged minister, who, more than fifty years before, had been by the same Presbytery and on the same day with himself, licensed to preach the Gospel, and whom, (they living in parts of the country remote from each other,) he had for the first time since met as a fellow-member in this Assembly, that that Body referred when they say; "The presence in this Body of two venerable fathers in Christ, who after more than half a century already spent in obeying their Master's last injunction, still feel impelled to devote the very twilight of life to the arduous work of missions, should make an irresistible appeal to ministers who are in the meridian of their vigour to enter upon this field.* Dr. Blythe returned home to prosecute this good work. In the following autumn, he originated in his own Synod a plan providing for the regular devotion by settled pastors of a portion of their time to missionary labours; and visited two neighbouring Synods to procure the adoption by them of the same plan. Thus, like old Nestor among the marshalled hosts of the well-booted Greeks on Ilium's shore, did this noble old man stimulate and urge on his junior comrades in the sacramental host of God to prosecute the warfare in which he himself had spent the vigour of his own days. Nay, rather like a good soldier of a Captain greater than Agamemnon, King of men, and in an infinitely nobler warfare than that waged by the Greeks against Troy, the language of his conduct was,—"I think it meet as long as I am in this tabernacle to stir you up, knowing that, shortly, I must put off my tabernacle." In this spirit our venerable friend habitually acted. Those among whom he went in and out, will not easily forget how favourite a theme with him during the last two or three years of his life, was this of the missionary operations at home and abroad for the spread of the Gospel, and the extension of the Kingdom of Christ;—how, everywhere,—in the pulpit, in the prayer-meeting, in the private circle, he urged its claims;—with what delight he hailed what he believed to be the morning rays of millenial glory;—how, when this was his theme, his imagination kindled, his bosom swelled with hope, his heart was enlarged with desire, his eyes were suffused with tears, and his supplications to the throne of grace gathered from every new occasion new fervour and importunity.

The *end* of this venerable servant of God was such as well became his course in life. During his last illness, I saw him daily,—sometimes oftener,—and left him about half an hour before his departure. From an early period of his illness, he regarded a fatal termination as a not improbable event. During life,

* Minutes of Assembly, 1841.

and even in his last years, while cherishing an abiding persuasion of his personal interest in Christ, he was not wholly exempt from the fear of death; and sometimes, in confidential intercourse, he gave expression to this apprehension in respect to the last enemy. From this fear, however, he obtained deliverance, and, from the beginning of his sickness, contemplated with composure his end. There were no visions of imagination travelling in the clouds, and no enthusiastic raptures of doubtful joy. But there was what was more satisfactory, along with deep views of sin, a direct and very decided acting of faith upon the righteousness of the Redeemer, as the ground of his acceptance with God, and a confiding repose on the promises of God in Christ. So resting, he possessed his soul in perfect peace. Repeatedly laying his hand upon his bosom, he would say,—"All here is peace," and express his gratitude for it. He spoke of the comfort brought him by prayers having special reference to his condition. Often he expressed the satisfaction he found in reposing directly upon the Word of God, in preference even to evangelical sentiment, when expressed in words of man's wisdom. On one occasion, reciting some popular lines expressive of repose on Christ, which are often on the lips of the dying, he said:—"Those are the words of man;" then quoted the Scripture promise,—"I will never leave thee nor forsake thee;" saying "*That* is the promise of God and I can rest upon it;" and again repeated a loose paraphrase of a passage in one of the Psalms; saying, "those are the words of man;" and then the words of the Psalm itself; "I shall be satisfied when I awake with thy likeness," adding, "*that* is the Word of God and it comforts me." In the earlier part of his illness, there was perhaps a prevalence of the natural desire of life, and some wish of further usefulness in the service of the Gospel on earth. But toward the close of his days, the desire of his inheritance in Heaven was predominant; and, as expressive of the state of his own mind, he referred to the declaration of the Apostle,—"I am in a strait betwixt two; having a desire to depart and be with Christ, which is far better."

So passed away this aged saint of God, and servant of Jesus Christ. Recognising and acting on the principle that he was under obligation to be consecrated to the service of Christ, he, in early youth, not only gave himself to the Lord, but devoted his life to the work of preaching the Gospel of the grace of God to men. In the work which thus engaged the morning of his days, he persevered through the meridian of life, and down to the evening of old age. Active, zealous, ardent, during a period of more than fifty years, he abounded in labours in establishing and conducting institutions of learning, and in planting and watering churches,—causing the wilderness to blossom as the garden of the Lord. Over many a field in this great Western land has he sown the good seed of the word, now waving with the harvest, and destined, as we trust, to bring forth their fruits in their season, while the earth shall remain, and the ordinances of Heaven endure. And herein is that saying true, "One soweth, and another reapeth; other men laboured, and we are entered into their labours." But in the end, the sower and the reaper together shall come from the field, bringing their sheaves with rejoicing.

I am, Rev. and dear Sir, with great respect,

Very truly yours,

E. D. McMASTER.

SAMUEL MILLER, D. D.*

1791—1850.

SAMUEL MILLER was the fourth son of the Rev. John Miller, and was born October 31, 1769, at the residence of his father, a few miles from Dover, De. His early literary training was under the parental roof; but in due time he was removed to Philadelphia, and became a member of the University of Pennsylvania. After passing through this institution, he graduated with high honour, July 31, 1789.

Having formed the purpose of devoting himself to the ministry, he entered upon the study of Theology, shortly after his graduation, under the direction of his father. But his father being removed before he had completed his theological course, he was licensed by the Presbytery of Lewes,—of which his father had long been a leading member,—on the 15th of October, 1791, and immediately after put himself, for the residue of his course, under the instruction of the celebrated Dr. Nisbet of Dickinson College. Here he continued for a number of months, and during this time not only enjoyed the best opportunities for literary and theological improvement, but formed an intimacy with his venerable instructer, which was a source of great pleasure, not only to himself, but to those to whom he imparted his cherished recollections, as long as he lived.

At a meeting of the Presbytery in April, 1792, a call was put into the hands of Mr. Miller to take the pastoral charge of the Congregation at Dover, then recently vacated by the death of his venerable father,—which, however, he ultimately declined. In the course of this year he was invited to visit a Church on Long Island, with a view to being heard as a candidate for settlement. On his way thither he stopped in New York, and preached to great acceptance. The result was, that, in the autumn of that year, he received a unanimous call from the united Presbyterian Churches of New York to become the colleague of Dr. Rodgers and Dr. McKnight. He has been heard to remark that he had never at that time aspired to anything beyond an ordinary country charge; and that nothing could have surprised him more than that he should have been thought of for such a public and important sphere of labour. He, however, after due deliberation, accepted the call, and was ordained and installed June 5, 1793. The Sermon on the occasion was preached by the Rev. Dr. McKnight.

From the commencement of his ministry in New York, he enjoyed a reputation in some respects peculiar to himself. Though Dr. Mason, and Dr. Linn, and Dr. Livingston, and other great lights were there, yet the subject of this notice was far from being thrown into the shade. Besides having the advantage of a remarkably fine person, and most bland and attractive manners, he had, from the beginning, an uncommonly polished style, and there was an air of literary refinement pervading all his performances, that excited general admiration, and well nigh put criticism at defiance. He was scarcely settled before his services began to be put in requisition on public occasions; and several of these early occasional discourses were published, and still remain as a monument of his taste, talents, and piety. One of his earliest published sermons was before a Society in the city of

* Communication from himself.—Presbyterian, 1850.

New York for the Manumission of Slaves; and it may well be doubted whether a more discreet, unexceptionable, and dignified sermon has been written on the subject since.

At the beginning of the present century, Mr. Miller preached a sermon appropriate to the time, reviewing some of the more prominent events and works of the century then just concluded. This sermon formed the nucleus of a work published in 1803, in two volumes octavo, which contained the most thorough account of the various improvements of the eighteenth century, which was then to be found in the English language. In executing this work he brought to his aid many of the most gifted and accomplished minds in various departments of learning; and in the favourable manner in which the book was received on both sides of the water, he had the most gratifying testimony that his labour had not been misapplied.

He was honoured with the degree of Doctor of Divinity, from the University at which he was graduated, in the year 1804. At that day it was uncommon, if not unprecedented, for a person so young to receive that honour; and he used sometimes, in sportively referring to it, to relate the following anecdote:—

He was travelling in New England with a clergyman who was well acquainted there, and they called, at the suggestion of the Doctor's travelling companion, to pay their respects to a venerable old minister, who lived somewhere on their route. The Doctor's friend introduced him as Dr. Miller of New York; and as the old gentleman knew that there was a distinguished medical practitioner of that name living there, and as he had not heard that the clergyman had been doctorated, and perhaps it had never even occurred to him that so young a man as he saw before him *could* be, he took for granted that it was the medical doctor to whom he had been introduced; and, after a few minutes, wishing to accommodate his conversation to the taste and capabilities of the stranger as well as he could, he turned to him, and asked him whether he considered the yellow fever, which had then just been prevailing in New York, contagious. Before the Doctor had time to reply, his friend perceiving the old gentleman's mistake, said, "This is not a medical doctor, Sir, but a Doctor of Divinity." The venerable minister gathered himself up, as if in a paroxysm of astonishment, and lifting up both hands, exclaimed, with a protracted emphasis upon each word, "*You don't!*"

In 1806, Dr. Miller was Moderator of the General Assembly of the Presbyterian Church.

In May, 1811, died the Rev. Dr. Rodgers, with whom Dr. Miller had served in the ministry, as a son with a father, for nearly twenty years. He preached a touching and impressive Sermon on the occasion of the death of his venerable colleague, and two years after published it, with an extended biography of him, in an octavo volume. As Dr. Rodgers had been identified with the Presbyterian Church more prominently, and for a longer period, than any other man, Dr. Miller, in writing an account of his life, was led almost of necessity to detail many events and scenes with which he was connected in common with many others; and hence there is probably more of the general history of the Presbyterian Church to be found in this volume than in any other biographical work that has been published. Independently of the peculiar interest that attaches to the subject, the work is quite a model in its department.

Dr. Miller is understood to have taken a deep interest in the establishment of the Theological Seminary at Princeton, from the first inception of the enterprise, though without the remotest idea that he was destined to be more intimately connected with it than many others of his brethren. When Dr. Alexander was inaugurated, in August, 1812, Dr. Miller preached the Sermon—and an appropriate and admirable sermon it was. When the chair of Ecclesiastical History and Church Government was to be filled, the eyes of the Church were directed to Dr. Miller; and in due time the judgment of the Church was pronounced in his being formally elected to that responsible place. The appointment was made in May, 1813; and having accepted it, he was inducted into office on the 29th of September following.

Here Dr. Miller continued discharging the duties of his office with great fidelity and ability, and to the entire acceptance of the Church, during a period of more than thirty-six years. Though he had not, in his latter years at least, any great vigour of constitution, and was obliged to nurse himself with more than ordinary care, yet he was able to go through with his prescribed duties in the Seminary, besides performing a good deal of occasional literary labour, until within about a year of his death. In May, 1849, the General Assembly accepted the resignation of his office, testifying, at the same time, in the strongest manner possible, their grateful appreciation of his services, and their high respect for his character. His health, which had been waning for a considerable time, failed after this more perceptibly, until at length it became manifest to all that his period of active service was over. He lingered a number of weeks, suffering not so much from positive pain as from extreme exhaustion and difficulty of respiration, but without a cloud to intercept the clear shining of the Sun of Righteousness. He felt that his work was done, and he was ready to enter upon his reward. The few friends who were privileged to see him during the period of his decline, especially after he had nearly reached the dark boundary, were not only edified but surprised at the expressions of humble, grateful, joyful triumph, that fell from his lips. He gently passed away to his reward, on Monday evening, January 7, 1850. His Funeral drew together a large concourse of clergymen and others from the neighbouring towns and cities, and an appropriate and characteristic Sermon was preached on the occasion, by his venerable colleague, Dr. Alexander.

In the autumn of 1801, Dr. Miller was married to Sarah, daughter of the Hon. Jonathan Dickinson Sergeant, a distinguished lawyer and member of Congress, of Philadelphia. They had ten children, one of whom died in infancy, and only six survived him. The eldest daughter became the wife of the Rev. Dr. John Breckenridge. Two of the sons are ministers of the Gospel, one is a surgeon in the Navy, and one a lawyer,—practising in Philadelphia.

Dr. Miller, as I have already had occasion to intimate, had much more than common advantages in respect to personal appearance. Of about the middle size, he was perfectly well proportioned, with a fine, intelligent and benignant countenance, which would not be likely to pass unnoticed in a crowd. His manners were cultivated and graceful in a high degree, uniting the polish of Chesterfield with the dignity and sincerity of a Christian minister. He was remarkably exact in his attention to little things; and though this may have sometimes given him, to a certain extent, an air of formality, it had undoubtedly much to do in giving a finish to both his manners and his character. His work on "Clerical Manners" could never have been written by one who was less considerate and exact than himself; and, indeed, but for his exceeding modesty, one might almost suppose that in writing it he was taking his own portrait. He was never thrown into any society so polished but that he was entirely at home in it, and while he was as far as possible from being enslaved to worldly usages, or cultivating a habit of too indiscriminate worldly intercourse, he never thought it beneath him to appear on all occasions as the accomplished Christian gentleman.

Dr. Miller's intellectual and moral character partook of the same beautiful symmetry that characterized his external appearance. How far this grew out of his natural constitution, and how far it was the result of discipline and habit, it may be difficult to decide; though he has been heard to say that he was originally of an impetuous turn, and that it had required severe efforts to school himself into all that moderation and self-control of which we saw him in possession. He had evidently by nature a kindly, sympathetic and generous spirit. His heart beat quick to the tale of distress, and his hand opened instinctively to administer relief. He had warm social affections, and received as well as imparted great pleasure in his intercourse with his friends. His mind was not, like that of Dr. Mason—bold, startling, I had almost said terrible in some of its demonstrations; but it was perfectly well balanced in all its faculties, calm and deliberate but certain in its movements, and worthy of being trusted wherever good taste, sound judgment, and high intelligence, were demanded. He might not have been selected as the man to electrify the multitude by a single effort, but there are few men who have an assemblage of intellectual and moral qualities, so well fitted as were his to form a dignified character, or to secure a course of honourable and enduring usefulness.

I have already alluded to the fact that Dr. Miller early took rank with the best preachers of his day. His sermons were generally written, but in the earlier periods of his ministry, as I have heard him say, were almost always committed to memory,—as the prejudice against reading in New York was so great, that it was at the peril at least of one's reputation as a preacher that he ventured to lay his manuscript before him. At a later period, however, especially after he went to Princeton, he generally read his discourses, but he read with so much ease and freedom, that, but for the turning over of the leaves, one would scarcely have been aware that he was reading at all. His voice was not strong, nor yet particularly musical, but it was pleasant notwithstanding; and so perfectly distinct was his enunciation that he could be heard without effort at the extremity of the largest church. His attitudes in the pulpit were extremely dignified, though perhaps somewhat precise; and his gesture, which was never otherwise than appropriate, was yet not very abundant. His utterance was deliberate,—possibly too much so to suit the mass of hearers; but it was marked by an evident sincerity and solemnity that were well fitted to make an impression. He would occasionally deliver a sentence with an air of majesty, and a degree of unction that would make it quite irresistible. I remember, for instance, to have heard him relate in a New Year's sermon on the text "How old art thou?" the well known anecdote of the Roman Emperor, exclaiming at the close of a day which had gone to waste, "Oh, I have lost a day!" and it seemed scarcely possible that the exclamation should have been uttered in a way to secure to it a higher effect. Still he could not be considered an impassioned preacher; and his manner was characterized rather by quiet dignity, and occasionally by genuine pathos, than by any remarkable versatility or vigour. But his discourses were decidedly superior to his manner of delivering them. He never shot at random: he always had a distinct object in view, and he went deliberately and skilfully to work to accomplish it. There was the same symmetry about his sermons as there was about his character—every thing was in its right place. If you did not expect to be thrilled by such overwhelming passages as you might sometimes hear from Mason or Chalmers, you knew that you would never be shocked by any thing of doubtful propriety. You expected that every thing in the service would be fitting and reverent, and every way up to the dignity of the pulpit; and you were never disappointed. No man was farther than Dr. Miller from that miserable affectation that throws together dry and doubtful speculations,—at best the refuse of philosophy, and then calls the heap of chaos that is thus produced a Gospel sermon. While his preaching was not common-place in any worse sense than the Bible is so, he had no ambition for originality that led him to stray beyond the Bible for the material of his discourses; and while he was satisfied with what he found there, his object seemed to be to work it up in a manner which should best subserve the great objects of his ministry.

As a Professor in the Theological Seminary, Dr. Miller was alike able and faithful. He gave to his work all the energies of his mind and body; and even after the infirmities of age had so accumulated upon him that he might have reasonably found an apology for relaxing, if not altogether discontinuing, his labours, he still continued to perform the full amount of service demanded by his Professorship. His lectures were always highly appropriate and instructive; and while they were evidently the result of much thought and investigation, and were so admirably perspicuous and well arranged that they could easily be remembered, they were written with excellent taste, and sometimes, where description was called for, were marked by great rhetorical beauty. In his intercourse with the students of the Seminary he was quite as much the Father as the Professor; and if a record of all his kind offices towards his pupils, many of which were a matter of profound secresy, could be displayed, I doubt not that it would greatly exceed any estimate which those who appreciate his beneficence most highly, have ever formed.

Dr. Miller was an honest, vigilant and devoted friend of what he believed to be the true interests of the Presbyterian Church. In the controversy which issued in its division he was inflexibly with the Old School, though he had many warm friends on the other side with whom he continued to maintain the most friendly relations. Indeed it was impossible for him to be otherwise than bland and courteous even towards an adversary. Not a small part of his writings are, in a greater or less degree, of a polemical character; but they are generally marked by great caution and dignity, and I have never heard a more hearty tribute paid to him as an author, than by one eminent man who held with him a somewhat vigorous controversy.

Dr. Miller's highest attraction, after all, was that he was great in goodness. Not only was he endowed by the God of nature with superior moral qualities, but these qualities were moulded by the God of grace into an exalted specimen of Christian excellence. He was eminently conscientious, disinterested and devout. Condescending in indifferent matters, he always stood firm to his own convictions, where any thing important was involved. He was meek, humble, patient and forgiving. He moved about in society, exhibiting the graces of nature in attractive combination with the higher graces of the Spirit. In his latter years, he was reverenced as a Patriarch, and there was wide-spread and hearty mourning when he went down to his grave.

The following is a list of Dr. Miller's publications:—

VOLUMES.

A Brief Retrospect of the Eighteenth Century, 2 vols. 8vo., 1803. Letters on the Constitution and Order of the Christian Ministry, addressed to the Members of the Presbyterian Churches in the city of New York, 12mo., 1807. A Continuation of Letters concerning the Constitution and Order of the Christian Ministry, being an Examination of the Strictures of the Rev. Doctors Bowden and Kemp, and the Rev. Mr. How, on the former series, 12mo., 1809. Memoirs of the Rev. John Rogers, D. D., 8vo., 1813. Letters on Unitarianism, 8vo., 1821. Letters on Clerical Manners and Habits, 12mo., 1827. An Essay on the Warrant, Nature, and Duties, of the Office of the Ruling Elder in the Presbyterian Church, 12mo., 1831. Letters to Presbyterians on the Present Crisis in the Presbyterian Church in the United States, 12mo., 1833. Infant Baptism scriptural and reasonable, and Baptism by Sprinkling or Affusion the most suitable and edifying mode: Two Sermons [originally preached at Freehold, N. J.], 12mo., 1834. Presbyterianism the truly Primitive and Apostolical Constitution of the Church of Christ, 1835. Life of Jonathan Edwards, (Sparks, American Biography,) 12mo., 1837. Memoir of the Rev. Charles Nisbet, D. D., 12mo., 1840. The Primitive and Apostolic Order of the Church of Christ Vindicated, 12mo., 1840. Letters from a Father to his Sons in College, 12mo., 1843. The Warrant, Nature, and Duties, of the Office of Ruling Elder in the Presbyterian Church: A Sermon preached in Philadelphia, with an Appendix, 18mo., 1843. Thoughts on Public Prayer, 12mo., 1849.

PAMPHLETS.

A Sermon preached in New York, on the Anniversary of American Independence, 1793. A Discourse before the Grand Lodge of the State of New York, 1795. A Discourse Commemorative of the Discovery of New York, by Henry Hudson, (New York Historical Collections,) 1795. A Sermon delivered in New York, on the nineteenth Anniversary of the Independence of America, 1795. A Discourse delivered before the New York Society for the Manumission of Slaves, &c., 1797. A Sermon delivered in the city of New York, on a day of National Humiliation, Fasting, and Prayer, 1798. A Sermon delivered in New York, on a Day of Thanksgiving, Humiliation, and Prayer, observed on account of the removal from the city of a malignant and mortal disease, 1799. A Sermon occasioned by the death of General Washington, 1799. A Sermon before the New York Missionary Society, 1802. Two Discourses on Suicide, preached in the city of New York, 1805. A Sermon for the Benefit of a Society in New York, for the relief of Poor Widows with Small Children, 1808. A Sermon preached in New York, on the Divine Appointment, the Duties, and Qualifications, of Ruling Elders, 1809. A Discourse delivered in New York, on the Burning of the Richmond Theatre, 1812. A Sermon delivered at

Princeton, at the Inauguration of Rev. Archibald Alexander, D. D., as Professor, &c., 1812. A Sermon delivered at Baltimore at the ordination and installation of Rev. William Nevins, 1820. A Letter to the Editor of the Unitarian Miscellany, in reply to an attack on the Sermon at the ordination of Mr. Nevins, 1821. A Sermon delivered at New Haven, at the ordination of Rev. Messrs. William Goodell, William Richards, and Artemas Bishop, as Evangelists and Missionaries to the Heathen, 1822. Reply to Professor Stuart on the Eternal Generation of the Son, 1822. A Sermon entitled "The Literary Fountains Healed," preached in the Chapel of the College of New Jersey, 1823. A Sermon delivered at the opening of the new Presbyterian Church in Arch Street, Philadelphia, 1823. A Sermon preached at Newark, before the Synod of New Jersey, for the benefit of the African School under the care of the Synod, 1823. An Introductory Lecture addressed to the Theological Students at Princeton, on the Utility and Importance of Creeds and Confessions, 1824. A Discourse delivered at Princeton, before the Literary and Philosophical Society of New Jersey, 1825. A Letter to a gentleman of Baltimore, in reference to the case of the Rev. Mr. Duncan, 1826. A Sermon delivered in Baltimore, at the installation of the Rev. John Breckenridge, 1826. Two Sermons in the National Preacher, (Nos. 8 and 9,) on the Evidence and Duty of being on the Lord's Side, 1826. An Introductory Lecture addressed to the Students of the Theological Seminary at Princeton, on the Importance of the Gospel Ministry, 1827. An Introductory Lecture to the Students of the Theological Seminary at Princeton, on the Importance of Mature Preparatory Study for the Ministry, 1829. A Sermon preached at Albany, at the installation of the Rev. W. B. Sprague, 1829. Two Sermons in the National Preacher, (Nos. 98 and 99,) on Religious Fasting, 1831. A Sermon on Ecclesiastical Polity, (one of the Spruce Street Lectures,) 1832. A Sermon in the Presbyterian Preacher, (Vol. I. No. 1,) on the importance of Gospel Truth, 1832. A Sermon entitled, "A Plea for an Enlarged Ministry," preached in Philadelphia, before the General Assembly's Board of Education, and published in the Presbyterian Preacher, (Vol. III. No. 1,) 1834. A Sermon delivered at Pittsburg before the Association of the Alumni of the Theological Seminary at Princeton, 1835. Two Sermons in the National Preacher, (Nos. 198 and 199,) on the Importance and Means of Domestic Happiness, 1835. A Sermon preached at Baltimore, before the American Board of Commissioners for Foreign Missions, 1835. A Sermon preached at Princeton, in memory of the Rev. George S. Woodhull, 1835. A Sermon preached at Baltimore, at the installation of the Rev. John C. Backus, 1836. Two Sermons in the National Preacher, (Nos. 230 and 231,) on Christ our Righteousness, 1836. A Sermon on the Dangers of Education in Roman Catholic Seminaries, preached in Baltimore and New York, 1837. A Sermon preached in Philadelphia, before the Board of Foreign Missions of the Presbyterian Church, 1838. An Address delivered at Elizabethtown, at the dedication of a Monument to the memory of the Rev. James Caldwell, 1845.

In addition to the preceding, Dr. Miller published a Biographical Sketch of Edward Miller, M. D., prefixed to his works; an Essay introductory to Lectures to Young People, by W. B. Sprague; a Letter appended to Lectures on Revivals, by W. B. Sprague; Contributions to the Biography of Mrs. Margaret Breckenridge, &c., &c.

FROM THE REV. JAMES CARNAHAN, D D

PRINCETON, February 16, 1855.

Rev. and dear Sir: Several months ago you did me the honour to request that I would furnish you with some of my reminiscences of the late Rev. Dr. Miller of this place. You are aware that personal affliction and consequent derangement of domestic affairs have since occupied my attention, so that I could think of little else. And now, though I would gladly pay my tribute of affectionate respect to the venerable man, whose virtues and usefulness you wish to embalm, I confess I am at a loss where to begin and what to say. For half a century Dr. Miller occupied a very prominent place in the Presbyterian Church in this country, so that his biography in his public relations would be, to a great extent, the history of his denomination, for more than fifty years. It is to be hoped that this important service to the Church will ere long be performed by some competent hand—all that I can attempt, and I suppose all that you desire, will be a few general remarks.

Fifty years ago, I knew Dr. Miller from reputation and from his published works, especially from his Review of the Eighteenth Century and his Defence of the Validity of Presbyterian Ordination. Since that time the productions of his pen have been numerous and various, so that, as a writer on theological subjects, he is as well and as favourably known in Europe and America as any author in our country of the same period. In every thing he has written there is a clearness of thought, and a purity and precision of diction, which render his style as fair a specimen of good old English as our country affords. We find in his writings no laboured effort to involve in mist a common thought, in order to give it the air of novelty; much less do we find, as is too much the fashion of the present day, involved sentences consisting of high sounding words laboriously strung together, in order to give to the superficial reader the idea of profound thought, when in truth there is no intelligible meaning conveyed.

If Dr. Miller proposed no new theory on the subject of religion or morals, and stamped his name on the doctrine taught, he did all that we have a right to expect any one to do at the present day for the benefit of the Church—I mean that he stated in a perspicuous manner the teachings of the Bible, and met what he regarded the prevailing errors of the day, with the courtesy of a Christian gentleman. In this respect he may be considered as a model controvertist. He never substitutes personal abuse of an opponent for argument in refutation of his doctrines. While he states with all fulness, and maintains by fair argument, what he believes to be the truth, he never attempts to render ridiculous or odious those who hold different opinions.

Until 1823 my personal acquaintance with this excellent man was transient. From that time until his death, a period of twenty-seven years, it was my happiness to live in his neighbourhood, and to have frequent and almost daily intercourse with him; to see him in the pulpit, in the Presbytery, in the Board of Trustees of the College, in the social circle, and in private interviews; and I must say that the respect and admiration with which I regarded him both as a man and as a Christian, increased every year until he was removed from this world.

In the pulpit, I have heard men who, by the ardour of their utterance, the brilliancy of their imagery, and the energy of their action, would rouse the attention and excite the feelings of a popular audience in a higher degree than Dr. Miller; but for solid Gospel truth, presented in a distinct and logical manner, and expressed in chaste and appropriate language, he was certainly distinguished above most of his brethren. He loved to preach,—not for the sake of human applause; for he continued to occupy the pulpit, whenever an opportunity offered, long after he had reached the zenith of his fame. When his services were not required in the Seminary, or College, or Church in Princeton, he would frequently ride to some neighbouring congregation, and volunteer his services, which were always acceptable both to the pastor and to the people. In leading the devotions of the large congregation, or of the social meeting, he was peculiarly happy. There was a simplicity and reverence in his manner and language, and an appropriateness in the topics which he introduced, which were admirably fitted to awaken devout feeling in the hearts of his auditors. Though he was not given to repetition in prayer, he sometimes, from the fulness of his heart, violated the rule which he prescribed to his pupils on this subject—*to be brief.* No matter at what time or place he was called on, he was always ready to engage in prayer in a solemn and devout manner; nor was it difficult for him to make the transition from social and cheerful conversation, in which he greatly delighted, to acts of devotion. His whole demeanour in public and in private indicated that he habitually acted under a sense of the Divine presence; but his devotional spirit was as far as possible from any thing like a gloomy habit of mind. He was a most genial and cheerful companion, abounding in rich and appropriate anecdotes, while he never descended to any thing unbecoming a Christian or a minister of the Gospel.

For several years the Professors of the Theological Seminary and the officers of the College were in the habit of meeting at each others' houses once in two weeks, for the purpose of spending the evening in easy and familiar conversation on subjects chiefly connected with the interests of education and religion. In these meetings Dr. Miller took a lively interest; and he contributed greatly to make them profitable and pleasant, not only by drawing largely from his own rich and varied stores, but also by eliciting from others whatever each one might know on the subject under consideration. I remember with what skill he would touch the key-note which would open the lips of his distinguished and venerable colleague, Dr. Alexander, or of the gifted and lamented Professor Dod, or of others whose presence helped to give interest to the meeting. He delighted to receive and to impart instruction by oral communication; yet it is remarkable that his fondness for social intercourse, and the solicitude of his friends to enjoy his company, were never allowed to interfere with his studies. The pleasant companion neglects his books—the student becomes a recluse. In Dr. Miller both these characters were most happily blended. Whoever has read or even glanced at his numerous publications, must be convinced that he was a laborious and successful student; and when we take into view his preparations for the pulpit, and for the daily instruction of his class in the lecture room, it is just matter of surprise that any man could perform so much intellectual labour, especially when it is remembered that Dr. M. did not enter on the performance of any public duty without full and accurate preparation. The great secret of his being able to do so much and to do it so well, was that he did every thing systematically. He had a time for every duty; and one duty was not suffered to encroach upon another. In his study he did not lounge, and permit his thoughts to wander from the subject before him. For the purpose of preserving his health, or perhaps as an excitement to mental exertion, he did all his writing, standing at his desk. In early life, and indeed to the close of life, he had a tendency to pulmonary disease. To counteract this tendency he was temperate in all things. Before he came to Princeton, and for some time after, he was in the habit of taking a single glass of wine at dinner, believing that it assisted digestion and promoted health. But he considered that his example might be injurious to others; and at that period of life when many think that artificial stimulants are necessary to sustain declining nature, he denied himself his former moderate indulgence, and abstained entirely from all kinds of intoxicating drinks. He adopted this practice, not because he thought the moderate use of alcoholic drinks in all cases in itself wrong, but from an apprehension that his example might have an injurious effect upon others. He, however, often remarked that he never experienced the least injury or inconvenience from the change.

Believing that daily exercise in the open air was necessary for his health, he permitted no weather or engagement to prevent his walking or riding out, at least once every day. I have seen him in the most inclement weather in summer and winter, wending his way to the Post-office, or to make a necessary call, or to breathe the fresh air without any other object. While he carefully avoided a current of air coming upon him from a window or a door, he dreaded neither cold nor heat, nor snow nor rain, in an atmosphere freely circulating on all sides. I cannot doubt that this daily contact with the open air, connected with regular and temperate habits, was the means of sustaining to an advanced age a constitution not naturally strong.

In his personal habits and dress he was remarkably neat, without any thing, however, of undue precision. From the use of tobacco in all its forms, it was a matter of conscience as well as of *taste* with him carefully to abstain; for he believed not only that it was positively injurious to health, but that it tended to create a thirst for intoxicating drinks. In his manners he was polished and graceful, and duly attentive to all those proprieties which confer dignity upon social intercourse. Of the "clerical manners" which he recommended in his invaluable work on that subject, he was himself an admirable example. His own fine manners were no doubt to some extent the effect of culture—of having been accustomed from early life to mingle much in refined society; but they were still more to be referred to the legitimate acting of his benevolent affections. His words and actions were the unstudied expressions of a warm and generous heart. He was ready to assist a friend, not only when it was convenient to himself, but at the expense of his own convenience; and he did it with a heartiness and good will which made the kindness doubly valuable.

In the management of his secular and domestic concerns, he was well worthy of imitation. Economy in all his personal and household expenses was conspicuous; and if his creditor could be reached, he permitted no debt, great or small, to remain unsatisfied a week or a day. His private means, independent of his salary as a Professor in the Theological Seminary, were probably equal to the frugal expenses of his family; yet he did not permit his property to accumulate—he acted on the principle which he frequently inculcated—namely, that a large inheritance is generally a curse to children. It is impossible to estimate how much he distributed every year to good and charitable purposes; because he made no display of his charities by giving to particular objects large sums, worthy of being displayed as examples of liberality. But it could not be concealed that he refused aid to no object that he considered worthy of public or private beneficence. He used to say that he loved to have a nail in every building intended for the glory of God or the good of man.

At the time of his decease, Dr. Miller had been forty-three years a Trustee of the College of New Jersey, and he had seldom been absent from the meetings of the Board, and was always an active and influential member. A short time before his death he attended a meeting of the Trustees, and, before the business was finished, he rose, and, on account of the feeble state of his health, asked leave of absence the remainder of the session; at the same time stating that he did not expect ever to meet the Board again. His work, he said, was done; and, lifting his feeble hands, he prayed that the blessing of God might rest on the Trustees, the Faculty, the students, and all connected with the venerable and beloved institution. This was the final benediction of one who for several years had been the Senior Trustee. It was truly an impressive and solemn scene—not to be forgotten, I am sure, by any one who witnessed it.

Leaving it to some one of Dr. Miller's numerous pupils to say what he was in the Lecture room, I will only add that the crowning excellence of his character was his humble and devoted piety, his attachment to the great truths of the Gospel, his earnest desire to honour his Lord and Saviour, and to extend to his fellow-sinners that precious Gospel by which he was himself so wonderfully sustained and comforted in the evening of his days.

I am, my dear Sir, with great respect,

Yours very truly,

JAMES CARNAHAN.

FROM THE REV. NICHOLAS MURRAY, D. D.

ELIZABETHTOWN, January 15, 1853.

My dear Sir: I cannot possibly refuse your request for my recollections of our late beloved and venerated Dr. Miller; and yet, as I am well aware that your own long and intimate acquaintance with him qualifies you to render every testimony that could be desired concerning his character, I shall limit myself to an account of an interview that I had with him a short time before his death—an interview rendered memorable to me not only by the fact that it was the last, but from its having witnessed to one of the most remarkable exhibitions of the very sublimity of Christian triumph, that have ever come within my knowledge.

The Historical Society of New Jersey had met at Princeton, now a place of patriotic, and classic, and sacred associations. It was a noble gathering of men distinguished in their various professions as Jurists, Advocates, Professors, and Divines; and there was a most cordial greeting and commingling of these historic associates. All differences in sentiments, professions, and politics, were laid aside, while in the pursuit of the one common object of honouring New Jersey by collecting materials for its history, and rescuing from oblivion the names of her many heroic and distinguished sons.

But one was absent who had rarely been absent before, and who was one of the founders and Vice President of the Society; one whose bland and polished manners always attracted regard, and whose venerable aspect always left an impression. His absence from the meeting, and in the town of his residence, excited inquiry; and when it was announced that Dr. Miller was very seriously ill, there was a universal expression of sorrow and sympathy. It was solemnly felt by all that in those historic gatherings we should see his face no more.

Dr. Miller's son conveyed to me a message from him that he would like to see me on the morning of the next day, if convenient. The hour of our interview was fixed; and, as other engagements required punctuality, I was there at the moment.

But, as the barber had just entered the room, he was not quite ready to see me, and he sent a request that I would wait half an hour. This my other engagements absolutely forbade; and, on sending him word to that effect, he invited me to his room. As I entered it, the scene which presented itself was truly impressive. The room was his library, where he had often counselled, cheered, and instructed me. There, bolstered in a chair, feeble, wan, and haggard, was my former teacher and friend,—one half of his face shaven, with the soap on the other half, and the barber standing behind his chair. The old sweet smile of welcome played upon his face, and having received his kind hand and greetings, he requested me to take a seat by his side. His communication was a brief one: he had written a history of the Theological Seminary for the Historical Society, which was not yet printed, and he wished an unimportant error into which he thought he had fallen to be corrected; and that there might be no mistake, he wished me to write it down,—thus showing his ruling passion for even verbal accuracy. When his object in sending for me was gained, he then, in a most composed and intensely solemn manner, thus addressed me:

"My dear brother, my sands are almost run, and this will be, probably, our last meeting on earth. Our intercourse, as Professor and pupil, and as ministers, has been one of undiminished affection and confidence. I am just finishing my course; and my only regrets are that I have not served my precious Master more fervently, sincerely, and constantly. Were I to live my life over again, I would seek more than I have done, to know nothing but Christ. The burdens that some of us have borne in the Church will now devolve upon you and your brethren—see to it that you bear them better than we have done, and with far greater consecration; and as this will, no doubt, be our last interview here, it will be well to close it with prayer. As I am too feeble to kneel, you will excuse me if I keep my chair."

I drew my chair before him, and knelt at his feet. The coloured barber laid aside his razor and brush, and knelt by his side. As he did not indicate which of us was to lead in prayer, I inferred, because of his feebleness, that it would be right for me to do so; and while seeking to compose my own mind and feelings to the effort, I was relieved by hearing his own sweet, feeble, melting accents. His prayer was brief, but unutterably touching and impressive. He commenced it by thanksgiving to God for his great mercy in calling us into the fellowship of the saints, and then calling us into the ministry of his Son. He then gave thanks that we ever sustained to one another the relation of pupil and teacher, and for our subsequent pleasant intercourse as ministers of the Gospel. He thanked God for the many years through which He had permitted him to live and for any good which He had enabled him to do. "And now, Lord," said he, "seeing that thine aged, imperfect servant is about being gathered to his fathers, let his mantle fall upon thy young servant, and far more of the Spirit of Christ than he has ever enjoyed. Let the years of thy servant be as the years of his dying teacher; let his ministry be more devoted, more holy, more useful; and when he comes to die, may he have fewer regrets to feel in reference to his past ministrations. We are to meet no more on earth; but when thy servant shall follow his aged father to the grave, may we meet in Heaven, there to sit, and shine, and sing, with those who have turned many to righteousness, who have washed their robes and made them white in the blood of the Lamb. Amen."

I arose from my knees, melted as is wax before the fire. My full heart sealed my lips. Through my flowing tears I took my last look of my beloved teacher, the counsellor of my early ministry, the friend of my ripening years, and one of the most lovely and loved ministers with which God has ever blessed the Church. Every thing impressed me—the library, his position, the barber; his visage, once full and fresh, now sallow and sunken; his great feebleness, his faithfulness, his address, and, above all, that prayer, never, never to be forgotten! He extended his emaciated hand from under the white cloth that hung from his breast to his knees, and, taking mine, gave me his parting, his last benediction. That address—that prayer—that blessing, have made enduring impressions. It was the most solemn and instructive parting interview of my life.

When I next saw him, he was sleeping in his coffin in the front parlour of his house, where he often, with distinguished urbanity and hospitality, entertained, instructed, and delighted his friends. That parlour was crowded by distinguished strangers, and by many of his former pupils, who mourned for him as for a father—for a father he was to them all. And as they passed around to take a parting view of his countenance, from which even death could not remove its accustomed placid, benevolent smile, their every bosom heaved with intense emotion, their eyes were suffused with tears; and could the tongue have uttered the emotions of the heart, it would have been in the language of Elisha when he gazed on Elijah ascending before him into Heaven,—"My father, my father, the chariot of Israel, and the horsemen thereof!"

His death was as calm and triumphant as his life was pure, disinterested, and lovely; and as pious men carried him to his burial, and as we covered up his remains under the clods of the valley, the prayer arose at least from one heart, "May I live the life of this righteous man, and let my last end be like his!"

There are many scenes in the life of Dr. Miller that memory frequently recalls—scenes in the class-room, in the General Assembly, in the Synod of New Jersey, in the pulpit, in the social party—scenes which occurred during the conflicts of parties, and in the frank and unrestrained intercourse of social life. In them all Dr. Miller was pre-eminently like himself. But the scene by which I most love to recall him, and which memory most frequently brings back, is that parting scene in his study. Oh, may that last prayer be answered!

With great regard, very sincerely yours,

NICHOLAS MURRAY

ARCHIBALD ALEXANDER, D. D.*

1791—1851.

Archibald Alexander was of Scotch Irish extraction,—his grandfather, Archibald Alexander, having emigrated from Ireland to Virginia in 1737. His father, William Alexander, was a person of great worth and respectability, and was one of the original Trustees of Liberty Hall Academy, which has since become Washington College. The subject of this sketch was born near Lexington, Rockbridge County, Va., April 17, 1772, and was the third of nine children. Among the incidents of his early life, he used to relate that, on his arrival at Liberty Hall, where he went to pursue his studies, he found, on unpacking his trunk, a copy of Soame Jenyns on the Evidences of Christianity, which his mother had placed there without his knowledge. He became at once deeply interested in the work, and did not lay it aside till he had finished reading it.

In 1788, a very unusual attention to religion prevailed in the Congregations in Virginia, South of the James River, and East of the Blue Ridge. In August, 1789, the Rev. William Graham, Rector of Liberty Hall, in compliance with an invitation from the Rev. John Blair Smith, then President of Hampden Sidney College, made a visit to Prince Edward, to attend a Communion in the Briery Congregation. He was accompanied by several of his young students, who, he hoped, might find the visit profitable to them. Archibald Alexander was one of the number; and the following incidents of the visit are related by himself:—

"The sermon of Mr. Graham on the text—'Comfort ye, comfort ye my people,' &c., was the first sermon that he preached, on his first visit to Prince Edward, when I accompanied him. It was preached at Briery, immediately after the administration of the Lord's Supper; and Dr. Smith said to me that he had never heard more than one sermon which he liked as well, and that one was preached by the Rev. James Mitchel. I did not

* Memoir by his son, Rev. J. A. Alexander, D. D.—Presb. Mag., II.—Foote's Sketches of Va., 2d Series.

hear the first part of this discourse, for there being a prospect of rain, the Communion was administered in the house, and the non-professors, to which number I belonged, were requested to remain under the arbour, and hear sermons from the Rev. Nash Legrand, and the Rev. Samuel Houston.* But the rain came on and drove us into the house, as many as could press in. I remember the peculiarly solemn appearance of the congregation when I entered the house. The speaker was then addressing such as were not the people of God; and he commenced every paragraph with 'Oh comfortless ye!'"

It was during this revival that Archibald Alexander, as he believed, first became experimentally acquainted with the power of religion. He returned home with a joyful, and as he trusted, a renovated heart. Mr. Graham, on his return, preached at Lexington, and after the sermon called upon two young men, one of whom was Mr. Alexander, to lead in prayer. The effect upon the congregation was very perceptible, and a revival of great power immediately commenced, which extended to almost every Presbyterian Church in the Valley of Virginia. Mr. Alexander made a public profession of his faith in the autumn of 1789.

Several young men who were the subjects of this revival, directed their attention to the study of Theology, under the superintendence of Mr. Graham and of this number was young Alexander.

In the spring of 1791, Mr. Alexander, at the suggestion, and by the earnest desire, of his Preceptor, Mr. Graham, consented to go to Philadelphia to attend the General Assembly, in the capacity of a ruling elder. There were many highly interesting incidents attending his journey and visit, but he seems to have felt ill at ease on account of his extreme youth; and what he undertook then not without great reluctance, he regarded in after life, as having been at best an ill-judged and awkward affair.

On the 1st of October, 1791, when he was nineteen years of age, he was licensed to preach the Gospel by the Lexington Presbytery. The text of his trial sermon before the Presbytery, which was given him by the Rev. Samuel Houston, was "But the Lord said unto me, say not I am a child: for thou shalt go to all that I shall send thee, and whatsoever I command thee, thou shalt speak." Jer. i. 7. Mr. Graham listened to the sermon with the deepest interest; and, at the close of it, expressed to a few friends a most favourable opinion of the character and prospects of the young man

* SAMUEL HOUSTON, the son of John and Sally (Todd) Houston, was born within the limits of the New Providence Congregation, Va., and completed his education about the time of the removal of Liberty Hall Academy to the neighbourhood of Lexington. In 1781, when he was in his twenty-third year, he served for a while in the army of the Revolution. In November of that year, he was received by the Hanover Presbytery as a candidate for the ministry; and on the 22d of October, 1782, was licensed to preach the Gospel. On the 20th of May, 1783, he accepted a call from the Providence Congregation, in what is now Tennessee, and was ordained on the third Wednesday of August following. When the Presbytery of Abingdon was formed in August 1785, Mr. Houston became one of its members. In common with most of his brethren at the time, he seems to have mingled a good deal in civil affairs, and was a zealous advocate for the formation of a new State to be called Franklin. Owing to various circumstances, he returned to Virginia, sometime before the State of Tennessee was formed; and on the 24th of October, 1789, was admitted a member of the Lexington Presbytery. On the 20th of September, 1791, he accepted a call from Falling Spring for two-thirds of his time; and here and at High Bridge he performed the duties of a minister with great fidelity until he was disabled by the infirmities of age. He was, for many years, a popular and successful teacher of a classical school. He attended the Synod of Virginia for the last time in October, 1837, listened to the debates with great interest, and finally gave his vote to sustain the Exscinding Acts of the General Assembly of that year. He died on the 20th of January, 1839, aged eighty-one years. He is represented as having united great modesty with great intrepidity and benevolence.

who had delivered it. During the winter succeeding his licensure, he was occupied, partly in gratuitous missionary labour, and partly in supplying the pulpits of his friends,—the Rev. Nash Legrand and the Rev. William Hill, one of whom was absent on a journey, the other confined by illness.

The General Assembly having directed each of the Synods to recommend "two members well qualified to be employed in missions on our frontiers, for the purpose of organizing churches, administering ordinances, ordaining elders," &c., the Commission of the Synod of Virginia, on the 19th of April, 1792, appointed Mr. Alexander, then a probationer under the care of the Lexington Presbytery, to carry out the purpose of the Assembly, by engaging in the missionary work. In fulfilling this appointment, he laboured in several of the destitute counties of Virginia, and wherever he went, was greatly admired, as well for his quiet and unassuming manner, as for his simple and sparkling eloquence. In this missionary tour he was occupied about six months, during which time he visited fifteen or sixteen counties in Virginia, and several in North Carolina.

The Rev. John Blair Smith having accepted a call to Philadelphia, the Congregations of Briery and Cumberland, together with the Trustees of Hampden Sidney College, invited Mr. Graham to take charge of both the College and the Churches; and upon his returning a negative answer, the attention of the people was directed to Mr. Alexander. All the Presbyterian Congregations in that neighbourhood were then vacant,—namely, Cumberland including the College, Briery, Buffalo, and Cub Creek including Charlotte Court House; but for the two first named, the Rev. Drury Lacy, then acting President of the College, was a regular supply. It was agreed, upon consultation, to call two ministers, who should serve these several churches in rotation; and Mr. Lacy and Mr. Alexander were the two designated, both of whom signified their acceptance. They were to preach in six different places,—their field being not less than sixty miles in length, and thirty in breadth; and their travelling was all on horseback. This arrangement, however, proved inconvenient to the pastors, and unsatisfactory to the people; in consequence of which, a division of the field was soon effected, and Mr. Alexander received for his share the Churches of Briery and Cub Creek. He was ordained at Briery, November 7, 1794, and was dismissed from Cub Creek, April 11, 1797, and from Briery, November 16, 1798.

Mr. Lacy having resigned the Presidency of the College in 1796, Mr. Alexander accepted a call to become his successor; and though the institution, owing to various causes, was at that time in a depressed and languishing state, he, by his great wisdom and untiring industry, soon imparted to it a more healthful and vigorous tone, as well as greatly increased the number of its students. His combined influence in the College and in the pulpit, at this period, was at once very powerful and very extensive.

In 1796, Mr. Alexander went as a delegate to the General Assembly at Philadelphia; and such was his popularity as a preacher, that the Pine Street Church, then vacant by the removal of Dr. John Blair Smith to the Presidency of Union College, invited him to become their Pastor. He, however, declined the invitation.

About the year 1797, Mr. Alexander became seriously doubtful in respect to the authority of infant baptism. The occasion of this was what he afterwards regarded as "too rigid notions as to the purity of the Church, with a belief that receiving infants had a corrupting tendency." He frankly stated the embarrassment he felt on the subject, to his people and his Presbytery; and by both was tolerated in the omission to administer the ordinance to infants for a year or two; but he subsequently became satisfied that his scruples were not well founded, and returned to his former practice.

In 1801, he was sent a second time to the General Assembly. His health had now become considerably reduced, in consequence of his arduous labours, and he felt the need of relaxation and rest. Accordingly, after the Assembly had closed its sessions, he proceeded to New England, as a delegate to the General Association of Connecticut, and continued his journey as far East as Portsmouth, N. H. He preached in various places, and there are still persons living in New England, who will speak in raptures of the wonderful effect which his eloquence produced upon them. On his return home, he preached in the Third Presbyterian Church in Baltimore, and shortly after received a call to settle there, as the successor of Dr. Allison, but declined it.

In 1806, he received a second call from the Pine Street Church in Philadelphia; which, owing to the weight of his duties in the College, in connection with some other circumstances, he determined to accept. He was received a member of the Presbytery of Philadelphia on the 21st of April, 1807, and was installed on the 20th of the next month,—the Sermon on the occasion being preached by the Rev. George C. Potts.* Here he continued, an eminently faithful pastor and popular preacher, for about six years.

In 1807, at the age of thirty-five, he was chosen Moderator of the General Assembly. The next year he preached the opening Sermon on the text—"Seek that ye may excel to the edifying of the Church;" (1 Cor. xiv. 12;) and on this occasion he made a suggestion in regard to the importance of a Theological Seminary, which is supposed to have had an important bearing on the ultimate action of the Church in establishing the Seminary at Princeton.

In 1810, the degree of Doctor of Divinity was conferred upon him by the College of New Jersey.

In 1812, the Assembly having decided on establishing a Seminary at Princeton, Dr. Alexander, on the 2d of June, was chosen to the Professor-

* George Charles Potts was a descendant of an English officer by the name of Potts, who, when the army of Cromwell made its memorable incursion into Ireland, (1649,) remained in the Island and became the head of an Irish house. He was born in Clontibret, County of Monaghan, in 1775; was educated at the University of Glasgow; and was licensed to preach the Gospel by the Presbytery of Monaghan. He entered with great ardour into the memorable struggle for freedom; joined the Society of United Irishmen; and in 1795 visited Paris as the bearer of an important communication to the French National Convention. While on this embassy, he travelled as far as Switzerland. But being satisfied that he could not remain with safety in his native country, he directed his course to the United States, and arrived here in July, 1797. After preaching for some time to various vacant churches in Pennsylvania and Delaware, he chose Philadelphia as the field of his permanent labours, and, with the sanction of the Presbytery, gathered a new Church in the Southern part of the city. In June, 1800, he was ordained and installed Pastor of the Fourth Church; which, from a small beginning, grew to a large and well established congregation. Here he continued in the faithful discharge of his duties, for thirty-six years, when, on account of his increasing infirmities, he resigned his charge. For three years preceding his death, he was an invalid, and occasionally a great sufferer. He died, sustained to the last by the glorious hopes of a better life, on the 23d of September, 1838, in his sixty-fourth year. Without any high degree of popularity as a preacher, he was distinguished for soundness of judgment; for the kindliness of his spirit and manners; for the most faithful attention to his pastoral duties; and for a cordial sympathy in every enterprise designed to promote any of the great interests of humanity. He was the father of the Rev. George Potts, D. D., Pastor of the Church in University Place in the city of New York.

ship of Didactic and Polemic Theology. He accepted the appointment, after considerable deliberation, and was inaugurated on the 12th of August following,—an appropriate Sermon on the occasion being preached by the Rev. Dr. Miller, which, in connection with Dr. Alexander's Inaugural Address, was published.

Here he continued in the laborious discharge of his duties till near the close of life. About a month before he died, he was attacked with dysentery, which had been prevailing to some extent in that region; and his friends, from the commencement of his disease, were somewhat apprehensive of a fatal result. He continued to sink gradually, until it became apparent to all, and to none more than himself, that he had nearly done with the world. He contemplated the approaching event with the utmost calmness, and felt that the circumstances of his departure were all ordered in great mercy. It was a source of special gratification to him that his son, the Rev. Dr. James W. Alexander, who had been passing a few months in Europe, reached Princeton, on his return, a week before his father's death. He died in perfect peace on the 22d of October, 1851. The Synod of New Jersey, which was in session at Princeton at the time, attended his Funeral on the 24th,—an appropriate Sermon being preached on the occasion by the Rev. Dr. McDowell, whom Dr. Alexander himself had designated to perform the service.

Dr. Alexander was married on the 5th of April, 1802, to Janetta, daughter of the Rev. James Waddel, D. D., of the county of Louisa,—a connection with which no small part of the happiness of his future life was identified. Mrs. Alexander died, after a brief illness, on the 7th of September, 1852. They had seven children who survived them,—six sons and one daughter. Of the sons, three are ministers of the Gospel, two are lawyers, and one is a physician.

The following is a list of Dr. Alexander's publications:—

VOLUMES.

A Brief Outline of the Evidences of the Christian Religion, 1825. 12mo. The Canon of the Old and New Testament ascertained; or the Bible complete without the Apocrypha and unwritten Traditions, 1826. 12mo. A Selection of Hymns, adapted to the Devotions of the Closet, the Family, and the Social Circle, and containing subjects appropriate to the Monthly Concerts of Prayer for the success of Missions and Sunday Schools, 1831. (Seven hundred and forty-two hymns.) 32mo. The Lives of the Patriarchs, published by the American Sunday School Union, 1835. 18mo. History of Israel. 12mo. Biographical Sketches of the Founder and Principal Alumni of the Log College; together with an account of the Revivals of Religion under their Ministry, 1845. 12mo. A History of Colonization on the Western Coast of Africa, 1846. 8vo. A History of the Israelitish Nation from their Origin to their Dispersion at the destruction of Jerusalem by the Romans, 1852. 8vo. Outlines of Moral Science, New York, 1852. 12mo.

PAMPHLETS.

A Sermon at the opening of the General Assembly, 1808. A Discourse occasioned by the burning of the Theatre in the city of Richmond, Va., 1812. A Missionary Sermon before the General Assembly, 1813. An Inaugural Discourse delivered at Princeton, 1814. ASermon to Young Men, preached in the chapel of the College of New Jersey, 1826. Suggestions in vindication of Sunday Schools, 1829. Growth in Grace: Two Sermons in the National Preacher, 1829. A Sermon before the American Board of Commissioners for Foreign Missions, 1829. The Pastoral Office: A Sermon preached in Philadelphia, before the Association of the Alumni of the Theological Seminary at Princeton, May 21, 1834. The House of God Desirable: A Sermon in the Presbyterian Preacher, 1835. The People of God led in Unknown Ways: A Sermon Preached in the First Presbyterian Church, Richmond, 1842. An Address delivered before the Alumni Association of Washington College, Va., on Commencement day, 1843.

He published Introductions to Matthew Henry's Commentary, Works of the Rev. William Jay, and Dr. Waterbury's Advice to a Young Christian.

The following books and tracts, as well as some of those mentioned above, are issued by the Presbyterian Board of Publication:—

Practical Sermons; to be read in Families and Social Meetings, 8vo. Letters to the Aged, 18mo. Counsels of the Aged to the Young, 18mo. Universalism false and unscriptural, 18mo. A Brief Compend of Bible Truth, 12mo. Divine Guidance; or the people of God led in Unknown Ways, 32mo. Thoughts on Religious Experience, 12mo. The Life of the Rev. Richard Baxter, (an abridgment,) 18mo. The Life of Andrew Melville, (an abridgment,) 18mo. The Life of John Knox, the Scottish Reformer, (an abridgment,) 18mo. The Way of Salvation familiarly explained in a conversation between a Father and his Children, 32mo.

To which must be added the following Tracts:—

The Duty of Catechetical Instruction. A Treatise on Justification by Faith. Christ's gracious Invitation to the weary and heavy-laden. Ruth, the Moabitess. Love to an Unseen Saviour. Letters to the Aged. A Dialogue between a Presbyterian and a Friend (Quaker). The Amiable Youth falling short of Heaven. The Importance of Salvation. Future Punishment Endless. Justification by Faith. Sinners welcome to Jesus Christ. The following Tracts have been published by the American Tract Society:—The Day of Judgment. The Misery of the Lost.

FROM THE REV. JOHN HALL, D.D.

TRENTON, March 28, 1855.

My dear Sir: It would give me great pleasure to make the slightest contribution to the materials for illustrating the character of Dr. Alexander; but I do not find any thing in my recollections or impressions that seems to have any original value. Such as they are, however, they are at your service.

My first recollection of Dr. Alexander is as the Catechist of the children of his congregation in Philadelphia. Through the only winter which I was old enough to attend, we were assembled on Saturday afternoons in the main aisle of the church. Our seats were the baize-covered benches used by the communicants, when sitting at the Lord's table. The aisle was paved with bricks, and with the gravestone of Dr. Duffield, a former Pastor of the Church. A large tin-plate stove in the middle, was the only heater. Near it the Pastor took his seat, by a small table, and put the class through the Shorter Catechism. The older children were required to bring written proofs of certain points assigned. I was scarcely out of my infancy when the Doctor left Philadelphia for Princeton, and cannot revive any impressions of his course as a Pastor beyond the incidents of the middle aisle on Saturdays; but I could not have passed so much of my life among those who never ceased to speak of his ministry with fond recitals of its extraordinary value, without receiving some idea of its characteristics. Imagine then, a man of Dr. Alexander's knowledge, wisdom, and piety, placed over a people of plain habits, but of religious dispositions,—to whom he would and easily *could* accommodate his bearing and language at all times and in all places; always simple, affable and in good humour, but never light, familiar or undignified; inexhaustible in conservation, yet not exciting a thought that he loved to talk or to be heard; suiting himself to each one's intellectual and spiritual condition with equal facility; delighting most to serve the poor and ignorant, and adapt himself to them, but just as well qualified, and as much at home, in serving those who stand highest in the social or mental ranks; in preaching, actuated by no ambition of greatness, and yet attaining it by the very talent of making every class of hearers interested and pleased; so living among his people that all could confide in him as their best friend and counsellor in private as well as in the pulpit; accustomed to have their tenderest emotions kept in action by the sagacity and force with which his sermons, prayers, exhortations, and conversations were perpetually penetrating their hearts, and having no eccentricities or habits that would qualify the general tenor of so much excellence—imagine such a Pastor, and you will not wonder how a plain congregation could *love* as well as, or even more than, *admire* him.

As is so often the case with the most effective preachers, no printed sermons of Dr. Alexander's can give an adequate conception of the interest which belonged to their delivery, especially when he preached without a manuscript. It was the naturalness of his manner,—the getting up and talking rather than a formal oration or lecture,—the sweetness of his voice and the delightful modulations of its tones, in which feeling and understanding, instead of the rules of elocution, were obviously exercising the whole direction—that captivated the ear, even when the matter made no impression. He had very peculiar cadences—tones now so tender, and now so solemn, and now so long-drawn, and always so unaffected, that one who did not know the language he spoke, must have been moved by the very sound and manner. So his gestures were peculiar. They were not graceful, neither were they ungraceful; but they were natural and significant. The fore-finger pressed on the chin at the pause of a sentence which called for serious reflection—the head thrown down, and eyes peering forth in silence, as if expecting that what he had said *must* be that moment taking effect,—every look and tone indicating that *his* soul was in what he was saying, and that he was moving the souls he addressed,—many more such unstudied, unaffected traits of his manner in preaching can be recalled by those who heard him, than they can describe to the apprehension of those who never enjoyed this privilege. The words were not remarkable for rhetorical excellence, except the utmost simplicity of expression, adapted to all classes of hearers, be admitted to be such an excellence in the pulpit. Hence his universal acceptance. I have before me a family letter, written by my father in June, 1818, who, on his way to the seashore at Long Branch, stopped for the Sabbath at the little village of Eatontown, in the neighbourhood. This was six years after Dr. Alexander left Philadelphia, when we were his parishioners. He writes,—" We had the pleasure of hearing Dr. Alexander preach yesterday. It was in a neat Methodist Church about three miles from this town. The Doctor had a ride of four miles. The preacher of the place finished about twelve o'clock, and our Doctor began in about fifteen minutes afterwards. His intention was to make a short address; but as he advanced in the discourse he seemed to become interested, and a more animated, eloquent discourse I never heard from him. His text was, 'Take my yoke upon you,' &c. His audience, though at times very noisy, (I suppose this alludes to the audible demonstrations of sympathy often heard in churches of this denomination,) were very attentive, and seemed to feel the word preached. His sermon was nearly an hour and a quarter long, and when he finished, though unusually late, the good people seemed to be in no haste to go. They tarried about the door till he came out, and I believe the whole congregation stood looking at him, as if wondering who he was." It will be admitted by those who knew the Doctor's temperament and characteristics, that this was just the occasion for one of the most striking manifestations of his power, and such will readily believe that the extempore discourse that so charmed a plain, country congregation, would have proved equally fascinating and impressive to the most cultivated persons who might have been present, if their hearts had the least sympathy with Divine subjects. Indeed the youngest of his hearers were often kept attentive by the manner so direct and colloquial, in which he often preached. A relative, who was but sixteen years old when the Doctor removed to Princeton, informs me that he has never forgotten the substance of many of his discourses, and recognises several passages in the volume of "Practical Sermons" as once heard in Pine Street.

The vivacity, intelligence, and inquisitiveness, of Dr. Alexander's conversation will be remembered among his most agreeable qualities; and I have often been reminded of a remark I heard when a child, from my mother, that, whatever was the business or calling of any one with whom he conversed, one would have supposed that the Doctor was of the same pursuit, and had lived in the same place. Though always seeking information from every one he encountered, he seemed already to be familiar with the leading facts, and generally with details. A friend of mine once said to me that while a student at the Seminary, he was often foiled in trying to communicate to his teacher in their familiar interviews something new or uncommon that occurred to him in his reading or observation, and had to content himself with the resolution to be constantly receiving every sort of information from him without imparting any in return. After leaving the Seminary, however, he spent ten years in India, and upon his return, he went, as he said, with some confidence that he could now find something to say that Dr. Alexander did not know beforehand; but, after a long conversation, he came away with the disheartening impression that he knew more, even about India, than himself.

But the more I strive to give expression to my views of his peculiarities, the more confident I become that he was one of those uncommon men whose traits cannot be communicated by description, and who must be seen and heard to be at all appreciated, or to have the secret of their influence and popularity understood.

Very respectfully yours,

JOHN HALL

FROM THE REV. H. A. BOARDMAN, D. D.

PHILADELPHIA, April 9, 1855.

Rev. and dear Sir: It has given me very great pleasure to learn that you were engaged in writing a series of biographical sketches of the leading ministers of our country, and I cannot deny your request when you ask me for a letter to be inserted in your account of the late venerable Dr. Alexander. It was my privilege to be a good deal in the society of our revered Professor, during the three years I spent at Princeton; and I was in the habit of meeting him not unfrequently, down to the close of his life. But I have had no advantages above those enjoyed by many of my brethren, for supplying the sort of reminiscences you desire; nor can I write any thing which *I* should regard as a fitting tribute to the memory of this patriarchal man. But I am quite willing to say just what occurs to me on the subject; and you must allow me to say it in the most desultory manner.

If I were to attempt to account for Dr. Alexander's great influence both in the Seminary and out of it, I should say, first of all, that it was not owing to any assumption of superiority on his part. For, aside from the fact that pretensions of this kind are apt to defeat their own end, all who knew him are aware that entire exemption from such claims was one of his prominent characteristics. No one could be more unassuming in manner and disposition than he was. Nor was his influence to be ascribed altogether, or even chiefly, to the splendour of his abilities. For, although his talents and attainments were of a very high order, they were not of so extraordinary a cast as to place him in this view above all his contemporaries. But the secret of his power over men lay in the singular *combination* of excellencies which his character presented—in his blended piety and wisdom; his simplicity and consistency; his sound sense and his spirituality; his never saying nor doing foolish things, and his hearty sympathy with every thing good, and kind, and useful; and above all, or as pervading all, his deep experimental knowledge of the human heart, and of the Gospel as the only remedy for its corruptions. None who were in the habit of hearing him preach, will wonder at the sway he exercised over those brought in contact with him. For how can we help reverencing a man, whom we feel, as soon as he begins to speak, busy about our hearts, and who goes on opening one ward after another, until we begin to fear that there is not a secret chamber that he will not enter, and expose all that is in it? This was what Dr. Alexander did—he addressed himself so much to the consciences of people,—came home so thoroughly to their own varied experiences, that they must have been either more or less than human not to be moved by it. He seemed to have studied every phase of character, and to be equally at home in every part of the wide field of experimental religion. It mattered not whether the subject were joy or sorrow, temptation or triumph, submission or rebellion, trust or despondency, faith or works, the flesh or the spirit, life or death—you soon saw, in listening to him, that it was familiar ground to *him*, and that wherever you were, he had been there before you. His discursive *talks* at the Sabbath afternoon conferences in the Seminary, if gathered up by a stenographer, would have formed a body of practical and casuistical Divinity, inferior to nothing of the kind in the language. His students, in all their doubts, and conflicts, and fears, felt at full liberty to consult him, and they always found him perfectly accessible. He could penetrate the nature of their spiritual difficulties from a hint or two, as readily as Cuvier, the great naturalist, could identify a skeleton from a single joint. He was quick in discerning, and gentle but firm in administering, the antidote which every case required. And then his counsels carried such *authority* with them that they were far more effective than they would have been, had the same sentiments been expressed by another person. The feeling was, that it was not safe to disregard the views of one, who evidently enjoyed in so high a degree the presence of the Holy Spirit. And so strong was this feeling that many a conscientious student has had his hope revived by an encouraging word from his revered teacher, while others of doubtful piety have been led by his paternal and faithful suggestions to turn aside into some more suitable profession.

There was a charm about Dr. Alexander's public ministrations that no one who ever heard him can forget. His unique and inimitable manner—so simple, so vivacious, so earnest, was sure to rivet the attention. His discourses were replete with instruction drawn fresh from the fountain of wisdom. A mere rhetorician might have criticised them as deficient in ornament, but no one felt this in listening to him. He had the rare faculty of making didactic and familiar topics interesting even to persons of no religion; for his sermons partook of the vitality and freshness of his mind, which was like a perennial fountain sending off its sparkling waters. They abounded in terse apothegms, and gleamed with pithy and pleasant sayings, like the bright flowers which light up the rich green of a prairie. You could not possibly suppress a smile sometimes, at the lively turns and sprightly sallies which occurred in his discourses; nor less at the felicitous expressions with which, in a single sentence, he would put before you a vivid transcript of what was passing in your own breast. You smiled, not from lightness of feeling, but from pure pleasure—a pleasure blended with deep seriousness, and often with the spirit of devotion. This simplicity and animation won the hearts of his hearers, and they followed whithersoever he chose to lead them, not because they *resolved* to follow him, but because they were too much interested to resolve any thing about it. As there was no ostentation in his manner, no pretension, no demand for applause, criticism was disarmed and led captive. Men of all classes felt his power alike. Beyond any minister of his day, his preaching was equally acceptable to the learned and the illiterate, the old and the young, the untutored and the refined. For the *nature* of all men is the same, and Dr. Alexander was one of Nature's preachers. He was so simple that children could understand him; but his simplicity never degenerated into *silliness*—it was the graceful but invisible mould into which the instinct of his nature, and the habit of his life, made him cast the richest ore of Divine truth.

There is no greater element of power in the pulpit than the capacity of exciting religious emotion. This must take precedence of intellectual prowess, of learning, of brilliancy of imagination, of logical astuteness, and of all the graces of oratory. Dr. Alexander possessed it in combination with several of these qualities in a most remarkable degree. He could set forth the Gospel in its adaptation to the endlessly diversified states of human feeling, with a skill and effect truly wonderful. And the facility with which he could awaken emotions of gratitude, praise, contrition, joy and the like, gave him a rare control over any *Christian* auditory. Nor did his sermons die with the occasion; they combined with the radical principles and affections of his hearers, and went to strengthen and perpetuate their reverence for him.

Besides the elements of power to which I have already referred, Dr. Alexander's great influence was to be ascribed, in no small measure, to his earnest sympathy with his kind. A stranger, to look in upon him in his study,—an old man half doubled in his big chair, engaged with his books and manuscripts, and occupied professionally as a teacher of Theology, might have conjectured, at first sight, that he was as much isolated from the great Babel in feeling as he was in situation. But this was not the case; and the whole Church knew it. He never sank the man in the philosopher, nor the citizen and patriot in the divine. His sterling common sense formed a bond of union between himself and his fellowmen, which neither his scholastic pursuits, nor his high spiritual attainments, ever weakened or tarnished. There was no chasm to be bridged over before you could approach him;—no mailed coat of professional dignity to be pierced;—no steps to climb up to the high official chair where he sat in state. You could not hear him in the pulpit nor meet him in social life, without feeling that there was a common ground for you to stand upon; that there were numerous points of contact between you and himself; and that you could talk with him as freely as with any other man. There was assurance of this, not only in his genial sympathies, but in that native cheerfulness and mother-wit, which made him a delightful companion. His wit, using the term in its broad philosophical sense, revealed itself often in his discourses. But when he was in full health, and no *adverse winds* depressed his spirits, it would sometimes play in the class-room, and in the social circle, like the Aurora Borealis. If the scintillations of it which have been preserved by his students could be collected, they would make a brilliant and substantial volume. But his wit never degenerated into coarseness, nor his cheerfulness into levity. It is not probable that a minute scrutiny into his ministerial life would bring to light an act or an expression that was inconsistent with the dignity of his sacred office. And while he pleased in private life, he instructed. Persons who were drawn around him by his vivacity, seldom retired without carrying away some wholesome truth or valuable suggestion. It was his high vocation to do good; and he seemed never to lose sight of it, nor ever to prosecute it as a task.

I must not omit to say that another source of Dr. Alexander's great power was his eminent piety. And yet I hardly need expatiate upon this, as a distinct attribute; for it was to his character what the soul is to the body—the pervading, life-giving, governing principle; and it would be difficult to speak of him in any of his relations or pursuits without recognising the fact of his singular attainments in holiness. It was his rare fortune to maintain an unsullied reputation for superior piety, wisdom, benevolence, and consistency, throughout a ministry of nearly sixty years. This entire period he spent, not in the seclusion of a remote rural parish, but in the most prominent and responsible situations—as the President of Hampden Sidney College, the Pastor of a Church in this city, and the Senior Professor at Princeton. It was a period, too, of great excitement, marked by a succession of momentous changes in the politics and commerce of the world, and with incessant conflicts in Theology and morals. Yet, with such fidelity to his Master, and with such meekness of wisdom, did he carry himself throughout, that the most violent controvertists have rarely ventured to breathe a word of censure against him.

But it is more than time for me to close. I have simply glanced at some of the most prominent traits of Dr. Alexander's character, without attempting a full delineation of it. If these familiar sketches should afford you the least assistance in finishing your portrait of one whom we all revered as a Master in Israel, it is all I could expect or desire.

I remain, my dear Sir,

Sincerely and affectionately,

Your friend and brother,

HENRY A. BOARDMAN.

FROM THE REV. WILLIAM E. SCHENCK.

PHILADELPHIA, April 6, 1857.

Dear Sir: It gives me pleasure to comply with your wish that I should furnish you some personal reminiscences of the late venerated Dr. Archibald Alexander. His biography has been so well and so thoroughly written, that it seems almost presumptuous to attempt any thing in addition. If, however, any of the following impressions or incidents can be of the least service, they are placed at your disposal very willingly.

I have always accounted it one of the most distinguished privileges of my life, to have lived from early childhood in the near vicinity of two such men as Dr. Samuel Miller and Dr. Archibald Alexander. They were, to my youthful mind, both in and out of the pulpit, very models of ministerial excellence and dignity. The impression made by them respecting the elevation of goodness and of usefulness to which an ambassador of Christ may attain, has not yet worn away, and never can.

During my boyish years, Dr. Alexander was held in profound reverence, mingled with strong affection. Although not then specially interested in the great subject of religion, I can yet recall the feelings of peculiar delight with which I always saw him rise in the pulpit and heard him preach. His simplicity, vivacity, and directness of speech, were such as always to rivet attention, afford pleasure, convey instruction, and secure conviction, even to a child's understanding. It was not, however, until I had become a theological student, that I enjoyed frequent access to him, and almost daily opportunities of hearing and observing him.

As a lecturer, Dr. Alexander was always profound, philosophical, instructive. His lectures, as I heard them, were written out with great care, yet he never confined himself to his manuscript. Assuming an easy position in his chair, with his forefinger pressed against his cheek, he read deliberately and critically, just as if perusing for the first time the production of another mind, in which he might possibly detect some error. Frequently a sentence would suggest remarks not found upon the paper, when he would enter upon an extemporaneous discussion of that point, and after a while would come back to his manuscript. There was so much in his manner that was conversational, fresh and easy, that the attention of any hearer seldom was seen to flag. When attending to the performances of the students, they always had his careful and undivided attention. When criticising their productions, his remarks were pointed, brief, apt and judicious. Hundreds of these brief and sententious criticisms still live in the memories of his students, and many a preacher's whole style of pulpit performances has been revolutionized by a single one of them.

I have heard it hinted that Dr. Alexander was sometimes tart in his remarks to the students, and even at times unnecessarily severe. This, I believe, is a mistake. Although gifted with the power of uttering prompt and scathing sarcasm, when occasion called for it, he was exceedingly chary in the use of this formidable weapon. During a somewhat intimate acquaintance of over twenty years, and after seeing him in every variety of circumstances, I cannot remember to have heard him utter a single sharp remark, which my own judgment did not regard as entirely suitable and called for by the occasion. Indeed there was only one class of his students with whom he ever used sarcasm. They were *the self-conceited.* For them he agreed with Solomon that severe remedies alone could be expected to do any good. With these his remarks were sometimes like the point of a pen-knife, thrust into an inflated balloon. Many a mortifying yet beneficial collapse has followed them. But to the self-distrustful and the humble, his words were uniformly full of kindness and encouragement. The students always found in him a ready, patient and wise adviser. They knew that they could resort to him in every emergency in their affairs, and however busy he might be, if they did not receive as ample expressions of tender sympathy as in some other quarters, they were sure to receive advice that was full of practical sagacity, and genuine pious wisdom. Many a pupil of his, now even past the meridian of life, not seldom wishes in his exigencies that he could still resort to him for guidance.

Few things caused more astonishment to Dr. Alexander's clerical visiters than his extensive and accurate knowledge of the ministers and churches of his own denomination. He was acquainted not only with their present condition, characters, and prospects, but was familiar also with their histories from the beginning. This was the case not only with the more important churches in the cities and larger towns, but with even the obscurest missionary churches. I have heard him discourse at length about the little preaching places in the Pines of New Jersey, and along the sea shore, or back in the mountains of Pennsylvania, until I marvelled how he could possibly either acquire or retain all his information.

After my settlement as Pastor of the First Church in Princeton, he was uniformly one of the kindest and most attentive of parishioners. Although to one so conversant with the whole circle of biblical and theological science, I knew that the truth to which he listened was familiar as the alphabet, yet I never could have inferred from his manner that it was not to him as fresh and new as to the most illiterate among my hearers. When his help, either pecuniary or ministerial, was needed to advance the interests or efficiency of the Church, it was promptly and cheerfully extended.

The depth of experimental piety, and the clearness of philosophical discrimination, which were so remarkbly conjoined in him, made Dr. Alexander's unstudied and devotional exhortations always very precious to pious hearers. It was a common feeling among the theological students that his Sabbath afternoon talks in the conference meetings were among the most profitable of all his religious instructions. For the same reason every one rejoiced to hear him at the Communion table. There he was perfectly at home, and thence his Christian hearers would go away, after listening to his words of wisdom, feeling that they had been refreshed and strengthened by partaking of the very best of the old wine of the Gospel. His very last public service was of this description. On Sabbath, September 14, 1851, he took his place at the Communion table by my side, and delivered a beautiful and most touching address to the communicants,—exhorting them *as pilgrims* to a faithful and hopeful performance of their duties. Before the next Communion season had come round, his own pilgrimage was terminated, and he had, as we cannot doubt, entered joyfully upon his eternal rest.

Early in the spring of 1850, a little more than a year before Dr. Alexander's death, it pleased a gracious God largely to pour out his Spirit upon Princeton and its institutions of learning. Just preceding this, there had been a brief season of unusual coldness. On a Communion occasion, a few weeks before the revival commenced, not a single soul was added to the First Church. Dr. Alexander occupied the platform with the Pastor, and made a few very pointed and solemn remarks to the Christians then present on their duty in the existing state of religion. I have always believed that those remarks were instrumental, under God, of bringing believers to the throne of grace to supplicate more earnestly for a revival of religion. In a few weeks it was graciously granted. And when it came, no one took a livelier interest in it throughout than Dr. Alexander. For six or seven weeks, religious services were maintained every evening except Saturday, and the house was thronged with eager listeners. During this course of services, he repeatedly preached, and although now nearly eighty years of age, it was with all the richness, unction, and power, which had characterized the days of his very prime. One of these sermons was on the parable of the Prodigal Son, and was peculiarly rich in discriminating and pointed practical remark. More than one new convert afterward said to me that that sermon had been blessed as a means of bringing him to the great decision. After these meetings had been held some weeks, Dr. Alexander was consulted about the expediency of continuing them longer. He advised that they should be kept up as long as the people continued manifestly to hunger for the word. "Divine truth," he would say, "never yet surfeited a hungry soul. Only be careful to let it have nothing but truth."

The annual meeting of the Synod of New Jersey was to be held in October, 1851, at Princeton. Before the time came, Dr. Alexander had been stricken down with the illness which terminated his life. You have requested me to give you especially some account of my last interview with him. Directly after this interview occurred, I wrote out with some care a full account of it, with no thought that it would ever meet any other eye than my own. It was, however, afterwards, in part, inserted in the Life of Dr. Alexander by his son, and I prefer to extract the account as then published rather than attempt to rewrite it.

"It was on the morning of the Thursday preceding Dr. Alexander's death, that I called to inquire after his health. My inquiries having been answered at the door, I was about to leave when I was called back by one of his sons, who said that his father had heard I was at the door, and desired to see me. As I entered the study, he was lying on the sofa in his usual dress, but supported by pillows. He extended his hand in a very cordial manner—on taking it I found it icy cold. He at once said to me in a very warm and tender tone, 'My dear young friend, I have much desired to see you once more, and am glad to have this opportunity. I wish to bid you farewell. You will see me no more in this life.'

"I was so greatly overcome by this address that I hardly knew what to reply. I merely said, 'I trust and most earnestly hope, dear Sir, that you may yet be mistaken. Should it be so, we are confident it would be your inexpressible gain; but it would be a sorrowful day indeed for all of us that should survive.'

"'I feel confident,' said he, 'that I am not mistaken; I shall not live long. Nor have I any wish to stay longer. I have lived eighty years, which is more than the usual term of human life, and, if I remain, I have little to look forward to but infirmity and suffering. If such be the Lord's will, I feel thoroughly satisfied, and even would prefer, to go now. My work on earth I feel is done. And it does seem to me (he added with great earnestness) as if my Heavenly Father had in great mercy surrounded me with almost every circumstance which could remove anxieties, and make me feel that I can go without regret. My affairs have all been attended to, my arrangements are all completed, and I can think of nothing more to be done. I have greatly desired to see my son James before my departure, and sometimes feared I should not have that privilege; but the Lord has graciously brought him back in time to see me, having led him safely through much peril on the ocean. My children are all with me. The Church of which you are Pastor is prosperous and flourishing. The Seminary Faculty is again full, and the institution is in an excellent condition. The more I reflect upon the matter, the more all things seem to combine to make me perfectly willing to enter into my rest. The Lord has very graciously and tenderly led me (he added, closing his eyes and clasping his hands in a devotional manner) all the days of my life. Yes, all the days of my life. *And He is now with me still. In Him I enjoy perfect peace!*' The last sentence he uttered in a quick, earnest and happy tone of voice, such as was peculiar to him in certain moods. Pausing a moment or two, as if to recover breath, he then said:—

"'I have much desired to see you that I might bid you farewell, and once more invoke God's blessing upon you and your ministry. You have had a strong hold upon my affections, and I have felt much satisfaction in your preaching. Continue as you have begun, and have done thus far, to preach Christ and Him crucified, scripturally, plainly, earnestly, and God will continue richly to bless your ministry, even as here He has so lately done.' He lifted his hands as if to pronounce a benediction. I fell on my knees beside the sofa, with my head bowed and weeping bitterly; nevertheless I tried hard to restrain my feelings, while, with his hands extended over me, he offered a short and fervent prayer, closing with these words: 'God greatly bless his servant in his person, in his family, and in his ministry. May it please God to give him great usefulness and success. May many souls be saved through his efforts; and when his work is done, may we be permitted to meet again in a happier world, Amen.'

"As I arose from my knees, he reached out his hand, as if to bid me farewell.

"'I cannot go,' (said I,) 'until I attempt to thank you, which I do with my whole heart, for your long and unvarying kindness to me. You have been to me the best and most valued of earthly friends.'

"'You must thank God for that' (said he, quickly); 'all kindness and all friends are his gifts. Give my love to your wife and children.'

"The last sentence he repeated when I had reached the door, and very slowly, as if he were very loath to have me leave him.

"'Give my love and a very affectionate farewell to your wife and children.'"

"As I walked away from the house, I could not repress my tears, and a sense of utter desolation came over me for a little while, as I thought that I had probably received the last words of affectionate counsel from that beloved and venerated friend to whom I had been accustomed to resort, and on whose counsels I had been accustomed to rely, as on those of no other man on earth. But soon my feelings grew calmer. I felt that I had been breathing an atmosphere redolent with the very fragrance of Heaven. The room that I had left seemed to have been perfumed with holy composure and immovable confidence in a glorified but present Redeemer. As I reflected upon the scene, I gained new views of life, of death, and of Heaven. I felt, as I had never felt before, how 'sure and steadfast' is that anchor of Gospel hope which 'entereth into that within the veil.' I could not help asking myself,—'Is it possible to die so? Does the Lord Jesus give his people such complete and quiet victories over the grim King of Terrors?' There was nothing excited, nothing exultant; and yet it seemed to be thoroughly triumphant; a calm, believing, cheerful looking through the gloomy grave into the glories of the eternal world. It was the steady, unfaltering step of a genuine Christian philosopher, as well as an eminent saint, evincing his own thorough, heartfelt and practical belief in the doctrines he had so long and so ably preached, as he descended into the dark valley and shadow of death. And I could not help praying, as I had never prayed before,—'Let me die the death of the righteous, and let my last end be like his!'"

On Thursday, the 23d of October, 1851, Dr. Alexander's precious remains were deposited in the cemetery at Princeton, made venerable by the ashes of the many great and good which there await the Resurrection morn. It was a scene never to be forgotten. Just as an unclouded sun was sinking to the Western horizon, a group was gathered around his open grave, such as had seldom been gathered in one spot in any part of our land. There were the students and Faculty of the College of New Jersey, and those of the Theological Seminary, the entire Synod of New Jersey, and many members of the Synods of New York and Philadelphia, besides a crowd of other spectators, a numerous company of God's ministers and people, all feeling that a great man in Israel had fallen.

Ever most respectfully yours,

WILLIAM EDWARD SCHENCK.

JOHN POAGE CAMPBELL, M. D.*

1792—1814.

JOHN POAGE† CAMPBELL, a son of Robert Campbell, was born in Augusta County, Va., in the year 1767. In 1781, when about fourteen years of age, he removed to Kentucky with his father, who settled first in Lexington, and afterwards in Mason County, where he became an elder in the Smyrna Church. He was a descendant, on the mother's side, of the celebrated Scottish divine, Samuel Rutherford,—one of the members of the Westminster Assembly, and author of the work well known as "Rutherford's Letters." In his early youth, he gave evidence of uncommon talents, which led his father, notwithstanding he was in moderate circumstances, to resolve on giving him a liberal education; and, after studying some time with Messrs. Hamilton and McPheeters in Rockbridge, and afterwards with Mr. Rankin‡ in Lexington, he was entered as a pupil in the Transylvania

* Davidson's Hist. Presb. Ch., Ky.—Foote's Sketches of Va., 2d Series.

† He took the name of *Poage*, as a memorial of a bosom friend and connection by marriage, who died about the time of his settlement in the ministry.

‡ ADAM RANKIN was born, March 24, 1755, near Greencastle, Pa.,—his ancestors having emigrated from Ireland, and at a more remote period, from Scotland. At the age of eighteen, he became hopefully pious, and shortly after commenced the study of the languages, at Mr. Graham's Academy in Virginia. Having been prevented from entering the College of New Jersey by its being in possession of the British troops, and having lost a year's study by dan-

grammar school, under the care of Mr. Rice. He subsequently studied with Mr. Archibald Scott, in his native county; and, at the age of nineteen, was himself Preceptor of an Academy at Williamsburg, N. C. Here he imbibed infidel opinions, but, not long after, renounced them in consequence of reading Soame Jenyns' Treatise on the internal evidences of Christianity. And he was not only a speculative but practical convert; and though he had before engaged in the study of medicine, he now resolved on giving himself to the work of the ministry. He graduated at Hampden Sidney College in 1790. He prosecuted his theological studies, first under the Rev. William Graham, and afterwards under the Rev. Dr. Moses Hoge. then of Shepherdstown; and was licensed to preach in May, 1792. So acceptable was he as a preacher that he was immediately associated with his theological teacher, Mr. Graham, as Colleague Pastor of Lexington, Oxford, New Monmouth, and Timber Ridge, Congregations. He continued, however, in this relation but a short time, by reason, it has been said, of "some of those jealousies and partisanships which are not uncommon in collegiate charges."

In 1795, he went to reside in Kentucky, and first took the pastoral charge of the Churches of Smyrna and Flemingsburg, in Fleming County. He afterwards exercised his ministry in Danville, Nicholasville, Cherry Spring, Versailles, Lexington, and Chilicothe; and in 1811, he officiated as Chaplain to the Legislature. His salary was altogether inadequate to the support of his family; so that they were actually sometimes in a state of abject want. With a view to remedy this evil in some degree, he took up the practice of medicine. One of his friends, hearing the fact misrepresented, and being informed that he had given up his profession with a view to entering political life, wrote him a letter of expostulation; which drew from Dr. Campbell an honest statement of the case, including also the necessity which had dictated the measure.

Dr. Campbell died near Chilicothe, November 4, 1814, at the age of forty-seven. His death was occasioned by exposure while he was preaching. He had great tranquillity in his last hours, and expressed the utmost confidence in the truth of the doctrines which he had preached.

gerous illness, he subsequently prosecuted his studies under the Rev. Archibald Scott, of the Hanover Presbytery, and completed his course at Liberty Hall, about the year 1780. On the 25th of October, 1782, he was licensed to preach by the Hanover Presbytery. He received three calls from the neighbourhoods of Holstein and Nolachuckey, but declined them on account of disputes on the subject of Psalmody; and the next year he visited Kentucky, and receiving a call from Lexington, removed thither with his family in 1784, and shortly after opened a school. His opposition to singing any other than Rouse's version of the Psalms seems to have become a sort of monomania; and in 1792, after having been involved in protracted difficulties growing out of this opposition, he seceded from the Presbyterian Communion, and joined the Associate Reformed Church. But in this connection he was not more happy than he had been in the other; for his pugnacious propensities brought on at last a judicial investigation, and a Commission of the General Synod, of which Dr. J. M. Mason was one, were deputed to sit in Lexington upon the case. Though Mr. Rankin declined their jurisdiction, the trial proceeded, and he was suspended from the office of the ministry on the charge of "lying and slandering his brethren." But he refused to respect the decision, and he and his congregation became independent. He seems to have been pre-eminently a victim to fanatical impulses. Either from a dream, or from the study of the prophecies, or perhaps from both, he became impressed with the idea that the time for rebuilding the Holy City was at hand, and he took a solemn farewell of his flock, and set off on a journey to Jerusalem; but died on the way, in Philadelphia, November 25, 1827, aged seventy-two years. He published several things, the most important of which was "Dialogues pleasant and interesting on the Government of the Church," designed as an Answer to Dr. Mason's "Plea for Catholic Communion." His writings evince considerable talent, but are greatly lacking in the Christian spirit. Notwithstanding the fury of his polemic zeal, he is said to have been amiable in his private relations, and to have possessed in a high degree the affections of his people.

Dr. Campbell was married three times. His first wife was a Miss Crawford of Virginia; his second a Miss Poage of Kentucky; his third a daughter of Col. James McDowell, of Lexington. His last wife survived him several years, and died in 1838, in the vicinity of Maysville, under peculiarly distressing circumstances. She had become entirely deaf and quite infirm; and, being left alone for a few minutes, her clothes took fire. Her daughter instantly ran to her rescue, but the attempt proved worse than abortive; for both mother and daughter were burnt to death. Dr. Campbell, on his demise, left behind him a family of nine children.

The College of New Jersey was about to confer on him the degree of Doctor of Divinity, when death prevented the intended honour.

Dr. Campbell was an accomplished scholar and an elegant writer. Few, if any, of his day, especially in the part of the country where he resided, spoke so frequently or so effectively as he, through the press. The following is a list of his publications:—

A Sermon on Sacred Music, 1797. The Passenger, 1804. Strictures on Stone's Letters on the Atonement, 1805. Vindex: or the doctrine of the Strictures vindicated, 1806. Essays on Justification. An installation Sermon, 1809. Letters to the Rev. Mr. Craighead, 1810. A Sermon on Christian Baptism, 1810. The Pelagian detected: a Reply to Mr. Craighead, 1811. Letters to a gentleman of the Bar, published in the Evangelical Record, 1812. An Answer to Jones, and Review of Robinson's History of Baptism, 1812. A Sermon preached on the opening of the Synod, 1812.

In the year 1812, while I was a member of Yale College, Dr. Campbell visited Connecticut, and passed a few days in New Haven. Dr. Dwight, contrary to his ordinary practice, asked him to preach in the College chapel; and I have now, at the distance of thirty-eight years, a perfectly distinct recollection of his appearance and manner, and to some extent, of his sermon. He was tall and slender in person, of a strongly marked countenance, but rather pale complexion, and altogether more than commonly attractive in his appearance. He preached without notes, and apparently extempore, but was graceful and animated in his delivery. His sermon, as I now remember it, was designed to show the harmony of true Philosophy with Christianity; and the subject seemed to have been chosen with special reference to the character of his audience. I am confirmed in the impression that it was no ordinary performance by the fact that I have, in latter years, found a number of persons who remember it, and whose recollections fully agree with my own estimate of its merits. Dr. Dwight expressed great satisfaction in making Dr. Campbell's acquaintance, and spoke of him as a remarkably accomplished scholar and divine.

FROM THE HON. C. S. TODD,

AMBASSADOR FROM THE UNITED STATES TO RUSSIA.

NEAR SHELBYVILLE, Ky., 9th October, 1849.

Rev. and dear Sir: I had known Dr. Campbell in my youth; but my acquaintance with him was more marked and intimate in the summer of 1814, during the period I was stationed at Chilicothe, O., as the Adjutant and Inspector-General of the Western army. Such was the feebleness of the church, and the low standard of religion, at that boisterous period of public affairs, that this eminent divine was under the necessity to practise medicine in connection with his clerical duties. It was my good fortune to enjoy his society, and to be permitted to profit by the rich stores of intelligence with which his fertile and cultivated mind abounded. His intercourse with me was unreserved, and I was impressed with intense admiration, as well by the fine qualities of his heart and the fascination of his colloquial powers, as by the splendour of his eloquence in the pulpit. In the estimate of his character as a pulpit orator, my subsequent acquaintance with Dr. Archibald Alexander, and the late Dr. John Breckenridge, leads me to say that Dr. Campbell combined many of the excellencies of each; especially the simplicity and vigour of the former with the energy and affectionate pathos of the latter. I think I have rarely, if ever, heard a preacher whose discourses were so profound, and at the same time so chaste and elegant, as those of Dr. Campbell; and this is the more creditable to him, as the congregation he addressed was of such a mixed character in a new country as might be expected to lead the preacher to some degree of carelessness in the style, arrangement, and general execution, of his discourses.

I was greatly delighted by the reference which he once made to sundry letters he had addressed to that gifted, though eccentric, orator, Col. Joseph Hamilton Daviess, who fell at Tippecanoe. This distinguished lawyer was touched with the prevailing Deism of that day, and Dr. Campbell exerted his great genius and acquirements for the purpose of impressing him with proper notions in reference to the Christian religion. Dr. C. was a correspondent of my sister-in-law, the late Mrs. McDowell, and eldest daughter of Governor Shelby, a lady of uncommon mind and attainments; and it will be difficult for me to give you a better idea of his fine powers and exalted character than by sending you one of the letters he addressed to her.

I am, as ever, yours in Christian bonds,

C. S. TODD.

MATTHEW LYLE.

1792—1827.

FROM THE REV. DRURY LACY, D. D.

RALEIGH, N. C., 22d June, 1853.

Rev. and dear Sir: I resided in the same neighbourhood with the Rev. Matthew Lyle many years; but was so young, and so little observant of men and manners, that I should be disposed to distrust my early impressions of his life and character, did I not enjoy the advantage of having them confirmed by one who knew him intimately, from early life. Having occasion lately to revisit the old neighbourhood in which he lived, and laboured, and died, I made known your wishes to a surviving member of the family, who kindly furnished me a letter of sympathy and condolence from the late venerable Dr. Alexander to Mrs. Lyle, on the decease of her husband,—an extract from which I shall take the liberty to subjoin to this communication. Whilst in the neighbourhood, I collected the following facts concerning him, which perhaps may suffice as an outline of the history of his life.

MATTHEW LYLE was born in what was then Augusta County, in Virginia, but is now Rockbridge—in that part of the County, called Timber

Ridge, on the 21st of October, 1767. He was the son of James Lyle, who was a respectable farmer, and of Hannah, his wife, who was a daughter of Archibald Alexander, one of the first and most highly esteemed settlers of this part of Virginia. Matthew was the second son of his parents, and, as the Rev. John Brown was the Pastor of Timber Ridge Congregation when he was born, there can be no doubt that he was baptized by him.

In his youth, he was reckoned a very steady boy, and was of a very kind and friendly disposition. Until he was grown up, he received no other than an English education, and was occupied with his brothers on his father's farm; but when he was about eighteen years of age, he commenced his classical learning, and, possessing a good capacity and persevering diligence, he made rapid progress; and in a shorter time than usual became a respectable scholar. But whilst at Liberty Hall, (now Washington College,) he fell into the company of some dissipated and immoral young men, whose influence upon him was very pernicious. For some years he lived an irreligious and irregular life. But when the great revival, which spread over so large a part of Virginia in 1789, reached Rockbridge, he was among the first who were seriously impressed. His convictions were deep and pungent, and he did not remain long in this state before he found relief by believing in the Lord Jesus Christ; and the hope and comfort which he now received, remained with him till his dying day. But he was never disposed to say much about his own private exercises; and he has left no journal or diary, from which any thing can be learned on this subject. His piety was deep and solid; and no man was more regular and conscientious in attendance on all religious duties, private and public. His life was uniform and consistent; and he always took a deep interest in every thing which was connected with the advancement and enlargement of the Church of Christ.

After going through a course of theological study, under the direction of the Rev. William Graham, he put himself under the care of the Presbytery of Lexington; and, having passed through all the usual trials preparatory to the work of the ministry, was licensed to preach the Gospel on the 28th of April, 1792. For about two years, he was engaged in missionary labours, both in the Northeastern and Southwestern part of Virginia. He was sent several times into the Northern Neck, where his labours were highly appreciated by the people, especially in the County of Lancaster.

On the 5th of March, 1794, he was married to Sarah Lyle, the youngest daughter of Samuel Lyle, Esq., a man of uncommon worth and extensive reading. Soon after his marriage, he visited Prince Edward County, and, having received a call, on the 4th of October, 1794, from the Congregation of Briery for one half of his labours, and from the Congregation of Buffalo for the other half, he accepted the same, and was ordained as Pastor of these two Churches by the Presbytery of Hanover, shortly after. The late Rev. Archibald Alexander, D. D., of Princeton, was his colleague in Briery. Here he remained in the unremitted and faithful exercise of his ministry for thirty-three years. During this whole period, until within a few weeks of his death, he was seldom prevented from taking his place in the pulpit. His decease occurred on the 22d of March, 1827, when he had reached his sixtieth year. Although he had been indisposed for some time yet his departure might be said to be sudden, as he had been scarcely at all confined to his bed. On this account, his friends were deprived of the privilege of hearing from him the views which he entertained of death, when that awful but honest hour had arrived.

As a man, Mr. Lyle was by nature endowed with a sound, discriminating mind, and was possessed of inflexible firmness and great energy and decision of character. Honesty was the very texture of his soul. To deceit and flattery he was a perfect stranger. If he entertained an ill opinion of any person, he never attempted to conceal it. This was not the way to conciliate every body, but was the way to keep a good conscience. No man ever called his sincerity in question. His friendships, too, were select, but faithful and lasting. The utmost dependance could be placed on his prudence, secrecy, and fidelity. In domestic life, he was affectionate and uniformly indulgent; as a neighbour, peaceable, kind and obliging.

But he appeared to the greatest advantage in the pulpit. His sermons were remarkable for clearness, conciseness, and energy; and they were always truly evangelical. By some judicious hearers he was preferred to all other preachers. He was, perhaps, never known to deliver an indifferent sermon; nor did he ever fall into confusion or embarrassment. He uniformly preached without notes,—rarely, if ever, taking even a skeleton of a sermon with him into the pulpit. The only faults which were ever found with his preaching were a want of sufficient variety, and a want of persuasive tenderness; but no one preacher ever possessed every kind of excellence.

In social intercourse, Mr. Lyle had a benignity of manner, and a lively pleasantness of remark, accompanied with sallies of wit, which rendered him an exceedingly agreeable companion, when surrounded by friends in whom he had confidence. His departure left a wide chasm in the society of which he was so long the guide and ornament.

The following is the extract from Dr. Alexander's letter, above referred to:—

"I have not, for a long time, been so much affected with the departure of any friend; for although I heard from time to time that he was sick, yet I never conceived that his sickness was unto death. I never dreamed that I should see his face no more in the land of the living. Many a time we took sweet counsel together, and always our intercourse was of the most cordial kind. He was my earliest friend—when, a small boy, I was sent to board at his father's, to go to school, he took me under his special protection. He never failed to defend me when I was assaulted by larger boys, and from that day to the day of his death, he acted the part of a sincere friend. Indeed, I never knew a man who was more incapable of insincerity. As he feared no man, so he never assumed an appearance of attachment which he did not feel. Since his conversion to God, his course has been uniformly steady and consistent. He did not serve his Divine Master by *fits*, but *always*. And I need not say to you, how attentive he was to all the duties of religion, even the most secret. He was never very communicative of his religious experiences and feelings, which arose in part from the natural reserve of his temper, and more, I believe, from deep humility; but I have reason to think that, during life, he cherished uniformly a lively hope of the Divine favour. I have no doubt that his soul is at rest, and that he now beholds without a mist, the glory of God in the face of Jesus Christ. As a preacher, his constant endeavour was to be faithful in delivering the message of God, and with him the trumpet of the Gospel never gave an uncertain sound."

With great respect, very truly,

Your sincere friend and brother,

DRURY LACY.

CPSIA information can be obtained
at www.ICGtesting.com
Printed in the USA
BVHW04*1444070818
523683BV00034B/1351/P

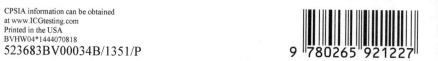

9 780265 921227